ENCYCLOPEDIA YEAR BOOK 1977

Grolier
INCORPORATED
NEW YORK

Editor in Chief	EDWARD HUMPHREY
Executive Editor	JAMES E. CHURCHILL, JR.
Senior Editor	HALLBERG HALLMUNDSSON
Art Director	FRANKLIN N. SAYLES
Editors	JUDITH A. GLICKMAN
	WAYNE JONES
Indexer	VITRUDE DeSPAIN
Layout Artist	ROBERT REDDY
Production Supervisor	HARRIET L. SMITH
Picture Research	MARGARET L. SKAGGS, Head
	NATALIE GOLDSTEIN
Editorial Assistant	NILSA JIMENEZ

GROLIER INCORPORATED

HOWARD B. GRAHAM
Senior Vice-President, Publishing

WALLACE S. MURRAY
Vice-President and Editorial Director

CONTENTS

CONTRIBUTORS   Page 6

PREFACE   Page 10

CHRONOLOGY   Page 11

FEATURE ARTICLES OF THE YEAR

THE U. S. PRESIDENTIAL ELECTION   Page 24

Contributor—Marquis Childs. As the year began, people were referring to Jimmy Carter as Jimmy Who? As the year ended, the former Georgia governor, now president-elect, was busy selecting his administration and preparing to move into the White House. A veteran analyst of many presidential campaigns discusses this most unusual election.

THE BICENTENNIAL   A time for reflection   . Page 32

Contributor—Mike Mansfield. The Senator from Montana presents his interpretation of the meaning of the 200th birthday of the United States. Full-color photographs and description of some of the various celebrations held in honor of the event are included.

THE STATUS OF THE THREE R's   Page 37

Contributor—Merrill Sheils. Educators, parents, and the general public have become concerned over the inability of some youngsters, teenagers, and even adults to read, write, and add. Consequently, a "back to basics" movement has arisen in our schools. Newsweek's education specialist probes the situation, analyzing the arguments pro and con.

MONARCHIES: A new lease on life?   Page 44

Contributor—John Grigg. The feature explains how it is no longer self-evident that monarchy is an antipopular system of government and that in fact it is increasingly evident that the reverse is true.

UNITED NATIONS CONFERENCE ON THE LAW OF THE SEA   Page 50

Contributors—H. S. Amerasinghe, James E. Andrews, Jon L. Jacobson, and Henry Charnock. The conference president outlines the responsibilities of this important international meeting. Experts discuss the subjects of the conference's committees—The Ocean Floor, Jurisdiction and Navigational Rights, and Scientific Research and Pollution Control.

THE QUICK FOOD CHAINS   Page 61

Contributor—Jane Bradford. In recent years the quick food chains have become the fastest growing segment of the restaurant industry. The feature not only gives the fascinating statistics involved but also the history of the quick food chains and the reasons for their growth.

MULTINATIONAL BUSINESS ETHICS   Page 65

Contributor—Eugene R. Black. The former president of the World Bank discusses corporate bribery, the multinational corruption phenomenon, which has gained so much attention of late, and considers the problems that may hamper efforts at reform.

THE ALPHABETICAL SECTION

Articles listed below are in the Review of the Year section, which begins on page 71, and are grouped in broad subject categories. Separate entries on the continents, the major nations of the world, U. S. states, Canadian provinces, and chief cities will be found under their own alphabetically arranged headings.

ECONOMICS, BUSINESS, AND INDUSTRY

Advertising	73	Fashion	212	Labor	285
Agriculture	81	Food	217	Mining	339
Automobiles	112	Foreign Aid	220	Publishing	415
Banking	114	Housing	244	Stocks and Bonds	482
Consumerism	171	Industrial Review	257	Taxation	488
Economy, U. S.	185	Insurance	260	Telecommunications	490
Energy	195	Interior Design	261	Transportation	508
Engineering, Civil	201	International Trade and Finance	263	Travel	515

GOVERNMENT, LAW, AND POLITICS

Censorship	151	Disarmament and Arms Control	183	Postal Service	409
Civil Liberties and Civil Rights	166	Law	292	Prisons	410
Crime	172	Military Forces	335	United Nations	525
				U. S.: The Carter Cabinet	534

HUMAN WELFARE

Cities and Urban Affairs	163	Ethnic Groups	208	Religion	424
Environment	203	Older Population	390	Social Welfare	435
		Population	407	Women	553

HUMANITIES, ARTS, AND HOBBIES

Architecture	95	Gardening and Horticulture	225	Photography	400
Art	102	Libraries	297	Recordings	421
Canada: Culture	147	Literature	300	Sports	449
Coin Collecting	167	Motion Pictures	347	Stamp Collecting	481
Dance	179	Music	353	Television and Radio	491
Education	190			Theater	500

SCIENCE AND MEDICINE

Anthropology	91	Drug Addiction and Abuse	184	Microbiology	331
Archaeology	92	Genetics	226	Oceanography	386
Astronomy	108	Geology	227	Physics	403
Biochemistry	117	Marine Biology	317	Polar Research	406
Botany	134	Medicine	320	Space Exploration	442
Chemistry	154	Meteorology	325	Zoology	559

MISCELLANEOUS

Accidents and Disasters	72	Obituaries	372	Prizes and Awards	412
Biography	118				

SPECIAL REPORTS

Canada: The Inuit	146
Cuba's New International Role	176
Economy, U. S.: Economic Thought—1976	188
Environment: The UN Conference on Human Settlement	205
Great Britain's War Against Inflation	239
Medicine: The Swine Flu Vaccination	322
Publishing: The Daniel Schorr Case	417
Theater: Britain's New National Theatre	506
Transportation: The Concorde	510

CONTRIBUTORS

ADAMS, GEORGE, Formerly, Legislative Reference Librarian, Connecticut State Library: CONNECTICUT

ADRIAN, CHARLES R., Professor of Political Science, University of California, Riverside: CALIFORNIA; LOS ANGELES

ALEXANDER, ROBERT J., Professor of Economics, Rutgers University: ECUADOR; GUYANA; URUGUAY

ALLER, LAWRENCE H., Professor of Astronomy, University of California, Los Angeles; Author, *Atoms, Stars, and Nebulae; Abundance of the Elements; Nuclear Transformations, Stellar Interiors and Nebulae:* ASTRONOMY

AMBRE, AGO, Economist, Bureau of Economic Analysis, U. S. Department of Commerce: INDUSTRIAL REVIEW

AMERASINGHE, H. SHIRLEY, Ambassador of Sri Lanka to the United Nations: UNITED NATIONS CONFERENCE ON THE LAW OF THE SEA—*Responsibilities of the Conference*

AMSPOKER, JOANNE, Professor of History, Oregon College of Education: OREGON

ANDREWS, JAMES, Department of Oceanography and Hawaii Institute of Geophysics, University of Hawaii: UNITED NATIONS CONFERENCE ON THE LAW OF THE SEA—*The First Committee*

BALLINGER, RONALD B., Professor of History, Rhode Island University: BIOGRAPHY—*Ian Smith, B. J. Vorster;* RHODESIA; SOUTH AFRICA

BANKS, RONALD F., Professor of History, University of Maine, Orono: MAINE

BECK, KAY, School of Urban Life, Georgia State University: GEORGIA

BENEDICT, BURTON, Professor of Anthropology, University of California, Berkeley; Author, *Indians in a Plural Society, Mauritius: Problems of a Plural Society,* and *People of Seychelles:* SEYCHELLES

BERGEN, DANIEL P., Professor, Graduate Library School, University of Rhode Island: LIBRARIES

BEST, JOHN, Chief, *Canada World News,* Ottawa: NEW BRUNSWICK; PRINCE EDWARD ISLAND

BISSELL, RICHARD E., Research Associate, Foreign Policy Research Institute; Managing Editor, *Orbis:* AFRICA

BITTON, LIVIA E., Associate Professor, Department of Classical and Oriental Languages, Herbert H. Lehman College, City University of New York: RELIGION—*Judaism*

BLACK, EUGENE R., Consultant to the Board of Directors, American Express Company; Author, *The Diplomacy of Economic Development, Alternative in Southeast Asia:* MULTINATIONAL BUSINESS ETHICS

BLACK, KENNETH, JR., Regents Professor of Insurance, Georgia State University; Coauthor, *Life Insurance* and *Property and Liability Insurance:* INSURANCE

BLANCHARD, LLOYD G., Editor, Polar Information Section, Division of Polar Programs, National Science Foundation: POLAR RESEARCH

BLOODSWORTH, DAVID R., Assistant Director, Labor Relations and Research Center, University of Massachusetts: POSTAL SERVICE

BÖDVARSSON, HAUKUR, Editorial Assistant, *Iceland Review:* ICELAND

BOLUS, JIM, Sports writer, *The Courier-Journal;* Author, *Run for the Roses:* SPORTS—*Horse Racing*

BOND, DONOVAN R., Professor of Journalism, West Virginia University: WEST VIRGINIA

BOULAY, HARVEY, Assistant Professor of Political Science, Boston University: BOSTON; MASSACHUSETTS

BOVEY, JOHN A., Provincial Archivist of Manitoba: MANITOBA

BOWERS, Q. DAVID, Columnist, *Coin World;* Author, *Collecting Rare Coins for Profit, Coins and Collectors,* and *High Profits from Rare Coin Investment:* COIN COLLECTING

BRADDOCK, BILL, Sports Department, *The New York Times:* BIOGRAPHY—*Julius Erving, Rosi Mittermaier;* SPORTS—*Basketball, Boxing, Football, Golf, Sailing, Swimming, Track and Field, Summary*

BRADFORD, JANE, Assistant Producer, CBS News: THE QUICK FOOD CHAINS

BRAMMER, DANA B., Associate Director, Bureau of Governmental Research, University of Mississippi: MISSISSIPPI

BREWERTON, DAVID, *The Daily Telegraph,* London: LONDON

BRODIN, PIERRE E., Director of Studies, Lycée Français de New York: LITERATURE—*French*

BROEG, ROBERT, Sports Editor, *St. Louis Post-Dispatch:* SPORTS—*Baseball*

BURKS, ARDATH W., Associate Vice President for Academic Affairs and Professor of Political Science, Rutgers University: JAPAN

BURLINGAME, MERRILL G., Professor of History, Montana State University; Author, *The Montana Frontier;* Coauthor, *A History of Montana:* MONTANA

BUSH, G. W. A., Senior Lecturer in Political Science, University of Auckland: NEW ZEALAND

BUSTIN, EDOUARD, Professor of Political Science, Boston University; Author, *Luanda Under Belgian Rule: The Politics of Ethnicity:* ANGOLA; GUINEA-BISSAU; MOZAMBIQUE; ZAIRE

BUTWELL, RICHARD, Dean for Arts and Sciences and Professor of Political Science, State University of New York at Fredonia; Author, *Southeast Asia: A Political Introduction, U Nu of Burma,* and *Southeast Asia Today and Tomorrow:* BURMA; CAMBODIA; LAOS; PHILIPPINES; VIETNAM

CAIRNS, JOHN C., Professor of History, University of Toronto: FRANCE

CAMMACK, PAUL, St. Antony's College, Oxford: BOLIVIA

CANN, STANLEY, Consultant, *The Forum,* Fargo: North Dakota

CHALMERS, J. W., Faculty of Education, University of Alberta: ALBERTA

CHARNOCK, HENRY, Director, Institute of Oceanographic Sciences, England: UNITED NATIONS CONFERENCE ON THE LAW OF THE SEA—*The Third Committee*

CHILDS, MARQUIS W., Contributing Editor, *St. Louis Post-Dispatch;* author of several books, including *Washington Calling; This is Democracy;* editor, *Witness to Power;* coeditor, *Walter Lippmann and His Times:* U. S. PRESIDENTIAL ELECTION

CHRIEN, ROBERT E., Senior Physicist, Brookhaven National Laboratory: ENERGY—*Nuclear*

CLARK, LOIS CARTER, Freelance writer and resident of Oklahoma City; Former teacher, Oklahoma City Public Schools: OKLAHOMA

COCKRUM, E. LENDELL, Professor, Department of Ecology and Evolutionary Biology, University of Arizona: ZOOLOGY

COHEN, SIDNEY, Clinical Professor of Psychiatry, University of California, Los Angeles; Author, *The Drug Dilemma, The Beyond Within: The LSD Story:* DRUG ADDICTION AND ABUSE

COLE, CAROLYN J., Assistant Vice President, Research, Paine, Webber, Jackson & Curtis, Inc.: STOCKS AND BONDS

COLLINS, ROBERT J., Sports Editor, *The Indianapolis Star;* Author, *The Best of Bob Collins, Boilermakers: The Story of Purdue Football;* Coauthor, *What's It Like Out There?:* SPORTS—*Auto Racing*

CONRAD, ED, *The Gazette,* Montreal: SPORTS: *The Summer Olympics; Hockey*

COPPAGE, NOEL, Contributing Editor, *Stereo Review:* MUSIC —*Popular;* RECORDINGS—*Popular*

CORLEW, ROBERT E., Chairman, Department of History, Middle Tennessee State University: TENNESSEE

CORNWELL, ELMER E., JR., Professor of Political Science, Brown University: RHODE ISLAND

CRAWFORD, MALCOLM, Economics Editor, *Sunday Times,* London: GREAT BRITAIN: *War Against Inflation*

CURTIS, L. PERRY, JR., Professor of History, Brown University: IRELAND

DANIELS, ROBERT V., Professor of History, University of Vermont: VERMONT

DARBY, JOSEPH W., III, Assistant City Editor, *The Times-Picayune,* New Orleans: LOUISIANA

DAVIS, WILLIAM A., Travel Editor, *Boston Globe:* TRAVEL

DELZELL, CHARLES F., Professor of History, Vanderbilt University: BIOGRAPHY—*Enrico Berlinguer;* ITALY

DOBLER, CLIFFORD, Professor of Business Law, University of Idaho: IDAHO

DOLAN, PAUL, Professor of Political Science, University of Delaware; Author, *Government and Administration of Delaware:* DELAWARE

DORPALEN, ANDREAS, Professor of History, The Ohio State University: GERMANY

DOUGLAS, CARLYLE, Formerly, Associate Editor, *Ebony Magazine:* OBITUARIES—*Paul Robeson*

DRACHKOVITCH, MILORAD M., Senior Fellow, The Hoover Institution, Stanford University: YUGOSLAVIA

DRIGGS, DON W., Chairman, Department of Political Science, University of Nevada, Reno: NEVADA

DUFF, ERNEST A., Professor of Political Science, Randolph-Macon Woman's College; Author, *Agrarian Reform in Colombia, Violence and Repression in Latin America:* COLOMBIA

DURRENCE, J. LARRY, Department of History, Florida Southern College: FLORIDA

ELGIN, RICHARD, Editorial Writer, *The Patriot-News,* Harrisburg: PENNSYLVANIA

ELKINS, ANN, Fashion Director, *Good Housekeeping Magazine:* FASHION

EL-MALLAKH, RAGAEI, Professor of Economics, University of Colorado; Author, *Energy and Development, Economic Development and Regional Cooperation: Kuwait:* ENERGY —*Survey, Natural Gas*

ETCHESON, WARREN W., Associate Dean, Graduate School of Business Administration, University of Washington: WASHINGTON

EWEGEN, BOB, Staff Writer, *The Denver Post:* COLORADO

FENNELL, LEE C., Associate Professor of Political Science, University of the Pacific: BIOGRAPHY—*Jorge Videla*

FISHER, PAUL, Director, Freedom of Information Center, University of Missouri: CENSORSHIP

FOLEJEWSKI, ZBIGNIEW, Professor and Chairman, Department of Slavic Studies and Modern Languages, University of Ottawa: LITERATURE—*Soviet*

FRANC, HELEN M., Formerly, Editor-in-Chief of Publications, The Museum of Modern Art; Author, *An Invitation to See: 125 Paintings from The Museum of Modern Art;* Coauthor, *Bright Stars: American Painting and Sculpture Since 1776:* OBITUARIES—*Alexander Calder*

FRIDLEY, RUSSELL W., Director, Minnesota Historical Society; Author, *The Uses of State and Local History, Minnesota: A Student's Guide to Localized History:* MINNESOTA

FRIIS, ERIK J., Editor and Publisher, *The Scandinavian-American Bulletin;* Author, *The American-Scandinavian Foundation 1910–1960: A Brief History;* Editor, *The Scandinavian Presence in North America;* Co-editor, *Scandinavian Studies:* DENMARK; FINLAND

FURIE, KENNETH A., Music Editor, *High Fidelity Magazine:* MUSIC—*Classical;* RECORDINGS—*Classical*

GAILEY, HARRY A., Professor of History, San Jose State University: NIGERIA

GEIS, GILBERT, Professor, Program in Social Ecology, University of California, Irvine; Author, *Man, Crime, and Society:* CRIME

GELMAN, DAVID, General Editor, Media, *Newsweek* Magazine: PUBLISHING—*Daniel Schorr Case*

GJESTER, THOR, Editor, *Economic Review,* Oslo: NORWAY

GLANVILLE, BRIAN, Soccer Columnist, *Sunday Times,* London: SPORTS—*Soccer*

GOODMAN, DONALD, John Jay College of Criminal Justice, City University of New York: PRISONS

GORDON, MAYNARD M., Editor, *Motor News Analysis:* AUTOMOBILES

GOUGH, BARRY M., Associate Professor of History, Wilfrid Laurier University, Ontario; Author, *Royal Navy and the Northwest Coast, To the Arctic and Pacific with Beechey,* and *Canada:* BIOGRAPHY—*Joseph Clark;* CANADA—*National and International Affairs*

GRAYSON, GEORGE W., Associate Professor of Government, College of William and Mary: BIOGRAPHY—*Mario Soares, Adolfo Suárez González;* PORTUGAL; SPAIN

GRIGG, JOHN, Political Journalist and Author; Author, *Two Anglican Essays* and *The Young Lloyd George:* MONARCHIES: A NEW LEASE ON LIFE?

GROTH, ALEXANDER J., Professor of Political Science, University of California, Davis; Coauthor, *Contemporary Politics: Europe:* POLAND

GRUBERG, MARTIN, Professor of Political Science, University of Wisconsin, Oshkosh; Author, *Women in American Politics:* CIVIL LIBERTIES AND CIVIL RIGHTS

GULICK, LEWIS, Staff Consultant, U. S. House of Representatives International Relations Committee: FOREIGN AID

GUNN, JOHN M., Formerly, Professor of Radio-TV-Film, State University of New York at Albany: TELEVISION AND RADIO

HAKES, JAY E., Associate Professor of Political Science, University of New Orleans: KENYA

HAND, SAMUEL B., Professor of History, University of Vermont: VERMONT

HANNA, WILLIAM J., Professor of Electrical Engineering, University of Colorado: ENERGY—*Electricity*

HARVEY, ROSS M., Assistant Director, Department of Information, Government of the Northwest Territories: NORTHWEST TERRITORIES

HAYDEN, DOROTHY, Prairie History Room, Regina Public Library, Sask.: SASKATCHEWAN

HAYES, KIRBY M., Professor of Food Science and Nutrition, University of Massachusetts: FOOD

HEAD, HOWARD T., Partner, A. D. Ring & Associates, Consulting Radio Engineers: TELEVISION AND RADIO—*Engineering*

HELMREICH, E. C., Thomas B. Reed Professor of History and Political Science, Bowdoin College: AUSTRIA

HELMREICH, PAUL C., Professor of History, Wheaton College, Norton, Mass.: SWITZERLAND

HELMS, ANDREA R. C., Associate Professor of Political Science, University of Alaska: ALASKA

HERBERT, WALTER B., Consultant on Canadian Cultural Matters; Fellow of the Royal Society of Arts: CANADA— *Cultural Affairs*

HERSHEY, ROBERT D., JR., Washington Correspondent, *The New York Times:* BANKING

HERSHKOWITZ, LEO, Professor of History, Queens College, City University of New York; NEW YORK; NEW YORK CITY

HINTON, HAROLD C., Professor of Political Science and International Affairs, George Washington University; Author, *Communist China in World Politics; An Introduction to Chinese Politics; Three and a Half Powers: The New Balance in Asia:* BIOGRAPHY—*Hua Kuo-feng;* OBITUARIES—*Chou En-lai*

HODGES, RALPH W., Associate Technical Editor, *Stereo Review:* RECORDINGS—*Audio Equipment and Techniques*

HOGGART, SIMON, Political Correspondent, *The Guardian,* Manchester: BIOGRAPHY—*James Callaghan;* GREAT BRITAIN

HOOVER, HERBERT T., Professor of History, The University of South Dakota; Author, *To Be An Indian, The Chitimacha People:* SOUTH DAKOTA

HOPKO, THOMAS, St. Vladimir's Orthodox Theological Seminary: RELIGION—*Orthodox Eastern Church*

HOPSON, JANET L., Biology/Chemistry Editor, *Science News* Magazine: BIOCHEMISTRY

HOTTELET, RICHARD C., United Nations Correspondent, CBS News: OBITUARIES—*Mao Tse-tung*

HOWARD, HARRY N., Board of Governors, Middle East Institute: TURKEY

HUTH, JOHN F., JR., Reporter-Columnist, *The Plain Dealer,* Cleveland: OHIO

IMPERATO, PASCAL J., First Deputy Commissioner, New York City Department of Health; Assistant Clinical Professor, Departments of Medicine and Public Health, Cornell University Medical College; Author, *The Treatment and Control of Infectious Diseases in Man* and *What To Do About the Flu:* MEDICINE—*The Swine Flu Vaccination*

JACOBSON, JON L., Professor of Law and Director of the Ocean Resources Law Program, University of Oregon; Coauthor, *The Future of International Fisheries Management:* THE UNITED NATIONS CONFERENCE ON THE LAW OF THE SEA—*The Second Committee*

JAFFE, HERMAN J., Department of Anthropology, Brooklyn College, City University of New York: ANTHROPOLOGY

JARVIS, ERIC, Department of History, University of Western Ontario: TORONTO

JEWELL, MALCOLM E., Professor of Political Science, University of Kentucky; Coauthor, *Kentucky Politics, The Legislative Process in the United States:* KENTUCKY

JOHNSON, LINDA, Acting Territorial Archivist of the Yukon Territory: YUKON TERRITORY

JOHNSON, WILLIAM OSCAR, Senior Writer, *Sports Illustrated:* SPORTS—*The Winter Olympics*

JOHNSTONE, J. K., Professor of English, University of Saskatchewan; Fellow of the Royal Society of Literature; Author, *The Bloomsbury Group: A Study of E. M. Forster, Lytton Strachey, Virginia Woolf, and Their Circle:* LITERATURE—*English*

JONES, H. G., Curator, North Carolina Collection, University of North Carolina Library: NORTH CAROLINA

KARSKI, JAN, Professor of Government, School of Foreign Affairs, Georgetown University: BULGARIA; HUNGARY

KATZ, EUGENE R., Associate Professor of Biology, State University of New York at Stony Brook: GENETICS

KEHR, ERNEST A., President, Philatelic Press Club: STAMP COLLECTING

KELLER, EUGENIA, Managing Editor, *Chemistry* Magazine: CHEMISTRY

KENNEDY, ROBERT E., JR., Associate Professor, Department of Sociology, University of Minnesota; Author, *The Irish: Emigration, Marriage and Fertility:* POPULATION

KIMBALL, LORENZO K., Chairman, Department of Political Science, University of Utah: UTAH

KIMBELL, CHARLES L., Physical Scientist, Office of Technical Data Services, United States Bureau of Mines: MINING

KING, PETER J., Associate Professor of History, Carleton University: ONTARIO; OTTAWA

KLAUSLER, ALFRED P., Editor at Large, *Christian Century:* RELIGION—*Protestantism*

KNERR, CHARLES R., Department of Public Administration, University of Texas, Arlington: TAXATION

KOLLEGGER, JAMES G., President and Publisher, Environment Information Center, Inc.: ENVIRONMENT

KOSAKI, RICHARD H., Professor of Political Science, University of Hawaii at Manoa: HAWAII

KRANGLE, KARENN, Reporter, *The Vancouver Sun:* ENVIRONMENT—*The UN Conference on Human Settlement*

LAI, CHUEN-YAN DAVID, Associate Professor of Geography, University of Victoria, B. C.: HONG KONG

LANDSBERG, H. E., Professor Emeritus, University of Maryland: METEOROLOGY

LARSEN, WILLIAM, Professor of History, Redford College; Author, *Montague of Virginia, The Making of a Southern Progressive:* VIRGINIA

LAURENT, PIERRE-HENRI, Department of History, Tufts University: BELGIUM

LAWRENCE, ROBERT M., Professor, Department of Political Science, Colorado State University: DISARMAMENT; MILITARY FORCES

LEE, STEWART M., Professor and Chairman, Department of Economics and Business Administration, Geneva College; Coauthor, *Economics for Consumers:* CONSUMERISM

LEIDEN, CARL, Professor of Government, University of Texas at Austin: BANGLADESH; EGYPT; PAKISTAN; THAILAND

LEVIN, RUBEN, Editor, *Labor* Newspaper: LABOR

LEVITT, MORRIS J., Professor, Department of Political Science, Howard University; Coauthor, *State and Local Government and Politics:* WASHINGTON, D. C.

LINDAHL, MAC, Harvard University: BIOGRAPHY—*Thorbjörn Fälldin, Carl XVI Gustaf;* SWEDEN

LLOYD, ROBERT M., Director of Management Services, South Carolina Appalachian Council of Governments: CITIES AND URBAN AFFAIRS

LOBRON, BARBARA, Journalist, Editor, Photographer: PHOTOGRAPHY

LONSFORD, MIKE, *The Houston Chronicle:* HOUSTON; TEXAS

LOTT, LEO B., Professor of Political Science, University of Montana; Author, *Venezuela and Paraguay: Political Modernity and Tradition in Conflict:* PARAGUAY; VENEZUELA

MABRY, DONALD J., Associate Professor of History, Mississippi State University: BIOGRAPHY—*José López Portillo;* MEXICO

MACAULAY, NEILL, Professor of History, University of Florida; Author, *The Prestes Column:* BRAZIL; LATIN AMERICA

MANDEL, RUTH B., Director, Center for the American Woman & Politics, Eagleton Institute of Politics, Rutgers University: WOMEN

MANSFIELD, MIKE, United States Senator from Montana: THE BICENTENNIAL—*A Time for Reflection*

MARGOLIS, JOSEPH, Editor, *African Update,* African-American Institute: ALGERIA; MOROCCO; SUDAN; TUNISIA

MATTHEWS, JOHN R., JR., Professor of Economics, College of William and Mary: ECONOMY—*Economic Thought; International Trade and Finance*

McCORQUODALE, SUSAN, Associate Professor, Department of Political Science, Memorial University of Newfoundland: NEWFOUNDLAND

McGILL, DAVID A., Professor of Ocean Science, U. S. Coast Guard Academy: OCEANOGRAPHY

MARCOPOULOS, GEORGE J., Associate Professor of History, Tufts University: CYPRUS; GREECE

MATHEWS, THOMAS G., Professor, Institute of Caribbean Studies, University of Puerto Rico: CARIBBEAN; PUERTO RICO; VIRGIN ISLANDS, U. S.

MESSNER, STEPHEN D., Head, Department of Finance and Director, Center for Real Estate and Urban Economic Studies, School of Business Administration, University of Connecticut; Author, *Effective Business Relocation, Industrial Real Estate, Marketing Investment Real Estate: Finance, Taxation, Techniques:* HOUSING

MEYER, EDWARD H., President and Chairman of the Board, Grey Advertising Inc.: ADVERTISING

MEYER, RALPH C., Associate Professor of Political Science, Fordham University at Lincoln Center: ASIA

MILLER, LUTHER S., Editor, *Railway Age:* TRANSPORTATION—*Railroads*

MITCHELL, GARY, Professor of Physics, North Carolina State University at Raleigh: PHYSICS

MOORE, CHARLES W., Professor of Architecture, University of California, Los Angeles; Coauthor, *The Place of Houses:* ARCHITECTURE

MURPHY, OWEN J., JR., Editor, *The Catholic Free Press,* Worcester, Massachusetts: RELIGION—*Roman Catholicism*

MURPHY, THOMAS, Author, *Urban Politics in the Suburban Era, The Politics of Congressional Committees, The New Politics Congress:* MARYLAND

NEILL, R. F., Associate Professor of Economics, St. Patrick's College, Carleton University: CANADA—*The Economy*

NEWSOM, DONALD W., Professor and Head, Department of Horticulture, Louisiana State University: BOTANY; GARDENING AND HORTICULTURE

NIENABER, JEANNE, Assistant Professor, Department of Political Science, University of Arizona; Coauthor, *The Budgeting and Evaluation of Federal Recreation Programs:* ARIZONA

NOLAN, WILLIAM C., Associate Professor of Political Science, Southern State College: ARKANSAS

NORRIS, DAVID, Journalist, *The Sunday Telegraph,* London: THEATER—*Britain's National Theatre*

O'BARR, JEAN, Lecturer, Department of Political Science, Duke University; Author, *Cell Leaders in Tanzania, Language and Politics:* TANZANIA; UGANDA

OCHSENWALD, WILLIAM L., Professor, Department of History, Virginia Polytechnic Institute and State University: SAUDI ARABIA

OTT, MARVIN C., Assistant Professor of Political Science, Mount Holyoke College: INDONESIA; MALAYSIA; SINGAPORE

PALMER, NORMAN D., Professor of Political Science and South Asian Studies, University of Pennsylvania: INDIA; SRI LANKA

PANO, NICHOLAS C., Associate Professor of History, Western Illinois University: ALBANIA

PARKER, FRANKLIN, Benedum Professor of Education, West Virginia University; Author, *George Peabody, A Biography, Battle of the Books: Textbook Censorship, Kanawha County, W. Va., 1974–75, Who Controls the Schools;* Co-editor, series on *American Dissertations on Foreign Education; A Bibliography with Abstracts:* EDUCATION

PEARCE, JOHN B., Director, Ecosystems Investigation, Sandy Hook Laboratory, National Oceanic and Atmospheric Administration: MARINE BIOLOGY

PEARSON, NEALE J., Associate Professor of Government, Texas Tech University: CHILE; PERU

PERKINS, KENNETH J., Assistant Professor of History, University of South Carolina: LIBYA; RELIGION—*Islam*

PERRY, HARRY, Private Consultant, Resources for the Future, Inc: ENERGY—*Coal*

PHEBUS, GEORGE E., Supervisor, Processing Laboratory, Department of Anthropology, National Museum of Natural History, Smithsonian Institution: ARCHAEOLOGY—*North America*

PHILLIPS, JACKSON, Executive Vice President, Moody's Investors Service, Inc.: ECONOMY, U. S.

PIPPIN, LARRY L., Professor of Political Science, Elbert Covell College, University of the Pacific: ARGENTINA; PANAMA

PLATT, HERMANN K., Associate Professor of History, St. Peter's College, Jersey City: NEW JERSEY

PLISCHKE, ELMER, Professor of Government and Politics, University of Maryland; Author, *Conduct of American Diplomacy, American Government: Basic Documents and Materials,* and *International Relations: Basic Documents:* UNITED STATES—*Foreign Affairs*

POLK, IRWIN J., Director of Children's Allergy Service, St. Luke's Hospital, New York City, Freelance Medical Writer: MEDICINE

POPKIN, HENRY, Professor of English, State University of New York at Buffalo: THEATER

PORTER, J. R., Professor and Chairman, Department of Microbiology, College of Medicine, University of Iowa: MICROBIOLOGY

POULLADA, LEON B., Professor of Political Science, Northern Arizona University; Fulbright Professor in Afghanistan, 1976–77; Author, *Reform and Rebellion in Afghanistan:* AFGHANISTAN

PRICHETT, C. HERMAN, Professor of Political Science, University of California, Santa Barbara: LAW

PUMPHREY, RALPH E., Professor of Social Work, Washington University, St. Louis; Co-editor, *The Heritage of American Social Work:* OLDER POPULATION; SOCIAL WELFARE

QUIRK, WILLIAM H., North American Editor, *Construction Industry International* Magazine: ENGINEERING, CIVIL

RAGUSA, ISA, Research Art Historian, Department of Art and Archaeology, Princeton University: ART

RAYMOND, ELLSWORTH L., Professor of Politics, New York University; Author, *Soviet Economic Progress* and *The Soviet State:* UNION OF SOVIET SOCIALIST REPUBLICS

RICARD, FRANÇOIS, Associate Professor, Department of French Language and Literature, McGill University: LITERATURE—*Canadian Literature in French*

RICHARD, JOHN B., Department of Political Science, University of Wyoming; Author, *Government and Politics of Wyoming:* WYOMING

RICHMOND, ROBERT W., State Archivist, Kansas State Historical Society; Author, *Kansas: A Land of Contrasts:* KANSAS

RODRIGUEZ, ALFRED, Professor of Romance Languages, University of New Mexico: LITERATURE—*Spanish*

ROMAN, JAMES R., JR., President, Lynn Machine and Tool Co.; Associate Professor of Business Administration, The George Washington University: TRANSPORTATION—*Survey, Highways, Mass Transit, Shipping*

ROSE, ERNST, Author, *A History of German Literature;* Professor Emeritus, New York University: LITERATURE—*German*

ROSS, KENNETH O., Editorial writer, *Chicago Tribune:* CHICAGO; ILLINOIS

ROSS, RUSSELL M., Professor of Political Science, University of Iowa: IOWA

ROWLETT, RALPH M., Professor of Anthropology, University of Missouri, Columbia: ARCHAEOLOGY—*Africa, Asia, Australia, Europe*

RUFF, NORMAN J., Assistant Professor of Political Science, University of Victoria, British Columbia: BRITISH COLUMBIA

SADLER, LOUIS R., Associate Professor of History, New Mexico State University: CENTRAL AMERICA; CUBA

SALSINI, PAUL, State Editor, *The Milwaukee Journal:* WISCONSIN

SANDER, GORDON F., Specialist in Benelux Affairs; Contributor to *The New York Times:* LUXEMBOURG; NETHERLANDS

SAVAGE, DAVID, Lecturer, Department of English, Simon Fraser University: LITERATURE—*Canadian Literature in English*

SCHNEIDERMAN, RONALD A., Editor, *Consumer Electronics Daily:* TELECOMMUNICATIONS

SCHWAB, PETER, Associate Professor of Political Science, State University of New York at Purchase; Author, *Decision-Making in Ethiopia:* ETHIOPIA

SCOTT, EUGENE L., Publisher, *Tennis Week;* Author, *Tennis: Game of Motion:* BIOGRAPHY—*Björn Borg;* SPORTS—*Tennis*

SETH, R. P., Associate Professor, Mount Saint Vincent University, Halifax: NOVA SCOTIA

SHEILS, MERRILL M. L., General Editor, *Newsweek* Magazine: CURRENT STATUS OF THE THREE R'S

SHINN, RINN-SUP, Senior Research Scientist, Foreign Area Studies, The American University, Washington, D. C.; Coauthor, *Area Handbook for North Korea, Area Handbook for South Korea:* KOREA

SHOGAN, ROBERT, National Political Correspondent, Washington Bureau, *The Los Angeles Times;* Author, *A Question of Judgment: The Fortas Case and the Struggle for the Supreme Court:* BIOGRAPHY—*James Earl Carter, Robert Dole, Gerald R. Ford, Walter F. Mondale*

SIMMONS, MARC, Author, *New Mexico, A Bicentennial History, Spanish Government in New Mexico* and *The Little Lion of the Southwest:* NEW MEXICO

SIMS, JOHN F., United Press International: BIOGRAPHY—*Mikhail Baryshnikov, Natalia Makarova;* DANCE

SLOAN, HENRY S., Associate Editor, *Current Biography:* BIOGRAPHY—*H. S. Amerasinghe, Anne Armstrong, Saul Bellow, Sarah Caldwell, Barbara Jordan, James Slattin Martin, Jr., Barbara Walters, Robert Penn Warren;* OBITUARIES—*Howard Hughes*

SQUIRE, C. B., Contributing Editor, *International Oil News:* ENERGY—*Petroleum*

STACKS, JOHN F., Washington Correspondent, *Time* Magazine; Author, *Stripping: The Surface Mining of America:* UNITED STATES—*Domestic Affairs*

STERN, JEROME H., Associate Professor of English, Florida State University: LITERATURE—*American*

STOKES, W. LEE, Professor, Department of Geology and Geophysics, University of Utah; Author, *Essentials of Earth History;* Coauthor, *Introduction to Geology:* GEOLOGY

STOUDEMIRE, ROBERT H., Director, Bureau of Governmental Research, University of South Carolina: SOUTH CAROLINA

STRINGER, JERRY R., Information Officer, Polar Information Section, Division of Polar Programs, National Science Foundation: POLAR RESEARCH

SYLVESTER, LORNA LUTES, Associate Editor, *Indiana Magazine of History,* Indiana University: INDIANA

TABORSKY, EDWARD, Professor of Government, University of Texas at Austin; Author, *Communist Penetration of The Third World:* CZECHOSLOVAKIA

TAFT, WILLIAM H., Professor of Journalism and Director of Graduate Studies, University of Missouri, Columbia; Author, *American Journalism History:* PUBLISHING

TAN, CHESTER C., Professor of History, New York University; Author, *The Boxer Catastrophe* and *Chinese Political Thought in the Twentieth Century:* CHINA

TAYLOR, WILLIAM L., Associate Professor of History, Plymouth State College, Plymouth, New Hampshire: NEW HAMPSHIRE

THEISEN, CHARLES W., Staff Writer, *The Detroit News:* MICHIGAN

THOMAS, JAMES D., Professor of Political Science, Bureau of Public Administration, University of Alabama: ALABAMA

THOME, PITT G., Deputy Director for Earth Observations Flight Program, National Aeronautics and Space Administration: SPACE EXPLORATION

TURNER, ARTHUR CAMPBELL, Professor of Political Science, University of California, Riverside: IRAN; IRAQ; ISRAEL; MIDDLE EAST

VALESIO, PAOLO, Professor of Italian Linguistics, Yale University: LITERATURE—*Italian*

VLIET, GARY C., Associate Professor of Mechanical Engineering and Solar Energy Program Coordinator, Center for Energy Studies, University of Texas at Austin: ENERGY—*Solar*

VOLSKY, GEORGE, Center for Advanced International Studies, University of Miami: CUBA—*New International Role*

WALLOT, JEAN-PIERRE, Vice-Dean Academic, Faculty of Arts and Sciences, University of Montreal: MONTREAL; QUEBEC

WEBB, RICHARD E., Former Director, Reference and Library Division, British Information Services, New York: UNITED NATIONS

WEEKS, JEANNE G., Member, American Society of Interior Designers; Coauthor, *Fabrics for Interiors:* INTERIOR DESIGN

WELCH, CLAUDE E., JR., Professor of Political Science, State University of New York at Buffalo; Author, *Soldier and State in Africa: A Comparative Analysis of Military Intervention and Political Change:* GHANA

WENTZ, RICHARD E., Coordinator, Religious Studies Program, Arizona State University: RELIGION—*Survey, Far Eastern Religions*

WESTERN, JOE, Senior Editor, *The National Observer:* AGRICULTURE

WETMORE, WARREN C., Engineering Editor, *Aviation Week & Space Technology:* TRANSPORTATION—*Air, The Concorde*

WILLARD, F. NICHOLAS, Department of History, Georgetown University: JORDAN; LEBANON; SYRIA

WILLIAMS, DENNIS A., Associate Editor, *Newsweek* Magazine: ETHNIC GROUPS

WILLIS, F. ROY, Professor of History, University of California, Davis; Author, *The French in Germany, 1945–1949, France, Germany and the New Europe, 1945–1967,* and *Italy Chooses Europe:* EUROPE

WILLNOW, RONALD D., News Editor, *St. Louis Post-Dispatch:* MISSOURI

WILSON, ALAN, Chairman, Canadian Studies Program and Professor of History, Trent University, Peterborough, Ontario; Author, *John Northway, A Blue Serge Canadian, The Clergy Reserves of Upper Canada,* and *A Canadian Mortmain:* CANADA—*The Inuit*

WILSON, JOHN S., Jazz Critic, *The New York Times* and *High Fidelity* Magazine; Author, *Jazz: The Transition Years, 1940–1960:* RECORDINGS—*Jazz*

WOLF, WILLIAM, Film Critic, *Cue* Magazine; Former Chairman, New York Film Critics; Lecturer, New York University and St. John's University: MOTION PICTURES

WOODS, GEORGE A., Children's Books Editor, *The New York Times:* LITERATURE—*Children's*

YOSHIZAKI, HIROTAKA, Staff Reporter, Tokyo Bureau, *The New York Times:* TOKYO

YOUNGER, R. M., Author, *Australia and the Australians, Australia! Australia! The Pioneer Years, Australia's Great River:* AUSTRALIA; BIOGRAPHY—*Malcolm Fraser;* OCEANIA

YUDELL, ROBERT J., Urban Innovation Group, Los Angeles: ARCHITECTURE

ZABEL, ORVILLE H., Professor of History, Creighton University: NEBRASKA

ZACEK, JOSEPH F., Professor and Chairman of History, State University of New York at Albany: RUMANIA

PREFACE

Senator Mike Mansfield, who retired Jan. 3, 1977, after 24 years in office, 16 of them as majority leader, saw the 200th birthday year of the United States as a "time for contemplation and reflection," a time of looking backward with some pride, to be sure, but also a time to look forward, seeking renewal.

In the United States, the presidential election campaign that coincided with the national birthday brought a brand new face into the political arena. When the fireworks and the oratory were done, a man who had never before held federal office remained, stage center, to take the presidential oath. A former governor of Georgia, he had captured one of the world's toughest jobs by hard, long campaigning across the 50 states. With the simple introduction, "My name is Jimmy Carter and I'm running for president of the United States," the one-time naval officer unhesitatingly emphasized his newness, his freedom of Washington connection. Americans in sufficient number liked the approach and accepted the man.

Queen Elizabeth II used the occasion of her after-dinner remarks to the guests gathered in the White House Rose Garden on July 7 to observe that "interdependence is a feature of the modern world, a world that has become smaller, yet more complex. Today no nation can stand alone. We depend, as never before, upon each other. . . . We live in times of uncertainty, even of apprehension, and with forces that we cannot allow to escape from our control."

Events elsewhere bore witness to a wide concurrence in these beliefs. On the continent of Africa the winds of change seemed at last to be strong enough to move some of the most intractable adversaries into conference and the search for justice. Purposeful convening to promote cooperation and share experience took place in British Columbia, where the Habitat conference focused international attention on housing, and in Sri Lanka, where the nonaligned nations made it clear that their number one concern is economic: the uneven distribution of the world's wealth.

Renewal in its most mundane sense preoccupied the populations of places as far apart as Guatemala, northern Italy, Turkey, and China, where terrifying earth movements shook vast areas of the inhabited world into dust. In China the devastation coincided with the national search for new leaders, following the deaths of Chou En-lai and Mao Tse-tung.

Seeking answers to extraterrestrial questions is as old as man. With Viking 1 and 2 scientists moved a giant step closer to an understanding of Mars, but the nagging question of whether life exists on that planet continued to puzzle them. On earth, they showed more readiness not just to develop new technology, but to understand its impact on the quality of our life.

Thoughtful people, contemplating the business that many sports have become, felt uneasiness about the future. Could amateurs continue to test their excellence in olympic meets if the politicizing of the games continued unchecked? Could professional sports survive the players' growing demands for ransomlike salaries?

Accepting the Nobel Prize for Literature, Saul Bellow restated and expanded upon Senator Mansfield's theme: "Out of the struggle at the center has come an immense, painful longing for broader, more flexible, fuller, more coherent, more comprehensive account of what we human beings are, who we are, and what this life is for."

The pages that follow will, it is hoped, contribute to the fuller account.

WIDE WORLD

Queen Elizabeth II of Great Britain and her husband Prince Philip made an official visit to the United States in honor of its 200th birthday. A highlight of the trip was a televised state dinner at the White House. President and Mrs. Gerald R. Ford received the royal couple at the North Portico.

CHRONOLOGY 1976

JANUARY

CHOU EN-LAI DIES IN CHINA

STEELERS RETAIN NFL TITLE

CEASE-FIRE BEGINS IN LEBANON

S	M	T	W	T	F	S
				1	2	3
4	5	6	7	8	9	10
11	12	13	14	15	16	17
18	19	20	21	22	23	24
25	26	27	28	29	30	31

1 Venezuela formally nationalizes its oil industry.

7 In Italy, the cabinet of Prime Minister Aldo Moro resigns.

8 Chou En-lai, prime minister of China since the Communists assumed power on the mainland in 1949, dies.

11 In Ecuador, Guillermo Rodriguez Lara is removed as president in a peaceful military coup.

12 In Thailand, the coalition government of Prime Minister Kukrit Pramoj resigns. King Bhumibol Aduldej calls for national elections for April. ● In Norway, Odvar Nordli, who had been named to succeed Trygve Bratteli as premier, announces a new 12-member cabinet.

18 The Pittsburgh Steelers retain the National Football League title by defeating the Dallas Cowboys, 21–17, in the 10th Super Bowl game.

19 U.S. President Gerald R. Ford delivers the State of the Union address.

21 President Ford sends his budget for fiscal year 1977 to the U.S. Congress. A deficit of about $43 billion is estimated.

22 Lebanon's President Suleiman Franjieh announces an agreement ending the nation's nine-month civil war.

24 The United States and Spain sign a five-year Treaty of Friendship and Cooperation.

26 The United States vetoes a UN Security Council resolution establishing new conditions for negotiating a Middle East peace settlement.

28 Addressing a joint session of the U.S. Congress, Itzhak Rabin, prime minister of Israel, reaffirms his nation's willingness to negotiate with any Arab state but not with the Palestine Liberation Organization (PLO). ● In Spain, Prime Minister Carlos Arias Navarro outlines a plan to move toward a "Spanish democracy."

29 The U.S. House of Representatives votes to withhold the final report of the House Committee on Intelligence until it has been censored by the Executive Branch. ● Morocco announces that its military forces have defeated Algerian soldiers and members of the Algerian-backed Saharan independence movement following three days of fighting in the Spanish Sahara.

30 The U.S. Supreme Court upholds government financing of presidential campaigns and campaign contribution disclosure rules, but strikes down limits on political expenditures (except for presidential candidates accepting federal subsidies). Ceilings on political contributions are also upheld, but the Federal Election Committee is declared unconstitutional as presently organized.

UPI

A resident of the British colony of Hong Kong reads of the death of Chou En-lai. The Communist Chinese prime minister died in Peking on January 8.

FEBRUARY

S	M	T	W	T	F	S
1	2	3	4	5	6	7
8	9	10	11	12	13	14
15	16	17	18	19	20	21
22	23	24	25	26	27	28
29						

TRUDEAU TOURS LATIN AMERICA

CENTRAL AMERICA HIT BY QUAKE

WAR ENDS IN ANGOLA

2 Canada's Prime Minister Pierre Elliott Trudeau concludes a nine-day Latin American tour.

4 A major earthquake strikes Guatemala and Honduras, killing about 22,000 and injuring about 75,000 persons. ● U. S. Secretary of Transportation William T. Coleman, Jr., rules that Britain and France can fly the Concorde supersonic jet airliner to Washington, D. C., and New York on a limited 16-month trial basis.

5 Testifying before the U. S. Senate Banking Committee, James E. Smith, comptroller of the currency, declares that the national banking system is sound but that there are 28 national banks in financial trouble.

7 Communist China reveals that Hua Kuo-feng is appointed acting prime minister, succeeding the late Chou En-lai.

10 A one-party minority government is formed in Italy. Aldo Moro retains the prime ministership. ● President Ford signs a $112.3 billion defense appropriation bill, containing a ban on further aid to forces opposing Soviet and Cuban factions in Angola's civil war. ● W. J. Usery, Jr., is sworn in as U. S. secretary of labor, succeeding John T. Dunlop.

11 The Organization of African Unity recognizes the government proclaimed by the Popular Movement for the Liberation of Angola (MPLA) as the legiti-

mate government of Angola and admits the People's Republic of Angola as its 47th member. (Earlier the Soviet and Cuban-supported MPLA had captured several key Angolan cities.)

13 Following the assassination of Gen. Murtala Ramat Muhammed, Nigeria's chief of state since July 1975, in an unsuccessful coup attempt, Lt. Gen. Olusegun Obasanjo is named head of state.

15 In Innsbruck, Austria, the 12th Winter Olympic Games come to a close.

17 President Ford announces a widespread reorganization of the U. S. intelligence agencies.

22 Joseph C. Clark is named leader of Canada's Progressive Conservative party.

24 Soviet Party Chairman Leonid Brezhnev addresses the opening of the 25th Congress of the Soviet Communist party.

26 In Portugal, military and political leaders sign an agreement ending military rule and establishing a democratic system. ● Spain withdraws all Spanish officials from its former Spanish Saharan colony as Saharan representatives ratify the annexation of its territory by Morocco and Mauritania.

29 Former President and Mrs. Richard M. Nixon conclude an eight-day visit to Communist China.

UPI

A major earthquake struck Central America on February 4. At right, in Tecpán, Guatemala, a young boy guards his family's land; their home was destroyed.

MARCH

FIGHTING RENEWED IN LEBANON

HAROLD WILSON RESIGNS

MRS. PERON IS REMOVED IN COUP

S	M	T	W	T	F	S
	1	2	3	4	5	6
7	8	9	10	11	12	13
14	15	16	17	18	19	20
21	22	23	24	25	26	27
28	29	30	31			

4 Mike Mansfield (D-Mont.), U.S. Senate majority leader since 1961, announces that he will not seek reelection in November 1976.

5 The 78-seat Northern Ireland Convention, elected in May 1975 to arrange a peace settlement between Catholics and Protestants in the province, is dismissed. Britain's Secretary of State for Northern Ireland Merlyn Rees announces that Britain will govern Northern Ireland.

11 Eleven miners are killed in an explosion in a mine near Whitesburg, Ky. It is the second such explosion in the mine in three days; fifteen miners were killed in a blast on March 9.

15 William W. Scranton, former governor of Pennsylvania, is sworn in as U.S. representative to the United Nations, succeeding Daniel P. Moynihan who resigned.

16 Great Britain's Prime Minister Harold Wilson announces his resignation.

19 In Rhodesia, talks between the white minority government of Ian Smith and the African National Council (ANC) faction, headed by Joshua Nkomo, reach an "impasse" and are broken off. ● In Great Britain, a statement from Kensington Palace announces that Princess Margaret and her husband Lord Snowdon are separating.

20 Patricia C. Hearst is found guilty of armed robbery by a jury in San Francisco, Calif. ● The government of Thailand orders the United States to close its remaining military installations in Thailand and to withdraw its military personnel, excluding 270 military aid advisers, within four months.

24 The three commanders of Argentina's armed forces assume control of the government following the overthrow of President Isabel Martínez de Perón.

25 The United States vetoes a resolution in the UN Security Council deploring Israeli policies in Jerusalem and the occupied areas in the West Bank of the Jordan River. ● In Lebanon, a general offensive by Muslim military units forces President Suleiman Franjieh to vacate the presidential palace. (Heavy fighting between Lebanon's Christian and Muslim forces had broken out again earlier in March.)

29 Lt. Gen. Jorge Rafael Videla becomes the 39th president of Argentina; a cabinet of six military officers and two civilians is also sworn in. ● The University of Indiana wins the National Collegiate Association basketball championship.

30 Six Arabs are killed and some 70 persons are wounded as a general strike by Israeli Arab citizens turns into violent clashes with security forces.

In Argentina, the government of Isabel Martínez de Perón was overthrown by the military on March 24.
UPI

Following the coup, Lt. Gen. Jorge Videla was installed as the 39th president of Argentina on March 29.
UPI

APRIL

S	M	T	W	T	F	S
				1	2	3
4	5	6	7	8	9	10
11	12	13	14	15	16	17
18	19	20	21	22	23	24
25	26	27	28	29	30	

NEW BRITISH CABINET NAMED

HUA KUO-FENG CHOSEN IN CHINA

ELECTIONS OCCUR IN PORTUGAL

5 Great Britain's Foreign Secretary James Callaghan is elected to succeed Harold Wilson as leader of the Labour party and prime minister.

7 In China, Teng Hsiao-ping is deposed as deputy prime minister; Hua Kuo-feng is named prime minister and first deputy chairman of the Communist party.

8 Anthony Crosland is named as Great Britain's new foreign secretary.

9 Syrian troops begin moving into Lebanon as the Lebanese civil war continues.

11 Ray Floyd wins the 40th Masters Golf Tournament.

12 Communists, Syrian Baathists, and candidates sympathetic to the PLO sweep to victory in municipal elections on the Israeli-occupied West Bank.

14 Thomas S. Gates is sworn in as head of the U. S. liaison office in China. ● A new government is announced in Cambodia; Khieu Samphan is named chairman of the state presidium and Tol Saut is the new prime minister. ● Morocco and Mauritania sign an agreement dividing the disputed Spanish Sahara between themselves.

15 The Indian government announces that it is sending an ambassador to China for the first time in 15 years.

21 A nationwide strike by U. S. rubber workers begins. ● Representatives of Egypt and China sign a military protocol in Peking.

22 In Thailand, a four-party coalition government, headed by Seni Pramoj, is sworn in. The previous governing coalition of Premier Kukrit Pramoj was defeated in April 4 national elections.

23 U. S. Secretary of State Henry Kissinger begins a 12-day tour of 7 African nations.

25 In Portugal's first free parliamentary elections in half a century, the Socialists win a plurality. ● Voters in North and South Vietnam elect a joint National Assembly with no opposition members.

26 The U. S. Senate Select Committee on Intelligence Activities issues its report, proposing legislation outlining the "basic purposes" of U. S. intelligence agencies.

27 Pope Paul VI announces the appointment of 21 new members to the College of Cardinals.

28 The U. S. Department of Agriculture announces additional grain sales to the Soviet Union.

29 Dmitri F. Ustinov, a civilian, succeeds the late Andrei A. Grechko as Soviet minister of defense.

30 The Italian government of Aldo Moro resigns.

UPI

A new Labourite government took over in Britain in April: James Callaghan (*above*) is the new prime minister and Anthony Crosland is the foreign secretary.

UPI

MAY

GISCARD VISITS THE U.S.

NATO FOREIGN MINISTERS MEET

DISARMAMENT TREATY SIGNED

S	M	T	W	T	F	S
						1
2	3	4	5	6	7	8
9	10	11	12	13	14	15
16	17	18	19	20	21	22
23	24	25	26	27	28	29
30	31					

1 Bold Forbes wins the 102d running of the Kentucky Derby.

5 The British Treasury and the nation's trade union leadership agree to a new wage control policy. ● The U. S. Senate upholds President Ford's veto of a $125 million bill on child day care. ● Delegates from 153 nations assemble in Nairobi, Kenya, for the fourth UN Conference on Trade and Development.

6 A powerful earthquake strikes northeastern Italy, killing more than 900 persons.

8 Elias Sarkis, a conservative banker and civil servant, is elected president of Lebanon.

10 Jeremy Thorpe resigns as leader of Britain's Liberal party.

13 The New York Nets win the American Basketball Association title.

14 India and Pakistan agree to resume diplomatic relations (suspended since December 1971).

15 The Conference of Islamic States concludes its seventh annual meeting in Istanbul, Turkey.

16 The Montreal Canadiens capture hockey's Stanley Cup by defeating the Philadelphia Flyers, 4 games to 0.

18 Addressing a joint session of the U. S. Congress, French President Valéry Giscard d'Estaing urges the United States to "show the same confidence in us [West Europe] that we have in you."

19 Four days of violent anti-Israel riots by Arabs in the West Bank and Jerusalem come to an end; three Arabs are killed by Israeli soldiers during the disturbances.

21 In Martinez, Calif., a school bus on a bridge ramp smashes through a guard rail and plunges 30 feet (9 meters) to the ground, killing 28 members of a high school choir. ● A two-day meeting of 15 foreign ministers of the North Atlantic Treaty Organization ends in Oslo, Norway.

24 The Concorde, the British-French supersonic jet, begins trans-Atlantic passenger service to Washington. ● The U. S. Supreme Court rules that states cannot prevent pharmacists from advertising the prices of prescription drugs.

25 U.S. Rep. Wayne L. Hayes (D-Ohio) acknowledges that he has had a "personal relationship" with Elizabeth Ray, but denies her claim that she was paid $14,000 a year from public funds to be the Congressman's mistress.

28 The United States and the Soviet Union sign a treaty limiting the size of underground nuclear explosions detonated for peaceful purposes and calling for some on-site inspection.

29 Nadine Chaval, daughter of Belgium's ambassador to Mexico, is released in Mexico City after being held by kidnappers since May 25.

31 The UN Conference on Human Settlement or Habitat opens in Vancouver, B. C.

UPI

U. S. President Gerald R. Ford and French President Valéry Giscard d'Estaing confer in the White House Rose Garden on May 18. Later the French president addressed the U. S. Congress.

JUNE

S	M	T	W	T	F	S
		1	2	3	4	5
6	7	8	9	10	11	12
13	14	15	16	17	18	19
20	21	22	23	24	25	26
27	28	29	30			

U.S. ENVOY KILLED IN BEIRUT

BLACKS RIOT IN SOUTH AFRICA

COMMUNISTS GAIN IN ITALY

1 The foreign ministers of Iceland and Great Britain sign an interim agreement ending the "cod war," a dispute over fishing rights.

3 Egypt's Foreign Minister Ismail Fahmy condemns Syria's intervention in Lebanon's civil war.

5 Rep. Carl B. Albert (D-Okla.), speaker of the U. S. House of Representatives, announces his retirement at the end of the current session. ● In Idaho Falls, Idaho, a corner of the new Teton Dam collapses, killing at least 9 persons, leaving 30 missing, and forcing 40,000 to evacuate their homes.

6 The Boston Celtics win the National Basketball Association title, defeating the Phoenix Suns four games to two in the final play-offs.

7 The United States and a group of other industrialized nations agree to lend Great Britain $5,300,-000,000 to help bolster the pound.

12 In Uruguay, President Juan Maria Bordaberry is ousted by the military.

15 The Chinese government announces that Mao Tsetung will no longer receive foreign guests.

16 Francis E. Meloy, Jr., U. S. ambassador to Lebanon, Robert O. Waring, the embassy's economic counselor, and their driver are shot to death in Beirut.

19 Three days of the worst racial violence in South Africa's history come to an end; more than 100 persons, most of them black, are killed. The disturbance began as a protest against a government regulation requiring the use of Afrikaans as a teaching language in South African schools.

20 The U. S. Navy evacuates more than 250 Americans and other foreign nationals from Beirut.

22 Final results of Italy's parliamentary elections are released—the Christian Democrats remain the nation's largest party; the Communists gain an additional 49 seats in the Chamber of Deputies and 23 seats in the Senate.

23 In the UN Security Council, the United States vetoes Angola's application for UN membership.

24 The first session of the National Assembly of reunified Vietnam opens.

25 The Polish government cancels an announced plan to increase food prices, following major protests.

27 Gen. António Ramalho Eanes, Army chief of staff, is elected president of Portugal.

28 Concluding a two-day economic conference in San Juan, P. R., leaders of seven industrialized nations agree on a policy of sustained economic growth.

29 The Seychelles, a group of islands in the Indian Ocean, become an independent republic.

30 Leaders of 29 European Communist parties conclude a two-day conference in East Berlin.

UPI

The bodies of Francis Meloy, U. S. ambassador to Lebanon, and Robert Waring, economic counselor, arrive at Andrews Air Force Base, Md. The two officials were killed in Lebanon June 16.

JULY

ISRAEL RESCUES HOSTAGES

U.S. MARKS 200TH BIRTHDAY

DEMS NAME CARTER-MONDALE

S	M	T	W	T	F	S
				1	2	3
4	5	6	7	8	9	10
11	12	13	14	15	16	17
18	19	20	21	22	23	24
25	26	27	28	29	30	31

2 North Vietnam and South Vietnam are reunited officially, with Hanoi as the capital. ● By a 7–2 vote, the U.S. Supreme Court rules that capital punishment does not violate the Constitution's ban of cruel and unusual punishment.

3 Israeli commandos land at Entebbe Airport, Uganda, and free 91 passengers, mainly Israelis, and 12 crew members of an Air France plane hijacked by pro-Palestinian guerrillas June 27.

4 The United States marks its 200th birthday. ● José López Portillo is elected president of Mexico.

5 In Spain, Adolfo Suárez González is sworn in as prime minister, succeeding Carlos Arias Navarro.

6 The U.S.S.R. launches Soyuz 21, with Col. Boris Volynov and Lt. Col. Vitaly Zholobov aboard.

7 David Steel is elected leader of Great Britain's Liberal Party.

8 The Indonesian government announces that the death toll from an earthquake that struck West Irian Province on the island of New Guinea, causing landslides, has surpassed 9,000 persons.

14 In Uruguay, the ruling National Council names Aparicio Mendez president.

15 At the Democratic National Convention in New York City, former Georgia Gov. Jimmy Carter and Minnesota Sen. Walter F. Mondale accept the party's nominations for president and vice president, respectively.

16 In Canada, legislation limiting the use of capital punishment is enacted.

17 The Olympic Games open in Montreal.

20 The unmanned U.S. spacecraft Viking I lands on Mars and begins transmitting photos of the planet.

21 Britain's Ambassador to Ireland, Christopher T. E. Ewart-Biggs, is killed as a land mine explodes underneath his moving automobile.

23 The new Portuguese government of Prime Minister Mário Soares takes office. (Gen. Antonio R. Eanes had assumed the presidency on July 14.)

27 In Japan, former Prime Minister Kakuei Tanaka is arrested and charged with accepting funds that were brought into Japan illegally.

28 Two powerful earthquakes strike Peking, China, causing "great losses to people's lives and property." ● The British government severs diplomatic relations with Uganda.

29 By a vote of 381–3, the U.S. House of Representatives votes to reprimand Rep. Robert L. F. Sikes (D-Fla.) for financial misconduct.

30 In Italy, a new minority government, led by Giulio Andreotti as prime minister, is sworn in.

UPI

Lt. Gen. Mordechai Gur, Israel's chief of staff, uses a map to explain his nation's rescue of hostages at Entebbe Airport, Uganda.

AUGUST

S	M	T	W	T	F	S
1	2	3	4	5	6	7
8	9	10	11	12	13	14
15	16	17	18	19	20	21
22	23	24	25	26	27	28
29	30	31				

2 AMERICANS KILLED IN KOREA

GOP TICKET IS FORD AND DOLE

BRITAIN THIRSTS FOR RAIN

1 Thirty-eight U. S. citizens and their 11 Vietnamese dependents—about the last American in Vietnam—are permitted to leave Saigon.

7 Uganda's President Idi Amin and Kenya's President Jomo Kenyatta sign document promising to resume normal diplomatic relations, reduce the threat of war, and restore trade. ● The United States and Iran sign a pact calling for the sale of $10,000,000,000 worth of U. S. arms to Iran.

9 H. Guyford Stever is confirmed as director of the U. S. Office of Science and Technology Policy.

11 At Istanbul, Turkey, airport, pro-Palestinian guerrillas explode grenades and fire machine guns among passengers waiting to board an Israeli jetliner for Tel Aviv; 4 persons are killed and at least 30 are wounded.

12 An estimated 35–40 persons are killed following a week of rioting by blacks in South Africa.

16 Leaders of the nonaligned nations begin four-day conference in Colombo, Sri Lanka.

18 Two American military officers are killed and four American enlisted men and five South Korean soldiers are wounded during a clash with North Korean forces in the demilitarized zone.

19 At the Republican National Convention, Gerald Ford defeats former California Gov. Ronald Reagan for the presidential nomination and selects Sen. Robert Dole of Kansas as his running mate.

20 In Argentina, 46 persons are murdered, apparently by right-wing extremists in reprisal for the assassination of a retired Army general.

24 British Prime Minister Callaghan holds an emergency cabinet meeting to discuss the nation's worst drought on record.

25 France's Trade Minister Raymond Barre succeeds Jacques Chirac as the nation's premier.

26 Prince Bernhard of the Netherlands resigns almost all of his military and business posts after a three-man government commission concludes that the prince had allowed himself to be tempted to take unacceptable initiatives.

30 The report of a U. S. Senate subcommittee investigating Medicaid in eight cities terms the administration of the program "abysmal." ● La Soufrière volcano on the Caribbean island of Guadeloupe explodes. ● In London, England, more than 400 persons are injured during a riot at a West Indian fair.

31 William and Emily Harris are given "indeterminate sentences" after being convicted of armed robbery, kidnapping, and auto theft. ● The Mexican government allows the peso to float in world currency markets.

American and South Korean soldiers clash with North Korean forces in the demilitarized zone, August 18.
UPI

SEPTEMBER

MAO TSE-TUNG DIES IN PEKING

SOCIALISTS LOSE IN SWEDEN

FORD-CARTER DEBATE ISSUES

S	M	T	W	T	F	S
			1	2	3	4
5	6	7	8	9	10	11
12	13	14	15	16	17	18
19	20	21	22	23	24	25
26	27	28	29	30		

1 A state of emergency is declared in the Republic of Ireland so as to avoid a constitutional crisis over proposed legislation increasing prison sentences for members of the Irish Republican Army and convicted terrorists. ● In Uruguay, Aparicio Méndez is installed as president.

3 The lander of the Viking II spacecraft touches down on the planet Mars. ● In Barbados, J. M. G. Adams is sworn in as prime minister after his Barbados Labor Party won 17 of 24 seats in House of Assembly elections September 2.

4 President Ford announces that Clarence M. Kelley will maintain his post as director of the Federal Bureau of Investigation. On August 31, Kelley had admitted that some of his home furnishings had been provided by the FBI without charge and that he had received gifts from top aides.

6 The U. S.-led United Nations Command and North Korea agree to partition the joint security area at the Panmunjom truce site in the demilitarized zone. The accord is intended to avoid clashes. ● A Soviet Air Force lieutenant flies a Soviet MiG 25 to Japan and requests asylum in the United States.

9 Mao Tse-tung, chairman of the Chinese Communist Party, dies in Peking at the age of 82. ● An economic austerity program is announced in Portugal.

10 Following the resignation of Britain's Home Secretary Roy Jenkins, Prime Minister Callaghan reshuffles his cabinet.

12 Jimmy Connors wins the men's singles tennis title of the U. S. Open at Forest Hills, N. Y. Earlier, Chris Evert had captured the women's crown.

14 Canada's Prime Minister Trudeau announces a shake-up of his cabinet.

16 The Episcopal Church formally approves the ordination of women to the priesthood.

20 In Malta, final returns of September 17–18 elections give the Labor Party of Prime Minister Dominic Mintoff a three-seat margin in the 65-member House of Representatives. ● Sweden's Prime Minister Olof Palme resigns after his party is defeated in parliamentary elections.

21 H. S. Amerasinghe of Sri Lanka is elected president of the 31st session of the UN General Assembly.

23 Elias Sarkis is sworn in as the sixth president of Lebanon.

24 Rhodesia's Prime Minister Ian Smith accepts British-U. S. plan for transferring government's power to black majority rule.

U. S. presidential candidates Ford and Carter hold the first of a series of TV debates, September 23.

UPI

OCTOBER

S	M	T	W	T	F	S
					1	2
3	4	5	6	7	8	9
10	11	12	13	14	15	16
17	18	19	20	21	22	23
24	25	26	27	28	29	30
31						

GERMAN VOTERS BACK COALITION

HUA KUO-FENG SUCCEEDS MAO

RHODESIAN CONFERENCE IS HELD

1 The second session of the 94th U. S. Congress adjourns.

3 Parliamentary elections are held in West Germany; the coalition of Chancellor Helmut Schmidt's Social Democratic Party wins a narrow majority.

4 U. S. Secretary of Agriculture Earl Butz resigns with an apology for the "gross indiscretion" of a racist remark.

5 The U. S. Federal Energy Research and Development Administration reports that radioactive fallout from a recent Chinese nuclear explosion has been detected in the eastern United States.

6 In Thailand, Premier Seni Pramoj and his cabinet are deposed in a coup; the military, led by Adm. Sa-ngad Chaloryu, takes control of the government. ● A Cuban passenger jet falls into the Caribbean Sea after one or more bombs explode on board; all 73 passengers and crew members are killed. Cuban exiles and Venezuelans, opposing Fidel Castro, are blamed for the incident.

8 In Sweden, Thorbjörn Fälldin of the Center Party names a 20-member cabinet.

12 The appointment of Hua Kuo-feng as successor to Party Chairman Mao Tse-tung is confirmed.

15 U. S. vice presidential candidates Robert Dole and Walter Mondale hold a televised debate.

17 The West German mark is revalued upward against six other Western European currencies.

21 The Cincinnati Reds defeat the New York Yankees, 4 games to 0, to win baseball's World Series.

22 Hsinhua, the official Chinese press agency, announces that the Communist Party Central Committee has crushed a coup attempt led by Chiang Ching, Mao's widow, and three other members of the party's radical faction. ● In Thailand, a new 17-member cabinet takes over; a new constitution, giving Premier Thanin Kraivichien absolute power is approved. ● Cearbhall O Dalaigh resigns as president of the Republic of Ireland.

26 A two-day Arab League summit conference adjourns. At the meeting, proposals for enforcing a truce in the civil war in Lebanon were discussed. A cease-fire agreement had been reached earlier in Riyadh, Saudi Arabia. ● The Republic of Transkei is proclaimed independent of South Africa.

28 Prime Minister Ian Smith and leaders of Rhodesia's four black nationalist groups meet in Geneva to formulate a plan for the transfer of government power to Rhodesia's black majority.

Under the chairmanship of Britain's Ivor Richard (left), the Conference on Rhodesia opens in Geneva, October 28.

UPI

NOVEMBER

CARTER ELECTED PRESIDENT

QUEBEC SEPARATISTS TRIUMPH

VIETNAM DENIED UN MEMBERSHIP

S	M	T	W	T	F	S
	1	2	3	4	5	6
7	8	9	10	11	12	13
14	15	16	17	18	19	20
21	22	23	24	25	26	27
28	29	30				

After winning an extremely close presidential election, Jimmy Carter takes a vacation at St. Simons Island, Ga.

2 In U. S. elections, James Earl (Jimmy) Carter, Jr., defeats President Gerald R. Ford; Democrats retain control of both houses of Congress; San Juan Mayor Carlos Romero Barcelo of the pro-statehood New Progressive Party defeats Puerto Rico's incumbent Gov. Rafael Hernandez Colon. ● India's lower house of Parliament passes a set of constitutional amendments increasing the powers of the prime minister and legislature.

6 Benjamin L. Hooks is named to succeed Roy Wilkins as director of the National Association for the Advancement of Colored People.

7 The Soviet Union commemorates the 50th anniversary of the Bolshevik Revolution.

8 Canadian destroyers seize three Cuban fishing boats for violating Canada's 12-mile fishing limit. ● Robert S. Strauss announces his resignation, effective Jan. 21, 1977, as chairman of the Democratic National Committee.

9 Patrick J. Hillery is declared president-elect of the Republic of Ireland.

10 In Japan, the 50th anniversary of the reign of Emperor Hirohito is marked. ● Following the overthrow of Burundi's President Michel Micombero in a bloodless coup on November 1, Col. Jean-Baptiste Bagazi is appointed to the post.

11 Alexander Calder, 78-year-old American artist, dies in New York City.

12 In Paris, U. S. and Vietnamese diplomats hold their first formal talks since the Communists capture of Saigon in the spring of 1975.

15 In provincial elections in Quebec, the Parti Québécois, headed by René Lévesque, captures a majority of National Assembly seats. ● The United States vetoes the admission of Vietnam to the United Nations.

22 President Ford and President-elect Carter discuss the transition of leadership. ● Mary Louise Smith resigns, effective January 1977, as chairman of the Republican National Committee.

24 A major earthquake ravages eastern Turkey, killing an estimated 4,000 persons.

26 In Italy, the government and the Vatican agree on proposals revising the concordat that has governed church-state relations since 1929. Under the agreement, Roman Catholicism will no longer be recognized as the state religion of Italy.

28 Australia devalues its currency by 17.5%.

DECEMBER

S	M	T	W	T	F	S
			1	2	3	4
5	6	7	8	9	10	11
12	13	14	15	16	17	18
19	20	21	22	23	24	25
26	27	28	29	30	31	

PORTILLO INSTALLED IN MEXICO

OPEC INCREASES OIL PRICES

FUKUDA TAKES OVER IN JAPAN

1 José López Portillo is sworn in as the 60th president of Mexico.

3 Hsinhua, the Chinese press agency, announces that Huang Hua, China's delegate to the UN, has succeeded Chiao Kuan-hua as foreign minister. ● President-elect Carter names Cyrus R. Vance as secretary of state. ● The U.S. Department of Labor announces a November unemployment rate of 8.1%.

5 As a result of elections for Japan's lower house of Parliament, the ruling Liberal-Democratic Party loses its majority.

6 Thomas P. O'Neill, Jr. (Mass.) and Jim C. Wright (Texas) are elected speaker and majority leader of the U.S. House of Representatives of the 95th Congress.

7 The UN Security Council approves the nomination of Kurt Waldheim for a second term as secretary general. ● The U.S. Supreme Court rules that private employers with workmen's compensation programs for employees absent from work because of disabilities may refuse to pay women for absences caused by pregnancy or child birth.

9 An interim cabinet, headed by Selim al-Hoss, is formed in Lebanon. ● The UN General Assembly calls for the reconvening of the Geneva Conference on the Middle East before March 1, 1977.

12 Local elections are held in Portugal. The ruling minority Socialist Party government receives 33.11% of the total vote, a qualified vote of confidence.

15 The British government announces a series of new moves aimed at improving the economy. ● Voters in Spain approve a referendum calling for free elections in the spring of 1977. ● In Jamaica, the People's National Party of Prime Minister Michael Manley wins an overwhelming majority in parliamentary elections.

17 Meeting in Doha, Qatar, representatives of the Organization of Petroleum Exporting Countries (OPEC) announce that the price of petroleum from Saudi Arabia and the United Arab Emirates will increase by 5%, while the price of oil from the 11 other OPEC nations will rise by 10%.

20 Israel's Prime Minister Yitzhak Rabin resigns from office after calling for the dissolution of Parliament and new elections. He will remain head of a caretaker government until the elections are held. ● Richard J. Daley, mayor of Chicago, dies of a heart attack.

21 Egypt and Syria announce the formation of a "united political leadership."

24 Takeo Fukuda is elected prime minister of Japan by a narrow parliamentary margin.

UPI

José López Portillo acknowledges the applause rendered him as Mexico's new president. In his inaugural speech, the new chief executive called for a "democratic alliance for production."

The 31st Republican National Convention was held in Kemper Arena in Kansas City, Mo., August 16–19, 1976.

U.S. PRESIDENTIAL ELECTION

By Marquis Childs, Contributing Editor, *St. Louis Post-Dispatch*

In one of the strangest presidential elections in American political history a candidate who two years before the balloting was almost totally unknown outside his native Georgia won the Democratic nomination and then, by a narrow margin in the electoral college, the election in November. Jimmy Carter, even as the primaries began in February, was laughingly known as "Jimmy Who." But with a capacity for organization and a tireless and incessant effort he went through 31 primaries to become the inevitable choice of his party at the Democratic Convention in Madison Square Garden in New York City in July.

Election Trends. The election in the bicentennial year of the United States underscored several major trends of past years. One was the domination of American political life by television. The television news created a melodrama out of one primary after another, making them sound as though they were boxing matches with the winner's hand held high for all to see. More often than not the hand was that of the peanut farmer from Plains, Ga. The smile with the remarkable display of teeth, the stern blue eyes, the slightly tousled rust-colored hair, was the image seen on millions

At the Democratic National Convention in New York City, a Georgia delegate displays the party's campaign slogan.

of television screens, triumphing over the veterans of Washington politics. As Carter said after his election victory, he would not have won if it had not been for a series of televised debates with his opponent, President Gerald Ford.

A principal theme that Carter accentuated throughout the year was his freedom from all the commitments and entanglements of Washington. In the aftermath of Watergate, of the conviction and sentencing of President Nixon's principal aides, and of a presidential resignation for the first time in history, this had a powerful appeal.

Still another trend was the unprecedented number of primary contests. The primaries began in the snows of New Hampshire when it seemed that there were almost more reporters, commentators, and TV technicians than voters who would decide the outcome. Carter had already gained national publicity by winning 27% of the caucus vote in Iowa. Without the primaries and the stamina to fight them through in one corner of the country after another, Carter would never have won the nomination. He was certainly not the choice of the party bosses or the Washington panjandrums.

New Hampshire was the beginning, too, of President Ford's struggle. It was in itself an extraordinary fact that an incumbent president, granted he had never been elected by a nationwide vote, was forced to meet a serious challenge for the nomination of his party. The challenge came from Ronald Reagan, two-term governor of California, the most populous state in the Union. Reagan had an enthusiastic following in the Republican Party and he came close to crowding President Ford out of the GOP nomination.

The Primaries. But New Hampshire crowned Ford and Carter as victors, and the nearly year-long race was on. If Ford, who several times crisscrossed New Hampshire, had lost to Reagan his position would have been far from easy from the start. Similarly, if Carter had come in second

On May 5, former California Gov. Ronald Reagan catches up on the latest news—his victories in the Indiana, Alabama, and Georgia Republican primaries. Reagan gave the President a good fight, but lost the nomination to Ford on the first ballot.

President and Mrs. Gerald Ford present the vice presidential nominee to be, Sen. Robert Dole of Kansas, and his wife, Mary Elizabeth, to the press.

UPI

or third to one or more of the half dozen Democrats then running he would have had a much more difficult time ahead. He could more or less ignore the Massachusetts primary that followed and let it go to Sen. Henry Jackson without loss of stature.

The big test was Florida, the third principal primary. At least a year before any candidate had begun to think about 1976, Governor Carter was laying his plans for that state, knowing he must beat Gov. George Wallace of Alabama there without alienating Wallace's followers. He had visited the state more than 40 times before the opening bell of the campaign even sounded. This is part of the Carter story that will intrigue political historians for a long time to come.

Wallace had won his biggest victory of 1972 in Florida. Now he was crippled from the waist down by an assassin's bullet and confined to a wheelchair except when with great effort and determination he struggled to his feet to speak behind a bulletproof rostrum. This serious handicap was one of the reasons for the prediction that Wallace's strength had sharply declined. But Carter took nothing for granted. He campaigned from one corner of the state to another as the date of the primary approached. He had the help of some northern liberals, including Leonard Woodcock of the United Auto Workers who came in search of an antiracist candidate who could capture the South. When he had run successfully for governor of Georgia in 1970 Carter had taken a conservative stance with kind words for Wallace and Lester Maddox, the ardent segregationist who was then governor of the state.

Carter won a 3 percentage-point victory over Wallace in Florida and that word *momentum* became part of the political vocabulary. His television image rapidly expanded with relatives in Plains enhancing the picture of a simple, honest, deeply religious, "twice born" man of the soil who wanted to be president. The candidate's mother, soon known as Mizz Lillian, his eight-year-old daughter, Amy, and his wife, Rosalynn, who campaigned across the country with a zeal comparable to that of her husband, sharpened his image. Carter was a supersalesman, putting himself across with promises never to lie and to represent all the people. Issues were a comparatively minor part of his performance.

The Democratic presidential team—Jimmy and Rosalynn Carter and Joan and Walter Mondale—wave to the convention crowd.

The Republican candidate was meeting with serious difficulties in a party that, according to the polls, could claim the allegiance of only 20% of the voters. Ford's choice of campaign managers was unfortunate. Howard (Bo) Calloway, a Georgian who had been secretary of the army, began what seemed to be a calculated attack against Vice President Nelson Rockefeller. Calloway hit at Rockefeller's liberal views and his age in July 1975. This came to a head with Rockefeller's announcement in November 1975 that he would not under any circumstances be a candidate for election as vice president. He followed this with a press conference in which he scarcely concealed his bitterness over the Calloway attack.

Earlier, in September 1975, a dozen Republican senators, liberals and moderates, men like Mathias of Maryland, Percy of Illinois, and Javits of New York, called on the President. They went to the White House to remind him that there were those in the party who did not share the conservative views of Ronald Reagan. As their contest progressed President Ford was allowing Reagan to push him more and more to the right until he began to sound like an echo of the former California governor. If the mission of the moderate-liberal senators had any impact it was not visible as the campaign against Reagan increased in rancor.

Ford openly declared that the American people would never accept a candidate with views as ultraconservative as those of Reagan. In the Florida primary Reagan made a strong chauvinistic appeal to keep United States sovereignty over the Canal Zone in Panama with no recognition of the fact that the Ford administration had for nearly two years been conducting negotiations with the government of Panama over surrender of at least a share of control of the Zone. Far from repudiating this attack on his policy the President seemed to sanction it. Ford up to this point had won four primaries while Reagan had taken none. Friends of Reagan believed he was ready to withdraw. But angered by Ford's attacks he entered the North Carolina primary where he won a surprise victory and the contest, so disastrous to party unity, went down to the convention in Kansas City.

During this time Carter's supersalesmanship, his sermon of political faith healing and restoration in the wake of Watergate, was working well.

In his quest for the presidency, Jimmy Carter depended on his family for assistance on the campaign trail. His mother, Mizz Lillian, received wide attention.

The 1976 campaign introduced something new to the political scene—a televised debate between the vice presidential candidates. Senators Mondale and Dole debated the issues in Houston's Alley Theater, October 15.

He carried Pennsylvania with its critical 103 delegate votes, proving that a southerner could take a large industrial state even though organized labor had held out for Sen. Hubert Humphrey, an unannounced candidate. Similarly Ohio fell into his column. But often he won by a small percentage of eligible voters. The conspicuous example was in Michigan where he was challenged by Rep. Morris Udall, virtually the only remaining Democratic contestant. Despite the help of the United Auto Workers Carter won by only half of one percent out of 709,000 votes cast.

The Conventions. In the last set of primaries on June 8 he picked up an additional 200 delegates, enough to give him more than the 1,505 required for nomination. But this had not been accomplished without some suspense at the end. California Gov. Edmund G. Brown, Jr., a belated entry in the primary race, had carried three state primaries, including Maryland and a sweep of his own California. Brown was a new face, newer than Carter. Sen. Frank Church of Idaho had carried Nebraska, Oregon, Montana, and his home state. But Carter had won the day, having repeatedly asserted that he would get the nomination and persuading the public that he spoke the truth. The Democratic national convention was something of an anticlimax although the able national chairman, Robert Strauss, had livened it up with historic movies of the Truman triumph of 1948 and with appearances by Democratic bigwigs. When Carter came on in the grand finale with his opening, "My name is Jimmy Carter and I'm running for president of the United States," the Garden broke into wild emotion.

In the interval following the meeting of the Democrats in mid-July the polls were to give what proved to be a wholly false picture of the standing of the Democratic candidate. They showed him with a lead of 37 to 40 points over either Ford or Reagan. This may have given the little group around Carter from the very beginning—Jody Powell and Jordan Hamilton, among others—a spurious self-confidence, while at the same time they may not have been wholly aware of the major task they faced. Their man had to be converted from the simple country boy to a national leader capable of directing the nation in the turbulent years ahead.

Meeting a month later, the Republicans were embroiled in the Ford-Reagan quarrel. The Reagan strategists forced a vote on a change in the

"...I believe that we must now put the divisions of the campaign behind us and unite the country once again in the common pursuit of peace and prosperity."
President Gerald R. Ford Nov. 3, 1976.

Jimmy Carter won the presidency by personally campaigning across the country. The nation's high unemployment rate was a frequent theme of the former governor.

UPI

rules requiring a nominee for president to declare his vice president prior to his own nomination. Two weeks before, Reagan had named Sen. Richard Schweiker of Pennsylvania, a moderate, as his vice presidential candidate, with a varied reaction as between conservative and moderate Republicans. Embodied in Resolution 16-C, the proposed change was defeated by the Ford delegates by 112 votes. It was an unmistakable sign of how the vote would go for the nominee. But measured by enthusiasm and decibels of sound it was a Reagan convention.

To the surprise of many of his followers Ford designated Sen. Robert Dole of Kansas as his vice presidential running mate. Carter had chosen Sen. Walter Mondale of Minnesota whom conservative Democrats considered too liberal. Dole immediately began an active campaign starting in his home town of Russell, Kans., with Ford at his side. But he devoted so many of his appearances to wisecracks and one-liners that even in the White House the feeling grew that he was a handicap.

The Polls and the Campaign. The polls immediately began to narrow. Incidentally, the importance of the polls was another trend of the bicentennial election. Pollster Peter Howard predicted before the campaign began, in an extended nationwide survey, that the turnout of eligible voters would be the lowest in history. This had an immediate effect on the strategy of the campaign. Carter's allies in the labor movement and the black community set out to try to ensure the largest possible turnout. This was also Republican strategy.

Certain polls had predicted prior to the Kansas City convention that if Reagan were the nominee as many as 30% of the Republican voters would turn to Carter or stay home on election day, and conversely Reaganites would be turned off by the nomination of Ford. The President in the first part of the campaign decided the most advantageous course would be to stay in the White House and convince the electorate that he was attending to the affairs of the nation. From the Rose Garden of the White House, and before the television cameras, he signed bills, named appointees to high office, and gave press conferences. The Democrats dubbed him the Rose Garden candidate, and Ford found himself, as had incumbents in the past, damned if he went on the campaign trail and damned if he didn't.

"We'll set priorities, we'll work hard to accomplish all of our goals, but there has to be a realization it's a shared responsibility among the people of this country."
President-elect Jimmy Carter Nov. 4, 1976.

THE ELECTORAL VOTE

297 □ CARTER
240 ▭ FORD
● REAGAN

WASH. 8 ●
ORE. 6
MONT. 4
N.D. 3
MINN. 10
WIS. 11
N.H.
VT. 4
ME. 4
IDAHO 4
WYO. 3
S.D. 4
IOWA 8
MICH. 21
MASS. 14
N.Y. 41
NEV. 3
UTAH 4
COLO. 7
NEB. 5
ILL. 26
IND. 13
OHIO 25
PA. 27
R.I. 4
CONN. 8
CALIF. 45
KAN. 7
MO. 12
KY. 9
W. VA. 6
VA. 12
N.J. 17
DEL. 3
ARIZ. 6
N.M. 4
OKLA. 8
ARK. 6
TENN. 10
N.C. 13
MD. 10
D.C. 3
S.C. 8
MISS. 7
ALA. 9
GA. 12
TEXAS 28
LA. 10
FLA. 17
ALASKA 3
HAWAII 4

UPI

Carter began a drive across the country discovering as he traveled that in many states the Democratic organization was weak or nonexistent, indifferent to his fate. He also had a problem of identity. To many Democrats he was still an unknown. What does he stand for? they asked. In this respect, a series of four debates was a boon, particularly when he was belligerent and when, as in the debate on foreign policy, the President said in effect that Poland and the other Eastern European states were free of Soviet domination. Taking six days to confess his error, it was a blooper from which Ford never really recovered. In an interview with *Playboy* magazine in which lust and pride were discussed, Carter made a similar boner that was to plague him through the rest of the campaign.

In state after state he appeared with Democratic candidates for the Senate whose pulling power was far greater than his, as the election returns were to show. Edward Kennedy in Massachusetts, Hubert Humphrey, despite his recent recovery from a serious cancer operation, in Minnesota, Lloyd Bentsen in Texas, were returned with far larger majorities than Carter's. Sen. Harrison Williams won reelection to a fourth term with a sizable majority in New Jersey although Carter failed to carry that state. In California, Brown made at best a minimal effort for the national ticket as Reagan did for Ford. Both men had swept the California primaries with larger majorities than their respective parties captured in November. And Carter lost California as he did every state of the Far West.

The Outcome. It was, in short, a regional election with similarities to 1940 and 1944 when Franklin Roosevelt had won with a strategy based on the solid South and the discontents of certain northern industrial states. A striking fact was the turnout of the black vote, which in the past has been low. An estimated 94% of the blacks voted and except for a small fraction these were mostly Carter votes. With the vote close in some southern states statistical analysis may well show that it was the black vote which swung it. Carter carried Mississippi, for example, by a squeaker of 13,000 votes. The pride of the South in electing one of their own, in addition to the loyalty of the blacks, had not a little to do with the outcome. Carter was the first southerner from the old Confederacy to be elected since Zachary Taylor in 1848. From the outset his strategy had been based on winning the electoral votes of the old South, and it paid off.

As November 2 drew near there was no doubt that it would be an extremely close election. For the principals, election night was a long torment as the returns wavered from one state to another. Not until after 3:30 in the morning of November 3 did the networks project Carter as the winner. At that hour Carter had 297 electoral votes to 235 for Ford.

THE POPULAR VOTE

Carter	40,827,394
Ford	39,145,977
McCarthy	745,042
Others	963,505
Total	81,681,918

Oregon, still undecided as the counting continued, finally went to Ford with its six electoral votes bringing the Ford total to 241. Running as an independent candidate, former Sen. Eugene McCarthy received in four states a fraction of the vote that would otherwise have gone to Carter. These states were Maine, Iowa, Oklahoma, and Oregon. Ohio was so close that a recount was ordered.

But the closeness of the presidential election was no measure of the disaster to the Republican Party. It was left with only twelve governors. While it had been expected that the Republicans would defeat many of the freshman class of 43 in the House, the balance was not significantly changed. The new Congress has 292 Democrats to 143 Republicans. In the Senate the Democratic majority will remain the same, 61 Democrats, 38 Republicans, and 1 Independent. Only one or two personal upsets marked the general score. In California, S. I. Hayakawa, a 70-year-old former semantics scholar at San Francisco State College, defeated Democratic Sen. John Tunney who was running for a second term. In New York, James Buckley, the only Conservative Party candidate who also ran on the Republican line, was defeated by Daniel Patrick Moynihan. In state legislatures the Democrats came out of November 2 with control of both houses in 36 states, the Republicans having both houses in only five states.

In races that drew national attention, Dixy Lee Ray (D) was elected governor of Washington and Daniel Patrick Moynihan (D) defeated Sen. James Buckley of New York. *Below,* a post-election cartoon.

COPYRIGHT 1976 BY HERBLOCK IN "THE WASHINGTON POST"

"THEY CAN'T SAY I'M NOT CONCERNED"

THE BICENTENNIAL

a time for reflection

By Senator Mike Mansfield

On July 4, 1976, the United States celebrated the 200th birthday of a nation that has lived longer under a single written constitution than any nation in history. For most Americans the Bicentennial was a time of celebration. But it was also a time for reflection and contemplation.

It was a time for rejoicing in the success of the most endurable political experiment ever conducted. It was a time when Americans were encouraged to reflect on the wisdom of our Founding Fathers who had the foresight to construct a system of self-government that is both stable enough to free us from day-to-day anxiety and flexible enough to adjust to the needs and priorities of an ever-changing nation and world.

The Bicentennial was a time to rejoice that we are at once the most prosperous and generous of nations and that, while we are the most powerful, we are also the most open and compassionate society on earth.

But Americans did and must do more than celebrate the beginning of the third century of independence. Our Bicentennial was also a time of national self-reflection, self-criticism, honest reassessment of our past, and thoughtful contemplation of our future. Nineteen hundred and seventy-six was a period of great soul-searching after the momentous events and crises of the past decade: a divisive and tragic war in Southeast Asia, the resignations of a president and a vice president, and the abuses of power by persons in positions of public trust.

As we enter our third century of independence, our citizens long to restore the fundamental assumptions on which our society has endured: that our leaders can be trusted and believed; that our public and private institutions are responsive to the needs of those whom they are established to serve; and that our public policies are designed and implemented to serve the general welfare.

We, as did our forebears, have faith in the future. We celebrate their courage, their commitment to liberty, and their political wisdom. As they were optimistic of survival in the past, we are optimistic that we will survive human imperfection and national misfortune and continue to bring to fruition the great ideals on which our nation was founded.

As Abraham Lincoln said on July 4, 1858:
> "We hold this annual celebration to remind ourselves
> of all the good done in the process of time, of how
> it was done and who did it and how we are historically
> connected with it. And we go from these meetings in
> better humor with ourselves, as we feel more attached
> the one to the other and more firmly bound to the
> country we inhabit."

It is this sense of shared national experience that has made our nation great and that will keep us, on this and on each of our birthdays, "more firmly bound to the country we inhabit."

FRED WARD, BLACK STAR

Philadelphia received an eight-tiered birthday cake.

BICENTENNIAL INDEPENDENCE DAY

A Proclamation

By the President of the United States of America

"The Continental Congress by resolution adopted July 2, 1776, declared that thirteen American colonies were free and independent states. Two days later, on the Fourth of July, the Congress adopted a Declaration of Independence which proclaimed to the world the birth of the United States of America. . . .

"In recognition of the two-hundredth anniversary of the great historic events of 1776, and in keeping with the wishes of the Congress, I ask that all Americans join in an extended period of celebration, thanksgiving, and prayer . . ."

The Declaration of Independence (*left, above*), as well as the Constitution and the Bill of Rights, were on display in the National Archives, Washington, for 76 straight hours during the July 4 weekend. In Boston, the Declaration of Independence was read during ceremonies at the Old State House.

MARTIN LEVICK, BLACK STAR

OFFICE OF CULTURAL AFFAIRS, BOSTON

C. PETER JORGENSEN

JEAN-CLAUDE LEJEUN, BLACK STAR

Along the Charles River in Boston, 400,000 people heard Arthur Fiedler conduct Tchaikovsky's *1812 Overture*. Ringing church bells, shots from howitzers, and fireworks accompanied the performance.

A Revolutionary War battle was reenacted in Western Springs, Ill. The "Spirit of '76" was the theme of a parade in the village of Wellington, Ohio.

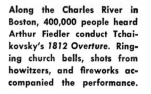

FRANK ALEXSANDROWICZ, BLACK STAR

TED HARDIN, BLACK STAR

BOB LEBAR

OPERATION SAIL:
Stately Ships Mark July 4

Hundreds of vessels, including 16 of the world's tallest old windjammers, participated in Operation Sail, New York City's tribute to the bicentennial. More than 225 sailing ships under 31 flags paraded from New York Harbor up the Hudson River to the George Washington Bridge. Millions of Americans, including President Ford on board the *Forrestal,* witnessed the nautical array. At the same time, a 22-nation fleet of 53 naval units held the International Naval Review. Vice President Rockefeller was the official reviewer. Following Op Sail, large crowds (*below*) inspected the sailing ships, which were docked at the city's piers.

The ships had left Plymouth, England, for Bermuda in May, and had sailed from Bermuda to Newport, R. I. (*above*), before leaving for New York and the big day.

BERT MILLER, BLACK STAR

THE STATUS OF THE THREE R's

By Merrill Sheils
General Editor
Newsweek *Magazine*

MIMI FORSYTH, MONKMEYER

Despite recent innovations in education, testing remains the basic instrument to determine a pupil's mastery of learning skills.

In 1976, the United States spent more than $110,000,000,000 on the education of its citizens. That huge sum—$500 for every man, woman, and child in the country—was the highest in American history. But even as the money spent on schooling has more than doubled in recent years, studies of how much Americans learn have turned up gloomy evidence that the students of today do not perform as well on basic tests as their counterparts did a decade ago. Standardized tests of reading, writing, and arithmetic indicate that many youngsters simply do not seem to be mastering the skills that are fundamental to further learning.

Alarmed by these data, many taxpayers and educators have begun to ask some tough questions about American education. Why is it that Johnny doesn't seem to read, write, and add as well as he once could? Have schools stopped insisting that he learn? Has the modern world changed so much that the three R's are less important than they used to be? Should parents and government officials start demanding that schools get back to the basics?

Some Troubling Signs. The signs that students are having difficulties with the three R's are many and well-documented.

Scores on the Scholastic Aptitude Tests, which measure the verbal and mathematical abilities that students need for good performance in college, have been falling steadily for more than a decade. In 1963, the average math score for high-school juniors and seniors was 501; by 1975, it was 472. Verbal scores fell from 480 to 435 over the same period. Some educators explain this decline in terms of the vast expansion of the student population taking the tests. In the early 1960's, the argument goes, only a scholastic elite tried to get into college in the first place, whereas today, pupils from all socioeconomic groups aspire to higher education. But officials of the College Entrance Examination Board, which administers the tests, point out that it is not just the average score that has been going down. There are also fewer students today who earn very high marks on the exams, a fact that suggests that even the best pupils may be poorly prepared.

At an expensive prep school, the library is a focal point. Many educators still believe that the best way to learn to read is by reading.

A recent study conducted for the U. S. Office of Education found that more than 23 million Americans—one out of every five adults—cannot read, write, or compute well enough to function effectively in the modern world, and that 40 million more possess just the minimum skills necessary for survival. Researchers at the University of Texas, who spent four years compiling their data, explored the performance of adults on 70 questions and tasks that almost everyone faces in everyday life. They found that more than 12% (14 million) cannot address an envelope in a manner adequate to get it through the postal system; 26% (30 million) do not know what the expression "credit check" means; and one fifth of all adults do not understand the meaning of a sign that says "We Are an Equal Opportunity Employer."

The Association of American Publishers recently prepared a pamphlet designed to help college freshmen get the most from their textbooks. Its compilers were startled to find that the pamphlet's "readability level"—aimed at 12th-grade reading skills—was far too high for students about to enter college. They rewrote their handbook at the 9th-grade level.

Since 1969, the National Assessment of Educational Progress (NAEP) has been studying the achievement of Americans between the ages of 9 and 35 in a number of educational areas including reading, writing, and mathematics. The NAEP's findings have been mixed. In reading, their results have been slightly higher than the specialists expected; still, nearly 11% of all 17-year-olds, NAEP data show, are functionally illiterate—unable to read a newspaper, a driver's license, or the label on a medicine bottle. In writing, NAEP experts note a decline in coherency and an increase in awkwardness and run-on sentences, especially among 17-year-olds. Math tests administered by the National Assessment show that the majority of students are fairly proficient in addition, subtraction, multiplication, and division, but have serious difficulties with percentages, decimals, and word problems. These findings are particularly worrisome in view of the fact that everyday consumer transactions often involve percentages or the ability to translate a word problem into simple arithmetic terms. What's more, a thorough understanding of decimals will be essential if the United States is soon to adopt the metric system.

Standardized tests given annually to elementary and secondary school-children across the country indicate, in many areas, that students are passed along from grade to grade without mastering the skills considered appropriate to each level. Particularly in the inner cities, a large majority of pupils read one, two, and even three full years behind their grade levels. And according to a report to the U. S. Office of Economic Opportunity, based on research by the Hudson Institute, recent years have seen significant drops in achievement levels even in affluent suburban schools.

Other Indications. Beyond the hard test data, there are more amorphous indications that something is wrong with the three R's. College and university professors are complaining that their freshmen—even those who have graduated near the very top of their high-school classes—seem to lack essential skills. To remedy this problem, nearly every institution of higher education in the country has instituted sweeping remedial programs. Once, such courses were populated by students, usually from inferior schools, whose admission to college had been a borderline question to begin with. Now, however, colleges report that topnotch students from schools with excellent reputations are having to take remedial training. And while college officials blame secondary schools, personnel officers in commerce and industry claim that the colleges and universities themselves are turning out workers who cannot read, write, and compute with any real proficiency.

New Focus of Teaching. Has something happened to the teaching of reading, writing, and arithmetic? There are no easy answers to the question. Teachers say they have never ceased teaching the basic skills, and they suggest that perhaps the standardized tests simply do not measure children's talents well enough. "They no longer test what the schools are teaching" is the response of many ·teachers' groups to parental complaints about test scores, and to a large extent, that explanation seems to be true.

MIMI FORSYTH, MONKMEYER

A city high school: urban educational leaders are concerned that scores on some standardized tests are lower in the cities than in nearby suburbs.

During the 1960's, the American educational system grew by unprecedented strides. More money than ever before was spent on the research and development of new and better ways to handle schooling, and reforms were instituted that in many areas resulted in a major change in American educational philosophy. The focus of teaching, the reformers insisted, should be "the whole child." Rote learning, drills, and memorization, they protested, were outdated techniques that had the effect of drying up a child's interest in exploring his or her world. Students should be encouraged to pursue talents and interests that they had already developed, rather than told that they must measure up to other people's assessment of what they should learn and become. The "affective" sphere of education, the child's subjective reaction to his school experience, was promoted as most important; the objective content of an education, the reformers argued, would follow automatically, as the student gained interest, broader outlook, and a feeling for learning. "Individualized instruction" became the order of the day. Since not all students are alike, why should they be expected to meet identical standards?

Automatic Promotion. The specific changes in classroom procedure that followed this shift in philosophy have been many and complex. For one thing, curriculums have been broadened enormously at almost every level of elementary and secondary education. No longer, for example, do all 3d-graders in all schools read similar primers, do standard grammar exercises, and engage in spelling bees. Some schools threw out these traditional methods entirely; others kept them for some pupils but ceased requiring them of everyone. For another, school districts virtually abandoned the practice of keeping students back a grade if they had not mastered the material as well as their classmates. No matter how poorly a 5th-grader performed, under the new system, he would be promoted to the 6th grade along with his classmates. To hold him back, it was thought, would simply discourage him and stifle for all time his confidence in his learning ability.

The open classroom approach to elementary education emphasizes the "whole child" and encourages each to pursue individual talents and interests.

One effect of these policy changes was to alter dramatically a student's relationship—as measured by standardized tests—to others in his or her age group. With every individual pursuing learning at his own pace, a "3d-grade level of performance," mandated by an exam, became a meaningless standard.

Little Time for Reading. Despite these factors, individualized instruction was still aimed at ensuring that every student would be equipped with basic skills. If, in fact, pupils are not learning those fundamentals, the fault may well lie with an entirely different set of developments. One frequently-cited villain in the verbal skills area is the ubiquitous television set. No thorough studies have yet been completed of the TV generation to determine exactly what effects television has on learning abilities, but at least one fact is indisputable: the average child spends three to four hours a day in front of the screen—and that is time that he or she does not spend with books. Reading as a form of recreation is rare among modern children, and it is not surprising that lack of practice at home should show up in diminished capabilities in school.

Indeed, even in the classroom the children of today do not spend as much time actually engaged in the activity of reading as students did a decade ago. Many of the modern educational materials are of the "audiovisual" variety—filmstrips, tapes, and electronic presentations that require little or no decoding of printed symbols. The libraries in many schools have been renamed "resource centers," and books are by no means their primary commodity. Outside the English classroom, students can often get by with doing almost no reading or writing at all, and an English teacher determined to make students get plenty of practice in verbal skills is often a lonely crusader among science and social-studies colleagues who are converts to the multimedia approach.

New Math and Calculators. The field of mathematics has been similarly influenced by developments in technology. First came the "new

Teenagers attend a woodworking class at a vocational high school. Supporters of the "back to basics" movement believe that the 3 R's must be given a new priority in such institutions.

math," a revolutionary approach to the subject that deliberately deemphasized the basic how-to skills of arithmetic in favor of teaching *why* mathematics works as it does. By 1973, 85% of all schools were using new math—and scores on math achievement tests, which still demand that children perform basic computations, were plummeting. Mathematicians answered the protests of bewildered parents with the contention that, in fact, their children were being taught to understand far more about math than students of the past ever learned through rote drills. Besides, said the educators, calculators would soon be so widespread—and so cheap—that every student would have one, and none would have to rely on the accuracy of his own calculations.

That prediction has practically come true. Calculators are now widely used in schools, and teachers say they are extremely useful in keeping the interest of students who once despised the drills of basic computations. In 1976, the National Council of Teachers of Mathematics overwhelmingly endorsed calculators as a learning tool. Even if modern students turn out to be ill-equipped to do elementary problems without their calculators, they insist, the students will understand the abstractions of math, and calculators will be at hand whenever they need them.

New Basics for Old? Many teachers admit that underlying all these new developments in education there is a common assumption: in the Electronic Age, a facility in reading, writing, and computing, once considered essential to education, may simply no longer be necessary. If the huge majority of communications among people are to be conducted in the future by screen and tape, is it absolutely necessary that youngsters concentrate on the written word? Would they not be better equipped for modern life by thorough training in the electronic arts? And if calculators and computers are to be the commonplace tools of average citizens, why insist that students master arithmetic skills they may never have to use?

Differing Remedies. So far, however, proponents of this brave new world have failed to convince the ordinary citizens who pay the school bills—particularly the parents who want to know why their own Johnnies

EDWARD BARNARD, PHOTO TRENDS

In recent years, some educators have come to rely heavily on audiovisual aids. Such items require little or no involvement with printed symbols.

are not learning to read, write, and add as well as they themselves did. In 1976, a new movement was afoot in school districts and state legislatures across the country, a movement demanding that students be sufficiently trained in the three R's to meet standards of "minimal competency." The requirements vary from district to district. Maryland officials, for example, drew up a scheme that requires all public-school students to pass yearly tests, from second grade on, in order to be eligible for promotion. Florida legislators enacted a law that requires proficiency testing in the 3d, 5th, 8th, 11th, and 12th grades. Any student who fails must take extra tutoring and remedial work at state expense. In Oregon and Los Angeles, the new rules deny a high-school diploma to any student who cannot prove that he or she has mastered certain fundamental reading and mathematical skills.

In addition, parents in many local school districts have banded together in a "back-to-basics" movement. These parents do not believe that the three R's have been emphasized enough in recent years, and they have asked school boards to set up "fundamental schools" that stress reading, writing, and arithmetic above all other areas of education. In some communities, like Pasadena, Calif., the fundamental schools stand side by side with modern experimental institutions, and parents can choose which kind of classroom their children attend.

Reform or Reaction? Thoughtful proponents of renewed attention to the three R's stress the fact that their importance runs far deeper than simple questions of how "useful" they are in the modern world. To be able to read well, for example, is to have access to all the sources of Western civilization that preceded this century and to build habits of understanding and analysis that are quite different from the "quick-impression" talents engendered by audiovisual communication. To be able to set down one's thoughts in writing one has to organize and clarify those thoughts in a way that is not required by the ephemeral transactions of speech. To develop the accuracy and discipline demanded by elementary mathematical computations is to master skills that are invaluable in many other areas of learning.

A consensus is growing among those responsible for educational policy that while schools should continue to broaden the materials and options they offer students, they should not do so at the expense of fundamental skills. On the other hand, many distinguished educators warn that the reaction against innovations and the burgeoning local efforts to improve test scores and revive basic skills, could result in throwing out many of the most valuable innovations of recent years—especially the notion that education is more than memorization and drill and should mean expanding every student's horizon enough to make him want to learn more.

To provide some answers in the debate over the three R's, the College Entrance Examination Board has asked a panel of educational experts to investigate why the verbal and math scores on the college boards keep going down. This group will study what kind of education modern students are receiving, how their teachers are prepared to pass on basic skills, and exactly why the students seem to be having trouble with the tests. Whatever they find out, the debate will certainly continue for some time. In the end, it may result in a useful public discussion among educators, parents, students, and politicians about what they want from the schools— and how, in the future, they should spend the enormous sums of money that they pay for them.

MARGOT GRANITAS,
PHOTO RESEARCHERS

Personal measurements, such as height and weight, help children realize the importance of basic math.

MONARCHIES:

a new lease on life?

BY JOHN GRIGG, *Political Journalist and Author*

One of the main reasons for the emergence of a republican form of government 200 years ago was the identification of the old monarchical system with autocratic rule. Government "by the people" was the new ideal, and republicanism has since swept the world. Today, however, it is no longer self-evident that monarchy is an antipopular system of government; rather, it is increasingly arguable that the reverse is true. For while most of the world's remaining monarchies are of the constitutional sort, in which the actual government is democratically based, most of the world's republics are autocracies or oligarchies of one kind or another.

The Hold-Outs and the Drop-Outs. In 1914 the world was still largely monarchical. Apart from the great empires, such as the British, German, Russian, Habsburg, Ottoman, and Japanese, most of the small countries of Europe and Asia were monarchies. Among major powers, only the United States and France were republics, though Latin America reflected the republicanism of the United States and there were also recently established republics in China and Portugal.

CIFRA GRAFICA, PHOTO TRENDS

Spain's royal couple, Juan Carlos I and Queen Sofia, on a formal occasion in Catalonia. Though the latest among European royalty to ascend a throne, the Spanish king probably wields more actual power than any of his colleagues.

A colorful array of European royalty gathered in Stockholm in the summer of 1976 to witness the wedding of King Carl XVI Gustaf of Sweden to Silvia Sommerlath, a German commoner. Prominent examples of the world's monarchies, the Scandinavian countries are also among the most firmly entrenched democracies.

Coming from the altar of Stockholm Cathedral on June 19, 1976, King Carl XVI Gustaf leads his new queen past the smiling figures of King Baudouin and Queen Fabiola of the Belgians.

Queen Juliana and Prince Bernhard of the Netherlands in an official photograph taken before international business scandals forced the prince to resign all his military positions in August 1976.

Tradition, pomp, and ceremony surround the British royal couple, Queen Elizabeth II and Prince Philip, wherever they go on their official functions.

During World War I the whole scene was revolutionized, and since 1918 the world has been predominantly republican. Britain and Japan have remained unfaltering in their monarchism, and so, among lesser powers, have Holland, Denmark, Norway, and Sweden in the West, Nepal and Thailand in the East. In the Middle East, Iran is an ancient monarchy which has made considerable material progress under a new dynasty, and among successor states of the Ottoman empire Jordan, Saudi Arabia, and a few Persian Gulf sultanates are monarchies. In the Commonwealth of Nations a number of states are monarchies with the British queen as their sovereign, notably Canada, Australia, New Zealand, and Jamaica; and Malaysia has its own indigenous monarchy. Finally, among former dependencies of France, Morocco is a kingdom.

But that is just about all. Most of the new countries that have emerged from the break-up of European empires are republics. Indonesia, the Indian subcontinent, and practically all of black Africa have gone republican (Lesotho and Swaziland are still kingdoms). During or since World War II monarchies have been overthrown in Italy, Yugoslavia, Rumania, Bulgaria, Albania, Greece, Egypt, Iraq, Libya, Ethiopia, Cambodia, and Laos. South Africa, formerly a monarchy within the Commonwealth, has become a republic, and so has even part of the British Isles, southern Ireland. Beyond question, the monarchical form of government is thoroughly abnormal in the modern world. But is it doomed?

The Spanish Test Case. An interesting case of monarchical revival, which may well prove to be a test case, is that of Spain. In 1931 Alfonso XIII fell after local elections in which—it is significant to recall—the countryside and small towns voted monarchist, though the big cities voted republican. In the civil war of 1936–39 the republic in turn was brought down and the personal regime of Generalissimo Franco established. Franco was a monarchist who had no intention, however, of restoring any king during his own lifetime. In 1947 he proclaimed Spain a monarchy but left the throne empty while continuing himself as head of state. In 1969 he designated as his successor, in the event of death or retirement, Alfonso XIII's grandson, Prince Juan Carlos, and when Franco died, in November 1975, Juan Carlos duly became king.

Though he had been educated in Spain under Franco's auspices and was to a considerable extent identified with the Franco regime—since he had to pay formal allegiance to it as the price of being chosen by the dictator to succeed him—Juan Carlos was acceptable not only to moderate supporters of the regime, but also to many of its opponents, as the person most likely to preside over an orderly transition from dictatorship to representative and responsible government. At the time of writing, considerable progress has been made toward that objective, and there are solid grounds for hoping, though certainly not for assuming, that by gradual stages it will be attained.

Already there has been a dramatic liberalization of the press, and political parties—with the notable exception of the Communists—have been legalized. Mayors are to be elected, as a preliminary to more far-reaching moves toward democracy. One motive assisting the cause of reform is that even conservative Spaniards tend to be very eager for their country to become a member of the European Community and are well aware that it will never be admitted unless and until its institutions are made to conform to Western democratic standards.

Backers of the restored monarchy fall into two distinct categories, known in Spain as monarchists *de corazón* (from the heart) and monarchists *de razón* (for reasons of expediency). The second group includes a large number of old republicans, including Salvador de Madariaga and even a few Anarchist leaders (who yield to none in their hostility to the Communists). But merely rational and opportunistic support for the monarchy may become more heartfelt as time goes on, and already there is plenty of evidence that Juan Carlos has strong popular appeal. Even in Catalonia he has been received with great enthusiasm, partly because of his ability to speak Catalán. But Basque nationalism is still largely unappeased, and since it often takes a violent form, the danger of assassination can never be discounted.

Belgium Revitalized. Another European country in which the monarchy has acquired a new lease on life is Belgium. The Belgian monarchy did not have to be restored, though it came very near to falling as a result of King Leopold III's surrender to the Germans in 1940 and the unpopularity of his second wife, the Princess de Réthy. But since his abdication in 1951 the monarchy has been revitalized by his son, Baudouin, and perhaps even more by Baudouin's admirable wife, Fabiola—by birth a nonroyal Spaniard. Were it not for the outstanding success of this dedicated pair, not only might the Belgian monarchy have collapsed, but Belgium itself might have disintegrated.

Lacking ethnic, linguistic, or cultural unity, Belgium has always de-

LEMOINE, SYGMA

Good horsemanship rounds out the many-faceted education of Charles, Prince of Wales, the heir to the British throne.

On Christmas Day 1976 Emperor Hirohito of Japan, shown here with his wife, Princess Nagako, completed 50 years of reign over his nation—which makes him the longest-reigning monarch in the world.

pended to a large extent upon the monarchy for its cohesion, and it is one of the major achievements of Baudouin and Fabiola that they have bridged the gap between the two principal communities in the country, since they are both bilingual in French and Flemish. Though unfortunately they have no children, the succession is assured through Baudouin's brother, Albert, and his children.

The British Monarchy and the Commonwealth. The monarchy which commands the widest allegiance, and whose influence has been most pervasive, is the British. Elizabeth II is queen of 11 countries, including the United Kingdom, and she is also titular head of a commonwealth consisting of 36 countries. This unique phenomenon reflects a process of adaptation that has gone on for well over a century, since Lord Durham in 1839 proposed that Canada should have responsible self-government under the Crown. First, the Crown was, as it were, multiplied to take account of colonial independence and then, after World War II, a new formula was evolved to enable the British sovereign to preside symbolically over an association containing republics as well as monarchies.

Commonwealth nations are to be found in every part of the world, and its people represent all the world's important racial groups and subgroups. Certainly it is not a solid bloc or amalgam of power, and to the extent that it can be said to be united at all, its unity is limited and tenuous. All the same, it does exist as a political entity of sorts, and one of the bonds holding it together is the House of Windsor.

The queen has traveled a good deal in the Commonwealth, but to most of its people she is still no more than an occasional visitor. In Commonwealth countries of which she is the sovereign she is permanently represented on the spot by a governor general, who is nowadays nearly always a citizen of the country in question. It is arguable that she should pay more frequent and informal visits, at least to the principal nations of the Commonwealth overseas. But Prince Philip, the Prince of Wales, and other members of her family are assiduous travelers, and during her reign the monarchy's impact outside the United Kingdom has undoubtedly been growing, even though most of her time is spent at home.

In Britain republican sentiment is negligible. Though the queen was loyally criticized earlier in her reign for certain defects in her performance, she has since shown considerable signs of having heeded the criticism. As she attains her silver jubilee (1977), she is an immensely popular and respected figure, though it is a vital feature of British monarchism that it has never—or never for long—taken the form of a quasi-religious cult. This is less true of Japanese monarchism, though to Japan, as to Britain, the monarchy has been of incalculable value, helping the country through many vicissitudes, including the destruction of Hiroshima and Nagasaki.

Drawbacks and Advantages. One stock objection to monarchy is that it encourages snobbery, and so in a sense it does. But there is little evidence that snobbery is confined to those who live under monarchical constitutions, and it may even be thought that in the absence of the particular types of snobbery associated with monarchy other and even less desirable types are apt to prevail.

The specific advantages of constitutional monarchy, which the modern world has by no means rendered obsolete, may be listed as follows. It provides a head of state whose succession is automatic and not determined by electoral or any other form of contest. It separates what the British 19th-century social philosopher Walter Bagehot called the "dignified" aspect of government from what he called the "efficient" aspect. (This also happens in those republics where the president is only a figurehead, but there the "dignified" aspect of government is often not sufficiently dignified). Since monarchy involves not only the person of the monarch but his or her family as well, the system enables people of different ages, tastes, and interests to participate in the beneficent functions of the office. Finally, monarchy appeals to the esthetic side of human nature. The pageantry and the myth that surround it give it not only the splendor lacking in most lives but also a kind of fairy-tale quality that appeals to people of all classes. After all, who has not, at one time or another, dreamed of being king or queen?

CLAUDE SALHANI, SYGMA

King Khalid of Saudi Arabia rules the wealthiest and most influential of the Arab kingdoms.

SIPA-PRESS, LIASON

A survivor of numerous intrigues, plots, and pressures, King Hussein of Jordan enjoys a vacation of Alpine skiing with his third wife, Alia Toukan.

Y. NAGATA, UNITED NATIONS

H. Shirley Amerasinghe, president of the Conference on the Law of the Sea, opens its fourth session (*opposite*) on March 15, 1976. He is flanked by Secretary General Kurt Waldheim (*left*) and David Hall, conference secretary.

UNITED NATIONS CONFERENCE ON

THE LAW OF THE SEA

RESPONSIBILITIES OF THE CONFERENCE

BY H. S. AMERASINGHE
President of the Third United Nations Conference on the Law of the Sea

A stable international legal order for the use of the world's ocean and its immensely valuable resources is one of the most precious legacies that statesmen of today can bequeath to posterity. This is the monumental task on which the Third United Nations Conference on the Law of the Sea, with the participation of the largest number of sovereign states ever brought together in an international parley, has been engaged since December 1973.

One of the principal responsibilities of the Conference is to fashion a new order that would preserve the ecological balance of the ocean, protect it from pollution, and prevent the reckless depletion of its living resources, which provide an irreplaceable means of sustenance for mankind. Another of its responsibilities is to substitute for the existing legal order, which grants almost exclusive privileges and opportunities to a minority of powerful nations, a new regime which would be equitable, both in theory and fact, to the technologically and economically weaker nations that comprise the overwhelming mass of humanity.

The Conference is also charged with the duty of establishing, for the benefit of all nations, an international authority for the exploration and exploitation of the ocean floor and its subsoil beyond the limits of national jurisdiction. This area and its resources have been declared the common heritage of mankind. The new authority should give life and substance to this concept in a manner which would help reduce the glaring economic disparity that now exists between the developed and the developing countries. That is the essence of the New International Economic Order which the United Nations is striving to create. It is designed to ensure social justice in the world's trading and financial relations.

The world requires and deserves a new, comprehensive law of the sea founded on justice and equity—one which, through its almost universal acceptability, could survive far into the future. The only alternative to such a law is the rule of ruthless competition and unbridled licence, which could spell disaster for all mankind.

The First Committee: THE OCEAN FLOOR

The ocean covers 71% of the earth's surface, and beneath its waters the ocean floor is slowly revealing its secrets. Even today it remains the largest unexplored area of the earth's surface. While man has been drawing maps and charting the resources of the land for centuries, it is only within the last 100 years that the study of the ocean floor has been undertaken, and only within the last 25 years that any degree of understanding has been obtained. Yet our picture of the ocean floor is still only a most general one, lacking the detail which is taken for granted in the simplest studies of land areas.

Two Zones. What, then, is the ocean floor? It is that portion of the earth's surface which lies beneath the sea, and it can be described as two distinct regions—the deep basin and the continental margin. The deep basin has an average depth of 5,000–6,000 m (15,000–18,000 ft) and contains many shallower structures, often of volcanic origin. The continental margin is the submerged edge of the continent, and the zone of transition from continental to oceanic rocks in the earth's crust.

The two zones of the ocean floor are quite different in form, origin, and resource potential. The continental margin consists of a continental shelf of varying width at relatively shallow depth (the drowned edge of the continent), and a continental slope (the edge of the continental block, and the connection between the shelf and the basin floor). The shelf extends from the shoreline to depths of 100–200 m (300–600 ft). Its width varies around the world from 10 km (6.5 mi) to as much as 1,200 km (750 mi). Often the shelf is cut by submarine canyons, drowned river valleys, and—in high latitudes—glacially carved basins. At its outer edge, the slope of the ocean floor increases abruptly toward the basin, marking the beginning of the continental slope. The shelf shares many of the geological features of the adjacent land area and has been the most exploited part of the ocean floor.

The basin floor lies at depths of 2,000–6,000 m (6,000–18,000 ft). Prominent features of the basin are the mid-ocean ridges and the volcanic

By James E. Andrews
*Professor
of Oceanography,
University of Hawaii*

island and seamount groups. The ridges form a nearly continuous structure extending throughout all of the ocean basins. They are zones of elevated topography (about 2,000 m, or 6,000 ft, in depth at the crest) and frequent, concentrated earthquake activity.

Creative and Destructive Processes. Since 1960, marine geologists and geophysicists have shown that this activity (and the topography) results from the systematic and continuous formation of ocean basin crust along the axis of the ridge system. Sometimes the volcanic activity involved in the process is directly observable, as in Iceland which lies on the crest of the Mid-Atlantic Ridge. Iceland is slowly being torn apart by the movement of the new crust away from the ridge axis. Shallow earthquakes along the axis are associated with the spreading of the crust away from the ridge. As the earth is not growing in size there must be a corresponding zone of crustal destruction, and this is found in the deep sea trenches. At the trenches, the ocean basin crust is sinking back into the interior of the earth at the same rate at which it is being formed at the ridges. This sinking is accompanied by intense volcanic activity and shallow- to deep-focus earthquakes. The shape of the trenches themselves—long, linear troughs up to 11,000 m (33,000 ft) deep—is created by the forces which are bringing the crust back into the deeper layers of the earth. Most of the trenches are located in the Pacific Ocean; in fact, the Atlantic and Indian oceans are slowly widening at the expense of the Pacific Ocean. It is this global pattern of formation and destruction of ocean floor that is the source of the major catastrophic events affecting our living areas—events such as the San Francisco earthquake, the Alaska Good Friday earthquake, the more recent San Fernando Valley earthquake, and the major event of the last century—the explosion of Krakatoa.

This evolution of the earth's crust has been more complex in the past than it appears today. At present we find a single major ridge in each ocean basin—the Mid-Atlantic Ridge and the East Pacific Rise in the Atlantic and Pacific oceans, respectively, and the Carlsberg-Indian-Antarctic Ridge in the Indian Ocean. Extinct spreading centers and shifting boundaries of the crustal plates have left complex patterns in the older parts of the ocean basin. The basins, however, are younger than the continental areas; the oldest part of the ocean floor is perhaps slightly more than 150 million years old.

Wealth of the Ocean Floor. The resources of the continental shelf have been exploited for over a century. These include sand and gravel (for use in construction industries), oil, shell deposits (for lime production), bottom-dwelling fish, and heavy mineral placer deposits. Placer deposits are concentrations of heavy minerals in sediment deposits, created by changes in the energy of the stream, current system, or wave patterns which transport the material. They include deposits of diamonds off South Africa, tin and gem stones off Southeast Asia, and gold and platinum in areas such as Alaska.

Oil is one of the major resources of the shelf; more than 16% of the world's production of oil comes from offshore areas such as the Gulf of Mexico, the California shelf, the Cook Inlet of Alaska, the East African shelf, Southeast Asian waters, and the North Sea. Bottom fisheries are also a resource of the shelf in areas such as the Grand Banks and Georges Bank. The exploitation of the fish and oil resources was the first to raise international legal questions about ownership, and these questions have become more nagging as technology has permitted exploitation of the

An underwater television camera on the launch ramp of an ocean-mining vessel. The prospect of tapping the ocean's riches is sprouting a whole new technology as well as legal concepts.

resources farther and farther from shore, in some cases threatening their depletion. The oil, sand and gravel, and placer industries raised some of the first environmental concerns with their extremely visible local pollution.

Ocean Mining. The potential for exploiting the resources of the deep basin, especially the extensive deposits of manganese nodules on the basin floor, has been recognized only recently. The nodules were first discovered in the 1870's, but the great extent of the deposits and their value as a source of needed metals have been clearly defined only in the past 15 years. Manganese nodules are small concretions of manganese and iron oxides, irregularly spherical in shape and measuring 2–8 cm (.75–3.25 in) in diameter. They grow on the ocean floor by the slow addition of material from sediments and from the waters above the ocean floor. (Slow in this case means a rate of growth for the nodules of approximately 1 mm, or less than $\frac{1}{16}$ of an inch, per million years.) Included, as the nodules grow, are varying amounts of other metals in addition to the iron and manganese. The most important of these for economic purposes are copper, nickel, and cobalt. The nodules occur throughout all the ocean basins but are most abundant at depths greater than 4,000 m (12,000 ft). They rest on the ocean floor as a single layer of varying density—forming one of the more unusual ore bodies known. Only rarely are they found buried in the sediments, and mining will involve simply scraping them off the ocean floor and bringing them to the surface.

General distribution of the nodule deposits and their metal content are controlled by the geology of the ocean basin, its sedimentation, and the circulation of the ocean waters. The richest deposits in terms of copper and nickel are found in a band north of the equator in the Pacific Ocean. The average metal contents of these nodules are 30% manganese, 5% iron, 1.4% copper, 1.5% nickel, and 0.3% cobalt. Most land-based mines producing copper and nickel have ores of about 1% metal value.

Where metal contents such as these occur, with 10 kg/m² (2 lb/ft²) or more of nodules over several tens of square kilometers of ocean floor, a potential mine exists. In addition, the area must have gentle enough topography to permit mining systems to remove the nodules efficiently. The percentage of the ocean floor having a suitable combination of all of these parameters is small and limits the choice of mining zones. But future demands for the metals and developments in technology may make more of the ocean floor available for deep-ocean mining.

Problems of Control. Major obstacles facing future and present ocean miners are technological, environmental, and legal. The problems of raising 3–5 million tons of nodules per year from 4,000–5,000 m (12,000–15,000 ft) depths are being solved, but the dredging will have to be done within a framework of environmental understanding. In the continental margin, the effects of pollution from mining and oil wells are obvious, partly because of the small area in question, partly because of the restriction of circulation, and partly because of the closeness of the effects to human presence. In the deep ocean the situation is not so clear, and no adequate description of the basic environmental patterns exists for the development of control guidelines. The National Oceanic and Atmospheric Administration is currently conducting baseline studies for the needed data, and will use these as a guide to monitor pilot mining operations.

Metal-bearing nodules may be scooped from the ocean floor by dredges, but environmental hazards are unclear.

A rope through a hole cut in its fin will secure the whale to the craft. Whaling is restricted for ecological reasons.

PHOTO BY B. J. NIXON, DEEPSEA VENTURES, INC.

THOMAS D. W. FRIEDMAN, PHOTO RESEARCHERS

The legal questions are equally complex. For the continental margins the doctrines of territorial limits have been gradually extended from the early three-mile range to more recent limits of up to 200 miles. These limits have been applied mainly to questions of fisheries control and navigation rights. Control of the resources of the ocean floor, other than bottom fisheries, was first dealt with at the First U. N. Law of the Sea Conference in 1958 which led to the Continental Shelf Convention. Unfortunately, an adequate definition of the shelf's seaward limit proved impossible because of its widely different widths and depths in various parts of the world. The conference gave two alternative criteria for the outer limit of the shelf: (a) the line connecting those points at which the sea floor first reaches a depth of 200 m (600 ft)—that is, the 200-m isobath; or (not and) (b) the distance from shore at which the water is still shallow enough to permit exploitation of the natural resources. With the possibility now of recovering manganese nodules from depths of 5,000 m (15,000 ft) or more, the second criterion could conceivably permit the total partition of the ocean floor among the coastal states.

In the shallow North Sea this has in fact been done for the purpose of oil development, but it is a restricted area and properly speaking on the continental shelf. Although the United Nations has proposed a moratorium on exploitation of the deep ocean floor and has declared the resources to be the "common heritage of mankind," there exist in fact no legal bars at the present time to deep-ocean mining. At the same time, there is no legal protection other than the "freedom of the high seas" for groups undertaking such activities. Thus, while development of mining systems and identification of mine sites is continuing, it is not likely that large-scale exploitation will be undertaken until a legal regime is established either by the United Nations or, lacking global agreement, the nations most involved in ocean development. It is precisely such a regime that the Third U. N. Conference on the Law of the Sea has been striving to formulate.

The Second Committee: JURISDICTION AND NAVIGATIONAL RIGHTS

BY JON L. JACOBSON
*Professor of Law,
University of Oregon*

The Second Committee of the Law of the Sea Conference was assigned the bulk of the agenda items—those concerned with the redefinition of traditional ocean zones and boundaries. During 1976, events both within and outside the conference halls clearly indicated the basic shape of the ocean regime to come.

In many important respects, 1976 was a watershed year. Ocean politics, for several centuries, have been a struggle between the rights of coastal nations to their adjoining waters and those of maritime nations to unrestricted use of the entire world ocean. On the whole, the maritime nations have had the upper hand since the early 17th century, when Dutch jurist Hugo Grotius formulated the "freedom of the seas" concept. By the late 18th century, it had nevertheless become a clear international doctrine that coastal nations were entitled to a narrow band of *territorial sea* along their shores. Even so, nonhostile navigation, or *innocent passage,* was to be unimpeded within territorial seas.

In recent years, things have become more complicated. The now common claims by sea-bordering nations to exclusive fishing zones up to

200 miles (370 km) wide have led to confrontations such as the three "Cod Wars" between Iceland and Britain. New discoveries of resources, combined with advanced ocean technologies, have also led to new legal directions. Offshore oil deposits have prompted many countries to assert exclusive rights to the resources of their continental shelves. Since the First U. N. Law of the Sea Conference in 1958, these rights have been recognized in international law. In 1976 it became clear that they will be expanded.

Part II of the Revised Informal Single Negotiating Text, produced by the Second Committee, is the most heavily negotiated portion of that document. It follows closely the draft treaty articles prepared by a group of international legal experts led by the highly respected Norwegian lawyer Jens Evensen. For that reason, Part II may be viewed as a prediction of the resolution of the long struggle between coastal and maritime nations. On the basis of Part II and some indicative events, the ocean geography of the future can now be generally described. As will be seen, the coastal interests are winning many important rights.

Territorial Sea. All sea-coast countries will be allowed an adjoining 12-mile-wide (22 km) ocean belt, called the territorial sea and properly viewed as an extension of the sovereignty exercised by the coastal nation over its land territory. Traditionally, the only real exception to this total control has been the doctrine of innocent passage, which allows foreign-flag vessels to navigate unimpeded through the territorial sea. Certain activities, however, including fishing and underwater navigation, have been considered non-innocent and subject to exclusion or restriction by the coastal country. Aircraft have always been denied a right of passage over territorial seas of other nations.

Innocent passage will pretty much retain its present status. But a new concept, called *transit passage,* is receiving growing recognition. As defined, transit passage would allow *all* foreign vessels *and* aircraft to travel freely (not just "innocently") through a strait used for international navigation, as long as the transit is "continuous and expeditious," *even though the strait is entirely within the territorial seas of countries bordering the strait.* The transit passage rule would primarily affect the movements of submarines and aircraft. Where planes were formerly prohibited and submarines required to surface and show their flags, air navigation and submerged transit would be allowed by the new doctrine. The United States is the strongest proponent of the transit passage concept. The new 12-mile standard for territorial seas means that such important straits as Gibraltar and Hormuz will be covered by one nation or another's sovereignty; without free transit passage, U. S. military mobility would be severely restricted.

Another new notion would allow nations made up of groups of islands, such as the Philippines, to place some control on traffic through and over their inter-island *archipelagic waters.*

High Seas. Until the early part of this century it could be said that international law recognized only one major ocean zone other than the territorial sea: the high seas. Covering the vast majority of the ocean, the high seas supposedly belonged to the world community, though in practice it was the domain of those nations capable of sailing the world ocean. In the high seas, it was thought, no nation could control navigation, fishing, or any other activities of another nation's citizens.

By the time of the First U. N. Law of the Sea Conference in 1958, it

USCGC *Storis* (small craft, left) catches Soviet trawlers *Lamut* and *Kolyvan* fishing within the U. S. 12-mile limit off St. Matthews Island in the Bering Sea.

U. S. COAST GUARD

had become clear that customary international law recognized at least one or two exceptions to the absolute "freedom of the high seas." On the basis of this customary understanding, the 1958 Geneva conventions established a *contiguous zone* and a *continental shelf zone.* Both concepts granted certain limited jurisdiction to coastal countries beyond their territorial seas. With these qualifications, the 1958 conventions recognized high-seas freedoms of vessel and air navigation, fishing, and laying of cables and pipelines on the sea floor. The 1976 Revised Text shows how far we have come, for—as will be seen—several important, and some drastic, limitations on what have been free high-seas activities are now being acknowledged.

Continental Shelf. Following the lead of the United States in 1945, many nations claimed sovereign rights to the minerals located in and on the continental shelves off their coasts. Since the average width of the continental shelf is nearly 50 nautical miles (92 km), these claims generally reached far out under high-seas waters. The 1958 Continental Shelf Convention ratified these claims, granting coastal countries sovereign rights to the natural resources, other than fish, of the adjacent seabed out to a depth of 200 m (600 ft) or to the limit of exploitability.

The 1976 Revised Text, if adopted as a treaty, would extend these rights to the edge of the continental *margin,* that is, down to the ocean floor or to a distance of 200 miles, whichever is farther. Where, however, mineral exploitation occurs in the margin beyond 200 miles, the coastal nation would be required to contribute a portion of the proceeds to the International Sea-Bed Authority.

Exclusive Economic Zone. The proposed 200-mile *exclusive economic zone* is the greatest departure from the traditional scheme of ocean order. In 1952, when three South American countries first claimed the right to control fishing within 200 miles of their shores, the claims were hardly taken seriously, certainly not as a portent of things to come. In the intervening years, rather narrow fishing-zone claims were common; only a few nations, mostly in Latin America, emulated the 200-mile claimants. Yet, in 1976, a worldwide system of national 200-mile resources zones was ensured—not by the Law of the Sea Conference but by the unilateral action of the United States. The Fishery Conservation and Management Act of 1976, to take effect on March 1, 1977, asserts U. S. jurisdiction over all fish and fishing within 200 miles of the U. S. coast and over fishing for U. S.-source salmon species throughout their migratory routes. It is expected that many other countries will use the U. S. action, and similar ones by Mexico and Canada, as precedents for making 200-mile claims. Such claims will almost certainly proliferate until the 200-mile limit is an established fact of ocean jurisdiction. The principal holdouts were the Soviet Union and Japan, whose world-ranging factory-vessel fleets in large measure caused the 200-mile reaction. Yet even the USSR has now joined the new order, if only "temporarily," pending a global agreement.

It is possible that this pattern of unilateral claims will be superceded by international agreement. If so, the substance of the 200-mile jurisdiction will probably resemble closely the one outlined in the 1976 Revised Text. Each coastal nation will have sovereign rights to the living and nonliving natural resources within its exclusive economic zone. Where its own fishermen do not have the capacity to harvest the entire allowable catch, it may be obligated to grant fishing licenses to foreign fishermen. Highly migratory fish and anadromous species (mainly salmon) are treated separately. It is important to note that the 200-mile economic zone will not affect the traditional freedoms of navigation and overflight and of laying submarine cables and pipelines.

Landlocked and "Geographically Disadvantaged" Nations. Throughout the sessions of the Law of the Sea Conference, the landlocked nations and those (calling themselves "geographically disadvantaged") which otherwise have unfavorable access to the sea and its resources have formed a vigorous negotiating bloc. As a result, the 1976 Revised Text includes provisions granting landlocked countries access rights to the ocean across their coastal neighbors' territories and further granting landlocked and "disadvantaged" nations rights to participate in living-resource harvests from the economic zones of their neighbors.

The Third Committee: SCIENTIFIC RESEARCH AND POLLUTION CONTROL

By HENRY CHARNOCK
Institute of Oceanographic Sciences, England

Marine researchers are accustomed to making observations anywhere in the ocean, without hindrance. They justify the high cost of their work by pointing out that the ocean acts as a support for ships, a source of food, a sink for waste, and a regulator of climate: knowledge about such an important resource is bound to prove valuable.

It now looks as if their freedom will soon be over. At least so far as a 200-mile (370-km) coastal zone is concerned, the Law of the Sea may soon require them to seek permission of the appropriate coastal state before they can make measurements or take samples of the water, the ocean floor, or living organisms. Such applications may not always be considered on their merits but can be capriciously refused or hedged about with conditions so restrictive as to make the work not worth attempting.

How has this come about? Is it justified? What is likely to happen? These are some of the questions now worrying marine scientists. Unambiguous and dispassionate answers are not to be expected. Nevertheless some of the background can be recognized and some possible consequences foreseen.

Recent decades have seen a great increase in the number of independent nations, many of them previously colonies or dependencies of what

U. S. COAST GUARD

Control of pollution in the
world ocean is one of the
vital issues facing mankind.
The wrecked tanker (above)
left an oil spill 14 inches
(35 cm) thick outside San
Juan Harbor and blackened
11 miles (18 km) of seashore.

were once great powers. Most of these new countries are at an early stage
of their industrial development; few of them have, as yet, a capacity for
independent marine research. As long as oceanography was the interest
of only a few eccentric scientists this caused no difficulty, but as it developed and became useful for military and commercial pursuits, it seemed as
if it might be one of the many activities which perpetuated, or even increased, the disparity between rich and poor nations. It was thought that
great wealth was readily available to anyone who could dredge it from the
floor of the ocean; unanswerable questions were raised about the ownership
of the hypothetical bonanza of marine resources. This was in an era when
the extraction of offshore oil began to be of greater commercial value than
fishing; when the great powers took to transporting their hydrogen bombs
in nuclear submarines.

The discussions of the Law of the Sea Conference have taken place
against this background. The conference has acted as a focus for the hopes
and fears of many nations not previously concerned with maritime matters,
some of them without coastlines. Most discussion has been on economic
and military matters, with marine science often being regarded as a pretext
by means of which the predatory rich can get an early sight of the wealth
to be taken. Present indications are of a zonation of the ocean, the parts
nearest land to be controlled by coastal states, the open ocean to come
under a more general control committed to exploiting it for the common
good.

It is not, perhaps, surprising that the idea of a broad economic zone,
controlled by the coastal state, has replaced the old notion of narrow territorial limits. The word 'economic' reflects the main preoccupation of the
long legal discussions which have taken place.

It may be argued that, since the typical width of our ocean far exceeds
200 miles, plenty is left for scientists to study, but it happens that many
of the most important and most interesting phenomena occur at the edge.
Processes close to land have a disproportionate effect: one has only to
think of western boundary currents like the Gulf Stream and the climatic
effect of its huge transport of warm water poleward, to realize that we cannot understand the ocean until we understand what is going on at its edges.

If it is admitted that scientists need access to the near-shore zone as
well as the open sea, there would appear to be no reason why a coastal
state should not allow them to work within its economic zone. Yet all the

indications are that research vessels will not be allowed merely to notify the state concerned, but will have to make a detailed formal application. This is presumably a safeguard against commercial or military activity, though neither seems likely to present a major difficulty; almost any nation can contrive sufficient surveillance to be aware of any major exploitation, while military demonstrations of any importance are increasingly the prerogative of a few large powers—powers which indeed might with impunity prefer not to ratify any treaty that is negotiated. Some developed nations prefer to remain ignorant of any resource within their economic zone until they are technically capable of exploiting it.

It may be that many nations are ready to slow down the pace of marine research in the hope that their own capability will become comparable with that of the present leaders. Because such decisions are unilateral and not based on a wish to promote natural knowledge, there seems no way in which they can be delegated to an international authority, even if one could be found, or created, which was capable (and seen to be capable) of distinguishing between bonafide science and resource reconnaissance. That marine research will be slowed down seems inescapable, for not only will lack of reasonable access have a direct effect but, more important, the bright young people on whom progress depends will naturally prefer a branch of science within which freedom to make observations does not depend on unpredictable bureaucratic decisions. Altogether the prospect for freedom to attempt to understand the properties, populations, and processes of the ocean is less favorable than it has been for many years. Of course there is much to do in the open sea, and many nations are sufficiently cooperative to make interesting work possible closer to land. But what some find the main attraction of marine research—its combination of personal effort with international cooperation—seems doomed to fade.

It is ironic that this should be so at a time when everyone is becoming more conscious of the need to protect man's environment. If it is desirable that we should use the ocean, it is vital that we should use it wisely. Of all the substances in the world, water is the one most magically related to the evolution of man, yet our knowledge of the sources, the cycles, and the sinks of substances in the ocean is not sufficient to allow us to predict the effects of even small changes in concentrations of particular elements. We are rightly concerned over the dumping into the ocean of radioactive waste, there are scares about metals such as mercury, worries about increasing amounts of lead from automobile exhausts, about DDT, and a host of other substances. About half the amount of potential pollutants reaches the ocean through rivers, the other half being transported by the wind. In either case the effect is felt in the ocean as a whole and not only in the near-shore zone. Marine pollution is caused mainly by the developed nations, for there is a marked connection between the amount of industrial waste and the gross national product.

Scientific research and pollution control were discussed by the same committee of the Law of the Sea Conference, but they have little in common. It is true that only scientific research can inform us whether a particular substance is a serious pollutant and provide us with a sound basis on which to estimate the likely concentration for a given matter. But pollutants are man-made and their control a matter for legislation.

Sensible legislation is clearly desirable. International groups of able scientists and lawyers are working on problems of definition and detection, but they will be much hindered if scientific research is made more difficult.

THE QUICK FOOD CHAINS

The Fastest Growing Segment of the Restaurant Industry

BY JANE BRADFORD, *Assistant Producer, CBS News*

Americans now eat one of every three meals outside the home. In the 1950's, only a few cents of the average family food dollar went for meals eaten out. Today the figure is 35 cents. The restaurant industry accounted for 4.5% of the U. S. gross national product, or $64,000,000,000, in 1974. The industry is number one in retail outlets, with more than 500,000 serving units across the United States. In other words, there are more restaurants than any other business.

In recent years, one segment of the industry, the quick food chains, has exceeded all others in growth. With 35 cents here and 35 cents there, the quick food restaurants are serving $11,500,000,000 worth of meals a year. Today there are an estimated 45,000 quick food stands. Such places exist not only in the United States, but are dotting the globe as well.

Hamburger places are the most popular, with more than 25,000 units; chickens are second with nearly 6,000 units; and pizza and taco establishments are third and fourth respectively. Seafood stands bring up the rear, but are marching forward rapidly in terms of the number of customers. There are over 3,700 McDonald's restaurants; some 4,700 Kentucky Fried Chickens; 2,400 Pizza Huts; 1,600 Burger Kings; 925 Burger Chefs; 900 Hardees; 800 members of the Jack-In-The-Box chain; and 500 Arby's. Indeed, for better or for worse, the world is becoming linked not so noticeably by communication satellites as by golden arches, pizza huts, and the smiling face of a Kentucky colonel.

History. In the 1880's, the Industrial Revolution sent vast numbers of men and women into factories and offices. They had to be fed quickly and inexpensively. To meet the need, the first cafeteria opened in New York City in 1885. With the cafeteria, restaurants were brought within the financial reach of all. The Industrial Revolution continued. The automobile assembly line developed. Additional ways of feeding people en masse were explored, especially during World Wars I and II.

A result of World War II was the postwar baby boom. An effect of the baby boom was the quick food restaurant. The kids had to eat. Time for the assembly-line burger had come.

McDonald's. In the late 1940's in San Bernardino, Calif., two brothers, Maurice "Mac" McDonald and Richard McDonald, opened a hamburger stand . . . with arches. Later the brothers decided to serve only hamburgers, drinks, and French fries. They also eliminated all the usual restaurant frills and even some "necessities"—silverware, glasses, dishes, and long menus. The new emphasis was on cleanliness and uniformity. The McDonald's business honed its performance to deal with heavy volume in a short amount of time. The formula worked. Soon they had franchised six other stores in California.

While the brothers were the creators of McDonald's, Ray Kroc was the promoter, the dynamo. A piano player, a music director of a Chicago radio station, a lot salesman in Florida, and a seller of milk-shake machines, Ray Kroc knew what he wanted. And when a hamburger stand in San Bernardino wanted eight of his milk-shake machines, he wanted the hamburger stand. Initially selling McDonald's franchises for a commission, Ray Kroc eventually bought the contract.

By the end of 1965, there were 710 McDonald's. Today there are some 3,700. In 1975, McDonald's sales volume accounted for about 20% of the quick food market. It sold $2,500,000,000 worth of quick food. In food volume, it surpassed the U. S. Army.

Kentucky Fried Chicken. In his early years, Harland Sanders was neither a colonel nor a millionaire. He was born in 1890 on a farm in Henryville, Ind. At the age of six, following the death of his father, Harland became cook and head of the household while his mother worked. Later he worked as a railroad fireman, insurance agent, streetcar conductor, steamboat promoter, and service station attendant. While

The recent success of the quick food chain is due in part to rapid customer turnover, self-service operation, and a flexible labor force with a high percentage of part-timers.

BURGER KING CORP.   FOODMAKER, INC.

MURRAY GREENBERG, MONKMEYER

operating a service station in Corbin, Ky., Harland decided to make some homemade snacks to serve the travelers . . . homemade chicken snacks. The Sanders' Cafe was born. The food became so renowned in the 1930's that Kentucky Gov. Ruby Laffoon gave Harland the title colonel in recognition of his contribution to Kentucky's cuisine. The Sanders' Cafe thrived until the mid-1950's when the two roads on which the restaurant stood were bypassed by a new highway. The cafe was sold at auction.

Rather than live on social security and whatever savings he had, Colonel Sanders set out in 1956, at age 66, to sell his recipe. "Let me cook chicken for you and your staff," he told restaurant operators. "If you like the way it tastes, I'll sell you my seasoning, teach you how to cook it, and you pay me a four-cent royalty on every chicken you sell." They liked the taste.

By 1960, Sanders had 400 franchises in the United States and Canada. By 1962, he had close to 600. By 1963, he had enough. He sold the company to investors for $2 million with the proviso that he receive a lifetime salary and remain in charge of quality control. Heublein, the food and liquor conglomerate, acquired Kentucky Fried Chicken in 1971 for $285 million. Today there are 4,700 KFC stores, grossing over $1,000,000,000 a year. Some 2.5 million "finger lickin' good" dinners are served daily.

Burger Chef. Like the other quick food hamburger restaurants, Burger Chef began in the years following World War II and blossomed in the 1960's. The first Burger Chef restaurant was started by an Indianapolis restaurant equipment company looking for a place to display its wares. By 1964, there were over 300 Burger Chef restaurants. Today there are some 925. The restaurant did better than the equipment.

In the 1960's, the ripest areas for all of the quick food restaurants were the suburbs and heavily traveled roads. By the mid-1970's, such restaurants had moved into the inner cities.

Ownership and Franchising. While many of the quick food chains were begun by individuals, today most are owned by the huge food conglomerates. Burger King is owned by Pillsbury; Burger Chef is a subsidiary of General Foods; Kentucky Fried Chicken is owned by Heublein; Jack-In-The-Box belongs to Ralston Purina.

Value, speed of service, cleanliness, and uniformity of product all contributed to the growth of the quick food chains. But in the 1960's one policy in particular, franchising, gave the quick food chains the money and manpower to expand beyond all expectation. The franchisee brings to the quick food company his money, talent, interest, and energy. What does he get? He gets a recipe. He gets a nine-week course leading to a bachelor of "hamburgerology" degree from Hamburger University if he opens a McDonald's. He gets a three-week training course at Whopper College if he opens a Burger King unit. But no matter what company he joins, he gets a name.

What is in a name? Referring to a Burger King restaurant in New York City, Frederick H. Guterman, chairman of the N. Y. restaurant chain of Horn & Hardart, claims: "I could walk down there today, take down the Burger King sign, and put one up that read Fred's Burgers, and volume would drop 60% before the end of the day." In the year before it acquired franchising rights to Burger King in Manhattan, Horn & Hardart lost $10 million on sales of $29 million. With eight Burger King units, Horn & Hardart earned $115,000 on sales of $48 million in 1975. Obviously, quite a lot is in a name.

According to the U. S. Department of Commerce study, "Franchising In The Economy," there were 44,724 fast food establishments in 1975—11,121 company owned and 33,603 owned by franchisees. Despite these facts, a new trend seems to be arising—several of the larger quick food chains are beginning to eliminate franchising. Some are buying back franchises, especially from the individual. Economics is also forcing the individual out of the quick food industry. Each unit of Burger King, for example, costs over $200,000 for the building, equipment, and franchise fees.

Costs. At McDonald's, a Big Mac hamburger, French fries, and a "thick shake" cost about $1.75. In fact, the average quick food meal costs under $2.00. If one prepared the food at home, it might cost more. How do the quick food restaurants maintain such prices and still make a profit?

For one thing, there is the limited, uniform menu. For another, the restaurants are self-service. Not only do you get the food yourself, you are encouraged to clear away the used containers. In addition, most of the labor force at the quick food chains are high school and college students and housewives—as many as 90% working part-time. This enables the restaurants to increase their staffs during peak hours and decrease them at other times. The workers are generally paid the minimum wage with few fringe benefits. The restaurants also depend on a rapid customer turnover. Seats, in fact, are designed to be hard enough so that customers will not linger.

Conclusion. In a National Restaurant Association Consumer Attitude Survey, conducted in 1975, Americans were asked to reveal their reasons for dining out. "Nobody has to cook or clean up" and "a change of pace" were frequent answers to the question. "Enjoy good food," was number *eleven*. To be fair to American standards of taste, however, the most common complaint of the diners-out was "poor food quality."

In conclusion, a caution is in order. Although most quick food meals supply ample amounts of protein and energy to satisfy the daily requirements of the body, they lack sufficient nutrients and are excessively high in calories. No more than one third of our daily calories should come from fat. In fast food meals, however, almost half the calories come from fat. As a result, nutritionists warn the frequent visitor of quick food establishments to make sure that other meals include vegetables and fruits.

MULTINATIONAL BUSINESS ETHICS

By Eugene R. Black
*Former President
of the World Bank*

During 1976, in the wake of the political scandals known collectively as Watergate, the world learned that large numbers of U. S. business enterprises were making illegal or questionable payments to businessmen and government officials both at home and abroad. The phenomenon swiftly gained such labels as corporate bribery and multinational corruption, and it attracted the attention not only of businessmen, regulators, legislators, and the press, but also of foreign governments, international organizations, and students of the changing shape of world trade.

Some Proposals for Reform. Opinion is divided on the question of just what steps are necessary to control unethical corporate payments. Plans for corrective action seem to reflect the broader perspectives of the various interests involved. At one extreme of opinion, there have been calls for legislation that would define certain international payments as criminal offenses under United States statutes—although the problems of enforcement, given the number of jurisdictions sharing authority over the matter, are immense. At the opposite extreme, a few businessmen have dismissed the problem as either too commonplace or too trivial to worry about and have bitterly criticized the hypocrisy of government officials around the world; for it is government officialdom that has often been the prime mover of corporate bribery.

Meanwhile, proposals less extreme than either global legislation or total indifference have included the suggestions:

—that individual corporations monitor their international marketing procedure much more carefully;

—that corporations subscribe to common and specific codes of conduct;

—that all payments by American companies to foreign officials be disclosed to the U. S. government;

—that the Securities and Exchange Commission, overseer of many other aspects of business life, set precise guidelines for the disclosure of funds disbursed to government officials abroad;

In July, former Japanese Prime Minister Kakuei Tanaka (*above*) was arrested on charges of violating Japan's foreign exchanges rules. Special editions of Tokyo newspapers (*left*) reported the case.

—that "slush funds" and similar irregular accounts be eliminated.

Without a doubt, some of these steps will be instituted in the United States and other countries. The desire is widespread both to improve the reputation of multinational corporations and to enable them to engage in vigorous world trade.

The Lockheed Scandal. Perhaps the best-known case of an American company that has offended people all over the world with its questionable and/or illegal methods of marketing is that of the Lockheed Aircraft Corporation. During 1976 it became apparent that Lockheed had spent tens of millions of dollars in secret payments to officials of foreign governments for the purpose of securing or continuing the sale of Lockheed's aircraft. When the payments were uncovered the outcry was particularly loud in the United States because the federal government had just spent hundreds of millions of dollars in special loans and grants to Lockheed in attempts to save the company from bankruptcy.

Lockheed's bribes caused a sensation everywhere. Vague reports that the company had paid off an Italian prime minister were partly responsible for the resignation of the Christian Democratic government of Premier Aldo Moro. Most spectacular of all were the multimillion dollar payments to various Japanese officials, businessmen and lobbyists—including former Prime Minister Kakuei Tanaka, who in late July went to jail for not reporting international currency transactions, a clear violation of Japanese law. The Lockheed scandal was Japan's worst since World War II.

In the Netherlands, Prince Bernhard was forced to resign his military and business posts in part because of his relationship with Lockheed. A three-member commission spent six months investigating the Prince's case and concluded that he had "allowed himself to be tempted to take initiatives, which were completely unacceptable and which were bound to place himself and the Netherlands procurement policy . . . in a dubious light."

Finally, as one further illustration, it was reported that a private citizen of Saudi Arabia, Adnan Khashoggi, received more than $100 million from Lockheed in commissions between 1970 and 1975.

The Lockheed case, though more bizarre and in some instances more deeply reprehensible than any other multinational corporate scandal, was not the only one in which laws were broken, the relations between nations strained, the reputations of American businesses compromised, and the general level of cynicism raised. By the summer of 1976, more than 150 companies had either been accused of comparable behavior or had voluntarily submitted to the Securities and Exchange Commission accounts of questionable payments. These companies included some of the most prestigious in the United States: the Aluminum Company of America, the Armco Steel Corporation, the General Tire and Rubber Company, the Inmont (chemical specialties) Corporation, the Squibb drug company, the Occidental Petroleum Corporation, the United Brands company, and many others. It became clear that bribes and kickbacks, although in some cases small and infrequent, were a nearly universal practice.

American companies were not alone, of course. Other industrial nations were similarly embarrassed—when they were exposed at all. Certain Japanese firms, for instance, are among the most notorious dispensers of money and favors—this in a country which has recently experienced the "shocks" of American corporate misconduct.

What Is a Bribe? The specific problems that emerged from all these cases were interpreted differently by different commentators. A few themes, however—some ethical, some political, some diplomatic, and others strictly economic—were mentioned over and over again.

Bribery—to start with the most obvious theme—is universally frowned upon. There are laws in other countries, just as there are in the United States, that exact criminal penalties for the payment of money and other valuables to public officials for the purpose of securing special favors. Some observers of the recent multinational scandals have pointed to this fact as reason for maintaining a hard-line attitude toward questionable corporate payments.

In many cases, however, defining what constitutes bribery is not at all simple. For if outright bribery is frowned upon in all civilized societies, gifts are not. Nor are tips, bonuses, retainers, commissions, expediting fees, and similar considerations. When passed under the table, of course, they may be known as *la mordida* ("the little bite" of Latin America), or as "grease." Yet many countries engage in such practices all the time. So do many people in the United States.

The ambiguity in the meaning of bribery has suggested to some observers that guidelines and codes of conduct rather than new laws are the best means to reform multinational business ethics. Moreover, the universal prohibition against outright bribery of government officials has suggested to some that no *additional* laws are required. If the payments are truly bribes, in other words, they are illegal, and no one should be in any doubt about them; if discovered, presumably, they will result in prosecutions, fines, and similar sanctions. If the payments are not bribes, and if the corporations break no laws or local customs, then they are at worst unethical, and any company or individual exposed for such actions would suffer a certain degree of ill-will.

International Backlash. There are other problems, however, that could have serious repercussions for American business. Corporate pay-

UPI

Adnan Khashoggi, a private citizen of Saudi Arabia, is said to have received from Lockheed more than $100 million in commissions between 1970 and 1975.

ments of a questionable nature could have a very bad effect, first, on America's international reputation (the inevitable guilt by association), and second, on the conduct of American foreign policy. The American public, moreover, probably has a right to know if the behavior of powerful corporations reflects poorly on the United States. There can be no doubt that some such dishonor has already soiled the nation. It has not improved its morale. Nor has it escaped the attention of those abroad who are either undecided about what to think of the United States, or who already carry its condemnation in their pockets. As a Washington lawyer, Lloyd Cutler, said in a speech before the Tri-Lateral Commission of American, European, and Japanese businessmen: "Nothing we have recently done to ourselves has helped more [than corporate bribery] to discredit private enterprise, both in the United States and abroad—especially multinational private enterprise—and to speed the spread of the corporate state." In other words, government intervention will tend to follow any truly irresponsible behavior in the free market system.

This is a point, incidentally, that most multinational corporations understand without being told, and it helps explain why the directors of hundreds of companies have taken steps to investigate and reform their organizations' questionable marketing tactics.

On a more immediate level of foreign policy, revelations that foreign leaders have been the recipients of cash payments and the tools of foreign interests could easily lead to their downfall. Situations like that are to be avoided. They could dangerously muddle America's interests.

Other Facets of the Problem. Several other themes became prominent with the recent disclosures. One of them is the suggestion that American business behavior in the world is worse than it used to be and worse than that of other countries. This would be a difficult thesis to prove. Indeed, it is probably untrue. American business conduct abroad is more standardized, more carefully accounted for, and far more open to scrutiny than it used to be, and its integrity, for the most part, is at least equal to that of other countries. Certainly, there are other nations whose business standards are generally considered below those of the United States. Some of the most virulent criticism of American business conduct, by the way, has come from precisely those countries.

If the recent disclosures, some of which are undeniably sordid, reflect any powerful new trend, it is not that moral standards are plummeting or that multinational corporations are peculiarly unscrupulous but that an enormous and unprecedented amount of business is being conducted. The growth of world trade in recent years has been staggering, and many of the acts that have been disclosed date back to the beginnings of that surge—notably to the late 1960's and early 1970's. Competition has been sharp and is getting sharper, and the pressures on American companies— on their affiliates, subsidiaries, salesmen, forwarding agents, and so on— have been intense. It does not make such strain any more bearable that the products of these companies are second to none produced in other nations and, indeed, better than most. In retrospect, it might have been equally surprising to have watched a huge new international business system conducted without the shadow of a kickback as it has been to see scandals reported almost daily in the press.

The Role of Government Officials. There are other problems as well. One of the most disturbing—and least amenable to internal business reform—concerns the role of government officials in the whole matter of

Sen. Frank Church (*right*) served as chairman of the Senate Subcommittee on Multinational Corporations. David J. Haughton resigned as Lockheed's chief executive officer following reports that the company paid millions of dollars to foreign government officials to promote arms sales.

business ethics. Even in the United States, the heavy-handed tactics of campaign fundraisers for Richard Nixon are not the only, nor the latest, examples of corrupting official pressures on corporate conduct. The situation is no better, and often it is far worse, in many of the countries in which multinational corporations do business. Some political candidates and government officials have put their hands out; some corporations have agreed to fill them.

The precise threats made, or the promises given, tend to vary with circumstances, yet the essential fact remains that government officials can, if they so choose, prevent a corporation from doing business. (That many foreign business enterprises are actually agencies of their governments only enlarges the field of possible government extortion.) As John J. McCloy expressed the matter in testimony before the Senate Banking Committee: "In practically all these questionable payment situations, one finds a government somewhere in the woodpile."

Criminalization or Forced Disclosure. Proposals for dealing with the problems of international corporate ethics are in a state of flux—a state that reflects both the complexity and the ideological controversy that suffuse the subject. Some general remedies have already been mentioned. A few more specific proposals for reform should also be noted.

Sen. William Proxmire, Democrat of Wisconsin and chairman of the Senate Banking Committee, introduced a bill that would make it a crime to offer bribes to foreign government officials. This approach to the problem, widely publicized, is strongly urged in some quarters, and Theodore C. Sorensen has recommended it on the grounds, among others, that it would make corporation representatives overseas less susceptible to the outstretched hands of government officials. A simple U. S. law would tell them not to oblige. As *The Washington Post* has editorialized, however, "to 'criminalize' bribery, when prosecution would depend on witnesses and information beyond the reach of the U. S. judicial process, would be of dubious benefit."

Less stringent than the proposal to make overseas bribery a crime in the United States was the plan put forward by President Ford's administration to require American companies to disclose all payments made to foreign officials or their associates for the purpose of furthering business interests. The hope behind this plan is that companies would never bribe anyone in the first place if they were compelled by law to announce the fact. Their disclosures, in any case, would go to the State Department, which might reveal the payments to the foreign governments involved and to the public, thus embarrassing the corporations and exposing them to possible prosecution abroad. Simple failure to disclose, if discovered, would result in prosecution at home.

This plan has encountered less criticism than the Proxmire proposal, but it, too, has been called imperfect. As *The New York Times* editorialized (in defense of criminal statutes): "Any firm bent on continuing payoff relationships with foreign authorities or buyers could manage to conceal the payments. . . ."

Some business leaders also oppose forced disclosure—in general because it would represent yet another intrusion by government into the private sector, but more specifically because it might put American corporations at a serious disadvantage in the competitive arena of world trade. Yet, some system of disclosure will very likely be instituted. It is widely believed, for instance, that accounting procedures which allow the existence of "slush funds" and other off-the-books accounts must be reformed—by the corporations themselves and also by law. This was one of the conclusions of John J. McCloy when he was chairman of the Gulf Special Review Committee that investigated approximately $5 million in illegal campaign contributions by the Gulf Oil Corporation to political candidates in the United States. McCloy also emphasized the responsibility of legal counsel, accountants, auditors, audit committees, and directors to demand full information on just what kinds of payments are being made.

Global Solution Needed. The problems of unethical corporate behavior in international trade have also attracted attention outside the United States. The United Nations has focused on the issue, and so have the 24 industrial nations in the Organization for Economic Cooperation and Development (O. E. C. D.). The United Nations' Economic and Social Council, acting on an initiative from the United States, plans by early 1977 to draw up an accord on bribery that may or may not be included in a more general code of conduct being developed by the Commission on Transnational Corporations, another agency of the United Nations. The O. E. C. D., meanwhile, has already devised such a code for multinational corporations.

Such global efforts to come to terms with the realities of multinational business are much needed, and it is to be hoped that they are seriously undertaken; it is clear that international trade requires international attention. None of these large-scale codes, however, will amount to much unless American businessmen clean up their own shops. Fortunately, many corporations have taken actions to do just that.

If anything is in danger of being forgotten amid all the concern over corporate misbehavior, it is the fact that these companies have been the agents of industrial and organizational progress throughout the world. They have also added to the prosperity of many millions of people. It is true that some multinational corporations have acted reprehensibly, and no appeal to the complexities and competitive pressures of trade can exonerate them. But it is also true that most companies have conducted the large bulk of their business honorably—and indeed more productively and straightforwardly than most governments, east or west.

UPI

Mao Tse-tung, a founder of the Chinese Communist Party and one of the most powerful men in the world, died in Peking on Sept. 9, 1976, at the age of 82. During the 27 years that Mao led the People's Republic of China, massive pro-Mao demonstrations such as the one that took place in April (photograph) were a common occurrence.

REVIEW OF THE YEAR

ACCIDENTS AND DISASTERS

On May 21, in Martinez, Calif., a school bus crashed through a guard rail and plunged to the ground. Twenty-eight members of a high school choir were killed.

UPI

AVIATION

Jan. 1—Middle East Airlines Boeing 707 crashes in Saudi Arabian desert, killing all 82 aboard.

Jan. 3—Soviet TU-134 airliner crashes on takeoff at Vnukovo airport, Moscow, killing all 56 aboard.

April 14—Plane owned by the Argentine state oil company crashes in southern Argentina, killing all 37 passengers.

April 27—American Airlines jetliner crashes on landing at Charlotte Amalie in the U. S. Virgin Islands, killing 37 and injuring 51 survivors.

May 9—Iranian Air Force 747 cargo aircraft crashes near Madrid, killing all 17 crew members.

June 4—Air Manila jet strikes truck during takeoff from Guam airport, killing 45 passengers and the truckdriver.

June 6—Plane crash on the island of Borneo kills 11, including the entire leadership of Sabah, the east Malaysian state formerly known as North Borneo.

July 28—Czechoslovak airliner crashes into a lake while on a landing approach at Bratislava airport, killing 70 of the 76 people aboard.

Aug. 3—Plane crash in Missouri kills U.S. Congressman Jerry L. Litton, his wife, two children, and two others.

Sept. 4—Venezuelan plane carrying a choir to Spain crashes in the Azores, killing 68 persons.

Sept. 10—British and Yugoslav airliners collide above Zagreb, Yugoslavia, killing 176 persons.

Oct. 6—Cuban jetliner crashes into the Caribbean just off Barbados, killing all 73 persons aboard.

Oct. 12—Indian Airlines jet crashes at Bombay airport, killing all 95 passengers.

Oct. 13—Cargo jet plunges into one of the main thoroughfares of Santa Cruz, Bolivia, and kills 100 people.

Nov. 23—Greek airliner crashes in northern Greece, killing all 50 persons aboard.

Nov. 29—Soviet airliner crashes during takeoff from Moscow airport, killing at least 72 passengers.

EARTHQUAKES

Nov. 24—A major earthquake strikes eastern Turkey, killing some 4,000 persons.

(For a listing of earthquakes occurring earlier in the year see page 228.)

FIRES, EXPLOSIONS, AND BUILDING CAVE-INS

Jan. 1—Flash fire sweeps through a Belgian dance hall, killing 15 persons and injuring 33 others.

Jan. 10—Explosion and fire destroy a hotel in Fremont, Neb., leaving at least 18 dead.

Jan. 30—Fire spreads through a nursing home in Chicago, killing 18 elderly residents.

April 11—Fire sweeps through a hotel in Abu Dhabi, killing at least 5 persons and injuring 9 others.

April 13—Explosion at an ammunition factory in Finland kills 45 workers and injures 70 others in Finland's worst industrial accident.

Sept. 9—Six-story apartment building in Karachi, Pakistan, collapses, leaving more than 80 dead.

Oct. 24—Fire in New York social club kills 25 young party-goers and injures 24 others.

Nov. 19—Three fire fighters are injured as fire rages through a high-rise office building in Los Angeles.

Nov. 21—An explosion rips through a factory in New York City, killing four and injuring more than 45 workers.

LAND AND SEA TRANSPORTATION

Jan. 9—Chicago Transit Authority train plows into a parked commuter train, killing one and injuring 400.

Mar. 9—A ski-lift cable car plunges 200 feet (60 m) to ground near Cavalese, Italy, killing 42 of 43 aboard.

Mar. 26—At least 45 wedding guests are killed when their tractor-drawn wagon plunges into a canal in Pune, India.

April 15—Survival capsule launched from a sinking oil rig in the Gulf of Mexico capsizes, drowning 13 men; passenger bus skids into a deep pond near Gonda, India, drowning 50 persons.

April 21—Express train hits bus in central Taiwan, killing 40 bus passengers and injuring 42 others.

May 4—Dutch commuter train collides with the Rhine Express near Rotterdam, killing 23 passengers.

May 23—Speeding fuel truck and train collide in Seoul, South Korea, killing at least 19 people.

June 14—Passenger and freight train collision in Bulgaria kills 10.

June 27—Train derailment in Belgium leaves 11 vacationers dead and 29 injured.

July 13—Commuter train crash in New Canaan, Conn., kills 1 and injures 24.

Aug. 8—Ferryboat capsizes off southern Thailand; 26 persons drown.

Sept. 11—Two passenger trains collide in south Cameroon, killing nearly 100 persons.

Oct. 15—Two runaway freight cars plow into a crowded bus near Havana, Cuba, killing 54 bus passengers; a cargo ship with a crew of 37 is reported missing and believed sunk in an area of the Atlantic Ocean known as the Bermuda Triangle.

Oct. 20—Ferryboat on the Mississippi River capsizes, north of New Orleans, La., after being rammed by a Norwegian tanker; 77 bodies are found.

Nov. 3—Express train rams passenger train in southern Poland, killing 25 people and injuring 60 other passengers.

Nov. 11—Nineteen crewmen are lost as a Japanese lumber vessel sinks in the Pacific Ocean northwest of Honolulu.

Nov. 14—Bus plunges into the Urubu River near Manaus, Brazil, killing 38 passengers.

Nov. 29—At least 12 people are killed as express train plunges into a river at Kathekani, Kenya; bus and taxi collide in Van, Turkey, killing 25 people and seriously injuring 15.

STORMS AND FLOODS

April 10—Tornado in Bangladesh kills 19 and injures more than 200.

May 20–24—Typhoon sweeps northern Philippines causing four days of torrential rains and floods, claiming 215 lives and leaving about 630,000 homeless.

May 22—Typhoon in Guam leaves 80% of the island's buildings in ruins and 3 people dead.

June 6—Floods caused by the collapse of the Teton Dam in Idaho kill 11 and leave 30,000 homeless.

July 31—Flash floods in the Big Thompson River canyon near Denver, Colo., kill 139 people.

Aug. 10—Monsoon floods in the Punjab region of Pakistan kill at least 150 and damage about 140,000 homes.

Sept. 13—Typhoon in southern Japanese island of Kyushu kills more than 160 and leaves nearly 325,000 persons homeless.

Oct. 1—Hurricane Liza strikes Baja California, Mexico, killing more than 600 persons.

Oct. 6—Rain-swollen waters break through a dike in Pereira, Colombia, killing at least 47 people.

Nov. 13–14—Floods caused by heavy rains in eastern Java leave 14 persons dead and more than 30 injured.

Nov. 21—At least 29 people die as a cyclone hits the state of Andhra Pradesh on India's east coast.

ADVERTISING

Advertising volume in the United States during 1976 showed the strongest growth rate (18%) in 30 years, well ahead of the gross national product. Unusual spending was fueled by special events—the bicentennial, the Olympics, national election campaigns. New product introductions received aggressive ad support, as did newly-hot categories from CB radios to pet food. Escalating media costs, especially in television, prompted advertisers to test new media mixes or alternate solutions. Self-regulatory efforts toughened, as advertising increasingly attracted legal and regulatory action.

Law and Regulation. A landmark U. S. Supreme Court decision awarded advertising First Amendment protection as "commercial" speech. Pressure mounted to allow professionals, such as lawyers, to advertise. Ad spending and practices were key issues in a Federal Trade Commission (FTC) case against major cereal makers. Self-regulation underwent an FTC probe on effectiveness. Industry-wide efforts included stricter scrutiny of ad abuses and guidelines on portrayal of such groups as the elderly and women. Individual industries, such as banking, also developed self-policing codes. Meantime, regulatory action hit new areas from testimonials to cold remedy ingredients and claims.

Copy. Clashes of comparative product claims escalated in categories from leading colas to non-aspirin analgesics. These tough head-on confrontations aroused industry concern and prompted issuance of FTC rules. Sober, fact-oriented copy, promoting product benefits uncovered by consumer research, continued as the hallmark of many campaigns. Advocacy advertising promoted causes ranging from returnable beverage containers to energy conservation; the Advertising Council even mounted an effort on behalf of the U. S. economic system.

Media. Television, the major medium for top advertisers, was the center of controversy on costs. Pressure increased for a fourth network, as advertisers moved to control pricing and program environment through nationwide syndication of their own shows. Fierce competition saw ABC, long the third-place network, take the lead from CBS, a 20-year front-runner.

Magazine successes ranged from gossipy tabloids, including *People* (the first mass periodical to make it in years), to new regional—especially sunbelt—entries. Specialized publications zeroed in on such target groups as working women and gourmets, or those adopting alternate life styles, including homosexuals and marijuana smokers. Newspapers fought local television incursions with aggressive drives for co-op dollars. With circulation lagging behind population, owners tried livelier formats and new features. Radio's multimedia study helped counter the medium's weakness in audience research, gaining new advertisers.

© GENERAL FOODS CORPORATION 1976

New product innovations, including Cycle 4 dog food, received aggressive advertising support in 1976. Fact-oriented copy (*example below*) pointed out product benefits uncovered through consumer research.

© 1975 NO NONSENSE FASHIONS INC.

Advertising Volume. Total spending surged to $33,200,000,000 from 1975's $28,300,000,-000, with national advertising ($18,200,000,000) growing faster than local ($15,000,000,000). Newspaper ads were $10,000,000,000, while television spending spurted to $6,700,000,000 (up 26%). Direct mail ads reached $4,800,000,000; outdoor $3,900,000,000; and radio $2,300,000,-000. Magazine advertising, reversing 1975's dip, rose 21% to hit $1,800,000,000, while business publications first topped $1,000,000,000. All other media—from catalogues to car cards—totaled $6,400,000,000.

Canada. The first year of government-mandated wage-and-price controls was rocky for advertisers. Increased government regulation on both provincial and federal levels included legislation (1) disallowing business deductions for ads in Canadian editions of U. S. publications and on U. S. television; (2) requiring French only or both English and French on outdoor ads in Quebec; and (3) defining "misleading" advertising more strictly. A bill introduced in Quebec would ban all advertising to children.

Total expenditures rose 21% to $618,000,-000, largely because of media rate increases. Television captured 51% of all spending, or $342,000,000 (up 31%). Other media grew less dramatically: newspapers got $129,000,000 (up 17%); weekend papers $31,000,000 (up 12%); and radio $60,000,000 (up 6%). Magazines, constant at $50,000,000, reflected tax action against Canadian editions of U. S. publications.

EDWARD H. MEYER, *Grey Advertising, Inc.*

AFGHANISTAN

The Republic of Afghanistan celebrated its third year amid political calm.

Politics. As 1976 ended, the long-awaited Constitution was still awaited, and the country continued to be ruled by presidential decree. Politically conscious elements showed remarkable apathy and no overt resistance to the authoritarian regime of President Mohammed Daud. Rumors of underground disaffection remained.

Daud disarmed his potential opponents by pursuing moderate and centrist policies. Early speculation that he was a stalking horse for procommunist elements disappeared. He effectively neutralized his more leftist supporters by removing them from influential government posts and assigning them to harmless duties in the provinces or abroad. He replaced them with moderate colorless technocrats whose principal qualification is complete loyalty to Daud.

Except for tax and land reforms, Daud issued no decrees that might provoke popular resistance. In effect, he blunted opposition by offering no targets to potential opponents. The government remained centralized and authoritarian.

Economics. The year saw the tightening of government controls over the private sector. Increased taxes, strict regulation, official harass-ment, and collection of alleged back taxes, plus a general government attitude unsympathetic to private initiative, slowed business activity. As a result, there was a sharp drop in demand for foreign currencies to finance imports. This caused the U. S. dollar to drop 25% against the afghani, and, in turn, made Afghan exports more expensive and less attractive. The 1975 nationalization of the Banke Milli, the principal private bank with many commercial subsidiaries, contributed to the loss of confidence in the business community.

In the public sector of finance the government was more successful. An extensive subsidy kept food prices low, thus avoiding popular discontent. Revenues increased because of stricter tax collections. New controversial land reform and tax legislation were promulgated but the effects will not become evident for some years. A new Seven-Year Plan went into effect with expenditures of $312,000,000 in the first year. A substantial proportion of this money will come from foreign aid.

Afghanistan successfully diversified and increased its sources of aid. No longer is it principally dependent on the economic cold war rivalry between the USSR and the United States. Future substantial aid will probably come from Iran and other oil producing nations, as well as international financial institutions. The only question is whether the republican regime will absorb and utilize these large amounts better than the previous royal government.

Foreign Relations. The republic scored its most significant successes of 1976 in foreign affairs. At the Colombo Conference and in and out of the UN, it consolidated its nonaligned position with the Third World. It maintained friendly ties with the Soviet bloc, China, and the United States. Most importantly, it took an important step in normalizing its relations with Pakistan. The exchange of visits between Pakistani Prime Minister Bhutto and President Daud resulted in easing tensions over a long-standing dispute involving the status of tribal groups which straddle the border.

LEON B. POULLADA
Northern Arizona University

—— AFGHANISTAN • Information Highlights ——

Official Name: Republic of Afghanistan.
Location: Central Asia.
Area: 250,000 square miles (647,497 km²).
Population (1976 est.): 19,500,000.
Chief Cities (1973 est.): Kabul, the capital, 534,000 (met. area); Kandahar, 140,000; Baghlan, 111,000.
Government: *Head of state and government,* Mohammed Daud Khan, president and prime minister (took office July 1973). *Legislature*—Shura (dissolved July 1973).
Monetary Unit: Afghani (45 afghanis equal U. S.$1, June 1976).
Gross National Product (1975 est.): $1,560,000,000.
Manufacturing (major products): Textiles, cement, processed fruit, carpets, furniture.
Major Agricultural Products: Wheat, cotton, fruit and nuts, karakul pelts.
Foreign Trade (1973–74): *Exports,* $212,400,000; *imports,* $182,900,000.

UPI

"Long Live the Just Struggle of the People of Zimbabwe" is the translation of one of the thousands of wall paintings in Maputo, Mozambique, expressing support for the Rhodesian nationalist guerrillas.

AFRICA

Africa in 1976 became a focus of great power interests. The competing factions in Angola sought increasing amounts of aid and armed assistance from any outside sources. The festering conflicts in Rhodesia, South West Africa, and South Africa attracted the attention of U. S. Secretary of State Henry Kissinger, who engaged in a short spate of "shuttle diplomacy." The French indicated their clear intention to withdraw from the Horn of Africa, thus setting in train a reconsideration of allies by the various states in East Africa. The Organization of African Unity (OAU) and the smaller African states were pushed to the sidelines, to concentrate on their internal economic problems. The prices of imports rose faster than those of exports, and yet little instability ensued. There were few changes of power.

THE USSR IN AFRICA

Angolan Civil War. At the beginning of the year the Soviet Union had several hundred military advisers in Angola, supplemented by some 10,000 Cuban regular troops. Large weapons shipments were being dispatched to the regime in Luanda, the Popular Movement for the Liberation of Angola (MPLA). The Soviet presence on the African continent was made famous by the 122 mm. rocket barrages ("Stalin's organs") that effectively decimated the untrained forces opposing the MPLA rise to power. Much spec-

ulation occurred over the relationship between the Cubans and the Soviet Union, with observers unclear as to which was closer to the MPLA regime of Agostinho Neto.

U. S. President Ford considered a cutoff of grain sales to the Soviet Union in January, to retaliate for the Soviet role in Angola. Within days, however, he rejected the idea as ineffectual. The Soviet Union and the MPLA maintained a tough line on the possibility of a negotiated solution and turned back any mediating body, including the OAU, which attempted to reconcile the parties fighting the civil war.

Soviet Bases. Soviet activity around established and proposed bases continued to provoke anxieties among the Western nations. The air and sea patrols from the USSR's bases in Guinea proved to be useful in the support of Soviet and Cuban activities in Angola. Similar activities from Somali bases ensured the approval by the U. S. Congress of construction funds for, a matching American base on the Indian Ocean island of Diego Garcia.

Much concern centered, however, on the potential for Soviet bases in the independent states of southern Africa, particularly Angola and Mozambique. By the end of 1976, the oft-rumored option of the Soviet Union to obtain a base in Angola, in exchange for the aid given during the civil war, had not been exercised. In Mozambique, there was greater cause for interest, as Russian technicians directed construction of a runway at Bazaruto, an island off the coast in the Mozambique Channel. The completion of

UPI

Angolan President Agostinho Neto bids farewell to Soviet President Nikolai Podgorny after a visit to the USSR.

prompted by the open and massive shipment of Cuban troops to Angola.

With the faltering of the official U.S. effort in Angola, various private groups picked up the pace of mercenary recruitment in the United States and Britain. The black Congress of Racial Equality (CORE) acknowledged plans to recruit Americans to support the forces—The National Union for the Total Independence of Angola (UNITA). CORE's plans were damaged by public rumors of the involvement of the Central Intelligence Agency in the recruitment of mercenaries. With the subsequent splitting of the black community in the United States, opinion moved rapidly against CORE's plans.

But small groups of mercenaries, recruited under other auspices, made it to the Angolan front. Mercenaries captured by the MPLA were placed on trial in June, and three Britons and an American were executed in July. The U.S. government indicated its inability to do anything other than protest. By the end of the year, the United States had not yet established diplomatic relations with the Angolan government. In June the United States vetoed the admission of Angola to the United Nations. However, when the vote came up again in December, the United States abstained and Angola became the 146th member of the world body. The U.S. action was in deference to the desires of most African nations to see Angola admitted to the UN.

Reconsideration of U.S. Policy. In April, Kissinger visited several friendly African states to obtain advice on a new U.S. foreign policy. The Ford administration decided to strengthen the military posture of two traditional allies, Zaire and Kenya. A visit by Secretary of Defense Donald Rumsfeld to Kinshasa and Nairobi in late June resulted in the public announcement of the sale of sophisticated weapons to both countries: helicopters and antitank weapons to Zaire and F-5 fighter planes to Kenya. Each sale was said to be only to match previous Soviet buildups, in Angola and Somalia respectively.

Minority Rule in Southern Africa. By the end of the summer, the situation in Rhodesia and South West Africa had deteriorated to the point where Kissinger felt the United States would have to mediate, or abandon the field to Cuban-supported guerrilla troops. Talks with South African Prime Minister John Vorster in Geneva, during the first week of September, proved to be productive. Kissinger offered to undertake shuttle diplomacy between the white-ruled states and the "front-line" black states of Tanzania, Mozambique, Zambia, and Botswana. American domestic support for Kissinger's initiative was of wavering quality, as public opinion polarized over the need to provide diplomatic support for the white governments of southern Africa.

Shuttle diplomacy occupied the rest of September, as the key heads of state appeared to become Prime Minister Ian Smith of Rhodesia, President Kenneth Kaunda of Zambia, President

some work there in October gave rise to panic headlines in South Africa over the potential for Soviet interference with shipping lanes around the Cape of Good Hope.

Soviet Diplomacy. In general terms, the Soviet Union had its share of gains and losses. An attempted coup in Sudan in July, although instigated by Libyan agents, caused President Numeiry to look to the United States for political and economic support. The involvement of domestic Communists in the revolt was enough to implicate the Soviet Union. In the continuing problem of the former Spanish Sahara, the Soviet Union backed its Algerian allies, apparently the losing side.

UNITED STATES AND AFRICA

Southern Africa. Secretary of State Henry Kissinger never escaped from African problems in 1976. Fully embroiled in the Angolan civil war in January, he was preoccupied with Rhodesia and South West Africa by the end of the year.

The Angolan war divided the American government, with Congress approving an amendment to a defense appropriations bill to block all aid to pro-Western factions. President Ford signed the bill with regret on February 10, in the process accusing the Congress of "losing their guts." The secretary of state then attempted to draw the OAU into a mediating role, but found that the military superiority of the MPLA gave it a decisive negotiating edge. A major casualty of the dispute was the possible normalization of relations between the United States and Cuba,

Julius Nyerere of Tanzania, and Vorster of South Africa. By the end of September, however, Kissinger turned the Rhodesian problem back to the British, with the latter chairing the Geneva negotiations between the Smith government and the various black Rhodesian nationalist leaders.

INTRA-AFRICAN RELATIONS

OAU. The annual summit meeting of heads of state was held in Port Louis, Mauritius, at the beginning of July, just after the Council of Ministers meeting of June 24–29. Only seven heads of state attended, one of the poorest records in recent years, as the political developments in Africa were clearly dominated by forces other than the OAU. It appeared that the year-long presidency of the OAU held by Uganda's Idi Amin had damaged the already low prestige of the organization.

The invasion of Uganda by Israeli forces to rescue the Entebbe hostages had done little to increase Africa's pride, and Field Marshal Amin as a symbol of African leadership was making Africa a laughingstock.

Angola. On the issue of the just-completed civil war in Angola, the Organization of African Unity ratified the point of view taken by the MPLA, namely the "inalienable right of Angola to adopt the political regime that suits it and establish relations of cooperation with all countries it may choose." It also named the South Africans as the principal aggressors in Angola, thereby retreating into the formulas that had provided unanimous majorities in the OAU in the past. Thus the impotence of the OAU shown in the emergency session held in January to deal with Angola was brushed aside.

Spanish Sahara and Djibouti. On these two sticky decolonization issues, where African states have competing claims on the same territory, the OAU did its best to avoid taking sides. All members were in favor of independence, but since neither territory is self-sufficient economically, some neighboring states will achieve dominant presence. Neither issue, however, was considered important enough, nor the role of the organization so central, as to encourage more heads of state to attend the OAU summit meeting in July.

Transkei. The independence granted to the Transkei bantustan by South Africa on October 26 occurred without problem, and without international recognition. The fact that Transkei's independence took place within the framework of South Africa's apartheid policy led the OAU to pass a resolution at its July meeting asking all African states to refuse diplomatic relations with the newly-independent state. Transkei's Prime Minister Chief Kaiser Matanzima expressed disappointment, but stated that "the Transkei would ignore the political sanctions by unreasonable countries and would continue along its chosen path of achieving freedom by peaceful means."

At the Independence Day celebrations, Matanzima described a future course of multiracialism for the Transkei, a distinct departure from South African laws.

SUBREGIONAL PROBLEMS

War of the Western Sahara. The continuing dispute over the Western Sahara between Morocco and Mauritania on one side and Algeria on the other provoked difficulties in the northwestern corner of Africa. The official Spanish withdrawal from the Western Sahara (formerly known as Spanish Sahara) came on February 26, even though the course of events for some months previously had been determined by the Moroccan government. Morocco divided the area under its control into three provinces—Al-Aaium, Smara, and Bojador. The southern part of the territory, controlled by Mauritania, was incorporated into that nation's normal administrative structure.

On February 27 the Polisario, the rebel movement fighting for independence for Western Sahara, proclaimed the territory the Saharan Arab Democratic Republic. The republic received recognition from ten generally radical African states within the first month. The republican government was based in Algeria.

The Algerian government gave unmistakable signs of militancy: a 20% increase in the Al-

Mozambique railwaymen were armed to help repel attacks by Rhodesian forces chasing nationalist guerrillas.

UPI

gerian defense budget, rapid shipments of Russian weapons to Algeria, and the appearance of Cuban army advisers to train units of the pro-Algerian Polisario guerrilla forces. Coming in the immediate wake of the Cuban/Russian success in Angola, these moves generated much concern in late January and early February. The Polisario forces, which continued to demand independence for the Western Sahara instead of the enforced partition, were not able to draw in the regular Algerian army units, and the immediate reinforcement of Morocco's military forces with American weapons created a stalemate.

For the remainder of the year, the dispute simply simmered, with the Algerians supplying weapons to the Polisario and the Moroccan troops doing what they could to eliminate the guerrilla bands, estimated at no more than 5,000. The rich phosphate mines at Bou Craa, which would further support Morocco's position as the dominant force in world phosphate prices, could not be worked.

Morocco's interest in working the mines had diminished, to be sure, following the severe drop in world prices during 1975 and 1976. The Polisario forces, however, also repeatedly cut the 50-mile (80-km) conveyer belt that carried the phosphate output to the coast. The Moroccans were thus exporting no phosphate from the former Spanish mines.

French Withdrawal from the Horn of Africa. The French Territory of the Afars and Issas (FTAI), dominated economically by the city and harbor of Djibouti, went through several critical stages in 1976. At the beginning of the year, the French were negotiating with various Somali nationalist parties with a view to granting autonomy but retaining the military installations as a French base. But violence instigated by forces in exile in Somalia convinced the French that it was more important simply to withdraw

from the area sometime during the early months of 1977.

Especially traumatic was the incident in February, when guerrillas belonging to the Front for the Liberation of the Somali Coast (based in Somalia) kidnapped a group of French school children in the FTAI, taking them in a school bus across the Somali border. Many lives were lost in the ensuing battle, and the reconsideration of French policy resulted in a movement toward negotiation without conditions with the nationalists.

The predominant political force to emerge during the negotiations was the Union Nationale pour l'Independence (UNI), headed by Ali Aref Bourhan, president of the government council until the French forced his resignation in July. The increasingly disorderly French withdrawal was occurring without serious provision for the economic survival of the independent nation. Since 50% of the territory's revenue had derived from the presence of French forces, the ability of the government to maintain stability in 1977 was not considered good. The other major problem faced by the granting of independence was the creation of a legitimate roll of voters. The nomadic way of life in the area makes it difficult to determine the true inhabitants of the new country, and ethnic balances are close enough for the issue to provoke serious tensions.

The governments of Somalia and Ethiopia continued their verbal battles over the future of Djibouti. Ethiopia's only rail outlet to the world ends at Djibouti harbor, a link it is very anxious to maintain. The Ethiopians supported a government-in-exile, called the Djibouti Liberation Movement, to maintain their interest in Djibouti. At the same time, the Ethiopians quietly conceded that they would settle for the creation of a government truly independent from Somalia, so that the strategic railroad line could not be cut.

UPI

Transkei became the first of South Africa's black "homelands" to attain independence in October. Ceremonies marking the event were presided over by South African President Nicolaas Diederichs and Transkei Premier Kaiser Matanzima.

INFORMATION HIGHLIGHTS ON THE COUNTRIES OF AFRICA

Nation	Population (in millions)	Capital	Area (in sq mi)	Head of State and/or Government (as of Dec. 1, 1976)
Algeria	17.3	Algiers	919,662	Houari Boumédienne, president
Angola	6.4	Luanda	481,351	Agostinho Neto, president
Benin (Dahomey)	3.2	Porto-Novo	43,483	Mathieu Kerekou, president
Botswana	.73	Gaborone	231,804	Sir Seretse Khama, president
Burundi	3.9	Bujumbura	10,747	Jean-Baptiste Bagaza, president
Cameroon	6.5	Yaoundé	183,569	Ahmadou Ahidjo, president
Cape Verde	.3	Praia	1,557	Aristides Pereira, president
Central African Republic	1.8	Bangui	240,535	Jean Bedel Bokassa, president
Chad	4.1	N'Djamena	495,754	Felix Malloum, president
Comoro Islands	.31	Moroni	838	Ali Soilih, president
Congo	1.4	Brazzaville	132,047	Marien Ngouabi, president
Egypt	38.1	Cairo	386,660	Anwar el-Sadat, president
Equatorial Guinea	.32	Malabo	10,831	Francisco Macías Nguema, president
Ethiopia	28.6	Addis Ababa	471,777	Tafari Banti, chairman, Provisional Military Administration Committee
Gabon	.53	Libreville	103,346	Albert-Bernard Bongo, president
Gambia, The	.54	Banjul	4,361	Sir Dawda K. Jawara, president
Ghana	10.1	Accra	92,099	Ignatius K. Acheampong, head, National Redemption Council
Guinea	4.5	Conakry	94,926	Ahmed Sékou Touré, president
Guinea-Bissau	.53	Bissau	13,948	Luíz de Almeida Cabral, president
Ivory Coast	6.8	Abidjan	124,503	Félix Houphouët-Boigny, president
Kenya	13.8	Nairobi	224,959	Jomo Kenyatta, president
Lesotho	1.1	Maseru	11,720	Moshoeshoe II, king Chief Leabua Jonathan, prime minister
Liberia	1.6	Monrovia	43,000	William R. Tolbert, president
Libya	2.5	Tripoli	679,360	Muammar el-Qaddafi, president, Revolutionary Command Council
Malagasy Republic (Madagascar)	7.7	Tananarive	226,657	Didier Ratsiraka, president
Malawi	5.1	Lilongwe	45,757	H. Kamuzu Banda, president
Mali	5.8	Bamako	478,765	Moussa Traoré, president
Mauritania	1.3	Nouakchott	397,954	Mokhtar Ould Daddah, president
Mauritius	.89	Port Louis	720	Sir Raman Osman, governor general Sir Seewoosagur Ramgoolam, prime minister
Morocco	17.9	Rabat	172,413	Hassan II, king
Mozambique	9.3	Maputo	302,328	Samora M. Machel, president
Niger	4.7	Niamey	489,190	Seyni Kountche, head of military government
Nigeria	64.7	Lagos	356,668	Olusegun Obasanjo, head of government
Rhodesia	6.5	Salisbury	150,803	John Wrathall, president Ian D. Smith, prime minister
Rwanda	4.4	Kigali	10,169	Juvénal Habyalimana, president
São Tomé and Príncipe	.08	São Tomé	372	Mañuel Pinto da Costa, president
Senegal	4.5	Dakar	75,750	Léopold S. Senghor, president
Seychelles	.06	Victoria	107	James R. Mancham, president
Sierra Leone	3.1	Freetown	27,700	Siaka P. Stevens, president
Somalia	3.2	Mogadishu	246,200	Mohammed Siad Barre, president, Supreme Revolutionary Council
South Africa, Rep. of	25.6	Pretoria and Cape Town	471,444	Nicolaas Diederichs, president B. J. Vorster, prime minister
Sudan	18.2	Khartoum	967,497	Jaafar al-Numeiry, president
Swaziland	.51	Mbabane	6,704	Sobhuza II, king
Tanzania	15.6	Dar es Salaam	364,899	Julius K. Nyerere, president
Togo	2.3	Lomé	21,622	Gnassingbe Eyadéma, president
Tunisia	5.9	Tunis	63,170	Habib Bourguiba, president
Uganda	11.9	Kampala	91,134	Idi Amin, president
Upper Volta	6.2	Ouagadougou	105,869	Sangoulé Lamizana, president
Zaire	25.6	Kinshasa	905,565	Mobuto Sese Seko, president
Zambia	5.1	Lusaka	290,585	Kenneth D. Kaunda, president

UPI

Polisario guerrillas in the Western Sahara are fighting for independence from Morocco and Mauritania.

From Decolonization to Majority Rule. The nature of the disputes in southern Africa changed between 1975 and 1976. No longer was one able to speak of decolonization, since non-African powers had been excluded from the subregion with the withdrawal of the Portuguese in late 1975. The issue then became one of white rule versus black rule or, in the terminology of some commentators and experts, majority rule versus minority rule.

Zambia played a key role in the subregion, as it extricated itself from involvement in the Angolan war and gradually became an important transit zone for guerrillas fighting in South West Africa and Rhodesia. Zambia's President Kaunda, who had been instrumental in encouraging the "détente" with South African Prime Minister Vorster, took an increasingly hard line with Vorster, who in turn made it clear to Rhodesia's Ian Smith that compromise through negotiation was the best solution. In addition, the increasingly public involvement of Botswana's Sir Seretse Khama, who had been careful not to offend the South Africans in the past, made it clear where the future lay—black rule, or at least multiracial rule.

Zambia's economy was not in a strikingly strong condition to carry out these diplomatic initiatives. The price of copper was very low, and the transport facilities were still not adequate despite the opening of the Chinese-built Tanzam railway, linking the country with the Tanzanian port of Dar es Salaam.

However, progress was made to move Rhodesia and South West Africa away from white rule. The Rhodesian talks in Geneva opened in late October, although with uncertain probabilities of success. The South West African problem made less progress, in a real sense, toward multiracial rule. But the prognosis for ultimate success was greater, since the South African government could impose a solution at a time of its choosing.

The South West African transition was beset by a simple problem: the constitutional talks being held in Windhoek, capital of South West Africa, were conducted without the presence of the representatives of the South West Africa People's Organization (SWAPO), the principal liberation movement recognized by the United Nations and the OAU.

Even within those talks, controversies erupted occasionally, as in early October when the tribal representatives walked out over allegedly racist remarks by the white delegates. An additional long-term problem was highlighted by Vorster's statement in September that South Africa would retain Walvis Bay as an integral part of South Africa.

See all VARIOUS INDIVIDUAL COUNTRY ARTICLES, Biography: Ian Smith, J. B. Vorster; UNITED NATIONS.

RICHARD BISSELL
Foreign Policy Research Institute

The Somalis, on the other hand, pressed their case for the incorporation of the FTAI into Somalia. In March, American intelligence officials revealed that more than 600 Cuban troops from Angola had been infiltrated into Somalia to begin stepping up the guerrilla war against the French authorities in the FTAI. Others felt that the Cubans were simply present as a contingency, in case the Ethiopian government collapsed due to internal opposition, in which case the Somalis could assert their long-stated desires to reclaim the Ogaden region of Ethiopia. Tensions between Ethiopia and Somalia never reached the point, however, of an actual outbreak of armed conflict.

The larger issue discussed during 1976 was the meaning of Djibouti to the no-African powers with interests in the region. The continuing American aid to Ethiopia, balanced by Soviet assistance to Somalia, and complemented by French control of Djibouti, had provided for a sharing of interests in the lower Red Sea area. The most obvious disruptions to this system of interests were the impending French withdrawal and the growing doubts in the United States regarding support of an unstable Ethiopian regime. Pressures for change came from several sources.

In early May, it was revealed that the U. S. State Department had ignored an offer from the Saudi government to displace the Soviet Union from Somalia as a major aid donor. Within Ethiopia, it was revealed that the Israelis had returned in 1976 to help train certain units of the Ethiopian Army. In Sudan, the attempted coup by dissident units in July, supported covertly by the Libyans and Russians, caused President Numeiry to turn to the United States for major aid programs. All these shifts in alignment introduced instability and greater chances for war.

AGRICULTURE

In 1976 world food production increased in both the developing and the developed countries. In the United States total farm output was at near record levels in spite of adverse weather conditions.

World Agriculture

The Food and Agriculture Organization (FAO) of the United Nations in a 1976 report concluded: "There has been a distinct improvement in the immediate food situation of many developing countries, but the basic world food situation remains as insecure as before, with the long-run production trends still inadequate."

Even so, fears of world food shortages and of overpopulation faded from the headlines in 1976. The year's crops were larger, due mainly to more favorable weather conditions throughout most of the developed and developing nations. The once soaring rises in retail food prices slowed in many lands. World agricultural trade expectations, particularly in grain, were being revised downward slightly, although demand continued strong.

FOOD PRODUCTION

The U. S. Department of Agriculture (USDA) reported that world grain production was up in 1976. In its periodic survey, World Agriculture Situation, the Department of Agriculture concluded: "This suggests that the tight international grain supply situation of the last four years has begun to ease."

World sugar production was up, but production of green coffee fell sharply. Tobacco production in 1976 was expected to remain near 1975's record level. Production of most oil-seeds rose substantially. Global production records were achieved for fats and oils and for high protein meals (animal feed). Cotton output recovered from the low levels of 1975, but strong demand kept prices high.

According to the FAO, world output of grains in 1976 was about 6% higher than in the previous year. It estimated wheat output at about 401 million metric tons, up 13% from 1975. Production of coarse grains (mostly animal feeds) was placed at 697 million tons, 5% above 1975 totals. Rice production of 227 million tons was 2% less than the 1975 record.

The generally improved food situation in 1976 was due to favorable weather in regions that frequently have natural disasters—India, North Africa, the Sahelian Zone of Africa, the Near East, and the Soviet Union.

World stocks of wheat, milled rice, and coarse grains could increase as much as two fifths to about 144 million tons—about 10–12% of projected annual world consumption. Many grain importing countries appeared to be making a greater effort than in the past to build up stocks, although the major exporters will still carry by far the largest share.

World trade in meat was again restricted. In the beef exporting lands of the Southern Hemisphere, slaughter rates were increasing, and herd numbers were leveling off or declining, as in the United States where a downward adjustment in cattle inventories was under way.

UPI

West German farmers use a new type of machine to gather straw. The large bundles are easy to move.

UPI

Despite drought and insect infestation, the U. S. wheat crop reached a record 2.1 billion bushels.

Although the economic recovery in developed countries continued, the specter of renewed inflation haunted food and industry policy makers. But prices of many farm products fell in August as prospects for increased food and fiber output brightened.

WORLD FARM OUTPUT

Western Europe. Drought conditions plagued this region from spring through summer in spite of temporary relief in late July. The total 1976 grain harvest of nearly 124 million metric tons was 5% below the previous year's crop and 9% lower than the 1971–75 average. France and Spain suffered the greatest losses.

Because of the drought, livestock slaughter increased, particularly in France, West Germany, and Italy. Hog and poultry production continued to rise. Milk output was down somewhat.

Australia. A drought in southeastern Australia sharply cut wheat harvest expectations to about 7.8 million tons from about 12 million tons. In addition, pasture conditions were disastrous for dairy, beef, and sheep. The U. S. Department of Agriculture said owners sacrificed many dairy cattle and sold beef animals at tremendous discounts.

Canada. Favorable weather helped produce a wheat crop of about 20 million tons, the largest since 1966. Coarse grain production also was about 20 million tons, up a bit from 1975. Hog numbers were increasing slowly, with total inventories up 4% from a year earlier. Beef output was running at about 11% above the previous year's level.

USSR. Soviet farm output continued to be hampered by poor feed supplies and distress slaughtering. Crop production in 1976 was near record high, but output of livestock products, particularly meat, was well below the records set in 1975. Soviet farmers planted about 319 million acres (129 million hectares), up from 316 million acres (128 million hectares) in the previous year. The 1976 acreage was the largest grain area in 10 years. Total Soviet meat production was about 2 million tons less than the 15.2 million-ton record of 1975.

Eastern Europe. Grain yields in this region were reduced by drought. The estimated production of 85 million tons was less than in any of the previous four years. The drought also reduced the harvest prospects of such crops as sugarbeets, potatoes, forages, vegetables, and fruits, jeopardizing domestic food and feed supplies.

To conserve feed supplies, measures included a ban on burning of straw everywhere in Eastern Europe. Nevertheless, distress slaughter of livestock became widespread. Food shortages caused hoarding, especially of sugar and flour. The region faced the necessity of food rationing or of importing large quantities of supplies.

People's Republic of China. USDA analysts reported that Chinese efforts to expand output far exceeded those of any previous year, but unfavorable weather disappointed farmers and officials. According to USDA's preliminary estimate, early harvested grain crops were slightly less than in 1975. Late harvested crops were mixed, with improving weather a helpful factor. No official information was available on most industrial crops, of which cotton is the most important. But weather and a claimed increase in acreage led experts to assume output was about the same as in 1975.

Asia. Elsewhere in Asia, drought in most countries curtailed farm production, lowering rice estimates in India, Indonesia, Thailand, and Sri Lanka. But generally food and fiber output was good, as rains later in the year fell in time to save many crops. Good weather prevailed in Bangladesh and the Philippines.

Prolonged drought in Java, Indonesia, following earlier floods and pest infestations, threatened the country's vital rice crop. Production was estimated to be only marginally above the 15.3 million tons of the previous year. The country was expected to import large quantities of rice. Drought also hurt Thailand's rice harvest, but rainfall throughout the rest of the season saved most of the crop, which probably totaled 9.6 million tons.

Latin America. Farm output recovered in these lands, approximating the population growth rate of 2.7%. Adverse weather cut harvests of Brazilian coffee and Argentine feed grains sharply below 1975 levels, and prospects for later crops were reduced by bad weather in Argentina, Chile, Venezuela, Guyana, and northeast Brazil. Persistent dry conditions continued to limit irrigation water supplies in northern Mexico. Growing conditions remained favorable in other Latin American areas.

Plantings of food and export crops continued to expand in response to higher prices and other incentives in most countries. The recovery trend was strengthened by a general improvement in the livestock situation, associated in part with higher beef exports.

Argentina's small harvest of corn and sorghum will limit exports, but larger soybean and sunflowerseed crops promised increased exports of those commodities. A recovery in beef production more than doubled 1975 export supplies.

Brazil's frost-damaged coffee crop was less than one half of the 1.4 million tons grown in 1975. Production of corn and rice was up sharply above previous records. The soybean area continued a record expansion. Sugar crops recovered from recent poor yields.

Mexico's agricultural production had recovered to record levels in 1975, and output in 1976 was estimated at near record amounts. But heavy July rains and flooding of croplands in central Mexico hurt the output of corn and other basic food crops.

Production in other Latin American areas was up, and export supplies of coffee, sugar, and bananas probably will increase. Chilean grain and oilseed harvests were reduced by unusually dry weather and later by rains and flooding. Venezuelan and Guyanan rice crops suffered from wet weather. Favorable growing conditions in Colombia, Peru, and Ecuador boosted farm output, and Central America and Caribbean agriculture recovered from the adverse weather of 1975.

Africa. In North Africa, the excellent 1976 cereal harvest in Morocco, Algeria, and Tunisia sharply reduced the need for imports. Farm output in Egypt was up more than the 1% gain of 1975. Ghana moved to boost cocoa and coffee prices to producers as incentives to increase production. In an effort to modernize the nation's agriculture, Nigeria announced plans to establish 25,000-acre (10,000-hectare) plantations for grains and beef and dairy cattle.

Precipitation in Kenya was subpar, with corn and wheat harvests down as much as 15% from 1975. Angola, struggling to recover from civil war, was expected to offset lower food production with larger imports. Drought hurt Malagasy Republic's rice crop. Mozambique, once self-sufficient in rice, faced the need for importing this important grain. In Zaire, total food output was falling behind needs stemming from rapid urbanization.

West Asia. Iran had a good agricultural year. Wheat output reached a record high of 5.5 million tons, up 10% from 1975. Rice output was unchanged. Farm production in Iraq was up sharply from the previous year. Wheat production was almost double the 1975 level.

Drought cut the wheat harvest in Israel 25% below that of 1975. Jordan's wheat crop of 68,000 tons was up 36% from the disastrous crop of 1975. Turkey enjoyed a record wheat crop of 12.5 million tons, surpassing the previous high of 1975 by 8.7%. Sugarbeet production also reached a record high.

The "Green Revolution" Slows. USDA analysts reported that the "green revolution," the developing world's switchover from traditional varieties of wheat and rice to new high-yielding strains, lost some momentum in 1975. Experts said that although the area planted to high-yielding varieties of wheat and rice continued to increase, the rate of expansion has slackened, probably because of 1974/75's fertilizer shortage.

In the noncommunist nations of Asia and the Near East, total area put to the new varieties grew 8% in 1974/75, surpassing the 100 million-acre (40 million-hectare) mark for the first time. The expansion was 18% in each of the two previous years.

EARL BUTZ

JOHN KNEBEL

PHOTOS UPI

A racial slur forced Earl Butz to resign as U. S. secretary of agriculture in October. John Knebel became acting secretary.

But the USDA study said expansion probably would continue. One reason is that new varieties being developed for a broader array of environmental conditions could greatly widen the potential for spreading the green revolution. A summary of the USDA report said: "Perhaps the fate of the green revolution ultimately lies with the people who started this movement in the first place."

U. S. Agriculture

Although acreage planted in major crops expanded again in 1976 and livestock and products output rose, food and fiber production only matched the previous year's large output. The main reason was adverse weather conditions, which plagued crops in key growing areas.

Nevertheless, total farm output in the United States was second only to the record high of 1973. Record production was achieved in such major commodities as corn, broiler-chicken and turkey meat, and beef.

The USDA reported in a new study that more new cropland is developed each year in the United States than is lost to urban development. The USDA's survey said that 1.3 million acres (526,000 hectares) are added annually to the nation's cropland, while only about 500,000 acres (202,000 hectares) are lost to urban uses.

The long-term decline of the U. S. farm population continued in 1976, but again at a slow rate. In the previous year, the USDA estimated the decline at about 400,000 persons, to a total of approximately 8.9 million. Between 1970 and 1975 the number of farm children declined by one fourth, but there was an increase in the proportion of young adults 20 to 34 years old living on farms.

Production. In 1976, U. S. farm output of crops and livestock reached an index number of 111 (1967 = 100), almost the same as in 1975 and slightly below the record 112 of 1973. Plantings for harvest of major crops expanded to 335.2 million acres (135.6 million hectares) in 1976, up more than 10 million acres (4 million hectares) from the previous year. But yields per acre for most major crops were below those of 1975.

August weather was brutally hard on most U. S. crops. Subnormal temperatures blanketed the nation except in the northern and central Great Plains. Precipitation varied greatly. Dry conditions hurt the Great Plains, much of the corn belt, and other areas. But northern California and Oregon received more than five times normal precipitation.

Nevertheless, corn production of 5.9 billion bushels was 2% larger than the previous year's record. Wheat output was a record 2.1 billion bushels, slightly larger than in 1975. Crop production reached an index number of 118, down from the record 122 in 1975, mainly because of smaller production of soybeans, rice, peanuts, and grain sorghums (livestock feed).

Exports. U. S. agricultural exports reached records in both value and tonnage in the fiscal year that ended June 30, 1976. The value was nearly $22.2 billion, up 3% from the record of the previous year. Tonnage shipped rose to 103 million metric tons, up 20% from the previous year. The sharply increased volume more than offset lower prices.

Wheat export volume was up 12% and feed grains (corn, grain sorghums, oats, and barley) were up more than 30%. Livestock and meat products, up sharply in value, rose to $1.7 billion, up by more than $250 million. The export value of poultry meat increased by 79% to $135.2 million.

The record large export earnings more than offset agricultural imports of more than $10 billion, producing a record surplus of over $12 billion. This offset a nonagricultural trade deficit of $8 billion, putting the nation's trade balance in the black by $4 billion.

Livestock and Poultry. In 1976, livestock and livestock products rose to a production index number of 103, up from 100 in the previous year, and second only to the record of 108 attained in 1971 and 1972.

Record beef and veal output more than offset a decline in pork output and in lamb and mutton. Late in 1976, hog production turned upward from 1975's low levels. Broiler production was up 10–14% over a year earlier. Turkey output was up 26% early in 1976, but declined somewhat in the last half. Nonetheless, record volumes of poultry meat resulted in a cost-price squeeze for producers that was expected to continue.

Income and Consumption. Realized farm net income during 1976 was up slightly from the previous year's $23 billion, and far below the record of $32.2 billion in 1973. But per capita food consumption was up about 2.5% from 1975 and probably exceeded the record high of 1972 by a small margin. Most of the increase was of beef, poultry, fish, sugar, and vegetable oil. These increases more than offset declines for fresh potatoes and coffee. Rising consumer incomes, generally plentiful food supplies, and a slowing of retail-price boosts accounted for the rise in per capita intake.

Assets and Land Values. Farm real estate values rose 14% in the year ending March 31, 1976, raising the U. S. average to $403 per acre from $354 a year earlier. The total value of U. S. farm real estate was $421 billion, up $51 billion in a year. The average value of an operating farm unit rose 15% to $165,000.

Corn belt and northern plains states led the advance in farm land values. Highest boosts were in Iowa and Nebraska—both up 26%. Land values in the Far West, Northeast, and Southeast increased the least.

JOE WESTERN
Senior Editor
"The National Observer"

ALABAMA

The necessity for comprehensive prison reforms was a major problem confronting the Alabama state government in 1976.

Judicial Actions. The federal court for the Middle District on January 13 ordered the state to carry out a program of prison reform. The order was based on the finding that the conditions of their confinement deprived state prisoners of basic constitutional rights. It set standards that the State Board of Corrections must meet and established a Human Rights Committee to monitor the program's implementation. Later, the legislature created an investigative task force which recommended measures to revise prison operations. Perhaps the most important of these to become law was one that altered the manner in which sentence reductions for good behavior are made. The new arrangement was expected to provide an incentive for good behavior lacking under the old rules and to alleviate conditions' of overcrowding by the early release of exceptional prisoners.

In October the federal court for the Southern District ordered the city of Mobile to change its government from a three-man commission to a mayor-council form, with the council elected from one-member districts, as a means of giving blacks representation in city affairs. Unless the order is overturned on appeal, it will become effective in August 1977.

It is of interest to note that on October 25 the state granted a pardon to Clarence Norris, the only surviving defendant in the controversial "Scottsboro Trials" of the 1930's.

Legislative Developments. The legislature convened on May 4, meeting for the first time under the rule of regular annual sessions established by a 1975 constitutional amendment. A new law set meeting dates for legislative sessions. As of 1977 they will begin on the first Tuesday in February during the first three years of the legislators' term and on the second Tuesday in January in the final year.

When the legislature met, it was thought that problems of funding the education, highway,

UPI

Jimmy Carter visited Governor Wallace in June. In November Alabama was won by the Democratic team.

prison, mental health, and Medicaid programs would be unusually severe. As it turned out, the state ended its fiscal year on September 30 with a surplus in the treasury.

Significant new legislation included a measure designed to improve the state budget administration and a "Sunset Law" providing for regular legislative reviews of state government agencies. Under the latter measure, state agencies unable to justify their programs could be terminated.

Elections. As usual, primary elections were held in May. Delegates to the national conventions were elected under a new system which mandates that the presidential candidate to whom a delegate candidate is pledged must be listed on the ballot with the delegate candidate's name. The new measure also shifted the primary election to a date in September, with a run-off if necessary.

In the general election on November 2 Alabama for the first time used the presidential "short ballot," showing the names of the presidential and vice presidential candidates, rather than those of candidates for presidential electors. The state was carried by the Democratic candidates, Carter and Mondale. State Sen. Ronnie G. Flippo (D) of Florence won the congressional seat vacated by retiring Rep. Bob Jones (D). All three of Alabama's incumbent Republican congressmen were reelected.

JAMES D. THOMAS
The University of Alabama

ALABAMA · Information Highlights

Area: 51,609 square miles (133,667 km²).

Population (1975 est.): 3,614,000.

Chief Cities (1970 census): Montgomery, the capital, 133,386; Birmingham, 300,910; Mobile, 190,026.

Government (1976): *Chief Officers*—governor, George C. Wallace (D); lt. gov., Jere L. Beasley (D). *Legislature*—Senate, 35 members; House of Representatives, 105 members.

Education (1975–76): *Enrollment*—public elementary schools, 384,947 pupils; public secondary, 374,399; nonpublic (1976–77), 56,400; colleges and universities, 146,653. *Public school expenditures,* $779,984,-000 ($1,038 per pupil).

State Finances (fiscal year 1975): *Revenues,* $2,317,-561,000; *expenditures,* $2,332,629,000.

Personal Income (1975): $16,779,000,000; per capita, $4,643.

Labor Force (July 1976): *Nonagricultural wage and salary earners,* 1,191,500; *insured unemployed,* 46,-800 (5.1%).

Construction of the Alaskan oil pipeline continues. Despite a clamor over faulty welds in 1976, the pipeline is expected to open on or close to schedule, July 1977.

UPI

ALASKA

During 1976, Alaskans were primarily concerned with the continued impact of construction of the oil pipeline. The estimated final cost of construction was $7,700,000,000.

Pipeline Construction. A major problem developed when the integrity of nearly 4,000 of approximately 30,000 welds was questioned. The affected welds were repaired, but full inspection of all welds, some of which are buried, would have delayed completion by a year and raised the cost to $8,400,000,000.

Pipeline employment peaked at 20,000, and dropped to 8,000 in October as the construction season ended. Gov. Jay Hammond declared an end to housing emergencies in Fairbanks, Anchorage, and Valdez, and disbanded the Emergency Rent Control boards in each city. There was considerable debate over the future of the 360-mile (580-km) haul road from the Yukon River to Prudhoe Bay. The road will be open to commercial traffic only.

Offshore Constructors, Inc. paid a $5,000 fine for a minor oil spill in Kachemak Bay that occurred when the drilling rig *George Ferris* went aground in the late spring. The minimum fine was imposed because the company cooperated fully in the clean-up. Kachemak Bay is a major crab and shrimp fishery area.

New Capital. On November 2, Alaskans selected a new site for their capital—Willow, a small town 70 miles (113 km) north of Anchorage. The choice was made in accordance with a 1974 initiative calling for the capital to be moved from Juneau to a location closer to the state's population and commercial center. The move is scheduled to begin by 1980.

Politics. Alaska's three electoral votes were won by President Ford with 60% of the vote. In addition, the state's Republican representative was reelected. Republican Governor Hammond weathered a series of legislative challenges.

Economy. The legislature approved a $681 million budget for fiscal 1977. A study by the governor's Management and Efficiency Review team proposed a series of changes in various state activities that would save $70 million an-

nually if implemented. With the $900 million from the 1969 North Slope lease sales nearly exhausted, new methods of financing public programs and realizing economies are needed.

Other Resources. The U. S. Geological Survey estimated reserves of coal in northern Alaska at over 3,000,000,000 tons. Uranium and thorium sites north of the Yukon River appeared to be more plentiful than previously indicated.

The planned federal lease sale of lower Cook Inlet gas and oil fields generated concern about shellfish, birds, and salmon in the area. There was an increase in red salmon catch in 1976 compared to the last several years.

The largest timber sale in U. S. history was abandoned when the Champion Paper Co. withdrew because of increased costs and continued conflict with conservation groups. The sale would have involved some 8,000,000,000 feet of spruce and hemlock.

Mountain Climbing. During the summer, climbing accidents increased on Mt. McKinley and neighboring peaks. By July 31, four persons had died on McKinley and 30 had been injured. Six members of a Japanese climbing team died on Mt. Foraker between May and August.

Two of the Chugach Mountains were named for Reps. Hale Boggs of Louisiana and Nick Begich of Alaska, who disappeared in October 1972 while campaigning in Alaska.

ANDREA R. C. HELMS, *University of Alaska*

─────── **ALASKA · Information Highlights** ───────

Area: 586,412 square miles (1,518,807 km²).
Population (1975 est.): 352,000.
Chief Cities (1970 census): Juneau, the capital, 6,050; Anchorage, 48,081; Fairbanks, 14,771.
Government (1976): *Chief Officers*—governor, Jay S. Hammond (R); lt. gov., Lowell Thomas, Jr. (R); *Legislature*—Senate, 20 members; House of Representatives, 40 members.
Education (1975–76): *Enrollment*—public elementary schools, 51,094 pupils; public secondary, 38,201; nonpublic (1976–77), 1,900; colleges and universities, 13,831. *Public school expenditures*, $176,225,000 ($1,982 per pupil).
State Finances (fiscal year 1975): *Revenues*, $696,085,-000; *expenditures*, $833,911,000.
Personal Income (1975): $3,324,000,000; per capita, $9,448.
Labor Force (July 1976): *Nonagricultural wage and salary earners*, 190,100; *insured unemployed*, 6,400 (5.4%).

ALBANIA

The year 1976 marked the 35th anniversary of the ruling Albanian Party of Labor (APL) and the 30th of the People's Socialist Republic of Albania.

Political Developments. The purge of top-level government and party officials, begun in 1974, apparently ran its course with the ouster of Education Minister Thoma Deljana and Agriculture Minister Pirro Dodbiba in April 1976. Tefta Cami succeeded Deljana and Themie Thomaj replaced Dodbiba.

At the 7th Albanian Party of Labor (APL) congress, November 1–7, Enver Hoxha was reelected First Secretary and all 12 Politburo incumbents were also reelected to their posts. In his address to the congress Hoxha confirmed that Defense Minister Beqir Balluku and his associates had been purged in 1974 for plotting to seize power, and emphasized there would be no changes either in Albania's domestic or foreign policies. He indicated the Ideological and Cultural Revolution, which is to eliminate all remaining "bourgeois" and "non-Marxist" influences in Albania, will continue and stressed that the new draft constitution, soon to be formally adopted, is intended to prevent the emergence of "Soviet-style revisionism" in Albania.

Foreign Relations. The deaths of Chou En-lai and Mao Tse-tung, the purge of the Chinese "radicals," and the apparent reduction in Peking's economic aid to Albania raised some doubts about the future of Albania's relationship with China. Albania, however, rejected Soviet overtures to restore commercial and diplomatic ties between the two nations. The Albanians also refused any détente with the United States.

Economy. Albania failed to achieve the economic goals for the 1971–75 Five-Year Plan. Industrial production increased by 52%, instead of 61–66%; agricultural output rose by 33%, about half the planned level.

For the 1976–80 plan period industrial production is scheduled to increase by 41–44% and agricultural output by 38–41%.

NICHOLAS C. PANO
Western Illinois University

ALBERTA

For Alberta, 1976 was a year of high employment and prosperity despite continued inflation. Relative tranquility prevailed on the labor scene, although by year-end the situation had been unsettled by Anti-Inflation Board wage roll-backs.

Agriculture. Meager winter precipitation created dry seeding conditions. But summer rains and warm weather resulted in excellent growth, followed by near perfect harvesting conditions. Alberta experienced top quality crops without the marketing problems of recent years. A decline in prices did not dampen grain growers' general prosperity. However, beef producers suffered from persisting low prices.

Energy Resources. Work advanced on a second major oil sands project, but plans for further development were suspended pending clarification of the political-economic atmosphere. Studies continued on extraction of heavy oil by steam or hot water injection. Significant new natural gas extraction has begun in southeastern Alberta. Renewed attention was given to the province's vast coal deposits, despite ecological and other opposition.

Industry. Based on oil and gas resources, decentralized development of secondary industry proceeded rapidly. Although lumbering stagnated, urban building construction again promised to reach record levels, especially in home building. But housing continued tight.

Government. Alberta M. P. Joseph Clark was elected leader of Canada's Progressive Conservative Party in February. Federal-provincial relations remained strained over the control of natural resources, the legality of provincial purchase of a regional airline, and amendment of the Canadian constitution.

Education. Increased enrollments, spending restrictions, and inflation hampered provincial post-secondary institutions, resulting in a 25% tuition fee increase and some limitation of registrations. The provincial government decided to continue with the development of Athabasca University as an alternative institution.

JOHN W. CHALMERS
University of Alberta

ALGERIA

The crash industrialization program to turn Algeria into "the Japan of the Arab world" slowed in 1976 as technical, financial, and agricultural troubles piled up.

Economy. The country's second four-year plan (1974–77), which calls for a $27,500,000,000 outlay, pinned its hopes on the rapid development of vast natural gas reserves. But exploitation of the reserves, estimated by the World Bank at 4,000,000,000,000 cubic yards (3,000,-000,000,000 m³) bogged down.

A gas liquefaction plant had been scheduled for completion near Oran in April, but after steep cost overruns and production problems the original contractor, Chemico, pulled out. Completion was pushed back to autumn 1977 with another American contractor, Bechtel International. The plant is designed to liquefy 1,000,-000,000 cubic feet (28,000,000 m³) of natural gas per day, all of it destined for the U. S. market. Two other plants are on the drawing boards for 1980, but costs have almost tripled and the three plants together will cost about $2,700,-000,000.

Earnings from oil, which account for 90% of Algeria's export revenues, had been expected to pay for the natural gas development, but production was disappointing. Output rose slightly over 1975's 45 million tons to an estimated 46 million in 1976, and oil experts said the country was producing at its maximum. Production eventually will reach the peak level of 1973's 51 million tons by the end of the decade, still a long way from the 1977 target of 59 million tons.

Oil prices dropped below 1974 expectations, selling at between $12.70 and $12.90 a barrel, and the cost of goods Algeria imports increased. The 1976 balance of trade deficit was put at between $900,000,000 and $1,800,000,000. Overall foreign debt was $6,300,000,000, five times more than in 1971. Interest payments rose from 8% to 15% of the $5,000,000,000 annual budget.

Defense. Some revenues were diverted to defense in 1976 because of tension with Moroc-co over Western Sahara, the former Spanish Sahara territory. Defense spending increased by 20% to $350 million, the biggest jump in 11 years. Algeria backs the Polisario Front insurgents who seek independence for the former Spanish colony, which was annexed by Morocco and Mauritania under an agreement with Spain. Military ties were strengthened with Libya, which also supports Polisario.

Agriculture. Besides rapid industrialization, Algeria made land reform a cornerstone of its socialist revolution. However, 13 years after the introduction of land reform in the largely agricultural nation, there is still widespread resistance from herders and small landowners. Even though government-sponsored cooperatives began in 1963, at least half the estimated 12 million acres (5 million hectares) of farmland remain privately owned.

Although roughly half the population earns its living from agriculture, food production has dropped as much as 25% since independence in 1962. In 1976, food imports to feed the steadily growing population accounted for almost 30% of oil revenues.

President Houari Boumédienne has been trying to impose land reform on the tradition-bound fellahin, or peasantry, through persuasion rather than force. Boumédienne mobilized 10,000 student volunteers to live briefly on the farms, explain the principles of reform, and bring back to Algiers suggestions for improving the system. The slow progress in 1976 was blamed on "the complexity and restraints of the rural environment" and the "appalling lack" of skilled labor.

The fellahin continued to leave the countryside and crowd into the cities where they joined the ranks of the unemployed. Skilled labor is so desperately needed in the cities that the government began a campaign to encourage the estimated 50,000 Algerians with skills who live in France to return home. But the only Algerians who want to return are among the 400,000 without skills living in poverty.

Politics. In November, the Algerian revolution entered a new phase with elections for a president and the national assembly signaling a retreat of the military's preeminence over civilians. The military has been a staple of political rule since the army overthrew President Ahmed Ben Bella in 1965.

The start of more open political activity occurred in June, when Algerians voted on a new national charter in a referendum whose outcome was considered an overwhelming endorsement of Boumédienne's policies. The charter will form the basis for a constitution that will return power to civilians. One far-reaching result of the charter was the proposed granting of equal rights to women, although Islam is the national religion.

Although the favorable vote had been expected, what was unusual was the wide-ranging discussion that preceded it. Boumédienne elim-

---

ALGERIA · Information Highlights ———

Official Name: Democratic and Popular Republic of Algeria.
Location: North Africa.
Area: 919,662 square miles (2,381,741 km²).
Population (1976 est.): 17,300,000.
Chief Cities (1974): Algiers, the capital, 1,000,000; Oran, 330,000; Constantine, 254,000.
Government: *Head of state and government,* Houari Boumédienne, president (took office June 1965).
Monetary Unit: Dinar (4.20 dinars equal U. S.$1, July 1976).
Gross National Product (1974 est.): $8,800,000,000.
Manufacturing (major products): Processed foods, textiles, leather goods, liquefied natural gas, cement, petroleum products.
Major Agricultural Products: Wheat, citrus fruits, wine grapes, cork, olives, dates, figs, tobacco, fish, livestock.
Foreign Trade (1975 est.): *Exports,* $4,442,000,000; *imports,* $5,300,000,000.

inated the usual restrictions on open discussion and a flood of response followed. With few previous opportunities for saying in public what they thought, Algerians by the thousands met across the country and freely attacked and praised the government. Criticism was directed at the ruling Revolutionary Council, which was accused of having become "middle class." Charges of favoritism, corruption, and maladministration were also leveled at the government. There was no disagreement, though, with the government's basic socialist program and no quarrel with Boumédienne's rule.

JOSEPH MARGOLIS
"African Update," The African-American Institute

ANGOLA

The year 1976 was one of civil war and reconstruction for Angola. When it became independent from Portugal in November 1975 the likelihood of a protracted struggle for power seemed ominously high. In fact, the civil war turned out to be much shorter than anticipated despite (or because of) the extent of direct foreign intervention.

Civil War. When Portugal pulled out, the Communist-backed MPLA (Movimento Popular de Libertação de Angola), which controlled the capital city of Luanda, immediately proclaimed the People's Republic of Angola (PRA). MPLA leader Agostinho Neto was named president. The two rival Western-backed movements—UNITA (União para la Independência Total de Angola) and FNLA (Frente Nacional de Libertação de Angola)—countered by proclaiming their own People's Democratic Republic of Angola. But differences between the FNLA and UNITA had been only papered over, and personal rivalries continued between their leaders, Holden Roberto (FNLA) and Jonas Savimbi (UNITA).

The FNLA and UNITA were supported by U. S. aid and by South African and Zairian troops. The MPLA received an influx of Soviet equipment and was aided by Cuban troops. As the year began the tide had turned in favor of the MPLA, and in January the U. S. Congress passed a bill prohibiting aid to any Angolan faction.

It was the extent of South African intervention on their behalf that ultimately damaged UNITA's and FNLA's claim to speak for the Angolan people, and prevented their government from being recognized even by those nations that actively supported their cause. The Organization of African Unity (OAU) held an emergency session on Angola, January 10–12. But it was deadlocked, split evenly (22 to 22, with Uganda and Ethiopia abstaining) between those favoring immediate admission for the MPLA government and those insisting that all factions be included in a government of national unity.

In the meantime, the military situation in Angola had taken a decisive turn in favor of the MPLA. A last-ditch attempt by the anti-MPLA coalition to raise a mercenary force turned into a fiasco. The improvised mercenary contingent failed to stem the advance of MPLA troops, and several of the white soldiers of fortune were promptly captured and displayed to foreign press correspondents, thus further damaging the already tarnished image of the anti-MPLA coalition. Early in February the country's major towns and cities fell to the MPLA forces without any serious resistance. On February 11 the MPLA-led People's Republic of Angola was admitted to the OAU after it had been recognized by a majority of the members.

Foreign Affairs. The MPLA victory sent shock waves throughout the continent. But more startling was the swift adjustment to the new situation by Angola's neighbors and former adversaries. Zaire expelled Holden Roberto and was formally reconciled with the PRA government

UPI

Col. Samuel Chiwale, commanding officer of UNITA troops, marches victoriously with some of his soldiers in January. By mid-February the anti-MPLA forces had been defeated.

Captured white mercenaries, who had fought with anti-MPLA forces, were tried by the Angolan government in June. All were convicted and four were later executed by firing squad.

UPI

by the end of February. The Zambian government recognized the PRA in April. Even South Africa negotiated the withdrawal of its last contingents from Angola at the end of March and was permitted to resume construction of the Cunene hydroelectric project on the Angolan border with South West Africa (Namibia).

The new government of Angola showed no signs of wanting to intervene beyond its own borders, and insisted that it would not allow any foreign bases to be set up on its territory. The continued Cuban presence (which the United States invoked to veto Angola's application for membership in the United Nations) was explained in terms of their assistance in reconstruction tasks, and of the continuing activity of anti-MPLA guerrilla units in the south. At the end of the year "mopping up" operations were still going on. Another source of preoccupation for the government was the extensive counterinsurgency campaign initiated by South Africa along South West Africa's 1,000-mile (1,600-km) boundary with Angola.

─────── **ANGOLA · Information Highlights** ───────

Official Name: People's Republic of Angola.
Location: Southwestern Africa.
Area: 481,351 square miles (1,246,700 km²).
Population (1976 est.): 6,400,000.
Chief Cities (1973): Luanda, the capital, 540,000; Huambo, 89,000; Lobito, 74,000.
Government: *Head of state,* Agostinho Neto, president (took office Nov. 1975). *Head of government,* Lopo do Nascimento, prime minister (took office Nov. 1975).
Monetary Unit: Escudo (25.00 escudos equal U. S.$1, Nov. 1976).
Manufacturing: Chemicals, foodstuffs, tobacco products, cotton textiles, petroleum products.
Major Agricultural Products: Coffee, cotton, sisal, corn, sugar, palm oil.
Foreign Trade (1974): *Exports,* $1,202,000,000; *imports,* $614,000,000.

Meanwhile, Angola had become a member of the group of five "front line" African states directly involved in seeking a negotiated solution to the Rhodesian problem. Partly in recognition of Angola's role, the United States withdrew its opposition to the PRA's bid for UN membership, and Angola was admitted to the world body on December 1.

Economy. The government of President Neto also was faced with the monumental task of rebuilding a shattered economy. Coffee production had deteriorated from its pre-1974 level of 3.5 million bags to 1.5 million in 1975–76. In June, the government mobilized 150,000 workers to harvest the coffee crop in the region formerly controlled by the FNLA.

The government also had to cope with food shortages and with what it regarded as the "demagogic" and "ultra-leftist" demands by some urban labor groups. One of the government's first decisions was to cut the salaries of top-ranking civil servants in the name of austerity. But it was not until July that it ventured to put a firm lid on any further wage increases "not warranted by a rise in productivity." The decision was clearly unpopular with organized labor and apparently widened some rifts within the MPLA.

Under pressure from the U. S. State Department, Gulf Oil had suspended its operations in Cabinda in December 1975. But after the MPLA victory the U. S. government dropped its objections to the retroactive payment of royalties by Gulf Oil, which thereupon released $120 million to Angola. Pumping was not resumed until May, however, after Gulf Oil had been threatened with immediate forfeiture of its assets. Continued oil exports are crucial.

EDOUARD BUSTIN, *Boston University*

ANTHROPOLOGY

The year 1976 brought announcements of major discoveries of fossil forms of the genus *Homo* which may change prevailing views on the age and direction of hominid evolution. A new concept, so-called Media Anthropology, holds increasing interest for anthropologists.

New Hominid Finds. In an announcement made late in 1975, Dr. Mary Leakey, widow of Louis Leakey, the Kenyan paleoanthropologist, said that she had found the jaws and teeth of at least 11 creatures that appear to belong to the genus *Homo*. Dated at almost 3.75 million years, they were found in a remote region called Laetolil, south of Olduvai Gorge in Tanzania.

Dr. Leakey believes that the new fossils are of a species clearly different from *australopithecus*, a form that was previously thought to have been ancestral to *Homo sapiens*. If Richard Leakey's "1470" fossil, reported upon last year, belongs to the same species as the Laetolil specimens, then there is strong evidence that the human lineage has had a separate line of evolution for at least 4 million years and that there were transitional forms, older still, as yet undiscovered.

At a joint conference held March 8, 1976, by Richard Leakey, director of the National Museum of Kenya, and Dr. Donald C. Johanson, curator of physical anthropology at the Cleveland Museum of Natural History, both researchers said the new fossils proved conclusively that *australopithecus* was only a contemporary of the early *Homo* fossils and eventually died out. Leakey also reported the discovery of the most complete skull, including the face, yet found of *Homo erectus*, a species of human being, known from finds in Asia, Europe, and Africa. The most famous example of the species is the Peking Man, *Homo erectus pekinensis*, found some 50 years ago and believed to be about 500,000 years old. The new skull, found by Leakey's assistant, Bernard Ngeneo, and dated at 1.5 million years was discovered in Koobi Fora, northern Kenya, on the eastern shore of Lake Turkana. In addition, another specimen of "1470" was found, unambiguously indicating a major phase of hominid evolution between 2 and 4 million years ago. Dr. Johanson announced discoveries from the Afars region of Ethiopia of the remains of what may have been a family of early hominid forms, representing perhaps two children about four or five years of age and three to five adults. The fossils, which are strikingly modern in form, were in sediments which appear to be about 3 to 3.5 million years old.

Teaching and Publishing Projects. The Committee on Art and Anthropology of Harvard University has initiated a five-year pilot project to develop teaching, research, and exhibition of the arts of Native America, Black Africa, and Oceania. The committee is chaired by the heads of the anthropology and fine arts departments, David Maybury-Lewis and John Rosenfield.

To commemorate the 75th anniversary of the American Anthropological Association (AAA) in 1977 the association is publishing two volumes of selected papers from the *American Anthropologist*, journal of the association, spanning the years 1921–45 and 1946–70. These will accompany the reissue of a similar volume covering 1888–1920.

Media Anthropology. An issue of *Human Organization* (Vol. 35, No. 2), journal of the Society for Applied Anthropology, was devoted to Media Anthropology. The occasion was the rising awareness that anthropology has not effectively utilized the communications media to present its insights into the nature of society to the American population. The participants in the symposium, whose papers comprise the contents, feel that the perspectives of anthropology with its holistic, cross-cultural, and objective viewpoints of human culture, could, if communicated to people at large, serve to increase understanding of ourselves and our society.

Death. Harry Hoijer, professor emeritus of anthropology at UCLA and former president of AAA, died March 4, 1976, in Santa Monica.

HERMAN J. JAFFE
Brooklyn College, City University of New York

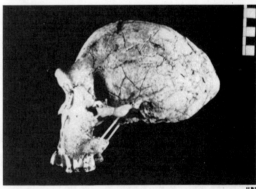

UPI

In 1976, a 1,500,000 year-old skull, a near duplicate of Peking Man, and 3,000,000 year-old fossil bones were found in Kenya and Ethiopia respectively.

UPI

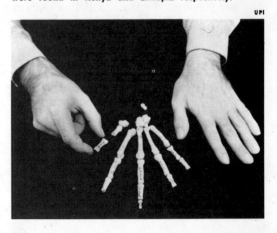

Archaeologists search near La Jolla, Calif., for the remains of North America's oldest human inhabitants.

ARCHAEOLOGY

Archaeological activities during 1976 continued to shed new light on early civilizations. In North America some remaining questions about the Cahokia (Ill.) culture were finally settled; in the Old World archaeologists claimed to have found the burial site and remains of Gautama Buddha.

North America

Traditionally, man's arrival in the New World has been associated with the appearance and reappearance of a Bering Sea land bridge during the last 50,000 years of the Pleistocene Epoch. To date, the preponderance of archaeological evidence has pointed to a relatively recent migration, about 10,000 B. C., labeled as Paleo Indian. Current research, however, is focusing on the question of possible earlier migrations. During the summer of 1976 several archaeological programs tested the belief that man's history in the New World may go as far back as 20,000–50,000 years.

California. Near La Jolla, a major effort is under way to locate and analyze the remains of North America's oldest human inhabitants. The search is spurred by a new dating technique utilizing the properties of amino acids, which has resulted in the dating of the famous Del Mar skull at 48,000 years, nearly 30,000 years older than any previous estimates. In 1976 a team of researchers from various disciplines and institutions concentrated their efforts on locating living sites comparable in age to the Del Mar skull.

Arkansas. A unique archaeological discovery was described in 1976 by members of the Arkansas Archaeological Survey. A cache of forty lithic tools, unquestionably associated with and dateable to the little-known Trans-Paleo Dalton Period, was recovered from a terrace of the appropriately named Cache River near Jonesboro. The Dalton period, or aspect, of the Paleo-Indian Transitional period, circa 7000 B. C., has been magnified by this assemblage which includes 18 projectile points of the Dalton type, end scrapers, adzes, abraders, chisels, blades,

and preforms. Researchers have labeled the cache a "Dalton base settlement tool kit."

Minnesota. Excavations of the peninsular Shakopee Bridge site in Mille Lacs County produced a significant inventory of features and specialized artifacts related to the harvest of wild rice. Although stratigraphic disturbance obstructed the identification of each sequential cultural horizon, occupation beginning in the late Middle Woodland period (c. 1000 A. D.) and continuing into the Late Woodland (c. 1200 A. D.) was confirmed. Much attention was given to a unique sub-surface feature labeled "rice-jigs."

Illinois. Archaeological research at the Cahokia site near St. Louis has produced data that finally settle questions about the development, climax, and decline of that great North American complex. Studies indicate occupation of the general area during the period 600–900 A. D., near the end of which a significant change in house construction is noted, accompanied by changes in ceramic technology.

About 900 A.D. a growth into a major urban configuration began; this was associated with definite ceremonial structures and the primary construction of Monks Mound. Flint hoes, found in quantity, have been interpreted as a key to the agricultural expansion that became necessary to provide for Cahokia's increasing population.

By 1050 A. D. the Cahokia complex was basically complete, with Monks Mound, massive stockades, and smaller game and ceremonial features added to the grounds. Mississippian Ware dominated the ceramic style, and the "weeping eye" motif appeared as a new art element. The number of ceramics from other regions implies growing commerce.

About 1150 A. D. Cahokia's culture became formalized and the term "climax" is applied to this time. Large, rectangular, communal dwellings were in vogue, and artifacts are somewhat standardized.

After 1250 A. D. the aspects of a formalized society began to disappear, and the character of the city took a more individualistic direction.

Evidence suggests a clash of socio-religious ideologies that culminated in the collapse of Cahokia society. Following 1500 A. D. the occupation of Cahokia dwindled rapidly. Later, the mounds were reused by historic Indians as mortuary sites.

The maximum population for Cahokia, including satellite towns and the major urban ceremonial center, is placed at 25,000.

Apart from agricultural products, the principal sources of food were the white-tailed deer, fish, and water fowl.

Canada. Systematic archaeological survey of the Milk River in southern Alberta has been reported by the University of Calgary. Archaeological sites are described as stone circles, campsites, kill sites, workshops, lookouts, and ceremonial grounds. The cultural sequence begins about 6000 B. C., although earlier settlement of the region is suspected.

Near Ft. Erie, Ontario, a joint team from the University of New York at Buffalo and the National Museum of Canada completed excavations at the Orchid site. Principally a salvage project, the Orchid site excavations revealed a complex of individual and multiple pit burials. The mortuary features were attributed to the Late Woodland and the Historic Iroquois (c. 1700 A. D.) periods, in the latter instance readily identified by glass beads and copper artifacts. An abundance of notched sinkers suggests the site was favored for its fishing. Levanna triangular projectile points and cord-on-cord pottery characterize the Late Woodland occupation.

GEORGE PHEBUS
Smithsonian Institution

ARKANSAS ARCHAEOLOGICAL SURVEY

Members of the Arkansas Archaeological Survey recover a cache of lithic tools from a terrace near Jonesboro.

Africa, Asia, Australia, Europe

Economic conditions slackened the pace of Eastern Hemisphere archaeology in 1976, but some significant finds were recorded, including additional evidence of early metallurgy.

Oldest Fireplaces? Researchers at Lake Rudolf in Kenya have announced that thermoluminescence tests indicate that discolored spots of soil at the australopithecine site there were made by fire. Highly localized, such controlled fires would presumably have been the hearths of early man about 2.6 million years ago. Flake tools and choppers lay around the evident fireplaces.

Stone Age Travelers. A cave on Hunter Island, off the north coast of Tasmania, yielded the residues of the oldest known inhabitants of Tasmania—bones, shells, stone tools, and hearths. Charcoal from the latter was dated about 19,000 B. C., a time during the last glaciation period when the sea was at its lowest, creating land bridges to Asia.

By the North Sea near Wilhemshaven, West Germany, a settlement of Linear Ware people has come to light. Previously, it had not been thought that these first farmers of transalpine Europe had penetrated so far north and west with their slash-and-burn agriculture. Their appearance after 5,000 B. C. helps explain the manufacture of pottery and the taming of wild oxen by the more northern Ertebølle people shortly thereafter.

Neolithic collective chamber tombs in north and west Europe nearly always contain skeletons, but a long dolmen at Sjørup, Denmark, dated about 3000 B. C., contained instead four cremations, two adults with two children. The dolmen is wider at one end than the other, rare for Denmark, but more common in the countries of Poland and England.

Precocious Metallurgy. The Vinca Culture of Yugoslavia has been considered the epitome of European stone-age farming, but hoards of "neolithic" pots have now been discovered in ancient galleries following copper-ore veins at Rudna Glava, in the mountains of northeastern Serbia. These archaeological finds, typical of the late Vinca-Plocnik period (c. 4000 B. C.), help explain the origin of the precocious bronze-using Bodrogkeresztur Culture of Hungary about 3500 B.C.

The 126 graves excavated at Ban Chiang, Thailand, not only confirm bronze metallurgy in Southeast Asia in the fourth millenium B. C., but other graves have produced iron tools dated to 1400–1600 B. C. This date is coeval with the Hittites of Asia Minor, who were also early iron smelters.

An idol of Buddha and other artifacts were uncovered by Indian archaeologists at the village of Piprahwa.

Lost Cities. A lost city of the ancient Sumerians, the world's first urbanites, was discovered in Syria by an Italian-American archaeological team. Some 1,500 clay tablets were found bearing cuneiform inscriptions in Sumerian and a previously unknown Semitic language, related to Biblical Hebrew and dubbed Eblalite. Carbonized furniture were found in the ruins of the commercial center, conquered in 2250 B. C. by Akkadians.

A temple in a city as old as those of ancient Sumer was brought to light by Soviet archaeologists in Armenia. The temple, dated to 3,000 B. C., yielded important ceramics and clay statuettes. The building and its neighboring structures were evidently destroyed by an earthquake in ancient times.

Iron Age Rites. Besides unusual neolithic and Bronze Age graves, the Iron Age burial site at Garton Slack, Humberside, England, revealed much ritual activity. Besides a chariot burial and a female interred with an iron mirror, there was a rectangular ditch enclosure filled with decapitated chalk figurines of Iron Age warriors. Alongside burials of deer and cows in galloping position was a double human grave. In a chariot-sized hole, but without the vehicle, were a youth of 19 and a woman of about 30, impaled through the arms with wooden stakes. Below the woman's pelvis was the skeleton of a 3-month premature baby: was it an execution for prehistoric adultery?

Indian archaeologists claim to have recovered the remains of Buddha. At the village of Piprahwa, Uttar Pradesh, a soapstone urn containing pieces of human bone and ashes carried an inscription in ancient Indic script, stating it contained the remains of Prince Siddhartha. The site had already been hypothesized as that of the city Kapilvastu, home of the Buddha during his first 29 years.

One of the most extensive Pictish sites ever found was detected under water by sonar during the search for the Loch Ness monster. The structures mapped include a stone wall, a possible fortified island, and several ancient stone burial mounds.

Catastrophes of Roman Times. Spaces formed by 11 bodies lying together were found on the outskirts of Pompeii, destroyed by an eruption of Mt. Vesuvius in 79 A. D. Archaeologists preserved the shapes of the bodies by injecting plaster into the hollow spaces formed by the decomposition of the bodies, thus obtaining casts of the unfortunates.

Pit dwellings, walls, granaries, pottery, and human skeletons, found at an important river crossing on the Tiza River in northern Yugoslavia, bear witness to a settlement of Sarmatians, a herding people, originally from southern Russia, who invaded about 100 B. C. The site was later used by the notorious Huns and could possibly be Attila's previously unfound capital.

From Procurator to Christians. An enormous Roman villa, surely the palace of the Roman governor of Belgica, was unearthed by a road construction team near Echternach, Luxembourg. Excavations traced the walls of a structure 400 feet (120 m) long and 200 feet (60 m) wide, including cellars with ceilings supported by stone columns. Erected in the time of Augustus, it was remarkably well built. Apparently, this is the villa later converted into a monastery cited in early Christian documents and used as a base by the English St. Willibrord, who served as a missionary to the low countries and Saxony in the 8th century.

Constructive Vandals. The large Roman baths at Thuburbo, Tunisia, were rebuilt, modified, and furbished with lavish mosaic designs from the 1st through the 3d centuries A. D. Eventually the baths deteriorated, but after Vandals conquered the area in the 5th century, the baths were shored up, especially the *frigidarium,* or cold bath, to help the northern immigrants cope with the hot climate. Finally, however, the 500-year-old building was too dilapidated to maintain, so the Vandals reworked the interior into a stable, fitting in grain-grinders (from inverted column bases) and watering troughs for their chargers.

Double Find. Archaeological divers from the British Museum have discovered two sets of antiquities at once. The warship "Colossus," sunk off the Scilly Isles in a storm in 1798, is a find in its own right, but the ship's cargo was a priceless collection of classical artifacts gathered by Sir William Hamilton, whose previous collection had been one of the bases for the British Museum. The objects seem to include Greek and Roman coins and more than 200 Greek pots dating from the years 700 to 400 B. C.

RALPH M. ROWLETT
University of Missouri

ARCHITECTURE

With building starts in sharp decline and construction costs approaching an annual increase of 10% it is not surprising that much of the year's energetic thinking in architecture was manifest in exhibitions, competitions, conferences, legislation, and research, while active building has languished. It was a year to retrench and reconsider, a year in which the simplified version or facile answer was shunned. Architects and builders looked in many directions for parts of answers, often opting for incremental and modest solutions. Besides a greater interest in learning from the past, there was the growth of a new pluralism in which many styles and paths of expression were welcome. Economic and ecological pressures persisted as our worst nemeses and while the Mideast oil embargo and energy crisis were forgotten, the ecological awareness that they helped to foster remained.

Energy. In the domain of energy conserving technology, theory has begun to move into the specifics of built experiments and legislative proposals. The federal government has considered programs to establish demonstration projects in such areas as solar heating and cooling, and wind power. They have, as well, shaped legislation to provide grants to cities and states for "retrofitting" public buildings with solar energy systems and to generate incentive for homeowners installing energy efficient materials and devices.

Enthusiasm in privately sponsored projects grew apace. The United Auto Workers initiated an experiment to use wind, sun, and water power to supplement energy needs at its Onaway, Mich., family resort. Solar collectors will heat swimming pool water, while wind power is converted to store electrical energy and river water is used in a cooling system. In Jacksonville, Florida Junior College has undertaken a bold experiment in building: a translucent air-supported roof will incorporate solar collecting cells and house botanical gardens and offices. And, in a more visionary gesture, Paolo Soleri of Arcosanti, Ariz., has exhibited his scheme for an arcology (city based on architecture and ecology) which is designed and sited to exploit the natural convection effects of the sun.

Urban Development. In June representatives of 131 nations met in Vancouver, B. C., for the U. N. Conference on Human Settlement (Habitat) to consider the massive questions of human settlement as related to the quality of life and to local, national, and international problems and relations. Architects, planners, environmentalists, lawyers, sociologists, economists, and politicians came together with common interests and, while politicizing and propaganda frustrated some, their expression of concern and recognition of the need for a common effort was a

Columbus East High School in Indiana won an AIA award for Mitchell/Giurgola Associates.

critical beginning. Featured at the conference were the results of the International Design Competition for the Urban Environment of Developing Countries. New Zealand architect Ian Athfield was first prize winner with an innovative scheme that stressed low-technology, energy-conserving systems (windmills, methane producing waste disposal units, and solar collectors) and light, non-polluting industries topped by communal gardens and in close proximity to housing. The whole was meant to help establish self sufficiency in poor urban neighborhoods of the world.

Alternatives. The search for alternatives to totally new construction sparked creative use of historic resources and a complementary interest in architecture of the past. Congress passed the Buckley bill supporting the preservation of public buildings of historic or architectural significance. An exhibition of the architecture of the École des Beaux Arts sponsored by New York's Museum of Modern Art generated national interest as architects awakened to some of the lost treasures of 18th and 19th century projects. Two American Beaux Arts works by McKim, Mead, and White won victories in the struggle for survival in New York City: the landmark status of Grand Central Terminal was upheld in state court and the Villard Houses were granted a partial preservation in accommodations with developers of a proposed high rise hotel.

Other distinguished buildings were guaranteed new vitality. Frank Furness' dazzling Pennsylvania Academy of Fine Arts, built for the centennial of 1876, was restored in time for the 1976 festivities. In Boston Benjamin Thompson Associates restored the abandoned 1820's Quincy Market to its original use with interior and exterior stalls for food vendors.

On a larger scale, cities explored schemes for weaving pieces of new construction into

The Pennsylvania Academy of Fine Arts, designed by Frank Furness in 1876, was restored for the bicentennial, a year that saw a deep interest in the architecture of the past.

PHOTOS HARRIS AND DAVIS, PENNSYLVANIA ACADEMY OF FINE ARTS

the salvageable urban fabric. In Cincinnati a two block neighborhood was skillfully revived by Woollen Associates to provide recreation and social services facilities with a maximum use of existing structure. And, in a previously decaying section of Bedford-Stuyvesant, N. Y., Arthur Cotton Moore Associates developed a neighborhood center by a similarly sensitive accommodation to existing conditions. Cities were, as well, rediscovering their abused and neglected natural resources. In New Orleans planning proceeded for an International River Center incorporating convention, recreation, and travel facilities on a river site formerly overlayed with railroad yards. And Philadelphia retrieved part of its Delaware River waterfront, undertaking construction of a boat basin and extensive public gardens.

Urban mass transit continued to be viewed as a means of integrating and enlivening the city but cost overruns on underground systems spurred the search for alternatives. The Washington, D. C., Metro opened a 4.6 mile (7.4 km) run of an anticipated 98 mile (158 km), $4.6 billion system. In both the cities of Decatur, Ga., and San Francisco, Calif., plans for subway stops stimulated concepts for additional amenities: the Decatur station will be developed with a below grade pedestrian mall and the San Francisco subway stop will relate to landscaped recreation spaces.

Buffalo, N. Y., began planning for a light rail network with a combination of above- and below-ground tracks that yields a system less expensive than the conventional subway. Detroit revived its abandoned trolleys as many city administrators saw that recently obsolete form as an affordable transit solution. In a surprising turn, the taxi was given new attention. The Museum of Modern Art exhibited prototypes for taxis that would be nonpolluting, energy-efficient, and vastly more comfortable than current models.

Institutional and Corporate Building. In spite of the economic downturn, well financed private institutions have been able to commission a modest number of "high style" works of architecture. The office of Roche and Dinkeloo continues to produce finely detailed objects of powerful imagery. Both their Richardson-Merrell Headquarters in Wilton, Conn., with its weathering steel and glass façade, and the Worcester County Bank building in Mass., with its mirrored glass prisms, are structures of unrelenting integrity in both conception and construction. This year's recipient of the American Institute of Architects' "Architectural Firm Award," Mitchell/Giurgola Associates of Philadelphia, exhibited equal skill in buildings such as the Columbus East High School in Indiana. That work was one in a series of public structures whose architectural fees were paid by local philanthropist J. Irwin Miller. His guidance has literally transformed that small midwestern city into a vital museum of outstanding architecture. The Courthouse Center and Commons complex by Cesar Pelli of Gruen Associates is another of the Columbus collection. There an indoor "piazza" and shopping center are wrapped in a sleek prismatic envelope of glass as Pelli extends the peculiarly American exploration of manipulating the sheer glass wall.

The focus of much establishment architecture is now the Arab nations. Large firms have undertaken major projects such as international hotels, technical institutions, medical clinics, and entire new universities.

Celebrations. Two major celebrations gave the stimulus for much absorbing construction. In Montreal, the site of the 1976 summer Olympics, buildings such as the Olympic Stadium and Velodrome by French architect Roger Taillibert displayed dramatic cantilevers and structural gymnastics appropriate to the occasion.

The U. S. Bicentennial brought the completion of a series of especially commissioned buildings. Philadelphia proudly opened its Liberty Bell Pavilion and Living History Center by Mitchell/Giurgola as well as the Visitors Center by Cambridge Seven and Franklin Court Museum designed by Venturi and Rauch and dedicated to Benjamin Franklin.

Aalto. The end of an era was marked by the passing of Finnish architect Alvar Aalto. He died on May 11, the last towering master of modern architecture, leaving a legacy of buildings which have already influenced generations. His works in the United States include Baker House dormitory at the Massachusetts Institute of Technology (1947) and Mount Angel Abbey Library in Oregon (1970).

See also CITIES, ENVIRONMENT, HOUSING, and OBITUARIES.

CHARLES W. MOORE and ROBERT J. YUDELL

KEVIN ROCHE JOHN DINKELOO AND ASSOCIATES

Roche and Dinkeloo continued to design buildings of powerful imagery and unrelenting integrity. New examples of their work include the Worcester County Bank in Massachusetts (*above*) and the Richardson-Merrell Headquarters in Wilton, Conn.

KEVIN ROCHE JOHN DINKELOO AND ASSOCIATES

Following the ouster of Argentina's President Isabel Perón in March, soldiers, fully prepared for battle, guard the presidential palace.

UPI

ARGENTINA

In Argentina, the major event of 1976 was the overthrow of President Isabel Martínez de Perón in a bloodless military coup on March 24. Following the coup, a de facto military regime hastily addressed itself to the most pressing problems inherited from the hapless Peronist government.

Government and Politics. The armed forces named Lt. Gen. Jorge Rafael Videla to head the government replacing that of the deposed Isabel Perón. Videla had been the army commander. The new administration was composed mainly of military appointees, but it included two civilians —José A. Martínez de Hoz and Ricardo Bruera who were named ministers of economy and education respectively. All members of the supreme court were removed. Organized political activity was suspended and labor unions were placed under military control.

Many political and union leaders, identified with the Peronist governments between 1973 and 1976, were detained, including Mrs. Perón herself. She was removed to an Andean resort area while the charges against her were investigated. Former President Héctor Cámpora (May–July 1973) took asylum in the Mexican embassy. Raul Lastiri, his successor in the presidency (July–October 1973), was awaiting trial by the military regime.

Of immediate concern to the Videla government was suppression of the political terror that had claimed 1,700 lives during the Perón presidency and was to claim 400 more victims during the first two months of military rule. A most telling blow against leftist subversives was struck in July, when official units ambushed the leadership of the People's Revolutionary Army (ERP). Those who fell in the shootout included Mario Roberto Santucho, organizer and leader of that Trotskyite guerrilla organization since 1970. Few triumphs were registered in an attempted neutralization of the dissident Perónist Montoneros, whose tactics included bombings, kidnappings of businessmen, and subversion of industrial operations. As for terror on the right, several dozen police officers were arrested, after being linked with right-wing death squads. Capital punishment had been reinstituted on March 24.

In his efforts at reorganization, General Videla had to surmount opposition within the nation's armed forces. The hard-line generals favored military responses to Argentina's persistent problems, while moderates preferred constitutional solutions.

──── **ARGENTINA · Information Highlights** ────

Official Name: Argentine Republic.
Location: Southern South America.
Area: 1,072,158 square miles (2,776,889 km²).
Population (1976 est.): 25,700,000.
Chief Cities (1970 census, met. areas): Buenos Aires, the capital (1974), 8,925,000; Rosario, 810,840; Cordoba, 798,663.
Government: *Head of state and government,* Jorge Videla, president (assumed office March 1976). *Legislature*—Congress: Senate and Chamber of Deputies.
Monetary Unit: Peso (243.90 pesos equal U.S.$1, Nov. 1976).
Gross National Product (1975 est.): $120,400,000,000.
Manufacturing (major products): Iron and steel, automobiles, machinery, processed foods, chemicals, petroleum products, packed meat.
Major Agricultural Products: Wheat, corn, grapes, sugarcane, oats, sunflower seeds, sorghum.
Foreign Trade (1975): *Exports,* $2,961,000,000; *imports,* $4,000,000,000.

Labor Restiveness. After assuming executive and legislative power, the junta issued warrants for Lorenzo Miguel, labor leader, and Casildo Herreras. The General Labor Confederation (CGT) and a group of powerful organizations were taken over by the regime. Also, almost all union activities, including the right to strike and to bargain collectively, were suspended. Wages of the workers remained frozen. The harsh treatment of the unions produced unauthorized strikes in the auto industry and the publicly-owned electricity company. Other reactions to state repression of the laborers included work slowdowns and sabotage. Encouraged by the Montoneros, some workers in Cordoba and Buenos Aires formed clandestine resistance committees within the CGT, advocating wildcat strikes, slowdowns, sabotage, and absenteeism.

Talks with union leaders, initiated by the government in September and aimed at a new labor code, were not productive. Regime hardliners adamantly opposed any concessions that could result in a restoration of power to the CGT. The economy minister maintained that there was no possibility of additional wage increases in 1976. A team of economic experts advocated the firing of 300,000 workers in publicly-owned activities (railways, docks, and petroleum) in order to reduce the fiscal deficit for the year.

Finance. An inflation rate of 600% and a budgetary deficit equivalent to $3,000,000,000 were projected for the year. To correct this fiscal crisis which the Videla regime inherited, Martínez de Hoz pushed for decreased public spending, reduced domestic consumption, increased production, additional foreign investment, and removal of price, exchange, and import controls. A few days after taking office, the new economy minister was able to obtain a $127,500,000 credit from the International Monetary Fund. Its purpose was to help cover a balance of payments deficit.

Private foreign banks in the United States and in Europe agreed to short-term extensions on payments due in 1976. Foreign exchange reserves reached $1,200,000,000 in May (up from $371,000,000 in February), partly due to a bumper wheat harvest. Acreage topped 17,000,-000 (6,868,000 hectares) in comparison with only 14,600,000 acres (5,900,000 hectares) planted in 1975. The yield increased by 43%.

A new foreign investment law was issued in August, providing increased investment opportunities for foreign capital. Under its provisions covering repatriation, profits of up to 12% could be repatriated without tax. Foreign firms would be allowed greater access to local credit.

Foreign Affairs. President Videla launched a foreign policy that was designed to regain the prestige that Argentina formerly enjoyed. His first encounter with a foreign head of state occurred in September when Videla and Aparicio Méndez, his Uruguayan counterpart, inaugurated a new international bridge linking the two countries at the Argentine town of Puerto Unzue. Videla scheduled a state visit to Santiago, Chile, in November, becoming the first head of state to accept an invitation from General Augusto Pinochet. The Argentine chief executive also visited Bolivia.

Relations with Great Britain deteriorated when the Perón government revived Argentine claims to the British-held Islas Malvinas (Falkland Islands). Both London and Buenos Aires withdrew their respective ambassadors. Support for the Argentine position came from the Inter-American Judicial Committee of the Organization of American States. The committee declared its support for Argentina's "unassailable right to sovereignty" over the islands.

Argentina reopened the sovereignty case after the British government had sent an economic mission to the islands, following reports of oil deposits in that area. Some 50 companies have requested exploration rights in the islands from the British government.

LARRY L. PIPPIN
Elbert Covell College
University of the Pacific

UPI

Argentina's chief notary public administers the oath of office to the new junta. It included (left to right): Emilio Massera (Navy), Jorge Videla (Army), and Orlando Agosti (Air Force).

ARIZONA

The year 1976 was characterized in Arizona by legislative stalemate, an upward trend in the economy, increased concern with the problems of organized crime, the retirement of Sen. Paul Fannin (R), and an insufficient water supply. The state participated in the national trend toward an economic revival, with unemployment dropping to 7.7%, a figure below the national average. Arizona maintained its position as the nation's most rapidly growing state.

Crime. The state's battle against organized crime came to national attention with the murder of Don Bolles, an investigative reporter for the *Arizona Republic*. Bolles died of severe injuries on June 13, eleven days after a bomb placed beneath his car blew up. At the time of his death, Bolles was writing a story concerning the involvement of several prominent Arizona politicians in land fraud. In February, Ed Lazar, a suspected Mafia associate, was shot to death the evening before he was to testify to a grand jury concerning land fraud in Arizona.

The Bolles tragedy sparked the state legislature into immediate action. It passed several strong anti-organized crime bills designed to reveal the participants in so-called blind real estate transactions and to allocate special funds to investigate murders of this nature. The state attorney general also stepped up his investigation into organized land fraud.

The Legislature. The Arizona state legislature surpassed its 1975 record by remaining in session 165 days. The failure to pass much-needed legislation, however, was due primarily to the stalemate produced by a Democratic-controlled Senate and a Republican-controlled House. Gov. Raul Castro criticized the legislature for spending the taxpayers' money on a long session while failing to reach a decision on many important issues. The list of bills which again failed to become law included ground water law reforms, a revised tax structure, county home-rule, and collective bargaining for teachers, police, and firemen. The collective bargaining bill was intended to settle a series of strikes and threatened strikes by police and firemen in Tucson and Phoenix. The legislature also refused to ratify the federal equal rights amendment. A state Medicaid program was finally enacted.

Water Supply. Arizona's long-standing water problems have been exacerbated in recent years by a rapid increase in population and no reform of existing state water laws. Studies were under way in 1976 to measure more precisely the amount of ground water left in Arizona.

The proposed Central Arizona Project, a controversial solution to the water shortage problem, was given serious consideration. The project would divert water from the Colorado River to the Phoenix and Tucson areas through a massive construction effort carried out by the Bureau of Reclamation. It was first conceived in the late 1940's, but actual construction was delayed by engineering and funding problems. Proponents of the project claim that it will substantially alleviate the state's water shortage problem and provide additional jobs and income. Opponents are well-organized, and maintain that the project is too expensive and environmentally damaging.

Political News. Dennis DeConcini (D) was elected to succeed Sen. Paul Fannin (R). President Ford received the state's electoral votes. In races for the House of Representatives, incumbents Morris Udall (D) and John J. Rhodes (R) were reelected; Bob Stump (D) and Eldon D. Rudd (R) were elected. A proposal to impose strict controls on the state's nuclear power industry was defeated.

JEANNE NIENABER, *The University of Arizona*

ARIZONA • Information Highlights

Area: 113,909 square miles (295,024 sq km).
Population (1975 est.): 2,224,000.
Chief Cities (1970 census): Phoenix, the capital, 581,-562; Tucson, 262,933; Scottsdale, 67,823.
Government (1976): *Chief Officers*—governor, Raul H. Castro (D); secretary of state, Wesley Bolin (D). *Legislature*—Senate, 30 members; House of Representatives, 60 members.
Education (1975–76): *Enrollment*—public elementary schools, 349,831 pupils; public secondary, 143,164; nonpublic (1976–77), 56,200; colleges and universities, 139,631 students. *Public school expenditures,* $650,850,000 ($1,330 per pupil).
State Finances (fiscal year 1975): *Revenues,* $1,622,-386,000; *expenditures,* $1,597,045,000.
Personal Income (1975): $11,908,000; per capita, $5,355.
Labor Force (July 1976): *Nonagricultural wage and salary earners,* 732,000; *Insured unemployed,* 25,100 (4.3%).

Don Bolles, 47-year-old investigative reporter for the "Arizona Republic" was killed in June.

UPI

ARKANSAS

During 1976, Arkansas was unable or unwilling to continue full support of constantly expanding government programs. Retrenchment in some areas took place as revenue increases failed to keep pace with inflation. Gov. David Pryor proposed reducing state financing of local government activities.

Environmental protection and consumer advocacy programs met with mixed success as utilities continued to increase rates and some legislators attacked environmental regulations.

Elections. Arkansas returned to the Democratic fold. For the first time since 1964 the state cast its presidential vote for a Democrat, Jimmy Carter. Democrats, unopposed in most other contests, also won all state offices and three of the four Congressional seats. One of the few contests to generate much enthusiasm was the election of popular state Attorney General Jim Guy Tucker to the U. S. House seat vacated by Wilbur D. Mills.

Two of the three proposed constitutional amendments were approved by the voters. One raised the constitutional limits on the annual salaries of elected state officials; that of the governor was increased from $10,000 to $35,000. The other removed intangible property such as stocks and bonds from the tangible property tax rolls, thus negating the attempts of consumer groups to force via court suits the taxing of intangibles by counties. Labor's bid to legalize the union shop through the amendment process was defeated. Voters also approved the calling of a constitutional convention.

The Governor. David H. Pryor, elected to the customary second two-year gubernatorial term, followed a policy of keeping state expenditures within state revenues and discouraging additional state taxes. He imposed a short moratorium on hiring new state employees, reduced the 1978–79 budget requests of some departments below their existing appropriations, recommended only a 5% budget increase for state universities with no new construction funds, and threatened to veto a proposed 1¢ state sales tax increase.

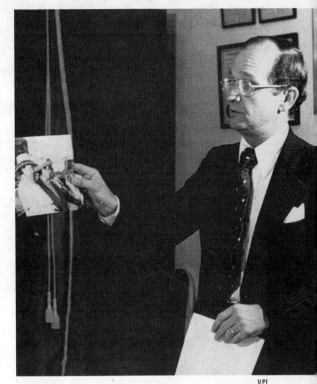

UPI

During the bicentennial, Lt. Gov. Joe Purcell took 1,000 photos of a wagon train in Arkansas.

Pryor startled local government officials and legislators by recommending that some state turnback funds to counties and cities be discontinued. To make up the difference, he proposed that county quorum courts be empowered to levy additional taxes, subject to popular referendum, and that state income taxes be reduced 25% within two years to make increased local taxes more palatable. Local officials opposed the proposals. The Arkansas Education Association withdrew its endorsement of Pryor.

The Legislature. The 70th General Assembly had circumvented the constitutional restraint upon annual sessions by refusing in March 1975 to adjourn *sine die* its regular 60-day biennial session and by extending its session for 17 calendar days in January 1976. Among the statutes passed during the extended session were a bill permitting public school teachers to conduct a brief period of silent prayer; an appropriation for an Arkansas trade office in Brussels, Belgium; and a sales tax exemption on electricity used by the Reynolds Metal Company to persuade the company to resume full production in Arkansas.

The governor called a special session in September to pass only one bill—an authorization of overtime pay for some state employees, which previously had been based on a federal act voided by the U. S. Supreme Court.

WILLIAM C. NOLAN
Southern Arkansas University

ARKANSAS • Information Highlights ———

Area: 53,104 square miles (137,539 km²).
Population (1975 est.): 2,116,000.
Chief Cities (1970 census): Little Rock, the capital, 132,483; Fort Smith, 62,802.
Government (1976): *Chief Officers*—governor, David H. Pryor (D); lt. gov., Joe Purcell (D). *General Assembly*—Senate, 35 members; House of Representatives, 100 members.
Education (1975–76): *Enrollment*—public elementary schools, 242,794 pupils; public secondary, 213,909; nonpublic (1976–77), 20,800; colleges and universities, 61,977 students. *Public school expenditures,* $363,001,000 ($837 per pupil).
State Finances (fiscal year 1975): *Revenues,* $1,231,020,-000; *expenditures,* $1,240,596,000.
Personal Income (1975): $9,755,000,000; per capita, $4,620.
Labor Force (July 1976): *Nonagricultural wage and salary earners,* 635,900; *insured unemployed,* 23,-600 (4.5%).

A Yale University Art Gallery exhibition for the bicentennial featured Chippendale-style furniture and Copley portraits.

ART

The U. S. bicentennial was the occasion for innumerable exhibitions sponsored by both private and public organizations, national and international, during 1976.

Bicentennial Exhibitions. The year began with a major international show at the National Gallery in Washington, "The European Vision of America," organized by the Cleveland Museum in collaboration with the National Gallery and the Réunion des Musées Nationaux, Paris. It moved to Cleveland in May and to Paris in September. It is fortunate that the wealth of material brought together, including drawings, prints, porcelains, tapestries, and clocks, as well as paintings and sculptures, will be preserved in the form of the beautifully illustrated and scholarly catalogue. The show revealed a fresh view of America ranging from the fabulous to the scientific, from the romantic to the realistic, according to the traditions of successive European observers and travelers.

Much publicity accompanied the Spanish government's salute to America. Eight paintings by Goya that had never before left their home were sent from the Prado. The fact that the two so-called *Majas*—the clothed and the nude—supposed portraits of the Duchess of Alba, were included in the group was enough to ensure a steady flow of visitors to the National Gallery and then to the Metropolitan Museum, New York. Clearly, the generous loan of these valuable paintings was to mark a new era of friendship between the United States and Spain after the long period of cool relations. This became apparent when pictures of the new king and queen of Spain viewing the paintings while on their state visit in Washington, D. C., were widely circulated. In contrast, there was the

modest but touching exhibition of pictures by 75 children on the theme "How do I see America," sent by Austria as a token of gratitude for the aid received after World War II. It was shown only in the U. S. Senate Building in Washington.

More closely tied to the birth of America was the National Gallery's own exhibition about the author of the Declaration of Independence, "The Eye of Jefferson." His influence on the nation went far beyond the political role he played as the writer of the Declaration. A man of unusual intellect and culture, whose interests ranged from horticulture, astronomy, and chemistry to painting, architecture, and rare books, Jefferson literally determined the appearance of America in the first century of its existence. In an exhibition memorable for the pleasure it afforded as well as the information it imparted the National Gallery recreated the ambiance of his time. The predominant classical influence was represented by a reproduction of a small temple designed by Jefferson. It contained the Medici Venus, on loan from the Uffizi, the very statue the nation's third president considered the quintessence of the classical.

The unique place held by Philadelphia in the history and culture of the United States was suitably marked by the exhibition "Philadelphia: Three Centuries of American Art," which inaugurated the newly renovated galleries of the Philadelphia Museum. It was probably the largest bicentennial show in the country, with hundreds of different objects. The early period of U. S. history was featured in the Yale University Art Gallery's exhibition "American Art, 1750–1800, towards Independence." Among other museums that reviewed American art achievements were the Whitney Museum in New York with two shows, "200 Years of American Sculpture" and "American Art from the Collection of Mr. and Mrs. John D. Rockefeller 3rd," and the Museum of Modern Art in New York with the show "The Natural Paradise."

Losses of Works of Art. The continuation and even escalation of the destruction, theft, and vandalism of art was the most disturbing fact of the year. It is not yet known how much of Angkor Wat in Cambodia (threatened even in good times by the encroaching jungle) was damaged during the civil war there, nor how much of the necessary restoration will be carried out by the new government. In Lebanon there has been fighting in the impressive Roman ruins of Baalbek, where only a few years ago the international *beau monde* met to enjoy the music festivals.

And, as if man's own irrational fury were not sufficient, natural disasters have added to the destruction. The series of earthquakes in the Friuli seriously damaged that area of Italy least touched by modernization. The loss is not so much that of individual monuments as the whole environment of medieval and renaissance towns which can never be restored. In addition, there is the constant attrition caused by pollution and by careless inhabitants and tourists in such cities as Florence where whole areas are like an outdoor museum. For example, comparison of the state of sculptures on church facades in photographs taken just after World War II with their present conditions shows alarming deterioration of surfaces, as well as missing parts.

Thefts have become so commonplace that only those of the best known and most valuable objects are reported in the newspapers. The ever increasing value of works of art and the publicity given this aspect by news headlines announcing the sale of yet another million-dollar

THE CLEVELAND MUSEUM OF ART

Jean-Antoine Houdon's sculpture of Robert Fulton was part of "The European Vision of America" show.

painting have undoubtedly contributed to the rise in thefts. However, there is nothing new about art thefts or the methods used to gain access to supposedly well guarded premises; it is the extent of the losses that is so alarming. Public and private collections, churches, and small wayside chapels all over the world are victims. In 1976 the Ducal Palace in Urbino lost its famous Piero della Francescas and its Raphael (fortunately soon recovered by the police); 119 Picasso paintings valued at $1.5 million were stolen from the Museum of the Palace of the Popes at Avignon; the Boston Museum's Rembrandt portrait valued at $500,000

The National Gallery's "The Eye of Jefferson" exhibition included a Venus de Medici, installed in a garden temple designed by Thomas Jefferson, the President's telescope and stand, and David's painting *Lavoisier and his Wife*.

PHOTOS NATIONAL GALLERY OF ART, WASHINGTON, D. C.

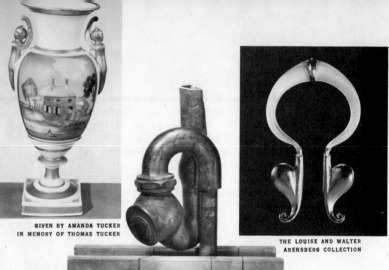

The Philadelphia Museum highlighted such American objects as William Rush's painted pine eagle, a Tucker and Hemphill vase, a 1917 mixed-media sculpture, and a 1972 necklace.

was taken (also subsequently recovered); and even the Soviet Union reported the theft of paintings and drawings worth about $1.5 million, belonging to the largest private collection in that country, owned by George Costakis. It is clear that present safety measures are no longer sufficient. By means of ingenuity and skill the robbers circumvent alarm systems, sometimes imitating the exploits recorded in popular movies, and because of human failure to recognize the gravity of the situation even the best alarm systems are valueless. Thus, when the Gallery of Modern Art in Milan was the victim of a major robbery twice within a short period, investigation revealed that the night guards were in the habit of turning off the alarm in order to enjoy uninterrupted sleep.

But these are only the events that make the headlines; it is the continuing losses of works of all kinds, and from less well known collections, that add up to the staggering statistics. It has been estimated by the International Foundation for Art Research that close to $1,000,000,000 worth of stolen or smuggled art is now in circulation. In 1976 this organization proposed the establishment of a central archive for stolen art that would make available the data to help identify the works and prevent their purchase by innocent buyers. However, this is only part of the solution as it would save only those works that eventually find their way into legitimate channels of distribution. Prevention of the theft is the best answer, especially because all works suffer to a degree when forcibly removed from their controlled environment. Many works have already been removed for safety from church altars and sacristies to local museums, which at least makes them still available though it deprives them of the special meaning inherent in their position. The ultimate solution is, of course, the safety vault, but then art is reduced to a financial asset, losing its esthetic and

spiritual value. Continued investigations into the problem are indeed required.

As if to compensate in some way for all the losses, a few works reappeared. The Cleveland Museum, for example, acquired Caravaggio's *Martyrdom of Saint Andrew* that had hung unrecognized in a private collection in Spain. The price was rumored to be $2 million. In England a long lost Donatello bronze tondo known as the *Chellini Madonna* suddenly surfaced in the home of an English nobleman. With the help of contributions from the public the Victoria and Albert Museum was able to keep it from being sold out of the country. But the greatest excitement was probably generated by the discovery of a series of drawings possibly by Michelangelo in a basement room of the New Sacristy of San Lorenzo in Florence. Plans are also being made in Florence to search for traces of the frescoes painted by Leonardo da Vinci in the Palazzo Vecchio.

Museum Finances and Business Ventures. Like many other American institutions museums are finding it more and more difficult to balance their budgets in the face of higher operating costs and lower yields from endowments. The traditional way of making money by the sale of catalogues and postcards is now being expanded to the point where questions about the validity of increasing commercial activity by museums are being raised. A New York *Times* art critic (July 25, 1976) accused museums of ignoring the essential character of a work of art and, in effect, diverting the museum visitor from the esthetic experience felt in the presence of a work of art by flooding the museum with "counterfeit art." The counter selling postcards and catalogues has been continuously enlarging, and merchandises books and gift items that often have very little to do with the museum's own collection and nothing with its primary function of preserving and displaying its holdings. The

Metropolitan Museum now plans to expand its activities in this field even further, with a project of a large-scale publishing venture, the production to be housed within its walls. The Museum of Modern Art also plans to branch out—into a $30-million construction venture! The main part of its funds is to be used for a real estate development, the building of a 40-story condominium apartment tower over the southwest corner of the original museum building on 53d Street. The tower would provide space for expansion of the museum as well as income from the luxury apartments. The City Board of Estimate approved a deal to permit diversion from the city to the museum of about $1 million a year in real estate taxes on the condominium units. This plan is considered vital to the museum's existence. The question is whether this will set a precedent for other cultural organizations to divert taxes on business ventures, and how far a non-profit organization can go in competition with taxpaying business, causing justified resentment in the private business sector.

The Rothko Estate. When the abstract expressionist painter Mark Rothko committed suicide in 1970, his estate consisted mainly of his paintings. Most of these were disposed of by the executors of his will to the London dealer Marlborough (headed by Frank Lloyd) for a total of $1.8 million. Rothko's children, believing they had been defrauded, instituted a lawsuit that was finally concluded in December 1975, after four years of litigation and an eight-month trial that heard testimony from many famous art critics and historians.

According to some of the witnesses the actual value of Rothko's estate at the time of his death was $14.5 million and would now be equal to $32 million. It was also maintained that two of the executors had ties to Marlborough and were therefore less than disinterested. In his decree the judge ordered the executors of the estate removed, the daughter of Rothko to be appointed sole administrator, the sale to Marlborough to be rescinded, and damages assessed against the executors and Mr. Lloyd of $9 million. It was also discovered that during the period of litigation Marlborough had continued selling paintings from the estate, taking advantage of the publicity to raise prices. In a cloak-and-dagger sequel to the trial a short time later private detectives located a huge cache of paintings in a warehouse in Toronto, which they claimed was about to be shipped secretly to Europe by Marlborough to avoid seizure in satisfaction of the judgement. As a result, 41 paintings were returned to the estate. Litigation continues on new charges against Lloyd and his associates in connection with contempt, and an appeal of the entire case is pending.

Museum and Gallery News. Of major significance is the reappearance of the remarkable collection amassed during the last century by the Misses Hewitt and formerly inadequately dis-

played in the Cooper Union building at Astor Place in New York. The survival of this important collection of decorative arts was in doubt until the Smithsonian Institution acquired it a few years ago. Fortunately, it will remain as an entity at the Carnegie mansion on Fifth Avenue at 90th Street in New York, where its true extent can at last be seen. Comprising vast collections of glass, ceramics, textiles, prints, drawings, and photographs, it rivals such world-famous collections as those of the Victoria and Albert Museum in London and the Musée des Arts Décoratifs in Paris.

The Guggenheim Museum in New York proudly produced a monumental catalogue of its paintings from 1880 to 1945 to coincide with a retrospective exhibition. Written by Angelica Rudenstine with extraordinary scholarship and thoroughness, it is the only complete catalogue of a museum of modern art.

Contemporary art in gallery exhibits revealed no single direction. Generally speaking, there is a continuation of realism on the one hand and abstraction on the other. One of the liveliest shows, and one that struck out on its own, was "Ruckus Manhattan 1975–76" at the Marlborough Gallery. Produced by Red Grooms, with collaborators, it was a kind of comic-strip reconstruction of parts of New York with three-dimensional buildings, including a version of the World Trade Center towers. The labor involved in its production was recorded on film by Peter Hutton and shown with the exhibit.

See also OBITUARIES: Alexander Calder.

ISA RAGUSA, *Princeton University*

A show of ingenious contemporary art was "Ruckus Manhattan 1975–76" at the Marlborough Gallery.

PHOTOGRAPH BY RICHARD L. PLAUT, JR.,
COURTESY MARLBOROUGH GALLERY, NEW YORK

In February, leaders of the five anti-Communist nations comprising the Association of Southeast Asian Nations (ASEAN) sign a Treaty of Amity and Cooperation in Southeast Asia and a Declaration of Concord.

ASIA

The year 1976 in Asia was characterized chiefly by a rebuilding of better regional relations, increased local autonomy, some economic progress, and the continued rejection of liberty and acceptance of increased governmental authority.

From Conflict to Normalization. The resumption of normal diplomatic relations was a frequent occurrence throughout Asia. China and India, the two largest nations, exchanged ambassadors after 14 years of diplomatic tension. India also reestablished diplomatic and trade relations with Pakistan.

Vietnam established relations with the Philippines and Thailand, but relations with Cambodia were still strained. Cambodia and Thailand recognized each other, and in November Vietnam and the United States began to talk of normalizing relations.

No progress was made relieving the cold war relations between China and the Soviet Union, although China's new regime sent the Soviets a softer than usual message on the anniversary of the Bolshevik Revolution. Relations between North and South Korea also remained about the same. Trade between Japan and China declined, but this was more a result of political instability and adverse economic conditions than of an alteration of diplomatic attitudes. Thai-Laotian

relations were tense. Nevertheless, a clear trend toward stabilization and mutual acceptance of differences had begun throughout Asia.

Recognizing the necessity for coexistence in a regional power framework, Australia's prime minister visited China at midyear.

From Dependence to Political Autonomy. The U. S. military presence in Asia continued to decline. Only a few hundred U. S. advisers were left in Thailand by the end of the year. U. S. troops in Taiwan were reduced to around 20,000 in accordance with the 1972 Shanghai agreement.

Negotiations over the retention of U. S. bases in the Philippines went slowly, and it was clear that President Ferdinand Marcos did not want U. S. forces to leave very rapidly. The Japanese published a White Paper stating that they had no intention of building up a large defense establishment, so U. S. presence there was likely to continue. Also, the new U. S. naval base on the tiny island of Diego Garcia in the Indian Ocean began to function.

Britain pulled its last troops out of Singapore after a 157-year stay. The Soviet Union increased its aid to Laos and Vietnam, and succeeded in negotiating some bases, but it was understood to be concerned by India's rapprochement with mainland China.

Several Asian states significantly increased their military prowess. Iran continued to purchase planes and ships, although at a slower pace because of its declining oil revenues. India built its army to around 900,000 men, making it the third largest army (behind the Soviet Union and China) in the World. Vietnam increased its power by quickly unifying the two Vietnams and integrating their military equipment and potential manpower.

China, Japan, India, and Iran continued to be the primary Asian powers in the region, with Vietnam a secondary power. But the Soviet Union and the United States still possessed the option to influence many Asian events financially, militarily, and diplomatically.

From Stagnation to Development. Economic progress was not uniform throughout the region. Japan was still suffering from the effects of the oil embargoes and the world recession. The nation's unemployment figure reached a record level, rising 26% to over one million. The investigation of the involvement of major political figures in the Lockheed Corporation payoffs held back foreign purchases. At midyear total output was up 15% from the previous year, but the recovery was still considered slow by Japanese standards.

Burma was, as usual, hindered by governmental mismanagement. Once a rich rice producing area, Burma now has the lowest rice yield per area unit in Southeast Asia. Most goes to the blackmarket, and it is estimated that 70% of Burmese commerce now takes place in the blackmarket. Inflation has risen 250% in three years.

Vietnam, Laos, and Cambodia were still trying to recover from the war, and the various governments were attempting to impose very radical changes upon their respective social and economic structures. All were engaged in moving hundreds of thousands of people from Saigon, Phnom Penh, and Vientiane to build canals and to increase agricultural production in the countryside. Both Saigon and Vientiane are believed to have shrunk in population by about one third during 1976. In Cambodia, fewer than 200,000 people are believed to remain in the capital, which once had 2.5 million. At least one of every 15 Laotians fled their country, although some had no choice but to return later on.

The most radical changes were occurring in Cambodia, where an attempt was being made to rely on the barter system. The underlying cause was that money, wages, private shops, indeed all private ownership had been abolished.

India, Pakistan, Sri Lanka, and Bangladesh contain 60% of the world's poor. In the first three, 40% of the people are chronically malnourished; 70% are in Bangladesh. Development is not just desirable there, it is imperative. Fortunately the monsoons were favorable and 1976 was a reasonably good year. There appeared to be some improvement in Bangladesh. India had a record harvest of 116 million tons of food grain, inflation declined from 30% to 2%, and total production increased 5.5%. Pakistan's economy grew at a faster rate, without Bangladesh to drag it behind.

Nepal's income from its Gurkha troops serving in the British army had declined significantly in recent years, but aid from India and tourism seemed to be providing substitute sums. Iran's growth in 1976 declined to about 17% from 1974's 42% level, a decline other Asian nations would happily accept.

Some further steps were taken toward population control. Pakistan provided more pills and condoms than before. India announced a much more extensive plan involving increased payments for vasectomies and the withholding of loans to civil servants with more than two children. Some Indian states were trying forced sterilization after three children. China was also experimenting with forced operations.

From Liberty to Authority. The trend toward political control and coercion was stronger than ever. The heads of North Korea and India appeared to be grooming their sons for succession, and Marcos in the Philippines was promoting his wife. Repression of the press increased in such countries as Cambodia, India, Indonesia, South Korea, and Vietnam. In India the mighty *Indian Express* was pressed with claims for back taxes and the traditionally provocative journal *Seminar* could no longer attract policy critics.

Reports of prison torture emanated from Iran, India, and the Philippines, but the practice was surely more widespread. India released some top opposition leaders, but estimates of the number of political prisoners reached or exceeded 100,000. Preventive detention for political prisoners was extended a year. Elections were delayed for an equal time. In Laos nearly 600 political prisoners escaped, and only half were caught. Reeducation programs for the old political elites were common in Southeast Asia.

Thailand's military clamped down heavily and reversed the democratic trend of the previous three years. In a bloody coup the military, led by Adm. Sa-ngad Chaloryu, proclaimed martial law on October 6 after a student protest in Bangkok. Although elections were promised it seemed far more likely that democracy was now dead in Asia, save in Japan.

China Regroups. With much of Asia trying more radical measures to solve its problems, China seemed to be controlled by moderates. Soon after Premier Chou En-lai died in January, Hua Kuo-feng was named acting premier. Following the death of Mao Tse-tung in September, Hua first became head of the Communist Party politburo and then the party chairman. Mao's widow and three other prominent leftists were arrested and charged with such crimes as fabricating Mao's will and betraying state secrets. Pragmatism may have won over radicalism, and the internal intelligence agency over the army, but no outsider could be certain.

See also articles on the individual nations of Asia.

RALPH C. MEYER
Fordham University at Lincoln Center

ASTRONOMY

Some of the most exciting 1976 developments in astronomy involved our solar system, especially Mars, Venus, and Jupiter.

Mars. Both the Viking I and Viking II missions to the planet Mars were strikingly successful. The landers arrived at the Martian surface with negligible damage and were able to carry out their experiments successfully. Meanwhile, the orbiters secured excellent photographs of Martian surface features with resolutions ranging from .06 mile to 0.6 mile (0.1 km–1 km). The terrain of Mars appears to be very old. Eroded stream beds seem to have been caused by water flowing perhaps hundreds of millions of years ago. Some areas of the surface, heavily pocked by impact craters, may actually have lain virtually undisturbed for billions of years, thus resembling the moon. Even small craters have survived, showing that wind erosion is inefficient.

For the first time, direct chemical composition measurements of Martian atmosphere and soil have become possible. The Viking tests have shown that the soil contains familiar metals, such as iron, calcium, and titanium, in proportions similar to those in terrestrial basalts. The atmosphere was found to be 95% carbon dioxide, 2–3% nitrogen, 1–2% argon, and less than 1% oxygen. There are also traces of heavier inert gases, such as helium, and extremely small quantities of water vapor. The reddish color of the rocks has been attributed to limonite, probably produced by photooxidation of certain minerals by solar ultraviolet radiation in the presence of the small amounts of water on Mars. The Martian sky is orange-red due to suspended dust particles. Occasionally, very thin clouds, which may consist of water ice, appear. The polar caps contain more water ice than previously thought.

The search for life on Mars was certainly of greatest interest. The Viking landers conducted a number of experiments, which, it was hoped, might reveal microscopic life forms. In the gas exchange experiment, liberation of gases from a sample exposed to a nutrient would be consistent with the presence of life, but could also arise from inorganic chemical processes. In the labeled release experiment, a sample containing living organisms supplied with nutrients tagged with radioactive C^{14} atoms would be expected to release some of these marked atoms. But a lifeless Martian soil exposed to ultraviolet radiation might contain unstable radicals that would react strongly with water and nutrients, thus mimicking to some degree the performance of living cells. In fact, results thus far seem to bear all this out. A third necessary condition for the existence of life is the presence of fairly complex organic compounds. To date, more complicated compounds have been found in the inhospitable depths of interstellar space than on Mars.

Well-defined erosion patterns indicate that water flowed on the planet at some time in the past. The phenomenon must have been temporary, possibly caused by sudden melting of permafrost. There never were any oceans or seas, and the atmosphere was never more than about ten times its present mass for significant periods.

Venus. In October 1975 the Russian probes Venera 9 and Venera 10 had descended through a haze of sulphuric acid-like droplets about a micron in size to land on the rock-strewn surface of Venus. The planet's atmospheric pressure was found to be about 100 times that at the earth's surface and the local temperature was about 386° F (470° K). Evidence has been found for the presence of volcanoes.

The Solar System. Saturn and especially Jupiter have been revealed as exceptionally interesting objects. Saturn actually radiates more energy from internal sources than it receives from the sun, and Jupiter almost as much. The early development of these planets presumably resembled the evolution of low-mass stars, except that nuclear sources were never turned on. The net energy emitted was supplied by gravitational contraction. Both planets are now slowly cooling down. Corroborative evidence for an early star-like evolution of Jupiter is supplied by the Galilean satellites, whose mean densities decrease steadily from the innermost, Io, to the outermost, Callisto.

The chemical compositions and surfaces of the outer bodies of the solar system have been intensively studied. Water ice (but not other frozen gases)' has been found on the surfaces of several of Saturn's satellites—Iapetus, Rhea, Dione, and Tethys. The surface of tiny Pluto appears to contain frozen methane ice, which sublimes at about 373° F (48° K). The actual size of Pluto may be smaller than the moon, thus placing it—in size at least—in the satellite class.

Comet West, discovered by Richard West on Sept. 24, 1975, reached perihelion on Feb. 25, 1976. It was a beautiful naked eye object in the March predawn sky with its spectacular, bright-banded, diffuse dust tail. The unstable nucleus split into four fragments that separated and faded.

There were no total lunar eclipses in 1976. An annular eclipse visible from North Africa to central Asia occurred on April 22. The track of the solar eclipse of Oct. 23, 1976, which started south of Lake Victoria in East Africa, crossed the Indian Ocean and passed over southeastern Australia, including the city of Melbourne where totality lasted about three minutes.

Some of the most exciting advances in stellar astronomy have been in X-ray work. So far, X-rays have been detected from supernovae remnants, old novae, white dwarfs, flare stars, binary stars, and combination variables that show great ranges in temperature in a single source. Some sources of X-rays have not been identified with any optical object.

Interstellar Medium. New molecules found in the Sagittarrius B2 cloud include cyanimide (NH_2CN) and cyanidoacetylene (HC_5N), thus approaching in molecular weight and complexity the simplest amino acids, which, however, have not been found. Acetylene (C_2H_2) has been found in extended clouds of material around old, carbon-rich stars.

Galaxies. From studies of the 21 cm radiation of atomic hydrogen in the direction opposite to the galactic center, it has been suggested that the galaxy has a dwarf companion, three times nearer than the Magellanic clouds. The object presumably has a small mass and appears to be suffering from tidal disruption effects.

Cosmology. The weight of evidence for the origin and evolution of the universe is now tipping strongly in the direction of the Big Bang as distinct from the steady-state hypothesis. Likewise, it appears that the universe is "open," that is, it will go on expanding forever. From a

comparison of radio and optical spectra from a quasar, it appears that at least for about a third of the age of the universe there has been no change in the numerical values of fundamental physical constants.

LAWRENCE H. ALLER
University of California, Los Angeles

AUSTRALIA

In a year of sharp political redirection, Australia moved away from the permissive economic and financial policies of the 1972–75 Labor Party administration to acceptance of more orthodox and austere measures designed to curb a dangerous inflation. Real wages declined, social advancement was accorded a lowered priority, and the crucial issues revolved around the prevailing slackness in consumer spending and a consequent hesitancy among businessmen to invest.

The year opened with many expressions of confidence in the new government, and a buoyant stock market that rose 18% in the first months. With wider appreciation of the underlying economic problems stemming from the high cost structure, sustained inflation, and a 4.5% unemployment, business confidence subsided in the second half and the stock market moved lower.

In the international sphere Australia espoused more active identification with the United States within the framework of the 1951 ANZUS Treaty, while at the same time supporting the concept of a middle power's ability to pursue an "independent" foreign policy.

The Economy. Facing problems of an economy debilitated by the sharp and sustained cost increases of recent years, the newly elected Liberal-National Party coalition led by Prime Minister Malcolm Fraser adopted a series of measures to draw down the inflation rate and halt the job-destroying escalation of wages, while simultaneously reducing federal income tax.

To reinforce austerity measures designed to dampen federal spending, the government directed that the number of federal employees be reduced. A ban on recruitment, combined with the attrition of retirements and resignations, brought the number of federal employees down by nearly 3% by midyear, and the process continued. As a means of breaking the wage/price spiral, the wage determining court was asked to drop automatic increases tied to the consumer price index, and this resulted in a tapering index of wage rises. The inflation rate fell below 12%. Deficit spending was reduced, and the money supply increase was held at under 12%. GNP, excluding rural production, rose 4%. Drought and poor prices for beef pared farm output.

Treasurer Phillip Lynch presented a budget providing for expenditures of $30,400,000,000 (up 11.3% compared with a 23% increase in fiscal 1976) and receipts of $27,100,000,000, leaving a deficit of $3,253,000,000, including a

UPI

During one of several foreign trips, Prime Minister Fraser met with Japan's Prime Minister Takeo Miki.

domestic deficit of $1,754,000,000. As a means of stimulating the economy and especially investment, tax concessions were provided for business and changes were made in income tax arrangements for mining and oil companies. Personal income tax was also eased. On the expenditure side, increases were provided for defense (up 17% to $2,723,000,000), education and social welfare, and overseas aid. Lower expenditure was provided for health (due to changes in government-run Medibank, which became partially funded from a special tax levy), urban and regional development projects, and public works.

The budget's thrust was intended to lighten the burdens on business as a basic means of encouraging a reduction in unemployment.

A leading financial authority described the budget as endorsing the government's readiness to administer "unpalatable medicine" by placing a firm limit on the growth of money supply and by indicating that increased consumer demand would have to be financed largely out of reduced

——— AUSTRALIA · Information Highlights ———

Official Name: Commonwealth of Australia.
Location: Southwestern Pacific Ocean.
Area: 2,967,900 square miles (7,686,848 km²).
Population (1976 est.): 13,800,000.
Chief Cities (1974 est., met. areas): Canberra, the capital, 200,000; Sydney, 2,900,000; Melbourne, 2,620,000.
Government: *Head of state,* Elizabeth II, queen; represented by Sir John Kerr, governor general (took office July 1974). *Head of government,* Malcolm Fraser, prime minister (took office Dec. 1975). *Legislature*—Parliament: Senate and House of Representatives.
Monetary Unit: Australian dollar (0.98 A. dollar equals U.S.$1, Nov. 30, 1976).
Gross National Product (1975 est): $79,056,500,000.
Manufacturing (major products): Petroleum products, steel, machinery, chemicals, automobiles, meat products.
Major Agricultural Products: Wool, sugarcane, barley, fruit, tobacco, dairy products, sheep.
Foreign Trade (1975): *Exports,* $11,575,000,000; *imports,* $9,811,000,000.

household savings instead of through the "artificial impetus" of government spending. Unless inflation was controlled, there was grave risk to the fundamental basis of Australia's political, economic and social system.

Increased loan raising abroad maintained a high level of foreign currency reserves. Exports were buoyant, remaining well above imports, with earnings from minerals continuing to rise in spite of the decline in metals prices.

International Affairs and Defense. Fraser expressed concern over the possible dangers of détente and pointed to expansion of Soviet military power "beyond the requirements of mere defense," especially in the Indian Ocean. In July, Fraser visited Washington to reinforce Australia's close relationship with the United States. Other important visits were made to the People's Republic of China, Japan, and Indonesia.

Following new defense assessments, the government disagreed with assumptions of the previous Labor government, and moved to strengthen Australia's capability through a five-year $15,000,000,000 program to update weaponry and maintain more adequate forces. The current level of defense forces—16,155 Navy, 31,352 Army and 21,223 Air Force—was considered inadequate.

In October, Australia's biggest peacetime military exercise was held in the Tasman and Coral seas, and along the eastern coastal area. The 17-day war games involved about 11,000 troops, 40 ships, and 250 aircraft from the three ANZUS nations.

In his first address to the UN General Assembly as Foreign Minister, Andrew Peacock said that the distinction between the political and the economic aspects of international politics was being narrowed. He saw a need for the UN to reappraise its "tasks and methods" so that it made the fullest contribution in the changing environment, especially economic questions.

The long-awaited basic treaty of Australia/Japan Friendship and Cooperation was signed in June and was followed by extensive talks by leading industrialists, financiers, and businessmen who examined important aspects of trade between the two countries.

In international discussions Australia urged adoption of a 200-mile (370-km) coastal economic zone and expressed a determination to apply this in Australia's case.

General. Fraser's declared policy of moving away from Labor's centralizing concepts was in evidence in the "new federalism" under which a revised formula assured the state governments of enhanced tax-funded revenues from the federal government. Fraser also created a 22-member advisory council, modeled on the U. S. Advisory Commission on Intergovernmental Relations, to enhance cooperation among federal, state, and municipal levels of government.

R. M. YOUNGER
Author, "Australia and the Australians"

AUSTRIA

Continued recovery from the worldwide recession characterized Austria in 1976. Social and political conditions were generally stable, marred only by agitation by some Slovenes in Carinthia.

Political Events. On January 1 a law establishing equal rights for husband and wife went into effect. It continued a series of measures reforming family law begun in 1949. A law passed on July 7 will allow minority groups, when they constitute at least 25% of the population, to use their own language in government, business, schools, and on signposts. The law aroused opposition among Slovenes in Carinthia, who feared growing influence by German minorities in Slovene-dominated areas. It was enacted only after the ruling Social Democratic party agreed to hold a national language census on November 14. The census became a focus for attack by certain Slovenes who sought and received political support from Yugoslavia.

Chancellor Bruno Kreisky attended the meeting of European Socialist and Social Democratic parties in Oporto, Portugal, on March 13–14. Two months later the Austrian Socialists held their 23d party congress in Vienna, and Kreisky was again elected chairman. The congress adopted reforms in the party structure, backed the policy of détente, called for support of national liberation movements in the Third World, and condemned Cuban and South African intervention in the Angolan War.

Economic Developments. While Austria experienced a 2% drop in gross national product in 1975, preliminary figures indicated a growth of more than 2.5% in 1976. Economic recovery was attributed primarily to consumer spending, although it was definitely helped by the government's three-point program of public construction, credit and tax rebates to encourage private investment, and financial credits for exports. Unemployment was about 2.6%, in part controlled by reduction in the number of foreign workers: 155,000 in March 1976 compared with 250,000 in 1973. Inflation averaged about 8%.

UPI

The Alps and the Austrian countryside made a beautiful setting for the 1976 Winter Olympics.

On July 13 the Austrian central bank allowed the schilling to float on the international market, and it soon rose in value.

Traffic in Vienna and on the Danube was seriously disrupted on August 1 when the Reichsbrücke, a 790-foot suspension bridge spanning the Danube near the center of the city, mysteriously collapsed, killing four people.

Foreign Affairs. During the year Yugoslavia repeatedly charged Austria with violating the rights of the Slovene and Croatian minorities guaranteed by the State Treaty of 1955. On February 17–19 Chancellor Kreisky was in Prague, the first time an Austrian head of government had visited Czechoslovakia since World War II. The resulting talks led to some easing of communications between the two countries.

Austria played host to the Winter Olympics in Innsbruck in February. In early April the Vienna Philharmonic gave a series of nine concerts in the United States in recognition of the American bicentennial. As a mark of gratitude for aid received under the Marshall Plan, Austria announced an official bicentennial gift to the United States of an endowed chair for Austrian studies at a major U. S. university.

An Anniversary. Vienna's historic Burgtheater celebrated its bicentennial in 1976. The first official performance at the theater, which has been called the "Court and National Theater," was on Feb. 17, 1776.

ERNST C. HELMREICH, *Bowdoin College*

AUSTRIA • Information Highlights

Official Name: Republic of Austria.
Location: Central Europe.
Area: 32,374 square miles (83,849 km²).
Population (1976 est.): 7,500,000.
Chief Cities (1975 est.): Vienna, the capital, 1,650,000; Graz, 253,000; Linz, 207,000; Salzburg, 132,000.
Government: *Head of state:* Rudolf Kirchschläger, president (took office July 1974). *Head of government,* Bruno Kreisky, chancellor (took office April 1970). *Legislature*—Federal Assembly: Federal Council and National Council.
Monetary Unit: Schilling (17.09 schillings equal U. S.$1, Oct. 1976).
Gross National Product (1975): $33,189,000,000.
Manufacturing (major products): Processed foods, chemicals, textiles, iron, steel, electrical goods, machinery, paper, wood products.
Major Agricultural Products: Rye, wheat, barley, potatoes, sugar beets, oats, forest products.
Foreign Trade (1975): *Exports,* $7,518,000,000; *imports,* $9,391,000,000.

111

The 1977 Ford Granada includes a new seat trim and sports steering wheel. The '76 Granada was one of the year's most popular models.

AUTOMOBILES

The U. S. domestic auto industry recorded its second highest production run of all time with 1976 models, recovering from two successive downturns since its record performance in 1973.

Output and Sales. Output of '76 cars reached 8,320,000, up nearly 30% from the 1975 run total of 6,523,880. The record high achieved in 1973's model run, prior to declines occasioned by the Arab oil embargo and the 1975 sales recession, was 9,915,802.

By contrast with earlier model runs, the 1976 cycle was marked by strength in so-called "regular-size" and intermediate cars. This proved to be the case despite substantial price increases in the fall of 1975 on new models in all size groupings. Several of the Detroit-headquartered industry's newer compacts also enjoyed strong sales years, but the lowest-priced subcompacts and minicompacts fell below expectations. Most imported cars failed to equal their 1975 U. S. sales.

As top producer of regular-size models, General Motors benefited from the 1976-model upsurge to the extent that its share of production rose 2.07 percentage points to 56.86%. Ford, although its Granada and Monarch compacts were again among the sales leaders, fell 1.51 points to 26.08%. Chrysler Corp. held its share of '76-model output to 13.56%, thanks to keen demand for its two new compact entries—the Plymouth Volaré and Dodge Aspen. American Motors, concentrating on compacts and subcompacts, fell 0.56 of a percentage point to 3.50%.

1976 Model Production. Though shares of model run varied, all of the four domestic auto producers boosted their volumes above comparable '75-model totals. GM production was up 32.08%; Chrysler, 27.26%; Ford, 20.26%; and AMC, 9.8%.

Indicative of the swing to intermediate-size models in 1976 was the fact that the production leader for the first time was not the standard-size Chevrolet Impala/Caprice but GM's Oldsmobile Cutlass intermediate, of which more than 490,000 were built. The Cutlass volume exceeded its '75-model total by more than 170,000, while the regular Chevrolet slid nearly 20,000 to 333,000. Ford Granada, a compact introduced as a '75 model, finished second to Cutlass.

However, Chevrolet easily outproduced Ford to retain its long-held divisional production leadership. Chevrolet built more than 1,900,000 '76 models in 10 distinct nameplates, compared with Ford's 1,500,000 in nine marques. Chevrolet surpassed Ford in output of intermediate and regular-size models, but Ford was ahead in compacts and subcompacts.

In a "big-car year," producers identified with larger autos achieved significant production gains contrasted with Chevrolet and Ford. Oldsmobile jumped to 864,000 from 593,000; Buick from 480,000 to 727,000; Pontiac from 514,000 to 708,000; Cadillac from 264,000 to 309,000; and Lincoln-Mercury from 487,000 to 565,000. Chrysler Corp. added more than 200,000 cars to its volume, reaching nearly 1.1 million. Two long-produced Chrysler Corp. compacts, the Plymouth Valiant and Dodge Dart, were discontinued after the 1976 season. AMC built 25,000 more cars in 1976, totaling 280,000.

The 1977 Models. Economy and fuel efficiency became predominant considerations as GM drastically reduced the weight and length of its regular-size, largest models. The new Federal Energy Act, requiring that every auto manufacturer's fleet attain a mileage-per-gallon average of 18 (28.8 km) starting with 1978 models, was the impetus for GM's "downsizing" program. The new standard Chevrolet Impalas and Caprices, for example, were 11 inches (279 mm) shorter in overall length and almost 700 pounds (317 kg) lighter in curb weight. All largest-size Buicks, Oldsmobiles, Pontiacs, and Cadillacs—except for the front-wheel-drive Oldsmobile Toronados and Cadillac Eldorados—were also reduced in length and weight for 1977. GM said that interior roominess was at least the same.

As a result of the engineering surgery on top-of-line series, together with elimination of heavy V-8 engines, GM claimed that its corporate fleet average for 1977 models was 18.1 miles (28.9 km) per gallon, above the standard mandated for '78 cars. Chrysler and Ford, by contrast, made only one "downsizing" change for 1977—that being in a transfer of Ford's Thunderbird from a full-size body to an intermediate—and miles-per-gallon averages for Ford and Chrysler fleets fell short of the initial target. Automakers face stiff penalties if they fail to reach goals of 18 miles (28.8 km) per gallon on 1978 models, 19 MPG (30.4 km) on 1979 models and 20 MPG (32 km) on 1980 cars.

In responding to the GM model overhaul, Ford and Chrysler set forth a marketplace challenge based on their retention of standard-size models in size "packages" which once were the top U. S. sellers. Despite the announced intentions of U. S. auto producers to raise prices of 1977 models from 5% to 6% to offset inflationary cost increases, the Big Three all were bullish in forecasting 1977-model sales of 11 million to 11,250,000, including imports, up at least 10% from the projected final 1976 totals.

Imported Cars. Sales of foreign-built cars in the United States dropped 165,000 units to 978,000 in the first eight months of 1976. Volkswagen and other European products were hardest hit by price increases and Americans' preference for larger models. Volkswagen joined Volvo in announcing plans to build cars in the U. S. Volvo's plant at Chesapeake, W. Va., and VW's at New Stanton, Pa., were both scheduled to enter production in 1977. For the second year in a row, Toyota and Datsun outsold VW. Honda's year-to-year sales gain was imports' largest.

MAYNARD M. GORDON
Editor, "Motor News Analysis"

WORLD MOTOR VEHICLE DATA, 1975

Country	Passenger car production	Truck and bus production	Motor vehicle registrations
Argentina	185,162	54,874	3,125,903
Australia	362,384	93,783	5,900,000
Austria	284	7,415	1,787,471
Belgium	196,776	25,400	2,819,019
Brazil	524,203	405,602	6,101,823
Canada	1,044,822	379,184	10,472,124
Czechoslovakia	175,411	35,662	1,528,880
France	2,952,824	346,796	17,434,000
Germany, East	160,000	40,000	2,214,189
Germany, West	2,907,819[1]	278,389	18,658,239
Hungary	...	12,075	575,827
India	31,232	43,024	1,337,150
Italy	1,348,544	110,085	15,435,963
Japan	4,567,854	2,373,737	26,781,306
Mexico	238,743	121,935	2,692,272
Netherlands	60,528	11,570	3,797,000
Poland	173,200	85,200	1,355,279
Portugal	...	278	1,092,000
Rumania	54,000	46,000	136,000
Spain	696,124	118,040	5,299,387
Sweden	316,386	50,403	2,809,165
Switzerland	200	1,300	1,899,511
United Kingdom	1,267,695	380,704	15,864,400
United States	6,717,043	2,264,537	129,943,087[2]
USSR	1,201,000	763,000	8,288,200
Yugoslavia	183,182	22,385	1,486,146
Total	25,365,416[4]	8,071,378[4]	314,334,563[3]

[1] Includes 268,925 micro-buses. [2] U. S. total includes 104,898,256 cars and 25,044,831 trucks, excluding Puerto Rico (607,830 and 124,506, respectively); Canal Zone (17,569 and 461); and Virgin Islands (32,000 and 6,000). [3] Registration total includes all countries, of which non-producing countries exceeding 1 million registrations were: Venezuela, 1,199,209; Denmark, 1,475,048; Finland, 1,076,208; Norway, 1,043,697; New Zealand, 1,320,521; and South Africa, 2,733,823. Total includes 248,609,010 cars and 65,725,553 trucks and buses. [4] Excludes 1,556,744 car and 452,565 truck and bus assemblies, principally in Belgium, South Africa, Venezuela, Taiwan, and Iran. Source: Motor Vehicle Manufacturers Association of the United States, Inc.

PHOTOS UPI

Most 1977 models of large-size autos, including the Cadillac Seville (below), were reduced in size and weight. The Oldsmobile Toronado (top) was an exception.

BANGLADESH

Two factors were overwhelmingly important to Bangladesh's survival in 1976. The weather improved enough to permit two good grain crops, cutting the price of rice by at least 50% over 1974. And Maj. Gen. Ziaur Rahman, the ruling strongman, succeeded in establishing a measure of stability and order.

Domestic Affairs. In November 1975 the military overthrew the regime of President Khondakar Mushtaque Ahmed, who had taken power in an earlier coup. A three-man junta of officers was established, headed by army chief of staff Maj. Gen. Ziaur Rahman, who quickly demonstrated his dominance over colleagues and civilian leaders. Former Chief Justice Abu Sadat Mohammed Sayem was named president. General Ziaur attacked with some success the perennial problems of Bangladesh—corruption and political ineptitude. He promised to hold elections in 1977, but observers believe that they will be postponed.

Support for General Ziaur was not unanimous; armed dissidents and guerrillas were active.

Several secret trials were held of individuals accused of "antistate" activities. One army officer was executed and a number of long prison sentences were imposed. Dutch journalist and social worker Peter Custers received a 14-year sentence, but was pardoned and deported.

Bangladesh is one of the most storm- and disaster-ridden areas of the world, but for once good weather characterized much of the year. This meant good crops, which lessened not only starvation but inflationary pressures. Relative "prosperity" contributed to popular support of the military regime.

General Ziaur initiated a serious program of birth control. Bangladesh has over 76,000,000 people with a birthrate of 46 per thousand. Although sterilizations averaged some 8,000 a month, births exceeded 300,000 per month.

The most virulent form of smallpox has been absent from Bangladesh for more than a year, and the World Health Organization hopes that the disease has at last been erased from the earth. (A milder form persists in Ethiopia.)

--- **BANGLADESH • Information Highlights** ---

Official Name: People's Republic of Bangladesh.
Location: South Asia.
Area: 55,126 square miles (142,776 km²).
Population (1976 est.): 76,100,000.
Chief Cities (1974 census): Dacca, the capital, 1,320,-000; Chittagong, 458,000; Khulna, 436,000.
Government: *Head of state,* A. S. M. Sayem, president (took office Nov. 1975). *Head of military junta,* Maj. Gen. Ziaur Rahman (took office Nov. 1975).
Monetary Unit: Taka (14.954 takas equal U. S.$1, June 1976).
Gross National Product (1973 est.) $5,880,000,000.
Manufacturing (major products): Jute products, cotton textiles, processed foods, wood products.
Major Agricultural Products: Rice, jute, sugarcane, tea, oilseeds, pulses, forest products.
Foreign Trade (1975): *Exports,* $311,000,000; *Imports,* $710,000,000.

Foreign Affairs. Relations with India were generally correct but certainly not friendly. The government continued to accuse India of fomenting subversive activity within Bangladesh. There were apparently several armed clashes between border troops in April. A major source of conflict was the continuing bitter quarrel over the new Indian dam at Farakka, which diverts some of the water of the Ganges River. Bangladesh claimed that the diversion has had serious consequences on its economy.

CARL LEIDEN
The University of Texas at Austin

BANKING

The most sweeping bank legislation since the Depression was considered by the U. S. Congress during 1976, including proposals to permit banks to pay interest on checking accounts, to consolidate federal regulation in one new superagency, and to trim the powers of foreign banks in the United States. But virtually nothing was enacted into law. Intense lobbying by bankers and labor was instrumental in forcing the House of Representatives to strip the legislation of real substance, and what remained died in the Senate.

Bank Regulation. Combining bank supervision in one agency was an idea that developed from the well-publicized "problem bank" situation. Many institutions had gotten into difficulty during the recession from bad loans, particularly those involving real estate. The so-called watch lists maintained by the Federal Reserve Board, the Comptroller of the Currency, the Federal Deposit Insurance Corporation, and the Federal Home Loan Bank Board swelled to or approached record levels.

These agencies came under fire for allegedly lax supervision as Congress worried that stress in the financial system might lead to a dangerous wave of bank failures. However, except for the collapse in February of the holding company of which the $400 million Hamilton National Bank of Chattanooga was the main component, no major banks fell and concern faded as the economy continued to improve. Fourteen of the nation's 14,700 banks failed during 1976, compared with 13 the year before. Robert Barnett, who took over as head of the FDIC when Frank Wille completed his six-year term, suggested that consideration be given to removal of the $40,000 ceiling on FDIC insurance, thereby fully protecting deposits of all sizes.

There was also a change in comptrollers. When James E. Smith resigned in July, he had ridden out the criticism of his agency and had installed new procedures to monitor bank performance. Stanley E. Shirk, a retired accountant whose specialty is banks, was nominated by President Ford to the post. But the Senate failed even to hold hearings on his confirmation and the year ended with an acting comptroller still in office.

To attract business, U. S. banks depend heavily on appealingly designed offices. Philadelphia's new Central Penn National Bank features many plants and modern wallhangings.

THE KLING PARTNERSHIP: KLING/INTERIOR DESIGN

Another bill that failed to pass was one to set up a government-funded $1.25 billion institution to finance consumer cooperatives. It was sponsored by consumerists, including Ralph Nader, who described banks as unfamiliar with co-op lending and disinterested in dealing with nonprofit enterprises. Nader also published a study that he said showed that the entry of bank holding companies in nonbanking businesses was weakening their banks and causing undue concentration in the other fields.

Banks continued to make inroads in 1976 into the securities business despite vigorous opposition from brokers. The most dramatic plan was that of New York's Chemical Bank to offer its checking account customers a cut-rate stock brokerage service that could save typical individual investors up to 90% on their transactions. But the plan quickly ran into difficulty with government authorities responsible for investor protection. The Securities and Exchange Commission, for example, expressed its view that banks should not be permitted to have a competitive advantage by doing things prohibited to brokers or done under different ground rules.

The banks lost in an attempt to prevent the Federal Trade Commission from putting into effect in May a rule that struck down the long-established holder-in-due-course doctrine. This had allowed banks to finance the transactions of such merchants as automobile dealers and home-improvement contractors without incurring any liability for customer dissatisfaction with the product. The new FTC rule forces banks, by making them subject to suits, to take a major role in policing the marketplace. As a result many banks stopped lending to merchants they thought would cause a problem and raised their interest rates to such businesses.

Monetary Policy. The Federal Reserve was quite successful in producing the growth in the nation's money supply that it desired—between 4½% and 7% for most of the year. Its discount rate—that charged member banks for temporary loans—was reduced to 5½% in mid-January and to 5¼% later during the year. There was plenty of money available for savings banks and savings and loan associations to cover their lagging demand for mortgages, but these interest rates dropped only slightly to 8½ to 9¼%.

The problem banks caused the Federal Reserve to worry early in the year that other banks might become overcautious in their lending and thereby threaten the nation's economic recovery. Indeed, the banks did rebuild their financial positions but were able to do so without denying needed credit. They raised capital in healthy stock and bond markets and generated good earnings gains in the second half of the year by holding their lending rates firm as their cost of money declined.

When it became evident that economic growth had slowed during the third quarter there was criticism that the banks' strategy had made credit on reasonable terms unavailable to some second-echelon borrowers. But Federal Reserve chairman Arthur F. Burns said he found no evidence this had occurred. The prime rate held in a narrow 6½–7¼% range all year despite weak loan demand at big-city banks that did not pick up until fall.

The SEC adopted guidelines under which banks would significantly expand the data they make public, particularly those involving the risk of loan portfolios and their various non-banking activities.

ROBERT D. HERSHEY, JR.
The New York Times

UPI

King Baudouin addressed Parliament in 1976 for the first time, celebrating 25 years as Belgium's king. He established a new foundation as a jubilee gift.

BELGIUM

Persistent economic recession and ethno-linguistic conflict continued to plague Belgium in 1976.

Economy. The inflation rate lingered above 10%, slightly lower than the 11% of 1975 and 15% of 1974. This third year of severe economic ills saw higher consumer prices and an unemployment rate of more than 8%. Low domestic demand and diminished exports resulted in further debilitating the economy, primarily because Belgium's export position became more vulnerable. "Stagflation" reduced foreign investments, and the energy crisis pointed up the nation's dependence on external sources of power. Dwindling coal reserves and the rising price of crude oil meant no expansion of steel production. A trade surplus did emerge in 1976, after two years, but it was not so sizeable as predicted. With foreign trade heavily based on the European economy, Belgium's comparative position with her main trading partners, the Netherlands and West Germany, declined.

Government recovery measures had only limited results. Since 1975, public investments programs for specific regional development and a tighter incomes policy have rekindled the language war. Counterinflationary devices, such as relaxed monetary restrictions, reduced income taxes, expanded lending, and lower interest rates failed to check the significant decline in borrowing. Despite major job-creating programs, Belgium was left with the second highest jobless rate in the European Community and its highest youth unemployment. The new expansionary monetary policy and price-restraint mechanisms were widened in late 1976. Although few economic indicators were bright, long-range stimulative efforts suggest that Belgium may participate more fully in the general European recovery in 1977.

Elections. The politics of the language controversy were reflected in the October 10 election to determine whether to fuse the nearly 2,400 municipal councils into less than 600. The right-center coalition government of Leo Tindemans supported the bigger administrative units and the diminution of influence and power of city hall politics in Belgium. The 12,500 seats filled by the election strengthened the Social Christian party and opposition Socialists at the expense of Tindemans' two partners, the Party of Liberty and Progress and the Rassemblement Walloon. Single-issue language parties lost ground, while the left gained in economically depressed Walloon areas in the south, and the right in the sector-development-aided Flemish areas of the north. Since the regional boards had limited political power, a true, comprehensive regionalization plan was seen by many, particularly Socialists, as a political means of resolving the linguistic tribalism.

The bicultural battle was further heightened by the question of amnesty for World War II collaborators, rejected in the Parliament in March, but pressed on King Baudouin in his silver anniversary year. The issue of collaboration (prevalent among both Walloons and Flemings during the war) intensified the tensions between the two communities, which were already aggravated by educational policies.

Prime Minister Tindemans, following in the footsteps of other Belgian "Europeanists," Paul-Henri Spaak and Jean Rey, produced a major report on European Union. His design for the future of the Economic Community was the primary subject of debate and analysis throughout the nine countries of the community in 1976.

PIERRE-HENRI LAURENT
Tufts University

——— **BELGIUM • Information Highlights** ———

Official Name: Kingdom of Belgium.
Location: Northwestern Europe.
Area: 11,781 square miles (30,513 km²).
Population (1976 est.): 9,800,000.
Chief Cities (1975 est.): Brussels, the capital, 1,100,000; Antwerp, 670,000; Liège, 440,000.
Government: *Head of state,* Baudouin I, king (acceded 1951). *Head of government,* Leo Tindemans, prime minister (took office 1974). *Legislature*—Parliament: Senate and Chamber of Representatives.
Monetary Unit: Franc (37.35 francs equal U. S.$1, Oct. 1976).
Gross National Product (1975): $66,400,000,000.
Manufacturing (major products): Steel, metals, textiles, cut diamonds, chemicals, glass.
Major Agricultural Products: Sugar beets, potatoes, wheat, oats, barley, flax, hay.
Foreign Trade (includes Luxembourg, 1975): *Exports,* $28,807,000,000; *imports,* $30,688,000,000.

BIOCHEMISTRY

Molecular biology—particularly recombinant genetic engineering—continued to create much excitement during 1976. However, important new findings and techniques were reported in other areas of biochemical research, as well.

Artificial Genes. The first functioning artificial genes were synthesized and reported in 1976. Nobel laureate Har Gobind Khorana's group completed nine years of research by demonstrating that a chemically synthesized tyrosine transfer RNA gene, including promoter and terminator regions, would function when transferred to a mutant bacterial virus, then into *Escherichia coli* bacterial cells.

A second group, headed by Herbert W. Boyer, synthesized the operator region of the familiar lactose operon and demonstrated its activity when incorporated in plasmids (small circular pieces of DNA), then in *E. coli* cells.

Work with these artificial genes promises better understanding of gene control and function, plus safer gene transfer techniques.

Mammalian-Bacterial Hybrides. Four research groups, using recombinant genetic techniques, successfully integrated a portion of the gene coding for rabbit hemoglobin protein into *E. coli*. This represents the first recombination of mammalian and bacterial genes. Genes from frogs, fruit flies, and sea urchins had already been transplanted to bacteria.

Historic Guidelines. Such genetic manipulation experiments promise better understanding of biological mechanisms and future medical, agricultural, and pharmaceutical applications. But they have also engendered concern that recombinant organisms might escape the laboratory, with unforeseeable and perhaps uncontrollable consequences. The National Institutes of Health, therefore, released a set of guidelines to govern gene manipulation research. The guidelines ban certain types of experiments; require special justification for each piece of research; establish levels of physical and biological containment to match estimated potential hazards of each experiment; and assign responsibilities to investigators, institutions, and NIH.

Many, however, are still concerned that the research may be excessively risky. The city of Cambridge, Mass., imposed a three-month moratorium on moderate and high risk recombinant DNA experiments pending review by a panel of local citizens and scientists—an action viewed by many scientists as a bad precedent for academic freedom. Two U. S. Congressmen called for a White House directive or a law to assure compliance with the NIH guidelines.

It is clear from these advances and regulatory actions that the development of powerful new gene manipulation techniques will continue to arouse extreme caution.

Photosynthesis. An organism without chlorophyll has been shown to carry on a new kind of photosynthesis. The system was discovered in the purple membrane of the salt-loving bacterium *Halobacterium halobium*. Walther Stoeckenius and colleagues discovered a purple, light-absorbing pigment protein similar in structure to rhodopsin, the visual pigment in animal retinas. They named the protein "bacteriorhodopsin." This membrane pigment can capture light energy, store it chemically, and use it to drive metabolic processes. This finding may shed light on the evolution of vision and provide a harnessable system for large-scale energy production.

Brain Opiates. Highly specific opiate receptors were discovered several years ago in the brains of various vertebrates, including man, and an intensive search was begun for opiate-like substances in the brain that might interact with those receptors. Brain opiates were subsequently found and named "endorphins." Recent studies on the structure and function of endorphins have identified several pituitary peptides that can interact with opiate receptors. One current hypothesis holds that endorphin deficiency—perhaps an inherited condition—could predispose a person to narcotic addiction. Several groups are now developing radioimmune assays to test this hypothesis.

Oncogene. Evidence has accumulated during the past five years to suggest that certain tumor viruses contain "oncogenes"—cancer genes responsible for transforming normal tissue into the malignant state and maintaining the resulting tumors. Recent research on one oncogene from the Avian Sarcoma Virus (responsible for certain bird tumors) revealed that all vertebrates—from primitive fish to human beings—contain a DNA sequence closely resembling part of the ASV oncogene. This is the most dramatic demonstration to date that oncogenes and normal DNA are intimately related and suggests, further, that the ASV oncogene evolved from normal vertebrate DNA. It is not yet clear what role the vertebrate oncogene sequence may have in tumor initiation, but research to ascertain that role is now under way.

Ribosome Structure. Cellular information flows from DNA to RNA to proteins. Small spherical organelles called ribosomes are the sites of protein synthesis and are thus strong links in the chain from genetic information to new cellular material. Since structure is strongly related to biological function, the molecular structure of ribosomes is a major research goal.

An analytic technique called neutron scattering is used to map the precise structure of ribosomes, and the location of four proteins in the ribosomal subunit were reported in 1976. This technique should produce a complete map within the next few years and, together with data on activated ribosomes, should reveal the exact process by which genetic information is translated into living proteins.

JANET L. HOPSON, *"Science News"*

BIOGRAPHY

A selection of profiles of persons prominent in the news during 1976 appears on pages 118–132. The affiliation of the contributor of the biography is listed on pages 6–9. Included are sketches of:

Amerasinghe, H. S.
Armstrong, Anne
Baryshnikov, Mikhail
Bellow, Saul
Berlinguer, Enrico
Borg, Björn
Caldwell, Sarah
Callaghan, James
Carl XVI Gustaf
Carter, James Earl, Jr.

Clark, Charles Joseph
Dole, Robert Joseph
Erving, Julius
Fälldin, Thorbjörn
Ford, Gerald Rudolph
Fraser, John Malcolm
Hua Kuo-feng
Jordan, Barbara
López Portillo, José
Makarova, Natalia

Martin, James S., Jr.
Mittermaier, Rosi
Mondale, Walter F.
Smith, Ian
Soares, Mário
Suárez González, Adolfo
Videla, Jorge Rafael
Vorster, B. J.
Walters, Barbara
Warren, Robert Penn

AMERASINGHE, Hamilton Shirley

Since 1973, Hamilton Shirley Amerasinghe, a veteran diplomat and U. N. official from Sri Lanka (formerly Ceylon), has presided over the Third United Nations Conference on the Law of the Sea, which ended its 5th session in September 1976 in a deadlock. The conference, which has been called the most ambitious project ever undertaken by the United Nations, is charged with drawing up a treaty to replace the 17th-century code governing use of the seas, which cover 71% of the earth's surface and contain natural resources of inestimable value. Among the questions under debate by delegates of more than 150 countries were those involving jurisdiction of coastal waters, ownership of fish and mineral resources in the oceans, the extent of permissible marine research, control of marine pollution, free passage through strategically located straits, and access of landlocked countries to their share of the oceans' wealth. At the urging of Amerasinghe, who is known as a skilled negotiator and master of teamwork, a tentative draft treaty was drawn up at Geneva in May 1975. A seven-week session held in New York in the spring of 1976 made little progress toward agreement. But although serious differences remain—notably, between underdeveloped countries seeking a strong international agency favorable to their interests, and industrial nations wanting greater freedom for private and national deep-sea enterprises—Amerasinghe is optimistic about the prospects for eventual conclusion of the treaty. In September, Amerasinghe was elected president of the newly convened 31st session of the U. N. General Assembly.

Background. Amerasinghe was born in Colombo, Ceylon, on March 18, 1913. He was educated at the Royal College in Colombo and at Ceylon University College and obtained his B. A. with honors from the University of London in 1934. After entering government service in 1937 he occupied various posts, including secretary to the minister of health, controller of finance, and secretary to the minister of transport. From 1950 to 1952 he was manager of the Gal Oya Development Board, a water and power agency, and from 1953 to 1955 he served as counselor at the Ceylon embassy in Washington. He was director of the Bank of Ceylon in 1962–63, high commissioner to India from 1963 to 1967, and ambassador to Brazil in 1973. Since 1967 he has been his country's permanent representative to the United Nations. In 1969 he headed a committee to investigate human rights in Israeli-occupied Arab territory. From 1962 to 1967, Amerasinghe served as chairman of the U. N. committee to study peaceful uses of the ocean floor beyond the limits of national jurisdiction. In 1973 he became chairman of an ad hoc committee on the Indian Ocean, and that same year he was named president of the U. N. Law of the Sea Conference.

HENRY S. SLOAN

ARMSTRONG, Anne

Anne Armstrong, who was sworn in as U. S. ambassador to the United Kingdom of Great Britain and Northern Ireland on Feb. 19, 1976, is the first woman to represent the United States at the Court of St. James's. A former cochairman of the Republican National Committee and a counselor to Presidents Nixon and Ford, she presented her credentials to Queen Elizabeth II on March 17. Ambassador Armstrong sees as the dominant theme in Anglo-American relations "the harmonizing of national efforts to achieve a common purpose."

Background. The daughter of a coffee importer of French Creole background, and the great-granddaughter of a Texas lieutenant governor, Anne Armstrong was born Anne Legendre in New Orleans, La., on Dec. 27, 1927. She was student body president and class valedictorian at the Foxcroft School in Middleburg, Va., and received her B. A. degree from Vassar College. After working as an assistant editor of *Harper's Bazaar*, she married Tobin Armstrong in 1950.

Mrs. Armstrong became vice chairman of the Texas Republican party in 1966 and served as a delegate and member of the platform committee at the 1964 and 1968 national conventions. From 1968 to 1973 she was a Republican national committeewoman, and in 1971 she became one of the party's two cochairmen. In December 1972, President Nixon named her a White House counselor with cabinet status, making her the first woman to serve in that capacity. As a counselor, she acted as liaison in matters concerning women, youth, Hispanic Americans, and the Bicentennial Commission. She founded the Office for Women's Programs in the White House and served as a member of several committees. She resigned her White House post in November 1974 because of family commitments. Ambassador Armstrong, who has served on the board of directors of several corporations, and her husband are the parents of five children.

HENRY S. SLOAN

Anne Armstrong, an active member of the GOP, was appointed ambassador to Great Britain early in 1976.

UPI

BARYSHNIKOV, Mikhail

Mikhail Baryshnikov achieved maximum critical acclaim during 1976, even eclipsing Rudolf Nureyev by being described as the world's best male dancer. Baryshnikov spread his talents wide during the year, making his mark in modern ballet as well as excelling in the classical roles for which he was trained in the Soviet Union. He became the acknowledged star of the American Ballet Theater and continued the rise to superstardom that began in the years immediately after his defection to the West in 1974. In addition to his roles in *Giselle*, *Coppélia*, and *La Bayadère*, Baryshnikov danced the intricate modern choreography of Twyla Tharp's *Push Comes to Shove* and a special *Pas de Duke* created by Alvin Ailey to the music of Duke Ellington. Baryshnikov also partnered Natalia Makarova in the pas de deux *Other Dances* choreographed for them by Jerome Robbins to music by Chopin. In addition to his work with the American Ballet Theater, Baryshnikov made guest appearances all over the world, notably with London's Royal Ballet.

Baryshnikov made his home in New York and announced his intention of trying all dance styles. Dance critics raved over his impeccable technique and particularly his *ballon*, the moment when a leaping dancer appears to rest suspended in midair.

Background. Baryshnikov received his early dance training in Riga, Latvia, where he was born on Jan. 27, 1948, of Russian parents. When he was 12 his mother, a great lover of the ballet, entered him in the School of the Theater Opera Ballet in Riga. After three years he abandoned early dreams of becoming a pianist to concentrate on ballet.

At the age of 15 he was taken to Leningrad with a group of other young dancers, but applied on his own for an examination at the Vaganova School. He studied there for three years under the great teacher Alexander Pushkin. Baryshnikov joined the Kirov Ballet of Leningrad at the age of 18 as a soloist, skipping over the usual apprenticeship of the corps de ballet. A week after his acceptance at the Kirov he made his professional debut in the Peasant pas de deux in *Giselle*. Two years later he was a principal dancer with the Leningrad company. In 1966, he won the gold medal at the International Ballet Competition in Varna, Bulgaria.

While touring Canada as a guest artist with the Bolshoi Ballet in 1974, Baryshnikov defected in Toronto. His first performance after breaking away from the Soviet Union, and his first performance in the United States, was as Albrecht in *Giselle* with the American Ballet Theater.

JOHN SIMS

BELLOW, Saul

"For human understanding and subtle analysis of contemporary culture that are combined in his work," a Canadian-born novelist was awarded the 1976 Nobel Prize for literature.

Saul Bellow, who has been called the most intellectual of contemporary fiction writers and "the novelist laureate of Jewish life in America," also received the Pulitzer Prize for fiction for his book, *Humboldt's Gift*. The novel parallels the career of the successful Jewish-American writer Charlie Citrine with that of his mentor, the tragic poet genius Von Humboldt Fleisher, whom the author modeled upon the late Delmore Schwartz. It is written with humor and insight into human frailty.

Background. The youngest of four children of Russian-Jewish immigrants, Saul Bellow was born in Lachine, Quebec, Canada on July 10, 1915. His family moved to Chicago—which he considers his real home—when he was 9. He studied sociology and anthropology at the University of Chicago and at Northwestern University, where he was graduated with honors in 1937. He briefly undertook graduate study at the University of Wisconsin but dropped out to devote himself to creative writing. Bellow worked for a time with the WPA Writers

Mikhail Baryshnikov, the "world's best male dancer," performed throughout the world during 1976.

Project, taught at a Chicago teachers' college, and served on the *Encyclopedia Britannica* editorial staff.

Bellow's first two novels, *Dangling Man* (1944) and *The Victim* (1947) brought him some favorable reviews. With his third book, *The Adventures of Augie March* (1953), Bellow adopted the free-wheeling colloquial style that characterized his later work. It was followed by *Seize the Day* (1956), a volume of stories, and *Henderson the Rain King* (1959), a novel about an eccentric millionaire's spiritual odyssey in Africa.

Herzog (1964), Bellow's most personal novel, has as its protagonist a tragicomic intellectual, a sort of "contemporary Jewish Everyman," who ultimately comes to terms with his human condition. In *Mr. Sammler's Planet* (1970) Bellow dissects the social turmoil of the 1960's. His play, *The Last Analysis*, a satire on Freudianism, had a brief run on Broadway in 1964. His newest work, *To Jerusalem and Back*, telling of the problems of Israel, was published in late 1976.

Among the distinctions that Bellow has won are a Guggenheim fellowship, 3 National Book Awards, a National Institute of Arts and Letters Award, and the Prix International de Littérature. He has taught at the universities of Minnesota, New York, and Puerto Rico, and at Princeton and Bard College. A member of the University of Chicago faculty since 1962, he became chairman of its Committee on Social Thought in 1970. Bellow, who has 3 sons from his earlier marriages, makes his home in Chicago with his fourth wife, Alexandra.

HENRY S. SLOAN

BERLINGUER, Enrico

Enrico Berlinguer, the soft-spoken general secretary of the Italian Communist party, emerged in 1976 as that country's freshest political figure. The experience of

Allende in Chile had convinced Berlinguer that Communists must not try to govern by themselves in a strongly Catholic country like Italy. Instead, he called for a "historic compromise" with the Christian Democrats, who have headed Italy's governments for the past thirty years amid growing economic troubles and charges of corruption. In the June 20 parliamentary elections, the Communists gained 49 seats for a total of 228, while the Christian Democrats lost 3 (leaving them 263) in the 630-seat Chamber of Deputies. Although the Communists were excluded from the new Christian Democratic minority government of Giulio Andreotti, the latter promised to consult them on major issues. Berlinguer's Communists in parliament hold a virtual veto power.

On the larger European stage, Berlinguer was becoming the continent's most articulate and independent Communist leader. In a speech in Moscow on February 27, Berlinguer, while not criticizing the Soviet Union directly, drew a clearly independent line, declaring that use of the multiparty democratic system is the correct route to power. At the conference of European Communist parties, held in East Berlin on June 29–30, Berlinguer won the support of Yugoslav, French, and Spanish party leaders and torpedoed Soviet efforts to get the Western parties to reaffirm "proletarian internationalism" (a euphemism for the Brezhnev Doctrine). Thus, Berlinguer has ushered in a new era of "Eurocommunism."

Background. Enrico Berlinguer was born on May 25, 1922, in Sassari, Sardinia, to a family descended from Catalan nobility. He is married to a practicing Roman Catholic and has four children. His father, Mario, a Socialist lawyer, was appointed in 1944 to head the commission to enforce the purge decrees of the post-Fascist Italian government. Enrico joined the Communist party in 1943. A year later he was jailed for three months on charges of instigating a bread riot in Sassari. Acquitted, he started but did not finish college. In 1944 he became the protégé of Palmiro Togliatti and rose rapidly in the party, being elected in 1945 to the Central Committee. He was secretary general of the party's youth movement in 1949–56 and chairman of the World Federation of Democratic Youth in 1950–53. In 1958 he became chief of the party's Organizational Department. From 1968 to 1972 he was deputy secretary of the party. In the latter year he succeeded the ailing Luigi Longo as secretary general. He has been an elected member of the Chamber of Deputies since 1968.

CHARLES F. DELZELL

BORG, Björn

Björn Borg, the Swedish wonder kid, was the world's number one tennis player for 1976. Winning over $300,000 in 1976 alone, Borg became the richest 20-year-old in the sport's history. He so dominated the early part of the season, winning World Championship Tennis, Wimbledon, and the U. S. Professional title (for the third successive year), that even his loss to Jimmy Connors in the finals of the U. S. Open did not disturb his premier position one eyelash. No one reached Borg more than once in these four matches.

Borg flashed on the tennis scene like a junior meteor in 1972 by beating New Zealander Onny Parun in his Davis Cup debut at age 15. In 1974, he won the French and Italian championships (which the players themselves consider the toughest in the world) and was runner-up to John Newcombe in the WCT finals. The next year he won the French Open again, lost to Ashe in the WCT final, and single-handedly led his country to a Davis Cup victory (Sweden's first) in the Challenge Round. By this time Björn was making so much prize money on tour that he left the harsh tax bite of his native Sweden to live in Monte Carlo.

Borg for the first time proved during 1976 that he is a master on all surfaces. WCT is played indoors on a medium-fast artificial rollout rug, Wimbledon on slick grass, and the U. S. Pros and Forest Hills on slow clay.

UPI

Swedish tennis star Björn Borg captured the cup at Wimbledon and became a very wealthy 20-year-old.

Borg has become the complete player with a fine kicking serve, violently topspun forehand, and super mobility. And his on-court disposition is cooler than the North Sea—a particularly valuable asset in this time of racquet kicking, cursing, and obscene gestures by many of the circuit stars.

Background. Borg was born in Södertälje near Stockholm on June 6, 1956. He is still coached by the mentor of his teens, Lennert Bergelin, the famed former Swedish Davis Cup player. Bergelin has groomed his blond prodigy so well that he has never lost to a younger player. It's hard to find anyone on the circuit younger than Borg, let alone someone who can match two fisted backhands with him. And Jimmy Connors will be a veteran before Björn reaches his prime.

EUGENE L. SCOTT

CALDWELL, Sarah

Sarah Caldwell, who has been called the "first lady of American opera," made her debut with New York's Metropolitan Opera on Jan. 13, 1976, becoming the first woman conductor ever to mount its podium. She had been engaged for the 1976 season to conduct 11 performances of *La Traviata,* 8 of them starring soprano Beverly Sills who had personally requested Caldwell's services. As the artistic director of the Opera Company of Boston, which she founded in 1957, Caldwell is noted for her innovative and ingenious productions and is considered by some to be the most creative opera director in the United States. She had made her mark as a symphonic conductor with the Milwaukee Symphony Orchestra and the New York Philharmonic in 1975. "I don't think of myself as a 'woman conductor,' but as a conductor," she said, "and I hope my abilities will speak for themselves."

Background. The daughter of a university professor, Sarah Caldwell was born about 1928 in Maryville, Mo., and grew up in Fayetteville, Ark. Encouraged by her mother, a pianist and music teacher, Sarah was considered a prodigy both in music and mathematics by

Sarah Caldwell, the "first lady of American opera," made her debut with the Metropolitan Opera in 1976.

the time she was four. After completing high school at 14, she attended the University of Arkansas for two years and then entered the New England Conservatory of Music. On completion of her studies there, she turned down offers to play the violin with the Minneapolis and Indianapolis symphony orchestras. Having become passionately devoted to opera, she accepted an invitation from Boris Goldovsky to become his assistant in directing the New England Opera Theatre. During her 11 years with Goldovsky, she spent many of her summers at the Berkshire Music Center in Lenox, Mass., both as a student and a faculty member. During the 1950's she became head of the opera workshop at Boston University, where she staged the American premiere of Hindemith's *Mathis der Maler*. In 1957 she and a group of friends established the Boston Opera Group, later renamed Opera Company of Boston. As a result of Caldwell's researches, the company performed little-known operas as well as the standard works. Its repertory has included Offenbach's *Voyage to the Moon*, Schoenberg's *Moses and Aaron*, Kurka's *The Good Soldier Schweik*, Schuller's *The Fisherman and his Wife*, Smetana's *Bartered Bride*, Berlioz's *The Trojans*, and a modern version of Stravinsky's *The Rake's Progress*. In 1967–68 she directed the American National Opera Company and in 1973 she staged Henze's *The Young Lord* and Strauss's *Ariadne auf Naxos* for the New York City Opera Company.

HENRY S. SLOAN

CALLAGHAN, James

James Callaghan, British foreign minister since 1974, was elected leader of the Labour party and thereby became prime minister on April 5, 1976. He succeeded Harold Wilson who had announced his resignation the previous month. Callaghan was the first choice of only a minority of Labour's members of Parliament, but the exhaustive ballot system tends to favor the man who is at least acceptable to the greatest number. A right-winger in Labour party terms, he beat off a strong challenge from the left-winger Michael Foot, but has

subsequently consolidated his position by keeping close links with the party's rank and file.

Callaghan immediately won support from both party and members of Parliament, and opinion polls demonstrated his popularity in the country as a whole. His air of candor and refusal to pretend that he had any miracle cure for Britain's ailments struck a chord with voters, and his successful efforts to reunite left and right within his own party appealed to politicians. But these successes could not obscure doubts about his earlier performance. As chancellor of the exchequer—finance minister—from 1964 to 1967 his tenure was marked by dithering and a failure to devalue the pound sterling early enough. He became home secretary in 1967 and alienated many in his own party by putting the first restrictions on entry to Britain for East African Asians who had British passports. On the other hand, during a short period in charge of the problems of Northern Ireland he was generally agreed to have tackled an impossible situation with courage and sympathy.

Background. Callaghan was born on March 27, 1912, the son of a chief petty officer in the Royal Navy, who died when the boy was nine. His mother had no pension and they lived in penury for some years. In 1929 he became a civil servant in the inland revenue. He volunteered for the Royal Navy in 1942 and served as an ordinary seaman and lieutenant.

Callaghan joined the Labour party in 1931 and was first elected to parliament for Cardiff South in 1945. He held a number of minor posts in the 1945–51 Labour governments, but rose to authority within the party during its 13 years of opposition, 1951–64. He married Audrey Moulton in 1938; they have a son and two daughters and eight grandchildren.

SIMON HOGGART

CARL XVI GUSTAF

For young King Carl XVI Gustaf of Sweden 1976 was a busy year. On April 2 he arrived with his entourage at Kennedy Airport, New York, beginning a month-long visit to the United States in honor of the bicentennial. Stopping in more than a dozen cities, he covered points from Williamsburg, Va., in the East to Seattle, Wash., in the Northwest, the tour highlighted by a meeting with President Gerald Ford in the White House on April 3. The king returned home on his 30th birthday, April 30. Seven weeks later, on June 19, he married German-born Silvia Sommerlath in Stockholm Cathedral. It was the first wedding of a reigning Swedish monarch in 179 years. The royal couple then left for a honeymoon that took them as far as the Hawaiian islands.

Background. Born at Haga Palace, Stockholm, King Carl XVI Gustaf is a descendant of Napoleon's famous marshal, Jean-Baptiste Bernadotte, who was elected crown prince of Sweden in 1810. Carl Gustaf has four elder sisters. His mother, Princess Sibylla, died in 1972.

Carl Gustaf became crown prince when his grandfather, Gustaf VI Adolf, acceded to the throne in 1950; his father, Prince Gustaf Adolf, having died in an air crash three years earlier. He became king on Sept. 19, 1973, and chose as his motto "For Sweden in Keeping With the Times." The young monarch has gained the confidence of a broad section of the population in his socialist country. His duties are only ceremonial.

MAC LINDAHL

CARTER, James Earl ("Jimmy"); Jr.

The rise of Jimmy Carter to the leadership of the Democratic party and his election to the presidency is one of the most remarkable success stories in the history of American politics.

When Carter announced his candidacy for the presidency in December 1974 the event was little noticed. Carter is a Southerner, and no citizen of a Southern state had been nominated for the presidency by a major political party in more than a century. His tenure as

UPI

Democratic presidential nominee Jimmy Carter demonstrated driving energy and great self-confidence.

governor of Georgia was about to end, leaving him without the prestige and perquisites of public office. He was almost unknown outside his own state. And he could not rely on the support of any of the powerful interest groups that ordinarily dominate the Democratic party.

Yet Carter managed during the ensuing campaign to turn all these apparent drawbacks into advantages. As a son of the South, his efforts stirred the deep pride of that long alienated region which ultimately became the cornerstone of his support. As an ex-governor, he could spend all his time on his campaign. His relative obscurity made him a new face to voters tired of the familiar presidential contenders. Without obligation to organized constituencies or political power brokers, he could cast himself as an outsider and an underdog.

But the wellspring of Carter's appeal was his distinctive personality, shaped by his upbringing in the rural South. He did not inherit great wealth or a celebrated family name. But his early experience stamped him with attributes which were to prove just as important to his success—boundless ambition, driving energy, self-confidence bordering on cockiness, and an abiding faith in his Southern Baptist religion.

Carter's 1974 appointment as Democratic campaign chairman gave him the contacts around the country which helped him get his own campaign off to a strong start. He made two important strategic decisions early. One was to compete for delegates in nearly every state, while his opponents picked and chose where they would run. The other was not to focus on specific issues, which might divide his potential supporters, but rather to concentrate on broad, unifying themes, such as the need for trust and compassion in government. He campaigned tirelessly, promising never to tell a lie and emphasizing the love and goodness of the American people. His strong appeal to black voters, buoyed by the endorsements of such prominent black leaders as the Rev. Martin Luther King, Sr., won over many Northern liberals suspicious of his Southern origins.

Carter's successes in the primaries, climaxed by his big June 8 victory in Ohio, assured him of the nomination a month before the convention. This gave him time to placate the opposing factions in his party and achieve a remarkable state of Democratic unity. After the convention, to underline his separation from the Washington establishment, he set up his campaign headquarters in Atlanta, in his home state.

Background. James Earl Carter, Jr. (who prefers the folksier "Jimmy" in public life) was born on Oct. 21, 1924, the first of four children of James Earl Carter, Sr., and his wife Lillian. Carter, Sr. was a relatively successful farmer. But living conditions on the farm and in the tiny nearby town of Plains were primitive by today's standards. Moreover, in the 1930's, when Carter came of age, times were hard. As he later wrote in his self-revealing memoir *Why Not the Best?*, "My life on the farm during the Great Depression more nearly resembled farm life of 2,000 years ago than farm life today."

Comforts were few and hardships abounded. For years the family used an outdoor privy and drew their water with a hand pump. As a small boy, Carter rose with the hired hands at 4 A. M. to begin his chores. Amid this Spartan existence both young parents set examples of enterprise. The father ran a store near their home, and the mother, a registered nurse, worked at nearby hospitals or in the homes of patients. By the time he was six, Carter was selling boiled peanuts on the streets of Plains, an experience which, he wrote later, helped him distinguish between good and bad people. "The good people, I thought, were the ones who bought boiled peanuts from me." Later, of course, he learned more sophisticated standards for judging people. But the impact of his farm youth stayed with him, leaving him disciplined to meet the physical demands of his ambitions and deeply wedded to the work ethic.

Carter, who since childhood had yearned to go to the U. S. Naval Academy, was admitted there in 1943. When he was graduated, in 1947, he was conscious of the fact that he was the first member of his family to have earned a college degree. At his father's death, in 1953, Carter resigned from the Navy and together with his wife, Rosalynn, whom he had married in 1947, returned to Plains. Using the family farm as a base, Carter specialized in the sale of seed peanuts. The business flourished and made him a wealthy man.

In 1962, after a bitter campaign, he won election to the Georgia State Senate. But in 1966, when he sought the Democratic nomination for governor, he was beaten, a setback which left him bitterly disappointed. In his distress he sought the guidance of his evangelist sister, Ruth Carter Stapleton. The result was a religious experience which Carter has described as being "born again" and which reaffirmed his faith.

In 1970 Carter sought the governorship again, and this time, after a vigorous handshaking campaign, he won. He soon made his mark on Georgia. In his inaugural address he bluntly declared, "The time for racial discrimination is over." To dramatize the point, he had a picture of Martin Luther King, Jr., hung in the state capitol. And he jolted the bureaucracy by launching a massive drive to reorganize the state government.

Some critics, recalling Carter's effort in his gubernatorial campaign to win the votes of supporters of George Wallace, doubted his commitment to civil rights. Others contended that he was too rigid and dogmatic, particularly in dealing with the state legislature. Nevertheless, he received national acclaim as a prime example of the "new breed" of Southern politicians. Barred by the Georgia constitution from seeking reelection, he then turned his attention to the national scene and to the presidency. By 1972 his advisers had already laid out a rough outline of a strategy for gaining the 1976 Democratic presidential nomination.

The Carters have three sons, John William (Jack), 29, James Earl III (Chip), 26, and Donnel Jeffrey (Jeff), 24, and a daughter, Amy Lynn, age 9.

ROBERT SHOGAN

CLARK, Charles Joseph

Joe Clark, member of Parliament and leader of the opposition in the Canadian House of Commons, is the youngest Canadian ever to take charge of a major national political party. On Feb. 22, 1976, at the age of 36, he was elected by the Progressive Conservative Party convention in Ottawa as its 14th leader, succeeding Robert Lorne Stanfield who retired after eight years in that office. Clark won on the fourth ballot with a slender margin over Quebec's Claude Wagner.

Clark is regarded by fellow Conservatives as a progressive. He is critical of Liberal welfare programs as expensive and inefficient. He favors and has voted for the abolition of capital punishment, supports the Official Language Act for the bilingualization of the Federal Civil Service, and believes in government decentralization, with Ottawa being "a partner, not a bully" in its relations with the provinces. Bilingual himself, Clark is highly respected as a party organizer. During his tenure as leader he has worked hard toward healing rifts within his party and reaching accommodation with dissident members. An attractive and tough political performer, he hopes to present a unified front against the Liberal, New Democratic, and Social Credit parties in the expected 1978 election.

Background. Charles Joseph Clark was born on June 5, 1939, the son of Charles Clark, editor and publisher of the High River, Alberta, *Times*. After public school education in High River, he was graduated with a bachelor of arts degree in history from the University of Alberta; studied law for a brief period at the University of British Columbia; and returned to Alberta for a master's degree in political science. In 1959 he became private secretary to W. J. C. Kirby, leader of the Alberta Progressive Conservatives. He was a two-term (1962–65) national president of the Conservative Students' Federation and a founding chairman of the Canadian Political Youth Council. In 1966 he became director of the Conservative party organization that later elected Peter Lougheed to power in Alberta. In 1967 he was made executive assistant to Stanfield and in 1972 ran for federal office and was elected member of Parliament for the Rocky Mountain riding. He was reelected in 1974. In 1973 he married Maureen McTeer of Cumberland, Ontario.

BARRY M. GOUGH

DOLE, Robert Joseph

During 26 years in politics, Kansas Republican Senator Robert J. Dole had established himself as a forceful defender of conservative principles and a slashing critic of his Democratic opponents. It was evidently this reputation, more than any other quality, that was responsible for President Ford's surprising choice of the senator as his vice presidential running mate. Ford needed someone to placate the conservative supporters of Ronald Reagan, whom he had just defeated for the GOP nomination. And he also wanted someone who could take the offensive against the Democratic ticket which at the time of the Republican convention held a commanding lead in the polls.

Dole appeared ideally suited for the job. From his early days in the Senate in 1969 he had taken a prominent position as a defender of President Nixon on controversies ranging from Supreme Court appointments to policies in Indochina. His voting record won him high remarks from the conservative Americans for Constitutional Action and a correspondingly low rating from the liberal Americans for Democratic Action.

From Ford's point of view he also had other assets. The two men had established a personal relationship in 1961–68 when Dole served in the House under Ford's leadership. And as a Kansan, Dole seemed likely to help the Republican ticket in the farm-belt states, where success was essential to GOP prospects.

Although the senator staged a tough campaign, the Ford-Dole ticket was defeated on November 2.

Background. Robert Joseph Dole was born in Russell, Kans., on July 22, 1923. He was educated at the University of Kansas, where he got his bachelor's degree, and at Washburn Municipal University in Topeka, where he studied law. On completing law school he enlisted in the U. S. Army and served as a platoon leader in Italy until he was severely wounded by a shell burst. Recovery took three years and left him with a withered and almost useless right arm. It also left him with a continued interest in programs to aid the handicapped.

Dole won his first campaign, for a seat in the Kansas legislature, in 1950. Two years later he was elected to the first of four two-year terms as Russell County attorney. He won a seat in the U. S. House of Representatives in 1960 and moved up to the Senate after the election of 1968.

His aggressiveness as a defender of the Nixon administration won him national attention and the gratitude of the president, who in 1971 recommended him for chairman of the Republican National Committee. In that post Dole was a loyal Nixon partisan. During the early stages of the Watergate scandal he sought to rebut attempts to link it to the White House, but his independence and outspokenness evidently offended some Nixon aides; after the 1972 elections he was asked to leave the chairmanship. This turned out to be a blessing in disguise since it removed Dole from direct connection with the White House during the most politically damaging phase of the Watergate scandal. Even so, Dole had to wage an uphill battle to retain his Senate seat in 1974. He won, in part, by accusing his Democratic opponent of trying to smear him by linking him to Watergate.

Dole's most notable characteristic is his biting wit, which he generally uses against Democrats. He labeled former Georgia Gov. Jimmy Carter, the 1976 Democratic presidential nominee, as "Southern fried McGovern," a reference to the liberal 1972 Democratic nominee, Sen. George McGovern of South Dakota. But fellow Republicans, and sometimes Dole himself, have also been targets for his edged humor. During his 1974 reelection bid, Dole noted that he had not asked Nixon to campaign for him in Kansas, but added he would not object "if Nixon flew over the state." And after Ford pardoned Nixon, Dole quipped that Ford had "thrown him an anchor."

In 1948 Dole married Phyllis Holden, a physical therapist, who first met him at the hospital where he was recovering from his war wounds. The marriage ended in divorce in 1972, and in 1975 Dole married Mary Elizabeth Hanford, a member of the Federal Trade Commission. He has a daughter, Robin, by his first marriage.

ROBERT SHOGAN

ERVING, Julius

The many admirers of Julius Erving fall into three classes—those who think he is great, those who think he is the best basketball player in action today, and those who believe he is the best of all time. The ranks grew in all three categories during the 1975–76 season, especially during the American Basketball Association play-offs.

Erving was voted the most valuable player in the A. B. A. for the third straight year (he shared the honor with George McGinnis of Indianapolis in 1975). He had won the scoring title for the third time in four years with 2,462 points, an average of 29.3 per game. He was the most valuable player in the play-offs in leading the New York Nets to the championship. Actually, he practically took over the final series against the Denver Nuggets with spectacular scoring and defensive plays.

It is the éclat with which Erving performs that makes him the most exciting basketball player of the era. Doctor J, as he is known to his admirers, operates as well high off the floor as others do with both feet on the court. Erving has the ability to leap about 15 feet and slam-dunk the ball in the basket. While air-borne the 6-foot-7-inch (2 m) forward can switch the ball from one hand to the other for a shot or a pass to a teammate or he can whirl clear around. He is equally adept on defense, blocking shots and stealing as well as rebounding.

Background. Julius Winfield Erving began playing basketball as a boy in Hempstead, N. Y., where he was born Feb. 22, 1950. After starring at Roosevelt (N. Y.) High School, he played for the University of Massachusetts and led all college players for two years in rebounding. After his third season, he quit college and signed a four-year contract for $500,000 with the Virginia Squires. In his first year, 1971–72, he was sixth in scoring and was named to the A. B. A. rookie team. The next season he paced the league's scorers with 2,268 points, 31.9 per game. He then agreed to play for the Atlanta Hawks of the National Basketball Association, but the deal was stalled because Milwaukee claimed N. B. A. rights to him. A federal court ruled that he was the property of the Squires, thwarting his bid to jump.

The Nets, whose base is near Erving's home, settled the controversy by giving the Squires $750,000 and another star player for Erving and paying $100,000 to Atlanta. His new contract was for eight years at about $350,000 per season. In 1973–74 he led the Nets to the A. B. A. title, pacing the scorers again with 2,299 points, 27.4 per game, and was named m. v. p. The next season he shared the top award with McGinnis, a 2,343 total. He carried a five-year total of 11,626 points and an average of 28.5 into action in the N. B. A. The older league had acquired the most exciting player by absorbing the Nets and three other A. B. A. teams in June 1976. However, a contract dispute forced the Nets to trade Erving to the N. B. A.'s Philadelphia 76ers.

BILL BRADDOCK

FÄLLDIN, Thorbjörn

Thorbjörn Fälldin—the surname is pronounced Fell-dean—was designated prime minister of Sweden in early October 1976. He thus became head of the first non-socialist government in the country in 44 years. It is a three-party coalition made up of the Center (formerly the Agrarian), the Moderate (formerly the Conservative), and the Liberal parties—the so-called bourgeois parties—which defeated the Social Democrats in the general election on September 19, winning an 11-seat majority.

"Now we are going to lead Sweden step by step toward decentralization," said Fälldin at his first press conference after the election. "We are going to break the power concentration. It will not happen overnight, but I promise that our supporters will not have to wait long before noticing results," he added. Fälldin and his cabinet face many problems, one of them being the defeated government's nuclear energy program, which he strenuously opposed during his campaign. Once in office, however, he considerably modified his stance against the spread of nuclear power plants.

Background. Thorbjörn Fälldin, leader of the Center Party, comes of a family of farmers. He was born in Högsjö in northern Sweden on April 24, 1926, and since 1956 he has lived with his family on a nearby hilltop farm where he raises sheep, grows potatoes, and cuts timber. Upon completion of his formal education at age 19, he became an officer in the infantry reserve, and for two subsequent years (1949–51) was an ombudsman in his native district's section of the Swedish Agrarian Youth Organization.

He was a member of Parliament from 1958 until 1964, when he lost his seat by 11 votes; he was reelected in 1967. He became first vice chairman of the Center party in 1969 and its leader in 1971. A member of the government's environmental committee from 1963 to 1971, he also held a post on the labor market board. Since 1971 he has been on the board of directors of the private Svenska Handelsbanken

(Swedish Commercial Bank). He married in 1956 and has three children. Maintaining a one-room apartment in Stockholm, Fälldin spends as many weekends as possible and every holiday on his farm.

MAC LINDAHL

FORD, Gerald Rudolph

"I'm a Ford, not a Lincoln," Gerald Ford once told his countrymen. This self-appraisal, with its characteristic candor, neatly suggests the strengths and weaknesses of the first man to become president of the United States without winning a national election. Like the legendary Model T's, which once rolled off Henry Ford's assembly lines, Gerald Ford is sturdy, reliable, and unpretentious. What he seemed to lack, as the 38th president of the United States, was the vision, the eloquence, or the inspirational force which made Lincoln a great leader.

Until his succession to the presidency, under unprecedented circumstances, Ford had managed to fashion his life and career to take maximum advantage of his assets and to minimize his limitations. For 25 years in the U. S. House of Representatives, he had been a competent politician and efficient representative of his Michigan constituents, personally well regarded by his colleagues in both parties. The presidency, an office he did not seek, presented a different and more demanding challenge to his character and intellect.

Background. Gerald Rudolph Ford was born on July 14, 1913, in Omaha, Nebr., to Leslie Lynch and Dorothy King and christened Leslie King at birth. When he was two, his parents were divorced, and the mother later married Gerald Ford, a Grand Rapids, Mich., paint manufacturer, who adopted the child and gave him his name.

Young Ford's boyhood in the 1920's was typical of middle-class, Midwestern America. His home life was stable and relatively comfortable until the Depression cut into his father's paint business and forced the Fords to tighten their belts. The young man took odd jobs in town to help pay for his education. His athletic prowess helped, too. Young Ford excelled in football at high school and won a football scholarship to the University of Michigan where he starred as center on the Wolverine team. After graduation from Michigan in 1935 he went on to Yale Law School, where a job as an assistant football and boxing coach helped finance his education over an extended six-year program. He finished in the top third of his class.

Ford began a modest law practice in Grand Rapids, but when the United States was plunged into World War II he enlisted in the Navy. In 47 months of active service he won 10 battle stars in the South Pacific and rose to the rank of lieutenant commander. Back in Grand Rapids he resumed his law practice and, in 1948, won the Republican nomination for Congress in Michigan's fifth congressional district. Ford easily defeated his Democratic opponent, the first of 13 successive victories in the district.

In October of 1948, just before the election, Ford married Elizabeth Bloomer Warren, whose previous marriage had ended in divorce. In 1949 the young couple moved to Washington where they were to rear four children—Michael, now 26, Jack, 24, Steve, 20, and Susan, 19.

As a young representative, Ford's positions were in the standard mold of conservative Midwest Republicanism. But he did support internationalist views, and in 1952 he was one of the 18 Republican congressmen who urged Dwight Eisenhower to seek the Republican presidential nomination against the competition of conservative Ohio Sen. Robert A. Taft.

Except for the first two years of Eisenhower's first term, the Democrats maintained control of both houses of Congress, a situation which frustrated Republicans in general. But Ford's own career progressed, as his diligence and congeniality won him many friends among his Republican colleagues. He was elected to his first leadership post, chairman of the House GOP Conference, in 1963. And in 1965, after the resounding Republican defeat in the 1964 elections, he was elected minority leader of the House.

After the 1972 elections, when the Republicans remained in the minority in Congress, despite Nixon's landslide presidential victory, Ford told friends that he planned to make one more effort to help elect a Republican Congress, in the 1974 elections. If that hope failed, he intended to retire at the end of 1976.

But events intervened, dramatically. On Oct. 12, 1973, President Nixon named Ford to replace Vice President Spiro Agnew who had been forced to resign under a criminal indictment for taking kickbacks and evading income tax. Ford was confirmed by large majorities in both houses of Congress and sworn in as vice president in December. He was the first man to become vice president under the 25th Amendment.

Eight months later, in August 1974, Nixon, whom Ford had steadfastly defended, was forced to resign to avoid almost certain impeachment because of his involvement in the Watergate scandals. Ford immediately won widespread support from a scandal-weary nation by the simplicity of his inaugural speech in which he declared, "Our long national nightmare is over." But a month after he became president he unexpectedly pardoned Nixon for any federal crimes he might have committed while in office and brought down a storm of protest on his own head. In the subsequent elections the Republicans suffered a severe defeat, for which the Nixon pardon was partly blamed. Ford's appointment of Nelson Rockefeller as his vice president angered conservatives and further weakened Ford's support in his party.

Other problems loomed, too. The economy dipped drastically, and the country headed into the worst recession since the 1930's. Abroad, the Communists scored a victory over the South Vietnamese regime the United States had long supported.

In May 1975 Ford's standing in public opinion polls climbed after he ordered a military action to recover the *Mayaguez*, a U. S. merchant ship seized by Cambodia. But the improvement was only temporary. The recession deepened and complaints grew louder that Ford lacked leadership qualities. Emboldened by Ford's apparent weakness, former California Gov. Ronald Reagan challenged him for the Republican nomination. Reagan campaigned in primaries across the nation and carried the battle to the floor of the GOP convention in Kansas City. Ford, however, prevailed by 1,187 votes to 1,070.

Though the party he led seemed weak and divided, and though he himself trailed his Democratic opposition in the polls, Ford remained determined and outwardly confident. His acceptance speech to the convention was probably the most impressive political address he had ever made. The president cited the accomplishments of his two-year presidency in maintaining peace and fostering economic recovery. And he broke precedent as an incumbent president by challenging his Democratic opponent, Jimmy Carter, to a face-to-face debate on the major issues confronting the nation.

Following a series of widely watched and discussed television debates, Ford was unsuccessful in his bid for a full term.

ROBERT SHOGAN

FRASER, John Malcolm

Backed by the largest parliamentary majority in Australia's history, 46-year-old Liberal Prime Minister Malcolm Fraser, in his first year in office, moved along orthodox fiscal and monetary lines to deal with the country's economic ills of spiraling inflation and stubborn recession. Honoring the pledge on which he came to power in December 1975, Fraser reduced deficit spending, halted the tax spiral, and reined in federal expenditures after three years of rapid growth under a Labor administration. He set lower ceilings on departmental budgets and trimmed the federal payroll by more

UPI

In part, President Gerald Ford campaigned for a full term by staying and working at the White House.

than 3% in the first 12 months. Seeking to reduce centralized decision-making, he also initiated a "new federalism" to improve the status of state governments and municipal authorities.

The first Liberal party leader in 10 years to enjoy unchallenged loyalty, Fraser impressed people with his sincerity and dedication. In his quiet bearing he contrasted sharply with the prime minister whom he had succeeded, Labor party leader Gough Whitlam.

Background. John Malcolm Fraser was born in Melbourne on May 21, 1930, into a well-to-do family in which politics had long been a dominant force. As a schoolboy he was industrious and a good student. From Melbourne Grammar School he went on to Magdalen College, Oxford, and in 1953 graduated in philosophy, politics, and economics. Choosing to pursue a political career, he was endorsed by the Liberal party for the rural constituency in which his family lived. He was narrowly defeated in 1954 but won handsomely in 1955. He held his first ministerial post at 36 and retained portfolios until he resigned in 1972 after a clash with the Liberal leadership. He became parliamentary leader of the Liberal party in March 1975.

R. M. YOUNGER

HUA Kuo-feng

Before the death of Chinese Premier Chou En-lai on Jan. 8, 1976, few people in the West had ever heard the name of Hua Kuo-feng. It had been widely expected that First Vice Premier Teng Hsiao-p'ing, who had borne the brunt of administrative responsibility during Chou's final illness, would succeed him; instead, that was when he began to get into political difficulties. Nevertheless, it came as a complete surprise to western observers when in early February, Hua Kuo-feng, since January 1975 an obscure minister of public security and one of many vice premiers, was informally revealed to have become the acting premier. On April 7, two days after a remarkable demonstration in Chou's memory, for which Teng Hsiao-p'ing was officially blamed, Hua was formally named both premier and first vice chairman of the Chinese Communist party's Central Committee—the latter title never before used.

Following the death of Mao in September, Hua was selected to succeed Mao as party chairman. At the same time, he retained the posts of prime minister and chairman of the party's military commission. No other Chinese official had ever held all three positions simultaneously. In addition, he was named editor of Mao's works.

While it is too early to assess him as chief executive of the world's largest nation, Hua appears in reality to hold essentially moderate views. Generally considered a pragmatist, Hua seems to emphasize the themes of party unity, discipline, and production.

Background. Hua Kuo-feng was born in the province of Shansi about 1920, but nothing is known, outside China, of his early life and career. He got his real start in 1955 when he was appointed secretary of the Communist party committee of Hsiangtan, Mao Tse-tung's home town in Hunan. Hua was careful to associate himself publicly with this political holy place, for instance by building a hall to memorialize Mao's early life in the town, and by the 1960's he had become active and influential in Hunanese politics at the provincial level. He was elected a senior member of the Revolutionary Committee—a Cultural-Revolution-model provincial government—of Hunan at the time of its formation in April 1968. On Mao's birthday, (December 26) 1970, when Hunan became the first province to reestablish its party committee in the post-Cultural Revolution period, Hua was elected its first secretary.

At the same time he had begun to emerge as a national figure. During the Ninth Congress of the Communist party (April 1969) he was elected to its Central Committee; at the Tenth Congress (August 1973) he was elected to the ruling Political Bureau. He was appointed vice premier and minister of public security in January 1975. In October of that year he made a key speech at an important conference on agriculture in which, characteristically, he summed up and tried to harmonize the divergent views of the Maoist radicals and the moderates.

HAROLD C. HINTON

JORDAN, Barbara

Democratic Representative Barbara Jordan of Texas, who in 1972 became the first black woman to be elected to the U. S. Congress from the Deep South, delivered a keynote address at the 1976 Democratic National Convention. The first of her race and sex to present a convention keynote speech, she electrified her audience with her appeal for "a national community . . . in which all of us are equal." Representative Jordan asserted that "we cannot improve on the system of government handed down to us by the founders of the Republic, but we can find new ways to implement that system and to realize our destiny." Rejecting efforts by the Black Caucus to nominate her for vice president, she urged support for the candidate chosen by the Democratic presidential nominee, Jimmy Carter.

Background. Barbara Charline Jordan, the daughter of a Baptist minister, was born in Houston on Feb. 21, 1936. Encouraged by her parents to strive for excellence, she was graduated *magna cum laude* from Texas Southern University in 1956. After obtaining her LL. B. degree from Boston University in 1959, she was admitted to the bar in Massachusetts and Texas. While engaged in private practice in Houston, she worked as an administrative assistant to a county judge and became active in Democratic politics.

After unsuccessful bids for a seat in the Texas House of Representatives in 1962 and 1964, she won election in 1966 to the state Senate. She helped to sponsor legislation establishing the Texas Fair Employment Practices Commission.

She was elected to the U. S. House of Representatives from the 18th Congressional District of Texas in 1972 and reelected in 1974 and 1976. Representative Jordan is a constant champion of civil rights and the war against poverty.

UPI

Barbara Jordan became the first woman and the first black to deliver a convention keynote speech.

As a member of the House Judiciary Committee, she was among those who approved the articles of impeachment against President Nixon in July 1974. It was at this time that she first came to the attention of many Americans.

Representative Jordan is single and lives with her mother.

HENRY S. SLOAN

LÓPEZ PORTILLO, José

José López Portillo was sworn in as president of Mexico on Dec. 1, 1976, to serve a single, six-year term, his first elective public office. The candidate of the government's Institutional Revolutionary party, he faced no opposition in the July election, the first such occurrence since 1928. Nevertheless, Dr. López campaigned vigorously to make himself known to the public and to gather information on citizen problems and demands.

The candidate promised to continue the Mexican revolution by promoting social justice for the masses, maintaining Mexico's independent foreign policy, and achieving economic balance. In office, the new president is expected to make national government more efficient, less corrupt, and better planned while continuing support of Third World positions and friendliness to the United States in foreign affairs.

Dr. López' path to the presidency was a minor departure from traditional political practice. Although a member of the government party, he had a technical rather than a political career. Instead of coming to the presidency from the Interior Ministry, he came from Finance. Like his childhood friend and predecessor Luis Echeverría, he is a Mexico City native, unusual in a system that seeks regional balance. López Portillo was chosen to bring order to governmental finance and promote economic development without alienating the left or right.

Background. José López Portillo was born on June 16, 1920, the son of a prominent family. He earned a law degree from the national university in 1946 and later received the Ph. D. in administrative science. Leaving his private law practice in 1959 to serve as a technical consultant in the National Patrimony Ministry, he subsequently rose to be undersecretary. He held similar high posts in the Presidency Secretariat and the Federal Electrical Commission before becoming secretary of finance in 1973. He is married and has three children. The new president runs a mile daily, does calisthenics, and is fond of U. S. football and music. A former university professor, he has authored several books on public administration.

DONALD J. MABRY

MAKAROVA, Natalia

Natalia Makarova in 1976 finally was given the sole distinction she complained she had not received since her defection from the Soviet Union in 1970—a modern ballet designed specifically for her. Choreographer Jerome Robbins created the pas de deux *Other Dances* specifically for Makarova and Mikhail Baryshnikov for performance within the American Ballet Theater season.

When Makarova defected during a London tour with Leningrad's Kirov Ballet, she said she wanted greater artistic freedom than was offered in the Soviet Union. Nevertheless, she continued to dance mainly the classical roles she had sought to escape, and complained that no Western choreographer had created a role especially for her. Robbins' creation was an extended pas de deux for her and Baryshnikov to piano music by Chopin. It won her critical acclaim.

She also was successful in the classical roles for which she has become best known. For the American Ballet Theater, Makarova also took on the dual role of Odette-Odile in Swan Lake, and one performance was broadcast live nationwide by the Public Broadcasting System. Dance experts labeled her as possibly the best dancer in the world.

Background. Makarova was born on Nov. 21, 1940, in Leningrad. At the age of 12 she joined the Young Pioneers, a Communist Party youth movement, and received her early training in one of their dance classes. Her first professional training came at the Vaganova School in Leningrad and she joined the Kirov Ballet in 1959. As a principal dancer with the Kirov her major role was Giselle. On the occasion of breaking away from the Kirov Ballet Makarova said Soviet ballet choreography was stagnant and she wanted to try new roles.

Natalia Makarova won an additional honor in 1976— a modern ballet was designed specifically for her.

UPI

She made her debut with the American Ballet Theater in 1970, but attached herself principally to the Royal Ballet of London. Since her marriage to businessman Edward Karkar on Feb. 22, 1976, Makarova has concentrated more on her American commitments. (She was previously twice divorced from Russians.) In 1976 she reconstructed the last act of *La Bayadère* for the American Ballet Theater and danced in a new production of *Sleeping Beauty.*

Makarova has homes in London and San Francisco, but saw both only briefly during a busy 1976 of guest appearances all over the world.

Her favorite hobby is painting.

JOHN SIMS

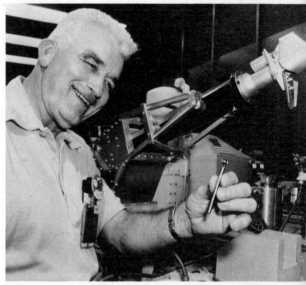

UPI

Former research engineer James S. Martin, Jr., directed the successful Viking I and II missions.

MARTIN, James S., Jr.

The success of Project Viking, which accomplished the first landing of a man-made apparatus in working order on the planet Mars on July 20, 1976, is largely owed to the efforts of its project director, James S. Martin, Jr. Observing the completion of the 11-month, 212,000,000-mile (341,000,000-km) journey of the instrument-laden landing craft of the spacecraft Viking I, Martin exclaimed: "We have a touchdown! This has got to be the happiest time of my life. It's incredible to me that it all worked so perfectly." Despite some initial mechanical malfunctions, the photographic, geological, chemical, and meteorological data sent back by Viking I substantially increased man's knowledge of the "red planet."

A second spacecraft, Viking II, landed in a different area of Mars on September 3. Following the missions, project scientists continued to seek answers to the question of whether life exists or has existed on Mars.

Background. The son of an electrical engineer, James Slattin Martin, Jr., was born on June 21, 1920, in Washington, D. C., and grew up in Springfield, Ill. After graduation from the University of Michigan in 1942 he worked for Republic Aviation where he helped design the P-47 Thunderbolt and the F-84 jet fighter. After World War II, Martin became chief research engineer, and later manager of space systems requirements, at Republic Aviation.

Martin joined the National Aeronautics and Space Administration in 1964, and as manager of the Lunar Orbiter Project he was responsible for the five successful photographic missions of unmanned spacecraft that were completed in 1966 and 1967. He then worked at NASA's Langley Research Center in Virginia, and in 1968 he was named project director of the newly initiated Viking program.

Martin, whose permanent residence is in Seaford, Va., is making his home in Glendale, Calif., with his wife and two of their four children until the completion of the Viking project.

HENRY S. SLOAN

MITTERMAIER, Rosi

Just the time it takes to blink an eye separated Rosi Mittermaier from the finest possible achievement in Alpine skiing at the Winter Olympics. The 25-year-old West German finished second in the grand slalom only twelve-hundredths of a second slower than the winner after capturing the downhill race and the slalom. No woman had achieved a sweep of the three events as two men had done. But at Innsbruck not far from her home in Winklmoosalm, Miss Mittermaier did post the best Olympic performance for a woman by winning two gold medals and a silver for second place.

Because of her gregariousness, her infectious smile, and her humility, Miss Mittermaier was affectionately called "Granny" by the others in the World Cup entourage of which she was the eldest. Her victories were rousingly applauded because of a feeling of empathy for Miss Mittermaier who was competing in the Olympics for the third time and had not yet won a medal. When the games began in early February, she was leading World Cup competition in overall points, although she had not won any event. When she finally finished first in the Olympic downhill, the world's best skiers felt it was time for Granny to capture the cup.

Miss Mittermaier attributed her Olympic victories to deeper concentration and to more relaxation because of her experience. She continued to improve her concentration and completed her 10th year in World Cup competition by winning the overall championship. She finished first in the slalom, third in grand slalom, and ninth in downhill. She clinched the cup with victories in the slalom and grand slalom at Copper Mountain in Colorado. During the competition, she so captivated the crowds with her skill and personality that the Colorado resort management renamed the slalom course "Rosi's Run."

Although proud of her Olympic achievements, Miss Mittermaier said that "the World Cup triumph is more important to a ski racer because it requires good performances in all three disciplines throughout the year." In May she retired to do a series of commercial promotions.

Background. Rosi Mittermaier was born in Reit im Winkl, Bavaria, Aug. 5, 1950. Her parents were hotel owners and she was brought up on the ski slopes. She became a member of the West German team at the age of 16 joining her older sister, Heidi, and competed for the World Cup in 1967, the year of its inception. Her early performances were only mediocre, but she is the only woman to score points in all 10 years. She was 6th overall in 1972, 4th in 1973, 7th in 1974, and 3d in 1975. A younger sister, Evi, became her teammate in 1975.

BILL BRADDOCK

MONDALE, Walter Frederick

When Walter Mondale withdrew from the race for the 1976 Democratic presidential nomination in November 1974, the decision pointed up two important aspects of the Minnesota senator's character. One was his natural sense of balance and perspective, which helped him realize he had only a slim chance of gaining the nomination. On the other hand, his withdrawal reinforced the view of some critics that he tends to be overly cautious and to shy away from the rigors of political combat. However, in the judgment of Democratic standard bearer Jimmy Carter, who selected Mondale as his running mate from a long list of leading Democrats, this implied flaw was far offset by strengths. Mondale's background appealed to Carter chiefly because it served to fill gaps in Carter's own political profile. Mondale is a favorite of Democratic liberals, many of whom were unenthusiastic about Carter's candidacy. He had had a long and close relationship with his fellow Minnesotan, Hubert Humphrey, whose strong support would be helpful to the Democratic ticket. And his 12 years in the U. S. Senate had given him the sort of direct experience in the federal government which Carter lacked. But if Mondale's career and philosophy differed from Carter's, the two men had enough in common to make them, as Carter put it, "compatible." And on November 2, the American electorate selected Governor Carter and Senator Mondale for the nation's two highest offices.

Background. Walter Frederick Mondale, or "Fritz," as his friends call him, was born in Ceylon, Minn., on Jan. 5, 1928, and reared in nearby Elmore; both are small towns like Carter's home town of Plains, Ga. Religion has been a strong influence in Mondale's life, as it has been in Carter's. His father was a Methodist minister, and his wife, Joan, whom he married in 1955, is the daughter of a Presbyterian minister. Though he lacks Carter's evangelical bent, much of Mondale's rhetoric has a strong moralistic tone. He is a fervent believer in the family as an institution, and his greatest interest in the Senate has been his work on the Senate Subcommittee on Children and Youth.

Mondale broke into Minnesota politics in 1948, at age 20, when he helped to manage Hubert Humphrey's successful campaign for the U. S. Senate; he has remained a Humphrey protégé since. In 1958, two years after obtaining a degree from the University of Minnesota Law School, Mondale ran Gov. Orville Freeman's reelection campaign. He was duly rewarded in 1960, when Freeman named him to fill a vacancy as state attorney general, a post to which he was elected later in the year and reelected in 1962. In late 1964 another and bigger vacancy opened up when Humphrey resigned from the Senate to become vice president. Mondale was appointed to fill the seat and was returned to it by big majorities in the 1966 and 1972 elections.

In the Senate, Mondale became a leading spokesman for liberal views on a wide range of domestic issues, particularly urban affairs, civil rights, education, and child care. He played a major role in passing the Housing and Urban Development acts of 1968 and co-sponsored the open housing provisions of the 1968 civil rights act.

As chairman of the Senate Select Committtee on Equal Education, Mondale vigorously opposed legislative proposals to restrict court-ordered busing for purposes of desegregation. When challenged on his stand on this controversial issue during the Democratic national convention, he contended that he did not favor busing as such, but added, "I am opposed to repealing the 14th Amendment."

In 1975, at the opening of the 94th Congress, Mondale led a successful fight to ease Senate rules for stopping filibusters, which in the past had been used to kill civil rights legislation. More recently he was a member of the Senate Select Committee to Study Governmental Operations With Respect to Intelligence Activities, probing into allegations of illegal activity by the intelligence agencies.

Partly because of his close association with Humphrey, Mondale did not take a strong stand against the Vietnam War until the late 1960's, a delay which he later acknowledged to be "the biggest mistake I've made since I began my public life."

Mondale still has close ties to his native Minnesota and his favorite relaxation is a fishing or hunting trip in his home state. The Mondales have two sons, Theodore, 19, and William, 14, and a daughter, Eleanor Jane, 16.

ROBERT SHOGAN

DARQUENNES, SYGMA

For Rhodesia's Prime Minister Ian Smith, 1976 was a year of crisis and intense diplomatic activity.

SMITH, Ian Douglas

In 1976, as black nationalist guerrilla activity continued to escalate, Prime Minister Ian Smith of Rhodesia faced his most serious crisis. It was his 12th year as leader of the Rhodesian Front government and the 11th since he and his party, in an effort to ensure continued white rule, unilaterally and illegally declared the colony's independence from Great Britain. Throughout these years, supported by the overwhelming majority of the 278,000 whites, he has searched unsuccessfully for international legitimacy, an end to U. N. sanctions, and—above all—escape from the increasing pressures to accept a definite and short timetable for the transition to black majority rule. The pattern has become familiar: constitutional talks, conflicting if cautious expectations, protracted negotiations, and then breakdown on the issue of black rule. It was repeated in March. After nearly four months the so-called "last ditch" talks between Smith and African National Council leader Joshua Nkomo reached an impasse on the issue of black rule. Earlier that month President Machel of Mozambique closed the frontier with Rhodesia, and guerrilla activity subsequently escalated across the 750-mile (1,200-km) border, as well as the Zambian border in the north. Even the Botswana frontier in the west became vulnerable. Smith responded with the country's largest military mobilization, an extension of the draft, and the introduction of a wartime system of censorship. At the end of April he appointed four chiefs as government ministers and three other blacks as deputy ministers. At the same time he announced that the whites had no intention of surrendering their position.

In September, Prime Minister Smith accepted a British-American plan for majority rule in Rhodesia within two years. The plan was the basis for negotiations between blacks and whites at a conference in Geneva, beginning in late October.

Background. Ian Douglas Smith was born at Selukwe in Southern Rhodesia on April 8, 1919, the son of a Scottish pioneer. He was educated at Selukwe and Chaplin School, Gwelo, and Rhodes University, South Africa. He interrupted his studies to serve as a fighter pilot in the Royal Air Force, seeing combat in North Africa, Italy, and Germany. After the war he followed his father into farming but also entered politics and won election to the Southern Rhodesian Legislative Assembly in 1948. In 1953 he was elected to the Federal (Rhodesia and Nyasaland) Parliament as a member of the United Federal party. He became chief government whip in 1958 but resigned in 1961 after rejecting the 1961 Southern Rhodesian constitution which granted 15 of 65 seats to blacks. A founder member of the new Rhodesian Front, he became deputy prime minister when that party swept the 1962 elections and prime minister of Southern Rhodesia on April 13, 1964. He married Janet Watt in 1948, and they have a daughter and two sons.

RONALD B. BALLINGER

SOARES, Mário

On July 16, 1976, Mário Soares was named prime minister of Portugal by the country's first democratically elected president in 50 years. As leader of the Socialist party which won a plurality in the April 1976 parliamentary contests, Soares assembled a cabinet of socialists, independents, and military officers to confront the massive unemployment, inflation, and labor unrest besetting the Iberian nation of nine million.

Soares is accustomed to adversity. In 1975 he pulled his party out of a coalition government to protest limitations on press freedom and the growing role in the media, government, and economy of Portugal's Communist party, which had aligned itself with radical officers. He subsequently led a series of marches to protest the country's slide toward left-wing totalitarianism, inspiring moderate officers to purge the government of extremists and require free elections for the nation's presidency and parliament.

As presented to the freely-elected Parliament on Aug. 2, 1976, Soares' plan to revive Portugal's economy envisioned "competitive coexistence between capitalism and socialism." It stressed the urgency of responding to the housing, health, and educational needs of Portugal's five million "have-nots." At the same time, it urged credit, tax, and investment incentives to resuscitate the country's ailing private sector.

Background. Mário Alberto Nobre Lopes Soares was born in Lisbon on Dec, 7, 1924, and attended the University of Lisbon before studying law at the Sorbonne. Son of a prominent Catholic educator who held a

The prime objective of Portugal's new Prime Minister Mário Soares was the revival of the economy.

NUNO DE MENDONCA, SYGMA

cabinet post during the short-lived republic (1910–26), he joined his father's struggle against the dictatorship of António Salazar.

Soares helped found the Democratic Youth Movement in 1946 and later defended political prisoners (among whom were Communists, Progressive Roman Catholics, and African Nationalists), while joining various underground opposition movements. He participated briefly in the Communist Youth Organization but left it because of the intolerance and inflexibility of party leader Alvaro Cunhal. Soares ran for deputy in 1965 and 1969, both times unsuccessfully.

For his articulate activism, Soares was jailed 12 times and banished from the country on at least two occasions. One of the first moves of Marcello Caetano, who replaced the stroke-afflicted Salazar in 1968, was to permit Soares to return home. But he failed to still the tongue of the tall, stocky lawyer; within a year, Soares was again forced from the country because of persistent attacks on the dictatorship and support for self-determination in Portugal's African possessions. He spent this exile in France where he taught university courses, and renewed friendships with Europe's Socialist leaders. In 1973 in West Germany, Soares founded Portugal's own Socialist party. He was the first political figure to return to Portugal after the surprise coup by young army officers of the Armed Forces Movement in April 1974 and became foreign minister in the first revolutionary government. As such, he presided over the liquidation of Portugal's colonial empire.

GEORGE W. GRAYSON

SUÁREZ GONZÁLEZ, Adolfo

Anxious to have his own man as head of government, King Juan Carlos I on July 3, 1976, selected his friend Adolfo Suárez González as prime minister of Spain, thereby replacing an appointee of the late Generalissimo Francisco Franco. Although himself a life-long Francoist, Suárez readily acceded to the king's announced intention of converting the nation into a "modern democracy." He played a key role in gaining parliamentary approval for a bill legalizing political parties (except Communists and separatists); he pledged amnesty for political prisoners; he met with opposition political leaders; and he has revised Spain's relations with the Vatican by renouncing the privilege of naming bishops. In addition, the suave, articulate prime minister reaffirmed an inherited commitment to hold general elections in 1977, while seeking to strengthen his country's relations with the European Economic Community and NATO, both of which Spain now hopes to join as part of its reentry into the mainstream of European life after four decades of dictatorship.

Despite Suárez' assurance that "reforms will continue," liberals regard him with suspicion. Five progressive cabinet members immediately informed the king of their refusal to serve under his designee. They apparently felt that Suárez represented Francoism in new clothes and would become an instrument of the conservative, affluent businessmen associated with Opus Dei, the semi-secret Catholic lay organization to which he is known to have close ties. The youngest prime minister in modern Spanish history, Suárez cobbled together an undistinguished cabinet composed mainly of youthful, inexperienced technocrats. The fate of his government depends on its response to the twin challenges of reforming Spain's antiquated political system and improving an economy lashed by inflation and unemployment.

Background. One of five children of a state prosecutor, Adolfo Suárez González was born on Sept. 25, 1932, in the small Castilian town of Cebreros, and studied law at the University of Salamanca. A dutiful, hardworking professional, he was rewarded for his loyalty to the Franco regime with a series of minor administrative posts before being appointed governor of Segovia Province in 1968. The following year he was made head of the state-run television network. In spite

UPI

Prime Minister Adolfo Suárez González, a friend of King Juan Carlos, promised Spain a "modern democracy."

of hopes that there would be more openness in news reporting, the medium then, as now, presented a strictly official point of view.

The young administrator later received a key leadership post in the National Movement, the only legal political party during the dictatorship and the keystone of Spain's corporative state, and developed his links with the politically influential Opus Dei.

Prior to Franco's death in November 1975, Suárez left government service to promote the Union of the Spanish People, a new right-of-center political association committed to pluralism and gradual reform. The philosophy of this organization closely parallels that of the new prime minister, who has stated: "I believe in change without trauma, for change is indispensable. In my opinion, extremes pose the greatest threat, and there is no better remedy against that than thoroughgoing reforms."

GEORGE W. GRAYSON

VIDELA, Jorge Rafael

Lt. Gen. Jorge Rafael Videla became the 38th president of the Argentine Republic following the March 24, 1976, military coup which overthrew the administration of Isabel Martínez de Perón. A career soldier who had been commander-in-chief of the army since the previous August, 51-year-old Videla is Argentina's 15th president of military origin.

The first months of Videla's administration were devoted primarily to battles against leftist guerrilla movements and a seriously deteriorating economy. Significant successes were recorded on both fronts, but terrorism from the left continued to plague the government which also confronted increasing counter terrorism from the right. Despite Videla's reputation as a political moderate and his pledge to oppose all terrorist activity with equal vigor, critics repeatedly accused the government of bearing down harshly on the left while ignoring much of the terrorist activity from the right. Moreover, Videla's government came under increasing attack internationally because of alleged violations of human rights in the campaign against leftist guerrillas and politicians.

Videla is widely regarded as a moralistic and tough-minded, but ideologically moderate, officer who had never sought political power. As recently as December 1975, the army commander had opposed plans by other high-ranking officers for a coup, urging instead that a constitutional solution be sought for the nation's problems. By late March, however, the continued deterioration of the economy and the inability of the government to control guerrilla activity apparently had led to a change of mind.

Background. Son of an army colonel, Videla was born Aug. 2, 1925, in the Buenos Aires provincial city of Mercedes. He graduated from the national military academy, the Colegio Militar, in 1944 and served for the next 25 years in a series of army positions both in Argentina and abroad. Videla taught at the Colegio Militar several times, and following his 1971 promotion to general he was put in charge of the academy. Two of Videla's seven children are cadets at the Colegio Militar.

LEE C. FENNELL

VORSTER, Balthazar Johannes (John)

John Vorster entered on his 10th year as prime minister of South Africa with a status and popularity among the white electorate probably unequalled by any of his six predecessors. In November 1975 a white opinion poll showed that 87% approved of his performance. He has long been noted for his political toughness, his image as a "man of granite," his unswerving dedication to white security and to his predecessor's policies—Dr. Verwoerd's separate development. But it was the promise held out by his détente initiatives and his personal diplomatic successes between mid-1974 and the end of 1975 that fired the imagination and hopes of the electorate. As an international statesman, he seemed to South Africa's whites the embodiment of a new flexibility and pragmatism,

B. J. Vorster entered his 10th year as prime minister of South Africa. For him, it was a tense period.

UPI

fully alive to the grave dangers of the region and equal to them. But aside from his part in the negotiations on Rhodesia, 1976 brought him few successes and the country no relief from tension. In the wake of his Angolan intervention, the resumption of guerrilla activity in Rhodesia, and the slow progress on Namibian (South West African) self-rule, little was left of détente. At home, the Soweto riots and racial unrest underscored his government's failure to implement the antidiscrimination promise and undermined the image of domestic stability so important to his foreign policy. Vorster and his party placed great emphasis on the granting of independence to the Transkei in October, but the pressing internal problems arising from racial discrimination remained; so did inflation and the fallen price of gold.

Background. Balthazar Johannes Vorster was born in Jamestown, Cape Province, on Dec. 13, 1915, the 13th of 14 children of a sheep-farming family. He was educated at Sterkstroom and Stellenbosch University, from which he received a law degree in 1938 and where he was prominent in the Nationalist Youth movement. He practiced law in Port Elizabeth and in 1940 became a leader in the popular, para-military, and increasingly National-Socialist-inclined Afrikaner movement known as the *Ossewabrandwag*. In 1942 he was arrested for antiwar activities and interned until 1944. He then moved to the Transvaal and ran unsuccessfully for Parliament as an Afrikaner party independent in 1948. Subsequently accepted as a National party candidate, he won a seat in 1953 and has represented the same constituency ever since. He was appointed deputy minister of education, arts, and sciences in 1959 and minister of justice in 1961. He became prime minister and leader of the National party in September 1966, following the assassination of Dr. Verwoerd. In 1941 he married Martini Steyn Malan; they have two sons and a daughter.

RONALD B. BALLINGER

WALTERS, Barbara

Television's "most influential woman," Barbara Walters, made media history in April 1976 when she was hired by the ABC network to co-anchor its *Evening News* with veteran newscaster Harry Reasoner. Her salary of $1 million a year for five years makes her the highest-paid journalist in history. She is also the first woman to broadcast evening news regularly over a major network. Her contract also requires her to anchor at least 4 prime-time specials a year and to act as occasional host on ABC's *Issues and Answers* series and other documentary and news programs. Although some broadcasting officials had misgivings about the lucrative contract, noting that it further obscured the tenuous line between journalism and show business, there was general agreement about Walters' capabilities and high standards of professionalism.

During her 13 years on NBC's early morning *Today* show, Walters established her reputation as a skilled interviewer, capable of making her guests feel at ease while eliciting from them answers to questions of interest to audiences. She has also hosted her own syndicated series, *Not for Women Only*, filled in for Johnny Carson on his *Tonight* show, and acted as commentator on NBC radio's *Monitor* program.

Background. Barbara Walters, the daughter of nightclub impresario Lou Walters and his wife, Dena, was born in Boston on Sept. 25, 1931. She attended the Fieldston School and Sarah Lawrence College, where she received a B. A. degree in 1954. Although she originally planned to become a teacher, she drifted into television and public relations work and was employed for several years by NBC and CBS, eventually rising to the rank of producer. In 1961 she was hired by Dave Garroway as a writer for NBC's *Today* show, and within three years she was appearing regularly before the cameras, conducting interviews with such celebrities as Mamie Eisenhower, Truman Capote, Robert Kennedy, Mrs. Martin Luther King, Jr., Golda Meir, Prince Philip,

Barbara Walters, TV's "most influential woman," left NBC's *Today* show after 15 years and joined ABC.

Warren's poetic works include *Thirty-six Poems* (1936), *Brother to Dragons* (1953), *You, Emperors, and Others: Poems, 1957–1960* (1960), *Audubon: A Vision* (1969), and *Selected Poems: New and Old, 1923–1966* (1966), which earned him a Bollingen Prize. Among his works of fiction are *Night Rider* (1939), *At Heaven's Gate* (1943), *The Circus in the Attic and Other Short Stories* (1948), *Bands of Angels* (1955), *The Cave* (1959), and *Meet Me in the Green Glen* (1971). His nonfiction works include *John Brown: The Making of a Martyr* (1929), *Segregation: The Inner Conflict in the South* (1956), *Selected Essays* (1958), *Who Speaks for the Negro?* (1965), and *Democracy and Poetry* (1975). Warren also co-edited with the critic Cleanth Brooks two influential textbooks, *Understanding Poetry* (1938) and *Understanding Fiction* (1943).

Warren has taught at Southwestern College, Vanderbilt University, Louisiana State University, the University of Minnesota, and other institutions. In 1950 he joined the faculty of Yale University where he has been professor emeritus since 1973. A founder of the *Southern Review* and a member of its editorial staff from 1935 to 1942, he has also served as an advisory editor of the *Kenyon Review*. In 1944–45 Warren occupied the chair of poetry at the Library of Congress, and in 1959 he was elected to the American Academy of Arts and Letters. He is married to the writer Eleanor Clark, and has a son and a daughter.

HENRY S. SLOAN

Robert Penn Warren was honored by the Academy of American Poets for *Or Else—Poem/Poems 1968–1974.*

and Henry Kissinger. In 1974 she was named co-host of the *Today* show.

Among the many honors that Barbara Walters has received is a mass media award of the American Jewish Committee and a 1975 Emmy award. Her book *How to Talk With Practically Anybody About Practically Anything* was published in 1970. Divorced from Lee Guber, a theatrical producer, she makes her home in New York City with her 8-year-old adopted daughter, Jacqueline. She is a past honorary chairperson of the National Association for Help to Retarded Children.

HENRY S. SLOAN

WARREN, Robert Penn

Robert Penn Warren, one of the most versatile and productive of American men of letters, was honored on May 10, 1976, with the Copernicus Award presented by the Academy of American Poets. The occasion of the award was Warren's most recent book, *Or Else—Poem/Poems 1968–1974.* While he is known as a major figure in the Southern Literary Renaissance, his provincialism is transcended by his moral concern with mankind. Warren's works include 10 volumes of verse, 9 novels, a play, short stories, critical essays, and sociological studies. The only writer ever to receive the Pulitzer Prize for both fiction and poetry, Warren won the award for *All the King's Men* (1946), a novel inspired by the life of Huey Long, and for the volume *Promises: Poems 1954–1956* (1957).

Background. Robert Penn Warren was born in Guthrie, Ky., on April 24, 1905. He attended Vanderbilt University where he was an editor of *The Fugitive,* and from which he was graduated summa cum laude in 1925. He received his M. A. degree from the University of California in 1927 and then, as a Rhodes Scholar at Oxford, earned a B. Litt. degree in 1930.

BOLIVIA

The year 1976 proved difficult for the Bolivian military government and for President Hugo Banzer Suárez, who in August celebrated five years in power. It was a time of a prolonged political crisis, the repercussions of which were still felt as the year drew to a close.

Economy. While it had been possible in 1975 to hold inflation to 8%, reduced income from exports of oil and tin turned the big trade surplus of 1974 into a balance of payments deficit of $50 million. Net foreign exchange reserves fell to $117 million by the end of 1975, while outstanding foreign debts more than doubled to $1,650 million. However, an ambitious program of public investment produced a 6.8% growth rate in the gross domestic product, and the steady inflow of foreign loans reflected the excellent credit standing of the government. Nevertheless, the 1975 deficit and forecasts of a similar one in 1976 led to stringent measures, including import deposits and controls, higher tariffs, and a ban on the importing of passenger cars.

Political Crisis. The difficult economic situation contributed to a political crisis. A strike of factory workers in Cochabamba in January over threatened reductions in the work force won backing from miners and students, and dismissal notices were withdrawn. Demands in February from students in La Paz for a dialogue with the authorities, and later for an amnesty for political prisoners and exiles, led to the closing of the universities, the arrest of more than 250 students, and a sympathy strike by the Miners' Federation. At the same time, nine "conspirators" were sent into exile, including Col. José Patino Ayoroa, a member of the dissident Ayoroa clan which had helped Banzer to power. Against a somber background marked by the assassinations of Gen. Joaquín Zenteno Anaya (military commander of the Santa Cruz zone when Che Guevara was killed there) by leftwing extremists in Paris, and of former President Torres, ousted by Banzer in 1971, by right-wing terrorists in Argentina, the

UPI

La Paz, Bolivia's largest city, experiences urban expansion—heavy traffic, tightly grouped buildings.

Miners' Federation challenged the government directly. It summoned a congress in defiance of a ban on trade union activity, called for the tripling of wages and for political amnesty, and reelected its exiled leader Juan Lechín Oquendo as general secretary. The news of Torres' death was followed by a declaration of periods of mourning by miners and students and strikes in all the major mines to back up the wage demand. The government responded by declaring a state of siege. On June 8, 24 miners' leaders were arrested and, with the collaboration of the Chilean junta, deported to confinement in southern Chile. Food supplies to the mining areas were cut off, and in July the miners accepted the original government offer of a 30% pay raise. The Miners' Federation was subsequently proscribed and replaced by a government-backed federation: although sporadic protests continued through August and September, Banzer had emerged with his authority confirmed. He had won agreement from the military in March that he should continue in office until 1980, and in June civilian Finance Minister Carlos Calvo Galindo announced a five-year plan aiming at an annual growth rate of 8%, investments totalling $3,500 million, a fivefold increase in oil production, and higher yield from the declining tin mines. The ambitious, improbable targets reflect Bolivia's confidence and relative prosperity and the country's appeal to foreign investors.

PAUL CAMMACK
St. Antony's College, Oxford

--------- **BOLIVIA • Information Highlights** ---------

Official Name: Republic of Bolivia.
Location: West-central South America.
Area: 424,163 square miles (1,098,581 km²).
Population (1976 est.): 5,800,000.
Chief Cities (1974 est.): Sucre, the legal capital, 90,000; La Paz, the actual capital, 700,000; Cochabamba, 245,000.
Government: *Head of state and government,* Hugo Banzer Suárez, president (took office Aug. 1971). *Legislature*—Congress (suspended Sept. 1969): Senate and Chamber of Deputies.
Monetary Unit: Peso (20 pesos equal U.S.$1, Oct. 1976).
Gross National Product (1975 est.): $2,155,000,000.
Manufacturing (major products): Processed foods, textiles, leather goods, cement.
Major Agricultural Products: Sugar, cotton, corn, potatoes, wheat, rice, coffee, bananas.
Foreign Trade (1975): *Exports,* $518,000,000; *imports,* $558,000,000.

In Boston, court-ordered school desegregation entered its third year; clashes between students and police were common.

BOSTON

Continuing problems with school integration, bicentennial festivities, and municipal fiscal issues were major events in Boston during 1976.

School Desegregation. The city school system began its third year of court-ordered desegregation in an atmosphere of increasing calm, although acts of violence—racially motivated and otherwise—kept political officials and law enforcement authorities on edge. September saw the start of "Phase II-B" of city-wide busing to secure racial balance in the public schools. Under Judge W. Arthur Garrity's third-year plan the numbers of students transported and the areas of the city affected were held roughly constant from last year. Overall school attendance was up from the previous year.

Peace March Follows Violence. In April a number of violent incidents occurred in which groups of white and black youths fought, stoned cars, and attacked people. Several of those attacked were seriously injured. These episodes were followed by a large bomb blast at the downtown Suffolk County Court House on the morning of April 22. Eighteen persons were injured. The bombing was apparently unrelated to the city's racial problems, but Mayor Kevin H. White, in an effort to stem the violence, called for a peace march the next day. Led by city and state officials, thousands of people marched through the streets to City Hall where a prayer vigil was held. Racial violence quickly subsided. On July 2, however, an Eastern Airlines plane was destroyed by a bomb at Logan Airport, and another bomb damaged a National Guard armory in the Dorchester section. Several persons were arrested for the two attacks.

Bicentennial Events. In sharp contrast to the violent incidents, Boston's bicentennial celebrations greatly pleased the hundreds of thousands who attended the many events during the week of July 4–11. Highlighting the festivities were the arrival of the "Tall Ships" regatta in Boston Harbor on July 10 and a visit by Queen Elizabeth II on July 11. On the 4th of July itself a crowd estimated at 400,000—the largest in the city's history—gathered on the Esplanade by the Charles River to listen and watch as 82-year-old Arthur Fiedler conducted Boston musicians in a gala concert. For Fiedler it was the 47th anniversary of his first Esplanade concert.

City Property Taxes Increase. In September Mayor White announced a 28.5% rise in the property tax, the first such increase in four years. Growing school costs associated with desegregation were a major cause. The City Council, trying to improve the fiscal situation, passed an ordinance requiring city employees to live in Boston; it was immediately contested by city employee unions.

HARVEY BOULAY, *Boston University*

BOTANY

According to the Smithsonian Institution there are 100 plants of the continental United States, including Alaska, that are "probably or possibly extinct" or "extinct in the wild but cultivated." Another 1,999 plants are endangered, or likely to become so shortly.

Endangered Species Act. Concern for endangered wildlife in the United States has been widely publicized. Until recently, however, little concern has been manifest about endangered or threatened native flora. In fact, the National Environment Policy Act of 1969 completely excluded plants from protection. Congress did pass the Endangered Species Act in 1973, giving the Smithsonian authority to compile a list of endangered, threatened, and recently extinct plants and to issue recommendations for conserving these species. If the institution's listing is approved by the Department of the Interior and ratified by Congress, plants included will be protected by the Endangered Species Act.

Botanists and other scientists are currently trying to determine whether endangered or threatened species can be successfully cultivated and subsequently reintroduced into the wild. Unless they develop techniques that are effective in saving these species and unless the federal government protects the habitats of endangered or threatened species that grow on federally owned land (60–70% of all such flora), many of these species will become extinct in the foreseeable future.

"Vinegar" Rain. Botanists have also become concerned that acid rain is causing ecological damage by killing plant tissues, altering their growth, and making nutrients unavailable. Dr. Gene Likens, Professor of Ecology at Cornell University, was among the first to study this problem. He has reported that automobile and industrial pollutants are responsible for acid rain. These pollutants, according to Likens, may be carried great distances in the atmosphere before getting entrapped in raindrops and returning to the earth. Rainfall data from New York City, collected in the 1920's, shows that rainwater then was only slightly acid, whereas today its acidity may be as high as that of household vinegar.

In addition to the immediate direct effects of acid rain on plant growth, there may be other indirect effects. Plants require large quantities of nitrogen but can neither synthesize it nor extract it from the atmosphere. Bacteria in the soil and on the roots of some plants convert atmospheric nitrogen into a form agreeable to plants. Increased soil acidity resulting from acid rain apparently reduces the efficiency of nitrogen-fixing bacteria, thereby diminishing the available nitrogen.

DONALD W. NEWSOM
Louisiana State University

BRAZIL

Brazil had its worst year economically in nearly a decade as the growth rate of its gross national product fell from 4% in 1975 to around zero in 1976. By the end of the year, however, recovery appeared to be under way. The government of President Ernesto Geisel survived the economic troubles, as well as political challenges from left and right, and came through the year stronger than ever. Overruling adamant opposition from within the military establishment, Geisel permitted municipal elections throughout Brazil in November.

Economic and Social Conditions. While the rate of economic growth fell, the rate of inflation rose, from 38% in 1975 to around 45% in 1976. In May 1976 the government decreed a 44% increase in the minimum wage, the second year in a row that such an increase has exceeded that of the cost of living in the preceding 12 months. But the gains wage-earners received from this measure were, by the year's end, practically wiped out by accelerating inflation. Nevertheless, President Geisel's efforts to raise the purchasing power of the masses and his attempts to identify himself with the populism of the late President Getúlio Vargas, distinguish him from the other generals who have ruled Brazil since 1964.

Despite the president's efforts, social conditions deteriorated due to the economic slump and a drought in the northeast. Migrants from the drought-stricken countryside flocked to the cities, where they put severe pressure on urban social services. It was estimated that there were 3.5 million abandoned children in the nation, including one million in the city of Rio de Janeiro. A moderate decline in the national birth rate, from 3.1% in 1961 to 2.6% in 1976, was offset in urban areas by the arrival of increasing numbers of impoverished country people. The government of the industrial state of São Paulo, which has experienced phenomenal population growth in recent years, in 1976 launched a birth-control program which was seen as a pilot plan for the nation. After years of insisting that Brazil needed more, not fewer, people, the country's military regime seemed to be preparing to order an about-face.

Politics. In January President Geisel acted with astonishing speed and firmness in removing General Ednardo D'Avila Melo from command of the powerful Second Army in São Paulo. D'Avila Melo was fired only hours after the president learned of the death of a political prisoner, Manuel Fiel Filho, a metalworker, at a Second Army interrogation center. The death, termed "suicide" by the investigators, recalled that of the noted journalist Vladimir Herzog, in October 1975, under similar circumstances. Like Fiel Filho, Herzog had been in the custody of the Second Army for alleged Communist activi-

——— **BRAZIL · Information Highlights** ———

Official Name: Federative Republic of Brazil.
Location: Eastern South America.
Area: 3,286,478 square miles (8,511,965 km²).
Population (1976 est.): 110,200,000.
Chief Cities (1975 est.): Brasília, the capital (1974), 545,000; São Paulo, 7,200,000; Rio de Janeiro, 4,860,000; Belo Horizonte, 1,560,000.
Government: *Head of state and government,* Ernesto Geisel, president (took office March 1974). *Legislature*—National Congress: Federal Senate and Chamber of Deputies.
Monetary Unit: Cruzeiro (11.43 cruzeiros equal U. S.$1, Oct. 1976).
Gross National Product (1975 est.): $72,800,000,000.
Manufacturing (major products): Processed foods, chemicals, textiles, automobiles, metals, petroleum products, paper, fertilizers.
Major Agricultural Products: Coffee, soybeans, rice, corn, sugarcane, wheat, oranges, cacao.
Foreign Trade (1975): *Exports,* $8,656,000,000; *imports,* $13,558,000,000.

UPI

Brazilian officials, led by President Geisel (*right*), and U. S. Secretary of State Kissinger enjoy a soccer game.

ties, but the charges were disbelieved by civic and religious leaders, who accused the regime of torturing and murdering him because of his denunciations of government violations of human rights.

Anticipating a similar outcry over the Fiel Filho affair, Geisel lost no time in removing the Second Army commander. The president's swiftness stunned other hard-line anticommunists in the military and left Geisel more firmly in control of the government than at any time since taking office two years before. In the months that followed, Geisel consolidated his position by retiring or otherwise undermining the power of potentially dangerous generals. At the same time, the president demonstrated his intention to maintain political repression by suspending the political rights of several outspoken Congress members of the opposition party, the Brazilian Democratic Movement (MDB). Opposition newspapers continued to be censored, and a law was enacted prohibiting radio or television broadcasting of electoral propaganda.

In August President Geisel permitted what turned out to be the first mass demonstration against the government since 1964. The occasion was the funeral in Brasília of former President Juscelino Kubitschek (see OBITUARIES). Over the objections of military hard-liners, who considered Kubitschek a subversive, Geisel decreed three days of official mourning for him. In the funeral procession some 60,000 Brazilians marched through the streets of the capital chanting antigovernment slogans.

The daily *Estado de São Paulo,* which speaks for powerful banking and industrial interests, usually supports Geisel, and is one of the few newspapers in the country not subjected to censorship, embarrassed the government with revelations of corruption and personal extravagance at public expense among high-ranking officials.

This was part of its campaign in favor of private enterprise and against statism. Energy Minister Shigeaki Ueki, a civilian, seemed to share the *Estado's* viewpoint and suggested selling part of the government's oil monopoly, Petrobrás, to private investors. The Minister of Industry, Gen. Severo Gomes, was strongly opposed, and his position, that of the military nationalists, prevailed. President Geisel, however, did take action against high-living officials and grafters, to the point of suspending the political rights of five members of the government party, the National Renovation Alliance (ARENA); previously, this punishment had been reserved for opposition politicians.

As the date for the November municipal balloting approached, extreme right-wing elements mounted a terrorist campaign, apparently aimed at forcing the cancellation of the elections. Members of the clandestine Brazilian Anti-Communist Alliance assaulted the liberal Catholic bishop of Nova Iguaçú, planted bombs in Rio and São Paulo, and distributed leaflets denouncing Geisel as "The Red President."

The MDB conducted a deliberately low-key campaign, emphasizing the steep inflation rate and other economic issues. It fielded candidates in little more than half the total number of municipalities, thus assuring victory for the government's ARENA even before the voting started.

Foreign Relations. During the year President Geisel made official visits to France, Britain, and Japan, seeking to assure governments and businessmen that Brazil still offered opportunities for profitable investment. U. S. Secretary of State Henry Kissinger journeyed to Brazil in February and pleased the government by signing an agreement providing for consultation between the United States and Brazil on the foreign-minister level at least twice a year.

NEILL MACAULAY, *University of Florida*

BRITISH COLUMBIA

Government and Politics. Governmental changes during 1976 included the introduction of the office of auditor general, preliminary consideration of the post of ombudsman, a new provincial Buildings Corporation, a provincial Ferry Corporation, and a Government Employees Relations Bureau. The creation of a Department of the Environment was followed in October by a reorganization of cabinet portfolios.

The province also entered into an agreement to participate in the federal program to fight inflation.

A June 3 by-election in Vancouver East resulted in the reentry of former New Democratic party Premier David Barrett into the legislature. Party standings are now 35 Social Credit, 18 New Democratic, 1 Liberal, and 1 Progressive Conservative.

Finances. Provincial revenues for the fiscal year 1975–76 amounted to $2,973 million and total expenditures were reported at $3,378 million. Revenue from lands and forests continued to decline and a budgetary cash deficit of $261 million was shown. The new provincial government emphasized its policy of restraint in the budget for 1976–77. Revenues were estimated at $3,587 million and expenditures at $3,615 million. The shortfall is to be met from six special purpose funds. The budget featured increases in sales, corporation, personal income, cigarette, and tobacco taxes and in liquor license fees. Provincial hospital insurance charges were also increased. Royalties on mineral production were replaced by a profits tax. In addition, considerable increases were made during 1976 both in automobile insurance rates under the Insurance Corporation of British Columbia Autoplan, and in the fares for the British Columbia ferry system.

Economy. Adverse economic conditions, particularly in British Columbia's export markets, have slowed the economic growth of the province. The labor force grew at a rate of 4.8% and exceeded the average 1975 level of employment of 1,009,000 by 94,000.

NORMAN J. RUFF
University of Victoria

BULGARIA

As in previous years, life in Bulgaria was marked by rigid controls and planning, efforts to increase the nation's productivity, and aloofness from western influences. Any criticism of either the Communist party or the state—both headed by 64-year-old Todor Zhivkov—continued to be forbidden.

Domestic Affairs. On May 30, the 7th National Assembly was convened, and it unanimously reelected Zhivkov chairman of the State Council. Stanko Todorov was reelected chairman of the Council of Minister.

According to the Central Committee of Bulgaria's Communist party, there were 788,200 party members in 28,850 party organizations by the end of 1975. This means that one out of every eight Bulgarians over 18 is a party member. The Central Committee criticized party cadres for sluggishness, lack of realism in their projects, and frequent primitivism. It called for a higher standard of living, better housing, industrialization, and more ideologically oriented education and culture. Ludmila Zhivkova, minister of culture and Zhivkov's daughter, called for "formation of moral and esthetic features of a Communist personality."

With substantial Soviet assistance, the country continued to develop its economic base, bringing up its annual production very considerably.

Some 60% of capital investments during the current 1976–1980 plan, had been earmarked for the existing industries and general modernization. In 1976, Bulgaria had already developed strong shipbuilding and electronic industries and modern factories producing a variety of textiles, furniture, canned goods, and industrial vehicles.

Foreign Affairs. The leading slogan in foreign policy in 1976 was "eternal friendship with the Soviet Union." Bulgarian politics and economics thus continued to be most closely linked to the Soviet Union. Almost 80% of Bulgaria's foreign trade was conducted with the Soviet-bloc countries and 60% with the Soviet Union itself.

JAN KARSKI
Georgetown University

— BRITISH COLUMBIA · Information Highlights —

Area: 366,255 square miles (948,597 km²).
Population (April 1976 est.): 2,486,000.
Chief Cities (1971 census): Victoria, the capital, 61,761; Vancouver, 426,256.
Government (1976): *Chief Officers*—lt. gov., Walter S. Owen; premier, William R. Bennett (Social Credit party); chief justice, John L. Farris. *Legislature*—Legislative Assembly, 55 members.
Education (1976–77): *Enrollment*—public elementary and secondary schools, 540,790 pupils; private schools, 20,450; Indian (federal) schools, 2,790; post-secondary, 50,620 students.
Public Finance (1975–76 est.): *Revenues,* $2,973,000,-000; *expenditures,* $3,378,000,000.
Personal Income (1974 est.): $12,870,000,000; average annual income per person, $5,374.
(All monetary figures are in Canadian dollars.)

——— BULGARIA · Information Highlights ———

Official Name: People's Republic of Bulgaria.
Location: Southeastern Europe.
Area: 42,823 square miles (110,912 km²).
Population (1976 est.): 8,800,000.
Chief City (1973 est.): Sofia, the capital, 870,000.
Government: *Head of State,* Todor Zhivkov, chairman of the State Council and first secretary of the Communist party (took office July 1971). *Head of government,* Stanko Todorov, chairman of the Council of Ministers (took office July 1971).
Monetary Unit: Lev (0.87 lev equals U. S.$1, Oct. 1976).
Gross National Product (1975 est.): $20,600,000,000.
Manufacturing (major products): Processed foods, machinery, chemicals, steel, tobacco products.
Major Agricultural Products: Corn, wheat, barley, fruits.
Foreign Trade (1975): *Exports,* $4,614,000,000; *imports,* $5,324,000,000.

BURMA

President Ne Win's regime was threatened by internal and external enemies in 1976. An attempted coup by junior army officers—the first such action in 14 years of military rule—was thwarted. But Chinese-supported Communists and a variety of ethnic rebels expanded their revolts against the Rangoon government.

Politics. The conspiracy to unseat President Ne Win and his chief lieutenants, heir apparent Gen. San Yu and intelligence chief Col. Tin Oo, was led by Capt. Ohn Kyaw Myint. Announcing discovery of the plot, the president blamed a "worship of personality" cult, a reference to another Tin Oo, a popular general who was removed as defense minister earlier in the year. But there was no evidence of Gen. Tin Oo's involvement in the coup attempt, and he was not arrested.

Discontent with the regime also was reflected in March student demonstrations, which caused the government to close the country's universities for the fourth time in two years. Three grenade-throwing incidents in Rangoon, the capital, in August were blamed on right-wing opposition elements.

Economy. Economic conditions continued to worsen. June monsoon flooding destroyed large amounts of crops and cattle and made more than 200,000 persons homeless. Inflation was estimated at an annual rate of over 40%. A highly successful black market accounted for 90% of domestic commerce.

Insurgencies. The Ne Win regime believed its Communist rebels were being supplied with surplus U. S. arms left behind in Vietnam. Nine non-Communist ethnic minorities, long in revolt, in July formed a "National Democratic Front" against the government.

Foreign Relations. The major foreign policy development was the government's willingness to give a sympathetic hearing to World Bank proposals for aid and advice. Previously, Burma had limited such cooperation with the West.

RICHARD BUTWELL
State University of New York College at Fredonia

BURMA • Information Highlights ———

Official Name: Socialist Republic of the Union of Burma.
Location: Southeast Asia.
Area: 261,789 square miles (678,033 km²).
Population (1976 est.): 31,200,000.
Chief Cities (1975 est.): Rangoon, the capital, 2,100,-000; Mandalay, 417,000; Moulmein, 202,000.
Government: *Head of state,* U Ne Win, president (took office March, 1974). *Head of government,* U Sein Win, prime minister (took office March 1974). *Legislature* (unicameral)—People's Assembly.
Monetary Unit: Kyat (6.83 kyats equal U. S.$1, June 1976).
Gross National Product (1975 est.): $2,700,000,000.
Per Capita Gross National Product (1974 est.): $90.
Manufacturing (major products): Processed foods, textiles, tobacco products, wood products.
Major Agricultural Products: Rice, groundnuts, sesame, tobacco, sugarcane, millet, cotton, forest products.
Foreign Trade (1975): *Exports,* $158,000,000; *imports,* (1974), $128,000,000.

CALIFORNIA

The 1976 election produced a major upset when first-term U. S. Sen. John V. Tunney was defeated by S. I. Hayakawa, 70-year-old retired president of San Francisco State University. In the June primary, Tunney had had a difficult time defeating Tom Hayden, former anti-Vietnam War "activist." Hayakawa won the Republican nomination with only 38% of the primary vote in a desultory three-man contest.

Elections and Issues. Gerald R. Ford carried California in his losing try for the presidency, with 49.7% of the vote to 48.0% for Jimmy Carter. Five other candidates received scattered votes. In California's 43-member congressional delegation, the Republicans lost one seat. Voters were called upon to make choices in 15 referendum issues in the primary and a like number in the general election. Politically, the most important was one which would have adopted policies regarding management-labor relations in agriculture and placed these beyond the ability of the legislature to amend. Gov. Edmund G. Brown, Jr., gave strong support to the proposal, but it received only 37.8% of the vote. Another proposal, to allow pari-mutuel betting on dog racing, lost 3 to 1. Bingo was legalized under certain conditions. A proposal to restrict the construction of nuclear-energy plants was defeated 2 to 1. Seven propositions providing for bonding or state-loan programs were defeated.

Legislation. A major action of the legislature was the enactment of a law to control urbanization and land-use along the state's 1,070-mile (1,725-km) coastline. However, no permanent action was taken on malpractice insurance reform. Nor was any land-use plan adopted to preserve prime agricultural land.

The state's 59-year old indeterminate-sentence law, originally adopted as a progressive reform, was repealed in favor of definite terms, now advocated by reformers. Several laws providing for safety in nuclear-energy production were adopted. Many health measures were enacted, including one designed to discourage inefficient or wasteful construction of hospital fa-

---

CALIFORNIA • Information Highlights ———

Area: 158,693 square miles (411,015 km²).
Population (1975 est.): 21,185,000.
Chief Cities (1970 census): Sacramento, the capital, 257,105; Los Angeles, 2,809,596; San Francisco, 715,674.
Government (1976): *Chief Officer*—governor, Edmund G. Brown, Jr. (D); lt. gov., Mervyn M. Dymally (D). *Legislature*—Senate, 40 members; Assembly, 80 members.
Education (1975–76): *Enrollment*—public elementary schools, 2,653,818 pupils; public secondary, 1,765,-753; nonpublic (1976–77), 437,800; colleges and universities, 1,404,866 students. *Public school expenditures,* $5,660,100,000 ($1,301 per pupil).
State Finances (fiscal year 1975): *Revenues,* $18,801,-572,000; *expenditures,* $17,712,038,000.
Personal Income (1975): $139,337,000,000 per capita, $6,593.
Labor Force (July 1976): *Nonagricultural wage and salary earners,* 7,967,800; *insured unemployed,* 342,100.

In California, S. I. Hayakawa (*right*) defeated incumbent Sen. John Tunney.

cilities. Other laws passed provide for equal pay for equal work for men and women and eliminate provisions of existing laws said to discriminate against women.

Crime. On July 12, seven persons were shot to death in the library of California State University, Fullerton. A custodian was seized and charged with the crime. Four days later, 26 schoolchildren and a bus driver were kidnapped from their school bus in the San Joaquin Valley. They were held in a buried moving van, but all escaped unharmed. Three sons of well-to-do families in suburban San Francisco were arrested and charged with the abduction.

William and Emily Harris of the "Symbionese Liberation Army" were convicted in Los Angeles on charges of kidnapping, robbery, and car theft. Later, the two went on trial in Berkeley on charges of aiding in the kidnapping of Patricia Hearst in 1974. In a separate trial, Hearst was sentenced to prison for her part in a San Francisco bank hold-up and still awaited trial in Los Angeles on the same charges of which the Harrises were convicted in that city. In November, however, she was released in her parents' custody on $1.5 million bail.

CHARLES R. ADRIAN
University of California, Riverside

CAMBODIA

Cambodia's Communist rulers established new instruments of government and generally consolidated their political control over the country in 1976, their first year in power. Economically, however, they continued to have serious problems. A persisting food shortage resulted in widespread chronic malnutrition and starvation, and tens of thousands of Cambodians died.

Total Mobilization. Cambodia was said to be in a state of total mobilization by the few foreigners allowed to visit the country. Refugees

who crossed over into Thailand confirmed this description. A large-scale movement of population was reported in the early months of 1976 as it had been in the wake of the Communists' April 1975 take-over. The capital city of Phnom Penh, which formerly had 2½ million inhabitants, reportedly had dropped to 100,000 residents by the end of 1976.

Refugees charged that 500,000 to 1,000,000 persons have lost their lives since April 1975. This was said to be the result of starvation; forced labor; reprisal executions of middle class and other sympathizers of the previous Lon Nol administration; and the outright abandonment of many old, ill, and crippled persons.

The government announced a lifting of the ban on marriages it had instituted in 1975 to control population growth and, reportedly, to conserve energy for farm work.

Politics. The Communist leadership kept tight military control over the country. But significant progress apparently was registered in the establishment of new governing institutions and in the distribution of power among the chief ruling figures. A new constitution, approved by a 1,000-member national congress in December 1975, went in effect on January 5. The country was renamed "Democratic Cambodia," and a new national anthem and flag were adopted.

Elections were held on March 20—the first in any of the three Indochinese Communist countries since the take-overs in 1975—for a 250-delegate People's Representative Assembly. There were 515 candidates for the 150 seats for farmers, 50 for soldiers, and 50 for "workers." A reported 98% of the 3.6 million eligible voters participated. Among those gaining seats were Chief of State Prince Norodom Sihanouk and his chief lieutenant, Premier Penn Nouth.

Sihanouk and Nouth resigned their government positions in April, when the People's Representative Assembly, which will meet only once a year, held its first session. Khieu Samphan, believed by many to be Cambodia's top Communist, became the country's new chief of state as its first president. Tol Saut, a previously obscure leader of rubber plantation workers, succeeded Nouth as premier.

However, who really ruled Cambodia was still not clear. Saut was subsequently replaced as premier, for reasons of health, by Muon Chea, chairman of the standing committee of the People's Representative Assembly (which acts on behalf of the assembly between its annual sessions). Refugee reports, meanwhile, indicated that Saloth Sar, secretary general of the Cambodian Communist Party, might be the country's real leader, ruling through an unpublicized five-man committee.

Economy. Reports respecting economic developments under Cambodia's new Communist rulers were contradictory. President Samphan declared in April that a record rice crop had been harvested in the just-ended dry season, and the rice ration was increased in March to 500 grams (little more than a pound) a day. As for meat, it was reported that a pig was allotted for each 10 people every 10 days. But Premier Tol Saut said in July that the country had barely enough food. Refugees told of widespread starvation and resulting deaths by the thousands. Planes from China were known to have flown in large quantities of rice.

There was no doubt as to the government's goals, however. Construction gangs worked to build dams and irrigation canals to restore Cambodia's once substantial rice surplus with which to earn foreign currency to buy and build factories. Reestablishment of the country's formerly prosperous rubber plantations also was begun.

Private ownership was totally abandoned. There were no shops at all and no private plots for peasants to cultivate—not even money or wages. Rations were the sole means by which the population got its food.

Foreign Relations. Only a few diplomats from some of the other Communist countries were resident in Phnom Penh. The Chinese were Cambodia's almost exclusive source of foreign assistance, and replaced the Vietnamese as advisers to the country's military forces. Foreign Minister Ieng Sary visited Peking in August, while relations with Hanoi remained strained.

RICHARD BUTWELL
State University of New York College at Fredonia

CAMBODIA · Information Highlights

Official Name: Democratic Cambodia.
Location: Southeast Asia.
Area: 69,898 square miles (181,035 km²).
Population (1976 est.): 8,300,000.
Chief Cities (1976 est.): Phnom Penh, the capital, 100,000.
Government: *Head of State,* Khieu Samphan, president (took office April 1976). *Head of government,* Muon Chea, acting prime minister (took office Sept. 1976). *Legislature* (unicameral)—People's Representative Assembly.
Monetary Unit: Riel (1,111.11 riels equal U.S.$1, Dec. 1976).
Gross National Product (1972 est.): $680,000,000.
Manufacturing (major products): Paper, textiles, tobacco products, sawnwood.
Major Agricultural Products: Rice, corn, rubber, beans, sweet potatoes and yams.
Foreign Trade (1973): *Exports,* $10,000,000; *imports,* $51,000,000.

Anti-Khmer Rouge guerrillas attend a training meeting in a jungle clearing, about 25 miles (40 km) inside the territory of western Cambodia.

J. F. CHAUVEL, SYGMA

UPI

Prime Minister Trudeau and Governor General Léger introduce new Canadian cabinet. Included are (l-r): Iona Campagnola, Francis Fox, Monique Begin, John Roberts, Anthony Abbott, Léger, Trudeau, L. Marchand, and J.-J. Blais.

CANADA

In 1976 the federal government's guidelines on prices and wages as regulated by the Anti Inflation Board (AIB) continued to be the focus of national politics. The Liberal government, led by Pierre Elliott Trudeau, prime minister since 1968, continued to come under attack and was hurt by allegations and scandals involving members of the government. A major election in Quebec, labor unrest, and controversial legislation on language rights in Quebec and in the civil service provided significant, divisive issues of a national and provincial nature.

Amid the gloom of high unemployment and lower productivity, Canada hosted the 1976 Summer Olympics, a successful event not marred by violence as the 1972 games in Munich were, but were stressed at the outset by the attention focused on the matter of Taiwan's admissibility under the flag of the Republic of China and a boycott by most African states on the issue of race relations. Canada undertook a number of initiatives to make itself less dependent on the United States as a trading partner.

DOMESTIC AFFAIRS

The new year opened with Trudeau's announcements that government would intervene further in the economy. This drew heated criticism from members of his Liberal party, and sparked debate among members of the business community and especially labor. Trudeau's policies were defended by his cabinet colleagues on grounds that such measures were needed to control inflation and buttress the AIB guidelines

introduced in the fall of 1975. Trudeau's remarks prompted a political shift toward free enterprise, and by the fall parliamentary session Trudeau announced that government intervention would be kept to a minimum. This reflected his response to a growing concern in Canada about the overabundance of government, the rise in levels of taxation, and the mounting unpopularity of the Liberals and corresponding rise in popularity of the Progressive Conservative Party whose new leader, Joe Clark (see Biography), announced that if he should become prime minister he would streamline federal welfare and spending programs and reduce the government's heavy emphasis on bilingual programs.

The Supreme Court of Canada approved the AIB guidelines on July 12 on the grounds that they were necessary to meet the nation's economic crisis. In March the guidelines were extended to construction, trucking, grain handling, longshoring, and shipping.

Labor Unrest. Meanwhile, labor unrest continued. In March the Canadian Labour Congress (CLC), the leading union organization, representing 2.3 million rank-and-file workers, rejected the AIB controls at its annual meeting. The CLC withdrew from the Canadian Labour Relations Council and the Economic Council of Canada. CLC demonstrations were held outside Parliament. Joseph Morris, CLC president, denounced government policy as "callous and brutal treatment for all who toil for a living." The CLC's national "day of protest" on October 13 was a mixed success because the Public Service Alliance representing 177,000 employees refused to join the walkout and other union organizations would not be bound by the CLC. The day

UPI

Under its new leader Joe Clark, the Progressive Conservative Party enjoyed renewed popularity.

of protest divided the union cause in Canada and tended to undermine the CLC's role as union spokesman. The strike brought major public protest, especially from interest groups such as the Canadian Manufacturers' Association. The Supreme Court of Ontario ruled the strike illegal; the British Columbia Supreme Court ruled it legal. Above all the day of protest increased the Canadian public's suspicions about the role of unions at a time of economic uncertainty.

Responses to Canadian government economic policies came in other ways. On June 3, 5,000 Quebec dairy farmers rioted on the steps of Parliament, pelting Agricultural Minister Eugene Whelan with eggs, butter, and milk in protest against reduced federal subsidies on milk production. The Royal Canadian Mounted Police suppressed the disturbance. Teachers' strikes in Toronto and Montreal were long-standing. Disruptions in the postal service continued.

─────── CANADA · Information Highlights ───────

Official Name: Canada.
Location: Northern North America.
Area: 3,851,809 square miles (9,976,185 km²).
Population (1976 est.): 23,100,000.
Chief Cities (1974 met. est.): Ottawa, the capital, 626,-000; Montreal, 2,798,000; Toronto, 2,741,000.
Government: *Head of state,* Elizabeth II, queen; represented by Jules Léger, governor general (took office Jan. 1974). *Head of government,* Pierre Elliott Trudeau, prime minister (took office April 1968). *Legislature*—Parliament: Senate and House of Commons.
Monetary Unit: Canadian dollar (1.02 C. dollars equal U. S.$1, Nov. 1976).
Gross National Product (2d quarter 1976 est.): $182,-860,000,000.
Manufacturing (major products): Pulp and paper, petroleum products, iron and steel, motor vehicles.
Major Agricultural Products: Wheat, barley, oats, rye, potatoes, forest products, livestock, furs.
Foreign Trade (1975): *Exports,* $31,881,000,000; *imports,* $34,306,000,000.

Another strike, that of the Air Traffic Controllers Association of Canada, went to the root of the sensitive question of language rights. Trudeau said it formed the most critical political issue between the founding races since the conscription crisis of 1944. The Quebec wing of the Air Traffic Controllers sought an extension of the use of French to all airplanes flying in Quebec air space. The English-speaking and national wings of the same organization argued that such a regulation would make flying unsafe since English was the customary language on domestic and international flights. The federal Ministry of Transport first backed the French position but when the Air Traffic Controllers went on strike in late June in defense of its position, the government backed down and appointed a judicial committee to report on the use of French in the air and its implications for safety. The nine-day strike came to an end with Ottawa's promise that English would be the language used on all national and international flights. French was allowed in only six small Quebec airports. Jean Marchand, Trudeau's longtime associate, resigned as minister of the environment, saying he could not defend the government's position in his home province. Later he resigned as a member of parliament and ran as a Liberal in the Quebec provincial election.

Bilingualism. Ottawa's bilingualism policy served to further alienate Western Canada and the provinces of Atlantic Canada where deep-seated suspicion of Trudeau's policies already existed. These attitudes were further prompted by reports from the Commissioner of Official Languages, Keith Spicer, that the government's program for making the civil service bilingual was unsuccessful and costly, that bilingual civil servants were to be paid higher salaries than their unilingual counterparts, and that science work was being slowed by bilingualism.

In March Trudeau announced intentions of bringing the British North America Act, Canada's constitution, home from Westminster. This would effectively introduce a new constitution in which English and French language rights would have to be explicitly defined. Trudeau remained committed to enshrining French language rights in the new constitution, with Quebec having veto powers over any future legislative changes involving languages. Trudeau and the provincial premiers held meetings on the subject throughout the year. A formula whereby the constitution could be repatriated was sought at such meetings. In October Defence Minister James Richardson resigned in protest.

Trudeau, meanwhile, attacked Robert Bourassa, the Quebec premier, declaring the controversial legislation Bill 22 on French being the official language of Quebec as "politically stupid." Protest against the legislation from Greek and Italian immigrants in Montreal mounted. In early November, during the provincial election campaign in Quebec, Bourassa proposed modi-

PHOTOS UPI

Prime Minister Trudeau listens to the demands of the Canadian Labour Congress, which staged a massive protest against the government's anti-inflation program in March.

fying the legislation to soothe immigrant communities who wish to learn English and to pacify English-speaking citizens. However, on November 15, Bourassa's Liberal party was defeated by the Parti Québecois, a separatist party.

Under the leadership of René Lévesque, a 54-year-old journalist, the Parti Québecois had emphasized during the campaign the economic problems facing Quebec rather than the independence issue. Lévesque promised that there would be no unilateral move toward independence until a referendum on the subject had been held. At the same time it was clear that the party would seek negotiations with the federal government for greater local responsibility. The separatist victory was bound to have wide effects

in the province and in the nation, as well as for Prime Minister Trudeau personally. Even before the election, critics had charged that Trudeau had overacted regarding bilingualism.

Criminal and Judicial Proceedings. In 1976 law enforcement, prisons, and justice attracted much national attention and became leading political issues. Ottawa abolished capital punishment after lengthy debate. Toronto police were accused of brutality. Dr. Henry Morgentaler, who was convicted in 1975 of performing an illegal abortion, was released from prison after the Quebec Supreme Court upheld his appeal. Major prison riots occurred at the British Columbia Penitentiary, Dorchester, Laval, Millhaven, and elsewhere, sparking a national debate

UPI

Quebec dairy farmers carry a paper-mâché cow to Parliament Hill to show their discontent with prices for milk and butter.

on the questions of rehabilitating criminals and treating hard core offenders.

In April five prominent individuals, including Sen. Louis Giguere and National Hockey League President Clarence Campbell were arraigned on charges of conspiring to influence the government to extend the lease on a duty-free airport concession operated by Sky Shops Export Ltd. In the course of the year one cabinet member, André Ouellet, was found guilty of contempt of court, and another, Charles Drury, resigned after a report by the Quebec Chief Justice pointed toward interference in judicial decisions. These resignations plus others brought major changes to a cabinet that was further modified by a cabinet reshuffle on September 15.

Defense and Energy. As Canada continued to strengthen its defenses and meet its NATO commitment, the nation purchased 18 long-range patrol aircraft from Lockheed. It was a $1 billion purchase, the largest in Canadian military history.

Canada continued to pursue policies designed to make the nation self-sufficient in energy. Oil and natural gas exports to the United States were reduced while prices for these commodities rose. The Sarnia-to-Montreal pipeline began operation, and plans were laid for a pipeline from Kitimat, B. C., to Edmonton, Alta. The crown corporation PetroCanada purchased ARCO Canada for $335 million.

INTERNATIONAL AFFAIRS

In July Canada signed an agreement with the European Economic Community whereby its ties with Western Europe were strengthened. In June Trudeau attended an economic summit of seven leading industrial nations in Puerto Rico to pursue policies for developed countries. Trudeau also undertook diplomatic tours to Cuba, Mexico, Venezuela, and Japan to promote trade links. His Latin American tour was marred by the behavior of his wife Margaret whose informal dress, impromptu speeches, and unusual songs prompted wide international comment.

Canada proclaimed legislation whereby on Jan. 1, 1977, the 200-mile offshore limit would come into effect. In November Canada seized Cuban fishing vessels within the existing 12-mile international limit.

U. S. Relations. Trade relations between the United States and Canada remained strong. A pipeline treaty was ratified, committing each government not to impede the flow of oil or natural gas destined for the other. Canada and the United States also signed an extradition treaty to control airplane hijacking, terrorism, and narcotics traffic. In July, as a bicentennial gift from the Canadian people, Trudeau presented President Ford with a copy of *Between Friends/Entre Amis,* an attractive photobook about life on the Canadian-American border.

The Canadian-American Committee, an independent body of businessmen, reported in July that relations were strained between the two countries, and that a widespread belief existed in the United States that Canada was hostile to United States investment. The report asked Canada to discriminate between "what is politically desirable in the short run and what is economically necessary in the long run."

BARRY M. GOUGH
Wilfrid Laurier University

THE CANADIAN MINISTRY
(According to precedence, December 1976)

Pierre Elliott Trudeau, Prime Minister
Allan J. MacEachen, President of the Queen's Privy Council for Canada; House Leader
Donald C. Jamieson, Secretary of State for External Affairs
Jean Chrétien, Minister of Industry, Trade and Commerce
Robert K. Andras, President of the Treasury Board
Jack S. G. Cullen, Minister of Manpower and Immigration
Monique Begin, Minister of National Revenue
James H. Faulkner, Minister of State for Science and Technology
J. Judd Buchanan, Minister of Public Works
Jean-Jacques Blais, Postmaster General; Deputy House Leader
John Roberts, Secretary of State for Canada State
W. Warren Allmand, Minister of Indian Affairs and Northern Development
Francis Fox, Solicitor General of Canada
Anthony Abbott, Minister of Consumer and Corporate Affairs
Leonard S. Marchand, Minister of State to the Minister of Industry, Trade and Commerce
Iona Campagnolo, Minister of State to the Minister of National Health and Welfare
Roméo LeBlanc, Minister of Fisheries and Environment
Donald S. Macdonald, Minister of Finance
John C. Munro, Minister of Labour
Stanley R. Basford, Minister of Justice; Attorney General of Canada
Barnett J. Danson, Acting Minister of National Defence; Minister of State for Urban Affairs
Otto E. Lang, Minister of Transport
Jean-Pierre Goyer, Minister of Supply and Services
Alastair W. Gillespie, Minister of Energy, Mines and Resources
Eugene F. Whelan, Minister of Agriculture
Marc Lalonde, Minister of National Health and Welfare
Daniel J. MacDonald, Minister of Veterans Affairs
Jeanne Sauvé, Minister of Communications
Raymond Perrault, Leader of the Government in the Senate
Marcel Lessard, Minister of Regional Economic Expansion

In disagreement with the prime minister, James A. Richardson resigns as federal defence minister.

UPI

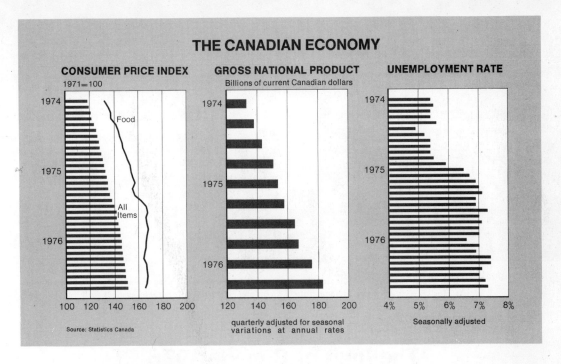

THE CANADIAN ECONOMY

CONSUMER PRICE INDEX
1971=100

GROSS NATIONAL PRODUCT
Billions of current Canadian dollars

UNEMPLOYMENT RATE

Source: Statistics Canada

quarterly adjusted for seasonal
variations at annual rates

Seasonally adjusted

THE ECONOMY

The general picture for the Canadian economy in 1976 was one of slow and uncertain recovery. At midyear the gross national product had increased by 21.2% to $182,860,000,000 and by 6.7% in real terms. The rate of increase in the consumer price index fell to 6% throughout the year from 11% in the fall of 1975. Most of the decline was accounted for by lower food prices which in September were down 0.5% from one year earlier. Nonfood prices were up 9% over the same period. The unemployment rate rose unevenly to 7.3% in September. Employment rose 4.8% over midyear 1975. Jobs in goods producing industries were up 3.7%, in the service sector 1.8%, and in government 1.1%. Of those who were unemployed 75% were men and women under 25 years. In 1960 this group constituted only 40% of the unemployed. Average earnings (wages) rose 12% in 1976, down from 18% in 1975. Nonunion earnings (44% of labor) advanced 6.6%.

In September pretax profits at $18,780,000,-000 were 10% higher than one year earlier. The Bank of Canada held to its target of a 10%–15% increase in the money supply over the first seven months of the year, and in August lowered the target to 8%–12%.

Commodity exports increased unevenly, leaving the October figure ($3,400,000,000) 15% higher than in 1975. Beginning in March 1976 the deficit in foreign commodity trade that marked 1975 was reversed. This improvement was outweighed by an increasing deficit in services which reached $5,000,000,000 in 1976, and by a deficit in direct investment.

The success of the 1975 wage and price control program was not evident. In fact that program, together with the budget of May 1976, which attacked inflation with both monetary and fiscal instruments, probably caused much of the difficulty. Wage and price controls were imposed in line with Galbraithian theories of cost-push related to concentrations of economic power. The opponents of controls blamed inflation on the growth of government and of the money supply. The May budget took account of their arguments by freezing the relative size of the public sector and by reducing welfare payments and conditional grants to the provinces. There may have been some overkill at the expense of the public sector, the unemployed, welfare recipients, and the have-not provinces.

Strains in the economy were reflected in organized protests by both labor and business, and by the usual provincial attempts to rectify all problems by manipulating natural resources. British Columbia, generally depressed economically, sold increasing amounts of coal ($340 million, up from $8 million in 1967) mostly to Japan. Alberta did well on oil, reducing unemployment to 3% and raising per capita income at the fastest rate in the country. Still it had to subsidize its lagging cattle industry with $40 million. Saskatchewan forced the sale of potash companies to the provincial government, and Manitoba withdrew its support from federal wage and price controls because the rules were ill suited to resource producing industries in the north. The Maritime provinces had no success with oil and fell further into the doldrums as federal aid began to dry up.

R. F. NEILL, *Carleton University*

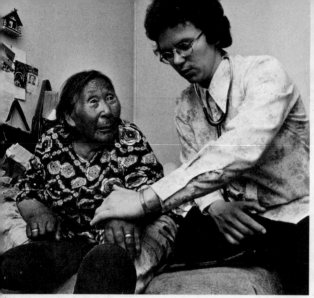

PHOTOS CANADIAN CONSULATE

In recent years, the Inuit of Canada have gradually become more accustomed to present-day health-service facilities, and have demonstrated a greater awareness of their distinct cultural heritage.

SPECIAL REPORT:

The Inuit of Canada 1976

The Inuit of Canada number 19,000 in the Northwest Territories, northern Quebec, and Labrador. Living in six distinct regions, they share a remarkably similar culture and a basic language, Inuktitut, itself divided into several regional dialects. Although their traditional way of life has for centuries been nomadic and the focal point of their society the family, recent events have greatly accelerated the erosion of these certainties. They have also stirred a new consciousness of the distinct Inuit heritage and bred new means for its preservation in a transitional era.

The Inuit face advancing urbanization, mechanization, health services (and disease), education (and inadequate curriculums), changed communications, federal supervision, territorial councils, and—most controversial—exploration for oil and other resources. All this has brought a mixture of relief and apprehension to a simple, scattered, and vulnerable people. The fragile northern environment has been increasingly threatened, but in the testing, Inuit society and tradition have proved strong and responsive. The Inuit now focus their defensive organization on five concerns: language and communication; schools; social habits; land; and regional organization and coordination.

Written Inuktitut. Inuit oral traditions are older and stronger than their written culture. Recently, both have changed. Technical and production innovations by the Canadian Broadcasting Corporation—in both radio and television, and in the Inuit dialects—have proved crucial. They have dramatically extended northern communications networks, prompting im-

portant exchanges of ideas and increasing Inuit awareness of common interests. In September 1976, Inuit leaders, meeting at Frobisher Bay, unanimously recommended adoption of a standardized writing system, replacing the five different systems currently in use. A dual form in both syllabics (qaniujaaqpait) and Roman characters (qaliujaaqpait) would preserve tradition and satisfy regional interests. The recent communications revolution may thus be vastly extended.

Schools. There has also arisen an even stronger reaction against the North's traditional school system based on religious denominations. Its varied "centres" have for years disrupted traditional family patterns by forcing youths to move to distant places (sometimes hundreds of miles away) in pursuit of an increasingly obsolete education. The Inuit insist upon regional schools and a curriculum to meet Inuit particular needs and aspirations. Like the "quiet revolution" of 20 years ago in the province of Quebec, demands for secular, relevant, regional schooling are most important elements in the northern movement.

Social Demands. Among demands for social change, two are preeminent. Better housing and an ecologically safe sanitation system are considered essential if the nomadic life is to yield yet more to settlement. Improved public health facilities are generally demanded, but the greatest emphasis—on prohibition—has deeper cultural implications. Successively, Inuit communities are opting for prohibition, not only as a health measure but as a symbolic gesture of resistance to one of the worst characteristics of southern white and—significantly to them—of Indian culture.

Nunavut. The land and adjoining seas, however, remain the focal point of the new Inuit movement. Nunavut (Our Land) symbolizes freedom, dignity, and permanence. With southern professional help but Inuit direction, scientific land-use surveys have affirmed that the preservation of Nunavut and its people rests in freedom of movement and a conservation-conscious life style that requires, by southern Canadian standards, a vast territorial extent. Land and sea together form the principal medium of Inuit culture. Their protection must be the Inuit's first concern. Indifference to native landed and cultural interests—such as in Quebec's James Bay Project—have alerted the eastern Inuit and driven them to common cause with those in the western Arctic, particularly in the Mackenzie River basin.

The Inuit Taparisat. The chief sponsor of these land surveys, of reviews of northern business opportunities, of new wildlife studies, of legal aid programs, of nonprofit housing projects, and of an Inuit management-training scheme is the Inuit Taparisat of Canada (ITC, the Eskimo Brotherhood), founded in 1971. Its offices, in Ottawa since 1972, have become the rallying center for many specialized and regional Inuit organizations. These include the important western body, the Committee for Original People's Entitlement (COPE). The ITC has also created an impressive network of northern social workers in local chapters. Their effect has been to raise the consciousness, pride, and coordination of the Inuit. A major decision was taken in September 1976 to consult even more intensively the wishes of thousands of individuals and local communities. Further examination of the bases and implications of Inuit land claims has been demanded, and there are those who are not satisfied with the moderate, accommodating spirit of the ITC's approach to date. The question is whether the Inuit will have time to prolong their inquiries and consultations, for the petroleum industry, the government, and other resource and energy interests are impatient for decisions and action.

At Pond Inlet, N.W.T., in November 1975, the ITC adopted a historic declaration of objectives and strategy. A chief consequence was the proposal to Ottawa on Feb. 27, 1976, that it should recognize an Inuit territory or quasi-province, Nunavut. This move was not a separatist threat, but a responsible first step toward Inuit administrative and political maturity. Although the ITC has since revised its proposals, their fiscal provisions are based on recognition that Nunavut the land is the property of the Arctic's first citizens. The expectation of a 3% return for leasing its use cooperatively is a moderate, responsible challenge to southern Canadians.

ALAN WILSON

CANADA: CULTURAL AFFAIRS

Belt tightening was the official theme for everybody in Canada in 1976, and cultural grants from all sources were frozen at the 1974 level. Nevertheless, it was a reasonably rich cultural year throughout the country.

One event that could have been big turned out to be a fizzle—the Olympics Cultural Program in August. It was planned as a glittering display of Canada's artistic talents, but management and promotion of the program were poor and basic publicity was neglected. Some of the invited performing companies refused to show up. Others played to almost empty houses.

In October, Donald MacSween was named to succeed Hamilton Southam as director general of the National Arts Centre.

Theater. The 1976 theater season was marked by a lack of boldness in both programming and production, mainly as a result of worrisome financial constraints. However, box office results were generally good and several companies announced optimistic plans for 1977.

The Stratford Festival, with record-breaking ticket sales exceeding $3 million, ran for 22 weeks with 318 performances of 10 plays. Montreal's Théâtre du Nouveau Monde (TNM) celebrated its 25th anniversary in October. There was much nostalgic excitement, but the icing on the birthday cake was a report that a $4.5 million renovation of the old TNM playhouse would commence at once. The Neptune Theatre in Halifax, which has grown in ten years to be one of Canada's major drama theaters, had a very successful season artistically, but the financial outcome was woeful.

Stratford Festival, 24th season: Maggie Smith and Keith Baxter starred in *Antony and Cleopatra*.

ZOE DOMINIC, STRATFORD SHAKESPEAREAN FESTIVAL FOUNDATION OF CANADA

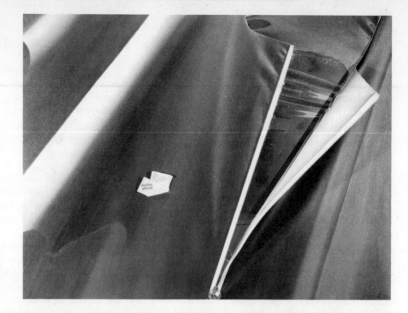

For the first time, in 1976, a large collection of paintings, prints, tapestries, and silkscreens by artists from the province of Quebec were displayed in New York City. Included in the exhibit were the acrylic painting "Hommage à Dali" by Solange Léveillé (right), the polyester sculpture "Cube Québec" by François Brosseau (below, left), and the lithograph "Sauna" by Eudice Garmaise.

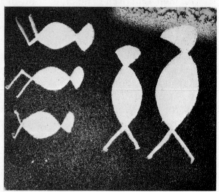

PHOTOS COURTESY GALERIE SIGNAL
SOCIÉTÉ DES ARTISTES PROFESSIONNELS DU QUEBEC

The Redlight Theatre, a Toronto group devoted entirely to staging plays by and about women, was given use of the old, deserted city morgue for $1 a year. The Centaur, a well-established company playing on two stages in Montreal's downtown financial district, enjoyed a good year and partially pulled itself out of a financial hole. The Canadian Mime Theatre undertook the longest tour ever made by a Canadian performing arts company, travelling to New Zealand, Australia, Malaysia, England, and Scotland.

In October, the country's oldest regional company, the Manitoba Theatre Centre in Winnipeg, did its first Shakespeare production in ten years. Vancouver's major group, Playhouse Centre, surprised the community when it made a "unique package ticket deal" with the local professional football club. The Citadel Theatre in Edmonton opened its new $6 million premises in November with an astonishing 12,000 subscribers.

Music. The 90-member Tokyo Symphony Orchestra made its international debut in Vancouver, B. C., in September. Under the direction of Kazuyoshi Akiyama (who also directs the American Symphony in New York City), the Japanese group played three highly successful concerts jointly with the Vancouver Symphony, a spectacular type of musical twinning rarely attempted. Major orchestras in other Canadian cities had artistically satisfying seasons.

Opera was the only truly vigorous and entertaining musical form in 1976, enjoying what may have been the peak of a five-year explosive growth. Toronto's Canadian Opera Company provided a lavish and robust 28th season with *La Bohème, Tosca, Die Walküre*, and *The Grand Duchess of Gerolstein* to delight SRO houses at home and on tour. A smashing production of Tchaikovsky's opera *The Queen of Spades*, performed in Ottawa's National Arts Centre in August, was a hit with full-house audiences.

Dance. The current worldwide surge of popular interest in all forms of dance has been apparent in Canada since the late 1960's, and in 1976 it almost reached a state of beneficent turmoil. In spite of generous financial aid from both the public and private sectors, irresistible growth pushed expenditures far above income for most dance companies. Unhappiness developed concerning how the money pie should be divided. Claimants for priority were the performing companies, training schools, individual dancers and choreographers, scholars, and journals.

On the whole, dance groups enjoyed an exciting year, with much innovative choreography. The big three—the Royal Winnipeg Ballet, The National Ballet Company of Toronto, and Les Ballets Canadiens in Montreal—each had a big, glossy season with normal 1976 financial echoes.

Winnipeg's prestigious Contemporary Dancers faced up to money troubles by soliciting and receiving $35,000 from local supporters, after the Manitoba government had agreed to match that amount. Le Groupe de la Place Royale in Quebec and the Anna Wyman Dancers in Vancouver, with enlarged repertoires featuring works by Canadian and foreign choreographers, won bigger and bigger followings.

An indication of Canadian taste for dance could be seen in the enthusiastic welcoming of many visiting companies in 1976, including The Dutch National Ballet, Cologne Dance Forum, Ballet D'Espana, Israel's Inbal Dance Theatre, and Mexico's Ballet Folklorico.

Visual Arts. Canada's painters, sculptors, and allied fine craftsmen have, with few exceptions, been strangely quiet and unenterprising. Most of the art news has been related to institutions and big business.

The Montreal Museum of Fine Arts reopened after a hiatus of three years. A $10 million renovation produced a 5-story addition to the venerable old building, 34 impressive galleries, a new auditorium, and a substantial reference library. The richness and diversity of the museum's collections are now visible for the first time to artists, patrons, scholars, and the general public. Not related to the opening was the resignation in October of Dr. David Giles Carter, director since 1964.

Following its bicentennial gesture to a number of cities in the United States, the superb collection of master paintings from the Soviet Union's Hermitage and State galleries stopped over for exhibitions in Winnipeg and Montreal before returning to Leningrad in December.

People. Dr. Jean Boggs resigned as director of the National Gallery of Canada. Her departure seemed to stem from an unwillingness to adapt her professional concepts to the federal government's new policy of museum's management. The appointment of Christopher Youngs as director of the Canada Council's Art Bank was a matter of great interest. The bank, which was established with federal funding to provide practical encouragement for painters and sculptors, buys $1 million worth of contemporary works each year and rents its holdings to government departments and agencies for display in public areas. Early in the summer Robin Phillips, the sensational young director of the Stratford Festival, caused some consternation when

he announced his irrevocable decision to quit. However, he signed a new 5-year contract in September and many North American theater buffs sighed with relief.

The whole Canadian cultural community was shocked and deeply saddened by the sudden death in October of Herman Geiger-Torel, the great man of opera in Canada. He had retired in July after 25 years of service as director of the Canadian Opera Company.

WALTER B. HERBERT
Consultant on Canadian Cultural Affairs

CARIBBEAN

Drought, politics, and growing Cuban interest in the neighboring islands characterized events in the Caribbean during 1976.

Alternating Extremes. The 1976 weather patterns were marked by the imbalance between floods and drought which has been noted since 1973. Severe drought hit all the islands of the Greater Antilles during the first eight months, followed by heavy rains in the remaining third of 1976. Jamaica suffered under the worst dry spell in decades, which left Kingston with scarce water supply during most of the summer months. In Haiti, now accustomed to long months without rain, the farmers have practically given up any agricultural pursuits in the two peninsulas which jut out westward in the north and the south. As in previous years, the drought was ascribed by meteorologists to the dust clouds which crossed the Atlantic from the Sahara desert. When rains finally did arrive in the region, with the tropical depressions and storms of September and October, the flooding, particularly in the Dominican Republic, was notable. Although hurricanes continue to come out of the Atlantic, none penetrated the Caribbean Sea and none affected directly any of the islands. The hurricanes either moved off to the north of the area or were formed late by storms moving from the Caribbean into the Gulf of Mexico.

In mid-1976 the 4,869-foot (1,484-m) volcano, Soufrière, on the French West Indian island of Guadeloupe threatened to erupt. As a precaution against any tragedy, like that which hit Martinique in 1902, some 74,000 people were evacuated from the area around the base of the large mountain. For the months of July and August the volcano rumbled and fumed, but no major eruption occurred, and the people slowly returned to the small farms and towns located between the sea and the mountain.

Finances. Bad weather, falling prices for agricultural products, and an increased U. S. import tax on sugar all combined to have an adverse affect on agricultural development in the Caribbean. The United States loaned $10 million to the Caribbean Development Bank, bringing to $42.3 million the total U.S. contribution to that institution. The recent loan is expected to be used to improve the production of agriculture in the less developed islands and to extend credit to small farmers in the larger islands. New Zealand also made a contribution of $600,000 to the Caribbean Development Bank; it was expected to provide technical aid for small agricultural communities.

In July 1976 the Eastern Caribbean Currency Commission severed the long-time connection between the East Caribbean dollar and the British pound sterling. This action was prompted by the falling value of the pound on the international monetary market. The East Caribbean and the United States dollars were tied at a parity of E.C.$2.70 to U.S.$1. The islands affected by this decision were the West Indian Associated States: Dominica, St. Kitts-Nevis, Antigua, St. Lucia, and St. Vincent; and the two British colonies of Montserrat and Anguilla.

Politics. Elections were held in 1976 in many of the Caribbean islands, bringing about changes of one kind or another. In addition to Puerto Rico and the Virgin Islands, elections were held in Anguilla, Antigua, Barbados, and Trinidad and Tobago. Ronald Webster, who successfully led the fight to separate Anguilla from St. Kitts and Nevis, succeeded in capturing six out of the seven seats in the Anguillan legislature for his People's Progressive party.

In Antigua the voters narrowly rejected a bid for full independence from Great Britain by defeating the party in power, led by George Walter, who had promised to ask for independence if returned to the post of premier. The victorious Antigua Labor party, led by Vere Bird, had been defeated in 1971 by Walter's Progressive Labor Movement. Although the election was extremely close, the Labor party captured two thirds of the 17-seat parliament of the associated state. The new government acted quickly to explore charges of misuse of funds by three former cabinet ministers and to repeal the repressive tax laws, which the Inter-American Press Association had condemned as being against freedom of the press on the island.

In September the Democratic Labor party, which had governed Barbados for 15 years, was narrowly defeated by the Barbados Labor party. Errol Barrow, who retained his seat in parliament, saw his party's representation drop from 16 seats to seven. The Barbados Labor party, which captured 17 of the 24 seats of parliament, is led by John Michael Geoffrey ("Tom") Adams, son of the island's first prime minister, Sir Grantley Adams, who was also the only prime minister of the short-lived West Indian Federation (1958–62). There is little of substance to distinguish between the two labor parties.

Contrary to the cases of Antigua and Barbados, the elections in Trinidad and Tobago did not bring about a change in government; nevertheless, the results produced an even more profound change than in the other two islands. Dr. Eric Williams and his People's National Movement won an easy victory, capturing 24 seats in the 36-seat parliament. The most striking result of the election was the virtual disappearance of the long-time opposition party composed mostly of East Indians, the Democratic Action Congress; it captured only two seats. In turn, the role of chief opposition passed to the newly formed and militantly left-wing United Labor Front, which elected 10 representatives to Parliament. Thus, the two conservative groups in Trinidad, the East Indians and the pro-Williams creoles, have united behind the People's National Movement. The United Labor Front has been successful in building a broad Marxist-Leninist political movement among the industrialized workers of the country's oilfields. Shortly after the election, Trinidad and Tobago, which will retain its membership in the Commonwealth of Nations, declared itself a republic.

Jamaican Violence. The island of Jamaica was torn by almost continuous outbreaks of violence for a five-month period beginning in January. The turmoil did not ease until mid-June, when the government declared a state of emergency to last throughout October. The violence was centered in the slum areas of Kingston, the capital, and took the lives of more than 100 persons, including the Peruvian ambassador to the country. It apparently originated in roving rival gangs belonging to opposite political parties.

Until the emergency was declared the rivalry between the island's two major parties was extremely intense. The opposition party accused the government in power of provoking the unrest to justify a suspension of the democratic process and bring about the establishment of a Communist state patterned after Cuba. The party in power, in turn, accused the opposition of cooperation with subversive elements, financed by the United States, for the purpose of destroying the stability of the pro-Cuban, socialist government of Prime Minister Michael Manley.

The state of emergency evidently had some quieting effects, since the incidence of violence was cut by half during the first month. More than 2,000 people were arrested on suspicion of participation in the violence and some 20 people were sentenced to life imprisonment for illegal possession of firearms.

Elections to the House of Representatives, held on December 15, resulted in a resounding victory for Manley, whose party captured 48 out of the 60 contested seats—a gain of 11.

Not only in Jamaica but elsewhere in the Caribbean the influence of Cuba among its neighbors is noticeable. When Cuba air-lifted its troops to Angola, bases for refueling were utilized in Guyana and Barbados. Only the latter protested, and the practice was halted.

On October 6 a Cuban airline DC-8 exploded shortly after take-off from the airport in Barbados. A Cuban exile group announced that it was responsible for the Barbados tragedy.

THOMAS G. MATHEWS
University of Puerto Rico

CENSORSHIP

Groups which in 1976 submitted annual reports on the status of freedom in the world found an increase in the number of countries restricting it. The International Federation of Journalists said that "hardly two dozen countries still enjoy press freedom," while the rest enjoy it only as defined for them by their governments. By its criteria of freedom, the International Press Institute found half the world without a free press.

Freedom House estimated that only 19.8% of the world's population lived in freedom in 1976, as against 35% a year before, a decline largely explained by the loss of India from the list of free countries.

India, which now rigidly censors its own press, has also imposed limits on the freedom of foreign correspondents to report. In this action it joins many Third World countries which have made reporting by correspondents either extraordinarily difficult by restricting their movement while in the countries or completely impossible by virtue of totally disallowing entry.

By the strength of their number, Third World countries at meetings sponsored by the United Nations Educational, Scientific, and Cultural Organization have been able to publicize proposals for the control of communications, based on their broad contention that the state should have the responsibility of determining the content of mass media. The media are envisioned as tools that developing countries should use to build economies and to protect cultures against richer, more developed nations of the world, not as vehicles for the flow of information free of governmental limitations. To these ends, Third World countries in several regional meetings have planned establishment of wire services to be financed by consortiums of governments. A Soviet-sponsored resolution declaring that "States are responsible for the activities in the international sphere of all mass media under their jurisdiction" was narrowly averted at the UNESCO conference in Nairobi, Kenya, in November.

Censorship at the Source. The quarter-century effort to limit bureaucratic secrecy continues. Virtually every state now has both open-meetings and open-records statutes. The recently amended Freedom of Information Act has made records of federal agencies more accessible to citizens. A 1976 statute (the "Sunshine Act") makes it mandatory, though with certain exceptions, that more than 50 federal agencies conduct their meetings in public.

The House of Representatives and, more recently, the Senate have adopted rules that greatly increase the openness of congressional committee meetings, including those of conference committees which long have been bastions of secrecy. While it is still possible for committees to vote to close, a continuing study by *Congressional Quarterly* has found that only 7% of all committee meetings were closed in 1974; this compared with 40% as recently as 1972.

Trial judges, following the practice of recent years, have continued to issue orders restricting coverage by the press of criminal proceedings. The press, however, won an important victory in 1976, when the U. S. Supreme Court found a Nebraska court's order that the news media suppress facts concerning a pending sensational case to be unconstitutional on grounds of prior restraint. The Supreme Court called this "the most serious and least tolerable infringement on First Amendment rights," especially "as applied to reporting of criminal proceedings."

The court, however, left the door ajar for a possible imposition of prior restraint under other circumstances, declaring that "Reasonable minds can have few doubts about the gravity of the evil pretrial publicity can work. . . ." The Nebraska case had simply not demonstrated the gravity of the evil with "the degree of certainty our cases on prior restraint require."

Censorship and Community Standards. The Supreme Court continued to pass obscenity problems on to states and localities for solution. Now that local rather than national standards may determine whether a publication is obscene or not, publishers are discovering how widely standards vary. Thus, the much litigated movie, *Deep Throat,* plays uninhibited in some cities while it is banned in others.

The Supreme Court has upheld the constitutionality of local zoning ordinances that restrict "adult" movies and bookshops within set areas. In a 5–4 decision, the court ruled prior restraint was not an issue since dissemination of information was not limited but only the place of dissemination.

Book battles raged on between civil-libertarian and parental groups. The issue reached a federal appellate court whose ruling gave comfort to both factions. The court found no constitutional violation in the choice of textbooks by a local school board, even though the choice was contrary to faculty desires. Nor did it find that a school must provide a library. However, the court said, a library, once established, is "an important privilege created by the state for the benefit of the students in the school" that is "not subject to being withdrawn . . . by school boards whose members might desire to 'winnow' the library for books the contents of which occasioned their displeasure or disapproval."

The theory that advertising—"commercial speech"—is not protected by the First Amendment was rejected by the U. S. Supreme Court when it struck down a Virginia statute prohibiting advertising by pharmacists. The court ruled that truthful, nondeceptive, commercial speech, relative to lawful activities, falls within the protection of the First Amendment.

PAUL FISHER
Director, Freedom of Information Center
University of Missouri

CENTRAL AMERICA

The principal developments of 1976 in Central America included a devastating earthquake in Guatemala, improved relations between Honduras and El Salvador, political unrest in Costa Rica, and congressional elections in El Salvador. (For a discussion of 1976 events in Panama see page 395.)

On February 24, U. S. Secretary of State Henry Kissinger met with the foreign ministers of Costa Rica, El Salvador, Guatemala, Honduras, and Nicaragua in San José, Costa Rica. Clearly referring to possible armed intervention by Cuba, the secretary said that the United States would "not tolerate a challenge to the solemn treaty principle of nonintervention in this hemisphere." Pressing domestic matters within Guatemala, El Salvador, and Honduras were given as the reason for the cancellation of a planned conference between Kissinger and Central American heads of state.

Before returning home, Kissinger stopped off in Guatemala, where he pledged additional U. S. reconstruction aid for the country's earthquake victims.

Costa Rica. Normally a tranquil nation, Costa Rica experienced signs of political unrest common to other Central and Latin American nations in 1976. Bombings, strikes, and clashes between strikers and the police occurred during the year. In addition there were allegations of plots against the government. President Daniel Oduber was forced to increase his own security force. Some of the tensions were thought to be caused by an austerity program launched by the government in order to reduce the country's endemic balance-of-payments deficit.

In early July, a crisis developed within the ruling National Liberation party (PLN). Unsuccessful in an attempt to change a constitutional provision preventing the nation's chief executive from serving two consecutive terms, PLN leader José Figueres Ferrer, a former president of Costa Rica, formed a splinter party. A simultaneous general strike by the nation's electricity workers complicated the crisis. The strike was declared illegal.

Earlier in the year, about 100 persons were arrested in San José, the nation's capital, for rioting in front of the presidential home. The disturbance was a protest against a proposed 25% increase in urban transit fares. President Oduber stated that the Communists were responsible for the unrest.

In the area of foreign affairs, Costa Rica renewed trade relations with Cuba and established full diplomatic relations with reunified Vietnam. As of May 31, 1976, Costa Rica claims a 200-mile territorial waters limit.

El Salvador. President Arturo Armando Molina's National Reconciliation party captured all 52 congressional seats in the elections held on March 14. It had earlier held about two thirds of the legislative seats. The party also won the mayoral offices in all the country's 261 municipalities. Although the National Opposition Union had withdrawn its candidates to protest the law governing the elections, its withdrawal was not officially acknowledged, and the candidates remained on the ballots.

While the government, reorganized early in the year, thus seemed solidly ensconced, it was badly shaken only two months after the elections, when the chief of staff of the armed forces and the third most powerful individual in the nation, Col. Manuel Alfonso Rodríguez, was arrested by U. S. federal agents in New York City and charged with conspiracy to sell 10,000 submachine guns to the mafia and to defraud the U. S. government. He was dismissed from his post on May 22, and Col. Armando Leonidas Rojas was named to replace him.

Relations with neighboring Honduras, jittery ever since the "soccer war" of 1969, took a turn for the better in 1976. Having reached some agreement at a meeting in Poy, a border post, on February 24, President Molina and Honduran President Melgar Castro on June 14 signed a document intended to resolve the seven-year conflict. On October 6, after a series of border clashes during the summer, the countries took a further step toward peace, when they agreed to submit their dispute to a mediator.

Guatemala. One of the worst earthquakes in Latin American history devastated much of Guatemala on February 4. The major damage occurred in Guatemala City and in neighboring departments, where many towns and villages were completely leveled. More than 500 tremors shook the area in the week that followed, causing new landslides and the collapse of buildings damaged in the first quake. Terrified residents slept in the open air. The death toll was estimated at 25,000 persons and more than 74,000 were injured. Some 1,277,000 people—about one fourth of the population—were left homeless.

CENTRAL AMERICA · Information Highlights

Nation	Population (in millions)	Capital	GNP (millions U. S.$)	Head of State and Government
Costa Rica	2.0	San José	$1,125 (1973)	Daniel Oduber Quirós, president
El Salvador	4.2	San Salvador	$1,970 (1975)	Arturo Armando Molina, president
Guatemala	5.7	Guatemala City	$3,860 (1975)	Gen. Kjell Laugerud García, president
Honduras	2.8	Tegucigalpa	$1,000 (1975)	Col. Juan Melgar Castro, president
Nicaragua	2.2	Managua	$1,190 (1974)	Anastasio Somoza, president
Panama	1.7	Panama City	$1,650 (1974)	Demetrio Lakas Bahas, president Omar Torrijos Herrera, chief executive

UPI

In February, a devastating earthquake in Guatemala killed some 25,000 persons, injured more than 74,000, and left more than 1,000,000 homeless. Above, the process of rebuilding begins in the town of San Bartolomé.

The Guatemalan army headed the relief action. The United States, many nations of Latin America and Europe, and foreign relief agencies provided and distributed food, clothing, and medical assistance. Relief to outlying areas was hampered by landslides and ruined bridges. Despite the severity of the disaster there were few reports of looting or public disturbances.

Relations remained tense with Belize, a semi-independent British colony that Guatemala claims as its territory. Consequently, Guatemala refused relief aid from Britain, but contributions from private British groups were accepted.

Honduras. Honduras began the year with the words of their president ringing in their ears: the country would remain under the control of the military until the end of 1979, at the least. After that, President Juan Alberto Melgar Castro announced in his New Year's message, a consultative council, made up of members of trade unions, student organizations, political parties, and business associations, would be established to advise the government on policies. Mindful of the bloody clashes of 1975 between peasants and landowners, the president also reiterated the government's intention to step up its land-reform program.

Revelations of bribes paid to Honduran officials by United Brands resulted in a new anti-corruption law in 1976. The law provides for sentences of 3–12 years' imprisonment for public officials convicted of taking bribes.

Still not recovered from the ravage of the 1974 hurricane Fifi, Honduras suffered another natural assault when an earthquake destroyed the greater part of three towns near the Guatemalan border on February 4. Although damage was not on the same scale as in Guatemala, electric power was cut in at least a dozen cities, while broken water and sewer mains flooded some communities. (For the country's rapprochement with El Salvador, see page 152.)

Nicaragua. The year was a generally quiet one for the government of President Anastasio Somoza. But National Guard units continued to have encounters with guerrillas of the Sandinista National Liberation Front. In October, the newspaper *Novedades,* owned by President Somoza, accused the Jamaican government of allowing Cuban guerrilla groups to pass through Jamaica on their way to Nicaragua.

A new program to aid campesinos (small farmers) was established in 1976, financed jointly by the government and the U. S. Agency for International Development (AID). Known as INVIERNO (Institute for Campesino Development), the program was intended to provide campesinos with agricultural training, marketing facilities, lines of credit, and reasonable conditions governing the repayment of loans.

Following a visit by the Spanish minister of trade, Spain announced in October that it would grant substantial credits to Nicaragua.

LOUIS R. SADLER, *New Mexico State University*

CHEMISTRY

A continued controversy over aerosol spray cans, the search for life on Mars, new discoveries regarding superheavy elements, and a new toxic substances control law were among the 1976 developments in chemistry.

Aerosol Spray Cans. Uncertainty remained about whether or not chlorofluorocarbons (Freons) used in aerosol spray cans and as refrigerants damage the stratospheric ozone layer that filters out dangerous ultraviolet rays from the sun. Freons are said to release chlorine (Cl-) which reacts with ozone to form oxygen. The fate of the chlorine was uncertain. A group of scientists found less hydrogen chloride (HCl) in the stratosphere than predicted. This suggested that chlorine was not being released. Later, these scientists said that calibration of their equipment was faulty and that HCl content was nearly 100 times greater than predicted.

Chlorine oxide (ClO) is an intermediate in the ozone reaction. Another scientific group found that its stratospheric content was also 100 times greater than predicted by theory. This suggested a large natural source of chlorine and that the effects of Freons were negligible. But new results showed concentrations only twice as high. Still another suggestion was that chlorine combines with nitrogen oxides to form chlorine nitrate ($ClONO_2$). But sensitivity of instruments is lower than the concentration of chlorine nitrate, and some scientists claim that it is not important in stratospheric chemistry. Nevertheless the National Academy of Sciences recommended that the use of freons in aerosol spray cans be phased out by January 1978.

Life on Mars. Results from experiments to detect life on Mars were ambiguous, but created some excitement. In one Viking I experiment, radioactive carbon monoxide and dioxide were added to a soil sample. Scientists hoped that microbes, were they present, would consume these materials and incorporate them into their bodies. Then the test chamber was flushed out with helium gas and the sample was heated to high temperatures to convert the organisms to gases. When monitored for radioactivity, the gases showed levels six times that predicted if no life were present. Then a sample was sterilized to kill organisms and heated to high temperatures. If no organisms had been present radioactivity should have been low and it was, but not low enough to discount presence of life —21 counts compared with 96 in the first test.

In another test, nutrients labeled with carbon-14 were added to a soil sample and incubated. Radioactivity of gases, such as carbon dioxide possibly emitted by metabolism of organisms, rose sharply. A second test using a sterilized sample was negative, suggesting that organisms once present had been killed. One suggestion was that a peculiar soil chemistry caused the semi-positive results. Similar experiments done on soil from Antarctica showed lower radioactive peaks than the Martian soil.

Superheavy Elements. Superheavy elements, those having atomic numbers much greater than that of uranium (92), are not known to exist in nature. But existence or synthesis of some has been predicted. In 1976, evidence was found that elements 116 and 126 once existed in monazite (thorium-bearing rocks) estimated to be a billion years old. Giant halos, 80 to 100 micrometers in diameter, caused by damage from alpha radiation, were found. These are much larger than those caused by lighter radioactive elements. The method used to obtain this evidence was bombardment of monazite crystals with proton (hydrogen nuclei) beams. This caused the crystals to emit X-rays having energies of 20 to 30 million electron volts, values which matched closely those calculated on the basis of theory for elements 116 and 126. Also scientists at the University of Chicago were studying tiny fractions of the Allende meteorite that fell in Mexico during 1969, to discover if element 114 once existed in the solar system.

Toxic Substances. After some five years of debate, the United States enacted a toxic substances control bill. The bill gives the administrator of the Environmental Protection Agency wide discretionary powers to decide if a chemical should be banned, or restrict its manufacture, distribution, or disposal. He can also require testing of new chemicals or old chemicals for new uses. Not everyone was happy with the legislation. A labor leader said that it was worse than none. Some small chemical companies said it would put them out of business. An environmentalist said that the problem of chemicals in the environment was so urgent that some type of legislation was needed immediately.

However, the EPA seemed to be bogged down by previous responsibilities—administering the federal pesticide law, Congressional inquiries, court suits, complex regulations, and staff shortages. A pesticide industry spokesman said that excessive regulations had skyrocketed costs. For example, the 1967 cost of discovering and marketing a new pesticide was about $3.4 million; in 1976 it was $8 million.

Cigarette Smoking. While the campaign to induce people to stop smoking continues, the National Cancer Institute announced development of a low-hazard cigarette. The work, supported by $8 million in federal funds, started with chemical analyses of the tobacco. Next, a cigarette was smoked in a smoking machine and the smoke was collected and tested for toxic properties on animals. Flavor components were identified and tested for toxicity. Finally, results of chemical analyses, animal tests, and flavor were correlated. Although the scientists had learned how to make low-hazard cigarettes, the smoke tasted mostly of hot air. The problem is to achieve flavor without risk.

EUGENIA KELLER, *Managing Editor, "Chemistry"*

CHICAGO

Richard J. Daley, mayor of Chicago since 1955, died in December. Michael A. Bilandic was named acting mayor pending a special 1977 election.

Faced with a $47.5 million deficit and unable to obtain extra funds from the state, Chicago public schools closed 16 days early in June. This resulted in an 8.5% salary loss for the system's 43,000 employees. The early closing, however, threatened the schools with the loss of $53 million in state funds because of a provision which penalizes schools 1% of their state funds for each day they fall short of the minimum 177-day school year.

After Gov. Daniel Walker vetoed a school package passed in the summer because the General Assembly failed to approve a tax speedup plan of the governor's, the legislature was called into special session in September. The package would have reduced Chicago's penalty by $22 million. During the special session, the legislature approved a compromise which returned $23 million of the penalty to Chicago by changing the formula upon which penalties for not completing a 177-day school year are assessed. Chicago schools continued to face serious problems in the 1976–77 year, however. Unless additional state funds were forthcoming, a deficit of $116 million was likely.

Fares of the Chicago Transit Authority and suburban and commuter railroad operations under the jurisdiction of the six-county Regional Transportation Authority increased about 11% in September. The increase resulted from a battle between the five city and four suburban members of the RTA board. The fight led to a $24 million cut in state funds and delayed approval of the fiscal 1977 RTA budget.

Periodic racial violence broke out during the summer in Marquette Park in a predominantly white area on the Southwest Side. Whites protested marches by blacks who support open housing. In the largest of the outbreaks on July 17, 33 persons were injured and 63 arrested.

On May 4, Mayor Richard J. Daley said the city would enforce a 1927 ordinance requiring city employees to live in Chicago. An estimated 10% of the 43,000 employees lived in the suburbs.

In September, a federal judge lifted a racial and sexual quota on hiring by the Chicago police department, imposed in 1974. He accepted a city compromise based on ratios existing on the police eligibility roster. The act freed $47 million in federal revenue sharing funds which had been held up because the city had not complied with the judge's earlier quota.

The city's celebration for the bicentennial was an international trade fair and folk festival at the restored Navy Pier on the downtown lakefront. The LaSalle Hotel in the city's financial district closed at the end of June.

KENNETH ROSS, *Chicago Tribune*

Augusto Pinochet, president of Chile since 1973, waves to crowd during Independence Day parade.

UPI

CHILE

For Chile the most significant events of 1976 were the passage on June 18 of a mild resolution by the Organization of American States (OAS) urging Chile "to continue adopting measures to assure the observance of human rights," Chile's proposals to provide Bolivia with access to the Pacific Ocean, and indications that the economic depression and high inflation might soon end.

OAS. The human rights issue dominated the sixth General Assembly of the OAS in Santiago, June 4–18. Prior to the meeting, human rights units of the United Nations and the OAS, as well as the governments of Great Britain, Italy, the United States, and Venezuela, continued to charge Gen. Augusto Pinochet Ugarte's regime with torture and other abuses. Chile released 300 political prisoners in May—49 of them on

─────── **CHILE • Information Highlights** ───────

Official Name: Republic of Chile.
Location: Southwestern coast of South America.
Area: 292,257 square miles (756,945 km²).
Population (1976 est.): 10,800,000.
Chief Cities: Santiago, the capital, 2,661,920 (1970 census, met. area); Valparaiso, 292,850 (1970 est.).
Government: *Head of state and government,* Gen. Augusto Pinochet Ugarte, president (took power Sept. 1973). *Legislature*—Congress (dissolved Sept. 1973).
Monetary Unit: Peso (13.92 pesos equal U. S.$1, Aug. 1976).
Gross National Product (1974 est.): $7,940,000,000.
Manufacturing (major products): Iron and steel, petroleum products, pulp and paper, chemicals.
Major Agricultural Products: Wheat, sugar beets, potatoes, corn, grapes, citrus fruits, rapeseed, fish.
Foreign Trade (1975): *Exports,* $1,661,000,000; *imports,* $1,811,000,000.

William E. Simon confers with General Pinochet and Minister of the Treasury Jorge Cauas (center) in May. The U. S. treasury secretary told the Chileans that continued U. S. aid was dependent on the regime's respect for human rights.

UPI

the day before a visit by U. S. Secretary of the Treasury William Simon, who noted that further U. S. economic assistance was dependent upon Chile's respect for human rights. Addressing the OAS assembly June 8, U. S. Secretary of State Henry Kissinger hoped that the "obstacles" raised by the abuse of human rights "would soon end."

Chileans who fled abroad were not spared harassment, however. On June 11, right-wing terrorists—most likely off-duty policemen—kidnapped 25 foreign political refugees, of whom 23 were Chileans, in Buenos Aires, Argentina. They were released after protests to the Argentine government by the office of the United Nations High Commissioner for Refugees. On September 21, Orlando Letelier, a former cabinet minister and former ambassador to the United States, was killed in Washington, D. C., when a bomb exploded as he drove his car to work.

Government Attacks on the Church. After the government expelled three U. S. nuns and two Italian priests in November 1975 and denied a Dutch priest who left Chile in December permission to reenter, Archbishop Raúl Cardinal Silva Henríquez and three other bishops published a letter January 13 asking 1,398 foreign priests and nuns to stay despite the government's "unjustified" and "shameful" acts.

Church officials were further outraged August 15 when a crowd, including three secret policemen, threw rocks at a car carrying three bishops from the Santiago airport after their return from Ecuador. Subsequently, the church excommunicated four of the attackers. Although President Pinochet and church leaders had lunch together at the presidential palace August 18, the Episcopal Conference issued a statement condemning the August 6 expulsion of Jaime Castillo Velasco and Eugenio Velasco Letelier to Argentina. Both lawyers had defended political prisoners and represented the church's relief organization.

Cabinet Reshuffled. On January 3, General Sergio Arellano Stark, chief of the National Defense Staff, resigned after reports of military discontent with Pinochet. He was replaced by Rear Admiral Jorge Seburgo Silva. Following the resignation of the entire cabinet March 5, President Pinochet replaced his health, labor, and transportation ministers. The new cabinet was composed of eight civilians and six military men.

On January 23, the government permitted distribution of a booklet by former President Eduardo Frei Montalvo that criticized the military regime's social and economic policies.

Foreign Policy Matters. On January 6, the Foreign Ministry published its proposals providing Bolivia with a corridor to the Pacific north of Arica in territory seized from Peru in the 1883 War of the Pacific. In return, Bolivia would have to cede an equal area of territory and make other concessions, and Chile would gain exclusive use of the River Lauca's water, a question which ruptured relations from 1962–1975. In March, Chile and Peru appointed negotiators for talks between those countries because former Peruvian territory is affected.

The U. S. Congress barred the sale of arms to Chile in fiscal 1977. Limited U. S. economic assistance was provided.

Although militantly anticommunist domestically, the Pinochet regime bought antitank rocket launchers from the USSR through a Czechoslovak agency in February. The decision was probably a reaction to Peruvian purchase of Soviet tanks and U. S. armored personnel carriers.

Economics. Prices for Chilean copper, which fluctuated between 53–63 cents a pound in 1975, rose to 66–72 cents in April–October 1976. Copper, which accounted for 76–79% of Chilean exports in 1973–1974, declined to 58.2% of the nation's exports in 1975. Nontraditional exports —such as fruit, lumber, and mutton—increased.

While the inflation rate (340.7% in 1975), one of the world's highest, was reduced to about 210% annually by July 1976, unemployment in Greater Santiago continued to creep upward to an unprecedented 19.1% in August. The country's inflation was also reflected in the decline of the peso.

In October, Chile withdrew from the Andean Pact, a regional economic pact. Chile's action resulted from a dispute with the five other member nations over rules governing foreign investment and import tariffs.

NEALE J. PEARSON, *Texas Tech University*

PHOTOS UPI

Following the death of Mao Tse-tung, a fierce power struggle occurred in China. Hua Kuo-feng was named as Mao's successor; four leftists, including Mao's widow, were arrested, which set off demonstrations of approval.

CHINA

China, the world's most populous nation, remains divided under opposing regimes: the People's Republic of China (Communist China) on the mainland, and the Republic of China (Nationalist China) on the island of Taiwan.

PEOPLE'S REPUBLIC OF CHINA

Chairman Mao Tse-tung's death in September 1976 ended the long era during which he dominated the Chinese Communist party and the nation. A fierce power struggle ensued, resulting in the arrest of Chiang Ch'ing, Mao's widow, and three other leftist leaders. Premier Hua Kuo-feng was appointed chairman of the party, succeeding Mao Tse-tung. He had the support of moderate party bureaucrats and army commanders.

The new leadership called for speedy economic development, as had been advocated by the late Premier Chou En-lai. The policy was expected to stimulate the economy, which had slowed down in 1976. Peking continued to stress struggle against the Soviets and adopt a conciliatory attitude toward the United States.

Mao's Death. Mao Tse-tung, chairman of the Chinese Communist party and supreme leader of the nation, died on Sept. 9, 1976, at the age of 82. Rising to predominance in his party in 1935, he led the Communist revolution to victory and founded the People's Republic in 1949, beginning the Maoist era that ended only with his death. His regime was marked by massive re-

construction as well as violent purges. It brought the country to its feet, ending a century of foreign oppression, and restored it to its traditional place as a great nation.

The chairman had been ill for a long time. He had not appeared in public since 1973, although he continued to receive foreign leaders until June 1976. The official announcement did not specify the nature of his illness, but it was believed that he had long been suffering from Parkinson's disease.

In the statement of September 9 the Central Committee of the party appealed for unity and pledged to carry on "the cause left by Chairman Mao." It called for continued class struggle, the strengthening of the centralized leadership of the party, deepening the criticism of Teng Hsiao-p'ing, and continuation of Mao's revolutionary line and foreign policies.

The government proclaimed an eight-day mourning period, with the last day, September 18, set for a commemorative mass rally to be held in T'ien An Men Square in Peking. It was estimated that during the first seven days 300,000 people, including a large number of foreigners in Peking, paid their respects to the chairman lying in state at the Great Hall of the People; about a million Chinese took part in the rally that ended in a wave of weeping.

There was no designation of Mao's successor as chairman of the party in the statement of September 9. For some time a collective leadership, consisting of radicals and moderates, appeared to be in charge. But the political situation was far from stable. Of the nine-member

Standing Committee of the Politburo, four had died before Mao, including Premier Chou En-lai in January, and Chu Teh, the famed military leader, in July. With Mao's death, the Standing Committee was left with four members, namely, Hua Kuo-feng, the new premier; Wang Hung-wen, the youthful Shanghai leftist; Chang Ch'un-ch'iao, a Cultural Revolution leader; and the 78-year-old Yeh Chien-ying, the minister of defense. Premier Hua Kuo-feng appeared to be the central figure in the transitional leadership. He had been named premier of the State Council and first vice chairman of the Central Committee of the party after the purge of Teng Hsiao-p'ing, the first deputy premier. Teng had been purged during the Cultural Revolution of 1966–69, but was later rehabilitated, largely through the efforts of Premier Chou En-lai. He was then denounced as the chief motivator of the T'ien An Men Square riots on April 5, when 100,000 people gathered to protest the removal of several hundred wreaths placed at the Monument to the People's Heroes to commemorate the late Premier Chou En-lai. According to the official report, the demonstrators "hoisted the ensign supporting Teng Hsiao-p'ing and directed their spearhead at Chairman Mao." The rioters were finally suppressed, and at Mao's proposal the Politburo dismissed Teng Hsiao-p'ing from all posts both inside and outside the party.

Premier Hua Kuo-feng was a relatively little known leader. He had been chief of the Communist party branch in Chairman Mao's home district in Hunan province. He was generally regarded as a moderate and appeared at that time to be a compromise candidate chosen for his lack of strong factional involvement.

Arrest of Leftist Leaders. Factional disputes that had raged up to the eve of Mao's death now took an abrupt turn. On October 6, Chiang Ch'ing, Mao's widow, and three other leftist leaders—Wang Hung-wen, Chang Ch'un-ch'iao, and Yao Wen-yuan, the party's chief propa-

gandist—were arrested. Six days later Peking announced that Premier Hua Kuo-feng had been elected chairman of the Chinese Communist party. He was then acclaimed the leader of the nation at a rally of one million people in Peking on October 24, thus affirming the victory of the moderates over the leftists in the bitter struggle for power.

The arrest of the four leftists was officially confirmed on October 22, when Peking announced that the party Central Committee, under the leadership of Hua Kuo-feng, had "shattered" an attempt by the "anti-party clique" to "usurp party and state power." No details of the leftist "conspiracy" were given, but posters in Peking and other cities accused the four of a wide range of crimes—from planning an armed uprising and conspiring to kill Hua Kuo-feng to forging Mao's documents and disrupting economic progress. Although some provinces demanded severe punishment of the "gang of four," Peking was silent on their fate.

New Leadership. The leadership shake-up put Hua Kuo-feng at the top of the party hierarchy. He was named not only chairman of the party, succeeding Mao Tse-tung, but also chairman of the Military Commission. He was apparently supported by moderate senior party leaders and army commanders.

Among the influential leaders who stood by his side were Li Hsin-nien, a longtime associate of the late Chou En-lai and a deputy premier in charge of economic affairs; Yeh Chien-ying, the defense minister; and Ch'en Hsi-lien, commander of the Peking military region. Peking reported that the new leadership would carry out the program of economic development set forth by the late Premier Chou En-lai—widespread modernization that would bring forth a powerful, modern, socialist China by the end of the 20th century.

Earthquakes. A powerful earthquake struck Peking on July 28, at 3:45 A. M. According to

During the official mourning period, the body of Mao Tse-tung lay in state in the Great Hall of the People. Some 300,000 persons viewed the body. Later it was announced that a mausoleum for the body would be built in Peking.

UPI

Following the dismissal of Teng Hsiao-p'ing, soldiers gathered at the base of the Monument to the People's Heroes in Peking's T'ien An Men Square.

UPI

the U. S. Geological Survey in Golden, Colo., it registered an intensity of 8.2 on the Richter scale, making it the strongest quake in the world since 1964. A series of afterquakes followed, the strongest of which was recorded at 7.9.

The earthquake was centered in Tangshan, an industrial city of one million people about 90 miles (145 km) southeast of Peking. The Chinese government announced that the quake had caused great loss of life and property and that Tangshan in particular suffered "extremely serious damage." No indication of the number of victims was offered, but foreign observers believed that Tangshan was very largely destroyed and that many thousands could have lost their lives in the city. The earthquakes sent Peking's six million people into the streets. They slept in tents and make-shift shelters which lined every street of the capital.

Economy. China's economy showed signs of slowdown in 1976. Preliminary figures for the first half of the year indicated an industrial growth of 7%, compared with an average 10% annual growth in the preceding 15 years. The slowdown was partly attributable to factional quarrels over the policy of economic development. The pragmatists, such as Teng Hsiao-p'ing, emphasized professionalism and modern technology for developing a comprehensive economic system, but the leftists adhered to Chairman Mao's principles of hard work, self-reliance, and mass enthusiasm. As the struggle mounted against Teng Hsiao-p'ing, the economic plans prepared under him necessarily lacked vigorous support for implementation.

Foreign trade registered a decrease in the first half of the year, ending a two-year expansion. Peking canceled all orders for American wheat and corn and cut its purchase of Japanese steel by 75%. Exports of oil to Japan and the Philippines were also reduced.

China's move was attributable to the anti-rightist campaign, which certainly unnerved the economic planners. But bona fide economic factors also played a role. The buying spree during the two previous years, 1974–75, had resulted in a deficit of $730 million in trade with Japan, China's largest partner, and $145 million with the United States. This was incompatible with China's standing policy of maintaining an even balance of trade and Chairman Mao's call for self-reliance rather than purchase of foreign technology. The new emphasis on economic development, however, was expected to change the situation. On October 27 Peking announced resumption of large-scale foreign trade in 1978.

Nixon's Visit. On February 21, after repeated Chinese invitations, former U. S. President Richard Nixon arrived in Peking for a second visit. His first visit in 1972 had initiated contact between the United States and China after 23 years of antagonism. Though no longer president, Nixon was treated as a virtual head of state by the Chinese. He had three long sessions with Premier Hua Kuo-feng and a friendly talk with Chairman Mao Tse-tung. In Peking Nixon supported the Chinese position against Soviet expansionism.

The reasons for Peking's eagerness to have Nixon revisit China were complex. The Chinese were not pleased with the U. S. policy of dé-

— COMMUNIST CHINA • Information Highlights —

Official Name: People's Republic of China.
Location: Central part of eastern Asia.
Area: 3,705,396 square miles (9,596,961 km²).
Population (1976 est.): 836,800,000.
Chief Cities (1974 est.): Peking, the capital, 7,600,000; Shanghai, 10,800,000; Tientsin, 4,000,000.
Government: *Chairman of the Chinese Communist Party,* Hua Kuo-feng (took office Oct. 1976). *Head of government,* Hua Kuo-feng, premier (took office April 1976). *Legislature* (unicameral)—National People's Congress.
Monetary Unit: Yuan (2.00 yuan equal U. S.$1, Nov. 1976).
Gross National Product (1974 est.): $245,000,000,000.
Manufacturing (major products): Iron and steel, machinery, cotton textiles, fertilizers, electronics, pharmaceuticals, instruments, transportation equipment.
Major Agricultural Products: Rice, wheat, sweet potatoes, sorghum, corn, cotton, tobacco, soybeans, barley, tea.
Foreign Trade (1974): *Exports,* $6,300,000,000; *imports,* $7,400,000,000.

New brick housing with roofing of a traditional style is built for fishermen in Hsinghua province.

In a cotton field of a commune in south-central China, plant-protection workers instruct peasants on the advantages of pest control.

"Hsihu," China's major new oil tanker, is launched at a northeastern shipyard in August.

PHOTOS UPI

tente with the Soviet Union, and the continued recognition of Taiwan was a disappointment to them. Bringing in Nixon, the symbol of building a great bridge between the two countries, might impress on the United States the importance of Sino-American relations and make clear to future Chinese leaders Mao's basic policy of normalizing relations with the United States.

U. S. Relations. At a news conference on September 9, Secretary of State Henry A. Kissinger said that he did not think Chairman Mao's death would set back Sino-American relations. He added that the United States for its part would continue to strengthen the ties with Peking in accordance with the Shanghai Communiqué, issued at the end of former President Nixon's visit, which called for normalization of relations.

On October 15 Kissinger further stated that the United States would consider it "a grave matter" if China were threatened by an outside power. This was a strong enunciation of U. S. interest in China's security, and it was intended as a reassurance to the new Chinese leadership. The statement was followed by a Washington announcement that President Ford had approved the sale to Peking of a computer system capable of defense as well as industrial uses.

Soviet Relations. Sino-Soviet relations showed no signs of improvement in 1976. In February Peking reported an armed clash between Chinese militia and Soviet troops along the Sinkiang border in the northwest. The Chinese accused the Soviet troops of intrusions, but Moscow denied any such clash.

On September 14 Peking rejected messages of condolences from the Soviet and East European Communist parties on the death of Chairman Mao. A Chinese spokesman said that the messages were unacceptable because the Chinese Communist party did not have relations with its counterparts in eastern Europe.

China's nuclear test on September 26, only two and a half weeks after Chairman Mao's death, showed that Peking would continue to strengthen its defense against any Soviet military threat. At a UN meeting on October 5, Chinese Foreign Minister Ch'iao Kuan-hua spurned Soviet attempts to normalize relations. He denounced Soviet imperialism as "the biggest peace swindler and the most dangerous source of war today."

Western Europe. Peking intensified its efforts to expand trade in western Europe, welcoming the visits of West German and French officials to hold trade conferences in China. Though actual trade between the two areas was relatively small, Chinese purchase of West European merchandise was clearly on the rise. Special attention was given to West Germany, where the Chinese did not hesitate to mix business with politics. They encouraged Bonn to work for an economic and military union of Europe to balance the Soviet power.

Japan. For some time China has been negotiating a peace treaty with Japan to bring a formal end to World War II. One of the demands made by Peking is that the treaty should include a provision stating that both countries oppose the efforts of any third nation to achieve hegemony in Asia. Asserting that the provision was aimed at the Soviet Union, Moscow in 1976 warned that it would be forced to "reconsider" its relations with Japan if Tokyo acceded to the Chinese demand. Although Japanese Premier Takeo Miki declared on January 13 that Japan would agree to the Chinese request on the subject of "hegemony," Sino-Japanese negotiations showed little progress.

Others. Peking gave Premier Kaysone Phoumvihan of Laos an enthusiastic welcome when he visited China in March; he was received by Chairman Mao. An agreement on economic and technical cooperation was concluded, under which China gave Laos an interest-free loan.

In April Peking agreed to India's proposal that the two countries exchange ambassadors. Since the border dispute in 1961, each had sent the other a chargé d'affaires rather than an ambassador. Peking's efforts to curb Soviet expansion appeared to be a major factor in the shift of its India policy.

Peking signed a military protocol with Egypt on April 21, a month after Cairo abrogated its friendship treaty with the Soviet Union. It was reported that Peking was to supply spare parts to Egypt for its Soviet-make MiG fighters. The conclusion of the treaty was regarded as a significant success for China.

REPUBLIC OF CHINA

Political stability continued to prevail in Taiwan, and the government was becoming less remote to the people. It maintained adequate economic growth, despite slow world economic recovery. The Nationalists showed uneasiness over relations with the United States as the American presidential election drew near. They were afraid that the United States might normalize relations with Peking and sever its ties with Taiwan.

Throughout the year Taipei made extensive efforts to promote trade with countries with which it had no diplomatic relations.

Government. The continued political stability in the Republic of China was attributed to sophisticated control, positive leadership, and economic progress which furnished the average citizen a rising income and a better standard of living. Corruption was eliminated at high levels; top officials worked hard and lived modestly. Under Premier Chiang Ching-kuo the government was far less remote than before; the premier frequently went out to meet people in an informal way, making a point of talking to the peasants and the country folks.

A partial reshuffle of the cabinet was ordered on June 9. Chang Feng-shu, former mayor of Taipei, was named minister of the interior; Walter H. Fei, former secretary general of the Executive Yuan, was appointed minister of finance; Wang Tao-yuan, former vice minister of justice, was promoted to be minister of justice; and Lin Chin-sheng, former interior minister, became minister of communications.

Economy. Taiwan was subject to considerable pressure from the world recession, but it managed to maintain adequate economic stability. Taiwan's economic growth was expected to reach 10% in 1976. The optimistic estimate was based on the speedy recovery in many countries and the stimulation provided by the major construction projects under implementation. In the program approved by the Ministry of Economic Affairs for fiscal 1977 (which started on July 1, 1976) emphasis was laid on price stability, pro-

---

—NATIONALIST CHINA • Information Highlights—

Official Name: Republic of China.
Location: Taiwan, island off the southeastern coast of mainland China.
Area: 13,885 square miles (35,961 km²).
Population (1976 est.): 16,300,000.
Chief Cities (1974 est.): Taipei, the capital, 1,900,000; Haohsiung, 784,502; Taichung, 428,426.
Government: *Head of state,* Yen Chia-kan, president (installed April 1975). *Head of government,* Chiang Ching-kuo, premier (took office May 1972). *Legislature* (unicameral)—Legislative Yuan.
Monetary Unit: New Taiwan dollar (36.36 NT dollars equal U. S.$1, Nov. 1976).
Gross National Product (1975 est.): $16,100,000,000.
Manufacturing (major products): Petroleum products, processed foods, textiles, electrical machinery, electronics, chemicals, apparel.
Major Agricultural Products: Sugarcane, bananas, mushrooms, pineapples, rice, tea, vegetables.
Foreign Trade (1974): *Exports,* $5,530,000,000; *imports,* $7,000,000,000.

motion of rural reconstruction, development of the heavy and chemical industries, and expansion of the transportation and communication systems. The Nationalist Chinese government expected that in six years Taiwan would become a developed nation.

Taiwan's foreign trade during the first half of 1976 increased 38.8% over the same period of 1975. It registered a favorable trade balance of $125.7 million in the six months, compared with a deficit of $277.9 million for the same period of 1975. Efforts to reduce imports from Japan continued but were not very successful. On the other hand, Taiwan's exports to the United States in the first half of the year reached $1,324,000,000, an all-time high that provided a favorable trade balance of $493 million. Among the exports, agricultural products made up 5.2%, processed agricultural products 7.8%, and industrial products 87%. Among the imports, capital goods aggregated 31.4%, raw materials 62%, and consumer goods 6.6%. Textiles remained the nation's leading export, amounting to $1,158,000,000, an increase of 68.5% over the 1975 figure.

Extensive efforts were made to expand trade with countries that did not recognize Nationalist China. Special attention was given to international exhibitions, which local manufacturers were given official assistance to attend. Nationalist manufacturers thus took part in trade exhibitions held in the United States, West Germany, and France.

Foreign Relations. As the American presidential election drew near, Taiwan showed growing uneasiness over its ties with the United States. Officials and businessmen felt that after the election the United States would seek to normalize relations with Communist China. Since Peking insisted on a one-China formula, Washington might have to sever diplomatic relations with Taiwan. If that should happen, it would be impossible for the United States to maintain its security treaty with and defense commitments to Nationalist China. And Taiwan's trade with the United States, its largest partner, might be adversely affected, even though some kind of trade relations would continue. All of these various factors could seriously impair Taiwan's security and economic growth.

Those who were more optimistic, however, did not think that the situation was so hopeless. They pointed out that President-elect Jimmy Carter had said that he would be reluctant to give up relationship with Taiwan without assurances that it would be free of military pressure or domination from mainland China.

On August 29 the Nationalist government denied American reports that Taiwan had been reprocessing spent uranium fuel for possible use in producing nuclear weapons. Earlier, Premier Chiang Ching-kuo had stated that it would be unthinkable to use such weapons against the Communist Chinese because of the loss of life to his countrymen on the mainland.

Canada's threat to ban Taiwan from the Olympic Games touched off a strong American protest. Apparently under pressure from Peking, the Canadian government in July announced that it would not allow the Taiwanese team to enter Canada under the name of the Republic of China, to display its Nationalist flag, or to play its anthem. The U. S. Olympic Committee then threatened to pull its athletes out of the games if Canada did not reconsider its decision. The Canadian government finally modified its stand and proposed to allow Taiwan to participate with its own flag and anthem on the condition that its athletes did not call themselves representatives of the Republic of China. The U. S. Olympic Committee accepted this modification, but the Nationalist government decided to withdraw from the games.

The Republic of China strengthened its relations with Saudi Arabia in March when Dr. Mahsoun Bahjat Jalal, director of the Saudi Fund for Development, signed an agreement to provide Taiwan with a low-interest loan of $50 million to finance the construction of highways. He also announced that another loan of $30 million would be made for railway electrification on the island. Saudi Arabia pledged to continue its supply to Taiwan of crude oil. In return, the Nationalist Chinese government agreed to send technicians to assist Saudi Arabia with its economic modernization, particularly urban and rural electrification and improvement of railway and harbor systems.

See also BIOGRAPHY: Hua Kuo-feng; OBITUARIES: Chou En-lai and Mao Tse-tung.

CHESTER C. TAN
New York University

Taiwanese track star Chi Cheng, a bronze medalist in 1968, reads of the Olympic Committee's decision to go along with Canada and ban Taiwan from the games.

UPI

Renaissance Center, Detroit's $337-million, publicly financed development, consisting of office buildings, a hotel, and stores, nears completion.

UPI

CITIES AND URBAN AFFAIRS

Unfavorable events and trends have a way of attracting attention and making news. In 1976, the cities made news when fiscal problems caused lay-offs of municipal workers, or encouraged strikes by them, and when violent gangs of youthful thugs terrorized innocent citizens in the streets.

Such news does not tell the whole story of the cities, however. Every year, cities show their resiliency and ability to address and solve problems. The difficulties may vary somewhat from year to year, but the problems of one city are never vastly different from those of others. Each has to make certain, by means of an adequate tax base, that it can pay for services and that the services provided will ensure adequate safety, transportation, and welfare for its citizens. Put somewhat simplistically: when a city fails to provide services or cannot pay for them, it is most likely to attract attention.

Financial Problems. Financial troubles continued to head the list of notable urban problems in 1976. A report released by the U. S. Conference of Mayors in June revealed that of 136 surveyed communities, with populations exceeding 30,000, only 21 did not cite financial plight. In the extreme, the City of Monroe, La., became the first U. S. city in six years to default on its

payroll; only an emergency federal grant saved the city. As complex as the urban financial condition is, solutions to the problem can be lumped into two broad categories—increasing revenues and decreasing expenditures. A number of events emphasized that fact.

Labor problems hit many cities as wage and benefit demands of workers placed local budgets in precarious positions. Policemen and firemen struck in Youngstown, Ohio, over pay demands while the "blue flu," a malady common to disgruntled policemen, plagued New Orleans. The issue there was holiday overtime pay.

With the beginning of the school year, more than 20,000 teachers in 11 states went on strike. School children from Manchester, N. H., to Seattle, Wash. were affected. Sixteen municipal hospitals in New York City suffered a walkout by 18,000 workers. Garbage collectors in Philadelphia, Pa., Raleigh, N. C., and Chattanooga, Tenn., interrupted service by striking.

City governments almost stopped adding to their work forces. The U. S. Census Bureau reported that municipal employment grew by the smallest percentage (0.6%) in 14 years. Still, the payrolls for workers employed by city governments grew.

In New Jersey, budgetary increases by local governments were limited by a state law signed by Gov. Brendan Byrne.

A tramway transports residents of the new community of Roosevelt Island, Queens, N.Y., to Manhattan.

Local governments, particularly those of larger cities, stressed productivity—getting better results with the same or fewer resources. This solution appealed to politicians and taxpayers alike. But achieving it proved difficult. A National Center for Productivity and Work Quality was established for that end.

The business community took a significant step when the Business Roundtable, a group of top corporation executives, urged their colleagues to take part in the solution of urban problems. This could be achieved, they claimed, by investment within cities, lobbying for urban legislation, and promoting better, more productive management practices.

New York City, which had spent most of 1975 trying to save itself from financial ruin, in 1976 made progress toward financial reform. The city continued to receive federal loans, while the U. S. Treasury Department monitored the city's implementation of the financial reforms which were a condition for receiving the loans. The city's audit for the most recent financial year, released in late October, revealed that New York's budgetary deficit, while still nearly $1,-000,000,000, was $83 million less than had been anticipated. Still, the fact that the city was having increasing difficulty keeping up with the three-year schedule for balancing its budget indicated that the remaining period of budget-cutting would be tougher. To make matters still worse, a court of appeals ruled in November that the moratorium on the city's short-term notes, one of the cornerstones of its recovery plan, was unconstitutional. A congressional report claimed that the Ford Administration's handling of New York City's fiscal crisis had cost the nation's cities more than $1,000,000,000 in higher borrowing costs. Administration officials denied this.

Federal Actions. The federal government continued to have a major effect on the state of the cities and the ability of their governments to deliver services. The fight by city, county, and state governments to achieve renewal of the federal revenue-sharing program ended successfully in October when a 3¾-year extension was signed into law. The program will continue to distribute federal tax money to eligible governments according to their relative tax effort, population, and per capita income. Few changes resulted from congressional deliberations over the extension. Those that were made were designed primarily to assuage critics of the program, who had alleged, with some justification, that citizens did not have much say in how revenue-sharing funds were to be spent and that civil-rights violations were not adequately investigated or eliminated by the federal agency responsible.

The effort to achieve passage of a program to alleviate recessionary pressures on state and local governments was not so smooth. The concept—that the federal government should distribute funds to jurisdictions with high unemployment rates because they were subject to reduced tax collections and consequent cutbacks in services—twice met with a presidential veto. The second veto was overridden by Congress, however, and the promise of even more tax money for facility construction and maintenance of basic services was good for another year, until September, 1977.

Despite substantial criticism of the record of the federal law enforcement assistance program which has provided grant funds to local police agencies for service improvement for eight years, Congress passed a comprehensive three-year extension of the legislation, ensuring federal support for this local function.

Another significant action of Congress extended for one year the public service jobs program established to hire unemployed persons as staff for city and county governments.

In the presidential election campaign, urban issues appeared to take a back seat to economic ones. Some observers blamed this inattention on the fact that the problem of the cities was too complicated to address. The U. S. Conference of Mayors claimed that a unified national urban policy was necessary to replace the inadvertent one that they alleged had existed since the end of World War II. A special post-election meeting of the big-city mayors was held to develop an urban agenda for the incoming Carter administration. The mayors named stimulating employment and stemming emigration from the cities as major issues.

On June 24, the U. S. Supreme Court issued a decision on a challenge by the National League of Cities and other groups to the 1974 amendments to the Fair Labor Standards Act. A 5-4 majority held that the amendments, which extended the minimum wage and hour requirements of the act to the employees of state and local governments, were unconstitutional.

The opinion was significant for several reasons. First, it rewarded an effort by subnational governments to contest federal authority. Second, it bore strongly against the attempt by the federal government to extend requirements for collective bargaining to state and local governments.

Another Supreme Court decision affected cities, although it was not immediately clear how extensively. The court upheld the power of municipalities to require certain public workers to live within the city limits. Many observers felt the decisions of the Supreme Court expressed the independence of state and local governments from federal regulation. Several appeals to the high court asked that the actions of local governments be ruled invalid. In many of the cases, however, the opposite rulings were achieved.

Crime and Violence. The crime problem got worse. Data released by the Federal Bureau of Investigation cited a 9% nationwide rise in crime. However, the increases in rural areas and suburbs exceeded those in inner cities. Only one reported crime in five ended in an arrest. Jobless inner-city youth were cited as a particularly troublesome group. Of those arrested, 45% were under 25. The availability of firearms continued to be a source of concern as two thirds of all murders were committed with firearms and more than half with handguns.

Crime, however, was not the only trouble the police had. A national study revealed that physical fitness among police officers was a problem, and that only 14% of the local law enforcement agencies surveyed had a program to assure personnel fitness.

One city where downtown violence was notable was Detroit. Budget problems forced the city to lay off 450 of its police, but after gangs of hoodlums terrorized and vandalized the inner city, the police were called back in an attempt to get the situation under control. The city government also passed a 10:00 p. m. curfew ordinance for youths under 18.

Bizarre occurrences happened in cities, too. In Philadelphia, a tape-recorded message found in City Hall threatened that 1,000 gallons of oil would be dumped into the city's water supply unless the city paid $1 million. In Baltimore, an irate citizen stormed into city council offices and shot several officials. A city councilman was killed.

Race Relations. Boston, which entered its third year of court-ordered busing to achieve racial integration, endured less violence than in previous years, and school attendance figures rose after the jitters of the first few days of the new school year. In Omaha, Nebr., and Dallas,

Texas, extensive public media campaigns emphasized that court-ordered busing in those cities was the law and that citizens would do themselves and their city a favor by exerting every effort to make the busing plans work.

A court in Chicago took under consideration a case involving the zoning policies of the village of Arlington Heights, Ill. It was alleged that its zoning laws excluded blacks.

Bicentennial. The nation's bicentennial was marked in most cities. The celebrations brought people together in vast numbers, although some cities did not have as many as anticipated. Washington, D. C., for example, did not have nearly so many visitors as expected, apparently because some would-be tourists stayed closer to home to avoid the crowds. In other cities, the gatherings were large and exuberant. Some 400,000 went to hear a 4th of July hometown concert by the Boston Pops, while thousands of others crowded the shores of New York Harbor to see the hundreds of sailing "Tall Ships" honor the nation's birthday.

City Politics. City politics, as usual, had its share of controversial happenings. Philadelphia's Mayor Frank Rizzo spent much of the year struggling to avoid recall. A petition urging such action circulated during the summer and received 122,000 signatures, but the City Commission rejected many of these as invalid.

ROBERT M. LLOYD
South Carolina
Appalachian Council of Governments

City workers in San Francisco were on strike in March. Urban labor problems were common in 1976.

UPI

Supporters of the federal equal rights amendment staged a rally at the Illinois State Capitol in May.

UPI

CIVIL LIBERTIES AND CIVIL RIGHTS

Since Earl Warren left the U. S. Supreme Court, civil libertarians have maintained an apprehensive watch on the national judiciary. Would the Nixon appointees undertake a constitutional revolution, or would the Burger court perpetuate its predecessor's major rulings? With the departure of William O. Douglas in late 1975, there was no doubt that conservatism was ascendant on the supreme tribunal. Yet, tallying the line-up of judges from case to case, the analyst would conclude that here was a court of nine individuals rather than two blocs of partisans. The court in 1976 did, however, enunciate some themes: restricting the rights of criminal defendants, reinforcing states' rights, refusing to expand privacy rights, and curtailing access to the federal courts. Whereas the Warren bench gave citizens enlarged standing to challenge a range of national and state statutes, the Burger panel decreed that federal courts should only prevent local officials from violating the constitution when there are "extraordinary circumstances."

Defendant's Rights. In 1972, in a 5–4 ruling, the court declared that the death penalty contained in laws then on the books gave too much discretion to judges and juries. The majority, though, did not rule that capital punishment was constitutionally forbidden as cruel and unusual. In the aftermath, 35 states and the federal gov-

ernment reenacted the death penalty. In 1976 the Supreme Court (7–2) upheld the death penalty in some cases, where it was not mandatory and where standards were provided for the penalty's imposition. However, in a companion ruling (5–4), the court struck down measures which did not call for judges and juries to consider specific circumstances before deciding the penalty. Inasmuch as the 1976 cases dealt with capital punishment for murder, opponents took some hope in the possibility that subsequent cases could rule out death as a penalty for such crimes as arson and rape.

In another set of cases, the majority modified the exclusionary rule, the "law and order" justices refusing to bar from use in trials evidence damaging to defendants even though the data were improperly obtained.

Though civil libertarians had their setbacks before the nation's highest tribunal, they chalked up victories elsewhere. The effort in the U. S. Senate to put through a federal criminal code (S.1), containing numerous statist features, was stymied. In Alabama a federal district court judge issued an unprecedented order, listing in detail minimum constitutional standards for state prisons. Within all branches of the government and in the press, attention was directed to uncovering, punishing, and preventing unconstitutional excesses by the Central Intelligence Agency, the Federal Bureau of Investigation, and the rest of the federal intelligence apparatus.

Civil Rights. The record of the Supreme Court on matters of racial discrimination was mixed. It refused to overturn the federal district court order that led to the busing of 26,000 Boston pupils. However, it also ruled that school boards were not required to revise their busing plans annually to keep up with changing racial patterns and thereby prevent black majority schools.

The nation's highest court also decided that private schools could not refuse to admit black children because of their race, that blacks who had been denied jobs in violation of the Civil Rights Act of 1965 must be given retroactive seniority once they succeeded in getting those jobs, that white workers were as fully protected from racial discrimination on the job as black workers, and that the judiciary could require federally subsidized public housing in the suburbs in order to relieve racial segregation within the cities if the government had contributed to the segregation.

Though the Equal Rights Amendment was still four states short of ratification, a number of federal and state legislative, executive, and judicial policies were adopted to bring about equal treatment of women.

First Amendment. In 1971, Chief Justice Warren Burger wrote that "The line of separation [of church and state], far from being a 'wall,' is a blurred, indistinct and variable barrier depending on all the circumstances of a particular relationship." This fuzziness was exemplified in a 5–4 decision (*Roemer* v. *Maryland Board of Public Works*) which allowed church-related colleges to be included in a Maryland program of subsidies for higher education. In another church-state case, a three-judge federal court voided a New York state law that provided aid to nonpublic schools for the costs of administering state-required paperwork.

The Supreme Court struck down a court order barring the Nebraska press from reporting testimony heard in open court in a sensational murder case, limited the protection of the press against libel suits, overruled parts of the new campaign financing law on the ground that the regulations restricted First Amendment rights, and upheld the use of zoning to restrict proliferation of movie theaters that show sexually explicit movies. In 1976 Chicago became the first major American city to prohibit persons under 18 from seeing films containing scenes of "harmful" violence.

Sexual Conduct. A constitutional amendment to ban abortions was tabled in the Senate. The Supreme Court, in its first major decision on the subject since 1973, ruled that states may not require a woman to obtain the consent of her husband, or a girl under 18 to receive permission from a parent, to get an abortion.

Without hearing oral arguments or issuing an opinion, the Supreme Court affirmed that states could prosecute consenting adults for private homosexual conduct.

Government Workers. Public employees had a difficult year. Though the Supreme Court ruled that they could not be fired just because they belonged to the party out of power, other decisions went against them. The courts ruled that their municipal employers could require them to live within the cities, that the Fair Labor Standards Act did not apply to nonfederal public employees, that employers could set standards for personal grooming, and that public employees had no property or constitutional rights to a job or to an impartial hearing unless those rights were agreed to in a union contract.

The Economic Crisis. Although the economy was recovering, 1976, for racial and other minorities, and women, was a year during which their needs were on the back burner of benign neglect. Affirmative action programs were at best slowing down the process of hiring those who had previously been favored. Cutbacks of social services by financially troubled cities and states left the poor and unemployed the victims of retrenchment, confronting daily denials of due process and equal rights in Medicare, food stamp, and welfare programs.

MARTIN GRUBERG
University of Wisconsin, Oshkosh

COINS AND COIN COLLECTING

The year was an exciting one in numismatics. By 1976 the bicentennial designs, released for the U. S. quarter, half dollar, and silver dollar in 1975, were a common sight. The special designs are to be discontinued in 1977.

Sets of specially minted proof coins featuring the cent, nickel, and a special 1776–1976 design for the quarter, half dollar, and silver dollar were offered for sale to collectors. By March the orders totaled a record 4,100,000 sets—the largest number of proof sets ordered in U. S. Mint history. A wide array of numismatic souvenirs was distributed for the bicentennial observation. Considerable controversy resulted when an official gold medal was issued for $4,000. Bronze and silver strikings were available at much lower prices, however.

On April 13, 1976, a new $2 note, a denomination which had been discontinued, appeared. The note has a special reverse design by John Trumbull. In an unprecedented arrangement, the U. S. Post Office offered first-day-of-issue cancellations for the $2 note. Additional special cancellations were offered by post offices on July 4th. By year-end the $2 bills were more of a novelty than an actual currency instrument. In September the U. S. Mint revealed that a modification of the silver dollar was being designed, perhaps to a new small size format slightly larger than a quarter. It was believed that a small-size silver dollar would be of greater

UPI

A 100 billion mark note, highest denomination note issued in Germany during the chronic inflation of the 1920's, was auctioned in April in London.

use. The three U. S. operating mints—Philadelphia, Denver, and San Francisco—produced more than 14,000,000,000 coins in 1975, of which 74% were of the one cent denomination.

In February, Louis Eliasberg, 80, owner of the most comprehensive collection of U. S. coins ever formed, died. Later the Eliasberg Collection was put on special loan exhibition for the bicentennial at the Philadelphia Mint.

World Coins. In January the Netherlands Antilles issued its first gold coin with motifs to salute the U. S. bicentennial. In February the Bahamas released one of the most expensive new issues ever produced, a $2,500 gold coin containing 12 ounces of the precious metal.

Israel announced the release of a special 1976 25 lirot independence day commemorative issue and a medal honoring the Entebbe rescue.

The Olympics in Montreal furnished the occasion for the climax of a series of special commemorative coins. Struck in silver and in the $5 and $10 denominations, over $300 million of these coins were sold. The Canadian government also announced that a special $100 face value Olympics gold coin would be struck. The Royal Canadian Mint inaugurated its new facility in Winnipeg. In June the highest price ever realized for a Canadian coin was set when the McKay-Clements specimen of the extremely rare 1911 Canadian silver dollar pattern was sold at auction for $110,000.

Q. DAVID BOWERS, *Columnist, "Coin World"*

COLOMBIA

Events in Colombia in 1976 followed much the same pattern as in the past few years—gains for the economy, coupled with a high rate of inflation; a continuation of urban and rural violence, as well as infighting among the Liberal and Conservative elites; and growing disenchantment with political institutions.

Politics. August marked the mid-point in Liberal President López Michelsen's four-year term of office. López could point to some real achievements, especially during the first months of 1976. His government had instituted many of the reforms promised at his inauguration, such as lowering the voting age to 18, legalizing divorce for persons married in civil ceremonies, and making 51% Colombian ownership of banks mandatory. By midyear, labor and student unrest, which racked the country from February through April, had tapered off, so he could lift the state of siege he had imposed during the previous year. And tax reform measures, which he instituted in 1975, had resulted in an increase of 60% in direct tax revenues, while reducing taxes for most taxpayers.

López was unable, however, to bring an end to the endemic urban and rural violence. In August new student riots in major cities, coupled with a renewed rash of bombings in Bogotá, testified that civil peace was still a long way off.

In departmental and municipal elections in April, the Liberal and Conservative parties swept more than 90% of the vote, the remainder divided among three opposition parties. Fully 76% of the qualified voters, however, failed to cast their ballots. To most observers, this indicated a massive disillusionment with the workings of the political system. In addition, the factionalism which has long plagued the Liberal party was again manifest in the elections. Candidates favoring President López received about 19% of the vote, those favoring former Foreign Minister Cesar Turbay Ayala captured 29%, while candidates supporting former President Carlos Lleras Restrepo won 21%. Both Turbay and Lleras are already vying for the Liberal nomination for the presidency in 1978. Allegations that President López was a virtual prisoner of military men and rightists in his administration were softened somewhat in early September, when Cornelio Reyes, the hard-line interior minister, resigned. Other reshuffling of army and police personnel indicated that López was moving to place his own people in important posts.

Economy. Inflation remained a major problem. The government had predicted a 15% rise in the consumer price index during 1976, but by midyear it had already risen by 17.5%. The fact that during 1976 Colombia became a net importer of petroleum for the first time only increased the country's economic woes. A new pricing policy adopted in May tended to ameliorate some of the effects but also resulted in a complete stoppage of prospecting in the country. On the bright side, higher world prices for coffee, Colombia's major export, produced a trade surplus of more than $70,000,000,000, and the Colombian economy grew at an adjusted estimated rate of some 6% during 1976.

So-called minor exports also increased by more than 20%. The growth in export earnings brought about some relaxation of Colombia's import restrictions. Although there were no tariff reductions, many administrative controls on imports were eliminated.

ERNEST A. DUFF
Randolph-Macon Woman's College

─────── **COLOMBIA · Information Highlights** ───────

Official Name: Republic of Colombia.
Location: Northwest South America.
Area: 439,736 square miles (1,138,914 km²).
Population (1976 est.): 23,000,000.
Chief Cities (1975 est.): Bogotá, the capital, 2,800,000; Medellín, 1,100,000; Cali, 920,000.
Government: *Head of state and government,* Alfonso López Michelsen, president (took office Aug. 1974). *Legislature*—Congress: Senate and Chamber of Representatives.
Monetary Unit: Peso (34.84 pesos equal U. S.$1, June 1976).
Gross National Product (1975 est.): $13,400,000,000.
Manufacturing (major products): Textiles, beverages, iron and steel, petroleum products.
Major Agricultural Products: Coffee, bananas, rice, cotton, sugarcane, tobacco, potatoes, corn.
Foreign Trade (1975): *Exports,* $1,358,000,000; *imports,* $1,558,000,000.

COLORADO

The Colorado elections received national attention as voters crushed efforts to repeal the state Equal Rights Amendment (ERA), restrict nuclear power, and virtually prohibit tax increases. Proposals to abolish the state sales tax on groceries and require a nickel deposit on beverage containers were also defeated.

Other Election Results. Republicans, who had controlled the state Senate, kept their edge and won back control of the previously Democratic state House. Democrats salvaged their existing 3–2 margin in the congressional delegation.

The state ERA, originally passed in 1972, won a 61% approval on its second test. Women's leaders said the vote would spur efforts to add such an amendment to the U. S. Constitution. The defeat of the nuclear power and bottle deposit initiatives was a further sign of weakening in Colorado's once-powerful environmental lobby. Industry groups spent nearly $1 million—a state record—to oppose the two plans.

The tax limitation plan had key backing from the John Birch Society. It would have required a majority of the total registered electorate to approve any increase in taxes or fees. Under such a plan, registered voters who stayed home would be automatically counted as "no" votes. A coalition of governmental groups and employee organizations said such a restriction would "paralyze" Colorado and trounced it 3–1. Voters gave a narrow approval for a state sweepstakes, but that measure may face a court test.

Governor's Troubles. The defeat of the food sales-tax repeal, by a 3–2 margin, was a major setback for Democratic Gov. Richard D. Lamm. The issue had been Lamm's top priority, and he backed a citizen initiative to bypass the Republican Senate to put it on the ballot. The once-popular governor had faced rising political troubles all year. Criticism of Lamm reached a crescendo when he addressed a group of seated journalism executives and said—within range of a microphone—"I want them to stand up, god-dammit!" The governor later apologized, but Republicans gleefully seized on the faux pas, calling it a sign of arrogance.

Arts and Leisure. Construction began on the Denver Center for the Performing Arts, which eventually will consist of seven structures worth $80 million. The project is funded by city and private monies. Leisure activities expanded. The Spurs of the World Hockey League folded, but Denver's new 17,000-seat sports arena found a new tenant in the National Hockey League Rockies. The Denver Nuggets of the now-defunct American Basketball Association became a thriving expansion club in the more prestigious National Basketball Association.

Miscellany. Conservative Coloradans were upset when four homosexual couples took out marriage licenses. But Atty. Gen. J. D. Mac-Farlane ruled that such marriages have no legal standing in the state. A series on governmental corruption in Trinidad by Denver *Post* reporters Norman Udevitz and Jay Whearley sparked a grand jury investigation and indictments of several local officials.

Population shifts continued to the crowded suburban ring around Denver. The suburban Jefferson County schools attracted so many young families that their students outnumbered Denver, though the city's total population is twice as large. The growth strained schools throughout the suburban ring. It combined with tax assessment problems to bring persistent calls for reform of the state's school-finance act.

BOB EWEGEN, *The Denver "Post"*

────── **COLORADO · Information Highlights** ──────

Area: 104,247 square miles (270,000 km²).
Population (1975 est.): 2,534,000.
Chief Cities (1970 census): Denver, the capital, 514,678; Colorado Springs, 135,060; Pueblo, 97,453.
Government (1976): *Chief Officers*—governor, Richard D. Lamm (D); lt. gov., George L. Brown (D). *General Assembly*—Senate, 35 members; House of Representatives, 65 members.
Education (1975–76): *Enrollment*—public elementary schools, 302,216 pupils; public secondary, 266,912; nonpublic (1976–77), 40,600; colleges and universities, 130,275 students. *Public school expenditures,* $750,000,000 ($1,361 per pupil).
State Finances (fiscal year 1975): *Revenues,* $1,863,-502,000; *expenditures,* $1,740,582,000.
Personal Income (1975): $15,168,000,000; per capita, $5,985.
Labor Force (July 1976): *Nonagricultural wage and salary earners,* 985,300; *insured unemployed,* 21,100 (2.9%).

UPI

In Loveland, Colo., rescue workers aid victims stranded by floods of the Big Thompson River. One hundred and thirty-nine persons lost their lives in the midsummer disaster.

UPI

Connecticut state employees protest a proposed bill that would extend their workweek from 35 to 40 hours.

CONNECTICUT

Cities beset by fiscal problems, low-income and minority housing, pollution, refuse disposal, and debate over Sunday store hours marked the year in Connecticut. Reduced state aid forced local tax increases. A federal court ordered redevelopment funds for eight Hartford suburbs held up for not providing low-cost housing.

Many towns faced refuse disposal crises, and construction design was begun for the first regional resources recovery and recycling facility in Bridgeport. Thames River dredging was halted for a pollution study, and a 9,000-job producing development at the mouth of the Housatonic River awaited a decision on its environmental impact.

The state's 300-year-old Blue Laws were relaxed by the legislature and in an October court decision they were declared unconstitutional, resulting in many stores opening on Sunday.

Economy. In January, a predicted $80 million budget deficit led Gov. Ella Grasso to lay off 500 state employees and tighten spending. But at the end of fiscal 1976 the state had a $34.7 million surplus. Increased collections from the 7% sales tax and from capital gains and dividends taxes helped create the surplus.

Connecticut ranked third in the nation in per capita income. There were 1,224,440 employed, 16,560 above the 1975 period, but the number of unemployed was 143,000 or 9.5% of the labor force, 2% higher than the national average.

In certain industrial areas unemployment was higher.

Legislature. The General Assembly enacted a $1,800,000,000 budget for fiscal 1976–77, a 7% increase over the previous year without significant new taxation. The only tax increase was for gasoline—from 10 to 11 cents per gallon. The legislature halved the 7% tax levies on business services and on machinery and equipment purchases.

The legislators failed to pass the governor's requested increase in the workweek of state employees from 35 to 40 hours, or to liquidate a special $29 million veterans' fund. The governor vetoed a bill lowering the penalty for possession of marijuana since it made no distinction for the amount possessed.

Elections. Although registered Democrats outnumbered Republicans, President Ford won Connecticut's eight electoral votes by a 71,000-vote plurality. Republican Lowell P. Weicker won reelection to the Senate, defeating Gloria Schaffer by 217,000 votes. All six incumbent representatives were reelected.

Republicans gained 31 more seats than they held in the 1976 General Assembly. The 1977 legislature will have 22 Democrats and 14 Republicans in the Senate and 93 Democrats and 58 Republicans in the House.

Abortion. Federal district courts struck down a law empowering the state to veto abortions for state wards under 18 and banned the withholding of Medicaid funds for welfare recipients' abortions.

Gambling. The state's first jai ali frontons opened in Hartford and Bridgeport. Off-track betting parlors opened throughout Connecticut in April. The state's semiannual, weekly, and new daily lottery brought annual revenue expectations to $70 million.

People and Events. Queen Elizabeth II and Prince Philip paid a bicentennial visit to New Haven in July. The 159-year-old Hartford *Times,* once Connecticut's largest newspaper, ceased publication on October 20.

GEORGE ADAMS
Formerly, Connecticut State Library

—— **CONNECTICUT · Information Highlights** ——

Area: 5,009 square miles (12,973 km²).
Population (1975 est.): 3,095,000.
Chief Cities (1970 census): Hartford, the capital, 158,-017; Bridgeport, 156,542; New Haven, 137,707.
Government (1976): *Chief Officers*—governor, Ella T. Grasso (D); lt. gov., Robert K. Killian (D). *General Assembly*—Senate, 36 members; House of Representatives, 151 members.
Education (1975–76): *Enrollment*—public elementary schools, 403,494 pupils; public secondary, 248,955; nonpublic (1976–77), 98,900; colleges and universities, 145,053 students. *Public school expenditures,* $1,002,479,000 ($1,540 per pupil).
State Finances (fiscal year 1975): *Revenues,* $1,972,-518,000; *expenditures,* $2,283,697,000.
Personal Income (1975): $21,584,000,000; per capita, $6,973.
Labor Force (July 1976): *Nonagricultural wage and salary earners,* 1,230,300; *insured unemployed,* 74,-100 (6.4%).

CONSUMERISM

Consumerism in the United States was a modest movement during 1976 compared with the activity in the consumer field of recent years. Inflation, even though somewhat slowed down, continued to be the major concern of consumers. Prices increased about 6% during 1976.

The Presidential Campaign. There were sharp differences between the consumer programs of presidential candidates Gerald Ford and Jimmy Carter. A major dispute centered on the Agency for Consumer Advocacy (ACA) bill, which had passed both the House and the Senate. Because President Ford promised to veto the bill, its sponsors decided not to send it to the President, but to reintroduce it into Congress in 1977. Instead of supporting the ACA bill, the President sent a memorandum to each of the 17 executive departments and agencies instructing them to appoint a consumer affairs advisor and establish procedures to handle consumer inquiries and complaints within each office.

Legislative Action. With the repeal of the "fair trade" (resale price maintenance) law in 1976, manufacturers no longer are allowed to fix retail prices. It has been established that this repeal measure could save consumers more than $2 billion a year through discount prices.

Legislation was passed giving the Food and Drug Administration the authority for the first time to regulate medical devices such as hearing aids, contact lenses, and heart pacemakers.

The passage of the Toxic Substances Act gave the government authority to require certain chemicals to be tested for safety before they are put on the market. An amendment to the antitrust law permits state attorneys general to sue on behalf of the general public for violations of antitrust laws and collect damages three times actual amounts involved.

The legislative charter of the Consumer Product Safety Commission was revised to strengthen the agency's legal powers. The commission was empowered to seek immediate injunctions to block the sale of hazardous products and to engage directly in legal proceedings, rather than work through the Justice Department.

Federal Trade Commission. As a result of many consumer complaints, FTC regulations now require that mail-order firms must either deliver goods on time or allow consumers to cancel their orders. The regulations placed the burden for late or nondelivery on the mail-order industry.

A new FTC regulation restricted the use of the holder-in-due-course provision in consumer credit transactions. Basically, the regulation made a third party to a credit transaction, such as a bank, which becomes a "holder-in-due-course" when it buys the contract from a creditor, liable to fulfill the contract terms if the original seller of the goods or services does not fulfill the agreement.

U. S. Supreme Court. The Court ruled that states may not prevent pharmacists from advertising the prices of prescription drugs. It ruled that advertising in general—even when it is "purely commercial," with the sole purpose of offering a product for sale—is entitled to at least some protection under the First Amendment's guarantee of freedom of speech.

U. S. Department of Agriculture. The USDA issued a regulation requiring that all new standards and revised standards established for fruits and vegetables must be labeled "Fancy," "No. 1," "No. 2," and "No. 3." This should gradually bring about a standardization in grade terminology, which had been almost meaningless in the past. For example, a grade designation such as "U. S. No. 1" had been used for the top grade, the second grade, and in some cases for the third grade in certain categories of fruits and vegetables.

Item Pricing. A major battle was brewing in 1976 between consumer advocates and supermarkets over the gradual introduction of electronic scanning checkout counters. With the use of these scanners, it is not necessary to have the price marked on each item. The supermarket industry contends that this would save money, while consumer advocates argue that this would take away a very basic right. The industry argues that if the price were on the shelf there would be no need for it to be marked on each package, while consumer advocates hold that it is essential to have the price marked on each item. Bills were introduced in many state legislatures and in Congress to require item pricing, but the pressure for this legislation eased when the supermarket industry capitulated and recommended that the price be retained on each item.

Canada. A series of open-dating requirements for meat products went into effect throughout Canada in 1976. Labels on all meat products must indicate the optimal period for consumption.

Canada's health minister announced that alcoholic products must carry a warning that they may be hazardous to health.

Britain. One of the main tasks during 1976 of the Office of Fair Trading (OFT) was to interpret and simplify the new Consumer Credit Act. The OFT also supervised the first major attempt to analyze consumer complaints on a nationwide basis. More than 142,000 complaints were made to local consumer agencies in a nine-month period. Major areas of complaint were: food and drink, 18,201; motor vehicles and accessories, 14,671; furniture and floor coverings, 10,934; and footwear, 8,138.

In spite of the need for extensive budget cuts throughout the economy, the British government continued to invest in consumer advice centers, which give the person-to-person help that is so often needed at a time of high inflation and unemployment.

STEWART M. LEE
Geneva College

CRIME

The bicentennial spurred a scholarly review of the history of criminal activity in the United States. Appearing in the January 1976 issue of the *Annals of the American Academy of Political and Social Science,* the symposium reached the verdict that there now is less mob violence than there formerly was, but that a much higher rate of individual crime prevails today compared to earlier times.

Historical View of U. S. Crime. Mob activity in the form of vigilantism, associated with the westward movement, the gun culture, and slavery, reached a peak in the United States during the 1830's. By 1976 it had virtually disappeared, except for sporadic urban race riots. On the other hand, the rate of crimes committed by single individuals or by small groups of persons has increased enormously during the life of the United States.

Historian Arthur Schlesinger noted that only 38 persons were convicted of murder in Pennsylvania from the time of the colony's settlement through 1775, a rate of one person every three years. The corresponding figure for burglaries was less than one a year. These low figures were registered despite a mixture of nationalities, continuing frontier disorders, the presence of a large number of felons who had been deported from Britain, and the temptation of the considerable amount of wealth located in the important city of Philadelphia.

In August, Emily and Bill Harris were convicted of kidnapping, robbery, and auto theft. They later began serving prison sentences of 11 years to life.

UPI

Conditions that might have contributed to the strikingly low crime rates in earlier days, as compared to present times, are instructive. Philadelphia, the largest colonial city, had a population of only 23,000 persons in 1760. Boston had but 16,000 residents. Behavior was restricted by networks of interdependence; a person's reputation in so small a world was a matter of great importance. Humiliation in the stocks and the pillory, two common early forms of punishment, induced conformity.

Most colonial offenses involved violations of religious rules, such as sexual dictates and the requirement to attend church regularly. Punishment for crimes of violence and theft was death, but such a harsh response was rarely invoked. The lesson from bicentennial retrospection seems clear: In the United States, impersonal massings of people in today's cities contributes significantly to escalating crime rates.

Crime by Women. In more recent years, there has been a particularly large increase in crimes committed by women. Murders carried out by women associated with Charles Manson and kidnappings and bank robberies by women members of the Symbionese Liberation Army have focused public attention on spectacular kinds of offenses by females. Women committed the two assassination attempts in California against President Ford in 1975.

An analysis of trend statistics conducted by educator Rita James Simon indicated, however, that it is crimes against property, not crimes of violence, that are being committed by more women than ever before in American history. "It is larceny, embezzlement, fraud, and forgery that are proving so attractive to women," Dr. Simon noted, "and not homicide, assault, and armed robbery." She believes that the larger percentage of women in the labor market is the single most important fact leading to their greater involvement in property offenses.

Strong words were exchanged during the year regarding the importance of the feminist movement in contributing to the rising number of criminal offenses by women.

A two-day March conference in Washington on women and crime, sponsored by the National League of Cities and the U. S. Conference on Mayors, heard Dr. Freda Adler of Rutgers University proclaim in a keynote address that "female offenders are striving for higher position in the criminal hierarchy." "It is apparent," Adler said, "that they are no longer willing to be second class criminals limited to 'feminine crimes' such as shoplifting and prostitution." She noted that the general arrest rate for women in the past 12 years has risen nearly three times more rapidly than that for males. Embezzlement, for instance, increased 280% for women, compared with 50% for men. She thought that the feminist movement, pressing for equality, contributed to the rising rates of crime being committed by women.

PHOTOS UPI

The July 15 kidnapping, near Chowchilla, Calif., of 26 children and their school bus driver gained national headlines. The victims were held in an underground van (see photos) for 16 hours until they managed to release themselves. Three men were later arrested and charged with the crime.

Karen DeCrow, president of the National Organization of Women, disagreed sharply with Adler's position, calling it "outrageous." According to DeCrow, "most people who are arrested are poor, uneducated, and not interested in any kind of social movement. If, in fact, the female crime rate is going up, you have to remember that it remains very low anyway." She insisted that opponents of feminism, intent upon keeping women "in their place," were seizing upon crime figures to sidetrack the feminist drive. DeCrow believes that in the long run feminism will contribute to a crime rate reduction, particularly in regard to crimes of violence, because it will chip away at the "masculine macho trips that lead men to prove that they are tough guys . . . by sticking a knife into someone else."

Rape. Whatever its contribution, if any, to the rates of female crime, the feminist movement clearly had a pronounced impact in 1976 on aspects of the crime of rape. Feminists have insisted that rape is an act of violence, not a sexual offense. They maintain that rape victims are "twice traumatized," once by the offense and then again by discriminatory and harsh treatment within the criminal justice system, particularly by male police officers and insensitive court officials.

Most states have dropped the requirement that corroboration is necessary for conviction of rape, bringing the standard of proof for rape into line with that for other criminal offenses. Inquiries into the previous sexual history of the complainant have also largely been barred, except in cases in which there was previous association between the defendant and the complainant.

The notorious cautionary instruction in rape cases, first enunciated in England in the 1600's, has now almost universally been abandoned. It specified that as the charge of rape is easily made and once made, difficult to defend against even if the person is innocent, the testimony of the female involved therefore should be examined with caution before being acted upon. However, despite feminist pressures, there have been no changes in the statutory stipulation that rape cannot be committed by a husband against his wife.

A pioneering rape reform law enacted in Michigan in 1974 established different degrees of rape, and included all the reforms noted above. But an examination in 1976 of the law's operation indicated that new statutes may not by themselves be sufficient to bring about basic changes in rape prosecutions. For example, the inclusion of different degrees of rape was employed to induce more plea bargaining (that is, pleas of guilt to lesser offenses than rape), an outcome not anticipated by the framers of the law.

In Britain, public agitation was aroused by the 1976 report of the Advisory Group on the Law of Rape, which upheld the decision of the law lords that a person could not be convicted of rape if he believed that the victim had consented, even if his belief was not one that would be held by a "reasonable" person. The case under review involved three members of the Royal Air Force. They had raped the wife of a companion who told them that she enjoyed sexual violence, despite any protests that she might make. Their conviction was not reversed, because the law lords did not believe that they truly accepted the story. On the other hand, the defendant in a case later in the year was acquitted when he maintained that he believed a woman who "consented" to intercourse with him, even though her consent had been induced by earlier threats made against her by her husband, out of the presence of the defendant.

In July, a jury awarded singer Connie Francis $2.5 million in damages based on her claim following a rape attack that a motel had been negligent in not providing an adequate lock on her door. Her husband was awarded $150,000 in connection with the case. An appellate court in September upheld her award but reduced her husband's to $25,000.

Crime Statistics. The feminist drive in regard to rape was expected to produce an increase in the number of such crimes becoming known to the police, since women would be encouraged to submit reports. Figures released by the Federal Bureau of Investigation covering 1975 indicated, however, that there was only a 1.3% increase in reported cases of rape over 1974, well below the 9.8% overall increase in the number of serious crimes known to the police.

The largest crime rise in 1975 was in larceny-theft, which showed a 13.6% jump. Burglary rose 7%, the next sharpest increase. The only decline was for murder, which dropped 1%. The 20,510 murders committed during 1975 showed a regional pattern ranging from a high of 12.7% per 100,000 persons in the southern states to a low of 7.6% per 100,000 in the northeast. Handguns continued to figure in the largest number of murders (51%), followed by cutting or stabbing weapons (18%), shotguns (9%), and rifles (6%).

Capital Punishment. The U. S. Supreme Court declared that the death penalty did not violate constitutional guarantees against cruel and unusual punishment. The decision was limited to murder convictions and the court still has to decide if capital punishment is acceptable for crimes that do not take a life, such as kidnapping, rape, and armed robbery.

The majority opinion in the 7–2 decision stated that judges and juries may impose death sentences so long as they have been given adequate legislative and judicial guidance to determine whether the sentence is appropriate in the particular case. Thirty-five states as well as the federal government now have capital punishment laws, and about 300 of the more than 600 persons on death rows could be executed under the court's ruling.

In Britain, a move to restore capital punishment, but only for persons taking a life through terrorist activity, was defeated in Parliament. The first execution in France since 1973, of the murderer of an 8-year-old girl, was carried out by guillotine in July in Marseilles. All European countries except Belgium, France, Greece, the Soviet Union, and Spain now have eliminated capital punishment, and Belgium has not executed anyone since the 1860's. In July, Canada abolished the death penalty for all civilian crimes.

Crime in the News. The major criminal event of the year was the July 15 kidnapping, near the town of Chowchilla, Calif., of 26 children and the driver of their school bus. Three persons— James and Richard Schoenfeld and Frederick Woods—were later charged with the crime. The kidnap victims were imprisoned in an underground van until they managed to release themselves. Later in the year, Patricia Hearst, herself at one time a kidnap victim, was sentenced to a 7-year term in connection with a bank robbery in which she had participated. She was released on bail in November.

GILBERT GEIS
Professor, Program in Social Ecology
University of California, Irvine

FBI Director Clarence Kelley displays a replica of a letter bomb. An unusually large number of corporations received extortion demands in 1976.

UPI

CUBA

For the Cuban government of Prime Minister Fidel Castro the year 1976 was marked by military and political triumphs abroad. Serious economic problems plagued the island.

Angola. The most noteworthy Cuban activity was the successful use of an estimated 15,000 Cuban troops in the former Portuguese colony of Angola. Beginning in the fall of 1975, Cuban army units were airlifted to Angola, apparently at the behest of the Soviet Union, to spearhead the military forces of the Soviet-backed Popular Movement for the Liberation of Angola (MPLA). By late February 1976 the MPLA had won the civil war, with Cuban troops given the principal credit for defeating the two Western-backed factions. At the end of the year more than 5,000 Cuban troops remained in Angola.

Economy. Cuba faced serious and growing economic problems during the year. Castro conceded the difficulties, warning his people that they must again be prepared to "make sacrifices." The economic problems principally revolved around the declining price of sugar on the world market, which meant that Cuban export earnings would drop to about $3,000,000,000 in 1976 (down some $400 million from the previous year). Aggravating the problem was a rise in Cuban imports to about $3,900,000,000 (up $100 million from 1975), thus creating a $900 million balance of payments deficit.

The production of sugar, which accounts for about 85% of Cuba's exports, was estimated in 1976 at about 6 million tons, an increase of approximately 500,000 tons over the previous year. A dry spell, which began in 1974, continued into its third year, slicing the sugar yield that under normal conditions would be in excess of 6.5 million tons.

Significantly, late in the year Cuba refused to pick up shipments of railway equipment that had been ordered from Argentina, indicating a scarcity of funds. Most economic forecasters familiar with the Cuban economy suggest that these problems will persist in the future.

Constitution. On February 15, Cuban voters went to the polls to ratify a new constitution. Castro boasted that 97.7% of the voters approved the new document, which apparently opened the way to a more decentralized government. The new constitution provides for the reorganization of the 6 existing provinces into 14 new ones, and the establishment of elected assemblies from the provincial to the national level. In essence, the new constitution institutionalizes the Castro government while providing for some decision-making at the local level.

Foreign Relations. Cuba continued to receive a high level of economic assistance from the Soviet Union. The Soviet government was elated at the successful use of Cuban troops as surrogates of Soviet foreign policy in Angola.

U. S.-Cuban relations became more frigid during the year, with the Cuban intervention in Angola cited as the most important factor. In addition, Cuban officials were angered by two events. The first was an attack on two Cuban fishing vessels on April 6, apparently by Cuban exiles from Miami; the second, a crash, caused by a terrorist-planted bomb, of a Cuban airliner on October 6 near Barbados.

Late in 1976 Castro and his brother Raul, the armed forces minister, stated that Cuba was looking for signs of a more friendly attitude from the United States under the Carter administration.

The Cuban-supported government of Prime Minister Michael Manley won reelection on the neighboring island of Jamaica. In accord with a 1975 Jamaican-Cuban technical cooperation agreement, by 1976 there were some 300 Cuban physicians, engineers, and technicians in Jamaica to assist the Manley government.

LOUIS R. SADLER
New Mexico State University

Diplomatically, Cuba had an active year. Canada's Prime Minister Trudeau visited the island in January.

UPI

CUBA • Information Highlights

Official Name: Republic of Cuba.
Location: Caribbean Sea.
Area: 44,218 square miles (114,524 km²).
Population (1976 est.): 9,400,000.
Chief Cities (1970 census): Havana, the capital, 1,755,-400; Santiago de Cuba, 276,000; Camaqüey, 196,-900.
Government: *Head of state,* Osvaldo Dorticos Torrado, president (took office July 1959). *Head of government,* Fidel Castro Ruz, premier (took office Feb. 1959).
Monetary Unit: Peso (0.83 peso equals U. S.$1, 1976).
Gross National Product (1973 est.): $3,400,000,000.
Manufacturing (major products): Sugar products, tobacco products.
Major Agricultural Products: Sugarcane, tobacco, rice, oranges and tangerines, sweet potatoes and yams.

SPECIAL REPORT:

Cuba's New International Role

After several years of being relatively inactive in foreign affairs, the Cuban government considerably expanded its international role in 1976. Militarily and politically, Cuba's involvement in the Angolan civil war was highly successful for the Havana government. The country also has won increasing acceptance from other Latin American nations.

Angolan Intervention. Cuba's interest in Africa was not new. For more than a decade the leaders of black African nations and of African "national liberation movements" have visited Cuba. At international forums, the Cuban government has repeatedly voiced its support for the anticolonial struggle in black Africa.

Cuba began sending combat troops to Angola late in 1975 to aid the Popular Movement for the Liberation of Angola (MPLA) in its struggle for supremacy against two Western-supported factions. According to Prime Minister Fidel Castro, the decision to send troops to Africa was made by his government on Nov. 5, 1975 "at the urgent request" of MPLA leader Agostinho Neto, then hard pressed by enemy battalions marching on the capital, Luanda. However, other reports strongly suggested that the initiative to send abroad an expeditionary force of some 15,000 men, about 15% of the country's regular armed forces, was not Castro's own. Western observers said that Cuban soldiers, carrying only light weapons, flew to Angola aboard Soviet planes. They were then equipped in Angola with Russian tanks, artillery, trucks, and other war matériel transported there at the same time from the Soviet Union.

The Cubans turned the tide in the Angolan conflict, and as a result the MPLA government, with Neto as president, became firmly entrenched. In July, President Neto traveled to Havana to thank Castro personally for the military assistance and to discuss future relations between the two countries. Castro, promising to "spare neither resources, nor cadres needed to organize the Angolan army," said that Cuban troops would remain in Angola during "the time that is strictly necessary to aid in the defense of the Angolan people and until the army is organized and supplied."

By the end of the year, about 5,000 Cuban soldiers were said still to be stationed in Angola, where they continued to assist government forces against guerrilla attacks. In addition, observers believed that Cuba had troops in a few other African countries, among them Congo, Mozambique, and Guinea-Bissau.

The Cuban intervention in Angola caused apprehension elsewhere in Africa and in Latin America, and the Havana government tried to assuage those fears. In a speech in April, Castro said that "no country in Latin America, regardless of its social system, will have anything to fear from the armed forces of Cuba." Proclaiming his peaceful intentions, he added that Cuba would even be willing to maintain normal relations with the United States.

Cuban-U. S. Relations. Havana recognized that the two countries could not begin talking about normalizing relations until after the U. S. election. Castro's prerequisite for such talks continued to be the lifting by Washington of its 16-year-old economic embargo against Cuba. The United States insisted that Cuba, first of all, must stop interfering in the domestic affairs of Puerto Rico. President Ford, visiting Puerto Rico in June, warned Cuba against interfering in U. S.-Puerto Rican relations. The United States also criticized Cuban intervention in Angola.

There were many more issues to be negotiated by the two countries, among them the extension of the 1973 bilateral antihijacking agreement. But following the midair explosion of a sabotaged Cuban plane off Barbados on October 6, Castro announced that the agreement would be terminated April 15, 1977. He accused the U. S. Central Intelligence Agency of complicity in what appeared to be a terrorist attack by Cuban exiles, and said that cessation of these activities would be his condition for the pact's renegotiation.

Relations with the Third World. Militant posture in Africa if anything enhanced Cuba's influence among the countries of the Caribbean. Prime Ministers Forbes Burnham of Guyana and Michael N. Manley of Jamaica endorsed Cuban relations in Angola. On his part, Castro, with Moscow's support and encouragement, continued to cultivate friendships in the Third World, attempting to make Cuba the leader of nonaligned nations. At the same time, Castro faithfully followed the Soviet line in international affairs and scathingly attacked the Chinese leadership.

Castro's Travels and Visitors to Cuba. Castro addressed the 25th Congress of the Soviet Communist Party in Moscow on February 25. It was the first time he had attended a Soviet congress. After his visit to the Soviet Union he traveled to and conferred with the leaders of Yugoslavia, Bulgaria, Algeria, and Guinea.

Gen. Omar Torrijos Herrera, the head of Panama's military junta, visited Cuba from Jan. 10–15. Among the issues discussed was Panama's negotiations with the United States over the future of the Panama Canal. Later in January, Prime Minister Pierre Trudeau of Canada visited Cuba as part of a Latin American tour to stimulate trade. Castro declared that relations between their two countries were "better than ever."

GEORGE VOLSKY, *University of Miami*

Left-wing Cypriot students, carrying a Palestinian flag and anti-Syrian placards in Greek, English, and Arabic, demonstrate in Nicosia in October.

CYPRUS

Cyprus remained divided during 1976, the Turkish government retaining control of about 40% of the island in the north. The Turks conquered this territory in 1974. The Greek Cypriots lost all voice in the governance of the Turkish-held area.

Negotiations. The United Nations maintained a peace-keeping force on the island of Cyprus during the year, and under the aegis of UN Secretary General Kurt Waldheim efforts were made to promote formal talks between the Greek and the Turkish Cypriots on the island's future. Four such rounds of talks had been held in 1975. A fifth round was held at Vienna, Austria, in February 1976. Glafkos Clerides, speaker of the Cyprus House of Representatives negotiated for the Greek Cypriots; the Turkish Cypriots were represented by their leader, Rauf Denktaş. Results were inconclusive, and the negotiations subsequently broke down.

Clerides had submitted his resignation in January but was persuaded to remain. A storm of criticism faced him, however, when it was learned that he had kept some details of the February negotiations secret from President Makarios. Under fire, Clerides resigned as negotiator in April and was replaced by Tassos Papadopoulos. He remained speaker of the House until late July, when Papadopoulos succeeded him in that post also. Umit Süleyman Onan took over duties as Turkish negotiator.

Elections. Clerides formed a new political party, the Democratic Rally, in May 1976. He represented the point of view that meaningful accommodations with Turkey should be reached as soon as possible. (Conversely, President Makarios spoke of a "long struggle" to remove Turkish influence from the island.)

Although Clerides' party received as much as 30% of the votes cast in elections for the House of Representatives on September 5, he won no seats because of Cyprus' electoral system. A combination of three pro-Makarios parties, including the Communists, captured 34 out of 35 seats at contest. Tassos Papadopoulos, an independent, won the 35th.

In the Turkish-held territory, which in February 1975 had been unilaterally proclaimed the "Turkish Federated State of Cyprus," elections were held on June 30, 1976. Denktaş was elected president, and 40 members were chosen for an assembly. Neither the Federated State nor the voting was recognized by the Makarios government, which considered itself the only lawful government of Cyprus.

Sampson's Trial. In July a sentence of 20 years' imprisonment was given by the Criminal Court at Nicosia to Nicos Giorgiades Sampson for his role in the coup that temporarily toppled President Makarios in 1974. The coup set off the chain of events which led to the Turkish invasion and occupation.

Population Shifts. Turkish efforts to entrench their control were evident during 1976. Aside from the occupation forces and the native Turkish Cypriots, numerous mainland Turks were resident on Cyprus; some figures showed the latter to number around 40,000.

In addition, Greek Cypriots remaining in the north were pressured to emigrate south, while some 200,000 refugees who had fled before the Turkish onslaught in the summer of 1974 were not allowed to return to their homes. This state of affairs continued to be a major obstacle to a peace settlement acceptable to the Greek Cypriot majority.

GEORGE J. MARCOPOULOS
Department of History
Tufts University

--------- CYPRUS · Information Highlights ---------

Official Name: Cyprus.
Location: Eastern Mediterranean.
Area: 3,572 square miles (9,251 km²).
Population (1976 est.): 640,000.
Chief Cities (1973 est.): Nicosia, the capital, 112,000; Limassol, 48,000
Government: *Head of state and government,* Archbishop Makarios III, president (took office Aug. 1960). *Legislature*—House of Representatives.
Monetary Unit: Pound (0.42 pound equals U. S.$1, June 1976).
Gross National Product (1973 est.): $807,300,000.
Manufacturing: Food and beverage processing, nonmetallic mineral products.
Major Agricultural Products: Potatoes, grapes, citrus fruits, wheat, barley, carobs, sheep, goats, pigs.
Foreign Trade (1975): *Exports,* $151,000,000; *imports,* $306,000,000.

CZECHOSLOVAKIA

The two main events of 1976 were the 15th congress of the Communist party and the elections to representative bodies on federal, state, and local levels.

Party Congress. Meeting on April 12–16, the congress was characterized by the usual attacks on "right-wing opportunism" and "revisionism," coupled with professions of unswerving loyalty to the Soviet Union and "proletarian internationalism."

Gustav Husák was reelected secretary general and so were all full and alternate members of the Presidium of the Central Committee (except ailing former President Ludvík Svoboda) and all secretaries of the Central Committee. The Central Committee was enlarged from 115 to 121 members, of whom some 30% were new. It was announced that the party had 1,382,000 members—a 200,000 increase since the 14th congress in May 1971.

The keynotes of the congressional proceedings appeared to be unity, stability, continuity, and moderation. They accounted also for the only surprise of the five-day session, namely, the conspicuous absence of most of the hard-liners from the roster of speakers.

Elections. On October 22–23 elections were held to choose members of the Federal Assembly, the Czech and Slovak National Councils, and all levels of people's committees. Only candidates approved by the Communist-controlled National Front were placed on the ballot and Communist-controlled commissions supervised all phases of the elections. Needless to say, all the candidates were overwhelmingly elected.

Economy. The Sixth Economic Five-Year Plan was launched in 1976. It calls for the following increases in 1976–80: national income, 27–29%, mostly from increased labor productivity; industrial production, "around" 34%; construction, more than 35%; agricultural production, 14–15%; capital investments, 31%; average wages, 13–15%; and real income, 23–25%.

Increases achieved in the first half of 1976 (over the same period in 1975) were as follows: overall industrial production, 6%; construction, 6.4%; labor productivity in industry and construction, 5.4%; freight transportation, 4%; average wages, 2.6%; monetary income of the population, 3.6%. But a decrease occurred in the construction of apartments, of which 2,621 fewer were built than in the corresponding period of 1975. Harvest and livestock levels and milk and meat production were below 1975.

Foreign Affairs. Czechoslovakia's foreign policy continued to adhere rigidly to the Soviet line. The first anniversary of the Helsinki conference brought out a spate of statements hailing it as a victory of "progressive peace forces" over "reactionary circles of imperialism." A polemic developed with Yugoslavia over the treatment of Yugoslav workers in Czechoslovakia, and the Yugoslav daily *Politika* recalled its correspondent from Prague, claiming he was prevented from carrying out his work. On the other hand, Czechoslovakia's endeavors to improve relations with non-Communist countries continued in 1976 with an official visit of Premier Strougal to Turkey and Foreign Minister Chnoupek to Great Britain, and visits to Prague by the Austrian chancellor, the foreign ministers of Greece, Cyprus, and Iceland, and by a Vatican delegation.

EDWARD TABORSKY
University of Texas at Austin

—CZECHOSLOVAKIA · Information Highlights—

Official Name: Czechoslovak Socialist Republic.
Location: East-central Europe.
Area: 49,370 square miles (127,869 km²).
Population (1976 est.): 14,900,000.
Chief Cities (1975 est.): Prague, the capital, 1,165,000; Brno, 355,000; Bratislava, 335,000.
Government: *Head of state,* Gustav Husák, president (took office 1975). *Head of government,* Lubomir Strougal, premier (took office 1970). *Communist party secretary general,* Gustav Husák (took office 1969). *Legislature*—Federal Assembly: Chamber of Nations and Chamber of the People.
Monetary Unit: Koruna (5.41 koruny equal U. S.$1, Nov. 1976).
Gross National Product (1975 est.): $44,300,000,000.
Manufacturing (major products): Machinery, chemicals, petroleum products, glass, textiles, iron, steel.
Major Agricultural Products: Sugar beets, wheat, potatoes.
Foreign Trade (1975): *Exports,* $8,358,000,000; *imports,* $9,081,000,000.

UPI

At the United Nations, Czechoslovakia's Foreign Minister Bohuslav Chnoupek (*right*) meets with Czech diplomats Ladislav Smid (*left*) and Jaromir Johanes.

DANCE

Mikhail Baryshnikov and Judith Jamison perform in "Pas de Duke," choreographed by Alvin Ailey to music by jazzman Duke Ellington.

MARTHA SWOPE

The bicentennial provided the theme for much of what happened on the ballet scene in 1976. All the major American companies offered either special bicentennial productions or revivals of specifically American works to mark the anniversary. Several foreign ballet companies made visits to join the celebrations. The visitors, including the royal ballets of Britain and Denmark, brought some of the best dancing available in the world. But the American Ballet Theater (ABT) and the New York City Ballet more than held their own, and the latter scored a considerable hit in a bicentennial visit to Paris.

Makarova and Baryshnikov. The stars of the year were without question the two former Kirov Ballet stars, Natalia Makarova and Mikhail Baryshnikov. Although both concentrated their efforts on the classical productions of the ABT, they also extended their ranges. Baryshnikov performed in several new works, including *Pas de Duke,* choreographed for him and Judith Jamison by Alvin Ailey to music by Duke Ellington. Another choreography created for Baryshnikov was *Push Comes to Shove* by Twyla Tharp, a delightful spoof of ballet. In his first effort at choreography, Baryshnikov staged a highly praised new production of Tchaikovsky's *The Nutcracker* for the ABT. Makarova staged the Kingdom of the Shades segment of Petipa's *La Bayadère* for the ABT.

The two stars danced together in several works, including a pas de deux created for them by Jerome Robbins of the New York City Ballet. The duet, *Other Dances,* was set to music by Chopin and allowed both dancers to demonstrate their considerable skills. The dance, however, did not greatly advance the state of the art. But it was welcomed by Makarova, who had complained that no choreographer had developed a dance specifically for her.

Bicentennial Visits. Britain's Royal Ballet led the bicentennial visitors, making its 15th visit to the United States since it was founded in 1931. It is often said the Royal Ballet dances better in New York than in London. Certainly the company offered several dazzling productions during its stay, notably *Romeo and Juliet* choreographed by Kenneth MacMillan and designed by Nicholas Georgiadis. Anthony Dowell and David Wall, the company's young principals, alternated the roles of Romeo and Mercutio and both scored successes in both roles. Canadian-born Lynn Seymour proved the best interpreter of Juliet, especially with her lithe "dead" act in the tomb pas de deux. Wayne Sleep was a delight in his featured solos in both *Romeo* and the company's version of *Manon.* The tiny dancer gave a virtuoso athletic performance in every role he offered. MacMillan's *Manon* brought Rudolf Nureyev back to the company. The Royal Ballet also performed Frederick Ashton's *A Month in The Country, La Fille Mal Gardée,* and *The Dream,* as well as MacMillan's more modern productions, *Elite Syncopations, Rituals,* and *Song of the Earth.*

The Royal Danish Ballet was making its first visit to the United States in more than 10 years. It offered a chance to see again the classic style of August Bournonville not practiced anywhere else in the world. Bournonville became director of the Royal Danish Company in the early 19th century and his ballets have remained virtually untouched since then.

The Danish company has not stood still, however, and has added several modern works to its repertoire. It brought a mix of the old and new to the United States. The Bournonville ballets were *Napoli, Act III, The Guards of Amager,* and *La Sylphide.* The more modern productions included John Neumeier's unsatisfying *Romeo and Juliet* and *The Lesson, The Four Seasons* and *The Triumph of Death,* all choreographed by Flemming Flindt, the current director of the Copenhagen company. *The Triumph of Death* brought nude ballet to the stage of the Metropolitan Opera House for the first time, and achieved a small *succès de scandale.*

The Australian Ballet, also visiting for the bicentennial, brought its new music-only version of Franz Lehar's *The Merry Widow.* Margot Fonteyn starred in what may become a perfect vehicle for her fading skills.

The National Ballet of Canada came for a brief season, helped by Nureyev and Erik Bruhn. However, it probably would not have sustained interest without the two stars.

The Netherlands' cultural contribution to the bicentennial included the first visit to the United States of the Amsterdam-based Dutch National Ballet. In its one-week visit, the company managed to squeeze in seven modern ballets. The best offering was an evening consisting of Rudi van Dantzig's *Ginastera,* Hans van Manen's *Adagio Hammerklavier,* and Toer van Schayk's *Before, During and After the Party,* in three widely varied styles that showed the company's flexibility and elegance.

U. S. Companies. The American Ballet Theater provided most of the fireworks of the season, offering several important revivals and a look at the greatest galaxy of foreign and home-grown talent. The company's roster for the year read like a who's who of great dancers in the world: Baryshnikov, Bruhn, Fernando Bujones, Eleanor d'Antuono, Gelsey Kirkland, Ivan Nagy, Terry Orr, Martine van Hamel, Makarova, Carla Fracci, Alicia Alonso, Marcia Haydee, Lynn Seymour, Paolo Bortoluzzi, and Nure-

yev. At the end of the year Cynthia Gregory, one of America's best native talents, announced she was returning to ballet after a one-year retirement. The ABT offered a wide range of ballets, from the classical *Swan Lake* to Agnes de Mille's newest work *Texas Fourth.* The company excelled in all styles and maintained its position as the world's premiere dance group.

The New York City Ballet of George Balanchine was a great success at home and abroad. During a season in Paris, French critics called the company the best they had seen. Balanchine's big new offering—and bicentennial tribute—was *Union Jack.* The piece is the second in a series of three labeled *Entente Cordiale.* The first, *Stars and Stripes,* premiered three years ago. The third will be *Tricolore,* a tribute to France scheduled to debut on July 4, 1977. *Union Jack* is in three parts: the first an evocation of Scotland filled with marching groups in dress tartan kilts; the second a costermonger duet; and the third dedicated to the Royal Navy. The music is a pastiche of traditional British airs arranged by Hershy Kay.

The Alvin Ailey City Center Dance Theater continued pulling together Ailey's tribute to the late composer Duke Ellington. The tribute finally was presented in August and offered more than a dozen ballets set to Ellington's music. The quality of the ballets varied but the whole was considered a success. Ailey said of Ellington: "He wrote the heartbeat and rhythms of this century and, more than that, celebrated the beauty and uniqueness of man." Ailey's principal ballerina, Judith Jamison, continued to inspire the company with her verve. At year's end she debuted in a new solo created for her by John Butler.

The Joffrey Ballet's bicentennial offering already had been presented in 1975 but continued to prove a popular success. *Drums, Dreams and Banjos* took its music and inspiration from the works of Stephen Foster. Joffrey paid another tribute to the past by reviving several ballet's by German Kurt Jooss, including *The Green Table, A Ball in Old Vienna, The Death of an Infanta,* and *The Big City.* The polemics in some of the pieces appeared a little outdated but the works were well received. One of Joffrey's up and coming ballerinas, Ann Marie de Angelo, received a special diploma for modern interpretation at the 1976 International Ballet Competition in Varna, Bulgaria.

Modern Dance. Modern dance continued to burgeon, although one of the better known groups—the Paul Taylor Dance Company—went out of business for lack of funds. The Dance Roundabout in New York continued to feature a long series of smaller groups. One of the more interesting experiments was the presentation of *Spirit of Denishawn* mounted by the Joyce Trisler Danscompany in a tribute to the modern dance pioneers of the 1930's.

JOHN F. SIMS, *United Press International*

As a bicentennial tribute, George Balanchine's New York City Ballet offered the three-part "Union Jack."

MARTHA SWOPE

DELAWARE

In 1976 Delaware was concerned with two absorbing statewide events: The celebration of the national bicentennial, which coincided with that of the state, and the November state elections for governor, U. S. representative, and U. S. senator.

Celebrations. The bicentennial got under way with the creation of a Delaware American Revolution Bicentennial Commission composed of several of the state's leading citizens. The celebrations were highlighted by a number of events commemorating national and state independence, organized and directed by the University of Delaware.

Elections. The nomination of Pierre S. Du Pont, IV, as the Republican candidate for governor and the renomination of Sherman W. Tribbitt, the Democratic incumbent, in midsummer started the political campaign that attracted the attention of the citizenry. The races for representative and senator, as well as those for state legislature and "line" offices, were of lesser importance, but they provided a series of lively debates.

The voting in November resulted in the election of Du Pont as governor, Thomas B. Evans, Jr. (R) as U. S. representative, and William V. Roth, Jr. (R) as U. S. senator. Both houses of the state legislature remained Democratic. Governor Carter won the state's electoral vote.

Two of the issues addressed by the gubernatorial candidates had to do with (1) with the financial difficulties experienced by the Farmers Bank of the State of Delaware, a private institution which has long served as the depository of state funds; and (2) with the precipitous rise in the state debt, which at year's end exceeded $700,000,000, one of the largest per capita state debts in the Union.

The legislature was caught in the throes of the bank issue because nine of its members served on the bank's board of directors. Eventually, the legislature was forced to borrow funds to meet the exigencies of the bank's difficulties; otherwise, the state's deposits would have been placed in serious jeopardy.

UPI

Delaware's Governor-elect Pierre S. Du Pont, IV, and his family celebrate his election victory.

Correction. The legislature was also faced with continued problems in the state prison, where a series of escapes has occurred. Several legislators demanded the resignation of the prison's director. In October the governor named his successor.

Finances. The state budget rose more than 10%, and this fact brought forth charges that the legal requirement that expenditures be met by revenue was being circumvented. Short-term borrowing increased as a result of growing expenditure and lowered state income. The state lottery was finally established on a paying basis. It was hoped that this would augment revenue.

Education. Satewide school strikes were avoided, although some local districts had momentary labor problems. In September, the U. S. District Court decreed that cross-district busing to establish more equitable ratios between black and white pupils in the public schools of New Castle County (which includes the city of Wilmington) be instituted, beginning in 1977. The decision was appealed to the U. S. Supreme Court.

Economy. Unemployment, which had reached 11% in 1975, began to recede in 1976. By late summer it stood at 7.5%. Both the auto and construction industries showed improvement, and gross farm income displayed a slight increase over that of the previous year.

PAUL DOLAN
University of Delaware

DELAWARE · Information Highlights

Area: 2,057 square miles (5,328 km²).

Population (1975 est.): 579,000.

Chief Cities (1970 census): Dover, the capital, 17,488; Wilmington, 80,386; Newark, 21,078.

Government (1976): *Chief Officers*—governor, Sherman W. Tribbitt (D); lt. gov., Eugene D. Bookhammer (R). *General Assembly*—Senate, 21; House of Representatives, 41 members.

Education (1975–76): *Enrollment*—public elementary schools, 64,512; public secondary, 62,964; nonpublic (1976–77), 18,700; colleges and universities, 29,956 students. *Public school expenditures*, $187,750,000 ($1,491 per pupil).

State Finances (fiscal year 1975): *Revenues*, $550,565,000; *expenditures*, $568,653,000.

Personal Income (1975): $3,908,000,000; per capita, $6,748.

Labor Force (July 1976): *Nonagricultural wage and salary earners*, 231,400; *insured unemployed*, 8,800 (4.3%).

UPI

Denmark's Queen Margrethe II and Prince Henrik walk New York City streets during a bicentennial visit.

DENMARK

The Danish economy continued to sag in 1976, leading the government to inaugurate an austerity economic package and devaluate the krone.

Economy. On August 19 the Folketing (parliament) passed an austerity plan aimed at reducing a record foreign trade deficit. The package limited wage increases to a maximum of 6% for the next two years and boosted consumer taxes. It also included a reduction in public spending and strict price-and-profit controls. Thousands of workers took part in wildcat strikes on August 19–23 to protest passage of the austerity plan.

Another result of the difficult economic situation and the balance of payments deficit was the devaluation of the Danish krone. The decision was taken at a meeting of Danish and West German finance ministers and national bank directors in October. Primarily a devaluation vis-à-vis the West German mark, the result was a 4% reduction of the krone. A price, wage, and rent freeze was enacted in December.

Nuclear Power. A debate in the Folketing in May showed conclusively that there was a majority for the introduction of nuclear energy as a major source of power. Preliminary plans called for the construction of five atomic power plants at a cost of 17,600,000,000 kroner. The first plant is scheduled to begin operations in 1985. In addition, 12,000,000,000 kroner will be invested in energy-saving projects, which are expected to save about 40,000,000,000 kroner in energy costs. The Folketing turned down a Progressive Party proposal to hold a referendum to decide if nuclear energy should be introduced into Denmark.

Social Welfare. A new law on social welfare and assistance went into effect on April 1. One of the largest legislative complexes adopted in Denmark for some time, it superseded former laws dealing with public assistance, aid to children and young people, help to mothers, and day care. Under the new law all public assistance will be channeled through the social offices of local municipalities and rural communities.

Foreign Relations. The foreign ministry announced in October that it had requested the recall of the North Korean ambassador and three of his senior staff members. The reason given was the discovery that the North Korean diplomats had sold narcotics, alcoholic beverages, and cigarettes in contravention of Danish law.

Queen Margrethe II and Prince Henrik visited with President and Mrs. Ford at the White House during a bicentennial tour of the United States in May and early June. They also became the first Danish royalty to travel to the Virgin Islands, the former Danish West Indies.

"Free State." The so-called "Free State of Christiania," an area taken over by some 700 hippies inside the city of Copenhagen, was supposed to be cleared by April 1, according to a decision of the Folketing. In existence since the late 1960's, the squatters' "state" had been given three years to disband. In April, the ministers of defense and justice turned the case over to the Copenhagen Bailiff's Court, which passed the problem over to a higher court.

Obituaries. Prince Knud, uncle of Queen Margrethe, died on June 14 at the age of 75. He had been heir apparent to his brother, King Frederick IX, until the constitution was changed in 1953 to permit female succession. Viggo Kampmann, prime minister from 1960 to 1962, died on June 3 at the age of 65.

ERIK J. FRIIS
Editor, "The Scandinavian-American Bulletin"

――――― **DENMARK • Information Highlights** ―――――

Official Name: Kingdom of Denmark.
Location: Northwest Europe.
Area: 16,629 square miles (43,069 km²).
Population (1976 est.): 5,100,000.
Chief Cities (1975 est.): Copenhagen, the capital, 1,300,-000; Aarhus, 246,000; Odense, 169,000.
Government: *Head of state,* Margrethe II, queen (acceded Jan. 1972). *Head of government,* Anker Jørgensen, prime minister (took office Feb. 1975). *Legislature* (unicameral)—Folketing.
Monetary Unit: Krone (5.92 kroner equal U.S.$1, Nov. 1976).
Gross National Product (1975 est.): $41,900,000,000.
Manufacturing (major products): Beverages, processed foods, machinery, ships, chemicals, furniture.
Major Agricultural Products: Barley, oats, sugar beets, dairy products, cattle, hogs.
Foreign Trade (1975): *Exports,* $8,716,000,000; *imports,* $10,366,000,000.

DISARMAMENT AND ARMS CONTROL

Arms control and disarmament specialists were concerned about three basic problems in 1976. These were the failure of the Soviet Union and the United States to agree upon further limitations on strategic arms, the inability of advanced and developing nations to agree on means to prevent the proliferation of nuclear weapons, and the increasing sales of U. S. arms to many nations.

American-Soviet Negotiations. Negotiators from the two superpowers spent much of the year in Geneva attempting to formalize a new set of nuclear arms agreements referred to as SALT II (Strategic Arms Limitation Talks II). There was some urgency in the negotiations because a portion of the SALT I accords, the part that places quantitative limitations upon strategic offensive weapons, will expire on Oct. 3, 1977. The basis for the negotiating efforts is an agreement in principle, reached by President Gerald Ford and Chairman Leonid Brezhnev in the fall of 1974, known as the Vladivostok Declaration. In this statement the United States and the Soviet Union agreed to work for the implementation of two types of ceilings upon offensive weapons.

One is a limitation of 2,400 on strategic offensive weapons, SLBM's (submarine-launched ballistic missiles), ICBM's (intercontinental ballistic missiles), and for the first time long range bombers. The second ceiling is 1,320 on missiles equipped with MIRV's (multiple individually targeted reentry vehicles). The hopes expressed in the United States early in the year that the Vladivostok guidelines could be converted into a treaty failed to materialize.

A basic cause for the failure was disagreement between Moscow and Washington about whether two weapons systems should be included in the limitations. The Soviet weapons system that the Americans wanted to include in the 2,400 limitation was the Backfire bomber. Many in the Pentagon argued it was a long range bomber because it could reach the United States on a one-way mission, or if it used inflight refueling from a tanker aircraft. The Soviets argued for exclusion of the Backfire, claiming that it was not a long range bomber. The United States said that its new cruise missile, capable of being carried by bombers or fired from submarines and surface ships, should not be included under the 2,400 ceiling unless the Backfire was also. As the year ended, arms controllers were pessimistic because it appeared that a compromise might permit each superpower to deploy some of the new weapons.

Nuclear Weapons Proliferation. Vying with the SALT II negotiations as a high priority arms control issue was the growing concern over the spread of nuclear technology. Many feared that the new technology would lead to the proliferation of nuclear weapons beyond the six nations that have demonstrated the ability to construct nuclear explosives. These nations are the United States, the USSR, England, France, Peoples Republic of China, and India. In addition, it is widely suspected that Israel has developed but not tested atomic weapons.

The heart of the proliferation problem is the increasing frequency with which nations are seeking to replace the energy obtained by burning oil and natural gas with electricity produced by nuclear reactors. A byproduct extracted from the wastes of such reactors is plutonium. Plutonium is one of several elements that can be used to construct atomic weapons. Plutonium can be separated from reactor wastes by a chemical reprocessing technique. Chemical reprocessing is difficult, but technically much easier than separating weapons grade uranium from ordinary uranium. It is for this reason that presidential candidates Gerald Ford and Jimmy Carter stressed that the United States should increase its efforts to control the spread of plutonium reprocessing technology.

Currently the basic strategy to control the proliferation of nuclear weapons is to convince nations to ratify the Non-proliferation Treaty, requiring non-nuclear-weapon signatories to accept inspections to preclude the diversion of plutonium for military purposes. Additional measures are under examination. For example, there is a plan to have an international authority manage plutonium reprocessing plants at regional locations around the globe. Plutonium thus obtained would be kept under international control. Another possibility is for nations, such as the United States, which supply uranium fuel for reactors, to buy back the reactor wastes so that the plutonium can be reprocessed and safeguarded by major industrialized nations. Still another possibility would be for the United States to join other nations in imposing sanctions upon those nations that misuse civil nuclear technology that they have obtained from the advanced nations.

U. S. Arms for the World. Increasing concern was voiced in 1976, particularly in the U. S. Congress, regarding the growing supply of arms made available by the United States to a number of other nations. The government defended the arms sales by citing several justifications. It was argued that American allies in the effort to contain Communism had to be supplied with armaments. Secondly, those sympathetic to the struggle of the Israelis against numerically superior Arab forces argued for continued military assistance to the Jewish state. It is also pointed out that the United States should not antagonize oil producing Arab states by refusing to sell arms to them. Lastly, some defend the government's arms sales by noting that if the purchasing nations could not buy arms from the United States they would get them somewhere else, probably from the Soviet Union.

ROBERT M. LAWRENCE
Colorado State University

Former drug addicts and abusers erect temporary living facilities along the Hudson River in Albany, N. Y. The group said that they would stay in the "City of the Forgotten" until the state restored cuts in the drug programs.

DRUG ADDICTION AND ABUSE

The anticipated White Paper on Drug Abuse, issued as a report to the president by the Domestic Council Task Force, became available in 1976. It made a number of observations and recommendations that summarize the current drug-abuse situation and approaches to its solutions.

Supply Reduction. One favored approach is to make abused drugs difficult to obtain, costly, and risky to sell, possess, or consume. It has been demonstrated that when drug-taking is hazardous, inconvenient, or expensive, fewer people will form the habit and many will give it up.

The federal government spends $350 million a year on supply reduction efforts, but no such program can be completely effective. It is estimated that only 10–15% of all illegal supplies are confiscated. Nevertheless, it is believed that efforts to control availability must remain a central element in the government's strategy.

Major Recommendations by the Task Force. 1. Balance should be maintained between the efforts to reduce the supply of drugs and those aimed at diminishing the demand for them. The two approaches are complementary and interdependent.

2. Total elimination of drug abuse is unlikely, but governmental action can contain the problem and limit its adverse effects. Drug abuse is a long-term problem requiring a long-term commitment.

3. All drug use is not equally destructive. Containment efforts should be centered on drugs that have a high addiction potential. Priority of treatment should be given to those using high-risk drugs and to compulsive users.

4. Existing programs to reduce supply and demand must be broadened. To diminish supplies, more emphasis should be put on stopping the diversion of drugs from legitimate production and on international cooperation to curtail illicit production. Efforts at reducing demand should focus on prevention and vocational rehabilitation.

5. The federal government leads the battle against drug abuse, but it cannot do the job alone. Aid and encouragement from state and local governments, private businesses, and community organizations are essential.

Additional Recommendations. The president's proposal for mandatory minimum sentences for those trafficking in hard drugs was endorsed. It was suggested that these penalties be extended to dealers in barbiturates and amphetamines. Other enforcement recommendations were: consecutive rather than concurrent sentences for multiple convictions; parole revocation upon rearrest on a narcotics trafficking charge; and the use of the Internal Revenue Service to prosecute drug dealers for violation of income tax laws.

The fostering of international cooperation, especially with Mexico, to prevent illicit production of drugs was given a high priority. Intensified diplomatic efforts to heighten other governments' concern about violations of drug treaty obligations were recommended. Crop substitution was suggested as a method of eliminating supplies of raw materials like opium. The study of *Papaver bracteatum* (which is similar to the oriental poppy) instead of morphine-containing *Papaver somniferum* (opium poppy) for the production of codeine should be accelerated.

Heroin, barbiturate, intravenous amphetamine, and polydrug abusers were recommended for priority of treatment at drug-abuse centers. Community mental health centers were suggested as the site for treatment of lesser types of drug abuse. The use of hospital beds for treatment is to be severely restricted because of cost. The use of the long-acting methadone (1-alphaacetylmethadol) instead of regular methadone was favored as soon as its safety and efficacy were assured. Training to enhance the skills of paraprofessional workers should be expanded. A recommendation was also made that schools of medicine, social work, psychology, and vocational rehabilitation teach drug-abuse treatment.

SIDNEY COHEN, M. D.
Clinical Professor of Psychiatry
University of California, Los Angeles

Although credit buying was a prevalent trend in the United States during 1976, some retailers offered a discount to cash customers.

UPI

ECONOMY, U. S.

The year 1976 was replete with a host of notable and often dramatic economic developments. Although the thrust of the business pattern which evolved in 1976 proved favorable on balance, some negative remnants of the preceeding recession/inflation dilemma continued to serve as glaring reminders that the U. S. economy had not completely recovered.

One of the triumphs recorded was that the economy succeeded in moving out of the most severe recession since the depression of the 1930's. Industrial activity, spurred by an accommodative Federal Reserve money and credit policy and rising demand, picked up considerably. Corporate profits rose appreciably, contributing to vastly improved levels of corporate cash flow. The resurgence of business activity, coupled with lingering recession-induced attitudes on the part of business and the consumer, enabled a modest restoration of liquidity to occur in most sectors of the economy.

Spotty areas of weakness, however, persisted throughout the year. The most serious weak spots appeared to be the problems of high unemployment, lagging residential construction, and the inability to control inflation adequately. The initial surge of total output during the first quarter proved unsustainable and the rate of advance eased over subsequent periods. As the year progressed, some price relief brightened consumer attitudes. By year-end record savings —flows into thrift institutions and lower mortgage rates—caused a considerable improvement

in the housing picture. Business spending for plant and equipment showed great difficulty in getting untracked, but some signs of a modest revival began to be noticeable.

As the year began to draw to a close the generally uncertain economic environment was further complicated by the election of a new president. The exaggerated fears stemming from the election, which were evident in some business quarters, were quickly dispelled. Although many questions remained unanswered at year-end, a greater emphasis on economic stimulation was expected under the Carter administration.

Total Output. The nation's output of goods and services surged ahead in the first quarter of 1976, and the gross national product (GNP) soared to around $1,640,000,000,000. This represented a total gain of over 12%, on a seasonally adjusted annual basis, of which about 9% was in real terms. The following period, a slower rate of increase in consumer spending, a significantly lesser quarter-to-quarter rise in net inventory accumulation by business, and a modest pickup in price inflation, pared the real GNP advance to a shade below 4.5%. In spite of more robust consumer expenditures in the third quarter, as well as a diminution of inflationary pressures, this trend remained largely in effect so that the growth rate was further reduced to below 4%. By year-end there was little evidence that the business recovery was ready to resume anything approaching boom proportions, but the GNP, after price adjustment, nevertheless appeared to have registered a healthy rate of expansion for 1976 as a whole.

Industrial Production. Industrial output, as measured by the Federal Reserve Board's index, continued along a generally rising path, a trend which was already in full swing by the middle of 1975. The index rose to over 130 (1967=100) late in the second half of the year, compared with a 117.8 average for 1975. Although industrial activity slowed in September and October, relatively high manufacturers' new orders kept the index at a respectable level, and for the year as a whole it succeeded in chalking up an increase in the general area of 10%.

Production strength was concentrated in the manufacturing sector, while the output of mines and utilities traced a relatively flat path for much of the year. Both durable and nondurable industries contributed heavily to the advance. In the hard goods area, production of building products and transportation equipment was well maintained, as was that of steel before it began to falter toward the end of the third quarter. The revival of automobile output was a significant detail in the total picture; auto production soared to nearly 138 on the 1967 index basis by August, compared with around 101 for 1975 as a whole. In 1976, more than 8 million units were produced domestically, up substantially from the depressed 6.7 million unit level of 1975.

Domestic Investment. Business fixed investment pushed ahead of the depressed 1975 level and by the third quarter was nearly 11% higher than the previous year's average. But the tempo of such outlays proved to be below expectations and this contributed to a measure of restraint on the part of many business leaders regarding future expansion plans, a development which, however, is subject to rapid change. As far as total business investment is concerned, the quickest and largest change was in the accumulation of inventories. Stocks began to be built up at a seasonally adjusted annual rate of nearly $15,000,000,000 in the first quarter and net accumulation remained at high levels throughout the year. The future course of business capital investment, a key ingredient in the more mature stage of any business recovery, will be closely tied to future economic expectations of business, corporate cash flow, the cost and availability of external financing, and the conditions prevailing in the securities markets.

Personal Income and Employment. In spite of a pickup in overall economic activity, the problem of high unemployment refused to disappear in 1976, and in fact worsened later in the year, surpassing 8% of the civilian labor force. In addition to a moderately tight labor market, the jobless rate was strongly influenced by growth of the labor force as more women and teenagers began to seek employment.

The slack employment situation contributed to less rapid growth of personal income and, together with lingering inflation, was responsible for tempering consumer attitudes from time to time. Per capita after-tax income rose less than 6%, to $5,528, from the end of 1975 through the third quarter of 1976. Adjusted for inflation, however, such income registered only a nominal increase of slightly more than 2%. In spite of employment and price problems, the consumer appears to have endeavored to preserve his living standard by maintaining fairly healthy outlays. To some extent this was accomplished by the assumption of increased debt burdens and by drawing on savings.

Government Spending. Government expenditures continued to increase in 1976 but at a slower pace than they had in the previous year. Some restraint in certain areas, particularly defense spending, was noticeable. Outlays for nondefense goods and services rose at a relatively higher rate, but were also subdued when compared with 1975 spending. Fiscal 1976, however, was characterized by a much larger increase in federal outlays than in receipts so that the budget deficit swelled to over $65,000,000,000, compared with under $40,000,000,000 in fiscal 1975. State and local government spending was also fairly robust, but the rate of increase was somewhat below the 12.5% pace of calendar 1975. Nevertheless, municipalities carried out a record amount of financing in the markets. Such municipalities gathered momentum as the initial impact of New York City's fiscal difficulties lost much of its sting.

Stocks and Bonds. The financial markets generally mirrored the mixed reactions of investors to background economic developments throughout most of the year, but a healthier tone prevailed on balance. Stock prices rose sharply in the beginning months of 1976 and subsequently proceeded along a horizontal direction, but at relatively high levels. Bond prices began to edge up in the early months of 1976, faltered around midyear, and rose fairly consistently thereafter. During the second half of 1976, the credit markets benefited from the accommodative policy of the Federal Reserve, modest short-term credit demands, and manageable supplies of new corporate and government debt issues in relation to the amount of investable funds.

The Outlook. The year closed on a mixed note, and a consensus concerning the economic outlook was difficult. While a distinct improvement in business activity from the previous year was a reality, the pace of such activity had slowed. The inflationary problem had not been fully resolved, and some indications were pointing to the possibility of greater price inflation pressures ahead. At the same time, the unacceptably high rate of unemployment continued. The new Carter administration was thus faced with the distasteful and difficult problem of trying to balance political, social, and economic priorities, not an easy undertaking in the U. S. system of government.

JACKSON PHILLIPS, *Executive Vice President*
Moody's Investors Service, Inc.

THE U.S. ECONOMY

GROSS NATIONAL PRODUCT

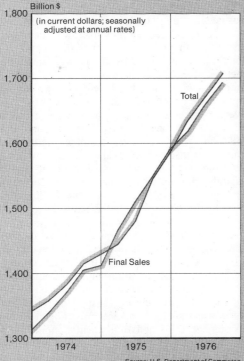

Billion $

(in current dollars; seasonally adjusted at annual rates)

1,800

1,700

Total

1,600

1,500

1,400

Final Sales

1,300

1974   1975   1976

Source: U.S. Department of Commerce

UNEMPLOYMENT RATE

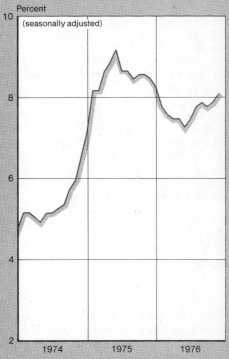

Percent

10

(seasonally adjusted)

8

6

4

2

1974   1975   1976

Source: U.S. Department of Labor

INDUSTRIAL PRODUCTION

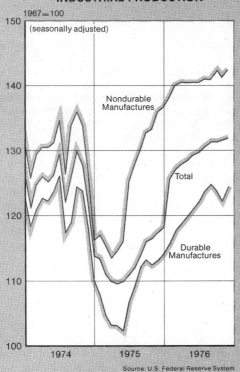

1967=100

150

(seasonally adjusted)

140

Nondurable Manufactures

130

Total

120

Durable Manufactures

110

100

1974   1975   1976

Source: U.S. Federal Reserve System

CONSUMER PRICE INDEX

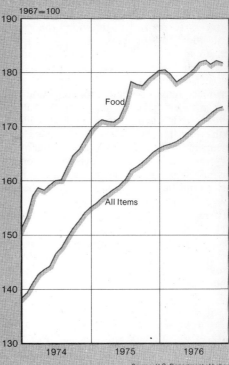

1967=100

190

180

Food

170

160

All Items

150

140

130

1974   1975   1976

Source: U.S. Department of Labor

SPECIAL REPORT:

Economic Thought—1976

Prior to the Great Depression in the United States economists of the "classical" and "neoclassical" schools were the dominant influence. They believed that the economy was self-stabilizing and ever moved toward full-employment equilibrium. With flexible prices and wages, unemployment of resources would be temporary. Beyond the temporary periods, changes in aggregate demand and supply would affect prices, not output and employment. Government stabilization policies had no role in the classical schema. But classical macroeconomics could not adequately analyze the Great Depression in which 25% of the industrial labor force was unemployed. The market mechanism was not getting people and resources together, and the economy was in equilibrium at far less than full employment.

In 1936 John Maynard Keynes attacked the major tenets of classical economic theory. He showed that savings and investment are undertaken by different groups with dissimilar motives and are not determined by a single variable such as the rate of interest. If planned investment were less than savings at full employment, actual savings and investment would be made equal via a fall in income out of which savings occur, and this equality could exist below full employment. Flexible wages would not guarantee full employment because a fall in money wages would reduce consumer demand and so lower the derived demand for labor and other resources. Hence, Keynes provided the theoretical justification for the use of government action to influence the gross national product (GNP). His theories aided the passage of the U. S. Employment Act of 1946, mandating that government must use both monetary and fiscal policy to meet the goals of relatively full employment and stable prices, and provide for growth. Fiscal policy takes the form of direct government expenditures and/or changes in taxes which affect private demand; monetary policy affects investment as well as capital movements in the balance of payments by changing the level of interest rates.

There is a multiplier process in Keynes' model whereby any autonomous change in any GNP component induces further changes in the income stream so that GNP increases (or decreases) by a multiple of the original injection (withdrawal). Initially Keynesian analysis focused on how monetary and fiscal policies could be used to combat business cycles. Any departure from full employment led to either an inflationary or deflationary gap; the gap was closed by decreasing or increasing aggregate demand.

The second phase of Keynesian analysis began in the late 1950's and early 1960's when the focus shifted to lowering the unemployment rate. Following World War II the amplitude of business-cycle fluctuation had been small but the average rate of unemployment was between 5 and 6%. In terms of the analytical concept of the Phillips-curve trade-off between unemployment and inflation, it was concluded that unemployment could be brought down by the proper use of monetary and fiscal policies. However, if lower unemployment was given priority it would be necessary to accept some price inflation. Early Keynesians thought of the "full-employment" level as a relatively narrow range. As time went by, economists came to see the "stabilization band" as having a wider range, and this view is encompassed in the Phillips curve.

The 1970's in the United States have created questions about Keynes and the Phillips curve because economic problems do not divide themselves neatly into inflationary (deflationary) gaps or a smooth unemployment-inflation swap-off. Stagflation, with inflation and high unemployment occurring simultaneously, cannot be handled by manipulating aggregate demand. Economists are seeking explanations and policy tools to combat the stagflation phenomenon.

Some depict the Phillips curve as shifting outward because of inflationary expectations; this would cause wages to rise along with higher rates of unemployment. In this case the inflationary psychology must be weakened via direct price controls, if necessary. Rising food and materials prices could also cause price increases in the absence of rising aggregate demand. If these increases are passed on, you have cost-push causation, especially if they occur in firms with power to set prices without much concern for demand. In such cases, Keynesian economics *per se* has little applicability. Monetary and fiscal policy which primarily affect aggregate demand and competitive markets would exacerbate the situation without affecting cause. Other factors weakening the link between monetary and fiscal policies include welfare programs and minimum wage laws.

Moreover, the U. S. economy has become increasingly subject to international influences. The worldwide economic boom of the 1970's, crop failures abroad, and devaluations of the dollar, contributed to U. S. inflation. These events were followed by a high increase in energy prices. Some who emphasize institutional factors and market imperfections advocate some kind of incomes policy. Most economists favor some type of "structural" reform, eliminating many of the institutional features that contribute to any inflationary bias or reduce the response of wages and prices to stabilization policies.

JOHN R. MATTHEWS, JR.

The junta that deposed Ecuador's President Guillermo Rodríguez Lara in January 1976 included (*left to right*): Gen. Guillermo Durán, Rear Adm. Alfredo Poveda, and Gen. Luis Leoro.

UPI

ECUADOR

For Ecuador, 1976 was a year of political turbulence and economic uncertainty.

Military Coup. Trouble began on January 5, when a transport strike was called to protest opposition to a 20% increase in bus fares. This provoked resignation of the cabinet. On January 9 the armed forces took control of the government. They deposed the president, Gen. Guillermo Rodríguez Lara, and established a junta presided over by Adm. Alfredo Poveda. It restored the 1945 constitution and promised an elected civilian government within two years.

Civilian politicians demanded a quicker return to elected government. The *Junta Civica,* including the Conservative, Liberal and Christian Democratic parties, demanded immediate elections. When the interior minister was removed in June, the parties again demanded quick elections, but the government merely reiterated its election schedule.

In August the government issued an appeal to the opposition parties for a dialogue. Although the parties rejected the idea, their opposition began to disintegrate in the last months of the year, as several factions broke with this intransigent position.

Strikes. The month of June was marked by strikes and political disturbances. On June 20 a strike of coffee and banana workers began, supported by government-employed agronomists and veterinarians. Some 600 agronomists were dismissed on June 29. A nationwide walkout of heavy transport workers took place between June 21 and 25, ending only when the government threatened to arrest the strikers. On June 21 the high school students of the port city of Guayaquil struck for 48 hours. This came after a week of riots that followed the police shooting of a 14-year-old student on June 15.

On July 15 another kind of disturbance hreatened the government—a one-day strike by policemen in Quito, demanding a pay increase. It resulted in the arrest of 13 senior police officers on July 17.

Economy. The country faced considerable economic difficulties during the year, particularly in its petroleum industry, the principal source of exports. For a while, the government embargoed oil export by the Gulf Oil Corporation until it paid supposedly owed taxes of $25 million. By September the government was announcing its intention to nationalize foreign oil firms operating in the country.

The government, however, sought to continue the country's economic development. In March, Ecuador received a loan of some $90 million from 21 U. S. banks, headed by the Bank of America. This loan was for improvements of transport, education, and medical care. Another measure was a program for the Guayaquil area, which projected an investment of $128 million in the area's agriculture and industry.

Clash with Clergy. On August 12, the government arrested more than 50 Catholic priests and laymen meeting in Río Bamba at the invitation of the local bishop. This was a parley of the Conference of Latin American Bishops (CELAM) to discuss social problems on the continent, and it was also attended by several clerics from the United States. Among those arrested were 37 foreigners and 15 bishops. The government accused the conferees of circulating "subversive" documents. The action was denounced by U. S. and Venezuelan bishops, as well as by Pablo Cardinal Munoz Vega, primate of the Ecuadorean Church, and by CELAM. The arrested clerics were deported on August 14.

ROBERT J. ALEXANDER, *Rutgers University*

─────── **ECUADOR • Information Highlights** ───────

Official Name: Republic of Ecuador.
Location: Northwest South America.
Area: 109,483 square miles (283,561 km²).
Population (1976 est.): 6,900,000.
Chief Cities (1974 est.): Quito, the capital, 557,000; Guayaquil, 814,000.
Government: *Head of state and government,* Alfredo Poveda Burbano, president of military junta (took office Jan. 1976). *Legislature*—Congress (dissolved Feb. 1972).
Monetary Unit: Sucre (25 sucres equal U. S.$1, Aug. 1976).
Gross National Product (1975 est.): $4,300,000,000.
Manufacturing (major products): Processed foods, textiles, petroleum products.
Major Agricultural Products: Bananas, coffee, cacao, rice, potatoes, sugarcane, cotton, forest products.
Foreign Trade (1975): *Exports,* $884,000,000; *imports,* $943,000,000.

EDUCATION

Continued retrenchment characterized U.S. education at all school levels in 1976. Money shortages further limited programs already affected by enrollment decline. Typical problems were New York City's public school and higher education cutbacks, New Jersey's search to equalize educational funding, and continued efforts to make desegregation work.

U.S. ELEMENTARY AND SECONDARY SCHOOLS

New York City. The city's 1.1 million pupil public school system, the nation's largest, opened in September 1976 with a reduced budget, shortened school days, larger pupil-teacher ratios, and fewer teachers (43,630, 1976; 56,623, 1975). Reduced services embittered many in the city's nearly 1,000 public schools. Suspensions, largely among the ⅔ black and Puerto Rican pupil majority, reached 25,253 in 1975–76, despite the use of 1,400 school security officers. On August 23, New York State Supreme Court's veto of the Stavisky-Goodman bill to provide more funds for the city's schools led to the layoff of 3,500 teachers. New York City's high welfare and city service costs, 72.9% of total expenditure, forcing a low 27.1% school expenditure, was a problem common to other large cities.

New Jersey. The State Supreme Court closed New Jersey's 2,500 schools July 1 to force the legislature to increase taxes to equalize state-wide school expenditure. The court agreed with a 1970 lawsuit charging unequal school finance from widely varying property taxes in 578 school districts. It ordered the legislature in 1973 to meet the constitutional requirement for "thorough and efficient" schools. The legislature resisted passage of an income tax until forced by court closure of schools. On July 10 the legislature passed an income tax expected to raise $775,000,000, $374,000,000 of which will go toward school cost equalization. Other states with similar school finance equalization problems watched the unprecedented case.

Boston. Boston's third year of court-ordered integration began with fewer incidents than in 1975, as 22,000 of its 76,000 students were bused to school. Opening day attendance was 69.4% (59% in 1975). Clashes occurred at South Boston High School, center of busing resistance, which Federal District Judge W. Arthur Garrity, Jr., put under court protection. White family flight took 17,216 students from Boston's public schools to private and suburban schools, bringing Boston schools' ratio to 47% white, 41% black, 12% other minorities.

The U.S. Supreme Court's refusal on June 14 to review lower court-ordered integration plans upheld Judge Garrity's Boston plan, modified since mid-1974. Boston's Mayor Kevin White urged peaceful acceptance of Garrity's plan.

The court's decision muted President Ford's request in May that Attorney General Edward H. Levi find in Boston or elsewhere a test case for the court's intervention to limit busing for integration. Democrats, whose election platform supported busing, civil-rights leaders, and others criticized Ford's antibusing stand as playing politics with an explosive issue. Likewise, Ford's bill to limit "excessive" busing for integration, sent to Congress on June 24, did not receive major support.

Civil Rights Commission Report. On August 24, the U.S. Commission on Civil Rights reported progress in school integration in communities where leaders worked to make it succeed. The report faulted Ford's antibusing statements as encouraging community resistance and said that, while half of all school children ride buses for normal transportation, only 7% of all public school children and 3.6% of all school children were bused for integration. Critics cited the report's false optimism as based on only eight relatively easily integrated small school systems. They named Detroit, Baltimore, Cleveland, New York City, Chicago, and Washington, D.C., as economically shaky, black-dominated cities with still segregated schools.

Private Schools. A U.S. Supreme Court ruling on June 25 prohibited private nonreligious schools from excluding blacks. The 7–2 ruling, based on the 1866 Civil Rights Act, arose from two recent suburban Virginia cases. Observers felt the ruling might discourage further growth of all-white academies and dampen white flight from integrated city schools. Most all-white academies in the South, enrolling 1 of every 10 white students, advertise open admission to retain tax-free status, knowing that high tuition costs bar poor minorities.

U.S. HIGHER EDUCATION

CUNY Cutbacks. City University of New York's 20 collegiate units opened September 1976 with the first tuition charges in the university's 129-year history. A fee of $750 was charged for freshmen and sophomores, and $900 for juniors and seniors. New York State increased its contribution to $195,000,000; New York City lowered its contribution to $160,-000,000. This formula plus tuition allowed the 155,040 student body (271,000, 1975–76) to operate under a 1976–77 austerity budget of $470,000,000 ($539,000,000, 1975–76). Forced into midyear budget cuts, CUNY closed May 28, two weeks before the spring term's end. State aid of $24,000,000 enabled it to finish the year and grant over 30,000 degrees. Financial agony led to cuts in faculty (down 19% from 1975), enrollment (down 17% from 1975), programs, and open admissions (CUNY's unique remedial program for salvaging academically weak students).

New York State Disputes. New York Gov. Hugh Carey signed a bill July 29 making decisions by the state's Commissioner of Education

Schools in Louisville, Ky., open peacefully in September, contrasting sharply with 1975 racial turmoil.

Ewald B. Nyquist subject to court review. Tension grew from Nyquist's unpopular integration orders but was also caused by money, enrollment, and other problems.

The state's Board of Regents 1976 master plan for higher education evoked a clash over control between the Regents and State University of New York officials.

Church College Aid. On June 21, the U. S. Supreme Court, by a 5–4 vote, upheld Maryland's aid to church colleges for secular purposes only. Proponents said states may now constitutionally aid financially desperate private colleges. Opponents feared encroachment on traditional separation of church and state.

West Point Cheating. In March, most West Point juniors (class of 1977) had a take-home electrical engineering test to solve individually. Of 823 test papers turned in, one marked "I received help" initiated investigations of the honor code's statement, "A cadet will not lie, cheat, or steal, or tolerate those who do." Of 229 cadets accused of cheating, 65 implicated nearly 700 others as violators in the 174-year-old U. S. Military Academy's third major cheating scandal since 1951.

As of September 13, 104 of the 229 accused cadets had resigned; of these nearly 90 are under a special offer of possible readmission; 40 appealed; the rest were cleared.

Some thought the honor code too rigid in not allowing lesser penalties than dismissal or resignation for minor infractions and first offenses. Others felt that take-home tests invited collaboration, a practice now stopped. Others said abuse was inevitable in competitive class rankings which determine future military assignments.

U. S. ENROLLMENTS, COSTS, GRADUATES

The Health, Education, and Welfare Department issued the following 1976–77 statistical estimates (1975–76 comparisons in parentheses):

Enrollments, kindergarten through grade 8: 34,200,000 pupils (34,700,000, down over 1%); high school: 15,800,000 + (increase of under 1%); colleges and universities: 10,100,000 (9,700,000, up 4%); total, 60,100,000 students (60,200,000).

Expenditures, elementary and secondary, $81,500,000,000 ($75,300,000,000); colleges and universities, $48,800,000,000 ($44,500,000,000); public schools, all levels, $105,800,000,000; private schools, $24,500,000,000; total, $130,000,000,000 + ($120,000,000,000).

Number of teachers, elementary and secondary, 2,500,000 (small increase); colleges and universities, 687,000 (670,000, up 3%). Graduates, high school, over 3,100,000; bachelor's degrees, 918,000; first professional degrees, 60,000; master's, 338,000; doctorates, 37,000.

Education directly involves 63,600,000 people or 3 out of 10 Americans; expenditure of about 8% of the 1975 gross national product, divided in 1976–77 among state governments, $45,000,000,000, 34.5%; local, $38,200,000,000, 29.3%; federal, $13,400,000,000, 10.3%; private and other sources, $33,700,000,000, 25.9%.

A City University of New York employee receives a note instead of a paycheck. A financial crisis forced CUNY to close in May and charge tuition in the fall.

In March, some 15,000 French students demonstrate against a government plan to reform higher education.

ENGLAND AND WALES

School Leaving Exam. On July 8, Britain's Schools Council voted 57–6 to accept the Certificate of Education (CE) examination to replace both the traditional secondary school leaving exam, the General Certificate of Education (GCE), and the Certificate of Secondary Education (CSE, begun 1965). Students currently start courses toward either GCE or CSE exams at age 14 and take one of these examinations at the age of 16.

Direct Grant Schools End. To end education inequalities, the Labour government will phase out direct grant schools. These 170 private secondary schools received state grants for offering up to 25% free places for bright but poor students from the Local Education Authorities (LEA's). One hundred and nineteen of these schools plan to remain independent, while 51, mainly Roman Catholic, will become state schools.

Comprehensive Secondary Schools. In 1965 the Labour government asked all LEA's to prepare comprehensive secondary education plans rather than rely on selective and hence socially divisive private grammar schools. A May 25 council election in Tameside, near Manchester, was won by Conservatives on a pledge to retain grammar schools. Education Minister Fred Mulley ordered Tameside to follow its comprehensive plan. The council's appeal was upheld by the House of Lords Judicial Committee on August 2. Seven Conservative councils refuse to go comprehensive; thirty other British councils remained undecided.

Progressive-Traditional Clash. A Lancaster University research report in May added fuel to the controversy over comprehensive state schools versus selective private schools. The report showed that traditionally educated students scored higher on tests. This finding, still being debated at year's end, contradicted the government's Plowden Report (1967) that endorsed progressive methods and influenced "Open Education" in Britain and the United States.

University Costs. A study showed that Britain spent $100,000,000 a year educating overseas students, among them 3,400 Americans who pay $640 annual tuition, or $360 more than British students pay but only a fifth or sixth of American college costs. In 1976 the government raised tuition costs by 30% for all 4,500,000 students in Britain's 44 universities. Foreigners are mainly affected since British students can apply for scholarships according to need.

Tyndale School. A July 28, 1976, report on William Tyndale Junior School (ages 7 to 11) in working class Islington, north London, described alleged conservative reaction to hasty and arbitrary progressive teaching methods. Strong factionalism developed, teachers went on strike, parents withdrew their children. Falling enrollment led to the much publicized report which criticized some actions of the headmaster, teachers, board of managers, and Inner London Education Authority.

CANADA

Bilingualism. The Secretary of State provided C$134,000,000 to provincial education for second language teaching in renewed effort to stress Canada's official bilingualism. In practice this move means more use of French. A University of Montreal report on bilingualism issued August 17 preferred early second language teaching in school over spending money to teach middle-aged civil servants a new language.

Science. For 1976–77 the National Research Council of Canada awarded C$11,000,000 graduate student grants to promote science and its application to national needs.

Ontario. From 1977, foreign students at Ontario universities will pay C$1,500 (was C$585) per two-term year and C$750 (was C$250) at colleges of applied arts and technology.

OTHER INTERNATIONAL DEVELOPMENTS

France. In March–April some 100,000 of France's 850,000 university students boycotted classes to protest higher education reforms set for 1977. The reforms include more selective admissions, less time to earn higher degrees, industry and business involvement to tie courses to job needs, and more emphasis on scientific and technical programs for national development. Half of the 200,000 annual graduates of France's 76 universities study humanities and liberal arts. Only 1 in 8 now finds a job, mainly as a state-paid teacher. The changes aim to combat oversupply and underemployment of French university students who double the number of students in England, which has the same population, and exceed the number in West Germany, which has more population. Student discontent focused on Secretary of State for the Universities Alice Saunier-Seïté, who backed the reforms proposed in January by Education Minister René Haby. University presidents voted for reconsideration of the reforms. But President Giscard d'Estaing said they would go forward.

Israel. A program to educate low IQ children of uneducated Israeli immigrants from the Middle East and North Africa was declared successful. Hebrew University Education Professor Carl Frankenstein used "the most difficult materials that are available," taught by well-trained, sympathetic teachers determined not to write off slum students as nonachievers. The program secured university entrance for 50% of the students in the experiment.

Medical Education Cooperation. In a New York State-Israeli sponsored program of medical education at Tel Aviv University, the state pays $6,000 a year for eligible New York students, each of whom pays another $6,000 a year in tuition and can apply for scholarships. Teaching is in English for two years and then in Hebrew. Graduates must practice medicine 3 or 4 years in a New York State area of need.

West Germany. School policy was an issue in West Germany's elections. Middle class voters feared lowered educational quality because of the Social Democrats' goal of ending educational elitism and including more children of workers and farmers in universities. In September parents in Hesse took that state's education minister to court to stop his plan to eliminate some required senior high school courses. Current university enrollment is 23% of the relevant age group, compared with 8% in 1960.

Australia. Since 1971 about 2,000 U.S. teachers have been selected to teach mainly in New South Wales and Victoria. Australia's teacher training has since greatly expanded, an oversupply has resulted, and reaction has set in. Teachers' unions resent job competition and Americans' special privileges: tax-free status, free U.S.-Australia transportation, low-cost housing, and migrant status.

USSR. The USSR's current 5-year plan (1976–80) includes new school construction for 7 million students, more than half of it to bring rural schools up to urban standards. In 1972, 12 million students were in universities and technical colleges and 5 million studied in night schools.

See also feature article on the 3 R's, pages 37–43.

FRANKLIN PARKER, *West Virginia University*

UPI

In Montreal, children of Italian descent attend a kindergarten class taught by their parents. The action was in defiance of the Official Language Act Bill 22, making French the official language of the province of Quebec.

In October Egypt's President Anwar el-Sadat was sworn in for a second six-year term. Later he discussed a new cabinet with Premier Mamdouh Muhammad Salem and Vice President Muhammad Hosni Mubarak (*right*).

EGYPT

In many ways 1976 was a return for Egypt to the pre-Nasser days of the early 1950's, with a relatively free economy, a lessened preoccupation with Israel, but an increased concern with "Arab" politics.

Domestic Affairs. In late October Egypt held its first free election since the days of King Farouk (ousted in 1952). Nearly 1,700 candidates competed for 347 seats in the People's Assembly. Although no formal political parties were permitted, factions of the Arab Socialist Union played the role of parties. The election was marred by disturbances and violence (at least three dead), but it brought victory to the faction supporting President Sadat and his prime minister, Mamdouh Salem. The fact that there was competition at all made this election unique in modern Egyptian history. President Sadat won reelection, without competition, to a six-year term in September and was sworn into office on October 16.

The economy was variously described as "troubled," "burgeoning," "liberalized," and "westernized." Indeed, Sadat continued to free the economy of the Nasserite restraints that characterized it in the 1960's. One inevitable consequence was that the economy moved in unpredictable ways. A real-estate speculative boom pushed some land in Cairo to as much as $1,000 per square yard, and a new crop of millionaires (about 500) has come into being. In August Sadat stated that labor strikes would not be permitted and that production must rise. Although in some ways the old social and economic habits still characterize Egypt, new changes are evident. In March the government secured religious support for new and liberalized rights (including divorce) for women. Not all was well on the political front, however. The extremist Muslim Brotherhood, banned since 1948 and literally broken up in 1954 (after an attempt on Nasser's life), was once again active in Cairo. And in June, Nasser's old intelligence chief, Salah Nasr, was convicted of torturing prisoners and sentenced to ten years at hard labor.

Arab Affairs. In late February the final step in Egypt's Sinai accord with Israel took place, and Egyptian forces occupied the last portions of territory that Egypt was to obtain under the agreement. The pact continues to ensure a lull in the dispute between Egypt and Israel, but it also acts as an irritant in Egypt's relations with other Arab states.

The great crisis in the Arab world in 1976 was the civil war in Lebanon, where the unlikely scenario of Syrian military intervention in support of right-wing Christian groups but against Muslim and Palestinian liberation forces was played out. Israel quietly aided those perceived to be its "friends," Libyan money was also involved. All this affected Egypt in numerous ways. Sadat continued to demand a role in Palestinian affairs and paid lip service at least to the Palestinian cause against Israel; consequent-

---

EGYPT • Information Highlights

Official Name: Arab Republic of Egypt.
Location: Northeastern Africa.
Area: 386,660 square miles (1,001,449 km²).
Population (1976 est.): 38,100,000.
Chief Cities (1975 est.): Cairo, the capital, 8,400,000; Alexandria, 2,500,000.
Government: *Head of state,* Anwar el-Sadat, president (took office Oct. 1970). *Head of government,* Mamdouh Muhammad Salem, prime minister (took office April 1975). *Legislature* (unicameral)—People's Assembly.
Monetary Unit: Pound (0.39 pound equals U. S.$1, Sept. 1976).
Gross National Product (1975 est.): $11,700,000,000.
Manufacturing (major products): Cotton textiles, processed foods, fertilizer, iron and steel.
Major Agricultural Products: Cotton, forage plants (berseem), rice, wheat, sugarcane, millet, corn, fish.
Foreign Trade (1975): *Exports,* $1,402,000,000; *imports,* $3,951,000,000.

ly, he strongly objected to the role played by Syria. Personal competition with Syrian President Hafez al-Assad also gave Sadat uneasy moments. He journeyed throughout the Arab world to promote Egyptian views of the Lebanese events; but his travels were also designed to obtain further financial support for the Egyptian economy. The year's end found Syrian prestige in Lebanon undiminished, but in other ways Sadat's Arab ventures were fruitful. Relations with Libya, however, were typically bad.

In January Libyan students in Cairo, undoubtedly with Egyptian support, forcibly occupied their country's embassy, denouncing events in Benghazi. In March Libya was accused of sending agents to Cairo to kidnap dissident Libyan political leaders. In early August Libya was blamed for terrorist bombings in Cairo and Alexandria; later in the same month an abortive hijacking of an Egyptian airliner was also put to Libya's account. The usual military confrontation was staged along the Libyan-Egyptian border, but few Lybians or Egyptians seemed very concerned. The Qaddafi-Sadat dispute is of long standing; although it does not go away, it has not yet resulted in war. Egypt was on good terms with Saudi Arabia and the rest of the Arab world.

Foreign Affairs. Relations with the United States were generally good during 1976. Secretary of the Treasury William Simon visited Cairo in March, promising $1,800,000,000 in economic aid. While this was welcomed, Egypt equally desired "defensive" weapons to beef up its armed forces, still lacking in equipment since the 1973 war with Israel. But there was considerable opposition to this in Congress—even to the sale of a half dozen C-130 military transport planes. Egypt said, however, that it would be satisfied with 40% of the U. S. arms that went to Israel; little of any "military" equipment has actually gone to the Egyptians. There was some disappointment with the outcome of the American presidential elections with regard to expected aid.

Egyptian-Soviet diplomatic relations were up and down during the year. Although President Sadat in March called for an end of the "friendship" pact of 1971, in May relations had once again improved and condemnations of the Soviet Union in the Egyptian press had ceased. In October the Egyptian and Soviet foreign ministers met in Bulgaria to attempt ironing out their differences. In April it was announced that mainland China had agreed to the sale of MiG parts and other military equipment to Egypt. President Sadat toured western Europe in the spring to build support for his position in the Middle East.

See also MIDDLE EAST.

CARL LEIDEN
University of Texas at Austin

ELECTIONS, U. S. See pages 24–31.

ENERGY

SURVEY

The consumer nations' indecision over long-term energy policies, growing U. S. dependence on the Organization of Petroleum Exporting Countries (OPEC), and the question of how to pace economic growth, both domestic and international, and its consequent rise in energy demands, characterized the 1976 energy scene.

Although some of the uncertainty prevalent in 1975 lingered on, the year presented a more realistic view of the U. S. petroleum sector and the energy potential in general. The major concerns continued to be (a) resistance to increased domestic drilling and well completion and (b) the need for greater capital spending for new oil and gas projects as the primary moves to meet short- and medium-range energy requirements.

U. S. Energy Trends and Policies. Two major changes in the composition of U. S. oil imports occurred in 1976. In March, the United States, although a net importer of both oil and natural gas for some years, for the first time recorded oil imports in excess of domestic output: Second, the importation trend shifted toward the Eastern hemisphere, with the Arab oil-producing nations furnishing the largest portion of U. S. petroleum imports. The demand for petroleum by American consumers was climbing to the 1973 pre-embargo level, if not higher. In 1976, imports were expected to average about 43% of total U. S. oil consumption.

Failure to develop alternative energy sources as planned, unsuccessful energy conservation measures, a tight capital market, and a continued reduction in domestic production are responsible for the changing U. S. import pattern. Materials and water shortages and other physical limitations also acted as deterrents to hopes, outlined in Project Independence and by the Energy Research and Development Administration (ERDA), of lowering dependency on foreign supplies through enlarged production of conventional energy sources and development of new sources. Dr. John Fallon of ERDA estimated that the energy source pattern with petroleum's large share will be primarily unchanged until about the year 2000 because of technical and economic constraints in the development of shale, geothermal, and solar energy.

As a result of this situation, Frank Zarb, the administrator of the Federal Energy Administration, proposed an energy strategy package to include: (a) energy use reduction from a 3.5% annual growth rate to 2.5%; (b) support of policies to maximize petroleum and gas production and development largely through induced incentives to the petroleum sector; (c) a doubling of coal production by 1986; (d) developing nuclear power to supply 26% of electrical requirements

Representatives of the Organization of Petroleum Exporting Countries hold a general meeting in Paris in January. As petroleum becomes a more scarce commodity, the power of OPEC increases.

UPI

from the present 9% level; and (e) creation of a 1,000,000,000-barrel stockpile of petroleum. The latter oil reserve would represent only a small amount of oil compared to global and OPEC trade volumes; therefore, it is thought more beneficial for the United States to seek the lowest prices for its petroleum purchases through international trade with a concomitant saving of U. S. tax dollars and a reduction in possible intergovernmental friction.

A strong correlation exists between growth of the gross national product (GNP) in the United States and the increased use of energy. Yet Zarb believes optimistically that growth in energy usage could be curtailed by up to 14% without lowering the living standard or the per capita income. Nonetheless, a 1976 International Energy Agency study noted that, unlike most other industrialized nations, the United States has failed to cut energy waste. Moreover, the price control on domestic production and relatively low taxes have kept oil prices below those of other OECD (Organization for Economic Cooperation and Development) states, thereby hindering conservation in the United States. Despite the 1973–74 OPEC price hikes, American auto users still pay only one half to one third of the price that their European counterparts pay for gasoline.

New Proposals. A goal to require all cars to operate at 20 miles per gallon (mpg) (32 km pg) by 1980 and at 27.5 mpg (44 km pg) by 1985 received increased support. Dr. Stephen Berry of the University of Chicago foresees a doubling of average gas mileage in U. S. autos by 1985 leading to a saving of 7% of the U. S. annual energy requirements, i. e., some 1,200,-000,000 barrels of oil.

Of critical importance to domestic energy development, supply, and pricing was the 1976 Congressional attempt to force the breakup of major integrated oil companies, that is, firms which engage in the full range of petroleum activities from exploration and production, to pipelines, transport, refining, and marketing. Proposed legislation would have required such companies to divest themselves of various

UPI

Within two years Ford Motors plans to introduce a six cylinder engine that can switch to a three cylinder operation. Officials predict a 10% fuel savings.

branches and concentrate on a specific activity; the legislation might also break up "energy companies," requiring a firm to participate in only one energy source, such as coal or oil, but not both. Supporters of this legislation believed lower energy prices could result. Opponents contended such action would bring about higher prices through loss of economies of scale and tremendous problems in meeting financial obligations and in acquiring needed investment for research and development programs caused by the proliferation of smaller entities.

RAGAEI EL MALLAKH
Professor of Economics
University of Colorado

COAL

Coal is the most abundant of the fossil fuels found in the United States. While the exact quantity is unknown, it will last for hundreds of years at current consumption rates.

The oil embargo imposed on the United States in 1973 raised serious concerns about the security of supply of U. S. energy sources. A new government policy was announced that appeared to move toward maximizing the use of indigenous resources, which would result in a wider utilization of domestic coal. Although coal production has increased somewhat since 1973, the growth rate has not been as great as anticipated, and oil imports are increasing.

The fact that coal production has not grown at the expected rate is due in part to the environmental impacts of the mining and use of coal and in part to the impossibility of directly substituting coal for oil and natural gas in transportation and some industries. There is still a sharp difference of opinion whether commercial technology exists for the control of sulfur oxides, a major air pollutant released by the combustion of high-sulfur coals. The use of low-sulfur coals, which meet sulfur-oxide standards and which can be strip-mined at low cost in the western United States, has been delayed by federal leasing policies and uncertainties about the cost and practicality of land reclamation in regions of limited rainfall.

Cleaner and more efficient methods for burning coal at industrial and utility plants are being studied, but until coal can be mined and used in an environmentally acceptable manner, its use will be limited, even where it could be substituted for fuels that are in short supply.

More than half of the coal produced in the United States is used at electric generating plants. Most of the balance is either used at domestic industrial plants or exported. Increased use of coal is expected in all of these markets. The growth of coal use at electric generating plants depends on questions, unresolved as the year came to an end, about comparative costs of coal and nuclear fuels.

New uses for coal are anticipated in the production of synthetic gas and oil. Both have been made from coal in the past, but production costs have been much higher than those of domestic oil and natural gas and even the artificially high world price of oil. No new processes for reducing these high costs have been proved to be commercial.

Prospects for increased coal production in the United States remain favorable, but quantities will depend mainly on international oil import policies.

HARRY PERRY
Author, "Coal Conversion Technologies"

ELECTRICITY

Electricity, though not in itself an energy source, is a convenient and popular medium for the use of energy in the coal, natural gas, petroleum, water power, and nuclear fission from which it is produced. The United States doubles its use of electricity about every ten years. In 1976 normal industrial expansion was maintaining its growth rate, and decreasing supplies of petroleum and natural gas were raising produc-

tion costs and forcing increased use of coal and nuclear fission energy. Unfortunately, these were the only practical sources of energy available to industry, and both were under heavy attack in the United States and elsewhere for environmental and social reasons.

Urban expansion and environmental concerns make it increasingly difficult to locate sites for power plants and transmission lines. This fact and the increasing demand for electricity make it necessary to construct larger generators and operate transmission lines at higher voltages —up to 746,000 volts in 1976 and 1,100,000 expected in the near future.

Much research is being performed in areas such as solar energy, nuclear fusion, wind and geothermal power, and ocean thermal gradients for electricity production, but the technology was not available in 1976 to make major use of them. Magnetohydrodynamics (MHD), for the direct conversion of heat to electricity, was showing promise as a means of extracting more electricity from the energy in coal. Cryogenics, the field of extremely low temperature research, suggested a new means for transmitting very large amounts of electrical energy underground for long distances. Developments in cryogenics may make it possible to store electricity directly for use at a later time more efficiently than in pumped-storage systems.

The per capita consumption of electricity for household use was about the same in the United States as in other developed nations. The overall consumption was higher than elsewhere (about 35% of the world production). As other countries of the world develop, their use of electricity increases, resulting in a need for continuing expansion of the world's generating and transmission facilities.

WILLIAM J. HANNA
University of Colorado

NATURAL GAS

Natural gas continued in 1976 to be the second largest source of energy used in the United States.

In an attempt to avoid shortages in the supply of this commodity which were foreseen by the Ford administration in 1975, deregulation of the price of natural gas was sought. During 1976 the Federal Power Commission (FPC) raised the ceiling price of natural gas sold in interstate commerce, hoping to alleviate the predicted gas shortages. After the higher prices for new gas sales were set, deregulation action was tabled. However, the issue is likely to be revived following the inauguration of the new Carter administration, particularly in light of declining domestic production and reserves.

Those favoring deregulation point out that efficiency is better ensured through the functioning of free market forces of supply and demand effecting the proper balancing, or equilibrating, price for natural gas. Deregulation backers also

NATURAL GAS CONSUMPTION AND WORLD GAS RESERVES, 1975

Region	Consumption (Est.)	As % of Total Consumption
North America	620 Mrd m³	51
U.S.S.R.	270 Mrd m³	22
Western Europe	180 Mrd m³	15
China and Eastern Europe	60 Mrd m³	5
Rest of world	80 Mrd m³	7
Total	1,210 Milliard (10⁹)m³*	100

Region	Reserves	As % of Total Reserves
North America	8,000 Mrd m³	13
U.S.S.R.	23,000 Mrd m³	36
Middle East	15,200 Mrd m³	24
Africa	5,800 Mrd m³	9
Western Europe	5,100 Mrd m³	8
Far East	3,200 Mrd m³	5
South America	2,200 Mrd m³	3
China and Eastern Europe	1,000 Mrd m³	2
Total	63,500 Milliard (10⁹)m³**	100

* Equivalent to approximately 20.5 million b/d of oil.
** Equivalent to approximately 400 milliard barrels of oil.
Source: Shell International Petroleum Company Limited, Information Handbook 1976–7 (London, 1976), p. 84.

hold that inefficiency has developed due to a free market for intrastate sale of natural gas while interstate sales have been regulated by ceiling prices. Consumer groups represent the majority of those seeking the strengthening of federal control of price setting for natural gas, arguing specifically for control of intrastate gas sales and lower prices.

Supporters of the FPC's higher price for interstate sales of natural gas feel that the new higher prices justify explorations, both onshore and offshore, which were previously uneconomic. Industrial affiliates hope for decontrol of both onshore and offshore price setting.

RAGAEI EL MALLAKH
University of Colorado

NUCLEAR ENERGY

As 1976 came to a close, the U. S. nuclear power industry was subjected to a virtual moratorium on new power plant construction. The moratorium came as the result of the U. S. Nuclear Regulatory Commission's (NRC) response to a July 21 Court of Appeals decision calling for a more thorough consideration of waste management and conservation issues in the licensing of plants. The NRC subsequently prepared a documented environmental survey on the costs of fuel reprocessing and waste management and began to draft new licensing rules.

Eleven plants scheduled for construction were held up by the licensing moratorium. At year end the United States had 211 reactors either operating, or under construction, with a total electrical output of 206,835 megawatts. The 59 operational had a total capacity of 41,183 megawatts. This represented about 8% of the total U. S. electricity output.

About 50% of the planned or operating nuclear power production in the world is in the United States. The remarkable growth of the commercial nuclear power industry in the last decade was slowed markedly in 1976 by a combination of environmental concerns—especially on radioactive waste disposal—and lack of capital funds. The most visible public reaction occurred in Sweden, where Thörbjorn Fälldin's party was elected to power in September after Fälldin promised a halt of nuclear power plants. As prime minister, however, Fälldin withdrew his opposition to a new reactor to be commissioned in southern Sweden, and appointed a special group to study the whole question of nuclear power plants.

UPI

Employees examine Unit 1 of the Sequoyah Nuclear Power Station being built at Daisy, Tenn., by the Tennessee Valley Authority. As a result of a court decision calling for greater consideration of the environment, new power plant construction was at a virtual standstill as the year came to an end.

In California, voters rejected a proposal that would have banned new plant construction and reduced power output of existing reactors by a 2 to 1 margin. Initiatives controlling nuclear-power plant development were defeated in Arizona, Colorado, Montana, Ohio, Oregon, and Washington in November.

Radioactive fallout from a September 26 Chinese test caused abnormally high levels of I-131 in milk supplies in the northeast United States about one week later. While the activity levels were not considered dangerous by most experts, they exceeded by a large margin what is delivered to the atmosphere from a nuclear power plant.

About 13.5% of the Energy Research and Development Administration's proposed 1977 budget of $5,266,000,000 was devoted to fission reactor development, and some 48.9% was nuclear-related. Included were such additional topics as fuel cycle and nuclear safeguards, uranium enrichment, environmental control technology, basic energy science, space nuclear systems, and fusion power. Some 51.1% was non-nuclear or military, and in this category fossil-fuel research, solar power, geothermal power, and conservation were included.

A prominent new development in nuclear fusion research surfaced in 1976 with the suggestion to use beams of heavy ions—highly charged atoms—directed onto deuterium-tritium fuel pellets to initiate thermonuclear reactions. The concept promises to join two other fusion schemes—those of magnetic confinement and of laser-induced fusion—in the forefront of the U. S. energy research programs.

ROBERT E. CHRIEN
Brookhaven National Laboratory

PETROLEUM

With no major crude oil price increase imposed during the year by the Organization of Petroleum Exporting Countries (OPEC), 1976 turned out to be a year of reflection and consolidation for the world oil industry.

Governments of the oil producing countries were working out new relationships with the oil companies—in some cases taking over total ownership of oil wells and working out "service contracts" under which the oil companies continued to produce the oil.

The industrial nations, free for the moment of sharp upward surges in the cost of the oil on which their economies depend, took the first faltering steps toward lessening their dependence on imported oil, by encouraging lower consumption of petroleum products and developing alternate sources of energy. But in the United States, the picture was quite different: petroleum products demand was up, refineries were working at a higher rate than in other countries, but domestic crude production was down. Thus, the United States was importing oil at the highest rate in its history, with crude oil imports in 1976

UPI

The search begins for oil and gas deposits off Cape Cod. Such offshore exploration slumped in 1976.

equal to nearly 45% of the country's crude oil consumption.

The memory of long lines of automobiles at gasoline pumps in the winter months of 1973–74 and of shortages of heating oil in parts of the country had failed to lessen demand for the country's main source of energy.

By mid-1976, a worldwide slump in offshore "wildcatting"—the search for oil in new areas —was beginning to be felt. Of the world's 425 offshore drilling rigs, 66 were in layup, and 29 new rigs—ordered in a more optimistic time— were due to enter the market without any prospects of work, to join 33 rigs completing contracts, also with no jobs lined up.

Through September world crude production was up by about 4.8%, to 43,493,000 barrels a day. But the OPEC countries as a group accounted for nearly all of the increase, with a total output of 29,265,000 barrels a day, up 7.2% from the year earlier.

In the United States, despite the definite increase in demand for petroleum products, crude production was actually down by 3.1%—a situation blamed on an $8 per barrel ceiling on the average price of domestic crude, against about $12 for OPEC oil.

Two new major oil-producing areas were being readied in 1976 to start moving crude to market. One of these areas, the North Sea off the northwestern coast of Europe, would be proving substantial amounts of crude to European refineries, starting in 1977—despite lower demand for products in Europe and a 60% refinery operating rate there. But the advantages to such countries as Britain and Norway of using their North Sea oil were indeed great, for it would conserve the foreign exchange spending for the OPEC oil their North Sea production would displace.

The other giant stirring on the oil scene was Alaska, where a pipeline was being built to move vast quantities of crude from the northern coast to a warm-water port at Valdez on the southern coast. From there, the oil would be moved to the U. S. West Coast by tanker. Production of Alaskan crude is due to start in 1977 and soon reach a rate high enough to displace about a third of total U. S. oil imports.

West Coast refineries will not be able to use all this Alaskan crude, however, so plans are being worked out to move the oil to other U. S. refining areas. One such plan would involve a little-used natural gas pipeline from West Texas to the Los Angeles area. The line would be reversed and used to move Alaskan oil to connections in Texas with other pipelines to refineries in the Middle West and East.

There was little major refinery construction during 1976. European refiners modernized their equipment so as to produce more gasoline and light heating oil and less heavy fuel oil.

Many countries—particularly the OPEC states, which wanted to upgrade their crude into higher-valued products before exporting it—still had ambitious plans for large-scale refinery construction. But few of these projects moved into the construction stage, and a U. S. government midyear report concluded that even longer range refinery construction plans "have failed to become any firmer than they were a year ago."

In the United States, even though refineries were operating at better than 80% of capacity and petroleum products demand was up, virtually no new refineries were being built. Environmental opposition, especially on the East Coast, and construction costs were blamed for the lag.

C. B. SQUIRE, *Contributing Editor*
"International Oil News"

Solar cells gather in the sun's rays and convert them to electricity to control rail protection devices.

UPI

WORLD CRUDE OIL PRODUCTION AND PROVEN RESERVES, 1975*
(in percentage)

Country/Region	Production	Reserves
U.S.	18.0	5.5
Canada	3.1	1.2
Rest of Western hemisphere	7.9	4.3
Europe	1.1	3.2
Africa	9.1	8.1
Middle East	35.5	62.7
Far East/Australia	4.0	2.6
U.S.S.R., Eastern Europe, China	21.3	12.4
	100.0	100.0

*Production figures include that of crude oil and natural gas liquids.
Source: Shell International Petroleum Company Limited, Information Handbook 1976–7 (London, 1976), pp. 58–61.

SOLAR ENERGY

Public interest in solar energy has grown along with its technical and commercial development. Commercialization at the present is limited largely to water heating and, to a lesser degree, space heating. The Energy Research and Development Administration (ERDA) has the major role in defining and administering the U. S. solar energy program. The major emphasis has been on solar heating and cooling and on solar generation of electric power. However, other energy development programs are being carried out.

The solar water heating industry has shown significant development because it is the only one using solar energy which is economically viable throughout the United States. Solar space heating is attractive in many regions of the country but not everywhere. Solar cooling (in conjunction with space and water heating) is presently not competitive with other methods due to high initial costs.

In the first phase of the residential solar heating and cooling demonstration program, administered by the Department of Housing and Urban Development, 55 projects consisting of 143 units, mainly involving heating, were funded. In the second phase, beginning in the fall of 1976, approximately 102 demonstration projects were to be funded.

A 5-Mw thermal test facility is being developed at Sandia Laboratories in Albuquerque, N. Mex. It is intended as a pilot for a 10 Mwe (megawatts of electricity) solar electric power plant, with a central receiver, designed under ERDA contract. Proposals from 9 utilities to install and manage such a 10 Mwe facility were submitted to ERDA in September 1976. The most recent cost of solar cells purchased by ERDA contract was $15 per peak watt—a 25% reduction over six months earlier. When used with a concentrating collector, these costs are, of course, considerably reduced.

The location and specific role of the Solar Energy Research Institute (SERI) had not been decided by the year's end.

GARY C. VLIET
University of Texas at Austin

PHOTOS LEE W. NIELSEN, U. S. BUREAU OF RECLAMATION

Nambe Falls Dam, a thin-arch double-curvature concrete type completed in 1976, is located just north of Santa Fe, N. Mex. It is the first prestressed arch dam to be built in the United States.

ENGINEERING, CIVIL

While the construction industry in 1976 suffered from insufficient funding, many civil engineering achievements were recorded both in the United States and abroad.

BRIDGES

United States. The first bridge over the Yukon River in Alaska is a dual-purpose span for vehicles and pipeline. Located 100 miles (160 km) north of Fairbanks, the $31.5-million bridge consists of twin orthotropic steel-box girders supporting a 30-foot (9-m) wide roadway. Its 2,280-foot (695-m) length includes four spans at 410 feet (125 m) and two end spans at 320 feet (97.5 m). Hung below the deck are two pipelines, 48 inches (122 cm) in diameter, in which oil will flow south from Prudhoe Bay 798 miles (1,284 km) to Valdez. The dual-service bridge was completed in 1976.

In Alabama a 7-mile (11-km) twin bridge is being built to carry Interstate 10 over Mobile Bay. Each 43-foot (13-m) wide concrete trestle consists of piles, caps, and deck sections, with spans averaging 66 feet (20 m) in length.

England. The world's longest single-span bridge is being built over the Humber River estuary, upstream from Hull, England. Its 4,626-foot (1,410-m) main span is 368 feet (112 m) longer than the Verrazano-Narrows Bridge in New York City. The Humber's two side spans of 919 and 1,739 feet (280 and 530 m) give the bridge a length of 7,284 feet (2,220 m) between anchorages. Its two 508-foot (155-m) high towers are slip-formed of concrete, while the bridge's superstructure consists of steel-box girders supported by two 27-inch (682-mm) diameter cables. Started in 1973, the $125-million structure is expected to open in 1979.

Egypt. The Rameses Bridge over the Nile River at Cairo, Egypt, is part of the 1.5-mile (2.5-km) Sixth of October crossing that passes over the narrower west branch of the river, Gezira Island, and the broader 1,608-foot (490-m) east branch of the Nile. The Rameses Bridge east branch crossing has five spans and a 105-foot (32-m) wide roadway. The project started in 1969 and was completed in 1976.

South America. Also opened in 1976 was the 7,741-foot (2,359-m) prestressed concrete vehicular bridge over the Río Uruguay, about 170 miles (274 km) north of Buenos Aires. Jointly owned by the nations of Uruguay and Argentina, which it connects, the $10-million bridge replaced a ferry. The main channel is crossed by a 472-foot (144-m) center span, and two 318-foot (97-m) side spans.

CANALS

In the United States the Bureau of Reclamation is planning a $496-million combined irrigation and water-supply system in North Dakota. The Garrison River diversion project will include 1,800 miles (2,900 km) of canals to carry water to 14 communities. The Bureau of Reclamation will also dig a 14.3-mile (23-km) canal for the Central Arizona project to carry Colorado River water from Lake Havasu near Parker, Ariz., to a service area in the Gila River Basin. The concrete-lined aqueduct will have a bottom width of 24 feet (7.3 m) and a depth of 16.4 feet (5 m).

Germany. In 1976 the 72-mile (114-km) Elbe Lateral Canal opened to barge traffic, linking the Elbe River at Hamburg with the Mittelland Canal that crosses northern Germany from west to east. The 180-foot (55-m) wide waterway shortens the water route from Hamburg to Berlin by 79 miles (127 km).

The Teton Dam, near St. Anthony, Idaho, ruptured only a short time after it was finished in 1976. Damage was estimated at $1,000,000,000.

DAMS

The Army Corps of Engineers is building Gathright Dam in Virginia to retain spring floods that threaten Richmond and other communities along the Jackson and James rivers. The $68-million rock-and-earthfill project is scheduled for completion in 1978. It will be 1,250 feet (381 m) long, 257 feet (78 m) high, and contain more than 3,000,000 cubic yards (2,200,000 m³) of selected material.

In 1976 the U. S. Bureau of Reclamation completed Nambe Falls Dam, the first prestressed arch dam in the United States. A double-curvature structure, 136.6 feet (42 m) high and 332.5 feet (98 m) long, it is 5 feet (1.5 m) thick at the crest and 15.2 feet (4.6 m) at the base. It is located 16 miles (25 km) north of Santa Fe, N. Mex., and provides irrigation water.

Work had only recently been completed on Teton Dam on the Teton River near St. Anthony, Idaho, when the dam burst on June 5, 1976, flooding the upper Snake River Valley. The break killed 11 people and injured 2,000. Damage was estimated at $1,000,000,000. Built by the U. S. Bureau of Reclamation with earth and rockfill, the Teton Dam was 305 feet (93 m) high and 3,050 feet (930 m) long. It contained 9,500,000 cubic yards (7,300,000 m³) of material and cost $60,000,000.

South America. Brazil and Paraguay started in 1976 to construct Itaipu Dam, designed to be the world's largest hydroelectric structure. The $6,000,000,000 project is on the Paraná River, forming the border between the nations, about 8.5 miles (14 km) upstream from Iguaçú Falls. The dam will be a concrete buttress type, flanked by earth-and-rockfill embankments. The central concrete gravity dam and intake structure will be 580 feet (177 m) high and 4,945 feet (1,507 m) long; it will contain 10,000,000 cubic yards (7,600,000 m³) of concrete. Scheduled for completion by 1983, the dam will have a generating capacity of 12,600 Mw from a powerplant with 18 generators of 700 Mw each.

TUNNELS

United States. One of the nation's lengthier tunnels currently under way is the 11-mile (17.7-km) sanitary sewer running from west to east under Austin, Tex. The $20-million project has a finished diameter of 84 inches (2.13 m) at its upper end, increasing to 96 inches (2.44 m) at the lower end near the treatment plant. The sewer will be in operation by mid-1977.

Pakistan. Construction is continuing on the 3.1-mile (5-km) Lowari Pass vehicular tunnel to connect the Dir and Chitral valleys, Pakistan. The bore is 30 feet (9 m) wide by 25 feet (7.6 m) high and lies at an elevation of 7,877 feet (2,401 m) in the Hindu Kush mountains. The present road, over a 2-mile (3.2-km) high pass, is snowbound during the wintertime. Started in 1975, the tunnel is scheduled for completion in 1979.

New Zealand. After nearly seven years of construction, workers in 1976 holed through the 5.5-mile (8.9-km) Kaimai railway tunnel in New Zealand. The country's longest, it bores through the 2,500-foot (760-m) high Kaimai Range on North Island, cutting 32 miles (51.5 km) from the freight route from Hamilton to the port of Tauranga. The 21-foot (6.4-m) diameter bore, lined with concrete, cost more than $56 million.

Egypt. Construction has started on the first of three highway tunnels under the Suez Canal to link the undeveloped Sinai with the western bank. The initial bore, 6 miles (10 km) north of the city of Suez, will be 1.7 miles (2.7 km) long, and is scheduled for completion in 1979.

WILLIAM H. QUIRK
"Construction Industry International" Magazine

Chicago's water pollution control samples lake water at various depths.

ENVIRONMENT

Global efforts to stem decay of the environment inched forward in 1976, despite some economic and political setbacks which threatened to disrupt progress at the international level.

WORLD ENVIRONMENT

Policy-makers continued to focus their attention on the task of developing machinery to solve environmental problems identified in previous years. The slow pace of progress caused pessimism among many observers who felt that advances should come more swiftly, but when the year's successes are contrasted against the almost total lack of environmental awareness that prevailed only four years ago, there is good cause for optimism.

Progress. Before the World Environmental Conference was called in Stockholm in 1972, only 20 nations—all of them industrialized countries—had environmental agencies. The Stockholm Conference sparked an international environmental awakening, and by 1976 more than 100 nations—most of them developing countries—had instituted such agencies. In 1972, concerns were largely national in scope; by 1976, international and regional cooperation had begun. A pact for the protection of the Mediterranean was signed, and similar treaties covering the West African coast, the Persian Gulf, and the Caribbean were in the drafting stage. In 1972 the World Bank and UNESCO were the only UN agencies with an environmental mandate. By 1976 nearly all UN agencies were invested with some environmental mission, spearheaded, of course, by UNEP (United Nations Environmental Program). Unfortunately, other attempts to mobilize world efforts deteriorated into media events, with more evidence of posturing than of problem-solving.

Stalemate. Two major meetings, the Law of the Sea Conference and the Habitat Human Settlement Conference, were nearly paralyzed by fighting between industrialized and developing nations. Many delegates left the Habitat Conference frustrated, wondering if it might be the last of the great world conferences. (See *Special Report*, p. 205.) Delegates to the Law of the Sea Conference found themselves preoccupied with efforts by the Group of 77 to insure that its member nations, many of which are landlocked, would have equal access to and control over seabed resources. (See special feature beginning on p. 50.)

Lack of Funds. Limited resources—although of another kind—preoccupied UNEP this year. Contributions to the UNEP fund fell far short of the sums originally pledged by supporting nations. The United States delivered only $25 million on a pledge of $40 million, and other nations, including the Soviet Union, paid their shares in soft currencies which are in effect nonconvertible. Substantial expected contributions from the swollen treasuries of oil-producing nations never materialized. UNEP was accused of spreading itself too thin and incurring excessive overhead expenses.

Despite its financial woes, UNEP outlined an ambitious program for the coming year. The agency allocated $2 million for a study of the impact of waste heat and pollutant emissions and for an evaluation of energy development strategies. Future projects will focus on the Caribbean, human settlements in Latin America, and cyclone monitoring in Asia.

Various Efforts. The outlook for more regional cooperation improved in 1976. A pact to clean up and protect the Mediterranean Sea was adopted in Barcelona by 18 Mediterranean nations. EEC (European Economic Community) nations increased their efforts to protect water quality. Among developing nations environmental efforts progressed at a more fundamental level as attempts to provide adequate food, clothing, and shelter for Third World inhabitants continued. The new UNEP director, Mustafa Kamal Tolba, stressed in his "state of the environment" report that for much of the world, including his native Egypt, ". . . environmental problems are still those associated with poverty."

The year also witnessed a growing reluctance of several nations to press on with the development of nuclear power. A report by a British royal commission urged that further proliferation of nuclear plants be postponed as long as possible, and Swedish voters ousted Prime Minister Olof Palme and his government partly because of his strong support for nuclear energy.

U. S. ENVIRONMENT

In the United States 1976 was a grim year for environmentalists as many new signs of decay became visible. In Pittsburgh 14 people died during an air pollution emergency. Tons of sewage—apparently from New York City—fouled Long Island beaches which had to be temporarily closed. Fishing was banned in the Hudson River and in rivers and lakes in South Carolina and Georgia, the result of PCB (polychlorinated biphenyl) contamination. In Idaho a dam that had been a source of contention among environmentalists and geologists collapsed.

Nuclear Power. Numerous other environmental events received wide publicity, but the attention focused on them produced few answers to the questions they raised. The explosion of buried nuclear waste at an underground depository in Hanford, Wash., and the defeat of "Proposition 15," California's nuclear moratorium initiative, sparked new controversy over nuclear power, but neither Congress nor President Ford proposed a plan for rational nuclear power development. In the absence of a federal initiative six states took steps of their own by placing questions on continued nuclear power development on the November ballots.

(Supersonic transport again aroused considerable interest as citizens' groups voiced bitter objection to its use in the United States. See TRANSPORTATION: *Special Report*, p. 510.)

The Ozone Layer. Ozone was much in the news again. New evidence was reported that fluorocarbons from popular spray cans are contributing to the depletion of the earth's ozone layer. Scientists maintain that the result could be an increased incidence of human skin cancer, as well as untold climatic changes.

Candidates' Stands. The presidential candidates generally skirted environmental issues per se, but they did bring into focus the issue that looms behind all environmental controversies: economics versus environment. Democratic candidate Carter maintained that environmental preservation and economic growth were not incompatible. President Ford insisted that stricter environmental controls would result in a loss of jobs. The positions reflected the stands adopted in their party platforms, as well as the split in the nation as a whole.

Polluters Penalized. Notwithstanding the inactivity induced by election-year politicking, new strides were made in 1976. Major polluters were forced to pay for their environmental abuses. Allied Chemical Co. was ordered by the courts to pay $13.3 million—the largest award of its kind—in damages for polluting the James River with the highly toxic chemical Kepone. In another major case the General Electric Co. agreed to pay $4 million to help finance the cleanup of PCB's that it discharged into the Hudson River. The settlement was viewed as an important precedent-setter because G. E. was forced to pay for cleanup even though it had been issued a permit to discharge the toxic substance. A $91-million suit was filed against Chrysler Corporation on the grounds that Chrysler installed faulty smog control devices in 9,100 automobiles.

Preservation of Natural Areas. Environmentalists active in wilderness preservation successfully thwarted construction of dams along the New River in North Carolina and the Snake River in Idaho. An attempt by a consortium of electric companies to build a coal-fired power plant that would have emitted 300 tons per year of air pollutants into a region that included eight national parks and three national recreation areas was also defeated. A new law was enacted to prevent two million acres (800,000 ha) of wilderness from falling under the jurisdiction of the Bureau of Land Management. Departing from past positions, the Council on Environmental Quality recommended the preservation of entire ecosystems rather than individual species.

Toxic Substances. New measures were taken in 1976 to reduce the amount of hazardous substances released into the environment. The Food and Drug Administration banned the use of red dye no. 4 and carbon black in food products.

(Continued on page 206)

SPECIAL REPORT:

The UN Conference on Human Settlement

Habitat, the UN Conference on Human Settlement, brought together 500 official delegates from 131 nations to discuss living conditions and land use around the world. The delegates met in Vancouver, B.C., from May 31 to June 11, 1976. Several distinguished individuals—including author and scientist Buckminster Fuller, anthropologist Margaret Mead, and economist Barbara Ward—addressed the conference.

Planning. The idea for Habitat was proposed by the UN Conference on Human Environment held in Stockholm, Sweden, in 1972 and accepted by the UN General Assembly in 1973. In January 1975, a 56-member preparatory committee began planning an agenda and framework for the conference and in December 1975 the assembly approved them. The preparatory committee met with various government officials, and worked out basic areas for study and debate.

Organization. Habitat opened with a warning from UN Secretary General Kurt Waldheim that the world's living conditions, which he said were already unsatisfactory, would deteriorate rapidly unless solutions were found immediately. Conference Secretary-General and chief organizer Enrique Peñalosa, formerly administrative manager of the Inter-American Development Bank, said that settlement problems must not be set aside simply because they do not seem as urgent as other world issues. Barnett (Barney) J. Danson, Canada's urban affairs minister and head of the Canadian delegation, was unanimously elected conference president.

Also at Habitat's first sessions were Mexico's outgoing President Luis Echeverria, Canada's Prime Minister Pierre Elliott Trudeau, and U.S. Secretary of Housing and Urban Development Carla Hills. Echeverria told the gathering that the UN must strengthen itself and pay attention to the Third World in order to preserve peace. Trudeau called for greater sharing among nations. Mrs. Hills said that the United States was prepared to offer technological assistance to the poorer nations for their development and that all countries share an obligation to help the world's poor.

The conference itself was divided into the main plenary session and three committees. At the plenary meetings, chaired by Danson, representatives from each country discussed their own settlements and ideas for a world plan. Committee I, chaired by George Kamau Muhoho, director of Kenya's environment secretariat, considered the draft declaration of principles and the programs for international cooperation. Committee II, led by Iran's Minister of Housing Homayoun J. Ansari, studied ways in which countries could organize themselves to deal with policies, planning, and management of settlements. The third committee, chaired by Diego Arria, governor of Caracas, Venezuela, looked at the components that make up the body and maintain the functions of communities—shelter, infrastructure, services, and land.

On June 6, the world's first Water Day rally was held. Following a 1.5-mile (2.4-km) walk, during which participants carried buckets of water, Danson, Peñalosa, and others vowed to work for a cleaner water supply by 1990.

Results. Following two weeks of deliberations, more than 100 proposals intended to improve community life were approved. Included among the proposals, which had to be ratified by the UN General Assembly, were recommendations calling for land to be managed as a public resource, not as a profit-making commodity; for a redistribution of land in the world's poor nations; and for a more equal distribution of wealth. The conference specifically stated that "land, because of its unique nature and the crucial role it plays in human settlement, cannot be treated as an ordinary asset, controlled by individuals and subject to the pressures and inefficiencies of the market."

The conference also adopted two resolutions, supported by Arab, Communist, and Third World nations, obliquely criticizing Israel. The first resolution, which passed by a 69–8 vote with 26 abstentions and 28 nations absent, said that "in occupied territories the uprooting of native population and the establishment of new settlements for intruders is inadmissible."

The second resolution, adopted by an 89–15 vote with 10 abstentions and 17 nations absent, said it was "the duty of all people and governments to join the struggle against any form of colonialism, foreign aggression and occupation, domination, apartheid and all forms of racism and racial discrimination referred to in the resolutions" adopted by the UN General Assembly. Nations voting against the resolution, which clearly referred to the UN's resolution of 1975 equating Zionism with racism, were the United States, Canada, Britain, Australia, New Zealand, Israel, Netherlands, Norway, Denmark, France, West Germany, Italy, Ireland, Belgium, and Luxembourg.

In addition, Panama's attempt to debate the United States over the Panama Canal was unsuccessful. The U.S. delegate simply moved that the Panamanian proposal relating to the canal be "adopted by consensus."

The main conference was paralleled by Habitat Forum, a meeting of nongovernment organizations held in old air force hangars at Vancouver's Jericho Beach Park. The forum urged a role for the world's poor in improving their settlements.

KARENN KRANGLE, *"The Vancouver Sun"*

"Oleanic," a system capable of recovering 50 tons (45 metric tons) of oil spillage per hour, is demonstrated off Portsmouth, England.

UPI

Congress passed the Toxic Substances Control Act, which authorizes the EPA (Environmental Protection Agency) to require testing of new chemicals for adverse environmental and health effects and also empowers it to order labeling of such substances as dangerous or, if necessary, to prohibit their sale. The act also calls for a complete halt to production of PCB's within two years.

Air Pollution. In an encouraging report issued in 1976 the Council on Environmental Quality said that the nation's air quality was steadily improving. Although many states have yet to achieve the air-quality objectives established for mid-1975 by the Clean Air Act, the council reported that most regions would be in compliance by the early 1980's. On the dismal side the council noted that the level of air pollutants in New York City and Los Angeles was still unacceptable.

Proposed amendments to the Clean Air Act died in filibuster. One of the the most controversial of them would have delayed implementa-

tion of stringent new auto-emission standards. As a result of its defeat 1978-model cars must comply with stricter standards than manufacturers had anticipated. Auto makers, however, began to certify their 1978 models according to current standards in the expectation that next Congress will manage to push the amendments through.

EPA ordered 45 states to adopt stronger plans for implementing federal air-quality standards. Also, the Supreme Court ruled that EPA cannot consider economic or technological feasibility when reviewing state implementation plans. When New York City attempted to set aside its implementation plan, environmentalists sued and won two signal victories. The court ordered the city to reinstitute its clean-air plan and, in doing so, confirmed the right of citizens' groups to force compliance with federal regulations by suing in court.

Water Pollution. In the area of water pollution control 1976 was a year of mixed results. On the positive side, thousands of millions of dollars were released to finance wastewater treatment installations. On the negative side, the Council on Environmental Quality reported that of 12 rivers monitored over the past several years only five showed improvement. To the elation of environmentalists, an amendment to the Federal Water Pollution Control Act, which would have eliminated federal control over most of the nation's wetlands, was killed in committee. However, environmentalists suffered a setback when President Ford vetoed a jobs bill which would have provided $700 million for the construction of wastewater treatment facilities.

Land Use. The Coastal Energy Impact Bill was passed in 1976, receiving mixed reviews from environmentalists. The law appropriates $1,200,000,000 to aid coastal states with growth problems resulting from the development of offshore oil and gas fields. Some critics charged that the bill was merely designed to win over local governments opposed to offshore development. California adopted stringent legislation, placing all development taking place in an area extending from three miles (5 km) offshore to

Sludge, the solid waste remaining after water is removed from sewage, is checked at a treatment plant.
UPI

five miles (8 km) inland, along the entire coast, under the jurisdiction and supervision of a commission composed of state citizens and public officials. The commission is mandated to preserve natural areas and farmlands and insure public access to the shoreline.

Environmentalists were foiled when Congress failed to override President Ford's veto of legislation prohibiting strip-mining, and they fared only slightly better when Congress passed a bill giving the Department of Agriculture control over clear-cutting in U. S. forests.

Energy. To the surprise of few but the regret of many, the nation again failed to develop a rational energy policy in 1976. There was not, however, complete inactivity. Congress and the president volleyed the politically explosive issue of oil and gas prices back and forth. The result was a bill providing for an immediate reduction in domestic oil prices, followed by periodic price hikes. When Congress failed to act on natural gas prices, the Federal Power Commission raised them administratively. The only initiatives taken during the year were in the area of automobile efficiency standards and tax breaks for home-builders who employed energy-efficient construction materials. The Alaska oil pipeline inched toward completion, plagued by 3, 955 bad welds and ruptures during a trial run. Concern over its timely completion managed to obscure questions regarding the environmental impact of future spills and its present impact on the wildlife habitat.

JAMES G. KOLLEGGER
Environment Information Center, Inc.

ETHIOPIA

In 1976, the Provisional Military Administrative Committee initiated and then canceled a peasant march on the secessionist province of Eritrea, announced plans for the future formation of political parties, executed several opponents of the regime, and came into conflict with students who opposed its methods.

Eritrean-Ethiopian Violence. Attempting a final defeat of the Eritrean secessionist movement in order to keep Ethiopia intact, the government initiated a major offensive against Eritrean rebels in May. Predominantly Christian farmers and landless peasants were promised land if they would march into Eritrea in a "holy war" against the rebels, more than half of whom are Muslims. During May and June the untrained and unorganized peasant army of 50,000 was transported to the Eritrean borders only to be decimated by the rebels. With fear spreading because of continuous routing, many of the peasants fled back to their home provinces. On June 19 the "holy war" was called off. It was a dismal failure.

The junta also tried a carrot and stick policy during May and June, promising amnesty to Eritrean political prisoners, financial assistance to the region, and a closer integration between Eritrea and the rest of Ethiopia if the rebels would halt their war of secession. The separatist leadership turned down the offer.

Domestic Politics. The patriarch of the Ethiopian Orthodox Church, Abuna Theophilos, was arrested and removed from office on February 18. He was accused by the military junta of crimes against the Ethiopian people, including the accumulation of millions of dollars. The arrest of Theophilos was part of the junta's policy of politically neutralizing officials associated with the regime of the late Emperor Haile Selassie.

On April 21, the government announced that political parties would, at some unspecified future date, be permitted in Ethiopia. Political parties have never existed in the country. The junta claimed this would help create a "People's Democratic Republic." A 15-member civilian commission will coordinate the establishment of political parties.

Eighteen military leaders, including the third-ranking member of the ruling committee, were executed by the regime on July 13. They were accused of plotting a coup. On July 25 two more army officers were executed for allegedly inciting soldiers to rebel against the government. On August 21 the government released 209 political prisoners, all of whom were minor officials under the regime of Emperor Haile Selassie.

Ethiopian students by the thousands have sought refuge in the Sudan, Kenya, and Somalia after becoming disillusioned with the tactics of the junta. Many claim they were beaten, arrested, and hounded out of the country. The government maintains that the students were unwilling to participate in the Ethiopian revolution.

Foreign Affairs. The United States in 1976 signed a $246-million arms sale agreement with Ethiopia; delivery will be spread over a number of years. An annual $10-million military grant for troop training and spare-part replacement was also authorized by the United States. Ethiopia established diplomatic relations with Cuba on August 14.

PETER SCHWAB
State University of New York at Purchase

ETHIOPIA • Information Highlights

Official Name: Ethiopia.
Location: Eastern Africa.
Area: 471,777 square miles (1,221,900 km²).
Population (1976 est.): 28,600,000.
Chief Cities (1974 census): Addis Ababa, the capital, 1,083,420; Asmara, 296,044.
Government: *Acting head of state and government,* Tafari Banti, chairman of the Provisional Military Administrative Committee (took office Nov. 1974).
Monetary Unit: Birr (2.09 birrs equal U. S.$1, Oct. 1976).
Gross National Product (1974 est.): $2,400,000,000.
Manufacturing (major products): Processed foods, textiles, cement, leather and shoes.
Major Agricultural Products: Coffee, cotton, sugarcane, corn, millet and sorghum, oilseeds, pulses, cattle, sheep.
Foreign Trade (1975): *Exports,* $238,000,000; *imports,* $310,000,000.

ETHNIC GROUPS

Developments in education and economics balanced out to something of a stalemate where minorities were concerned in 1976. But in politics, the labors of the past impressively bore fruit as a sizable black vote helped elect Jimmy Carter, a Southern white man, president of the United States.

The Election. From the beginning of his long-shot quest for the presidency, former Georgia Gov. Jimmy Carter counted on a measure of black support to help establish his credibility with the rest of the country. Some blacks, including U. S. Congressman Andrew Young of Atlanta, a former lieutenant of Martin Luther King, Jr., originally backed Carter, a moderate, as a means of heading off George Wallace in the Southern primaries. But eventually, Young and others became committed to Carter and served as a link to the black community as well as to Northern liberals.

That support was demonstrated when Carter made the first major mistake of his campaign. In April, Carter told a white audience that he was in favor of preserving the "ethnic purity" of urban neighborhoods. Many observers thought the remark signaled an intent to support de facto segregation in such areas as housing and education. Carter apologized for the remark, and at an Atlanta unity rally was photographed in an all-is-forgiven handshake with black patriarch Martin Luther King, Sr. "Ethnic purity" was defused as an issue.

At the Democratic convention in New York in July, Rep. Barbara Jordan, a black from Texas who is remembered for her eloquence before the House Judiciary Committee during the Watergate crisis, delivered a stirring keynote address that was a highlight of the convention. Andrew Young gave one of Carter's nominating speeches, and the convention closed with a rousing benediction by "Daddy" King and an emotional singing of "We Shall Overcome."

On election day, voters turned out in fairly heavy numbers and this favored the majority Democrats. Nearly seven million black voters went to the polls, 92% of them casting their ballots for Carter. According to many analysts, the black turnout made a crucial difference. The Joint Center for Political Studies in Washington determined that black voters gave Carter a clear margin of victory in seven states with a total of 117 electoral votes. (With 270 electoral votes needed to win, Carter outpolled President Ford 297–241.) Three of those states were among the so-called "Big Ten" with the most electoral votes: Ohio, Pennsylvania, and Texas. In Ohio, for example, Carter received 282,000 black votes to win by a scant 7,000. Ford actually won a majority of white votes in Carter's supposedly solid South, but the heavy black vote kept every Southern state except Virginia in the Carter column.

Most significantly, the 1965 Voting Rights Act, which was prompted by the civil rights activity of the 1960's, had resulted in an election in which black people played an active and critical part. It was clear that those voters would in turn expect a new administration conscious of and responsive to the needs of the nation's minorities.

The Economy. The economic news for minorities was disappointing in 1976 after encouraging trends in earlier years. According to a U. S. Census Bureau report, the median income for black families had risen to a new high of $8,779. But those black families still earned only about 60% of what their white counterparts earned. The proportion of blacks living below the poverty line increased, as did the number of black households headed by a woman. Some experts suggested that a majority of black families could now be considered middle class on the basis of their earnings, but that conclusion was questionable. While the general jobless rate was considered high at over 7%, the minority rate was over 13%. Teenage minority unemployment was over 40%, more than twice that for white youths. Politicians were generally careful not to suggest 1960's-style recovery programs aimed at minorities. They judged the mood of the country, particularly in fiscal matters, to be conservative.

Education. In the spring, University of Chicago Professor James S. Coleman, the "godfather" of school busing for racial integration, presented the results of a new study suggesting that busing as practiced was, for the most part, a failure. Coleman contended that forced busing had polarized many urban communities and provoked a pattern of "white flight"—white families leaving the city or patronizing private schools to avoid busing. Coleman offered his revised views before a special session of the Massachusetts state legislature, at about the same time that the city of Boston was shaken by an outbreak of racial violence.

But despite Coleman's reversal, busing continued. Boston entered its third year of court-ordered busing in the fall with improved attendance and markedly less student violence. The antibusing demonstrations that troubled Louisville in 1975 were ineffective the second time around, and school attendance in that city was up to 96% within a week. Five years of planning in Detroit finally culminated in a fairly smooth integration of that city's schools. Dallas and Dayton also saw peaceful beginnings of well-planned busing programs, and Milwaukee initiated a new busing plan based on voluntary cooperation and specialized inner-city schools to attract more white pupils.

The issue, however, was not resolved. In November, the U. S. Supreme Court said it would review the power of federal courts to impose remedies for segregation, such as busing. At the same time, the justices blocked enforce-

PHOTOS UPI

The year's black newsmakers include Benjamin L. Hooks, a member of the FCC, who was named executive director of the NAACP, and Sylvia E. Mathis, who was the first black woman to be recruited as a special agent for the FBI.

ment of a California Supreme Court ruling that would eliminate special minority admissions programs in state medical schools. The delay was to remain in effect until the court could consider the issue of special admissions itself.

In May, Dr. Bernard D. Davis of the Harvard Medical School published a letter in the *New England Journal of Medicine* that questioned the success of such special admissions programs. Although the number of minority students in medical and law schools has increased remarkably since 1970, those students still suffer higher attrition rates than their white classmates and account for a disproportionate number of failures on state professional licensing exams. Dr. Davis made the point that too often, perhaps, well-meaning institutions graduate minority students who—according to the test results —may not be qualified to practice professionally. Supporters of special admissions suggested, on the other hand, that the problem may be not with the students but with the exams, which tend to measure basic skills rather than professional competence. Minority professional students, it was noted, may lag behind whites in some scholastic skills because of inferior early education, but they are no less capable when it comes to practicing medicine or law. However, financial problems were forcing many schools to restrict special admissions programs.

Civil Rights. In a Mississippi court, the National Association for the Advancement of Colored People lost a lawsuit brought by a group of local white merchants over a boycott demonstration in 1966. The plaintiffs charged that in conducting the boycott, the NAACP supported an illegal black business monopoly. The judgment against the association amounted to $1 million. In order to appeal the decision, the NAACP was required to post a bond totaling $1.6 million. Frantic fund raising efforts were conducted until the association was granted a delay of the appeal deadline, allowing more time to raise the bond.

That legal squeeze, which was unresolved at year-end, came during a time when the NAACP was in the midst of a rare leadership crisis. Executive Director Roy Wilkins, who had headed the nation's oldest civil rights organization for 31 years, had announced his retirement but then postponed it, prompting internal discord over the date of his departure and the identity of his successor. Finally, the NAACP announced that its new leader would be Benjamin Hooks, a Memphis lawyer, minister, onetime judge, and a member of the Federal Communications Commission. Hooks was to assume his post in January, with Wilkins leaving at midyear.

Migrant Farmworkers. United Farm Workers head Cesar Chavez pressed the union's struggle for the rights of the mostly Chicano migrant farm workers of California. With the support of liberal Gov. Edmund G. Brown, Jr., Chavez initiated Proposition 14, a ballot referendum that would strengthen the controversial 1975 Agricultural Labor Relations Act. The proposition was defeated in November but the legislation remained in effect, offering some hope of a resolution of the bitter dispute between growers and migrant farmworkers.

DENNIS A. WILLIAMS
Associate Editor, Newsweek

Representatives of Western Europe, Canada, Japan and the United States attend an economic summit conference at Dorado Beach, Puerto Rico, in June.

UPI

EUROPE

Lingering problems, despite economic recovery, plagued western Europe in 1976, while the southern part of the continent took some encouraging steps toward democratization.

Recovery From Recession. The recession provoked by the five-fold increase in oil prices imposed by the Organization of Petroleum Exporting Countries (OPEC) and deepened by the subsequent rise in commodity prices from Third World countries came slowly to an end in 1976. The revival of the American economy reopened Europe's principal market for exports. The OPEC countries helped the revival by freezing oil prices and by use of oil royalties for vast purchases of manufactured goods, European real estate, and shares in European companies. Large-scale government investment, especially in France and Germany, provided direct stimulus in the public sector. As a result, the gloomy record of 1975, during which many European countries suffered a decline in gross national product, was reversed. By June, unemployment in the Common Market had been reduced by 5%. By the end of the year, it was predicted, West German gross national product would increase by at least 5.5%, and even the chronically weak British economy would post a slight gain. Progress in dealing with the high rates of inflation that had hampered recovery in 1975 was also made in a number of countries. West Germany's inflation rate was barely 4%; and the British rate of 12% represented a reduction by more than half of the rate of 1975.

Weakness Within the Common Market. It was clear, by the time the heads of government and the finance ministers of the Common Market held their summit meeting in Luxembourg in April, that Britain, Italy, and to a lesser degree France, were not keeping pace with the recovery of West Germany or the Benelux countries. In the days before the meeting, the Italian lira fell by 8% and the French franc by almost 4%, while the value of the British pound slipped to less than $2. The French government was compelled to withdraw from the "snake" (the agreement of eight European countries to hold their currency values within 4.5% of each other), to which it had returned only in 1975. In these unfavorable circumstances the summit achieved nothing. The bickering partners could not even agree on their relative shares of seats in the European Parliament which, in accordance with the decision of their summit meeting in Rome in December 1975, was to be popularly elected in 1978. As German Chancellor Helmut Schmidt remarked, "Those who were expecting nothing had every reason to be satisfied."

At the economic conference of government heads of seven major industrial states, held in Puerto Rico in June, Italy and Britain were pressured to reduce inflation by cutting government spending; but it was clear that only large international loans could prevent the collapse of their currencies. Britain, which had received a credit of $5,300,000,000 from the industrial nations in the Group of Ten in June, failed to halt the downward slide of the pound; and in October, while the pound neared the $1.50 mark, it was compelled to ask the International Monetary Fund for a credit of $3,900,000,000. As their currencies declined during the summer, Britain, Italy, and France saw their hopes of a record harvest destroyed by one of the worst droughts of the century. French agriculture expected losses of $1,000,000,000, and a fall in the grain harvest throughout Europe was expected to raise fodder prices, force slaughter of herds, and bring higher meat prices by the year's end. Inflation was thus likely to fire consumer discontent, even in those countries where the economic recovery was strong.

At the second summit meeting in Brussels in July, most members expressed skepticism of the ability of the Common Market to affect the basic divergencies between the economies of its stronger and weaker members. The ministers did, however, succeed in apportioning the 410 seats of the European Parliament among the nine members, and it seemed probable that elections could be held in 1978 as planned. In that case, many observers felt, the Common Market might be jolted into more action by the presence in the European Parliament of prestigious politicians and, perhaps, by a large Communist delegation. It was also recognized that the Common Market's administration would be improved by implementation of the integrative measures proposed in a large-scale reorganization plan drawn up by Belgian Prime Minister Leo Tindemans, while the appointment of Roy Jenkins, the most pro-European member of the British Labour government, as chairman of the Commission in 1977 would strengthen that body's influence.

Retreat From Authoritarian Rule. Politically, the most positive feature of European development was the continuing democratization of Greece, Portugal, and Spain. Greece's political stability under the government of Constantine Karamanlis's New Democracy party, which had replaced the military dictatorship in 1974, was sufficiently advanced for the Common Market to agree to begin negotiations for full Greek membership within two years. The Common Market also showed its support for the democratization of Portugal by granting a loan of $187 million; the Socialist parties of Northern Europe, which had given advice and financial aid to the Portuguese Socialists headed by Mario Soares, welcomed his nomination as prime minister by António Ramalho Eanes who was elected president in July. In both parliamentary and presidential elections, the Communist party was decisively repudiated. To many western Europeans, King Juan Carlos's dismantling of the authoritarian controls in Spain, after Generalissimo Franco's death in November 1975, seemed slow; but some progress was made. Large numbers of political prisoners were freed by two amnesties. A referendum in October on a democratized constitution was to be followed by national elections in 1977. And Adolfo Suárez González, a younger political moderate, replaced Carlos Arias Navarro as prime minister in July.

National Roads to Communism. Throughout western Europe, except in Portugal, Communist parties made gains by emphasizing their determination to work for reform of the existing social system in alliance with Socialist and even Catholic political parties. French Communist party leader Georges Marchais joined pioneering Italian party chief Enrico Berlinguer in renouncing the dogma of dictatorship of the proletariat and emphasized that their parties proposed to come to power through free elections. Many west European Communist leaders openly criticized Russian policy and denounced the notion of a monolithic Communist movement in Europe. The direct gains from this policy were most evident in Italy in national elections in June, when the Communist party was able to increase its representation in the Chamber of Deputies from 179 to 228 and gain influential committee chairmanships. Communist influence was so great that Christian Democratic Prime Minister Andreotti could win a vote of confidence for

his new cabinet only by relying on Communist abstention.

The Italian delegation took the lead at the Conference of European Communist parties, held in East Berlin in July, in demanding that national parties be permitted to adjust their strategy to differing national conditions; and Soviet party chief Leonid Brezhnev was compelled to accept many of the demands for greater autonomy expressed by an emerging coalition of the French, Italian, and Spanish parties with the Rumanian and Yugoslav parties.

Socialist Government Under Pressure. A third significant political development in western Europe was growing pressure on Socialist governments in power from conservative forces. In Sweden, where Socialist governments had been in power for 44 years and created one of the most complex and costly systems of state services in the world, Social Democratic Prime Minister Olof Palme was ousted in national elections by a coalition of three non-Socialist parties. In Britain, disillusionment with the economic record of the Labour government was largely focused upon the power of the trade unions. Although the unions agreed in May to restrict pay increases to 4.5%, a shipping strike in September was averted only by granting fringe benefits beyond the guideline. Finally, even in prosperous West Germany, Socialist Chancellor Schmidt won only a narrow victory, with reduced representation, in October elections.

F. ROY WILLIS
University of California, Davis

Posters urge Italians to vote Communist in parliamentary elections. The Communists gained new seats.

UPI

FASHION

LONDON DAILY MAIL-ESCHAVE ASSOC.

Yves St. Laurent's elegant peasant style, featuring wide skirts and luxurious fabrics, was the newest look in 1976.

Fashion in 1976 was divided into contrasting trends in day wear and evening wear. Fashion went from functional by day to fantasy at night, grit to glamour, reason to romance.

WOMEN'S CLOTHES

Functional for Day. For women, daytime was spent in classic haberdashery looks, authentic work clothes, or fashions and fabrics from the great outdoors. Suits tailored with Saville Row precision in flannel or gabardine, many with vests and man-tailored shirts, gave a sharp, businesslike look to the liberated woman. At the same time, suppliers of hunting, fishing, and backpacking gear as well as riding outfitters were inundated with orders for the "real" hard-wearing, hard-working, sporting classics.

Fantasy for Night. After five, women became soft, sexy, and glamorous. Costumes rather than clothes took over. Opulent fabrics in vivid colors transformed her from the efficient executive or fresh-faced outdoor girl into a rich peasant or a czarina.

Fashion Trends. Skirts were strong, especially softly gathered dirndls or narrow tubes with slits or kick pleats front or back. Kilts, a happy combination of classic, costume, and authentic, were popular.

The traditional pants look was out. Fashion pants were represented by culottes or pants skirts, jodhpurs, and harem pants either tied or gathered at the ankle to blouse gently. When worn with boots, the 1975 traditional straight leg pants were tucked in to achieve the newer look.

Dresses were strong in retail sales figures that, overall, were not spectacular. The "Big Dress" of 1975 had narrowed to a tube, slim and soft, side slit to double as a tunic over pants or the straight skirt. For evening the tube dress was often strapless or one shouldered, an elegant column of satin, crepe de chine, or jersey.

Bare shoulders were part of the city summer look when sundresses took over as the hot weather uniform. A popular style that did double duty had wide shirring across the bosom and was strapless. Pulled down, with the shirring hugging the hips and topped with a T-shirt, the sundress became a patio skirt. Other sundresses had wide straps and were worn over shirts in the manner of a jumper.

The T-shirt reached a saturation level and was used as *the* gift and giveaway promotional item by advertisers and manufacturers. Consequently, at the retail level, sales were down.

The dress as tunic spawned the tabard, a "sandwich-board" styled garment that was shown for fall in almost every length. Open at the sides, it was tied or toggled under the arms and at the waist to float over the body and layer over dresses, pants, or skirts.

The tabard added a medieval touch to sportswear as did the giant cowls seen on sweaters and the many hoods that were part of the coat and poncho trend. The importance of the poncho was apparent in its wide use for day and night.

The cloth coat had a renaissance in the blanket cloth. Often unlined, wraps and reefers were at their most fashionable when done in blanket fabrics, striped in American Indian or Bedouin motifs, in plaids like camp blankets, lap robes, or buffalo checks, or soft pastel baby blankets. Extending the blanket coat idea was the "downer," which could best be described

Evening lounge wear was dominated by fluid fabrics, like this Matisse-inspired floral pattern.

Lanvin's layered look featured checked pants with tunic, shirt, and scarf, all in different stripes.

One of the most popular daytime fashions was a Dior blanket plaid suit topped by a loose cape.

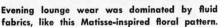

as a walking sleeping bag. Ciré jackets in bright colors, quilted and stuffed with down or fiberfill became Arctic gear turned sportswear for the young and thin.

Fabrics and Colors. Fabrics followed the day/ night split. Gray, beige, and pin-striped flannel was in short supply because of its popularity in couture to chain store lines. All the heavy duty, outdoor fabrics were popular for day— melton, cotton flannel, chino, corduroy, Harris tweed, herringbone, blanket cloth, and gabardine. Basic colors such as gray, brown, beige, khaki, and forest green were relieved by bright or deep red in plaids, buffalo checks, or blanket stripes.

The turnabout for evening came in the focus on fragility and opulence. Chiffon, lamé, crepe de chine, satin, and lace were the beginnings of glamour and drama. The only full-bodied fabric seen at night was crisp taffeta, in black or in tartan plaids. In full-gathered, long skirts taffeta was mated with softly styled peasant blouses or shirts and velvet vests.

Accessories. Functional for day also was fulfilled in accessories. Businesslike and rugged, bags took the form of briefcases, camera totes, musette bags, and duffles. Sporting goods store creels and rucksacks were models for fashion versions designed in buckskin, pigskin, canvas or linen.

Man-tailored oxfords, ghillies, and wing tips were worn by the woman in the gray flannel suit. The woman in more casual sportswear took to the hiking boot or sleek English-styled riding boot with its lowered heel, straight leg, and instep strap. Berets, watch caps, and fedoras covered the head as did the babushka or the hood of a coat or poncho.

"Real" jewelry was back. The declining price of gold made it an attractive material to use for the classic costume pieces that were being revived. Lapel pins, button and hoop earrings, fine gold chain necklaces, and link bracelets were the proper touches for 1976 fashions. Diamonds were worn in unshowy ways as delicate stud earrings or spaced between lengths of delicate chaining. The ankle bracelet was the newest jewelry item. Rhinestones provided the only razzle-dazzle in art deco-inspired jewelry adaptations and trimmings on evening clothes and their accessories.

The luxe look in evening accessories continued in delicate evening bags designed to be hand held or to hang from fine gold chains.

Sundresses were the hot weather uniform, making bare shoulders and backs part of the city look for summer.

© 1976 BY THE CONDÉ NAST PUBLICATIONS INC.

Many were made from satin or suede, often trimmed with ribbon, braid, or jeweled clasps. Small gold or antique painted boxes were also used as evening bags. Gold and silver sandals were luxe fashion footwear.

MEN'S WEAR

Return to Tradition. Men's fashions were more unified than women's clothes. Casual looks were being sharpened and pulled together in a more middle-of-the-road way. The jean suit was replaced by the traditional slack and sport coat combination. Neatness counted. Even the looks that were based on the workwear or outdoor gear that influenced fashion were well-fitted, well-coordinated, and well-styled.

The vest, in single and double breasted versions, was a major item in the man's wardrobe. As part of a three piece suit, it was often contrasted in pattern or color. Sweater vests gave a relaxed look to suits and separates.

Sportswear. Jackets were adaptations of active sportwear styles. Windbreakers, baseball jackets, hunting shirts, pea coats, and duffles were the shapes for the leisure suit jacket. All were easy fitting and well made with action backs, raglan sleeves, or saddle shoulders and detailed with ribbed cuffs and waistbands, patch pockets, and saddle stitching. Many were hooded or had drawstring waists and were often zippered or had toggle closings.

Sweaters were neat, classic pullovers done with interesting textures and stitches in tweeded yarns, bouclés, or shetlands. Cable, rib, garter, and stripe stitches in monochrome prevailed.

Dress Shirts to Polo Shirts. The traditional dress shirt was low key in plain fabrics or refined stripes or patterns. The collars were softer and wider with elongated points. The cuffed short sleeve sport shirt was back as a fashion item. The newest shirt for casual wear was the comfortable unfitted top, which took the form of rugby or polo shirts, farmer's shirts or smock tops, and yachting or sailor middies. They copied the authentic fabrics, colors, and stripes of the original.

Accessories. Accessories were underplayed. The flamboyant touches of jewelry and scarves were replaced by the conservative digital watch and newly narrowed tie or ascot. Shoes and boots were in soft leathers, rich in color with narrower toes. Platforms and high heels were gone. Slip-ons, moccasins, espadrilles, and ankle boots were refined, clean, and elegant. The shoe for casual wear was a jogger, desert, or cowboy boot.

In general, men's wear came out of its peacock period and returned to classic traditional tailoring, fabrics, and styling. Men's fashion retained only the comfort, easy fit, and coordination of the separates that were so much a part of previous year's experimentation and liberation.

ANN M. ELKINS
Fashion Director, "Good Housekeeping"

FINLAND

A political crisis, the travels of President Urho Kekkonen, and establishment of a new investment bank were major news stories in Finland.

Politics. In mid-May 1976, Prime Minister Martti Miettunen tendered the resignation of his coalition cabinet to President Urho K. Kekkonen, the apparent reason being the inability of the government to cure such economic ills plaguing the country as the balance of payments deficit (about $2,000,000,000) and the rate of unemployment (4%). Also, numerous strikes, among them a police strike lasting 17 days in February and a dock laborers' stoppage which for three weeks closed all ports, added to the country's economic woes.

One main reason for the cabinet's failure to formulate plans and programs that might alleviate the situation was the tension and disagreement within the cabinet. It consisted of ministers representing the Center Party, the Social Democrats, the Swedish Party, the Liberals, and the Communists. President Kekkonen, however, refused to accept the resignation of the Miettunen cabinet; it remained in office throughout the summer until a seemingly insoluble conflict arose between the Communists and the other four parties in regard to the 1977 budget, involving unemployment measures and farm and housing policies.

On September 29 a new government took office, with Martti Miettunen retaining the premiership and Dr. Keijo Korhonen, also of the Center Party, becoming foreign minister. The new coalition consisted of 9 Center Party members, 3 from the Liberal Party, 4 from the Swedish People's Party, and one non-party member. The Communists were left out of the new coalition.

Local elections, for governing councils of municipalities and rural communities, were held on October 17. The elections did not result in major surprises. The People's Democratic League (Communists) advanced by 1% of the total vote, while the Social Democrats and the

UPI

Finland's Prime Minister Martti Miettunen (*left*) submits his government's resignation to President Urho Kekkonen. Miettunen later formed a new cabinet.

Socialistic Workers' Party suffered minor losses compared to the 1972 elections. The major winners, compared to 1972, were the Conservatives (who gained 2.4%) and the Center Party (who gained 1.2%).

With a view to the presidential elections in 1978, most of the big political parties went on record in 1976 as supporting the reelection of President Kekkonen. Two of the smaller groupings, however, the Constitutional People's Party and the Unity Party, decided at their annual meetings eventually to nominate separate candidates for the nation's highest office.

Presidential Travels. President Kekkonen, an inveterate traveler, attended the wedding of King Carl XVI Gustaf of Sweden and Miss Silvia Sommerlath and also visited Norway, Hungary, and the Soviet Union. He later went to the United States for the bicentennial, where he was the guest of President Ford.

In May he played host to Queen Elizabeth II and Prince Philip of England and to President Julius Nyerere of Tanzania. The latter nation has benefited greatly from Finnish commercial and technical aid.

A New Bank. In May the Finnish Parliament agreed to the establishment of a Nordic Investment Bank. The bank will be charged with tasks of implementing various economic projects and promoting exports from the Scandinavian countries. Its headquarters will be in Helsinki.

Aalto. World-famous architect and designer, Alvar Aalto, died on May 11 at the age of 78. Perhaps more than any other architect of our time he left his imprint on many lands.

ERIK J. FRIIS
The Scandinavian-American Bulletin

FINLAND · Information Highlights

Official Name: Republic of Finland.
Location: Northern Europe.
Area: 130,120 square miles (377,009 km²).
Population (1976 est.): 4,700,000.
Chief Cities (1975 est.): Helsinki, the capital, 499,500; Tampere, 165,050; Turku, 163,050.
Government: *Head of state,* Urho Kaleva Kekkonen, president (took office March 1974 for 4th term). *Head of government,* Martti J. Miettunen, prime minister (took office November 1975). *Legislature* (unicameral)—Eduskunta.
Monetary Unit: Markka, or Finnish mark (3.88 markhas, equal U.S.$1, July 1976).
Gross National Product (1975 est.): $27,600,000,000.
Manufacturing (major products): Wood and paper products, ships, machinery, chemicals, metals, textiles, cement.
Major Agricultural Products: Oats, potatoes, sugar beets, barley, rye, wheat, forest products.
Foreign Trade (1975): *Exports,* $5,487,000,000; *imports,* $7,602,000,000.

FLORIDA

The continuing rate of unemployment had a decisive impact on politics and public policy in 1976, as Florida's economic recovery lagged.

Economy. The unemployment rate was approximately 11% in January, but dropped below 9% in October. This was partly due to a 10% increase in tourism. Home construction and sales improved somewhat, as new residents came into the state in growing numbers. Farm income, which set new records in 1975, appeared strong; however, citrus producers were concerned that the expected bumper crop would cause prices to plummet.

Legislature. The legislature introduced a record number of bills but passed only 11.3% of them into law. All tax increases were rejected, and the budget remained balanced. Bowing to widespread public pressure, the legislature repealed the 1974 law which granted automatic cost-of-living pay increases to county officials. Legislators attempted to help consumers by authorizing, for the first time, the advertising of eyeglass prices, and they passed another bill requiring pharmacists to use the less expensive generic drugs in filling prescriptions. Noting that the number of state employees had increased twice as rapidly as the population since 1960, the legislature passed an amendment to restrict the number of state employees to 1% of the population. At the urging of Governor Askew, the voters rejected this amendment in November.

Former Sen. Edward J. Gurney (R-Fla.) faces newsmen after being acquitted of remaining felony charges.

UPI

Environmental issues were casualties; the legislature seemed determined to remove any potential obstacle to business growth. A new law virtually prohibits state environmental regulations more stringent than federal ones. Several measures designed to protect Florida's beaches and wetlands met with such stiff opposition from business interests that they died in committee. Bills to prohibit nonreturnable beverage containers died without a hearing. But a program to restore the Kissimmee River basin to its natural state was initiated; another law requires the restoration of drilling areas by petroleum companies.

The legislature again refused to ratify the Equal Rights Amendment; however, it did order the university system to eliminate sex discrimination in its pay scales. It also passed new laws attempting to control the cost of malpractice and automobile insurance and added new rules to protect consumers from unscrupulous real estate developers.

Politics. The presidential campaign of Jimmy Carter and the reelection bid of Sen. Lawton Chiles dominated the political stage. Carter, who had demonstrated unexpected strength at the Democratic state convention in November 1975, showed it was no fluke when he won the state presidential preference primary. Carter, George Wallace, and Sen. Henry Jackson, who had the support of the popular Governor Askew, received 34%, 32%, and 24% of the vote, respectively. Florida followed the rest of the South, save Virginia, in giving its electoral votes to Governor Carter in November.

Lawton Chiles, who literally "walked" himself into the U. S. Senate in 1970, won handily over Dr. John Grady. Chiles' victory may be attributed to his limited success in getting Congress to adopt a "government in the sunshine" policy. Voters also approved of his moderate stance on issues. However, his policy of limiting campaign contributions to $10 per person did most to rally the voters to his camp. It was hailed as a courageous attempt to restrict the influence of special interest groups.

J. LARRY DURRENCE, *Florida Southern College*

FLORIDA • Information Highlights

Area: 58,560 square miles (151,670, km²).
Population (1975 est.): 8,357,000.
Chief Cities (1970 census): Tallahassee, the capital, 72,586; Jacksonville, 528,865; Miami, 334,859.
Government (1976): *Chief Officers*—governor, Reubin O'D. Askew (D); lt. gov., J. H. Williams (D). *Legislature*—Senate, 40 members; House of Representatives, 120.
Education (1975–76): *Enrollment*—public elementary schools, 793,708; public secondary, 757,665; nonpublic (1976–77), 147,600; colleges and universities, 295,703 students. *Public school expenditures,* $2,018,772,000 ($1,298 per pupil).
State Finances (fiscal year 1975): *Revenues,* $4,666,797,000; *expenditures,* $4,901,551,000.
Personal Income (1975): $47,055,000,000; per capita, $5,638.
Labor Force (July 1976): *Nonagricultural wage and salary earners,* 2,665,700; *insured unemployed,* 97,700 (3.7%).

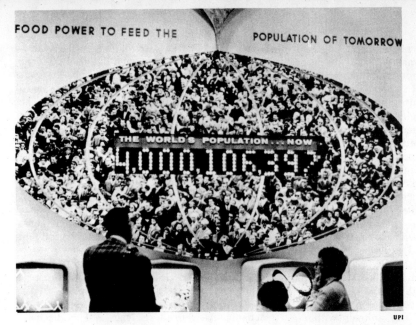

FOOD POWER TO FEED THE POPULATION OF TOMORROW

THE WORLD'S POPULATION . . . NOW
4,000,106,397

Visitors to the Museum of Science and Industry in Chicago listen to an explanation of the institution's population clock. Feeding the world's population of over 4,000,000,000 is a growing problem.

UPI

FOOD

While the world food situation did not make equal headlines with political upheavals and natural disasters in 1976, in terms of quantity, quality, and location of supplies the situation had not improved, but had worsened.

The world's population was estimated to be growing at a rate of about 2% per year. Although food production has doubled since 1950, while the population has increased by about 50% to approximately 4,000,000,000, the shortage of food persists, the result of pockets of surplus and deficit areas throughout the world. This situation, along with the concurrent problems of starvation and malnutrition, was not confined to developing countries alone but also could be found within developed countries.

GLOBAL FOOD SUPPLY

The need for food throughout the world is increasing. Scarcities and rising prices have compounded the problem both in developing and developed countries, leading to intensive efforts by all nations to increase food production and provide a higher level of nutrition to their citizens.

The food imbalance in the world has been worsening over the years. Preliminary world grain production figures for 1975/76 put the year's grain crop at 1,220 million metric tons, or roughly 20 million tons above the depressed 1974/75 level. This increase, however, was below that of the 1973/74 record by approximately 31 million metric tons. Based on these figures, the grain supply coupled with demand has remained nearly even, with little easing of price structure or increase in the supply of grains for emergencies.

Growing Conditions. Weather conditions in 1976 adversely affected crops and cattle production in Britain, Western Europe, the U.S.S.R., the United States, and Australia. While the U.S. corn and wheat harvests were predicted to be near record levels, oat and barley growing areas were hard hit by drought, with harvests expected to be down nearly 20%.

In much of Britain, Europe and Australia one of the worst droughts in years was expected to reduce drastically harvests of grain, sugar beets, and potatoes. The Soviet Union's 1975/76 wheat, milled rice, and coarse grain crops were reported at 134 million tons, as compared with 186 million tons in 1974/75 and 213 million tons in 1973/74. The European Economic Community harvest was approximately 99 million tons, compared with a 108 million-ton average in the previous three years. In addition, cattle (dairy and meat) herds in parts of Europe and Australia were being drastically reduced as a result of lack of water and high feed costs.

In other areas, production was about 77 million tons above the 1974/75 level. The per capita grain production within most developed and centrally planned countries was at near record levels. In the developing countries the increases either slowed or halted the drop in per capita production and reduced the dependence on imported grains. Preliminary forecasts for the 1976/77 outlook were optimistic, suggesting a possible increase of 7%, or 83 million tons, above the 1975/76 level.

Of great importance was the rise in rice production throughout most of Asia. As a result of the increase in the 1975/76 production, supplies of rice were under reduced pressure, at least until the crop reports for 1976/77 are known. Record rice harvests were reported in the United States, Brazil, and other producing areas.

Although production figures appeared promising, the consumption of grains and other foods by human beings is dependent upon not only supply but also upon price, ability to pay, trade barriers, and demand for grain for livestock feeding. With the world population rising at an annual rate of approximately 2%, the larger producers of food cannot continue to supply deficit producing areas. In order to prevent further starvation and malnutrition, it is imperative that food production in lesser developed areas be raised by increased technological assistance from developed areas and by a willingness of governments and their people to become self sufficient. A number of countries, such as China, which were formerly deficit producing nations, have turned into self-sufficient or self-supporting food countries. Nevertheless, with a rising population, the world has been consuming food from a diminishing supply provided by a few.

As a number of food experts have pointed out, the solution to world feeding is not increased productivity by a few, but a realization that agriculture from within must be given priority. Deficit producing countries must increase food yields from crops and animals within a relatively short period.

Grain Trade. Recent experience has shown that large purchases of grain on an irregular basis can disrupt the market. The Soviet Union purchased 2.5 million tons of grain in 1972 and secretly purchased nearly 13 million tons in 1973. In 1975 the United States and the Soviet Union reached a five-year agreement to regularize Soviet purchases at a minimum of 6 million tons annually.

U. S. FOOD INDUSTRY

The American food supply was again the most abundant and varied in the world in 1976. But although its food supply was of high quality, consumers and governmental agencies continued to investigate and regulate many of its activities. Among the major concerns of the industry were safety, food additives, microbiological quality, costs, and inflation.

Food Costs. Inflation in 1976 rose at a rate about half that of the previous year, with the result that food costs rose at a more predictable rate. The cost of food to consumers rose slightly to about 17.1% of their income after taxes. The latest available figures (1972) prior to these showed that food costs represented 16.3% of after-tax income in the United States, 23.4% in France, 24.2% in West Germany, 25% in Japan, 29.8% in Britain, and 35% in the Soviet Union.

Low-cost food in the United States results from the combination of farm productivity and the efficiency of the food processing industry. Food processing as a component of the food industry has been growing larger. In 1975, 42 cents of each consumer dollar spent for food at retail prices went to the farmer and 58 cents went to the food processing sector. The largest cost in handling and processing food is for labor, followed by packaging, and transportation.

Regulatory Actions. In a move that had been anticipated, the Food and Drug Administration (FDA), as of February 1977, banned the widely-used dye Red No. 2 as an additive in food. The decision was based on an FDA study that was severely criticized for its statistical methods. Red No. 40 was the most likely substitute. The Canadian Food and Drug Directorate stated that Canada would not ban Red No. 2 since the study did not disprove its safety, and would not approve the use of Red No. 40 in Canada. In a related action, the U.S. Department of Agriculture (USDA) delisted Violet No. 1 as an approved denaturant on carcasses, meats, and food products. The controversy on food colors has sparked much research in natural food pigments derivable from grapes, beets, and other highly colored products.

In an effort to utilize more meat from animal carcasses, the USDA issued an interim regulation in April establishing nutritional criteria and limits of use in processed meat products of mechanically-deboned red meat. The mechanical deboning process strips bones clean of all meat more efficiently than traditional hand deboning. As a similar system for poultry had done, the process was calculated to add nearly one billion pounds of meat to the supply. But when a coalition of consumer groups and a court restraining order challenged the regulation, the USDA withdrew it on September 14, halting production by mechanical deboning. It was not known if mechanically deboned poultry meat would be affected in the future.

In another action relating to meat, the USDA issued interim standards for products made from traditionally cured meat to which have been added nonmeat products containing protein. The standards were issued in response to the increased use of soy protein and milk products in combination meat products.

In other moves, the FDA published proposed requirements to ensure safe manufacturing, processing, and packing procedures for pickled, fermented, and acidified foods. The proposal was designed to ensure that these foods will be subject to the same regulations as thermally processed low acid foods. The proposal will also require operating supervisors to complete a course of instruction. The FDA also issued a proposal outlining the policies and procedures that it follows and that regulated food firms should follow in the conduct of product recalls. In addition, the FDA published proposed good manufacturing practice (GMP) regulations for tree nuts and peanuts. This action followed an FDA evaluation that indicated existing industry procedures were not sufficient to assure production of safe and sanitary products.

An economic impact study done for the Occupational Safety and Health Administration (OSHA) reported that its proposals to reduce worker exposure to industrial noise might cost food processors as much as $1.7 billion a year. Public hearings to discuss on-the-job noise exposure were held in late summer.

Industry Advances. Container technology advanced with the introduction of two different plastic "cans." One is made of clear acrylonitrile resin while the other is of high density polyethylene (HDPE). Both can accept normal can ends to form hermetic seals. The acrylonitrile can is designed for high acid (pH 4.5 or less), hot-filled foods while the HDPE is for frozen juices. In each case, existing can lines may be used with minor modifications.

Another development was the introduction of a high fructose corn syrup. While fructose syrup is not new, the increase from 42% to 90% fructose is. The chief benefits of the syrup are lower calorie content for a given degree of sweetness, improved flavor of some foods, improved handling, and shipping weight savings. Its use will be in beverages, salad dressings, jams and jellies, and other products where sweetening is needed.

Producers of frozen foods have been revising retail packages to include directions for microwave cookery. Some 6.2% of U.S. homes had microwave ovens in 1976. It is estimated that 26.5% will by 1980.

NUTRITION AND THE CONSUMER

In a supermarket survey on consumer attitudes and buying habits, the results showed that 55% were worried about the cost of food (down from 76% in 1975), 33% were pressed by the economy, and 45% chiefly blamed the government, not the farmers, for high food prices.

High Fiber Diet. Consumers reacted strongly to widely publicized medical studies reporting apparent health benefits from diets high in fiber. Interest in fiber came from a British report indicating that rural Africans whose diets are high in fiber-containing foods have a very low incidence of diseases such as appendicitis, hemorrhoids, diverticular disease, and cancer of the colon. These diseases are more prevalent in the United States and Western Europe.

As a result, total pound sales of ready-to-eat bran cereals increased 20% in 1976. A new high-fiber bread was introduced containing 30% fewer calories than regular white bread and providing comparable amounts of nutrients, but with 400% more fiber than whole wheat bread. On the negative side, some scientists cautioned that extensive research was needed to determine if the fiber theories were correct.

Government Actions. The Senate Select Committee on Nutrition and Human Needs released a report entitled "Nutrition and Health," which expanded on recommendations and testimony given at the 1974 National Nutrition Policy hearings. Basically, the report examined nutrition evaluation and counseling, a method for monitoring the national nutrition status, and proposals for establishment of a Food and Nutrition Policy Board.

The FDA proposed to regulate baby foods more closely by requiring percentage labeling of all ingredients present at levels of 5% or higher and requiring descriptive terms in the common or usual name. Target date for the regulations was Jan. 1, 1978.

See also AGRICULTURE.

KIRBY M. HAYES, *University of Massachusetts*

Experts estimate that a total of 56 persons is fed by the average U. S. farmer.

UPI

FOREIGN AID

Reports issued in 1976 indicated a rise in economic assistance from industrialized nations to developing countries and relatively good growth in the developing world. In the world's poorest countries, however, economic improvement hardly kept pace with population increases.

The 17-nation Development Assistance Committee (DAC), whose members provide most of the foreign aid from the industrialized world, reported that concessional Official Development Assistance (ODA) rose to $13,600,000,000 in 1975, 20% above the year before in dollar volume and 10% above in real terms when adjusted for inflation. As a percentage of gross national product of the donor countries, this ODA climbed to .36% in 1975 from .33% a year earlier (but still far short of the DAC target of .7%). Counting private and nonconcessional flows to developing countries, the total from DAC nations increased 39% to $38,800,000,000 in 1975, for an average of 1.02% of donors' GNP compared with .81% in 1974. This marked the first time the DAC target of 1% of GNP for total flows had been reached.

Members of the Organization of Petroleum Exporting Countries (OPEC) were reported to have substantially increased their aid outlays. The flow of concessionary and nonconcessionary disbursements by OPEC states to developing countries was estimated to have climbed from about $922,000,000 in 1973 to $4,600,000,000 in 1974 and $5,600,000,000 in 1975.

Among the developing countries, the World Bank's 1976 annual report noted that economic growth rates continued at a reasonably high annual average of 5.4% during 1973–75 (as against 6.0% during the previous five years). The gain was registered despite problems posed by inflation and recession. Positive factors included external assistance and improvements in domestic agricultural production. However, the poorest countries, mainly nations in South Asia and sub-Sahara Africa, registered an annual GNP gain averaging only 2.8% during 1973–75, which was largely offset on a per capita basis by population growth.

Multilateral Aid. The principal worldwide development assistance institutional group, the World Bank, recorded lending and investment commitments totaling nearly $6,900,000,000 in fiscal 1976, $769,000,000 (12.5%) above the record level of 1975. However inflation eroded nominal gains to the extent that, if measured in constant 1976 dollars, the real-term increase in IBRD and IDA commitments was a more modest 6% in 1976. About 39% of these commitments was extended to the world's poorest countries. Agriculture and rural development projects received some 25% of the total, more than any other single category.

U. S. Aid. ODA by the United States rose to $4,000,000,000 in 1975 (0.27% of GNP), up from $3,400,000,000 (0.24% of GNP) the year before. The United States, while the largest single contributor, was in 12th place among the 17 DAC donors in terms of percent of GNP contributed.

With Congress already having authorized U. S. economic development assistance for two years in 1975, the principal legislative focus in 1976 was on military and security-related economic aid to U. S. friends and allies. A bill authorizing $4,400,000,000 for such aid in fiscal 1976 and containing various policy provisions passed Congress but was vetoed by President Ford on the grounds that the restrictions encroached on presidential foreign policy authority and were unwise.

Congress then passed a two-year authorization for fiscal 1976 and 1977 with some modifications to meet the president's objections, but still containing significant restrictions, and President Ford signed the bill into law June 30 despite "serious reservations." The new legislation authorized $6,900,000,000 in arms and security-supporting assistance for the two years including the transition quarter, with heavy emphasis on funds for the Middle East (total aid and sales-credit authorized for Israel was about $4,300,-000,000; economic aid to Egypt was authorized at $1,450,000,000). Significant policy provisions included termination of U. S. military grant assistance and military advisory groups abroad by the end of fiscal 1977, tightened Congressional and governmental control over foreign military sales, and restrictions aimed against human rights violations abroad, nuclear proliferation, and discrimination against U. S. citizens on the basis of race, religion, or sex.

Communist Aid. According to the Central Intelligence Agency, communist economic assistance to developing countries in 1975 totaled some $1,852,000,000 including $1,264,000,000 from the USSR, $319,000,000 from East European countries, and $269,000,000 from China. Communist arms accords with the Third World (developing nations) in 1975 were put at $925,-000,000, of which $725,000,000 were by the USSR, $175,000,000 by East Europe, and $25,-000,000 by mainland China.

International Conferences. The dialogue between industrialized nations and developing countries over Third World proposals for more favorable economic treatment made some progress during 1976. A May 5–30 United Nations Conference on Trade and Development (UNCTAD) in Nairobi, Kenya, attended by more than 2,000 delegates from 153 countries, ended with adoption of a compromise proposal to set up a fund to stabilize commodity prices, to be negotiated in 1977. A plan, proposed by Secretary of State Kissinger, for a $1,000,000,000 raw materials development bank was rejected.

LEWIS GULICK
Staff Consultant
House International Relations Committee

President Giscard, *left*, enjoys a light moment with his friend, Chancellor Helmut Schmidt of West Germany, during a Common Market summit meeting in Luxembourg early in the year.

UPI

FRANCE

Clouds hung on the political and economic horizons through 1976. Two cabinets wrestled uncertainly with long-standing financial and social problems. The regime seemed already to be living in anticipation of the 1978 elections which, in theory, could change the shape of the republic.

DOMESTIC AFFAIRS

With polls showing almost half the voters dissatisfied with his performance, President Valéry Giscard d'Estaing shuffled a few portfolios on January 21 and went on to protect the authority of his office. The challenge came from his hard-line prime minister, Jacques Chirac, leader of the diminished but still powerful Gaullists (174 seats in the National Assembly). Chirac pressed Giscard to abandon the tactic of wooing moderates from the Communist-Socialist alliance, which won 56% of the vote in local elections in March. Initially giving way, Giscard announced on March 24 that Chirac would henceforth "coordinate and animate" the parties of the ruling coalition, an ambiguous concession which avoided Chirac's demand for control of domestic affairs. Clearly, the prime minister and his party wanted a return to a thoroughly Gaullist government, while paradoxically trying to reduce the presidency, which had been its predominant feature, because it was held by an Independent Republican, who had failed in loyalty to de Gaulle.

The struggle lasted five months. Narrowly elected in 1974, Giscard was labeled "le gagman" for his political gimmicks. Chirac was known in parliamentary franglais as "le bulldozer." But power rested with the president, if he chose to use it. A series of financial, political, and foreign policy disagreements moved

him to cut Chirac down. Resigning on August 25, Chirac complained privately that Giscard was "monarchical" and publicly that he had been denied the powers he needed to do his job. Giscard's version was that Chirac was overly ambitious and mistaken in seeking national elections immediately.

As Giscard had failed to rally the Gaullists to join his own Independents and various centrist groups in a strong presidential coalition, his future seemed uncertain. But in getting rid of Chirac he was only doing what two previous presidents had done to their prime ministers. The difference was that he was no Gaullist, had no Gaullist majority, and thus ended the Gaullist nature of the regime.

For prime minister he chose the politically colorless foreign trade minister, Raymond Barre, a distinguished economist who also took the finance portfolio. The career diplomat Louis de Guiringaud replaced Jean Sauvagnargues as foreign minister. The centrist leader Jean Lecanuet moved from justice to national development. Françoise Giroud became secretary of state for culture; her previous post for women's affairs,

─────── **FRANCE • Information Highlights** ───────

Official Name: French Republic.
Location: Western Europe.
Area: 211,207 square miles (547,026 km²).
Population (1976 est.): 53,100,000.
Chief Cities (1975 census): Paris, the capital, 2,291,000; Marseille, 908,000; Lyon, 457,000; Toulouse, 383,000.
Government: *Head of state,* Valéry Giscard d'Estaing, president (took office May 1974). *Chief minister,* Raymond Barre, prime minister (took office Aug. 1976). *Legislature*—Parliament: Senate and National Assembly.
Monetary Unit: Franc (4.98 francs equal U. S.$1, Nov. 1976).
Gross National Product (1975 est.): $359,200,000,000.
Manufacturing (major products): Steel, machinery, metals, chemicals, automobiles, airplanes, processed foods, beverages, clothing, textiles.
Major Agricultural Products: Wheat, barley, oats, sugar beets, vegetables, apples, grapes, cattle.
Foreign Trade (1975): *Exports,* $52,214,000,000; *imports,* $54,247,000,000.

which had proved ineffective, was abolished. The Gaullist Yvon Bourges remained at defense, and Gaullist Olivier Guichard became minister of justice. Giscard's friend, Michel Poniatowski remained in the powerful Interior Ministry. It was a slightly smaller cabinet, and its support from the Gaullist Union of Democrats for the Republic (UDR) was shaky.

Every party speculated about the looming 1978 elections. The Gaullists' strength was ebbing, and in the face of a strong Union of the Left they chose to support Giscard. By opposition, they could compel early elections and possibly save many of their seats before further strength evaporated. For the moment, however, they preferred conditional support of Barre.

The Socialist party was much more optimistic. Dramatically rebuilt in the past five years, it was the most formidable single group. At the moment it might command 30–35% of the popular vote, hence obtain close to a majority of assembly seats, at least doubling its 1973 performance. Evidently, First Secretary François Mitterrand expected to become prime minister in 1978. But the Socialists believed this eventuality depended on their collaboration with the Communists in the Union of the Left, though experience showed that it was hard to get both parties to adhere to the rules of the game.

At its 22d congress, February 4–7, the Communist party emphasized its independence of Moscow. Secretary General Georges Marchais attacked "repressive measures" in Russia, declared the concept of the "dictatorship of the proletariat" outmoded, and insisted that "our road to socialism" was "a French road." The pitch was for cooperation with the salaried middle classes, and the style was borrowed from other European Communists (notably the Italians). Some thought the change a mere mask, some fundamental. What was new was the public display of intra-party differences. Backed by some 20% of the electorate, the party might well have the opportunity of clarifying its position as part of a ruling coalition.

The triennial (cantonal) elections on March 7 and 14 in some 1,863 districts showed substantial Socialist and Communist gains. Not normally considered significant of national trends, these general council elections, however, produced an unusually high voter turnout; though remaining in majority, the government took the challenge seriously. President Giscard affected calm: after the first round of balloting, he concluded a cabinet dinner not with a strategy session but with a round of gin rummy.

Reforms and Scandals. It was a poor year for ~ocial reform. The government's capital gains ~ bill met an unfortunate end. No sooner was ~resented to the assembly, in April, than the ~ial community denounced it as discouraging ~nvestment. Chirac and the Gaullists were ~ the Communists and Socialists found it ~ rich. The result was 375 amend-

ments to the bill as passed on June 23. Emasculated, the new law would bring in a mere $100 million a year (while income tax fraud is estimated at $13,000,000,000). The fate of a government bill to give workers representation on company boards was no happier. The unions were critical; the employers were hostile. A Socialist-sponsored bill to tax individual and corporate fortunes above $400,000 at 0.5% (rising to a maximum of 2%) was almost unanimously rejected. A report in August by the Organization for Economic Cooperation and Development showed that the gap between the very rich and the very poor was greatest in France, even if there had been some improvement in the situation since 1945.

Françoise Giroud's five-year plan for the improvement of the position of women was accepted in principle. It would cost about $4,000,-000,000. But Giroud's post was abolished and the plan relegated to the new prime minister's office. In the climate of austerity now decreed, it was unlikely that the plan would be realized. By contrast, university reforms generated so much student and professor protest that the government retreated from them in April.

Scandal, as always, hovered on the edges of politics. The press reported corporate wrongdoing, envelopes distributed at election time, price rigging, cheating on taxes. But the left failed to get parliamentary investigation; mutual charges of corruption from left and right canceled each other out. A secret Finance Ministry report of procurement rivalries, waste, and malpractices involving defense agencies and arms manufacturers was leaked without creating serious demands for investigation. Judicial authorities taking their investigations further than multinational corporations thought wise were suddenly transferred.

Strikes and Protests. Strikes occurred throughout the year. The wine-growers demonstrated repeatedly against Spanish and Italian imports, attacking depòts and bottling plants. They bombed and sacked government offices in Narbonne on March 1 and battled police there two days later, leaving two men dead and others wounded. Troops and armored cars were airlifted into the Montpellier district. Road and rail traffic was disrupted and rolling stock set ablaze. Much of the uproar was caused by the devaluation of the lira which permitted cheap Italian wine to undersell French.

Millions of public employees disrupted services on March 9 to back annual wage demands. Students protesting suggested government reforms curtailed instruction in universities for weeks. Violent clashes with the police occurred in the Paris Latin Quarter in March and April. Police expelled the occupants of the arts faculty at Nancy on May 7. The Paris bus and subway systems were struck in January for better hours and wages. The subway shut down on June 1 to protest the rising incidence of robbery and as-

Named prime minister in August, economist Raymond Barre (*right*) put together a non-Gaullist cabinet of experts. Career diplomat Louis de Guiringaud (*above*) became minister of foreign affairs, while child psychologist Nicole Pasquier (*top right*) was called upon to handle women's concerns.

sault. Paris newspapers were disrupted over a plant modernization scheme until agreement was reached in July among 16 major dailies, the printers' union, and four plants.

Economy. Plagued by drought and inflation, despite revised forecasts of a slightly higher gross national product (GNP), the economic and financial situation deteriorated. After a massive central bank support of the franc, pressure finally led to a middle-of-the-night decision on March 15 to free it from the joint currency float of July 1975. The seventh five-year economic and social development plan (1976–80), adopted by the cabinet on April 21, proposed a $40,000,000,000 "priority action" to create one million additional jobs, raise the GNP by 6%, and increase workers' purchasing power by 3%. Of major concern was a 12% inflation (twice the rate of France's competitors) on top of heavy unemployment. On September 22 the government froze prices until the year's end,

proposing a 6.5% ceiling on 1977 increases. "France is living above its means," Barre told the nation. The economy showed "serious weakness." Taxes were raised on income, alcohol, automobiles, and gasoline. The Communists attacked all this as "a plan for social regression," and called a 24-hour strike for October 7 (in which six million participated) on the grounds that the government should not now be applying the brakes. But Giscard asked for worker restraint. "The slogan of the French Republic," he told the nation, "cannot be liberty, equality and selfishness."

Defense. France's return to cooperation with NATO continued to be politically sensitive. Armed Forces chief of staff Gen. Guy Méry created a Communist-Socialist and Gaullist storm on June 1 by stating that France must be ready to fight a forward battle with NATO in event of attack from the east. Giscard endorsed the view as "good common sense," while Rear Adm. Antoine Sanguinetti was dismissed for criticism of the policy.

FOREIGN AFFAIRS

Remnants of France's former empire continued to move toward independence. The Territory of the Afars and the Issas was scheduled for independence by year's end, though French troops would remain in Djibouti to discourage Soviet-backed Somalian designs. On June 5 the islands of St. Pierre and Miquelon, though 3,000 miles (4,800 km) from Europe, became France's 100th metropolitan department.

Relations with Great Britain were good. When Giscard addressed Parliament during his three-day state visit in June, he announced that he and the British prime minister would meet annually, and their ministers periodically, to coordinate policies. On November 2 it was announced that the Concorde project would be terminated with the 16th aircraft. No more orders had come in. Despite regular flights to the Americas, the enterprise was to be written off as a prestigious but ruinous success.

Relations with Russia remained cool following Giscard's 1975 disagreement with Soviet interpretation of the Helsinki accord. Foreign Minister Gromyko visited France in April, and Brezhnev, despite criticisms from French Communists earlier in the year, gave a friendly interview on French television on October 5.

In the Middle East France unsuccessfully tried to play a major role. A second good-offices mission went to Lebanon in April (the first had gone in November 1975), but Giscard's offer on May 21 to send peace-keeping forces brought no request from the Lebanese government.

Relations with Iran were good, marked by Giscard's state visit in October, when he concluded agreements to cooperate in transport and nuclear power developments. Previous agreements to build nuclear plants in Libya and South Africa, coming after such sales to Pakistan, raised criticism both in France and abroad. The president set up a high council to examine details of further such deals.

Relations with the United States were cordial but with a normal complement of friction. Washington was angered by the publication in a Paris newspaper of names and addresses of 32 alleged CIA agents attached to the U. S. embassy in Paris. Warnings against admission of Communists to government posts (still a long way off, at best) brought condemnation of President Ford and Secretary Kissinger for their "absolutely intolerable intrusions." The two states had rival approaches to aid for developing nations. Giscard permitted himself public anxiety about U. S. hesitations over what to do in Angola. But during his state visit in May he stressed the two nations' unity. Nevertheless, polls showed that neither the French nor the American people had much faith in one another's capacity to bring peace and stability to the world.

JOHN C. CAIRNS, *University of Toronto*

Strikes and protests proliferated in 1976 as the French economy deteriorated and austere new restrictions were imposed. In October, a one-day nationwide strike was highlighted in Paris by a workers' protest march.

UPI

GARDENING AND HORTICULTURE

A Gallup poll has indicated that, for the first time since World War II, more than half of all American households had vegetable gardens during the summer of 1976. A prominent seedsman, David Burpee, ended a 56-year-old search for a white marigold when he bought the white selection from Mrs. Alice Vonk, a home gardener from Sully, Iowa. The purchase reportedly made the white marigold the costliest flower in the world. In addition to the $10,000 payment, the cost of research to develop a white marigold totaled more than $250,000.

All-America Selections. A trio of beautiful roses, developed by Reimer Kordes, a German breeder, received All-America Rose Selection Awards during 1975–1976. It is the first time in history that one breeder has had three such winners in a two-year period.

Prominent, a grandiflora, is Mr. Kordes's third award winner. It is a brilliant, hot orange, shaded yellow at the base of the petals. The flowers are comparatively small, measuring about three inches (7.5 cm) across, but beautifully shaped; they maintain their bright color throughout their life on the bush. The blooms often last ten days when cut, and this makes Prominent outstanding as a cut flower. It generally produces typical grandiflora candelabra-type stems and blooms; however, in Europe, it often yields hybrid-tealike, single-stem roses.

Prominent is a tall, vigorous grower, with abundant dark-green foliage clothing the plant from the ground up. It forms a shapely, upright bush, which bears many clear, orange-red blooms throughout the season. It has good disease resistance and is an excellent hot-weather plant. Prominent has also received numerous awards in Europe.

First Edition, the award-winning floribunda, brings to the garden a true floribunda growth habit, with eye-catching bloom coloring. The flowers seem to have a fluorescent glow that makes them stand out, even on a cloudy, dark day. This cultivar produces great clusters of perfectly shaped, 2.5-inch (6.3-cm) blooms, in which the yellow, orange, and red shades blend to yield a distinctive coral. First Edition has the highly desirable floribunda characteristic of constantly bearing its masses of blooms throughout the growing season, the color deepening as the nights become cool in the fall. The pointed buds open to well-formed blooms, of which one spray will make a beautiful indoor bouquet and one plant a magnificent outdoor display. Plants of First Edition develop into broad, mounded 2.5-foot (75-cm) bushes, well covered with medium-sized, glossy, bright-green foliage. Because of its consistent, compact habit and masses of blooms, this floribunda should have many uses, both in the garden and as a landscape plant. This cultivar should also be well adapted for a showy hedge. It provides color all summer long.

ALL-AMERICA SELECTIONS

Prominent, a beautifully shaped, hot orange grandiflora, won an all-America Rose Selection Award for 1975–76.

Double Delight is probably one of the most outstanding hybrid teas produced in many years. When the long, pointed, creamy-white buds reach the first unfolding stage, they begin to appear as though the tips had been dipped in ruby-red paint. As the flower continues to open, it discloses large areas of bright, carmine red, unevenly splashed along the margins of the petals. As the bloom matures, the red areas begin to merge until, at the time of petal drop, Double Delight becomes practically a red rose. Its blooms are very large, averaging 5.5–6 inches (14–15 cm) across in most gardens, with 35–45 broad, thick petals making up the shapely flower. The roses, held erect on long, strong stems, are produced continuously throughout the season. The formal, high-centered blooms have a pleasing fragrance—a blend of spice and anise. The growth habit of Double Delight is upright-spreading, quite bushy, and above average height. The foliage is abundant, of a deep, glossy green, and holds well to the ground. This cultivar is the result of cross breeding between Granada and Garden Party, which bring into its ancestry such famous roses as Peace, Charlotte Armstrong, Tiffany, Crimson Glory, Margaret McGredy, and Talisman. Double Delight will make a striking garden rose, and its well-formed flowers and attractive perfume should make it most satisfactory as a cut flower.

DONALD W. NEWSOM
Louisiana State University

Dr. Har Gobind Khorana and a group of his colleagues at MIT synthesized the first gene that is fully functional in a living cell. The achievement, announced in August 1976, gives geneticists a new means of studying genes and a variety of diseases.

GENETICS

Normal human males are distinguished from females by one pair of chromosomes called the sex chromosomes. Female cells contain two copies of a large chromosome called the X, whereas males contain one X and a smaller chromosome called the Y.

The X Y Y Male. Once in a while, by an error in cell division, males are produced containing two Y chromosomes in addition to the X—the so-called XYY males. The incidence of the type has been estimated at roughly 1 per 1000 live born males. In recent years numbers of studies have suggested that there is an elevated frequency of XYY males among the inmates of penal and penal-mental institutions. This has led to the hypothesis that the XYY chromosome complement is somehow associated with "aggressive" behavior.

In 1976 the results of a major new study of XYY males were reported by a scientific team made up of geneticists, psychologists, and statisticians. In this study the chromosome constitutions of more than 4,000 men were examined and for each man his general intelligence and criminal record were also recorded. The first results confirmed earlier findings: the 12 XYY men identified in the study tended to be taller than average and had a higher incidence of criminality. In addition, however, the study found that the XYY men were significantly less intelligent than average, which raised the possibility that the criminality associated with XYY was simply due to their lack of intelligence and had nothing to do with "aggressive" behavior. Partial answers came by (1) looking in detail at the kinds of crimes committed by the XYY's and (2) examining the incidence of criminal activity among XY men in the study of the same intelligence range as the XYY group.

The first study found no evidence that the crimes committed by XYY men were any more violent or more closely associated with "aggressive" behavior than those of the normal XY population. The second study found that there was a higher than normal frequency of criminal records among the less intelligent XY males but still not as high as that of the XYY group. The authors leave open the possibility that with better intelligence testing they might be able to account for all the differences between the groups.

Recombinant DNA. Biologists have developed methods by which single genes from almost any organism can be inserted into a bacterium, producing so-called "recombinant DNA" (deoxyribonucleic acid, the essential genetic material). The foreign gene can replicate and function along with the bacterial host and can be studied in a variety of ways not otherwise available. Molecular geneticists see unlimited potential in these methods for the study of the structure and function of the genetic material.

These same biologists were the first to point out the potential dangers in these methods. It is not always possible to know what gene is being put into the bacterium, and it is possible that a harmful gene could inadvertently be inserted. Since the host bacterium in all these studies is *Escherichia coli,* a bacterium normally found in the human intestine, the danger is that an *E. coli,* carrying such a harmful gene, could "escape" from the laboratory and rapidly spread through the human population with catastrophic effects. The biologists themselves proposed a moratorium on certain types of recombinant DNA experiments until the National Institutes of Health could draw up guidelines to govern these kinds of experiments. These guidelines were released in 1976 and designated four types of recombinant DNA experiments, each associated with a different degree of potential danger. For each class they defined the kinds of containment facilities to be used to insure that a potentially harmful bacterium could never "escape."

The controversy over the recombinant DNA experiments moved out of the laboratory and into the political arena when the Cambridge, Mass., city council declared a three-month moratorium on the experiments until a review board had a chance to study the issue and make recommendations on whether recombinant DNA research should be allowed in Cambridge.

EUGENE R. KATZ
State University of New York at Stony Brook

GEOLOGY

The year 1976 was one of unusual geologic events and discoveries. The unmanned landings on Mars and a number of destructive earthquakes on earth were front-page news. Exploration of the ocean basins continued, and advances of a more routine nature were made on all fronts.

The Viking Missions to Mars. Two unmanned Viking spacecraft were launched Aug. 20, and Sept. 9, 1975. After a journey of about 210,-000,000 miles (390,000,000 km) Viking 1 touched down July 20 in the Chryse Planita basin of Mars; Viking 2 landed September 3 on the Utopia Planita (Utopian Plains) about 4,500 miles (7,350 km) from Viking 1. These spacecraft are possibly the most sophisticated instruments ever put together and their performance was excellent. Numerous photographs were taken and sent from the orbiters (transmission time about 19 light-minutes), and information of a more varied nature came from the landers.

Mars is proving to be a much more complex and dynamic body than the moon. There have been surprises at every step as tantalizing information has poured in from the Viking missions. So diverse and alien is the topography of Mars that an entirely new classification of land forms has been invented to classify them. One scheme suggests: 1) *pitted* and *etched,* mainly due to scouring by wind; 2) *fretted,* due to a variety of actions including melting of frozen subsurface; 3) *troughed,* caused by systematic collapse or subsidence accompanying withdrawal of magma, melting of ground ice, or splitting under crustal tension; 4) *hollowed,* uncertain origin; 5) *chaotic,* caused by slumping, collapse, and subsidence with no apparent pattern. Dense or sparse craters are superimposed on all types of terrane and are, of course, due to external, haphazard impacts.

Paradoxical is the absence of surface water together with evidence of vast ancient floods. Great canyons with branching tributaries, dendritic drainage patterns like earth badlands, wide braided channels cutting into and around streamlined "islands" give evidence of what geologists call catastrophic floods. Adding to the puzzle is the scarcity of sediment-filled basins and rounded pebbles.

Evidences of volcanic action abound. The great mountain, Olympus Mons, 15 miles (24 km) high, is the greatest volcanic cone known in the solar system. Smaller cones and lava fields show overlapping flows and sheets of debris. One collapsed lava tube is traceable for 250 miles (400 km), much longer than any known lava tube on earth. Much of the landscape has been shaped by wind action and there are both destructional and constructional features. The dunes and streamlined sand trails seen in the vicinity of Viking 1 lander are very earth-like. Possibly the least understood of all

UPI

Venzone, Italy, suffered severe quake damage in May.

Martian landscapes is due to frozen water both on the surface and in the subsurface. Melting of the icecaps may be the source of the catastrophic floods in the distant past, while melting of subsurface ice appears to account for the collapse and disruption of vast tracts at all latitudes. Among the most significant of the Viking findings is that the polar cap is water ice and that nitrogen, argon, and krypton are present in the atmosphere.

The Viking spacecraft took many separate experiments to Mars. Most of these may be said to be biologically-oriented. So far the presence or absence of life has neither been confirmed nor denied.

Seismology. The study of earthquake and other earth vibrations, seismology is making rapid strides. Geologists are placing increasing confidence in the theory of plate tectonics as a frame of reference within which causes and effects can be discussed. Thus the earthquake that struck Guatemala in February is explained without question by its location exactly on the boundary between the west-moving North American plate and the east-moving Caribbean plate. There is a strong suspicion that there has been a recent general north and east movement of the African and Indo-Australian plates toward the Eurasian and Pacific plates. Some consider this motion to have been rather abrupt and hold it responsible for the rash of earthquakes along the zone of potential collision. China is a somewhat special case, but it is probable that the pressure of India against Tibet is being transmitted northeasterly into China which seems to be a mosaic of uneasy smaller blocks.

Earthquake Warnings and Predictions. China obviously has much to gain from successful earthquake prediction. Major efforts are being put forth in this field. Past lessons have been harsh. The greatest loss of life of any earthquake was in 1556 when at least 820,000 were killed in Shensi province; in 1920, 180,000 died in a quake in Kansu province. Seismology in China is a "peoples science." It is reported that over 10,000 persons cooperate in routine observations. Also, about 250 seismic stations and 5,000 "observation points" have been established. Amateurs measure changes in the electrical conductivity of the ground, note the behavior of animals, and pay particular attention to what goes on in water wells. Professionals must carry on the more sophisticated measurements of magnetic fields and radon gas. The involvement of citizens everywhere and the long history of earthquake awareness have given prediction a status in China that may not be possible to match in the United States.

In the United States tentative steps toward earthquake prediction and protection are being taken. The National Research Council stated that reliable prediction is an achievable goal within 10 years if long-term research is undertaken immediately. Bills have been introduced in the Senate and House to finance the improvement of quake-resistant buildings and the possibilities of predictive studies. The U. S. Geological Survey is responsible for prediction and warnings.

Volcanoes. Volcanoes and predictions of volcanic activity were also in the news. Soufrière volcano on the island of Guadaloupe in the Caribbean showed ominous signs of eruption in August and 72,000 residents were ordered out of the vicinity. There were terrifying sounds and trembles together with extrusion of stones, gas, steam, and mud prior to the anticipated eruption on August 30. Geologists took advantage of the lively situation to study volcanic action first hand. A major eruption of Mauna Loa Volcano, island of Hawaii, some time before July 1978 is predicted. The volcano has not erupted since June 1950 and its 25-year "rest" is the longest in recorded history.

Deep Sea Drilling. The Deep Sea Drilling project continued to make major contributions. With Leg 42B, the Black Sea was sampled for the first time. Legs 43 and 44 in the North Atlantic completed the phase of shallower drilling. The research vessel *Challenger* entered drydock in September, 1975 and was refitted for the International Phase of Ocean Drilling, IPOD, aimed at penetrating and sampling the oceanic crust to depths of several kilometers. Legs 45 and 46 were conducted on the Mid-Atlantic Ridge. Forty-seven, 48, and 49 obtained data in the eastern Atlantic off European coasts and Leg 50 is to drill one hole, near the northwest coast of Africa, to a record depth of about 10,000 feet (about 3,000 meters).

W. LEE STOKES
University of Utah

EARTHQUAKES 1976: A PARTICULARLY ACTIVE YEAR

Tens of thousands of persons were killed and extensive destruction occurred as a result of a series of earthquakes on at least three continents in 1976.

In many parts of the world, including the United States, the magnitude of an earthquake is measured by the Richter scale (photo, below). The scale was devised by U. S. seismologist Charles F. Richter in

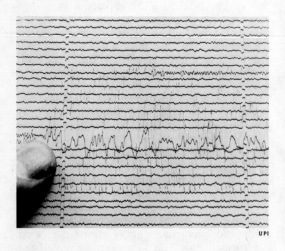

UPI

1935. An increase of one point on the scale means that the ground's motion is 10 times greater. Any earthquake measuring 7 or more on the scale is considered a major one.

Mercalli's scale, developed in 1902, is a qualitative assessment of perceived shock and damage.

Location	Date	Magnitude	Death Toll
Iceland, north-eastern	Jan. 13	6.0-6.5	—
Central America, 120 miles (190 km) northeast of Guatemala City	Feb. 4	7.5	25,000
Friuli, northern Italy	May 6	9.5[1]	1,000
Uzbekistan, USSR	May 17	7.3	6
Bismarck Sea, off New Guinea	May 23	6.7	—
Northern Solomon Sea	June 3	6.8	—
Philippines, east-southeast of Manila	June 7	6.5	—
Near Simeulue Island, Indian Ocean	June 20	7.2	—
Indonesia, about 85 miles (140 km) south of Djajapura	June 26	7.1	450[2]
Molucca Sea, near Talaud Islands	June 26	6.6	—
West Irian province, New Guinea	July 8		9,000
Bali Island, Indonesia	July 19	5.6	500
China, about 100 miles (160 km) southeast of Peking	July 28	8.2	est. 100,000
Transcaucasia, USSR, 800 miles (1,280 km) southeast of Moscow	July 28	6.3	—
New Hebrides Islands	Aug. 2	6.9	—
Szechuan province, China	Aug. 16	7.2	—
Celebes Sea, Mindanao, the Philippines	Aug. 17	7.8	8,000
China, Great Snow Mountains	Aug. 18	7.2	—
China, north-central	Aug. 23	6.7	—
Italy, northeast	Sept. 11	7.5[1]	1

[1] Mercalli scale (after Giuseppe Mercalli, an Italian priest).
[2] 1,500 persons killed in related landslides.

GEORGIA

Presidential politics dominated Georgia affairs in 1976. A former governor was elected president and another former governor was also a presidential candidate.

Presidential Politics. Former Gov. Jimmy Carter became the first Georgian to be elected president. Aided by the Peanut Brigade, a group of Georgians who paid their own expenses to campaign in various states, Carter won a majority of the primaries, including Georgia's. He won the Democratic nomination on the first ballot. After his nomination, Carter's hometown of Plains (population 682) was transformed from a farm community into a tourist area.

Carter won Georgia's 12 electoral votes, carrying the state with 67% of the vote. He made his victory speech at a party attended by 25,000 people in the World Congress Center, a new state-owned convention and trade show facility in Atlanta. The Democrats retained all 10 Congressional seats.

Former Gov. Lester Maddox, self-styled segregationist, reemerged on the political scene and gained national attention as the presidential nominee of the American Independent Party. He claimed that he was the only candidate representing the conservative position.

Economy. Georgia's unemployment rate continued to rise. However, the outlook for economic recovery was optimistic, primarily because of the growth in the food processing and electrical equipment industries.

Rich's Inc., the venerable department store chain headquartered in Atlanta for 109 years, announced a proposed merger with Federated Department Stores of Cincinnati, Ohio. If approved by the Federal Trade Commission, the city's largest home-based retail concern would be acquired for $106 million.

Legislation. The General Assembly passed a court reform measure dividing the state into 10 judicial districts supervised by an administrative judge who would allocate court caseloads. Other major 1976 legislation allowed employers access to the criminal records of potential employees working in sensitive positions; transferred the jurisdiction of marijuana possession offenses from state to municipal courts, thereby reducing the maximum penalty; permitted tax breaks on solar energy equipment; and allowed Atlanta restaurateurs to sell mixed drinks on Sunday.

Georgia physicians won two major legislative victories in the battle to hold down the cost of medical malpractice insurance. In order to reduce publicity, attorneys were barred from listing the exact amount of malpractice suits above $10,000. In addition, the two-year statute of limitations on medical suits was redesigned to begin on the date of occurrence, rather than the date of discovery.

Constitutional amendments passed by the legislature and approved by the voters will allow Gov. George Busbee and future chief executives to seek a second four-year term, barred legislators from voting themselves pay raises, approved a local option freeport tax exemption on goods in transit, and legalized bingo games for nonprofit organizations.

Center for Disease Control. The CDC in Atlanta was the focus of much national attention and controversy as researchers there sought to identify the baffling "legionnaire's disease." The CDC also was responsible for developing and defending the swine flu vaccine.

KAY BECK, *Georgia State University*

After the Rev. Clennon King of Albany, Ga., was barred from services at the Plains Baptist Church, the congregation voted to drop its ban on membership by blacks. Jimmy Carter is a member of the church.

UPI

───── **GEORGIA • Information Highlights** ─────

Area: 58,876 square miles (152,489 km²).

Population (1975 est.): 4,926,000.

Chief Cities (1970 census): Atlanta, the capital, 497,-421; Columbus, 155,028; Macon, 122,423.

Government (1976): *Chief Officers*—governor, George D. Busbee (D); lt. gov., Zell Miller (D); atty. gen., Arthur Bolton (D). *General Assembly*—Senate, 56 members; House of Representatives, 180 members.

Education (1975–76): *Enrollment*—public elementary schools, 653,771 pupils; public secondary, 436,521; nonpublic (1976–77), 71,200; colleges and universities, 165,595 students. *Public school expenditures,* $1,101,337,000 ($1,035 per pupil).

State Finances (fiscal year 1975): *Revenues,* $2,932,-388,000; *expenditures,* $3,036,002,000.

Personal Income (1975): $25,052,000,000; per cápita, $5,086.

Labor Force (July 1976): *Nonagricultural wage and salary earners,* 1,749,800; *insured unemployed,* 46,300 (3.3%).

It was an election year in West Germany. The Christian-Democratic Union, led by Helmut Kohl (*left*), reduced the ruling coalition's majority. Chancellor Schmidt (*above, right*) needed the support of Foreign Minister Hans-Dietrich Genscher (*above, left*) and his liberal Free Democratic Party to remain in power. Former Chancellor Willy Brandt (*below, right*) and President Scheel discuss the new government.

GERMANY

Germany is divided into two different states. One is the Federal Republic of Germany, or West Germany, a parliamentary democracy allied with other western nations in the North Atlantic Treaty Organization (NATO) and the European Community. The other is the German Democratic Republic, or East Germany, which is, in effect, a Communist one-party state. It is a member of the Warsaw Pact and the Council for Mutual Economic Assistance (COMECON).

FEDERAL REPUBLIC OF GERMANY
(West Germany)

On October 3 the country elected a new *Bundestag*. The "social-liberal" coalition government of Social Democrats (SPD) and Free Democrats (FPD), headed by Chancellor Helmut Schmidt, emerged victorious over the conservative opposition. However, the Christian-Democratic Union (CDU) and its Bavarian offshoot, the Christian-Social Union (CSU), led by the minister-president of Rheinland-Pfalz, Helmut Kohl, managed to reduce the coalition's majority from 46 seats to 10. This setback to the government was due in large part to the twin problems of inflation and unemployment, although both were relatively low (4.5% and 4%, respectively) by non-German standards. On the other hand, CDU and CSU could offer no plausible alternative to the government's carefully balanced policy of partial retrenchment, higher taxes, and a limited public-works program. Neither did their electoral theme of "Freedom or Socialism" prove persuasive enough. Likewise, last-minute charges connecting CSU leader Franz-Josef Strauss, a one-time defense minister, with the Lockheed bribe scandals had no effect; the CSU won a 60% majority in Bavaria.

It was indicative of the prevailing political climate that the radical parties on both right and left received all together less than 1% of the vote. Similarly, political terrorism, a major prob-

lem only a year before, appeared to have come to an end. With their leaders either dead or in jail, the remnants of the urban guerrillas were paralyzed. The trial of the Baader-Meinhof group dragged on. In May Ulrike Meinhof hanged herself in her cell.

Economy. The economy in 1976 began to recover from the recession of the two preceding years. Efforts to reduce unemployment even further were hampered by a considerable outflow of capital, primarily to the United States. Some industries found it more profitable to manufacture goods for the American market in the United States rather than in West Germany.

Some of the economic difficulties are due to the growing costs of the comprehensive health insurance system. The government will have to decide between cutbacks of some of the services or increased taxes. At the same time additional funds must be found for more adequate old-age pensions and for retraining and other programs to fight unemployment.

Social Conditions. If the country remained calm despite unemployment and rising prices—unlike 1966–67 when recession drove considerable numbers into the neo-fascist National Democratic party—a major reason may well have been the generous benefits (68% of the regular pay) to which the unemployed are entitled. Nonetheless, as an official investigation revealed, some two million families—six million people—were living below the poverty level. Those affected were largely households of old-age pensioners or of five or more members.

The presence of large numbers of foreign workers created not only economic, but social problems as well. These workers, who for legal reasons cannot be returned to their homelands, tend to settle in urban areas. Between 16 and 19% of the population in Munich, Stuttgart, and Frankfurt are Turks, Greeks, Yugoslavs, Spaniards, and Portuguese. Local governments have been authorized to refuse residence permits to foreign workers if their number surpasses 6% of the population. To what extent this power will be applied will depend, however, on the influence of those industries in which West Germans are not anxious to work—hotels, restaurants, construction, and mining.

Foreign Policy. Bonn's foreign policy was dominated by economic concerns. In the face of worldwide difficulties Chancellor Schmidt held up his country as a model of sound economic policies. He berated West Germany's partners in the European Community for lack of thrift and stability and for the time being opposed any further integration. Italy also was warned that if it formed a government including Communists, it could not expect any western help. Schmidt's undiplomatic outspokenness may have been a campaign tactic aimed at his domestic audience, but it caused considerable dismay in the countries he criticized. Yet, anxious to help out European nations in need, West Germany revalued the *Deutschmark* upward in favor of Norway, Sweden, Denmark, the Netherlands, Belgium, and Luxembourg.

Bonn signed an agreement with the United States, releasing the Federal Republic from its obligation to contribute to the upkeep of American forces on West German soil. Introduced in the late 1950's to relieve U. S. balance-of-payments difficulties, this international agreement had become unnecessary because of the large outflow of West German capital to, and the increase of West German imports from, the United States.

A prolonged wrangle over the adoption of a standardized tank by the U. S. and West German armies was finally settled; both American and West German manufacturers will contribute to the equipment of the agreed-upon model.

West Germans celebrated the bicentennial of the American Revolution in some 4,000 events of their own, including balls, exhibitions, and even a rodeo. The high point was a ceremony in the *Paulskirche* in Frankfurt—a shrine of German democracy as the seat of a constituent assembly during the Revolution of 1848.

Relations with the Soviet Union were, on the whole, calm. Trade between the two countries kept growing and is expected to reach an annual volume of $10,000,000,000 by 1980. West Germany provides especially steel, chemical plants, pipelines, and industrial tools and machinery. To help build the world's largest steel plant near Kursk, some 3,000 West German engineers and mechanics and their families will be transferred there. A special settlement, including schools and hotels, is being built in order to accommodate them.

So far, West German imports from the USSR —mostly raw materials—amount only to one half of the exports. Attempts to increase them are hampered by Moscow's reluctance to spend much on advertising and marketing. As the West German weekly *Die Zeit* noted, one West German exhibition of industrial machinery in Moscow last spring took up 10 times as much

West German Finance Minister Hans Apel (*left*) and Federal Bank President Karl Klasen inform the press October 18 that the German mark is being revalued.

UPI

— WEST GERMANY · Information Highlights —

Official Name: Federal Republic of Germany.
Location: North-central Europe.
Area: 95,790 square miles (248,096 km²). West Berlin, 186 square miles (481 km²).
Population (1976 est.): 62,100,000.
Chief Cities (1975): Bonn, the capital, 285,000; Hamburg, 1,735,000; Munich, 1,325,000.
Government: *Head of state,* Walter Scheel, president (took office July 1974). *Head of government,* Helmut Schmidt, federal chancellor (took office May 1974). *Legislature*—Parliament: Bundesrat and Bundestag.
Monetary Unit: Deutsche Mark (2.42 D. Marks equal U. S.$1, Nov. 1976).
Gross National Product (1975 est.): $441,600,000,000.
Manufacturing (major products): Mechanical engineering products, automobiles, chemicals, iron and steel.
Major Agricultural Products: Rye, oats, wheat, barley, potatoes, sugar beets, hops, forest products.
Foreign Trade (1975): *Exports,* $91,620,000,000; *imports,* $75,565,000,000.

UPI

The ninth congress of the East German Communist Party was held in the new Palace of the Republic in May. The session emphasized economic affairs and promised social reforms.

space as all Soviet economic exhibitions in the Federal Republic during an entire year.

Politically, there were some flare-ups over the status of West Berlin. In this context an agreement that West Germany build a nuclear power plant in the USSR in return for supply of electricity from that plant to West Germany and West Berlin was canceled. Apparently, the plan was called off because the Soviets wished the transmission lines to bypass West Berlin and feed electricity to that city through a special connecting line, lest it be regarded as a part of West Germany. This was unacceptable to the West Germans since West Berlin *is* economically tied to West Germany.

GERMAN DEMOCRATIC REPUBLIC
(East Germany)

The main political event of 1976 was the ninth congress of the (Communist) Socialist Unity party (SED). The speeches, with their emphasis on the need for increased productivity and the more economical use of raw materials, reflected the continuing difficulties of the country. The congress promised long-expected social reforms; a week later increases in minimum pensions and wages, reduction of the work week to 40 hours by May 1977, and longer maternity leaves were announced.

On October 17 elections were held for the *Volkskammer*. The various parties and other participating organizations were united in a National Front and sent deputies to the chamber according to a prearranged key. While the SED

was allotted only a plurality, its control of the nation was assured through its domination of the participating unions and youth, cultural, and other associations.

Ideology. On June 30 and July 1 East Berlin was host to a meeting of European Communist parties. SED chief Erich Honecker sided with his Soviet counterpart, Leonid Brezhnev, in denouncing the decision of the French and Italian parties to forgo the dictatorship of the proletariat and enter government coalitions with bourgeois parties. Honecker warned that such cooperation would strengthen the capitalist system. However, the meeting decided to let each party proceed as it wished.

--- **EAST GERMANY · Information Highlights** ---

Official Name: German Democratic Republic.
Location: North-central Europe.
Area: 41,768 square miles (108,178 km²).
Population (1976 est.): 16,800,000.
Chief Cities (1974 est.): East Berlin, the capital, 1,090,-000; Leipzig, 573,000; Dresden, 507,000.
Government: *Head of state,* Willi Stoph, chairman of the Council of State (took office 1973). *Head of government,* Horst Sindermann, minister-president (took office in 1973). *First secretary of the Socialist Unity (Communist) party,* Erich Honecker (took office 1971). *Legislature* (unicameral)—Volkskammer (People's Chamber).
Monetary Unit: Ostmark (2.54 ostmarks equal U. S.$1, 1976).
Gross National Product (1975 est.): $43,700,000,000.
Manufacturing (major products): Iron and steel, machinery, chemicals, transport equipment, electronics.
Major Agricultural Products: Rye, potatoes, sugar beets, wheat, oats, barley, livestock.
Foreign Trade (1975): *Exports,* $10,088,000,000; *imports,* $11,290,000,000.

Economy. The new Five-Year Plan, adopted in 1975, stresses investments and production for exports at the expense of consumer goods. This choice of priorities became imperative because of price increases for vital imports (oil, natural gas, iron ore). Moreover, due to crop failures, some 3 million tons of grain had to be imported, mostly from the United States. While food was available at low, state-subsidized prices, industrial products—furniture, refrigerators, and fabrics—were often in extremely short supply.

To encourage the repair of old household goods and reduce the purchase of new ones, the remaining private craftsmen and craftsmen's cooperatives are being provided more generously with credits, supplies, and apprentices—a reversal, presumably temporary, of the policy of phasing them out altogether.

Social Conditions. As in previous years, special attention was paid to the housing situation. During the years 1971–75, some 609,000 homes were either built or renovated, 109,000 more than anticipated. During the 1976–80 period 750,000 homes are to be built or restored. An entire new suburb for 100,000 near East Berlin is to be completed by 1990.

Many East Germans still are trying to move to the West. Except in cases of a family reunion, however, few permanent departures of persons under 60 have been permitted. In 1975, about 10,000 left. Late in 1976 the exit regulations were further tightened. Among those who departed were a number of discouraged Lutheran clergymen. One pastor, Oskar Brüsewitz, set himself on fire in the market square of Zeitz, a small industrial town in Saxony, in protest against religious repression.

Olympics. East Germany took second place among all the competing nations at Montreal, winning 40 gold, 25 silver, and 25 bronze medals. This astonishing success was due to the careful selection and rigidly supervised training of athletes at state expense. To improve their performance, in many cases sex hormones and steroids were administered; however, such biochemical manipulations, practiced also by other countries, probably played a minor part in the East German victories.

WEST BERLIN

This isolated city continued to struggle with a declining birth rate, an unending exodus of residents, reduced investments, and a corresponding erosion of jobs. Small businesses have decreased from 5,200 to 3,000 during the last 10 years, the work force at the Siemens electrical concern has shrunk from 38,000 to 28,400, that of the rival AEG/Telefunken from 29,000 to 15,500. In 1975 alone West Berlin lost almost 40,000 people, or 2% of its population. Tax incentives, special bonuses, and moving allowances have attracted only few West Germans to the city.

However, life for West Berliners has improved inasmuch as they can now travel more easily to both East and West Germany. For Sunday recreational outings they can also go to East German areas of Berlin's vicinity, thus avoiding the crowded parks and resorts on West Berlin's territory.

EAST-WEST GERMAN RELATIONS

Relations between the two German states had their ups and downs. On the positive side almost 8 million West Germans and West Berliners visited East Germany in 1975 while 1.37 million East Germans headed west, among them 40,000 below the age of 60 who were granted permits to attend to urgent family business. Mail and telephone services increased markedly, and transit traffic between West Berlin and West Germany kept moving almost without interfer-

During 1976, the 15th anniversary of the Berlin Wall, a new concrete wall was built inside East Berlin.

ACHTUNG!
BAUSTELLE
Kranarbeiten

ence. New *Autobahnen,* financed jointly by Bonn and East Berlin, are being built between West Berlin and Hanover and Hamburg, respectively. Trade, too, keeps expanding.

On the other hand, there were recurrent border incidents, due to shootings by East German border guards. Other clashes were caused by defiant West Germans, one of whom tried to defuse land mines laid to prevent escapes from East Germany. When a CDU youth organization, in a widely publicized move, tried to send delegations across East Germany to attend a protest meeting in West Berlin on the 15th anniversary of the Wall, its buses were stopped at the border. The East Germans considered the trips a deliberate abuse of the transit agreements; the West Germans on their part accused East Germany of having violated these agreements by barring the buses.

A leading West German public opinion poll found that the emotional estrangement of West Germans from East Germans keeps increasing. Only 52% of those interviewed still looked on the East Germans as fellow nationals (68% in 1970), while 29% considered them foreigners (20% in 1970). There were indications that family ties across the border were also weakening.

ANDREAS DORPALEN
The Ohio State University

GHANA

Gen. I. K. Acheampong's hold on power was increasingly challenged during 1976 by restiveness within the military and in the eastern part of the country, and by a sluggish economy. Ghana remained active in the Organization of African Unity.

Politics. The major focus of unrest was former British Togoland, incorporated formally into Ghana after a 1956 UN-sponsored referendum. The National Liberation Movement of Togoland was banned in March, undoing the amnesty extended seven months earlier. A series of arrests followed as government spokesmen said their patience had been exhausted. Death by firing squad was set by a September decree as the penalty for organizing or promoting secession.

─────── GHANA · Information Highlights ───────

Official Name: Republic of Ghana.
Location: West Africa.
Area: 92,099 square miles (238,537 km²).
Population (1976 est.): 10,100,000.
Chief Cities (1973 est.): Accra, the capital, 848,800; Kumasi, 249,000.
Government: *Head of state,* Gen. I. K. Acheampong, chairman of the National Redemption Council (took office Jan. 1972). *Legislature*—National Assembly (dissolved Jan. 1972).
Monetary Unit: New cedi (1.15 new cedis equal U. S.$1, Sept. 1976).
Gross National Product: (1974 est.): $3,660,000,000.
Manufacturing (major products): processed agricultural products, wood products, cement.
Major Agricultural Products: Cocoa, corn, cassava, groundnuts, sweet potatoes, forest products.
Foreign Trade (1975): *Exports,* $720,000,000; *imports,* $805,000,000.

Tensions within the armed forces, linked in part to regional and ethnic issues, occupied government attention. Eight persons (including two retired and three active duty officers) went on trial in May on charges of having plotted a coup d'état in December 1975. All the accused were Ewe, the dominant group in the affected area. Their ten-week trial resulted in death sentences for five of the accused, who were convicted of conspiracy to commit subversion. Defense lawyers claimed confessions had been extracted by force.

Other trials also occupied public attention. Subversion charges were brought against four officers in August. They claimed during their trial that they had been unfairly passed over for promotion after the 1972 coup d'état.

Ghanaian writer Dr. Kofi Awoonor, a former university lecturer in the United States, was jailed on charges of harboring the alleged leader of a plot to overthrow the government. Most of his trial was devoted to determining whether a statement admitting complicity was given under duress. The visa granted an observer of Amnesty International was cancelled without explanation. Awoonor received a 12-month prison sentence, but was pardoned in October and allowed to resume his teaching post at Cape Coast University.

All three Ghanaian universities were closed in April by student disturbances arising from food complaints. The government named a five-man commission of inquiry, and announced that in the future students must serve their own food and wash their own dishes. Although Acheampong mentioned occasionally that he intended to return Ghana to civilian rule, no concrete steps were taken during 1976.

Economy. Inflation continued to take its toll. According to the governor of the Bank of Ghana, the rate of inflation rocketed from 18% in mid-1975 to 30% in mid-1976 to nearly 50% in September 1976. This rapidly increasing rate resulted largely from escalating costs for domestic food and imported products. Cocoa remained the mainstay of the Ghanaian economy, although the nation's share of world production continued to decline. The government boosted the price paid cocoa farmers to record levels in order to encourage greater plantings.

Foreign Relations. U. S. Ambassador Shirley Temple Black left Ghana in June, after a successful two-year stint. Ghana served on the UN Security Council and remained active in the Organization of African Unity, particularly in the Liberation Committee. Together with other African states, Ghana withdrew from the Montreal Summer Olympics. Ghana cancelled a planned visit in April by U. S. Secretary of State Henry Kissinger. U. S. spokesmen considered Soviet pressure to be the main reason for the cancellation.

CLAUDE E. WELCH, JR.
State University of New York at Buffalo

Britain had an active political year. Following the sudden resignation of Harold Wilson (*right*) as prime minister and Labour party leader, James Callaghan (*above, center*) was chosen for the post. David Steel (*below*) succeeded Jeremy Thorpe as leader of the Liberal party.

GREAT BRITAIN

PHOTOS UPI

It was a year of almost unrelieved gloom for the British economy, a year in which for the first time the British people seemed to turn against their Labour government as the scapegoat for their misfortunes. As 1976 came toward its end, the economic pointers seemed worse than ever, with only the hazy prospect of the nation's vast supplies of oil offering some hope for the 1980's. Diplomatically, the nation was involved in seeking a solution to the thorny problem of transfer to black rule in Rhodesia.

The Economy. All the various economic and financial problems were coming together to make the country's situation week by week more perilous. As the value of the pound sterling dropped from $2.02 at the beginning of the year to just over $1.60 in November, the country's imports became more expensive with exporters failing to cash in on the opportunities offered by the falling pound. The balance of payments deficit for the year was heading toward £1,900 million sterling.

In turn the flight from the pound forced the government to raise interest rates to a record 15%, so placing in hazard an industrial recovery which depended on heavy investment. British manufacturing requires substantial quantities of imported raw materials, so the cost of the recovery would have been much greater, even if adequate finance had been available in the first place.

At the end of the year, more bad news came with the suggestion—not denied by finance ministers—that the government would have to borrow 11,000,000,000 pounds in 1977 instead of the predicted 9,000,000,000 in order to finance its spending. This in turn was almost certain to fuel inflation, which had risen to 14.7% per year

in November—a marked rise instead of the longed-for drop toward single figures.

The increase in prices, particularly for such essentials as food (running at 22% inflation), was thought likely to put fresh strain on the "social contract", the informal but largely successful agreement between government and the labor unions. Under this pact, the government promised various social reforms and benefits for union members and other workers, in exchange for severe restrictions in wage demands. During the summer the figure negotiated was a belt-tightening 5% rise, with a minimum increase of £2.50 per week and a maximum of £4. Politicians doubted whether a similar figure could be arrived at in 1977, when standards of living would be markedly lower for the great majority of the British people.

At the same time, unemployment rose to 1,375,000, one of the highest figures since the great slump. This continued to produce surprisingly little social pressure on the government, partly because the rates of benefit now enable the average family to live not perhaps in comfort but at least with some dignity. In November the government raised the rates to keep pace with inflation, costing another £1,400,000,000 per year, though it proposed to start taxing state handouts, which may recover some money from the less poverty-stricken.

From the left-wing of the Labour party, and increasingly from moderate economists, there came a louder demand for a change in economic strategy and the imposition of import controls. These controls would protect the more inefficient industries from the devastating competition of such nations as Japan and West Germany, and hopefully enable greater efficiency to be created behind the safe walls of protectionism.

But the government remained resolutely opposed for the time being, arguing that controls would bring swift and terrible retaliation from other industrial nations, as well as cut Britain out of the world financial community. Government leaders also felt that protection for inefficient industries would merely allow them to remain inefficient, without tackling the root causes of the problem.

As if in silent sympathy, Big Ben, the huge bell which sits atop the clock tower in Parliament, groaned to a halt in August. For generations the sound of the bell tolling the hours on radio and later TV had symbolized the continuity of British life; now scientists were baffled by the breakdown and nuclear experts were called in.

The continuing economic crisis began to convince the government that Britain might not be able to rescue itself without social upheavals which could damage the fabric of the whole nation. Prime Minister James Callaghan, reacting to Opposition demands for huge cuts in public spending, said that such cuts would "rend this country in two." He was slightly buoyed by continual public support from Helmut Schmidt, West German chancellor, who often stated that the pound sterling was undervalued. One popular government theory was that the Western Alliance could not afford to let the British economy be destroyed, a point made by Mr. Callaghan when he warned that further difficulties would force Britain to withdraw from some of its NATO commitments.

One possibility being suggested was a massive "super-loan" for Britain, which would provide the pound with enough stability to give time for industrial recovery.

Political Developments. In Britain, the general measure of a government's fortunes with the electorate comes with by-elections, which follow the death or the resignation of a member of Parliament. After a series of by-elections in which the Labour government did surprisingly well, considering the nation's economic problems, it suddenly suffered two crushing defeats in Labour strongholds.

One, Workington, was in a seat which Labour had held continuously since World War I. In another, a massive swing from Labour to

Tory of 22% gave the industrial heartland of Walsall to the Conservatives. The defeats were a tremendous psychological blow to the government, whose supporters in Parliament were only barely encouraged by Prime Minister Callaghan's frequent announcements that he intended to carry on, regardless. The government's majority in the House of Commons, on which its survival largely depends, was wiped out in one night, and it found itself relying on the votes of a collection of minor parties, including socialist Scottish separatists and extreme Republicans from Northern Ireland, in order to push its legislation through.

However, the very proliferation of minor parties in Parliament, a recent feature of British political life, gave the government hope of hanging on for some months. The 13-man Liberal party was in almost as battered a state as Labour and was unwilling to precipitate a general election. The various nationalist parties were keen to harry the government while keeping it in office long enough to pass the "devolution" bill, designed to go through Parliament in 1977 and give considerable domestic autonomy to Scotland and Wales. The government even had the paradoxical support of Enoch Powell, a maverick Northern Ireland MP more famous for right-wing populism than for any commitment to the social democratic cause.

Callaghan himself arrived at the top job in British politics after one of the most startling announcements of recent years: the sudden decision on March 16 by Harold Wilson to resign the office of prime minister. Wilson had been the longest-serving peace-time premier Britain had ever had; hated by his political opponents and deeply suspect to large sections of the Labour party, he was nevertheless loved by thousands of supporters who saw him as the man who had made Labour the "natural" party of government. He had won four of five elections as party leader. In his 13 years as leader, eight as prime minister, Britain had become less prosperous compared to its neighbors, though better off in real terms. Certainly it had not moved significantly to the left, as the Conservatives

---

———— GREAT BRITAIN • Information Highlights ————

Official Name: United Kingdom of Great Britain and Northern Ireland.

Area: 94,226 square miles (244,046 km²).

Population (1976 est.): 56,100,000.

Chief Cities (1973 est.): London, the capital, 7,281,000; Birmingham, 1,004,000; Glasgow, 836,000; Liverpool, 575,000.

Government: *Head of state,* Elizabeth II, queen (acceded Feb. 1952). *Head of government,* James Callaghan, prime minister (took office April 1976). *Legislature*—Parliament: House of Lords and House of Commons.

Monetary Unit: Pound (0.61 pound equals U. S.$1, Nov. 1976).

Gross National Product (1975 est.): $226,000,000,000.

Manufacturing (major products): Iron and steel, motor vehicles, aircraft, textiles, chemicals.

Major Agricultural Products: Barley, oats, sugar beets, potatoes, wheat.

Foreign Trade (1975): *Exports,* $43,760,000,000; *imports,* $53,262,000,000.

Security personnel search men and women as they enter the Ideal Home Exhibition in London's Olympia. Some 80 persons were injured by a bomb explosion at the exhibition center in March.

UPI

claimed; at the same time it had become a slightly more just and equable society.

The nation spent months trying to fathom the reason for Prime Minister Wilson's sudden departure. The cynical believed he had got out before the economy crumbled; there were others who believed his own claim that he had planned the date years in advance.

His going signaled a three-week struggle for succession, marked by an amazing lack of vindictiveness among the candidates. Left-winger Tony Benn, and rightists Roy Jenkins and Anthony Crosland were knocked out early. (Jenkins went on to become president of the European Commission and Crosland became foreign minister.) Chancellor Denis Healey polled poorly. The contest resolved itself into a struggle between the centrist Callaghan and a revered, middle-aged left-winger, Michael Foot, who polled 137 MPs' votes to Callaghan's 176.

The party swiftly closed ranks until its disastrous fall conference, when the gaping split between the leftist policies of the party rank and file and the more orthodox policies of the government led to open clashes. Chancellor Healey was even booed when he arrived to seek support for his austere policies—designed to secure a massive $3,900,000,000 loan from the International Monetary Fund.

For another party leader, the year was even worse. Jeremy Thorpe, for nine years leader of the small Liberal party and the man who won it nearly 20% of the popular vote, was forced to resign after months of an old-fashioned British sex scandal. In January, an unemployed man named Norman Scott alleged that he had had a sexual relationship with Thorpe in his youth; enough of Scott's mud seemed to stick, and after weeks of diligent research by journalists, Thorpe was forced to resign. Admittedly, he was helped on his way by his lack of popularity among his own colleagues. His fate was sealed by his own publication of two letters written to Scott in which affection was clearly displayed.

Thorpe's demise led to two agonizing questions: should the press invade private life in this manner, and should homosexuality, proved or not, be a bar to public office? The affair did, however, have one good result: the Liberals set out to be the first British political party to have a grass roots democratic election of their party leader, instead of leaving the job solely to MPs.

The resulting campaign, between a quiet and shrewd Scottish MP named David Steel and a more rambunctious economist named John Pardoe, was marked by much acrimony which, however, ended as the result was announced—a huge victory for Steel.

Another scandal loomed toward the end of the year with the discovery that a number of MPs who might have been prosecuted for corruption had escaped because of an ancient law that protects MPs from criminal proceedings to do with their duties. After a wave of protests, a committee of MPs was set up to investigate the allegations, all of which involved the web of corruption established in the 1960's by a jailed architect, John Poulson.

Race Relations. Relations between the races, which Britain had thought for so long were improving, looked set to burst again. Even as Parliament was passing a new bill designed to provide more stringent penalties for discrimination, a riot broke out during a West Indian carnival in the London district of Notting Hill. The riot, which lasted for hours, was mainly directed against the police, and did not involve any interracial civilian fighting; the omen however was serious.

Racist parties such as the National Front began to score heavily in elections, winning occasional local government seats, and taking up to 8% of the poll in some by-elections. The Conservative party called for stricter controls against immigration while Labour and the labor unions joined to fight racism. The feared mass disturbances did not materialize, though there were ominous warnings.

Drought. But for millions of British people the main event of the year was the great drought —a three-month spell of almost no rainfall unknown in living memory. The traditional damp English summer was replaced by continuous blazing sunshine and, by British standards, a heatwave which sent temperatures soaring into the nineties. Crops failed, cattle had to be destroyed, water was severely rationed, and the government exhorted citizens to save water.

Then, shortly after the appointment of a new minister for water, Denis Howell, the skies opened, and for two months the country suffered the wettest fall in living memory. The rain, though welcome, was not enough or sufficiently prompt to bring crops back to their normal level.

Northern Ireland. Northern Ireland suffered another bloody year; hopes of peace seemed as distant as ever. Violence shifted away from attacks on the British army—though some continued—toward vengeful sectarian violence. An example was the murder of Mrs. Maire Drumm, a grandmother who headed the IRA's political action wing in Belfast. Mrs. Drumm was in a hospital bed when a Protestant gang, one member in a white coat, burst in and killed her.

The British government pursued its policy of leaving the Northern Ireland politicians to sort out a solution for themselves, refusing to offer any initiatives. Though there were desultory talks between leading Protestant and Catholic politicians, both sides felt too entrapped by their supporters to offer any meaningful compromise. Meanwhile, calls for an independent Northern Ireland grew on both sides—an option which has already begun quietly to attract a weary British government.

See also feature article MONARCHIES, pages 44–49; AFRICA; BIOGRAPHY: James Callaghan; METEOROLOGY.

SIMON HOGGART, *Political Correspondent*
"The Guardian," Manchester

Shoppers in London, including many foreign tourists, take advantage of bargains caused by the falling pound sterling. The value of the pound dropped to just over $1.60 in November.

UPI

As the British Trades Union Congress votes to accept a 4.5% maximum pay increase agreement, demonstrators demand the right to work and the resignation of the Labour government.

SPECIAL REPORT:

Britain's War Against Inflation

Great Britain entered 1976 with the highest rate of retail price inflation of all the major developed nations. During 1975, the inflation index had risen 25%, and even that was below the peak of 26.9% reached during the 12 months to August 1976.

In July 1975, the government and the unions had jointly launched a program of wage restraint, in which a limit on wage and salary increases was agreed to (and more or less enforced) at £6 a week. This represents an increase of about 10% on average basic rates. The program was succeeded a year later by a second stage, also to run for a year, in which increases were limited to 4.5% or 5%, depending on income level. The implication of stage one for weekly earnings was estimated by the government as 13%. This rather gradualist objective appears to have been just narrowly missed, as wage earnings rose 13.9% in the twelve months to July 1976. Private estimates of what stage two means for weekly labor earnings range from 6.5% to 9%, and while no official forecast was announced, it is known to lie within this range.

Prices have been subject to an extensively detailed form of control since 1972. This operated, until late 1975, in a way that tended to reduce profit margins. Since then, two liberalizations (the major one in July 1976) were found necessary owing to the critical state of profitability in industry. The rate of return on industrial assets, after depreciation and stock appreciation but including interest, is officially stated at 3.9% for 1975, the lowest figure on record. While the easing of price control is unlikely to have had much effect on prices before mid-1976, it is expected to add at least 1% to inflation in the year to mid-1977. The government has predicted that retail prices will rise by only 7% over that period provided the wage restraint policy holds; but private predictions cluster around 10%. This would imply a fall in real wages.

Although the wage and price controls are the main instruments of counter-inflationary policy, the Chancellor of the Exchequer, Denis Healey, maintained that fiscal and monetary policies were consistent with the anti-inflation goals. He pointed with pride to the fact that the broadly-based money supply (M_3) increased by only 8% during 1975. However, this was largely a recession phenomenon for banks' reserve assets rose 16.8%. During the first eight months of 1976, M_3 rose at an annual rate of 13.5%. And the pace of domestic credit expansion was greater than that, since £3,500,000,000 (nearly 9% of the money supply) left the country in the form of official support for the exchange rate.

The policy of supporting the rate so as to damp inflation, chiefly by borrowing foreign currency, began to crumble as early as April 1975. Between then and the end of 1975, sterling fell 10%, and then dropped a further 20% in the nine months to September 1976. Even so, British export prices became less and less competitive right up to the first quarter of 1976, and even the subsequent sharp fall in the rate may not have restored their pre-1974 ratios to other countries' export prices. A maximum drawing from the International Monetary Fund was sought, to support the pound and finance the current account deficit.

While economic policy since mid-1975 has emphasized fighting inflation, a gradualist approach has been deemed necessary owing to high unemployment. By September 1976, however, the unemployment rate had not started to fall. Consequently, the inflation fighting objective came to seem second in importance to the related goals of greater stability of prices and exchange rate. Assuming that the IMF drawing is effected, the surveillance of the Fund will powerfully reinforce the priority of those economic goals.

MALCOLM CRAWFORD
Economics Editor, "The Sunday Times"

Greece's Minister of Foreign Affairs Dimitrios S. Bitsios and U. S. Secretary of State Kissinger initial agreement providing for continued use of U. S. military bases in Greece and additional U. S. aid.

UPI

GREECE

During 1976 Premier Constantine Caramanlis built up his country economically, politically, and militarily while the possibility of a clash with Turkey loomed.

Internal Affairs. Caramanlis ruled Greece democratically as he had done since July 1974, when he assumed the premiership after the ignominious fall of the military regime. During 1976, particular emphasis was put on strengthening the economy; the inflation rate was kept within reasonable limits, and foreign capital was attracted to the country. National defense needs were also given high priority. All the while, the premier underscored his intention to bring Greece into the European Economic Community.

Greco-Turkish Relations. Greece's relations with Turkey—severely strained since the 1974 Turkish invasion of Cyprus—grew further exacerbated over the rights of each nation in the Aegean Sea. Influenced by the discovery of oil near the Greek Island of Thasos several years before, the Turkish government claimed that the location of the continental shelf on its Aegean seashore gave it rights even around the many Greek islands nearby. In addition, there was a matter raised by Turkey about who should control air-space rights over the Aegean. In July, Turkey sent a ship to make geologic explorations in the seabed of the disputed area. The Greek government considered this a provocation and appealed the dispute to the UN Security Council and to the International Court of Justice at the Hague. The Security Council passed a resolution on August 25, asking Greece and Turkey to reduce tensions and negotiate the matter. But the Hague court, in a September 12 ruling, evaded the major substantive issue. Greek and Turkish deputations then opened two separate negotiations at Paris, France, and Berne, Switzerland, on November 2. The first was to discuss Aegean air rights; the second, the Aegean continental shelf.

American Aid. When U. S. Secretary of State Henry Kissinger and Turkish Foreign Minister Ihsan Caglayangil on March 26 reached an agreement, subject to congressional approval, to give Turkey $1,000,000,000 in aid, spread over four years, anti-American feelings in Greece were vehemently expressed, particularly among elements of the parliamentary opposition. There was a widespread belief that Kissinger and the American government had not only failed to stop the Turkish invasion of Cyprus in 1974, but were also giving assistance which would prolong the Turkish occupation. Foreign Minister Dimitrios Bitsios, however, on April 15 initialed an agreement with Kissinger to give Greece $700 million in aid over four years. When strong anti-Turkish elements in the U. S. Congress blocked passage of the Turkish aid bill, a step which won favor in Greece, Premier Caramanlis indicated that his government had negotiated the Greek aid agreement in order to maintain parity with the Turks, and that he would not be displeased if both pacts failed to be ratified. The 94th Congress adjourned before the November elections, having approved neither pact. Similarly, though Greco-American negotiations had been conducted on the status of American bases in Greece, a final agreement was not reached before the U. S. elections.

Foreign Affairs. Foreign leaders who visited Greece during the year included Tito of Yugoslavia, Ceausescu of Rumania, and Zhivkov of Bulgaria. Various trade and economic pacts and protocols were signed during these visits.

GEORGE J. MARCOPOULOS, *Tufts University*

--------- **GREECE · Information Highlights** ---------

Official Name: Hellenic Republic.
Location: Southeastern Europe.
Area: 50,944 square miles (131,944 km²).
Population (1976 est.): 9,000,000.
Chief Cities (1971 census): Athens, the capital, 867,-023; Salonika, 345,799; Piraeus, 187,458.
Government: *Head of state,* Constantine Tsatsos, president (took office June 1975). *Head of government,* Constantine Caramanlis, premier (took office July 1974). *Legislature*—Parliament.
Monetary Unit: Drachma (36.71 drachmas equal U. S.$1, June 1976).
Gross National Product (1975 est.): $20,800,000,000.
Manufacturing (major products): Construction materials, textiles, chemicals, petroleum products, processed foods, metals, ships.
Major Agricultural Products: Tobacco, grapes, cotton, wheat, olives, citrus fruits, tomatoes, raisins.
Foreign Trade (1975): *Exports,* $2,288,000,000; *imports,* $5,457,000,000.

GUINEA-BISSAU

It was essentially a year of consolidation for this former Portuguese colony.

Union with Cape Verde Islands. Steps were taken during the year to further the goal of political unification between Guinea-Bissau and the Cape Verde Islands. The impulse comes from the fact that both nations are ruled by the same political party, the PAIGC (African Party for the Independence of Guinea and Cape Verde).

Following a protocol signed on April 13, the two countries now share a judiciary and penal system, and their legal systems are to be made uniform. In September, Aristides Pereira, secretary general of the PAIGC and president of Cape Verde Islands, chaired a five-day session of the party's political bureau, and set up an inter-governmental body that will meet twice a year until the two countries are fully unified. The third PAIGC congress (July 1977) is expected to come up with a program of integration, but the issue will also be submitted to the peoples of both nations in referendums.

Relations with Portugal. Guinea-Bissau's ties with Portugal have not been totally ruptured. A major bone of contention has been Guinea's national debt. The PAIGC government made it clear that it had no intention of assuming responsibility for the debts incurred by the colonial regime. In late February, Guinea-Bissau decided to create its own currency, the peso, to replace the Portuguese escudo. Portugal retaliated by freezing Guinean assets in Portugal. By the end of June, however, tension had abated, and Portugal agreed to provide Guinea-Bissau with two loans, totaling about $7.5 million.

Other Foreign Relations. Although relations with Sekou Touré's Guinea remained cordial, they were no longer exclusive. During 1976, Guinea-Bissau signed a trade agreement with Gambia, and a series of bilateral pacts with Senegal. In May, Guinea-Bissau was the only non-Francophile nation to attend a summit conference convened by the French government.

Guinea-Bissau continued to diversify its economic links and to receive aid from a variety of Communist and non-Communist sources.

ÉDOUARD BUSTIN, *Boston University*

UPI

Cheddi Jagan and 12 members of his People's Progressive Party returned to Parliament, ending a boycott.

GUYANA

Nationalization of important parts of the economy and a rapprochement between the government and the opposition marked 1976 in Guyana.

Economy. In January an agreement was announced that the government would purchase Sprostons (Guyana) Ltd., a subsidiary of Aluminium of Canada, whose bauxite mining investments had been nationalized several years earlier. Much more significant was the nationalization of the Bookers firm. Bookers was the principal grower and shipper of sugar, the country's principal crop, and controlled about 40% of the nation's exports. Negotiations, completed before the transfer of ownership, resulted in agreement that Bookers would be paid $18 million, most of it in promissory notes of 20 years' duration.

With the transfer of Bookers to the Guyanese government, the latter controlled about 80% of the national economy, and the handful of banks and insurance companies still under foreign ownership were faced with strong competition from government firms.

GUINEA-BISSAU • Information Highlights

Official Name: Republic of Guinea-Bissau.
Location: West African Coast.
Area: 13,948 square miles (36,125 km²).
Population (1976 est.): 530,000.
Chief City (1975 est.): Bissau, the capital, 75,000.
Government: *Head of state and government,* Luiz de Almeida Cabral, president (took office Sept. 1974). *Legislature* (unicameral)—National People's Assembly.
Monetary Unit: Peso (30.77 pesos equal U. S.$1, Nov. 1976).
Gross National Product (1975 est.): $105,000,000.
Major Agricultural Products: Groundnuts, rice, millet, coconuts, palm oil.
Foreign Trade (1973): *Exports,* $3,160,000; *imports,* $43,000,000.

GUYANA • Information Highlights

Official Name: Cooperative Republic of Guyana.
Location: Northeast coast of South America.
Area: 83,000 square miles (214,970 km²).
Population (1976 est.): 810,000.
Chief City (1973 est.): Georgetown, the capital, 195,000 (met. area).
Government: *Head of state,* Arthur Chung, president (took office March 1970). *Head of government,* Forbes Burnham, prime minister (took office Dec. 1964). *Legislature* (unicameral)—National Assembly.
Monetary Unit: Guyana dollar (2.55 G. dollars equal U. S.$1, July 1976).
Gross National Product (1975 est.): $370,000,000.
Major Agricultural Products: Sugarcane, rice, corn.
Foreign Trade (1975): *Exports,* $359,000,000; *imports,* $342,000,000.

Politics. The nationalization of Bookers was a major factor in the final rapprochement between Burnham's People's National Congress and the principal opposition group, the People's Progressive party, headed by Cheddi Jagan. Although he remained critical of Burnham's supposedly pro-Chinese position, Jagan admitted that the government's policies were "socialist."

Foreign Affairs. International relations were important in Guyanese affairs during 1976. For one thing, the Soviet Union sent its first resident ambassador to Guyana. For another, Guyana had several run-ins with the United States, which held up economic aid because of Guyana's vote in the United Nations condemning Zionism as racism. Guyana's representative on the UN Security Council also repeatedly voted for resolutions vetoed by the United States. In July Guyana was one of 32 countries that withdrew from the Olympics in Montreal because of the presence of New Zealand, which had sent its national rugby team to play in South Africa.

ROBERT J. ALEXANDER, *Rutgers University*

HAWAII

In 1976 Hawaii joined the nation in celebrating the bicentennial year. A major special event was the voyage of the *Hokule'a,* a replica of an ancient Polynesian canoe, which was navigated from Hawaii to Tahiti by the sailing methods of the early Polynesians. But the year was generally uneventful, as the economy, except for tourism, showed little growth.

On the political front, the state awaited the results of the elections, a major report from its Government Organization Commission, and a state plan from its Department of Planning and Economic Development.

There were continuing concerns over environmental problems, and efforts were renewed to protect the shoreline and to preserve open spaces. But the increase in automobiles continued unabated, and the tourists came to Hawaii in unprecedented numbers.

Economy. Tourism, Hawaii's major industry, enjoyed a banner year. Every month of 1976

HAWAII • Information Highlights

Area: 6,450 square miles (16,706 km²).
Population (1975 est.): 865,000.
Chief Cities (1970 census): Honolulu, the capital, 324,-871; Kailua, 33,783; Kaneohe, 29,903; Hilo, 26,353; Waipahu, 22,798.
Government (1976): *Chief Officers*—governor, George R. Ariyoshi (D); lt. gov., Nelson K. Doi (D). *Legislature*—Senate, 25 members; House of Representatives, 51 members.
Education (1975–76): *Enrollment*—public elementary schools, 93,342; public secondary, 83,088; nonpublic (1976–77), 34,300; colleges and universities, 37,677 students. *Public school expenditures*, $251,461,000 ($1,417 per pupil).
State Finances (fiscal year 1975): *Revenues,* $1,113,-975,000; *expenditures,* $1,166,897,000.
Personal Income (1975): $5,674,000,000; per capita, $6,658.
Labor Force (July 1976): *Nonagricultural wage and salary earners,* 347,600; *insured unemployed,* 15,300 (4.8%).

---

showed the arrival of record numbers of tourists; August had a high of 305,700. But the construction industry indicated no signs of regaining its high peaks, and its sluggishness contributed to the state's unemployment rate, which climbed to 9%. The decline of sugar prices also adversely affected the islands, as sugar still remains Hawaii's major agricultural product. This drop was blamed on the expiration of the federal Sugar Act, and a campaign was mounted to reenact similar legislation. Governmental efforts to promote diversified agriculture continued, but the results were mixed.

Transportation. Economical and efficient movement of people and goods among the islands of Hawaii remains a challenge. To supplement the two major air carriers, hydrofoil passenger service was initiated between the islands. Plans for greater dispersal of Hawaii's population to islands other than Oahu (which has more than 80% of the populace) and for larger interisland ships have not gone much beyond the discussion stage. Meanwhile, a new and larger "reef" runway is nearing completion at the Honolulu International Airport.

Energy. Hawaii is heavily dependent on oil, all of it imported, as its energy source. Research projects have been under way to attempt to harness the forces of the sun, wind, ocean currents, and volcanoes. Noteworthy were the positive initial test results for geothermal energy on the island of Hawaii.

Race Relations. While the residents continued to appreciate the harmonious relationships among Hawaii's great diversity of races, ethnic imbalances in terms of occupational groups and employment practices were more frequently mentioned in the public media, and native Hawaiians asserted their identity and claims to their ancestral lands in more active ways. Congressional hearings were held on the various islands to gather testimony on the land claims and reparations for native Hawaiians.

Politics. Democrats won all the major races. The state voted for Jimmy Carter and the following: for the U. S. Senate, Spark Matsunaga; for the House of Representatives, Cecil Heftel and Daniel Akaka. The Democrats maintained their heavy majority in the state legislature and in the county governments. The electorate also voted to convene a constitutional convention.

RICHARD H. KOSAKI, *University of Hawaii*

HONG KONG

Recovery from the 1974–75 economic recession, begun in the autumn of 1975, accelerated in 1976. Hong Kong hosted the Miss Universe Pageant in 1976 for the first time.

Economy. Figures for the year beginning July 1975 showed value increases of 31.1% for domestic exports, 26.2% for imports, and 20.8% for reexports, over the preceding year. In the first six months of 1976, the export trade had

UPI

A vast fire during the lunar New Year's holiday destroyed a squatters' area of Hong Kong's Aldrich Bay. Despite the extensive damage, particularly to property, there was no loss of life.

an average growth rate of 50%. The previously predicted deficit for 1975–76 turned out to be a surplus of $45 million because of an unexpected yield due to the stock market revival.

An Apprenticeship Ordinance came into effect in July, requiring manufacturers in "designated trades" to give their apprentices time off with pay to study at technical institutes. The number of statutory holidays for workers increased from 6 to 10 days but it is still lower than in Japan (14), Taiwan (13), and Singapore (11).

The Loans for Small Industry Scheme, instituted in 1972, was discontinued in 1976 because it was ineffective. The first industrial estate in Hong Kong is being built at Tai Po.

Police. The Independent Commission Against Corruption has been making investigations into syndicated corruption in the traffic department of the police. About 300 policemen of various ranks applied and were approved for resignation or early retirement in the first half of 1976. Crimes in the colony during that time totaled 26,608, an increase of 3.4% over the same period in 1975.

Mass Transit Railway. After a Japanese consortium pulled out in January 1975, the government took over the construction of the Mass Transit Railway (MTR). The modified initial system will run from Kun Tong to Shamshuipo and along Nathan Road, under the harbor, to Chater Road on Hong Kong Island; its cost is estimated at $1,160,000,000. In June, the MTR Corporation issued $80 million in 10-year bonds carrying an interest of 9⅜%.

Typhoon Ellen. Some 16.4 inches (41.6 cm) of rainfall brought by typhoon Ellen on Aug. 25, 1976, caused widespread flooding, landslides, and loss of human life.

See also ACCIDENTS.

CHUEN-YAN DAVID LAI
University of Victoria, British Columbia

─────── **HONG KONG · Information Highlights** ───────
Location: Southeastern coast of China.
Area: 398 square miles (1,034 km²).
Population (1976 est.): 4,400,000.
Chief City (1976 est.): Victoria, the capital, 1,100,000.
Government: *Head of state,* Elizabeth II, queen (acceded Feb. 1952). *Head of government,* Sir Murray MacLehose, governor (took office 1971).
Monetary Unit: Hong Kong dollar (4.85 H. K. dollars equal U. S.$1, Oct. 1976).
Gross National Product (1975 est.): $7,200,000,000.
Manufacturing (major products): Textiles, clothing, furniture, jewelry, electronic components.
Foreign Trade (1975): *Exports,* $6,019,000,000; *imports,* $6,757,000,000.

With the U.S. housing industry improving but below peak, a southern California developer opened a new community by holding a lottery for the right to purchase the first homes. With a low deposit required, the community's first homes were completely sold.

THE IRVING COMPANY

HOUSING

It was estimated in 1976 that one third of the world's population is without housing or is living in substandard dwellings. In the United States, the year provided gradual and geographically mixed improvement in the housing industry.

U. S. Developments

U.S. housing starts reached an annual rate of 1.5 million by the end of the year. This represented a substantial improvement over the low annual rate of 880,000 in late 1974, but was a far cry from the peak production rate of 2.7 million which was reached in February 1972. Housing production also fell far short of federal targets, but then little in the way of new programs or legislation was initiated by the public sector to stimulate the industry.

As 1976 drew to an end, it was clear that the three-year depression in housing was coming to a halt, but not without some concern for the slow pace of the recovery and the persistence of the inhibiting factors of high interest rates on mortgage loans and inflation in housing prices. The rates on new mortgage money hovered around 9% for most of the year, reflecting sustained demand for mortgage money as well as intense pressures on the money markets from the nonhousing sectors.

Home buyers faced much higher housing prices as well, in spite of only modest levels of demand. House prices had risen over 13% in 1975 following two years of falling demand and the building of large inventories. In 1976, house prices rose by over 20%, surpassing the rate of increase in incomes, and putting conventionally constructed, single-family houses out of the reach of even more prospective home buyers.

Multifamily Housing. Apartments continued to lag behind the general recovery. Even though construction of new units was well above that of 1975, fewer than 400,000 units were completed, a number some 60% below the 1973 level. No single cause could be identified for this level of production, but housing experts cited the fact that government subsidies for low-income dwellings were virtually frozen in 1973, and new apartment construction had suffered since. In addition, large inventories of unsold multifamily units, especially condominiums, were created through 1973 by the combination of continued construction during a period of declining demand. This overbuilding created large inventories that will take years to absorb, especially in such places as south Florida and Atlanta, Ga.

Mobile Homes. The mobile home continued to represent the primary source of single-family housing for the low- and moderate-income families. All indicators pointed to the fact that the mobile home industry would play an even more important role in the future. With the median price of the conventionally constructed, single-family home and site reaching nearly $45,000 in 1976, the mobile home's median price of under $12,000 meets a unique need in the housing market. The trend of the mobile home industry has been toward larger and larger units. The standard of the industry began with the 8 by 30 foot (2.4 by 9 m) unit; the 10 foot (3 m) wide was introduced in 1954, the 12 foot (3.6 m) in 1962, and the 14 foot (4.2 m) in 1969. In recent years, double-wide units (typically, two 12-foot, 3.6 m, widths) have become increasingly popular. In 1976, nearly one third of all units sold were double-wide units, which average 1,400 square feet (130 m²)—very close to the median size new home sold in America today.

The late 1960's and early 1970's were banner years for the mobile home industry, with shipments reaching a record 576,000 in 1972. As the U.S. economy turned downward, however, mobile home production plummeted to an annual rate of just over 200,000 by late 1974, and 1975 being declared by industry officials as their worst year ever. The year 1976 saw substantial gains, with shipments approaching 300,000 units.

Two critical problems remained to be solved before the industry could achieve significant inroads into the middle-priced segment of the housing market. The first and most critical problem was financing, which continues to plague potential mobile home buyers who must generally borrow at higher interest rates and on a relatively short-term basis as compared with the typical home mortgage loan. The other problem rested with public opinion as expressed through local zoning regulations. Industry officials often complain that the least desirable sections of urban areas are most often zoned for mobile homes. Manufacturers were attempting to cope with the problems by making mobile homes less mobile and more conventional in appearance.

They are growing larger, being placed on permanent foundations, and being designed so that the exterior looks like the home next door with the familiar shingle, pitched roof, and wooden siding.

Public Housing. Across the nation the approximately 2,800 Public Housing Agencies (PHAs) faced ever increasing costs during 1976. As national unemployment failed to decline substantially (in fact, actually increased in absolute terms), public housing projects faced increased demand without significantly increased funding. Federal reports showed increased vandalism, deteriorating facilities, and generally lower levels of housing quality in public housing.

The one bright spot in public housing was the initiation of the Target Projects Program (TPP). TPP was created to improve conditions in a limited number of the nation's worst PHAs, with a special emphasis on general management and maintenance. The total program has planned funding of $35 million per year for three years, which represents expenditures over and above the current operating subsidies and moderniza-

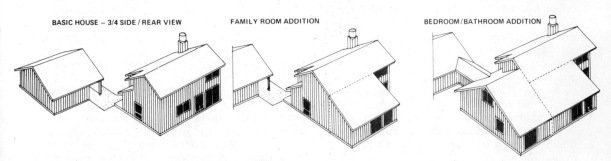

BASIC HOUSE – 3/4 SIDE / REAR VIEW FAMILY ROOM ADDITION BEDROOM/BATHROOM ADDITION

To try to counteract rising U.S. housing prices, the American Plywood Association and the editors of "Family Circle" magazine produced an efficient and economical "House with a Built-in Future."

AMERICAN PLYWOOD ASSOCIATION

tion funds that have been available for some time. By year end, there was guarded optimism for the program as a result of success with 35 PHAs. In 1977, three times as many agencies will be included in the program, but the potential impact on the total stock of public housing is limited; only a massive effort can produce improvements in the nation's public housing.

Federally Sponsored New Towns. The federal government has initiated or supported a variety of programs to help solve the nation's housing ills. One such program was designed to create model communities with balanced and systematic housing construction. Since 1970, the U. S. Department of Housing and Urban Development has encouraged the development of "new towns" by guaranteeing nearly $300 million in bonds to support 13 such communities. The new town concept was employed to introduce order to the common hodgepodge construction patterns.

During the latter months of 1976, HUD took steps to assume direct management responsibilities for seven of the 13 new town projects. Four of the remaining six projects were shaky financially. At year-end, only two of the 13 original projects were meeting their interest-on-debt payments, and the future looked dim for this form of federal program.

Although several reasons were cited for the apparent failure of this program, the most obvious was the turndown in general U. S. economic conditions. Particularly hard hit during the cyclical decline was the real estate industry; hundreds of thousands of condominiums remained in inventory unsold; and single-family construction dropped by over one million units.

International Developments

In terms of the international housing market, it is most alarming that the rate at which new units are being added falls far behind the rate at which existing housing becomes uninhabitable. Also, population gains increase demand.

Great Britain. Private house building in Great Britain has been in a deep economic slump for some time and this was further exacerbated by the serious drought of 1976 and by depressed economic conditions. Although starts were up slightly during the early months of the year, they were still 50% below the 1972 construction boom level.

Surprisingly, with so few new houses coming on the market, the volume of mortgages approached boom period levels during the first half of the year, and dropped off during the last half of the year. The financing of older homes is the primary reason for this phenomenon, and thus only a small portion of available funds is being used to support new home construction. The cost of mortgage loans dropped somewhat during 1976 to a level of approximately 10.5%, but this level is still relatively high for most Britons who faced governmental wage-increase restrictions.

The most serious setback to Britain's housing industry was the lack of government support for public housing. At year-end, the Labour government announced plans to make significant cuts from the more than $7,000,000,000 annual budget for public housing. In past years, Britons have depended heavily upon the public sector to supply housing when the private sector was depressed; in fact, a majority of the new housing units produced in 1975 was public housing units. Thus, the news of public housing cutbacks was received with a great deal of concern that its eventual impact would further depress the housing market. Only strong and direct governmental action, coupled with an improved economy, could hope to create substantial and sustained improvements in the quality and quantity of housing in Britain.

Canada. Housing has long been an area of concern for Canada, in spite of an impressive record of production and improved quality for over 20 years. In 1969, the federal government set a goal of one million new homes for the period 1969–1973, and surpassed this goal by 150,000 units. Although housing starts turned down during the period 1974–1975, Canada was better off than most other countries which were also experiencing general economic downturns and depressed housing production.

Perhaps the most serious and chronic housing problem that Canadians faced in 1976 was the continuation of increasing costs. The Ministry of Urban Affairs announced that over 800,-000 Canadian families pay more than one quarter of their income for housing, with one third of these families paying more than one half. With housing costs rising faster than income, low-income families and even middle-class Canadian families, with yearly incomes between $12,000 and $18,000, found it increasingly difficult to purchase acceptable housing. Even mortgage rates in Canada rose to levels well in excess of 10%.

Disasters. Over 400,000 refugees from Angola and Mozambique flooded into Portugal during late 1975 and the early months of 1976, creating a critical housing problem. Many of the refugees moved into hotels and other temporary shelters, pushing the existing housing supply to the absolute limit. Portugal's housing shortage had been estimated at over 500,000 units prior to the refugee problem. During 1976, the Portuguese public sector housing agency, the Fundo de Fomento da Habitacão (FFH) designed a national program to provide housing for refugees on an integrated basis and for all Portuguese needing improved housing.

The catastrophic earthquake that killed more than 22,000 persons and injured at least 76,000 in Guatemala in 1976 destroyed or damaged over 200,000 homes. The National Housing Bank of Guatemala took immediate action.

STEPHEN D. MESSNER
The University of Connecticut

HOUSTON

The death of a world-famous billionaire recluse (see OBITUARIES: *Howard R. Hughes,* p. 374), changes among top City of Houston personnel, politics, and three disasters were among the major events in Houston in 1976.

City Hall. In the wake of continuing problems within the police department, Mayor Fred Hofheinz on January 5 named Capt. B. G. "Pappy" Bond chief of police, succeeding Carrol Lynn, who was reassigned. Acting Fire Chief Joe Perino, despite an overwhelming vote of no confidence among city firemen, later was appointed fire chief. And City Attorney Jonathan Day resigned on July 23 to return to private practice. He was succeeded by Otis King, 43, dean of the Texas Southern University law school.

Politics. On August 24, following the Republican National Convention, James A. Baker III, 46, a Houston attorney and a relative newcomer to politics, was named by President Ford to head his national campaign for the November election. John Connally, former Texas governor, former secretary of the Navy and the Treasury, and onetime counselor to President Nixon, said on September 6 that he would head Ford's Texas campaign.

In local politics, Dr. Ron Paul (R) defeated attorney Bob Gammage (D) in an April 3 runoff to fill the unexpired term of Representative Bob Casey, who resigned in December 1975 to take a post on the Federal Maritime Commission.

Disasters. On February 22, grain dust in a grain elevator on the Houston Ship Channel exploded, killing eight persons. On May 11, a speeding ammonia tank truck crashed through a freeway interchange guard rail and exploded on the lane beneath. Seven persons died and 200 more were injured by the ammonia fumes.

Massive rains, measuring up to 13 inches (33 cm) in some parts of the city, caused widespread destruction on June 15. Seven persons died in the flooding. Damage was in the tens of millions of dollars and was especially severe at the Texas Medical Center.

Urban Ills. On February 10, the U. S. Census Bureau announced that Houston was the fifth largest city in the United States. Along with that designation, however, came these subsequent reports: cost of living up 8.1% in 1975, compared with 6.8% nationally; a housing boom which saw permits double the 1975 rate also saw the cost of home building increase by 22%; serious crime in 1975 was up 20%, double the national average; and costs of water, natural gas, and electricity soared, spurring much controversy.

Education. Houston's "magnet school" plan failed to achieve the degree of racial integration in its first year of operation that school officials had predicted, according to a July 4 report filed in federal court.

MICHAEL LONSFORD
"The Houston Chronicle"

HUNGARY

Throughout 1976, Hungary continued its course of political restraint and economic flexibility.

Domestic Affairs. Except for the taboo on criticism of the basic tenets of socialism, the Communist party, the Soviet Union, and foreign policy, individual freedoms remained relatively unrestrained. Profit motives and market-demand economics continued to be tolerated. Privately owned enterprises, mainly in the field of service and artisanship, seemed to prosper. As in previous years, a liberal travel policy allowed some 3 million Hungarians to go abroad, mostly to the Soviet-bloc countries. About 10 million tourists were admitted. A larger number of western magazines and newspapers were on sale.

In pursuing economic reforms, initiated in 1968, the economy remained largely decentralized, and individual state enterprises maintained their autonomy. Economic planning continued to be highly adaptable. Among the ills, lack of adequate housing was most felt. Rents were raised, and new accommodations were built for sale rather than rental. High prices and the high cost of credit resulted in discontent, reflected in mass media and party resolutions.

In December 1975, the parliament, after extensive discussion, enacted the fifth five-year plan (1976–1980). The discussion centered on low productivity, adverse balance of payments, consumption exceeding national income, and measures to improve housing conditions.

Foreign Affairs. As before, Hungary supported Soviet foreign policy. The press as well as party resolutions echoed Soviet attitudes and its arguments on détente, peaceful coexistence, ideological struggle, and condemnation of "capitalist imperialism." But there was also a noticeable tendency to demand more freedom for Hungary to pursue its own course. Various articles appeared in the press which, analyzing French and Italian Communist parties, pointed out the advantages of their "independent" course.

Trade with the Soviet Union continued satisfactory, and Hungarians won some concessions.

─────── **HUNGARY · Information Highlights** ───────

Official Name: Hungarian People's Republic.
Location: East-central Europe.
Area: 35,919 square miles (93,030 km²).
Population (1976 est.): 10,600,000.
Chief Cities (1975 est.): Budapest, the capital, 2,039,-000; Miskolc, 190,000; Debrecen, 173,000.
Government: *Head of state,* Pál Losonczi, chairman of the presidential council (took office April 1967). *Head of government,* György Lázár, premier (took office 1975). First secretary of the Hungarian Socialist Workers' party, János Kádár (took office 1956). *Legislature* (unicameral)—Parliament.
Monetary Unit: Forint (19.61 forints equal U. S.$1, Oct. 1976).
Gross National Product (1974 est.): $19,500,000,000.
Manufacturing (major products): Machinery and tools, vehicles, chemicals, pharmaceuticals.
Major Agricultural Products: Corn, wheat, potatoes.
Foreign Trade (1975): *Exports:* $6,091,000,000; *imports,* $7,176,000,000.

In Oslo, Norway, representatives of Iceland and Great Britain agree to settle the cod war.

The Soviet Union became the principal purchaser of high-quality horned cattle. It bought more than 120,000 head of fattened animals in 1976 and paid in dollars at world prices.

Hungary continued to lean heavily on western technology, credit, and trade; some 35% of its foreign trade is now conducted with the West. Still, prominent economists called for an increase, preferably to 50%. By the end of 1976 some 1,000 economic agreements with foreign governments or private corporations were in force. However, sluggish western markets contributed to an adverse balance of trade, and the limit of 49% on foreign equity investments in Hungarian enterprises unfavorably affected the flow of foreign capital.

In August an Exhibition of Agriculture and Food Industry Machinery was opened in Budapest. More than 2,000 items provided by 132 exhibitors from 20 countries were displayed. Thirteen western countries, notably the United States, were represented. The exhibition was successful and many contracts were signed.

JAN KARSKI, *Georgetown University*

ICELAND

Cod War III and an economic upturn made the biggest headlines in Iceland during 1976.

Fisheries Jurisdiction. Iceland's 200-mile fisheries zone was contested by Great Britain which sent naval escorts for its trawlers. There were intermittent clashes at sea, with considerable damage on both sides, but no loss of life. Public sentiment mounted in Iceland, and some called for withdrawal from NATO as a protest against the British action, but the dispute was finally ended on June 1 at a ministerial parley in Oslo, Norway. Iceland ceded a 6-month interim fishing quota to Britain in return for the lifting of Common Market trade sanctions against Icelandic exports. The settlement was hailed as a victory in Iceland. British trawlers left the Icelandic zone on December 1, pending further agreement on quotas.

Economy. Prices for Icelandic fish exports improved, particularly in the vital U. S. market,

and this signaled a moderate economic upturn; a gain of 1.8% in real gross national product was forecast. The tonnage of fish caught through August was down, however—in part because of a two-week general strike in February, but also because of deliberate cutbacks in order to protect the cod stocks from overfishing. Capelin operations were pursued in the summer for the first time, with good results, but other attempts to diversify the fishing industry were less fruitful. The herring appeared to be recovering, so the quota was liberalized to a degree, and new findings on the cod stock afforded some relief.

As debt service on foreign loans has become an economic drain, tight monetary policy was agreed on between the Central Bank and the commercial banks, but there were doubts whether general credit increases for 1976 could be held within the announced 16% ceiling. The inflation rate, having somewhat abated, was estimated at 25–30%, but the government was trying to find ways of further depressing it.

Energy. Work to harness domestic sources of energy to replace imported oil continued at an accelerated pace. The Sigalda hydroproject was nearing completion, as was the Krafla geothermal station, though there were alarms at the latter site because of earth tremors and the presumed danger of a volcanic outbreak.

HAUKUR BÖDVARSSON
Coeditor, "Iceland Review"

——— ICELAND · Information Highlights ———

Official Name: Republic of Iceland.
Location: North Atlantic Ocean.
Area: 39,768 square miles (103,000 km²).
Population (1976 est.): 220,000.
Chief City (1976 est.): Reykjavík, the capital, 85,000.
Government: *Head of state,* Kristján Eldjárn, president (took office for 3d 4-year term Aug. 1976). *Head of government,* Geir Hallgrímsson, prime minister (took office Aug. 1974). *Legislature*—Althing: Upper House and Lower House.
Monetary Unit: Króna (187.50 krónur equal U. S.$1, Oct. 1976).
Gross National Product (1974): $762,500,000.
Manufacturing (major products): Fish products, aluminum, cement, fertilizers, clothing.
Major Agricultural Products: Hay, potatoes, dairy products, sheep.
Foreign Trade (1975): *Exports,* $308,000,000; *imports,* $487,000,000.

IDAHO

Disaster made the headlines in Idaho on June 5 when the new Teton Dam gave way. It was a 305-foot (93-m) earth and rockfill structure built by the Federal Reclamation Bureau. Sugar City (pop. 617) and Rexburg (pop. 9,761) were devastated by a 10-foot (3-m) wall of water that killed 11 persons and 6,000 cattle and did $1,000,000,000 damage. Congress authorized funds to pay compensation. Several groups had tried to prevent the building of the dam because they felt the site did not have a suitable foundation.

Environment. The Hells Canyon Recreation Area was dedicated. The Chamberlain Basin, a 400,000-acre (162,000-ha) focal point of dispute between environmentalists and loggers, was added to the Wilderness Area by President Ford. Dredging of the upper St. Joe River for minerals was banned. A referendum on the building of an $800,000,000 coal-fired electric generating plant 30 miles (48 km) east of Boise showed voters opposed to the plant.

There is growing support for letting fires burn in the forests, on the grounds that exclusion of fire upsets the ecological balance. A proposal to draw Dworshak Reservoir down 155 feet (47 m) to produce power was opposed by Gov. Cecil Andrus. Steelhead and salmon runs have been seriously reduced by dams. Fishing is now allowed on only a short section of the Snake River. Idaho is suing Oregon and Washington to force its way into the Columbia River Compact.

Elections. Republicans did very well in the elections. President Ford won the state handily, as expected. Representatives Steve Symms and George Hansen, both Republicans, were returned. No U.S. senators or state officers were on the ballot. Republicans increased their advantage in the State House from 43 to 48 but lost one seat in the Senate.

The Legislature. The legislative session was the 4th longest in history, lasting 75 days. Appropriation increases were: general fund, from $222.5 million to $251.7 million; higher education, from $49 million to $52 million; and public schools, from $86.3 million to $103.6 million. Gasoline taxes were increased by 1¢ per gallon and automobile registration fees by $9 per year. A law was passed, providing for loss of liquor license of establishments with topless dancers.

Passed also was a law prohibiting paying for abortions for people on welfare; a court declared that unconstitutional. Defeated were bills requiring the teaching of the free enterprise system in public schools, collective bargaining for public employees, combining the state's universities into a single system, three new "land-use" bills and one that would have repealed the land-use bill passed in 1975, minimum streamflow legislation, and a fourth attempt to withdraw Idaho's ratification of the equal rights amendment.

Miscellany. Gov. Andrus was elected chairman of the National Governor's Conference. Later in the year he was appointed U. S. secretary of the interior by President-elect Jimmy Carter.

The Boise District Court ruled that the governor has 10 days from passage of a bill to sign it, even though he did not receive it for five days. The decision is on appeal.

Unemployment, while high, is below the national average. Idaho's Unemployment Fund is one of four in the nation that are in excellent financial condition.

A very cool summer delayed maturity of the crops by three weeks, but a warm, dry September allowed them to be harvested.

CLIFFORD DOBLER, *University of Idaho*

Idaho's new Teton Dam burst in June. Sugar City and Rexburg (*below*) were devastated by the disaster.

UPI

IDAHO · Information Highlights

Area: 83,557 square miles (216,413 km²).
Population (1975 est.): 820,000.
Chief Cities (1970 census): Boise, the capital, 74,990; Pocatello, 40,036; Idaho Falls, 35,776.
Government (1976); *Chief Officers*—governor, Cecil D. Andrus (D); lt. gov., John V. Evans (D). *Legislature* —Senate, 35 members; House of Representatives, 70 members.
Education (1975–76): *Enrollment*—public elementary schools, 99,922; public secondary, 96,694; nonpublic (1976–77), 4,800; colleges and universities, 35,347 students. *Public school expenditures*, $204,380,000 ($1,112 per pupil).
State Finances (fiscal year 1975): *Revenues*, $616,837,-000; *expenditures*, $599,781,000.
Personal Income (1975): $4,234,000,000; per capita, $5,159.
Labor Force (July 1976): *Nonagricultural wage and salary earners*, 284,000; *insured unemployed*, 9,000.

ILLINOIS

Politics dominated Illinois news in 1976. It was a bad year for Chicago Mayor Richard J. Daley, whose handpicked candidate for governor was defeated. Daley died on December 20, after more than 20 years in office.

Politics. Mayor Daley's candidate, Secretary of State Michael J. Howlett, defeated Gov. Daniel Walker in the March primary for the Democratic gubernatorial nomination. Walker, an independent Democrat, had feuded with Daley and the Illinois General Assembly from the time of his election in 1972.

But in the November election Howlett was trounced by Republican James R. Thompson, who received 65% of the vote and carried 100 of the state's 102 counties. It was Thompson's first try for elective office. He had gained prominence as a U. S. attorney when he obtained the conviction of several of Daley's top lieutenants. Thompson will serve a two-year transition term as the state changes to off-presidential years for the gubernatorial election.

Illinois' 26 electoral votes were won by President Ford, who carried the state 51% to 48%. His victory upset the state's 60-year habit of giving its electoral votes to the winning presidential candidate. Democrats maintained control of both houses of the General Assembly, although Republicans reduced the margin in the House.

Economy. The question of finances dominated state government. Governor Walker proposed a $9,900,000,000 budget for fiscal 1977, $224 million below the previous year as the result of reducing construction bond authorization and cutting state education funds. He also sought to improve the state's cash position temporarily by a one-time speedup in tax collections, which would have moved $95 million in receipts from fiscal 1978 to 1977. When the legislature rejected the governor's proposals he used his amendatory veto power to cut $84.5 million from a school aid package approved in June. A compromise school package was approved in September, but Walker's tax speedup proposal was cut in half.

Although unemployment ran below national levels, it remained high by historic standards, veering from a high of 9.3% in January to 6.8% in June and back to 7.4% by fall. Unemployment generally was highest in the Rockford and East St. Louis areas. The Illinois Chamber of Commerce announced plans for a three-year program to improve the state's business image. Businessmen claimed that increases in workmen's compensation insurance and talk of a change in the eight to five corporate/personal income tax ratio had caused a loss of manufacturing jobs to other states since 1967.

Illinois, the nation's leading corn and soybean producer, again had good crops in those commodities, 1,136,000,000 and 291,810,000 bushels respectively. However, both were down modestly from the record levels of 1975. Per acre yields varied throughout the state, but generally were down because of a lack of rainfall.

U. S. Transportation Secretary William T. Coleman, Jr. selected Waterloo-Columbia, Ill., 19 miles (31 km) south of St. Louis, Mo., as the site for a new St. Louis metropolitan area airport. His decision was opposed by Missouri officials, who favored expansion of the existing Lambert Field in St. Louis. But even if the decision stands, the new airport cannot go into operation before 1992 unless Illinois and Missouri officials agree on an earlier date.

KENNETH ROSS, *"The Chicago Tribune"*

--------- **ILLINOIS · Information Highlights** ---------

Area: 56,400 square miles (146,076 km²).
Population (1975 est.): 11,145,000.
Chief Cities (1970 census): Springfield, the capital, 91,753; Chicago, 3,369,359; Rockford, 147,370.
Government (1976): *Chief Officers*—governor, Daniel Walker (D); lt. gov., Neil F. Hartigan (D). *General Assembly*—Senate, 59 members; House of Representatives, 177 members.
Education (1975–76): *Enrollment*—public elementary schools, 1,538,579 pupils; public secondary, 731,-313; nonpublic (1976–77), 412,400; colleges and universities, 481,260 students. *Public school expenditures,* $2,952,549,000 ($1,322 per pupil).
State Finances (fiscal year 1975): *Revenues,* $7,488,-996,000; *expenditures,* $7,842,927,000.
Personal Income (1975): $75,666,000,000; per capita, $6,789.
Labor Force (July 1976): *Nonagricultural wage and salary earners,* 4,494,800; *insured unemployed,* 191,000 (5.2%).

UPI

James R. Thompson (R) and his wife, Jayne, enjoy election night victory. In the Illinois governor's race, the former U. S. attorney defeated Michael J. Howlett, Mayor Daley's chosen candidate.

Indian troops carrying guns and riding camels create a majestic appearance during Republic Day ceremonies.

INDIA

By the 10th anniversary of Mrs. Gandhi's selection as prime minister of India, in January 1976, it was apparent that the "temporary" emergency proclaimed on June 26, 1975, had become a permanent one. The events of 1976 confirmed this judgment. The improvement in the economic situation, which had begun in 1975, continued. Highlights of a very busy year in foreign policy were improved relations with Pakistan and China and Mrs. Gandhi's visit to the Soviet Union.

Constitutional and Legal Affairs. In January the Indian Parliament, dominated by Mrs. Gandhi and the Congress party, enacted sweeping measures which made the strict press censorship permanent and extended to one year the period during which the government could detain political prisoners without trial. In June this period was extended to two years. In May the government introduced a constitutional amendment that bans court review of censorship regulations.

On April 29 the Indian Supreme Court upheld the right of the government to imprison political opponents without trial. This decision confirmed the government's claim that its emergency powers superseded certain fundamental rights guaranteed in the Constitution. It was described by critics as "a milestone in the dismantling of India's democracy."

In March the Congress party appointed a Committee on Constitutional Reforms, headed by Swaran Singh, former minister of defense.

After lengthy hearings and deliberations, the committee recommended extensive changes in the Constitution. It suggested further limitations on the courts and on judicial review, stricter provisions for the disqualification of members of Parliament and state legislatures, and more power for the central government vis-à-vis the states. These recommendations, somewhat modified, were approved by the All-India Congress Committee in late May. Many of them were embodied in an omnibus Constitution (44th Amendment) Bill, introduced in the Lok Sabha (lower house of Parliament) by the law minister on September 1. The 59 clauses included provisions for the expansion of the Directive Principles of State Policy in the Constitution; further subordination of fundamental rights to the need for social and economic reforms; a new ten-point code of "Fundamental Duties"; legislation by Parliament banning "anti-national" activities and associations; powers to the president, acting at the prime minister's direction, to amend the Constitution, virtually at will, for two years; further restrictions on the powers of judicial review, making constitutional amendments unchallengeable in any court of law; and extension to one year (unless revoked earlier) of an emergency proclamation approved by Parliament. On November 2 the Lok Sabha approved these sweeping changes by a vote of 360 to 4. Three days earlier the government, for the second time since the emergency was proclaimed, announced that national elections would be postponed. These actions seemed to confirm the view that the "temporary" emergency had become permanent.

PHOTOS UPI

In January 1976 Indira Gandhi filled her tenth year as prime minister of India. A huge sign in downtown New Delhi emphasizes her 20-point program. Sanjay Gandhi, Mrs. Gandhi's 29-year-old son, has been called "a new star rising in the political firmament of India."

Politics. With Mrs. Gandhi in almost total control of the country and Parliament and most of her chief opponents still in custody or under close supervision, the political opposition remained weak and fragmented. Three top opposition leaders were released—Asoka Mehta, president of the Congress party, Atal Behari Vajpayee, former president of the Jana Sangh party, and Charan Singh, chairman of the Indian People's party—and one, George Fernandes, chairman of the Samyukta Socialist party, who had been underground since the emergency was proclaimed, was apprehended; he was brought to trial in October on charges of conspiracy to overthrow the government. Late in May the leaders of four opposition parties and some political independents formed a new party, under the leadership of Jayaprakash Narayan, the chief political opponent of Mrs. Gandhi. After the introduction in Parliament of the Constitution (44th Amendment) Bill, the leaders of the new party and prominent lawyers announced the formation of the People's Union for Civil Liberties and Democratic Rights, also headed by Narayan. But these moves had little impact. Narayan was seriously ill, his movements were closely watched, and few people came to see him for fear of reprisals.

President's rule (that is, direct rule by New Delhi) was proclaimed in the state of Tamil Nadu on January 31, ending nine years of government by the Dravida Munnetra Kazhagam, an important local party. On March 12 the same thing happened in Gujarat, where an opposition Janata Front government had been in power. President's rule was ended in Uttar Pradesh, India's most populous state, on January 21, and a Congress government was installed. On March 28 president's rule in the Union Territory of Pondicherry was extended for another year. The dominance of the Congress party was virtually unquestioned in all of the 22 states, and it was strengthened in March by indirect elections of one third of the members of the Rajya Sabha (upper house of Parliament). This gave the party 18 more seats and a two-thirds majority, the number required for passage of constitutional amendments.

Restrictions on foreign journalists were somewhat eased in 1976, but the net effect of various measures affecting the Indian press was that of further restrictions. In February four independent news agencies were merged into one mo-

--------- **INDIA · Information Highlights** ---------

Official Name: Republic of India.
Location: South Asia.
Area, 1,269,438 square miles (3,287,590 km²).
Population (1976 est.): 620,700,000.
Chief Cities (1973 est.): New Delhi, the capital, 3,600,-000; Bombay, 6,000,000; Madras, 2,500,000.
Government: *Head of State,* Fakhruddin Ali Ahmed, president (took office Aug. 1974). *Head of government,* Mrs. Indira Gandhi, prime minister (took office Jan. 1966). *Legislature*—Parliament: Rajya Sabha (Council of States) and Lok Sabha (House of the People).
Monetary Unit: Rupee (8.79 rupees equal U. S.$1, Sept. 1976).
Gross National Product: (1975 est.): $89,700,000,000.
Manufacturing (major products): Iron and steel, industrial machinery and equipment, chemicals.
Major Agricultural Products: Rice, wheat, groundnuts, barley, sesame, sugarcane, corn, rubber.
Foreign Trade (1975): *Exports,* $4,365,000,000; *imports,* $6,094,000,000.

nopoly news service under the name of Samachar. The last two major English-language newspapers that had maintained some degree of objectivity, *The Statesman* and the *Indian Express,* were brought under control by a variety of pressures, including forced changes in ownership and editorial direction.

Family Planning. In a tough speech on January 2 Mrs. Gandhi declared that the government would have to promote family planning with some "strong steps which may not be liked by all." Efforts by the central government and a few of the states to initiate such "strong steps" attracted international attention. In February plans were announced to penalize central government employees and New Delhi residents who did not limit their families to two children. In late April a new birth-control program was announced, giving "top priority" to measures to reduce the population growth. It embraced raising the age of marriage and paying people for having themselves sterilized. A few states even introduced legislation for compulsory sterilization of those who had more than two or three children. This caused protests and rioting.

Economy. In 1976 both the World Bank and the 13-nation Aid India Consortium reported a marked improvement in India's economic situation and commended the government for its economic measures and policies to control inflation. The reports called attention to the record harvest in 1975–76 (amounting to at least 115 million tons of food grains), the slight improvement in the balance of trade (still negative by $1,600,000,000), the marked increase in foreign exchange reserves (about $2,000,000,000 by the end of April), the decline of both wholesale and consumer prices, the sharp rise in the production of coal and oil, the improved performance of

public-sector enterprises, and an overall growth rate of about 6%. The reports emphasized the need to increase investments and expand exports more rapidly. The World Bank report concluded that "conditions are once again ripe for an upturn in the growth rate of the economy." But the Aid India Consortium estimated the country's foreign assistance needs for the fiscal year 1976–77 at $1,800,000,000.

On March 15 Finance Minister Subramaniam presented the 1976–77 budget, the first since the proclamation of national emergency. It envisioned an expenditure of $18,000,000,000, of which nearly $10,800,000,000 would be allocated for development expenditures—an increase of more than 31% over 1975–76. Defense expenditure was increased only slightly, to $3,800,000,000. Although a sizeable budgetary deficit—some $500 million—was contemplated, income and wealth taxes were reduced and excise concessions were made on consumer items.

Efforts to encourage investment and increase exports were central features of India's economic direction in 1976. In April a new import policy was instituted. It was designed to promote the import of essentials, notably food, fertilizers, and petroleum. On September 25 the Fifth Five-Year Plan (1974–79), with an outlay of $54,-140,000,000, was finalized.

India's record of reducing inflation, from a staggering 30% in early 1975 to less than 10% by the spring of 1976, was particularly impressive. This was due mainly to the favorable monsoons, which resulted in a record harvest in 1975, and to greater national discipline induced by the government. In mid-1976, however, prices of many basic products began to rise, and by the end of the year the general economic picture seemed less bright.

UPI

In the presence of Prime Minister Gandhi, young men pledge that they will not accept a dowry when they marry. Indian legislation prohibits the custom, popular for centuries.

Foreign Policy. India embarked on a new orientation in foreign policy by fostering relations with its two main adversaries, Pakistan and China. A series of talks and agreements with Pakistan led to the normalization of relations, the resumption of road links, rail and air traffic and overflights, and the exchange of ambassadors in July. In April India announced that it would send an ambassador to China for the first time in 15 years. A Chinese ambassador to India was named in July.

Much to India's discomfiture, relations with Bangladesh became more strained in 1976. The main issue in contention was the sharing of the waters of the Ganges River, centering on the withdrawal of water by India at Farakka Barrage near the Bangladesh border. Bangladesh accused India of violating its treaty obligations by building the barrage. India attributed the breakdown of high-level talks in New Delhi in September to the "inflexible position" of the Bangladesh delegation and its unwillingness "even to consider any of India's proposals."

On March 28 India and Sri Lanka signed an important agreement on their maritime boundaries, resolving one of the long-standing issues in dispute between them.

Relations with Canada became strained because of its decision to end cooperation with India in the nuclear field. Announcing this turn of events in the Lok Sabha on May 18, Y. B. Chavan, minister of external affairs, expressed the government's regret and surprise. He stated that an agreement on continued nuclear cooperation between India and Canada had been initialed in March after two years of strenuous negotiations, and he charged that the Canadian decision amounted to unilateral abrogation.

Under the direction of Foreign Minister Chavan, India exchanged ambassadors with China and Pakistan.

UPI

In spite of its displeasure with the new turn in Sino-Indian relations, the Soviet Union remained, in Indian eyes, a "steadfast friend." In April a new five-year trade agreement was signed in New Delhi. On June 8–11 Mrs. Gandhi was in the Soviet Union on an official visit. Brezhnev, Kosygin, and Gromyko welcomed her on arrival at the Moscow airport, and she had long talks with Brezhnev. Her son, Sanjay Gandhi, whose influence in India was still rising and who had been viewed with suspicion both by the pro-Soviet Communist party of India and the Soviet leaders, was a member of his mother's official entourage.

Indo-American relations continued to be limited and ambivalent. American officials were instructed not to make "gratuitous criticisms" of the political changes in India, but strong criticisms were voiced in the American press and by many U. S. citizens. The groundswell of criticism of the United States in India, featuring charges of activities by the Central Intelligence Agency and other forms of "intervention," continued to mount. In February the U. S. government broke off talks with India on possible economic assistance, apparently as an indication of general disapproval of trends in India; yet the United States continued to support multilateral assistance to the country through the World Bank and the Aid India Consortium, to both of which it was a major contributor. In the fall T. N. Kaul returned to India after 3½ years of service as ambassador to the United States. He was promptly replaced by another senior diplomat, Kewal Singh. In November U. S. Ambassador William Saxbe left India after less than two years of service, leaving a *chargé d'affaires* in control until the incoming Carter administration in the United States could name a successor.

India took a special interest in the fifth summit conference of nonaligned nations, held in Colombo, Sri Lanka, in August. Mrs. Gandhi headed a 30-member delegation to the conference and played a leading role in it. In a major address on August 17 she affirmed that "nonalignment remains the bulwark of an ever-widening area of peace"; warned that "economic exploitation persists in old and new garbs"; called for the unity of nonaligned countries and "a new equilibrium of equitable interdependence"; complained that "the response of advanced countries to the compulsion of a new world economic order has so far been pathetic"; and called attention to the advantages of the new press-agencies pool of the nonaligned countries, the details of which had been worked out at a ministerial conference in New Delhi in July.

In addition to her visit to the Soviet Union in June, Mrs. Gandhi made official visits to East Germany and Afghanistan in July and to Mauritius, Tanzania, and Zambia in October.

NORMAN D. PALMER
University of Pennsylvania

INDIANA

Legislation. Despite the limited 30-day session and heightened political differences in a major election year, the Indiana General Assembly enacted significant legislation in 1976. Included were measures providing for the recodification of all state laws and the condensation of about 3,000 miscellaneous laws on crime into 300 categories, matching the nature and severity of the crime with the penalty. Legislators also approved a law requiring preelection reporting of campaign expenditures by candidates and setting limits on contributions by corporations and labor unions. Additional legislation included a law placing the gubernatorial and lieutenant gubernatorial candidates on the ballot as a team, thus preventing the election of a governor and a lieutenant governor of different parties.

Failing to pass the General Assembly were measures providing for collective bargaining and pension reform for police and firemen, regulations for lobbyists, and an aerosol ban. The legislature postponed until 1977 consideration of the state and federal equal rights amendments. Gov. Otis R. Bowen's veto of a bill, which provided that county councils and voters could authorize pari-mutuel horse race betting within the county where the racing facility would be built, was sustained by the Senate. Also vetoed by the governor as a violation of free enterprise were controversial measures that would have established minimum liquor and wine prices and mandated that beer sold by wholesalers be transported by them.

Budget. On the last day of the legislative session the General Assembly approved a $3,-400,000,000 budget for 1976–77. Included in this amount were $1,600,000,000 in general fund revenues to assure the continuation of a 20% property tax relief. An extra $20 million in general fund revenues for roads raised taxes and fees on highway users by that amount. The budget enabled state mental health institutions to maintain their current level of professional

UPI

Richard Lugar, a college professor and former Indianapolis mayor, defeated Sen. Vance Hartke (D-Ind.).

staff and add 33 security employees, and it provided $65 for each public school student in the state based on average daily attendance. Also included in the budget were $279.6 million for higher education and $2.39 million in dedicated funds for capital projects, such as the Patoka Reservoir, the William S. Culbertson mansion at New Albany, the Ernie Pyle home at Dana, and the governor's mansion at Corydon in the southeastern section of the state.

Election. By a record voter turnout and a fairly substantial margin Indiana supported Republican Gerald R. Ford in his unsuccessful bid to retain the presidency. Republican Gov. Otis R. Bowen was reelected by an even wider margin, and Richard G. Lugar defeated incumbent Democrat Vance Hartke who was seeking a fourth term as U. S. senator. Republicans also retained all state offices on the ballot. Democrats, however, were elected in 8 of the 11 congressional districts, a loss of only one: eight-term incumbent J. Edward Roush unexpectedly lost to Republican J. Danforth Quayle in the Fourth District. Democrats also captured the state Senate, 28 to 22; Republicans had held 27 seats. In the House Republicans took control, 52 to 48; they had previously been in the minority, 56 to 44.

Several Indiana counties recorded more than 70% voter turnout, and at least two precincts in southern Indiana reported a 97% turnout.

LORNA LUTES SYLVESTER, *Indiana University*

——— **INDIANA • Information Highlights** ———

Area: 36,291 square miles (93,994 km²).

Population (1975 est.): 5,311,000.

Chief Cities (1970 census): Indianapolis, the capital, 744,743; Fort Wayne, 178,021; Gary, 175,415; Evansville, 138,764.

Government (1976): *Chief Officers*—governor, Otis R. Bowen (R); lt. gov., Robert D. Orr (R). *General Assembly*—Senate, 50 members; House of Representatives, 100 members.

Education (1975–76): *Enrollment*—public elementary schools, 653,891 pupils; public secondary, 572,317; nonpublic (1976–77), 102,700; colleges and universities, 198,964 students. *Public school expenditures,* $1,251,000,000 ($1,092 per pupil).

State Finances (fiscal year 1975): *Revenues,* $3,099,-901,000; *expenditures,* $3,002,409,000.

Personal Income (1975): $30,023,000,000; per capita, $5,653.

Labor Force (July 1976): *Nonagricultural wage and salary earners,* 1,995,400; *insured unemployed,* 33,-000 (2.1%).

INDONESIA

During 1976, which saw the 10th anniversary of President Suharto's "New Order" government, Indonesia's chief priority was economic development.

The Economy. While there were some significant achievements, the economy encountered serious difficulties due to the collapse of the government oil conglomerate, Pertamina. President Suharto ousted its head, Maj. Gen. Ibnu Sutowo, March 4. With the corporation badly overextended, the government was forced to step in and assume $6,000,000,000 in debts. Consequently, national development plans were set back, infrastructure projects (such as refineries, chemical plants, steel mills) were curtailed, foreign exchange reserves were depleted, and the debt service ratio increased to a dangerous level.

The government reallocated investment for the remaining three years of the second five-year plan from capital construction to rural development. Some projects were shifted to private funding. Government revenue collecting was intensified so as to take in an extra $240,000,000, mostly from tighter enforcement of duties and excise and income taxes. An energetic anti-smuggling campaign was launched.

The government also demanded that foreign oil companies producing in Indonesia accept renegotiated contracts providing for a much larger government share in profits and a tougher cost

Used bicycle parts are on sale in Jakarta. Economic development was the government's chief priority in 1976.

UPI

recovery schedule. Although the companies appeared likely to acquiesce, there were indications that their future investment in oil exploration in Indonesia might be cut back.

The greatest long-term threat to the economy continued to be rapid population growth. Each year, 2,000,000 new job seekers enter the market, but the economy provides only 600,000–700,000 new jobs. The government has initiated a family planning program and a program to encourage migration from Java to Sumatra.

East Timor. Following the outbreak of civil war in East Timor and the breakdown of Portuguese authority in August 1975, Indonesian armed forces "volunteers" intervened in December 1975. This action generated considerable foreign criticism, including UN Security Council resolutions calling for Indonesian forces to withdraw and for the secretary general to send a fact-finding mission to the territory. Nevertheless, Indonesian forces consolidated their control, and on July 17, President Suharto signed a bill making East Timor Indonesia's 27th province. This ended nearly 500 years of Portuguese rule.

Elections. Preliminary steps were taken to prepare for May 2, 1977 elections of a national People's Consultative Assembly. As a consequence of government-sponsored efforts to simplify the political spectrum, the election will be contested by only three major political parties.

Corruption became an increasingly prominent political issue, with rumors and foreign press reports of profiteering by high-level officials, including the president, his wife, and their families. President Suharto issued a six-point statement denying the accusations.

Foreign Affairs. Indonesia took steps to dilute its close identification with the West. The Soviet Union agreed to help build two hydroelectric stations in Java and an alumina smelter on Bintan Island. Indonesia and Vietnam announced an exchange of economic delegations to investigate possible trade and cooperation. Foreign Minister Adam Malik announced that Indonesia planned to establish diplomatic relations with China after the elections.

MARVIN C. OTT, *Mount Holyoke College*

INDONESIA • Information Highlights

Official Name: Republic of Indonesia.
Location: Southeast Asia.
Area: 735,269 square miles (1,904,345 km²).
Population (1976 est.): 134,700,000.
Chief Cities (1974 est.): Jakarta, the capital, 5,000,-000; Surabaja, 2,000,000; Bandung, 2,000,000; Medan, 1,000,000.
Government: *Head of state and government*, Suharto, president (took office for second 5-year term March 1973). *Legislature* (unicameral)—Dewan Perwakilan Rakyat (House of Representatives).
Monetary Unit: Rupiah (415 rupiahs equal U. S.$1, Sept. 1976).
Gross National Product (1975 est.): $29,200,000,000.
Manufacturing (major products): Processed agricultural products, petroleum products, mineral products, cotton textiles, tires, cement.
Major Agricultural Products: Rice, rubber, sweet potatoes, cassava, copra, sugarcane, coffee.
Foreign Trade (1975): *Exports*, $7,103,000,000; *imports*, $4,708,000,000.

Members of the Supreme Soviet adopt a new five-year plan, calling for a 36% increase in industrial production during 1976–80.

UPI

INDUSTRIAL REVIEW

World industrial production recovered briskly in the first half of 1976, but the rate of growth slowed in the second half.

Data available through the third quarter of the year indicate production growth among industrialized countries was sharpest in France (12.5%) and Japan (11%), measured from September 1975 to September 1976. For the same time span, the industrial production growth was 7.5% for the United States and West Germany, and 8.5% for Italy. The United Kingdom lagged with a growth rate of 3.5%, and Canada registered a growth of 5.5%. Broad production measures did not surpass recession levels.

Among developing countries, available data indicate the following growth rates for the year ending roughly in mid-1976: South Korea 44%; Nigeria 31%; Taiwan 24%; India 19%; and Brazil 11%. Mexico showed a 3% decline.

Industrial production is turning increasingly international. And the United States is getting its share. Germany's Volkswagen looks to its U. S. plant, acquired in 1976, to boost sagging sales. Production will begin in 1978, with a top capacity of 200,000 cars. Michelin of France is building a tire factory in South Carolina. Britain's ICI is investing in a herbicides plant in Texas. In an interesting switch, a Japanese paint firm bought a factory in Seattle, Wash., to produce for the market in Japan.

What has made the United States more attractive for foreign firms, market growth aside, is political stability, and the fact that manufacturing pay in the United States is no longer the highest in the world. Average compensation per hour worked in manufacturing is higher in Sweden and Belgium, and is just about at the U. S. level in West Germany, Canada, and the Netherlands.

Soviet Production. The Soviet Union announced its tenth five-year plan, covering 1976–80. The industrial sector's growth was planned at 4.3% in 1976. Soviet defense expenditures claim about 13% of the country's total production, just about double the U. S. proportion. Use of considerable resources for defense will tend to slow down output growth in the civilian sector. Passenger cars are a case in point. Soviet production grew from 344,000 in 1970 to 1.2 million in 1975. The current plan allows for a 3% annual rise in production. Much of the total auto output is planned for export, as much as 35%. In 1975, about 25% of the Soviet auto production was exported. Steel shortages have been cited for the slow expansion of auto production. In 1975, the Soviet Union produced 140 million tons of steel, and the Five-Year Plan calls for a 21% increase in output, to 170 million tons by 1980.

Soviet energy production is scheduled to grow at an annual rate of 5%, which is slightly lower than the rate during 1971–1975. Energy exports are scheduled to grow at about 4.7% a year in the 1976–80 period, compared with the 7.3% rate of 1971–75. The Soviet Union, which became the world's leading oil producer in 1974, exports about 20% of its petroleum production, with a little over two fifths of it going to the West. Oil is the top earner of hard currency, which is needed to pay for imported Western technology. Oil output is likely to reach about 600 million tons by 1980, compared with the 491 million tons produced in 1975. Most of the planned increases are scheduled to take place in West Siberia, which will account for half of the Soviet oil production by 1980.

Soviet coal production is scheduled to rise to 790–810 million tons by 1980, from the 700 million tons produced in 1975. That seems a likely development. The same cannot be said for goals set for natural gas, which call for a 1980 production of 525,000,000,000 to 570,-000,000,000 yards³ (400,000,000,000 to 435,-000,000,000 meters³), compared with 378,000,-000,000 yards³ (289,000,000,000 meters³) pro-

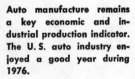

Auto manufacture remains a key economic and industrial production indicator. The U. S. auto industry enjoyed a good year during 1976.

duced in 1975. Soviet gas industry has had serious problems in coordinating field development with pipeline and gas treatment plant construction.

The first home air conditioner plant began production in the Soviet Union. Built by a Japanese concern, the production machinery was imported from Japan, West Germany, and the United States. By midyear 1976, daily production had reached 160 units, just about one tenth of the planned capacity. Among other consumer items, Soviet industry produced 5.6 million refrigerators in 1975, 3.3 million washing machines, 8.4 million radios, and 7 million television sets.

U. S. Production. U. S. industrial production averaged 10% higher in 1976 than in the preceding year. The Federal Reserve Board's industrial production index registered 130 (1967 = 100) for the year, according to preliminary estimates. It barely managed to climb over the prerecession high recorded for 1973. Manufacturing output increased a little over 11%, with the gain for durables slightly lower than for nondurables. Mining production increased during the year by 1%. Utilities increased their output by about 3.5%.

The industrial production index measures the physical volume of production of U. S. factories, mines, and utilities. It covers about two fifths of the nation's total output of goods and services, and reflects current trends in the economy.

The Board of Governors of the Federal Reserve System revised the index in 1976. It was the first general revision in five years, and the fifth since the index was first published 50 years ago.

The number of individual series increased from 227 to 235. Among the additions are separate series beginning with 1967 for large and small autos, consumer-type utility vehicles, and business vehicles. The revision incorporates benchmark data from the Censuses of Manufac-

tures and Minerals for changes from 1963 to 1967. A variety of other sources was used to adjust production levels from 1967 to 1973.

The revision centered on improving industrial production measures in oil and gas extraction and refining, in electric and gas utility operations, and in industries that produce chemicals, construction products, and motor vehicles. Measures of energy production by stage of processing were also developed.

The main effect of the revision was to raise slightly the production levels, mostly for business equipment and consumer goods. The new index shows that the boom in business and consumer investment during the 1972–74 expansion was greater than the old index had indicated. The new index also shows that the recovery from the sharpest post World War II recession was faster than registered by the old index.

Gains in manufacturing output were widespread. Durables production was paced by a 26% gain in motor vehicles and parts. The output of domestic cars reached 8.5 million, and truck production—at about 3 million—was close to the record set in 1973. Much of the boost in truck production came from heavy consumer demand for light trucks, such as vans, pickups, and utility vehicles. According to market studies, close to one half of the light trucks produced went for personal use in 1976, a sharp change from previous years. Consumers also showed a marked preference for big and intermediate size passenger cars, and left manufacturers no choice but to try to move stocks of small cars by offering cash rebates.

Despite the strong performance in the automotive industry, the gain for the transportation industry grouping was held to 13%, due mostly to a 2% decline in the output of aerospace and miscellaneous transportation equipment industries.

Lumber and lumber products gained 14%, as housing construction revived. That also helped the output of clay, glass, and stone products, which grew 13%. Furniture and fixtures registered a gain of 11%.

Primary metals showed a 13% gain. Steel producers poured 127 million tons of raw metal, a 9% increase from 1975. Steelmakers boosted their rate of manufacturing capacity utilization to 83%, a considerable improvement from the 76% in 1975.

Fabricated metal products and electrical machinery industries increased production by 11% in 1976. The gain in nonelectrical machinery output was a little over 6%. There was a substantial decline in ordnance production, as the index for the industry dropped 6.5%.

The output of nondurables was paced by rubber and plastic products industries, and apparel producers, which showed a 16% gain. Paper and paper products increased output by 14%, as did chemicals producers. Textile mill and leather goods production grew 12%. The gains in output of the food, tobacco, and petroleum products industries during the year were around 5–6%.

It was consumers, rather than business, who provided the impetus for industrial production growth in 1976. Among products, consumer goods output rose a shade over 10%, and business equipment production increased 5%. Government, as a customer for defense and space equipment, was a disappointment. Such production declined a little over 2%.

Aside from automotive products, where consumer goods output increased 21%, home goods also enjoyed a brisk demand, boosting output by 13%. The appliances, air-conditioning units, and TV sets were especially strong, with a 19% gain. Consumers went for a wide variety of products: digital watches, calculators, citizen band radios, and all kinds of boats. Private planes had their best sales in 10 years, with the unit count around 15,000. All told, consumer hard-goods production increased 16% in 1976.

Production of consumer soft goods increased 7.5%. Clothing production gained 15%, while the output of staples increased a little less than 6%. Production of consumer energy goods increased 2.5%.

Mining output in 1976 was held to a 1% gain by the 1.5% decline in oil and gas extraction. Coal output increased by a total of 1%. Metal mining output gained a little over 5%, and stone and earth minerals registered a jump of nearly 10% during the year.

A dramatic example of the interaction between technological innovation and industrial growth is the recent experience of the U. S. calculator industry. The first true commercial exploitation of the electronic calculator began in 1964 by the Japanese in their domestic market. In 1966, the Japanese products showed up in the United States, taking down 1% of the calculator market. The five vertically integrated U. S. electromechanical manufacturers did not change over to the new technology, so that the Japanese manufacturers captured 40% of the market by 1970.

Thanks to breakthroughs in integrated circuit technology, new U. S. firms—many of them small—jumped into the calculator field. With more than 40 of them active in 1971, price breaks were many. Several U. S. integrated circuit manufacturers entered the calculator field in 1972, helping boost U. S. producers' market share to 70% and send unit sales to 3 million. That in effect restored the importance of vertically integrated manufacturing to the calculator industry. U. S. firms had recaptured 80% of the calculator market by 1974, and by 1976 forced prices down to as low as $5 for simple units.

AGO AMBRE, *Bureau of Economic Analysis*
U. S. Department of Commerce

ALLEN REUBEN, DPI

Citizen band radios were the new "in" product of 1976. Over 5 million transceivers were put into service throughout the United States.

INSURANCE

During 1976 the U. S. economy struggled toward recovery. In this environment, the performance of the life insurance business was, on the whole, favorable. Property and liability insurance firms, on the other hand, lost more than $1,900,000,000 on their underwriting operations during the first half of 1976—this coming on the heels of 1975's underwriting loss, which was the largest in history.

PROPERTY AND LIABILITY INSURANCE

In 1975 the Insurance Information Institute recorded an overall statutory loss on underwriting operations of some $3,470,000,000. Factors contributing to the poor results included inadequate rate levels for many insurance lines, a growing number of costly lawsuits, and a continuing high rate of inflation of the costs of goods and services for which insurance must pay. The business continued to sustain large losses in the first half of 1976, but rate increases obtained late in 1975 and early in 1976 lessened the underwriting losses to some degree. Premiums written were projected to continue to increase to a level of about $42,000,000,000 during the year.

An improved securities market helped to boost policyholders' surplus to more than $25,-000,000,000, somewhat easing the concern over the financial stability of the business.

Insurance System Threatened. The very rate increases and restrictions on coverage that have strengthened the financial underpinnings of the business have raised questions about the future of the insurance system itself. The basic idea of insurance is that where a large number of people are exposed to a certain kind of risk, the losses are predictable and can be spread over the entire group through the premium system. If the risks and exposures cannot be stabilized, the government will have to intervene more and more, either by imposing constraints on the market or socializing the cost by spreading it through the tax system. In contrast to straight cost inflation, the real threat to the insurance business involves the enormous, unpredictable escalation of risks and exposures, which creates obligations that did not exist earlier. Malpractice is one example, product liability another. Product liability used to be a relatively small line, listed by the companies under "miscellaneous liabilities." Today it is an open-ended risk because the courts have extended liability to a wide range of cases in which the product was not the cause of the accident but was merely involved in it. Contingency fees make it worthwhile for a plaintiff's lawyers to go for an outsize award, no matter how much time and work it takes. It is not surprising that trial lawyers have been the center of opposition to no-fault automobile insurance, the first major effort to modify the old tort system.

Other Developments. The U. S. Justice Department began a review of all industry exemptions from federal antitrust laws—including those granted the insurance business by the McCarren-Ferguson Act. Fire losses in the United States during 1975 jumped 12% to $3,600,000,000, and authorities saw arson as a major contributing factor. U. S. insurers continued to expand their premium writings of insurance in foreign countries receiving more than $2,300,000,000 in premiums.

LIFE AND HEALTH INSURANCE

On balance, the performance of the life insurance business was favorable during 1976. As the economy struggled toward recovery, people continued to turn to life insurance, which has a history of reliability and stability in periods of great uncertainty. The average insured family in the United States increased its life insurance protection to a new high of $33,100 at the beginning of 1976. The development of the Individual Retirement Account (IRA) under the Employee Retirement Income Security Act of 1974 continued to be a significant factor in the performance of the business.

Purchases and Payments. New life insurance purchases in the United States amounted to $292,500,000,000 in 1975. Of this sum, $189,-600,000,000 represented individually purchased ordinary and industrial life insurance. New purchases of group life insurance totaled $96,-200,000,000. Life insurance companies paid $22,500,000,000 in benefits to policyholders, annuitants, and other beneficiaries. Such benefit payments were projected to be well over $23,-000,000,000 at the end of 1976.

Investments. Assets of 1,790 legal reserve life insurance companies were expected to total more than $300,000,000,000 at the end of 1976. Corporate securities accounted for 46.3% and mortgages for 30.8% of these investment holdings. Loans to policyholders declined to 8.5% of the total assets of insurance companies. The net pretax earnings rate on life insurance company investments in 1975 was 6.36%.

Health Insurance. More than 176 million people had health insurance through private organizations in the United States at the start of 1976. Private health insurance policyholders received an estimated $32,000,000,000 in benefit payments in 1975. The coverage was provided by insurance companies, Blue Cross-Blue Shield organizations, and other plans.

Other Developments. A sharp increase of 22.2% occurred in individual annuities which totaled 2.9 million at year-end. Some 225,000 of these were purchased for IRA's. Two major associations—the American Life Insurance Association and the Institute of Life Insurance—were merged under the American Council of Life Insurance on Jan. 1, 1976.

KENNETH BLACK, JR.
Georgia State University

An informal atmosphere dominates the headquarters of Kenneth Parker Associates, Philadelphia architects.

Interior Design

Humanism, according to Webster characterized by an individualistic, critical spirit and an emphasis on secular concerns for human interests or values, is a philosophy that asserts the dignity and worth of man. In architecture and interior design, humanism represents the designer's sensitivity to people and how they react to their environment.

Design in the mid-1970's is turning away from the concepts of the 1960's, which many found architecturally sterile and lacking in humanity. Balance of plan and color was more important than function. People inhabited spaces as if in a planned scheme. This was particularly true of institutional spaces, but too often also of sophisticated homes.

There is now a noticeable trend toward humanism in design. People are rediscovering the "joys and conveniences of fine and sensibly made things . . . , are returning to stable environments, and developing a requiting of normal human passions for individually crafted objects and more attractive ways to live and work" (Vincent Kling, *Interiors,* May 1975).

In an article on the new humanism (*Interiors,* November 1975), George Nelson hailed the presence of the atrium or galleria as a signal of

Walla Walla Community College, an open-registration institution, features a flexible, open space plan with movable furniture.

CROWN CENTER

Kaleidoscope, a children's museum in Kansas City, Mo., offers brightly painted walls and blown-up graphics.

the return to urban amenities. (The famed Milan Galleria has taken on a new significance as the prime example of the enclosed space designed as the hub of communal interaction and pleasure.) Nelson not only referred to architect John Portman's spectacular building-high atriums, incorporated into his hotel designs, but also to the many public plazas made possible by more humanistic zoning considerations.

Interiors (February 1976) is more specific in "Atrium Acrobatics," an article discussing the Ford and Earl Associates installation of the St. Louis Stouffers. An open, skylit interior central court, "that vestige of Roman gentility, encourages esthetic flights of fantasy...." The resurgence of the hotel lobby, designed as a grand place enjoyed by the user, once again realizes the human need for amenities in public spaces.

Schools. The new humanism in public schools is not defined by atriums. Design of educational institutions is keeping pace with new thoughts, curriculums, and teaching methods: open plans, colorful interiors, audiovisual aids, and machines. Schools, no longer laboratories of regimentation, now offer opportunities for individualism, and foster a sense of involvement, creativity, and advancement.

In Monterey, Tenn., the Uffelman Elementary School, designed by architects Yearwood & Johnson (C. Dale Carpenter, interior designer), found that space planning and graphics have directly influenced learning abilities. Children work and play in nooks and crannies, in groups or singly. Specific to the plan is the "Gymazo-

sanc," an enclosed maze and sanctuary incorporating carpeted levels, convex mirrors, unglazed windows, and such novel ways to enter or leave as rope ladders and knotted ropes.

Walla Walla Community College faces society's changing needs with open registration. The ebb and flow of enrollment led the designers, Environmental Concern, Inc., to create a flexible, open space plan with movable furniture systems. Partial barriers, carpeted for sound control, enclose the central planning cores; these open onto corridors that are color-coded to define high-traffic or common seating areas.

Museums. Kaleidoscope, the Hallmark children's museum in Crown Center, Kansas City, Mo., offers educational experiences by means of audiovisual and tactile learning. Children poke, stroke, listen, dip into art, or play musical instruments in an environment of brightly painted walls, blown-up graphics, and slide shows. They crawl through imaginative boxes that may reflect them as Charlie Brown or Lucy—characters from the *Peanuts* comic strip. The museum was conceived by Carolyn Yates, Sandra Johnson, and Rachem Chambers, who was the project director; Roger Thun was the principle in charge and Dale Brock the project designer.

Offices. Dental facilities share a common psychological obstacle—the perennial, ageless fear of the drill. Designers Smith/Yauch confronted the problem with a combination of color —a psychologically calming deep blue—and comfortable furnishings—padded, molded double seats lining three walls of the waiting room and covered in a striking acid green; a thick sound-absorbing carpet is midnight blue. The treatment room, a far cry from the clinical cubicle, features light-reflectant, shiny Mylar vertical blinds, and a molded, red plastic space-age treatment chair.

Architects Kenneth Parker Associates set up practice in a gutted building in one of Philadelphia's urban renewal areas. The interior, a triplex, has a relaxed, informal, home-like atmosphere. Spaces and levels are partially divided by glass, acrylics, or plantings. In fact, plants abound; a greenhouse extends one wall of the executive offices. The color scheme is keyed to natural woods and brick, coordinated with off-red upholstery. The furnishings, not specifically made for offices, present relaxed conversational surroundings.

Banks. John Ellis of the Vincent Kling office was given the problem of designing a Philadelphia bank without trendy clichés or institutional sterility. He employed a cheerful yellow, a series of flowering planters, and handsome, contemporary, textured wallhangings. The warm, friendly, and relaxed atmosphere is heightened by the soft glow of light from fixtures hidden behind soffits or the dropped central ceiling panel.

JEANNE WEEKS
Associate, American Society of Interior Designers

INTERNATIONAL TRADE AND FINANCE

By mid-1976 the world economy was recovering from recession but both unemployment and inflation were still high.

TRADE AND PAYMENTS

In the first half of 1976 volume rose at an annual rate of about 10%. The increase in volume and prices brought about a renewal of growth in export earnings of primary producing countries (oil exporters, non-oil developing countries, and the more developed countries) while the volume of imports was shrinking because of external financial strains and attempts to curb domestic inflation and protect balance of payments. Oil export earnings had been reduced by recession and the positive actions taken by importing countries in response to price increases, but the oil exporting countries themselves were under little restraint to curb imports. Hence, there was a reduction in their current account balance of payments surplus of about $32,-000,000,000 between 1974 and 1975. In the first half of 1976 under the impetus of recovery in the world demand for oil some rise in the surplus occurred. In the global pattern of current account balances, the main counterpart to the downward shift in the surplus of oil exporting countries from 1974 to 1975 was in the balance of payments of industrial countries.

Chou Hua-min was the head of China's delegation to the quadrennial session of UNCTAD held in Kenya in May.

UPI

The 1975 current account surplus of industrial countries was unevenly distributed: the United States and Germany more than accounted for the total, while several others, including Canada and the United Kingdom, had sizable deficits. Compensating capital flows in many instances kept pressures off exchange rates, with the exceptions of France which had reserve gains and appreciation in the exchange rate while Italy and the United Kingdom had reserve losses and exchange rate depreciation.

Early in 1976, the weakness of the Italian and British balance of payments positions became more obvious, and sharp downward movements of both the lira and pound dominated exchange rate developments during the first half of the year. The French franc also weakened during the period. The counterpart of these developments was the appreciation of other major currencies, combined with increased reserves. Exchange rate changes have become a more important means of balance of payments adjustment since the adoption of widespread floating in 1973. The experience since that time shows a strong correlation between relative rates of domestic inflation and changes in exchange rates.

By the first half of 1976, annual rates of increase in output over the second half of 1975 ranged as high as 6–9% for the three largest economies (United States, West Germany, Japan), as well as for Canada and France; the average was about 6.5% for the entire group of industrialized nations. On the inflation side, the overall rate dropped to 8.5% in the second half of 1975 and to 7% in the first half of 1976, but there was considerable disparity in rates of price increase. The lowest rates of price inflation were those in West Germany, United States, and Japan—3%, 4.5%, and 7.5%, respectively. These three countries also ranked highest in estimated growth in real gross national product (GNP). At the other end were Italy and Britain with 17% and 13%, respectively, and the lowest rates of output expansion (4.5% and 5%). France and Canada along with the other seven smaller industrial countries occupied intermediate positions.

Foreign trade prices typically showing the widest fluctuations are those for primary commodities. They were 5% above the 1975 average in the first half of 1976. By midyear, commodity prices in terms of Special Drawing Rights (SDR's) were about 23% higher than their late 1975 level. (One SDR equals U. S.$1.154).

Demand for metals and agricultural raw materials is especially dependent on the level of global activity and there was a firming of agricultural raw materials prices during the first half of 1976 while the market for metals was going through a period of adjustment associated with running down of inventories built up during the

1974–75 recession. The downward movement of prices for major foodstuffs was interrupted during 1975 because of substantial purchases of grain by the U. S. S. R. and because a severe frost in Brazil reduced the outlook for coffee supplies. However, the food price index as a whole was lower in the last half of 1975, and after an upswing in the first half of 1976 was expected to move downward with more ample supplies in the latter part of the year. In general, however, movements in foreign trade prices were relatively small and unit values of exports from industrial countries rose only moderately in terms of either local currencies or SDR's and declined vis-à-vis the U. S. dollar, reflecting its appreciation. During the first part of 1976 there was an upward movement of export prices reflecting recovery but this picture remained hazy at year's end because of adverse behavior in some economic indicators.

Capital Flows and Reserve Changes. The current account surplus of oil exporting countries of $35,000,000,000 in 1975 was concentrated in the four countries of Saudi Arabia, Kuwait, United Arab Emirates, and Qatar—nations with small populations and limited capacity to import. Most oil exporting countries use oil revenues in the following order: (1) development of their own economy; (2) assistance to developing countries, especially Arab; (3) investment in liquid assets (and to lesser extent in longer term securities) in industrialized countries, mainly the U. S.-Euro-dollar market and Britain.

Organization of Petroleum Exporting Countries (OPEC) investment in the United States amounted to $5,800,000,000 in the first six months of 1976, an increase of about $1,860,-000,000 over the comparable 1975 period. Of the total investment, $2,380,000,000 was in U. S. government bonds and notes; $736 million was invested in other long-term debt; and $1,140,-000,000 was in stock purchases. Long-term liabilities of banks to OPEC rose by $546 million. Short-term investment, such as bank deposits and U. S. Treasury bills, increased a little more than $1,000,000,000. In addition, there was important OPEC direct investment in production facilities and real estate. The estimated surplus on current account for major oil exporters in 1976 is $40,000,000,000.

For non-oil developing countries 1976 was another year of large current account deficits (around $32,000,000,000). The problem of external financing, though eased, remained. Capital inflows into these countries after 1973 came from sources not previously relied on to a great extent. The predominance of market borrowing, particularly from commercial banks, is important as this tends to increase debt charges as well as borrowings required to finance a given deficit. The increased availability to finance through banking channels reflected the recycling of oil exporters' surpluses and the dampening effect of recession on demand for bank loans. The

financing is viewed with concern because at mid-year U. S. banks and their major foreign branches had some $32,600,000,000 in loans outstanding to five developing nations.

The more developed primary producing countries also borrow heavily in international financial markets to cover current account deficits. These borrowings average $14,000,000,000–$15,000,000,000 a year but with relatively high incomes they can make adjustments by restraining imports and accepting lower growth rates in order to service debt commitments. The estimated deficit for these countries for 1976 is $10,000,000,000, reflecting a decrease in their borrowing needs.

UNCTAD. The fourth quadrennial session of the United Nations Conference on Trade and Development (UNCTAD) was held at Nairobi, Kenya, from May 3 to May 31, 1976. Major decisions taken by UNCTAD IV reflect a desire by its 112 members (called Group of 77) to influence the restructuring of the world economy as well as the economies of the developing countries which the members represent. The final acceptance of the need for structural changes in trade, aid, and technology depends on the political will of both rich and poor countries. Some of the major agreements achieved:

—to convene a negotiating conference in 1977 on a common fund for buffer stock financing, with commodity agreements finalized by the end of 1978;

—to integrate the commodity program to ensure stable conditions for commodity trade and development of export products;

—to study the debt problems of the developing countries with a view to providing guidelines for action in individual cases;

—to improve the generalized system of preferences granted by developed nations relative to tariffs and to extend its term beyond the originally envisaged ten years;

—to recommend to participants at Multilateral Trade Negotiations in Geneva that barriers to trade with developing countries be lifted or reduced;

—to urge the World Bank and regional development institutions to consider facilities to provide export credit refinancing for developing countries.

Exchange Rates and International Liquidity

By mid-1976 countries allowing their currencies to float dominated world trade and financial transactions. At year-end, the currencies of about 30 countries with 73% of world reserves were floating; their need to hold reserves was consequently less than it would be if they adhered to a par-value system. Members participating in the European common margin arrangements account for about 22% of world reserves. Participants in this arrangement are Belgium, Luxembourg, Denmark, West Ger-

The revaluation was intended to ease exchange rate pressures within the "snake" resulting from divergent rates of economic growth and inflation among these countries. German intervention to protect the "snake" had added almost $3,300,-000,000 to its international reserves between January and August.

Pound Problems. Sterling balances owned by foreigners, including foreign governments and oil-exporting countries, increased appreciably with the rise in oil prices in 1973. In 1975 oil-exporting countries and others began moving funds out of sterling and its value depreciated. This increased exports but also drove up import costs. It is estimated that for every 4% depreciation of the pound, prices rise by 1%. In April 1975, the pound was worth $2.40; in March 1976 it fell below $2.00 and kept falling until a consortium of countries provided an emergency loan of $5,300,000,000. At year-end it was worth a little over $1.60, having dropped one third of its value in 18 months.

U. S. Developments. Intervention in foreign exchange markets by the U. S. Federal Reserve between February and July amounted to an equivalent $270.4 million in sales and $301.4 million in purchases. Currencies sold were obtained through drawing on the reciprocal swap arrangements with the respective central banks. The amount of the facility available for use is about $20,000,000,000.

In late August the Mexican peso was set afloat as Mexican authorities terminated the 20-year-old fixed relationship of the peso to the U. S. dollar. The rate is now set by the foreign exchange market and by the end of the first week in September the peso had declined from 8 U. S. cents to 4.9 U. S. cents. The Mexican government introduced a series of measures to amplify the impact of the depreciation on the balance of payments and to minimize the impact on the domestic economy. There was also a $600 million U. S. loan to Mexico to help deal with disorderly conditions in the foreign exchange markets following the floating of the peso.

For the first quarter of 1976 a new format was used in reporting the U. S. balance of payments. The format was revised to take account of changes in the international monetary system and to eliminate some statistical problems. The Official Reserve Transaction balance and the Net Liquidity balance designed to measure direct and potential pressures on the U. S. dollar in foreign exchange markets, as reflected in changes in U. S. reserves and in liabilities to foreigners under fixed exchange rates, were eliminated as they had lost their meaning under current floating exchange rates. Also eliminated was the "basic" balance (current and long-term capital) that was designed to indicate long-term trends—the measure could be misleading because of the difficulties in defining "long-term" investment. Instead of the three overall balances, partial balances will be published along with an analysis

UPI

Brokers at the Frankfurt currency exchange are busy following the revaluation of the German mark. The action was intended to ease exchange rate pressures.

many, the Netherlands, Norway, and Sweden. France, Ireland, Italy, and Britain previously participated. Under the arrangement, called the "snake," when the exchange rate between two members reaches the margin of plus or minus 2.25% around its central rate parity, each country agrees to intervene in the currency of the other to prevent movement of the rate beyond the margin (intervention can also take place in dollars). All countries have at times intervened in foreign exchange markets with the degree of intervention differing. As a group, "snake" countries have intervened relatively little vis-à-vis nonparticipants but have intervened quite heavily in pursuit of common objectives.

"Snake" Problems. The Common Market's currency union weakened in March when France withdrew from the joint float. France had withdrawn initially in early 1974 but returned 18 months later only to drop out on March 15. Rising inflation and growing domestic economic difficulties kept Britain and Italy out of the float. The strength of the West German mark vis-à-vis the other currencies placed its value at the upper end of the permissible range. On October 17 Germany raised the value of the mark 2% relative to the Dutch guilder and Belgian franc, 3% relative to the Norwegian krone and Swedish krona, and 6% relative to the Danish krone.

UPI

In Manila in October, Philippine President Marcos addressed the annual meeting of the International Monetary Fund.

of particular categories of transactions. These partial balances which will be shown as memorandum items are merchandise trade balance; goods and services balance; balance on goods, services, and remittances; and the current account balance. The U. S. balance of payments under the new and old formats was showing continuing deficits in trade during the first half of 1976 while the other three memorandum items were slightly favorable. The cumulative trade deficit for the first nine months of the year came to $3,400,000,000.

The International Monetary Fund (IMF). The principal 1976 developments of the IMF relate to the meeting of the interim committee in Kingston, Jamaica, in January and the annual meeting of the boards of governors in Manila in October. The latter completed the first stage in the evolutionary reform of the international monetary system. Pertinent actions included:

1. Completion of negotiation on, and approval of, a comprehensive amendment for the Fund's Articles of Agreement. This amendment gives members freedom of choice in their exchange arrangements, e.g., legalize floating rates.

2. Completion of the Sixth General Review of Quotas providing for an increase of nearly SDR 10,000,000,000 to a total of SDR 39,000,-000,000. This change not only increases the Fund's resources but increases the voting power of the OPEC nations by about 5%.

3. Enlargement and extension of the oil facility through February 1977. Under this facility SDR 6,902,400,000 was borrowed from 17 lenders to finance oil purchases for 1974 and 1975 by 52 countries.

4. Establishment of a subsidy account to reduce the burden of interest payments under the oil facility for most seriously affected members. Objective of the account is to reduce by about 5% the effective rate payable in drawings under the 1975 oil facility.

5. Substantial liberalization of the compensatory financing facility to provide greater access by members with balance of payments difficulties caused by temporary export shortfalls, over which the country has no control.

6. Expansion, pending second amendment coming into effect, of the access by all members to the Fund's resources via increasing the size of each credit tranche (proportion of quota which can be used in a single year) by 45%—from 25% to 36.25%.

7. Agreement on arrangements to reduce the Fund's gold holdings by one third (50 million ounces): one half to be sold at public auctions for benefit of developing countries and the rest distributed proportionately to members at a price of SDR 35 per ounce. A concomitant of this is a change in the character and expansion of the uses of SDR's.

8. Establishment of a trust fund to be administered by IMF for the purpose of providing special balance of payments assistance to developing countries. Resources of the trust fund will consist largely of the profits from the sale of gold.

To implement the above it was expedient to abolish the official price for gold, to eliminate the obligation to use gold in transactions with the Fund and the Fund's authority to accept gold in transactions, and not to decrease other resources available to developing countries because of distribution of gold profits.

In addition, the 10 leading industrial nations in IMF agreed that (1) there would be no action to peg the price of gold, (2) the total stock of gold now in the Fund and the monetary authorities of the Group of 10 would not be increased, (3) they would respect any further condition governing gold trading that might be agreed to by their central bank representatives, (4) each would report semiannually to the Fund the total amount of gold bought and sold, (5) the arrangements would be reviewed at the end of two years.

It was decided that the sale of gold would be made over a four-year period with the profits (excess of receipts over official price of SDR 35 an ounce) accruing to the trust fund. Over the first two years, auctions are held every six weeks with the same quantity, approximately 780,000 ounces, to be offered in each of the 16 public auctions. The terms of sale, pricing method, etc., may be changed.

The peak price paid for gold in the market was $197.50 an ounce on Dec. 30, 1974; after the first IMF auction it sold for $121.85 an ounce. Following the second auction the market price fell to $107.75 an ounce. In August, prior to the third auction, a low of $103.50 an ounce was reached. In mid-November the gold price rebounded to $136.25 an ounce.

JOHN R. MATTHEWS, JR.
Department of Economics
College of William and Mary

IOWA

The 1976 Iowa corn crop was estimated to be 1,083,750,000 bushels (382,000,000 hl)—the fifth 1,000,000,000-bushel harvest in six years. The average yield of 85 bushels per acre (75 hl per ha) was 6% less than in 1975 and well below the record of 116 bushels per acre (101 hl per ha) in 1972.

The soybean yield of 203,360,000 bushels (71,600,000 hl) averaged 31 bushels an acre (28 hl per ha) and was some 14% less than the 1975 crop.

The reduced production was blamed upon the drought of July and August, when rainfall was the lowest in 40 years. Subsoil moisture was

still low in November, and there were fears for the 1977 crop unless heavy snow and spring rains replenished the soil moisture.

During 1975 the per capita income of Iowans rose to $6,077—$65 higher than the national average—and Iowa ranked 17th among the 50 states. Unemployment was 5%, well below the national average, for June, July, and August.

The 123d Iowa State Fair ended its 12-day run with a record turnout of 710,125 persons. The 1976 fair was also the longest ever. During the campaign, Democratic presidential candidate Jimmy Carter and Republican vice-presidential nominee Robert Dole both spoke before fair audiences.

Legislative Record. Several new records were established by the 1975–76 Iowa General Assembly. It made history as the longest legislature—the first session lasting 159 days and the second 139, or a total of 298 days. It adopted a record-high budget of $1,285,000,000 and, for the first time in modern history, did the budgeting on an annual basis. It was also the first Iowa legislature to operate without joint rules for the entire two-year session.

The major accomplishment of the two-year legislative session was the rewriting of the Iowa criminal code for the first time in more than 125 years. This measure, probably the longest single bill in Iowa legislative history, does not go into effect until January 1978, which allows the 1977 General Assembly to reexamine it and correct errors discovered before it is completely implemented.

No new taxes were imposed but the appropriations made will reduce the $240-million surplus in the state treasury.

Tax relief for the elderly was enacted; the adoption laws were updated; funds were made available to assist railroads; workmen's compensation and Iowa employee retirement benefits were improved; corporate farm laws were toughened; funding to meet basic needs of dependent children was provided; a state housing authority was created; and the election laws were revised. Also approved were some property-tax relief, funds to establish a foreign office to promote Iowa, salary increases for state employees, and funding for municipal transit systems.

Among the legislation approved but vetoed by Governor Ray was a "sunset law," which would have required periodical proof by each department of the need for its continued existence.

Elections. Iowa voters gave their eight electoral votes to President Gerald Ford. They reelected four out of five Democratic congressmen, and two Republicans were also sent to Congress. Neither of the two U. S. Senate seats was up for election.

The Democratic party continued to control both houses of the state legislature—the House 60–40, and the Senate 28–22. No state executive officers were on the 1976 ballot.

RUSSELL M. ROSS, *University of Iowa*

--- IOWA • Information Highlights ---

Area: 56,290 square miles (145,791 km²).
Population (1975 est.): 2,870,000.
Chief Cities (1970 census): Des Moines, the capital, 201,404; Cedar Rapids, 110,642; Davenport, 98,469.
Government (1976): *Chief Officers*—governor, Robert D. Ray (R); lt. gov., Arthur A. Neu (R). *General Assembly*—Senate, 50 members; House of Representatives, 100 members.
Education (1975–76): *Enrollment*—public elementary schools, 322,297 pupils; public secondary, 289,814; nonpublic (1976–77), 66,700; colleges and universities, 106,458 students. *Public school expenditures,* $817,966,000 ($1,368 per pupil).
State Finances (fiscal year 1975): *Revenues,* $2,003,254,-000; *expenditures,* $1,936,194,000.
Personal Income (1975): $17,440,000,000; per capita, $6,077.
Labor Force (July 1976): *Nonagricultural wage and salary earners,* 1,011,400; *insured unemployed,* 20,900 2.6%).

IRAN

For Iran the year 1976 was one of political stability and economic progress, marked by a general advance along established lines. The premiership of Amir Abbas Hoveida, entering its 12th year, continued, but the fundamental policy decisions were as before in the determined hands of Shah Mohammed Reza Pahlavi.

Oil Revenues. Like all countries whose major resource is oil, Iran is strongly affected by the rise and fall of economic activity in industrialized states. The government reported on February 3 that a sharp reduction in oil revenue, to $19,000,000,000 from an estimated $22,000,000,000, had lowered Iran's growth rate by two thirds and a budget deficit of $2,400,000,000 could be expected. But by October it was possible to make a much more optimistic forecast. It was likely that oil revenues would be up to $4,000,000,000 higher than envisaged in the budget, creating funds for development plans.

Long-term economic prospects, formerly thought doubtful because oil reserves were likely to run out in about 20 years, have improved. In July it was announced that the world's largest deposit of natural gas, estimated at 200,000,000,000,000 cubic feet (5,700,000,000,000 m³), had been discovered in the Persian Gulf. It is also becoming clear that Iran is much richer in minerals than had been supposed. Molybdenum is available in commercial quantities. Lead,

In Teheran, a planned apartment building was converted into Iran's first hospital that meets U. S. standards.

UPI

iron, and zinc are being increasingly mined. Coal reserves were recently discovered in the northeast. The most promising mineral developments, however, relate to copper. In the south, near Kerman, the $1,000,000,000 state-owned Sar Chesmeh copper-development complex is nearing completion. Iran expects to become an exporter of copper by 1978. The major difficulties with these plans (as with nearly all of Iran's development projects) are soaring initial costs, congestion at the ports, and lack of trained personnel.

Economic Agreements. Important technical assistance in development of the copper industry was expected to flow from the most impressive of the foreign economic deals concluded by Iran during the year—that with Krupp, announced on October 19. For an undisclosed sum Iran then acquired a 25.01% interest in the giant West German industrial firm.

Also in October, France and Iran reached trade accords running into thousands of millions of dollars. France is to construct two nuclear power plants at a total cost of $2,800,000,000, and may build up to six more. The French also agreed to build a railroad, a highway, 15,000 housing units, and an electric power plant for Tabriz. In November, the British state-owned aircraft manufacturer announced an oil-for-arms deal estimated at $676.8 million. British Aircraft Corporation will supply Rapier air defense systems and be paid in crude oil to be marketed overseas by Shell's British unit. A tentative deal by which Iran would have acquired an equity in Occidental Petroleum was announced on June 21 but abandoned on August 29.

Internal Affairs. Like other recent years, 1976 saw a long series of terrorist incidents, as well as firm attempts by the government to counter such activity. A number of occasions were reported on which terrorists (a total of several score) were either tried and executed, or shot in encounters with the police. Announcements were also made of the Shah's pardon and release of convicted terrorists.

The most disquieting incident was that on August 28, when gunmen in Teheran killed

---

IRAN • Information Highlights

Official Name: Empire of Iran.
Location: Southwest Asia.
Area: 636,294 square miles (1,648,000 km²).
Population (1976 est.): 34,100,000.
Chief Cities (1974 est.): Teheran, the capital, 3,930,000; Isfahan, 600,000; Meshed, 585,000; Tabriz, 560,000.
Government: *Head of state,* Mohammed Reza Pahlavi, shah (acceded Sept. 1941; crowned Oct. 1967). *Head of government,* Amir Abbas Hoveida, premier (took office Jan. 1965). *Legislature*—Parliament: Senate and Majlis (Lower House).
Monetary Unit: Rial (70.62 rials equal U. S.$1, Sept. 1976).
Gross National Product (1975 est.): $56,800,000,000.
Manufacturing (major products): Petroleum products, iron, steel, textiles, carpets, food products, caviar.
Major Agricultural Products: Wheat, rice, barley, cotton, tobacco, almonds, fruits.
Foreign Trade (1975): *Exports,* $19,978,000,000; *imports,* $10,343,000,000.

three U. S. employees of Rockwell International, the firm building the "Ibex" electronic surveillance installation. It is thought likely that foreign agents were involved.

Since the fall of 1975 the Shah's government has been attempting to combat inflation by a vigorous program of price control, with sanctions of heavy fines and severe sentences. The campaign has been reasonably successful; the rate of inflation has been much reduced. Another novel campaign, against corruption in public and private life, was proclaimed by the Shah in January. In February two undersecretaries of commerce were dismissed for dealings in sugar, and Rear Adm. Attaei, former commander of the Iranian Navy, and other officers were sentenced to fines and imprisonment for embezzling.

External Relations. During a visit to Iran in August U. S. Secretary of State Henry Kissinger signed an arms and trade pact, which will run until 1980 and amount to some $50,000,000,000. It included a provision for Iran to buy U. S. arms for $10,000,000,000 and civilian goods for $24,000,000,000.

In June the 1975 treaty settling outstanding differences with Iraq was ratified. A growing controversy between Iran and Arabs, who wish to rename the Persian Gulf the "Arab Gulf," led in January to the temporary withdrawal of six Iranian ambassadors from Arab states in or around the Gulf area.

ARTHUR CAMPBELL TURNER
University of California, Riverside

IRAQ

Iraq in 1976 continued on its individual way under the authoritarian hand of its Baath party government. Its policies are touchily nationalistic and fiercely independent, but tempered by a strong strain of common sense.

Oil Production. The foundation of Iraq's current success is its soaring oil production, particularly that of the North Rumaila field, developed with Soviet aid, which has added 800,000 barrels (102,000 metric tons) a day to oil output. The energetic search for new oil is spurred by the fact that since December 1975 all oil is nationally owned. Iraq now rivals Kuwait for third place among Middle East oil producers and has hopes of even surpassing Iran to become second only to Saudi Arabia. Iraqi oil production rose 17.1% in 1975, while it declined in all other Middle East countries. Oil revenues in 1975 totaled $7–$8,000,000,000, compared to $1,500,000,000 in 1971. The money is mostly devoted to domestic development, a new 5-year plan for which began in 1976. The ambitious program provides for investment in petrochemicals, agriculture, communications, and transport, as well as new schools, roads, hospitals, and factories.

Internal Affairs. A cabinet reshuffle was announced on May 10. Five ministers were dismissed, four new men were brought in, and six ministers were given different assignments. It was not, however, the sign of any major political change. Key ministries remained in the same hands, and Ahmed Hassan al-Bakr entered his ninth year in office in July.

Two new provinces were set up by a decree of February 7, and Kirjuk Province was renamed the Province of Tamin.

The Kurdish problem, presumably ended when Iran withdrew support for the rebellious Kurds in March 1975, continued to produce some echoes. A report in February said that the Kurdish Democratic party was attempting to organize Kurds inside and outside Iraq to renew the struggle, but it was doubtful if this constituted a serious threat.

Relations with the West. Iraq is violently anti-Israeli and a member of the "rejection front," opposing the step-by-step policy of U. S. Secretary of State Henry Kissinger. U. S.-Iraq diplomatic relations, severed by Iraq in 1967, have in theory not been resumed; in fact, an "interest section" of four U. S. officials has long been working out of the Belgian embassy in Baghdad. In June Iraq gave permission to double their number to eight. Political affinities are not allowed to influence economic decisions, which are pragmatic. Iraq receives abundant military hardware from the USSR, its closest friend, but in most fields prefers Western technology. The largest single contract ever signed by Iraq was that awarded in 1976 to the Lummus Company of Bloomfield, N. J., a $1,100,000,000 project to design and build a petrochemical complex near Basra.

Regional Policies. Iraqi relations with Iran remained reasonably good. The Iranian prime minister visited Baghdad in January, and the reconciliation treaty of June 1975 and protocols were ratified during a visit by the Iraqi foreign minister to Teheran in June. However, relations with neighboring Syria (which also has a Baathist regime) were bad, Iraq being intensely critical of Syrian intervention in Lebanon. There were also disputes over Syrian transit charges on Iraqi oil.

ARTHUR CAMPBELL TURNER
University of California, Riverside

--------- **IRAQ · Information Highlights** ---------

Official Name: Republic of Iraq.
Location: Southwest Asia.
Area: 167,925 square miles (434,924 km²).
Population (1976 est.): 11,400,000.
Chief Cities (1970 est.): Baghdad, the capital, 2,183,800 (met. area); Basra, 370,900; Mosul, 293,100.
Government: *Head of state and government,* Ahmed Hassan al-Bakr, president (took office July 1968).
Monetary Unit: Dinar (0.30 dinar equals U. S.$1, Sept. 1976).
Gross National Product (1975 est.): $13,400,000,000.
Manufacturing (major products): Petroleum products, processed foods, textiles, cigarettes, cement.
Major Agricultural Products: Barley, wheat, dates, rice, cotton, tobacco.
Foreign Trade (1975): *Exports,* $8,140,000,000; *imports,* $2,560,000,000.

IRELAND

The struggle over the fate of Northern Ireland continued to dominate Irish political life. The most dramatic reminder of that tragic conflict was the assassination on July 21 of the new British ambassador to Dublin, Christopher Ewart-Biggs. Several guerrillas detonated a bomb as the ambassador's car passed over a culvert on a road near his residence outside Dublin. The blast also killed Judith Cook, private secretary to Brian Cubbon, the senior civil servant in Northern Ireland, who sustained serious injuries.

Political Crisis. Spurred by this political murder, the coalition government (Fine Gael and Labour) asked the Dáil (House of Representatives) to approve an emergency powers bill which included a clause permitting the detention of suspects for up to seven days without formal charges. Although the Fianna Fáil party opposed certain clauses, the measure passed by a 70 to 65 margin. The bill touched off a political crisis, when President Cearbhall Ó Dálaigh, a constitutional scholar, questioned the legality of the measure. After the Supreme Court had declared the provisions constitutional, the president signed the bill into law. Several days later, on October 22, President Ó Dálaigh stunned the country by announcing his resignation from office because the minister for defense had criticized him in a speech for having delayed the

Patrick J. Hillery, 53-year-old doctor, is the youngest man ever to be named president of the Irish Republic.

UPI

measure. After nearly three weeks of turmoil, Dr. Patrick J. Hillery, a prominent Fianna Fáil politician, became president in an uncontested election on November 9.

Peace Movement. Perhaps the most positive, if precarious, political development of 1976 was the women's peace movement. Led by two courageous housewives from Belfast, the movement attracted thousands of supporters from the Roman Catholic as well as Protestant communities on both sides of the border. During the summer the movement spread well beyond Belfast, and on August 28 more than 20,000 people marched for peace in Dublin.

The peace crusade reflected the widespread aversion to the politics of the bomb and the bullet. It also angered the extremists on both sides. The Irish Republican Army (IRA) continued to advertize its strength by means of daring raids and dynamite. On July 15, four political prisoners blasted their way out of the Central Criminal Court where they were on trial. Police recaptured three of them, but one made good his escape.

The government intensified its campaign against illegal organizations by prosecuting known or suspected members of the IRA, but it could not prevent the level of sectarian violence from rising above that of 1975.

Economy. As in Great Britain, so, too, in Ireland the economy showed signs of serious decline: continuing inflation, mounting unemployment, and a depreciated currency. The erosion of the pound sterling aggravated an already adverse situation. On February 16, the government received a loan of $300-million from the European Community in order to cope with balance-of-payment problems. A strike by bank officials (the second in five years) forced the closure of the banks during July and August, causing untold difficulties for both individuals and businesses. On the energy front, the discovery of offshore oil by the Exxon Corporation in the Kinsale area was offset by the news that British Petroleum had found no large deposits of oil off the coast of Cork.

L. PERRY CURTIS, JR., *Brown University*

IRELAND • Information Highlights

Official Name: Ireland.
Location: Island in the eastern North Atlantic Ocean.
Area: 27,136 square miles (70,283 km²).
Population (1976 est.): 3,100,000.
Chief Cities (1973 est.): Dublin, the capital, 680,000; Cork, 224,000; Limerick, 140,000.
Government: *Head of state,* Patrick J. Hillery, president (took office Nov. 1976). *Head of government,* Liam Cosgrave, prime minister (taoiseach, took office March 1973). *Legislature*—Parliament; House of Representatives (Dáil Éireann) and Senate (Seanad Éireann).
Monetary Unit: Pound (0.60 pound equals U. S.$1, Sept. 1976).
Gross National Product (1975 est.): $7,800,000,000.
Manufacturing (major products): Processed foods, clothing, textiles, paper products.
Major Agricultural Products: Wheat, potatoes, sugar beets.
Foreign Trade (1975): *Exports,* $3,177,000,000; *Imports,* $3,768,000,000.

ISRAEL

No year is an easy one for Israel, but 1976 provided a respite from war and serious crises. The Sinai agreement between Israel and Egypt, one year old in September, was clearly working well. In November the mandate of the UN peace-keeping force in the Golan Heights was again renewed for six months. However, pressures were growing for solutions of fundamental problems—most likely, solutions unwelcome to Israel.

Premier Itzhak Rabin resigned on December 20 after expelling the National Religious party from his coalition government. He remained, however, as head of a caretaker cabinet, pending election in the spring of 1977. Rabin was confronted by myriad problems. Israel's situation has become more precarious and more dependent on U. S. support since the 1973 war.

Economy. Perhaps the most pressing problems facing Israel are those of its economy. It was a rapidly expanding one, with a healthy balance of payments, for the first quarter-century of the country's history. It began to stagnate and run a serious deficit in foreign trade in the 1970's. One reason is the prevalence of strikes in a union-dominated society. Any worker's grievance, however trivial, can balloon into a paralyzing strike. Thus, in one week in November, it was reported that a senior pilot of El Al airlines was grounded by the mechanics union because he had offended them; a senior merchant captain was indefinitely on the beach because he had a dispute with his bosun; hundreds of factory workers threatened with dismissal in Tel Aviv held the factory administration hostage; college students struck for three days to protest a rise in tuition; and also on strike, or threatening walkouts, were social workers, aircraft builders, hospital doctors, bank employees, and customs inspectors.

Inflation was running at about 35% per annum. Taxation is so ferocious that tax evasion is rewarding and widespread. The nomination in September of Asher Yadlin, a well-known establishment figure, to be governor of the central bank, and hence the second in control of the

UPI

Israel's newest nuclear test reactor was opened at the Weizmann Institute of Sciences in November 1976.

economy, was stalled in October when he was arrested on charges of evading taxes and receiving kickbacks. (He was later indicted for bribery and fraud.) The 1976–77 budget further added to the tax burden. To support outlays of $11,500,000,000, Israelis were to pay 70% of their incomes in state and city taxes, compared to 64% for 1975–76. A new value-added tax was to raise $300 million in revenue, and reductions in subsidies would lead to higher prices of many commodities and services. Finance Minister Rabinowitz said that security requirements accounted for 38% of the budget and 60% of the gap in the balance of payments.

Devaluations. The Israeli pound has been steadily sliding in value—in part a deliberate policy to make Israeli exports cheaper. Since June 1975 a ministerial committee has been empowered to devalue the currency up to 2% every month. This was done five times in the first seven months of 1976. On July 18 two other changes were announced. The exclusive link to the dollar was ended, and the currency was in the future to be linked to a "basket" of currencies of Israel's main trading partners: the United States, West Germany, Britain, France, and the Netherlands. Also, devaluation in the

---

ISRAEL · Information Highlights

Official Name: State of Israel.
Location: Southwest Asia.
Area: 7,992 square miles (20,700 km²).
Population (1976 est.): 3,500,000.
Chief Cities (1975 est.): Jerusalem, the capital, 345,000; Tel Aviv-Jaffa, 360,000; Haifa, 225,000.
Government: *Head of state,* Ephraim Katzir, president (took office May 1973). *Head of government,* Itzhak Rabin, premier (took office June 1974). *Legislature* (unicameral)—Knesset.
Monetary Unit: Pound (8.36 pounds equal U. S.$1, Sept. 1976).
Gross National Product (1975 est.): $12,100,000,000.
Manufacturing (major products): Polished diamonds, processed foods, chemicals, petroleum products, aircraft, electric and electronic equipment, textiles.
Major Agricultural Products: Citrus fruits, vegetables, cotton, eggs.
Foreign Trade (1975): *Exports,* $1,826,000,000; *imports,* $4,128,000,000.

future was to be made on an irregular basis to discourage speculation.

The general election due in 1977 was, by the year's end, already inhibiting any real drive for austerity and discipline. However, there were modest reasons for optimism. Prices of imported raw materials had dropped, export sales in agricultural products, electronics, and armaments had grown, and the balance-of-payments deficit was lessening.

West Bank Disturbances. A long series of outbreaks of violence took place in 1976 in the predominantly Arab West Bank territories, occupied by Israel since the 1967 war. These outbreaks, worse than any before, point to a severe dilemma for the Israeli government. Without the West Bank territories, Israel has an irregular, almost indefensible shape; yet there is little hope that Israeli rule there will be permanently accepted, even though it brings economic advantages. Rabin and others in 1976 indicated a willingness to make territorial concessions to buy a genuine peace.

The typical pattern was that of some kind of demonstration by young Arabs. Intervention by Israeli police to maintain order would then lead to Arab injuries, or even deaths (in the worst period of rioting, May 16–20, there were three). This would, in turn, lead to more rioting, answered by preventive detentions and enforced curfews. The West Bank disturbances began early in the year and persisted almost to its end. Among the triggering incidents were a two-day march by 20,000 militant Israelis at the end of April and an attempt in August to impose the new value-added tax, though Arab traders often do not keep books. There were

Brig. Gen. Dan Shomron led Israel's commando raid on Uganda's Entebbe airport to rescue hijacked hostages.

UPI

also symbolic religious incidents polarizing Jews and Muslims. But the long-term question is that of Israeli settlements. Since 1967 there have been about 100 of these established in the West Bank and Golan areas, some illegally. They are disapproved by most foreign governments since they clearly make reversion of the occupied lands less likely.

Terrorism and Entebbe. Israeli citizens were again victims of a number of terrorist attacks engineered by one or another Palestinian group. However, in one of the most spectacular incidents anywhere in the world in 1976, the Israeli armed forces scored a resounding victory over the forces of terrorism. This was the extremely efficient and operationally elegant rescue on July 4 at Entebbe Airport, Uganda, of hostages from an Air France jetliner, hijacked on June 27 on a flight from Tel Aviv to Paris. The Israeli task force, which made a seven-hour flight in six planes down the Red Sea to Uganda, consisted of 150 commandos and a team of 33 doctors. Seven of the guerrillas were killed in the operation, as were 20 Ugandan soldiers. The Israelis had one casualty, but three of the hostages also lost their lives.

The rescue, regarded in western countries as a magnificent achievement, gave a significant boost to Israeli morale and a clear warning to terrorists that they had no more safe sanctuaries.

Foreign Relations. There were no changes in the main lines of Israel's foreign relations. The great unsolved problem here is whether to continue the adamant refusal to deal with the Palestine Liberation Organization (which itself continues to be rigidly anti-Israel). The PLO receives increasing international recognition. Enjoying observer status at the United Nations, it was allowed to take part in the January Security Council debate, boycotted by Israel.

Israel's economic and military dependence on the United States inevitably continued, symbolized by Premier Rabin's long visit to Washington (Jan. 27–Feb. 6), and underlined by President Ford's decision in October to give Israel new, effective weaponry. Events in Lebanon, while of crucial concern, did not call for any Israeli intervention. Indeed, for most of 1976, there was a relaxation on the Lebanese-Israeli border. Israeli objections toward the end of the year to Syrian presence in the south of Lebanon were apparently effective. At the end of September there were Israeli-Soviet discussions at the United Nations, but diplomatic relations were not renewed. There was a distinct warming of relations between Israel and South Africa. Their reciprocal diplomatic missions were raised from consular to embassy status. Premier Vorster visited Israel (April 8–13), a trade agreement was made, and a standing joint committee created.

ARTHUR CAMPBELL TURNER
University of California, Riverside

In July, Giulio Andreotti (*left*) formed a new Italian government, made up solely of Christian Democrats. Tina Anselmi (with President Leone) was appointed labor minister and became the first woman to join an Italian cabinet.

ITALY

Italy's inflation-ridden economy in 1976 faced its worst crisis since World War II, while the Communist party sharply increased its strength in parliamentary elections held a year ahead of schedule.

ECONOMY

Along with Great Britain, Italy held the dubious distinction of having the sickest economy in the European Community (EEC). The inflation rate (about 18%) was the highest on the continent, and there was 7% unemployment. The country's trade deficit during the first nine months of the year doubled to $4,400,000,000, while the external debt approached $17,000,-000,000. The predicted growth in real gross national product was only 4.6%.

The chief causes of the crisis were pressures from the labor unions for higher wages without a corresponding increase in productivity, the quadrupling of oil prices since 1973, and the government's chronic inability to curtail expenditures. Italy has had to be bailed out repeatedly by loans from West Germany, the International Monetary Fund (IMF), and other foreign sources.

On February 16, the EEC approved in principle a $1,000,000,000 loan, to be financed mostly by recycled petrodollars from Saudi Arabia.

In the meantime, foreign currency reserves fell to less than $600 million as a result of speculation against the lira. By May 5, the lira had reached an all-time low of 915 to the U. S.$1, compared with 680 less than four months before.

Faced with this grim picture, the minority government of Premier Aldo Moro granted a formal consultative role to the Communist party on March 17 and, under growing pressure from foreign creditors, announced a series of austerity measures that it asked parliament to approve. But a cabinet crisis that led to new parliamentary elections on June 20 delayed consideration of these proposals until August, when a new minority government headed by Premier Giulio Andreotti resubmitted them. They went into effect in October, despite pressure from the unions to postpone them. On November 12, the Chamber of Deputies gave Premier Andreotti a vote of confidence on the measures.

The savage austerity package program included 25% higher gasoline prices and increased sales taxes on autos, movie tickets, alcoholic beverages, and other consumer items. A 15% increase in electric bills, a 25% hike in telephone rates, and higher bus fares will bring the government $1,250,000,000 more a year. Stepped-up controls on personal income tax returns and on business sales taxes will add another $5,000,000,-000. (Leftists estimate that evasion of direct and indirect taxes has cost Italy $12,000,000,000 a year.) Borrowing will cost 12% instead of

8%. The higher interest may entice back to Italy vast sums of money that have fled the country. Stiff curbs on foreign exchange dealings include a requirement that 50% of the amount of any transaction be deposited in the Bank of Italy for 90 days. The new deflationary measures could lead to zero economic growth in 1977.

In September Italy secured a renewal of the $2,000,000,000 loan from West Germany. In December Premier Andreotti conferred in Washington with President Ford and representatives of President-elect Carter in the hope of gaining additional credits. Italy was also approaching the EEC and Japan with the same intention.

In December Turin's hard-pressed Fiat automobile industry, controlled by Gianni Agnelli, surprised the world by announcing that the Libyan government was buying 9½% of its stock for $415,000,000.

Earthquakes. Italy's problems were compounded by a devastating series of earthquakes that rocked the mountainous Friuli-Venezia Giulia region in May and September. More than 1,000 people were killed and 120,000 left homeless. Thousands of refugees planned to relocate in Adriatic coastal areas. The government allocated several hundred million dollars of aid.

Ecology. On July 10 an explosion of a safety valve at high temperature in a Swiss-owned chemical plant north of Milan released a cloud of deadly dioxin (trichlorophenol) gas used for making defoliants. It killed a great number of animals and made scores of people seriously ill. Plant officials and regional authorities were slow to order evacuation of the town. Homes, trees, and shrubs in the afflicted area had to be burned with high-intensity flames to destroy the chemical. Because of the danger of deformed babies, couples were urged to avoid pregnancies for several months.

POLITICS

The shaky 13-months-old government of Premier Aldo Moro, made up of Christian Democrats and the small Republican party, came to an end on January 7 after the Socialist party withdrew parliamentary support. The Socialists

------ **ITALY · Information Highlights** ------

Official Name: Italian Republic.
Location: Southern Europe.
Area, 116,303 square miles (301,225 km²).
Population (1976 est.): 56,300,000.
Chief Cities (1974 est.): Rome, the capital, 2,856,000; Milan, 1,732,000; Naples, 1,224,000; Turin, 1,202,-000.
Government: *Head of state,* Giovanni Leone, president (took office Dec. 1971). *Head of government,* Giulio Andreotti, premier (took office July 1976). *Legislature*—Parliament: Senate and Chamber of Deputies.
Monetary Unit: Lira (864.30 lire equal U.S.$1, Dec. 1976).
Gross National Product (1975 est.): $177,500,000,000.
Manufacturing (major products): Automobiles, petroleum products, machinery, processed foods, chemicals.
Major Agricultural Products: Wheat, grapes, tomatoes, citrus fruits, rice, vegetables, olives, nuts.
Foreign Trade (1975): *Exports,* $34,821,000,000; *imports,* $38,366,000,000.

charged that their views on economic policy had been ignored by the Christian Democrats, who were instead consulting informally with the Communists. Moro tried unsuccessfully to form a new coalition that would include the Socialists, but the latter refused to join without the Communists, something the Christian Democrats would not tolerate.

Minority Government of Aldo Moro. At last, on February 11, Moro announced formation of a minority government (his fifth), made up of Christian Democrats only. This followed agreement from the Socialist, Social Democratic, and Republican parties not to oppose the new government in parliament.

On March 17, in an emergency meeting with political leaders on how to save the currency and economy from collapse, Premier Moro granted a formal consultative role to the Communists. It was the first time since 1947 that an Italian government had authorized such a step.

In April, the government faced a new crisis with the other parties over issues that included the depressed economy, Lockheed payoffs to politicians, political violence, and abortion. The Socialists insisted that parliamentary elections be held in the summer, a year ahead of schedule. This forced Moro to resign on April 30. Parliament was dissolved and new elections called for June 20. Moro was asked to remain as caretaker head of the government.

Parliamentary Elections. While calling attention to corruption in the government, the Communists, led by Enrico Berlinguer (see BIOGRAPHY, p. 119), campaigned on a platform of moderation that stressed commitment to the multiparty system and NATO. The elections produced impressive gains for them—34.8% of the popular vote for the Chamber of Deputies, compared with 27.2% in 1972. This put them close behind the Christian Democrats, who received 38.7%. All of the smaller parties lost strength, the Socialists faring the worst, winning only 9.7%. The Republicans got 3.1% and the neo-Fascists 3.4%. The Communists also gained 23 Senate seats, while the Christian Democrats barely held their own.

Early in July the Christian Democrats worked out a bargain by which a Communist, Pietro Ingrao, was elected speaker of the Chamber and a hardline Christian Democrat, Amintore Fanfani, president of the Senate. The Communist party also secured, for the first time, chairmanships of 7 of 27 parliamentary committees.

Giulio Andreotti Government. After a vain attempt to bring in the Socialists, Giulio Andreotti announced on July 29 formation of a new cabinet made up solely of Christian Democrats. It was dependent in parliament on the abstention of the Communists in key votes. The new government conspicuously excluded outgoing Premier Moro, former Foreign Minister Mario Rumor, and Treasury Minister Emilio Colombo. A woman was brought into the cabinet for the

UPI

Pope Paul VI confers with Diego Novelli, Communist mayor of Turin. Despite a major anti-Communist campaign by the Catholic Church, the party scored impressive gains in local and parliamentary elections.

first time—Tina Anselmi as labor minister. Arnaldo Forlani was named foreign minister, while Rinaldo Ossola was appointed minister of foreign commerce. The average age of the government leaders was below 50.

The new cabinet called upon parliament to approve a broad package of austerity measures. It also announced appointment of a parliamentary commission to investigate the Lockheed scandal. In addition, it called for reform of public administration through expansion of regional and local government. Andreotti promised more jobs, more investments in the South, reform in the police and intelligence services, a campaign against terrorism, a speed-up in the administration of justice, and improvement in the status of conscripts in the armed forces. With so many promises to fulfill, he conceded that spending could not be reduced, only held down.

Communist Misgivings. Berlinguer's policy of tacit cooperation with the government caused grumbling by elderly Communist Party President Luigi Longo and some labor leaders. Berlinguer responded by reassuring the rank-and-file that the party was not about to become Social Democrats. Moreover, he pressed for a "government of national emergency" that would include all democratic political forces—a move urged by Ugo La Malfa, leader of the Republican party.

Rome's Communist Government. As a result of local elections in Rome in June, a Communist became mayor of the city for the first time. Most regional and local governments in north-central Italy are now Communist-dominated.

FOREIGN RELATIONS

Some tension arose with the United States when the U. S. House of Representatives Select Committee on Intelligence revealed in January that the Central Intelligence Agency had funneled $6 million to individual anti-Communist politicians in an effort to prevent further Communist gains in the next election.

A summit conference of leaders of the seven major industrial nations of the free world, on June 29, resulted in a pledge to alleviate Italy's international payments problem by creation of a new multinational credit facility, possibly under the aegis of the IMF. But many Italians were infuriated a few weeks later when news was divulged in West Germany that Chancellor Schmidt and U. S. Secretary of State Kissinger had reached agreement, apparently behind Premier Moro's back in Puerto Rico, that additional loans to Italy would be dependent on the exclusion of Communists from the government.

At year's end, many Italians looked forward to the Carter administration in the United States, expecting it to be more flexible in dealing with their problems than Ford's had been. Andreotti was the first foreign leader to meet with representatives of the new president-elect.

CHARLES F. DELZELL, *Vanderbilt University*

"Banzai" cheers were given Emperor Hirohito and Empress Nagako on the 50th anniversary of his reign, celebrated on November 10, 1976.

JAPAN

Emerging slowly from a stubborn depression, Japan during 1976 experienced much of the same trauma as its ally, the United States. Japanese politics was rocked by the so-called Lockheed scandal, and the majority Liberal-Democratic party (LDP) faced a general election in December. On November 10 the Japanese public rather impassively marked the 50th anniversary of the emperor's accession to the throne. The press was more absorbed with speculation on the effect of the election of Jimmy Carter on U. S.-Japanese relations.

INTERNATIONAL AFFAIRS

The Foreign Ministry's *Blue Book on Diplomacy,* released in September, reflected Foreign Minister Zentaro Kosaka's emphasis on Japan's policy of pacifism. At the United Nations on October 4, Kosaka urged cooperation toward settlement of economic problems and peaceful solution of issues in the Middle East and Africa. He pointed to Japan's ratification of the nuclear nonproliferation treaty in June.

Relations with the United States. Speaking in Tokyo on November 8, Kosaka expressed hope that U. S.-Japanese relations would be further strengthened under the incoming Carter administration. Earlier, however, he had expressed concern over the firmness of the U. S. commitment to South Korea. In Washington, disclosures of wide-spread bribery of Korean officials had weakened the resolve to support what Americans regarded as the dictatorial regime of Park Chung Hee. Stability in the Korean peninsula was of direct concern to Tokyo for Japan's security.

Meanwhile, Japan was responding to American criticism that the value of the yen was being held down to increase Japanese exports. Japan's Ambassador Fumihiko Togo argued that the foreign exchange reserves ($15,900,000,000 in July) were increasing at an annual rate ($1,900,000,-000) less than that of the United States in 1975. At the economic summit meeting in Puerto Rico in June, Premier Takeo Miki urged developed nations to expand world trade in order to continue the current economic recovery.

Relations with the USSR. Japan's relations with the Soviet Union, which were normalized without a peace treaty in 1956, were severely strained when Lt. Viktor Belenko, without permission, landed a top-secret MiG-25 jet at Hakodate Airport on September 6 and promptly requested and received asylum in the United States. Moscow viewed Japanese cooperation with American military experts in the examination of the plane as a hostile act and further claimed that the Soviet officer defected to the United States against his will. Although Japan and the USSR worked out an agreement to turn over the plane on November 12 at Hitachi, Soviet officials unilaterally canceled the Japanese-Soviet Economic Committee's seventh joint session, scheduled in Tokyo on November 25.

Nonetheless, trade and transport ties between the countries steadily increased. The volume of trade grew 12% in 1975 over 1974 and reached a total of $2,546,000,000. Some 4,500 Soviet ships entered Japanese ports in 1975, and Aeroflot aircraft on the Moscow-Tokyo route carried 38,000 passengers.

--------- JAPAN · Information Highlights ---------

Official Name: Japan.
Location: East Asia.
Area: 143,689 square miles (372,154 km²).
Population (1976 est.): 112,300,000.
Chief Cities (1975): Tokyo, the capital, 11,500,000; Osaka, 2,800,000; Yokohama, 2,600,000; Nagoya, 2,000,000.
Government: *Head of state,* Hirohito, emperor (acceded Dec. 1926). *Head of government,* Takeo Fukuda premier (took office Dec. 1976). *Legislature*—Diet: House of Councillors and House of Representatives.
Monetary Unit: Yen (294.55 yen equal U. S.$1, Nov. 1976).
Gross National Product (1975 est.): $502,500,000,000.
Manufacturing (major products): Ships, automobiles, electronic components, textiles, iron, steel, petrochemicals, machinery, electrical appliances, processed foods.
Major Agricultural Products: Rice, wheat, barley, potatoes, vegetables, fruits, tobacco, tea.
Foreign Trade (1975): *Exports,* $55,844,000,000; *imports,* $57,881,000,000.

Relations with China. In somewhat similar fashion, Tokyo normalized relations with Peking in 1972, while the conclusion of a peace treaty was snagged on the Chinese insistence on an "anti-hegemony clause" aimed at the Soviet Union. Having officially expressed Japan's regret over the death of Mao Tse-tung, Ambassador Heishiro Ogawa returned to Tokyo for consultation on November 8. Prospects for resumption of talks aimed at a treaty seemed good, but Peking wanted to see the outcome of the Japanese election on December 5. Also, the new regime under Chairman Hua Kuo-feng continued to insist on the anti-hegemony principle.

With no formal diplomatic ties to the Republic of China, Japan still maintained a lively trade with Taiwan. The Japanese became excited over an *Asahi Shimbun* release on November 6, reporting that Taiwan emissaries and Peking officials had conferred in a meeting arranged by U. S. Secretary of State Henry Kissinger in Peking. Both U. S. State Department officials and Taipei denied the story.

Relations with Korea. In a speech delivered in Minneapolis on November 9, Ambassador Togo summed up the Korean dilemma facing Japan and the United States. He stated, "On the Korean peninsula the parallel existence of North and South Korea seems to be the only practical alternative in the present circumstances." Continued U. S. presence in the south, Togo said, is the safeguard against disruption of the precarious equilibrium in Korea.

However, both Tokyo and Washington were increasingly embarrassed by Seoul's actions. On

Premier Takeo Miki, at a special session of the Diet, rejected a "political settlement" of the Lockheed scandal.

UPI

August 28, despite earlier assurances made to Japan that opposition leader Kim Dae Jung would be freed, Park's regime sentenced Kim to eight years' imprisonment. In 1973 Kim had been abducted from a Tokyo hotel. Meanwhile, the Japanese openly speculated on the possible interconnections among their own Lockheed affair, the world-wide activities of the Korean Central Intelligence Agency, and the possible corruption of some 90 members of the U. S. Congress by a Korean businessman, Park Tong Sun, in Washington. Japan continued to be without formal relations with the Democratic People's Republic of North Korea.

Relations with Western Europe. Returning from a two-week mission to the European Community in late October, spokesmen for the Japanese Federation of Economic Organizations expressed alarm over the huge trade surplus with Western Europe, expected to top $4,000,000,000 in 1976. Japanese businessmen studied ways to limit exports without quotas and to expand imports of "attractive" items. The call for export restraint, however, was given a generally cool reception.

DOMESTIC AFFAIRS

In 1972 Premier Kakuei Tanaka met with President Richard Nixon in a summit conference in Honolulu. As part of their agreement, Japan undertook to purchase civil aircraft valued at $320 million. Later, in December 1974, Tanaka was forced out of office because of financial irregularities, but the stage had been set for the Lockheed affair which dominated all of Japan's politics during 1976.

The Lockheed Scandal. In July 1972 Vice Chairman A. Carl Kotchian of Lockheed told the Japanese press that he pinned his hopes for sale of the L-1011 TriStar Airbus on the Tanaka-Nixon summit meeting. On February 6, 1976, Kotchian testified before a U. S. Senate subcommittee that Lockheed had in fact expended large sums in Japan on consultant fees and outright bribes.

The difficulty faced by opposition parties and the press in Tokyo was that although President Ford promised Premier Miki on March 12 that U. S. agencies would supply Japan with information on the case, the agencies did so only on certain conditions. Thus, on March 24, Japan's Justice Ministry and the U. S. Department of Justice signed an agreement to supply "mutual assistance," providing that the information exchanged remained confidential, except in open-court proceedings.

From April 5 to 16 Japanese officials collected information from the Securities and Exchange Commission in Washington, but when they returned to Tokyo the data remained secret. The facts, however, as reconstructed by the Tokyo Public Prosecutor, gradually unfolded. It seemed that President Hiro Hiyama of Marubeni, Lockheed's sales agent, had called on Pre-

A rail strike in March forced many Japanese to walk to work, but some Tokyo office workers found a way to use the rails anyway.

UPI

Commuter traffic clogged the meandering freeways of central Tokyo during a general transit strike in April.

UPI

mier Tanaka twice in 1972. President Tokuji Wakasa of All Nippon Airways (ANA) had visited the premier's official residence on October 24, 1972. ANA announced its decision to purchase TriStars on October 30. On July 27, 1973, Lockheed had concluded a "consultant" contract with an ultra-rightist, Yoshio Kodama.

On March 23, 1976, Kodama's role was further dramatized when Mitsuyasu Maeno, a young actor, committed suicide by crashing a light plane into Kodama's Tokyo home. On April 2, in his first public statement since the Lockheed story broke, Tanaka informed his LDP faction that he was innocent. On May 10 Kodama was indicted for violating foreign exchange laws by accepting 440 million yen ($1.2 million) in cash from Lockheed's representative in 1973. Since he was reported to be ill, a Diet member investigating the case had to interrogate Kodama at his bedside. He denied that he had received any Lockheed funds other than 50 million yen ($180,000) annually as consulting fees. On July 2, however, his trusted aide, Tsuneo Tachikawa, was arrested.

Former Premier Tanaka was arrested on July 27 and indicted on August 16 in the Tokyo District Court for allegedly accepting a 500-million-yen ($1.8-million) bribe from Lockheed. The three channels for payoffs were said to be Marubeni, Kodama, and ANA, which purchased the airbuses. Public prosecutors filed additional charges against Marubeni's Hiyama. On August 21 Tomisaburo Hashimoto, former minister of transport and former secretary general of the LDP, was arrested on a charge of having received a 5-million-yen ($18,000) bribe through Marubeni.

In July and again on September 24 in the Diet, Premier Miki pledged all-out efforts to unravel the Lockheed mystery. Such statements won him support of public opinion, which favored strict law enforcement. On the eve of the election, however, the LDP was under severe pressure as 18 members were defined as "gray Dietmen" in a secret session of a lower house select committee. All had received Lockheed money but escaped indictment on technical grounds.

Party Politics and Elections. On June 14 six young members, led by Yohei Kono, seceded from the LDP to form a splinter party. As a result the LDP's majority shrank to 269 of 491 seats in the (lower) House of Representatives, with the remainder divided among the Japan Socialists (JSP, 114), the Communists (JCP), the Komeito, and the Democratic Socialists (DSP). In the (upper) House, the LDP had 128 of 252 seats.

In August both Deputy Premier Takeo Fukuda and Finance Minister Masayoshi Ohira called for Miki's resignation. Later, Fukuda left the cabinet to challenge Miki for the premiership. The campaign for the general election nominally began in Tokyo on November 15.

In the election, held on December 5, the LDP suffered its worst setback in 20 years, winning only 249 out of a new total of 511 seats. Only the support of nine independents salvaged the thin LDP majority. The biggest winners were the Komeito (55) and the DSP (29). Kono's New Liberals made proportionally large gains (17), the JSP modest ones (123). Premier Miki subsequently resigned, and in late December the Diet, in a new climate of coalition politics, selected Takeo Fukuda to be the new premier of Japan.

The Diet. The Lockheed scandal and factional infighting practically immobilized LDP leadership in the Diet. As late as April, the opposition JSP, JCP, and Komeito continued to boycott the legislature, insisting, in accordance with Diet resolutions, on complete disclosure of U. S.-supplied Lockheed data. The 77th regular Diet was able to pass the 1976–77 budget before adjourning its 150-day session on May 25. On September 16 the 78th extraordinary Diet opened without an agreement between the LDP and the opposition on a schedule. Nonetheless, by November, the government was able to pass pending bills on deficit-financing bonds and on higher rail fares and telephone rates.

The Cabinet. During the year Premier Miki obviously had to balance faction chiefs in order to maintain a viable cabinet. On September 11 a compromise was reached between pro- and anti-Miki forces within the LDP. This led to a cabinet reshuffle, followed by the extraordinary Diet, to be followed in turn by the general election. In a caretaker cabinet organized on September 15, the factional breakdown was identified by newspapers as follows: Miki 4, Fukuda 4, (Yasuhiro) Nakasone 3, Ohira 3, and, surprisingly, Tanaka 2. Miki retained Fukuda as deputy (until his defection) and Ohira as finance minister. Zentaro Kosaka, who had previously held the finance post, became foreign minister.

UPI

Sadaharu Oh of the Yomiuri Giants broke Babe Ruth's record with his 715th home run in October.

The Court. A legal ruling influenced the December election. On April 14 the Supreme Court held that the table of Diet seats had ceased to be consistent with the constitutional requirement of equal votes. All parties had to adjust their sights to an increase of seats from 491 to 511 in the election.

Economy. Like that of the United States, Japan's economy was emerging only slowly from recession. The gross national product (GNP) for fiscal 1975–76 grew at an inflation-adjusted rate of only 3.1%. Although the consumer price index in the Tokyo area dropped 0.9% in August, the overall Japan rate, because of increased transport fares, jumped 2.7% in September to reach an annual inflation rate of 9.7%. This was more than double West Germany's rate, but below Britain's and Italy's.

Fifty Years. On November 10, in the Nippon Budokan Hall in Tokyo, Emperor Hirohito attended a low-key ceremony to commemorate the 50th anniversary of his accession to the throne. (In fact he succeeded Emperor Taisho on December 25, 1926, but his coronation was held November 10, 1928). About 7,500 imperial family members, government officials, diplomats, and public representatives attended under security provided by 10,000 police, mobilized in Tokyo alone. Conspicuous by his absence, Tokyo Gov. Ryokichi Minobe joined the JSP in opposition to the celebration.

ARDATH W. BURKS, *Rutgers University*

JORDAN

For Jordan's King Hussein, 1976 was a year to consolidate the legitimacy he had gained in inter-Arab affairs as a result of the multifaceted alliance he negotiated with Syria's President Hafez Assad in August 1975. Making full use of the strength of the alliance while avoiding any overt involvement in the Lebanese civil war, the Jordanian monarch spent most of the year traveling to seek endorsement of the Arab formula for an overall peace settlement in the Middle East and to find diplomatic and financial support for his own regime.

Foreign Affairs. Hussein's consistent backing of the Syrian policy in Lebanon cost him some favor in the Arab world, but his willingness to tour the rest of the world, publicizing the Arab cause, more than made up for it. From the end of February to mid-April, Hussein and Queen Alia visited nine countries on the first leg of a year-long world tour. On March 3, in Australia, Hussein reiterated the Arab formula for Middle East peace: recognition of the national rights of the Palestinians, withdrawal of Israeli forces from all Arab territories occupied since 1967, and the right of all states to secure borders.

Hussein's support for Assad's policy in Lebanon enhanced the Syrian-Jordanian alliance. Meetings of the Syrian-Jordanian Joint Supreme Committee produced cooperative agreements in defense, industrial development, finance, education, tourism, and several other areas.

Hussein also maintained his traditionally firm relations with the West, though his ties with the United States were somewhat strained as a result of the game he played with Moscow and Washington over the sale of an advanced air defense system. Having called off the U. S. deal on April 14, when a $440-million price increase was announced, Hussein visited Moscow for 11 days in June to discuss the purchase of a Soviet system. In the ensuing months, negotiations with the United States were reopened, and on September 5 a deal financed by Saudi Arabia for $540 million in surface-to-air missiles and anti-aircraft guns was concluded.

UPI

Photographs taken during King Hussein's visit to Canada revealed that the monarch carried a handgun.

Internal Affairs. Jordan's economy, which has faltered badly in recent years, was buoyed by the input of thousands of millions of dollars in aid and investment capital from both the Arab and non-Arab worlds. A new $90-million airport will be built outside Amman, and Rumania agreed to construct a $500-million oil refinery at the Red Sea port of Aqaba.

Politically, a major change occurred when Prime Minister Zaid Rifai resigned in July. Cabinet member Mudar Badran was then named prime minister and asked to form a new government dedicated to building up Jordan.

F. NICHOLAS WILLARD, *Georgetown University*

——— JORDAN • Information Highlights ———

Official Name: Hashemite Kingdom of Jordan.
Location: Southwest Asia.
Area: 37,738 square miles (97,740 km²).
Population (1976 est.): 2,800,000.
Chief Cities (1974 est.): Amman, the capital, 615,000; Zarqa, 230,000; Irbid, 117,000.
Government: *Head of state,* Hussein ibn Talal, king (acceded Aug. 1952). *Head of government,* Mudar Badran, prime minister (took office July 1976). *Legislature*—National Assembly: Senate and House of Representatives.
Monetary Unit: Dinar (0.33 dinar equals U. S.$1, July 1976).
Gross National Product (1975 est.): $1,300,000,000.
Manufacturing (major products): Cement, petroleum products, cigarettes, vegetable oil, flour.
Major Agricultural Products: Wheat, tomatoes, barley, fruits, corn, olives, sorghum, grapes, tobacco.
Foreign Trade (1975): *Exports,* $158,000,000; *imports,* $731,000,000.

KANSAS

The economic climate in Kansas was healthy as 1976 began, for earnings in 1975 had been $346 million higher than predicted. The percentage of unemployed remained lower than the national average, and the only major disruption came during the national strike by rubber workers, which affected Topeka's huge Goodyear plant.

Agriculture. Wheat production in Kansas in 1976 was 327.5 million bushels (115,400,00 hl), 17.5 million (6,165,000 hl) below the 1975 crop. The corn harvest was estimated at 162.7 million bushels (57,300,000 hl), up 25 million (8,800,000 hl) from 1975. The sorghum grain crop was estimated at 157.15 million bushels (55,375,000 hl), up 9 million (3,170,000 hl) over 1975, but soybean production of 16 million bushels (5,640,000 hl) was down by 6 million (2,115,000 hl). Cattle numbers were trending downward to 6.4 million head, 4% under 1975, reflecting a somewhat depressed market, but hog production was increasing.

Weather. Kansas experienced another extended period of drought, spasmodically broken in scattered parts of the state. In some areas rains were heavy enough to cause flooding, while short distances away no precipitation occurred. The dryness, combined with high winds, damaged wheat in portions of western Kansas.

Legislation. The 1976 legislature appropriated $17 million more than Gov. Robert Bennett recommended—a total of $1,670,000,000. There were a minimal salary increase for state employees and a sizable increase in state aid to public schools. A bill was introduced to reimpose the death penalty but failed of adoption after long discussion and heated disagreement between the House and Senate. The state gasoline tax was increased to provide for highway improvements and new construction, and tax credits were given to new or expanding businesses. A dozen bills designed to reduce the incidence of medical malpractice claims were passed, as was a "tax increment system" of financing to revitalize blighted urban areas. The State Labor Department was reorganized into a new Department of Human Resources, assuming the manpower planning functions formerly in the governor's office. Mandatory prison terms were established for persons convicted of using firearms while committing crimes. A law to protect the rights of mental patients and offer them legal representation was also passed.

Election. President Ford and native-son vice-presidential candidate Sen. Robert Dole carried the state in the November elections, but eight-term Rep. Garner Shriver lost to Democrat Dan Glickman. Rep. Martha Keys (D) was reelected to a second term, and Republican incumbents—Joe Skubitz, Keith Sebelius and Larry Winn—won easily in the other congressional districts.

The Democrats took control of the House, while the Republicans retained control of the Senate with a 21–19 advantage. A constitutional amendment providing for assessment of agricultural land on a use-value rather than market-value basis won by a wide margin.

ROBERT W. RICHMOND
Kansas State Historical Society

KANSAS • Information Highlights

Area: 82,264 square miles (213,064 km²).
Population (1975 est.): 2,267,000.
Chief Cities (1970 census): Topeka, the capital, 125,-011; Wichita, 276,554; Kansas City, 168,213; Overland Park, 79,034.
Government (1976): *Chief Officers*—governor, Robert F. Bennett (R); lt. gov., Shelby Smith (R). *Legislature*—Senate, 40 members; House of Representatives, 125 members.
Education (1975–76): *Enrollment*—public elementary schools, 246,328 pupils; public secondary, 201,736; nonpublic (1976–77), 32,800; colleges and universities, 115,266 students. *Public school expenditures,* $618,614,000 ($1,386 per pupil).
State Finances (fiscal year 1975): *Revenues,* $1,386,715,-000; *expenditures,* $1,311,417,000.
Personal Income (1975): $13,655,000,000; per capita, $6,023.
Labor Force (July 1976): *Nonagricultural wage and salary earners,* 817,600; *insured unemployed,* 16,200 (2.6%).

KENTUCKY

Gov. Julian Carroll and Democratic presidential nominee Jimmy Carter, who won the state's electoral votes, made the year's dominant political news in Kentucky. The prosperity of the coal mining industry was overshadowed by a shocking double disaster in the Scotia Coal mine. Population increased in both urban and rural areas. The state lost its remaining professional sports team with the demise of the Louisville Colonels. The University of Kentucky basketball team moved into the mammoth new Rupp Arena in Lexington.

The Economy. Unemployment in the state remained below the national average because of the balance among agriculture, mining, manufacturing, and service. The state's economic growth provided for an increase of about 7% in total income. The state enjoyed its best agricultural year in history, with its largest grain crop and highest income from the tobacco crop. Animal prices were down, however,

Mining Disaster. Twenty-six men were killed in two explosions at the Scotia Coal Co. mine on March 9 and 11. Those killed in the second explosion included volunteers and three federal mine safety officials. The explosions were followed by controversy about the safety record of the company and the failure to recognize the dangerous condition of the mine at the time of the second explosion.

Desegregation. Controversy continued in Louisville over school desegregation and court-ordered busing. There were a number of demonstrations in the city, most of them peaceful. Opponents of busing put heavy pressure on the legislature and on local political leaders, but the court order remained in effect. When the schools reopened in Louisville in September, there was higher attendance and less disturbance than a year earlier. At the same time a number of private schools remained in operation.

Twenty-six miners were killed as a result of two explosions that struck Kentucky's Scotia Coal mine.

UPI

Area: 40,395 square miles (104,623 km²).
Population (1975 est.): 3,396,000.
Chief Cities (1970 census): Frankfort, the capital, 21,-902; Louisville, 361,958; Lexington, 108,137; Covington, 52,535.
Government (1976): *Chief Officers*—governor, Julian M. Carroll (D): lt. gov., Thelma Stovall (D). *General Assembly*—Senate, 38 members; House of Representatives, 100 members.
Education (1975–76): *Enrollment*—public elementary schools, 429,258 pupils; public secondary, 262,354; nonpublic (1976–77), 71,400; colleges and universities, 113,629 students. *Public school expenditures,* $633,000,000 ($917 per pupil).
State Finances (fiscal year 1975): *Revenues,* $2,394,-647,000; *expenditures,* $2,231,044,000.
Personal Income (1975): $16,541,000,000; per capita, $4,871.
Labor Force (July 1976): *Nonagricultural wage and salary earners,* 1,067,100; *insured unemployed,* 32,400 (3.9%).

Legislative Session. The regular session of the legislature was under the firm leadership of Governor Carroll. Among other things, it abolished the private bail bond business, defeated efforts to repeal ratification of the federal equal rights amendment, enacted the governor's package of consumer protection laws and a law regulating medical malpractice, and adopted the governor's budget. The budget included a substantial pay increase for public school teachers and a free textbook program. The legislature implemented the state constitutional amendment on the judiciary by establishing a new Court of Appeals, but a special session was required to implement reforms in the local court system.

Elections. Kentucky held its first presidential primary in May. With Governor Carroll's support, Jimmy Carter won an easy victory in the Democratic primary, while President Ford won a narrow victory over Ronald Reagan. Carter carried Kentucky in the November election with almost 53% of the vote, winning traditional Democratic areas, particularly rural counties, by large margins.

All incumbent congressmen, five Democrats and two Republicans, were reelected.

MALCOLM E. JEWELL
University of Kentucky

KENYA

Kenya's diplomatic and military posture toward neighboring states dominated the attention of President Jomo Kenyatta's government in 1976. Relations with Uganda plummeted in July after the Israeli raid at the Entebbe airport. But after several weeks of tension, Kenya-Uganda relations improved markedly.

Entebbe Raid. Israeli forces raiding Uganda's Entebbe airport to rescue hijacked Israeli and other citizens landed at Kenya's Nairobi airport to refuel before returning to Tel Aviv. Ugandan President Idi Amin charged that Kenya had collaborated with Israel to engineer the rescue. Kenyan Vice President Daniel Arap Moi denied that Kenya had cooperated with Israel, saying

UPI
Kenya's President Kenyatta (*left*) and Tanzania's President Nyerere meet for "very successful talks."

that Kenya too had been a victim of Israeli aggression. Despite Moi's denial, the incident provoked a state of near war for almost a month.

Uganda continued its verbal attacks on Kenya and threatened to seize areas of Kenya it had claimed earlier. More than 200 Kenyans residing in Kampala, Uganda, were reportedly killed.

Because Uganda is landlocked and relies on rail routes through Kenya, Kenya was able to retaliate by cutting off Uganda's supply of oil, thus virtually paralyzing Uganda's army and air force. Kenya demanded Ugandan traders pay for all rail shipments with Kenyan currency because of Uganda's mounting debts.

At meetings of Ugandan and Kenyan officials in Nairobi August 4–6 and September 16–21, however, most of the divisive issues were resolved. Both sides agreed to withdraw troops from border areas, cease threats to use force, and avoid issuing damaging statements against each other. Uganda also agreed to pay for goods and services from Kenya and to renounce claims on Kenyan territory.

American Visits. In April Secretary of State Henry Kissinger began his tour of Africa in Nairobi, where he said that he sought to identify "the aspirations of Africa with the aspirations of the United States." In Nairobi in June Secretary of Defense Donald Rumsfeld promised military aid in the form of 12 F-5 fighter planes to offset Soviet weapons in Somalia and Uganda.

JAY E. HAKES
University of New Orleans

Official Name: Republic of Kenya.
Location: East coast of Africa.
Area: 244,959 square miles (582,644 km²).
Population (1976 est.): 13,800,000.
Chief Cities (1973 est.): Nairobi, the capital, 630,000; Mombasa, 300,000.
Government: *Head of state and government,* Jomo Kenyatta, president (took office Dec. 1964). *Legislature* (unicameral)—National Assembly.
Monetary Unit: Kenya shilling (8.37 shillings equal U. S. $1, Sept. 1976).
Gross National Product (1975 est.): $2,800,000,000.
Manufacturing (major products): Construction materials, processed agricultural products, petroleum products.
Major Agricultural Products: Coffee, tea, sugarcane, sisal, corn, cassava, pyrethrum, fruits, livestock.
Foreign Trade (1975): *Exports,* $494,000,000; *imports,* $938,000,000.

KOREA

Two Americans were slain in August by North Korean guards at Panmunjom in a tree-trimming incident, a harsh reminder that Korea remains a most dangerous spot. After fruitless Red Cross talks, the two Koreas were again unable to reopen political dialogue. Both were braced for an uncertain 1977, South Korea because of its shadowy, influence-peddling scandals in Washington and North Korea because of economic tensions.

SOUTH KOREA

Economy. An export boom brought an impressive performance. A 50% increase in exports over 1975 plus good invisible transactions more than halved deficits in international balance of payments from an original estimate of $1,000,000,000. Gross National Product (GNP) growth soared 15% (8.3% in 1975). Per capita GNP was estimated at $690, up 30% over 1975. Foreign exchange reserves were $2,400,000,000 (predicted to be $1,500,000,000).

Seoul became a world-class overseas builder with $2,300,000,000 in contracts, mostly from the Middle East. Continued vigilance was dictated by heavy dependence on foreign resources in 1976: crude oil import cost $1,600,000,000; foreign loan repayments, $971 million (forecast for 1977: $1,340,000,000); and grain imports nearly $700 million. In 1975, 58% of imports were of raw materials. The discovery of oil announced in January proved untrue. In June, the government announced an outline of the 4th economic plan (1971–81) calling for average annual growth of 9%, a per capita GNP of $1,284 by 1981, and an inflow of $10,000,000,000 in foreign capital.

Politics and Repression. By year-end, the culture of silence was pervasive. In March, a group of dissidents issued a "Declaration on Democracy and National Salvation" urging President Park Chung Hee to resign, revoke his repressive constitution, and restore democratic rights. Eighteen persons charged with plotting to overthrow the government—a former presi-

UPI
Seoul policemen check the hair length of two young men. There is a ban against long hair in South Korea.

dent, an opposition leader who narrowly lost to Park in the 1971 election, a Quaker leader, a former foreign minister, and 14 other prominent patriots—were sentenced to 2 to 8 years in jail in August. The government described them as "a threat to national security."

Among other developments: 460 college professors were fired in March, 345 for political reasons. In July, Park claimed that the ideals of democracy enunciated in 1948 were brought closer to "concrete fulfillment for the first time today" under his constitutional system. In September, infighting within the moribund opposition New Democratic Party led to Lee Chol-sung's election as party leader. He pledged a dialogue with Park in lieu of his predecessor's "all or nothing" stance.

Defense and Foreign Relations. The government said that by 1978 it should be able to stop an invasion from the north "unaided" if its defense buildup continued on schedule. In June, it was reported in Japan that Seoul could make atomic bombs and acquire delivery technology by 1981. In external affairs, Seoul supported a renewed U. S. call for a four-nation (United States, China, North and South Korea) conference on Korea; Pyongyang insisted on "direct" talks with the United States.

As the year ended, Seoul appeared uneasy because of President-elect Jimmy Carter's campaign promise to phase out U. S. forces from the south and also because of an exposé of a South Korean lobby, which, masterminded by the Korean Central Intelligence Agency, sought to win U. S. Congressional support of Park's regime by "buying off" a number of Congressmen.

—— **SOUTH KOREA · Information Highlights** ——

Official Name: Republic of Korea.
Location: Northeastern Asia.
Area: 38,022 square miles (98,477 km²).
Population (1976 est.): 35,875,000.
Chief Cities (1976 est.): Seoul, the capital, 7,010,000; Pusan, 2,500,000.
Government: *Head of state,* Park Chung Hee, president (since December 1963). *Head of government,* Choi Kyu Hah, prime minister (took office December 1975). *Legislature* (unicameral)—National Assembly.
Monetary Unit: Won (484 won equal U. S.$1, Nov. 1976).
Gross National Product (1976 est.): $24,753,750,000.
Manufacturing (major products): Textiles, electronic equipment, petrochemicals, clothing, plywood, hair products, processed foods, metal products, furniture, ships.
Major Agricultural Products: Rice, barley, wheat, soybeans, sweet potatoes and yams, fish.
Foreign Trade (1976): *Exports,* $7,700,000,000; *imports,* $8,800,000,000.

U. S. Rear Adm. Mark Frudden, chief delegate of the United Nations Command, and North Korean representatives discuss the killing of two U. S. officers during an incident at Panmunjom. Subsequently, the Joint Security Area of Panmunjom was partitioned.

UPI

NORTH KOREA

Economy. Performance was sluggish because of the lingering effects of the oil crisis of 1973 and the ensuing collapse of markets for North Korean ferrous and nonferrous metals. Pyongyang's unfamiliarity with Western business practices and heavy defense spending exacerbated the problem. In 1975, Pyongyang defaulted on loan repayments to Western and Japanese creditors; in 1976, North Korea failed to meet payments on rescheduled debts. Its foreign debts (including those from communist block nations) were estimated at $1,500,000,000. An intensified economy drive was launched in January coupled with efforts to attain admittedly "unfulfilled" goals of the 6th year plan (1971–76). The plan had been declared completed in 1975 ahead of schedule.

In January, a Chinese-Korean oil pipeline was opened. Grain output in 1975 was placed at 7.7 million tons. In March, a "recent" discovery of coal, nonferrous, and precious metal deposits was announced. All nursery schools and kindergartens were said to be supported by state and public expenses beginning in June.

Politics. Foreign reports on a "succession crisis" in Pyongyang were speculative and overstated. President Kim Il Sung was active as a balancer among party ideologues, technocrats, and generals. His son, Chong Il, had yet to earn trust from senior Kim and other party elders; apparently, Kim Chong Il was not as yet a member of the party central committee. The ruling Korean Workers Party's members were officially numbered at two million in August 1976.

Defense and Foreign Relations. Defense outlays for 1977 were 16.5% of the budget. In March, Kim stated his intention not to have nuclear weapons or to ask for a foreign nuclear umbrella. He admitted that North Korea did not have enough money to make these weapons nor the place to test them anywhere in the north. His government took part in the nonaligned summit at Colombo in August.

When the North Korean killing of two American officers in August was met by a show of U. S. military power in and around Korea, Kim unprecedentedly expressed his regret to the United States, which termed his message "a positive step." After the incident, North Korea and the U. S.-led United Nations Command partitioned the Joint Security Area of Panmunjom into north and south. Military personnel from either side were banned from crossing the dividing line without prior consultation, but unarmed work crews, tourists, and journalists were permitted freedom of movement. In July, North Korea had reportedly established, apart from its 12-mile territorial waters, a 50-mile "security zone" off its shores.

Another showdown in the UN on Korea was averted in September. North Korea withdrew its draft resolution (similar to the one adopted in 1975), saying that it is the "will of many UN member states" not to have the Korean question debated this year. In October, North Korean diplomats in Scandinavian countries were charged with smuggling and black marketing and were declared *persona non grata*. Pyongyang denied the charges and declared that they were instigated by South Korea.

RINN-SUP SHINN
The American University

––––– **NORTH KOREA • Information Highlights** –––––

Official Name: Democratic People's Republic of Korea.
Location: Northeastern Asia.
Area: 46,540 square miles (120,533 km²).
Population (1976 est.): 17,008,000.
Chief Cities (1976 est.): Pyongyang, the capital, 1,300,-000; Chongjin, 322,500.
Government: *Head of state,* Kim Il Sung, president (nominally since December 1972; actually in power since May 1948). *Head of government,* Pak Song Chol, premier (took office April 1976). *Legislature* (unicameral)—Supreme People's Assembly. *The Korean Workers (Communist)* Party: General secretary, Kim Il Sung (since May 1948).
Monetary Unit: Won (1.03 won equal U. S.$1, Dec. 1975).
Gross National Product (1975 est.): $7,000,000,000.
Manufacturing (major products): Cement, metallurgical coke, pig iron and ferroalloys, textiles.
Major Agricultural Products: Rice, sweet potatoes, barley, soybeans, corn, livestock, fish.
Foreign Trade (1975 est.): *Exports,* $762,000,000; *imports,* $1,082,000,000.

Striking United Rubber workers and their supporters march down Main Street in Akron, Ohio. Some 60,000 employees at the "Big Four" U. S. rubber companies staged one of the longest walkouts of the year.

UPI

LABOR

Gains and setbacks marked the 1976 labor picture in most industrialized countries of the world. For much of the year there was refreshing economic progress, then came a depressing pause. Economic indicators reached a plateau, or trended downward, and labor in many sectors had to pull in its horns.

U. S. Developments. In the United States, the official unemployment rate declined during the first half of the year, then edged upward, hitting 8.1% in November. That was almost one percentage point below a year earlier, but substantially above the "less than 7%" predicted by Ford administration economists.

On the other side of the coin, the advance in living costs moderated. The Labor Department's consumer price index in October stood 5.3% above a year earlier. That was considerably below the double-digit inflation of 1974, and down from the 7% to 8% level of 1975. However, the wholesale price index jumped 0.9% in September and another 0.6% in October, presaging a new rise in the retail index.

In October, "real spendable weekly earnings"—calculated by subtracting from average earnings typical tax withholdings and adjusting this take-home pay for rises in living costs—was 0.4% below October 1975 and 6% below the peak reached by workers in October 1972.

Major collective bargaining settlements, those covering plants with 1,000 workers or more, had been expected to rise sharply in 1976 as the economy recovered, but they averaged less than in 1975, a depressed year. During the first nine months of 1976 these settlements produced wage increases of approximately 7% over the average 31.3 months' life of the contracts, down from 7.8% in 1975. As usual, these contracts were "front loaded," with average 8.9% increases in the first year, down from 10.2% in 1975.

Also, during the first nine months, all wages rose at an annual rate of 7.9%, compared with 9.5% in the corresponding 1975 period. These percentages incorporated new settlements as well as deferred increases and cost of living adjustments, the Labor Department reported.

The third quarter showed a slight bulge in average wage increases largely because of outsized settlements secured by the United Rubber Workers for 60,000 employees at the "Big Four" rubber companies, following strikes that lasted from 130 to over 140 days. These settlements were estimated at 36% over a three-year period, and included "catch-up" raises to offset the absence of a cost-of-living escalator clause in the previous three-year contracts.

One other large-scale strike of the year was that of the United Automobile Workers at Ford Motors, involving 165,000 employees. This lasted for a month at some plants, longer at others where additional time was required to settle local issues. In this dispute the UAW had placed more stress on winning shorter work hours than on wages. The final settlement yielded an additional 13 days off with pay annually —six in the second year of the three-year contract, seven more in the third year. Some UAW officials pictured this gain as a start toward an eventual four-day week, and said it would help halt the decline in auto industry jobs.

Wage increases in the settlement were de-

UPI

Lloyd McBride, the hand-picked candidate to succeed I. W. Abel in 1977 as leader of the United Steel Workers, meets with supporters at annual convention.

scribed as moderate—roughly 4% a year for production workers, more for skilled tradesmen, plus cost-of-living adjustments. Assuming a 6% annual inflation rate, the pact was expected to yield 27% in pay boosts over three years. GM and Chrysler settled on a similar basis.

Construction workers, usually in the forefront of the wage increase parade, trailed in 1976. Faced with heavy unemployment in the building industry, and by the escalation of non-union contractors, the building trades unions made modest settlements in most areas. In some cases, they signed contracts simply for relaxation of restrictive work rules.

For employees in the public sector, 1976 was also a bad year. Many cities, counties, and states found themselves in financial straits, and took a tougher than usual position in negotiations. Most public sector unions ended up with sparse wage settlements, and in some cases waived pay increases in order to avert layoffs.

In the industrial sector, working time lost by strikes was somewhat above 1975, but that was due in large part to the long stoppages by rubber and auto workers. In construction, strikes were down an estimated 50%.

A continued rise in Employee Stock Ownership Plans (ESOP's) was reported. A Washington attorney specializing in these plans estimated that 600 to 800 firms have now embodied them in whole or in part. The ESOP's have been spurred by congressional legislation that grants tax incentives to corporations setting up such plans and allocating stock to employees through worker stock ownership trusts. The labor movement has been cool to the idea.

Unionization among professional employees, such as teachers, doctors, nurses, and others, kept rising. It was estimated that 40% of such employees are now covered by collective bargaining agreements, compared with 25% in the labor force as a whole.

Organized labor also hailed a victory on the political front—that is, the election of the Jimmy Carter-Walter F. Mondale ticket. Labor conducted a big get-out-the-vote drive.

International Developments. Ferment marked the labor field in various nations outside the United States.

Canada. A major development of the year was the struggle by the Canadian Labour Congress against the wage curbs contained in the anti-inflation controls enacted in late 1975. The struggle culminated in a National Day of Protest on October 14, the first anniversary of the controls. The CLC had hoped to achieve the equivalent of a 24-hour general strike, but fell short of that goal. However, the CLC claimed that over a million of its 2.2 million members quit work for the day, making it the biggest labor demonstration in Canada's history.

Meanwhile, the government claimed success for the first year of the controls. The federal Anti Inflation Board reported that it had reduced negotiated wage increases by an average of 3.5% to bring the raises below the 10% maximum set by the controls, down from an average of 18% in 1975. Some of these reductions precipitated short-lived strikes.

Also, the government asserted that price boosts had been restrained, with the consumer price index registering a rise of 6.5% for the year, down sharply from a 10.6% rate. However, as in other countries, the pace of Canadian economic recovery, robust early in the year, slipped in the last half.

The unemployment rate stayed above 7%, reaching 7.3% in September, and higher in the winter months. Unit labor costs in Canada, including wages and fringes, were reported to have risen above the U. S. level by 13 cents an hour.

Japan. Through much of 1976 the Japanese economy moved toward recovery from the 1975 recession. However, industrial production fell in the August-October period, and the government announced a program of loans and other incentives to overcome the pause and to spur industrial expansion and housing construction.

The inflation rate, as measured by consumer prices, eased to 9% at midyear compared with 11% in 1975, but in the latter half prices began mounting and double-digit inflation was expected by year-end. The surge was blamed in part on poor weather that hurt vegetable production and a typhoon that cut rice output.

Moderate wage settlements reached during the junto, or spring "wage offensive" conducted by unions, helped to slow the inflation rate in the first half. Generally, unions settled for pay increases of about 9%, compared with 13% in the spring of 1975 and a whopping 33% in 1974. However, traditional summer bonuses were about 3% higher than in 1975.

The modest 9% wage settlements were reached on the basis of government promises to try to stabilize commodity prices and management promises to attempt to stabilize employment. Concern was voiced that failure to fulfill the promises could spark new labor unrest.

During the spring wage offensive, there were paralyzing strikes of up to two days on the railroads and other transport facilities; also in communications, mining, and other sectors. Some of these strikes, in government-owned facilities, were illegal, and resulted in employee dismissals or other penalties.

Japan's unemployment rate was officially estimated at a little over 2%, compared with a low of 1% in recent years. A big reason for Japan's low jobless rate is that under the tradition of "lifetime employment", many industries retain full forces during an economic downturn rather than lay off employees.

Latin America. Inflation, currency devaluation, military rule, joblessness, economic woes, and restrictions on labor dominated many nations of Latin America during 1976.

A military junta that toppled the regime of Mrs. Isabel Perón in March, imposed wage-price controls, barred strikes, and named "intervenors" to take over much of the union movement in Argentina. Several thousand local union activists were dismissed from their jobs. Inflation, running at a rate of up to 40% a month prior to the takeover, was trimmed to a range of 3 to 11% a month. Meanwhile, the controls and other austerity measures slowed the economy to recession levels. In response, the regime eased price controls to spur business and industry, but retained most wage curbs. As a result, "real" wages, in terms of purchasing power, fell.

Three successive devaluations of the Mexican peso—which cut its value in terms of U. S. currency by over 50%—disrupted price and wage relationships. Prices soared on many items following the first devaluation, and organized labor threatened strikes in late September for wage increases to offset the price jumps. The strikes were averted by pay raises of 16 to 23%.

In Chile austerity programs by the military regime reduced raging inflation. Wage increases were allowed in partial adjustment to prices. Chile's economy, hard-hit by earlier plunges in copper prices, brightened as those prices began rising again. Unemployment remained high—15% nationally.

Peru's military junta devalued currency 44% in July. Also, it began returning some nationalized industries to private ownership, while retaining provisions for workers sharing in ownership and decision making. Steep inflation and unemployment led to brief rioting in July and the government imposed a state of emergency. Strikes were banned and left-wing union leaders were arrested.

Strikes flared at Bolivia's government-owned mines in June. In the violence that followed seven persons died. The miners demanded 100% raises, but settled for 17 to 30% after many union leaders were arrested.

Efforts of Brazil's government to prod a lagging economy in late 1975 and early 1976 sparked a rise in inflation. The government then reversed course and put on the brakes. Nonetheless, a 50% inflation rate for 1976 was anticipated, compared with 30% in 1975.

Western Europe. Economic recovery during the early part of the year spurred inflationary trends, and most governments then reversed course and pressed deflationary measures which slowed down growth in the latter half of 1976.

A "social contract" between the British labor movement and the Labour government, designed

UPI

Striking members of the Canadian Press Wireservice convince Prime Minister Trudeau not to cross their picket line to hold a press conference.

to rein in wage-price increases, had substantial success for much of the year. The inflation rate was reduced from over 27% in 1975 to about half that rate. Strikes fell by 60%. However, plunges in the pound's value late in the year and consequent rising prices of imports jeopardized continuation of the "social contract."

As in past years, brief strikes marked the year in Italy. Some of them paralyzed transportation, business, and production from 2 to 24 hours at a time. As the inflation rate approached 20%, the government in October initiated austerity measures, including ceilings on salary increases, and boosts in utility and gasoline rates in order to reduce consumption. Protest strikes multiplied.

Efforts by the French government to limit wage increases, as part of an anti-inflationary program, stirred a rash of strikes, including a massive one in Paris in October that brought out 500,000 workers for six hours.

As heretofore, West Germany was a bright spot, compared with the rest of Europe. Its inflation rate dipped to 4% in the third quarter, the lowest in five years. The unemployment rate registered 4.3% in November, one of the lowest in Europe. Wage settlements were generally below 6%. Under a new law, labor representation on the supervisory boards of large industries rose from a third to half, but with the chairman chosen by the employer side.

Growth of free trade unionism continued in Spain and Portugal. Both countries struggled to hold down inflation and unemployment.

RUBEN LEVIN, *Editor, "Labor" Newspaper*

LAOS

Laos' first year as a "democratic republic" was tough, with severe food shortages causing growing disillusionment with the new Communist regime. Major aid from the government's main foreign friends—the Soviet Union, Vietnam, and, to a lesser extent, China—was necessary to head off starvation and to prevent the economy from collapsing. Politically, the country's leadership was not seriously challenged.

Politics. The "People's Democratic Republic of Laos," which came into being with King Savang Vattana's abdication in December 1975, turned out to be a fairly mild revolutionary regime in its first 12 months. No executions of former leaders were reported, and Prince Souvanna Phouma (premier in a coalition government until late 1975) was permitted to live in modestly comfortable retirement. Many onetime politicians, bureaucrats, and army officers, however, were taken off to a political re-education center at Viengsay, the former headquarters of the once insurgent Pathet Lao.

Top figure in the young regime was Kaysone Phoumvihan, who held both the prime ministership and the strategic post of secretary-general of the ruling Lao People's Revolutionary Party.

The premier, however, is half-Vietnamese and is reportedly regarded as too pro-Hanoi. Leaflets were circulated in Vientiane criticizing him for his partiality toward Vietnam—which still had 30,000 troops in Laos. Minister of Interior Somsume Kamphithoune, rarely seen and not widely known personally, was probably the second most important politician and reportedly the most radical. He had control of the national police. Prince Souphanouvong, titular head of the Pathet Lao in the insurgency years and half-brother of Souvanna Phouma, as president of the republic succeeded to the king's role as chief of state, but his political importance was limited.

The government's control did not extend throughout the countryside. Skirmishes with small opposition bands continued but diminished steadily in importance.

Economy. The government's economic aim was self-sufficiency, but the leadership's inexperience in economic affairs (and the flight of many persons with knowledge or competency) made its task a difficult one. Most peasants raised most of what they ate, but the residents of Vientiane experienced a severe meat shortage and had difficulty in obtaining even vegetables until the government changed some of its policies at midyear. Prices were high and rose steadily throughout the year.

More than one third of the shops closed down, their operators having fled abroad. Timber production, the nation's chief export, was down 80%. New *kip* notes were introduced, with an official exchange rate of 60 to U.S.$1.

Foreign Relations. The Soviet Union and Vietnam shipped large amounts of relief supplies in the first half of the year. The U.S.S.R., whose embassy staff officially numbered 230 (but was probably closer to 500), delivered 8,000 tons of desperately needed petroleum products. Moscow also agreed to a 50-year, $40 million interest-free loan to Laos.

Premier Kaysone Phoumvihan visited Moscow, Hanoi, and Peking. China provided relief rice and an interest-free loan. U.S.-Laotian relations were surprisingly good.

RICHARD BUTWELL
State University of New York College at Fredonia

LAOS • Information Highlights

Official Name: People's Democratic Republic of Laos.
Location: Southeast Asia.
Area: 91,429 square miles (236,800 km²).
Population (1976 est.): 3,400,000.
Chief Cities (1973 census): Vientiane, the capital, 177,000; Savannakhet, 51,000.
Government: *Head of state,* Prince Souphanouvong, president. *Head of government,* Kaysone Phoumvihan, prime minister. *Legislature* (unicameral)—National Assembly.
Monetary Unit: Kip (60 kips equal U.S.$1, Nov. 1976).
Gross National Product (1972 est.): $211,000,000.
Manufacturing (major products): Cigarettes, textiles.
Major Agricultural Products: Rice, corn, coffee, cotton, tobacco, cardamom, vegetables, forest products.
Foreign Trade (1974): *Exports,* $11,000,000; *imports,* $65,000,000.

LATIN AMERICA

The rightward march in Latin America continued in 1976 as Argentina fell under a military dictatorship, the Peruvian government cracked down on leftists, the new president of Mexico made overtures to the country's business community, and the voters of Barbados replaced a moderately nationalist government with a more conservative one. In Ecuador and Uruguay the military changed presidents and raised the possibility of a return to civilian rule at some future date. Cuba's success in the war in Angola frightened some Latin American governments and slowed the trend toward normalization of relations between the Communist island and other nations of the hemisphere. Economic troubles were reflected in the resumption of spiraling inflation in Brazil and drastic currency devaluations in Mexico and Peru.

Economic Associations. A sharp drop in the world market price of sugar, from 65¢ a pound ($1.43 per kg) in 1974 to less than 8¢ (18¢ per kg) in 1976, posed problems for Latin American producers, especially Cuba and the English-speaking islands that make up the Caribbean Common Market (CARICOM). Cuba was forced to revise its current five-year development plan, while CARICOM, already rent by squabbling between Jamaica and Trinidad and Tobago, did little to promote area development and economic integration during the year. Prospects for a revival of the Central American Common Market (CACOM) improved as Honduras and El Salvador, after a brief flare-up of fighting in July, moved closer toward settling their border dispute, which has disrupted CACOM since 1969.

Dissension among the Andean Pact countries —Venezuela, Colombia, Ecuador, Peru, Bolivia, and Chile—continued in 1976 as Chile virtually withdrew from the group. At issue was Chile's refusal to adhere to the pact's restrictions on foreign investment. Venezuela, the last member to join the group, seemed the most committed to making it work. Venezuelan President Carlos Andrés Pérez insisted that the pact's restrictions did not seriously limit the inflow of needed foreign capital. He was determined to prevent further defections and to preserve the group as a building block for the Latin American Economic System (LAES), which he and outgoing President Luis Echeverría of Mexico took the lead in promoting, and which 25 nations formally subscribed to in 1975. Little was done in 1976 to implement the LAES treaty.

Relations with the United States. U. S. Secretary of State Henry Kissinger, on a visit to Latin America in February, assured his hosts that Washington had no objection to LAES or any other regional groupings as long as they were not "used for confrontation" with the United States. Kissinger asked for more cooperation from his Latin American colleagues

UPI

Chile's President Pinochet (*center*) and the U. S. and Brazilian foreign ministers attend OAS conference.

and, for his part, promised to work to end U. S tariff discrimination against Venezuela and Ecuador. Kissinger also pledged to seek an early resolution of the Panama Canal question. But as the proposed canal treaty became a major issue in the campaign for the Republican presidential nomination in the United States, Washington suspended negotiations on the treaty. Talks were resumed after President Ford won the Republican nomination and Democratic nominee Jimmy Carter declined to take up the canal issue.

Some Spanish-American nations were disturbed when Kissinger signed an agreement with Brazil providing for twice-yearly consultations on the foreign-minister level between Brazil and the United States. This was seen as confirmation of the fears of many that the United States favored Brazilian hegemony on the South American continent. Increased U. S. economic aid to the rightist military dictatorship in Chile was also a source of concern to the few remaining civilian governments in Latin America. U. S. Secretary of the Treasury William Simon, on a visit to Santiago in May, responded to these concerns by warning the government of Gen. Augusto Pinochet that no more aid would be forthcoming unless the Chileans did a better job of safeguarding human rights.

The O. A. S. and Chile. The General Assembly of the Organization of American States met as scheduled in Santiago, Chile, in June. But other than lending some respectability to the Pinochet regime, it accomplished little. Only Mexico boycotted the session to protest the repressive policies of the host government. The rightward trend in the hemisphere in 1976 was putting an end to Chile's outcast status. The new military dictator of Argentina, Gen. Jorge Videla, visited Chile in November, becoming the first chief of state of a major Latin American nation to do so since the Chilean coup of 1973.

Terrorism. A rising tide of left and right terrorism, together with strikes and student demonstrations, preceded the overthrow of President

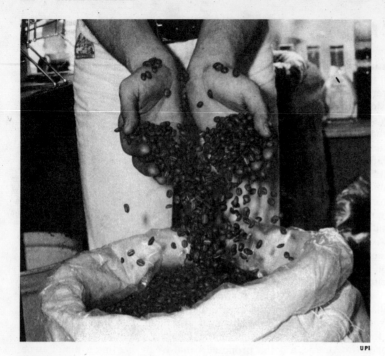

Coffee, a major product of such Latin American nations as Brazil and Colombia, was a valuable commodity during 1976. In the year ending March 31, global coffee shipments were the third highest on record.

UPI

Isabel Perón of Argentina in March. The military coup was conducted with great precision; President Perón and her principal collaborators were quickly rounded up and placed under arrest, and Gen. Jorge Videla was installed as president.

With the military firmly in control of the government, the army campaign against leftist guerrilla bands, in both rural and urban areas, was pursued with renewed vigor. Little, however, was done to curb rightwing terrorists, particularly the Argentine Anti-Communist Alliance (AAA), which continued to kidnap, murder, and torture suspected leftists, including many foreigners who had sought political refuge in Argentina during the Perón administration.

The AAA inspired a similar organization, the Anti-Communist Alliance of Brazil (AAB). The AAB in 1976 reintroduced terrorism to the cities of Brazil, which had been relatively quiet since the crushing of Marxist urban guerrillas in the early 1970's. While the AAB campaign did not attain the murderous intensity of its Argentine counterpart, its bomb blasts and physical assaults on suspected leftists were matters of concern for the moderate government of President Ernesto Geisel, whom the terrorists denounced as soft on Communists. Backed by disgruntled military men, the AAB sought to create a climate of disorder that would compel Geisel to cancel the November municipal elections or, perhaps, force his resignation. The elections, however, were held on schedule, and at the end of the year the greatest threat to the stability of the Brazilian regime seemed to come not from the AAB, but from a business slowdown coupled with a rate of inflation approaching 50%.

The effects of rightwing terrorism was felt in the Caribbean area and in the United States in 1976. In April two Cuban fishing boats were attacked in international waters by Cuban exiles apparently based in the United States; one fisherman was killed. Cuban Prime Minister Fidel Castro threatened to terminate his 1973 antihijacking agreement with the United States if it continued to allow U. S.-based terrorists to prey on Cuban vessels. The U. S. government launched an investigation but refused to condemn the attacks publicly. In October, after a terrorist bomb caused the crash of a Cuban airliner, killing all 73 persons aboard, Castro invoked the cancellation clause of the agreement.

Responsibility for bombing the airliner, which had taken off from Barbados on a flight between Venezuela and Cuba, was claimed by a Cuban exile group in Miami. Authorities in Barbados and Venezuela determined that the bomb had been placed on the plane by two Cuban exiles who boarded the flight in Trinidad and left it in Barbados. Venezuelan President Carlos Andrés Pérez denounced the atrocity and expressed his sympathy to Castro and the Cuban people for their loss. He promised a vigorous campaign against Cuban-exile terrorists in Venezuela, even though some suspects were naturalized Venezuelan citizens holding government jobs and a few had been associated with Pérez when he was fighting Cuban Communist subversion in the early 1960's as a member of the administration of Rómulo Betancourt. Earlier in the year Pérez had provided a burial place in Venezuela for Orlando Letelier, foreign minister of Chile under the Allende government, who was murdered in the United States, probably by Cuban exiles.

While President Pérez warmed up to Fidel Castro and Prime Minister Forbes Burnham of Guyana remained a staunch friend throughout 1976, Prime Minister Errol Barrow's government in Barbados, under U. S. pressure, put an end to the refueling there of Cuban military aircraft bound for Angola. Later, elections were held in Barbados, and Barrow was replaced as prime minister by the more conservative Tom Adams. Cuba, with its continued support for the independence and territorial integrity of Belize (British Honduras), in the face of Guatemalan claims, won no new friends among the governments of Central America, which backed Guatemala; after Cuba's Angolan victory, they feared that Belize might ask the protection of Cuban troops upon Britain's withdrawal.

Other Political Developments. In June the military ousted Juan María Bordaberry from the presidency of Uruguay and in September replaced him with another figurehead civilian, 72-year-old Dr. Aparicio Méndez. President Méndez promptly signed decrees formally depriving several thousand prominent Uruguayans of their political rights. The new administration claimed to be preparing the country for a return to constitutional rule in 1984.

In Peru, President Francisco Morales Bermúdez imposed tough economic stabilization measures, including wage freezes and a 31% currency devaluation. An attempt by some of his military colleagues to overthrow him in July gave Morales an excuse to place the country under martial law and crack down on leftists, who had nothing to do with the coup attempt.

Gen. Guillermo Rodríguez Lara was quietly deposed as president of Ecuador in January and replaced by a three-man military junta. The junta declared a general amnesty, promised a return to civilian rule by 1978, threatened to nationalize the holdings of Gulf Oil Corporation, and expelled a number of liberal Roman Catholic clergymen from the country.

Strikes, demonstrations, guerrilla activity, and military unrest plagued Colombia during 1976. Toward the end of the year a proclamation of a modified martial law, together with public fascination with a visit by King Juan Carlos of Spain, had the effect of cooling the civil disorder. The king also visited Venezuela and the Dominican Republic.

Before stepping down as president of Mexico at the end of his six-year term in December, Luis Echeverría decreed a devaluation of the peso by 39%, the first since 1954. His elected successor, José López Portillo, sought to overcome his own anti-business image and reassure investors that there would be an important and profitable role for private capital in Mexico under his administration. Echeverría, before leaving the presidency of Mexico, announced that he was a candidate for secretary general of the United Nations.

Natural Disasters. A severe earthquake struck Central America in February. While Honduras and El Salvador suffered some damage, the hardest hit was Guatemala, where as many as 22,000 people perished, mostly in rural areas. In September a Pacific hurricane came ashore in northwestern Mexico—a relatively rare occurrence—destroying property, disrupting communications, and killing more than 1,000 persons.

NEILL MACAULAY
University of Florida

UPI

In October a Brazilian policeman scuffles with a youth as customers wait to receive a rationed supply of black beans, a Brazilian staple. The government was forced to import the item from Chile.

In his first year on the U. S. Supreme Court, John P. Stevens (top, right) usually took an unpredictable but moderately conservative position. Other members of the court were (left to right, bottom): Justices White, Brennan, Burger, Stewart, Marshall; (top), Rehnquist, Blackmun, and Powell.

UPI

LAW

Events in law during 1976 included the active participation in U. S. Supreme Court deliberations of the newly sworn Justice John Paul Stevens and the court's affirmation of the constitutionality of capital punishment. Other legal developments are reviewed in the special feature on International Waters (page 50).

U. S. Supreme Court

The retirement of Justice William O. Douglas, the Supreme Court's most noted liberal, early in the 1975–76 term confirmed the increasingly conservative character of the present court. Particularly in the field of criminal punishment was the erosion of Warren court standards evident. The Burger court upheld capital punishment, limited federal habeas corpus proceedings, relaxed search and seizure restrictions on the police, made private papers and tax records subject to government subpoena, narrowed the famous *Miranda* rules, expanded powers of arrest, and limited access to federal courts to protect civil rights.

But the record was not entirely one-sided, as indicated by the fact that the court's most conservative member, Justice William H. Rehnquist, felt forced to dissent in 33 cases. While the court restrained school desegregation orders, it also held that private schools cannot deny access to black students. It did not retreat from its controversial 1973 abortion decisions, and

gag orders limiting press accounts of criminal trials were declared unconstitutional.

John Paul Stevens, a member of the Court of Appeals for the Seventh Circuit, was appointed by President Ford to succeed Douglas. He participated in only half of the term's decisions, yet registered 21 dissents. Taking an unpredictable but moderately conservative position, he tended to join with Potter Stewart and Lewis F. Powell in the court's center. William J. Brennan and Thurgood Marshall, the two remaining liberals, were in frequent and sometimes bitter opposition to the court majority, dissenting 58 and 53 times, respectively. Chief Justice Warren Burger recorded 15 dissents, Stewart 24, Byron White 22, Harry Blackmun 17, and Powell only 7. The court handed down 138 signed opinions, of which 50 (36%) were unanimous. The court also issued 37 per curiam opinions, 23 of them unanimous.

Criminal Prosecutions. After the court declared the death penalty unconstitutional in *Furman* v. *Georgia* (1972), it was widely assumed that revised statutes, eliminating the unpredictability and random imposition of the penalty to which the court had objected, would be constitutional, and 35 states adopted new death penalty laws. This evidence of "society's endorsement of the death penalty for murder" influenced the court, which ruled (7–2) in *Gregg* v. *Georgia* that the death penalty was not inherently cruel and unusual. The opinion also stressed improved procedures in the Georgia law, reducing the arbitrariness and possible racial prejudice condemned in *Furman.* Comparable Texas and Florida statutes were also upheld. But some states had eliminated all flexibility in their statutes and provided for mandatory death sentences for specific crimes. Thus, by vote of 5–4, the North Carolina, Louisiana, and Oklahoma laws were voided as "unduly harsh and unworkably rigid" (*Woodson* v. *North Carolina, Roberts* v. *Louisiana*).

Two major goals of Chief Justice Burger have been to limit habeas corpus review of state criminal convictions in federal courts and to end the exclusionary rule which forbids the use in court of evidence secured illegally. These concerns were combined in *Stone* v. *Powell,* in which the court held (6–3) that collateral attacks on state convictions through federal habeas corpus would no longer be permitted if the only challenge to the conviction was that evidence had been illegally secured. However, state courts were still obligated to enforce the exclusionary rule. Habeas corpus relief was also limited in *Francis* v. *Henderson,* which held that a defendant who failed to challenge the exclusion of blacks from the grand jury that indicted him, forfeited his right to make that challenge on habeas corpus.

The Warren Court's *Miranda* rules were held not to extend to witnesses before grand juries, even though they were criminal suspects (*United States* v. *Mandujano*), and *Michigan* v. *Mosley* gave police permission to resume inter-

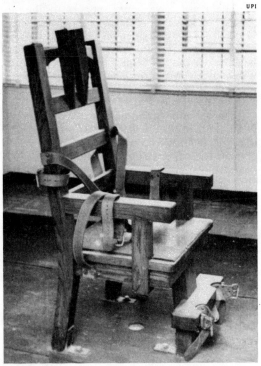

At the Raiford Prison in Florida, the electric chair was last used in 1964. In July 1976, the U.S. Supreme Court upheld the constitutionality of capital punishment.

UPI

rogation of a suspect after he had once exercised his right to remain silent. But *Doyle* v. *Ohio* held that if a suspect claimed his *Miranda* right during police questioning at the time of arrest, his silence could not be used to discredit his subsequent testimony on the witness stand.

Effectively reversing an 1886 decision protecting private papers and records under the Fourth and Fifth Amendments, the court held personal bank and tax records subject to subpoena by the government (*United States* v. *Miller, Fisher* v. *United States*). The court also sanctioned the use as evidence of material obtained in a warrantless search of an auto glove compartment while the car was impounded for parking violations (*South Dakota* v. *Opperman*).

Equal Protection. The principal racial discrimination case was *Runyon* v. *McCrary,* holding that refusal by private schools to admit qualified black children violated the Civil Rights Act of 1866. The same statute was applied to prohibit discrimination in private employment against whites as well as blacks (*McDonald* v. *Santa Fe Trail Transportation Co.*).

The court upheld a job qualification test given to applicants for the District of Columbia police which excluded a disproportionate number of blacks, because there was no intentional discrimination (*Washington* v. *Davis*). The court declined to hear a similar charge against the Georgia bar examination by blacks (*Tyler* v. *Vickey*).

In spite of the violence attending school integration in Boston and President Ford's pressure on the Justice Department to enter the case, the court declined to review Judge W. Arthur Garrity's busing orders (*White* v. *Morgan*). But the court did reverse a desegregation order in Pasadena, ruling that judges cannot require school authorities to readjust attendance zones each year to keep up with population shifts (*Pasadena Board of Education* v. *Spangler*).

A lower court finding that the Philadelphia police had systematically abused blacks and ordering remedial action was reversed by the court, which held that federal judges should not interfere with the internal operations of local police departments (*Rizzo* v. *Goode*).

An unusual number of cases concerned rights of aliens. The court held that resident aliens can be excluded from jury service (*Perkins* v. *Smith*) and upheld a California law making it a crime for employers to hire illegal aliens (*DeCanas* v. *Bica*) but invalidated a century-old Civil Service Commission regulation barring aliens from government employment (*Hampton* v. *Mow Sun Wong*).

Discrimination on the basis of age was sanctioned in two cases—a Louisiana law requiring all state employees to retire on their 65th birthday (*Cannon* v. *Guste*) and a Massachusetts law obliging state police to retire at 50 (*Massachusetts Board of Retirement* v. *Murgia*). The court also upheld a city ordinance requiring municipal employees to live within the city boundaries (*McCarthy* v. *Philadelphia Civil Service Commission*).

First Amendment Rights. A major decision by the court upheld the limits on campaign contributions imposed by the Election Campaign Act of 1974 and approved public funding of presidential campaigns, but the act's spending limits were found to violate the First Amendment guarantee of free expression (*Buckley* v. *Valeo*).

Major provisions of New York's fair campaign code, which forbade racial attacks in election campaigns, were invalidated as too broad and having a chilling effect on free speech (*Schwartz* v. *Vanasco*). *Elrod* v. *Burns* held that patronage dismissal of public employees because they belonged to the wrong political party was a violation of the First Amendment.

Reversing an earlier decision, the court held that the First Amendment does not protect labor union picketing on the grounds of a shopping center (*Hudgens* v. *National Labor Relations Board*). But *Hynes* v. *Oradell* struck down an ordinance requiring house-to-house canvassers for charitable or political causes to register with the local police. Providing new First Amendment protection for "commercial speech," the court invalidated a state law against advertising prices of prescription drugs (*Virginia Board of Pharmacy* v. *Virginia Citizens Consumer Council*).

The court unanimously nullified a "gag order" issued by a Nebraska judge to limit press reports about a pending criminal trial, holding that such orders are generally unjustified even though their purpose is to assure the defendant a fair trial by preventing prejudicial publicity. Three justices would have gone further, regarding gag orders as never justified (*Nebraska Press Association* v. *Stuart*). But the court refused to review a trial judge's order suppressing the film *Manson* in 26 California counties during selection of the jury for the trial of Lynette Fromme, a Manson "family" member, for her attempt on the life of President Ford (*Evans* v. *Fromme*).

The court attempted no further definition of obscenity but did affirm (5–4) a Detroit zoning ordinance, restricting the proliferation of movie theaters showing sexually explicit films (*Young* v. *American Mini-Theatres*). *Time, Inc.* v. *Firestone* held that a participant in a divorce proceeding is not a "public figure," no matter how notorious the case, and consequently need not prove malice against a publication, only negligence, to win a libel judgment. The court refused to order the American Broadcasting Company to give air time to a Polish organization for reply to a broadcast skit of "Polish jokes" (*Polish-American Congress* v. *Federal Communications Commission*).

Relaxing somewhat its opposition to state financing of religion, the court (5–4) upheld Maryland's financial grants to church-affiliated colleges, even though religion and theology were mandatory courses in the institutions (*Roemer* v. *Maryland Public Works Board*).

Privacy. The 1973 abortion decisions continued to generate litigation. The court held that states cannot force a married woman to obtain her husband's consent to an abortion, or give parents an absolute veto over abortions for unmarried daughters under 18 (*Planned Parenthood* v. *Danforth*). But *Greco* v. *Orange Memorial Hospital Corporation* permitted a private but government-funded hospital to forbid a doctor to do abortions there.

The court affirmed, without argument or opinion, a lower court decision that upheld a state law prohibiting homosexual acts, even by consenting adults in private (*Doe* v. *Commonwealth's Attorney*). In a different privacy area, the court rejected a federal civil rights suit (*Paul* v. *Davis*) brought by a man listed in a police flyer as an "active shoplifter." The court held that the due process clause protects only liberty and property, not reputation or good name.

Commerce and Environmental Problems. For the first time since the 1930's the court limited the commerce power of Congress, holding (5–4) that federal wage and hour standards for city, county, and state employees violated state sovereignty (*National League of Cities* v. *Usery*). *Michelin Tire Co.* v. *Wages* overruled a century-old decision which had limited the power of states and cities to tax imported goods.

A $25,000 damage award against an airline for barring Ralph Nader from an overbooked flight on which he had a reservation was upheld (*Nader* v. *Allegheny Airline*).

The court gave some support to the no-growth movement by declining to hear challenges to zoning regulations designed to limit growth in two California communities. It upheld an ordinance requiring property owners who want their land rezoned to secure approval of 55% of the city's voters (*City of Eastlake* v. *Forest City Enterprises*).

The way for strip mining of coal reserves in the northern Great Plains area was cleared by a ruling that the government did not have to prepare a regionwide environmental impact statement (*Kleppe* v. *Sierra Club*). The federal government was sustained in stopping ranchers from diverting water from a cavern in Nevada designated as a national monument to preserve prehistoric pupfish (*Cappaert* v. *United States*).

Ford Motor Co. v. *Coleman* upheld the federal law penalizing auto makers who fail to comply with orders to recall defective vehicles. Investors losing money in stock frauds cannot collect damages from accounting firms unless they can prove the accountants actively participated in the fraud (*Ernst & Ernst* v. *Hochfelder*).

C. HERMAN PRITCHETT
University of California, Santa Barbara

UPI

As civil war continues in Lebanon, the U. S. Navy in July evacuates some 300 persons from Muslim section of Beirut.

LEBANON

Lebanon's devastating civil war gripped the small mountainous republic in a murderous and seemingly endless state of anarchy during most of 1976. The duration, scope, and intensity of the fighting, which has cost Lebanon more than 35,000 dead and billions of dollars in property damage and lost revenues, overshadowed all other developments in the Middle East as its international implications jeopardized the peace of the entire region.

Issues and Implications. The regional implications of the issues dividing Lebanon's Christian right and Muslim left were more dangerous than the threat of a de facto partition of the state into Christian and Muslim enclaves. Although fought along primarily religious lines, the continued war was really over political, social, and economic issues.

The demands of the Muslim left for reform in the confessional system of representation were spearheaded by the loosely organized National Movement under the nominal control of Socialist leader Kemal Jumblat. These demands were apparently justifiable and long overdue: while Muslims constitute the majority of the population, there was a ratio of six Christian for every five Muslim deputies in Lebanon's unicameral legislature. Moreover, by an unwritten agreement, Lebanon could not have a Muslim president. At issue, however—and particularly as

the left began to demand complete secularization—was the role Lebanon would play in the region's future and how the nation would deal with the Palestinians living within its borders.

The Christian right, Israel, and Syria feared that Lebanon, if secularization should come about, would emerge as a radical, socialist state that would maximize its support for the Palestine Liberation Organization's (PLO) operations against Israel. Lebanon's rightists feared repeated Israeli reprisals, and both Syria and Israel recognized that a radical Lebanon could upset the Middle East's tenuous balance.

PLO and Syrian Intervention. Even though Palestinians had been the target of the incident which had polarized the country, and despite the right's objective to curtail, if not completely stop, the guerrillas' activities, the PLO had stayed clear of the fighting during 1975. However, when a Lebanese military aircraft strafed a PLO camp early in January 1976, PLO leader Yasir Arafat committed his troops to the Muslim left.

On January 20, some 2,500 regular troops of the Palestine Liberation Army (PLA), trained and controlled by Syria, entered Lebanon's Bekaa Valley from Syria and reinforced leftist operations. The Syrian intervention led to the announcement of a January 23 cease-fire to be policed by a six-member military commission made up of Lebanese, Syrians, and Palestinians. However, the military commission failed to operate, the poorly disciplined militias could not be restrained, and the cease-fire became the 23d such agreement negotiated and ignored since April 1975.

Political Reform. In the wake of the cease-fire's collapse and escalated fighting, Lebanese President Suleiman Franjieh, whose immediate resignation was demanded by the left, announced the terms of a new 17-point National Pact on February 14. The pact met the Muslim demand to abolish the Christian majority in the Chamber of Deputies, but because it called for the retention of the presidency by the Christian community, it was rejected outright by Socialist leader Kemal Jumblat.

Meanwhile, a leftist-Palestinian offensive in Beirut led to the complete deterioration of internal security. On March 11 and 12, Brig. Gen. Abdel Aziz Ahdab, commander of the military district of Beirut, resorted to radio and television to declare a state of emergency and to demand the president's resignation. Despite a March 13 parliamentary petition for his resignation, the president refused and barricaded himself in his palace. As the fighting worsened and Beirut was subjected to indiscriminate shelling, the legislature met on April 10 to pass a constitutional amendment allowing presidential elections up to six months before the incumbent's term expired.

On April 24 Franjieh signed the amendment but declared that, despite the elections, he would not step down until the fighting ceased or his term expired. On May 8, the Chamber of Deputies convened and elected Elias Sarkis, the Syrian choice, who had lost to Franjieh by one vote on the second ballot in 1970.

Syria's Role. The successes of the resurgent leftist-Palestinian alliance in March had induced Syria to shift its support to the badly sagging right in mid-April. Syria's inability to control the left and the right's failure to hold its own threatened Syrian President Hafez Assad's hope that a Lebanon in which Christians and Muslims shared power could survive. The wave of fighting that followed Sarkis' election compelled Assad to take direct action.

To curb the PLO and end the war, 100 tanks and 4,000 Syrian troops entered Lebanon on June 1. Within a week, 500 tanks and 12,000

Syrians were supporting the right in a three-pronged attack on leftist-PLO strongholds.

Inter-Arab Initiatives. Following the Syrian incursion, the Arab League met hastily in Cairo and approved a plan to send a 2,000-man peacekeeping force to separate Lebanon's antagonists. On June 21, the first contingent arrived in Beirut and took up positions between leftist and rightist lines in the downtown areas.

Until October, the war ground along despite all efforts to stop it. Initiatives by Saudi Arabia and Libya were as fruitless as those of Hassan Sabri Kholi, the Arab League's special envoy. By August the Christian right, buoyed by Syria's support, had established administrative bodies in the areas of the country it controlled, and on August 12 it achieved its most significant victory of the war when the emotionally symbolic Tell Zaatar Palestinian enclave in Beirut was overrun.

Sarkis Becomes President. When Franjieh's term expired on September 23, Elias Sarkis took office confronted by a conflict to which, apparently, there was only a military solution. The first half of the month had seen the failure of the 54th and 55th cease-fires of the war and the Muslim-PLO forces were savagely resisting the advance of rightists supported by a 22,000-man Syrian force. Negotiations stalled because the PLO refused to accept the Syrian demand that it abide by a 1969 Cairo agreement which limited its activities to certain areas and forbade interference in Lebanon's domestic affairs.

However, a diplomatic initiative by Saudi Arabia, on which Syria is financially dependent, combined with an October 12 Syrian-rightist push to remove the PLO from its positions east of Beirut and to isolate leftist-held Sidon in the south, led to a significant breakthrough.

On October 16, Syria's Assad, Lebanon's Sarkis and the PLO's Arafat flew to Riyadh, the Saudi capital, to confer with King Khalid, the emir of Kuwait, and Egypt's President Anwar Sadat. The day after, the six leaders announced a plan to return peace to Lebanon. Ratified on October 25 by 19 members of the Arab League, the plan's key features were the provision for a 30,000-member Arab League force, half of which was to be Syrian, to be placed under the command of President Sarkis, and the PLO's pledge to honor the 1969 Cairo agreement. A cease-fire went into effect on October 21 and held in spite of rightist efforts to block the return of PLO troops to the bases they occupied prior to their involvement in the civil war. When it was clear that the rightist objective could jeopardize the cease-fire, Syria shifted its support back to the PLO and aided the guerrillas in reoccupying their positions.

By mid-November the Syrian components of the Arab League force had moved in and occupied most of Beirut's key districts to pave the way for a political settlement.

F. NICHOLAS WILLARD
Georgetown University

LEBANON · Information Highlights

Official Name: Republic of Lebanon.
Location: Southwest Asia.
Area: 4,015 square miles (10,400 km²).
Population (1976 est.): 2,700,000.
Chief Cities (1974 est.): Beirut, the capital, 1,000,000; Tripoli, 128,000.
Government: *Head of state,* Elias Sarkis, president (took office Sept. 1976). *Head of interim government,* Selim al-Hoss, premier (took office Dec. 1976). *Legislature* (unicameral)—Chamber of Deputies.
Monetary Unit: Lebanese pound (2.23 pounds equal U. S.$1, July 1975).
Gross National Product (1974 est.): $3,700,000,000.
Manufacturing (major products): Processed foods, textiles, petroleum products, cement, tobacco products.
Major Agricultural Products: Cereals, fruits, vegetables, tobacco, wheat.
Foreign Trade (1974): *Exports,* $588,000,000; *imports,* $1,331,000,000.

LIBRARIES

During 1976 American librarians focused their attention on the progress of copyright legislation, on a remarkable series of organizational developments at the Library of Congress, and on a debate over the appropriate sources of funds for library service.

In attempting to revise the 1909 copyright law, Congress had to consider advances in the technology of copying as well as balance the rights of copyright proprietors against the national need for a broad dissemination of information. The new Librarian of Congress, Daniel Boorstin, created a task force to review the library's activities and also modified that institution's table of organization. Observers sought parallels for these actions in the early 1940's administration of Archibald MacLeish, a Librarian of Congress who, like Mr. Boorstin, was appointed to that position without previous professional experience in librarianship. Finally, both the National Commission on Libraries and Information Science and the Urban Libraries Council offered statements on the balance of funding for libraries from all governmental sources.

Copyright. On February 10 the Senate passed a revised copyright bill by a vote of 97 to 0. The Senate bill extended U. S. copyright protection to 50 years after an author's death and gave a public broadcaster the right to use a literary work provided a just royalty is paid. It also prohibited the "systematic" copying of copyrighted materials by libraries or archives, but left largely undefined what constituted "systematic" copying.

In August the judiciary committee of the House of Representatives reported its bill for the general revision of the copyright law. The committee agreed with the Senate that "the rights of reproduction and distribution . . . extend to the isolated and unrelated reproduction or distribution of a single copy or phonorecord of the same material on separate occasions. . . ." In an attempt to be more specific than the Senate, the committee insisted that the prohibition against "systematic" copying or reproduction did not prevent "a library or archives from participating in interlibrary loan arrangements that do not have, as their purpose or effect, that the library or archives receiving such copies or phonorecords for distribution does so in such aggregate quantities as to substitute for a subscription to or purchase of such a work." Concerned about controls on the use of photocopying or other techniques of reproduction in the course of interlibrary loan activity, librarians wondered just what "aggregate quantities" might substitute for a journal subscription or for the purchase of a book or phonorecord by a library receiving copies or reproductions of a particular work.

GIORGIO CAVAGLIERI ARCHITECT/PHOTO BY MARC NEUHOF

New award-winning libraries included the Jefferson Market Branch of the N. Y. C. Public Library (above) and the Pekin Public Library in Peoria, Ill.

JOHN HACKLER & CO.

Through their national associations and the National Commission on New Technological Uses of Copyrighted Works, librarians sought during the summer of 1976 a more precise delineation of "systematic" copying and argued that the burden of proving that "systematic" copying has occurred should be on the copyright proprietor.

Prior to adjourning in October, the House and Senate passed a final version of the copyright bill. The legislation extends protection to the life of the author plus 50 years, establishes criteria for reproduction, and provides protection for jukebox and cable television uses. The act covers published and unpublished works, and the term of copyright begins with the work's completion. In addition, it made the United States eligible for membership in the Bern Union, the international copyright agreement.

Library of Congress. In mid-January 1976, the Librarian of Congress created a staff Task Force on Goals, Organization, and Planning. Issues before the task force, which was to report on Jan. 15, 1977, included the quality of the library's service to Congress and the federal government; its existing and future roles as the *de facto* national library; its potential exploitation of information-processing technology; and its part in the promotion of freedom of communication. In a related organizational development, the reference department was divided into a department of reader services and a department of research on April 12, 1976. Not since the early 1940's, when the library was organized into five major departments—administration, reference, processing, the law library, and the copyright office—had there been such an important internal shift.

During February and early March 1976, it was decided that the James Madison Memorial Building of the Library of Congress would remain a library rather than serve as an office building for the U. S. House of Representatives. And on April 13, Thomas Jefferson's birthday, the Library of Congress Annex Building was renamed the Library of Congress Thomas Jefferson Building.

Library Funding. Early in 1976, the National Commission on Libraries and Information Science urged a reexamination of the financial support of library service and called for a more equitable local-state-federal partnership in such funding. Meanwhile, the Urban Libraries Council proposed a special program of federal aid to public libraries serving cities with populations of over 100,000. The council wanted more balanced intergovernmental funding of such libraries which heretofore had to depend too heavily on city resources.

In many financially pressed cities, including Detroit, a funding shift started to occur. The Detroit Public Library, 40% of whose users are nonresidents, was designated a state resource and its 1976 budget included more money from the state of Michigan than from the city of Detroit.

American Library Association. The Centennial Conference of the American Library Association was held in Chicago, July 18–24, 1976. Clara S. Jones, director of the Detroit Public Library, became president of the association. Eric Moon, president of the Scarecrow Press, was elected vice-president and president-elect. The proceedings were tinged with sadness because of the death on April 11, 1976, of Allie Beth Martin, director of the Tulsa City-County Library and ALA president, 1975–76.

The association was again sole sponsor of National Library Week, April 4–10. Its theme, "At the Library? At the Library! Come See What's New Besides Books," stressed the full

MAJOR LIBRARY AWARDS OF 1976

Beta Phi Mu Award for distinguished service to education for librarianship: Carolyn I. Whitenack, Purdue University

Randolph J. Caldecott Medal for distinction in picture book illustration: Leo and Diane Dillon, *Why Mosquitoes Buzz at People's Ears*

Melvil Dewey Medal for creative professional achievement: Louis Round Wilson, University of North Carolina, Chapel Hill

Robert B. Downs Award for promoting freedom of communication: Eli M. Oboler, Idaho State University

Grolier Award for achievement in stimulating the reading interests of young people: Virginia Haviland, Children's Book Section, Library of Congress

Joseph W. Lippincott Award for distinguished service to the library profession: Lester Asheim, University of North Carolina, Chapel Hill

John Newbery Medal for most distinguished contribution to children's literature: Susan Cooper, *The Grey King*

Irita Van Doren Award for promoting freedom of communication: Judith F. Krug, Office for Intellectual Freedom, American Library Association

---

range of services and print/nonprint materials offered by libraries.

Library Education. The number of graduate programs in librarianship accredited by the American Library Association increased to 66 in 1976 with the approval of master's degree offerings by the School of Library Media and Information Science at Clarion State College, Clarion, Penn., and the Department of Library and Information Science at St. John's University in New York. The Department of Librarianship at San Jose State University, San Jose, Calif., was denied accreditation following an appeal.

International Activities. It was proposed during 1976 that The Library Association of Great Britain be reorganized. The association was urged to make better provision for special interest groups while at the same time emphasizing that librarianship is a single, unified profession. In order that it might respond more directly to the concerns of librarians, the association was admonished to create standing committees on professional standards, career opportunities, and the conditions of employment for librarians, as well as one on library standards.

Meeting in Halifax, N. S., June 10–16, 1976, the Canadian Library Association voted to support government payments to authors based on the library circulation of their books, but only "in recognition of the cultural contribution of Canadian writers and not . . . of any legal recompense for the library use."

Lausanne, Switzerland, was the site of the forty-second general council meeting of the International Federation of Library Associations, Aug. 23–28, 1976.

DAN BERGEN, *Graduate Library School University of Rhode Island*

Col. Muammar el-Qaddafi (*left*) heads Libya's delegation at the nonaligned nations meeting in Colombo, Sri Lanka, in August.

UPI

LIBYA

Libya remained on uneasy terms with its neighbors throughout 1976 and antagonized many nations with its aid to revolutionary and terrorist movements. Prime Minister Abdul Salam Jallud conducted lengthy but futile negotiations to end the civil war in Lebanon. A large-scale development plan was initiated.

Disputes with Neighbors. Libyan-Egyptian relations were particularly tense, as presidents Sadat and Qaddafi each accused the other of plotting to overthrow his government. Egypt arrested several Libyans on espionage charges early in the year, and Libya retaliated by expelling several thousand Egyptian residents. Sadat expressed concern that the sophisticated weapons which the Soviet Union was supplying to Libya might be used against its neighbors.

Sudan's President Numeiry also accused Libya of actively supporting an abortive coup in Khartoum in July. Libya denied the charge, but the Sudanese government closed its borders with Libya in order to curtail Libyan influences.

Libya provided military and financial support to such revolutionary and terrorist groups as the Irish Republican Army, Philippine Muslim rebels, and antigovernment forces in Ethiopia, Chad, and Iran. Libyan aid, possibly amounting to $50 million, also bolstered leftist and Palestinian forces in the Lebanese civil war.

Truce Efforts. As tensions began to mount in Lebanon between Syria and the Palestine Liberation Organization (PLO) in the spring, Prime Minister Jallud arranged meetings aimed at reconciling the positions of Syrian President Assad and the PLO's Yasir Arafat. His attempts to align Syria with the "rejectionist" front failed when Assad agreed to renew the UN mandate to patrol the Golan Heights. In June, when Syrian troops invaded Lebanon, Jallud turned his attention to achieving a truce. Having temporarily succeeded, he volunteered to send Libyan soldiers to enforce it, but Syria claimed that Libya's sympathy for the PLO position disqualified it as a disinterested party able to police the settlement; a peace-keeping force under Arab League supervision was finally accepted. Jallud continued to mediate outstanding disputes, trying to preserve the fragile truce. His efforts ended in failure in late June, when the cease-fire collapsed. Returning to Libya, he vowed to aid leftist forces in Lebanon and to prevent the suppression of the PLO and the partition of the country. He again returned to Lebanon in July to supervise withdrawal of some Syrian troops and negotiate yet another short-lived cease-fire.

Economic Development. Libya's oil revenues in 1976 came close to $8,000,000,000 and were rising. From an average daily flow of nearly 1,900,000 barrels (255,000 metric tons) during the first seven months of 1976, production is expected to reach 2.4 million barrels (325,000 tons) a day in 1977.

Counting on continuing high income from its oil, the government in 1976 launched an ambitious five-year development plan, projecting an investment of $24,200,000,000. The largest share (17%) will go to agriculture in the hope that the country will be self-sufficient by 1985. The agricultural scheme calls for land reclamation, irrigation, water research, and forestation in addition to livestock production.

The second largest investment under the plan, 15% of the total, will go to industrial development, while 11% is to be spent on housing.

KENNETH J. PERKINS
University of South Carolina

--- **LIBYA · Information Highlights** ---

Official Name: Libyan Arab Republic.
Location: North Africa.
Area: 679,360 square miles (1,759,540 km²).
Population (1976 est.): 2,500,000.
Chief Cities (1975 est.): Tripoli, the capital, 295,000; Benghazi, 190,000.
Government: *Head of state*, Muammar el-Qaddafi, president, Revolutionary Command Council (took office 1969). *Head of government*, Abdul Salam Jallud, prime minister (took office 1972).
Monetary Unit: Dinar (0.30 dinar equals U.S.$1, June 1976).
Gross National Product (1975 est.): $12,200,000,000.
Manufacturing (major products): Petroleum products, processed foods.
Major Agricultural Products: Wheat, barley, tomatoes, dates, olives, peanuts, vegetables.
Foreign Trade (1975): *Exports*, $6,837,000,000; *imports*, $3,554,000,000.

LITERATURE

American Literature

The United States was honored by the award of the Nobel Prize for literature to Saul Bellow —the eighth American to win the prize. In other ways the U. S. bicentennial was distinguished by a large number of works of high quality.

Awards. The National Book Critics' Circle gave its first series of awards; E. L. Doctorow took the fiction prize with *Ragtime,* and R. W. B. Lewis' *Edith Wharton* won in nonfiction. The poetry award went to John Ashbery's *Self-Portrait in a Convex Mirror.* Paul Fussell's *The Great War and Modern Memory* received the critics' award and was also the National Book Award winner in the Arts and Letters category.

In response to varied criticism, the 1976 National Book Awards were reduced to six under the administration of the National Institute of Arts and Letters. In addition to prizes for Poetry and Arts and Letters there were awards for Fiction, bestowed on William Gaddis' *JR;* History and Biography, won by David Brion Davis' *The Problem of Slavery in the Age of Revolution 1770–1823;* Contemporary Affairs, captured by Michael J. Arlen for his reflective search for his past, *Passage to Ararat;* and Children's Literature, given Walter D. Edmonds' *Bert Breen's Barn.*

Poet John Ashbery won a National Book Award, a Pulitzer Prize, and a National Book Critics' Circle Award.

THOMAS VICTOR

The Pulitzer committee found itself in the ironic position of awarding its fiction prize to Saul Bellow's *Humboldt's Gift,* in which one of the main characters says "The Pulitzer is for the birds." Bellow had several times had the Pulitzer denied him despite critical recommendations. Paul Lamy won his second Pulitzer for history with *Lamy of Santa Fe.* The general nonfiction prize went to Robert N. Butler's *Why Survive? Being Old in America.* Michael Bennett and his collaborators took the drama award for their innovative musical, *A Chorus Line.*

Novels. An unusually large number of interesting first novels by women appeared in 1976. Ann Beattie's *Chilly Scenes of Winter,* a story of a man whose mother is insane, stepfather defeated, job boring, room-mate unemployed, and girlfriend married, would have been unbearably bleak had it not been for Beattie's finding of irony and hope in strange places.

Lisa Alther's satirical *Kinflicks* follows her heroine from her triumphs in high school through the archetypal experiences of the era, dropping out of college, radical politics, commune life, marriage, motherhood, and the search for God. In contrast to Alther's broad caricatures is Renata Adler's clinical *Speedboat,* a kaleidoscope of fragments of scenes overheard, observed, and reflected on. Adler skillfully utilizes sophisticated literary techniques to capture contemporary urban culture.

Rosellen Brown's *The Autobiography of My Mother* deals with the conflict between a mother, who is a successful, energetic civil-rights lawyer, and her daughter who can deal neither with her own life nor her illegitimate child's. In *Lovers and Tyrants* Francine du Plessix Gray tells of a cultured woman who refuses to accept the limits of existence and sets out on a strange odyssey through the American west. An unusual and successful first novel was Anne Rice's imaginative *Interviews With a Vampire* in which a somewhat poignant vampire recites into a tape recorder his life history and various adventures since 1791.

Two well received second novels were *Eva's Man,* a descent into a violent, nightmarish world by Gayle Jones, and *Meridian,* a penetrating study of paradoxes in the lives of some civil-rights activists.

American satirical novelists tend to work for a long time before they catch on. This was true of Kurt Vonnegut who released a new, whimsical, futuristic story, *Slapstick,* and of Richard Brautigan who called his self-conscious *Sombrero Fall-Out* "A Japanese Novel." Satirists whose reputations are still growing published interesting work. Stanley Elkin's *The Franchiser* is about the ultimate American businessman; Don de Lillo's *Ratner's Star* centers on a 14-year-old mathematical genius in a Pynchonesque world of scientists and philosophers; and Ishmael Reed's *Flight to Canada* has runaway slaves wandering through modern America.

In the fiction category, *Trinity*, Leon Uris' historically accurate tale of Ireland, was a best-seller.

Leon Uris

TRINITY

a novel of Ireland

JILL URIS

DOUBLEDAY & CO. INC.

Vance Bourjaily's long-awaited *Now Playing at Canterbury* uses the inauguration of a cultural center to try to make a statement about American culture. More successful was John Hawkes' narrowly focused *Travesty* which stays in the mind of one man, a driver bent on killing himself, his daughter, and his wife's lover. John Gardner concentrates on two characters in his moving *October Light*. An aging brother and sister, constantly feuding, living together on a mountain in Vermont, are set against an otherworldly book the sister is reading.

This was also the year of the unlikely novelist. William Buckley's *Saving the Queen,* John Lindsay's *The Edge,* John Ehrlichman's *The Company,* and Spiro Agnew's *The Canfield Decision* received attention more because of their authors than for their literary value.

Short Fiction. Some fine short story collections appeared in 1976. Cynthia Ozick's *Bloodshed and Three Novellas* are works of great imagination dealing with philosophical conflict between Jewish principles and western tradition. Bernard Kaplan's *Obituaries* dramatize individual alienation exacerbated by an alienated society. Frightening mysteries that quietly invade people's lives characterized Raymond Carver's *Will You Please Be Quiet, Please?* Vladimir Nabokov's fine stories written between 1924 and 1935 are translated in *Details of a Sunset.*

Poetry. Louis Zukofsky was 50 years at work on a 24-part poem which cryptically and suggestively reflects his world. *"A" 22&23* brings to completion this major work; he had already published the final section.

When a poet collects his scattered works, we can more easily study his evolution and weigh his importance. Archibald MacLeish's *New and Collected Poems 1917–1976* and Robert Penn Warren's *Selected Poems 1923–1975* demonstrate their long and fruitful careers. Robert

Lowell's *Selected Poems* cover less than 30 years but make clear why he is so often considered America's most important living poet. Edward Dorn's *The Collected Poems 1956–1974* and Diane di Parma's *Selected Poems 1956–1975* make their achievement visible.

By what they include and exclude, anthologies can shape literary history; *The New Oxford Book of American Verse,* compiled by Richard Ellmann, updates F. O. Matthiessen's influential 1950 edition and helps define poetry today.

The narrative possibilities of poetry are explored in James Merrill's widely acclaimed *Divine Comedies.* The volume is dominated by "The Book of Ephraim," an almost novelistic inquiry into the relationship between the real and the spirit world. These are autobiographical poems, as is Louis Simpson's *Searching for the Ox,* in which he dramatizes the conflict between intellect and sensuality.

The winner of last year's National Book Award, Marilyn Hacker, published her second volume, *Separations,* and a posthumous collection by Anne Sexton, *45 Mercy Street,* appeared, but neither contained their finest work.

Literary History and Criticism. Irving Howe's *The World of Our Fathers* is a learned and moving account of the migration of Eastern European Jews to the United States, the flowering of the Yiddish community, and its contribution to American political and cultural life.

In *Some Time in the Sun* Tom Dardis casts a new light on the Hollywood careers of Faulkner, Fitzgerald, Agee, Huxley, and Nathanael West. He shows how, contrary to the accepted myths that Hollywood destroys artists, they profited from their experiences. Meta Carpenter Wilde recalls her lengthy affair with Faulkner, which began in Hollywood, in *A Loving Gentleman.*

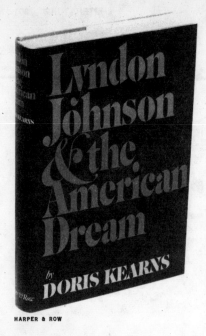

HARPER & ROW

JOAN BINGHAM

During Lyndon Johnson's last years, he spent a considerable length of time with Doris Kearns, a young Harvard instructor, telling her of his life, career, and philosophy. *Lyndon Johnson and the American Dream* is a personal memoir of this experience.

Dougald McMillan's *transition 1927–1938* is a history of that important avant-garde magazine. Long-time expatriate writer Henry Miller is vividly brought to our attention again by Norman Mailer in *Genius and Lust,* an anthology with critical commentary.

Several collections of notable essays appeared. The influential critic W. K. Wimsatt's essays on poetry, *Day of the Leopards,* appeared shortly after his death. Steven Marcus again demonstrated his ability to show the complex relations between literature and society in *Representations.*

Noam Chomsky, who almost single-handedly created modern linguistics, continued his speculations in *Reflections on Language.* And the Pulitzer-winning poet Richard Wilbur collected his essays on poetry in *Responses.*

David Perkins brought out *A History of Modern Poetry,* a work of great importance. The first of two volumes, it covers the period from the 1890's to what the author calls the "high modernist mode" and deals with more than 100 poets. Harold Bloom continues his argument that each generation of poets attempts to destroy the previous one in *Poetry and Repression.*

Carl Bode's huge collection, *The New Mencken Letters,* reveals that the cantankerous socio-literary critic was far more serious and kindly than his public persona. Giles Gunn's *F. O. Matthiessen: The Critical Achievement* demonstrates how the critic, who did so much to make America aware of its own literary riches, strove for both political and aesthetic ends.

Bill Henderson's *The Pushcart Prize,* a collection of the best works from America's small presses, demonstrates their continued vitality and their importance as a seedbed for future writers.

History and Biography. American historical writing is characterized by its changing approaches and insights. Striking examples appeared this year. *The American Revolution,* a collection of essays edited by Alfred Young, is a reexamination of that period by radical historians. William Appleman Williams' *America Confronts A Revolutionary World 1776–1976,* and Gabriel Kolko's *Main Currents in Modern American History* are both severely critical of many aspects of U. S. domestic and foreign policy on which Americans have long unhesitatingly congratulated themselves.

William Wise reconstructs a forgotten event; *Massacre at Mountain Meadows* tells of the Mormons' murder of more than 100 California-bound migrants. Thomas B. Marquis' exposé of the behavior of American troops at Custer's last stand, *Keep the Last Bullet for Yourself,* took 40 years to find a publisher. Anthony Scaduto argues in *Scapegoat* that the infamous Bruno Hauptmann, executed for the 1932 kidnap-murder of the Lindbergh baby, was innocent.

Literature and art are the source materials for two eminent intellectual historians. Sacvan Bercovitch in *The Puritan Origins of the American Self* examines rhetorical patterns in the writings of Cotton Mather and his peers in order to understand our early influences. Hugh Honour in *The New Golden Land* uses paintings of America to show how those images influenced America's view of itself.

The brilliant historian David M. Potter died in 1971, while working on a study of the causes of the Civil War; his book was completed by Don E. Fehrenbacher. *The Impending Crisis 1848–1861* is an important contribution to the understanding of that crucial period.

In contrast to those who argue that slaveowners either preserved or destroyed the black family structure, Herbert Gutman emphasizes the slaves' own resourcefulness in *The Black Family in Slavery and Freedom 1750–1925.*

Richard Kluger deals with more recent history in his deeply researched history of the battle for integrated schools, *Simple Justice.*

William H. McNeill's impressive *Plagues and People,* a study of man and the world as defined and changed by epidemic diseases, transforms our very notion of human history.

Some people have been so much written about that it seems doubtful that anything fresh can be added. That makes John Toland's mammoth *Adolf Hitler* all the more impressive. Toland convinced hundreds of people to grant him interviews and gained valuable new information.

Geoffrey Wolf beautifully recreated the 1920's in *Black Sun.* This is the life of Harry Crosby, a minor poet who helped found the Black Sun Press and in 1929 murdered his girlfriend and himself in a suicide pact.

In roughly same period Alexander Woollcott was becoming known as a public wit and making the Algonquin Hotel's round table part of U. S. history. In *Smart Aleck* Howard Teichmann tells the story of this strange man. Ring Lardner, another difficult person, is sympathetically portrayed by his son, Ring Jr., in *The Lardners,* a family biography. In *The Life of Raymond Chandler* Frank MacShane reveals the complexity of the mystery writer who took his work seriously despite critics' refusal to do so.

Mary Welsh Hemingway, Ernest's wife for his last 17 years, is the author of *How It Was,* an unusually perceptive, detailed, and well-rounded portrait that tells us much about her own literary talent. His youngest son, Geoffrey, has written an intelligent and affectionate memoir, entitled *Papa.*

C. David Heymann's *Ezra Pound: The Last Rower* at last supplies a detailed account of Pound's work for the Italian Fascists; the sad aftermath is recounted by Charles Olson in *Charles Olson & Ezra Pound: An Encounter at St. Elizabeth's* edited by Catherine Seelye.

Other Nonfiction. In *The Uses of Enchantment* Bruno Bettelheim penetratingly argues that fairy tales help children deal with their subconscious fears and fantasies.

Alex Haley, author of *The Autobiography of Malcolm X,* worked for 12 years on *Roots.* Subtitled "The Saga of an American Family," the book starts with Haley's own ancestors, traced back to 1750 in Gambia, West Africa. It then follows each generation, through abduction, slavery, and freedom. A mixture of historical accuracy and novelistic license, the book is, according to Haley, a "faction."

The chilling effect of the Vietnam War is distilled in C. D. B. Bryan's *Friendly Fire,* the story of an Iowa farm couple who attempt to discover the circumstances of their son's battlefield death in Vietnam but are baffled by Washington's impersonal, inept responses. Ron Kovic, a Vietnam veteran paralyzed from the waist down, tells of his experiences in *Born on the Fourth of July.*

Intimate information dominates Bob Woodward and Carl Bernstein's *The Final Days,* which covers the last two weeks of the Nixon presidency. Although criticized for questionable taste and lack of documentation, it is an extraordinary piece of American journalism.

JEROME H. STERN
Florida State University

Children's Literature

The number of individual children's books continued to decline in 1976. Early estimates placed the titles produced at 1,500—down 100 from the previous year. Again, the reasons cited were economic—paper and production costs, budgetary restraints on schools and libraries which are the primary purchasers of children's books. Production and promotion of paperbacks were more aggressive. Bidding for quality works among the larger paperback publishers was spirited, resulting in higher fees to authors.

Awards. Major awards were presented in 1976 for children's books published the previous year. The American Library Association's (ALA) John Newbery Medal for the most distinguished contribution to American literature for children went to Susan Cooper for *The Grey King,* the fourth in a series of five books on the struggle between the forces of darkness and light. The ALA's Randolph Caldecott Medal for the most distinguished picture book was given to Leo and Diane Dillon for their illustrations in *Why Mosquitoes Buzz in People's Ears,* a West African tale retold by Verna Aardema.

The National Book Award for children's books went to Walter D. Edmonds for *Bert Breen's Barn,* a lengthy novel about a boy's modest dreams and hard labor in upstate New York at the turn of the century. Carol Farley received the annual Child Study Association of America award for dealing realistically with young people's problems in *The Garden Is Doing Fine,* the story of a young girl who must come to terms with her father's long illness and death.

Bicentennial Review. The nation's celebration of its bicentennial prompted hundreds of volumes for all age groups dealing with early U. S. history and the Revolutionary War in particular. The most notable among these were two novels for teen-agers, Richard F. Snow's *Freelon Starbird* and James L. and Christopher Collier's *The Bloody Country.* For the 8-to-11-year-old group the most satisfying works were two brief, colorful biographies by Jean Fritz, *Will You Sign Here, John Hancock?* and *What's the Big Idea, Ben Franklin?* Worthy of mention also are two picture books, Steven Kellogg's illustrated *Yankee Doodle* and Robert Quackenbush's *Pop! Goes the Weasel and Yankee Doodle.*

Poetry and Nonfiction. Little of consequence or originality was to be noted in the half a hundred volumes of poetry other than N. M. Bodecker's *Hurry, Hurry, Mary Dear!,* a collection of nonsense poems, and Ted Hughes' *Moon-*

Whales, which possessed largely adult appeal. There were biographies of Sigmund Freud, Thomas Merton, Benedict Arnold, Bella Abzug, Mother Ann Lee of the Shakers, Lawrence of Arabia, and others, but none was of impressive artistic achievement. A reflection of U. S. society was to be noted in the many nonfiction works dealing with alcoholism, divorce, suicide, psychiatric counseling, death, grief, senility, venereal disease, and homosexuality.

For Younger Readers. Several picture books for four-year-olds and up stood out: Janet Quin-Harkin's retelling of an English ballad in *Peter Penny's Dance,* with exuberant illustrations by Anita Lobel; William Steig's 11th book for children, *The Amazing Bone,* in which a talking bone saves a bonneted pig from a debonnaire but villainous fox; Mary Rayner's *Mr. and Mrs. Pig's Evening Out,* in which ten piglets outwit a wolf in baby-sitter's clothes; Graham Oakley's *The Church Mice Spread Their Wings,* fourth in a series about those mischievous little rodents; Alice and Martin Provensen's handsomely illustrated *The Mother Goose Book;* and *Merry Ever After,* contrasting the feudal weddings of noble and peasant in beautifully executed paintings by Joe Lasker.

For children 6 to 10 the most noteworthy titles were: *Frog and Toad All Year,* the third in a series written and illustrated by Arnold Lobel; *The Golem,* a Jewish legend retold and richly illustrated by Beverly Brodsky McDermott; Randall Jarrells' *Fly by Night,* an oddly haunting, symbolic story illustrated by Maurice Sendak; and Margaret Musgrove's *Ashanti to Zulu,* describing the traditions and ceremonies of 26 African tribes, romantically and graphically illustrated by Leo and Diane Dillon.

The 9-to-12-year-old group received perhaps the most outstanding book of the year in another William Steig volume, *Abel's Island.* This Robinson Crusoe adventure of a mouse is witty, profound, and provocative. Other volumes of note for this group were: Alan Arkin's *The Lemming Condition,* about an individual having second thoughts over the species' destructive migration—an affecting parable on conformity; and William Mayne's *A Year and a Day,* a strange tale with a special resonance in the telling.

For Teen-Agers. For teen-agers the best books were: *Bible Stories You Can't Forget,* eight familiar stories from the Old and New Testaments, retold with wit and humor by Marshall Efron and Alfa-Betty Olsen; *Diving for Roses,* a powerful, literate story of alcoholism and pregnancy by Patricia Windsor; *Unleaving* by Jill Paton Walsh, a continuation of the author's previous *Goldengrove;* and a first novel by Sue Ellen Bridgers, *Home Before Dark,* in which a migrant family finds heartbreak and happiness in its new Carolina home.

Other novels of note for this age group were Paul Zindel's *Pardon Me, You're Stepping On My Eyeball!,* an energetic, madcap romp with a large cast of assorted eccentrics; Barbara Wersba's *Tunes for a Small Harmonica,* in which a tomboy type falls in love with her poetry teacher; and finally, Norma Fox Mazer's *Dear Bill, Remember Me?,* poignant short stories about young women at turning points in their lives.

GEORGE A. WOODS
Children's Book Editor, "The New York Times"

Major award winners: Leo and Diane Dillon captured the Caldecott Medal for Why Mosquitoes Buzz in People's Ears, and Susan Cooper took the Newbery Medal for The Grey King.

DIAL PRESS   ATHENEUM PUBLISHERS

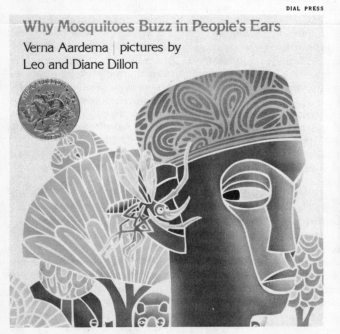

A Heritage of Canadian Art and Paul Duval's Ken Danby were cited for their illustrations and design.

PHOTOS CLARKE, IRWIN & CO., LTD.

Canadian Literature in English

Canadian writers again in 1976 demonstrated a great interest in Canadian subjects, be they politics, history, art, or cities. More biographies and autobiographies than usual appeared.

Nonfiction. C. P. Stacey's *A Very Double Life* draws on the diaries of Mackenzie King, long-time prime minister of Canada, to reveal his remarkable interest in spiritualism. Former Prime Minister John G. Diefenbaker continues his memoirs in *One Canada—The Years of Achievement, 1956–1962.* Joseph Schull's *Leader and Exile, 1881–1912* is the conclusion of his biography of Edward Blake, an early Canadian politician. The convention that chose Joe Clark leader of the Progressive Conservatives is the subject of *Winners, Losers* by Patrick Brown, Robert Chodos, and Rae Murphy.

Historian Donald Creighton is interesting and authoritative in *Canada: The Heroic Beginnings,* and Pierre Berton, in *My Country,* makes Canadian history anything but dull. Enid Mallory's *The Green Tiger* unfolds the life of James Fitzgibbon, a hero of the War of 1812. *The Donnelly Album* by Ray Fazakas is a painstaking account of the 1880 murders in Ontario of five members of the Donnelly family.

A Heritage of Canadian Art, designed by A. J. Casson, is an expansion of the 1973 *A Vision of Canada* and equally handsome. Paul Duval's *Ken Danby* is a well-illustrated study of a leading Canadian painter.

Canadian cities inspired several books. *The Toronto Book,* edited by William Kilbourn, is a collection of writings on Toronto. J. G. MacGregor tells an interesting story of growth in *Edmonton: A History.* Two books sing the praises of Vancouver. *The Vancouver Book,* edited by Chuck Davis, does it mainly in words, and *The City of Vancouver,* edited by Rudy Kovach, with text by Barry Broadfoot, does it mainly in pictures. Nick auf der Maur's *The Billion-Dollar Games* describes the "nightmare of bungling and escalating costs" that preceded the Olympic Games in Montreal.

Biographies included Ruby Mercer's *The Tenor of His Time,* about singer Edward Johnson. *The Far Side of the Street* is the splendidly written autobiography of Bruce Hutchison, perhaps Canada's best journalist.

Margaret Laurence, whom many view as Canada's most important novelist, writes personal essays in *Heart of a Stranger. Dual Allegiance,* the autobiography of Jewish businessman Ben Dunkelman, tells how he served both Canada and Israel in time of war.

In *Gringos from the Far North,* J. C. M. Ogelsby traces Canada's relationships with all other countries in North and South America. *The Arctic in Question,* edited by E. J. Dosman, gives the views of nine Canadian academics on Canada's Arctic sovereignty. *The Housing Crisis* by Gordon Soules is an expert examination of a world problem, with its possible solutions. *Between Friends/Entre Amis,* by the National Film Board of Canada, which was Canada's bicentennial gift to the United States, is a lavish photographic record of life along the border between the two countries.

The convention that selected Joseph Clark as Progressive Conservative party leader is the subject of *Winners, Losers,* by Brown, Chodos, and Murphy.

Poetry. Canada lost a fine poet with the death at 46 of Stanley Cooperman. His last volume, *Canadian Gothic,* published after his death, is his best.

Irving Layton's *For My Brother Jesus* is a plea in poetry for Jews to acknowledge Jesus as one of their prophets. *The Unwavering Eye* is a selection of Layton's poems since 1969. George Bowering increases his stature with his latest volume, *The Catch.* Al Purdy's *Sundance at Dusk* is typically robust and natural. In *Ice Age,* her 15th volume of poetry since 1928, Dorothy Livesay defies old age with lyric power.

George Woodcock, a prolific prose writer, turns to poetry in *Notes on Visitations. Signatures,* an anthology of Canadian poetry edited by Jim Head, John Laing, and Glen Miller, was well received. Less well received, though welcomed by some, was *Storm Warning 2,* a collection of poems by young Canadians, edited by Al Purdy.

Tom Wayman's third volume, *Money and Rain,* is about Vancouver and working there. Patrick Lane writes of South America in his *Unborn Things.* Susan Musgrave's *The Impstone* deals with a world of witches and torments. Bilingual Catherine Firestone, whose poetry in French has already been published, writes a volume in English, *Daydream Daughter.*

Fiction. Margaret Atwood's third novel, *Lady Oracle,* mixes satire with a strong measure of terror as it examines a woman's life. *Small Ceremonies,* by Carol Shields, is a convincing novel about a Canadian woman who is a wife and a writer. *Playground,* by John Buell, tells engrossingly how a city business executive saves himself in the wilderness with only his brains to help him. Another survival story, strong on

suspense, is David Morrell's *Testament.* Norman Hartley's *The Viking Process* is a fine thriller. In *Rerun,* Neil Crichton's promising first novel, a ball of light sends a man living in 1990 back in time to 1976, with the result that he knows all that will happen in the ensuing 14 years.

Ann Henry's *It's All Free on the Outside* tells of a prairie girl who leaves home to travel with a circus. It praises circus life and circus people. Jack Hodgins' *Spit Delaney's Island* is a collection of short stories, most of them set on Vancouver Island.

A trio of promising novels by Albertans appeared. Betty Wilson's *André Tom MacGregor* tells of the encounter of an Alberta métis boy with the white man's world. Randal Harker's *Adrift* chronicles a young man's failure in the city. Marie Jakober's *The Mind Gods* is science fiction set in 2350 A. D.

DAVID SAVAGE,
Simon Fraser University

Canadian Literature in French

In 1976, several important Quebec publishers folded: Les Editions du Jour, HMH, L'Aurore, and L'Actuelle. An enterprise as wealthy as Editions La Presse encountered setbacks it was not certain could be recovered. At the same time, Les Editions Quinze, a new publishing house brought to life by its writer-founders, gave promise of surviving. The crisis in publishing would be nothing, however, if it did not reflect a more profound crisis in Quebec literature itself.

In all literary fields it seemed to be a case of marking time. The important works published in 1976 were the product of already seasoned writers who made their mark ten, fifteen, or even twenty years ago. With rare exceptions, the voices of the current generation stay silent, as though, since 1970, some ideological barrier lay across any real resurgence of Quebec literature. It lay, so to speak, in the trough of the wave.

Novel. Two works by new authors are worthy of note: *L'Euguélionne* by Louky Bersianik (the pseudonym of Lucille Durand), a baroque feminist plea that has enjoyed immense commercial success, and *Mort et naissance de Christophe Ulric,* by Yvon Rivard, a poetic narration in carefully wrought prose full of rich and complex symbolism. But the really significant titles were the work of seasoned writers. Among the youngest of them are André Major, whose *Les Rescapés* makes the third (and possibly final) panel of his rustic fresco, *Histoires de déserteurs,* which began in 1974 with *L'Epouvantail;* Roch Carrier, author of *La Guerre, yes sir!,* who published a sort of fairy tale world, *Le Jardin des délices;* Marie-Claire Blais, whose *Une liaison parisienne* is her thirteenth and possibly her best novel; and Réjean Ducharme, who pursues in *Les Enfantômes* the linguistic adventure and the exploration of the evil of living that he began ten years ago in *L'Avalée des avalés.* Older still are Gilles Archambault, who created an excellent family chronicle in *Les Pins parasols,* and Jacques Godbout, whose fifth novel, *L'Isle au dragon,* is no less full of verve and humor than its predecessors. And lastly, there are the works of two writers launched in the period 1945–50: Gabrielle Roy, whose *La Petite poule d'eau* takes up once more the world, at once loving and distressed, which is the concern of the series of her novels collectively called *Un jardin au bout du monde,* and Anne Hébert, who, in *Les Enfants du sabbat,* has given us an odd story of love and sorcery.

Poetry. Save the collections of Gérald Godin (*Libertés surveillées*), of the inexhaustible Jacques Brault (*L'en dessous l'admirable*), and of Gaston Miron (*Courtepointes*), who has for the last fifteen years been the central figure among Quebec poets, nothing really first rate appeared. These three poets are among the established whom the newest poets are far from able to displace. But among the new poets mention should be made of Dominique Lauzon, whose first effort is *La Vie simple,* and Jean-Marc Fréchette, author of two fine collections, *Le Retour* and *L'Altra riva.* Given the ever more apparent exhaustion of the formal and neo-cultural schools that have dominated Quebec poetry in recent years, it appears that any renewal of poetry will have to come from these young poets working outside the established circle.

Essay. It is here that the domination by earlier generations is the most persistent and the least challenged, as though the essay were a literary form that the young neither understand nor dare to try. The five volumes that focused attention in 1976 are all from the pens of writers past forty. Four of the books are collections of political and literary pieces published by their authors some ten to fifteen years ago: *Escarmouches,* by Jacques Ferron, *Le Réformiste—textes tranquilles* by Jacques Godbout, *Chemin faisant* by Jacques Brault, and *Un génocide en douce* by Pierre Vadeboncoeur. The fifth, *Dictionnaire de moi-même,* is an autobiographical essay of Jean Ethier-Blais, a critic for the newspaper *Le Devoir.*

It was a year that consolidated past gains without pointing any new directions.

FRANÇOIS RICARD, *McGill University*

English Literature

One might expect English literature in 1976 to be affected by economic crises or by the continued terrorism in Northern Ireland and, occasionally, in London itself; but the effect of these events on British writing is, so far, apparently minor and indirect. Eugene McCabe's novel, *Victims,* about an Irish Republican Army raid on a mansion in Northern Ireland, is, significantly, by an Irish writer. Novels by David Hughes (*Memories of Dying*), Emma Tennant

(*Hotel de Dream*), and J. B. Priestley (*Found, Lost, Found, or The English Way of Life*) may be read as allegories describing an unsatisfactory present. There was perhaps more experimentation in the English novel in 1976 than there has been in recent years, and there was increased emphasis on the experience of characters in the transitional period between middle and old age. Otherwise, there was little change. The publication of interesting memoirs, biographies, and volumes of literary criticism, of competent, sometimes impressive, novels and short stories, and of collections of poems continued.

Nonfiction. Richard Crossman's *The Diaries of a Cabinet Minister* were awaited with interest, if only because the government had attempted to prevent their publication, as chronicled in Hugo Young's *The Crossman Affair.* The first volume of the *Diaries,* covering the years 1964 to 1966, is the verbatim record that Crossman dictated at the end of each week while he was minister of housing. *The Diaries of Evelyn Waugh,* edited by Michael Davie, were begun when Waugh was a schoolboy and continued until shortly before his death. Besides insights into Waugh's character, they record experiences that he used in his fiction.

The most various of several volumes of correspondence which appeared in 1976 was Kenneth Gregory's selection of letters published in *The Times* from 1900 to 1975. Nigel Nicolson and Joanne Trautmann edited the second volume of *The Letters of Virginia Woolf.* Jeanne Schulkind, in *Virginia Woolf: Moments of Being,* edited five previously unpublished autobiographical essays by Virginia Woolf. In *Violet Trefusis: Life and Letters,* Jullian Philippe wrote the biography of the woman who was the model for the Russian princess in Virginia Woolf's *Orlando,* and John Phillips edited a selection of Violet Trefusis's letters to Vita Sackville-West, with whom she "eloped" to France in the early 1920's. Another youthful friendship produced Noël Blakiston's *A Romantic Friendship,* an edition of letters written to Blakiston by Cyril Connolly, who became a well-known writer and book reviewer.

Two of the most interesting autobiographies of the year were *The Autobiography of Arthur Ransome,* edited by Rupert Hart-Davis, and Cecil Parrott's *The Tightrope.* Ransome, the author of *Swallows and Amazons* and other books for children, was a foreign correspondent in Russia during the Revolution. Parrott was a tutor of Prince Paul of Yugoslavia; he later became a British diplomat, and then a professor of history. In *Another World, 1897–1917,* Anthony Eden writes of his life at school and at war. This book is complemented by Sidney Aster's *Anthony Eden,* a biography. Another former prime minister, Lord Home, writes of his youth and his experiences in government in *The Way the Wind Blows.* Diana Petre's *The Secret Orchard of Roger Ackerley* describes her child-

UPI

Mystery writer Agatha Christie died in Wallingford, England, Jan. 12, 1976. Her last works, *Curtain* and *Sleeping Murder*, became best-sellers.

hood as a daughter of Ackerley's mistress. In *Joyce Grenfell Requests the Pleasure,* Joyce Grenfell tells of her life and stage career. The novelist Anthony Powell begins his autobiography in *Infants of the Spring,* and his wife, Violet Powell, continues hers in *Within the Family Circle. Coming Home* is the autobiography of the novelist Chaim Bermant; *The Marble Foot,* of the historian and editor Peter Quennell; and *A Cornishman Abroad* is the third volume of the autobiography of the historian A. L. Rowse.

Important biographies were John Watney's life of Mervyn Peake, the novelist and book illustrator, John E. Mack's *A Prince of Our Disorder: The Life of T. E. Lawrence,* Reginald Pound's *A. P. Herbert,* Christopher Hibbert's *Edward VII,* Denys Sutton's *Walter Sickert,* H. Montgomery Hyde's *Oscar Wilde,* Catherine Dupré's *John Galsworthy,* Winifred Gerin's *Elizabeth Gaskell,* and Sandra Jobson Darroch's *Ottoline,* a life of Lady Ottoline Morrell.

Significant historical and critical literary studies were Vernon Scannell's *Not Without Glory: Poets of the Second World War,* Frank Kermode's *The Classic,* John Bayley's *The Uses of Division,* and F. R. Leavis's *Thought, Words and Creativity.*

Fiction. Irish Murdoch's new novel, *Henry and Cato,* describes the return of two "prodigal sons," the one, Henry, to his father's estate,

which he inherits, the other, Cato, a priest, to a renewed faith in his church. On the way, both are tempted and misled, Henry by a girl, Cato by a boy, and Murdoch illustrates her subject: the difficulty of living happily and morally, and the need of experience if one is to have any hope of doing so.

In Muriel Spark's *The Takeover,* Maggie Radcliffe, a wealthy American, is an avatar of the goddess Diana, and Maggie's hanger-on, Hubert Mallindaine, of a priest of Diana, as described in Frazer's *The Golden Bough.* Maggie lives near Rome on the shore of Lake Nemi, once sacred to Diana. Robbed and swindled, she uses vigorous, if unethical, means to recover her fortune. Hubert, who is one of her robbers, defends himself with some success. Amid this comedy, Spark defends the wealthy on the ground that their needs enable others to live.

In *The Alteration,* Kingsley Amis plays with history, imagining that Henry VIII was defeated by Rome and that Luther, suborned by the offer of power and place, became Pope Germanian I.

David Storey's *Saville* is a solid developmental novel in the naturalist tradition. It describes the life from childhood to manhood of Colin Saville, a coal-miner's son, who grows up in a Yorkshire village, becomes a teacher, and leaves his village as the book ends.

John Braine's *Waiting for Sheila* is about another miner's son, now the manager of a department store, who reflects upon his own and his father's relations with women as he waits for his wife to return to his house.

Elizabeth Taylor's last novel, *Blaming,* completed shortly before her death, describes Amy Henderson's bereavement, the first year of her widowhood, her annoyance with Martha Laskin, a kind American novelist, and her feelings of guilt when Martha dies. Other novels about crises of middle age are Frank Swinnerton's *Some Achieve Greatness,* Philip Callow's *The Story of my Desire,* William Cooper's *You're Not Alone,* Chaim Bermant's *The Second Mrs. Whitberg,* and Elizabeth Sutherland's *Hannah Hereafter.*

J. I. M. Stewart continued his series of novels set in Oxford, *Staircase in Surrey,* with a third volume, *A Memorial Service.* Simon Raven concluded his impressive series, *Alms for Oblivion,* with a tenth volume, *The Survivors.*

Novels that are experimental or unusual in form, style, or subject matter were David Plante's *Figures in Bright Air,* Peter Vansittart's *Quintet,* Peter Redgrove and Penelope Shuttle's *The Glass Cottage,* Robert Nye's *Falstaff,* and N. F. Simpson's *Harry Bleachbaker.*

Poetry. An edition of the *Collected Poems* of W. H. Auden was a significant event in the publishing year. In the latter part of his life Auden revised many of his earlier poems, preparing them for republication in a definitive form. He entrusted the editing of this posthumous collection to Edward Mendelson, a member of the Department of English at Yale.

The *Collected Poems* of Kenneth Allott, most of whose poetry was published during the Depression and World War II, also appeared. Allott, like Auden, died in 1973. In witty and striking language, his poems deal with the erosion by time of things valued by the individual. Thomas Blackburn's *Selected Poems* are serious and stoical; Ronald Bottrall's *Selected Poems 1955–1973* are light and amusing.

Several important poets published volumes of new poems in 1976. In *Laboratories of the Spirit,* R. S. Thomas, a Welsh clergyman, finds the contemporary world a "laboratory" in which faith and the desire for excellence are severely tested. In *The Mountains in the Sea,* John Fuller contemplates Welsh scenery and man's solitude in verse that frequently pays tribute to Auden by echoing his tones. Roy Fuller meditates on common incidents in *From the Joke Shop* and considers more sinister aspects of everyday life in *An Ill-Governed Coast.* In *Living in a Calm Country,* Peter Porter considers himself and his surroundings objectively and sensitively. Ted Hughes's *Season Songs* is a modern *Shepherd's Calendar* for children and adults which sharply delineates the detail and significance of life in the countryside. The mood of Jon Silkin's *The Little Time-Keeper* is gloomy, as the poet looks at mechanical processes in the universe and violence and decay in life.

The poems of Adrian Mitchell, Alan Brownjohn, Gavin Ewart, and Donald Thomas are concerned with flaws in individuals and society. In *The Apeman Cometh,* Mitchell attacks capitalism with revolutionary zeal and attempts to illustrate Che Guevara's assertion that "The true revolutionary is guided by great feelings of love." Brownjohn satirizes the middle-class consumer society in *A Song of Good Life.* In *Be My Guest,* Ewart vigorously and humorously exposes his characters' faults and deflates their pretensions. Thomas observes the decadence of buildings, art, and people with affectionate irony in *Welcome to the Grand Hotel.*

Other interesting collections of poetry were Patricia Beer's *Driving West,* David Wright's *A View of the North,* Vernon Scannell's *The Loving Game,* F. T. Prince's *Drypoints of the Hasidim,* Richard Outram's *Turns,* and Michael Longley's *Fishing in the Sky.*

J. K. JOHNSTONE
University of Saskatchewan

French Literature

Four noted writers died in 1976: Paul Morand, one of the best story tellers of our time, who also created, during the 1920's, an elliptic, dynamic, and highly charged "XXth Century style"; Gaetan Picon, a brilliant essayist and critic; Kleber Haedens, who wrote some fine novels; and Audré Malraux, one of France's intellectual giants.

Fiction. Among books by well-known writers published in 1976, the following must be men-

tioned: Robert Merle's *Madrapour,* a kind of Sartrian *No Exit,* set in a plane which never lands; François Régis Bastide's *La Fantaisie du Voyageur,* a story about a romantic music-lover in the defeated Germany of 1945; Françoise Sagan's *Les Yeux de Soie,* a collection of short stories written with detachment and irony; Françoise Mallet-Joris's *Allegra* and Michèle Perrein's *Gemme Lapidaire,* both portraits of women who are stronger than men and have very little use for the male species; Bertrand Poirot-Delpech's *Les Grands de ce Monde,* a satire about politics and politicians, in which the author re-makes recent history; Maurice Genevoix's *Un Jour,* about an old man who lives in the woods, with love of life as its theme; Jean Cayrol's *Histoire d'une Maison,* about a man's dream ruined by the vicissitudes of history; Yves Berger's *Le Fou d'Amérique,* a love story set against the background of the discovery of America in which the country's geography and place names have a great impact on the characters; and Jean Cau's *Les Otages,* a ferocious, realistic fable. Among the works of "new" writers, Denise Roche's *Louve Basse,* an avant-garde novel, can be taken as a long cry against death; Pierrette Fleutiaux's fantastic *Histoire du Gouffre et de la Lunette,* received great applause for its originality.

Nonfiction. At the head of the list of best sellers during the summer of 1976 was *La Dérobade,* by Jeanne Cordelier, a former prostitute who in a highly realistic way tells of her unhappy experiences and the sordid milieux of her profession. Other interesting testimonies were Michel Leiris's *Frêle Bruit,* the memoirs of a well-known writer and poet; Claude Roy's *Somme Toute,* the recollections of a former Communist; Jacques Laurent's *Histoire Égoïste,* the memoirs of an anticonformist of the right; and, perhaps best of all, the *Journal* of Jean Monnet, one of the founders of the European Common Market.

Some of the best biographies published in 1976 were *La Fontaine ou La Vie est un Conte,* by Jean Orieux; *Diane de Poitiers,* by Philippe Erlanger; and *Portrait d'une Séductrice,* a book about Nathalie Barney, the American "Amazone" of the famous French writer Rémy de Gourmont, by Jean Chalon. The most notable essay was *Dieu est Dieu, Nom de Dieu,* by Maurice Clavel, a debated pamphlet about the Church.

Poetry. In the field of poetry, the most important publications were Claude Bonnefoy's 638-page anthology, *La Poésie Française des Origines à Nos Jours;* Jean-Pierre Amée's *Hébuternes,* a colorful work by a 22-year-old poet armed with daring and imagery; Jean Maxence's *Croix sur Table,* which incorporates angry leftism with Christian faith and somnambulism; and Danielle Jaeggi's *Me Sentir Femme,* short, simple, concrete poems motivated by her feminist point of view.

PIERRE BRODIN
Lcyée Français de New York

GERMAN INFORMATION CENTER

Max Frisch wrote the fictional autobiography _Montauk_.

German Literature

A generous output of novels and the discovery of new lyric talents marked the German literary scene in 1976.

Fiction. The traditional German novel was alive and well. New examples were Christine Brückner's nostalgic Prussian story, _Jauche und Levkojen;_ Manfred Bieler's prewar Prague tale, _Der Mädchenkrieg;_ Walter Kempowski's prison chronicle, _Ein Kapitel für sich;_ and Hermann Lenz's diary of a German counterpart of the good soldier Schweik, entitled _Neue Zeit._ More ambitious productions were Heinar Kipphardt's _März,_ whose hero embraces insanity as a release from contemporary civilization, Max Frisch's imaginary autobiography, _Montauk,_ and Martin Walser's anti-erotic _Jenseits der Liebe._ Siegfried Lenz and the Swiss Adolf Muschg brought out interesting short stories.

Nonfiction. _Der abwendbare Untergang,_ a profound analysis of the present international situation by Giselher Wirsing, appeared shortly after the author's death. Equally thought-provoking were Herbert Gruhl's indictment of worldwide industrial exploitation, _Ein Planet wird geplündert;_ Helmut Schelsky's sociological study, _Der selbständige und der betreute Mensch;_ and Klaus Mehnert's discussion of _Jugend im Zeitbruch._ Sensational programs for women's liberation were touted by Alice Schwarzer (_Der kleine Unterschied und seine grossen Folgen_) and Ernst Bornemann (_Das Patriarchat_).

Poetry. The climate for pure poetry continued to improve. New lyric talents were discovered in Godehard Schramm, Rainer Malkowski, and Karin Kiwus. Even the heavily engaged Hans Magnus Enzensberger returned to more descriptive political poems.

Drama. The Austrian Wolfgang Bauer achieved two successful premières, _Magnetküsse_ and _Gespenster,_ and Joseph Breitbach's department store play _Die Jubilarin_ enjoyed a good reception. But Rolf Hochhuth's dramatization of Ernest Hemingway's last days and Margarethe von Trotta's stage version of Heinrich Böll's shocker _Katharina Blum_ proved inept.

East German Literature. In its attempt to achieve a distinct identity the German Democratic Republic has shown itself to be temporarily willing to tolerate some nonconformity. This found expression in Adolf Endler's critical poems _Nacht mit Brille_ and in Gerti Tetzner's novel _Karin W._ Hermann Kant's story collection, _Eine Übertretung,_ willingly followed the party line.

ERNST ROSE
Author of "A History of German Literature"

Italian Literature

Interest in the established Italian literary prizes—as well as the quality of the works submitted—has continued to decline, and their story is by now a rather tired chronicle of good manners without much substance: Fausta Cialente won the Premio Strega for her novel, _Le quattro ragazze Wieselberger,_ while Mario Tobino gained the Premio Viareggio with his volume of short stories, _La bella degli specchi;_ the Viareggio prize for poetry went to Dario Bellezza for _Morte segreta,_ and that for critical essays to a volume by Sergio Solmi, _La luna di Laforgue._

The Publishing Climate. Meanwhile, the world of publishing was uneasy, and many traditional assumptions were questioned. About 15,000 books are printed each year in Italy, and a large publishing house receives an average of 2,500 manuscripts each year; but several authors now complain that insufficient attention is paid to the efforts of young or still unknown writers, and in general to experimental writing. One step toward satisfying this increased demand has been taken with the foundation of a _Cooperativa degli Scrittori,_ which has begun to publish fiction and essays with a novel approach. The problems of the daily press—as discussed, for instance, in the proceedings of a congress on _La stampa quotidiana tra crisi e riforma_—are even more grave. The dissatisfaction with traditional literary fare is manifested also, on a lighter level, by the appearance of an almost completely new genre: detective novels written in an idiom and environment which are recognizably Italian.

Historiography. Historical writing has become particularly important, especially because of the ongoing debate on the Fascist period. Thus, 1976 saw the publication of the 4th volume of Renzo De Felice's controversial biography of Mussolini and echoes of his polemics with other historians, as well as the appearance of the _Intervista sull'antifascismo_ by Giorgio

Amendola, of Umberto Terracini's clandestine correspondence from Fascist jails in the 1930's, and of monographs on special moments or figures of Fascist history, such as the short-lived Salò republic.

Encyclopedic Works. There was also an increase in encyclopedic compilations, like the *Enciclopedia Europea* edited by Garzanti. Einaudi's much-discussed *Storia d'Italia* was continued with the volume on *La cultura* by Alberto Asor Rosa. Collections like the proceedings of the *Primo Colloquio Internazionale del Lessico Intellettuale Europeo* also appeared, and there was continued activity in useful critical reissues of classic texts, such as the publication of Titian's letters on the occasion of the 4th centenary of the death of the great painter.

Obituaries. Alberto Mondadori, son of the founder of the publishing house and himself founder of the house "Il Saggiatore," died suddenly in 1976. The death of Enzo Paci deprived Italy of one of its leading philosophers, a creative interpreter of phenomenological thought; his intellectual influence went beyond the world of philosophy *stricto sensu,* and his writings were never disjoined from a fruitful teaching activity.

PAOLO VALESIO, *Yale University*

TASS FROM SOVFOTO

Georgi Markov's novel *Siberia* won the Lenin Prize.

Soviet Literature

People in the West do not generally realize how Soviet artists must constantly bear in mind the principles of Socialist Realism. Time and again, for nearly half a century, attempts have been made by artists and critics to broaden the interpretation of these principles, to create a more individual vision of the world. Each time the spokesmen of the Communist party have countered with a reassertion of the ideological doctrine and its implications. In 1975, which marked the 30th anniversary of the victorious war, there was a resurgence of patriotic themes which during the war had overshadowed ideology. The year 1976 saw a continuation of this trend. However, since it started with the 25th Congress of the Communist party, the emphasis on ideology was again more strongly felt in literary debates. Almost every issue of every journal and magazine contained editorials, lengthy articles, and reports on meetings devoted to the question what could be done to further the cause of Socialism. This was also the theme of numerous stories, plays, and poems published in journals or in separate volumes.

One of the perennial problems is that Soviet literature is in need of works giving a synthesis of contemporary life as a realization of the goals of Socialism. Though mostly stated in an indirect way, such problems continued to preoccupy writers and critics in 1976. While the debates of 1975 expressed mostly vaguely formulated hopes, the tone in the 1976 discussions was much more positive. One of the veterans of the debate on Socialist Realism, Vitali Ozerov,

saw a number of important achievements and more to come ("The Time of Great Achievements and Expectations," *Voprosy Literatury,* 2). In the discussions at the Sixth Congress of the Union of Soviet Writers, held in June, the novel *Siberia* by Georgi Markov was acclaimed as such an achievement and selected for the year's Lenin Prize. The novel is a broadly painted panorama of life, embracing various circles of society, but it is more of an excursion into the heroic past of the generation that made the revolution than a depiction of the present. Other works, old and new, were mentioned on various occasions as successful attempts at synthesizing contemporary problems in an epic vision. Among them were books of differing literary quality, such as Yuri Bondarev's *The*

Nobelist Aleksandr Solzhenitsyn, a nonperson in the USSR, spent part of the year studying at Stanford Univ.

UPI

Shore and Grigori Baklanov's *Friends*. Nevertheless, most writers produce more fragmentary depictions, choosing themes of the war, the conquest of nature, and the pride of every-day productive labor of an "average citizen." A typical example of the latter is Vladimir Popov's "All in a Day's Work" (*Sovietskaya Literatura,* 2).

There were no important poetic debuts in 1976, and only a few separate volumes by the known authors were published (Vsevolod Rozhdestvensky, Yevgeni Vinokurov). Yevgeni Yevtushenko published an aggressive long "sociopoem" on the Irish situation, "Safari in Ulster" (*Literaturnaya Gazeta,* 11), and he also appeared as a critic, praising the poetry of Nikolai Rubtsov.

It is interesting to note that Aleksandr Solzhenitsyn, a nonperson in the Soviet Union, was sharply criticized in an article, "Without a Tsar at the Head" (*Literaturnaya Gazeta,* 11), not for his writings (the publication of *Gulag Archipelago,* third part, was not even mentioned) but for his "monarchism."

Z. FOLEJEWSKI, *University of Ottawa*

Spanish Literature

The year 1976, one of great political and social turmoil in major areas of the Hispanic world (Argentina, Peru, Mexico, and Spain), will not go down as especially fruitful for literature. Under such trying, even desperate circumstances, an individual writer may flourish; a literature, however, must languish.

Narrative. Recipients of major narrative awards in Latin America included Mexico's Carlos Fuentes, who won the Xavier Villarrutia Prize for his novel *Terra nostra;* Ecuadorian novelist Gonzalo Ramón, who received his country's Unico Prize for *Guandal;* and Uruguayan novelist Juan Luis Cabo, winner of the Cáceres Prize for *La cuerda.* Prizes awarded to Spanish novelists included the Nadal Prize to Francisco Umbral for *Los ninfos,* which reconstructs the Spanish Civil War ambiance via an adolescent's account; the "Novelas y Cuentos" prize to Rodrigo Rubio for *Cuarteto de máscaras;* the Café Gijón Prize to Caty Juan for *La noche del calamar;* and the Ateneo de Sevilla Prize to José Luis Olaizola for *Planicio,* a surprisingly effective conventional narration.

Several other major novelists also published works in 1976, including Chile's José Donoso, whose daring *El lugar sin límites* effectively probes the darkest aspects of homosexuality; Argentina's Ernesto Sabató, whose *Abadón, el exterminador* was universally lauded; and Peru's Julio Ramón Ribeiro, whose political novel *Cambio de guardia* will surely have readers searching out roman à clef possibilities. Among well-known Spanish novelists publishing were Ramón Sender (*El fugitivo*), Francisco García Pavón (*Ya no es ayer*), and Manuel Ferrand (*Los farsantes*).

Noteworthy in the area of the short story were the prizewinning efforts of the Spaniard Luis Mateo Díez, whose *Cenizas* won the Ignacio Aldecoa Prize; the Argentinian Diego Angelino, whose collection *Con otro sol* received the La Nación Prize; and the Ecuadorian Raúl Pérez Torres, whose *Micaela y otros cuentos* was awarded his country's Premio Nacional del Cuento. Other significant short-story collections in 1976 were the Argentinian Eduardo Gudiño Kieffer's *La hora de María y el pájaro de oro,* the Peruvian Marco Antonio Rodríguez' *Historia de un intruso,* the Colombian Gustavo Alvarez Gardizábal's *La boba y el buda,* and the Spaniard Antonio Pereira's *El ingeniero Balboa y otras historias civiles.*

Nonfiction. Important essays published in 1976 included the Colombian Rafael Humberto Moreno-Durán's *De la barbarie a la imaginación* and works of the Spaniards José Luis Aranguren (*Talante, juventud y moral*) and Salvador de Madariaga (*Dios y los españoles*). Significant items under the heading of literary criticism included Jaime Alazraki's *José Luis Borges,* Francisco Mena Benito's *El tradicionalismo de Federico García Lorca,* Rafael Ferreres' *Aproximaciones a la poesía de Dámaso Alonso,* Joaquín Artiles' *El libro de Apolonio, poema español del siglo XIII,* and Julio Ramón Ribeiro's collection of critical essays *La caza sutil.*

Poetry. Spain's most significant prizes for poetry were awarded to José Luis Alegre's *Primera invitación a la vida* (Boscán Prize), Angel Sánchez Pascual's *Ceremonia de la inocencia* (Adonais Prize), Concha Saiz' *Paréntesis y cuevas* (Angaro Prize), Joaquín Fernández' *Zoon erotikon* (Aldebarán Prize), Francisco Toledano's *Trilogía interrogante* (Leopoldo Panero Prize), Francisco Mena Cantero's *Esta lluvia, esta húmeda respuesta* (Alcatraván Prize), and Laureano Jiménez' *Meditación vegetal* (Altolaguirre-Prados Prize).

Significant publications by major Spanish poets included Angel González' *Muestra de . . . ,* Justo Jorge Padrón's *Los círculos del infierno,* Alfonso Canales' *El año sabático,* Jaime Gil de Biedma's finally complete *Las personas del verbo,* and Luis Jiménez Martos' *Los pasos litorales.* Outstanding books from new poets were Rafael Osuna's *Sin orden ni concierto* and Santiago Casteló's *Tierra en la carne.*

Theater. The major Spanish prizes for new plays went to José Martín Recuerda's *El engañao* (Lope de Vega Prize), Manuel Alonso Alcalde's *Sólo se vive dos veces* (Pemán Prize), and Julio Martínez Velasco's *El microbusito Che* (Aguilar Prize).

Obituary. Two deaths were especially felt in the world of Hispanic letters: those of José Lezama Lima, a most significant modern Cuban poet; and Antonio Gaya Nuño, an outstanding Spanish critic and narrator.

ALFRED RODRIGUEZ
The University of New Mexico

LONDON

Economic difficulties in the United Kingdom continued to affect its largest city during 1976. Unemployment in London rose to around 200,-000, and special work creation programs were set up to deal with large increases in unemployed school leavers. Street battles between black youths and police erupted at the Caribbean Carnival in Notting Hill, scene of the 1968 race riots, in late August. Police presence was blamed for the violence, but police chief Robert Mark said there would be no "no-go" areas in his district. Deputy Greater London Council leader Illtyd Harrington said social deprivation was the root cause of violence and appealed for special urban aid for ghetto areas of inner London.

City Finances. In an attempt to keep within government guidelines, Greater London Council slashed spending committee budgets by £19 million for the year to April 1977. Housing was exempt from cuts, but all other services were reduced and 2,000 jobs were lost. Despite higher than market yield, a £100 million debt bond offer by Greater London Council was left with the underwriters. Bond dealers expressed fears that the council could be overtaken by bankruptcy as a result of record cost inflation which had hit city services.

Urban Development and Transportation. The central government agreed in outline to assist with £2,000 million rejuvenation of vast areas of redundant dockland to the east of the center of the city. Greater London Council wanted redevelopment to include new roads, factories, offices, houses, schools, and associated community facilities. Included in plans, implementation of which is unlikely to begin until the 1980's, is an extension to the subway train network to connect docklands to the city's center. Meanwhile the cuts in government spending reduced London's transportation budget for the period 1976–1981 by an estimated £300 million. Road improvements as well as train and bus services will be affected. Private real estate development was at a virtual standstill as developers wound up projects begun in earlier years and did not start new ones. There were signs, however, that the rental market had passed the worst, and the property investment market strengthened as the year progressed.

Tourism. Decline in the value of the pound, virtual cessation of IRA bombings, and fine weather brought a heavy influx of visitors from abroad. Hotels were full throughout the summer.

Water Shortage. Drought conditions meant water shortages and use restrictions for Londoners from August on as the Thames ran dry in upper reaches. Hot weather changed London habits—meals were taken out of doors; secretaries wore cooler clothes; and even their staid bosses discarded their jackets and ties.

DAVID BREWERTON, *City Office*
"The Daily Telegraph," London

LOS ANGELES

Conflicts over public salaries and property tax assessments occupied the attention of public officials in the Los Angeles area during 1976. So did problems of transportation, urban renewal, and school integration.

Government and Politics. Faced with sharp resistance to increased property taxes resulting from higher market values of homes, Mayor Thomas Bradley called for a "penny-pinching" fiscal policy. The City Council, responding to criticisms, froze the salaries of all top-ranking administrators. The City Administrative Officer had recommended increases of 11.5% for 19 high executives. Earlier, the council rejected a 10% increase for its own membership.

Transportation. On March 15 the California Department of Transportation began an experiment on the Santa Monica Freeway, which restricted one lane in each direction for use by buses and car pools. The experiment proved to be enormously unpopular. It reduced the actual carrying capacity of the freeway and increased accidents on adjacent surface streets by as much as 10%. In August the project was stopped by a federal judge on the grounds that federal and state guidelines for environmental impact evaluation had not been followed.

Urban Renewal. Richard Mitchell retired as administrator of the Los Angeles County Redevelopment Agency on June 30. Edward Helfeld, who had occupied a similar post in St. Paul, Minn., was hired to replace him.

Urban renewal continued to be a controversial area of public policy and threatened to become an important issue in the 1977 election. The Bunker Hill project, covering 25 blocks in the central city, remained less than 50% finished after 17 years. The huge 255-block downtown redevelopment project was stalled indefinitely by political conflict.

School Integration. The state supreme court ruled in June that the Los Angeles school district must proceed under earlier court orders to end de facto racial segregation. The court held that each school need not have a quota of students from each racial group, but must have a "reasonably feasible" integration plan.

Los Angeles Philharmonic. Zubin Mehta, music director of the Los Angeles Philharmonic Orchestra since 1962, announced in February that he would leave in two years for a similar position with the New York Philharmonic.

Sports. In football, UCLA upset Ohio State in the 1976 Rose Bowl, 23–10. Coach "Dick" Vermeil later left to become head coach of the Philadelphia Eagles; USC coach John McKay also left to take over the Tampa Bay Buccaneers. Terry Donahue and John Robinson were respective replacements. In basketball, the Lakers named former star Jerry West as new head coach.

CHARLES R. ADRIAN
University of California, Riverside

On the morning of October 20, a ferry and a Norwegian tanker collided near the Louisiana communities of Destrehan and Luling, killing at least 77 persons.

LOUISIANA

What was probably the greatest disaster on the Mississippi River in this century stunned Louisiana late in 1976 when at least 77 persons lost their lives in a ferryboat-tanker collision about 20 miles (32 km) north of New Orleans.

Disasters. Early on the morning of October 20 a ferry loaded with industrial plant and oil refinery workers was crossing the river between the communities of Destrehan and Luling when it collided with the Norwegian tanker *Frosta,* which was headed upstream to Baton Rouge. The ferry was hit amidships and capsized, knocking pedestrians and vehicles into the cold waters. Only 18 persons escaped alive from the ferry. A total of 77 bodies was recovered and at least 3 persons were missing. No one on the tanker was injured. One firm alone, Brown and Root, lost more than 30 employees. An autopsy on the ferryboat captain revealed that he had an alcoholic content of 0.9% in his blood at the time of death. In Louisiana, a content of .1% is sufficient to convict a person of driving while intoxicated.

In another disaster, 13 employees of the Tenneco Oil Co. refinery in Chalmette were killed and 6 others injured in a fire and explosion in August. The federal government later cited Tenneco for several safety violations.

Political Front. Gov. Edwin Edwards admitted in October that his wife, Elaine, had accepted a gift of $10,000 from Tongsun Park, a South Korean lobbyist and businessman. Edwards said the gift was made in 1971, when he was a congressman and a candidate for governor. He said his wife did not inform him of the gift until 1973 or 1974, when he was asked by the Internal Revenue Service to account for certain expenditures. The governor said the South Korean had offered him a campaign contribution, but when he refused the offer, Park presented Mrs. Edwards with a sealed envelope for her and the two Edwards daughters. The governor said he saw nothing wrong with the gift because he was unaware of it at the time, it was a personal present to his wife, and no political favors were asked of him in connection with it.

Park has been described by the press as a principal in a ring of South Koreans who spent up to $1 million annually in the early 1970's on gifts and favors to congressmen and other officials in exchange for legislative favors. The South Korean government later stated that Park acted in no official capacity.

Labor Developments. Early in the year a man was shot to death and four persons were injured when about 100 men, using a stolen forklift as a vehicle to ram through a fence, attacked a construction site at the Jupiter Chemical Co. plant in Lake Charles. The company charged that the plant was attacked by members of the Southwest Louisiana Building and Construction Trades Council, AFL-CIO, or persons under its direction. Additionally, an independent union, the American Federation of Unions, Local 102, whose workers were employed at the site, said in a civil suit that its members were intimidated by the AFL-CIO workers. Several persons were indicted in connection with the attack.

In July the legislature passed controversial right-to-work law, specifying that no worker could be forced to join a union in order to hold a job. On July 14, James Leslie, a Shreveport advertising executive who had handled the media campaign for the bill, was shot to death in Baton Rouge. The case was unsolved at year-end.

JOSEPH W. DARBY III, *Assistant City Editor*
"The Times-Picayune," New Orleans

------ **LOUISIANA · Information Highlights** ------

Area: 48,523 square miles (125,675 km²).
Population (1975 est.): 3,791,000.
Chief Cities (1970 census): Baton Rouge, the capital, 165,963; New Orleans, 593,471; Shreveport, 182,064.
Government (1976): *Chief Officers*—governor, Edwin W. Edwards (D); lt. gov., James E. Fitzmorris, Jr. (D). *Legislature*—Senate, 39 members; House of Representatives, 105 members.
Education (1975–76): *Enrollment*—public elementary schools, 592,479 pupils; public secondary, 254,723; nonpublic (1976–77), 165,900; colleges and universities, 148,335 students. *Public school expenditures,* $820,000,000 ($993 per pupil).
State Finances (fiscal year 1975): *Revenues,* $2,882,584,-000; *expenditures,* $2,796,126,000.
Personal Income (1975): $18,591,000,000; per capita, $4,904.
Labor Force (July 1976): *Nonagricultural wage and salary earners,* 1,193,400; *insured unemployed,* 39,-300 (3.8%).

LUXEMBOURG

Luxemburgers had little cause for worry in 1976. Despite a slight drop in iron and steel production—the mainstay of its economy—and a corresponding decline in the gross national product, the grand duchy remained one of the most economically secure places throughout Europe, with a minimal 11% rate of inflation, a basically contented work force, and no unemployment to speak of.

However, during the year, there were some minor sensations, principally in the area of foreign affairs.

In February *Time Magazine* reported that the Soviet mission to Luxembourg, with its large staff of 37, was in reality a regional headquarters for Soviet intelligence operatives and that the Soviets regularly used Luxembourg's unguarded borders to infiltrate into neighboring, allied countries. The revelation hardly surprised Luxemburgers but was embarrassing nevertheless.

Soviet operatives notwithstanding, Luxembourg's allies had little reason to question either its security or fidelity. Luxembourg, with its battalion-size army of 550 volunteers (which includes a 100-man band), is an active, if not overly significant, member of the North Atlantic Treaty Organization (NATO). Its troops eagerly and ably participated in the huge NATO Autumn Forge '76 maneuvers.

In July U. S. Secretary of State Henry Kissinger visited Luxembourg for a friendly chat with Prime Minister Gaston Thorn. Despite the spread of anti-American sentiment elsewhere in Europe, Luxemburgers still feel grateful to the United States for liberating them in World War II, and relations between the two countries remain particularly close.

Luxemburgers also remain fervent advocates of European integration. The duchy's commitment to the European Economic Community (EEC) was underlined when Finance Minister Raymond Vouel was appointed to be its representative on the EEC board of commissioners. Prime Minister Thorn was president of the EEC's council of ministers for the first half of 1976.

GORDON F. SANDER

--- **LUXEMBOURG • Information Highlights** ---

Official Name: Grand Duchy of Luxembourg.
Area: 999 square miles (2,586 km²).
Population (1976 est.): 358,000.
Chief Cities (1975 est.): Luxembourg, the capital, 78,-800; Esch-sur-Alzette, 27,700; Differdange, 18,300.
Government: *Head of state,* Jean, grand duke (acceded 1964). *Head of government,* Gaston Thorn, prime minister (took office June 18, 1974). *Legislature* (unicameral)—Chamber of Deputies.
Monetary Unit: Franc (38.88 francs equal U. S.$1, Aug. 1976).
Gross National Product (1975 est.): $2,200,000,000.
Manufacturing (major products): Iron and steel, chemicals, fertilizers, textiles, nonferrous metals.
Major Agricultural Products: Barley, wheat, oats, grapes, potatoes.

MAINE

In 1976, Maine joined the nation in celebrating its 200th birthday. Observers noted an unprecedented outpouring of community feeling and celebration during the months of July and August. It was the greatest peace-time commemoration in Maine's history. The year also saw much political activity.

Politics. Independent Gov. James B. Longley continued his domination of Maine's political life as he pursued his policies of cost-cutting in state government and his outspoken criticism of various interest groups.

In the November elections, Congressmen Dave Emery and Bill Cohen faced Democratic challenges from Rick Barton and Leighton Cooney. Both were reelected. Sen. Edmund Muskie gained reelection to a fourth term in the U. S. Senate, winning over Robert Monks, a wealthy businessman with roots in both Maine and Massachusetts.

The makeup of the Legislature remained the same, with Republicans controlling the Senate (21–12) and Democrats the House of Representatives (90–61). Voters overwhelmingly approved a returnable-bottle bill, which will require consumer deposits on bottles and cans when it becomes effective in 1978.

In June voters narrowly approved a proposal compelling the state to buy enough acreage to preserve Mt. Bigelow from private development.

Economy. The unemployment rate dropped from 10% to 8% during the year, as Maine slowly recovered from the recession. However, high fuel costs continued to hurt industry's competitive position.

The $17,000,000 Easton sugar refinery, which has been closed since 1970, was again in operation, supplied by some 12,000 acres (4,850 ha) of Maine and New Brunswick sugar beets. Its opening was made possible by a group of Aroostook potato farmers, incorporated as the Pine State Sugar Beet Growers, Inc., who purchased it from the state. An Austrian-Italian firm is operating the refinery.

Indian Suit. The major development of 1976 involved a threatened suit filed against the state of Maine by the U. S. Justice Department on behalf of the Penobscot and Passamaquoddy Indian tribes. The tribes are asking $300,000,000 in damages for two thirds of the state's land area which, they allege, was illegally taken from them.

If filed, the suit will contend that treaties between the tribes and Massachusetts (Maine was part of Massachusetts until 1820), which reduced their holdings to three reservations in Maine, are invalid because Massachusetts, and later Maine, never complied with the Non-Intercourse Act of 1790. That act required congressional approval of all treaties negotiated between states and their Indians, but Massachusetts, it is alleged, never received such approval.

UPI

Maine Sen. Edmund Muskie (*right*) and Idaho Sen. Frank Church enjoy a laugh at the Democratic convention.

By November, the state found itself in an extraordinary situation, as Boston and New York bond firms announced that they would not buy any state or municipal bonds marketed from Maine, because without clear title to the land, the solvency of both the state and municipalities was not at all certain. In addition, the validity of home mortgages was being questioned. The Farmers Home Administration announced that no new mortgages would be guaranteed by F. H. A. in Maine. By year-end, the entire fiscal structure of the public and private sectors was badly shaken with no prospect for a quick solution.

RONALD F. BANKS
University of Maine

MALAYSIA

As 1976 began, economic prospects brightened and there were clear indications that the government's target of 6% growth would be exceeded. Under the impact of the world recession, the Malaysian gross domestic product (GDP) had grown only 2.5% in 1975. Overseas demand for Malaysian primary exports (rubber, tin, palm oil, and timber) was strong in 1976. The Third Malaysia Plan (1976–1980) projects an average annual GDP growth rate of 8.5%, and places heavy emphasis on agriculture (25.5% of total outlays) to alleviate poverty in the rural, primarily Malay, areas.

Pernas, a government corporation, purchased a controlling interest in the London Tin Corporation, the world's largest tin company.

The Prime Ministership. On January 14, Tun Abdul Razak, prime minister since 1970, died of leukemia. His successor, Datuk Hussein bin Onn, deputy prime minister since 1973, announced that he would follow closely Razak's policies.

Scandal and Elections. Malaysia's most serious political scandal emerged with the conviction on corruption charges of Datuk Harun Idris, chief minister of Selangor state and leader of the youth section of UMNO, the nation's dominant political party. In Sabah State Assembly elections in January the Berjaya party captured 34 of 48 seats (6 appointed) and its leader, Tun Haji Mohammed Fuad Stephens, became chief minister. However, on June 6, he and three leading members of his Cabinet were killed in a plane crash. The premiership and party leadership were assumed by Deputy Chief Minister Datuk Harris Saleh. The year was marked by heightened concern regarding internal security.

Relations with Thailand. During a drive by Malaysian forces against communist guerrillas, airstrikes were conducted on targets across the Thai border. Thailand protested and Malaysia agreed to negotiate revisions in the 1964 accord permitting Malaysian counterinsurgency units to enter Thailand. Malaysian units stationed in the Betong area of Thailand were withdrawn.

MARVIN C. OTT, *Mount Holyoke College*

———— MAINE • Information Highlights ————

Area: 33,215 square miles (86,027 km²).
Population (1975 est.): 1,059,000.
Chief Cities (1970 census): Augusta, the capital, 21,945; Portland, 65,116; Lewiston, 41,779; Bangor, 33,168.
Government (1976): *Chief Officers*—governor, James B. Longley (I); sec. of state, Markham Gartley (R). *Legislature*—Senate, 33; House of Representatives, 151 members.
Education (1975–76): *Enrollment*—public elementary schools, 172,350 pupils; public secondary, 78,581; nonpublic (1976–77), 16,800; colleges and universities, 37,516 students. *Public school expenditures,* $272,000,000 ($1,120 per pupil).
State Finances (fiscal year 1975): *Revenues,* $801,433,-000; *expenditures,* $863,261,000.
Personal Income (1975): $5,071,000,000; per capita, $4,-786.
Labor Force (July 1976): *Nonagricultural wage and salary earners,* 370,200; *insured unemployed,* 21,400 (7.6%).

———— MALAYSIA • Information Highlights ————

Official Name: Malaysia.
Location: Southeast Asia.
Area: 127,316 square miles (329,749 km²).
Population (1976 est.): 12,400,000.
Chief Cities (1975 est.): Kuala Lumpur, the capital, 500,000; Pinang, 280,000; Ipoh, 255,000.
Government: *Head of state:* Sultan Yahya Putra (took office Sept. 1975). *Head of government,* Hussein bin Onn, prime minister (took office Jan. 1976). *Legislature*—Parliament: Dewan Negara (Senate) and Dewan Ra'ayat (House of Representatives).
Monetary Unit: Malaysian dollar (2.52 M. dollars equal U. S.$1, Sept. 1976).
Gross National Product (1975 est.): $9,500,000,000.
Manufacturing (major products): Petroleum products, refined sugar, rubber goods, steel, lumber.
Major Agricultural Products: Rubber, rice, palm oil and kernels, tea, pepper, coconuts, spices.
Foreign Trade (1975): *Exports,* $4,126,000,000; *imports,* $3,888,000,000.

MANITOBA

Political calm, government austerity, and agricultural prosperity characterized Manitoba in 1976.

Legislation. The Legislature sat from February 12 to June 11, passing 72 bills, few of which stimulated much controversy. Rent control legislation was approved without a dissenting vote, but amendments to the Trade Practices Inquiry Act met strong objections.

Government Austerity. On August 17 Premier Schreyer announced austerity measures to reduce expenditures in fiscal 1977 by up to $30 million. The provincial civil service was frozen at once and is to be reduced 10% by attrition.

Agriculture. Hot, dry weather continued all summer, but rain fell in sufficient quantities at the right time to ensure a record grain crop of 250 million bushels (88,100,000 hl). However, northern forests suffered from the drought; 750 forest fires broke out during the summer.

Anti-Inflation Program. In February Manitoba joined six other provinces in signing an anti-inflation agreement with the federal government. As the year progressed it came under increasing pressure from union supporters of the New Democratic party to repudiate this pact. Some 2,800 members of the United Steel Workers of America struck on June 15 after the Anti-Inflation Board reduced a negotiated wage increase from 18.11% to 12.9%. The strike ended 12 days later when the anti-inflation administrator ordered that the workers be paid the full amount. In August Liquor Commission employees were involved in a similar controversy.

Employment. About 18,000 persons were unemployed in mid-1976, giving Manitoba the third lowest provincial jobless rate in Canada, 4.1%.

Culture. The cultural highlight of 1976 was the exhibition in the Winnipeg Art Gallery of masterpieces from the Hermitage and Russian State galleries in Leningrad. Winnipeg was one of the two cities in Canada to display the 42 masterworks. The legislature passed a special "immunity from seizure" act to meet Soviet conditions. The exhibition attracted 93,000 paying viewers in 6 weeks.

JOHN A. BOVEY
Provincial Archivist of Manitoba

────── **MANITOBA • Information Highlights** ──────

Area: 251,000 square miles (650,090 km²).
Population (April 1976 est.): 1,026,000.
Chief City (1974): Winnipeg, the capital, 577,723.
Government (1976): *Chief Officers*—lt. gov., Francis L. Jobin; premier, Edward Schreyer (New Democratic party); chief justice, Samuel Freedman. *Legislature*—Legislative Assembly, 57 members.
Education (1976–77): *Enrollment:* public elementary and secondary schools, 216,050; private schools, 1,480; Indian (federal) schools, 5,910; post-secondary: 22,230 students. *Total expenditures,* $409,215,000.
Public Finance (1975–76 est.): *Revenues,* $1,021,000,000; *expenditures,* $1,027,000,000.
Personal Income (1974): $4,785,000,000; average annual income per person, $4,733.
(All monetary figures given in Canadian dollars.)

MARINE BIOLOGY

Marine scientists are becoming increasingly interested in the behavior of marine organisms. Thus, competition between individuals of the same species of gastropod snail has been shown to be a factor in controlling intertidal snail populations. High population densities hamper the growth of juveniles and increase the mortality of adults until their numbers are radically reduced. These findings are extremely important to the understanding and managing of the ecology of the marine coastal zone.

Aquaculture Studies. Scandinavian scientists are studying the special properties of Norwegian fjords. The investigations indicate that plankton populations in fjords are quite different from those in open ocean waters, a reflection of the stable conditions in sheltered fjords. Such basic studies provide the foundations for the future use of fjord waters for large-scale aquaculture.

Laser diffraction has been applied to measuring growth rates of the common blue mussel, *Mytilus edulis*. The investigator found that a minimum period of darkness is necessary for rapid growth. Another scientist, studying the relationships between water flow rate and the "pumping" (feeding rates) of the mussel, found pumping to be optimal under certain conditions of current flow. Pumping is in turn closely related to growth rates. Again, these basic findings are essential to the understanding and managing of marine organisms selected for aquaculture projects.

Parasitic Infections. It is known that infection by parasites can reduce growth rates of marine animals and induce sterility. For instance, certain free-swimming marine worms, called chaetognaths, become much larger and are sterilized when invaded by certain parasites. The great increase in size may be of interest to medicine and studies of growth enhancement.

Parasites are also being studied as biological "tags" to determine the origins and patterns of movement of marine finfish. Salmon from specific spawning areas harbor specific parasites. When these parasites are found on smolts in estuaries and open sea, the origin and pathways of movement can be identified.

Pollution. Scientists in California have reported that toxic lead is absorbed by marine algae and then transferred to abalone which feed upon them. This finding is important because of the worldwide distribution of lead by automobile exhaust gases and wastes discharged into coastal waters.

Scientists in Italy and other countries have studied how the hydrocarbons in petroleum enter living marine resources. They have found that hydrocarbons accumulated in mussel tissues are over 1,000 times the amounts found in their environment.

JOHN B. PEARCE
Sandy Hook Marine Laboratory

MARYLAND

Events in Maryland in 1976 were dominated by the trial of Gov. Marvin Mandel for corruption. Politics, including elections in November, and legislative actions were also newsworthy.

The Governor's Trial. In late 1975, Governor Mandel was indicted on 22 charges concerning actions taken while in office that allegedly benefited Mandel and some business associates. The charges dealt mostly with actions by the governor and the state legislature that enhanced the value of land or racing properties owned by Mandel's associates. The governor denied the charges and said he would prove his innocence in court. The trial began in federal court in Baltimore and ended in a mistrial in December.

Elections. Maryland's 10 electoral votes went to Jimmy Carter, who defeated President Ford in the state by a margin of 53–47%. In the race for the U. S. Senate, Democratic Rep. Paul Sarbanes decisively defeated Republican Sen. J. Glenn Beall with 57% of the vote. Earlier in the year Sarbanes had overwhelmingly defeated former Sen. Joseph Tydings for the Democratic nomination.

Sarbanes' congressional seat was won by Democrat Barbara Mikulski with 75% of the vote. The Republicans retained the seat of retiring Gilbert Gude with the victory of Newton Steers. Incumbents who sought reelection to Congress—four Democrats and two Republicans—were successful. The voter turnout for the election was 50%, a drop of 4% from 1974.

Baltimore Subway. Governor Mandel's 1976 budget included $120 million for phase one of a Baltimore city subway system. The proposed system would have a total length of 8 miles (13 km), and opponents argued that a trolley or light rail system would be just as effective and much cheaper. The opposition staged a two-week filibuster in the Senate, but it was eventually defeated by the governor's supporters who approved the $120 million appropriation.

One of the pressures operating to support the governor's proposal was the possibility that his office would cut off funds needed to complete the Washington Metro system. This potential threat was considered a factor in the favorable votes of most of the senators from the populous Washington suburbs of Maryland.

Legislation. Three major reform measures were debated in the 1976 legislature. A bill died that would have required much more extensive disclosure of lobbyists' expenditures. It had been heavily opposed by the lobbies that operate in the General Assembly.

A sunshine bill requiring open meetings of all government bodies in Maryland was passed over significant opposition. However, since the bill will not take effect until after the 1977 session of the General Assembly it is still open to amendment.

The third reform measure dealt with campaign financing. A bill passed in 1975 had provided partial public financing of all state and county elections beginning in 1978. However, the 1976 session provided no appropriation to carry out the law. A compromise attempt was made to amend the law to apply only to statewide office so that it would be more financially feasible, but the final outcome was no action at all.

The legislature passed a number of bills involving criminal law. Legislation was approved that will limit the ability of defense attorneys in rape trials to introduce evidence relating to the past behavior of the victim. New laws also established degrees of severity and punishment for sexual crimes. But a provision was rejected that would have eliminated laws against homosexuality involving consenting adults.

The city of Baltimore regained control over its own police department through legislation that transferred the power to appoint the city's police commissioner from the governor to the mayor.

The legislature also approved an appropriation for the start of construction of the Fort McHenry Tunnel and allowed Prince George's county to increase its tax on apartment rents. Bills to limit utility price increases were defeated.

Higher Education. The Maryland State Board for Higher Education replaced the Maryland Council for Higher Education. The new organization is to coordinate the activities of the separate boards of the state university, state college system, and the community college system. An attempt to combine those boards into one super board was defeated. The new unit has no final authority to change budget requests but receives and reviews the budgets of the three systems and submits a combined higher education budget to the governor.

The U. S. Supreme Court on June 21 upheld Maryland's program of assistance to private colleges, including certain church-related schools. It overruled objections based on the separation of church and state.

THOMAS P. MURPHY
University of Maryland (on leave)

--------- MARYLAND · Information Highlights ---------

Area: 10,577 square miles (27,394 km²).
Population (1975 est.): 4,098,000.
Chief Cities (1970 census): Annapolis, the capital, 30,-095; Baltimore, 905,759; Dundalk, 85,377; Towson, 77,799.
Government (1976): *Chief Officers*—governor, Marvin Mandel (D); lt. gov., Blair Lee III (D). *General Assembly*—Senate, 47 members; House of Delegates, 141 members.
Education (1975–76): *Enrollment*—public elementary schools, 459,731 pupils; public secondary, 421,196; nonpublic (1976–77), 133,600; colleges and universities, 175,622 students. *Public school expenditures,* $1,200,719,000 ($1,372 per pupil).
State Finances (fiscal year 1975): *Revenues,* $3,053,-387,000; *expenditures,* $3,410,574,000.
Personal Income (1975): $26,533,000,000; per capita, $6,474.
Labor Force (July 1976): *Nonagricultural wage and salary earners,* 1,458,300; *insured unemployed,* 39,-400 (3.5%).

MASSACHUSETTS

Economic and fiscal issues were among the dominant problems in Massachusetts in 1976. The statewide unemployment continued to be high; adjusted figures showed 8.8% of the labor force out of work in March. This level slowly dropped over the summer and autumn months. Concern over the jobless rate prompted some criticism of the business climate. Critics charged that the combination of high energy costs, taxes, and "lack of sensitivity" by government were driving firms out of the Bay State.

Economic concerns spread to state employees in June when the AFL-CIO alliance, representing 45,000 state workers, called a strike. The action disrupted many agencies in Massachusetts for four days, but legal action led the union to order a return to work on June 24. Bargaining went on for months after the strike, as issues of salary and working conditions were resolved very slowly.

Legislation. Increases in the state budget were the subject of much debate in the legislature which finally authorized $3,790,000,000. Among the more controversial items in the final budget were a 15% raise for legislators and a 5% cost-of-living increase for welfare recipients.

The legislature once again attempted to pass both a bill and a constitutional amendment restoring the death penalty. Gov. Michael S. Dukakis vigorously opposed the restoration, and the attempt failed, but sentiment for the death penalty among legislators remained very strong. A bill limiting the prisoner furlough program was passed after a heated debate but was vetoed by the governor after the legislature had adjourned in October.

Elections. As a heavily Democratic state, Massachusetts voters were carefully watched in the presidential primary on March 2. The election, however, was inconclusive: Sen. Henry M. Jackson won 23% of the vote, Rep. Morris K. Udall 18%, Alabama Gov. George C. Wallace 17%, and Jimmy Carter 14%. The fall elections went heavily to incumbents. Sen. Edward M. Kennedy, running for a third full six-year term made a very strong statewide showing in the September primary and easily defeated his Republican opponent in November. The congressional race in the Seventh District attracted an unprecedented number of candidates in the primary election after the death of Rep. Torbert Macdonald (see OBITUARIES) threw the contest open. Edward J. Markey won the seat. In the Fourth District, Rep. Robert Drinan was re-elected in a tight race against Republican Arthur Mason. In the presidential contest, Jimmy Carter emerged the victor.

Among important referendum questions in the November elections, were proposals banning the sale of beverages in disposable bottles, a graduated income tax to replace the 5% flat-rate tax on personal incomes, creation of a state electric power authority, and a complete ban on handguns, all of which failed. An equal rights amendment to the state constitution was approved.

Numbers. The Massachusetts State Lottery, one of the more successful in the nation, inaugurated a "numbers game" in April. The new scheme was designed to cut into the illegal "numbers racket," long a problem for law enforcement authorities. Concern over desegregation in Boston's schools led some communities in the area to reconsider or terminate their involvement with METCO, a voluntary metropolitan busing program.

HARVEY BOULAY, *Boston University*

— MASSACHUSETTS • Information Highlights —

Area: 8,257 square miles (21,386 km²).
Population (1975 est.): 5,828,000.
Chief Cities (1970 census): Boston, the capital, 641,071; Worcester, 176,572; Springfield, 163,905.
Government (1976): *Chief Officers*—governor, Michael S. Dukakis (D); lt. gov., Thomas P. O'Neill III (D). *General Court*—Senate, 40 members; House of Representatives, 240 members.
Education (1975–76): *Enrollment*—public elementary schools, 813,410 pupils; public secondary, 385,000; nonpublic (1976–77), 175,600; colleges and universities, 356,362 students. *Public school expenditures,* $1,710,000,000.
State Finances (fiscal year 1975): *Revenues,* $4,104,904,000; *expenditures,* $4,939,813,000.
Personal Income (1975): $35,568,000,000; per capita, $6,114.
Labor Force (July 1976): *Nonagricultural wage and salary earners,* 2,341,900; *insured unemployed,* 106,000 (5.5%).

Massachusetts Sen. Edward M. Kennedy and Sen. Hubert H. Humphrey celebrate the 65th birthday of the senator from Minnesota. Both key Democrats were reelected on November 2.

MEDICINE

The swine flu, some strange new diseases, including the "Legion Disease," new opinions regarding mammography, major developments in the Quinlan case and in the fields of dermatology and CAT scanning, and the marketing of various new drugs were among the items dominating 1976 medical news.

New Diseases. Diseases made the headlines in 1976. Most attention was given to an influenza virus isolated from young army recruits at Fort Dix, N. J. Tests of the blood of 308 persons at Fort Dix revealed that 68 of them had antibodies to the virus. This marked the first time in the history of modern virology that human-to-human transmission of an influenza virus resembling an influenza virus of swine had been confirmed. The new virus is similar to the one isolated in 1928 that is believed to have caused the 1918 influenza epidemic which resulted in millions of deaths. Accordingly, the U. S. government launched a campaign to produce and inoculate the entire American population with a vaccine against this new influenza virus (see page 322).

"Legion Disease" was another unusual illness reported for the first time in 1976. The disease developed in Philadelphia among people attending a convention of the American Legion at the Bellevue Stratford Hotel. The first symptoms appeared in legionnaires about July 21 and the last reported new case was on October 3. A total of 169 people was involved and at least 25 died. Symptoms of this bizarre illness included headache, muscle pain, and severe chills. About a quarter of the patients also had gastrointestinal symptoms including vomiting or diarrhea. Upper respiratory symptoms were conspicuous by their absence. The striking clinical features were the rapid onset of high fever, rapidly developing inflammation in the lungs, and rapid demise of the victim. Death was caused by respiratory failure. No infectious agents were identified nor was any toxic agent isolated. The cause of the illness remained unknown at year's end.

A third new disease was reported for the first time in the United States, mucocutaneous lymph node syndrome (MLNS). This disease was first reported in 1967 in Japan where 4,000 cases had occurred. The principal symptom is a fever ranging from 101° to 104° F (38°–40° C) which lasts from 1 to 2 weeks and does not subside after treatment with antibiotics. This is accompanied by reddening of the eyes, lips and mucous membranes of the mouth, drying and fissuring of the lips, and often swelling of the lymph nodes. A skin rash occurs which is variable. There is often reddening of the palms and soles after which swelling of the hands and feet may develop followed by scaling of the finger tips. Swelling of the lymph nodes of the neck is quite common. The only important compli-

cation of the illness involves the heart where inflammation of the heart muscle or the pericardium occurs.

About 1% of the children with MLNS suffer inflammation of the coronary arteries. Coronary thrombosis is the usual cause of death in patients who succumb to the disease. It may be confused with such usual diseases of childhood as scarlet fever or measles, and it resembles in some respects less common diseases, such as Rocky Mountain spotted fever or Steves-Johnson syndrome. The cause for MLNS is as yet unknown, and there is no specific treatment.

What may be a new form of arthritis was discovered in the New England area along the Connecticut River. The condition became known as "Lyme arthritis" after the area of Connecticut where it developed. Fifty-one patients reported episodes of joint swelling frequently accompanied by pain and sometimes by warmth and redness. A low grade fever was recorded in slightly more than half the patients as well as malaise and weakness in about a third. Headache, muscle aches, and pains develop in about one in seven. For most patients the episodes of joint swelling involved just one joint initially, frequently the knee. Many of the patients had recurrent attacks, usually about three but sometimes as many as ten. Some investigators suspect the disease to be infectious, perhaps with an agent carried by ticks.

Female Disorders. Management of women's disorders came under consideration. A report from the School of Public Health at UCLA recommended that mammography for routine screening of women in the 35 to 50 age group should be discontinued. Mammography is an examination of the female breast which uses X-ray technique. The report indicated that X-ray mammography led to a reduction of about 10–15% in the mortality from breast cancer. But all of this reduction in mortality occurred in women over 50 years of age. The report concluded that there is no measurable benefit from X-ray mammography for women under 50, and a slight risk develops from excessive exposure to X-ray.

Critics also raised their voices against the use of estrogen in treating the symptoms of menopause and as an ingredient of oral contraceptives. Estrogen is the female hormone responsible for secondary sex characteristics. It is available on prescription and was found in the sequential type of birth control pills that were removed from the market.

Oral contraceptives have been linked to increased heart attacks in young women and increased breast cancer in certain groups. At the same time, estrogen therapy for menopause symptoms has been linked to increased risk of cancer of the uterus. Breast cancer was found to be two and a half times more common in women who had been taking oral contraceptives than in women who had not. Likewise the inci-

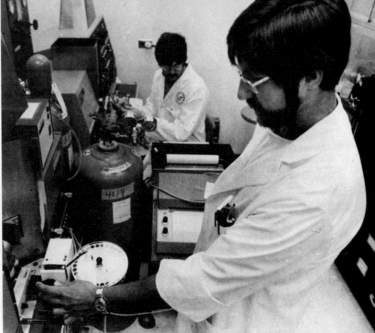

To fight its bad name, Gov. Shapp of Pennsylvania (*left*) stayed overnight at the hotel that was the focus of the "Legion Disease." Despite intensive research (*right*), the cause of the illness remained a mystery.

dence of cancer of the uterus in women of child-bearing age was reported to be significantly higher. Uterine cancer was five times more common in women who had been using estrogen for one to five years after the menopause. The increased risk was almost 14 times for women who had been using the hormone for seven years or more.

Convulsions and Birth Defects. A medicine used to prevent convulsions has been linked to birth defects. About 6,000 babies a year are exposed to hydantoin anticonvulsant drugs in the uterus. Ten percent of the mothers who had taken the anticonvulsant medicine throughout pregnancy developed signs of fetal hydantoin syndrome. These children showed one or more of the following abnormalities: developmental or mental deficiency, microcephaly, underdevelopment of the nails or fingers, finger-like thumb, positional deformities of the limbs, heart defects, hernia, scrotal deformity. In addition to the 10% of the children with these gross abnormalities another 20% show lesser degree of impairment of performance or abnormality in development. The mechanism of this process may be similar to that involved in folic acid deficiency. Women who take anticonvulsant compounds for long periods of time have decreased levels of folic acid in their blood. Folic acid deficiency is known to cause birth defects in pregnant rats.

Heart Disease. Surgery to bypass the blood flow to the heart muscle around a blocked artery has become popular as a treatment for heart disease that is a result of decreased circulation to the heart itself. About 60,000 such operations were performed in 1976 for patients with obstructive disease of the coronary arteries which had caused chest pain or previous heart attack. The operation is considered a safe one and results in relief of chest pain and increased tolerance of exercise in about three quarters of the patients. Improvement in the function of the heart takes place only in patients who have not had prior heart attacks. The criteria for this operation are quite strict and depend upon the condition of each individual patient.

A cooperative study was begun to find out if the regular daily use of moderate doses of aspirin will protect against heart attack in susceptible people. It is believed that one of the important early steps leading to heart attack is clumping of the blood platelets. This clumping is known to be prevented by use of aspirin. So a study, involving 16 American and 4 British clinical centers, was begun to see if patients with history of previous heart attack can be prevented from having another by regular daily doses of aspirin. Also included in the study is another drug, dipyramidole, used both with and without aspirin.

Skin Conditions. Interesting developments improve the outlook for patients with two common skin conditions, psoriasis and allergic eczema. For psoriasis, PUVA therapy continued to be highly effective. PUVA therapy is a combination of the oral medicine, psoralen, and ultraviolet-A light. In PUVA therapy, the medicine is given by mouth and the areas of the skin affected with psoriasis are treated with ultraviolet light two to three hours later. The amount of light used must be carefully regulated since an "overdose" of light amounting to perhaps 6 or 8 minutes of exposure can make the difference between satisfactory treatment of the psoriasis and a severe, blistering burn. Psoralen is a drug

SPECIAL REPORT:

The Swine Flu Vaccination

The National Swine Influenza Immunization Program was the largest single vaccination project ever undertaken in the United States and one of the most controversial. On March 24, 1976, President Ford announced a $135-million program to immunize the entire population against a possible epidemic of swine flu. From the beginning, however, the program was beset by problems. Many public health officials were skeptical about the possibility of a swine flu epidemic. Concern was voiced over the efficacy of the vaccine, and there was much apprehension about possible reactions to it. Many also doubted that the pharmaceutical industry could produce enough doses in time for the beginning of the flu season in October.

A malpractice issue arose in mid-June, when the four pharmaceutical houses producing the vaccine announced that they were losing their liability insurance coverage. They stopped producing and processing vaccine until late August, when Congress finally passed legislation indemnifying them and others participating in the program. Although the program was originally scheduled to begin in late July, it did not get under way until early October.

Background. In February and March 1976 a number of U. S. Army recruits at Fort Dix, N. J., came down with the flu. Officials of the New Jersey State Health Department conducted tests to find out the cause. They isolated the A/Victoria virus from most of the men. This was the strain of influenza A virus then prevalent in most of the United States. A dozen recruits, however, showed infection with a different virus, now scientifically called A/Swine/New Jersey/76, but popularly known as the swine flu virus. One of these recruits died after voluntarily participating in a difficult march although he had been ordered to bed. The others had a mild illness, and the one death was, in the opinion of many scientists, due in large measure to the strenuous exercise. Further studies of recruits at Fort Dix revealed that antibodies to the swine flu virus were present in many. This meant that they had been recently infected. But because many of them had not been ill at all, it also meant that the virus caused mild infections.

The swine flu virus was first isolated in 1928 by Dr. Richard Shope of the Rockefeller Institute. Since that time it has been generally accepted that this virus, which primarily infects swine, is a descendant of the influenza virus which caused the pandemic of 1918–19. During that pandemic, about 1,000,000,000 people fell ill, and 20,000,000 died. In the United States alone the death toll was half a million. The evidence linking the swine flu virus to the 1918–19 virus is indirect at best, since the latter was never identified.

The swine flu virus had occasionally infected human beings, but it had never, as far as was known, passed from one person to another. At Fort Dix it did this for the first time. This was viewed with concern by the proponents of the vaccination program. It meant that the swine flu virus had adapted to man and had epidemic potential. Those skeptical about the program pointed out the mildness of the disease at Fort Dix and in six volunteers experimentally infected in Great Britain. Proponents cogently argued that influenza viruses have been known to acquire virulence as they pass through the human population, so a mild beginning may not portend a mild epidemic course.

Vaccines. In April and May 1976 the four pharmaceutical companies—Parke Davis and Company, Merck Sharp and Dohme, Merrell-National Laboratories, and Wyeth Laboratories—began production of swine flu vaccines and conducted tests of them on 5,000 individuals. On June 21, U. S. Public Health Service officials

used for more than 25 years to increase skin pigment. It thickens the skin, causes inflammation, and increases the amount of pigment in the areas exposed to sunlight. It is available only by prescription.

Atopic dermatitis, sometimes known as allergic eczema, has been treated successfully with an ointment containing caffeine. Caffeine is one of a family of drugs that increases the amount of cyclic adenosine-three'-five'-monophosphate (cAMP). cAMP within the cell plays an important role in regulating the inflammatory and immunological functions of the white blood cells. Acute skin inflammations can be blocked by direct application of methylxanthine. Caffeine is a methylxanthine that is safe and readily available since it can be obtained from coffee. It was applied to the skin of patients in a controlled fashion, in an ointment containing 30% caffeine. There was marked improvement in most of these patients who underwent the treatment. Atopic dermatitis seems to be an inherited illness affecting about 3% of all children and up to 20% of the total population.

CAT Scanning. CAT scanning came of age in 1976. The abbreviation CAT stands for computerized axial tomography. This is a technique that makes possible precise diagnosis in many

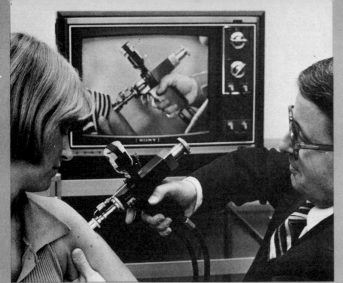

A pharmaceutical worker at a Merck Sharp and Dohme plant in West Point, Pa. (*right*), inspects eggs used in the production of the swine flu vaccine. In most clinics, the vaccine was administered by quick-working automatic jet injectors (*above*).

announced the results. The vaccines were found to be safe and effective in individuals 18 years of age and older. In younger persons, they caused more frequent and more severe side reactions and less than adequate protection.

Two major types of vaccines were used, a bivalent and a monovalent one. The bivalent vaccine contained both the killed swine flu virus (A/Swine/New Jersey/76) and the killed A/Victoria/75 virus. This vaccine was used in the "high risk" group—all individuals above 65 and those of any age suffering from chronic debilitating medical conditions. The monovalent vaccine, with only the swine flu virus, was used in the rest of the population over 18.

Program Administration. The immunization program was administered by the U. S. Public Health Service. The 50 states and New York City were given vaccine worth a total of $107 million and another $28 million to administer the vaccine. Each local jurisdiction received its allotment under a separate federal grant. The

monies allocated in these grants to administer the program averaged 13¢ per dose. Because the actual cost of vaccination was about 50¢, local health departments had to make up the difference. Local health agencies operated free clinics and distributed vaccines to hospitals, clinics, private physicians, and the medical departments of various public agencies and companies.

Much of the vaccine was administered in free public clinics with automatic jet injectors, which are capable of giving 1,000 inoculations per hour. Each person immunized was required to read and sign a detailed, informed consent.

A temporary scare occurred around mid-October, when three elderly people died after being vaccinated in Pittsburgh. Autopsies, however, found no direct link between the deaths and the vaccine. More serious was a possible link to cases of paralysis, reported in December. This led to suspension of the program, and it seemed dubious if it would ever be resumed.

PASCAL JAMES IMPERATO, M. D.

cases where the abnormality is unclear or undetectable by conventional X-ray or radioactive scans. CAT scans depict cross sections or slices of any region of the body as seen looking down through the patient, head to foot. This new technique using X-ray has revolutionized the examination of the contents of the skull and is now being widely used for examination of the chest and abdomen.

In CAT scanning, a moving beam of X-rays passes through the tissues and the transmission of the X-ray is changed by the density of the tissues. The X-ray beam is picked up on the other side of the body by sensitive crystal detectors.

The amount of X-ray that is received by these detectors is measured and analyzed by a computer. The computer is programmed to recover and analyze an enormous quantity of information that was previously lost by conventional X-ray methods. By solving equations having to do with absorption coefficients, a display is produced on a cathode-ray tube. This is a picture of the substance between the X-ray source and the crystal detectors, a view of a "slice" of tissue at a specific distance from the X-ray source. The depth of the slice-view can be adjusted. So by CAT scanning a series of pictures can be taken showing the structure of organs at different depths through the human body. A photograph is made of the display of the cathode-ray tube for permanent record.

CAT scanning originated in England and was initially reported in 1972. The first work with CAT scanning was done on the brain. It was found that this technique provided highly accurate information for diagnosis in such specific diseases within the skull as tumor, abscess, and stroke. But because tomography is a very slow process even the slight body motion of breathing interferes with accuracy of the pictures. However, 1976 advances in scanner technology permitted the examination of tissues within the chest and abdomen despite the body motion. This is accomplished by using faster and more sophisticated scanning equipment which has many crystal detectors in use at one time. From the data gathered, the computer can reconstruct various views of the body and give a clear picture of the internal organs.

Computer assisted tomography may be one of the greatest advances in medical diagnosis ever developed. The radiation exposure varies considerably with different units. The dose of radiation for 3 scans of the head may be as much as 2.0 rads and for the abdomen, 3 or more and sometimes as much as 18 rads. In comparison, a chest X-ray usually takes less than 0.1 rad. So the amount of radiation exposure is high enough to necessitate avoiding unnecessary use of the CAT scanner, even though the information supplied is more detailed than earlier methods provided. Each machine costs about $500,000. Additional large sums of money are needed to train technical and professional personnel and for installing the new devices.

Quinlan Case. The medical community and the public in general remained interested in the Karen Anne Quinlan case. The 22-year-old woman had suffered irreparable brain damage and had lived since April 1975 in an unconscious state with the aid of a respirator. Her parents argued that the respirator should be turned off and that their daughter should be allowed to die with dignity; the girl's doctors, fearing malpractice suits and unsure of the ethics involved in the case, disagreed. In late March the New Jersey Supreme Court ruled that the respirator should be turned off. The court also protected the hospital and the doctors from future civil or criminal action.

Miss Quinlan, however, continued to live without the respirator. This raised entirely new ethical and legal questions, including what constitutes extraordinary medical care.

New Drugs. Some new drugs of interest became available during the year. Beclomethasone was marketed for the treatment of bronchial asthma. This is a steroid drug taken by inhalation from a pressurized spray can. Steroid drugs have long been known to be useful in suppression of the symptoms of asthma but have had undesirable side effects. The new spray medicine is reported not to be absorbed into the body but works locally in the lungs. Accordingly, it is free from the systemic side effects of earlier steroid preparations. The drug has been used successfully in England, Canada, and Italy for many years, and has been approved for commercial distribution in the United States.

Psoriasis was reported to respond to another new drug recently released, Azaribine. This is a derivative of the antimetabolite 6-azauridine. It is believed to inhibit DNA synthesis and to suppress the overgrowth of skin cells that produce the psoriatic lesion. Results from the drug are quite satisfactory, but its side effects, including drowsiness, dizziness, nausea, diarrhea, and even heart and blood vessel complications, are quite severe. However, the drug shows promise for carefully controlled use.

Three new drugs for the treatment of arthritis, phenoprophine, naproxen, and tolmetin, were approved for marketing in the United States. All three are similar to drugs released previously, including ibuprofen and indomethacin. The new drugs are effective against pain and fever and are described as suppressing inflammation. Their mechanism of action is unknown. Gastrointestinal upset is the most common adverse effect but other adverse effects, including salt and fluid retention, ringing in the ears, and hearing loss, have been reported. The drugs work to calm the swelling and pain of arthritis in much the same fashion as aspirin. Like aspirin these agents can interfere with blood clotting. They are more expensive than aspirin but apparently safer and more effective.

Finally, the Food and Drug Administration was considering a new drug for the treatment of virus infections of the eye. The medicine, vidarabine, is applied to the eye in the form of drops. It is used in the treatment of herpes infections of the eye in much the same fashion as an earlier drug, idoxuridine. The new medicine is often helpful where the old one is not. It can also be used intravenously and is useful against virus infection deep within the eye. Earlier drugs could only be applied to the surface of the eye.

PVC and Fire Fighting. Of all the plastic polymers, polyvinyl chloride (PVC) causes the most serious problem in fire fighting today. This is due to the fact that PVC, a very common plastic, releases hydrogen chloride gas when burning. HCl in high concentration causes irritation of the throat after short exposure. Very high concentrations of HCl are dangerous even with brief exposure. The gas enters the upper respiratory tract and is inhaled into the lungs. Damage to the lungs may result from exposure to HCl and other gases released including chlorine, phosgene, benzene, toluene, naphthalene, and vinyl chloride. Carbon monoxide, well known to be a major cause of injury at fires, is also produced.

IRWIN J. POLK, M. D.
St. Luke's Hospital, New York City

METEOROLOGY

Weather modification and rain formation have remained the central areas of meteorological research.

Several years of study by the U. S. Forest Service of the reduction of lightning-induced forest fires by seeding thunderstorms with silver iodide have shown some success. The number of cloud-to-ground strokes has been decreased; in particular, the duration of current flow in the lightning channel has been shortened, thus reducing the sustained high channel temperature needed for ignition.

Hail and Rain Experiments. The U. S. National Hail Research Experiment in northeast Colorado has, however, yielded negative results for hail suppression; apparently, cloud seeding can, under certain circumstances, produce hail increases. In random trials during three seasons the mean hail mass on seeding days was 60–80% larger than that of non-seeded storms, but the results are still affected by considerable uncertainties.

Initiation of rain in clouds with subfreezing temperature has been well understood for many years. But indications are that rain initiation in warm clouds requires a different mechanism. Giant salt nuclei cause droplet formation. In moist air these grow rapidly to a large diameter. In maritime air fewer large droplets grow to raindrop size, in continental air too many drops frequently compete for the available water; hence, warm rain formation is less likely in those air masses. Oceanic bacteria have also been suspected as triggers for precipitation. The bacteria get into the air from the phytoplankton by bursting water bubbles and become active as freezing nuclei at a temperature of −3 to −5° C (27–23° F).

Instrumented flights through thunderstorms show that electrification begins when clouds reach temperature levels of −2° C (28° F). At that point the electric field increases rapidly from 100 volts per meter to 1,000 volts per meter. The glaciation of the cloud and the increases in the electrical field rapidly lead to the first lightning discharge and to precipitation from the cloud base. Charging and separation of charges are promoted by vertical motion of the air.

Shifting Tornado Centers. Tornadic storms have been observed by Doppler radar. The data yield wind speeds of 80 meters per second (179 mph) and vertical accelerations of 3g. The frequency and location of tornadoes in the United States seem to have undergone temporal changes. From their main location in the Midwest from 1911 to 1925 the center of activity moved, during the following two decades, to Georgia and Oklahoma, but in recent years the highest frequencies have again been in the Illinois and Ohio valley area.

Weather System Models. Fronts have become a new target for mathematical modeling of weather systems. Frontal circulations are often too small to be resolved by the large-scale general circulation models. The new models show convective and baroclinic instabilities to account for sharp temperature changes, and they also realistically depict ascending and descending air motion. Improved general circulation models now include both the ocean and the atmosphere and depict their interaction. Although models and input data are still imperfect, the limit of predictability of storms can now be placed at ten days.

Climate in the Last Ice Age. The fascination with climatic variations has resulted in a complete reconstruction of the earth's climate as it was 18,000 years ago, at the height of the last ice age. Data from cores taken on land and in the ocean floor and fed into a suitable model framework have led to the conclusion that global ocean-water temperatures at that time were only 2.3° C (4.1° F) below the present ones. But the sea level, because of the large mass of water frozen on land in North America and Eurasia, was 90 m (300 ft) below the present stage. Evaporation was reduced and global precipitation is estimated to have been 15% below what it is today. Analysis of the core samples also suggests that about 10,000 B. C., after a sudden re-advance of the continental ice sheets, catastrophically rapid melting occurred, flooding the water-free lowlands. Some have suggested this might be the great flood of biblical and other prehistoric legends.

Volcanic Effects on Climate. Volcanic explosions, long suspected as triggers for climatic fluctuations, have been theoretically examined with the conclusion that a few months after such an explosion the cooling by scattering of solar radiation back to space and the warming by absorption of infrared radiation from the earth will balance; hence, no notable changes in surface temperature will occur. Later, however, a remainder of fine dust and sulfuric acid mist in the stratosphere will cause cooling.

A Warming Trend. Analysis of data from 67 weather stations in the Southern Hemisphere, including 6 in the Antarctic, shows that a warming trend has been prevalent in the past two decades, particularly in subpolar latitudes. Evidence also shows that the Northern Hemisphere has been warming in the 1970's, whereas cooling prevailed in the prior two decades. This has revived an interest in the carbon-dioxide hypothesis of global warming. This gas has gradually increased in the atmosphere because of man's accelerated use of fossil fuels. Projections, by model studies, have been made for a doubling of carbon dioxide. They suggest an increase of 2–3° C (3.6–4.8° F) in global temperature, although the effect of concomitant changes in cloudiness has not, so far, been accurately considered.

Stratospheric Research. Concern about anthropogenic alterations of the climate has led to intensified surveys of pollutants in the atmosphere. Stratospheric measurements in the relatively uncontaminated Southern Hemisphere have revealed the existence of small droplets, which have been identified (by etchings and residues on copper plates flown on balloons) as sulfuric acid. Speculation attributes their origin to volcanic eruptions.

The controversy over man-made effects on stratospheric ozone has continued. Measurements have shown that chlorofluorocarbons do indeed get from the surface to the stratosphere.

Their dissociation, leading to the formation of chlorine, has been suspected of initiating an ozone-destroying chain reaction. However, much of the stratospheric chemistry of the process remains uncertain, and a vigorous research program to clarify the issue is under way.

Municipal incinerators, which contribute only 3% of the total aerosol in urban areas, account for nearly all of the several heavy metals, such as zinc, cadmium, antimony, tin, silver, and indium in the atmosphere. Some of these metals are real health hazards.

H. E. LANDSBERG
University of Maryland

In Great Britain, many reservoirs dried up in 1976 as a result of the worst drought in years. To deal with the problem, a special minister was named; Parliament passed emergency legislation; and Water Authority employees used T-shirts and posters to urge the public to conserve water.

PHOTOS UPI

Disasters Struck Many Areas

The big weather stories of 1976 were flash floods in the Rocky Mountains and an unprecedented drought in western Europe, especially in England.

December 1975–February 1976. Winter was very mild in most of the United States. Nearly the whole nation enjoyed above average temperatures. This was especially true of Montana, which had up to 10°F (5.5°C) above average, and Iowa, with 6°F (3.3°C) above average. Alaskan temperatures, however, were about 6°F below normal. Drought was conspicuous in the southern tier of states, from Arizona to the Carolinas and Florida. Less than 50% of the average precipitation fell in the Great Plains, snow cover was lacking, and this played havoc with winter crops. Most of California also missed its usual winter rainfall, and the resulting crop damage was estimated at $310 million.

The season had its share of severe weather. Heavy rains in the beginning of December caused damaging floods in British Columbia, Canada, and in the states of Washington and Oregon. A hurricane struck Port Hedland, Australia, with 135-mph (215-kmph) winds and 8 inches (20 cm) of rain, causing severe damage. In late December and early January a severe storm hit the Philippines, leaving 180,000 homeless. But the worst disaster was a double storm in western Europe, with up to 95-mph (150-kmph) gales, during the first week of January. It affected Ireland, England, Belgium, Holland, Germany, Denmark, and the Baltic states, caused 79 deaths, sank two vessels, disrupted electric service, and forced coastal evacuation in many sectors.

A record-breaking snowstorm in upstate New York on January 9 dumped 54 inches (137 cm), the heaviest since November 1900. Northern Mexico also had its first snow in eight years. February tornadoes caused casualties and severe damage in Mississippi, Louisiana, Alabama, Georgia, Tennessee, and North Carolina.

March–May. Spring started out with early warmth east of the Rockies, and April was unusually warm. Many areas in the Great Plains, the Midwest, and Northeast were up to 6°F (3.3°C) warmer than average, but May was cool there. The season was warmer than average from Montana to New England and along the Atlantic seaboard, where temperatures were 2–4°F (1.1–2.2°C) above average. Rainfall was very deficient, especially in western Texas, eastern Colorado, South Dakota, and Minnesota; most of these areas received less than 50% of the average. In the Canadian prairie provinces of Alberta, Saskatchewan, and Manitoba, many areas also received less than half their average.

Severe weather was widely experienced. A late-season snowstorm hit the upper Midwest and Great Lakes region early in March, leaving icy roads that led to fatal traffic accidents. In late March, tornadic activity caused some deaths and injuries in Oklahoma, Texas, Arkansas, Mississippi, Alabama, Florida, Illinois, and Missouri. The Washington, D. C., and Baltimore area was struck by 70-mph (110-kmph) wind gusts, while tornadoes killed 14 in Georgia and Kentucky, and gales lashed Pennsylvania, Delaware, and Michigan on March 22. In mid-May other tornadoes killed 4, injured 6, and caused heavy damage in North Carolina and Virginia. On April 11 tornadic winds to 100 mph (160 kmph) hit Bangladesh, killing 30, injuring 400, and leaving 30,000 homeless.

Also in the middle of April, floods in the Souris River of Montana inundated 400,000 acres and drove 13,000 from their homes. Floods in the Ceyhan River in Turkey and in Iran caused many casualties. In Micronesia and Guam typhoon Pamela caused devastation. Guam was declared a major disaster area because 80% of the dwellings were destroyed. The death toll there and in the Philippines was over 30. Droughts plagued northeastern Brazil and western Europe.

June–August. Summer was characterized by warm weather over the northern Great Plains. This area was also plagued by drought. Most of the area from southern North Dakota to the Texas border had less than 50% of its average rainfall. Elsewhere in the nation it was a fairly cool season, with rainfall close to normal. Despite fairly lively tropical storm activity, the Atlantic and Gulf coasts were spared severe collisions.

In June, floods in Guajarat state, India, killed a score and destroyed 16,000 homes. At the same time the Sylhet area of Bangladesh was also flooded, its rail and highway traffic cut. In the United States severe droughts threatened crops in Minnesota and promoted forest conflagrations in California. Destructive tornadoes hit North Dakota, Iowa, and Nebraska.

In July torrential rains of up to 12 inches (30 cm) in a day fell on Kansas and Missouri. At Joplin some 100 dwellings had to be evacuated. Heavy rains caused fatalities in eastern Japan, where the Izu peninsula, southeast of Tokyo, received 20 inches (50 cm) in 13 hours, flooding 2,700 homes. Rivers in Silao, Mexico, had the worst flood in two decades and sent hundreds fleeing; fatalities were about 150.

A severe flash flood on August 2 drove a 12-foot (3.6-m) high wall of water through the Big Thomson River Canyon in Colorado, causing at least 150 deaths. A week later rains flooded half of Lahore, Pakistan, killing 150, destroying 3,000 villages and 140,000 houses. And toward the end of the month typhoon Ellen dropped 16 inches (40 cm) of rain in 24 hours over Hong Kong, leaving scores of casualties and 3,000 homeless.

Yet, the great weather story of the summer was the drought in western Europe. It seared parts of England, Holland, Belgium, France, Portugal, West Germany, and Switzerland. Water rationing was instituted in many places. In southern England and Wales it was the worst drought since records began 250 years ago. In the United States the year from July 1, 1975, to June 30, 1976, was the driest in California since 1851. In Nebraska 40 counties were declared drought disaster areas.

September–November. Fall was a nasty season in many parts of the United States. Much of the country had temperatures far below average, and wintry weather started early in the central and eastern states. Both October and November had temperature deficiencies of 5–8°F (2.8–4.4°C) in the Great Plains and east of the Mississippi. Precipitation was ample in the central Appalachian region and southern California, where Pacific hurricanes were active. In the Great Plains and much of the East there were deficiencies of precipitation, but early snows enveloped the northern tier of states.

In western Europe the long-lasting drought was broken by ample rains. In September southern England had twice its average, and in Dublin, Ireland, it was the wettest September on record. Australia also experienced drought relief just in time for winter wheat to survive. Western Mexico was struck in October by Pacific hurricanes Liza and Madeleine, bringing torrential rains. They swept away homes, caused loss of life and major damage, but greatly improved soil moisture and reservoir water supplies.

Tropical storms savaged both Venezuela and Japan. In September typhoon Fran killed 114 persons, injured 351, and caused evacuation of hundreds of thousands in Kyushu. It sank 82 vessels and destroyed 240,000 homes.

At the end of October and in early November severe storms struck Italy, from Sicily to the Alps. Gale winds drove waves from the Adriatic onto St. Mark's Square in Venice. Flash floods in Frapani, Sicily, killed 10, caused an enormous mud flow, and made thousands homeless. In the Pacific wild gales sank ships and drove high wave walls up the beaches in Oahu, causing much coastal damage and forcing evacuation.

H. E. LANDSBERG

Presidential elections in Mexico: José López Portillo (*left*), the unopposed candidate, and outgoing President Luis Echeverría cast their ballots, July 4.

UPI

MEXICO

An attempt to break economic bottlenecks by a drastic devaluation of the peso overshadowed the uncontested presidential election of José López Portillo. Inflation, indebtedness, and declines in export earnings plagued the economy, although the rate of economic growth improved. Efforts were also made to protect the average person against the ravages of inflation.

Politics. In the July national elections, the government's Institutional Revolutionary party once again steamrolled the opposition. Elected with 93% of the vote for the 1976–82 presidential term was José López Portillo, the first unopposed candidate since 1928; the opposition National Action party refused to field a candidate. In his six-month national campaign, Dr. López, running for his first elective office, sought popular support to ratify his selection by Mexico's political bosses. He promised to continue liberal reforms, reorganize public administration and finance, and move the nation out of its economic difficulties. On the congressional level, 17% of the House seats went to opposition parties while the Senate gained its first opposition member since 1929. Female representation was increased in a move to give women a more prominent role in Mexican life.

Liberal editors of *Excelsior,* the major daily newspaper and one of the few critical of the government, were ousted in July by conservative employees, allegedly backed by the government. In October, the chief editor was charged with embezzlement.

The government continued its crackdown on terrorists, concentrating on the self-proclaimed Communist 23d of September League. The league was accused of several multiple murders during the spring, as well as the kidnapping of the Belgian ambassador's daughter in May. She was returned after payment of $400,000 contributed by relatives and concerned Mexicans. In August, the alleged leader of the league was shot by the

police and 30 others arrested. Also arrested during the year were more than 100 gang members who had terrorized university campuses.

Social Policy. Proposed legislation to control settlement patterns and urban development initially met stiff resistance from property owners, who feared it might mean government intervention in favor of the poor; it passed after amendments weakened the potential impact.

In February, the first tough consumer protection law passed Congress, creating a special prosecutor for consumer affairs, a national consumer protection institute, and strict rules on consumer transactions.

Natural Disasters. Hurricane Liza struck La Paz, Baja California Sur, in September, killing more than 650 persons when a dam burst. July floods in Tampico and central Mexico destroyed millions of dollars in property. A major earthquake in June, however, did little more than scare tourists out of Acapulco for a few days.

Economic Performance. Economic gains continued during the year, although the pace of real growth remained below the 30-year 6% average and the inflation rate hovered near 15%. Inflationary pressures were dampened by better control of government spending, a 19% rise in

---
MEXICO • Information Highlights

Official Name: United Mexican States.
Location: Southern North America.
Area: 761,602 square miles (1,972,546 km²).
Population (1976 est.): 62,300,000.
Chief Cities (1975 est.): Mexico City, the capital, 8,-592,000; Guadalajara, 1,561,000; Monterrey, 1,050,-000.
Government: *Head of state and government,* José López Portillo, president (took office Dec. 1976). *Legislature*—Congress: Senate and Chamber of Deputies.
Monetary Unit: Peso (24.39 pesos equal U. S.$1, Nov. 1976).
Gross National Product (1975 est.): $79,800,000,000.
Manufacturing (major products): Petroleum products, iron, steel, chemicals, transport equipment, aluminum, pharmaceuticals, cement.
Major Agricultural Products: Corn, cotton, sugarcane, wheat, vegetables, citrus fruits.
Foreign Trade (1975): *Exports,* $2,909,000,000; *Imports,* $6,631,000,000.

government revenue, and restriction of the money supply. In the first nine months, imports declined while exports rose 14% over the previous year. Income from tourism and border transactions was expected to reach $1,300,000,000 by the year's end. Direct federal expenditure for economic development increased to $3,230,000,000, of which 49% went to the industrial sector, 24% to rural areas, and 27% for transportation and communications. In addition, $720 million were spent on social assistance. The value of agricultural production rose to $3,480,000,000. Crude petroleum production reached one million barrels (133,400 metric tons) a day, and the first of three new refineries opened in Tula, Hidalgo. Installed electrical capacity doubled over the previous year. Mining production rose to $615 million. Steel production reached 10 million tons. Production gains in the first half of the year included petroleum (12.4%), petrochemicals (16.7%), electricity (8.9%), and construction (5.6%). Manufacturing lagged. Industrial production gains averaged 9% for the year.

Economic Policy. On August 31, the government announced that the peso would henceforth float on international money markets to fall to its true value, thus ending a 22-year policy of fixing the exchange rate at 12.5 pesos to the U. S. dollar. Free convertibility would be continued and the Bank of Mexico, with its $1,400,000,000 monetary reserves and more than $1,000,000,000 in Special Drawing Rights, would prevent wild fluctuations. In late September the bank stabilized the peso at 19.9 to the dollar but a month later was forced to let it fall to 26.5 to the dollar.

Devaluation was an effort to restore competitiveness of exports, stimulate tourism, and curtail imports and Mexican spending abroad. To protect the domestic economy and the wage earner from the effects of devaluation and inflation, the government took a number of decisive actions in September. Export subsidies were ended. Surcharges were placed on some exports to prevent domestic scarcity. Official prices on such key exports as petroleum were raised to international levels. Import tariffs were adjusted to reduce nonessential imports. Minimum wages, raised almost 22% in January, were raised about 23% on October 1, as were the wages and pensions of federal employees. With government aid, unionized workers in the private sector received increases of 16%–23%. Price controls on necessities were tightened. An excess profits tax was imposed to prevent speculation and subsidies were given to businesses hurt by the devaluation.

The new monetary policy signaled a change in economic development strategy from import substitution to export promotion and industrial competitiveness. Although foreign borrowing and direct investment will increase, the government, which accounts for 55% of all investment, will expand its economic role to stabilize the economy and discourage luxury and noncompetitive enterprises.

Foreign Relations. President Echeverría continued to take an independent, Third World stance in international politics. Although Mexico refused to apologize officially for equating Zionism with racism, U. S. Jewish organizations finally called off their tourist boycott early in the year; relations with Israel remained strained until March, however. In other actions, Mexico refused to play South Africa in the Davis Cup tennis competition and sought a permanent ban on South Africa. Some 30 Uruguayan leftists were granted asylum in the Mexican embassy in Montevideo. In October, Echeverría confirmed his long-expected candidacy for secretary general of the United Nations.

In June, Mexico proclaimed an exclusive maritime economic zone extending 200 miles from its shores and declared the Gulf of California its inland sea. Secretary of State Kissinger met with Mexican officials in June in an effort to ease tension. Outstanding issues separating the two nations included disputes over illegal Mexican aliens in the United States and a possible prisoner exchange, which would allow criminals to choose the country in which to serve their sentences. Agreement was reached on the latter.

As part of trade expansion efforts, Mexico hosted state visits from Canada's Prime Minister Trudeau in January and Yugoslavia's Marshall Tito in March. Both visitors inspected existing factories and discussed new trade and investment possibilities.

Mexico also helped create the 22-nation Group of Latin American and Caribbean Sugar Exporting Countries in March.

DONALD J. MABRY
Mississippi State University

October 27 newspapers tell of Mexico's decision to float the peso for the second time within two months.

UPI

MICHIGAN

A battle over bottles and crime in Detroit were major issues in Michigan during 1976.

A proposed ban on throwaway containers for beer and soft drinks was placed on the November 2 ballot as a result of a petition drive. The proposal was bitterly opposed by bottlers who mounted a million-dollar advertising campaign. Voters adopted the ban by a 2–1 margin. The measure requires nonreturnable containers to be phased out within two years.

Crime continued as a political and social issue in Detroit. One thousand policemen were among city employees laid off in midyear as a result of a budget crisis, but most were rehired by the end of October after a series of notorious crimes. A rampage at Detroit's Cobo Hall on August 19, when groups of young thugs terrorized patrons of a rock concert, led to a crackdown on juvenile gangs, which included a curfew on young people aged 17 and under.

Gov. William G. Milliken in August ordered the state police to begin patrolling Detroit freeways because of crimes against stranded motorists. These included the kidnapping and rape of a 19-year-old woman and several robberies. Some outstate communities complained that the police were taken from rural highway patrols, resulting in a sharp drop in traffic fines, which had benefited small-city treasuries.

Michigan farmers escort a dead cow to the state capitol to demonstrate their view that authorized levels of PBB (a flame retarding chemical) are deadly to cattle.

UPI

Forest Fire. A forest fire on July 30 in the Seney National Wildlife Refuge burned over 72,500 acres (29,300 ha) of the state's Upper Peninsula. Cost of fighting the fire was estimated at $7.4 million. State officials accused the U. S. Interior Department of allowing the fire to get out of control because of a policy of allowing forest fires to "burn themselves out." U. S. officials denied the allegation.

Elections. Michigan voters on Nov. 2 rejected a graduated state income tax, which had been proposed to replace the existing constitutionally required flat-rate tax.

Both presidential candidates campaigned in Michigan on the day before the national election when polls showed voters evenly split. But President Gerald R. Ford carried his home state by a 52–47% margin.

In a bitter mud-slinging campaign, Rep. Donald Riegle of Flint, a Democrat, was elected to the U. S. Senate to succeed Philip A. Hart, also a Democrat. Hart died in December.

Schools. Detroit public schools were faced with a $16-million deficit after two proposed tax increases were rejected by voters. A cost-cutting program included the elimination of all sports programs, teacher cutbacks, and course reductions. Football and girls' basketball were restored for one year with a $150,000 gift from Detroit's Bank of the Commonwealth.

Other Events. The Big Three automobile companies rebounded from an economic recession and reported healthy profits. The United Automobile Workers (UAW) struck the Ford Motor Company for 28 days before agreement on a new labor contract was reached. The UAW also signed labor contracts with the Chrysler Corporation and the General Motors Corporation.

A federal grand jury was investigating alleged corruption among top Detroit police officials as the year ended.

Detroit acquired its first black police chief, career officer William Hart. The first tenants moved into Detroit's $337-million Renaissance Center, which was heralded as the focal point of downtown revival.

CHARLES W. THEISEN, *The Detroit "News"*

─────── **MICHIGAN • Information Highlights** ───────

Area: 58,216 square miles (150,779 km²).
Population (1975 est.): 9,157,000.
Chief Cities (1970 census): Lansing, the capital, 131,-546; Detroit, 1,513,601.
Government (1976): *Chief Officers*—governor, William G. Milliken (R) lt. gov., James J. Damman (R). *Legislature*—Senate, 38 members; House of Representatives, 110 members.
Education (1975–1976): *Enrollment*—public elementary schools, 1,090,003 pupils; public secondary, 983,-285; nonpublic (1976–77), 220,100; colleges and universities, 414,450 students. *Public school expenditures,* $2,688,125,000 ($1,366 per pupil).
State Finances (fiscal year 1975): *Revenues,* $6,938,098,-000; *expenditures,* $7,688,334,000.
Personal Income (1975): $56,526,000,000; per capita, $6,173.
Labor Force (July 1976): *Nonagricultural wage and salary earners,* 3,135,300; *insured unemployed,* 158,-600 (5.6%).

MICROBIOLOGY

Several interesting and worthwhile discoveries occurred in microbiology in 1976, and these are recorded in the scientific literature. The following events were of most concern to the public.

Microbial Life on Mars. The landings in July and September 1976 of Viking 1 and 2 scientific laboratories on Mars, with special emphasis on the search for life, presented a paradox to microbiologists. Some of the biological experiments showed unusually large and rapid initial production of gases and then a decrease when Martian soil samples were treated with organic nutrients and water. Such activity was quite different from that in Earth soil samples. The discovery of small amounts of nitrogen, oxygen, krypton, and xenon in the Martian atmosphere made the microbiology tests tantalizing, but the question of life on Mars remained unanswered.

Microbial Genetic Manipulation. A breakthrough in the understanding of cellular function and the development of life came in 1976 with the announcement of the first man-made gene for bacteria.

The recent discovery of enzymes that cut and splice the hereditary material of living organisms with apparent precision may herald imaginative and far-reaching discoveries in microbiology and science in general.

Current research on excising deoxyribonucleic acid (DNA, the essential genetic material) segments carrying one (or more) gene from cellular material and splicing it to the hereditary substances in quite different organisms permits the construction of recombinant DNA molecules that may have beneficial or practical effects, as well as hazardous or harmful ones. Practical applications range from the possibility of transferring nitrogen-fixing genes of bacteria (rhizobia) to food crops other than legumes, thereby reducing the need for nitrogen fertilizer, to treating such human metabolic defects as diabetes. Microorganisms in the laboratory might even become the storehouse preserving genetic material from various endangered plant and animal species.

Many biologists believe the hazards associated with recombinant DNA experiments are remote, whereas others think the addition of foreign and potentially harmful genes (tumor-forming or toxin-producing, for example) to another bacterium or virus might cause catastrophies of great proportions if the organisms escaped from laboratories. During the year this topic was hotly debated in several communities and organizations. The U.S. National Institutes of Health and similar agencies in other countries therefore issued strict guidelines for conducting such research.

Influenza Immunization. Considerable scientific and political controversy arose over the national campaign to immunize the U. S. human population against swine influenza.

Several American and foreign microbiologists and health specialists questioned the desirability of the crash program for several reasons, including (1) the likelihood that a pandemic was too remote to justify mass immunization with what might be an ineffective viral vaccine, and (2) the fact that the vaccine might produce adverse side effects in some persons. Other scientists and public health officials discounted such criticisms, believing that if an influenza epidemic occurred an early and proper immunization with a multiple-strain vaccine would protect 85–95% of those over the age of 25. There was some evidence to support both these viewpoints. Each group admitted that young children (age 3 to 10) seldom develop antibodies when immunized with swine-influenza virus, and that there was some uncertainty about the dosage level needed to produce a protective antibody level in any age group.

Even though the U. S. government appropriated funds to pay for vaccine production, a problem arose about possible liability law suits by persons who might suffer adverse effects from the immunization. In August Congress passed an insurance protection bill. The bill applied only to swine-flu immunization and was not intended to set a precedent for similar protection against measles, polio, or other vaccines. (See also MEDICINE: *Special Report*, p. 322.)

Malaria and Schistosomiasis Immunization. The successful cultivation in 1976 of the malarial parasite in human red blood cells raised new hope that immunization against the disease will be possible. Malaria still strikes 96 million people annually, and a million die in Africa alone. However, much research with animals and human beings is required before immunization will be practical.

Schistosomiasis is a debilitating disease of an estimated 250 million people in the tropics. Interesting new research on the disease dealt with the production of an immune state that either limits further spread of the parasite in the tissues of persons already infected, or reduces the damage by later infection. Workers in a number of countries believe a vaccine can be produced to reduce the incidence or the harmful effects of this disease.

Microbial Protein from Methane. As protein shortages for food and fodder increase in the world, greater attention is focused on non-disease-producing microbes as supplements to other sources. Research in 1976 showed that methane is the most promising source of carbon for the industrial production of microbial protein; biomasses consisting of more than 65% protein have been obtained. Proposed technology may yield protein that is superior to all the traditional foods eaten today.

J. R. PORTER
University of Iowa

A Syrian Soviet-made T-54 tank rumbles down a hill in the Tell Zaatar Palestinian enclave in Beirut after the cease-fire in October.

UPI

MIDDLE EAST

With the one tragic exception of Lebanon, the Middle East in 1976 was an area of comparative quiet. It was difficult not to fear that the lull was merely a calm before another storm, such as a fifth Arab-Israeli war; yet there were conflicting indications that could justify either a pessimistic or an optimistic reading of the probabilities.

Sinai Agreement Holds. The cardinal fact about the Middle East in 1976 was that the Sinai agreement of Sept. 1, 1975, between Israel and Egypt, the masterpiece of Dr. Henry Kissinger's diplomacy as U. S. Secretary of State, had held up. The pact has not merely lasted well over a year (an achievement in itself in a part of the world where international agreements often prove to be "writ in water"), but has proved a resounding success. The agreement

Israeli soldiers load a U. S.-made *Lance* missile onto a launcher. Israel has rebuilt its forces since 1973.

UPI

has had its critics, but the benefits have, in fact, been considerable, even though it is admittedly just an interim agreement.

The Egyptian and Israeli armies are now separated by a 25-mile (40-km) wide buffer zone policed by the United Nations, and with radar stations manned by 164 U. S. technicians who watch for any unauthorized military activity. In these circumstances anything resembling the surprise attack that launched the 1973 war is extremely unlikely. The military provisions of the pact have, on the whole, been well observed. Israel has from time to time charged Egypt, apparently justifiably, with violations, but these have not been of a grave nature. Also, the promised ending of Egypt's propaganda and diplomatic offensive against Israel has not been observed since mid-1976.

Israeli Benefits. Nevertheless, the rewards promised to Israel by Secretary Kissinger as the price of its assent have been paid; indeed, both Israel and Egypt have derived substantial advantages. Israel has received the $2,300,000,000 pledged in U. S. aid. Israeli-bound cargoes move through the Suez Canal again without hindrance —an enormous gain. There has been a breathing space which has enabled Israel to rebuild its forces, equipping them with new arms from the United States and reorganizing them for greater combat effectiveness. There is reason to suppose that Israel is now militarily stronger than ever, even apart from the question of atomic weapons. It was revealed in April (by *Time* Magazine) that Israel has a small stock (13) of atomic bombs, which could be used in a desperate situation. Meanwhile, it is hoped, they will serve as a deterrent.

Also, less tangible but important rewards have been enjoyed by Israel in the form of solid diplomatic backing. The United States on January 26 vetoed a pro-Palestinian resolution in the UN Security Council and again on March 25 a resolution condemning Israeli occupation policies on the West Bank and in the Old City of Jerusalem. Similarly, on June 29, a Security Council resolution calling on Israel to withdraw from occupied Arab lands encountered another U. S. veto, the U. S. representative condemning the resolution as "totally devoid of balance." On December 11 a General Assembly resolution calling for the resumption by March 31 of the Geneva conference on the Middle East received 122 votes in favor, and two against—those of Israel and the United States. The United States also acts as intermediary between Israel and states with which it has no relations.

Egypt's Gains. The advantages accruing to Egypt have also been considerable. Israel relinquished the strategic Mitla and Gidi passes in the Sinai and returned to Egypt the Abu Rudeis oilfields, which earn Egypt nearly $1 million a day in hard currency. The threat of war having receded, Egypt is also rebuilding the ruined cities along the Suez Canal.

Lebanon. Any analysis of the Middle East in terms of stabilizing developments versus disruptive factors should note that events in Lebanon, which most of the year seemed beyond any hope of betterment, did in fact improve dramatically in the last quarter of the year. The appalling civil war, between the alliance of Lebanese Muslims and Palestinian radicals on one side and the Phalangist forces representing the hitherto economically dominant Christian element in Lebanese society on the other, had begun in April 1975. A conflict of great horror, it lacked clear battlelines and therefore also was without rear areas where life was safe and normal. The line-up of forces within the country was intensely complicated and sometimes contradictory. The destruction of life and property in the year-and-a-half of chronic, random violence was very great. The conflict came near to destroying the whole fabric of civilized life in Beirut; mail, telephone services, and utilities all became erratic or nonexistent. Beirut as a banking and commercial center was closed down. The government of Lebanon became a purely nominal entity and taxes went uncollected. The small Lebanese armed forces were themselves split.

Syrian Intervention. The new factor in 1976 was the Syrian intervention, which began tentatively in March and steadily grew until it became decisive. It also became a new divisive influence in the Arab world. President Hafez al-Assad's intervention was probably motivated by a desire not to let the situation in Lebanon get out of control. In particular, he did not care to become involved in hostilities with Israel because of Palestinian actions and not at his own decision. The intervention soon took the form of maintaining balance between the factions by heavy support on the side of the Christians, who had seemed doomed to defeat.

The Syrian aid finally became decisive. The Palestinian-Muslim forces were forced to retreat and were driven from their major strongholds.

UPI

Yasir Arafat, leader of the Palestine Liberation Organization (center, right) links hands in a victory gesture with Dr. George Habash of the People's Front for the Liberation of Palestine and two Lebanese soldiers of the Muslim left.

On October 19 the end of the long agony approached, when a meeting in Riyadh, Saudi Arabia, of six Arab leaders produced a peace plan and authorized an Arab peace-keeping force in Lebanon (in practice, largely the Syrian forces already there). A cease-fire (the 55th) was proclaimed on October 21 and, unprecedentedly, did become effective. In the last stages and aftermath of the civil war Israel was apprehensive of a Syrian move into south Lebanon, but in fact a boundary zone of some 15 miles (24 km) on the Lebanese side of the Israeli border remained free of Syrian forces.

The restoration of Lebanon to comparative tranquility was indeed a quasimiraculous improvement, but it is doubtful if the small country can ever again become "the Switzerland of the Middle East." A great many of the most highly-skilled Lebanese exponents of the free-enterprise economy are no longer there: they are in other Middle East countries, Cyprus, or western Europe, probably never to return.

Palestinians, Terrorism. One of the most significant results of the year's events, in Lebanon and elsewhere, was the decline in the power and influence of the Palestinian organizations— though it would be easy to exaggerate this. In some sense the Palestinian problem was still the great, central issue that inhibited a genuine peace; but, however high the movement may ride at the United Nations, a trend was discernible on the part of Middle Eastern governments to refuse to be jostled into policy decisions at the behest of the movement. What this meant was that, as a practical matter, the adamant opposition to the existence of Israel by some Palestinian leaders, such as Dr. George Habash, would not necessarily exercise a veto power on the diplomatic decisions of the Arab states—a modestly hopeful sign. The possibility that a small West-Bank Palestinian state might emerge as part of a general peace package had appeared over the diplomatic horizon. However, it should be noted that the Palestinian Liberation Organization (PLO) was granted full membership in the Arab League on September 6.

A similar, and parallel, recovery of nerve could be seen on the part of Middle East governments in their firmer attitude toward terrorists. This generalization, however, does not apply to Iraq, which organizes radical activity, nor to Libya, which approves and heavily finances terrorism. There is a profound and deepening split between radical and conservative governments in the Middle East.

Until recently, governments (apart from Israel) have shown a habitual and almost servile readiness to negotiate with the terrorists involved in any incident. This is no longer the case. On August 23 Egyptian paratroopers overpowered Arab hijackers holding more than 90 hostages captive on an Egyptian airliner at Luxor. On September 26 the Syrian government flatly refused to negotiate with raiders who took 90 hostages in the Semiramis Hotel in Damascus and put forward political demands. The building was stormed by Syrian troops. One of the raiders was killed (as were four hostages) in the subsequent battle. Another three of the raiders were publicly hanged the next day. The Syrian and Egyptian incidents were not isolated but clearly part of a general trend.

Entebbe. The most striking example of readiness to combat terrorist activity was, of course, the amazing rescue on July 3–4 at Entebbe, Uganda, of 103 passengers and crew of the Air France airbus that had been hijacked on June 27 by pro-Palestinian guerrillas. (See ISRAEL, UGANDA.) In this action Israel was true to the principle it has consistently followed of never negotiating with terrorists.

New Alignments in the Middle East. Syrian actions against the Palestinians afforded an opportunity for Sadat's Egypt to establish better relations with the PLO—though the latter's activities have never been tolerated in Egypt.

Also, on July 19 Egypt and Sudan announced a 25-year defense agreement which would "increase their ability to discharge their Arab and African responsibilities." The accord was considered to be designed to thwart further Libyan attempts against the Sudan, or Egypt, or any non-radical regime. Egypt also took a surprising step with Sadat's denunciation on March 14 of the 15-year treaty of cooperation signed with Russia in 1971, because of Soviet refusal to supply adequate arms to Egypt. However, it is probably wise to see in this no more than an Egyptian pressure play. Refueling rights for Soviet warships in Egyptian ports were not affected.

Soviet Influence. Though Soviet influence in the Middle East has been in eclipse during the high noon of Kissinger's diplomacy, it would be unwise to assume it cannot make a comeback. Iraq constitutes a strongly pro-Soviet bastion in the heart of the Middle East, with access to the Persian Gulf, and Libya also is an advanced base for Russian policies in the Mediterranean and Africa. The restoration of good relations with Egypt is by no means impossible. The flow of Soviet military components and spares to Egypt appears already to have resumed through third-country channels. The maintenance of the present preponderance of U. S. influence over Soviet influence in the Middle East will depend on the policies and the skill of the Carter administration.

Oil Price Split. The expected meeting of the Organization of Petroleum Exporting Countries to decide upon oil prices was held in Doha, Qatar, December 15–17. The surprising outcome was that the members agreed to disagree, Saudi Arabia and the United Arab Emirates raising their prices, as of Jan. 1, 1977, by 5%, while the 11 other countries posted a hike of 10%, with a promise of another 5% by July 1.

ARTHUR CAMPBELL TURNER
University of California, Riverside

UPI

Oil ministers of the Organization of Petroleum Exporting Countries had a gusty two-day meeting at Doha, Qatar, in mid-December. They raised oil prices by 5–10%.

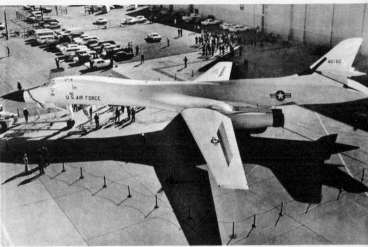

In 1976 U. S. military and government officials debated the merits of developing the B-1 strategic bomber, tested by Secretary of Defense Rumsfeld (*left*) in April. Final decision awaited the Carter administration.

MILITARY FORCES

As has so often been the case in the past, the major developments in the area of military forces were associated with the activities of the two superpowers. In the United States the time was approaching when a number of decisions would have to be made regarding which new weapons would be deployed, and which would be at least temporarily deferred. Such decisions about the "mix" of weapons for the late 1970's awaited the Carter administration. As for the Soviet Union, there was disagreement in the West regarding what inferences should be drawn from observable Soviet actions. The arms competition in the Middle East was second only to that between the United States and the Soviet Union in terms of total military scope and international intensity.

U. S. Forces. As in previous years controversy swirled about the B-1 bomber. The Air Force asked for production to begin on the first of 244 planes (several evaluation models have been built). President Ford supported the Air Force by including in his military budget request to the Congress a $1,000,000,000 item to enable production to begin in November. The Democratically controlled Congress, mindful that Democratic presidential candidate Jimmy Carter had expressed serious doubts about the utility of the B-1 program, refused the Ford request. By the fall Congress and the White House had worked out a compromise which postponed until February 1977 the decision whether to start B-1 production. This meant that the matter would await the new president. Congress did, however, authorize $87 million a month, starting in October, to be spent on the B-1 project. Much of this sum was intended for use by the plane's prime contractor, Rockwell International,

to keep together the several thousand persons comprising the core work force of the bomber production effort in case the 1977 decision is to initiate production.

Proponents of the B-1 argued that the aircraft was needed to replace the aging B-52's as the airborne component of what is known as the triad. According to the triad concept, the United States must confront the Soviet Union with the capability to retaliate after a Soviet attack upon the United States with three distinct types of weapons systems. These are land-based intercontinental ballistic missiles (ICBM's), submarine launched ballistic missiles, (SLBM's), and long range bombers. The theory supporting the triad mode of deployment is that the maintenance of three different weapons systems deters the Soviet Union from contemplating an attack because of the difficulty of having to destroy or substantially cripple three retaliatory systems. Another reason given for maintaining the triad is the belief that in this way the Soviet Union is forced to spread a limited amount of money and scientific talent further, thus reducing the support that can be given to other aspects of military preparations.

Those professing to see in Soviet missile deployment an increasing capability to strike first and destroy the U. S. land-based missile force were particularly insistent upon the B-1 development as a counter move. Their view was that bombers can be "flushed" from their airfields and gotten into the air where they would be safe before Soviet warheads could impact. Once in the air bombers can of course be recalled to their bases should the warning prove false. In either case bomber advocates emphasize the greater flexibility offered by aircraft in comparison with missiles. The latter would not normally be fired before Soviet warheads impacted and of course could not be recalled to

their silos after being fired. To the argument
that the B-1 might not be able to operate successfully in the Soviet airspace in the 1980's
bomber proponents reply that the B-1 has a
supersonic dash capability, and that it was designed to operate at low altitude, a zone where
it is generally felt Soviet radar systems are less
effective.

Those opposing the B-1 cited what they
claimed was the excessive cost of a single plane,
in the neighborhood of $88 million, and the
total cost of the 244 plane program, which is
estimated to be approximately $22,000,000,000.
B-1 opponents also argue that the United States
possesses sufficient retaliatory capability now
and that therefore the B-1 represents useless
and provocative "overkill" capacity. Their position is that even should attrition occur to the
1,054-missile ICBM force because of a Soviet
"first strike," there would remain sufficient retaliatory force in the 656 missile SLBM force,
and the B-52 fleet, to deter a Soviet attack.
Further, opponents of the new bomber point out
that the United States possesses a second line
of retaliatory strength in what is known as the
Forward Based Systems (FBS). Primary components of the FBS are aircraft carriers and
shorter-range aircraft and missiles, which are
based in several countries of Western Europe as
well as in South Korea.

While the B-1 controversy stole many of the
headlines in 1976, there were other important
disagreements about the Pentagon's plans for
development of other new weapons systems.
One such new program was also championed by
the Air Force. It is the proposal to build a
new missile twice the size of the Minuteman
III, currently the most advanced U. S. ICBM.
The new missile is designated the M-X. Several reasons account for the interest in the M-X.
Primary among them is the desire by the Air
Force to increase the invulnerability of its
ICBM force to the Soviet capability to destroy
missiles before they are launched. Some observers of the Soviet offensive missile program
fear that the increasing size of Soviet missiles,
and the presumed increase in their accuracy,
place in jeopardy the U. S. land-based missiles.
Thus it is argued that any new missile must have
improved prelaunch invulnerability. Prelaunch
invulnerability for the M-X missile may be
achieved in one of two possible ways. One
would be to carry 2 M-X's aboard large, so-
called wide-bodied, aircraft such as the C-5
which is currently in operation with the Air
Force. If this mode of deployment were to be
adopted the plane would be kept during periods
of low international tension at airfields in the
interior of the United States. Should tension
increase, particularly between the United States
and the Soviet Union, the planes could be rotated on airborne alert, thus increasing their
survivability in case of Soviet attack. The technique of launching an ICBM from a plane in

The USS "Tarawa," the Navy's newest and largest assault ship, undergoes sea trials in Gulf of Mexico.

flight was demonstrated in 1974 when a Minuteman ICBM was dropped by parachute from a
C-5 and was subsequently fired. Another means
of securing prelaunch invulnerability for the
M-X is adoption of what is known as the
"trench" configuration. This method of deployment would involve the placing of M-X missiles in a concrete cylinder buried in an underground trench, which could be 15 to 20 miles
(24–32 km) in length. Since an attacker would
not know where in the trench the missiles were
located, a successful attack would of necessity
have to involve an effort to destroy the entire
length of the trench. This would become a
formidable problem, particularly if multiple
trenches were used. In case of need the M-X
missiles would be blasted out of the trenches in
canisters from which they could be fired.

Still another major weapons system, the
size of which would await President Carter's
judgment, was the Trident submarine and the
new SLBM which it would carry. The first Trident, scheduled for launching in 1978, could be
the first of many such craft, or merely one of
several. In comparison with currently operating
missile submarines the Trident is larger, equipped
with more quietly running engines to lessen
acoustical detection, and it carries larger and
longer-range missiles. There was some speculation President Carter might favor the Trident
because of his former association with and ad-
miration for Admiral Hyman Rickover, the so-
called "father" of U. S. nuclear submarines. The

estimated cost for the Trident program would be approximately $25,000,000,000 to $30,000,000,-000.

As a hedge against the possibility that the SALT II talks would fail to place ceilings upon strategic weapons when the SALT I agreement expires in the fall of 1977, the Ford administration laid plans to replace some 60 Minuteman single warhead missiles with the MIRVed Minuteman III. This missile has three independently targeted warheads.

Another major decision which awaited Carter was the question of how many new generation jet fighters and fighter-bombers the nation will require in the late 1970's. The F-15, a Mach 2.5+ jet capable of air superiority missions or deep penetration raids, entered the Air Force inventory in 1974. The Navy F-14, designed for fleet defense, is currently operating from aircraft carriers. Either could be easily increased in numbers. The F-16, a multipurpose fighter plane, is not yet in service. First deliveries are expected in 1980. The F-18, and A-18, air superiority and fighter-bomber configuration of the same basic plane, are desired by the Navy but construction has not begun.

Whether or not to deploy the cruise missile constituted another defense debate in the United States. Proponents of the cruise missile, which is similar to a miniature unmanned jet plane, claim that it could offer a relatively cheap means to keep the aging B-52 fleet useful. Deployed on bombers, cruise missiles with a 1,500-mile (2,400-km) range could enable the bombers to remain safely beyond the range of Soviet anti-aircraft defenses when they released the cruise missiles. Cruise missiles could also be carried by the B-1 and can be fired from surface vessels and submarines.

MiG-25 pilot Viktor Belenko (left) is escorted to Tokyo airport for flight to asylum in the United States.

UPI

The size of the Navy was under debate. Rep. Les Aspin (D.-Wisc.), a frequent critic of Pentagon spending practices, alleged the Navy was "fudging the facts" in order to obtain funds for unneeded ships. The Navy disputed Aspin's claim that by 1980 the United States would have more surface combat ships than the Soviets, reversing a worrisome trend evident in the mid-1970's.

An interesting development, about which very little was said officially, was the possibility that the United States might supply military equipment to the Communist Chinese. Increased speculation about this resulted from remarks by former Secretary of Defense James R. Schlesinger that the Chinese defenses were not sufficient to stop a determined Soviet attack.

While discussions and arguments were underway about "how much is enough" in regard to various weapons systems, the United States quietly reduced its military posture in two areas. In Thailand the United States reduced its military presence to only several hundred advisers, down from some 50,000 during the Vietnam war. In North Dakota the first and possibly the last of twelve planned anti-ballistic missile sites was closed out. Thus ended a multibillion dollar program which had extended over two decades. The reason for the closing was the belief in Washington that the ABM defenses could too easily be swamped by the multiple warheads being adopted by the Soviets for their strategic missile force.

During 1976 two bizarre incidents occurred which involved advanced aircraft belonging to the two superpowers. Both demonstrated the sensitivity of each nation to the possibility of losing military secrets to the other. The first incident happened early in the fall when a Soviet MiG-25 jet interceptor was flown to Japan by a defecting Russian pilot. Despite demands from Moscow for its release, the plane was held several months as Japanese and American specialists examined it. The other incident involved an American F-14 jet fighter and the sophisticated Phoenix missile with which it was equipped. In September the F-14 was lost overboard from the aircraft carrier *John F. Kennedy* as the ship was participating in a NATO exercise in the North Atlantic. The plane sank in nearly 1,900 feet (580 m) of water. The Pentagon was concerned that the Soviets might engage in an underwater salvage operation to obtain the missile and the plane. To preclude this possibility the Navy located and recovered the missile and then the plane.

Just before Christmas, President-elect Carter named Harold Brown as his choice for secretary of defense in the new administration. At the time, Brown, a 49 year-old physicist, was president of the California Institute of Technology. He had served as secretary of the Air Force under President Johnson. Charles W. Duncan, Jr., was named deputy secretary.

The "Kiev," the Soviet Union's first full-fledged aircraft carrier, joined the Russian fleet in the Mediterranean Sea.

UPI

Soviet Developments. In the fall Secretary of Defense Donald Rumsfeld charged that the Soviet Union was attempting to acquire nuclear weapons superiority vis-à-vis the United States. Although the Soviets appear to be keeping within the numerical limits specified by the SALT I accords, Rumsfeld was concerned about the qualitative improvements being made in Soviet missiles, an area not covered in the SALT I agreements. Of particular concern were the new SS-17 ICBM, capable of carrying four warheads; the SS-19 with six warheads; and the very large SS-18 which is estimated to be capable of carrying eight warheads. Rumsfeld was also worried about a new intermediate range ballistic missile designated the SS-20. While probably not possessing the range to endanger the United States, this missile when deployed is expected to threaten the NATO nations of Western Europe. In contradiction of official Soviet statements, Rumsfeld stuck to Pentagon estimates that the Soviet Backfire bomber had intercontinental range and hence should be included in SALT II discussions.

Other Soviet activities caused concern in Washington. One was the announcement in midsummer that the *Kiev,* the Soviet's first fullfledged aircraft carrier, had joined the Russian fleet in the Mediterranean. Previously the ship had operated in the Black Sea. The *Kiev* is about the size of a World War II American carrier. In what could be a related event the Soviets were reported to have contacted the government of Western Samoa in the South Pacific, regarding the establishment of a fishing base on the island. The Pentagon, already worried over the presence of Soviet naval forces in the Indian Ocean, viewed the Soviet proposal with suspicion. One U. S. naval officer noted that experience suggested the Russians often open what appears to be a commercial operation that is actually a cover for military operations—in this case a possible move to outflank U. S. positions in Guam and the Marianas, some 3,000 miles (4,800 km) to the northwest. In Peru, other Soviet activities were being carefully observed by Washington. The concern was over the decision of the Peruvian government to purchase 36 swing-wing Sukhoi Su-22 jet fighter-bombers which have a top speed nearly twice that of sound. Consummation of the deal would represent the first sale of Soviet combat planes to a Latin American nation other than Cuba.

Still another disquieting development, one which in time could trigger a new Soviet-American arms competition, was the possibility that the Soviets were building "killer satellites." Such craft would have as their mission the destruction of U. S. reconnaissance satellites, and those used for communication and navigational purposes. So long as the Soviet satellites are designed to destroy with nonnuclear means no treaties would be broken. Should the Soviet activity be confirmed, there would exist strong pressures for the United States to develop some type of countermeasures. These would doubtless involve the capability to negate or destroy the Soviet craft. While this kind of arms competition in space would not involve the loss of life, it could become an expensive new form of military rivalry.

Middle East Developments. Almost as newsworthy as the military activities of the two superpowers was the weapons acquisition program carried on by some of the oil rich nations of the Middle East, and Israel. The situation was dramatized by the U. S. arms sales to the Shah of Iran. In 1976 Secretary of State Henry Kissinger announced that the U. S. would sell Iran between $10,000,000,000 and $15,000,000,000 worth of weapons by 1980. Iranian purchases may include the ultramodern F-16 jet. Already Iran has purchased F-4 Phantom jets and Spruance class destroyers, plus less sophisticated equipment. The Iranian sales are justified on the grounds that Iran must be secure against its northern neighbor, the U. S. S. R., and be able to provide stability in the oil producing Persian Gulf area. Also, further arms sales are said to soak up petrodollars which might be used to upset international monetary relations.

The United States also sells to other oil states and to Israel. So much equipment has been provided to Israel that Gen. George S. Brown, chairman of the Joint Chiefs of Staff, stated that Israel was something of a burden because equipment going to Israel drew down stocks needed by U. S. forces. The remark stirred substantial controversy and some suggested it showed an anti-Jewish bias, which General Brown subsequently denied.

See also DISARMAMENT.

ROBERT M. LAWRENCE
Colorado State University

A woman miner operates rock drilling machinery at a molybdenum ore mine in Grand County, Colo. The mine is near a newly built molybdenum ore processing plant.

UPI

MINING

The world's mining and mineral processing industry in 1976 apparently achieved a modest recovery from its 1975 slump, as many national economies registered upturns in overall industrial activity. As the year ended, however, it was impossible to ascertain whether declines in output levels for many commodities that were reported between 1974 and 1975 were made up or exceeded by 1975–76 growths. Clearly, however, general levels of consumption of mineral commodities were higher in 1976 than in 1975.

Value of World Output. Very preliminary estimates fixed the value of world crude mineral production (including fuel minerals) at $182,-000,000,000 in 1976 (in terms of 1973 constant dollars), compared with $180,000,000,000 in 1975, $183,000,000,000 in 1974, and $180,000,-000,000 in 1973. In terms of current (1976) dollars, the 1976 figure would be much higher, owing to the continued worldwide inflation.

Detailed country-by-country results were not available for 1974–76, but for 1973, the leading countries, and their percentage share of the total, were as follows: United States, 18.8%; U. S. S. R., 17.6%; Saudi Arabia, 5.7%; China, 4.9%; Iran and Canada, each 4.5%; Venezuela, 3.2%; West Germany, 3.1%; Libya, 2.7%; South Africa, 2.6%; and Nigeria and Kuwait, each 2.3%. These 12 nations accounted for almost 70% of the world mineral output total value in 1973.

Examining the same $180,000,000,000 total value for 1973 from the viewpoint of individual commodities' contribution, crude oil clearly ranked ahead of all others, accounting for 47.5% of the total, followed by anthracite and bituminous coal with 18.2%; natural gas with 7.0%; copper with 6.3%; iron with 4.4%; lignite coal with 2.0%; natural gas liquids with 1.9%; and zinc with 1.0%.

The Election and Minerals. Results of the 1976 U. S. general election had both direct and indirect relationships to the mineral industry. The most obvious direct relationship was the defeat, by wide margins, of referenda proposals to impose strict controls upon nuclear power plant development. Voters in Arizona, Colorado, Montana, Ohio, Oregon, and Washington rejected plans that varied in wording but which all had as their aim greater assurances of safety in nuclear power plant design before allowing additional construction. Earlier, in the California primary election, voters rejected an even stronger proposal which if approved would have provided not only more rigid control for future installations, but also for closing existing plants that failed to meet new requirements. Increase in nuclear power development can mean not only lessening requirements for coal, oil, and natural gas, but also could provide the opportunity for expanded nonfuel use of these traditional energy sources, specifically in the area of production of petrochemical feedstocks to support expanded production of plastics. Such substitution, in turn, would permit further substitution of plastic materials for metallic and nonmetallic construction and fabrication materials.

Ferrous Ores and Metals. Preliminary information suggests that world iron ore output closely approximated the 1975 level of 891.6 million tons. Partial 1976 results extrapolated to full year figures give the following estimated output levels for some major producers (in million tons): U. S. S. R., 237; Australia, 90; United States, 86; China, 70; Brazil, 60; France, 48; India, 47; Sweden, 31; Venezuela, 24. Data are insufficient to estimate Canada and Liberia, and to provide estimates of output levels for the ores of the major ferroalloying metals—manganese, chrome, and tungsten. Little change from the 1975 performance of these industries was expected.

World steel output in contrast was expected to show a modest increase over the 1975 level. On the basis of data for the first eight months of 1976, output in the U. S. S. R. was up by 3.1% relative to 1975, production in the United States was 3.5% above that of 1975; Japanese production was 2.1% higher than in 1975; West German output was 8.4% above the 1975 level; and output in China (although not reported) was believed to have advanced by 6% or more.

Nonferrous Ores and Metals. It was expected that an overall upturn in worldwide production of major nonferrous metals would be evident relative to 1975 results. Output for aluminum, copper, lead, and zinc would clearly exceed 1975 results and approach if not top those for 1974. Nickel, which alone among the major nonferrous metals proved to be an exception to the general downturn in output between 1974 and 1975, was expected to show further growth in 1976. The relative trends for minor nonferrous metals were unclear with the possible exception of mercury, which probably registered another decline in output. Mercury producers tended to restrain output in order to achieve more favorable market conditions.

Precious Metals. World output of both gold and silver registered declines between 1974 and 1975. Gold trended down for the fourth consecutive year, silver for a second year. Incomplete returns for 1976 indicate a further downturn in gold output and a very modest increase in silver production compared with 1975 results. The postulated downturn in gold is based primarily on continued declines in South African output, which seemed likely to continue into 1977 if plans announced in 1976 for economic rationalization of gold-mining there are carried out. The estimated upturn in silver output is based upon increased by-product recovery resulting from modest upturns in smelter output of major non-

ferrous metals in 1976 that in turn were related to the overall upturn in world-wide industrial activity. World platinum production in 1975 was estimated at about 5.1 million troy ounces, down slightly from the 1974 level of about 5.2 million ounces, with the U.S.S.R. and South Africa again ranking first and second, respectively, among producing nations, and together accounting for over 90% of the total.

Fertilizer Materials. Preliminary data suggest that 1976 world output of principal fertilizer materials (phosphate rock, potash, and nitrogen) closely approximated 1975 levels, but did not reach 1974 levels as market conditions did not improve substantially from those of 1975. World nitrogen output for the year ending June 30, 1975, totaled 43.1 million metric tons.

Miscellaneous. It seemed assured that the U. S. S. R. topped Canada in asbestos production for the second year in a row. Although Canadian output increased substantially with the end of the lengthy strike that had sharply restrained production in 1975, a substantial increase in Soviet production capacity in that year was sufficient to retain the U. S. S. R.'s rank as leading world producer. In contrast to many commodities, asbestos remained in a situation of tight supply on a worldwide basis through most of 1976 despite production growth.

Partial returns on 1976 world cement output suggest a recovery from the 1975 output level of 687.3 million tons, which was 2.4% below the 1974 level. Returns, however, were not sufficiently complete to fix the level of the world total. Principal 1976 gains were in the developing market economy countries and the centrally planned economy nations. The output situation in China was questionable for 1976 as a result of a major earthquake, but a subsequent upturn could be expected.

Preliminary returns indicated that world natural diamond output in 1976 closely approximated the 1975 level of about 41.1 million carats despite a shortfall in Angolan output as a result of the civil strife in that nation. The output of natural diamond was supplemented by the manufacture of diamond in several nations, most notably the United States, where output was presumed substantially to exceed the estimated figure of 17 million carats for 1973.

The downturn in industrial activity in 1975 that led to a 0.5% reduction in world sulfur output relative to that of 1974 apparently was more than compensated by development in 1976, despite poor market conditions in the industrial market economy nations. Preliminary results suggest that worldwide output probably topped both the 1974 and 1975 levels, setting a new record high, chiefly as a result of output increases in the less developed nations and the major producers of Eastern Europe, the U. S. S. R. and Poland.

CHARLES L. KIMBELL
U. S. Bureau of Mines

Dorothy Kathleen Benham, 20-year-old coed from St. Paul, Minn., begins her reign as Miss America 1977.

MINNESOTA

An extensive drought plagued Minnesota in 1976. The legislature enacted tax-relief measures for low-income and disabled persons.

Weather. Minnesota was afflicted by its driest summer and fall since the 1930's. Especially hard hit were the southwestern and west-central regions of the state. Forest and grass fires burned throughout the summer and fall and into December. More than 3,000 fires were counted, entailing a cost of $11 million in continual fire-fighting measures.

Economy. As a result of the lack of rainfall, farm income fell $500,000,000 in 1976. The manufacturing and commercial segments of the economy registered healthy gains, giving the state's overall economy a boost. The unemployment rate declined from 7.4% in 1975 to 5.2% in 1976. The state's fiscal position tightened but remained strong in comparison to other states. A surplus in the treasury dropped from $400 million in 1975 to $150 million at the end of 1976.

Environment. A dispute between the state and Reserve Mining Company over the discharge of asbestos-laden wastes from taconite processing into Lake Superior at Silver Bay remained unresolved. Reserve Mining indicated that it was willing to develop an on-land disposal site at Mile Post 7, a few miles from Lake Superior. The site was rejected by state environmental agencies and a state hearing officer, who took testimony in favor of a Mile Post 20 site, farther removed from the lake. U. S. District Judge Edward J. Devitt ruled that the plant would close on July 7, 1977, if the dispute is not resolved, leaving an uncertain future for the 3,000 employees of the facility.

Public Works. A national competition for the design of a new state historical center and an underground extension of the State Capitol was conducted. The competition attracted 256 entries and five were chosen to compete in the final phase. The project will cost an estimated $40 million and will conserve 52% in heating and 22% in cooling costs. The winning design will be selected in March 1977.

St. Paul was chosen as one of four U. S. cities to construct a downtown "people mover" transit system. The U. S. government will provide 80% of the $56-million funding.

Politics. Minnesota led the nation in the percentage of eligible voters who went to the polls— 75.4% or 1,978,286 Minnesotans voted. In winning reelection, Sen. Hubert H. Humphrey received 1,290,736 votes, the largest ever received by any candidate for public office in Minnesota. The Carter-Mondale ticket carried Minnesota by 56%. Walter F. Mondale became the second Minnesotan to be elected to the nation's second highest office. President-elect Jimmy Carter named 7th-district Congressman Bob Bergland to the post of secretary of agriculture. The division of seats in the U. S. House of Representatives remained the same—5 Democratic-Farmer Labor party members and 3 Independent-Republicans. The Democratic-Farmer Labor party increased its commanding margin in the state legislature, taking 49 of the 67 seats in the senate and 104 of the 134 seats in the House.

On December 29, Wendell R. Anderson, who was first elected governor in 1970, resigned midway in his second term. He was succeeded by Lt. Gov. Rudy Perpich. On December 30, Mondale resigned his seat in the U. S. Senate, and Perpich appointed Anderson to succeed him.

RUSSELL W. FRIDLEY
Director, Minnesota Historical Society

MINNESOTA • Information Highlights

Area: 84,068 square miles (217,736 sq km).
Population (1975 est.): 3,926,000.
Chief Cities (1970 census): St. Paul, the capital, 309,-828; Minneapolis, 434,400.
Government (1976): *Chief Officers*—governor, Wendell R. Anderson (D); lt. gov., Rudy Perpich (D). *Legislature*—Senate, 67 members; House of Representatives, 134 members.
Education (1975–76): *Enrollment*—public elementary schools, 426,779 pupils; public secondary, 453,165; nonpublic (1976–77), 100,200; colleges and universities, 176,011 students. *Public school expenditures,* $1,283,095,000 ($1,458 per pupil).
State Finances (fiscal year 1975): *Revenues,* $3,484,-007,000; *expenditures,* $3,139,168,000.
Personal Income (1975): $22,793,000,000; per capita, $5,807.
Labor Force (July 1976): *Nonagricultural wage and salary earners,* 1,510,700; *insured unemployed,* 40,-600 (2.9%).

U. S. Navy destroyers and amphibious assault ships move along a production line, right to left, at Litton Industries' Ingalls Shipbuilding division in Pascagoula. The facility is a major source of employment for southern Mississippi and the surrounding area.

UPI

MISSISSIPPI

A close presidential contest, a legislative session dominated by "tight money," and a major savings and loan crisis were items of particular interest to Mississippians during 1976.

Elections. Mississippi's electoral votes went to the Democratic presidential candidate for the first time since 1956, but the popular vote margin was so narrow that the negligence of some persons to vote for all electors pledged to their candidate generated considerable speculation that one or more of the state's seven votes would be assigned to the Republican nominee. The top elector pledged to Democrat Jimmy Carter received 49.6% of the record 769,000 votes cast, while President Gerald Ford's chief vote getter captured 47.7%. The remaining 2.7% was split among electors pledged to five other candidates. The Carter victory reflected a coalition of blacks, rural whites, and labor made possible by the meshing earlier in the year of the predominantly black Loyalist and the mostly white Regular factions of the state Democratic party.

John C. Stennis (D) was elected without opposition to a sixth term in the U. S. Senate, and all five incumbent congressmen (three Democrats and two Republicans) were returned.

Legislative Session. The major achievement of the 1976 legislature was the adoption of a balanced budget without an increase in taxes. Other important actions included establishment of a State Department of Corrections, approval of a plan to finance bridges (required by the Tennessee-Tombigbee Waterway Project), and enactment of small-business assistance legislation. Throughout the 125-day session ending May 9, new Gov. Cliff Finch (D) displayed an unusual willingness to cooperate with legislators.

Savings and Loan Crisis. In May, the largest state-chartered savings and loan association was forced into receivership, and six others experienced panic runs, triggering 30-day moratoriums on withdrawals. In an emergency session, called by Finch on June 18, lawmakers imposed a halt on the operations of all 34 state associations and authorized the immediate appointment of a conservator, with authority to determine if and when each association would be allowed to resume its activities. All institutions were directed to qualify for federal insurance by April 1, 1977, or face liquidation or consolidation.

Other Events. On August 9, a Hinds County chancery judge imposed a $1.25-million judgment against the National Association for the Advancement of Colored People (NAACP) and 147 individuals as the result of a late-1960's boycott of 12 Port Gibson merchants. On October 20, U. S. District Judge Orma C. Smith issued an injunction temporarily preventing the merchants from collecting damages and allowing the NAACP to appeal the judgment to the Mississippi Supreme Court without posting the $1.6-million bond required under state law.

On August 24, the U. S. Justice Department rejected as discriminatory against blacks an "open primary" law passed by the 1976 legislature. It was the second time that Mississippi legislation modifying the traditional party system of elections was disapproved under the Federal Voting Rights Act of 1965.

In the late summer, a three-judge panel of the Fifth U. S. Circuit Court of Appeals handed down a legislative reapportionment plan that placed all state House and Senate seats in single-member districts. The panel later rejected arguments that special elections be ordered prior to the 1979 effective date of the plan.

DANA B. BRAMMER, *University of Mississippi*

MISSISSIPPI · Information Highlights

Area: 47,716 square miles (123,584 km²).

Population (1975 est.): 2,346,000.

Chief Cities (1970 census): Jackson, the capital, 153,968; Biloxi, 48,486; Meridian, 45,083.

Government (1976): *Chief Officers*—governor, Charles C. Finch (D); lt. gov., Evelyn Gandy (D). *Legislature* —Senate, 52 members; House of Representatives, 122 members.

Education (1975–76): *Enrollment*—public elementary schools, 285,865 pupils; public secondary, 226,542; nonpublic (1976–77), 66,300; colleges and universities, 87,743 students. *Public school expenditures,* $478,309,000 ($943 per pupil).

State Finances (fiscal year 1975): *Revenues,* $1,623,648,000; *expenditures,* $1,578,478,000.

Personal Income (1975): $9,504,000,000; per capita, $4,052.

Labor Force (July 1976): *Nonagricultural wage and salary earners,* 682,600; *insured unemployed,* 19,400 (3.6%).

Missouri's newly elected Sen. John C. Danforth (R) (*left*) chats with Francis Valeo, secretary of the Senate. Danforth defeated former Gov. Warren E. Hearnes for the seat held by the retiring Stuart Symington.

UPI

MISSOURI

The death of a congressman in an airplane crash on the night he won the nomination for U. S. senator, the upset of an incumbent governor, the Republican national convention, and the most serious drought in more than two decades highlighted the year 1976 in Missouri.

Elections. Rep. Jerry Litton of Chillicothe won the Democratic nomination for U. S. senator in the August primary election, but before he knew of it, he, his wife, his two children, and two others died as they headed for Kansas City in a private plane to listen to returns.

The Democratic party picked former Gov. Warren Hearnes to replace Litton. Hearnes had been a surprise second-place finisher in the primary, but his reputation had been impaired by a lengthy federal probe of his eight-year administration, and he lost in the November election to State Atty. Gen. John Danforth.

The biggest surprise was the loss by Republican Gov. Christopher Bond in his reelection bid. Former Kansas City Prosecutor Joseph Teasdale defied opinion polls and won with a 12,000-vote margin. John Ashcroft, a Republican, was elected attorney general. Reelected were Lt. Gov. William Phelps, a Republican, and Treasurer James Spainhower and Secretary of State James Kirkpatrick, both Democrats. Jimmy Carter carried the state in November.

Because of retirements, Missouri's House delegation of 10 will have five new members. They are State Sen. Robert Young of St. Ann, St. Louis Alderman James Gephardt, State Sen. Ike Skeleton of Lexington, State Rep. Harold Volkmer of Hannibal and Thomas Coleman of North Kansas City. Coleman becomes the second Republican House member.

The Democrats retained control of the legislature. They picked up one Senate seat for a margin of 24 to 10 and lost only two House seats, reducing their margin to 112 to 51.

Four measures were placed on the ballot by petition drives, and voters approved two: an increase in the sales tax by ⅛% for conservation purposes and a ban on utilities' charging rate payers for construction in progress. Turned down were proposals to eliminate the sales tax on food and drugs and to provide specific state aid for private and parochial schools. Another initiative drive, to streamline the state court system, was stopped when the legislature presented a similar measure to the voters. The measure was approved.

Republican Convention. The Republicans brought their national convention to Kansas City, giving a boost to the area's economy. Most Kansas Citians, however, were more interested in their baseball team, the Royals, which won the American League Western Division championship.

Other Events. The battle over the St. Louis airport continued. Missouri state and local officials turned to the courts after U. S. Secretary of Transportation William Coleman decided a new airport to replace Lambert Field would be built in Illinois.

Missouri farmers suffered through the worst drought since 1954. Rainfall was about half the normal, and farmers saw their corn and soybean crops dry up and were forced to haul in water for their cattle.

RONALD D. WILLNOW
St. Louis Post-Dispatch

--------- MISSOURI · Information Highlights ---------

Area: 69,686 square miles (180,487 km²).
Population (1975 est.): 4,763,000.
Chief Cities (1970 census): Jefferson City, the capital, 32,407; St. Louis, 622,236.
Government (1976): *Chief Officers*—governor, Christopher S. Bond (R); lt. gov., William C. Phelps (R). *General Assembly*—Senate, 34 members; House of Representatives, 163 members.
Education (1975–76): *Enrollment*—public elementary schools, 514,997 pupils; public secondary, 450,363; nonpublic (1976–77), 141,200; colleges and universities, 205,929 students. *Public school expenditures,* $1,028,198,000 ($1,186 per pupil).
State Finances (fiscal year 1975): *Revenues,* $2,420,558,000; *expenditures,* $2,452,721,000.
Personal Income (1975): $26,244,000,000; per capita, $5,510.
Labor Force (July 1976): *Nonagricultural wage and salary earners,* 1,741,200; *insured unemployed,* 56,400 (4.0%).

MONTANA

The 1976 election was highlighted by the retirement of Mike Mansfield, distinguished U. S. senator. John Melcher, a Democratic representative from District No. 2 succeeded Mansfield. Ron Marlenee, a Republican, was elected to Melcher's seat. In District No. 1, incumbent Democrat Max Baucus won reelection by a large majority. Incumbent Gov. Tom Judge, a Democrat, was reelected, and Ted Schwinden was chosen as lieutenant governor. Republicans gained five seats in the state Senate and nine in the House. This means a 25-25 tie in the Senate, while Democrats hold a 58-42 majority in the House. As in other western states, President Ford won the electoral votes.

Election Measures. One constitutional amendment, which was adopted, calls for incorporating not less than 25%—and 50% after 1980—of the coal severence tax into a trust fund, the principal to remain inviolate unless appropriated by a three-fourths vote of each house of the legislature. A second amendment, proposing a limit of $275,000,000 on the state budget and a phaseout of all federal funds by 1984, was rejected. A proposition of a one-mill levy on all taxable property for a state library program also failed.

Three initiative measures were on the ballot. No. 71, prohibiting the choice of site for a nuclear facility until the facility had been approved by the legislature, failed. No. 72, permitting the governor to request appropriation by the legislature of a fund sufficient to repay taxes collected on the first $5,000 of the appraised value of each owner-occupied home, was approved. No. 73, proposing a recall procedure for persons elected or appointed to public office, was also approved.

Review of Local Government. The 1972 Constitution decreed that each county and municipality must offer to its citizens within four years, and thereafter each 10 years, an alternate form of government. Elected review commissions formulated alternate proposals. Sixteen communities voted in the July 1 primary election, and 146 on November 2. Relatively few changes were made. However, two county-city consolidated charter governments were adopted, Deer Lodge-Anaconda and Silver Bow-Butte; they are the first such combinations in Montana. Discussion of local government was much widened by a State Commission on Local Government which prepared a new 300-page code for presentation to the 1977 legislature.

Tax Reappraisal. The 1975 legislature enacted a statute requiring reevaluation of all taxable property every five years. The work was put on a five-year schedule, but as property was reevaluated it was placed on the tax rolls immediately. This led to suits based on inequitable taxation. The governor then declared a return to the 1974 evaluation until all property had been reevaluated. The shifting assessments created much confusion in budget making processes. The 1977 legislature will be asked for additional funds to speed up the reevaluation.

Continuing Issues. A continuing general fund surplus reached a high of $51,000,000, resulting in contention over beneficial expenditures and tax reduction. The most violent political issue of the year was the inconclusive investigation of alleged fraud in the workman's compensation division, begun in 1974 by the attorney general, who was the Republican candidate for the governorship in 1976.

MERRILL G. BURLINGAME
Montana State University

─────── **MONTANA · Information Highlights** ───────

Area: 147,138 square miles (381,087 km²).
Population (1975 est.): 748,000.
Chief Cities (1970 census): Helena, the capital, 22,557; Billings, 61,581; Great Falls, 60,091.
Government (1976): *Chief Officers*—governor, Thomas L. Judge (D); lt. gov., W. E. Christiansen (D). *Legislature*—Senate, 50 members; House of Representatives, 100 members.
Education (1975–76): *Enrollment*—public elementary schools, 114,646 pupils; public secondary, 57,142; nonpublic (1976–77), 8,800; colleges and universities, 29,812 students. *Public school expenditures,* $253,700,000 ($1,477 per pupil).
State Finances (fiscal year 1975): *Revenues,* $614,475,-000; *expenditures,* $554,721,000.
Personal Income (1975): $4,054,000,000; per capita, $5,422.
Labor Force (July 1976): *Nonagricultural wage and salary earners,* 245,100; *insured unemployed,* 8,900 (4.6%).

UPI

Montana Sen. Mike Mansfield (*right*) meets with Sen. Robert Byrd (D-W. Va.). Mansfield, a member of the Senate since 1953 and majority leader since 1961, did not seek reelection.

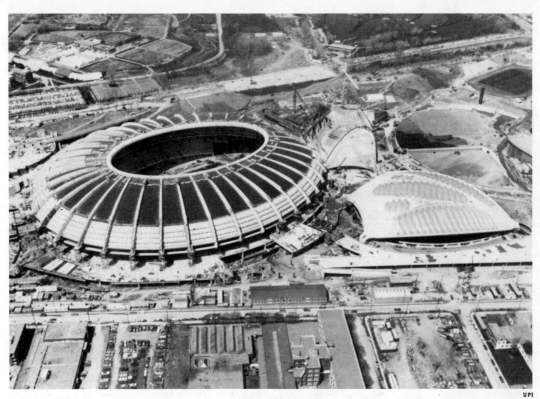

UPI

Montreal was host to the XXI Olympiad. French architect Roger Taillibert designed the stadium and velodrome (*right*).

MONTREAL

Economically, 1976 was not a good year for Montreal. Construction permits increased, and so did the manpower activity ratio, but most salaries remained lower than the Canadian average. Despite record crowds during the Olympics, the overall tourist inflow slowed in 1976.

Taxes and Services. There was a sharp rise in business, water, and regular taxes, yet a deficit of $200 million hung over the heads of Montreal taxpayers because the Quebec government refused to shoulder it. This led to many restrictions on public works and complaints about deteriorating services. The police especially, despite unification of forces throughout the island, complained of shrinking manpower, poor leadership, and low morale. Meanwhile, the crime rate continued to grow; of more than 70 Montreal murders by early September, less than half had been solved.

Urban Politics. On the political front, the opposition party (Rassemblement des Citoyens de Montréal), which holds 17 out of 55 City Council seats, was expecting a boost of aggressiveness with the return of its original leader, Jacques Couture, to municipal politics after a year's leave. Couture was rejected for a post as professor of social work at the University of Quebec in Montreal for what seemed to be ideological motives (he is not far enough left). The other municipalities of the island are fighting Montreal's leadership, opposing plans to centralize economic and commercial activities in downtown Montreal.

Education. In the summer of 1975 the Montreal Catholic School Board decided to send children whose mother tongue is not English and who do not score 60% in English tests to French schools. Later, the board allowed those scoring between 45 and 60% to proceed to English schools. This did not satisfy the parents, who are mostly of Italian descent. They sent a delegation to Quebec Prime Minister Bourassa (to no avail); nearly 1,000 of their children illegally entered English schools; and a group of Italian priests pressed the Catholic archbishop to intervene. Archbishop Grégoire, however, suggested that the government oblige all children whose mother tongue is not English to attend French schools.

The Press. The daily *Le Jour,* launched in February 1974 to spread separatist ideals, stopped publication at the end of August 1976. A financial gamble from the start, it failed, according to the newsmen, because of managerial incompetence and paternalism; according to management, the cause was the newsmen's irresponsibility and leftist activism.

Sports. The Montreal Canadiens won another Stanley Cup and provided the national hockey team with many of its players. The Canadian team won the Canada Cup.

JEAN-PIERRE WALLOT
University of Montreal

MOROCCO

Morocco's major concern in 1976 was to retain control of Spanish Sahara, the phosphate-rich territory on its southern border. The former Spanish colony was handed over to Morocco and Mauritania on February 26, two days ahead of schedule, but proved to be more of a burden than a blessing to Morocco.

Spanish Sahara. When the colony of Spanish Sahara was ceded to Morocco and Mauritania, the Polisario Front immediately declared the territory an independent nation, the Saharan Arab Democratic Republic. It sought recognition from the Organization of African Unity (OAU), which sidestepped the issue by saying it was up to member states to decide individually on recognition. Only nine African nations gave their formal recognition.

Morocco formally annexed about two thirds of the former Spanish colony, 70,000 square miles (180,000 km²) in April. It received the lion's share of the territory's resource wealth, the Bu Craa phosphate mines in the north. Spain sold Morocco a 65% interest in the mines, retaining 35% of its original $450 million investment. Morocco agreed to pay Spain about $120 million over the next four years.

Shortly before Morocco bought the Bu Craa mines, the market for Moroccan phosphates, which are used in fertilizers, dropped in the face of stiff American competition. The government of King Hassan II slashed posted prices by 29% to $45 a ton.

The acquisition of Bu Craa would have propelled Morocco into first place among the world's raw phosphate producers, ahead of the United States and the Soviet Union, except that no phosphate mined at Bu Craa during 1976 reached the coast for shipping to world markets. The Moroccan army reportedly was unable to secure the 60-mile-long (96-km) conveyor belt from constant sabotage by Polisario Front insurgents. Originally, the state mining corporation, Office Cherifien des Phosphates, had projected a 1976 production figure of approximately 2.8 million tons from Bu Craa.

Morocco had to keep an estimated 20,000 troops in the northern part of the territory, and despatched other forces to the south to bail out the hard-pressed Mauritanian army. Pitted against the two nations' armed forces, the Polisario Front waged a constant hit-and-run war from Land Rover vehicles, the updated version of camel transport. Armed by Algeria and Libya with sophisticated weaponry and advised by Cubans and Vietnamese, Polisario claimed to have inflicted heavy casualties on the Moroccan forces throughout the year. Morocco broke diplomatic relations with Algeria in March.

Economy. The financial burden of defending the former Spanish Sahara meant belt-tightening for Morocco's nearly 18 million people. Subsidies for food and other basic commodities were reduced by half and inflation cut into wages. In the cities, workers were told they would have to forego pay hikes until 1977.

Some $530 million, a third of Morocco's capital outlay, was earmarked for defense. At midyear, King Hassan announced a $227 million bond drive to finance defense and development expenditures in the Sahara territory. Among the development projects was a planned railroad from Marrakech to the Bu Craa mines. Work began on enlarging the road from Tan-Tan to Smara in the northern territory.

The decline in phosphate sales reduced planned revenues and put a crimp in Morocco's five-year (1973–77) industrialization program. Originally, 54% of the $6.3 billion plan was to have been financed from Moroccan sources, with a further 24% coming from overseas loans. In 1976, less than 40% was scheduled to come from domestic sources and the share from phosphate revenues fell from 12% of the total to less than 4%.

Politics. King Hassan permitted a series of local council elections, part of his "experiment in democracy" designed to restore a national assembly by the end of 1977. The assembly will have no real political power, however, and the king retained the right to dissolve it at will. In 1970 he disbanded the assembly one month after it had been elected. Opposition parties viewed the elections as academic because the king will continue to hold absolute power. All the parties taking part in the polls are pro-monarchy by law, even the Communists.

King Hassan said the elections were his reward to the opposition parties for their support on the Spanish Sahara issue. The king has been very popular at home since the spectacular march into the Sahara in November 1975, which generated renewed nationalism.

Local elections were held in November in the annexed Sahara region, partly aimed at pacifying the OAU and the United Nations, which had been pressing King Hassan to give the Saharaouis some measure of self determination.

JOSEPH MARGOLIS
"African Update," African-American Institute

--------- **MOROCCO** · **Information Highlights** ---------

Official Name: Kingdom of Morocco.
Location: Northwest Africa.
Area: 172,413 square miles (446,550 km²).
Population (1976 est.): 17,900,000.
Chief Cities (1973 est.): Rabat, the capital, 385,000; Casablanca, 2,000,000; Marrakesh, 330,000; Fez, 322,000.
Government: *Head of state,* Hassan II, king (acceded 1961). *Head of government,* Ahmed Osman, premier (took office 1972).
Monetary Unit: Dirham (4.50 dirhams equal U.S.$1, July 1976).
Gross National Product (1975 est.): $7,900,000,000.
Manufacturing (major products): Processed foods, metals, textiles, wine, cement, leather goods, chemicals and pharmaceuticals.
Major Agricultural Products: Barley, wheat, citrus fruits, vegetables, sugar beets, almonds, tomatoes, grapes, sheep, wool.
Foreign Trade (1975): *Exports,* $1,601,000,000; *imports,* $2,589,000,000.

FROM THE MOTION PICTURE, "ALL THE PRESIDENT'S MEN" COURTESY OF WARNER BROS., INC. © 1976

All the President's Men stars Robert Redford and Dustin Hoffman as *The Washington Post* reporters.

MOTION PICTURES

Most likely it was only coincidence, but in the bicentennial year many of the best and most widely discussed films were concerned with looking anew at America's past and worrying about its present. Customarily a broad time gap exists between controversial events and films attempting to deal with them, but the recent trauma of Watergate rapidly reached the screen.

The Past. Filmmakers long have shied away from the controversial McCarthy era of the 1950's, except for occasional passing references. Charlie Chaplin's *A King in New York,* made shortly after he had left the United States for exile, was the only nondocumentary theatrical feature to deal directly with these events. In 1976 *The Front,* starring Woody Allen in a mixture of comedy and tragedy, viewed the period of television blacklisting. Director Martin Ritt, screenwriter Walter Bernstein, and cast members Zero Mostel, Herschel Bernardi, Joshua Shelley, and Lloyd Gough all had been victims of the blacklist.

Blacklisting in Hollywood also was explored in 1976 in the documentary *Hollywood on Trial.* Combining film clips from the past and a series of reflective interviews, the picture contemplated the fate of the famed Hollywood Ten. They were imprisoned for contempt of Congress, after claiming their rights under the first amendment to the Constitution rather than disclose their politics to a Congressional committee and clear themselves by accusing others of Communist affiliations. Both *The Front* and *Hollywood on Trial* quickly engendered heated media discussion in which old wounds were opened and issues were reargued. In this new look taken on

screen, those who had been outcasts for upholding their principles emerged as heroes, those who had cooperated were seen as villains.

Another of the year's important films, *Bound for Glory,* achieved what relatively few films have been able to do: catch the flavor of the depression-ridden 1930's. Director Hal Ashby and cinematographer Haskell Wexler recreated the period with remarkable flavor in presenting Robert Getchell's film biography of Woody Guthrie, legendary folksinger and composer. David Carradine offered a muted, subtle portrayal of Guthrie. The film reflected the period's poverty, despair, and violence, but also the spirit and compassion that gave meaning to suffering and hope for the future. *Bound for Glory* became both an acknowledgment of America's ills and a testament to its enduring spirit.

Although far less successful, director Gordon Parks reached back into folk music with the biographical *Leadbelly,* the story of black folksinger and composer Huddie Ledbetter. The days of segregated baseball became the background for a comical but pointed story, *The Bingo Long Traveling All-Stars and Motor Kings.* Another film exploring events in the 1930's was *Voyage of the Damned,* a drama of a shipload of Jewish refugees from Nazi Germany who were denied admission to Cuba and the United States in 1939.

Films also continued to reexamine myths about the old West. Robert Altman's *Buffalo Bill and the Indians* presented Buffalo Bill as a product of publicity rather than a hero, and Sitting Bull as a tragic, heroic, and abused Indian leader. *The Missouri Breaks,* directed by Arthur

Penn and starring Jack Nicholson and Marlon Brando, viewed the conflict between rustlers and cattle barons as more complex than generally pictured in Westerns.

The Present. *All the President's Men,* based on the book by Bob Woodward and Carl Bernstein, loomed as one of the most effective films of 1976. Although it was really about investigative journalism and certainly among the best newspaper films ever made, it dealt forthrightly with Watergate and the persons implicated in the scandal. Robert Redford and Dustin Hoffman were widely acclaimed for their portrayal of the Washington *Post* reporters. Another tour de force was *Network,* a vigorous and outrageous satire written by Paddy Chayefsky and directed by Sidney Lumet. It depicted a deterioration in national values through a story about the news division of a mythical television network. The preoccupation with ratings and categorization of news as entertainment was carried to the extreme. Highlighting the film were outstanding performances, some of the year's best, by Peter Finch, Faye Dunaway, William Holden, and Robert Duvall.

Taxi Driver, another provocative American film, starred Robert De Niro as a New York cabbie in the throes of a mental breakdown and preparing to become an assassin. Through his contorted vision, the picture disturbingly conveyed the decay and frustrations devastating many of America's urban centers. The ongoing plight of coal miners in Kentucky was the sub-

***Seven Beauties,** starring Giancarlo Giannini, raises questions concerning the value of survival at all costs.*

COURTESY JOHN SPRINGER ASSOCIATES, INC.

ject of *Harlan County U.S.A.,* a documentary that brought cheers at the New York Film Festival. It was a first film for Barbara Kopple, who spent three years making the movie during a bitter strike and its aftermath.

Universal Themes. Marcel Ophuls, who changed the scope of documentary making with *The Sorrow and the Pity,* returned with another ambitious factual film, *The Memory of Justice.* The four and a half-hour film offered an examination of moral concepts related to the Nuremberg war crimes trials after World War II. Ophuls sought answers to questions about the difficulty of sitting in judgment and the relationship between atrocities committed by the accused in one time period and questionable actions of the accusers in other circumstances. The responsibilities of conscience were also explored in an open-ended manner that characterizes Ophuls' method of examining weighty, complicated issues.

In the fictional category could be found another heralded (and attacked) film, Lina Wertmuller's *Seven Beauties,* an Italian drama raising questions concerning what man must do to survive in this world, and whether the human being that results is worth preserving. Based on what Wertmuller says actually happened to someone, the film soars with an artist's insights into behavior during World War II and its link to the present. The film solidified Wertmuller's reputation as a major directorial talent, the first woman to achieve such exalted status on the international film scene.

Remakes. Producer Dino De Laurentiis, impressed by the fact that his daughter kept on her wall a poster depicting the 1930's film *King Kong,* reasoned it was time for a remake aimed at another generation. He decided to construct a giant mechanical ape instead of using blow-ups of a miniature; he created a lavish new spectacle at a cost of $23 million. By the time the film was released for Christmas, the build-up was so great (including a *Time* magazine cover) that the film seemed certain of box office success. Meanwhile, the producers of *Jaws,* the bonanza of 1975, apart from proceeding with *Jaws II,* were busy plotting the unthinkable—a sequel to *Gone With the Wind,* with Rhett and Scarlett meeting again later in life. All of the above was consistent with the trend toward making fewer, costlier, and potentially more profitable pictures.

Theater operators were finding it more difficult to lure audiences with attractions of modest appeal. The Loews chain closed five theaters in New York City for a month, claiming there was a film shortage. However, according to leaders in the field, the situation was more intricate. Many distributors typically were withholding films for holiday business or awaiting opportunities to place pictures in the most advantageous theaters. This meant a boon for some houses, with others unable to find strong enough films to attract audiences.

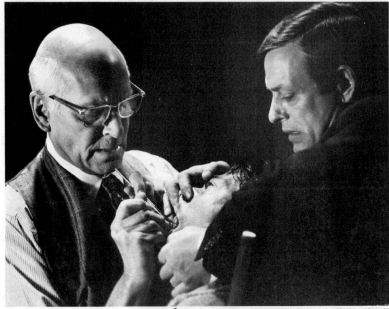

In *Marathon Man*, Laurence Olivier as a Nazi fugitive uses his dental skills to torture a graduate student played by Dustin Hoffman.

COLUMBIA PICTURES INDUSTRIES, INC.

Television blacklisting during the McCarthy era of the 1950's is the subject of *The Front*, starring Woody Allen and Andrea Marcovicci.

UNIVERSAL PICTURES

Alfred Hitchcock's *Family Plot* is played for laughs, with the pursuers also the pursued. William Devane plays a kidnapper and Karen Black his accomplice.

NOTABLE MOTION PICTURES OF 1976

*The following list of films released in the United States in 1976 presents a cross section
of the most popular, most typical, or most widely discussed motion pictures of the year.*

Alex & the Gypsy. Director, John Korty; screenplay, Lawrence B. Marcus based on novel by Stanley Elkin. With Jack Lemmon, Geneviève Bujold.

All the President's Men. Director, Alan J. Pakula; screenplay, William Goldman based on the book by Carl Bernstein and Bob Woodward. With Dustin Hoffman, Robert Redford, Jack Warden, Martin Balsam, Hal Holbrook, Jason Robards, Jane Alexander.

Alpha Beta. Director, Anthony Page; screenplay, E. A. Whitehead based on his play. With Rachel Roberts, Albert Finney.

The Bad News Bears. Director, Michael Ritchie; screenplay, Bill Lancaster. With Walter Matthau, Tatum O'Neal.

The Bingo Long Traveling All-Stars and Motor Kings. Director, John Badham; screenplay, Hal Barwood, Matthew Robbins based on novel by William Brashler. With Billy Dee Williams, James Earl Jones, Richard Pryor.

Bound for Glory. Director, Hal Ashby; screenplay, Robert Getchell based on the autobiography of Woody Guthrie. With David Carradine, Melinda Dillon, Ronny Cox, Gail Strickland, Randy Quaid.

Buffalo Bill and The Indians. Director, Robert Altman; screenplay, Altman, Alan Rudolph based on the play *Indians* by Arthur Kopit. With Paul Newman, Geraldine Chaplin, Burt Lancaster.

Bugsy Malone. Director, Alan Parker; screenplay, Parker. With Jodie Foster, Scott Baio.

Car Wash. Director, Michael Schultz; screenplay, Joel Schumacher. With Franklin Ajaye, George Carlin, Prof. Irwin Corey, Ivan Dixon, Richard Pryor.

The Clockmaker. Director, Bertrand Tavernier; screenplay, Jean Aurenche, Pierre Bost adapted from novel by Georges Simenon. With Philippe Noiret, Jean Rochefort.

Cousin, Cousine. Director, Jean-Charles Tacchella; screenplay, Tacchella. With Marie-Christine Barrault, Victor Lanoux, Marie-France Pisier, Guy Marchand.

Edvard Munch. Director, Peter Watkins; screenplay, Watkins. With Geir Westby.

Face to Face. Director, Ingmar Bergman; screenplay, Bergman. With Liv Ullmann, Erland Josephson.

Family Plot. Director, Alfred Hitchcock; screenplay, Ernest Lehman based on novel by Victor Canning. With Barbara Harris, Bruce Dern, Karen Black, William Devane.

The Front. Director, Martin Ritt; screenplay, Walter Bernstein. With Woody Allen, Zero Mostel, Herschel Bernardi, Andrea Marcovicci.

Grey Gardens. Directors, David Maysles, Albert Maysles, Ellen Hovde, Muffie Meyer; documentary.

Harlan County U. S. A. Director, Barbara Kopple. Documentary.

Idi Amin Dada. Director, Barbet Schroeder; documentary.

Jonah Who Will Be 25 in the Year 2000. Director, Alain Tanner; screenplay, John Berger, Tanner. With Jean-Luc Bideau, Myriam Boyer.

The Killing of a Chinese Bookie. Director, John Cassavetes. With Ben Gazzara.

King Kong. Director, John Guillermin; screenplay, Lorenzo Semple, Jr. With Jeff Bridges, Jessica Lange, Charles Grodin.

The Last Tycoon. Director, Elia Kazan; screenplay, Harold Pinter adapted from unfinished novel by F. Scott Fitzgerald. With Robert De Niro, Jack Nicholson, Jeanne Moreau, Robert Mitchum, Tony Curtis.

Leadbelly. Director, Gordon Parks; screenplay, Ernest Kinoy. With Roger E. Mosley.

Lumière. Director, Jeanne Moreau; screenplay, Moreau. With Moreau, Francine Racette, Lucia Bose, Caroline Cartier, Keith Carradine.

The Man Who Fell to Earth. Director, Nicolas Roeg; screenplay, Paul Mayersberg. With David Bowie, Rip Torn, Buck Henry, Candy Clark.

Marathon Man. Director John Schlesinger; screenplay, William Goldman based on his novel. With Dustin Hoffman, Laurence Olivier, Roy Scheider, William Devane, Marthe Keller.

The Marquise of O.... Director, Eric Rohmer; screenplay, Rohmer based on story by Heinrich von Kleist. With Edith Clever, Bruno Ganz.

The Memory of Justice. Director, Marcel Ophuls; documentary.

Mikey and Nicky. Director, Elaine May; screenplay, May. With John Cassavetes, Peter Falk.

Missouri Breaks. Director, Arthur Penn; screenplay, Thomas McGuane. With Marlon Brando, Jack Nicholson.

Murder by Death. Director, Robert Moore; screenplay, Neil Simon. With Eileen Brennan, Truman Capote, James Coco, Peter Falk, Alec Guinness, Elsa Lanchester, David Niven, Peter Sellers, Maggie Smith, Nancy Walker, Estelle Winwood.

Network. Director, Sidney Lumet; screenplay, Paddy Chayefsky. With Faye Dunaway, William Holden, Peter Finch, Robert Duvall.

Next Stop, Greenwich Village. Director, Paul Mazursky; screenplay, Mazursky. With Lenny Baker, Ellen Greene, Shelley Winters.

Nickelodeon. Director, Peter Bogdanovich, screenplay, Bogdanovich, W. D. Richter. With Ryan O'Neal, Burt Reynolds, Tatum O'Neal.

Obsession. Director, Brian De Palma; screenplay, Paul Schrader from story by De Palma, Schrader. With Cliff Robertson, Geneviève Bujold.

The Omen. Director, Richard Donner; screenplay, David Seltzer. With Gregory Peck, Lee Remick.

The River Niger. Director, Krishna Shah; screenplay, Joseph A. Walker based on his play. With Cicely Tyson, James Earl Jones, Lou Gossett.

Robin and Marian. Director, Richard Lester; screenplay, James Goldman. With Audrey Hepburn, Sean Connery, Nicol Williamson.

Rocky. Director, John Avildsen; screenplay, Sylvester Stallone. With Stallone, Talia Shire, Burgess Meredith.

The Sailor Who Fell From Grace With the Sea. Director, Lewis John Carlino; screenplay, Carlino based on novel by Yukio Mishima. With Sara Miles, Kris Kristofferson.

Seven Beauties. Director, Lina Wertmuller. With Giancarlo Giannini, Shirley Stoler.

The Seven-Per-Cent Solution. Director, Herbert Ross; screenplay, Nicholas Meyer based on his novel. With Nicol Williamson, Alan Arkin, Robert Duvall, Laurence Olivier, Vanessa Redgrave.

The Shootist. Director, Don Siegal; screenplay, Miles Hood Swarthout, Scott Hale based on novel by Glendon Swarthout. With John Wayne, Lauren Bacall.

Silent Movie. Director, Mel Brooks; screenplay, Brooks, Ron Clark, Rudy DeLuca, Barry Levinson. With Brooks, Marty Feldman, Dom DeLuise.

Small Change. Director, François Truffaut; screenplay, Truffaut, Suzanne Schiffman.

A Star Is Born. Director, Frank Pierson; screenplay, Joan Didion, John Gregory Dunne, Pierson based on a story by William Wellman, Robert Carson. With Barbra Streisand, Kris Kristofferson.

Taxi Driver. Director, Martin Scorsese; screenplay, Paul Schrader. With Robert De Niro, Harvey Keitel, Cybill Shepherd, Jodie Foster.

The Tenant. Director, Roman Polanski; screenplay, Polanski, Gerard Brach. With Polanski, Isabelle Adjani, Shelley Winters, Melvyn Douglas, Jo Van Fleet.

That's Entertainment, Part 2. Director of new sequences, Gene Kelly; narration written by Leonard Gershe. With Kelly, Fred Astaire, M-G-M stars.

Two Minute Warning. Director Larry Peerce; screenplay, Edward Hume based on novel by George La Fountaine. With Charlton Heston, John Cassavetes, Martin Balsam, Beau Bridges.

Voyage of the Damned. Director, Stuart Rosenberg; screenplay, Steve Shagan, David Butler. With Faye Dunaway, Oskar Werner, Orson Welles, Max von Sydow, Malcolm McDowell, James Mason.

An all-star cast is featured in *Murder By Death*, a spoof of detective stories in which an eccentric millionaire invites world-famous sleuths to his isolated mansion for "dinner and a murder."

Laughter. Mel Brooks kept his franchise on bellylaugh comedy with *Silent Movie,* his homage to pre-talkie screen humor. He took advantage of contemporary opportunities by applying music and sound effects to enhance his sight-gags. *Car Wash* played the *Grand Hotel*-type situation for laughs, with this center for lives in crisis a Los Angeles car wash. Neil Simon wrote *Murder by Death,* a witty spoof of detective stories and derivative films. *The Bad News Bears* satirized Little League baseball with hilarious results. *The Seven-Per-Cent Solution* combined adventure with humor in a fanciful encounter between Sherlock Holmes and Sigmund Freud. Peter Sellers returned as the bumbling police inspector in *The Pink Panther Strikes Again.*

Foreign Films. Swedish director Ingmar Bergman once again proved himself a master with *Face to Face,* the story of a woman psychiatrist, wracked by emotional problems and childhood demons, who attempts suicide. Liv Ullman's performance reaffirmed her position as one of the screen's great actresses. Bergman began working on a film in Germany after abandoning Sweden because of pressures from tax authorities.

A delegation of French filmmakers visited the United States to seek ways of increasing acceptance of French imports. There was little encouragement for any organized effort. However, several films from France won favor with the public in those cities where foreign language films have a following. Most notably, Jean-Charles Tacchella's *Cousin, Cousine* became the most popular French film in years. A comedy about a love affair between cousins through marriage, each having a spouse, the film was in keeping with an upheaval against convention. Other French films that enjoyed considerable success were Bertrand Tavernier's *The Clockmaker,* about the reactions of a man whose son suddenly is sought for murder, and François Truffaut's *Small Change,* a delightful look at children and their world. However, the importation of foreign language films remained economically precarious in the United States.

Censorship. What constitutes obscenity still had no clear-cut definition, if indeed any is possible. Hard core pornographic films flourished in various locales, while those seeking to eradicate explicit sex from the screen resorted to a federal tactic. The U. S. government pursued prosecutions on charges of conspiracy to transport obscene material across state lines. Among those convicted in the Memphis, Tenn., *Deep Throat* case was actor Harry Reems. Since he was only a performer and not involved in the distribution of the film, attention focused on his appeal, with many noted performers raising funds for his legal defense. Apart from the merits of his particular case, they saw Reems' conviction as a threat to any performer who appeared in a film that might be found obscene in some part of the country.

U. S. customs officials recalled the Japanese film *In the Realm of the Senses,* preventing it from being shown at the New York Film Festival. The film had passed through customs in California, but New York officials insisted on a look. A federal judge later barred customs from interfering with the exhibition of the film.

Festivals. The established film festivals found a frisky newcomer. Film enthusiasts in Toronto decided to establish a festival that would feature selections from festivals around the world. Plans for the Toronto Festival of Festivals were so ambitious as to engender local skepticism. However, the results astonished the city. During the festival week, 152 films were shown in five theaters to some 7,000 persons daily, morning and afternoon workshop sessions on filmmaking were crowded, a gala was held each evening, and Dino De Laurentiis showed a sample of *King Kong* and pledged 20 of his films for a retrospective next year.

A sore spot was the refusal of the major Hollywood studios to provide films. The snub added fuel to a revolt brewing in Canada. Since the U. S. majors take some $66 million in profits from Canada each year, Canadian filmmakers were calling with increased intensity for financial levies or quid pro quo arrangements that would aid distribution of Canadian-made films in the United States.

In New York, the Second Women's International Film Festival took place after a hiatus of four years, and received far more media attention than did the first edition. The highlight was Jeanne Moreau's debut as a director with *Lumière,* in which she also starred.

People. Alfred Hitchcock presented his 53d film, *Family Plot.* Barbar Streisand found her opportunity to follow Janet Gaynor and Judy Garland, playing in a remake of *A Star is Born,* this one with a rock music setting. Jack Nicholson won as Oscar for *One Flew Over the Cuckoo's Nest.* Audrey Hepburn made her first picture in nine years, *Robin and Marian,* playing Maid Marian to Sean Connery's Robin Hood. Sylvester Stallone, writer and star of *Rocky,* showed signs of emerging as a major new star.

WILLIAM WOLF, *Film Critic, "Cue" Magazine*

MOZAMBIQUE

Although faced with the monumental task of rebuilding a war-torn economy in 1976, Mozambique did not shrink from its proclaimed commitment to the cause of African liberation. As a result, it soon became embroiled in a direct military confrontation with Rhodesia's white minority regime. The capital city, Lourenço Marques, was renamed Maputo in February.

Conflict With Rhodesia. Beginning in January, Zimbabwe (Rhodesia) liberation forces, based mostly in Mozambique, sharply increased their attacks against Rhodesia. By the end of February, Rhodesian forces claiming the right of "hot pursuit" had launched the first in a series of retaliatory incursions into Mozambique. President Samora Machel immediately reacted by placing Mozambique on a war footing. He also imposed economic sanctions against Rhodesia, closing the border between the two countries and severing Rhodesia's rail links with the Mozambican ports of Beira and Maputo.

The cost of the break was expected to be substantial for Mozambique. The loss of revenue from port dues, rail freight, and other services was estimated between $63 million and $85 million annually. There was also the loss of some $22 million to $25 million in remittances formerly sent home to Mozambique by the 80,-000 Mozambican laborers employed in Rhodesia. The Organization of African Unity and a number of non-African states (including the United States) offered pledges of financial assistance totalling over $60 million to help Mozambique shoulder the cost of the sanctions.

U. S. Secretary of State Henry Kissinger's proposals for a settlement of the Rhodesian crisis brought a temporary lull in guerrilla activity. But border incidents flared up again at the end of June, and tension between the two countries continued to escalate during the second half of the year. On August 9 and October 31, Rhodesian forces launched major incursions into Mozambique and, according to Mozambican sources, indiscriminately massacred hundreds of villagers.

Foreign Relations. Tanzania reportedly seconded 1,500 of its own troops to Mozambique to enable the hard-pressed Mozambicans to maintain adequate deployment along the Rhodesian border. Zambian President Kenneth Kaunda visited Maputo in April. President Machel paid a visit to the Soviet Union in May. The country's relations with Portugal deteriorated, partly because of tension over the future of Portuguese residents in Mozambique.

Economy. Mozambique's economy is still in the process of trying to overcome the disruption caused by the 10-year struggle for national liberation. Agricultural production reportedly has dropped by 70% since 1974. Land and rental property were nationalized in February.

EDOUARD BUSTIN, *Boston University*

─── **MOZAMBIQUE • Information Highlights** ───

Official Name: People's Republic of Mozambique.
Location: East Africa.
Area: 302,328 square miles (783,029 km²).
Population (1976 est.): 9,300,000.
Chief City (1973 est.): Maputo, the capital, 383,775.
Government: *Head of state and government,* Samora Machel (took office June 1975). *Legislature* (unicameral)—People's Assembly.
Monetary Unit: Escudo (31.35 escudos equal U. S.$1, Nov. 1976).
Gross National Product (1972 est.): $2,000,000,000.
Manufacturing (major products): Petroleum products, beer, cement.
Major Agricultural Products: Cashews, cotton, sugar, copra, tea.
Foreign Trade (1974): *Exports,* $297,000,000; *imports,* $462,000,000.

The Bayreuth Festival marked its 100th anniversary with an uncompromisingly restaged "Ring."

MUSIC

During 1976, there was an unusual number of concerts, several American orchestras hired new conductors, and popular music developed its own theme, novelty.

Classical Music

In a year of ever-mounting financial pressures, good news must take precedence, and the news for New York concertgoers was very good when the new Avery Fisher (formerly Philharmonic) Hall opened on schedule in October. After 13 years of adjusting its acoustics, the entire interior was gutted and a completely new hall built inside the old shell. The work, masterminded by acoustician Cyril Harris, was accomplished in a remarkable five months, but the result was even more remarkable. Though a full assessment will require considerable experience of the hall, delighted first encounters with the rectangular auditorium—which bears no resemblance to the fan-shaped old one—suggest that it may prove one of the world's greatest.

Concert Premieres. No doubt spurred by the bicentennial, American concert life included an uncommonly generous assortment of new works. Among the composers represented were: William Bolcom (Piano Concerto, Seattle, March 8), John Cage (*Renga with Apartment House 1776,* Boston, October 1), Michael Colgrass (*New People,* Minneapolis, March 10), Donald Erb (Trombone Concerto, St. Louis, March 11), Ross Lee Finney (Violin Concerto, Dallas, March 31), Lukas Foss (*Folk Song for Orchestra,* Baltimore, January 21), Morton Gould (*Bicentennial Ballad,* New York City, April 24), Roy Harris (Symphony No. 10, Washington, D. C., February 10), Jean Eichelberger Ivey (*Testament of Eve,* Baltimore, April 21), Peter Mennin (*Voices,* New York City, March 28), Gian Carlo Menotti (*Landscapes and Reminiscences,* Milwaukee, May 14; Symphony No. 1, Saratoga, August 1), William Russo (*Sheet Music,* San Francisco, May 19), Kenneth Schermerhorn (*Monodrama,* Milwaukee, January 17), Robert Starer (*Journals of a Songmaker,* Pittsburgh, May 21), Jeffrey Steinberg (*A New Sound of Freedom,* Detroit, May 30), Morton Subotnick (*Two Butterflies,* Los Angeles, February 26), Lester Trimble (*Serenade,* New York City, April 23), and Robert Wykes (*Adequate Earth,* St. Louis, February 5).

The 1976 Pulitzer Prize for Music went to Ned Rorem for *Air Music,* a 30-minute set of orchestral variations first performed by the Cincinnati Symphony under Thomas Schippers on Dec. 5, 1975.

Appointments. Several major American orchestras engaged conductors to fill leadership vacancies. The tenure of the New York Philharmonic's music director Pierre Boulez ends with the 1976–77 season. He will be succeeded in 1978 (guest conductors will fill the gap) by Zubin Mehta, currently music director of the Los Angeles Philharmonic.

The San Francisco Symphony named principal guest conductor Edo de Waart to the post of principal conductor and artistic director, succeeding Seiji Ozawa, who had decided to devote full time to the Boston Symphony, of which he is also music director. The Dallas Symphony, which seemed permanently disbanded in 1974, appointed Eduardo Mata to assume the revitalized orchestra's music directorship in 1977.

One of the world's most distinctive opera houses has a new director. In East Berlin, Joachim Herz succeeded his mentor, Walter

Felsenstein, at the Komische Oper, which was run by Felsenstein from its founding in 1947 until his death in 1975. Felsenstein's other disciple Götz Friedrich, has been named director of production at London's Royal Opera House, Covent Garden, where he completed a staging of Wagner's *Ring* cycle in 1976. (Herz too completed a *Ring* in 1976, in Leipzig.)

Britain has a new master of the Queen's music: Australian-born Malcolm Williamson, subsequently made a CBE.

Opera in the United States. The presence of Sarah Caldwell is increasingly extending beyond her own Opera Company of Boston, whose 1976 undertakings included the first American staging of Roger Sessions' demanding *Montezuma*. In January, Caldwell made her Metropolitan Opera conducting debut in Verdi's *La Traviata* (with Beverly Sills, Stuart Burrows, and Ingvar Wixell). In October, she staged and conducted Rossini's *Barber of Seville* (also with Sills, and two outstanding basses, Donald Gramm and Samuel Ramey) for the New York City Opera.

The Metropolitan's 1976–77 season opened with Verdi's *Il Trovatore* (with Renata Scotto, Shirley Verrett, Luciano Pavarotti, Matteo Manuguerra, and James Morris), which featured the noteworthy house debut of veteran conductor Gianandrea Gavazzeni. Two of the six new productions planned for the ambitious 1976–77 season were unveiled in the fall: Massenet's *Esclarmonde* (with Joan Sutherland) and Wagner's *Lohengrin* (conducted by music director James Levine).

The New York City Opera's strike-shortened fall season included, in addition to the Caldwell *Barber*, Wagner's *Flying Dutchman*, designed and

For the U. S. bicentennial, La Scala brought Shirley Verrett to Washington, D. C., as Lady Macbeth.

NEW YORK TIMES PICTURES

directed by Robert Darling and conducted by Julius Rudel. Eve Queler and her Opera Orchestra of New York made history of a sort when their concert performances of Massenet's *Le Cid* (with Grace Bumbry and Placido Domingo) and Donizetti's *Gemma di Vergy* (with Montserrat Caballé) were recorded "live" by Columbia Records.

Increased interest in French opera could be seen throughout the United States. The Met repertory included operas by Gounod, Meyerbeer, Massenet, Saint-Saëns, and Poulenc. The San Francisco Opera and Chicago Lyric Opera seasons opened with, respectively, Massenet's *Thaïs* (with Beverly Sills and Sherrill Milnes) and Offenbach's *Tales of Hoffmann* (which was to have been conducted by the late Jean Martinon). *Thaïs* had been heard earlier in the year in Washington, D. C., with Noelle Rogers and Louis Quilico.

The Chicago Lyric season also dipped into the Russian repertory, with Mussorgsky's rarely produced masterpiece, *Khovanshchina*. The composer's much better known *Boris Godunov* was performed at the Colorado Opera Festival, while Tchaikovsky's *Maid of Orleans* (billed as *Joan of Arc*) was offered by the Nevada Opera Guild.

Enterprising fare heard around the country included Janáček's *Katya Kabanová* (Kentucky Opera Association), Schoenberg's *Moses und Aron* (University of Cincinnati College-Conservatory of Music), Richard Strauss' *Die schweigsame Frau* (Chautauqua Opera Association), and Josef Tal's *Ashmedai* (New York City Opera).

Two productions of Virgil Thomson's bicentennially apt *The Mother of Us All* (Gertrude Stein's vision of Susan B. Anthony) were preserved: the Santa Fe Opera's new production was recorded by New World Records for commercial issue; the young Chicago Opera Studio's revival of its inaugural production was filmed for possible public-broadcasting syndication. Among the American operas produced for the first time were Thomas Pasatieri's *Ines de Castro* (Baltimore Opera) and *Washington Square* (Michigan Opera Theater), Dominick Argento's *The Voyage of Edgar Allan Poe* (Minnesota Opera Company), Andrew Imbrie's *Angle of Repose* (San Francisco Opera), and Ulysses Kay's *Jubilee* (Opera/South).

International Opera. A few of the music festivals were torn by controversy. The greatest furor arose at West Germany's Bayreuth Festival. The Wagner shrine celebrated its centenary with a wildly controversial anti-capitalist staging by Frenchman Patrice Chéreau of the *Ring* cycle. (*Das Rheingold* substituted a hydro-electric dam for the Rhine, and prostitutes for the Rhinemaidens.) Pierre Boulez' scaled-down conducting had the orchestra members petitioning festival director Wolfgang Wagner (the composer's grandson) for permission to play louder.

The controversy at the Salzburg Easter Festival, whose director, conductor Herbert von

World-renowned musicians, including (l-r) Julius Bloom, Yehudi Menuhin, Dietrich Fischer-Dieskau, Mstislav Rostropovich, Vladimir Horowitz, Leonard Bernstein, and Isaac Stern, hold a "concert-celebration" in May in honor of the 85th anniversary of New York's Carnegie Hall.

LARRY MORRIS, NEW YORK TIMES PICTURES

Karajan, had just undergone back surgery, was more personal. Mounting tensions during the rehearsals for Karajan's new production of Wagner's *Lohengrin* led to the withdrawal of tenor René Kollo after the first performance.

In Paris and Milan, crises grew out of the respective governments' balking at the present level of subsidy given the opera houses. Both crises were solved, temporarily at least. At the Opéra in Paris, Georg Solti conducted new productions of Verdi's *Otello* and the first two operas of Wagner's *Ring*. The Otello was Placido Domingo, who repeated his tremendous 1975 Hamburg success. He then went to Milan to open the La Scala season in the same role. Among La Scala's more notable offerings, after Giorgio Strehler's controversial production of Verdi's *Macbeth,* was the fine Russian mezzo-soprano Elena Obraztsova in Massenet's *Werther.* Florence heard Gluck's *Orfeo ed Euridice* conducted by Riccardo Muti and the Italian premiere of Hans Werner Henze's early opera *König Hirsch.*

Henze's first new opera in ten years, *We Go to the River,* received a mixed greeting following its world premiere at London's Royal Opera House. The work was quickly taken up by the Deutsche Oper Berlin, whose season also offered Dietrich Fischer-Dieskau's first Hans Sachs in Wagner's *Die Meistersinger.* Covent Garden's revival of William Walton's *Troilus and Cressida,* featuring Janet Baker and conducted by André Previn, was recorded "live" by EMI. The BBC broadcast specially made tapes of Wagner's three little-heard early operas—*Die Feen, Das Liebesverbot,* and *Rienzi.*

Egon Seefehlner's administration of the recently troubled Vienna State Opera began September 1 with Verdi's *Don Carlos.* The season included such novelties as Berlioz' *Les Troyens* and the world premiere of Gottfried von Einem's *Kabale und Liebe.* Film director Roman Polanski made his operatic debut, directing Verdi's *Rigoletto* at the Bavarian State Opera.

KENNETH FURIE, *Music Editor, "High Fidelity"*

Popular Music

Reformations, revivals, and events seemed to have dominated popular music in 1976. It slipped away in several directions and ceased to be the unifying cultural force it had appeared to be a few years earlier. Changes in the culture and in the popular attitude about music gave it a different role—many roles, in fact—as the decentralization of the middle 1970's continued. Popular music was nominally the subject of a number of major events, the most extraordinary and unexpected being Bob Dylan's Rolling Thunder Revue tour. But event dynamics are predominantly visual and the music seldom seemed to dominate these convocations.

If the popular music environment had a theme, it was novelty, which of course is what underlies the appeal of an event. The idea of Dylan touring again, after spending a decade virtually as a recluse, was a novelty, and its character was colored by the old-fashioned "star-studded" aura of his Revue, which featured the Band, Joni Mitchell, Joan Baez, and Roger McGuinn. The idea of John Denver and Frank Sinatra teamed up to play the Nevada gambling palaces and television was a novelty. Also a novelty was the idea of Waylon Jennings, Jessi Colter, and Tompall Glaser touring together, putting most of the energy of the "progressive" or "outlaw" country-music movement on the same stage at the same time.

Neil Young and Stephen Stills, of America's favorite defunct supergroup, joined forces for a tour, as Graham Nash and David Crosby had done earlier. In addition, the Flying Burrito Brothers reformed themselves; Quicksilver Messenger Service tried for a comeback; Sandy Denny spent part of the year back with her old group, Fairport Convention; Marty Balin, founder of the Jefferson Airplane, was back with its successor, the Jefferson Starship; and Steppenwolf, another popular rock band of the late 1960's that had disbanded, was recording and touring again in 1976.

KEN REGAN. CAMERA 5

The Rolling Thunder Revue tour, featuring Bob Dylan, Joan Baez, and the Band, was seen throughout the United States.

But the music tended to sound anachronistic —as if it were still 1968, for example, the way Steppenwolf and Quicksilver played it—or, brought "up to date," it seemed catchy and breezy and removed from roots of any kind. Disco music, which Linda Ronstadt said sounded like advertising jingles, had considerable influence, and not merely among the established groups, such as the Bee Gees, who toyed directly with it. Disco eschewed ambition, commitment, or depth, favoring novelty, surface, and disposability. Novelty songs of the more conventional sort, from Larry Groce's *Junkfood Junkie* to various ones dealing with the Citizens Band radio craze, had a good year but were not as plentiful as the disco-influenced ones whose words did not have to be listened to at all.

Popular music's year was in part a salute to the old saw about soft entertainment for hard times. The economy was slightly but not much better, and behind the "soft entertainment" notion seemed to be a shift of emphasis, with music as a value losing ground to show business. "Being a musician" was becoming less of a goal than "being an entertainer." The rock group Kiss went from obscurity to fame during the year by wearing masks and playing a primitive and basically conservative rock style. A member of the group said charisma was one of the most important elements of the act. To some, it appeared to mean, among other things, that nostalgia for "glitter rock" had gotten started almost before glitter rock had died out.

On the other hand, there was reggae, quite a committed and political music—at least in its home islands in the Caribbean—having greater influence than ever before in the United States. And there were trend-ignoring musicians who emphasized craftsmanship. Followers of such non-gimmicky performers as Linda Ronstadt, Bonnie Raitt, Gordon Lightfoot, John Prine, and James Taylor seemed more loyal than ever to music based upon folk, country, and blues roots. Ronstadt, without taking on uptown trappings and decorations, emerged with a huge and fairly general audience. Lightfoot wrote some of his most literate and thoughtful songs. Waylon Jennings, Willie Nelson, and other "progressives" in country music had their greatest influence so far, and their music stayed close to root forms. They were trying to bring country music back to the basics, each performer seeking to establish a personal one-to-one credibility. New York's country-format radio station, WHN, finally established itself and its music as a success in the big city.

There were audiences for each of these styles and approaches, but there was also a sense that much of the audience was waiting for someone or something to point a way, for some innovation. Nothing seemed to occupy the center of popular music, no songwriter, no song, no genre. Popular magazines started the year by predicting great commercial success for the hybrid form called jazz-rock. Jazz pianist Keith Jarrett earned great respect if not riches in the pop market, and the Newport-in-New York Jazz Festival was an aesthetic success, but jazz-rock did not sweep the country. Broadway's most ambitious new musical production, *Rex,* sandwiched among various revival attempts, with lyrics by Sheldon Harnick and music by Richard Rodgers, was a major flop.

There was a desire to recapture something, perhaps encouraged by the bicentennial ceremoniousness, but that something was elusive if not lost completely. The year's "typical" new music was melodically a bit fancier than it had been for several years and lyrically it was plainer. Committed songwriters worked on refinements, speculative songwriters were decidedly bearish. Everyone waited.

See also RECORDINGS.

NOEL COPPAGE
Contributing Editor, "Stereo Review"

NEBRASKA

Lowered farm income, election of two Democrats to Congress, a controversial legislative session, and an increase in taxes concerned Nebraskans in 1976.

Agriculture. Nebraska farmers set no production records in 1976. While the national production increased, statewide drought dictated decline in all major Nebraska grain crops—corn, grain sorghum, soybeans, and wheat. Rapidly falling prices for both grain and livestock, coupled with lowered production and increased costs put most farmers in a financial squeeze.

Education. Enrollment in two- and four-year colleges increased 3.3% over 1975. Funding of higher education was the hottest issue of the 1976 legislative session. The legislature overrode Gov. Exon's veto of part of the proposed budget and thereby increased the university's state-provided funds by 25% over 1975. The governor's veto of an additional $15 million in state aid for elementary and secondary education was sustained.

Elections. President Ford carried Nebraska with 59% of the popular vote. More surprising was the election of popular Omaha Mayor Edward Zorinsky, a Democrat, to the U. S. Senate, replacing long-time Sen. Roman Hruska (R); not since 1934 had Nebraska elected a Democratic senator. Rep. John Y. McCollister (R), defeated in his Senate bid by Zorinsky, was replaced by John Cavanaugh (D). Republican Representatives Charles Thone and Virginia Smith defeated their Democratic challengers.

Omaha Mayor Edward Zorinsky (D) relaxes with his wife after being elected to the U. S. Senate in November.

WIDE WORLD

NEBRASKA • Information Highlights

Area: 77,227 square miles (200,018 km²).
Population (1975 est.): 1,546,000.
Chief Cities (1970 census): Lincoln, the capital, 149,-518; Omaha, 346,929; Grand Island, 31,269; Hastings, 23,580.
Government (1976): *Chief Officers*—governor, J. James Exon (D); lt. gov., Gerald T. Whelan (D). *Legislature (unicameral)*—49 members (nonpartisan).
Education (1975–76): *Enrollment*—public elementary schools, 167,440 pupils; public secondary, 148,229; nonpublic (1976–77), 45,300; colleges and universities, 66,040 students. Public school expenditures, $383,057,000 ($1,238 per pupil).
State Finances (fiscal year 1975): *Revenues,* $826,055,-000; *expenditures,* $866,032,000.
Personal Income (1975): $9,384,000,000; per capita, $6,087.
Labor Force (July 1976): *Nonagricultural wage and salary earners,* 563,000; *insured unemployed,* 9,000.

Of nine proposed changes to the Nebraska constitution, only two passed. One permits the legislature to consider individual items vetoed; the other allows the state to contract with private institutions for nonsectarian services to handicapped children. Defeated proposals included elimination of final reading of legislative bills, increase of salaries of legislators, and approval of state loans or grants to students at private colleges.

Legislature and Taxes. The annual session of the legislature again reflected conflict with Gov. J. James Exon, particularly over spending. The governor vetoed expenditures of some $30 million, and the legislature overrode $11 million, leaving a state budget of $451 million. Important legislation of the session included a medical malpractice act, increased appropriations for higher education, approval of an educational center and state office building in Omaha, and a "Sunshine Act," revamping laws on campaign reporting. Criminal code revision, coordination of higher education, and water resource management were unfinished business. The Board of Equalization raised income taxes as of January 1, 1976, from 13% of federal liability to 15%. On September 1 income taxes were raised again to 17%, retroactive to January 1, and the sales tax was raised from 2½ to 3%.

Miscellaneous. The courts played an important part in Omaha life in 1976, as public schools were peacefully integrated and the new lottery declared illegal. On January 10 a gas explosion and fire at the Pathfinder Hotel in Fremont killed 20 people and injured more than 40. Of interest was the parole of Caril Ann Fugate, who 18 years ago, as a 14-year-old girl, accompanied killer Charles Starkweather, later executed, on a rampage that left 11 people dead.

ORVILLE H. ZABEL, *Creighton University*

NETHERLANDS

On balance, 1976 was a year most Dutchmen would just as well like to forget. Their problems were largely domestic: the economy basically stagnated; the House of Orange was wracked by the worst scandal in its 140-year

In August, Prime Minister Joop den Uyl of the Netherlands addressed the Staten General on the inquiry into Prince Bernhard's involvement with the Lockheed Aircraft Corporation.

UPI

reign; and the center-left coalition government, its cracks widening, almost collapsed during bitter disputes over such issues as abortion—which is technically illegal, but tacitly condoned—and whether or not to supply parts for the building of a South African nuclear power station. (It was done.)

Economy. An upturn in world trade stimulated a partial recovery by the ailing Dutch economy. The gross national product (GNP), having dropped in 1975, increased by 3.5%, while the rate of inflation remained at a tolerable 8.5%.

Nevertheless, it was a gloomy year. The number of unemployed reached 230,000—7% of the labor force, a postwar high. Rising taxes and labor costs helped induce a marked decline in both foreign and domestic investments. Worried about the deterioration in the country's business climate, the chairmen of nine of the largest Dutch firms sent an open letter of protest to the government in February. They complained about high labor costs—including the employers' large social security contributions—and bemoaned the leftist government's apparent indifference to business.

The Hague responded by publishing a four-year plan for returning the country to prosperity by such devices as limiting the rise in public spending to 1% of the GNP per year and curtailing family allowances to households with more than average incomes. The plan was well received; nevertheless, Prime Minister Joop den Uyl's poor economic record is sure to be a major issue when he and his cabinet members stand for reelection in May, 1977.

Lockheed Scandal. Overshadowing the economic troubles was the controversy over Prince Bernhard's intimate relationship with the American aircraft industry. The prince's troubles began on February 6, when a former official of the Lockheed Aircraft Corporation told U.S. Senate investigators that in the early 1960's he paid a $1.1-million bribe to a "high official" of the Dutch government to secure the latter's aid in the sale to the Netherlands of numerous

Lockheed F-14 jetcraft. Clearly, the anonymous "official" was Prince Bernhard, who, as inspector general of the Dutch armed forces, had considerable influence over the nation's weapons procurement policy.

Still, it was hard to believe that long-accepted Bernhard could have had anything to do with the alleged pay-offs. A blue-ribbon commission was appointed by the prime minister to investigate the matter. On August 26, the commission's findings were finally issued. Although there was no hard proof that the wily prince actually accepted Lockheed's bribe, he was found to be "open to dishonorable requests and offers," and capable of "completely unacceptable initiatives."

The chagrined Bernhard was forced to resign virtually all of his business and military posts, including that of inspector general. The government, fearing a constitutional crisis, decided not to prosecute the matter. But the cloud over the House of Orange was not easily dispelled. As the year ended, Queen Juliana, smarting from her husband's disgrace, was said to be contemplating abdication.

See feature article on MONARCHIES beginning on page 44.

GORDON F. SANDER

——**NETHERLANDS · Information Highlights**——

Official Name: Kingdom of the Netherlands.
Location: Northwestern Europe.
Area: 15,770 square miles (40,844 km²).
Population (1976 est.): 13,800,000.
Chief Cities (1975 est.): Amsterdam, the capital, 758,-000; Rotterdam, 621,000; The Hague, 483,000.
Government: *Head of state,* Juliana, queen (acceded Sept. 1948). *Head of government,* Joop den Uyl, prime minister (took office May 1973). *Legislature* —Staten General: First Chamber and Second Chamber.
Monetary Unit: Guilder (2.57 guilders equal U.S.$1, Sept. 1976).
Gross National Product (1975 est.): $83,400,000,000.
Manufacturing (major products): Metals, processed foods, petroleum products, chemicals, textiles, machinery, electrical appliances, clothing.
Major Agricultural Products: Sugar beets, potatoes, wheat, barley, rye, oats, flax.
Foreign Trade (1975): *Exports,* $35,048,000,000; *imports,* $34,542,000,000.

NEVADA

For the first time since 1908, Nevada in 1976 gave its three electoral votes to the losing candidate in a presidential election.

Elections. President Ford received 53% of the popular vote in the state, despite almost a 2–1 Democratic edge in voter registration. Vice-presidential candidate Walter Mondale made two visits to Las Vegas, but neither Carter nor Ford went to Nevada during the final race. Both had campaigned in the state prior to the primary election—Nevada's first—in May, but finished second to Gov. Edmund Brown, Jr., and former Gov. Ronald Reagan, respectively. Under Nevada law, delegates chosen at state conventions are mandated to cast votes in accordance with the proportional breakdown of the popular vote for each candidate. Thus the Republican delegates cast 13 votes for Reagan and 5 votes for Ford; and the Democratic delegate votes were allocated 6½ for Brown, 3 for Carter, and 1 for Sen. Frank Church, with ½ vote uncommitted to represent the 5% who voted for "none of the above" on the primary ballot.

Sen. Howard Cannon was easily reelected to a fourth term, carrying 64% of the vote to 30% for former Republican Rep. David Towell. Democratic Rep. James Santini received a record-breaking 74% of the vote as he defeated Republican Walden Earhart and three minor-party candidates. Earhart backed into the final election contest after running second to "none of the above" in the primary. The Democrats picked up four additional seats in the state Assembly, swelling their margin to 35–5, while retaining a 17–3 advantage in the Senate.

Economy. Despite a brief strike by hotel workers in Las Vegas, the tourism and gambling industries continued to thrive in Nevada. Income from the gambling taxes for the 1975–76 fiscal year was up about 10% over the previous year, and sales-tax revenues increased by 12.7%. Thus the state treasury showed a healthy surplus of $33 million for the fiscal year. Despite the booming economy, unemployment reached 8.8% in both January and March. At the end of 1976

many in the state were concerned about the possible effects on Nevada's tourist economy of the approval of casino gambling in Atlantic City, New Jersey.

Sewer Bonds and Growth. A sharp controversy developed in the Reno area over a proposed bond issue to expand the sewer plant, which was working close to capacity. A group of citizens, who opposed the expansion unless the area adopted a limited growth policy, spearheaded the effort which defeated the bond question at the May election. The issue was placed on the ballot again in November and passed easily after a citizen's committee conducted extensive hearings and strongly recommended its passage on health grounds.

Education. Several school boards throughout the state were involved in prolonged salary negotiations during the year. Gov. Mike O'Callaghan refused to invoke binding arbitration in the two large-population counties, and the schoolteachers did less well than in recent years on salary matters. After several years of substantial growth, the University of Nevada at Las Vegas had only a slight increase in the fall of 1976, and the Reno campus had a slight decline.

DON W. DRIGGS
University of Nevada, Reno

NEW BRUNSWICK

The economy of New Brunswick, slowly recovering from the recession, got some encouragement in 1976 to help it along. A mildly stimulative deficit budget was introduced, but the thrust of government economic policy was toward controlling inflation.

Jobs for Moncton. The federal government's pension office, employing about 400 people, is to be moved from Ottawa to Moncton over a five-year period. The transfer, announced June 14, is in line with federal decentralization policies. Moncton has been suffering acute unemployment problems since the T. Eaton Co. closed its office there early in the year.

Budget. In his budget presentation to the legislature on March 16, Finance Minister Edison Stairs forecast an $82.1 million deficit for fiscal

--- NEVADA • Information Highlights ---

Area: 110,540 square miles (286,299 km²).
Population (1975 est.): 592,000.
Chief Cities (1970 census): Carson City, the capital, 15,468; Las Vegas, 125,787; Reno, 72,863.
Government (1976): *Chief Officers*—governor, Michael O'Callaghan (D); lt. gov., Robert E. Rose (D). *Legislature*—Senate, 20 members; Assembly, 40 members.
Education (1975–76): *Enrollment*—public elementary schools, 72,839 pupils; public secondary, 66,906; nonpublic (1976–77), 5,600; colleges and universities, 20,916 students. *Public school expenditures,* $570,-665,000 ($1,160 per pupil).
State Finances (fiscal year 1975): *Revenues,* $570,665,-000; *expenditures,* $499,259,000.
Personal Income (1975): $3,935,000,000; per capita, $6,647.
Labor Force (July 1976): *Nonagricultural wage and salary earners,* 285,400; *insured unemployed,* 11,000 (5.1%).

--- NEW BRUNSWICK • Information Highlights ---

Area: 28,354 square miles (73,437 km²).
Population (April 1976 est.): 687,000.
Chief Cities (1971 census): Fredericton, the capital, 24,254; St. John, 88,102; Moncton, 47,891.
Government (1976): *Chief Officers*—lt. gov., Hedard Robichaud; premier, Richard B. Hatfield (Progressive Conservative); chief justice, Charles J. A. Hughes. *Legislature*—Legislative Assembly, 58 members.
Education (1976–77): *Enrollment*—public elementary and secondary schools, 162,700 pupils; private schools, 270; Indian (federal) schools, 860; postsecondary, 12,580 students. *Total expenditures,* $217,081,000.
Public Finance (1976–77 est.): *Revenues,* $1,080,900,-000; *expenditures,* $1,163,000,000.
Personal Income (1974): $2,451,000,000; average annual income per person, $3,702.
(All monetary figures are in Canadian dollars.)

year 1976–77. Expenditures were estimated at
$1,163,000,000—$148 million more than a year
earlier. They included $11 million for the eco-
nomic growth department to help cover write-
offs of government investment in industrial development projects that failed.

Port Development. The federal and provincial
governments announced in August that they had
agreed to pay equal shares of a new $50 million
container facility in St. John harbor. Work has
been going on at the site since 1972.

Government. The legislature adjourned on
June 24 after members approved a bill creating
a New Brunswick lotteries commission to join
the other three Atlantic provinces in a regional
lottery. The spring session was marked by repeated Liberal opposition attacks on the government's spending-restraint program, part of Ottawa's national anti-inflation campaign. As a
result of protests by legislators as well as other
groups, the government agreed to provide more
funds for education.

Faced with a hard legislative battle and opposition from rural residents, the government
backed off from a controversial proposal to provide a new form of government for the province's unincorporated areas. The plan was designed for the 250,000 people—more than a
third of New Brunswick's population—living
outside the cities, towns, and villages.

JOHN BEST, *Chief, Canada World News*

NEW HAMPSHIRE

In the bicentennial year of 1976 politics
dominated the news. Starting in early January
and continuing through February 24, candidates
traveled through snow and cold seeking votes in
the first presidential preference primary. The
key in this primary was momentum, not delegates, for only 17 Democratic and 21 Republican delegates were at stake. When the tally was
complete, Jimmy Carter had 30% of the total
to runner-up Morris Udall's 24%. President
Gerald Ford won a close contest over former
Gov. Ronald Reagan, with 51% of the Republican vote. Ford carried the state again in November.

State Politics. The tax issue dominated the
state political scene. Gov. Meldrim Thomson
used the pledge of no new taxes to good advantage in both the campaign for the Republican
nomination and that leading to victory in November by a margin of more than 50,000 votes.
Thomson's stand put Harry Spanos, the Democratic nominee, on the defensive, forcing him to
indicate repeatedly that he would not propose
any income or sales tax.

Helping Governor Thomson achieve a third
term was the excellent condition of the state's
economy. The unemployment rate remained well
below the national average, dropping to 3.1%
in September. During the year several new
companies decided to locate in New Hamp-

shire. Unfortunately, most of them preferred
sites in the southern third of the state which
served to accentuate the imbalance between
southern New Hampshire and northernmost
Coos County, with its stagnant economy.

Energy and Environment. Environmental issues shared the headlines with politics throughout the year. None proved more volatile than
the construction by the Public Service Company
of a $1,600,000,000 nuclear power plant at Sea-
brook. Environmentalists and those opposed to
nuclear power fought the company, while it was
supported by those, including the governor, who
believe that New Hampshire will need the generating capacity of the Seabrook plant in the
1980's. The federal government, after long delays and deliberation, issued the necessary permits and licenses for construction to begin. Protest demonstrations followed; the most serious
one occurred on August 22, when 179 persons
were arrested. Construction has continued, and
completion is expected in the early 1980's.

An unresolved environmental issue, which
has its origins in the 1950's, is whether to build
a new highway through Franconia Notch. The
environmental impact statement was made public in late summer. After 90 days of public
comment, the state highway department began
preparing its recommendation to the Federal
Highway Administration. After the issuance of
the environmental impact statement, the federal
Environmental Protection Agency recommended
a two-lane parkway.

Another environmental controversy centered
on the location of a pulp mill in Walpole. The
town was of two minds whether a $200-million
plant should be located there. The cherished
principle of home rule triumphed at the March
town meeting, where voters rejected the proposal.

Bicentennial Honor. The bicentennial elicited
an enthusiastic response. New Hampshire
achieved 100% status in the Bicentennial Communities program of the American Revolution
Bicentennial Administration, indicating the public spirit of the people in the state.

WILLIAM L. TAYLOR
Plymouth State College

— **NEW HAMPSHIRE • Information Highlights** —

Area: 9,304 square miles (24,097 km²).
Population (1975 est.): 818,000.
Chief Cities (1970 census): Concord, the capital, 30,022;
  Manchester, 87,754; Nashua, 55,820; Portsmouth,
  25,717.
Government (1976): *Chief Officers*—governor, Meldrim
  Thomson, Jr. (R); secy. of state, Robert L. Stark
  (R). *General Court*—Senate, 24 members; House of
  Representatives, 400 members.
Education (1975–76): *Enrollment*—public elementary
  schools, 103,392 pupils; public secondary, 71,205;
  nonpublic (1976–77), 20,500; colleges and univer-
  sities, 37,190 students. *Public school expenditures,*
  $190,000,000 ($1,105 per pupil).
State Finances (fiscal year 1975): *Revenues,* $512,162,-
  000; *expenditures,* $559,338,000.
Personal Income (1975): $4,346,000,000; per capita,
  $5,315.
Labor Force (July 1976): *Nonagricultural wage and
  salary earners,* 321,200; *insured unemployed,* 10,600
  (4.3%).

NEW JERSEY

In New Jersey 1976 was the year of the income tax.

The Tax Issue. In a historic gesture on July 8, Gov. Brendan Byrne signed New Jersey's first law providing for a statewide income tax. This was the culmination of a political struggle that had been going on for several years and came to a head on July 1, when the state Supreme Court ordered the public schools closed because the legislature had not provided an alternative to the local property taxes for financing education. The tax was to be semi-graduated—a 2% levy on personal incomes up to $20,000 and 2½% on incomes above that figure. It was estimated that $775 million would be raised for the fiscal year ending June 30, 1977, with $374 million allocated for education and the rest for property tax relief.

Passage of the income tax law did not mean the issue was dead, however. Stipulation that it would be in effect for only two years gave the Federation of New Jersey Taxpayers, a leading antitax organization, a chance to mobilize its forces. The tax will be the major issue in the 1977 gubernatorial election.

Economic Conditions. During the first half of the year New Jersey did not keep pace with the rest of the country in recovery from the recession. In January there were over 400,000 out of

work, and the state had one of the nation's highest unemployment rates. The problem was compounded by a chronic depression in the manufacturing sector; the number of factory jobs in the state had declined by 160,000 between 1969 and 1976. Many agreed that reform in the business tax structure and programs to revive New Jersey's major cities were needed. Encouragement was seen in plans to construct urban industrial parks in Jersey City and Elizabeth, with the possibility that similar ventures might be initiated elsewhere. A further economic boost was the opening in September of the Meadowland Sports Complex, with a harness racing track and a football stadium. Casino gambling in Atlantic City, approved by the voters in November, was seen as another means to bring revenue to the state.

Election Campaign. New Jersey's presidential primary on June 8 had ramifications for the state Democratic organization. In giving early support to Jimmy Carter, Gov. Byrne opposed some of the leading members of his party, such as Sen. James Dugan and Jersey City Mayor Paul Jordan, who backed a slate of uncommitted delegates to the national convention. This slate won a narrow upset victory over the Carter ticket, weakening Byrne's statewide prestige. On the Republican side, President Ford won a substantial victory over Ronald Reagan. In the November elections President Ford carried the state by a margin of some 57,000 votes.

Senate and House nominations were also decided in the June 8 primary. Harrison Williams, the Democratic incumbent in the Senate, easily won renomination, and David Norcross, a Morristown lawyer and chairman of the New Jersey Election Law Enforcement Commission, was nominated over three Republican rivals. Williams was handily reelected in November. The most publicized congressional primary was in the Ninth District, where Democratic incumbent Henry Helstoski won, although he was under indictment for extortion. But he lost the November election to his Republican opponent, Harold C. Hollenbeck.

HERMANN K. PLATT, *St. Peter's College*

A secretary at Atlantic City's Convention Hall tries out a roulette wheel. On November 2, New Jersey voters approved casino gambling in the resort.

UPI

—— **NEW JERSEY · Information Highlights** ——

Area: 7,836 square miles (20,295 km²).
Population (1975 est.): 7,316,000.
Chief Cities (1970 census): Trenton, the capital, 104,-638; Newark, 382,288; Jersey City, 260,545.
Government (1976): *Chief Officers*—governor, Brendan T. Byrne (D); secy. of state, J. Edward Crabiel (D). *Legislature*—Senate, 40 members; General Assembly, 80 members.
Education (1975–76): *Enrollment*—public elementary schools, 924,000 pupils; public secondary, 534,000; nonpublic (1976–77), 300,800; colleges and universities, 264,655 students. *Public school expenditures,* $2,477,000,000 ($1,718 per pupil).
State Finances (fiscal year 1975): *Revenues,* $4,795,-353,000; *expenditures,* $5,217,884,000.
Personal Income (1975): $49,181,000,000; per capita, $6,722.
Labor Force (July 1976): *Nonagricultural wage and salary earners,* 2,686,800; *insured unemployed,* 130,200 (6.0%).

NEW MEXICO

New Mexicans enthusiastically joined in celebrating the nation's bicentennial throughout 1976. Santa Fe staged a two-day historical pageant honoring Spanish Gov. Juan Bautista de Anza, who ruled over the area in the late 1770's. The state contributed an entry to the Bicentennial Wagon Train and promoted activities commemorating the expedition of fathers Atanasio Domínguez and Vélez de Escalante through the Southwest in 1776.

Politics. The November 2 general elections brought an end to the 20-year congressional career of Sen. Joseph Montoya (D), who gained national attention for his part in the Watergate hearings. He was defeated by Harrison H. Schmitt (R), a 41-year-old geologist, engineer, and former astronaut from Silver City.

Voters in New Mexico soundly rejected a state constitutional amendment that would have allowed Gov. Jerry Apodaca and six other Democratic state officials to run in 1978 for second four-year terms.

Indians. In August the Indian Pueblo Cultural Center, a huge D-shaped structure modeled after Pueblo Bonito in Chaco Canyon, was opened in Albuquerque. Owned and operated by New Mexico's Indian people, the center offers educational, administrative, and exhibit facilities and provides a marketing outlet for Pueblo craftsmen. It was built at a cost of $2.1 million and is the only one of its kind in the nation.

Superintendent of Public Instruction Leonard De Layo began seeking recommendations from Indian leaders for appointments to the new division of Indian education created by the New Mexico legislature. This body will provide direct assistance to meet the special educational needs of Indian students.

House Bill 19, passed by the legislature and subsequently signed by Governor Apodaca, created a stir among New Mexico's Indians. The measure was aimed at taxing improvements on reservations made by non-Indians—business establishments or industrial plants, for example.

UPI

Harrison Schmitt (R), a former astronaut who walked on the moon, prepares to join the U. S. Senate. He defeated New Mexico's incumbent, Sen. Joseph Montoya.

Various tribes in the state complained that such taxation within a reservation constituted a direct encroachment on native sovereignty and jurisdiction. In protest, the Eight Northern Pueblos informed Governor Apodaca that they would withdraw from all participation in state bicentennial activities.

Environment and Energy. Members of the New Mexico Energy Resources Board announced that the natural gas supply in the state will be depleted within 10 years, and they recommended a speed-up of studies on alternate energy sources —solar, wind, geothermal, and nuclear.

Rapid expansion of uranium mining in the Grants region has brought with it new environmental problems. The U. S. Environmental Protection Agency (EPA) reported that the population in the active mining and milling areas may be exposed to harmful radiation. A study released by the EPA on water quality in the Grants uranium belt showed that levels of radium-226 and selenium in the water were intolerable. Little improvement can be expected in the future, however, since half the known uranium reserves in the United States are in this district, and exploration and development are expected to continue at a rapid pace. The city of Grants, meanwhile, with inadequate housing and utilities, is bracing for a large influx of population.

MARC SIMMONS
Author, "New Mexico, A Bicentennial History"

NEW MEXICO · Information Highlights

Area: 121,666 square miles (315,115 km²).
Population (1975 est.): 1,147,000.
Chief Cities (1970 census): Santa Fe, the capital, 41,-167; Albuquerque, 243,751; Las Cruces, 37,857; Roswell, 33,908.
Government (1976): *Chief Officers*—governor, Jerry Apodaca (D); lt. gov., Robert E. Ferguson (D). *Legislature*—Senate, 42 members; House of Representatives, 70 members.
Education (1975–76): *Enrollment*—public elementary schools, 133,681 pupils; public secondary, 140,931; nonpublic (1976–77), 14,000; colleges and universities, 50,542 students. *Public school expenditures*, $329,529,000 ($1,200 per pupil).
State Finances (fiscal year 1975): *Revenues*, $1,092,985,-000; *expenditures*, $907,961,000.
Personal Income (1975): $5,476,000,000; per capita, $4,775.
Labor Force (July 1976): *Nonagricultural wage and salary earners*, 389,600; *insured unemployed*, 11,300 (4.4%).

NEW YORK

A perennial fiscal crisis, aggravated by national economic woes—unemployment and inflation—as well as the precarious relationship between city and state, was again of uppermost concern to the citizens of New York State.

Budget Crisis. The state budget of $10,900,-000,000 mandated cuts in welfare costs, Medicaid, and other social programs, as well as a reduction of 11,000 in the state government's work force by January 1977. The budget was also balanced by such revenue devices as a new state lottery and the imposition of new fees. Short-term borrowing was carried out with the help of the state-employee pension system and treasury funds, but the state fell $300 million short of its goal of $2,850,000,000 from private credit markets. A $2,600,000,000 package of financial arrangements enabled the Housing Finance Agency to redeem past notes and finish current projects. In addition, the federal government agreed to provide insurance for certain housing-project mortgages held by the state.

Taxes. The state legislature passed New York City revenue measures that extended the surcharge on resident personal income and commuter taxes, increased transportation and corporation taxes, and put a surcharge on the stock-transfer tax. The legislators enacted state-tax abatements to businesses that expanded or rehabilitated plants and increased estate-tax exemptions for family farms. They also repealed $42 million in state and city corporate taxes on certain brokerage firms that were threatening to leave Wall Street. Five-year tax exemptions to those rehabilitating private homes were also added. A Republican-sponsored initiative to use any possible surplus revenues for business and personal tax abatement was killed.

Education. The state was expected to close the budget gap at the crisis-ridden City University of New York after the city government announced that by 1977 it would no longer support its senior colleges and its Graduate School and University Center. By year's end, however, no action had been taken to ensure the university's viability.

The legislature overrode Gov. Hugh Carey's veto of the "Stavisky Bill," requiring New York City to expend a certain percentage of its budget on public-school education during its three-year fiscal program. It was the first override in 104 years. The courts, however, found the measure illegal. Parents were permitted to remove children from sex-education classes if they thought that the subject and method of teaching was offensive.

Crime. Legislation providing for benefits to victims of crime was enacted; maximum aid was set at $20,000. An anti-loitering bill, aimed at prostitutes and their patrons, was passed. The administration offered a major juvenile-justice law, providing for a minimum sentence of two years and a maximum of five for 14- and 15-year-olds convicted of major felonies. The stringent Rockefeller drug laws were modified, but decriminalization of possession of less than one ounce (31 g) of marijuana was killed, as was an attempt to require a one-year mandatory sentence for illegal possession of a handgun.

Other legislative measures passed during the year reduced pensions for future state employees; enabled savings banks to offer checking accounts and overdraft privileges; and set noise limits at Kennedy Airport, effectively banning the SST.

Elections. Despite the efforts of Republican partisans, the generally liberal Democratic majority in the state supported the candidacy of Jimmy Carter; he drew 3,266,385 votes to President Ford's 3,016,058. The president's majority in the suburbs was not sufficient to offset severe losses in the city, where Carter outpolled him 2–1. Interestingly, Carter also had more votes upstate, in a traditionally Republican area, than did Ford; the vote was 1,198,120 to 1,158,522. This was reversed in the senatorial race.

In the race for the Senate, incumbent James L. Buckley (R-Cons.) jousted with Daniel P. Moynihan (D). Upstate districts were 1,423,451 in favor of Buckley and 1,182,828 for Moynihan. Surprisingly, however, Moynihan outpolled Buckley in the suburbs 737,386 to 729,484. Carter and Moynihan had an almost identically decisive vote in New York City. Moynihan had 1,369,575 to Buckley's 582,448, Carter 1,367,537 to Ford's 692,066. Democrats rode the crest of victory to gain two additional seats in the state Assembly—a total of 90 out of 150. In the state Senate, however, Democrats lost one seat. Their number there is 25, while Republicans have 35. All together, however, Democrats enjoyed more success at the polls than at any time since the 1930's.

The voters overwhelmingly approved so-called "Las Vegas Nights," a provision allowing nonprofit organizations to sponsor gambling events to raise funds.

LEO HERSHKOWITZ
Queens College, City University of New York

--- **NEW YORK · Information Highlights** ---

Area: 49,576 square miles (128,402 km²).
Population (1975 est.): 18,120,000.
Chief Cities (1970 census): Albany, the capital, 115,781; New York, 7,895,563; Buffalo, 462,768; Rochester, 296,233.
Government (1976): *Chief Officers*—governor, Hugh L. Carey (D): lt. gov., Mary Anne Krupsak (D). *Legislature*—Senate, 60 members; Assembly, 150 members.
Education (1975–76): *Enrollment*—public elementary schools, 1,753,293 pupils; public secondary, 1,647,-921; nonpublic (1976–77), 705,600; colleges and universities, 990,196 students. *Public school expenditures,* $6,616,954,000 ($1,962 per pupil).
State Finances (fiscal year 1975): *Revenues,* $17,206,-113,000; *expenditures,* $17,405,591,000.
Personal Income (1975): $118,958,000,000; per capita, $6,564.
Labor Force (July 1976): *Nonagricultural wage and salary earners,* 6,770,900; *insured unemployed,* 319,-100 (5.6%).

A total of 2,747 persons attended the New York Philharmonic's inaugural concert at the rebuilt Avery Fisher Hall in New York City. Some $6.4 million were spent to improve the auditorium's acoustics.

UPI

NEW YORK CITY

The attention of most New Yorkers in 1976 was riveted on the city's financial crisis, made worse by national problems—inflation, unemployment, and indifference to urban affairs by political leaders throughout the country.

Fiscal Affairs. The key to Mayor Abraham D. Beame's expense budget of $12,500,000,000 for the fiscal year beginning July 1 was austerity, which meant cuts of $379 million from the previous year. This was part of a three-year plan to achieve a balanced budget. Faced with declining revenues and a "cash-flow" crisis, New York's leaders asked municipal unions representing some 200,000 workers to take reductions in fringe benefits and to defer wage increases and raise productivity. Most city employees agreed to these requests. Transit workers, for instance, approved a pact which pegged raises to the cost of living. Policemen, however, refused to accept the inability of the city to grant wage increases; nor would they accept new work schedules designed to increase productivity. They staged noisy and sometimes unruly demonstrations. In December they won a court battle over a 1975 pay hike that had been "frozen" by the city.

Higher Education. Budget trimming resulted in the closing of the City University of New York for some two weeks in June. City officials withdrew from what had been a 50-50 cost sharing by city and state and terminated the city's commitment to the Graduate School and University Center and the senior colleges. By 1977, the mayor announced, the city would contribute support only to its community colleges.

Preceded by months of lay-offs, reduced paychecks, and bitter debate about the university's future, a decision was made in June to end the 129-year-old tradition of free tuition. Fees of $750–$900—a level comparable to that at the State University of New York—were set for some 170,000 undergraduates. The financial crisis caused dismissals of thousands of teachers and clerical staff.

Jobs and Race. The city's crisis was acerbated by dismal employment figures. By mid-summer the jobless rate was 10.6%, compared to a national average of 7.5%. At the same time it was estimated that it took $10,266 a year to maintain a family of four in New York at the lowest level of subsistence. These figures must be reviewed against the decline of the middle class white population, some 600,000 of which left the city between 1970 and 1975.

The Bronx became the first borough to have a majority black and Puerto Rican population. Minority students constituted 66.8% of all public-school enrollment in the city. Still, the black population increased by only 30,000 during this time, an increase caused by more black births than deaths. In fact, more blacks were leaving the city than arriving.

Upbeat Items. Despite the gloom, the "Big Apple" remained a vibrant community. The city celebrated the bicentennial with varied and exciting events. Millions of New Yorkers lined the waterfront on July 4 during "Operation Sail," when the tall vessels of many nations passed in review in New York Harbor. And as if to offset estimated losses to the city of $100 million for refurbishing Yankee Stadium, the New York Yankees in 1976 won their first American League pennant in 12 years.

From a low point in the 1950's, New York has seen a year-by-year increase in movies filmed on location in the city. In 1966, when a special office was created to aid film makers, 22 were shot. In 1976 the total rose to 50, highlighted by King Kong falling off the World Trade Center.

Elections. Politics held a particular interest in 1976 in view of the city's problems. In September former U. S. Ambassador to the United Nations Daniel P. Moynihan narrowly won over Rep. Bella Abzug for the Democratic nomination to the U. S. Senate. Moynihan, stressing the need for adequate representation from New York, handily defeated James L. Buckley, the Republican-Conservative incumbent. He carried the city by a vote of 1,369,575 to 582,-448. In the presidential contest the city gave Jimmy Carter margin enough to ensure President Ford's defeat in New York State. Carter's city vote was 1,367,537 to Ford's 692,066.

LEO HERSHKOWITZ
Queens College, City University of New York

NEW ZEALAND

Economic and industrial affairs continued to dominate attention as the government strove to correct the balance-of-payments deficit and to control inflation. Among the work force there was increasing restiveness over curbs on free bargaining.

Economy. The gravest problem was the unprecedented deficit in overseas exchange transactions. This reached $704,000,000 for the year ending June 1976. At this time unemployment stood at 11,824, the highest since the Great Depression. The government also faced a large deficit in its own accounts.

A tough policy to restrict external and public spending was unveiled in stages. Increased hire/purchase deposits on cars and TV sets were imposed; interest rates were raised; subsidies on staple foods were either abolished or cut; bread prices jumped nearly 50%; ceilings were fixed on staff levels in public service; import licensing schedules were cut 30%.

Top priority was given to the fashioning of an incomes policy. In May a conditional 7% general wage increase was awarded, but a wage freeze for a year was also imposed, and local bodies in New Zealand were prohibited from raising any new loans until April 1977. The creation of a completely new pay-fixing authority was foreshadowed.

Budget. Emphasis in the federal budget was laid on the need for a cut in the standard of living in the interest of the nation's future solvency. Most urgent was the need to steer resources into farming and export industries. State spending was to be reduced by 8%, but even then the estimated deficit of $847,000,000 was the highest ever.

Company and sales taxes on certain luxury goods were all raised. On the positive side, special livestock incentive and regional investment allowances were introduced. Social security benefits for the elderly were increased, and home ownership was encouraged. A leading national newspaper described the budget as a "combination of knife, lolly, and exhortation."

After the budget came a five-month freeze on prices and rents. A warning was issued that strong controls to deal with strikes would be adopted. In October the main industrial legislation entered Parliament. It proposed to make political strikes illegal and to introduce an element of voluntary trade unionism.

External Affairs. Prime Minister Robert Muldoon undertook a month-long tour of Great Britain, France, South Korea, Japan, and China in April. The chief objective was the improvement of trade opportunities. He was the first New Zealand leader to make an official visit to mainland China.

The national rugby team began a tour of South Africa just prior to the Olympic Games. Some 30 nations withdrew from the games in protest.

Domestic Affairs. In a by-election in March, the Labour party retained the Nelson seat with an increased majority. U. S. Vice President Nelson A. Rockefeller paid a brief visit in April. The chequered history of the rapid-rail scheme for Auckland took another turn down in April when it was announced that the government would never put money into the project. Toward the end of the year the visits of two nuclear-powered U. S. cruisers sparked substantial protests. The unions closed the ports concerned, and at Auckland, a "peace squadron" sought to block the harbor entrance.

G. W. A. Bush, *The University of Auckland*

After nearly seven years of construction, workers holed through New Zealand's Kaimai railway tunnel.

NEW ZEALAND CONSULATE GENERAL, NEW YORK

—— NEW ZEALAND · Information Highlights ——

Official Name: New Zealand.
Location: South Pacific Ocean.
Area: 103,736 square miles (268,675 km²).
Population (1976 est.): 3,200,000.
Chief Cities (1976 est.): Wellington, the capital, 360,-000; Auckland, 800,000; Christchurch, 325,000.
Government: *Head of state,* Elizabeth II, queen, represented by Sir Denis Blundell, governor general (took office Sept. 1972). *Head of government,* Robert Muldoon, prime minister (took office Dec. 1975). *Legislature* (unicameral)—House of Representatives.
Monetary Unit: New Zealand dollar (1.001 N. Z. dollars equal U. S.$1, July 1976).
Gross National Product (1975): $11,965,000,000.
Manufacturing (major products): Processed foods, meat, wood products, cement, fertilizers.
Major Agricultural Products: Wheat, potatoes, dairy products, sheep wool, forest products.
Foreign Trade (1975): *Exports,* $2,152,000,000; *imports,* $3,152,000,000.

A fishing village in Newfoundland. Prospects for the industry, a mainstay of the provincial economy, were good.

NEWFOUNDLAND

Financial difficulties, higher taxes, and low employment haunted Newfoundland in 1976.

Finances. The prime question before the House of Assembly seemed to be how to cope with financial constraints, national and provincial. Newfoundland was the first province to sign an 18-month agreement to the federal anti-inflation program. A provincial mini-budget, made public in November 1975, increased the personal income and sales taxes. When the regular budget was announced in March 1976, this trend continued. Gasoline and corporation taxes were increased, 200 hospital beds were taken out of use, 500 public service jobs were to be eliminated, and virtually all capital-works spending was halted in the province.

—— **NEWFOUNDLAND · Information Highlights** ——

Area: 156,185 square miles (404,520 km²).
Population (April 1976 est.): 550,000.
Chief Cities (1971 census): St. John's, the capital, 88,-102; Corner Brook, 26,309.
Government (1975): *Chief Officers*—lt. gov., Gordon Winter; premier, F. D. Moores (Progressive Conservative); *Legislature*—Legislative Assembly, 51 members.
Education (1976–77): *Enrollment*—public elementary and secondary schools, 156,540; private schools, 340; post-secondary, 8,350 students. *Total expenditures* (1972), $216,579,000.
Public Finance (1975–76 est.): *Revenues*, $770,000,000; *expenditures*, $937,000,000.
Personal Income (1974): $1,799,000,000; average annual income per person, $3,319.
(All monetary figures are in Canadian dollars.)

Economics. Unemployment in Newfoundland has always been the highest in Canada, running more than double the national average. This burden was made significantly heavier in March, when the oil refinery at Come-By-Chance, opened only 2½ years earlier, was declared bankrupt. The jobs of 350 employees disappeared. The province's second mortgage of $30 million was secured by assets, but debts to the Japanese firm of Ataka were more than $100 million. At the year's end no alternative financial support had been found, and the plant remained closed. Industrial development in two other areas is wavering. The provincially-owned linerboard mill at Stephenville is losing approximately $30 million per year, and the government is trying to make new arrangements. More disappointing still is the slowdown of the development of hydroelectric capacity in Labrador. The island portion of the province is facing an energy shortage but is unable to come to a financial arrangement with Quebec that would make the development and transmission of additional power feasible.

The fishing industry alone seems liable to improve. The government of Canada declared that it would establish a 200-mile offshore fisheries jurisdiction on January 1, 1977. This means sharing in a quota system seeking a sustained yield management of fish stocks. It is hoped that this will result in long-term improvements.

SUSAN MCCORQUODALE
Memorial University of Newfoundland

NIGERIA

Political instability continued to undermine the economy of Nigeria in 1976. Reforms of the army and state, proposed by the government, precipitated an abortive military coup. Although unsuccessful, the rebels killed the head of state, Gen. Murtala Muhammad. His second in command, Lt. Gen. Olusegun Obasanjo, was chosen to lead the nation and promised to carry on Murtala's programs.

The Attempted Coup. On the morning of February 13, a group of dissident officers, reacting to the government's plans to cut the armed forces to 100,000 men, attempted to seize power. Although the commissioner of defense, Maj. Gen. Bisalla, was among the plotters, the driving force was Lt. Col. Dimka; he led a group which killed Gen. Muhammad, seized the Lagos radio station, and broadcast the change to the nation. The rebels failed to assassinate other main government leaders. In contrast to those who overthrew the previous head of state, Gen. Gowon, seven months earlier, these plotters did not have the support of the bulk of the army. Most units remained loyal, and order was restored in a few hours. The new head of state acted swiftly, and within a week more than 125 persons were arrested. Most of the important plotters were tried by a military tribunal, and on March 11, Gen. Bisalla and 31 others were publicly executed at Bara Beach in Lagos. Dimka, whose testimony after his capture was so damaging to others, J. Gomwalk, the former governor of Benue-Plateau state, and five others were executed on May 16. Gen. Gowon, now a student at Warwick University in Britain, was also implicated in Dimka's testimony. Nigeria formally requested the British Foreign Office to return Gowon to Nigeria so he could be tried. Britain refused, and Gowon was subsequently declared a wanted person.

Political Developments. One of Murtala's pledges had been a return to civilian rule by the end of 1979. The constitutional panel making studies of the future form of government is expected to recommend a strong executive based partially upon the U. S. model. A decision was reached in July to restructure local government into units of 80,000 to 150,000 persons with civilian executive councils. The first elections to these councils were held in August.

In December 1975, two investigative panels reported favorably on moving the capital from coastal, overcrowded Lagos. These recommendations were accepted by the government, which announced in February that the new capital would be located near the center of Nigeria at the small city of Abuja. Although 3,090 square miles (8,000 km²) have already been obtained, it will be years before all the buildings and amenities in the federal enclave will be finished. The military government early in the

Murtala Muhammad, Nigeria's chief of state since July 1975, was murdered in an abortive coup in February.

year also accepted the report of a commission on new states and created seven new states within the federation. These are Imo, Ondo, Benue, Ogun, Gongola, Niger, and Bauchi. The names of three of the older states were also changed.

Economy. Nigeria's economy, despite its petroleum revenues, remained sluggish. Inflation and high unemployment were especially noticeable in the larger cities. Murtala's decision to cut the civil payroll by 11,000 and to reduce the outsized army contributed to the abortive coup. Despite recent construction, the transportation system is old and inefficient, the populations of the major cities continue to grow, and the port of Lagos remains so congested that unless a ship has priority to unload there may be a six months' wait. There are other more ominous general indicators. Although Nigeria is the world's sixth largest producer of petroleum, its trade surplus fell from $6,330 million in 1974 to $1,953 million in 1975. The federal budget was unbalanced, and in April Obasanjo cut back on proposed expenditures and placed an $8,800,-000,000 ceiling on spending. He also recast the figures for the third national development plan because of the continued high inflation rate and the revised estimates for petroleum production. It now appears that petroleum production by 1979 will be considerably below its present high of 2.3 million barrels (310,000 metric tons) per day. More devastating is the report by some experts that Nigeria's petroleum will last only until the early 1980's.

Foreign Affairs. Domestic problems kept Nigeria from assuming a dominant role in African affairs, although it still played its part in the Organization of African Unity and in such agencies as the Economic Community of West African States. Relations with the United States remained proper but cool. Many Nigerians believed that foreign states had a part in the abortive coup, and students stoned the U. S. embassy and the British High Commission. Relations with Britain remain strained largely because of the refusal to return Gen. Gowon.

HARRY A. GAILEY,
San Jose State University

NIGERIA • Information Highlights

Official Name: Federal Republic of Nigeria.
Location: West Africa.
Area: 356,668 square miles (923,768 km²).
Population (1976 est.): 64,700,000.
Chief Cities (1975 est.): Lagos, the capital, 950,000; Ibadan, 790,000; Ogbomosho, 400,000; Kano, 370,-000.
Government: *Head of state and government,* Lt. Gen. Olusegun Obasanjo (assumed power Feb. 1976).
Monetary Unit: Naira (0.63 naira equals U. S.$1, July 1976).
Gross Domestic Product (1974 est.): $22,800,000,000.
Manufacturing (major products): Processed foods, cotton textiles, cement, petroleum products.
Major Agricultural Products: Groundnuts, palm kernels, cacao, rubber, cotton, sweet potatoes and yams, forest products.
Foreign Trade (1975): *Exports,* $7,994,000,000; *imports* (est.), $6,041,000,000.

Raleigh, September 6: Some 4,000 demonstrators march in support of numerous causes.

UPI

NORTH CAROLINA

Politics, the economy, and the drought were the leading stories in North Carolina in 1976.

Politics. Stunned by the election of a Republican governor four years ago, the Democrats made a dramatic comeback in 1976. Lt. Gov. James B. Hunt, Jr., received the largest vote in the state's history as he won the governorship. Democrats also won all the Council of State offices and all but two congressional seats, and Jimmy Carter led Gerald Ford for the presidency by a smaller margin. Republicans retained only 10 of 170 seats in the General Assembly; blacks won 6 seats and women 23. In the Democratic runoff primary in September, Howard Lee received the largest vote ever given a black in his unsuccessful bid for the lieutenant governorship. Two women, Lillian Woo and former first lady Jessie Rae Scott, also received impressive votes in their losing campaigns for Council of State nominations.

Economy. Industrial investments of $701 million in 1975 softened the recession in 1976. Nevertheless, unemployment in the state stood at 6.0% in October, and tax collections for the fiscal year ending June 30 rose only 8.3% over the previous year. Despite the $23 million shortfall, the General Assembly granted a small salary increase to teachers and state employees. Optimistically, the new budget predicted an 11% increase in revenues in the coming fiscal year. *Business World* rated North Carolina second only to California as the state in which business firms are likely to build new plants in the coming decade.

Energy, Weather, and the Environment. The anticipated natural gas shortage did not materialize, but the price of power led to increased criticism of private power companies and the State Utilities Commission. Leading Democrats and Republicans, divided on most issues, joined in blocking construction of a proposed dam in Virginia which would have flooded the New River valley in several mountain counties.

A record drought led to crop damage and severe water restrictions in the northern Piedmont in late summer.

Education. The debate over the quality of public schools continued, and advocates of "back to basics" showed impressive strength (see pages 37–43). The National Center for the Humanities selected the Research Triangle Park for its new home, virtually assuring the continuation of the Raleigh-Durham-Chapel Hill triangle's national leadership in the number of Ph. D.'s per 1,000 population.

Sports. Dean Smith and Leroy Walker coached the medal-winning U. S. basketball and track teams, respectively, in the Olympics; and several North Carolinians won individual awards.

Names in the News. Louis Round Wilson, a distinguished library scholar, celebrated his 100th birthday with the publication of a new book. Edwin Gill, cultural leader and longtime state treasurer, announced his retirement; but Thad Eure, who was elected secretary of state in 1936 on the slogan, "Give a young man a chance," at the age of 77 put down the challenge of youthful contenders.

Terry Sanford, former governor, giving up his bid for the national presidency, returned to his job as head of Duke University. Ruby Murchison of Fayetteville was named "National Teacher of the Year." Gen. William C. Lee, "father of the airborne forces," was memorialized by a statue in his hometown, Dunn.

H. G. JONES
University of North Carolina

— NORTH CAROLINA · Information Highlights —

Area: 52,586 square miles (136,198 km²).
Population (1975 est.): 5,451,000.
Chief Cities (1970 census): Raleigh, the capital, 123,-793; Charlotte, 241,178; Greensboro, 144,076.
Government (1976): *Chief Officers*—governor, James E. Holshouser, Jr. (R); lt. gov., James B. Hunt, Jr. (D). *General Assembly*—Senate, 50 members; House of Representatives, 120 members.
Education (1975–76): *Enrollment*—public elementary schools, 817,537 pupils; public secondary, 367,459; nonpublic (1976–77), 56,800; colleges and universities, 187,155 students. *Public school expenditures,* $1,221,579,000 ($1,044 per pupil).
State Finances (fiscal year 1975): *Revenues,* $3,604,-808,000; *expenditures* $3,562,338,000.
Personal Income (1975): $26,995,000,000; per capita, $4,952.
Labor Force (July 1976): *Nonagricultural wage and salary earners,* 1,948,300; *insured unemployed,* 62,800 (3.8%).

NORTH DAKOTA

The major concerns in North Dakota in 1976 were politics, farm prices, and drought.

Politics. Democrats and Republicans each elected 50 members of the state House of Representatives and Democrats reduced the Republican Senate majority.

Voters supported President Ford in the November election. They also reelected U. S. Sen. Quentin Burdick, Gov. Arthur Link, and Lt. Gov. Wayne Sanstead—all Democrats—and Republican Congressman Mark Andrews. Three Republican and four Democratic incumbent state officers were reelected and two other Democrats were chosen to head state agencies.

North Dakotans approved constitutional amendments to ease the ban on gambling for charity by religious, fraternal, and patriotic organizations; extend the legislative term; revamp the judicial system; lower the qualifying age for legislators; and restructure the Board of Higher Education. They approved an initiated measure to cut the sales tax but rejected another to limit general fund spending.

Agriculture. North Dakota farmers planted and harvested a record wheat crop but reaped little profit from it. Distressed by falling farm prices, wheat growers organized. They first attempted an unsuccessful holding action, then toyed briefly with seeding cutbacks. Later they decided on fence-line to fence-line planting and seeded 11.9 million acres (4.8 million ha). Finally they formed a statewide marketing pool and pledged a portion of the record 293.9 million bushel (102.9 million hl) harvest for export.

The growing season was the state's driest in 50 years. All agricultural production was spotty, but rain fell at the right time in some heavily planted areas and resulted in a record sugar-beet harvest. Grain production fell below average. Fifteen of the state's best agricultural counties rated drought disaster tags.

Weather. Drought was not the only weather problem. Snow, floods, and hail caused widespread hardship and brought disaster area designations to 27 counties. A Mouse River flood

forced evacuation of 12,000 Minot residents and cost the city $2.3 million in property damage. Water covered portions of 9 counties.

Environment. Controversy continued over the environmental impact of the Garrison Diversion. Congress approved construction funding for the irrigation project and received a favorable report on return flow water quality. The International Joint Commission held hearings in North Dakota on possible pollution of Canadian waters from the project. The Audubon Society sued in federal court to halt construction pending further impact studies.

Coal development and use of water for expansion of energy production dominated the political scene. Governor Arthur Link's cautious policy was criticized by his Republican opponent, Richard Elkin, chairman of the Public Service Commission (PSC). The Democratic gains in the state House came from normally Republican coal and cattle areas where the United Plainsmen, an environmental group, put candidates into the field.

The PSC took jurisdiction over the siting of energy producing plants and transmission lines. Landowners protested the route of a power line and forced higher payments for right-of-way easements. But farmers and other foes of the power line told the PSC there would be confrontations in the fields and bitter court struggles over siting.

STAN CANN, *"The Forum," Fargo*

NORTHWEST TERRITORIES

Presentation of native land-claim proposals was the most significant development in the Northwest Territories in 1976.

Land Claims. In February, the Inuit (Eskimo) people presented a detailed proposal to Prime Minister Pierre Elliott Trudeau calling for the creation of a new territory called "Nunavut," in which the Inuit would have political control. The area involved would be basically the part of the present Northwest Territories that is above the tree line. Other highlights of the proposal included: outright Inuit ownership of 250,000 square miles (648,000 km²) of land surface; hunting, fishing, and trapping rights to an additional 500,000 square miles (1,295,000 km²) of land and 800,000 square miles (2,072,000 km²) of ocean; and a fair share of royalties from resources.

In October, the Indian people who refer to themselves as "Dene" presented the federal government with a land-claim statement of principles, which was meant to form the basis for detailed discussions. The statement called for creation in the Mackenzie Valley of a "Dene government" within the Canadian confederation with authority over matters now under the jurisdiction of the territorial or federal government. Other highlights included: Dene ownership of their traditional lands, establishment of

---

—— NORTH DAKOTA • Information Highlights ——

Area: 70,665 square miles (183,022 km²).
Population (1975 est.): 683,000.
Chief Cities (1970 census): Bismarck, the capital, 34,-703; Fargo, 53,365; Grand Forks, 39,008; Minot, 32,-290.
Government (1976): *Chief Officers*—governor, Arthur A. Link (D); lt. gov., Wayne G. Sanstead (D). *Legislative Assembly*—Senate, 50 members; House of Representatives, 100 members.
Education (1975–76): *Enrollment*—public elementary schools, 59,829 pupils; public secondary, 71,502; nonpublic (1976–77), 12,400; colleges and universities, 26,641 students. *Public school expenditures,* $153,000,000 ($1,167 per pupil).
State Finances (fiscal year 1975): *Revenues,* $589,826,-000; *expenditures,* $490,614,000.
Personal Income (1975): $3,652,000,000; per capita, $5,737.
Labor Force (July 1976): *Nonagricultural wage and salary earners,* 212,600; *insured unemployed,* 2,700 (1.8%).

—— NORTHWEST TERRITORIES · Information —— Highlights

Area: 1,304,903 square miles (3,379,699 km²).
Population (1976 est.): 40,000.
Chief City (1976 est.): Yellowknife, the capital, 8,500.
Government (1976): *Chief Officer*—commissioner, Stuart M. Hodgson. *Legislature*—Territorial Council, 15 elected members.
Education (Sept. 1976): *Enrollment*—elementary and secondary schools, 12,894 pupils. *Public school expenditures* (1975–76), $37,271,400.
Public Finance (fiscal year 1976–77 est.): *Revenues,* $206,445,300; *expenditures,* $206,445,300.
Mining (1975 est.): *Production value,* $181,787,000.
(All monetary figures are in Canadian dollars).

new federally financed Dene communities where Dene want to move out of predominately white communities, and federal compensation to non-Dene residents who wish to relocate.

Mackenzie Valley Pipeline. In November, Justice Thomas Berger completed his public hearings into the social, environmental, and economic aspects of building a multibillion dollar pipeline through the Mackenzie Valley.

Legislature. Two by-elections were held to fill vacated seats on the 15-member territorial council. In October, a third elected member was authorized for the territory's Executive Committee, which now has three elected members and three public servants. The council voted a budget of over $206 million for 1976.

ROSS M. HARVEY
Assistant Director of Information
Government of the Northwest Territories

NORWAY

Economy. Living standards continued to rise in 1976, and nearly full employment was maintained. The upturn of world business increased demand for several important Norwegian exports, such as metals and fish products. Companies in these industries saw their stocks return to more normal levels during the year. The shipping and shipbuilding industries, on the other hand, faced continued difficulties as a result of the prolonged world shipping slump. As in 1975, tanker shipping was particularly hard hit. Shipyards, though still busy in 1976, had few orders

—— NORWAY · Information Highlights ——

Official Name: Kingdom of Norway.
Location: Northern Europe.
Area: 125,181 square miles (324,219 km²).
Population (1976 est.): 4,000,000.
Chief Cities (1975 est.): Oslo, the capital, 465,000; Bergen, 214,000; Trondheim, 134,000.
Government: *Head of state,* Olav V, king (acceded Sept. 1957). *Head of government,* Odvar Nordli, prime minister (took office Jan. 1976). *Legislature*— Storting: Lagting and Odelsting.
Monetary Unit: Krone (5.26 kroner equal U.S.$1, Oct. 1976).
Gross National Product (1975 est.): $26,330,000,000; *per capita gross national product* (1974): $5,280.
Manufacturing (major products): Metals, pulp and paper, chemicals, ships, fish products.
Major Agricultural Products: Potatoes, barley, apples, pears, dairy products, livestock.
Foreign Trade (1975): *Exports,* $7,207,000,000; *imports,* $9,718,000,000.

beyond 1977. Oil platform building yards also lacked orders.

Offshore oil production rose, and was expected to reach some 103,585,000 barrels (14,-000,000 metric tons) in the year. The gross national product, at constant prices, was forecast to rise by some 5.9% from 1975.

The improving business outlook led the government to adopt more restrictive credit policies to prevent the economy from overheating. The interest rate was increased from 5% to 6%, and lending was curbed. Real incomes were allowed to go on rising, however. In the spring, the government intervened directly in collective bargaining between unions and employers, promising tax concessions and higher food subsidies if workers would accept relatively moderate pay increments. The aim was to give wage earners a 3% average increase over 1975 in real disposable income, while keeping price rises down to 9.2% over the year.

The budget for 1977, presented in October, proposed to continue this interventionist policy. It granted some tax relief to low- and middle-income groups and promised further concessions later, if workers again showed moderation in the spring wage bargaining. The high level of food subsidies was maintained. The government declared that it aimed at securing a 2.5% further increase in wage earners' real disposable income in 1977.

High government spending, coupled with heavy investment in the offshore oil industry, led to a further growth in the payments deficit. It was expected to reach a record $3,480,000,000 in 1976, which would bring Norway's accumulated foreign debt, at the end of the year, to $9,-770,000,000. Borrowing abroad to finance the

In January, Knut Frydenlund was reappointed foreign minister in Norway's new government led by Odvar Nordli.

UPI

During the year, Canatom MHG Heavy Water Ltd., in conjunction with Atomic Energy of Canada Ltd., was rebuilding the Glace Bay, N. S., heavy water plant, the first such operation to be constructed by a Canadian-owned company.

UPI

deficit was not difficult, however, because of the prospect of future oil and gas income.

Oil Industry. Delays were announced in development schedules for the important Frigg gas field and the Statfjord oil-and-gas field. Estimates of development costs also rose steeply. This led to some public debate about the wisdom of borrowing so heavily against future oil revenues. Delays and soaring costs, it was argued, might make the "oil adventure" less lucrative than first believed. A few more exploration licenses were allocated during the year.

Politics. Odvar Nordli became prime minister of the minority Labor government in January, upon the retirement of Trygve Bratteli. Nordli made some cabinet changes but in general continued to follow the moderate, Social-Democratic policies of his predecessor. Opinion polls showed a steady rise in the Labor party's popularity. In the autumn, Norway proclaimed a 200-mile economic zone around the mainland coast, effective Jan. 1, 1977, to protect fisheries and the livelihood of the coastal population.

THOR GJESTER
Editor, "Økonomisk Revy," Oslo

NOVA SCOTIA

Economic problems such as the energy crisis, inflation, rising unemployment, and labor unrest preoccupied Nova Scotians during 1976.

Legislation. The Liberal government enacted 92 bills of 138 proposed. Under an amendment to the Public Utilities Act, the publicly owned Nova Scotia Power Commission was required to have all future rates approved by the provincial Public Utilities Board. The Bridge Commission, under the Halifax-Dartmouth Bridge Commission Act, was authorized to create its own bonds and debentures for meeting future financial needs. The Rent Review Act established a commission with powers to review all rents and to protect tenants. Finally, an agreement between the provincial and federal governments brought all wage-and-price increases in the province under the jurisdiction of the Anti-Inflation Board in Ottawa.

Energy Crisis. Nova Scotians are facing a dramatic increase in their power bills. The power corporation has applied to the Public Utilities Board for rate hikes which, if approved, will boost domestic bills by as much as 65%. The province, meanwhile, has been unsuccessful in negotiating with the federal government for a power subsidy to keep power rates low. The power corporation has been exploring alternative sources of fuel.

Economy. Economic indicators in 1976 suggested that the provincial economy was recovering. Capital spending by business, government, and households was up by $1,000,000,000—a 19% increase over 1975. Housing starts touched a new high of 7,000. Although farm output increased only slightly, the farming community enjoyed gains in income. The manufacturing sector, despite strikes, remained strong; its factory shipments were up by 13% from 1975. And both exports and retail sales surged ahead. In spite of this, the provincial unemployment rate remained higher than the national average. The system was simply inadequate to cope with increases in the labor force, which averaged nearly 1,200 persons per month.

R. P. SETH
Mount St. Vincent University, Halifax

CHOU EN-LAI

Premier of the People's Republic of China: b. Kiangsu, China, 1898; d. Peking, January 8, 1976.

Chou En-lai was not only the most brilliant and, next to Mao Tse-tung, the most prestigious figure in the history of the Chinese Communist movement but also the most successful statesman in China, and perhaps in the world, during the 20th century.

Early Life. Chou was born into a well-to-do family of the gentry, whose ancestral home was in Chekiang province. During his student days in Shanghai, Shenyang (Mukden), Tientsin, and Tokyo, he was exposed to the major political trends then agitating the West and Japan. Like many other young Chinese, he became politically active at the time of the nationalist May Fourth Movement of 1919. Also like many others, he went to France in 1920 for study.

Rise in the Chinese Communist Party. While in France, Chou became a Marxist and joined the infant Chinese Communist Party (CCP). After his return to China in 1924, his intellectual and political brilliance, his magnetic personality, and his administrative ability soon brought him high office in the CCP, which at that time was allied with Chiang Kai-shek's Kuomintang (Chinese Nationalist Party). Chou specialized in the political aspect of military affairs.

After the bloody break between the CCP and the Kuomintang (1927), Chou, with his surviving colleagues, launched a revolutionary struggle against the Nationalists. He took a prominent part in the famous Long March in 1934–35, at which time he reconciled himself to Mao Tse-tung's leadership of the party. After that, the two men, whose personalities were markedly different and yet strangely complementary, worked together in harmony and mutual respect, at least to outward appearances.

During the Sino-Japanese War (1937–45), when the CCP again, to some degree, worked with the Kuomintang, Chou devoted himself to external relations and spent most of his time dealing very effectively with the Kuomintang and with American representatives in China.

Premier. From the time the Communists won a final victory in 1949 until his death, Chou served as premier of the People's Republic of China (PRC) and also, until 1958, as its foreign minister. Obviously, he deserves much of the credit for the regime's achievements in restoring order after a long period of warfare, launching a program of planned economic development, and establishing an important place for the PRC in the international community. He performed brilliantly in a diplomatic role at the Geneva Conference on Indochina (1954), the Asian-African Conference at Bandung (Java, 1955), and in negotiations with foreign leaders.

HENRI BUREAU, SYGMA

CHOU EN-LAI (1898–1976)
China's most successful statesman

The Cultural Revolution. In spite of the apparent closeness of their relationship, Chou was more moderate and pragmatic than the relatively radical Mao. Chou's finest hour came when Mao, for a variety of ideological and political reasons, launched his Cultural Revolution in 1965–66, one of whose main results was the disruption of the CCP's party apparatus and of Chou's governmental bureaucracy as instruments of political and administrative control over the country. Under very difficult conditions, Chou managed to avoid a break with Mao, while helping to stave off the chaos threatened by Mao's unruly Red Guards (organized radical students).

Last Years. After the end of the Cultural Revolution (1968–69), Chou played a leading role in restoring political and administrative stability to the country, reviving normal foreign relations, and facilitating a rapprochement with the United States. Following the death in 1971 of Defense Minister Lin Piao, for five years previously Mao's heir apparent, Chou ranked second only to Mao in the CCP. Whether he hoped to succeed Mao is not, and cannot be, known. He died after a year and a half of comparative inactivity because of illness, and was survived by his only wife, Teng Ying-ch'ao. Chou's memory is cherished by politically moderate Chinese, thousands of whom staged a unique demonstration in his memory in Peking on April 5, 1976.

HAROLD C. HINTON

[1] Arranged chronologically by death date

ROBESON, Paul Bustill

Singer, actor, political activist: b. Princeton, N. J., April 9, 1898; d. Philadelphia, Jan. 23, 1976.

Paul Robeson, renowned baritone, acclaimed Shakespearean actor, and controversial political activist, was one of the most famous Americans of his time and, toward the end of his career, one of the most tragic victims of a brief American hysteria called McCarthyism.

Born the son of a runaway slave, Robeson, as a member of the class of 1919 at Rutgers College (now university), earned a Phi Beta Kappa key and 15 varsity letters in four sports.

Singer and Actor. After graduation from Rutgers, Robeson moved to Harlem and enrolled in Columbia University Law School. At Columbia he met and fell in love with Eslanda Cardozo Goode, a brilliant chemistry student. At Eslanda's insistence he auditioned for and won a role in a YMCA production of *Simon the Cyrenian* in 1920. The YMCA role was a springboard into playwright Eugene O'Neill's Provincetown Players, a Greenwich Village group. In the next few years Robeson was hailed for his performances in O'Neill's *All God's Chillun Got Wings* and *Emperor Jones*. In 1921, Paul and Eslanda were married. She became and remained his manager until her death in 1965.

In 1925, Robeson gave his first formal concert, a program of Negro spirituals arranged by his lifelong accompanist Lawrence Brown, and found himself in demand as a singer as well as an actor. From the stages of New York's Broadway he moved to the theaters of London and the recital halls of Europe. In the role of Joe in Jerome Kern's *Showboat* in 1928, Robeson stunned London audiences with his rendition of "Ol' Man River," written for him by Kern. Robeson was identified with the song.

In 1930, Robeson played Othello opposite Sybil Thorndike's Desdemona to overwhelming acclaim in London. He went on to recreate his triumphant portrayal of Shakespeare's tragic Moor many times on both sides of the Atlantic. The moody giant's Shakespearean career reached its zenith in the 1943–44 season on Broadway, where, for a record (for Shakespeare on Broadway) 295 performances he starred opposite Uta Hagen.

In addition to his concert and theater bookings during these years, Robeson made 11 films, but abandoned the medium in the 1930's in protest of Hollywood's stereotyping of blacks.

Politics and Controversy. Because he found the racial climate of Europe more comfortable than that of the United States, Robeson made London his home from 1927 to 1939. He became a student of what he called "scientific socialism" and, after visits to the U. S. S. R., an outspoken defender of Soviet socialism.

PAUL ROBESON (1898–1976)
Magnificent artist

Back in the United States during and just after World War II, Robeson became a staunch supporter of organized labor and gave many concerts for the benefit of individual unions. Some of the organizations he supported were branded "Communist fronts" by Congressional investigators. As the Cold War intensified, Robeson was called before the House Committee on Un-American Activities. Asked if he was a member of the Communist Party, Robeson consistently refused to answer on fifth amendment grounds. Just as consistently, however, he privately denied being a Communist.

Even so, Robeson began to find U. S. concert hall doors closed to him. In 1950, European bookings, too, were put out of reach when the State Department revoked his passport because he refused to swear he was not a Communist. His politics, Robeson maintained, were nobody's business but his own. Blacklisted at home and unable to travel abroad, Robeson saw his income dwindle to less than $3,000 a year in the 1950's.

Robeson's passport was restored in 1958 when the U. S. Supreme Court ruled on a similar case, but his arteriosclerosis had by then advanced to the point that Robeson could make only a few more concert tours. He retired in 1961. Following his wife's death in 1965, the great baritone lived with his sister in Philadelphia until his death. He was survived by his son, Paul Jr.

CARLYLE C. DOUGLAS

1936

1952   1947   PHOTOS UPI

HOWARD HUGHES (1905–1976)
America's wealthiest recluse

HUGHES, Howard

American entrepreneur, industrialist, aviator, and motion picture producer: b. Houston, Tex., Dec. 24, 1905; d. en route from Acapulco, Mexico to Houston, Tex., Apr. 5, 1976.

Howard Hughes was one of the world's wealthiest men and also one of the most enigmatic. At his death he controlled an empire valued at $1,500,000,000 or more, including industrial enterprises, mining operations, hotels and casinos, landholdings, an airline, a television network, and an architectural engineering company.

Early Years. Howard Robard Hughes, Jr. was the only child of Howard Robard Hughes, a lawyer turned mining engineer, who developed important oil-well drilling equipment and founded the Hughes Tool Company in 1909. His mother, Alene (Gano) Hughes, died when he was 16. At school, Hughes was an indifferent scholar but demonstrated a remarkable mechanical aptitude. He later took courses at the Rice Institute in Houston and the California Institute of Technology but never earned a college degree. After his father's death in 1924, Hughes persuaded a Texas court to declare him of age and assumed control of the Hughes Tool Company. Eventually he parlayed the $750,000 family business into the multimillion-dollar Hughes Aircraft Company.

Motion Picture Producer. In the late 1920's, Hughes went to Hollywood where, after an initial failure, he scored a hit with the aviation film *Hell's Angels* (1930). Written, produced, and directed by Hughes, the film starred Jean Harlow, whom he had discoverd. By the early 1930's, Hughes had made about a dozen movies, including *Scarface,* starring Paul Muni, and *The Front Page,* with Pat O'Brien. His *The Outlaw,* featuring newcomer Jane Russell, became a success after some initial censorship problems in the early 1940's.

For a time Hughes owned the RKO Corporation outright, but he sold it in 1955. Among the Hollywood stars romantically linked with Hughes over the years were Katharine Hepburn, Olivia De Havilland, Lana Turner, Ida Lupino, Ava Gardner, and Ginger Rogers.

Aviator and Aircraft Designer. Hughes established a land speed record of 352 miles (566 km) per hour in 1935, flying his own H-1 racer. The following year he set a transcontinental record, and in 1938 he established a 91-hour record for a round-the-world flight, earning a Congressional medal. While test-piloting, Hughes experienced several close calls. During World War II he was involved in the development of the P-38 Lightning, the Lockheed Constellation, and improved machine guns for the B-17. But his "Spruce Goose," a huge troop transport plane made of plywood, proved to be impractical.

Later Activities. After World War II, Hughes Aircraft expanded its production to include missiles, lasers, and communications satellites. In 1954, Hughes relinquished his personal ownership of the company to the Howard Hughes Medical Institute, a nonprofit research organization. Among his profitable ventures was his development of Trans World Airlines, but litigation over its control caused him to sell his 78% interest for $566 million in 1966. Later that year he moved to Las Vegas, where he bought a multimillion dollar complex of properties. In 1972 he founded the Las Vegas-based Summa Corporation to oversee his interests.

During his last few years, Hughes was in virtually complete seclusion, staying at various times in Las Vegas, Vancouver, London, Managua, the Bahamas, and Acapulco, with only a small group of local attendants. Nevertheless, he continued to make news. In 1972 he was heard on the airwaves exposing author Clifford Irving's "autobiography" of him as a hoax; in 1974, Watergate investigators revealed that he had contributed $100,000 to Richard Nixon through Charles ("BeBe") Rebozo; and in 1975 he was reported to have provided a cover for the construction of the ship *Glomar Explorer,* commissioned by the Central Intelligence Agency to retrieve a sunken Soviet submarine.

Hughes, whose childless marriages to Houston socialite Ella Rice and actress Jean Peters ended in divorce, left no direct heirs.

HENRY S. SLOAN

MAO TSE-TUNG (1893–1976)
He conquered, pacified, and dominated China.

MAO Tse-Tung

Chairman of the Central Committee of the Communist Party of China: b. Shaoshan, Hunan province, Dec. 26, 1893; d. Peking, China, Sept. 9, 1976.

Mao Tse-tung fancied himself as a revolutionary theoretician, and he rose to power on his idea that in China revolution had to have its base in the peasantry, not in the proletariat. But history may, more likely, note him as a Chinese patriot who tried in his way to make his country united, powerful, and secure.

Background. Mao was born in the village of Shaoshan in Hunan province in central China on Dec. 26, 1893. Hard work, unyielding thrift, and a cold business sense had made his father a "rich peasant." These values also alienated his son. In his teens, Mao rebelled against his father and, thereby, against the ancient Confucian tradition of parental authority.

Mao was in school when Sun Yat-sen's nationalist movement overthrew the Manchu Dynasty in 1911. He cut off his pigtail and briefly joined the revolutionary army. After drifting a while, but reading voraciously, he spent five years in the Changsha normal school. In 1918 Mao's friends sent him to Peking. There he became a Marxist.

When the Communist Party of China was formed in Shanghai in 1921, Mao represented Hunan. Two Comintern representatives gave him his first contact with Soviet power. The Russians urged the new party to form a front with the Kuomintang, Sun Yat-sen's party, which was then pro-Soviet. The Russians supported the coalition until 1927 when Chiang Kai-shek turned on the Communists in Shanghai, destroying them or driving them out. Mao, then in Hunan and only a secondary figure in the hierarchy, became the mainspring of the party's survival and of its revolutionary purpose. When Chiang attacked in 1934, Mao led his surviving forces on the epic 6,000-mile (9,600-km) Long March to Yenan. In the isolation of Yenan, Mao developed his political concepts and married for the fourth and last time, Chiang Ching.

The war against Japan made the Communists and the Kuomintang allies once again. The United States tried, after World War II, to encourage a coalition government. When the effort failed, it backed Chiang Kai-shek. The Soviet Union also recognized and gave preference to Chiang. Stalin, who had retaken from Chiang the old Russian bases of Port Arthur and Dairen, showed no desire to see Mao win. Yet the Communists gained the support of the people and proclaimed the People's Republic of China in Peking on Oct. 1, 1949. Chiang and the Kuomintang had fled to Taiwan; Mao was party chairman.

Head of State. Mao's relationship with Moscow was not clearly perceived for some time. After a Sino-Soviet friendship treaty was signed in 1950, whatever hope there might have been for an improvement of relations with the United States was destroyed by the Korean War. At home and abroad, Mao appeared to follow a Soviet line. Class struggle was mercilessly pursued but Mao's impatience to reorder society led him into the blunder of the Great Leap Forward, a crash program of do-it-yourself development which utterly disjointed the frail economy.

In 1960 Moscow's sudden rupture of economic relations with China tore away the veneer of Communist solidarity. Mao accused the Soviet Union of following in the footsteps of the czars and seeking hegemony over China as part of a larger imperialism. Numerous incidents on the Sino-Soviet border and a pitched battle on the Ussuri River in 1969 reflected serious tension. Mao and Prime Minister Chou En-lai ordered a massive program of military preparedness, civil defense, and pragmatic economic development. They also moved to end Peking's isolation, taking China's seat in the UN and establishing contact with the United States.

Mao Tse-tung once described himself as "part monkey, part tiger." Others saw the same dichotomy, the romantic dreamer and the ruthless doer. He was a fanatic and a masterful maneuverer, a revolutionary in the deepest sense, whose goal seemed to be the reestablishment, in a new form, of eternal China.

RICHARD C. HOTTELET

UPI

ALEXANDER CALDER (1898–1976)
With Stabiles in Human Form

CALDER, Alexander (Sandy)

American artist: b. Lawnton (now part of Philadelphia), July 22, 1898; d. New York City, Nov. 11, 1976.

Alexander Calder was the most famous American artist of the 20th century. His international renown rests primarily on his two innovations in sculpture, the "mobile" and the "stabile." But his prolific output also included paintings and drawings, lithographs, book illustrations, posters, rugs and tapestries, fountains, jewelry, toys, household implements, stage sets, and decorations for airplanes and racing cars.

Life and Work. Calder's grandfather and father were successful sculptors and his mother was a portrait painter. After graduation from the Stevens Institute of Technology in 1919, he spent four years in various jobs related to mechanical engineering before making his decision to become an artist.

Calder studied painting at the Art Students League in New York and worked as a free-lance illustrator before making his first visit to Paris in 1926. There he created a miniature circus with movable wood and wire animals. The performances Calder gave with these marionettes quickly became the rage and brought him to the attention of leading advanced artists.

A crucial influence in Calder's development was the idea of the Russian Constructivist Naum Gabo that sculpture should abandon static mass and volume in favor of line expressing motion in time and space. Also decisive was a visit to the studio of the abstract painter Piet Mondrian in 1930. Calder was impressed by that master's flat, geometric shapes painted in black, white, and pure primary colors, but declared that he would prefer to see them move.

After making some abstract, manually cranked or motorized constructions, which Marcel Duchamp called "mobiles," Calder began to suspend light pieces of metal and other materials from wire, balancing them so that they were stirred into motion by currents of air. This reliance on natural forces to induce movement, rather than on machines that could be programmed, introduced into these constructions the element of chance. Calder hung some of the air mobiles from ceilings or walls. He provided others with standing bases, whose stability contrasted with the delicate motion of the elements they supported.

The "stabile," so christened by the artist Jean Arp, was Calder's second major invention. Instead of being set on a solid base, a stabile soars upward from the fewest possible points of contact with the ground. In a stabile, the movement inherent in a mobile is replaced by the action of the spectator. Walking around the object, he perceives different relationships between solid elements and the enclosed open spaces.

As his constructions increased in size and weight, Calder came to rely on foundries for their construction. Under his supervision, skilled workmen made enlargements from the models he provided, cutting, bending, and bolting together sheets of heavy metal to produce *tours de force* of engineering virtuosity.

Calder and his wife traveled widely, dividing their residence between Roxbury, Conn., and Saché, near Tours, in France. His work became known worldwide through many exhibitions, publications, and monumental pieces commissioned for modern buildings and public places. With their actual or implied movement and frequent allusions to flora or fauna, his objects seem to have an exuberant life of their own, to which one responds as to something existing in nature. They combine formal invention and technical skill with playfulness and wit.

Similar qualities of integrity, vitality, and humor characterized Calder's personality. At the time of his death, more people than ever before were realizing the scope and quality of his achievement, thanks to a current comprehensive exhibition of his work and a definitive book by Jean Lipman, both bearing the title *Calder's Universe*. The title was taken from one of Calder's frequently quoted statements: "The underlying sense of form in my work has been the system of the Universe, or part thereof. For that is a rather large model to work from."

HELEN M. FRANC, *Coauthor of Bright Stars: American Painting and Sculpture Since 1776*

The following is a selected list of some 170 prominent persons who died in 1976. Articles on major figures appear in the preceding pages.

Aalto, Alvar (78), Finnish architect: b. Kuortane, Finland, Feb. 3, 1898; d. Helsinki, May 11, 1976. One of the masters of modern architecture, he was often described as a humanist in his art, which emphasized man's relationship to nature. He studied in Helsinki where, drawing international attention with his sanitarium at Paimio, Finland, he soon had a thriving practice. He built the Finnish pavilions at the Paris and New York world fairs in 1937 and 1939 and subsequently taught at the Massachusetts Institute of Technology; he returned there in 1946, having spent the war years in Finland. By 1949, when he moved back to his native country, he was an acknowledged world master. His buildings in the United States include the Baker House dormitory at MIT.

Abdul Razak (53), Malaysian prime minister; a guerrilla fighter against the Japanese in World War II and one of the architects of his country's independence from Britain in 1957, he served as deputy prime minister for 13 years before assuming the prime ministry in 1970: d. London, Jan. 14.

Auchincloss, James C. (91), U. S. political figure; a three-term Republican mayor of Rumson, N. J., he won a seat in the U. S. House of Representatives in 1943 and held it until 1964: d. Alexandria, Va., Oct. 2.

Baddeley, Angela (71), English actress; sister of Hermione Baddeley, she achieved international recognition as Mrs. Bridges, the cook in the television series *Upstairs, Downstairs:* d. Essex, England, Feb. 22.

Bachauer, Gina (63), Greek-born pianist; a virtuoso musician who made her home in London, she played in concerts all over the world and was a regular guest performer with the New York Philharmonic orchestra: d. Athens, Greece, Aug. 22.

Bailey, Pearce (73), U. S. neurologist and author; studied with Freud, Jung, and Adler and became the first director of the National Institute of Neurological and Communicative Disorders and Strokes: d. Washington, D. C., June 23.

Baker, Sir Stanley (49), British actor, known for his portrayals of "tough guys" and soldiers of fortune; was knighted in May, 1976: d. Málaga, Spain, June 28.

Ballard, Florence (32), U. S. popular singer; was one of the original members of the Supremes trio that cut eight gold records in two years during the 1960's: d. Detroit, Mich., Feb. 22.

Bankhead, Dan (55), U. S. baseball player; was the first black to pitch in a major league game in 1947: d. Houston, Texas, May 1.

Barrett, William A. (79), U. S. legislator; represented the first district of Pennsylvania as a Democratic congressman from 1945 to 1947 and again from 1948 until his death: d. Philadelphia, Pa., April 12.

Berg, Helene (92), Austrian widow of composer Alban Berg; was generally thought to be the natural daughter of Emperor Franz Joseph: d. Vienna, Aug. 30.

Berkeley, Busby (80), U. S. choreographer; was best known for large, lavish productions in musical films, such as *42d Street, Footlight Parade,* and *Ziegfeld Girl:* d. Palm Desert, Calif., March 14.

Beyen, Johan Willem (78), Dutch banker and diplomat; instrumental in forming the European Coal and Steel Community, he was Dutch foreign minister from 1952 to 1958 and later held ambassadorial posts: d. The Hague, April 29.

Blair, David (43), British dancer and ballet master; a well-known choreographer for the American Ballet Theater, he had been recently designated director of the Norwegian ballet: d. London, April 1.

Bloomgarden, Kermit (71), U. S. theatrical producer; did many distinguished plays, including *Death of a Salesman, The Diary of Anne Frank, Look Homeward, Angel, The Music Man,* and *Equus:* d. New York City, Sept. 20.

Boswell, Connee (68), U. S. entertainer; one of the most celebrated singers on radio during the 1930's and 1940's, she made records that sold a total of 75 million copies; also appeared in movies and Broadway shows: d. New York City, Oct. 11.

Brailowsky, Alexander (80), Russian-born concert pianist: b. Kiev, Ukraine, Feb. 16, 1896; d. New York City, April 25, 1976. Internationally renowned as an interpreter of Chopin, he accomplished the feat of presenting the composer's entire number of piano works—169 in all—in a series of six recitals of consummate artistry. Described by critics as a born virtuoso, he performed his Chopin series for capacity audiences in Paris, Brussels, Zurich, New York, Mexico City, Montevideo, and Buenos Aires. He was a guest soloist with many major symphony orchestras and also made numerous recordings.

Britten of Aldeburgh, Edward Benjamin Britten, Baron (63), British composer: b. Lowestoft, Nov. 22, 1913; d. Aldeburgh, Dec. 4, 1976. Generally regarded as the greatest British composer since Henry Purcell, he is best known for his operas—*Peter Grimes, Owen Windgrave, The Turn of the Screw, A Midsummer Night's Dream, Billy Budd,* and others—and for his *War Requiem.* But he also wrote many smaller, more intimate works, as well as musical scores for documentary and feature films. He was granted a life peerage in June 1976.

Browning, Gordon (86), U. S. political figure; was congressman from Tennessee for six terms (1923–35) and governor of Tennessee for three (1937–39 and 1949–53): d. Huntingdon, Tenn., May 23.

Burnett, Chester Arthur ("Howlin' Wolf") (65), U. S. blues singer, guitarist, and harmonica player; the principal exponent of the Delta tradition, he influenced such later rock singers as Mick Jagger and the Rolling Stones: d. Chicago, Ill., Jan. 10.

Byrne, Donald (45), U. S. chess master; won the U. S. Open Championship in 1953 and was captain of the U. S. team at the 1966 and 1972 Chess Olympics in Havana: d. Philadelphia, Pa., April 8.

Cambridge, Godfrey (43), U. S. actor; a comedian and sometime civil rights activist, he starred in such movies as *Cotton Comes to Harlem* and *Watermelon Man* and on stage in Jean Genet's *The Blacks* and Ossie Davis's *Purlie Victorious:* d. Burbank, Calif., Nov. 29.

Casey, Richard Gardiner, Baron of Berwick (85), former governor general of Australia (1965–69); was member of the British War Cabinet during World War II and also served as Australia's first ambassador to the United States; held post of Australian minister of external affairs from 1951 to 1960 and was made life peer in 1960: d. Melbourne, Australia, June 17.

Cassin, René (88), French jurist and peace advocate: b. Bayonne, Oct. 5, 1887; d. Paris, Feb. 20, 1976. One of the foremost protagonists of peace and human rights since the end of World War I, he was awarded the Nobel Prize for Peace in 1968. He was the principal author of the Human Rights Declaration adopted by the United Nations and headed its Human Rights Commission. He was also one of the founders of UNESCO, a prominent campaigner for Jewish rights, and an ertswhile president of the European Court of Human Rights.

Alvar Aalto

Florence Ballard

Benjamin Britten

Godfrey Cambridge

PHOTOS UPI

Chu Teh   Lee J. Cobb   Richard J. Daley

Christie, Agatha (85), English mystery writer: b. Torquay, Sept. 15, 1890; d. Wallingford, Jan. 12, 1976. Probably the most widely read mystery writer of all time, she was the author of more than 100 books, with sales in excess of 100 million, and the creator of two of the most distinctive sleuths in detective literature—Hercule Poirot and Jane Marple. The virtues of her books lie in adroit plotting and sound characterization; some, such as *The Murder of Roger Ackroyd* (1926), rank among the classics of the genre. Dramatized, some of her yarns virtually acquired a life of their own. *The Mousetrap,* first shown on a London stage in 1952, is still running. She also wrote the autobiographical *Come Tell Me How You Live,* describing expedition life with her archeologist husband, Sir Max Mallowan.

Chu Teh (89), Chinese military leader: b. Ilung, Szechwan, Dec. 18, 1886; d. Peking, July 6, 1976. One of the great soldiers of history, he led the Chinese Red Army through three decisive stages: the Long March of 1934–35, the resistance to the Japanese, 1937–38, and the defeat of Chiang Kai-shek's Nationalist forces in 1948–49. A graduate of the Yunnan Military Academy, he was converted to Communism by Chou En-lai, and from 1928 on, when he joined his forces with those of Mao Tse-tung, he commanded the Red Army. After the Communist victory in 1949, he was named deputy chairman of the republic. Later, as chairman of the Standing Committee of the National People's Congress, he was the ceremonial head of state.

Cobb, Lee J. (64), U. S. stage and screen actor: b. New York City, Dec. 9, 1911; d. Los Angeles, Calif., Feb. 11, 1976. An actor of commanding presence, he was best known on stage as creator of the part of Willy Loman in Arthur Miller's *Death of a Salesman* and on the screen as the corrupt union chief in *On the Waterfront.* In the 1930's he was associated with the Group Theater in New York, where he appeared in such Clifford Odets plays as *Waiting for Lefty, Golden Boy,* and *Till the Day I Die.*

Combs, Earle (77), U. S. baseball player; a 12-season "Murderers' Row" New York Yankee (1924–35), he was elected to the baseball Hall of Fame in 1970: d. Richmond, Ky., July 21.

Costello, John A. (84), former Irish prime minister; a onetime attorney general of Ireland, he later led the Fine Gael party and headed the first Irish coalition government from 1948 to 1951; returned to office in 1954, serving until 1957: d. Dublin, Jan. 5.

Crawford, John (60), U. S. bridge player; set a series of records still unequaled: 24 victories in the three major national team championships and a total of 37 national titles; in 1957 he held simultaneously all five national titles: d. New York City, Feb. 14.

Cunningham, Imogen (93), U. S. photographer whose career spanned 75 years; was known for the wit and freshness of her pictures: d. San Francisco, June 24.

Curme, George O. (87), U. S. chemist; he was a pioneer in petrochemical research, facilitating the development of entire industries, such as synthetic fibers, plastic, polyesters, and agricultural chemicals: d. Oak Bluffs, Mass., July 28.

Daley, Richard J. (74), mayor of Chicago: b. Chicago, May 15, 1902; d. Chicago, Dec. 20, 1976. The last of the big-city bosses, for nearly a quarter of a century he was the unbeatable political power in Chicago (Cook County) and for any Democratic presidential aspirant a man to reckon with. He rose by hard work through the local Democratic organization, spent ten years in the Illinois state legislature (Assembly and Senate), and in 1953 became Cook County Democratic chairman. Two years later he was elected mayor of Chicago, and he jealously guarded both positions thereafter. While his grip was somewhat loosened after the unruly Democratic national convention in Chicago in 1968, he was still probably the single most powerful political leader in the country outside the White House.

Dam, (Carl Peter) Henrik (81), Danish biochemist: b. Copenhagen, Feb. 21, 1895; d. Copenhagen, April 17, 1976. Regarded as one of the world's leading nutritionists, he was awarded the Nobel Prize in physiology and medicine in 1943 for his discovery of vitamin K and its role in the coagulation of blood. He was professor of biochemistry and head of the biology department of the Polytechnic Institute in Copenhagen.

Davis, Meyer (81), U. S. band leader; a sought-after conductor at society gatherings, whose personal appearances were frequently booked many years in advance, he simultaneously presided over a musical empire that had as many as 80 bands, employing more than 1,000 musicians, on its payroll: d. New York City, April 5.

de Hory, Elmer (65), Hungarian painter, notorious as a master forger of French modern artists: d. Ibiza, Spain, Dec. 11.

Dennis, Patrick (55), U. S. novelist; was best known for his *Auntie Mame,* which was dramatized as a Broadway play and a movie, both starring Rosalind Russell (see below), and later as a Broadway musical: d. New York City, Nov. 6.

Dennison, David M. (75), U. S. theoretical physicist; discovered the spin of the proton, important to the understanding of molecular and nuclear structure: d. Ann Arbor, Mich., April 3.

Deschler, Lewis (71), retired parliamentarian of the U. S. House of Representatives; held the post for 46 years during which he was a powerful influence on some historic decisions: d. Bethesda, Md., July 12.

Dixon, Dean (61), U. S. conductor; the first black to lead the New York Philharmonic, he left the United States in 1949 to earn a reputation in Europe: d. Zurich, Switzerland, Nov. 4.

Döpfner, Julius (62), German cardinal; was archbishop of Berlin from 1957 to 1961, during which time he campaigned for religious freedom in East Germany; became cardinal at 45 in 1958 and was archbishop of Munich-Preising after 1961: d. Munich, Germany, July 24.

Douglas, Paul H. (84), three-term U. S. senator from Illinois; gained national reputation as an economist in 1930 with his book on *Real Wages in the United States,* followed four years later by *The Theory of Wages;* won a Senate seat in 1948 and became noted for his liberal views and his championship of civil rights: d. Washington, D. C., Sept. 24.

Dowling, Eddie (81), U. S. actor, director, and producer: b. Woonsocket, R. I., Dec. 9, 1894; d. Smithfield, R. I., Feb. 18, 1976. A versatile, energetic man whose accomplishments ranged from dancing in the Ziegfeld *Follies* to direction of Shakespearean drama, he was a force on Broadway for 40 years. Among the four of his productions that won the Drama Critics Circle Award was Tennessee Williams' *The Glass Menagerie* (1945), of which he also was co-director and creator of the part of the son-narrator. He was the original director of Eugene O'Neill's *The Iceman Cometh* in 1946.

Dushkin, Samuel (82), U. S. violinist who studied under Fritz Kreisler and Leopold Auer and was a frequent introducer of new works by Ravel, Prokofiev, and Stravinsky: d. New York City, June 24.

Dykes, James J. ("Jimmy") (79), U. S. athlete; was a major league baseball player and manager for 50 years and became known for his barbed wit, directed especially at umpires: d. Philadelphia, Pa., June 15.

Elazar, David (50), Israeli general; a hero of earlier wars, he commanded the Israeli forces during the Yom Kippur war of 1973 and was officially blamed for the country's unpreparedness: d. Tel Aviv, April 15.

Ernst, Max (85), German-born artist: b. Brühl, near Cologne, April 2, 1891; d. Paris, April 1, 1976. Having taught himself to paint while studying at the University of Bonn, he showed his work in the First German Autumn Salon in Berlin in 1913, where two of his co-exhibitors were Paul Klee and Marc Chagall. He served in the German army throughout World War I without receiving a scratch and managed to go on painting, too. After the war he joined the Dada movement in Cologne, later moving to Paris where he kept company with Surrealists. Condemned by the Nazis in the early 1930's, he fled France for America during World War II, settling in Arizona; he returned to Europe some years after the war. He was a provocative figure in 20th-century art, and his works may be found in all major museums on both sides of the Atlantic.

Ernst, Morris L. (87), U. S. lawyer; argued the case that in 1933 won publication rights in the United States for James Joyce's *Ulysses;* was long associated with struggle for literary and artistic freedom and a long-time counsel of the American Civil Liberties Union; a special counsel to the War Production Board during World War II, he also served on President Truman's Civil Rights Commission: d. New York City, May 21.

Evans, Dame Edith (88), British actress: b. London, Feb. 8, 1888; d. Cranbrook, Kent, Oct. 14, 1976. A legend of the English theater in her own lifetime, she was widely regarded as one of the two greatest actresses this century has known, the other being Dame Sybil Thorndike (see below). Though enormously versatile, she was perhaps most at home in the comedies of Shaw, Wilde, and the Restoration period. She also acted in many movies, and in 1968, at the age of 80, she captured all the acting awards for her old, friendless woman in *The Whisperers.* She was made Dame Commander of the Order of the British Empire in 1946.

Faith, Percy (67), Canadian-born U. S. conductor; a popular arranger and conductor on a succession of radio shows during the 1950's, he also wrote scores for Hollywood movies, winning an Academy Award nomination in 1955 for *Love Me or Leave Me:* d. Los Angeles, Calif., Feb. 9.

Farley, James A. (88), U. S. political figure: b. Grassy Point, N. Y., May 30, 1888; d. New York City, June 9, 1976. He was the strategist behind Franklin D. Roosevelt's election victories in 1932 and 1936. Having risen through the New York Democratic organization, he became chairman of the party's state committee in 1930 and the national committee in 1932. He was postmaster general in the first and second Roosevelt administrations, but resigned in 1940 over the issue of the president's third-term candidacy. He was the author of *Behind the Ballots* (1938) and *Jim Farley's Story* (1948).

Feather, Victor (68), British labor leader; a union negotiator for 40 years, he was general secretary of the Trades Union Congress from 1969 to 1973, and under him the labor movement became perhaps the most powerful estate in England: d. London, July 28.

Fierlinger, Zdenek (85), Czechoslovakian statesman; a prominent diplomat between the wars, he was the first post-World War II premier of Czechoslovakia under President Benes, but was later said to have engineered the Communist coup of 1948; became president of the National Assembly and a member of the Communist party Politburo and Presidium: d. Prague, May 2.

Folsom, Marion B. (82), U. S. businessman and cabinet officer: was the chief architect of the Social Security Act of 1935 and later served as undersecretary of the treasury (1953–55) and secretary of health, education, and welfare (1955–58); was associated with the Eastman Kodak Company from 1914 to 1969: d. Rochester, N. Y., Sept. 28.

Ford, Paul (74), U. S. stage and screen actor; won fame on Broadway as Colonel Purdy in John Patrick's *The Teahouse of the August Moon,* a role he later repeated for film and television. He also did a five-year stint on television as Colonel Hall in the *Sgt. Bilko* series: d. Mineola, N. Y., April 12.

Franklin, Sidney (72), U. S. bullfighter; began his career in Mexico in 1923 and was at his peak in the early 1930's, when he drew capacity crowds on both sides of the Atlantic; later operated a shop near Seville, Spain; wrote *The Bullfighter from Brooklyn* (1952), an autobiography: d. New York City, April 26.

Fuchida, Mitsuo (73), Japanese naval commander; led the attack on Pearl Harbor in 1941: d. Kashiwara, May 30.

Gabin, Jean (72), French film actor, equally known for his roles as gangster and detective, hobo and tycoon; among his many films were *Grand Illusion, The Human Beast, Les Misérables,* and *The Room Upstairs:* d. Neuilly, France, Nov. 15.

Gabrielson, Guy (84), U. S. political figure; was member of the New Jersey Assembly from 1925 to 1929 and Speaker of the House in 1929; served as chairman of the Republican National Committee from 1949 to 1952: d. Point Pleasant, N. J., May 1.

Gallico, Paul (78), U. S. writer; a one-time sports editor at the New York *Daily News,* he later wrote popular juvenile and adult novels, among which *The Snow Goose* and *The Poseidon Adventure* are the best known: d. Monaco, July 15.

Gambino, Carlo (74), reputed head of the largest, richest, and strongest Mafia "family" in the United States: d. Massapequa, N. Y., Oct. 15.

Geiger-Torel, Herman (69), German-born Canadian opera director; helped form the Canadian Opera Company in 1950, acting as stage director and producer; was general director of the opera from 1959 to 1976: d. Toronto, Oct. 6.

Getty, J. Paul (83), U. S. billionaire: b. Minneapolis, Minn., Dec. 15, 1892; d. Sutton Place, near London, England, June 6, 1976. Perhaps the world's richest private citizen, he made his first million at the age of 24 and later amassed a fortune of billions, mostly in oil. Besides being an entrepreneurial genius, he was an art collector of note who wrote *The Joys of Collecting* (1965). He was fluent in several modern languages and could read Latin and ancient Greek with relative ease. His influence, through his control of some 200 international business firms, was world-wide.

Ginsberg, Louis (80), U. S. poet and teacher; the father of poet Allen Ginsberg, he frequently appeared at poetry readings with his more famous son: d. Paterson, N. J., July 8.

Gordon, Kermit (59), U. S. economist and president of the Brookings Institution; a former Rhodes scholar and professor of economics at Williams College, he served as director of the U. S. Bureau of the Budget (1962–65) and in many other governmental capacities: d. Washington, D. C., June 21.

Jimmy Dykes

Max Ernst

Edith Evans

James A. Farley

PHOTOS UPI

Goulart, João (58), former president of Brazil; vice president from 1955, he was thrown into the presidency by the sudden resignation of Jânio Quadros in 1961 and out of it by a not so sudden military coup in 1964; he thereafter lived in exile: d. northern Argentina, Dec. 6.

Graham, Benjamin (82), London-born U. S. author and financier; generally regarded as the father of modern securities analysis, whose investments made him a millionaire before he was 35, he co-authored *Security Analysis* (with David L. Dodd, 1934), now a standard text in business schools and universities; he also wrote *The Intelligent Investor* (1949): d. Aix-en-Provence, France, Sept. 21.

Grechko, Andrei Antonovich (72), Soviet minister of defense: b. Golodayevka (now Kuibyshevo), Russia, Oct. 17, 1903; d. Moscow, April 26, 1976. A professional soldier since the age of 16, he was credited with the modernization of the Soviet armed forces, vamping them into a war machine of comparable efficiency to that of the United States. During World War II he distinguished himself in the defense of the Caucasus. He was appointed defense minister in 1967.

Gurevich, Mikhail I. (84), Soviet aircraft designer and mathematician; teamed up with Artem I. Mikoyan to design the MiG series of fighter planes: d. Nov. 21.

Hackett, Robert Leo ("Bobby") (61), U. S. musician; primarily known as a cornetist, he was described as an "extremely successful alloy of Beiderbecke and Armstrong" because of his mellow tone and graceful style: d. West Chatham, Mass., June 7.

Haddow, Sir Alexander (69), Scottish physician; was one of Britain's foremost cancer experts; demonstrated conclusively that chemicals can cause cancer and pioneered treatment of the disease with drugs: d. Amersham, England, Jan. 21.

Haig-Brown, Roderick L. (68), Canadian writer and environmentalist; he was the author of *Return to the River, A River Never Sleeps,* and more than 20 other books, mostly dealing with the outdoors: d. Campbell River, British Columbia, Oct. 9.

Harbage, Alfred (74), U. S. educator; considered among the most eminent American Shakespeare scholars, he authored *Conceptions of Shakespeare* and other studies of the poet and his time: d. Philadelphia, Pa., May 2.

Hart, Philip A. (64), U. S. senator from Michigan since 1959; b. Bryn Mawr, Pa., Dec. 10, 1912; d. Washington, D. C., Dec. 26, 1976. Often called "the conscience of the Senate" for the unwavering principle, courage, and honesty with which he discharged both his personal and official duties, he was a leading sponsor of most civil rights, consumer, and antitrust bills since the early 1960's.

Hastie, William (71), U. S. public official; served as governor of the Virgin Islands from 1946 to 1949; named to the U. S. Court of Appeals for the Third Circuit in 1949, the first black to attain a legal post of that rank, and served to 1971: d. East Norriton, Pa., April 14.

Heidegger, Martin (86), German philosopher: b. Messkirch, Baden, Sept. 26, 1889; d. Messkirch, May 26, 1976. Probably the most influential thinker of the 20th century, he was generally identified with existentialism, although he himself did not consider it his philosophy. He studied at Freiburg under Edmund Husserl whom he lated succeeded. In 1933, after the Nazis came to power, he accepted the post as rector of Freiburg, and he openly identified with the party until 1935. His major philosophical work was *Sein und Zeit* ("Being and Time"), published in 1927, but his ideas transcended the confines of philosophy, influencing scientific and scholarly endeavors ranging from physics to literary criticism.

Heinemann, Gustav (76), West German political figure; an early opponent of Nazism, he served as Social Democratic minister of justice in the "grand coalition" government of 1966–69, introducing far-reaching legal reforms; elected president of West Germany in 1969, he held office until 1974: d. Essen, July 6.

Heisenberg, Werner (74), German nuclear physicist: b. Würzburg, Dec. 5, 1901; d. Munich, Feb. 1, 1976. One of the century's foremost physicists, who received a Nobel Prize at the age of 31, he was the formulator of the indeterminacy principle, which maintains that the position and momentum of a subatomic particle cannot be precisely determined at the same time. He was prominent among those who, after World War II, pointed out the dangers of nuclear weapons.

Hoijer, Harry (71), U. S. linguist and anthropologist; was president of the American Anthropological Association (1958) and the Linguistic Society of America (1959); authored *Studies in Athapascan Languages* (1963) and *Introduction to Anthropology* (with Ralph Beals, 1965): d. Santa Monica, Calif., March 4.

Howe, James Wong (76), Chinese-born U. S. cinematographer; a pioneer and perfector of his craft, he was nominated for Academy Awards 16 times and won two Oscars, for *The Rose Tattoo* (1955) and *Hud* (1962): d. Hollywood, Calif., July 12.

Hubbard, DeHart (72), U. S. athlete; was the first black American to win an Olympic gold medal, for broad jump, in 1924: d. Cleveland, Ohio, June 23.

Hughes, Richard (76), English novelist and dramatist; was best known for *A High Wind in Jamaica* (1929), but also wrote plays and children's books: d. Talsarnau, Wales, April 28.

Ingersoll, Royal E. (92), U. S. admiral; commanded the U. S. Atlantic fleet for three years (1942–44) during World War II and subsequently served in the Pacific: d. Bethesda, Md., May 20.

Jackson, Quentin ("Butter") (67), U. S. trombonist; played with the bands of Cab Calloway, Duke Ellington, and Count Basie: d. New York City, Oct. 2.

Johnson, Malcolm (71), U. S. journalist who won a Pulitzer Prize in 1949 for his exposure of terrorism and racketeering on New York City's waterfront; reported for the New York *Sun* from 1928 to 1950, and later joined a public relations firm: d. Middletown, Conn., June 18.

Kampmann, Viggo (65), former Danish prime minister (1960–62): d. Copenhagen, June 3.

Kempe, Rudolf (65), German conductor; an internationally known musician and director of the Zurich Tonhalle, he was long associated with the London and Munich philharmonic orchestras: d. Zurich, Switzerland, May 11.

Kerner, Otto (67), U. S. public official; was U. S. attorney (1947–54), judge of Cook County (1954–60), governor of Illinois (1961–68), and judge of the U. S. Court of Appeals (appointed 1968); convicted of conspiracy, fraud, perjury, bribery, and income tax evasion (1973), sentenced to three years in prison, and fined $50,000; served seven months: d. Chicago, Ill., May 9.

Prince Knud of Denmark (75), eldest member of the Danish royal house and uncle of Queen Margrethe II: d. Copenhagen, June 14.

Konstanty, Casimer James ("Jim") (59), U. S. baseball player; a right-handed relief specialist, extraordinary with a slider and change-up, he was voted the National League's most valuable player in 1950: d. Oneonta, N. Y., June 11.

Kubitschek, Juscelino (73), former president of Brazil; a surgeon turned politician, he was president from 1956 to 1961 and as such responsible for the building of the new national capital of Brasília: d. (in a car crash) Rio de Janeiro, Aug. 22.

Kuhlman, Kathryn (in her 60's), U. S. popular evangelist; gained wide notoriety as a faith healer, although she disclaimed any such powers, saying their faith in God healed her followers: d. Tulsa, Okla., Feb. 20.

Lackey, Kenneth (74), U. S. vaudeville actor; was best known as one of the original Three Stooges slapstick comedy team: d. Columbia, Ohio, April 16.

Lang, Fritz (85), Austrian-born film director; b. Vienna, Dec. 5, 1890; d. Los Angeles, Calif., Aug. 2, 1976. One of the most notable film makers in Germany during the 1920's and early 1930's, he won fame with such classics as *Dr. Mabuse, the Gambler* (1922), *Metropolis* (1927), and *M* (1931). Loathing Nazism, he left Germany even before Hitler came to power. Going first to France, where he made *Liliom* (1934), he spent most of his remaining years in the United States. The most notable of his U. S.-made films is considered *Fury* (1936), a bold examination of mob violence. His own favorite was *While the City Sleeps* (1956).

Lavon, Pinhas (71), Israeli political figure; was defense minister in 1954 and the central figure in the so-called Lavon affair, a bungled Cairo sabotage operation which stirred the country's political life for years afterward: d. Tel Aviv, Jan. 24.

Lercaro, Giacomo (84), Italian cardinal; a long-time archbishop of Bologna, he was a driving force behind the Vatican's liturgical reforms: d. Bologna, Oct. 18.

Lehmann, Lotte (88), German-born operatic soprano and lieder singer: b. Perleberg, Feb. 27, 1888; d. Santa Barbara, Calif., Aug. 26, 1976. One of the most illustrious singers of the 20th century, she excelled as a Wagnerian soprano, though she was most often identified with the Marschallin in *Der Rosenkavalier*. She was a celebrated performer in Europe for 20 years before she made her American debut at the Chicago Civic Opera in 1930. She sang in every major opera house and under every major conductor in Europe and America. Her tenure with the Metropolitan Opera in New York lasted from 1934 to 1945, but she returned to the opera in 1962 to direct a production of *Der Rosenkavalier.*

Lotte Lehmann	**Margaret Leighton**	**Lin Yutang**	**André Malraux**

Leighton, Margaret (53), British stage and screen actress: b. near Birmingham, Feb. 26, 1922; d. Chichester, Jan. 13, 1976. Twice the winner of the Antoinette Perry (Tony) Award as best actress—for *Separate Tables* (1956) and *The Night of the Iguana* (1962)—she most often portrayed fragile, vulnerable women bruised by life. She was recruited for the Old Vic by Laurence Olivier and Ralph Richardson in 1944 and had her first role on Broadway in 1946. She appeared in 22 films, among them *The Winslow Boy* and *The Constant Husband.*

Leslie, Edgar (90), U. S. lyricist; wrote such popular songs as *Moon Over Miami* and—in collaboration—*For Me and My Gal;* was one of the prime movers in founding the American Society of Composers, Authors, and Publishers: d. New York City, Jan. 22.

Letelier, Orlando (44), Chilean leader of political exiles in the United States; was Chilean ambassador to Washington from 1971 to 1973, when he became foreign minister of the Allende administration; went into exile after the military takeover: d. (by bomb explosion in his car) Washington, D. C., Sept. 21.

Levy, Gustave (66), U. S. investment banker; headed the firm of Goldman, Sachs & Company and was actively involved in numerous civic endeavors; was fund raiser for the Republican party: d. New York City, Nov. 3.

Lhevinne, Rosina (96), Russian-born pianist and teacher: b. Kiev, Ukraine, March 29, 1880; d. Glendale, Calif., Nov. 9, 1976. The widow of renowned pianist Joseph Lhevinne, with whom she often played duos, she taught at the Juilliard School of Music in New York from 1924. She was by many considered the greatest piano teacher of the 20th century.

Lin Yutang (80), Chinese scholar, philosopher, novelist, and translator; resided in the United States from 1936 to 1966, producing a long series of highly regarded and popular books that included *My Country and My People* (1935), *A Leaf in the Storm* (1941), and *The Wisdom of China* (1949): d. Hong Kong, March 26.

Lippisch, Alexander M. (81), German aeronautical engineer; designed the first operational rocket-powered fighter plane, the Messerschmitt 163B; taken to the United States by the U. S. Army Air Force in 1946, he worked for the Air Force and Navy liaison office and in private industry: d. Cedar Rapids, Iowa, Feb. 11.

Lisagor, Peter (61), U. S. journalist; Washington bureau manager of *The Chicago Daily News,* he was one of the nation's best-known and most highly-regarded political commentators; often seen on public television, "Washington Week in Review": d. Arlington, Va., Dec. 10.

Litton, Jerry (39), U. S. representative from Missouri; a millionaire farmer at the end of his second term in Congress, he had just won the Democratic senatorial primary when his plane crashed shortly after take-off, killing his wife, Sharon, and his two children, Linda and Scott, as well: d. near Chillicothe, Mo., Aug. 3.

Lowenfels, Walter (79), U. S. poet and editor; shared the Richard Aldington Poetry Prize with e. e. cummings in 1931; later became editor of the Pennsylvania edition of *The Daily Worker;* convicted under the Smith Act in 1954; compiled 27 volumes of poetry and anthologies: d. Tarrytown, N. Y., July 7.

Lowry, L. S. (88), English painter; earned renown with his primitive canvases of drab industrial scenes and squalid suburbs; was a member of the Royal Academy: d. Glossop, England, Feb. 23.

Lyons, Leonard (original surname **Zucher**) (70), U. S. journalist; wrote "The Lyons Den," a syndicated Broadway gossip column notable for its lack of malice, which appeared in The New York *Post* and dozens of other papers for exactly 40 years (May 20, 1934–May 20, 1974): d. New York City, Oct. 7.

Lysenko, Trofim D. (78), Soviet geneticist; dominated Soviet agricultural sciences during the Stalin era, when he made controversial claims for man-induced hereditary changes in plants; a skilled political infighter, he avoided the status of an outcast even after he was found to be a fraud: d. Nov. 20.

McBride, Mary Margaret (76), U. S. radio personality; was for more than 20 years, beginning in 1934, the favorite five-days-a-week friend of millions of American radio listeners; conducted folksy, homespun-style programs and interviewed numerous famous and not so famous people: d. West Shokun, N. Y., April 7.

Macdonald, Torbert H. (58), U. S. congressman from Massachusetts; an outspoken critic of wealthy politicians "buying elective office," he served 21 years in Congress, where his principal interests were in legislation pertaining to broadcasting and television; was main author of the Federal Election Campaign Act of 1971: d. Bethesda, Md., May 21.

McKelway, Benjamin M. (80), U. S. journalist; a lifelong crusader for freedom of the press, he served the Washington *Star* for 43 years, the last 17 of them as editor in chief: d. Washington, D. C., Aug. 30.

MacLeod, Dame Flora (98), Scottish clan chief; was the only woman to head a clan and often traveled to the United States to meet clan members there: d. near Aberdeen, Scotland, Nov. 5.

MacMillan, H(arvey) R(eginald) (90), Canadian millionaire lumberman and philanthropist; at one time chief forester of British Columbia, he dominated the province's lumber industry for 50 years through his export company, formed after World War I; gave millions to the University of British Columbia and other universities: d. Vancouver, Feb. 9.

Malraux, André (75), French writer and war hero; b. Paris, Nov. 3, 1901; d. Paris, Nov. 23, 1976. A man of universal intellect, whose writings rank among the most distinguished in the French language, he was at the same time as much a man of action as of ideas. Having studied at the Paris School of Oriental Languages, he went to Indochina in 1923, where he eventually became incensed about the French colonial regime. After taking part in the 1927 uprising in China, he burst upon the literary world in 1933 with *Man's Fate,* which won him the Goncourt prize. During the rest of the 1930's he was active in European anti-fascist circles, and in the Spanish civil war he formed and led an air squadron for the Loyalists. As "Colonel Berger," he participated in the French resistance during the Nazi occupation. After the war he began a long association with Gen. Charles de Gaulle, during whose presidency he served as the government's spokesman and minister of culture. Among his other novels are *Man's Hope* (1937) and *The Walnut Trees of Altenburg* (1943). Equally distinguished were his books on the philosophy of art, such as *The Voices of Silence* (1951) and *The Metamorphosis of God* (1957).

Martin, Allie Beth (61), U. S. librarian and educator; served as director of the Tulsa city-county library system since 1963; authored a nation-wide study of public libraries entitled *A Strategy for Public Library Change* (1972); was president of the American Library Association: d. Tulsa, Okla., April 11.

Martinon, Jean (66), French conductor and composer; led the Chicago Symphony from 1963 to 1968 and conducted numerous other orchestras, world-wide; wrote the opera *Hécube,* four symphonies, and many smaller compositions: d. Paris, March 1.

Mauze, Abby Rockefeller (72), U. S. philanthropist; the only daughter of John D. Rockefeller, Jr., and the oldest of his six children, she was active in charitable and philanthropic causes, to which she donated millions of dollars: d. New York City, May 27.

Johnny Mercer   Martha Mitchell   Jacques Monod   Bernard Montgomery   Lily Pons

Meloy, Francis E., Jr. (59), U. S. ambassador to Lebanon; a career diplomat for 30 years, he served in many parts of the world, including Saudi Arabia, South Vietnam, Italy, Dominican Republic, and Guatemala: d. (murdered) Beirut, Lebanon, June 16.

Menshikov, Mikhail A. (73), Soviet diplomat; was ambassador to Washington from 1958 to 1962 and helped bring about a rapprochement in U. S.-Soviet relations: d. Moscow, July 21.

Mercer, John H. ("Johnny") (66), U. S. popular composer and songwriter; a four-time Oscar winner for the lyrics to *On the Atchison, Topeka and Santa Fe* (1946), *In the Cool, Cool, Cool of the Evening* (1951), *Moon River* (1961), and *Days of Wine and Roses* (1962), he also wrote the lyrics to such all-time winners as *Lazybones, That Old Black Magic,* and *Autumn Leaves:* d. Bel Air, Calif., June 25.

Merchant, Livingston T. (72), U. S. diplomat; served as assistant secretary for foreign affairs (1953–56 and 1958–59), ambassador to Canada (1956–58 and 1961–62), and under secretary of state for political affairs (1959–61): d. Washington, D. C., May 15.

Michaux, Lewis (92), U. S. bookseller and black nationalist; ran a bookstore that for 44 years was a Harlem landmark, tirelessly urging black people to discover "the impact of their heritage and of their own distinguished contribution to world civilization": d. New York City, Aug. 25.

Middleton, Troy H. (86), U. S. general and educator; commanded a regiment in World War I and led the VII Corps in the Battle of the Bulge in World War II; later served 11 years as president of Louisiana State University: d. Baton Rouge, La., Oct. 9.

Mielziner, Jo (74), U. S. stage and lighting designer; created sets and lighting for some 300 theatrical productions, including such well-known plays as *Winterset, A Streetcar Named Desire, Death of a Salesman,* and *Cat on a Hot Tin Roof;* co-designed with Eero Saarinen the repertory theater of New York's Lincoln Center for the Performing Arts: d. New York City, March 15.

Mineo, Sal(vatore) (37), U. S. screen actor: a high school drop-out who had his first walk-on role on Broadway at the age of 11, he achieved recognition and an Oscar nomination six years later for his supporting role in *Rebel Without a Cause;* was nominated again in the same category in 1961 for his part in *Exodus:* d. (of stab wound) West Hollywood, Calif., Feb. 12.

Mitchell, Martha (57), estranged wife of former U. S. Attorney General John Mitchell and sometimes outspoken critic of the Nixon administration's shadier dealings: d. New York City, May 31.

Monod, Jacques (66), French biologist; b. Paris, Feb. 9, 1910; d. Cannes, May 31, 1976. Perhaps best known for his uncompromising postulate that "chance alone is at the source of all novelty, all creation in the biosphere," he was the winner, with two co-workers, of the Nobel Prize for medicine and physiology in 1965 for research into the workings of the living cell. He joined the Pasteur Institute as a zoology instructor in 1931 and was named its director in 1971. Active in the French resistance during World War II, he was awarded both the Croix de Guerre and the American Bronze Star.

Montgomery of Alamein, Bernard Law Montgomery, 1st Viscount (88), British field marshal; b. London, Nov. 17, 1887; d. southern England, March 24, 1976. The most famous British soldier of modern times, he was the product of the Royal Military Academy at Sandhurst. He took part as a lieutenant in the battle of Ypres in World War I and won the Distinguished Service Order for courage and leadership. A major general at the outbreak of World War II, he got his outfit out of France through Dunkirk in relatively good shape and was later appointed to command the Eighth Army in Egypt. By his victory over German Gen. Erwin Rommel at El Alamein in late 1942, he turned the tide of the North African war. During and after the invasion of Normandy in 1944 he worked side by side with U. S. generals Eisenhower and Bradley and later served as commander in chief of the British occupation forces in Germany and military governor of the British zone. He was elevated to the peerage in 1946 and later that year made chief of the Imperial General Staff. When Gen. Eisenhower took command of the newly established NATO forces in Europe in 1951, Field Marshal Montgomery became his chief deputy, a post he held until his retirement in 1958. That same year saw the publication of his *Memoirs.*

Morand, Paul (88), French novelist and diplomat; was a member of the Académie Française since 1968: d. Paris, July 23.

Morison, Samuel Eliot (88), U. S. historian and naval officer: b. Boston, Mass., July 9, 1887; d. Boston, May 15, 1976. The undisputed grand old man of American historians, he combined a style of verve and gusto with impeccable scholarship, not only relating history but reliving it. Thus, in preparation for his *Admiral of the Ocean Sea: A Life of Christopher Columbus,* he made four voyages in sailing vessels, crossing and recrossing the Atlantic by routes followed by Columbus; and for *The History of U. S. Naval Operations in World War II* (15 vols.) he obtained a commission as lieutenant commander in the Naval Reserve (from which he retired a rear admiral in 1951), covering practically all the battle areas and naval operations of the war. He was a two-time winner of the Pulitzer Prize—for his life of Columbus in 1943 and for *John Paul Jones: A Sailor's Biography* in 1960.

Morton, Louis (61), U. S. historian and educator; one of the nation's foremost military historians, he was the general editor of the 21-volume series on *Wars and Military Institutions of the United States* and also edited the 11-volume *War in the Pacific: United States Army in World War II:* d. Burlington, Vt., Feb. 12.

Moss, Robert V. (54), U. S. clergyman, president of the United Church of Christ: d. Montclair, N. J., Oct. 25.

Nevers, Ernest A. ("Ernie") (73), U. S. athlete; won two all-American selections as fullback at Stanford University from 1923 to 1925; later played professionally and set an NFL record in 1929 for points scored in one game, running for six touchdowns and kicking four conversions for 40 points; admitted to the football Hall of Fame: d. San Rafael, Calif., May 3.

O'Brien, Henry J. (80), U. S. cleric; was the first Roman Catholic archbishop of Hartford, serving from 1953 to 1968: d. Hartford, Conn., July 23.

Ochs, Phil (35), U. S. folk singer and lyricist; gained reputation during the 1960's as the "troubadour of the new left," and his song *I Ain't Marching Anymore* (1963) was one of the first to protest the Vietnam War; also provided lyrics to other folk singers of the peace movement, such as Joan Baez and Bob Dylan: d. (suicide) Queens, N. Y., April 9.

Onsager, Lars (72), Norwegian-born U. S. chemist: b. Oslo, Nov. 27, 1903; d. Coral Gables, Fla., Oct. 5, 1976. Thought by some to be the greatest theoretical chemist the world has known, he won the Nobel Prize in 1968 for work he had made public in 1931, then merely 28 years old. His findings have been called the 4th law of thermodynamics or "the reciprocity relations of Onsager." European-educated, he moved to the United States in 1928 and later became one of the scientists involved in the development of the atomic bomb. His arguments for gaseous diffusion to produce the needed Uranium 235 isotope eventually prevailed.

Rosalind Russell   Alastair Sim

Ospina Pérez, Mariano (84), former president of Colombia; a three-time representative to the National Congress, he headed the Conservative party for nearly three decades; elected president in 1946, he served through the first two years of political warfare until 1950: d. Bogotá, Colombia, April 14.

Patman, Wright (82), U. S. congressman from Texas; a long-time chairman of the House Committee on Banking, Currency and Housing, he fought concentrated big-business and bank power and sponsored legislation establishing federal credit unions and the Small Business Administration: d. Bethesda, Md., March 7.

Prince Paul of Yugoslavia (93), expatriate brother of King Alexander I, who was assassinated by Croatian nationalists in 1934; ruled Yugoslavia as regent for his nephew, Peter II, from 1934 to 1941: d. Paris, France, Sept. 14.

Penfield, Wilder G. (85), U. S.-born Canadian physician: b. Spokane, Wash., Jan. 26, 1891; d. Montreal, April 5, 1976. One of the world's foremost neurologists, he devised a surgical method for treating epilepsy. A $1.2 million Rockefeller Foundation grant in 1934 enabled him to establish the Montreal Neurological Institute which under his direction (1934–60) became one of the world's most famous centers for brain surgery.

Phillips, Robert Allan (70), U. S. physician; a member of the Navy Medical Corps from 1940 to 1965, he conducted research leading to therapies that saved the lives of hundreds of thousands of cholera victims: d. Clark Air Base, Philippines, Sept. 20.

Piatigorsky, Gregor (73), naturalized U. S. cellist: b. Yekaterinoslav (now Dnepropetrovsk), Ukraine, April 17, 1903; d. Los Angeles, Calif., Aug. 6, 1976. One of the world's leading cellists, he was noted as a master of the 19th-century Romantic tradition. He became the principal cellist of the Bolshoi orchestra while still in his teens. In 1921 he fled the Soviet Union; he was first cellist and soloist with the Berlin Philharmonic from 1924 to 1928. After that he devoted himself mostly to virtuoso concerts around the world, making his U. S. debut in 1929. At the time of his death he had just completed a series of master classes in Switzerland.

Piston, Walter (82), U. S. composer; a two-time winner of the Pulitzer Prize (1948 and 1961) and professor at Harvard University, he wrote largely for orchestra and chamber ensembles: d. Belmont, Mass., Nov. 12.

Polyanyi, Michael (84), Hungarian-born chemist and philosopher; made the first interpretation of the X-ray diffraction patterns of natural plant fibers, which led to the rotating crystal method of X-ray analysis; later branched out into other areas of science and into social studies and philosophy; authored *Science, Faith and Society; Personal Knowledge; The Study of Man;* and *Beyond Nihilism:* d. Northampton, England, Feb. 22.

Pons, Lily (71), French-born U. S. coloratura soprano: b. Draguignan, near Cannes, April 12, 1904; d. Dallas, Texas, Feb. 13, 1976. One of the most glamorous opera stars of her time, she was a leading coloratura soprano at the Metropolitan Opera for more than 25 years and also enjoyed great popularity on the concert circuit and in films. Christened Alice Joséphine, she had been singing for a few years in France before auditioning at the Metropolitan Opera in 1930. Hired at once, she made her New York debut the following season as Lucia di Lammermoor. Her other roles, which she restricted to a total of ten, included Gilda in *Rigoletto,* Lakmé, and Philene in *Mignon.* During her 20-year marriage to conductor André Kostelanetz, her joint appearances with him on concert tours were enormously successful.

Queneau, Raymond (73), French novelist and poet, best known for his *Zazie dans le Métro:* d. Paris, Oct. 25.

Ray, Man (86), U. S. painter and photographer: b. (as Emmanuel Rudnitsky) Philadelphia, Pa., Aug. 27, 1890; d. Paris, France, Nov. 18, 1976. A member of such 20th-century art movements as Fauvism, Cubism, Dadaism, and Surrealism, he was an artist of inventive, impish wit and a photographer of great distinction. His so-called Rayographs were an important part of the development of abstract photography. An expatriate in Paris for some 50 years, he was praised by Jean Cocteau as "The great poet of the darkroom."

Red Fox (105), U. S. Indian chief (self-styled); achieved fame with *The Memoirs of Chief Red Fox* (1971), recalling the 1876 Battle of The Little Bighorn and the 1890 Massacre of Wounded Knee, which proved to be extensively plagiarized: d. Corpus Christi, Texas, March 1.

Reed, Sir Carol (69), English film director and producer; an early stage actor turned film director, he was known for his careful attention to details, his humane viewpoint, and his keen artistic judgment; among his outstanding successes were *The Fallen Idol, Odd Man Out,* and *The Third Man;* knighted in 1952: d. London, April 25.

Rethberg, Elisabeth (81), German-born soprano; described as "the world's most perfect singer," and "one of the greatest voices of her era," she sang at the Metropolitan Opera in New York for 20 seasons, from 1922 to 1942; while her public appearances after that were rare, records of some of her best work were released to critical acclaim in the early 1970's: d. Yorktown Heights, N. Y., June 6.

Richter, Hans (87), German artist and film director; an early member of the Dada group in Zurich, he is credited with making the first abstract film, *Rhythm 21,* in 1921; fled the Nazis to New York City in 1941 and was director of the Institute of Film Techniques at City College for 13 years; won a prize at the Venice Film Festival in 1947 for his *Dreams That Money Can Buy,* incorporating the surrealistic vision of his artist friends; wrote *Dada: Art and Anti-art* (1964), regarded as an authoritative work on the subject: d. Locarno, Switzerland, Feb. 1.

Robinson, Jim (86), U. S. jazz musician; played the trombone with the best New Orleans bands for more than 50 years: d. New Orleans, La., May 4.

Rose, Alex (78), U. S. labor figure and leader of the Liberal party: b. (as Olesh Royz) Warsaw, Poland, Oct. 15, 1898; d. New York City, Dec. 28, 1976. A power in New York politics for 40 years, he wielded influence felt on the national level. Though the Liberal party, which he led with a touch of autocracy, only had some 100,000 registered members, its sponsorship of candidates was frequently the decisive force that swept them into office. Considered by some a "kingmaker" and "political boss," he was, however, generally thought of as a promoter of liberal ideas and good government.

Russell, Rosalind (63), U. S. stage and film actress, best known for her portrayals of sophisticated, witty career women; her most famous role was that of *Auntie Mame,* which she played both on Broadway and in film version; among her other films were *His Girl Friday, My Sister Eileen, No Time for Comedy,* and *Picnic;* was four times nominated for an Oscar: d. Beverly Hills, Calif., Nov. 28.

Ružička, Leopold (89), Croatian-born Swiss chemist; was awarded the Nobel Prize for chemistry (together with Adolf Butenandt) in 1939 for his research into terpenes and large-ring organic compounds, which explained the structures of some important natural products, such as vitamin A and sex hormones: d. Zurich, Sept. 26.

Ryle, Gilbert (76), British philosopher, whose opinions were a central issue in modern philosophy for more than a quarter century: d. Yorkshire, England, Oct. 16.

Scott, Sir Arleigh Winston (76), governor general of Barbados since 1967: d. Georgetown, Barbados, Aug. 9.

Shelly, Mary Josephine (74), U. S. educator and military aide; a Bennington College administrator, she was given charge of the Navy's education for women in World War II, and she commanded the Women in the Air Force during the Korean War: d. New York City, Aug. 6.

Sim, Alastair (75), British stage and film actor; a master of comedy, he is remembered for such screen hits as *The Lavender Hill Mob* and *The Belles of St. Trinian's* and also as an accomplished dramatic actor both in Shakespearean stage roles and as Scrooge in the 1951 film version of *A Christmas Carol:* d. London, Aug. 19.

Slonim, Marc (82), Russian-born U. S. critic and educator; forced into exile by the Russian revolution, he lived in Florence, Prague, and Paris before moving to the United States in 1941; taught comparative and Russian literature at Sarah Lawrence College from 1943 to 1962; authored *Modern Russian Literature* (1953), *An Outline of Russian Literature* (1958), and *Soviet Russian Literature* (1964), as well as hundreds of articles: d. Beaulieu-sur-Mer, France, May 8.

Roy Thomson   Sybil Thorndike   Mark Tobey   Luchino Visconti   Adolph Zukor

Smith, Gerald L. K. (78), U. S. preacher and right-wing political crusader; was a follower of Huey P. Long and later founded the Christian Nationalist Crusade, a stridently anti-Communist, anti-Semitic, and anti-black fundamentalist organization: d. Glendale, Calif., April 15.

Smith, H. Allen (68), U. S. humorist; wrote *Low Man on a Totem Pole* (1941), which catapulted him onto the best-seller list he rarely left for the rest of the 1940's; produced 36 other books of humor, taking particular delight in skewering stuffed shirts and puncturing balloons: d. San Francisco, Calif., Feb. 24.

Smith, Howard Worth (93), U. S. political figure; served in the U. S. House of Representatives from 1931 to 1966 and became chairman of the Rules Committee; architect of the Smith Act of 1940, which made it a crime to be a Communist, he also used his chairmanship to block or water down many civil rights and welfare measures: d. Alexandria, Va., Oct. 3.

Spence, Sir Basil (69), British architect; erstwhile president of the Royal Academy, he is best known for his Coventry Cathedral: d. Eye, Suffolk, England, Nov. 18.

Stahlman, James (83), U. S. newspaper executive; was publisher and president of *The Nashville Banner* and twice president of the American Newspaper Publishers Association: d. Nashville, Tenn., May 1.

Strand, Paul (85), U. S. photographer: b. New York City, Oct. 16, 1890; d. Oregeval, near Paris, March 31, 1976. One of the most influential photographers of the century, ranking with Stieglitz, Steichen, and Cartier-Bresson, he won renown for still photos such as "Blind Woman Newsdealer" and "The Family" and such documentary films as *The Plow That Broke the Plains* and *The Wave*. Stressing the social contents of his art, he used his impressive talents for humanitarian goals.

Sullivan, Frank (83), U. S. humorist: b. Saratoga Springs, N. Y., Sept. 22, 1892; d. Saratoga Springs, Feb. 19, 1976. Creator of the character of Mr. Arbuthnot, expert on the cliché, he was the tireless spoofer of tired phrases, words, and ideas. He was long employed by New York City papers, especially *The World*. A member of the famous Algonquin Round Table of New York City wits, he wrote, from 1932 to 1974, an annual humorous poem at Christmas time for *The New Yorker*.

Thompson, Stith (90), U. S. folklorist and educator; won international recognition for *The Motif Index of Folk-Literature* (1935): d. Columbus, Ind., Jan. 10.

Thomson of Fleet, Roy Herbert Thomson, 1st Baron (82), Canadian-born British publishing tycoon; son of a barber, he built a media empire that included the London *Times* and *Sunday Times* and the Edinburgh *Scotsman*, as well as some 180 other newspapers, about 105 magazines, and numerous radio and television stations on four continents: d. London, England, Aug. 4.

Thorndike, Dame Sybil (93), British stage and screen actress: b. Gainesborough, Oct. 24, 1882; d. London, June 9, 1976. A performer of commanding stage presence and enormous versatility, she played every kind of role during her 70-year career. She received her early training in a Manchester stock company, went on to London's Old Vic, New York's Broadway, and tours of many other countries. George Bernard Shaw wrote the role of *Saint Joan* for her in 1923. In 1931 she was made Dame Commander of the British Empire. She played her last role at the age of 87, inaugurating a theater named for her at Leatherhead.

Tobey, Mark (85), U. S. abstract painter: b. Centerville, Wis., Dec. 11, 1890; d. Basel, Switzerland, April 24, 1976. He achieved fame with his abstract "white writing" or "whitetone" paintings, influenced by Oriental calligraphy. He was the winner of many prizes, and his paintings were coveted by museums and private collectors all over the world.

Toolen, Thomas J. (90), U. S. cleric and long-time archbishop of the Roman Catholic Diocese of Mobile-Birmingham; ended segregation in Alabama Catholic schools in 1964: d. Alabama, Dec. 4.

Trumbo, Dalton (70), U. S. screen writer and novelist; author of such films as *Kitty Foyle* and *Thirty Seconds over Tokyo,* he was jailed for a year and blacklisted for 13 for refusing to reveal his political leanings to the House Un-American Activities Committee in 1947; while blicklisted, won an Oscar under a pseudonym for the script of *The Brave One* (1957); won the National Book Award for his 1939 novel *Johnny Got His Gun* which he later turned into an award-winning film: d. Los Angeles, Calif., Sept. 10.

Visconti, Luchino (69), Italian film director; began as an assistant to French director Jean Renoir; later won worldwide renown with such films as *Rocco and His Brothers, The Leopard, The Damned,* and *Death in Venice:* d. Rome, March 30.

Prince Wan Waithayakon (85), Thai diplomat and statesman; was ambassador to Washington from 1947 to 1952 and chief delegate to the United Nations from 1947 to 1959; presided over the U. N. General Assembly in 1956–57: d. Bangkok, Thailand, Sept. 5.

Waring, Robert O. (56), U. S. diplomat; a Foreign Service careerist since 1944, he held administrative posts in various parts of Europe and North Africa before being stationed in Lebanon in 1972: d. (murdered) Beirut, Lebanon, June 16.

Warneke, Lon (67), U. S. baseball player; was an outstanding pitcher for the Chicago Cubs and the St. Louis Cardinals during the 1930's and early 1940's and then umpired for 10 years; later served as county judge: d. Hot Springs, Ark., June 23.

Weil, Joseph ("The Yellow Kid") (100), U. S. con artist; was so convincing that a detective taking him to jail on a swindling conviction bought $30,000 worth of "stock" from him: d. Chicago, Ill., Feb. 26.

Wheeler, Sir Mortimer (85), British archeologist; a pioneer of modern scientific archeology, he supervised field work at Mohenjo Daro, Pakistan, and is credited with having shed new light on the ancient Indus Valley civilization: d. Leatherhead, England, July 22.

Whipple, George Hoyt (97), U. S. physician: b. Ashland, N. H., Aug. 28, 1878; d. Rochester, N. Y., Feb. 1, 1976. He was one of three Americans who in 1934 shared the Nobel Prize in physiology and medicine for the discovery that a liver diet could control pernicious anemia, previously considered incurable.

White, Minor (67), U. S. photographer; a teacher, critic, and publisher in his field, he was considered one of the most important photographers of modern times: d. Boston, Mass., June 24.

Wiener, Alexander (70), U. S. serologist; was the co-discoverer, with Karl Landsteiner and Philip Levine, of the RH blood factor: d. New York City, Nov. 6.

Yakubovsky, Ivan I. (64), Soviet marshal; was commander of the Warsaw Pact forces since 1967: d. Moscow, Dec. 1.

Zenteno Anaya, Joaquín (53), Bolivian general and diplomat; led the force that captured and killed Ernesto ("Che") Guevara in 1967; was Bolivian ambassador to France: d. (assassinated) Paris, France, May 11.

Zukor, Adolph (103), U. S. motion picture executive: b. Ricse, Hungary, Jan. 7, 1873; d. Los Angeles, Calif., June 10, 1976. A shrewdly prescient businessman, he gave the American public the first look at a feature-length motion picture. He started out as a fur dealer, but, fascinated by movies, he invested in peepshow machines, and in 1912 he signed up Sarah Bernhardt to star in the first feature-length film, *Queen Elizabeth.* His company eventually grew into the giant movie empire known as the Paramount Picture Corporation.

OCEANIA

For the nations and islands of the South Pacific, 1976 was a year of review and restraint. The tone was inspired largely by the policies of the new conservative governments of Australia and New Zealand. In independent Papua New Guinea the main political development was an agreement arising from smouldering regional issues.

Regional Forums. The meeting of the nine-member South Pacific Forum at Rotorua, New Zealand, in March gave the area's leaders an opportunity to exchange views with the new prime ministers of Australia and New Zealand. Both Australia's Malcolm Fraser and New Zealand's Robert Muldoon urged an enlargement of U. S. military presence in the region. Under their leadership the forum adopted a weakened version of its policy supporting a "nuclear-free" South Pacific. The new policy would permit U. S. nuclear vessels and warships to travel freely in the region, but continued support for a campaign against nuclear testing in the area and the denial of nuclear bases to any power.

The forum met again in July in Nauru, where a major topic of discussion involved law of the sea issues. The members supported the concept of a 200-mile (370-km) economic zone in view of the potential of undersea mineral wealth and fishing resources. Meanwhile, stricter fishing surveillance was endorsed.

Australia's representative, Sen. Robert Cotton, raised the question of Soviet and Chinese involvement in the region. Cotton said Australia was concerned about the increasing Soviet activity in the South Pacific and feared that any development of large on-shore facilities to serve the Soviet fishing fleets could open the way for unwelcome longer-term developments.

The July meeting agreed to set up a Pacific Forum Line as a regional shipping force, initially by chartered vessels on main sea routes. The establishment of a regional civil aviation body was also discussed in an attempt to find a means of allocating routes to regional carriers that would replace bargaining between countries.

Political Developments. The Gilbert Islands were granted self-government by Britain as a prelude to complete independence. The decision failed to satisfy the hopes of the Banaban people of Ocean Island now living in Fiji, who sought to use their island's phosphate as a means of securing revenue to support a separate status for Ocean Island.

In the French territories, pressures for autonomy were in abeyance. In both French Polynesia and New Caledonia attempts to secure economic and defense commitments gained more support than "independence" efforts.

Secessionist Movement in Papua New Guinea. Papua New Guinea (PNG) faced a major challenge to its precarious unity in its first year of independence. The copper-rich island province of Bougainville sought to secede from the new republic and separatists began violent demonstrations in January. A compromise solution was reached following negotiations between Prime Minister Michael Somare and secessionist leader John Momis.

The agreement led to provincial autonomy for the newly created North Solomons provincial government, covering Bougainville and Buka. The agreement provided for a six-member policy secretariat under the provincial secretary, Leo Hennett. Although funded by the central government, the secretariat will be responsible to the newly-elected Provincial Assembly. Other public servants remained answerable to the national government while administering laws made by both the PNG and provincial legislatures.

Under the arrangement, the provincial government receives a share of the royalties and other revenues from Bougainville's copper deposits. The island's copper is the chief source of revenue for PNG.

Prime Minister Somare considered the establishment of the provincial government a victory for compromise. Most observers believe that PNG's future will depend on whether the concessions prove to be a foundation for a permanent settlement of the "separatist" issue or merely one more step by Bougainville toward secession.

Economic Developments. Economic activity was affected by static or falling prices for the area's products at a time of still rising costs. Tourism, which had declined after several years of rapid growth, showed only slight and scattered gains. Easter Island reported a steady stream of visitors coming and going on the weekly flights between Tahiti and Chile.

Papua New Guinea's first budget since independence was one of restraint, providing for revenues of $560 million and expenditures of $571 million. It relied heavily on Australia's contribution of $275 million as a first installment of a five-year budget-support pledge.

An $11.5 million sawmill to produce building lumber was opened on the PNG island of New Britain. It is a joint venture of Japanese interests, the PNG government, and local investors. With a 350-man workforce, the mill represented PNG's largest single investment since the establishment of the Bougainville copper mine.

Fiji reported a sharp increase in electronic data processing with the installation of three new computer services.

Commemorative Stamps. The stream of stamps to mark events and anniversaries continued. Western Samoa issued four subjects for the Summer Olympic Games in Montreal and Nauru honored the meeting of the South Pacific Forum. Norfolk Island released four stamps identifying American links with the island to mark the U. S. bicentennial.

R. M. YOUNGER
Author, "Australia and the Australians"

OCEANOGRAPHY

Since the ocean represents a common boundary between the major land masses, oceanography is an international science. Exchanges and cooperation between nations have been increasing as the discipline has grown. This was shown by the gathering in Edinburgh, Scotland, in September 1976 when over 700 participants from 40 countries met for the Joint Oceanographic Assembly.

The United States is a prominent participant in the International Biological Program (IBP) and the International Decade of Ocean Exploration (IDOE) which seek to increase our knowledge through multinational cooperation. Modern oceanography is also an interdisciplinary field in which the environment is studied.

Marine Geology. Marine geology has been an especially active field in recent years. In a continuing investigation of the sea-floor demarcation between major crustal plates, the submersible ALVIN from the Woods Hole Oceanographic Institution was used in 1976 to explore the 23,000-foot (7,000-m) deep Cayman Trough in the Caribbean Sea, which marks a major boundary between the North American and Caribbean crustal plates. It was slippage along this boundary that resulted in the earthquake in Guatemala in February 1976. Indeed, related aftershocks and small earthquakes along the boundary were recorded on the spot by this expedition. These first records of a shock along a subsea boundary are now being studied to learn their relationship to the spreading center—a 90-mile (144-km) section of the plate boundary running along the floor of the Cayman Trough where the two plates are actually moving apart in opposite directions. Cameras lowered from research vessels at the surface photographed a volcanic region in the center of the trough at a depth of 16,400 feet (5,000 m) with pillow lavas and other features almost identical to the Mid-Atlantic Ridge, another plate boundary previously studied by ALVIN. This is thought to indicate that the various spreading centers, which are nearly all on the ocean floor, are probably very similar. Dives in the Navy bathyscaphe TRIESTE to the spreading center and deeper parts of the scarps are scheduled for 1977.

In related studies, the Deep Sea Drilling Project (DSDP) continued its survey of the seabed into a new international phase involving full support by West Germany and the USSR in addition to the United States, Great Britain, and others. Recent bottom cores taken northwest of the British Isles have suggested that a great mountain range containing many volcanoes that once existed between Greenland and Europe began sinking about 80,000,000 years ago. It is now at a depth of 4,000 feet (1,220 m). Similarly, an ancient swamp has been found at the bottom of the Bay of Biscay at 10,000 feet (3,050 m) depth.

Physical Oceanography. Physical oceanographers have been involved with a U. S.-United Kingdom program called MODE-1 (the Mid Ocean Dynamics Experiment) that included an intensive field program in a small part of the western North Atlantic subtropical gyre in 1973, followed by extended experimental programs and mathematical modeling efforts. In 1976, a POLYMODE program was begun as a joint U. S.-Soviet plan for theoretical and experimental research which will reach its peak in 1977 and which will be coordinated with studies by many other countries. The data from MODE-1 provided the first full analysis of changes with time for a large block of ocean circulation. The major elements of the POLYMODE field program include a statistical/geographical experiment to explore and define eddy characteristics in different areas and a plan to follow a selected eddy for an extended time.

The Ocean and Weather Patterns. The effort to delineate world weather patterns continues. In 1976 some 50 drifting buoys for severe weather detection were tested in critical ocean regions that often spawn major disturbances. About 350 of the buoys are planned for use in the First GARP (Global Atmospheric Research Program) Global Experiment (FGGE) in 1977. Each buoy transmits atmospheric pressure, wind speed, and surface and water temperature to a Nimbus-6 satellite which has the capability of determining the position of each buoy as it drifts.

Studies of the ocean's role in the earth's climate have involved an extended examination of the polar regions, and especially of the role of the Antarctic Circumpolar Current that is driven clockwise around the continent of Antarctica by strong westerly winds. This work is part of the International Southern Ocean Studies (ISOS) program in which the South American nations of Chile and Argentina are cooperating with the United States.

Attention in 1976 was focused on the Drake Passage where the current is funneled between the tip of South America and the southern continent. The polar front, where young water that melts from the ice pack meets the older subantarctic water, is only about 30 nautical miles wide in the Drake Passage. The mixing of the two water types has important results to ocean circulation and heat balance throughout the ocean.

CUEA Program. The Coastal Upwelling Ecosystems Analysis (CUEA) program has continued to delve into details of this vital oceanic habitat, following the initial description of the unique functional aspects that define such areas. The goal now is to understand the specific factors in the major upwelling areas that are responsible for their differences in biological character. It now appears that relatively small differences in meteorology, topography, and water stability and circulation have large consequences in determining the presence and

UPI

The U. S. Navy's CURV III deep-sea recovery vessel is put in operation in San Diego.

abundance of species. Although they comprise only 1% of the ocean's surface, the major upwelling regions of the ocean (off the coasts of Northwest Africa, Baja California, Oregon, and Peru) provide more than 50% of all the protein harvested from the sea in fisheries. Thus, the value of an improved understanding of such areas is immense.

Our ability to detect large scale climatic and atmospheric changes that influence these areas, such as the *El Nino* disturbances off the west coast of South America, has been greatly increased. However, we are still lacking an ability to predict the biological response to variations of the nonbiological factors. Special attention is now being given to all components of the food chain, including the phytoplankton, zooplankton, and fish (both as larval forms and adults). Study of the Peru upwelling area continues to involve many U. S. institutions, working in cooperation with the Peruvian government.

JONSDAP 76 and Water Pollution. A Joint North Sea Informative Service (JONSIS), which collects data from a network of moored sensor stations and coastal observation sites, was expanded for 1976 into a 40-day data acquisition program called JONSDAP 76, using current meters, offshore tide gauges, plus ships and aircraft to study the area. Participation included institutes of Norway, Sweden, Denmark, West Germany, the Netherlands, Belgium, France, and the United Kingdom. The aim was to obtain

oceanographic and meteorological data for use as input to environmental predictive systems. The North Sea yields 5% of the world's total fish catch and is also a major center for gas and oil activity. It is of further importance as a recreation center and is the recipient of much water pollution. An intensive research effort is required to maintain the resources properly.

Man's pollution of the ocean has become an increasing concern. The problem is especially acute for the coastal countries surrounding some of the smaller ocean basins. A long-term plan to coordinate efforts by at least 17 of the 18 Mediterranean nations was prepared in Malta in 1975 and adopted at an intergovernmental meeting in Barcelona, Spain, convened by the United Nations Environment Program. A second Barcelona conference in 1976 considered specific protocols on combating pollution by oil and other substances and on prevention of pollution by dumping from ships and aircraft. Protocols from land-based sources and protection of seabed activities will be acted on later. Similarly, the nations around the Baltic Sea have coordinated their efforts to evaluate the population and pollution problems of that region, under the supervision of the Scientific Committee on Oceanic Research (SCOR) of UNESCO.

See also Law of the Sea feature, pages 50–60.

DAVID A. McGILL
Professor of Ocean Science
U. S. Coast Guard Academy

OHIO

Ohio became a national pivot in its June 8 primary, as it helped clinch the nominations for Democrat Jimmy Carter and President Gerald R. Ford. On November 2, the normally Republican state split down the middle, choosing Carter by 11,116 votes out of nearly 4 million.

Democratic Upturn. Sen. Robert A. Taft, Jr., lost his bid for a second term to Howard Metzenbaum, a Cleveland lawyer and businessman. Defeated by Taft in 1970, Metzenbaum had been appointed senator in 1973, when William Saxbe accepted a cabinet post, but lost the party nomination to John Glenn in 1974. Ohio Republicans held their 13–10 margin in the U. S. House of Representatives, but Democrats added two seats to their majority in the state House (61–38) and continued at 21–12 in the state Senate. The Assembly results promised difficulty for Gov. James A. Rhodes (R) with any controversial legislative program.

Issues. Four constitutional "consumer" amendments were defeated on November 2. They would have required greater safeguards in construction of nuclear power plants, created an official consumer-action group to fight utility rate increases, forced utilities to offer minimum monthly amounts of electricity and heating gas at lower rates, and eased requirements for placing initiative and referendum issues on statewide ballots. Three other changes—to order a line of

Howard Metzenbaum (D), a Cleveland lawyer and businessman, defeated Sen. Robert Taft, Jr., on November 2.

UPI

succession to a disabled governor; to remove obsolete references, such as to dueling, from the state constitution; and to avoid special Assembly sessions to hear final election results—were approved.

In the June 8 primary Ohioans approved team candidacy for governor and lieutenant governor, new voting rules for filling state office vacancies, and new estate-tax provisions. Proposals for new taxation were rejected.

Scandal. Investigations into workmen's compensation payments, begun in 1975 by *The Plain Dealer* in Cleveland, led to nearly 100 indictments in the summer of 1976. Most centered on allegations of fraud by lawyers, doctors, and others said to have framed claims for "employees" of nonexistent companies. The full extent of the scandal was not known by year's end, but estimates put the total wrongfully obtained at $600,000. In October the Ohio Senate ordered the removal of Gregory J. Stebbins, who had been chairman of the Ohio Industrial Commission. The commission supervises workmen's compensation claims in Ohio. An attorney named in the fraud investigation committed suicide.

Busing. U. S. District Judge Frank J. Battisti on August 31 ruled that the Cleveland and Ohio school boards had permitted segregation to exist and ordered the creation of a special panel to recommend changes. The Cleveland Board of Education appealed the verdict in September. There was much discussion about the cost of implementing changes. One view was that busing more than 50,000 Cleveland pupils would likely run to $75 million.

Rubber Strike. The economy of northern Ohio skidded somewhat with a strike of some 68,000 rubber workers, many of them in plants in Akron. The strike began in late April and did not end until four months later.

Sports. Again, Ohio athletes were stellar performers: the Cincinnati Reds of the National League won a second straight baseball world series, and Ohio State University's football team was again a power in the Big Ten.

JOHN F. HUTH, JR.
"The Plain Dealer," Cleveland

───── **OHIO · Information Highlights** ─────

Area: 41,222 square miles (106,765 km²).
Population (1975 est.): 10,759,000.
Chief Cities (1970 census): Columbus, the capital, 540,-025; Cleveland, 750,879; Cincinnati, 452,524.
Government (1976): *Chief Officers*—governor, James A. Rhodes (R); lt. gov., Richard F. Celeste (D). *General Assembly*—Senate, 33 members; House of Representatives, 99 members.
Education (1975–76): *Enrollment*—public elementary schools, 1,365,523 pupils; public secondary, 927,-124; nonpublic (1976–77), 284,100; colleges and universities, 367,776 students. *Public school expenditures,* $2,650,000,000 ($1,176 per pupil).
State Finances (fiscal year 1975): *Revenues,* $6,796,-066,000; *expenditures,* $6,824,242,000.
Personal Income (1975): $62,514,000,000; per capita, $5,810.
Labor Force (July 1976): *Nonagricultural wage and salary earners,* 4,044,400; *insured unemployed,* 96,200 (2.6%).

OKLAHOMA

Events in Oklahoma in 1976 were highlighted by the November elections, passage of a long-delayed prison construction bill, a congressional investigation, and two cases of "white-collar crime."

Elections. In the presidential race, Oklahomans gave their eight electoral votes to President Ford, casting 543,806 votes for Ford and 530,793 for Carter. Oklahoma Congressman Carl Albert, speaker of the House of Representatives, retired after 15 terms. First elected in 1946, he was a man of unassuming demeanor and quiet behind-the-scenes methods, which obscured his accomplishments as Democratic party whip for six years, majority leader for ten years, and speaker for six years. Wes Watkins, a Democrat, was elected to succeed him. Republican Mickey Edwards was chosen to succeed retiring veteran John Jarman, a Democrat. The state's four incumbent congressmen—all Democrats—were reelected.

Voters defeated a constitutional amendment that would have permitted the sale of liquor by the drink.

Legislation. The state legislature appropriated money for two new medium-security prisons, the first such funding in 66 years. The legislature also increased the money for education at twice the level of any previous two-year period.

After the U. S. Supreme Court struck down the state's 1973 mandatory death penalty in July, a special legislative session enacted a new capital punishment law. Under the new legislation a person charged with a capital crime will receive two trials, the first to determine guilt and the second to determine whether the defendent should receive a life or death sentence.

Agriculture. The state's wheat harvest in 1976 was one of the largest since the 1890's. But the cotton harvest was one of the poorest in Oklahoma history.

Natural Disasters. A tornado struck southeastern Oklahoma in March, resulting in three deaths and $1.5 million in property damage. Although it was a drought year for the state, spring rains in Tulsa killed three, damaged $12 million worth of property, and led to the evacuation of some 2,000 homes.

Scandals. A congressional investigation into the 1974 death of Karen Silkwood, an opponent of plutonium enrichment power plants, concluded that no foul play had been involved. She had died in a one-car accident on her way to meet with a union official and a New York *Times* reporter to tell of alleged safety violations at the Oklahoma nuclear power plant where she worked.

Executives of the now bankrupt Home-Stake Production Company pleaded guilty or no contest in U. S. district court during the year to charges of bilking some $40 million from persons who invested in their drilling programs in

UPI

District Attorney and Mrs. Joseph Wideman look on as their son tells reporters of being kidnapped by two youths demanding the release of an accused murderer.

1968–70. Alleged violations of the U. S. Securities and Exchange Commission as well as mail fraud were charged.

Three high-ranking officials of the Tulsa-based Phillips Petroleum Company were charged in U. S. district court with conspiracy to defraud the government by not paying corporate income taxes between 1963 and 1971 on some $3 million in assets.

Appointment. Dr. Robert Kamm, president of Oklahoma State University at Stillwater, was appointed to the board of UNESCO by President Ford in April.

LOIS CARTER CLARK
Free-lance Writer, Oklahoma City

--- **OKLAHOMA · Information Highlights** ---

Area: 69,919 square miles (181,090 km²).
Population (1975 est.): 2,712,000.
Chief Cities (1970 census): Oklahoma City, the capital, 368,856; Tulsa, 330,350; Lawton, 74,470; Norman, 52,117.
Government (1976): *Chief Officers*—governor, David L. Boren (D); lt. gov., George Nigh (D). *Legislature*—Senate, 48 members; House of Representatives, 101 members.
Education (1975–76): *Enrollment*—public elementary schools, 320,077 pupils; public secondary, 274,739; nonpublic (1976–77), 10,200; colleges and universities, 131,558 students. *Public school expenditures,* $627,000,000 ($1,072 per pupil).
State Finances (fiscal year 1975): *Revenues,* $1,747,-090,000; *expenditures,* $1,637,444,000.
Personal Income (1975): $14,237,000,000; per capita, $5,250.
Labor Force (July 1976): *Nonagricultural wage and salary earners,* 905,400; *insured unemployed,* 25,300 (3.6%).

UPI

Surrounded by HEW officials, President Ford signed a message to Congress requesting increased Social Security payroll taxes and new Medicare benefits.

OLDER POPULATION

Some measure of financial protection for older persons is provided by social security systems found in nearly all industrialized countries. In the United States, nearly 28 million persons receive benefits, of whom 16.7 million are retired workers and 2.9 million are spouses. Some of these people are included among the 2.3 million aged persons who also receive Supplementary Security Income.

Progress has been made in making health care available to the elderly through the Medicare program. But medical costs remain high, and nursing homes are expensive and the care sometimes inadequate. For many people, prolonged terminal illnesses are both financial and social burdens, especially with the introduction of new, costly life-support systems. New definitions of death and the legalization of "living wills" give promise for the future that these burdens may be eased in some cases. (See SOCIAL WELFARE).

Legislation. Late in 1975, when President Ford signed a bill extending the Older Americans Act for three years, he objected to some of the spending levels authorized by Congress. This was a forewarning of the fiscal battle that was precipitated by his budget message proposing widespread cuts in human service appropriations while increasing defense spending. Examples of

particular concern to the elderly were: 1) a decrease of $1.3 billion in Medicare outlays to be achieved by increasing co-insurance charges (which was not enacted); 2) a decrease of $52 million in Older Americans Act funding to be achieved by eliminating training programs and multidisciplinary gerontology centers, multipurpose senior centers, and the Senior Service Corps, which had 12,400 participants.

As Congress neared adjournment, prospects for legislation that would lift the financial burdens of older people became brighter. The supplemental appropriations bill that was passed in June supported all of the programs that were threatened with extinction by President Ford's proposed budget cuts in 1975. The Labor-HEW appropriations bill passed by Congress on September 30 over the president's veto went even further, including increased appropriations for services for the aging. The total funding for the Administration on Aging was increased by 65% to a new high level, more than double the amount in the budget message.

New legislation authorized $2.5 billion for housing units for the elderly during the next three years. The Department of Housing and Urban Development (HUD) was empowered to lend $750 million of the total allocation to nonprofit sponsors of 30,000 units in 1977.

In extending general revenue sharing programs, Congress included a prohibition against age discrimination, and inserted a requirement that states must provide elderly persons and senior citizen organizations with opportunities to be heard before the final disbursement of funds.

Tax Reform. The Tax Reform Act of 1976 included many provisions specifically affecting the elderly. Tax on gain from the sale of a personal residence by a person over 65 is now applied only when the sale price is over $35,000. Retirement income credits are restructured so that they are now available to single persons with an adjusted gross income of up to $12,500 and to an elderly couple with up to $17,500. A new unified estate and gift tax will provide credits equivalent to an exemption of $120,000 in 1977–78, increasing to the equivalent of $175,000 in 1981. These figures compare with the previous estate tax exemption of $60,000. The marital deduction is also increased, and it is estimated that only about 3% to 5% of all estates will be subject to federal estate tax.

A Trouble Year. Most of the apparent legislative program gains came just before the presidential election in November, and their operational effects will not be felt until 1977. Throughout 1976, Medicaid, nursing homes, and the food stamps program were all being criticized severely at both the national and state levels. Other programs were under clouds of uncertainty as federal appropriations were continued on a month-to-month basis with little assurance that they had a future. Furthermore, most states were experiencing severe financial problems as costs and demands went up while operating budgets remained the same. It was far easier for legislators to escape in searches for waste and fraud than it was to raise taxes. In New York City, municipal retirement funds were hard hit, setting off a wave of concern about inadequately funded pension plans for government employees and other workers. Many services to the elderly were also casualties at state and local levels. For instance, increased responsibilities for investigating child abuse led some state agencies to cut back on homemaker services for the elderly.

The ongoing programs at the local level, established during the past 10 years under the Older Americans Act, have fostered a much higher level of participation in activities by the elderly. This has led to a growing recognition of the needs and the potentialities of this segment of the population. The striking increase in the appropriation for the Administration on Aging is a clear indication that this development is a solid one which will continue to be an increasing force in the country.

RALPH E. PUMPHREY
Washington University, St. Louis

OLYMPICS. See SPORTS.

ONTARIO

During 1976 Ontario's minority government, the first in three decades, faced problems of inflation, mounting health costs, and growing concern over the quality of education.

Economic Policy. Treasurer Darcy McKeough saw a policy of restraint, with reduced government spending and smaller deficits, as the way to attack inflation. The 1977 budget (the fiscal year begins April 1) of $12,500,000,000 attempted to increase revenue by 19.4% while holding spending to a 10.4% increase over fiscal 1976. Taxes were raised on cigarettes, beer, and liquor; Ontario Health Insurance premiums were increased and charges for private or semi-private hospital care raised. Tax concessions were made to small businesses, and the sales tax on thermal insulation was removed as a conservation measure. Cuts were made in highway spending, and the civil service was to be reduced by 3.7%. A real economic growth rate of 5.3% was forecast, but unemployment was expected to remain at 6.3% due to an enlarged labor force in the province.

Health Costs. The raising of health charges reflected the growing cost of health, particularly that of hospital care. Health costs now total 28% of government expenditure. The Ministry of Health was prevented from closing several hospitals only by a court ruling that it lacked the necessary power. Since both the New Democrats and the Liberals opposed the closures, the minority government could not seek authority from the legislature.

The Perils of Minority Government. Premier Davis' Progressive Conservative government has survived by Liberal support. The Liberals, reduced to third-party status in 1975, seem reluctant under their new leader, Stuart Smith, to risk an early election. The Liberals supported the budget grudgingly, and although they joined the New Democrats to defeat the cabinet's farm income stabilization bill, they voted to sustain the government on a subsequent confidence motion.

The newly created ombudsman, Arthur Maloney, caused the government acute embarrassment with his first major report, which indicated gross inequalities in compensation for expropriated land paid to residents of the Pickering area. The responsible minister, John Rhodes, rejected the report of the ombudsman and demanded a completely new inquiry.

Education. With costs consuming some 26% of the budget and the number of students dwindling, education is becoming a major issue. Complaints are growing louder, especially from the universities, that Ontario high-schools are turning out illiterate graduates. In October Education Minister Thomas Wells announced that grades 9 and 10 will have required courses in English, mathematics, Canadian history or geography, and science; there will also be mandatory English courses for senior grades. This is sharp departure from the system of free electives introduced when Premier Davis was provincial education minister.

Provincial-Federal Friction. The Ontario government has been critical of federal failure to come to grips with economic issues, especially the failure to cut spending. It supported the federal anti-inflation program, but believes the program overemphasizes intervention and neglects economic stimulation.

As Canada's most industrialized province, Ontario opposes the federal policy of allowing oil prices to rise toward international levels, fearing it will injure Canada's competitive position abroad.

PETER J. KING
Carleton University

─────── **ONTARIO · Information Highlights** ───────

Area: 412,582 square miles (1,068,587 km²).
Population (April 1976 est.): 8,315,000.
Chief Cities (1971 census): Toronto, the provincial capital, 712,786; Hamilton, 309,173; Ottawa, the federal capital, 302,341.
Government (1976): *Chief Officers*—lt. gov., Pauline McGibbon; premier, William G. Davis (Progressive Conservative); atty. gen., Roy McMurtry; min. of educ., Thomas Wells; chief justice, Alexander Gale. *Legislature*—Legislative Assembly, 117 members.
Education (1976–77): *Enrollment*—public elementary and secondary schools, 1,979,700 pupils; private schools, 55,420; Indian (federal) schools, 7,380; post-secondary, 231,800 students. *Total expenditures,* $3,565,-253,000.
Public Finance (1975–76 est.): *Revenues,* $8,982,000,000; *expenditures,* $10,552,000,000.
Personal Income (1974): $44,997,000,000; average annual income per person, $5,559.
(All monetary figures given in Canadian dollars.)

As chairman of the House Ways and Means Committee, Oregon Rep. Al Ullman was a key spokesman on economic issues for the Democratic Party during 1976. He won reelection in November.

UPI

OREGON

Oregon saw an active election year in 1976. In May vigorous primary campaigns brought much maneuvering for nominations both in the U. S. presidential race and for state positions, and there followed six months of brisk contests.

Elections. The November voter turnout reflected the nationally heavy vote. Registration was the highest in the state's history, and more than a million of the 1.4 million registrants went to the polls. The last state in the nation to complete its tally because of prolonged tabulation of absentee ballots, Oregon gave Gerald Ford less than a 2,000-vote victory over Jimmy Carter—the state's closest margin in a presidential election since 1880.

Oregon's incumbent congressmen were easily returned to office, so that the state will continue to be represented in the U. S. House of Representatives by a wholly Democratic delegation: Les AuCoin, Robert B. Duncan, James Weaver, and Al Ullman, holder of the key position of chairman of the House Ways and Means Committee. Neither U. S. senator's term of office expired.

───── **OREGON · Information Highlights** ─────

Area: 96,981 square miles (251,181 km²).
Population (1975 est.): 2,288,000.
Chief Cities (1970 census): Salem, the capital, 68,856; Portland, 380,555; Eugene, 78,389.
Government (1976): *Chief Officers*—governor, Robert W. Straub (D); secy. of state, Clay Myers (R). *Legislative Assembly*—Senate, 30 members; House of Representatives, 60 members.
Education (1975–76): *Enrollment*—public elementary schools, 274,099 pupils; public secondary, 203,460; nonpublic (1976–77), 24,100; colleges and universities, 112,148 students. *Public school expenditures,* $640,000,000 ($1,399 per pupil).
State Finances (fiscal year 1975): *Revenues,* $1,941,-187,000; *expenditures,* $1,783,168,000.
Personal Income (1975): $13,201,000,000; per capita, $5,769.
Labor Force (July 1976): *Nonagricultural wage and salary earners,* 861,800; *insured unemployed,* 37,000 (4.8%).

State Offices. The Oregon secretary of state's position, which is second in importance only to the governor's and is often considered a stepping-stone to gubernatorial candidacy, was won by Norma Paulus (R) by a large majority. A lawyer who has served three very active terms in the state legislature, she will be the first woman to hold a state-wide elective office. She is seen by some of her supporters as having national potential. The position remains Republican as it has been for almost a century. Her opponent was State Senator Blaine Whipple.

The state treasurer's position was slimly won by Clay Myers (R), the outgoing secretary of state, who is constitutionally unable to succeed himself. The loser was Jewel Lansing (D), well-qualified for the position but a newcomer to Oregon politics. The attorney generalship race between two very able men was handily won by James A. Redden (D), state treasurer, over James W. Durham (R), who has been deputy attorney general since 1971.

Initiatives. The greatest petition activity since 1952 put 12 measures on the ballot by popular initiative. Both proponents and opponents spent large sums, totaling more than a million and a quarter dollars, on a proposition to impose severe restrictions before any more nuclear power plants could be built in the state (the existing Trojan plant west of Portland was excepted from the requirements). This paralleled similar measures in several other states. The voters rejected the proposal by nearly a 58% majority. A repeal of 1969 and 1973 laws which established comprehensive state-guided land-use planning and development was rejected by almost the same margin.

A proposal to lower the minimum age for eligibility to the state legislature from 21 to 18 was defeated by more than a 2–1 margin. A 1¢ increase in the state gasoline tax, as well as an increase in the weight tax for commercial vehicles, both to be used to finance maintenance and reconstruction of roads, was narrowly defeated. A ban on the addition of fluorides to any community water system also failed.

Economy. Beyond the elections, it was a rather calm year in Oregon. Unemployment in the state, alternately dropping and rising throughout the year from 9% to 9.5%, seasonally adjusted, remained more than 1.5% above national figures. Two relevant factors were the continued slowness of housing starts, which depressed lumber and wood products industries, and a rapid population growth, which meant more people seeking work. An apparent upturn in housing construction occurred late in the year.

JOANNE AMSPOKER
Oregon College of Education

OTTAWA

During 1976, Ottawa, Canada's capital and fourth largest city, found itself at odds with the federal government and beset with rising taxes, largely for education.

The Federal Presence. A parliamentary committee and a provincial commission, headed by Dr. Henry Mayo, studied government in the capital area, and both heard many criticisms of the federal presence. The focus of attack was the National Capital Commission (NCC), whose abolition or restructuring to include local politicians and direct elections was demanded. Dennis Coolican, chairman of the Ottawa-Carleton Regional Municipality, urged the parliamentary committee to end NCC planning powers and restrict its functions to federal lands. Particularly contentious is an NCC plan for a new satellite town of 100,000 at Carlsbad Springs, 10 miles (16 km) southeast of Ottawa, to deal with urban expansion. The region has rejected this site and plans expansion to the southwest.

Equally controversial is the federal policy of expanding the national capital by relocating federal departments in the Hull area across the Ottawa River in Quebec. Chairman Coolican made clear that Ottawa-Carleton had no interest in joining with the Outaouais Region in Quebec under a federal umbrella and did not want a "federal district" in any form. Jean-Marie Seguin, chairman of the Outaouais Council, similarly opposed joining the Ontario and Quebec sides. He also urged restrictions on NCC powers to acquire property and interfere with municipal planning. Fears have been expressed in Hull that the new federal complexes are destroying the character of the city and that the influx of thousands of English-speaking civil servants will submerge its French character. Mayor Lorry Greenberg of Ottawa charged that failure to consult with the city over the relocation could leave Ottawa a ghost-town oversupplied with recently-built but vacant office space, which would imperil the city's tax base. The mayor also raised the issue of the tax-exempt status of fed-

eral property, contending that the federal grants paid in lieu of taxes short-changed the city. His requests for an additional $2,500,000 in federal grants produced merely an increase of $200,000. Matters came to a head in May when the mayor refused to meet Edgar Gallant, NCC chairman, to discuss an NCC redevelopment project. Current federal fiscal policy ruled out any increased financial contributions.

Education. Large 1975 pay raises to teachers were reflected in 17% rises in the 1976 budgets of both the Ottawa and Carleton boards of education. French-language instruction was a major issue in Ottawa schools. After much debate, the Carleton board decided to maintain its experimental total-immersion program, although the separate school board has abandoned its own. A provincial report suggests that hostility to the program among some English-speaking teachers arises from fears of job security.

PETER J. KING
Carleton University

PAKISTAN

Political stability in Pakistan was weakened somewhat in 1976, although not upset, and the country continued to make economic progress. In foreign affairs, relations with India more and more returned to normal.

Political Affairs. Prime Minister Zulfikar Ali Bhutto kept tight rein on his government throughout the year. Political separatism based on language, long a smoldering issue in Pakistan, remained under control. But not untypically there were disturbances and political trials. Nearly 50 members of the Awami Party were tried in May for subversive and terroristic activity. The party, once an important opposition group to Bhutto's ruling Pakistan People's Party, had been banned in 1975. There was considerable political advantage in conducting the trial, which was indeed considered by many Pakistanis as being as much political as judicial. Corruption charges were brought in March against Mohammed Hanif Rammay, the former chief minister of the Punjab. A strong critic of Bhutto's government, he had resigned from the People's Party in 1975. In late October retired Air Marshall Asghar Khan, the leader of Pakistan's main opposition group, the Teherik-i-Istiqal Party charged that jails in Pakistan were "bursting" with an estimated 50,000 political prisoners.

In the fall, tribal uprisings in Dir District of the Northwest Frontier Province were crushed by army intervention. About 300 people reportedly were killed. Such disturbances as well as political trials and imprisonment are not uncommon in the brief history of Pakistan—founded in 1947 upon the breakup of British India.

Economy. Economically, Pakistan continued to make strides in 1976. Prime Minister Bhutto announced in July the nationalization of processing plants for the country's three major crops

PAKISTAN · Information Highlights

Official Name: Islamic Republic of Pakistan.
Location: South Asia.
Area: 310,403 square miles (803,943 km²).
Population (1976 est.): 75,000,000.
Chief Cities (1974): Islamabad, the capital, 250,000; Karachi, 3,500,000; Lahore, 2,100,000.
Government: *Head of state,* Chaudhri Fazal Elahi, president (took office Aug. 1973). *Head of government,* Zulfikar Ali Bhutto, prime minister (took office Aug. 1973). *Legislature*—Parliament: Senate and National Assembly.
Monetary Unit: Rupee (9.93 rupees equal U. S.$1, Sept. 1976).
Gross National Product (1975 est.): $10,100,000,000.
Manufacturing (major products): Textiles, processed foods, cement, petroleum products.
Major Agricultural Products: Wheat, cotton, rice, sugarcane, corn, millet, chickpeas, rapeseed, livestock.
Foreign Trade (1975): *Exports,* $1,005,000,000; *imports,* $2,125,000,000.

—cotton, wheat, and rice—as part of an effort to eliminate exploitation by middlemen.

One of the continuing and pressing problems facing Pakistan is the rapidly increasing population, estimated at about 75 million. Bhutto has continued the program of family planning begun in 1969 with subsidized prices of preventives—a month's supply of birth control pills or a dozen condoms for 2½ cents. The current birthrate is 2.4%, but the campaign to curb the country's population has begun to show progress. Pakistan has not resorted to the almost compulsory sterilization practiced in India.

The government has pressed a campaign to keep its most educated and talented citizens at home. An estimated 60,000 Pakistanis emigrate annually, primarily for more lucrative jobs in the Middle East. Although this emigration might seem to be a relief valve to population pressure, the country badly needs the skills of the professional and technical workers who are leaving.

The Bolan Dam, a principal source of irrigation in Baluchistan, collapsed on September 6 after weeks of torrential rains. Officials reported that 26 villages were washed away by the flood.

Foreign affairs. Not surprisingly, Pakistan's foreign relations continued to be dominated by India. Pakistan and India had broken off diplomatic relations in late 1971, after the war in which Bangladesh won independence. The principle of once again regularizing relations between the two countries was affirmed in the Simla agreement (1972). Very slowly, progress was made over the intervening years.

Bhutto wrote to Indian Prime Minister Indira Gandhi in late March 1976 suggesting that rail and air links be reestablished between the two nations. A conciliatory reply was received several weeks later. Formal discussions were opened in May, and by the middle of the month agreement was reached not only with respect to communications links but also on the need to reestablish formal diplomatic relations. New ambassadors were named by both India and Pakistan in late June. By July train and air service between Pakistan and India had been resumed. An Indian airlines plane was hijacked to Lahore, Pakistan, in September, but the incident blew over without repercussions.

In May, Prime Minister Bhutto visited China, where he received what was described as a warm welcome from Chairman Mao Tse-tung. Relations with the United States remained friendly, although Secretary of State Henry Kissinger traveled to Pakistan in August to argue against the Pakistani plan to purchase a nuclear processing plant from France.

CARL LEIDEN
University of Texas at Austin

WIDE WORLD

On arrival in Peking in May, Pakistan Prime Minister Ali Bhutto received a warm welcome.

A ship is lowered through the Miraflores locks. Negotiations for the eventual U. S. surrender of the Panama Canal continued intermittently during 1976.

UPI

PANAMA

Support for the regime of Gen. Omar Torrijos Herrera eroded rapidly in 1976, as Panama's economy became continually weaker and progress in canal treaty negotiations awaited political changes abroad.

Political Unrest. In September, General Torrijos sent heavily armed National Guardsmen to quell rioting in Panama City by previously loyal national university students. Perhaps as many as 500 students and looters were detained as Torrijos ordered the university closed indefinitely. Earlier in September, demonstrations had closed secondary schools for five days. The protesters complained about living costs and alleged government repression.

When dissident businessmen and stock growers, opposed to official policies, gathered at David in January, General Torrijos retaliated by

---

PANAMA · Information Highlights

Official Name: Republic of Panama.
Location: On the isthmus of Panama, which links Central America and South America.
Area: 29,209 square miles (75,650 km²).
Population (1976 est.): 1,700,000.
Chief City (1974): Panama, the capital, 393,000.
Government: *Military junta*, led by Gen. Omar Torrijos Herrera (took power Oct. 1972). *Head of state*, Demetrio Lakas Bahas, president (took office Dec. 1969). *Legislature:* unicameral—Peoples Assembly.
Monetary Unit: Balboa (1 balboa equals U. S.$1, Sept. 1976).
Gross National Product (1974 est.): $1,650,000,000.
Manufacturing (major products): Processed foods, petroleum products, textiles, wood products.
Major Agricultural Products: Bananas, vegetables, rice, forest products.
Foreign Trade (1975): *Exports*, $272,000,000; *imports*, $867,000,000.

---

exiling 15 businessmen to Ecuador. He shuffled his cabinet and offered to rewrite the nation's labor laws in an effort to placate complaints by the business community of leftist infiltration within the government.

Dissension over Torrijo's rule within higher echelons of the 10,000-man National Guard could no longer be confined to the barracks. The military has criticized the Torrijos regime for not acting more forcefully, at both the domestic and international levels, on mounting internal crises.

Economic Problems. A growth rate of only 1.7% was expected in 1976, reflecting the country's deepest economic slump in 20 years. To stimulate private investment in productive activities, General Torrijos announced in May that revisions would be made in the highly controversial labor code. Public investments of $473 million were planned for 1976, of which Panama expected to borrow $142 million abroad from several sources.

The Torrijos government pressed ahead with its $800-million Cerro Colorado copper project. Only 20% of the share capital for the project would be private. Panama expected to complete the financial arrangement for Cerro through bond issues, foreign loans, and direct allocations from the national budget. Local holdings of United Brands, the transnational banana firm, were nationalized in January.

The Bayano Dam was dedicated on March 16. Hydroelectric power from the new installation will save millions in foreign exchange, for Panama had been entirely dependent on imported fuel oil for the production of electricity.

Foreign Relations. Negotiations with the United States concerning a new canal treaty continued intermittently throughout the year, if only to deflect attention from the regime's domestic difficulties. Officials in Panama understood that further concessions could not be won until after general elections in the United States.

General Torrijos continued to rally foreign support for his Panama Canal negotiations through state visits. His travels took him to Cuba, Jamaica, Colombia, and Sri Lanka. President Tito of Yugoslavia visited Panama in March and was given a reception of unprecedented proportions. He reciprocated by endorsing Panamanian claims to the canal.

A ceremonial session of the council of the Organization of American States was held in Panama in June. It marked the 150th anniversary of the convocation on the isthmus by Simón Bolívar of the first inter-American Congress.

LARRY L. PIPPIN
Elbert Covell College
University of the Pacific

PARAGUAY

Church-state relations deteriorated in Paraguay in 1976 and political liberties suffered a setback as the government of Alfredo Stroessner responded to alleged threats to its 22-year-old existence.

Political Unrest. The national council of Roman Catholic bishops denounced the government for attempting to connect it with political disturbances in March and April, and for the harassment of its Christian Agrarian Leagues. The Church also accused the government of malicious oppression of students, priests, and peasants and of interference in its churches, seminaries, and university.

The government charged the Church with associating with the Military Political Organization, a new guerrilla force. The group is said to have units operating in urban centers to get funds by whatever means possible to carry on its battle with the Stroessner regime. As a result, much of Paraguay was under a state of emergency, a normal condition of affairs.

--------- PARAGUAY · Information Highlights ---------

Official Name: Republic of Paraguay.
Location: Central South America.
Area: 157,047 square miles (406,752 km²).
Population (1976 est.): 2,600,000.
Chief City (1974 est.): Asuncion, the capital, 400,000.
Government: *Head of state and government,* Gen. Alfredo Stroessner, president (took office Aug. 1954). *Legislature*—Congress: Senate and Chamber of Deputies.
Monetary Unit: Guarani (126 guaranies equal U. S.$1, Sept. 1976).
Gross National Product (1975 est.): $1,500,000,000.
Manufacturing (major products): Meats, leather, wood products, quebracho extract, vegetable oil.
Major Agricultural Products: Cassava, bananas, tobacco, cotton, soybeans, oilseeds, citrus fruits, cattle, forest products.
Foreign Trade (1975): *Exports,* $187,000,000; *imports,* $186,000,000.

Hemisphere reported the arrest of Miguel Chase Sardi, an eminent anthropologist. He is director of the Marandu project, which was established to help break down the barriers between the Indian population and the rest of society. The government regards any effort to change the status of the rural population as a menace to the political order. The police also cracked down on the Communist Party, arresting more than 100 of its members. The Uruguayan ambassador was killed in Asunción by a Croatian nationalist whose real target was the Yugoslavian ambassador.

The legislature passed a resolution in July calling for a constitutional convention to amend the 1967 charter to enable Stroessner to continue in office for another 10 years after the expiration of his fifth five-year term in 1978. This and other political actions brought the warring Liberal and Radical Liberal parties into a pact of unity. Both parties and the Febrerista Party refused to enter candidates for the convention and will cast blank ballots. With the suppression of *El Radical,* the opposition press has been completely silenced.

Foreign Affairs. Paraguay became involved in a dispute with Argentina over the supply of arms to Argentine guerrillas. The dispute caused President Stroessner to dismiss the head of the navy, a post that traditionally controlled the flow of arms to and from Paraguay. Stroessner visited Uruguay in March. A treaty of friendship and cooperation was signed with Brazil.

Economy. The inflation rate dropped in January from a 1975 high of 26.5% to 6.7%, one of the lowest rates in Latin America. A monetary stabilization policy was in part responsible. However, the national foreign debt amounted to a burdensome $616 million.

LEO B. LOTT, *University of Montana*

PENNSYLVANIA

The year 1976 was a time of rediscovery for Pennsylvanians. Throughout the Commonwealth people joined to commemorate the state's key role in the nation's birth. Communities of every size held celebrations; local histories were researched, compiled, and published, and historical sites of local or national significance (some long-forgotten, abandoned, and near ruin) were restored.

At the state level, the most inspiring undertaking was Pennsylvania's sponsorship of the Bicentennial Wagon Trains. From the far corners of the United States, 20th-century wagoners made their way back along the historical trails their forefathers had followed as pioneers. On the eve of Independence Day, the trains, composed of units from all the states, converged and settled at Valley Forge.

The bicentennial fervor might well have dimmed after July 4, but people's enthusiasm and efforts persisted. To the tourist industry, the

On January 1, the Liberty Bell was moved from Philadelphia's Independence Hall (*middleground*) to the new Liberty Bell Pavilion (*foreground*). The move was made to permit the maxi- mum number of persons to view the bell during the bicentennial.

ROLLIN R. LA FRANCE, MITCHELL/GIURGOLA ARCHITECTS

year was somewhat of a disappointment, but as 1976 drew to a close, Pennsylvanians for the most part held a deeper appreciation of their heritage and considered themselves far richer for the experience.

Health. Tragedy intruded in late July after a number of people attending the state convention of the American Legion in Philadelphia became mysteriously ill. When the crisis subsided several weeks later, the "Legion Disease" had claimed 29 lives and left 180 ill. Intensive investigations by scientists and health authorities failed to identify the disease.

The swine flu inoculations in October caused concern when three elderly residents of the Pittsburgh area died shortly after immunization. Programs in some states were discontinued briefly but resumed after health officials agreed the vaccine was not at fault.

Economy. Pennsylvania's economic outlook was bolstered by an agreement signed in September by Gov. Milton J. Shapp and officials of Volkswagen. The German auto maker soon will establish its first American assembly plant at New Stanton, near Pittsburgh. In return, the Pennsylvania Industrial Development Association has granted a $40-million loan and the state will spend another $20 million to complete a highway bypass near the site. Initial employment at the plant will total 2,000 but is expected to rise to 5,000 within two years. An estimated 23,000–35,000 workers will be needed in support industries.

Otherwise, the economy continued at a stable level, though unemployment in some chronically depressed industrial areas hovered near the 10%

mark. Agriculture, however, experienced a good year. Labor relations were peaceful for the most part, but differences over teachers' contracts interrupted classes in some districts.

Politics. Governor Shapp and Sen. Richard Schweiker fared badly in their quests for national office. Shapp withdrew from the race for the Democratic presidential nomination after a poor showing in the Florida primary. Ronald Reagan's selection of Schweiker, a liberal Republican, as a running mate on the eve of the Republican National Convention prompted a storm of criticism.

An attempt to recall Philadelphia Mayor Frank L. Rizzo ended with a court ruling that the petitions fell short of the necessary 145,448 valid signatures.

RICHARD ELGIN
Harrisburg "Patriot-News"

—— **PENNSYLVANIA** · Information Highlights ——

Area: 45,333 square miles (117,412 km²).
Population (1975 est.): 11,827,000.
Chief Cities (1970 census): Harrisburg, the capital, 68,-061; Philadelphia, 1,950,098; Pittsburgh, 520,117.
Government (1976): *Chief Officers*—governor, Milton J. Shapp (D); lt. gov., Ernest P. Kline (D). *General Assembly*—Senate, 50 members; House of Representatives, 203 members.
Education (1975–76): *Enrollment*—public elementary schools, 1,128,946 pupils; public secondary, 1,117,-272; nonpublic (1976–77), 467,900; colleges and universities, 429,628 students. *Public school expenditures*, $3,415,600,000 ($1,534 per pupil).
State Finances (fiscal year 1975): *Revenues*, $8,723,-817,000; *expenditures*, $9,475,515,000.
Personal Income (1975): $70,296,000,000; per capita, $5,943.
Labor Force (July 1976): *Nonagricultural wage and salary earners*, 4,430,900; *insured unemployed*, 225,-600 (6%).

PERU

Peru's most significant events in 1976 involved a shift to the right away from eight years of experiments in military-guided reform. The shift followed a series of economic austerity measures in January and June that provoked popular demonstrations and a cabinet reorganization in July. The anchovy catch continued to dwindle and a $1,000,000,000 gamble by foreign oil companies failed to find the oil in the Amazon jungles that the government had been counting upon to finance development and reform.

Economic Austerity. Faced with a heavy trade deficit and other serious economic problems, the government instituted a series of austerity measures in January and again in June. The June 28–30 economic package devalued the sol 44.4% (from 45 to 65 to the dollar), ended gasoline and food subsidies, froze wages, increased import and other taxes, and reduced government spending.

The June economic reforms led to widespread disorders in Lima and several provincial cities, following months of sporadic strikes protesting the January economic package. Popular reaction to the austerity measures was heightened by an increasing inflation rate of 50–60%, more than double the 24% increase in 1975.

Government Reorganization. The government declared a state of emergency on July 1 in an effort to end the disturbances. On July 9 troops suppressed a barracks rebellion led by Gen. Carlos Bobbio Centurión, the conservative commandant of the Peruvian Military Instruction Center, who tried to oust Prime Minister Gen. Jorge Fernández Maldonado. Bobbio acted after refusing an order by Fernández to retire.

President Francisco Morales Bermúdez fired four leftist generals from his cabinet on July 16 and replaced them with men considered more conservative politically. Among those dismissed was Fernández, who had been prime minister only since February 1 and was the architect of land reform programs and the expropriation of foreign mining and oil companies. He was re-

placed by Gen. Guillermo Arbulú Galliani, chairman of the joint chiefs of staff and an avowed anti-Communist. José de la Puente Radbill, a conservative economist and career diplomat, became foreign minister. He emphasized that Peru's relations with right-wing military regimes in Argentina and Chile would be strengthened.

Other Politics. Former President Fernando Belaúnde Terry visited Peru briefly in January, ending an exile that began in 1968 when he was ousted by the military. Although he praised President Morales Bermúdez, he also called for democratic elections. Belaúnde returned to Peru in May for the eighth national congress of his Popular Action party.

Foreign Relations. U. S. Secretary of State Henry Kissinger was received coolly when he visited Lima in February, although he announced on his arrival that the United States "understands and respects the objectives of the Peruvian revolution." U. S.-Peruvian relations improved after the July cabinet changes.

The June austerity measures were considered influential in obtaining a $240 million loan from 17 U. S. banks to help meet Peru's $400-million August debt payments. U. S. and Peruvian negotiators agreed on September 23 that Peru would pay the Marcona Mining Corporation $37 million in cash as compensation for properties nationalized in July 1975. In return, the San Francisco firm agreed to long-term purchases of Peruvian iron ore.

NEALE J. PEARSON, *Texas Tech University*

PHILIPPINES

President Ferdinand E. Marcos continued in full control of the Philippines in 1976, the fourth year of his martial law administration. A third referendum on the continuation of his rule carried overwhelmingly, but the environment in which it took place was far from free. Business ostensibly boomed, but there were several weak spots in the economy. Manila officially replaced adjacent Quezon City as the country's capital on June 24.

Politics. President Marcos appeared to enjoy success in several moves he took to consolidate his rule and control opposition to his continued leadership. In March, in his first major military shake-up since establishment of martial law, Marcos removed the commanders of the armed services and retired five other generals.

The Muslim separatist insurrection in the south, centered mainly on the island of Mindanao, appeared to have lost much of its thrust. However, although there was a surge of military action initiated by the rebels in midyear, the revolt did not seem to be succeeding in any of its objectives—to detach Muslim-ruled territory from the rest of the Philippines, to weaken Marcos' grip on power, and to weaken the government by draining away its economic resources.

───── **PERU · Information Highlights** ─────

Official Name: Republic of Peru.
Location: West coast of South America.
Area: 496,223 square miles (1,285,216 km²).
Population (1976 est.): 16,000,000.
Chief City (1972 census): Lima, the capital, 3,350,000 (met. area).
Government: *Head of state,* Gen. Francisco Morales Bermúdez (took office August 1975). *Head of government,* Gen. Guillermo Arbulú Galliani, prime minister (took office July 1976).
Monetary Unit: Sol (65.00 soles equal U. S.$1, Sept. 1976).
Gross National Product (1975 est.): $12,500,000,000.
Manufacturing (major products): Processed foods, textiles, chemicals, metal products, automobiles, fish meal, oil.
Major Agricultural Products: Cotton, sugar, rice, coffee, sheep, potatoes.
Foreign Trade: *Exports,* (1975): $1,301,000,000; *imports,* $2,329,000,000.

Members of the Philippine Volcanology Commission inspect a fissure spewing sulfur and methane gas on the slope of the Taal volcano. The activity followed a major earthquake that hit the Mindanao-Sulu region in August.

UPI

The Communist rebellion in the north on the key island of Luzon appeared to have all but expired, and "Captain Dante," leader of the "New People's Army," was captured in August. However, the growing ineffectiveness of the Communist insurrection, the proclaimed reason for the establishment of martial law, was not accompanied by any liberalization of Filipino politics.

Opposition to the October 16 referendum-plebiscite on the continuation of Marcos' rule was limited but active. In addition to one-time leading democratic political figures, the opposition to the referendum included the association of major religious superiors, which embraced one half of the 12,000 priests and nuns in the Roman Catholic country. However, more than 90% of an eligible 27 million persons participated in the referendum, and 90% of these indicated their approval of martial law. The effect was to allow President Marcos to "exercise legislative power until martial law is lifted."

In a move designed to undercut some of the opposition to his rule, Marcos authorized the 21-man national cabinet and the 91-member executive committee of the Association of Local and Provincial Assemblies to "share" legislative power with him.

Economy. The economy had its good spots and its bad ones. Business was visibly booming, inflation was kept down to less than 10%, the country's balance of payments deficit shrank from $264 million (in the first half of 1975) to $173 million (in the same period in 1976), and a bumper rice crop was harvested in the 1975–76 farming year.

But sugar, the country's leading export, fell nearly 50% in value in the first half of the year. The record rice crop depressed farmers' income as excessive supply forced down the price of the commodity. The minimum wage for workers, up to $1.40 a day, failed to keep pace with the rise in the cost of living. The gap between rich and poor appeared to grow. There was much criticism of the nearly $300 million spent on a dozen new luxury hotels.

Foreign Relations. U. S.-Filipino talks on continued American use of Clark Air Force and Subic Bay naval bases began in April, but quickly deadlocked. The Marcos government wants to exercise jurisdiction over U. S. airmen and sailors stationed in the Philippines if they violate Filipino law. The Philippines also sought a reduction in the size of the bases as well as in the length of their leases. Marcos declared his desire to "erase" all forms of Filipino "dependence" on the U. S. military. But his government was reported in October to be seeking thousands of millions of dollars in U. S. military equipment for continued use of the bases.

President Marcos paid an official visit to the Soviet Union, May 31–June 2. During his stay the two countries, which already had trade ties, agreed to establish diplomatic relations. Relations were also inaugurated with Vietnam and Cambodia during the year. The Philippines has established ties with 12 Communist nations since Marcos established martial law in 1972 to counter what he called a threatened Communist rebellion. Contact with the Communist states was not without its troubles, however, as evidenced by China's sudden cutoff of oil shipments in May.

The Philippines was host to 3,500 delegates from 128 countries for the annual joint meeting of the World Bank and International Monetary Fund.

RICHARD BUTWELL
State University of New York College at Fredonia

PHILIPPINES • Information Highlights

Official Name: Republic of the Philippines.
Location: Southeast Asia.
Area: 115,830 square miles (300,000 km²).
Population (1976 est.): 44,000,000.
Chief Cities (1975 est.): Manila, the capital, 1,459,000; Quezon City, 960,000; Cebu, 408,000.
Government: *Head of state,* Ferdinand E. Marcos, president (took office for 2d term Dec. 1969). *Head of government,* Marcos, prime minister (took office under new constitution Jan. 1973). *Legislature* (unicameral)—National Assembly.
Monetary Unit: Peso (7.43 pesos equal U. S.$1, Sept. 1976).
Gross National Product (1975 est.): $15,600,000,000.
Manufacturing (major products): Petroleum products, processed foods, tobacco products, plywood and veneers, paper.
Major Agricultural Products: Rice, corn, coconuts, sugarcane, abaca, sweet potatoes, lumber.
Foreign Trade (1975): *Exports,* $2,241,000,000; *imports,* $3,375,000,000.

PHOTOGRAPHY

While Americans continued their prolific image-taking to the tune of 7,000,000,000 pictures a year, the full-fledged arrival of automation, an explosion in the photographic press, and the coming of the golden age of color shaped the stories of 1976. Kodak made its long-awaited splash into instant cameras and prints as the electronization and sophisticated technology of equipment made the clearcut lines between amateur-oriented and professional machinery virtually disappear.

New Equipment. Previously on-the-verge, automation arrived full-blast during the year as many of the top-line SLR camera manufacturers brought out automatic exposure models well before the 1976 *photokina*, the international show held every other fall in Cologne, West Germany. Many followed the continuing trend toward size reduction, such as Konica's Autoreflex TC, whose body measures $5.5 \times 3.5 \times 1.8$ inches ($139.7 \times 88.9 \times 45.7$ mm) and weighs in at 25.6 ounces (725.7 grams) with the lens. The Olympus OM-2 represented a significant breakthrough in camera technology with its landmark feature of exposure automation based on monitoring the actual light reaching the film plane. The Canon AE-1 startled manufacturers and the public alike with its pro caliber electronic 35mm SLR, carrying an astonishing price tag of approximately $100. Meanwhile, Minolta broke through the heretofore impenetrable barrier between SLR and pocket camera design with its 110 SLR with a macro to zoom built-in lens. And a plethora of non-SLR pockets appeared with more advanced optical versatility. Leading the way was the world's first compact pocket zoom, the Fujica Pocket 350 Zoom from Fuji, with a 25–43mm lens. A dual-lens lineup was seen in Kodak's latest Tele-Instamatic, the 708, with a built-in four-element converter for turning the 25mm lens into a 43mm f/5.6 tele.

The 110 format and instant photography are the areas of greatest promise in market expansion and product development, according to the 24th annual *Wolfman Report of the Photographic Industry*. The report also noted the industry's economic recovery after the 1974–75 slump.

The big instant photography story was the long-awaited arrival of Kodak's film and camera system. The EK6 (listed at $69.50), an automatic film dispenser model, and the less popular EK4 ($53.50), the hand-crank model, used an E.1. 150 positive print film, ten to a battery-less pack, to produce a litter-free dry print after three minutes. In turn, Polaroid came out with a smaller, lower-priced version of the four-year-old SX-70, called the Pronto and competitively priced at $66, and sued Kodak for infringements of ten Polaroid patents.

Versatility was the big lens story in a slew of faster optics in compact, light-weight form—zooms, macros, wide-angles, long teles and super-speed normals with special attention to performance wide open, such as Leitz's Noctilux 50mm f/1. Many resulted from the technical fruition of the use of floating elements, new low-dispersion and other specialized optical glass, while the pressure on engineers to develop high-quality lenses at reduced price resulted in molded lens assemblies—which eliminate the cost of interior machining—in many of the 110s.

Other product trends included motor drives—even in Leitz's M4-2, an updated version of the Leica range finder 35; SLRs with the larger $1\frac{5}{8} \times 2\frac{1}{4}$ film format; improved meters that took into account the greater acceptance of electronic flash; modular build-it-yourself enlarger concepts; and from the Schneider Corp., the world's first zoom lens for enlargers. Many manufacturers brought out dryers especially for resin-coated paper and most of the super 8 cameras and projectors at *photokina* included XL "available light" shooting and the now routine in-camera sound recording capability.

A new technique called CPA, or concurrent photon amplification, was introduced in 1976 for exposing black-and-white film in "available darkness" while allowing for improved negative printability in terms of overall contrast. The method works by means of mini-lamps in the film gate, which boost sensitivity by the time-honored technique of "flashing" in-camera to irradiate film with weak illumination.

Color. At a time when 90% of all film purchased in the United States is color emulsion print, slide or instant, new color chemistry promises to reduce or eliminate most of the time-consuming drudgery. The three new processing contenders—Photocolor II, Unicolor Total Color, and the Kikuchi Family Color Kits—all do negs and prints using the same chemistry. Kodak entered the two-step color print processing race with Ektaprint 2. And manufacturers brought out a mass of equipment that makes it possible to make color prints on a kitchen table.

In color film, Kodachrome celebrated its 40th birthday while Kodak replaced its E-3 pro film with E-6 for improved color reproduction. Polaroid also improved its SX-70 film and came out with a Polacolor-2 8×10 instant color film.

William Eggleston's 75 prints of his native locale, northern Mississippi and Memphis, Tenn., splashed across the walls of the Museum of Modern Art in New York City. It was the first one-man color print show there in ten years, and the accompanying 48-print *Guide* was the museum's first color photographic book. *Newsweek* ran a major story and portfolio on color's "new frontier." Even black-and-white superstar Ralph Gibson translated his minimal abstractionistic viewpoint into hues, which appeared in the *1977 Photography Annual*. And at the Rochester Institute of Technology (RIT), a conference was held on color permanence and a second workshop on color photojournalism.

A trio of "first-generation master photographers" died during 1976. Minor White (*above*) developed the photo program at the San Francisco Art Institute; Paul Strand specialized in such subject matter as non-studio portraits, architectural designs, and landscapes; and Imogen Cunningham, 93, spanned the entire history of photography from the box-camera on.

Publications, Auctions, and Shows. A burgeoning photographic press opened up the boundaries long-retained by a quarter of major U. S. photo magazines. In New York, examples of the new publications included: *Photograph* and *Photo Review: A Critical Newsletter,* for more verbal criticism of *current* shows (while on the walls);

Fotofile, a newspaper showing images by many photographers; *Document,* for single portfolios; *The Flash,* a surrealist journal edited by photographer Charles Gatewood, "dedicated to high seeing." And on the continent of Europe, *Printletter* was produced in response to the heavy acceleration in print buying.

EASTMAN KODAK COMPANY

With the EK6, an automatic film dispenser model, Kodak made its splash into instant cameras in 1976.

The Photography Catalog, photography's first illustrated all-purpose source book on equipment, materials, techniques, and resources came out in time for the Christmas buying season. At RIT's well-attended weekend seminar on photographic book publishing, Gaylord Herron's new style book called *Vagabond* was heavily touted. The metaphorical collection of photographs, some paintings, and text was far removed from the "sterile purity" of the catalog-type, one-picture-to-a-page format made successful by *Aperture,* the granddaddy of the current longer-format publications. Yet even *Aperture* reacted to winds of change, as reflected in an issue of the quarterly that included eight pages of color by Helen Levitt and portfolios by an increased number of lesser-known photographers.

While periodicals stressed more current, encompassing, and critical coverage, books—and the shows that often ran concurrently—stressed documentation of previous eras and places, and the work of past photographers: *Street Life in London,* John Thomson's documentation of urban poverty in the 1870's; *The Last Empire: Photographs of Victorian India,* the 19th century record of how the British saw the India they ruled; *Alice's World: The Life and Photography of an American Original—Alice Austen, 1866–1952,* a photographer's diary of the wealthy society in which she lived.

Shows like "Remarkable American Women," which grew out of a *Life Special Report;* the Alaska Gold Rush; Timothy O'Sullivan's pictures of the Civil War; and a two-part showing from Stieglitz's *Camera Work* were a few of the many exhibits spurred on by the U. S. bicentennial.

Three New York auctions in the spring indicated photography's on-going boom in the art marketplace, with an intake of more than $500,-000 at Sotheby Parke-Bernet, and $60–70,000 and $90,000 respectively at the Swann Galleries and Martin Gordon's at the Hotel St. Moritz, the latter two new to the profitable scene pioneered by Parke-Bernet in 1967. And at Gordon's sale, the complete Edward S. Curtis "North American Indian" portfolio brought an astonishing $60,000 bid. The growing interest in collecting original photographs also resulted in a book called *The Photographic Print Collector's Handbook,* by Barbara and John Upton and gallery owner Lee Witkin.

A steady series of photographic shows continued almost unnoticed in the galleries that had formerly handled paintings and sculpture exclusively. And photographic galleries moved into the heart of the art scene: Witkin's to New York's 57th St., the Light Gallery to Fifth Avenue. The Soho cooperative enjoyed its sixth year of existence in new space with expanded show facilities, counted additional branches in Los Angeles, Philadelphia, and New Orleans, and honed plans for future expansion into Europe and Asia.

The trend in photographic content moved in an even more philosophical and spiritual direction, as evidenced in the increased popularity of Duane Michals' philosophical sequences, George Krause's special brand of photographic religiosity, and the rediscovery of the haunting multi-images of New Orleans' eccentric Clarence John Laughlin.

Obituaries. The end of an age was emphasized by the death of a trio of "first-generation master photographers."

Imogen Cunningham. At 93, this five-foot-tall, pixie-faced woman, who scampered around San Francisco with a black cape, cap, and peace symbol, "broke all the rules concerning how 90-year-old ladies should behave," observed one journal. She grew up with photography; printed for Edward S. Curtis from 1900 to 1909; mingled with Coburn and Stieglitz; and formed the "f/64" group of sharp, nature-oriented, realistic photographers with Edward Weston. She photographed male nudes at the turn of the century; earned her living from portraiture; and focused on horticultural studies. She was at work on a book on people over 90 when she died on June 24.

Paul Strand. At 85, this former student of Lewis Hine's was already a legend as a guiding influence in the new realism that broke with 19th century romanticism; the "brutal directness" Stieglitz saw in his work became a prototype for an entire generation of photography. Cubist abstractions, still lifes, non-studio portraits, and architectural and landscape renditions were his subject matter—in the black-and-white large format he used exclusively. His documentary approach as a filmmaker lives on in the classic films *The Wave* and *The Plow That Broke the Plains*.

Minor White. He died at 67, on the same day as Cunningham. Known as the modern-day dean of the Equivalence Photographers—a theme established by Stieglitz—he was well known as the most mystical and philosophical of the photographer/teachers. Along with Ansel Adams, he developed the photography program at what became the San Francisco Art Institute and was longtime photography head at the Massachusetts Institute of Technology. He wrote *The Zone System Manual,* helped found *Aperture* and was always its editor.

BARBARA LOBRON
Journalist, Editor, Photographer

PHYSICS

In physics, 1976 was a truly exciting year. Superheavy elements may have been discovered, and landmark advances were achieved in high-energy physics. Progress was made in the fields of controlled thermonuclear fusion, synchrotron radiation sources, and heavy-ion accelerators.

Superheavy Elements. Physicists have long predicted the existence of many more elements than those now occurring in nature. Elements 93 through 106 have been created artificially with large accelerators, but production of new elements is difficult. Physicists predict regions (or islands) of elements with increased stability against spontaneous decay. Elements in these regions, once created, might last long enough to be examined; such superheavy elements might even remain from primordial times.

Evidence of primordial superheavy elements has been presented by a group of physicists from Oak Ridge National Laboratory (ORNL), Florida State University, and the University of California at Davis. The elements were observed by bombarding small inclusions in a mineral sample and detecting the X rays emitted. The X-ray energies agreed with those predicted for several superheavy elements, with strongest confidence in element 126.

The apparent discovery was the outgrowth of an attempt to explain phenomena called giant halos that occur around monazite (a certain combination of rare earths and actinides) inclusions in some crystals. The halos are discolorations caused by radiation damage. If a radioactive element in the inclusion decays by emitting alpha particles, the halo results. The higher the alpha-particle energy, the bigger the halo. Giant halos appear to correspond to an exceptionally high alpha-particle energy, and thus, possibly, to a new element.

Another report concerns an extinct superheavy element 115 (or 114 or 113) which may have existed in a meteorite that fell in Mexico in 1969. The argument is a complex, inferential one based on the anomalously high amount of xenon in certain inclusions in the meteorite. The xenon is thought to be a fission product. Since the amount of xenon is anomalously high in locations that are rich in certain elements, the fission parent is assumed to be chemically similar to those latter elements. The best guesses are elements 113, 114, or 115.

Elementary Particles. New elementary particle discoveries abounded during the year. The whole field has been exceptionally active since the discovery in 1974 of a new particle by a group of researchers at Brookhaven National Laboratory and another group at Stanford Linear Accelerator Laboratory (SLAC). The particle was called J by the former group, psi by the latter. Another unusual particle (psi prime) was discovered a few days later at SLAC.

OAK RIDGE NATIONAL LABORATORY

Large radiation-damage rings, called "giant halos," in this photomicrograph suggest the existence of "superheavy" elements. The discovery was announced in July 1976.

A number of years ago it was proposed that many of the "elementary" particles actually consisted of subparticles, or quarks. Quarks were very useful in interpreting the large numbers of particles in the nuclear "zoo," but they were not (and have not been) observed directly. Originally, there were only three kinds of quarks. Later, a fourth quark was considered with a new property, called charm. When the psi particle was discovered, it was proposed that the psi consisted of a charmed quark and a charmed antiquark. The psi itself would not have charm, since charm was cancelled by the quark-antiquark combination; the new quark combination was called charmonium. Charmonium should have a whole spectrum of states, or related particles. Experiments at the Deutsches Elektronen-Synchrotron in Hamburg, West Germany, and later experiments at SLAC have found a number of these states; their properties agree well with predictions. Experimenters at the Fermi National Accelerator Laboratory and at SLAC now have definitely observed charmed mesons.

New Accelerators. The news of huge new accelerators usually comes from the field of elementary particles. Nuclear structure physics is also accelerator oriented, but traditionally on a much smaller scale. In the past few years, much interest within nuclear physics has turned to beams of heavy ions.

Until recently the two major centers for heavy-ion research were the Lawrence Berkeley Laboratory in California, and the Dubna Laboratory in the Soviet Union. A major new heavy-ion facility became operational in 1976: Gesellschaft für Schwerionforschung (GSI) near Darmstadt, West Germany. Acceleration of xenon nuclei is now routine, even uranium has been successfully accelerated. The cost of GSI ($60 million) is on the scale of particle physics and reflects the transformation now taking place in the field of nuclear physics. Other heavy-ion projects are also under way in Great Britain, France, and the United States, but the West Germans seem ready to take the leadership in heavy-ion physics for the near future. Not to be outdone, the particle physicists have begun negotiation for a new accelerator, so large and so expensive that not even the United States or the Soviet Union alone could fund the project.

Synchrotron Radiation. Accelerated charged particles emit synchrotron radiation, certain properties of which make the radiation very useful to molecular biologists, solid-state physicists, and many others. This source of high intensity, tunable ultraviolet, and X-radiation is ideal for studying such diverse topics as X-ray diffraction on crystals of protein, X-ray microscopy, and ultraviolet studies of solid surfaces. In practice the sources of synchrotron radiation serve as tunable X-ray and ultraviolet lasers. Synchrotron radiation users operate as secondary users at accelerators dedicated to particle physics, or at smaller facilities with less intensity. A new laboratory authorized in Great Britain, the Synchrotron Radiation Source, will be dedicated to this purpose alone; the new center will have intensities comparable to those at the largest existing facilities.

Magnetic Monopole. In 1931, P. A. M. Dirac developed the theory of a fundamental magnetic particle carrying a single magnetic charge (like a magnet with one pole). Since then, experimenters have searched fruitlessly for this magnetic monopole with particle accelerators and cosmic rays, in iron cores, ocean sediments, meteorites, and lunar rocks.

In 1975, a group of cosmic-ray researchers from the University of California at Berkeley and the University of Houston announced the discovery of a track they interpreted as that of a magnetic monopole. The particle detector was made up of a stack of films and plastic sheets, carried by a balloon to 130,000 feet (39,600 m), to search out heavy cosmic-ray particles. On etching the sheets, the investigators found them completely penetrated by one unusual track. The track indicated a particle of at least 600 proton masses with a charge 137 times larger than that of an electron. However, other physicists pointed out that to establish a new particle requires very strong evidence. It is not sufficient for the data to be consistent with the hypothesis of the new particle; other alternatives must be disproven before such a major discovery can be accepted. The identical alternative interpretation of the track was put forth independently: an initial platinum nucleus collided and was transformed twice in the plates. Without further evidence the existence of the magnetic monopole will remain unproven.

Controlled Thermonuclear Fusion. One basic world problem is the development of new energy sources. An ultimate alternative to the fission processes employed in present-day reactors is controlled thermonuclear fusion, but the practical problems in controlled fusion are monumental: the materials must be heated sufficiently for the fusion reaction to occur, and the reaction must be contained. The temperatures involved are in the range from 10 million to 100 million degrees Kelvin. At such extreme temperatures, the fusion materials form a plasma (ionized gas). Since no solid wall can contain plasma at such temperatures, researchers have used magnetic fields as a container.

Progress on many fronts, but no breakthrough, was reported in 1976. The optimists see the steady improvement of magnetic containment devices as gratifying and predict scientific breakeven by 1980. They are also heartened by evidence for fusion from laser-induced implosion. Even so, a practical fusion reactor is at least a generation off.

GARY MITCHELL
Department of Physics
North Carolina State University

POLAND

The domestic political situation in Poland became increasingly precarious in 1976. There were no major changes, however, in the leadership and organization of the ruling United Polish Workers' (Communist) party.

Government. In the early months of 1976 the party pursued a public debate of new constitutional proposals, which sought to link Poland even more closely with the Soviet Union; they emphasized the supreme power of the party over all other institutions and sought to curb the influence of religion on Polish life. The symbolism of these proposals met considerable opposition throughout the country, even among rank-and-file party membership. Several proposals were eventually watered down. The new constitution adopted in March gave implicit sanction to the Brezhnev doctrine. Henceforth, the Soviet alliance would be a constitutional obligation of all Polish governments.

More serious problems arose in June when the government announced food price increases averaging about 60%. Widespread strikes and rioting ensued. Workers tore up railroad tracks, halting the Warsaw-Paris express. The government did not employ nearly so much force as in the more serious previous outbreaks in 1956 and 1970, and it immediately rescinded the price increases. By July, the crisis in the factories and streets had eased. But the respite

seemed temporary because of the gravity of Poland's economic situation.

Economy. By mid-1976 the Gierek economic policy of financing rapid development at home through trade and credit from abroad appeared to be failing. Poland had accumulated an external debt estimated between $6,000,000,000 and $9,000,000,000 (the largest of any Communist state save the USSR), and there was a growing imbalance in the volume of trade; in 1976 imports exceeded exports by some $2,000,-000,000. Poland became, for the first time in its peace-time history, a net importer of foreign foodstuffs. The expected increases in productivity of Polish industries had not materialized. The government's policy of holding down food prices by artificial means contributed to low output by farmers and frequent shortages in stores. It also generated higher consumption than the state could afford to subsidize indefinitely. In the last quarter of 1976 the government was attempting to balance resources and consumer demands with piecemeal price increases, amidst tension and growing discontent.

Church-State Relations. There was considerable conflict between the regime and the Church over the new constitution. The episcopate succeeded in forcing the party to withdraw the most objectionable proposals for criminal punishment of people who "use religion for political purposes." The Church tacitly supported Polish intellectuals, led by the academician Edward Lipinski, seeking more individual liberties. In general, however, religious controversies were overshadowed by economic problems.

Foreign Affairs. Poland continued to seek foreign credit and trade opportunities abroad by special missions and diplomatic exchanges with France, Sweden, the United States, West Germany, and many smaller countries. There was continued improvement in Polish-West German relations as a result of the 1976 ratification by West Germany of the treaty for the exchange of 125,000 Germans living in Poland for low-interest credits of more than $400 million.

ALEXANDER J. GROTH
University of California, Davis

Poland's Foreign Minister Stefan Olszowski addresses the 31st session of the UN General Assembly.

UPI

POLAND • Information Highlights

Official Name: Polish People's Republic.
Location: Eastern Europe.
Area: 120,724 square miles (312,677 km²).
Population (1976 est.): 34,400,000.
Chief Cities (1975 est.): Warsaw, the capital, 1,410,000; Łodz, 787,000; Cracow, 668,000.
Government: *Head of state,* Henryk Jabłonski, chairman of the Council of State (took office 1972). *Head of government,* Piotr Jaroszewicz, chairman of the Council of Ministers (1970). *First secretary of the United Polish Workers' party,* Edward Gierek (1970). *Legislature* (unicameral)—Sejm.
Monetary Unit: Zloty (19.05 zlotys equal U. S.$1, Nov. 1976).
Gross National Product (1975 est.): $65,600,000,000.
Manufacturing (major products): Petroleum products, transport equipment, chemicals, machinery.
Major Agricultural Products: Rye, oats, potatoes, sugar beets, wheat, tobacco, livestock.
Foreign Trade (1975): *Exports,* $10,283,000,000; *imports,* $12,536,000,000.

A ski-equipped C-130 airplane damaged on the east antarctic plateau is repaired. The icebreaker *Polar Star* is tested for the first time off Alaska.

POLAR RESEARCH

Damage to three out of five of the U. S. antarctic program's ski-equipped C-130 airplanes limited research in Antarctica during the 1975–76 austral summer. However, a major earth-sciences investigation was completed near the main U. S. base, McMurdo Station, and researchers from the 10 nations active in year-round antarctic science continued to probe the region's ice, air, earth, and seas. In the Arctic, research centered on completing a major ice dynamics field program and continuing a large outer-continental-shelf program.

Antarctic. The C-130's were damaged in separate accidents while attempting to take off at the same site high on the plateau of East Antarctica. Called dome C (74°30′ S. lat., 123°10′ E. long., elev. 3,240 m, or 10,630 ft), the site is of special interest to glaciologists because its ice is among the thickest in Antarctica. There were no injuries to anyone aboard the three airplanes. Crews worked in average summer temperatures of around −30° C (−22° F) to recover two of the planes. The third was slated for repair and recovery in the 1976–77 season.

The Dry Valley Drilling Project, involving Japan, New Zealand, and the United States in a study of the geologic history of the McMurdo Sound region, completed its fifth season of deep-earth sampling. A core was obtained 188 m (617 ft) below the 2-m (6.5-ft) McMurdo sea ice, which served as a platform for the drill rig and camp.

Other antarctic research focused on the abundant life and the unique oceanography of the southern waters. Argentine and U. S. investigators continued their 5-year circumant-arctic oceanographic survey from aboard the Argentine research ship *Islas Orcadas*.

Some experts believe the day to be nearing when large-scale exploitation of the Antarctic's living and mineral resources becomes inevitable. With that in mind, biologists and others met at Woods Hole, Mass., in August 1976 for a conference on the living resources of the southern ocean. The session was held at the request of delegates to the eighth consultative meeting (1975) of the Antarctic Treaty to consider the future impact of major exploitation.

Also, delegates from the 12 Antarctic Treaty nations gathered in Paris in June 1976 for a special session on the question of exploration and exploitation of antarctic mineral resources. The discussion was to prepare for the ninth consultative meeting (London, September 1977), when this question is expected to be a major agenda item requiring a solution that is agreeable to all the signatories of the treaty.

Arctic. The 14-month main study of the Arctic Ice Dynamics Joint Experiment, or AIDJEX, ended on May 8, 1976. During the study, investigators worked at stations on ice floes approximately 640 km (400 miles) northeast of Point Barrow, Alaska, to learn more about air-sea-ice interactions. Instrumented airplanes provided remote sensing, and in April 1976 a nuclear submarine measured the roughness of the underside of the ice. An AIDJEX model is being refined to improve techniques of forecasting ice.

A federally funded environmental assessment of the outer continental shelf continued for the second year in the Beaufort Sea. The collected data will provide a basis for predicting the impact of oil and gas exploration and development on the marine environment. In 1976, there were more than 40 investigators conducting 45 projects that concerned mammals, birds, fish, benthos, plankton, microbiology, littoral zone, chemistry, physical oceanography and meteorology, ice, and geology.

The Coast Guard icebreaker *Polar Star*, which accommodates 10 scientists, was commissioned in January 1976 and tested in the Arctic. The ship had troubles with two of its three drive shafts during operations in the ice of the Bering Sea and had to undergo repairs in Seattle, Wash. As a result, its 1976–77 operation in antarctic waters was canceled.

JERRY R. STRINGER *and* L. G. BLANCHARD
Polar Programs, National Science Foundation

POPULATION

The world's population, estimated at 4,019,-000,000 in mid-1976, was calculated to be growing at a slower pace than was the case a few years earlier. Estimates of the annual growth rate have declined from 2.0% to 1.8%, lengthening the time it would take for the population to double to 8 billion from 35 to 38 years.

Recent declines in population have been due to lower fertility in many nations, including those with promising public birth control programs. But it has become apparent that future reductions in world population growth also may be the result of higher mortality due to setbacks in some death control efforts. In Pakistan, for example, malaria is making a comeback after once having been thought to be on the way to eradication. Reported cases in that country grew from only 9,500 in 1968 to 10 million in 1975. Other nations with increasing rates of malaria include Thailand, India, Sri Lanka, Vietnam, and Bangladesh.

Almost half of the world's population lives in just four countries. With an estimated 837 million persons, the People's Republic of China accounts for 21% of the world's total. India (621 million) has 15%, the Soviet Union, 6% (257 million), and the United States, 5% (215 million). If current trends continue, by the year 2000 the two most rapidly growing regions of the world—Latin America and Africa—will increase their combined share of the world's total from 18% today to 23%.

United States Trends. The large decline in fertility that occurred between 1970 and 1975 in the United States has produced intriguing contrasts between women now in their 40's and those in their 20's. In 1975 over one third of the former already had borne four or more children. But according to the U. S. Bureau of the Census, less than one tenth of the latter expect to have such large families. The most commonly desired family size among younger women now has become two children. Among women 18 and 19 years of age in 1975, for instance, 60% expected to have two children, 18% three children, 15% one or none, and 7% four or more. For the 12-month period ending in June 1976, the number of births per 1,000 population was 14.6. This was about 3% lower than the rate (15.0) for the corresponding period ending in 1975.

The mortality rate also declined, and fewer Americans died in 1975 than in any year since 1967. The death rate fell to 8.9 for each 1,000 persons during the 12 months ending in June 1976, compared with the previous low of 9.1 recorded both in 1954 and 1974. The continuing downturn is due to reductions in a number of causes of death. Interestingly, the greatest relative decrease among all causes of death from January–May 1975 to January–May 1976 was for homicide, down 17%.

The increase during the early 1970's in the proportion of persons who are divorced or separated is impressive. In 1975, among all ever-married persons 25 to 54 years old, 10% currently were divorced or separated, compared with 7% for the parallel group in 1970. The figures reflect the marital status of persons at the time they were interviewed by the Census Bureau, and thus do not include those who had remarried after divorce or had become reconciled after separation. The actual proportions who have experienced divorce or separation is higher, although exactly how much higher is not currently known.

Canadian Trends. Partly due to increased government restrictions on the admission of less-well-skilled immigrants, 14% fewer persons went to live in Canada in 1975 than in 1974. While the number of immigrants from all of the major sending countries and regions declined, the relative reductions were greatest among immigrants from Portugal (down 48%), the Netherlands (31%), Greece (28%), and the West Indies (25%). The smallest changes took place among persons emigrating from Italy (down 3%) and Germany (4%). Although somewhat reduced, immigration continues to be as important as fertility in adding to Canada's population, which reached an estimated 23.1 million on April 1, 1976.

ROBERT E. KENNEDY, JR.
University of Minnesota

PORTUGAL

In 1976 Portugal continued its precarious retreat from the shadows of a dictatorship that gripped the country for 48 years until April 25, 1974, when the Armed Forces Movement executed a coup d'etat which ousted Prime Minister Marcello Caetano.

In late June 1976 three fourths of the country's 6.5 million eligible voters went to the polls to select the first democratically elected president in more than 50 years. They gave a resounding mandate to Gen. António Ramalho Eanes, the sober, aloof army chief of staff, who enjoyed the backing of Portugal's three largest political parties—the Socialists, the Popular Democrats (now called the Social Democrats), and the Social Democratic Center (CDS).

General Eanes, who pledged to promote democratic socialism and bring law and order to this strife-torn nation of 8.5 million, received over 60% of the ballots cast. Thus, he overwhelmed Maj. Otelo Saraiva de Carvalho (16.5%), a radical populist who played a key role in the 1974 coup, Adm. Pinheiro de Azevedo (14.4%), the country's moderate prime minister who suffered a debilitating heart attack four days before the election, and Octavio Pato (7.6%), candidate of Portugal's Communist Party.

While a notable victory for democracy and socialism, the election proved a severe setback

UPI

In June, Gen. António Ramalho Eanes was elected president of Portugal, winning some 60% of the vote.

for the Communists. As close allies of the radical officers who took over the government soon after Caetano's overthrow, they gained dominance of the country's single labor confederation, control of a majority of local governments, and key positions in the mass media. However, pressure from the Roman Catholic Church, moderate officers, conservatives in Portugal's north, and European Economic Community leaders led to the downfall of the radical officers with whom the Communists' political fortunes were intertwined. During 1976 the Communists indeed lost ground.

The 41-year-old chief executive, a veteran of Portugal's protracted African wars, fulfilled his campaign promise and invited Mário Soares, the distinguished Socialist leader and former foreign minister, to form a government. The new cabinet, sworn in on July 23, 1976, is composed of 14 Socialists, 3 prominent independents, and 3 moderate officers.

In a speech to the legislative assembly, Soares committed his government to (1) civil liberties and the construction of a democratic state; (2) reorganization of the economy and stimulation of economic growth to achieve income redistribution and greater social justice; and (3) the pursuit of national independence and international cooperation for peace.

Despite resentment at not being invited to join a coalition, the Social Democrats and the CDS agreed to back Soares and his ministers.

Soares, a 51-year-old intellectual who was jailed a dozen times during the dictatorship, encouraged pluralism. During 1976, for example, his government abolished the single labor confederation as part of a labor reform that permits only unions to call strikes and forbids lockouts by management. He also called for elections on Dec. 12, 1976, to allow the Portuguese people to choose local governments.

The prime minister's major challenges are economic in character. His country is beset by a 50% rate of inflation, a 20% unemployment level, and a balance of payments deficit that could become chronic because of food and fuel imports. Moreover, the gross domestic product, which increased in 1973 (10.5%) and 1974 (3.9%), fell 3.6% in 1975 and may register an even larger decline when the 1976 figures are released.

To try to regain investor confidence that was badly shaken by the extensive expropriations of the post-coup period, Soares said that there would be no new nationalizations and the rights of ownership would be respected. However, private investors—both domestic and foreign—remained skeptical of the government's ability to achieve its twin goals of political stability and economic growth.

Because rural unrest and illegal land seizures had caused agricultural production to plummet at the very time there were more mouths to feed due to an influx of whites from Angola and Mozambique, Portugal imported half its food supply in 1976. In late September 1976, Soares' government ordered the eviction of peasants from 101 illegally occupied farms.

The Portuguese regime received strong economic assistance from countries anxious to see democracy and civil liberties take root in Iberia. Credits poured in from West Germany ($250 million), Switzerland ($50 million), Norway ($18 million), and the European Investment Bank ($240 million), an arm of the European Economic Community which Portugal hopes to join as soon as possible. The United States launched a $30 million aid program.

GEORGE W. GRAYSON
College of William and Mary

——— **PORTUGAL · Information Highlights** ———

Official Name: Portuguese Republic.
Location: Southwestern Europe.
Area: 35,553 square miles (92,082 km²).
Population (1976 est.): 8,500,000.
Chief Cities (1972 est.): Lisbon, the capital, 761,500; Oporto, 304,700.
Government: *Head of state,* António Ramalho Eanes, president (took office July 1976). *Head of government,* Mário Soares (took office July 1976). *Legislature* (unicameral)—National Assembly.
Monetary Unit: Escudo (30.77 escudos equal U.S.$1, Nov. 1976).
Gross National Product (1975 est.): $18,100,000,000.
Manufacturing (major products): Wine, canned fish, processed foods, textiles, ships.
Major Agricultural Products: Grapes, tomatoes, potatoes, wheat, figs, olives, fish, forest products.
Foreign Trade (1975): *Exports,* $1,939,000,000; *imports,* $3,840,000,000.

POSTAL SERVICE

The U. S. Postal Service continued to lose money in 1976. When the Post Office Department was reorganized on July 1, 1971, into the Postal Service, an independent establishment in the executive branch of government, it was anticipated that it would some day become a self-sustaining operation. But five years later these expectations had not been realized. During the fiscal year ending June 30, 1976, the Postal Service lost more money than in any previous fiscal year.

Total operating revenues in 1976, including congressional appropriations, increased by 10%, but off-setting increases in costs contributed to a net loss of $1,176,000,000. However, only $126 million of the deficit was incurred in the last half of the year, and some additional signs of financial improvement appeared in the quarter between the 1976 fiscal year and Oct. 1, 1976, when the Postal Service had a $15 million surplus. This was the first time the Postal Service operated in the black during an audited period. An intensified cost control program, unanticipated increase in mail volume, and continued reduction by attrition in the postal work force resulted in this healthy turnabout even though a deficit of $425 million originally had been projected.

Increased Volume. The increase in mail volume was the result of a three-month strike of employees of a private competitor, United Parcel Service. In the 15 affected states the Postal Service experienced a dramatic increase in the volume of parcel post, sack mail, and non-machinable items. Indeed, on Oct. 13, 1976, volume had increased by 225% when measured against a single day in the previous month. During the strike, bulk mail centers and regular postal installations increased the regular 8-hour work tours to 10 hours, and added two 10-hour shifts on Saturday and Sunday. Superb cooperation from its employees enabled the Postal Service to meet these new and unexpected demands with minimum delays in service.

Technological Study. Research was initiated into the possibility of the electronic transfer of mail. The Postal Service granted a contract for a two-year feasibility study to determine the technical and economic aspects of an electronic service system. The study will consider many alternatives, including employing communications satellites, terrestrial networks, facsimile devices, optical character readers, and word processing equipment. Such a system would be designed to accept a message in paper copy form, convert the material into a digital form, transport the message electronically to its destination, and convert the material back to paper copy form for delivery by a carrier.

Congressional Action. Proposed cutbacks in service ran into severe congressional opposition. During fiscal 1976 the Postal Service sought to eliminate small rural post offices and to reduce big-city downtown business mail deliveries from two to one daily. Additionally, the postal board of governors had authorized the legal preparations necessary for the elimination of Saturday mail deliveries everywhere at an estimated savings of $350 million a year. These reductions did not occur when the Postal Service received an additional appropriation from Congress.

Although congressional subsidies have averaged $1,500,000,000 yearly since 1972, the Postal Service has an accumulated debt of $3,000,000,000. Legislation signed by President Ford in September 1976 provided for an additional appropriation of $1,000,000,000 to be applied over a two-year period to the debt only and not to operating expenses. The bill also established a seven-member Commission on Postal Services to study and evaluate postal operations. The commission will examine services in terms of the economic and social benefits to the user and recipient, and the economic ability of users to absorb costs. In light of its findings the commission is expected to recommend which services should be provided for by tax dollars and which should be provided for by postal revenues. Increases in postal rates and reductions in service are frozen until the study group reports to the president on March 15, 1977.

Postal Improvements. Through mechanization, attrition, and other means, the Postal Service has reduced its work force by 50,000 over a five-year period. At the same time productivity of letter carriers increased by 23.8% and that of clerk mail handlers by 13.6%. Nevertheless, the personnel costs associated with a work force of 680,000 are most significant, representing 86.1% of the total expenses of the Postal Service, a slight increase over the expenses of the previous year.

By international standards the U. S. Postal Service has a commendable record. In comparing the productivity of U. S. postal employees with those of 10 other nations, it is found that U. S. productivity is in excess of 127,000 pieces of mail per year per employee, better than double that of postal workers in Great Britain and West Germany. Rates in the United States are generally lower as well. Although first class postage rates have increased by about 30% to 13 cents over the past two years, U. S. postage rates remain relatively low, second only to Canada, which will have a 12-cent first class stamp in 1977.

In fiscal 1976 the Postal Service maintained approximately 40,000 facilities and a motor fleet of 200,000 vehicles. In processing almost 90,-000,000,000 pieces of mail, it achieved for the second consecutive year its announced objective: to deliver local letter mail overnight at least 95% of the time.

DAVID R. BLOODSWORTH
University of Massachusetts

PRINCE EDWARD ISLAND

Developments in the political arena captured headlines in Prince Edward Island in 1976. The provincial Conservatives elected a new leader and the federal leaders of both major political parties visited the island. Economically, recovery from the recession remained sluggish, while heavy emphasis was placed on bringing inflation under control.

Politics. Prime Minister Pierre Trudeau encountered complaints, criticism, and some abuse when he visited Prince Edward Island for two days in September. The first day, while Trudeau was still closeted in his motel room, several Charlottetown residents called a radio open-line show to criticize him publicly. Farmers and businessmen who met him were courteous, though critical of his policies, but labor representatives brusquely rejected his invitation to discuss the federal government's anti-inflation wage and price controls program.

Angus MacLean, a former federal fisheries minister and a federal MP for 25 years, won the leadership of the province's Progressive Conservative party on September 25. He succeeded Melvin McQuaid, named earlier to the provincial Supreme Court. Among those attending the leadership convention in Charlottetown was federal Conservative leader Joseph Clark.

Economy. Prince Edward Island and Newfoundland entered the federal anti-inflation program together on February 2. Public-sector employees and agencies of the two provinces thus became subject to the restraint guidelines of the federal Anti-Inflation Board.

In the speech from the throne opening the spring session of the legislature, the Liberal government narrowed its priorities to two: energy conservation and public spending restraint.

Budget cutbacks resulting from the restraint program hit the University of Prince Edward Island, curtailing services. A number of vacant teaching positions were left unfilled.

Strikes by construction laborers and carpenters shut down 27 construction jobs in the province in June and July.

JOHN BEST, *Chief, Canada World News*

PRINCE EDWARD ISLAND • Information Highlights

Area: 2,184 square miles (5,656 km²).
Population (April 1976 est.): 120,000.
Chief Cities (1971 census): Charlottetown, the capital, 19,133; Summerside, 9,439.
Government (1975): *Chief Officers*—lt. gov., Gordon L. Bennett; premier, Alexander B. Campbell (Liberal); min. of justice, Alexander Campbell; min. of educ., W. Bennett Campbell; chief justice, Charles St. Clair Trainor. *Legislature*—Legislative Assembly, 32 members.
Education (1976–77): *Enrollment:* public elementary and secondary schools, 27,480 pupils; Indian (federal) schools, 50; post-secondary, 2,210. *Total expenditures,* $47,891,000.
Public Finance (1975–76 est.): *Revenues,* $182,000,000; *expenditures,* $192,000,000.
Personal Income (1974): $383,000,000; average annual income per person, $3,274.
(All monetary figures given in Canadian dollars.)

UPI

All U.S. federal prisons, except penitentiaries, are now required to employ women correctional officers.

PRISONS

The number of inmates in federal, state, and local prisons reached record levels in 1976. Overcrowding, often accompanied by smoldering tensions, became widespread. Genuine reforms were few, but some developments in sentencing and parole may indicate significant long-term policy changes.

Overcrowding. In March, the U. S. Justice Department announced that prisoners in federal institutions numbered 26,047, indicating that the prison system was operating at more than 22% above capacity. The continued climb of the crime rate and the trend among judges to give longer sentences have pushed many prisons to crisis conditions.

At the Lewisburg, Pa., penitentiary, which holds some of the toughest U. S. criminals, eight inmates were killed by other inmates within a two-year period. A board of inquiry, reporting in August, called attention to "an increase in the number of young, aggressive, immature, and criminalistic inmates," one fourth of whom were first arrested before they were 14, and nearly half of whom have served at least two previous prison terms.

A planned demonstration in August by prisoners at Attica, N. Y., site of the 1971 uprising and suppression which took 43 lives, remained nonviolent. Overcrowding had almost reached the 1971 levels and was one of the major grievances against which the inmates protested. The New York State prison population rose from 14,500 in March of 1975 to some 18,500 by the fall of 1976. Several new facilities were opened, but these only kept pace with the rising number of inmates and did not reduce pressures at existing facilities.

Serious altercations occurred at the Rahway and Trenton, N. J., prisons in February, and some prisoners were transferred to youth facilities and work camps throughout the state. All

The James V. Bennett Federal Prison in Burton, N. C., formally opened on May 13. Although designated for "serious" offenders, the innovative facility has no cell blocks or gun towers.

New Jersey prisons were crowded above capacity; the Rahway prison, designed for 800 men, contained 1,100.

Officials in several states acknowledged that inmates were at times assigned to nonexistent jobs and training programs so that the institution could receive state and federal funds. In March, the U. S. Labor Department, after surveying 560 institutions, declared vocational training for inmates inadequate and unrelated to civilian job markets. Prisons that did have training programs spent, on the average, only 7% of their budgets on them.

In the South, where severe overcrowding had been reported in previous years, some steps were taken to alter conditions. U. S. District Court Judge Frank M. Johnson, Jr., in Montgomery, Ala., ruled that state prisons had to meet specific minimum standards, including at least 60 square feet (5.6 m²) of living space per inmate and "a meaningful job" with instruction "designed to teach a marketable skill." Judge Johnson also ordered the state to increase the number of guards from 383 to 692 and balance the force's racial and cultural composition.

Sentencing and Parole. In March, Congress passed and the president signed into law a bill reorganizing the federal parole system. The changes introduced were intended to make it easier for an inmate who has followed prison regulations to obtain a parole. Prisoners sentenced to terms longer than one year will be presumptively entitled to parole after serving one third of their sentence. In cases of denial, prisoners will be provided with a written statement of the reasons.

Developments at the state level appeared to be moving in the opposite direction. Penal reforms during the 1920's introduced the indeterminate sentence coupled with a parole system. Judges were granted wide discretion in sentencing criminals for specific crimes, the prison time in many cases ranging from two years to life. When and if the prisoner showed evidence of rehabilitation, he could be released on parole. With the rising crime rate and general agreement that prisons do not rehabilitate, there has been a shift toward the deterrent concept. In May, a new program went into effect in Maine, requiring fixed sentences, under which the criminal has to spend a specific length of time incarcerated for a particular crime. A person convicted of armed robbery, for example, will go to prison for 10 years and serve a minimum of 6, with possible time off only for good behavior. There is no parole. It is clear that the new law means more time in prison, and it has already had the effect of raising the penal population. California and Indiana have enacted similar laws to become effective in July 1977. Many other states (Connecticut, Colorado, Ohio, and Washington) either have similar laws pending in their legislatures, or (as in Florida, South Dakota, and Virginia) have commissions studying proposals for fixed prison terms. In early 1976 a Twentieth Century Fund task force issued a report calling the prevailing systems of sentencing "perhaps the major flaw in the criminal justice system." There has been little opposition to the principle of fixed sentences, although there has been strong disagreement on the exact length of sentences.

Experiments on Prisoners. It was revealed in February that the Atomic Energy Commission had, during the 1960's, used 131 prisoners in radiation experiments. The program, to which the prisoners had given written consent, involved the beaming of X-rays into their testicles to see if heavy radiation caused sterility. After the experiments all the prisoners involved underwent vasectomies to avoid fathering deformed children as a result of damage inflicted by the tests.

DONALD GOODMAN
John Jay College of Criminal Justice
City University of New York

PRIZES AND AWARDS

NOBEL PRIZES

With the exception of the Peace Prize, which was with-held, all of the 1976 Nobel Prizes were won or shared by Americans. The awards, presented by King Carl XVI Gustaf in Stockholm, Sweden, on December 10, were valued at $160,000 each. The winners were:

Chemistry: William N. Lipscomb, Jr., Harvard University, for his studies on the structure and bonding mechanisms of compounds known as boranes, illuminating problems of chemical bondings.

Economics: Milton Friedman, University of Chicago, "for his achievements in the field of consumption analysis, monetary history and theory, and for his demonstration of the complexity of stabilization policy."

Literature: Saul Bellow, "for the human understanding and subtle analysis of contemporary culture that are combined in his works."

Medicine or Physiology: Baruch S. Blumberg, University of Pennsylvania Medical School, and D. Carleton Gajdusek, National Institute for Neurological Diseases, Bethesda, Md., were cited jointly for "their discoveries concerning new mechanisms for the origin and dissemination of infectious diseases."

Physics: Burton Richter, Stanford University, and Samuel C.C. Ting, Massachusetts Institute of Technology, shared the prize for their independent but almost simultaneous discovery of a new type of elementary particle known as psi or j.

ARTS

American Institute of Architects Awards: Anderson Notter Associates, Inc., for Old Boston City Hall, Boston, Mass.; Davis Brody and Associates, for Waterside, New York City; Myron Goldfinger, for Marcus House, Bedford, N. Y.; Gwathmey Siegel Architects, for dormitory, dining and student union facility, State University College, Purchase, N. Y., and Whig Hall, Princeton, N. J.; Hardy Holzman Pfeiffer Associates, for Columbus Occupational Health Center, Columbus, Ind.; William Kessler and Associates, for the Center for Creative Studies, Detroit, Mich.; Richard Meier and Associates, for Douglas House, Harbor Springs, Mich.; Miller Hanson Westerbeck Bell Architects, Inc., for Butler Square, Minneapolis, Minn.; C. F. Murphy Associates, for the Crosby Kemper Memorial Arena, Kansas City, Mo.

"Dance" Magazine Awards: Michael Bennett, Suzanne Farrell, E. Virginia Williams

National Academy of Recording Arts and Sciences Grammy Awards for excellence in phonograph records
 Album of the year: *Still Crazy After All These Years,* Paul Simon
 Broadway score: *The Wiz,* Charlie Smalls, writer
 Classical album of the year: *Beethoven: Symphonies (9)* (Solti)
 Classical vocal: Janet Baker: Mahler's *Kindertotenlieder*
 Country music song: *Another Somebody Done Somebody Wrong Song,* Chips Moman and Larry Butler, writers
 Female country vocal: Linda Ronstadt, *I Can't Help It* (If I'm Still in Love With You)
 Female vocal performance: Janis Ian, *At Seventeen*
 Group vocal performance: Eagles, *Lyin' Eyes*
 Male country vocal: Willie Nelson, *Blue Eyes Crying in the Rain*
 Male vocal performance: Paul Simon, *Still Crazy After All These Years*
 New artist: Natalie Cole
 Record of the year: *Love Will Keep Us Together,* The Captain and Tennille
 Song of the year: *Send in the Clowns,* Stephen Sondheim, writer

National Institute of Arts and Letters Awards
 Arnold W. Brunner Memorial Prize in Architecture: James Stirling
 Charles E. Ives Award: The Charles Ives Society and Music Library, Yale University
 Marjorie Peabody Waite Award: Rene Wellek
 Richard and Hinda Rosenthal Foundation Awards: Carl Nicholas Titolo; Richard Yates

Milton Friedman of the University of Chicago was awarded the Nobel Prize in Economics.

UPI

National Rock Music Awards
 Album of the year: *Fleetwood Mac,* by Fleetwood Mac
 Female vocalist: Linda Ronstadt
 Group: Fleetwood Mac
 Male vocalist: Paul McCartney
 Outstanding rock personality: Peter Frampton
 Single record: *Miracles,* by Jefferson Starship

Pulitzer Prize for Music: Ned Rorem

JOURNALISM

Drew Pearson Award: Seymour M. Hersh, *The New York Times*

Maria Moors Cabot Gold Medals for "distinguished journalistic contributions to the advancement of inter-American understanding": Bernard Diederich, Time-Life News Service; Jorge S. Remonda-Ruibal, La Voz del Interior, Cordoba, Argentina

National Magazine Awards
 Fiction Criticism: *Essence,* for "Isomx," a story of a black family
 Public Service: *Business Week,* for an article on women in business
 Reporting Excellence: *Audubon,* for article on a North Dakota irrigation project
 Service to the Individual: *Modern Medicine,* for a series on "Ethics, Genetics and the Future of Man"
 Specialized Journalism Reporting: *United Mine Workers Journal*
 Visual Excellence: *Horticulture*
 Special Award: *Time,* for its bicentennial issue

Overseas Press Club Awards
 Business news reporting from abroad: J. A. Livingston, *The Philadelphia Inquirer*
 Cartoon on foreign affairs: Tony Auth, *The Philadelphia Inquirer*
 Daily newspaper or wire service from abroad: Sydney H. Schanberg, *The New York Times*
 Daily newspaper or wire service interpretation of foreign affairs: Joseph C. Harsch, *The Christian Science Monitor*
 Daily newspaper or wire service photography reporting from abroad: K. Kenneth Paik, *The Kansas City Times*
 Magazine interpretation of foreign affairs: Arnaud de Borchgrave, *Newsweek*
 Magazine reporting from abroad: John J. Putman, *National Geographic*
 Radio interpretation of foreign affairs: ABC News and CBS News
 Radio spot news reporting from abroad: CBS
 TV interpretation or documentary: Howard K. Smith and Bill Seamans, ABC
 TV spot news reporting from abroad: Bruce Dunning, Mike Marriott, Mai Van Duc, CBS News
 Bob Considine Memorial Award: Sydney H. Schanberg, *The New York Times*
 Robert Capa Gold Medal: Dirck Halstead
 Madeline Dale Ross Award: Mayo Mohs, *Time*

Pulitzer Prizes for Journalism

Commentary: Walter W. (Red) Smith, *The New York Times,* for the "erudition" and "literary quality" of his sports column

Criticism: Alan M. Kriegsman, dance critic, *The Washington Post*

Editorial cartooning: Tony Auth, *The Philadelphia Inquirer*

Editorial writing: Philip P. Kerby, *Los Angeles Times,* for editorials against government secrecy and court-imposed censorship of trial proceedings

Feature photography: the photographic staff of *The Courier Journal/The Louisville Times,* Louisville, Ky., for a pictorial report of court-ordered school busing

General local reporting: Gene Miller, *The Miami Herald,* for stories leading to the exoneration of two men twice sentenced to death in Florida

International reporting: Sydney H. Schanberg, *The New York Times,* for his coverage of the Communist takeover of Cambodia

Investigative local reporting: *The Chicago Tribune* for uncovering and exposing abuses in federal housing programs and conditions that led to the closing of two hospitals

National reporting: James Risser, *The Des Moines Register,* for disclosing large-scale corruption in grain exporting

Public service: *The Anchorage Daily News* for its investigation into the growth and influence of the teamsters union in Alaska

Spot news photography: Stanley J. Forman, *The Boston Herald-American,* for a sequence of photographs of a fire

LITERATURE

Academy of American Poets Awards

Copernicus Award ($10,000): Robert Penn Warren

Edgar Allan Poe Award ($5,000): Charles Wright

Walt Whitman Award ($1,000): Laura Gilpin

American Library Association Awards: see page 298

Canada's Governor General's Literary Awards ($5,000 each): Brian Moore, Anne Hébert, Milton Acorn, Marion MacRae, Anthony Adamson, Louis-Edmond Hamelin, Pierre Perrault

National Book Awards

Arts and letters: Paul Fussell, *The Great War and Modern Memory*

Children's: Walter D. Edmonds, *Bert Breen's Barn*

Contemporary affairs: Michael J. Arlen, *Passage to Ararat*

Fiction: William Gaddis, *J R*

History and biography: David Brion Davis, *The Problem of Slavery in the Age of Revolution: 1770– 1823*

Poetry: John Ashbery, *Self-Portrait in a Convex Mirror*

National Institute of Arts and Letters Awards

E. M. Forster Award ($5,000): Jon Stallworthy

Gold Medal for Biography: Leon Edel

Loines Award for Poetry ($2,500): Mona Van Duyn

National Medal for Literature ($10,000): Allen Tate

Zabel Award for Criticism ($2,500): Harold Rosenberg

UPI

In May, James Risser of "The Des Moines Register" won the 1976 Pulitzer Prize for National Reporting.

Pulitzer Prizes

Biography: R. W. B. Lewis, *Edith Wharton: A Biography*

Fiction: Saul Bellow, *Humboldt's Gift*

General nonfiction: Robert N. Butler, *Why Survive? Being Old in America*

History: Paul Horgan, *Lamy of Santa Fe*

Poetry: John Ashbery, *Self-Portrait in a Convex Mirror*

MOTION PICTURES

Academy of Motion Picture Arts and Sciences ("Oscar") Awards

Actor: Jack Nicholson, *One Flew Over the Cuckoo's Nest*

Actress: Louise Fletcher, *One Flew Over the Cuckoo's Nest*

Director: Milos Forman, *One Flew Over the Cuckoo's Nest*

Film: *One Flew Over the Cuckoo's Nest*

Foreign language film: *Dersu Uzala,* USSR

Original dramatic score: John Williams, *Jaws*

Original screenplay: Frank Pierson, *Dog Day Afternoon*

Original song score and adaptation: Leonard Rosenman, *Barry Lyndon*

Screenplay based on material from another medium: Lawrence Hauben and Bo Goldman, *One Flew Over the Cuckoo's Nest*

Song: *I'm Easy,* Keith Carradine

Supporting actor, George Burns, *The Sunshine Boys*

Supporting actress: Lee Grant, *Shampoo*

Visual effects award: Albert Whitlock and Glen Robinson, *The Hindenburg*

Honorary Award: Mary Pickford

Jean Hersholt Humanitarian Award: Jules Stein

PHOTOS UPI

George Burns and Lee Grant were presented with Oscars as the best supporting actor and actress.

Cannes International Film Festival Awards
Actor: José Luis Gomez, *The Family of Pascal Duarte* (Spain)
Actress: Dominique Sanda, *The Ferramonti Heritage* (France); Mari Torocsik, *Where Are You, Madame Dery?* (Hungary)
Director: Ettore Scola, *Affreux, Sales et Méchants* (Disgusting, Dirty and Mean) (Italy)
Grand prize: *Taxi Driver*, directed by Martin Scorsese (United States)
Special prize: *La Marquise d'O*, directed by Eric Rohmer (West Germany); *Cria Cuervos*, directed by Carlos Saura (Spain)

PUBLIC SERVICE

Hall of Fame for Great Americans: Clara Barton, Luther Burbank, Andrew Carnegie
International League for the Rights of Man Human Rights Award: Carl Bernstein, Bob Woodward
Southern Christian Leadership Conference Martin Luther King, Jr., Award: Roy Wilkins
U. S. Medals of Freedom: Arthur Rubinstein, Martha Graham
Women's Hall of Fame: Abigail Adams, Margaret Mead, Mildred Didrikson Zaharias

SCIENCE

Albert Lasker Medical Research Awards ($10,000 each)
Basic Medical Research: Rosalyn S. Yalow, senior medical investigator, U. S. Veterans Administration
Clinical Research: Raymond P. Ahlquist, Medical College of Georgia; J. W. Black, University College of London
Special Award: World Health Organization (WHO)
American Chemical Society Awards
James T. Grady Award for interpreting chemistry: Gene Bylinsky
Irving Langmuir Award in Chemical Physics: John S. Waugh
National Medals of Science: John W. Backus, IBM; Manson Benedict, MIT; Hans Bethe, Cornell University; Shiing-Shen Chern, University of California, Berkeley; George B. Dantzig, Stanford University; Hallowell Davis, Washington University; Paul Gyorgy, University of Pennsylvania School of Medicine (posthumous); Sterling Brown Hendricks, formerly, U. S. Department of Agriculture; Joseph Hirschfelder, University of Wisconsin; William H. Pickering, California Institute of Technology; Lewis H. Sarett, Merck & Company, Inc.; Frederick E. Terman, Stanford University; Orville Alvin Vogel, U. S. Department of Agriculture; E. Bright Wilson, Jr., Harvard University; Chien-Hsiung Wu, Columbia University

TELEVISION AND RADIO

Academy of Television Arts and Sciences ("Emmy") Awards
Actor—comedy series: Jack Albertson, *Chico and the Man* (NBC)
Actor—drama or comedy series: Edward Asner, *Rich Man, Poor Man* (ABC)
Actor—drama or comedy special: Anthony Hopkins, *The Lindbergh Kidnapping Case* (NBC)
Actor—drama series: Peter Falk, *Columbo* (NBC)
Actress—comedy series: Mary Tyler Moore, *The Mary Tyler Moore Show* (CBS)
Actress—drama or comedy series: Kathryn Walker, *The Adams Chronicles* (PBS)
Actress—drama or comedy special: Susan Clark, *Babe*
Actress—drama series: Michael Learned, *The Waltons* (CBS)
Classical music program: *Bernstein and the New York Philharmonic* (PBS)
Comedy series: *The Mary Tyler Moore Show* (CBS)
Comedy-variety or music series: *NBC's Saturday Night* (NBC)
Drama series: *Police Story* (NBC)
Special—comedy-variety or music: *Gypsy in My Soul* (CBS)
Special—drama or comedy: *Eleanor and Franklin* (ABC)
Supporting actor—comedy series: Ted Knight, *The Mary Tyler Moore Show* (CBS)

Supporting actor—drama series: Anthony Zerbe, *Harry O*
Actress—comedy series: Betty White, *The Mary Tyler Moore Show* (CBS)
Supporting actress—drama series: Ellen Corby, *The Waltons* (CBS)
George Foster Peabody Awards for Radio: KDKB, Mesa, Ariz., "superior overall public service programming"; KMOX Radio, St. Louis, *Sleeping Watchdogs;* Jim Laurie, NBC News; Voice of America, Washington, *The Battle of Lexington*
George Foster Peabody Awards for Television: ABC-TV, New York, *ABC Theatre: Love Among the Ruins;* CBS News, New York, *Mr. Rooney Goes to Washington;* CBS-TV, New York, *Mash;* NBC-TV, New York, *Weekend;* WAPA-TV, San Juan, P. R., *Las Rosas Blancas;* WWL-TV, New Orleans, *A Sunday Journal*

THEATER

American Theater Wing, Antoinette Perry ("Tony") Awards
Actor (drama): John Wood, *Travesties*
Actor (musical): George Rose, *My Fair Lady*
Actress (drama): Irene Worth, *Sweet Bird of Youth*
Actress (musical): Donna McKechnie, *A Chorus Line*
Choreography: Bob Avian and Michael Bennett, *A Chorus Line*
Costume design: Florence Klotz, *Pacific Overtures*
Director (drama): Ellis Rabb, *The Royal Family*
Director (musical): Michael Bennett, *A Chorus Line*
Musical: *A Chorus Line*
Play: *Travesties*
Producer (drama): David Merrick, Doris Cole, Burry Fredric, *Travesties*
Producer (musical): Joseph Papp and The New York Shakespeare Festival, *A Chorus Line*
Score: Marvin Hamlisch and Edward Kleban, *A Chorus Line*
Supporting actor (drama): Edward Herrmann, *Mrs. Warren's Profession*
Supporting actor (musical): Sammy Williams, *A Chorus Line*
Supporting actress (drama): Shirley Knight, *Kennedy's Children*
Supporting actress (musical): Kelly Bishop, *A Chorus Line*
New York Drama Critics' Circle Theater Awards
American drama: *Streamers* by David Rabe
Musical: *Pacific Overtures* by John Weidman and Hugh Wheeler, music and lyrics by Stephen Sondheim
Play: *Travesties* by Tom Stoppard
Pulitzer Prize for Drama: *A Chorus Line*

Dinah Shore was the recipient of an Emmy Award for "Dinah!", which was named the best daytime talk show.

UPI

In September 1976, representatives of 67 nations attended the annual Frankfurt International Book Fair.

PUBLISHING

The U. S. Congress delayed additional postal rate increases—a concern throughout the publishing industry—by voting a billion-dollar subsidy for the Postal Service. It also called for a moratorium on rate hikes until more studies were completed.

Paper use was up, along with prices. Some magazines turned to lighter paper and used less coated stock. More standardization in widths was observed in the newspaper industry.

For the first time since 1909, Congress revised the copyright law, extending protection to authors and composers for their lifetime plus 50 years. The Library of Congress was authorized to preserve and maintain radio and television broadcasts of historic events. In addition, protection was provided for newer industries, such as cable television and photocopying.

Media criticism continued, sparked in part by the U. S. presidential campaign. John Mack Carter, editor of *Good Housekeeping,* attacked "journalistic pollution" in investigation journalism that dealt with "increasingly more intimate and irrelevant issues about who is sleeping with whom" in Washington. He compared the White House, FBI, and CIA transgressions in the name of "national security" to the press activities "in the name of the first amendment." The Daniel Schorr case (page 417) was also of major interest.

Books. Sales gained throughout 1975 and into 1976. The revenue increases, however, came from higher-priced books. The Association of American Publishers reported that 1975 sales reached $3,810,000,000, up 7.8% over 1974; paperbacks netted more than adult hardbounds.

Religious books recorded big gains. Billy Graham's *Angels: God's Secret Agents,* sold more than 1,600,000 copies. Sparked by inspirational and evangelical volumes, the religious market led all areas in growth in 1975, and the trend continued well into 1976. Publishers of *The Living Bible,* with total sales over 20,000,-000, issued its companion Catholic edition, *The Way.*

Politicians inspired many writers. Books about Jimmy Carter, pro and con, flooded the market. Richard M. Nixon was not overlooked. Bob Woodward and Carl Bernstein headed the best-seller list for weeks with *The Final Days.* Meanwhile, their earlier book, *All the President's Men,* sold well in paperback. Nixon's own words were promised for early 1977 with newspaper and magazine serialization rights sold to *The New York Times.*

Readers continued to be concerned with their own welfare, pushing Sylvia Porter's *The Money Book* and Herbert Benson's *The Relaxation Response* to the top of the list. Psychologist Wayne W. Dyer wrote *Your Erroneous Zones* and, after sales of 110,000 hardback copies, sold paperback rights for $1,100,000. Other readers turned to *TM: Discovering Inner Energy and Overcoming Stress, Total Fitness in 30 Minutes a Week,* and *Save Your Life Diet.*

Jaws continued to draw viewers to theaters and readers to the paperback racks; more than 9,000,000 copies were in print. *The Bermuda Triangle* returned to the top of the list where it had stayed two years previously. *Fear of Flying* approached 5,000,000, while *Once Is Not Enough* passed 4,500,000 copies in print. *The Joy of Sex* sold more than 3,000,000 copies, and *More Joy of Sex* was nearing its first million.

The People's Almanac by David Wallechinsky and his father, Irving Wallace, became a bestseller thanks to its unique subject matter. The traditional *Old Farmer's Almanac.* sold over 2,300,000 copies.

Publishers Weekly, the bible of the industry, reported on best-sellers in several categories. In addition to Agatha Christie's *Curtain* and Gore Vidal's *1876, Trinity,* the Leon Uris story about Ireland, led the fiction list for months. Previous hardcover leaders took over the paperback category, including *Helter Skelter, The Moneychangers, Rich Man, Poor Man, Shogun, Ragtime, The Omen,* and *Nightwork.*

The U. S. Department of Commerce predicted that by 1984 the book industry revenue would be $8,400,000,000, an annual growth rate of 8.4%. During 1975, book exports reached $270,000,000, an increase of 11% over 1974, with 44% of the business going to Canada. Revenues from mass market paperbacks surpassed those of hardcover books; some 380,000,-000 copies of the lower-priced volumes are sold annually.

Other 1976 highlights included an increase in the number of mergers of printing-publishing firms, the 50th anniversary of the William Morrow publishing firm, and higher profits for the first half of 1976 for many major firms. Singapore was "overtaking Hong Kong as the overseas base for low-cost, high-quality book production for Western publishers," according to *Publishers Weekly.* In recent years more and more books have been printed in Europe, South America, and other areas. Finland became a major bookbinding nation, and beautiful catalogs for American museums are printed in Switzerland.

Magazines. The magazine industry expects 1977–78 to be a peak period for ad revenues, paper consumption, and circulation income. Stephen E. Kelly, president of the Magazine Publishers Association, said that many publications would soon be selling for $1.50 per copy—and even higher for specials. He also noted the growth in single-copy sales and a growing involvement in business diversification by publishers.

TV Guide continued its domination in circulation and advertising. More than 20,500,000 copies were sold weekly. For the first half of 1976 ads produced $72,000,000, up 17% over 1975. *Reader's Digest,* with more than 18,000,-000 circulation, remained second. Its worldwide revenues were estimated at $600,000,000, half from outside the United States. Although ranking fourth in advertising, behind *Time* and *Newsweek, Reader's Digest* set a record with $8,500,000 worth of ads in its October 1976 edition.

Other magazines in the top ten in circulation were *National Geographic,* 9,200,000; *Family Circle,* 8,500,000; *Woman's Day,* 8,200,000; *Better Homes & Gardens,* 8,100,000; *McCall's,* 6,500,000; *Ladies' Home Journal,* 6,100,000; *Playboy,* 5,400,000; and *Good Housekeeping,* 5,300,000.

Indicative of the industry's success in 1976 was a report that 47 of the top 50 magazines increased their ad income.

Although *Time* trailed *Newsweek* in ad pages, it was ahead on ad income, $64,000,000 to $52,-000,000 for the first half of 1976. Time Inc. edged closer to becoming the first billion-dollar publishing firm as 1976 first half revenues reached $494,000,000. The firm's 1975 total revenue was $910,000,000. *People* reached 1,800,000 circulation; the firm sold some 25,-000,000 books; and *Life's* special editions attracted millions of sales. The firm did lose a libel suit to Alice Firestone and suffered a three-week strike in June.

New specialized publications arrived. *New West* created a controversy in which three firms claimed the title; of these *New York* staffers had the best-selling edition. Other newcomers were *Mother Jones,* "a magazine for the rest of us;" *C. B. Times,* and others in the citizen's band radio industry; *House Plants and Porch Gardens; Soap Opera People; Homegrown Fruits and Vegetables; Firehouse; Mariah,* for wilderness expeditions; *Residential Interiors; Paddle World; Pay Television; New Jersey; Rock; You; Pillow Talk; Spree;* and *Head,* for marijuana users, started after *High Times* reached 500,000 circulation with the same audience.

Woman's Day experimented by publishing an Octember issue—an extra between October and November. The *Country Gentleman* was revived. And the *Magazine Industry Newsletter* reported 56 mergers or acquisitions in the magazine and book fields for 1975, down slightly from 1974.

Playboy reported that its ad slide had been halted in mid-1976. Its sales, aided by a much-discussed Jimmy Carter interview, increased. *Hustler,* No. 3 behind *Playboy* and *Penthouse,* reached 1,500,000 circulation. To gain sales spots in supermarkets, *Viva* dropped total male nudity.

Newspapers. "Newspapers aren't doomed—they are the wave of the future," Speidel Newspapers' President Rollan D. Melton contended. Others were more alarmed as circulation declined, criticism increased, and production costs climbed. Still, profits were higher. The Newspaper Advertising Bureau, Inc., expected 1976 ad revenues for dailies to total $9,600,000,000, up 15% over 1975. *Editor & Publisher International Year Book* reported there were 1,756 dailies with circulation of 60,655,431, the lowest in a decade. Some 639 Sunday papers added 51,264,710 circulation. In Canada, the 117 dailies reported nearly 5,000,000 circulation, and 20 weekend papers added 2,586,421 circulation.

The Newspaper Advertising Bureau said Americans spent $3,900,000,000 and Canadians spent $300,000,000 for copies of daily and Sunday papers in 1975, up from 1974.

Newsprint reached the $300-a-ton neighborhood. Meanwhile, U. S. publishers planned a 150,000-ton newsprint mill in Georgia, estimated to cost $110-120 million, shared by Cox Enterprises, Knight-Ridder Newspapers, and Media General. The *Los Angeles Times,* the nation's largest user of newsprint in 1975, consumed 313,000 tons.

Publishers in 1975 spent $170,000,000 on production equipment and $80,000,000 for plant expansion and modernization. *Newsday* in 1976 contracted for $15,000,000 worth of new presses and folders. Major groups continued to expand. One of them, Gannett, acquired papers in Indiana, Missouri, New Mexico, Pennsylvania, and Oklahoma. *Family Weekly,* a Sunday supplement carried in over 300 newspapers, was

The Daniel Schorr Case

A growing furore over the leaking of government documents to the press took a fresh turn in February 1976, when *The Village Voice,* a New York City weekly newspaper with a reputation for antiestablishment crusading, published a House Intelligence Committee report on illegal activities of the Central Intelligence Agency. The *Voice* had obtained its copy of the report from Daniel Schorr, a CBS television correspondent who had been active in exposing intelligence scandals and frequently involved in controversy as a result.

During the previous year, findings by Congressional investigators that the CIA had plotted the assassination of foreign leaders and conducted domestic surveillance operations raised a public outcry for control of the agency. But continued leaking of the findings of the investigators created a parallel controversy over whether the disclosures posed a threat to national security. The argument was usually cast in terms of the government's need to conduct diplomacy in secret versus the public's right to be informed. But some saw it, more simply, as a sharpening of the traditional adversary relationship between an inquisitive press and a recalcitrant government establishment.

The assassination of a CIA station chief in Athens in December 1975, after his name had been disclosed in a self-styled watchdog publication, appeared to tip the balance of the argument toward those favoring secrecy. It was in this atmosphere that the House on Jan. 29, 1976, voted not to release the report of its own intelligence committee investigation.

The controversy flared anew on February 16, when the *Voice* published the text it had obtained from Schorr. As Schorr later told it, a source he would not name gave him his copy on January 25. In fact, he and *The New York Times* had already reported much of its contents, which included details of CIA operations in Italy and Angola. However, Schorr said, he still felt a "responsibility" to make the full text known. After exploring other possible outlets, he had arranged for publication in the *Voice,* in return for a contribution by *Voice* publisher Clay Felker to the Reporters Committee for Freedom of the Press.

Although the contribution was never made, the suggestion of payment tainted the transaction in the view of some of Schorr's colleagues. Others criticized him for electing to publish in what they considered a politically biased newspaper. With the tide apparently running against Schorr, the House, on February 19, voted an investigation by its Committee on Standards of Official Conduct—known as the Ethics Committee—to learn how Schorr obtained the report.

CBS suspended Schorr from his reporting duties pending the outcome. Over the next five months, committee investigators questioned more than 400 persons without managing to identify the source of the leak. Meanwhile, journalists who felt Schorr was being made a scapegoat to divert attention from CIA problems urged their fellow reporters to close ranks against what they perceived as a trend toward increasing restrictions on the press. Many rallied to Schorr's side.

On August 25, when it seemed the investigation was about to expire for lack of evidence, the 12-man committee voted 8 to 4 to subpoena Schorr himself. The subpoena was widely interpreted as a face-saving gesture, and one opposing member of the committee characterized it as purely "punitive." When he appeared on September 15, Schorr still declined to name his source, but his earnestness seemed to persuade most observers he was acting from conviction.

Although Chairman John J. Flynt (Dem.-Ga.) repeatedly warned Schorr that he could be cited for contempt, when the committee met again a week later it voted to take no action against Schorr. For the moment, at least, a direct confrontation between Congress and the media over first amendment free press rights had been avoided. Schorr subsequently resigned from CBS.

DAVID GELMAN
General Editor, Media, "Newsweek"

Prior to being suspended by CBS, Daniel Schorr (right) meets with CIA Director George Bush.

UPI

sold for $19,000,000 to four chains: Donrey Media Group, Hoiles Freedom Newspapers, Howard Publications, and Small Newspapers.

"Newspapers may one day let you pick the news you want," headlined the *National Observer*. This was one view being considered to counteract declining circulation. Other publishers blamed television. The Boston *Globe's* Thomas Winslip noted, "We're living in an age of audio-visually educated readers, and competing with much brighter visual products. Too many papers look dull in comparison."

Weeklies reported a decline to 35,000,000 circulation after a decade of steady growth. Suburban papers expanded, however. Magazines increased their readership.

Newsweek discussed "Jugular Journalism?" as the magazine reviewed the roles played by Bob Woodward and Carl Bernstein of the *Washington Post* in the Watergate case. *Newsweek* termed the "Woodstein Envy" a healthy affliction, prompting newsmen to become more aware of official malfeasance and to be "reluctant to take bureaucratic handouts at their slippery word." Others complain that "journalism has become excessively adversary-minded," out to "get" public figures.

U. S. News & World Report noted that "never has U. S. journalism enjoyed as much prestige as it does now . . . yet it is in growing trouble with the public, and talk of press curbs is on the rise." Traditional problems concerned privacy invasion, prejudiced or inflammatory reporting, and interpretations of the first amendment. *The New York Times* editorial-page editor John B. Oakes said, "The press is not going to retain, or regain, public confidence if it is perceived to be constantly arrogant, unwilling to recognize conflicting rights, or not too concerned about maintaining the most rigid standards to protect and preserve its own integrity."

Other than political news emanated from Washington. The "sex scandals" provided readable accounts even as newsmen debated the ethics involved in reporting such stories. The Associated Press called for more documentation beyond the "anonymous source" or "even a named source of doubtful reliability." Former Vice President Spiro Agnew continued his attack on the press, issuing a newsletter designed to "better balance the news." Columnist Jack Anderson, Hedrick Smith of *The New York Times*, and others sued former President Richard M. Nixon for invasion of privacy.

Samuel I. Newhouse acquired Michigan-based Booth Newspapers, plus Sunday magazine supplement *Parade* and suburban weeklies in Cleveland in a record sale exceeding $300,000,000. The New York *Post* was acquired by Australian publisher Rupert Murdock, who also began efforts to purchase *New York* magazine.

The Nebraska gag law was ruled unconstitutional by the Supreme Court, although Justice Byron R. White said additional cases must be reviewed before a general decision could be issued on such incidents. Gag problems existed elsewhere too. In Fresno, Calif., four *Bee* newsmen were jailed briefly for their refusal to reveal sources of grand jury transcripts. In Denver, a *Rocky Mountain News* reporter was cited for the same cause. Ohio Supreme Court justices urged judges to "exhaust all other possibilities for guaranteeing a fair trial before imposing restrictions on press coverage." Only three states —Colorado, Florida, and Alabama—permit cameras in the courtroom.

Under the Freedom of Information Act additional thousands of requests were made for government records. Many were by news sources seeking more data on such items as costs of congressional junkets and expenses of military equipment.

In September 1976, President Ford signed the sunshine bill that opened meetings of multi-headed federal agencies to the public under certain restrictions.

The Newspaper Guild and the International Typographical Union continued their merger talks as automatic devices, such as electronic composition equipment, reduced manpower needs.

WILLIAM HOWARD TAFT
University of Missouri

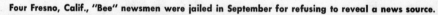
Four Fresno, Calif., "Bee" newsmen were jailed in September for refusing to reveal a news source.

UPI

PUERTO RICO

In June 1976, at the invitation of President Gerald Ford, the leaders of England, France, West Germany, Japan, Italy, and Canada met in a plush tourist resort on the north coast of Puerto Rico to discuss and coordinate the efforts to stimulate economic recovery. Although Puerto Rico and its leaders were only outside observers of the conference, the islanders were vitally concerned about its success, since Puerto Rico's economy had still to show any definite signs of recovery from the worst economic recession since the 1930's.

Economy. The official unemployment figures climbed to their highest levels: 21.9% in January, 20.6% in June, and slightly below 20% at the end of the year. For the sixth consecutive year more Puerto Ricans returned to their island than left it, swelling the rolls of the unemployed to more than 200,000.

All sectors of Puerto Rico's economy showed only the most feeble signs of recovery. Tourism was up about 2.5%. Some upturn was noted in the industrial sector; 38% more plants opened than in the previous fiscal year. Agriculture also gave some indication of growth, but the falling price of sugar prevented any real support from that sector. Construction continued to be a bankrupt industry on the island.

Austerity was the order of the day on all levels of the insular government. Wages were frozen and public payrolls were actually reduced 2%. Increased taxes on income and consumer items, established in previous years, provided funds for limited government operations.

In the face of such economic problems, serious social unrest has been prevented only by the federal food stamp program. More than 75% of the eligible families actually receive the stamps, compared to only 40% in the United States. Puerto Rico received more than $500 million in food stamps in 1976, twice as much as California, the top state in the Union.

Elections. Serious and widespread unemployment, the lack of any clear signs of strong economic recovery in any sector of the economy, and a government policy of austerity in public

UPI

Puerto Rico's newly elected governor, San Juan Mayor Carlos Romero Barceló, and his wife enjoy their victory.

spending—all combined to produce in an election year a voting population which was inclined to seek a change.

Four parties registered for the November 2 elections: the Puerto Rican Socialist party, a Marxist-Leninist group, which participated in the electoral process for the first time; the Puerto Rican Independence party, which has taken part in all elections since its foundation in 1946; the New Progressive party, which was defeated in 1972 by the party which controlled the island government from 1940 to 1968; and the Popular Democratic party, now in the hands of the second generation of young leaders who have followed its founder, Luís Muñoz Marín.

All told, 1,447,808 out of 1,751,000 eligible voters cast their ballots. The result of the election was extremely close. The Popular Democratic party of the government was defeated by the New Progressive party, led by young San Juan Mayor Carlos Romero Barceló. The vote was 686,387 to 646,810, giving a victory margin of about 2.8%. The winning party also succeeded in capturing both houses of the legislature and 41 of the 78 town halls on the island.

U. S. President Ford took Puerto Ricans by surprise on December 31, when he called for the admission of Puerto Rico as the 51st state of the United States. Most Puerto Ricans, however, received the president's suggestion coolly.

THOMAS G. MATHEWS
University of Puerto Rico

PUERTO RICO • Information Highlights

Area: 3,435 square miles (8,897 km²).

Population (1976 est.): 3,200,000.

Chief Cities (1975): San Juan, the capital, 471,400; Bayamon, 180,800; Ponce, 176,100; Carolina, 142,700.

Government (1976): *Chief Officers*—governor, Rafael Hernández Colón (Popular Democratic party); secretary of state, Juan Albors; attorney general, Carlos Rios. *Legislature*—Senate, 29 members; House of Representatives, 54 members.

Education (1974–75): *Enrollment*—public schools, 704,-106 pupils; nonpublic schools, 82,997; colleges and universities, 89,941 students.

Gross National Product (1975): $7,117,000,000.

Manufacturing (major products): Sugar, molasses, rum.

Major Agricultural Products: Sugarcane, coffee, coconuts, tobacco, pineapples.

Foreign Trade (1974–75): *Exports*, $3,138,000,000; *imports*, $4,951,000,000.

QUEBEC

Despite accurate polls, the Parti Québécois (PQ) victory in the hasty provincial elections on November 15 surprised most Canadians and Quebeckers. It catapulted the party from 30% of the vote and 6 assembly seats in 1973 to 41% and 70 seats, while Liberals fell to 34% and 27 seats (a loss of 75). The Union Nationale picked up 19% and 11 seats, and others won 2 seats. The "ethnic" minorities, nearly all English-speaking, made their weight felt by dividing their vote between the Liberals and the Union Nationale over language rights in the schools.

The Campaign. Former Premier Robert Bourassa had launched the elections to solicit massive support for his constitutional negotiations and labor policy. However, both these themes and his choice target, "separatism," were soon forgotten under the onslaught by other parties on maladministration, scandals, unemployment, and social problems. Defusing the sovereignty issue with the promise of a referendum, the PQ dominated the campaign with a strategy of sharp-shooting the government, while putting forth its own program piece by piece—on housing, unemployment, labor, and benefits for the old. New Premier René Lévesque culled a cabinet of moderates, who at once tried to calm public opinion. Despite Lévesque's promise to work inside the system, while aiming at complete sovereignty in the next few years, Prime Minister Pierre Elliott Trudeau and Quebec Liberals reacted nervously.

Pivotal Issues. The defeat of the Liberals has to be viewed against the backdrop of numerous problems that have plagued them in 1976: an enduring stalemate in all federal-provincial negotiations and a tongue-lashing of former Premier Bourassa by Prime Minister Trudeau in Quebec during the winter; the "dumping" of "used" federal ministers (Mackasey and Marchand) in the provincial elections; labor strife (about 50% of all days lost in Canada) involving such diverse categories as public service, for instance, schools (kept open by a special law), hospitals (where strikes and financial cuts dropped occupation below 50%), construction sites, Hydro-Quebec, two universities (Laval and Quebec at Montreal), and numerous other industries and services; scandals over "voluntary" gifts to the Liberal campaign funds from contractors; soaring costs at the Baie James and Olympics sites, without any serious inquiry into causes; the highest level (by 13%) of taxes in Canada and yet a projected deficit of $1,000,000,000; unemployment rising to 10%; scarce and costly housing in Montreal; and the lowest natality rate in Canada, resulting in stagnation of the population.

New Labor Leader. If labor strife was continuous, however, no civil disorder occurred in the province. And a new leader emerged: Norbert Rodrigue replaced Marcel Pépin as leader of the CSN (Confédération des syndicats nationaux), a confederation of labor that has thinned somewhat in the past several years because of ideological conflicts.

French in the Air. With the help of the Quebec government and private groups, French-speaking air controllers and Air Canada pilots have been waging a legal battle against English unilingualism in the air over Quebec. A partial victory was scored when Superior Court Chief Justice Dechêne ordered Air Canada to translate its manuals in two years and to authorize the use of French when security is not affected.

JEAN-PIERRE WALLOT
University of Montreal

Parti Québécois leader René Lévesque speaks to supporters following triumph in Quebec's Nov. 15 elections.

UPI

--------- **QUEBEC · Information Highlights** ---------

Area: 594,860 square miles (1,540,687 km²).
Population (April 1976 est.): 6,235,000.
Chief Cities (1974 est.): Québec, the capital, 190,000; Montréal, 1,215,000; Laval, 230,000.
Government (1976): *Chief Officers*—lt. gov., Hughes Lapointe; premier, René Lévesque (Parti Québécois); min. of intergovernmental affairs, Claude Morin; chief justice, Lucien Tremblay. *Legislature*—Legislative Assembly, 110 members.
Education (1976–77): *Enrollment*—public elementary and secondary schools, 1,318,800 pupils; private schools, 105,170; Indian (federal) schools, 4,700; post-secondary, 201,600 students. *Total school expenditures,* $2,824,519,000.
Public Finance (1975–76 est.): *Revenues,* $7,938,000,000; *expenditures,* $8,838,000,000.
Personal Income (1974): $27,626,000,000; average annual income per person, $4,504.

(All monetary figures are in Canadian dollars.)

RECORDINGS

In honor of the U. S. bicentennial, New World Records issued a survey of American music. Other major releases of 1976 included Arthur Rubinstein's recording of the five Beethoven concertos, the *Frampton Comes Alive!* album, and *Duke Ellington's Jazz Violin Session* issue. In addition, in the field of equipment, plans for a new tape format were announced.

CLASSICAL RECORDS

Given the recording industry's fondness for anniversary commemorations, the bicentennial year promised an outpouring of worthy Americana that, however, failed to materialize. The notable exception, thanks to Rockefeller Foundation financing, was New World Records' projected 100-disc survey of American music (nonclassical as well as classical). Otherwise, the most substantial contributions came from companies that have been mining Americana seriously for years—in particular Nonesuch, Columbia, and Vox.

While it would be hard to find any segment of the classical repertory unrepresented among the year's offerings, the mainstay remained the 19th century. Among conductors, for example, a set of the nine Beethoven symphonies has become mandatory, and the domestic catalogue saw new sets by Georg Solti (London), Rudolf Kempe (Seraphim), Rafael Kubelik (Deutsche Grammophon), and Bernard Haitink (Philips), with Eugene Jochum (Angel) and Colin Davis (Philips) working on theirs.

It was a good year for some of the music world's best-loved veterans. The nearly 90-year-old Arthur Rubinstein made his third, and in some ways best, recording of the five Beethoven concertos (RCA) and then, although virtually blind, undertook Brahms' grueling D minor Concerto (London). At the age of 94, Leopold

NOTABLE CLASSICAL RELEASES OF 1976

BACH: *Violin Partita No. 2; Sonata No. 3.* Kyung-Wha Chung, violinist (London)
BEETHOVEN: *String Quartets, Op. 18.* Végh Quartet (Telefunken)
CHOPIN: *Préludes.* Murray Perahia, pianist (Columbia)
HAYDN: *La Fedeltà premiata.* Lucia Valentini, Ileana Cotrubas, Frederica von Stade, Luigi Alva; Antal Dorati, conductor (Philips)
LISZT: *Hungarian Rhapsodies.* Michele Campanella, pianist (Philips)
MAHLER: *Symphony No. 2.* London Symphony Orchestra, Leopold Stokowski, conductor (RCA)
SCHOENBERG, SCHUBERT: *Songs.* Jan DeGaetani, mezzo-soprano; Gilbert Kalish, accompanist (Nonesuch)
STRAVINSKY: *Chamber Works.* Netherlands Wind Ensemble (Philips)
TIPPETT: *A Child of Our Time.* BBC Choruses and Symphony Orchestra, Colin Davis, conductor (Philips)
VERDI: *Luisa Miller.* Montserrat Caballé, Luciano Pavarotti, Sherill Milnes; Peter Maag, conductor (London)

Stokowski signed a new six-year contract with CBS, and among his half dozen new releases for the year was a stunning account of Mahler's huge *Resurrection* Symphony. Karl Böhm, now 82, showed no signs of age in Bruckner's Fourth Symphony (London) or the four Brahms symphonies (Deutsche Grammophon). Perhaps Nathan Milstein's achievement (the Bach solo violin sonatas and the Brahms concerto for Deutsche Grammophon) was more remarkable than Vladimir Horowitz' (a Schumann/Scriabin disc for RCA); both were born in 1904, but advancing years take their harshest toll of string players. Still, the Horowitz disc had the distinction of being assembled from live performances.

The booming interest in the pre-baroque period was, ironically, dominated by the brilliant young flutist/musicologist David Munrow, founder of the Early Music Consort of London. Most of the nearly dozen new recordings—from Angel, Archive, and Nonesuch—appeared after Munrow's tragic suicide in May, with more still to come.

More than a dozen operas received premiere recordings: from Philips, Haydn's *La Fedeltà premiata*, Rossini's *Elisabetta, regina d'Inghilterra*, and Verdi's *Il Corsaro;* from Angel, Bellini's *I Capuleti e i Montecchi*, Wagner's *Rienzi*, and Delius' *Fennimore and Gerda;* from Columbia, Donizetti's *Gemma di Vergy*, Massenet's *Le Cid*, Meyerbeer's *Le Prophète*, and Shostakovich's *The Nose;* from London, Massenet's *Esclarmonde* and Gilbert and Sullivan's *Utopia Limited;* from Deutsche Grammophon, Joplin's *Treemonisha;* from RCA, Beeson's *Captain Jinks of the Horse Marines*. In addition, infrequently recorded operas were heard again:

from London, Donizetti's *Maria Stuarda,* Verdi's *Luisa Miller,* Wolf-Ferrari's *Segreto di Susanna,* Tchaikovsky's *Yevgeny Onegin,* and Gershwin's *Porgy and Bess;* from Columbia, Charpentier's *Louise,* Schoenberg's *Moses und Aron,* and Tchaikovsky's *Queen of Spades;* from Angel, Massenet's *Thaïs.*

Among more standard fare, Wagner's elusive *Die Meistersinger* received new studio recordings by London and Deutsche Grammophon as well as live performances from the Bayreuth Festivals of 1943 (Electrola, conducted by Wilhelm Furtwängler) and 1975 (Philips). Philips also released a 1963 Bayreuth *Lohengrin.* The few new operatic-warhorse releases were dominated by star conductors: from London, Georg Solti's *Carmen;* from RCA, James Levine's *La Forza del destino;* from Deutsche Grammophon, Mstislav Rostropovich's *Tosca,* Claudio Abbado's *Macbeth,* and Carlos Kleiber's *Die Fledermaus.*

KENNETH FURIE
Music Editor, "High Fidelity"

POPULAR RECORDS

Carefully crafted throwaways dominated the popular record releases of 1976. The music industry drifted toward lightweight, message-free material and at the same time toward tighter control over production and engineering of the sound. This resulted in some brilliantly engineered recordings and in a few that seemed to have the spontaneity refined out of them. Overall it suggested a year in which it was easier to celebrate form than content.

Todd Rundgren's painstaking reproductions of rock-'n'-roll hits from his teen-age years resonated with this particular spirit of '76, as did Capitol Records' repackaging of mostly up-tempo (and mostly early) Beatles' hits as a two-disc album. The light but almost fussy sound of The Captain and Tennille resulted in high album sales and a television contract. Peter Frampton, continuing to write and perform what a critic called his I-love-you-baby songs, caught the public's fancy with his *Frampton Comes Alive!* album. Pleasant trivia from Steve Miller, such as *Take the Money and Run,* dominated AM radio programming for long

SELECTED POPULAR RELEASES OF 1976

JIMMY BUFFETT: *Havana Daydreamin'* (ABC)
BOB DYLAN: *Desire* (Columbia)
STEVE GOODMAN: *Words We Can Dance To* (Asylum)
WAYLON JENNINGS, WITH WILLIE NELSON, TOMPALL GLASER, JESSI COLTER: *Outlaws—Wanted* (RCA)
GORDON LIGHTFOOT: *Summertime Dream* (Reprise); *Gord's Gold* (Reprise)
BOB MARLEY & THE WAILERS: *Rastaman Vibration* (Island)
JONI MITCHELL: *The Hissing of Summer Lawns* (Asylum)
LINDA RONSTADT: *Hasten Down the Wind* (Asylum)
PAUL SIMON: *Still Crazy After All These Years* (Columbia)
DOC WATSON: *Doc and the Boys* (United Artists)

A & M RECORDS

stretches. John Sebastian styled a whole album after his title song for the television series *Welcome Back, Kotter,* celebrating the happy-go-lucky ambiance of high school. Neil Sedaka, virtually a symbol of lightweight craftsmanship, staged a heavily publicized "comeback."

Lurking behind this was disco music, which continued to have its main direct impact on dance halls. In the cities, discotheques were almost as effective as radio in exposing records to potential buyers. All surface and beat, disco was a force behind attitudes mostly, but it could also be heard directly now and then in a conventional radio-riding hit, such as Donna Summers' *Love to Love You Baby,* in which orgasmic groaning was the main part of "lyrics."

Coming from the opposite direction, and geographically from Jamaica, reggae had some influence on musicians, to the point where one song per album done reggae-style became routine. Political in its own context, reggae also had an engaging, undemanding surface (for the listener, that is; it is difficult to play well) pegged to a back-to-front orientation of the beat.

Performers trying to be serious in the mainstream folk-rock context had a more difficult time. Patti Smith attracted attention with her performances in New York, but her album *Horses* was not the artistic or commercial success expected. *Kate and Anna McGarrigle,* a startling, fresh, French-influenced album from sisters reared in Quebec, was a great favorite among critics, although it was unknown to most of the public. But deeper emotions and thoughts could be successfully presented, at least by certain performers already trusted, including Gordon Lightfoot's *Summertime Dream* and Linda Ronstadt's *Hasten Down the Wind.*

There was also a certain amount of experimentation. Joni Mitchell's *The Hissing of Summer Lawns* was a bold, complex, difficult album that examined, among other things, the stylized tension between the inner city and suburbia. Michael Oldfield, whose earlier *Tubular Bells* had been grafted into the soundtrack of *The Exorcist,* attempted a second rock-classical tone poem, *Ommadawn.* Stomu Yamash'ta composed and recorded a classical-rock-jazz tone poem

GRUNT RECORDS

ISLAND RECORDS

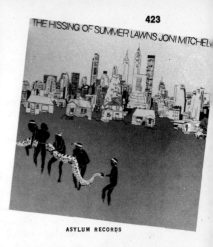

ASYLUM RECORDS

called *Go.* Both Oldfield's and Yamash'ta's albums were cinematic, or at least programmatic, and seemed to be the bases for future film or multimedia productions. Neil Diamond released *Beautiful Noise,* a cycle of songs about songwriting in the heyday of Tin Pan Alley.

In general, however, the Rolling Stones' journalist instincts tracked pop music's year. The Stones' album was called *Black and Blue,* and several songs on it sounded like disco music.

NOEL COPPAGE
Contributing Editor, "Stereo Review"

JAZZ RECORDS

During the past 20 years, sporadic jazz reissue programs have made records originally cut in the 1920's to 1940's available again. More recently, some jazz records of the 1950's and 1960's have become equally available. Until 1976, however, there were still large gaps in the reissues from these last two decades. Then, reprints were begun of the three major postwar jazz labels that were no longer in circulation—Savoy, Verve, and Bethlehem. This, along with earlier reissue series by Prestige-Fantasy, Blue Note, and Trip (covering Mercury and Em-Arcy), as well as the primarily prewar reissues of RCA Victor, Columbia, Decca (now MCA), and Biograph, has made the essential records from the entire era of recorded jazz concurrently available for the first time. The simultaneous appearance of the Savoy and Verve reissues was particularly welcome because, together, they document the rise and development of be-bop through the vital early recordings of Charlie Parker and Dizzy Gillespie.

At the same time, an unusual reissue series was begun by the Smithsonian Institution, which entered the jazz-record field in 1973 with a six-disc *Collection of Classic Jazz.* The success of that set inspired the institution to continue in the jazz field. Its first two releases, *King Oliver's Jazz Band/1923* and *Louis Armstrong and Earl Hines/1928,* focus on three major jazz figures of the 1920's at crucial periods in their long and prolific careers.

But there were more than just reissues in 1976. Arista Records, which put out the new

Savoy labels, also started Arista-Freedom which concentrated on avant-garde and contemporary jazz musicians—Cecil Taylor, Marion Brown, the Human Arts Ensemble, Andrew Hill, Roswell Rudd, Albert Ayler, Randy Weston—normally found only on obscure small labels. The recordings could give them wide exposure and distribution.

Among the significant individual releases of the year, two were further fillings in the gaps of jazz history. Paul Bley's *Live at the Hilcrest Club, 1958* (Inner City) carries the first recorded work of Ornette Coleman. *Duke Ellington's Jazz Violin Session* brings together Svend Asmussen, Stephane Grappelli, and Ray Nance—three strong, individual jazz violinists.

JOHN S. WILSON
"The New York Times" and "High Fidelity"

AUDIO EQUIPMENT AND TECHNIQUES

In 1976 three Japanese firms embarked upon an ambitious and chancy enterprise: the launching of a new tape format, the Elcaset.

Elcaset. Announced as a joint undertaking of Matsushita (Panasonic and Technics), Sony, and Teac, the Elcaset resembles an enlarged Philips cassette. It employs quarter-inch tape and is intended (though not bound) to operate at a speed of 3¾ inches per second. The Elcaset does not depend on its plastic case for the tape-guidance functions performed by the Philips cassette. Instead, it withdraws a broad loop of tape from the case and threads it onto external guides and tape-drive elements that contribute to more precise guidance. The first Elcaset machines were expected to appear on the market sometime in 1977.

Computers in Audio. Two 1976 products advanced the trend to computer techniques in home audio components. The ADC "Accutrac" turntable permits programing a lengthy sequence of commands that controls the order in which bands on a phonograph record are played. A computer memory in the Sherwood Micro/CPU 100 tuner stores the call letters for FM stations, displaying them in illuminated black letters as each station is tuned in.

RALPH W. HODGES, *"Stereo Review"*

RELIGION

General Survey

The General Convention of the Episcopal Church approved the ordination of women into the priesthood. The action may have an effect upon ecumenical relations with Eastern Orthodoxy and Roman Catholicism, where women priests are opposed on strong theological grounds. The Convention also gave preliminary approval to major revision of the Book of Common Prayer. Final adoption requires the approval of the General Convention of 1979.

The Lebanese civil war brought to world attention the Maronite Christians, an autonomous rite within the Roman Catholic Church. An Eastern Church that did not side with Constantinople during the schism of the 11th century, the Maronites are a militant force in the struggle with Muslims in Lebanon.

A renaissance of monasticism in the Coptic Church of Egypt was apparently under way. Reflecting the idea of desert seclusion historically associated with the East, the monastic revival was further evidence of a resurgence within Eastern Christianity.

In Lille, France, Archbishop Marcel Lefebvre, denounced the adulteration of Roman Catholic faith since Vatican II and began a crusade of Latinizing the Mass.

After seven years of preparation, the Vatican issued a "Declaration on Certain Questions Concerning Sexual Ethics." The statement was greeted with incredulity by those who feel that Rome's teaching on human sexuality is benighted and likely to be ignored by many Catholics.

The 41st International Eucharistic Congress of the Roman Catholic Church was held in Philadelphia in August. At least 1,000,000 persons were in attendance at the sessions, which were addressed by important church, political, and intellectual leaders. The theme was "Hungers of the Human Family."

The Rabbinical Council of America has sought Vatican recognition of Israel. Rome's position is that states are recognized only when their frontiers are officially outlined in a peace treaty. The Vatican earlier denounced an anti-Zionist declaration endorsed at the conclusion of a Christian-Muslim conference held in Tripoli, Libya.

The Unification Church of Sun Myung Moon purchased the 2,000-room New Yorker Hotel in New York City as a world mission center for the messianic cult that has been the subject of religious and political controversy. Thought by many to be a political movement in league with South Korea's reactionary government, the movement was also under fire for its mind control techniques.

The Soviet Union decided to use reason rather than terror in its attempt to stifle tradi-

French Archbishop Marcel Lefebvre denounced Vatican II reforms and created a stir in Catholic circles.

tional religion. A Leningrad study showed a considerable lack of positive response to atheism on the part of children.

RICHARD E. WENTZ
Arizona State University

Protestantism

During 1976, Protestantism throughout the world, and particularly the United States, was preoccupied with several major problems. The growth of the charismatic movement, the inroads made by the followers of the Rev. Sun Myung Moon and the Unification Church on the church's youth membership, the increasing tensions between conservative and liberal theologians, the systematic persecution of clergy and laity by repressive foreign regimes, and the ordination of women to the ministry were just some of the problems confronting Protestant leaders throughout the world.

Jimmy Carter's campaign for the presidency also raised several religious issues because, as a Southern Baptist, he had unequivocally stated he was a "born again Christian." While some Jews and Catholics expressed fears that Carter's conservative religion would create divisiveness, some Protestant voices expressed concern that he was mixing church and state.

Internal Problems. The Episcopal and Lutheran churches attracted attention during the year because of internal problems involving theology and church law.

At its triennial General Assembly, the Episcopal Church's House of Bishops and House of Deputies voted by large majorities to authorize

Reverend Moon, evangelist and industrialist, held a "God Bless America" rally in New York in June.

At a General Convention in September, the Episcopal Church voted to permit the ordination of women.

the ordination of women to the priesthood. The action followed several years of debate over the earlier invalid ordination of 11 women to the priesthood. Despite the assembly's decision, Episcopalians who disagreed may form a non-geographical diocese with a potential membership of 400,000. In the meantime, the Anglican (Episcopal) Church of Canada sanctioned the ordination of women and the first candidates were ordained in November.

The General Assembly also authorized the adoption of a newly-revised and rewritten *Book of Common Prayer.* Churches will use the new revision, the first since 1928, until 1979 when the church is expected to make the adoption official. The entire prayer book action was heatedly debated, with opponents arguing that the new versions contained liberal theology and poor English.

In the 2,800,000-member Lutheran Church-Missouri Synod, the synod's president, Jacob A. O. Preus, dismissed four district presidents (bishops) for their alleged refusal to accept his authority. Four other presidents, who stated they would not submit, were not removed. The actions by the synodical president sharpened up the theological debates that have raged in the synod since Dr. Preus assumed office in 1968. As a proponent of conservative theology and a literal interpretation of the Bible, Dr. Preus insisted on strict conformity to his views. During the year, an Association of Evangelical Lutheran Churches was organized to protest Dr. Preus' actions and to serve as an organizational center

for churches, districts, and individuals opposed to the synod's policies.

Evangelicals. In a Gallup poll, 34% of all Americans said they have had a "born again" experience. The poll also showed that four out of ten Americans believe the Bible "is to be taken literally, word for word." Another finding indicated that 58% of Protestants encouraged other people to believe in Christ. The swing to more conservative theology was also indicated by many mainline Protestant denominations, some of them considered theologically liberal. In January, a group of liberal Protestant theologians met in Boston to prepare a manifesto of concern for the drift away from social action in many churches. Their "Boston Affirmations" declared that a concern only for personal salvation is a basic denial of the Gospel.

Persecution. Protestant church leaders in South Korea and in several Latin American countries were either sentenced to long prison terms or driven into exile for allegedly conspiring against the governments and preaching social justice. Bishop Helmut Frenz, head of the Chilean Lutheran church, was declared persona non grata and denied a reentry visa because of his work with Chilean refugees and his criticism of the military regime. Protestant missionaries in some African countries were also expelled for alleged ties with the CIA. And in South Africa and Namibia, Protestant clergy who protested South Africa's apartheid policies were harassed or expelled from the country.

ALFRED P. KLAUSLER, *The Christian Century*

Roman Catholicism

Early in 1976, the Holy See excommunicated Archbishop Pierre Martin Ngo Dinh Thuc, the former archbishop of Saigon and brother of the assassinated Vietnam president, Ngo Dinh Diem, for illegally ordaining several men as priests and one man as a bishop in unauthorized rites in Spain. The excommunication was lifted in September after the Vietnam-born prelate expressed "repentance." By that time, however, Pope Paul and other Vatican officials were embroiled in a far more difficult controversy involving Archbishop Marcel Lefebvre, C. S. Sp., former head of the Holy Ghost Fathers and former archbishop of Dakar, Senegal.

An avowed traditionalist and critic of most of the reforms of the Second Vatican Council, particularly those dealing with interfaith and liturgical matters, Archbishop Lefebvre was suspended from both priestly and episcopal functions after he ordained 13 priests on June 29 at his ultraconservative seminary in Econe, Switzerland, in defiance of specific and personal papal orders. Before year's end the archbishop ordained 12 new deacons and a subdeacon and publicly celebrated the now banned Tridentine Rite Mass in Latin in French and German cities.

Bishop Donal Lamont, O. Carm., the Irish-born bishop of Umtali, Rhodesia, was sentenced to ten years at hard labor by a Rhodesian court after pleading guilty to charges of harboring black guerrillas and failing to report their activities. In the Philippines, South Korea, South Africa, Brazil, and Ireland, too, bishops lashed out against oppressive government policies.

But in Vietnam and in some parts of Eastern Europe conciliation was being attempted—particularly after Pope Paul named Archbishop Joseph Marie Trin Nhu Khue of Hanoi and Archbishop Laszlo Lekai of Esztergom (Budapest), Hungary, among 20 prelates raised to the cardinalate on May 24. The Vietnam prelate's elevation was a surprise. The Pope had named him "in pectore" (in the breast) until arrangements could be made for bestowal of the red hat. Among others elevated at the consistory were Archbishop William Baum of Washington, D. C., and Archbishop George Basil Hume, O. S. B., who was named to succeed the late John Cardinal Heenan as archbishop of Westminster (London) and primate of England.

The presence of four Latin Americans among the list of new cardinals did not ease church-state tensions in that hemisphere. The killing and imprisonment of bishops and priests who spoke out against social injustice became common. In mid-August Ecuadorian secret police broke into an international church meeting in Riobamba and arrested 57 persons—17 of them bishops, including four Americans—and held them for questioning in Quito.

Both the Pope and the Italian bishops' conference were rebuffed in their pleas to Catholic

India's Mother Teresa was a delegate to the 41st Eucharistic Congress. Its theme was world hunger.

voters not to vote for Communist candidates in June elections. Communists won impressive victories. The U. S. bishops' conference appeared to side with President Ford during the presidential campaign. The bishops said they did not endorse any candidate, however—despite their "encouragement" for the president's position relative to abortion. A position paper was released stating the relative positions of the bishops and the two party platforms on a variety of political, moral, and social issues.

The 41st International Eucharistic Congress was held in Philadelphia in early August. Its theme was the "Eucharist and the Hungers of the Human Family." Nearly 1.2 million persons participated in the week-long event.

Later in Detroit, the "most representative" deliberative assembly of American bishops, priests, religious, and laity ever assembled reaffirmed the commitment of the church to social justice. The 1,340 official delegates to the assembly expressed firm support of the direction of papal and episcopal teaching in most matters. But they voted in favor of an earlier statement by the Pontifical Biblical Commission that scriptural grounds alone were not enough "to exclude (the) possibility of ordaining women to the priesthood." They also asked for a reconsideration by the bishops of a married priesthood and discussions on matters involving sexual ethics.

OWEN M. MURPHY, JR.
Editor, The Catholic Free Press

Judaism

The year 1976 was one of grave concerns and challenges. The UN resolution of 1975 equating Zionism with racism was perceived by world Jewry as an assault on its prophetic-ethical tradition of social justice. Deterioration of Jewish conditions in the USSR, continued Arab terrorism, violent manifestations of anti-Semitism in several western countries, and Arab rioting in Israel caused collective concern. The successful Israeli rescue of hostages in Uganda on July 3–4, which was hailed by secular leaders as an act of courage and by Jewish religious authorities as the fulfillment of a Torah commandment—the redemption of captives—restored community morale. An unprecedented show of solidarity with the plight of Soviet Jewry, an upsurge of traditional observance, and a growing support for the religious Gush Emunim movement in Israel indicated a religious-emotional consolidation.

Challenges and Concerns. The largest international gathering on behalf of Soviet Jewry was held in Brussels. The meeting was prompted by news from the USSR of increasing publication of anti-Semitic propaganda, new restrictions on Jewish religious-cultural expression, and curtailment of emigration visas, and by a report by Amnesty International that Jews in Soviet prisons are singled out for abuse.

In Argentina, the publication of a rabidly anti-Semitic book was followed by bombings of Jewish religious institutions and by the appearance of a nationalistic group with avowed anti-Semitic aims. Similar bombings took place in France. In Mexico, anti-Semitic hate literature was traced to Arab publishers.

Israel. A growing nationalistic Gush Emunim movement committed to the preservation of "Biblical" borders staged a cross-country march in which 40,000 supporters participated. A magistrate's ruling permitting prayer services for Jews on the Temple Mount in Jerusalem touched off riots by Arabs who consider the area an exclusively Muslim shrine. In another riot, Arabs damaged Torah scrolls in the ancient Jewish shrine of Makhpela, which also houses a mosque. The defeat by the Knesset of a civil marriage bill preserved the Rabbinate's authority over marriage and divorce.

United States. Although religious and lay leaders warned of American Jewry's "extinction" because of low birth and high abortion and divorce rates, the threat seemed to be countered by the tendency, growing among Jewish youth, to identify with traditional values and practices.

The trend toward traditionalism was reflected within Reform Judaism by a sweeping revision of the liturgy and by the interest shown by rabbinical students at Hebrew Union College in the study of the basic texts of Judaism.

LIVIA E. BITTON, *Herbert H. Lehman College*
City University of New York

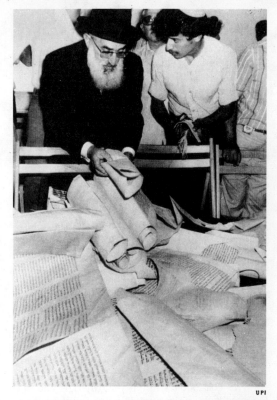

UPI

In Israeli-occupied Jordan, Rabbi Shlomo Goren inspects Torah scrolls damaged during an Arab attack.

Orthodox Eastern Church

The Greek Orthodox Church in America, an archdiocese of the Patriarchate of Constantinople, led by Archbishop Iakovos, was unsuccessful in its attempts to decentralize its administration into several metropolitanates. The Antiochene Church succeeded in integrating the dissident metropolitanate of Toledo into its ecclesiastical jurisdiction. The U. S. Supreme Court overturned an Illinois Supreme Court ruling that the Bishop of the Serbian Eastern Orthodox Diocese had been illegally defrocked by the mother church. The court also declared the reorganization of the diocese invalid.

For the first time in 40 years, an international Congress of Orthodox Theological Schools was held in Penteli Monastery outside Athens in August 1976. More than 100 official delegates from the 15 graduate faculties of theology in world Orthodoxy participated, including representatives of the schools of Halki in Turkey and Balamand in Syria, which had been closed because of political disruptions. The theme of the congress was "Orthodox Theology and its Application in Contemporary Life."

Metropolitan Meliton of the Patriarchate of Constantinople visited centers of Orthodoxy throughout Europe, calling for preparations for a general council of bishops of all Orthodox churches. Although preparatory work began,

Some 450 delegates from 40 Muslim nations attended the Seventh Annual Conference of Islamic Foreign Ministers in Istanbul in May.

politics prevent such a conference from occurring in the near future.

Meliton also visited the Vatican, and in a gesture of humility, Pope Paul VI kissed the foot of the Byzantine prelate. Delegates from virtually all Orthodox Churches had participated in the 5th Assembly of the World Council of Churches in Nairobi, Kenya, in late 1975. Metropolitan Mikodom of the Moscow Patriarchate was elected one of the six presidents of the body.

The official Anglican-Orthodox Dialogue, meeting in Moscow in 1976, noted Orthodox opposition to the ordination of women.

The Orthodox Church of America and the Church in Russia continued plans for the canonization of Father John Veniaminov (later Metropolitan Innocent of Moscow), a 19th century missionary.

THOMAS HOPKO
St. Vladimir's Orthodox Theological Seminary

Islam

Muslim spokesmen throughout the world protested what they termed the process of Judaization practiced by Israel in Jerusalem and other territories occupied after the 1967 Arab-Israeli War. The charge stemmed from a series of demonstrations during February and March in which Jews attempted to pray on parts of Jerusalem's Temple Mount reserved for Muslim worshippers. Israeli authorities banned the demonstrations and arrested many of the participants, but Muslim feeling continued to run high.

Political concerns highlighted the Seventh Annual Conference of Islamic Foreign Ministers held in Istanbul in May. The four-day meeting discussed economic and political problems in the Afro-Asian world, resulting in expressions of support for Palestinian and Turkish Cypriot Muslims. No progress was made, however, on a long-standing proposal for economic cooperation among Muslim states. Turkey, seeking support for its stand on Cyprus, accepted full membership in the organization, which it had previously declined because of the officially secular nature of the state. One new nation, the Comoro Islands, joined.

The increasing interest of Muslims in the spread of their faith, particularly in Africa,

where conversions have been most numerous in recent years, was shown by the formation of a powerful radio station, the Voice of Islam, supported by several Muslim groups. Its purpose is to broadcast information about Islam in Africa, foster Muslim solidarity on the continent, and offset Christian propaganda efforts there.

KENNETH J. PERKINS
University of South Carolina

Far Eastern Religions

South Korea has become a land of cults and repressive forms of religion designed either to maintain the status quo or to provide an escape from the pressures of the world. Since the end of the Korean War, numerous self-proclaimed messiahs have appeared. They tend to blend Asian mystical forms with Christianity, offering immediate salvation and economic security.

The Dalai Lama, exiled God-King of Tibet, selected a site in Central Kashmir for Dhukor Wangchen, the sermon of the Wheel of Time. Thousands of pilgrims went to hear Dhukor Wangchen, which is preached only a limited number of times during the life of a Lama. The eight-hour sermon expounds the doctrines of Tantric Buddhism, emphasizing mastery of esoteric knowledge as a means to salvation.

The hamlet of Meivazhichalai in South India was the scene of excavations to recover gold from the retreat center of a sect that has about 500,000 followers throughout India. The buried wealth was gathered at annual festivals when followers of the sect brought gifts to the hamlet.

In South Vietnam, Buddhist leaders have begun to support the Communist government, according to the *Giac Ngo,* the "voice of patriotic Buddhists." The magazine suggests that there is no governmental threat to Buddhism and that Buddhists must assist in the building of a new society.

The Indian Archaeological Survey reported that relics discovered in 1971 are part of the mortal remains of Prince Siddhartha, the Gautama Buddha, who died about 483 B. C. A soapstone casket, with an inscription identifying the contents as portions of the body of the founder of Buddhism, was unearthed in a village in Uttar Pradesh.

RICHARD E. WENTZ, *Arizona State University*

RHODE ISLAND

The state's slow recovery during 1976 from the economic recession was overshadowed in the news by political maneuvering in anticipation of the November elections.

Government. When the General Assembly convened in January it faced the necessity of raising taxes to finance even a relatively austere state budget. When it adjourned in late May, the sales tax was up from 5 to 6%.

Other action taken during the session included: legislation mandating open meetings for all public bodies, a statewide uniform building code, reform of malpractice insurance, reorganization of the Corrections Department, and the election of Speaker Joseph Bevilacqua as chief justice of the Supreme Court. Teacher strike legislation failed to pass.

Economy. Figures issued in the late summer showed slow economic improvement. Manufacturing employment increased by 4.6% in the first half of the year, a higher rate than in most other New England states. State tax revenue also surpassed projections.

October showed job figures continuing to increase and also brought the announcement that the Electric Boat plant on abandoned Navy land at Quonset Point would add 1,000 more to its existing work force of 4,000. With this addition, the state completed replacement of the 5,000 jobs lost by base closings. Additional hiring was also announced by Electric Boat's parent plant at Groton, Conn. Many of the new workers would be Rhode Islanders joining the 9,000 from the state already on the rolls there.

The highlight of the state's bicentennial celebration was both a patriotic success and an economic boon. "Operation Sail" brought the armada of square riggers first to Newport before it sailed to New York City for the 4th-of-July parade up the Hudson. Throngs of tourists greeted the stately vessels on their arrival the weekend of June 26 and witnessed their departure July 1. It is estimated that the state and Newport reaped a $15-million windfall in visitor expenditures. The tall ships may well have given a long-term boost to the tourist business, which —it is hoped—will replace the Navy as a source of revenue.

Politics. The decision of John O. Pastore not to seek reelection to the U. S. Senate launched the political season. Gov. Philip Noel, former Republican Gov. John Chafee and others made plans to seek the seat, as did Richard Lorber, a well-to-do Cadillac dealer.

The voters went to the polls on June 1 to choose national convention delegates. The Democrats divided their support about evenly among Jimmy Carter, Frank Church, and Jerry Brown. The Republicans had no real contest. In the hotly contested Democratic primary on September 14 Lorber defeated Gov. Noel by 100 absentee votes for the Senate nomination.

On November 2 an unusually large turnout of Rhode Islanders chose Carter over Ford by 56%, elected the whole Democratic slate of statewide officers, but preferred Chafee to Lorber for the U. S. Senate. By all odds, however, the biggest winner was Democratic Rep. Ed Beard, who had gained his first term in 1974 as an unendorsed challenger, won the 1976 primary again without party endorsement, and took 78% of the vote in the general election.

ELMER E. CORNWELL, JR., *Brown University*

—— RHODE ISLAND · Information Highlights ——

Area: 1,214 square miles (3,144 km²).
Population (1975 est.): 927,000.
Chief Cities (1970 census): Providence, the capital, 179,116; Warwick, 83,694; Pawtucket, 76,984.
Government (1976): *Chief Officers*—governor, Philip W. Noel (D); lt. gov., J. Joseph Garrahy (D). *General Assembly*—Senate, 50 members; House of Representatives, 100 members.
Education (1975–76): *Enrollment*—public elementary schools, 101,491 pupils; public secondary, 74,826; nonpublic (1976–77), 32,300; colleges and universities, 61,716 students. *Public school expenditures,* $234,935,000 ($1,403 per pupil).
State Finances (fiscal year 1975): *Revenues,* $750,736,-000; *expenditures,* $782,772,000.
Personal Income (1975): $5,413,000,000; per capita, $5,841.
Labor Force (July 1976): *Nonagricultural wage and salary earners,* 342,200; *insured unemployed,* 28,-300 (9.2%).

Ocean Victory, a giant offshore oil drilling rig, passes beneath Newport Bridge en route to a temporary berth at Quonset Point, R. I.

Rhodesia's Prime Minister Ian Smith (*extreme right*) and black nationalist leaders, including Robert G. Mugabe (*extreme left*) and Joshua Nkomo (*fourth from left*) meet in Geneva to seek an end to their struggle for control of Rhodesia.

UPI

RHODESIA

For Rhodesia 1976 was a momentous year. It was also a year of crisis, uncertainty and escalating guerrilla warfare. What was at stake—and remains so—was the future of the country itself. The question overshadowing all others was whether the government would bow to the mounting pressures, international as well as regional, and negotiate a specific timetable for transfer of power from the white minority to the black majority. The alternative was universally seen as a prolonged war with unpredictable consequences for the whole of Southern Africa. The major event of the year was Prime Minister Ian Smith's decision on September 24 to accept in principle the so-called Kissinger plan for black majority rule within two years.

The Geneva Conference. On October 28 Prime Minister Smith met in Geneva with four black nationalist delegations led by Joshua Nkomo, the Rev. Ndabaningi Sithole, Bishop Abel Muzorewa, and Robert Mugabe at a conference under the chairmanship of Ivor Richard, Britain's ambassador to the United Nations. The atmosphere was one of bitterness and suspicion, and negotiations were expected to be difficult and long. The consequences of failure were underlined, even as the conference sat, by the in-

tensification of guerrilla activity from Mozambique and Zambia bases and the heaviest retaliation yet by Rhodesian security forces on Mozambique camps. Hundreds of blacks were killed.

The background to the Geneva talks was the collapse of the South African détente initiative in the wake of the Angolan civil war and the abandonment in March, after four months, of constitutional talks between Smith and Nkomo. During his visit to Africa in April, U. S. Secretary of State Henry Kissinger outlined a 10-point plan for the resumption of talks and by September, after much shuttle diplomacy, secured the cooperation of all the détente states. Smith met Kissinger in Pretoria, South Africa, on September 19, while the latter was visiting Prime Minister Johannes Vorster. Smith was undoubtedly warned that no help from either could be expected in the event of foreign intervention if he refused to negotiate the transfer of power.

The Kissinger Proposals. In his September 24 address to the country Smith said the British-American plan his cabinet had accepted included majority rule in two years, a two-tier interim government with a Council of State equally divided between blacks and whites under white chairmanship, and a Council of Ministers with a black majority but the departments of defense and law and order under white ministers. The Council of State was to draft the new constitution. It is believed that there was provision for a $2,000,000,000 trust fund to be set up, both to provide compensation for whites wanting to leave and to assist the new government.

From the outset, two major difficulties confronted the conference. First, there was the lack of unity among the black leaders; and second, there was a difference of approach concerning the purpose of the conference. Smith regarded the proposals to which his cabinet agreed as settled; the black delegations considered all the terms negotiable. In fact, the first

─────── **RHODESIA · Information Highlights** ───────

Official Name: Rhodesia.
Location: Southeastern Africa.
Area: 150,803 square miles (390,580 km²).
Population (1976 est.): 6,500,000.
Chief Cities (1975 est.): Salisbury, the capital, 555,-000; Bulawayo, 339,000.
Government: *Head of state,* John Wrathall, president (took office Dec. 1975). *Head of government,* Ian Smith, prime minister (took office 1964).
Monetary Unit: Rhodesian dollar (0.61 R. dollar equals U. S.$1, Dec. 1976).
Gross National Product (1975 est.): $3,600,000,000.
Major Agricultural Products: Tobacco, sugar, tea, groundnuts, cotton, corn, millet, and sorghum.
Foreign Trade (1973): *Exports,* $654,000,000; *imports,* $541,000,000.

item finally agreed on was to set the time for black rule at March 1, 1978.

Domestic Affairs. The breakdown of the Smith-Nkomo constitutional talks was followed in April by increased guerrilla activity. Prime Minister Smith introduced new security measures. National service was extended to 18-year-olds, the army was placed on continuous alert, and virtual censorship was imposed under emergency powers regulations. The same week Smith appointed seven blacks to his cabinet—four chiefs from the Senate as ministers and three members of parliament as deputy ministers. No particular portfolios were announced. In June the minister of defense confirmed that a new guerrilla front had been opened on the Zambia border. But the heaviest fighting since 1972 came in October, culminating in Rhodesian "hot pursuit" across some 125 miles (200 km) of the Mozambique border at the turn of November.

Former Southern Rhodesian Prime Minister Garfield Todd was released from political detention on his farm in June, after four and a half years. But the whereabouts of Dr. Edson Sithole of the African National Council, abducted from Salisbury on Oct. 15, 1975, remains a mystery.

See also BIOGRAPHY: Smith, Ian.

R. B. BALLINGER, *Rhode Island College*

RUMANIA

The Rumanian Communist Party and Nicolae Ceauşescu, its secretary general and president of the republic, maintained their firm grip on state and society.

Domestic Affairs. There were few significant internal changes. In June, Ceauşescu carried out a shuffle of the Council of Ministers, replacing the defense minister and three other high officials. That same month, addressing a Congress of Political Education and Socialist Culture in Bucharest, he reminded the delegates that "all educational activities must be based on the principles of socialist ethics and equity."

Economy. A new five-year economic plan for 1976–80, announced on February 12, established extremely high production goals, with industrial output to increase by 70%. Rumania signed long-term economic and commercial agreements with China in January, Greece in March, Australia and the Philippines in April, and the United States in November.

Foreign Affairs. Rumania continued to maintain its stance of political and economic independence within the Soviet sphere of influence. In April, the Rumanian Communist Party daily, *Scienteia*, denounced the so-called "Sonnenfeldt Doctrine," interpreted as implying U. S. acceptance of permanent Soviet hegemony over Eastern Europe. Ceauşescu himself, attending the 25th Congress of the Soviet Communist Party in Moscow, February 24–March 5, stressed that his own party sought "the building of a new unity founded on respect for the right of each party freely to develop its political line, strategy, and revolutionary tactics, and to contribute in a creative fashion to the development of Marxism." This attitude was reiterated by Rumanian delegations to Communist Party congresses in Czechoslovakia in April and in East Berlin in May, and to the 30th session of the Council for Mutual Economic Assistance (COMECON) in East Berlin in July. Predictably, Rumania was pleased by the statement published at the conclusion of the meeting of 29 eastern and western Communist Party leaders in East Berlin, June 29–30, which rejected Soviet dominance over the world Communist movement.

Ceauşescu and Soviet leader Leonid Brezhnev exchanged conciliatory visits in the Crimea in August and in Bucharest in November. Ceauşescu publicly denied all Rumanian claims to territory in the Soviet republic of Moldavia, part of Rumania before 1940. It was announced in September that during 1978–83 Soviet spacecraft would also carry Rumanian astronauts.

The careful balance Rumania had tried to maintain between the Arab states and Israel was abandoned in 1976. At the United Nations, in the Security Council and the Committee on the Exercise of the Inalienable Rights of the Palestinian People, Rumania supported the pro-Palestinian position and called upon Israel to withdraw from all occupied Arab lands. In March, Rumania informed the Arab League's Boycott Office that henceforth it would boycott firms doing business with Israel.

Rumania participated, along with Greece, Turkey, Yugoslavia, and Bulgaria, in the first conference since World War II on intra-Balkan cooperation. Held in Athens from January 26 to February 5, the conference envisioned future multilateral cooperation in economic, technical, scientific, touristic, and cultural areas.

In another world arena, the Summer Olympics at Montreal in July, Rumania's amazing 14-year-old gymnast, Nadia Comaneci, won three gold medals and posted seven perfect scores, a unique achievement in Olympic history.

JOSEPH F. ZACEK
State University of New York at Albany

―――――― **RUMANIA • Information Highlights** ――――――

Official Name: Socialist Republic of Rumania.
Location: Southeastern Europe.
Area: 91,700 square miles (237,500 km²).
Population (1976 est.): 21,500,000.
Chief Cities (1974 met. est.): Bucharest, the capital, 1,682,000; Constanta, 262,000; Ploieşti, 233,000.
Government: *Head of state*, Nicolae Ceauşescu, president and secretary general of the Communist Party (took office 1965). *Head of government*, Manea Manescu, premier (took office March 1974). *Legislature* (unicameral)—Grand National Assembly.
Monetary Unit: Leu (4.88 lei equal U. S.$1, Dec. 1976).
Gross National Product (1975 est.): $41,000,000,000.
Manufacturing (major products): Construction materials, metals, chemicals, machinery, processed foods, textiles, petroleum products.
Major Agricultural Products: Corn, sugar beets, potatoes, wheat, rye, sunflower seeds.
Foreign Trade (1974): *Exports*, $4,874,000,000; *imports*, $5,144,000,000.

SASKATCHEWAN

The purchase by the Saskatchewan government of the potash mining operation of Duval Corporation for $128.5 million, was the top provincial news story in 1976. It marked the first step in the plan to take over at least half of the province's 10 potash mines, as a result of the alleged failure by the companies to pay some $30 million in taxes, and what a government spokesman termed "harassment in the courts" by the industry.

The Economy. A record grain yield of some 835 million bushels (294,000,000 hl) was harvested, and prices remained good. A depressed livestock market resulted in a substantial selling off of herds in the fall. The government budgeted $1 million to develop a farm income stabilization program.

The economy was working at nearly full capacity; the unemployment rate remained among the lowest in Canada. Saskatchewan enjoyed an excellent credit rating because of its fiscal record—14 years of budget surpluses.

Legislation. Full community college service in all areas of the province became a reality in 1976. An agreement was reached with the federal government to provide community college service to Indians on reserves and crown lands.

Despite proposed federal cutbacks in medical and hospital funding, $11 million was budgeted for further construction at the University Hospital in Saskatoon.

Major new initiatives in the area of housing included a program for the assembly and service of land for residential purposes.

Federal wage-and-price controls resulted in labor unrest and a succession of strikes, many of which protested rollbacks imposed by the Saskatchewan Public Sector Price and Compensation Board. Notable among these was a month-long strike by some 1,300 Saskatchewan Power Corporation electrical workers. While the province was the only one in Canada that did not sign an anti-inflation agreement with Ottawa, rent controls were imposed and the provincial board monitored wage and price increases.

DOROTHY HAYDEN, *Regina Public Library*

--- **SASKATCHEWAN** • Information Highlights ---

Area: 251,700 square miles (651,900 km²).
Population (April 1976 est.): 932,000.
Chief Cities (1971 census): Regina, the capital, 139,-469; Saskatoon, 126,449; Moose Jaw, 31,854.
Government (1976): *Chief Officers*—lt. gov., George Porteous; premier, Allan Blakeney; atty. gen., Roy Romanow; min. of educ., Ed Tchorzewski; chief justice, E. M. Culliton. *Legislature*—Legislative Assembly, 60 members.
Education (1976–77): *Enrollment*—public elementary and secondary schools, 216,050 pupils; private schools, 1,480; Indian (federal) schools, 5,910 students; post-secondary, 16,960 students. *Total expenditures,* $343,770,000.
Public Finance (1975–76 est.): *Revenues,* $1,197,000,-000; *expenditures,* $1,195,000,000.
Personal Income (1974): $4,265,000,000; average annual income per person, $4,702.
(All monetary figures are in Canadian dollars.)

UPI

Prince Saud ibn Faisal, Saudi Arabia's foreign minister, conferred with Egypt's President Sadat in May and was at the UN General Assembly session in September.

SAUDI ARABIA

Thanks to continuing high world prices for oil in 1976 Saudi Arabia was able to begin a major transformation of its domestic economy and to expand its influence in the Arab world.

Finance and Economy. The first stages of the ambitious $140,000,000,000 five-year plan (1976–80) were implemented during the year. Planning and construction work was concentrated on ports, electric generating facilities, and desalination plants. A new $231-million water purification plant for Riyadh and improvements in the Red Sea ports, costing $250 million, were announced in February. Plans for a port and industrial complex at Jubail were estimated in June to cost $15,000,000,000.

At the end of 1975 Saudi government reserves were at least $23,000,000,000 and growing rapidly. In April 1976 the Saudi Monetary Agency's investment in United States obligations was about $14,000,000,000. Large budgetary surpluses continued to accumulate.

In the first five months of 1976 oil production of the Arabian American Oil Company (ARAMCO) increased to an average of 7.9 million barrels (1,070,000 metric tons) per day compared with 6.8 million (970,000 tons) in 1975. Saudi Arabia is now America's largest foreign supplier of crude oil.

Negotiations to purchase the ARAMCO stock still owned by American oil companies were held in March 1976, but a Saudi takeover had not yet occurred as the year drew to a close.

——— SAUDI ARABIA • Information Highlights ———
Official Name: Kingdom of Saudi Arabia.
Location: Arabian Peninsula in southwest Asia.
Area: 830,000 square miles (2,149,690 km²).
Population (1976 est.): 7,400,000.
Chief Cities (1975 est.): Riyadh, the capital, 450,000; Jidda, 500,000; Mecca, 250,000.
Government: *Head of state and government,* Khalid ibn Abd al-Aziz al-Saud, king (acceded March 1975).
Monetary Unit: Riyal (3.53 riyals equal U.S.$1, June 1976).
Gross National Product (1974 est.): $40,000,000,000.
Manufacturing (major products): Petroleum products, cement, fertilizers, iron and steel.
Major Agricultural Products: Dates, vegetables, wheat.
Foreign Trade (1975), *Exports,* $27,754,000,000; *imports* (1974), $3,473,000,000.

Saudi oil policy continued to oppose new price increases by the Organization of Petroleum Exporting Countries.

Oil provided 89% of the 1976–77 budget. Expenditures and income balanced at $31,000,-000,000. Two thirds of the budget were allocated for new or continued development projects. Inflation remained high. The other chief economic problem was a shortage of skilled labor.

The new nation of the Seychelles joined the UN in 1976. President James Mancham (*left*), UN Secretary General Waldheim, and General Assembly President Amerasinghe attended the initial flag raising ceremony in New York.

UPI

Government. King Khalid retained supervision of the government while giving Crown Prince Fahd great influence in administration. On October 13 a new cabinet of 25 was announced, with seven brothers of the king in the chief posts. The al-Shaykh family, which is of high religious prestige, held three ministries. Sheikh Ahmed Zaki Yamani continued to be minister of petroleum. No basic changes were made in the internal political situation.

Foreign Affairs. Saudi Arabia in 1976 was successful in promoting its goals of peace among the Arab states and the preservation of conservative regimes in the Gulf. King Khalid met with the leaders of the Palestine Liberation Organization, Egypt, Syria, Jordan, the Sudan, and the Gulf states to try to compose intra-Arab rivalries. Saudi Arabia supported Syrian intervention in Lebanon. Long-lasting tensions with the People's Democratic Republic of Yemen and with Iraq were eased during the months of February and March.

Loans to foreign countries were estimated at $4,000,000,000 by the end of 1975. Aid in 1976 was given to Egypt for restoration of its Suez Canal cities.

Military. From July 1975 to July 1976 Saudi Arabia purchased $2,700,000,000 worth of arms and equipment from the United States. Large future sales of arms by America to Saudi Arabia became a political issue in the American presidential contest.

WILLIAM L. OCHSENWALD
Virginia Polytechnic Institute

SEYCHELLES

On June 29, 1976, Seychelles became a republic within the Commonwealth of Nations. This former British colony consists of more than 90 islands scattered over the western Indian Ocean. Mahe, the principal island, which sustains most of the population, lies about 4° south of the equator and some 1,100 miles (1,770 km) east of Mombasa, Kenya. About 90% of the population is of mixed Afro-European descent; the rest are Europeans (mostly of French and British origin), Indians, and Chinese.

Government and Politics. Seychelles is a parliamentary democracy with a president and a 25-member Legislative Assembly elected by uni-

——— SEYCHELLES • Information Highlights ———
Official Name: Republic of Seychelles.
Location: Indian Ocean.
Area: 107 square miles (277 km²).
Population (1976 est.): 60,000.
Chief City (1976 est.): Victoria, the capital, 15,000.
Government: *Head of state,* James R. Mancham, president (took office June 1976). *Head of government,* Albert Rene, prime minister (took office June 1976). *Legislature*—National Assembly (25 members).
Monetary Unit: Seychelles rupee (6.68 rupees equal U.S.$1, Sept. 1976).
Gross National Product (1974 est.): $31,000,000.
Major Agricultural Products: copra, cinnamon bark.
Foreign Trade (1974): *Exports,* $2,800,000; *imports,* $24,300,000.

Singapore's Premier Lee Kuan Yew (*right*) began the year by holding a series of talks with Philippine President Ferdinand Marcos.

versal franchise. The president selects 10 members of the assembly as his cabinet, including a prime minister. There are no elected local government bodies. There is a Supreme Court, consisting of a chief justice and a puisne judge, and two magistrate's courts.

The two major political parties are the Seychelles Democratic party (SDP) which has the support of the wealthier sections and inclines toward close ties with Britain and the West, and the Seychelles Peoples United party (SPUP) which looks more toward Africa. In the legislature the SDP has 18 seats and the SPUP 7. In the independence government James Mancham, head of the SDP, is president and Albert Rene, head of the SPUP, is prime minister.

Economy. Traditionally, Seychelles has depended on the production of copra and cinnamon for export and on grants from the United Kingdom. Only two passenger ships a month called at Seychelles until 1971 when a $14.5 million airport was completed on reclaimed land, opening the islands to tourists; 35,000 arrived in 1975. Hotels and other amenities were built, bringing a new prosperity. Seychelles must import most of its food, but its fishing industry is growing. Victoria, the capital, is a free port and is trying to establish itself as a tax haven and center for international banking. The country suffers from severe population pressures.

BURTON BENEDICT
University of California, Berkeley

SINGAPORE

Compared to most countries, Singapore weathered the global recession remarkably well in 1976. But its rate of growth was slowed.

Economy. Singapore's gross domestic product rose 6.1% in 1974 and 4.1% in 1975. This represented a considerable drop from the spectacular double digit figures of the late 1960's and early 1970's. The government target for 1976 was a modest 6–8%. There were several reasons for such caution. (1) Unemployment climbed from 3.9% in 1974 to 4.5% by mid-1975. (2) Unit labor costs increased faster than those in competing countries like Taiwan

and South Korea. (3) Foreign investment commitments declined 60% between 1974 and 1975. (4) World trade and the economies of Europe and North America remained sluggish. These were significant constraints, given Singapore's reliance on trade and large inflows of foreign capital and expertise.

The government responded with a policy of wage restraint and public spending to stimulate the economy. It launched Singapore's largest public works project, the $530,000,000 conversion of a former British Air Force base at Changi into the nation's international airport.

Domestic Affairs. Domestic political stability continued during the year. But in May the government announced discovery of a Communist attempt to launch a new phase of subversion in Singapore.

Foreign Affairs. Britain completed its military withdrawal from Singapore on March 31, ending a 157-year presence. As recently as 1963–65 the British force on the island had numbered 70,000 troops.

Prime Minister Lee Kuan Yew visited China in May. Both countries concurred that "more time" was needed to overcome the disputes of the past, but that cooperation could be expanded in fields where there was "basic agreement," such as trade.

Criticism from Western European Socialist parties concerning Singapore's attitude toward civil liberties forced the ruling People's Action Party to resign from the Socialist International.

MARVIN C. OTT, *Mount Holyoke College*

—— **SINGAPORE · Information Highlights** ——

Official Name: Republic of Singapore.
Location: Southeast Asia.
Area: 244 square miles (581 km²).
Population (1976 est.): 2,300,000.
Chief City (1974 est.): Singapore, the capital, 1,327,500.
Government: *Head of state,* Benjamin H. Sheares, president (took office Jan. 1971). *Head of government,* Lee Kuan Yew, prime minister (took office 1959). *Legislature* (unicameral)—Parliament.
Monetary Unit: Singapore dollar (2.46 S. dollars equal U.S.$1, Aug. 1976).
Gross National Product (1975 est.): $6,500,000,000.
Manufacturing (major products): Petroleum products, steel, textiles, tires, wood products.
Foreign Trade (1975): *Exports,* $5,376,000,000; *imports,* $8,134,000,000.

SOCIAL WELFARE

Social welfare programs in 1976 were enmeshed in politics in a number of countries, especially the United States, Canada, and Sweden. In the United States the tone was set by confrontations between President Ford and Congress, and legal and political balances of power permitted little legislation of significance to pass. Previous legislation, federal administrative policies, and budgetary crises intensified the deterioration of local and state programs that had been ongoing for several years.

WELFARE PROGRAMS AND SOCIAL SECURITY

The problem of dependent broken families is worldwide, and is dealt with in various ways by different countries. In Australia the government launches a study of family life. In Taiwan families with televisions or refrigerators are barred from relief.

"Welfare Reform." In the United States rhetoric about sweeping changes in the welfare system faded after Ronald Reagan unsuccessfully proposed that full responsibility for Aid to Families with Dependent Children (AFDC) be returned to the states. States vary in their ability and willingness to assume responsibility, and there is strong pressure for national standards. Failure to enact President Nixon's sweeping 1970 proposal for a "Family Assistance Plan" left proponents of change divided and unprepared to coalesce until they have strong, generally acceptable leadership. Their choices of reform proposals include federal assumption of welfare costs charged to cities; greater federal reimbursement of state expenditures; setting up one category with work incentives for persons in the labor market, and another without incentives for those unable to work; requiring able-bodied recipients to "work out" their grants; and limited experiments looking toward complete federalization.

The federal administration continued its efforts to reduce outlays through regulations requiring states to achieve arbitrary levels of perfection in case management, a trend away from considering individual differences in need toward dealing with recipients impersonally. Some attempt to counteract this mechanistic image appeared to be involved in the Department of Health, Education, and Welfare's (HEW) decision to seek greater public participation in the process of establishing its regulations. The department also announced plans to revise and simplify a multitude of regulations regarding assistance programs that have been promulgated since 1969 as a result of legislation and court decisions.

Complications continued to plague the federal Supplemental Security Income (SSI) program, which had replaced state-federal programs for the aged, blind, and disabled in 1974. Repercussions of earlier glaring computer and inter-governmental difficulties continued, with some new ones arising. Consequently, this initial experience with federalization of state public assistance programs has made both administrators and legislators cautious about sweeping changes in the remaining, much larger, public assistance and related programs.

Food Stamps. The furor over food stamps indicated the problems latent in attempts to ensure adequate aid to all in need. The public is confused because the eligibility requirements for food stamps provide wider coverage than either AFDC or SSI. Discrepancies frustrate apparently logical adjustments in HEW programs. In 1976, new limits were set on the eligibility of students and others popularly regarded as not needing aid. Fraud charges, including those against commercial vendors of the stamps, continued to create unfavorable publicity.

Jobs Legislation. High unemployment triggered a variety of proposals in the United States for public employment programs. Most comprehensive was the Humphrey-Hawkins bill, which sought a coordinated approach to assure balanced economic growth and full employment, with a goal of no more than 3% unemployment by 1980. The bill was supported in the Democratic Party platform. Conservatives, however, sided with President Ford, arguing that it would be inflationary, was unnecessary because unemployment was receding, and would create undue and unwanted controls on the economy. A rise in unemployment during the summer, which was contrary to optimistic economic predictions, was not sufficient to generate Congressional action. However, a modest public employment program was enacted over the president's veto.

Unemployment insurance reserves became depleted in many states, requiring higher taxes on employers. Also, persons exhausting their unemployment insurance benefits turned to the public assistance, food stamp, and social security programs for help.

In Common Market countries unemployment insurance payments to low-paid foreign workers have become controversial.

Social Security. A furor was generated early in the year when the official advisory committee, making its regular five-year report, pointed out that current social security tax revenues were not sufficient to meet current benefit payments, and that at the rate of outflow in fiscal 1975 the trust fund might be exhausted by 1980. Scare headlines threatened the 30 million beneficiaries with impoverishment and employed persons with loss of their tax investments in the program. Reasons for the cash flow deficit could be found in decreased revenues, more retirees due to unemployment, and to increases in benefits autorized in recent years. Congressional policy never has allowed the social security trust fund to become large enough to continue indefinitely in the face of long-lasting, adverse economic conditions.

Previous legislation had authorized the increase of taxable earnings by $1,200 a year each in 1976 and 1977, from $14,100 to $16,500. These increases will help the trust fund in the next few years, while the resulting higher retirement benefits will not begin to be felt as outgo for some years. With prospects of improved revenues for the fund from both increased employment and higher levels of taxable income, Congress declined to act on President Ford's recommendation of a tax rate increase, and he did not press an unpopular point.

Child Welfare. Political considerations also affected child welfare program decisions. A comprehensive bill introduced by Sen. Walter Mondale and Rep. John Brademas was attacked as socialist in origin and a threat to the family. A bill to implement child day care standards enacted in 1974 (as part of the new Title XX of the Social Security Act) was attacked and ultimately vetoed on the basis that standards should be set by the states. The veto was narrowly sustained in the Senate. But late in the session, when a similar bill passed by larger margins, the President signed it.

Allegations that day care was detrimental were refuted in controlled research studies, and parents who were able to afford the cost were using commercial day-care centers in such numbers that franchised national chains were becoming profitable.

Administration of Title XX involved a major readjustment of relationships among federal, state, and local government agencies as well as nonprofit and commercial organizations. The problem of insufficient funds was common. In New York City 49 day care centers serving 3,500 children were ordered closed in July, even though 75% of the cost would have been met by federal funds.

Part of the squeeze on day care and other traditional child welfare programs came from a mandate embodied in Title XX requiring all states to set up systems requiring physicians and other responsible persons to report cases of child abuse, so they could be investigated by a state agency. Previously-reported spectacular cases proved to be only the tip of an iceberg, and agencies with already insufficient staff had to divert their energies to this previously little-recognized problem.

Still another federal demand on state agencies was participation in a network of federal and state bureaucracies charged with tracing deserting parents of children receiving AFDC and collecting child support from them. The network's expenses are to be paid out of the collections, with the families ordinarily receiving no benefit beyond regular public assistance allowances. Optimistic proponents predicted that when the program is fully operational collections will exceed administrative costs by 4 to 1. However, during the start-up year, fiscal 1976, the results were less than 1.5 to 1, and the number of AFDC cases terminated because the collections were made was only 23,000 out of 3,600,000, about 0.6%.

HEALTH CARE

Contrary to expectations, no serious effort was made to bring any of the proposals for national health programs up for debate in Congress. However, health issues were constantly in the news.

Swine Flu. In February, President Ford proposed a plan to vaccinate all persons against swine flu. Some public health authorities both in the United States and abroad minimized the threat. But reminders of the great influenza pandemic of 1918 were enough to persuade Congress to support the preventive program.

Questions about the safety of the vaccine and fear of malpractice suits delayed the production and distribution of the vaccine until legislation established the government as the responsible party in dealings with the public. When immunization started early in October, public anxiety was stirred by reports of deaths among elderly persons who had received the vaccine. But the flu vaccine was declared safe. The program was suspended on December 16 because of concern that the vaccine might be linked to cases of paralysis. (See page 322.)

Malpractice. Temporary solutions of the malpractice insurance issues in many states eased tensions. As the nature of the problems and the range of possible solutions became clearer, legislatures, professional associations, and insurance carriers worked on permanent adjustments.

Right to Die. The problem of indefinite use of life-support devices became less pressing. Some publicized patients died in spite of life-support machines. In the much publicized case of Karen Anne Quinlan, a court authorized removal of life-supports did not result in death. She continued to survive in a nursing home.

The increased use of donated organs also highlighted the need for clearer medical and legal guidelines in determining death. Shifting the criterion from the nonfunctioning of the heart to nonfunctioning of the brain has been recommended by medical and legal authorities and is being considered in various state legislatures. Alternatively, in a "living will" an individual authorizes in advance the termination of life-support procedures at such time as it is determined that life can be prolonged only by artificial means. A law permitting the "living will" was enacted in California in the fall. Still, the boundaries between the right to die, euthanasia, and murder remained blurred.

Right to Life. At the other end of the life span, the issue of acceptable means of population restriction is a worldwide concern. The Netherlands considered legalizing abortion. In India slow response to contraceptive education and voluntary sterilization led to proposals for compulsory sterilization.

In the United States abortion became a political issue. A vocal, determined antiabortion campaign, in which Roman Catholic bishops assumed a leading role, put forward a candidate for president. The leading presidential candidates were examined on their views, and for a time it appeared that other issues were hardly to be considered. The House voted to ban the use of Medicaid funds for any abortions, while the Senate supported such use, in keeping with court decisions. In the final compromise on the HEW appropriations bill, use of Medicaid funds for abortions was limited to situations where the life of the mother is in danger. However, supporters of abortion claimed the restriction was unconstitutional. In November the Supreme Court suspended this provision pending review.

Medicaid. Assuring medical care for low income persons proved to be far more costly than anticipated, so Medicaid has been curtailed and subjected to intensive scrutiny. Typical localities where Medicaid expenditures are large have high proportions of low income persons who previously were never able to afford physicians except in emergencies. Hence physicians in these areas were few. Under Medicaid a relatively few physicians, laboratories, and pharmacies became the principal recipients of payments for services to thousands of new patients.

Suspicion of fraud was easy to generate, and state variations in regulations and procedures made a clear picture difficult to obtain. Congressional suspicions and frustration were highlighted by Sen. Frank Moss' personal exposure of allegedly poor quality service at "Medicaid mills" in New York City. Fraud indictments were brought against a number of Chicago physicians and others. In October, President Ford approved a bill creating an independent office of inspector general in HEW to ferret out fraud in both Medicaid and Medicare.

Health Systems Agencies. During 1976 a nationwide network of "health systems agencies" (HSA) was set up in accordance with 1974 legislation. These HSAs have replaced previous planning agencies and are to be responsible for health planning in their respective areas, ultimately with power to withhold federal grants and payments for services to enforce their decisions. Control of such power is a prize sought by the medical establishment, medical institutions, local and state politicians, and other special interests. Widely regarded as an important step toward establishment of a national health program, implementation of the law is threatened by a flood of law suits.

RALPH E. PUMPHREY
Washington University, St. Louis

Senators Frank Moss, Charles Percy, and Pete Domenici served on a subcommitte on long-term health care. Photos of Moss' investigations of the nation's "Medicaid mills" hang on the walls.

UPI

438

SOUTH AFRICA

For South Africa 1976 was another year of anxiety and crisis, as the Nationalist government struggled to come to terms with the changing political scene and the escalation of violence in Southern Africa.

Tensions and Protests. Growing pressure—international and regional, diplomatic and military—for the rapid transfer of power to black majorities in Rhodesia and South West Africa (Namibia) increased the tensions in the country and drastically altered Prime Minister Johannes Vorster's timetable for change. As the negotiations to achieve black rule move from the

general to the specific, both the pressures and the tensions may be expected to mount.

The year also witnessed the most serious crisis in domestic affairs since 1960—the year of Sharpeville. Protests, demonstrations, and violent rioting occurred first on June 16 in Soweto, the segregated black urban complex outside Johannesburg, and then spread to most of the nonwhite urban centers throughout the country; the death toll by November was close to 400. The universal condemnation of apartheid, which followed the initial disturbances, paralleled that following Sharpeville. It was another serious blow to Prime Minister Vorster's détente policy.

Apart from the shock to the country, the

DOMESTIC CRISIS IN SOUTH AFRICA

PHOTOS UPI

In 1976, South Africa experienced its most serious domestic crisis in over 15 years. Demonstrations and rioting in black areas of the nation were common. In light of the violence, the minister of police urged the white populace to arrange for their own protection (*below, right*).

Chief Gatsha Buthelezi, leader of the Zulu tribe, delivers a call for unity to tribesmen in the South African township of Soweto.

UPI

prolonged violence badly damaged the image of stability and peaceful race relations on which the government had been able to count in its diplomatic stance. It thrust apartheid to the fore again, with the other Southern African issues. So did the grant of independence to the Transkei on October 25, which was celebrated without disturbance but also without international recognition of the new state.

Foreign Affairs. During the first half of the year public attention was still focused primarily on external events. South African troops were not withdrawn from Angola until the end of March. The same month saw the breakdown of the Rhodesian constitutional talks, Mozambique's decision to close its frontiers and impose sanctions against Rhodesia, and the apparent collapse of Vorster's détente policy. Among the white electorate the failure of the West, and especially the United States, to take a stronger stand against the Russian-backed Cuban presence in Angola caused broad concern.

In an effort to keep the détente initiative alive Vorster met with U. S. Secretary of State

Henry Kissinger at Bodenmais, Bavaria, on June 24, and again in Zurich on September 4 and 5. A third set of meetings took place in Pretoria, beginning on September 17. Vorster saw the Rhodesian prime minister the same week. The government gave its support to Kissinger's ten-point plan for Rhodesia, outlined in his Lusaka speech in April, and to his proposal for a constitutional conference in Geneva to work out the transfer of power to the black majority within two years. At the same time, it seems, it accepted a two-year deadline for the independence of South West Africa. Rhodesian Prime Minister Ian Smith accepted the proposals in principle. Kissinger, during his visit to Zambian President Kenneth Kaunda in April, had publicly urged Vorster to use his influence with Smith for a speedy settlement of the Rhodesian question and to announce a definite timetable for South West Africa. He also warned that the time for peaceful change of apartheid policies was running out.

The United Nations. The campaign against South Africa was maintained. On March 31 the Security Council voted 9–0 (with 5 abstentions) to condemn South Africa alone for aggression against Angola. On June 19 it unanimously condemned the republic for "massive violence" against the inhabitants of Soweto. The council invited representatives of the two banned black South African political organizations, the African National Congress and the Pan-African Congress, to participate in the debate. On July 30 it further condemned South Africa for an armed attack on a Zambian village and refused its request for a fact-finding mission. And on October 20, after a six-weeks debate on the failure to meet the August 31 deadline for the handing over of South West Africa, another triple veto by Britain, France, and the United States saved South Africa from a resolution calling for a mandatory arms embargo.

--- **SOUTH AFRICA · Information Highlights** ---

Official Name: Republic of South Africa.
Location: Southern tip of Africa.
Area: 471,444 square miles (1,221,037 km²).
Population (1976 est.): 25,600,000.
Chief Cities (1970 census): Pretoria, the administrative capital, 543,950; Cape Town, the legislative capital, 691,296; Johannesburg, 642,967; Durban, 495,458.
Government: *Head of state,* Nicolaas D. Diederichs, president (took office April 1975). *Head of government,* B. Johannes Vorster, prime minister (took office 1966). *Legislature*—Parliament: Senate and House of Assembly.
Monetary Unit: Rand (0.87 rand equals U. S.$1, Sept. 1976).
Gross National Product (1975 est.): $34,600,000,000.
Manufacturing (major products): Textiles, iron and steel, chemicals, fertilizers, assembled automobiles, metals.
Major Agricultural Products: Sugarcane, tobacco, corn, fruits, wheat, dairy products, sheep, wool.
Foreign Trade (1975): *Exports,* $5,315,000,000; *imports,* $7,589,000,000.

The Windhoek constitutional talks, under South African auspices and without the participation of the South West Africa People's Organization or the UN, remain internationally unacceptable. On October 26 the UN General Assembly voted 134–0 to condemn the "sham independence" of Transkei and called on members to refuse to recognize it.

Domestic Affairs. A record budget of $9,000,-000,000, of which $1,550,000,000—an increase of $460 million over 1975—was for defense, and the new, virtually unfettered Parliamentary Internal Security Commission reflected Vorster's search for security. Analyses of nonwhite unrest all attacked aspects of apartheid, but all were overshadowed by the chain reaction of demonstrations and disorder across the country, which followed the Soweto riots. They were sparked by a regulation that Afrikaans must also be used as a medium of instruction in the black high schools. As late as October 2 the mayor of Johannesburg felt it necessary to cancel the 90th annual Mardi Gras parade for fear of violence. Leaders of the churches, industry, and commerce called for the abolition of the economic color bar and the pass laws, and Sir de Villiers Graaff, leader of the official opposition, suggested a "Save South Africa" program, beginning with the merger of the parliamentary opposition parties. He offered to resign if this would facilitate such a merger. Vorster continued to reiterate his commitment to the principle of separate development and his determination to grant blacks political rights only in their own homelands.

See also BIOGRAPHY: Vorster, J. B.

R. B. BALLINGER, *Rhode Island College*

SOUTH CAROLINA

For the first time since 1960, the Democrats won South Carolina's presidential vote, giving Jimmy Carter 56% of the total. His majority was boosted by a large black vote and strong support for a fellow Southerner. Many citizens declared that the Civil War was finally over. Democrats also scored victories in most other races, winning 5 of the 6 congressional seats, 155 of the 170 legislative positions, and most of the county and council offices. Republicans, correspondingly, suffered a defeat in most areas of the state—urban and rural.

Government. Due to the economy, governments have had to restrict budgets, leave vacant positions unfilled, and curtail salary increases. The state ended the year with a $15-million deficit.

The General Assembly enacted a uniform court system, increased the number of judges, merged the family courts with county courts, revised the consumer credit code, made slight increases in the liquor tax, and amended the medical malpractice insurance regulations. Because of two vetoes, a law to protect the coastal

UPI

Bobby Richardson (R) and his wife, Betsey, vote in Sumter, S. C. The former N. Y. Yankee star failed in his bid to unseat U. S. Representative Ken Holland.

zone was not enacted. All municipalities and most counties reorganized their governments under the 1975 local government law and employed many additional professional administrators. Major controversies arose between the governor and the Department of Social Services over welfare policies, control, and administration. The Department of Mental Health continued to build cottages to decentralize its patient care. The voters approved a new constitutional article on finance and taxation, which classifies property for taxation and provides restrictions on the issuance of bonded indebtedness.

Education. First-grade failures and dropouts in public schools declined in 1976, while many additional students were enrolled in vocational, adult, and special educational programs. The

---

— SOUTH CAROLINA · Information Highlights —

Area: 31,055 square miles (80,432 km²).
Population (1975 est.): 2,818,000.
Chief Cities (1970 census): Columbia, the capital, 113,-542; Charleston, 66,945; Greenville, 61,436; Spartanburg, 44,546.
Government (1976): *Chief Officers*—governor, James B. Edwards (R); lt. gov., W. Brantley Harvey, Jr. (D). *General Assembly*—Senate, 46 members; House of Representatives, 124 members.
Education (1975–76): *Enrollment*—public elementary schools, 382,693 pupils; public secondary, 247,036; nonpublic (1976–77), 49,400; colleges and universities, 121,265 students. *Public school expenditures,* $605,000,000 ($963 per pupil).
State Finances (fiscal year 1975): *Revenues,* $1,884,-803,000; *expenditures,* $2,033,096,000.
Personal Income (1975): $13,014,000,000; per capita, $4,618.
Labor Force (July 1976): *Nonagricultural wage and salary earners,* 1,019,200; *insured unemployed,* 34,-200 (4.4%).

State Department of Education has set long-range goals to improve public education and teacher certification. The new medical school at the University of South Carolina will admit students in the fall of 1977. Both public and higher education experienced serious monetary problems.

Economy. Although it fluctuated, the economy in general improved. Tax collections increased significantly, even though projections were not met. Unemployment, while high, was below the national rate, and industries made some important gains, especially through foreign capital. Salary increases were granted by the large textile industry. The state took strong action against several companies which were releasing dangerous elements into the upstate lakes and rivers. Despite variations between excessive rains and droughts, agricultural production was good, especially tobacco and peaches. Several major hotels and recreational facilities were opened along the beaches and on coastal islands.

Other Developments. Congress provided funds to buy and preserve the Congaree Swamp, with its virgin timber and record-size trees. Four coastal islands were deeded to the state, adding significantly to areas preserved for wildlife and natural growth. Land was purchased in the mountainous area for a state park.

All parts of the state, and especially the small towns, participated in bicentennial celebrations.

ROBERT H. STOUDEMIRE
University of South Carolina

SOUTH DAKOTA

After several years of drought and a reduction in livestock prices, South Dakotans in 1976 expressed their desire for fiscal restraint by voting Republican. American Indians chose moderate leaders to manage their affairs.

Elections. Voters awarded their four electoral ballots to Gerald Ford and Robert Dole. They reelected Larry Pressler and James Abdnor, both Republicans, to Congress, with majorities of 81% and 70% respectively, and gave Repub-

licans more than two thirds of the seats in the state legislature.

Desire for popular participation in governmental decisions was evident in other returns as well. Voters across the state rejected six proposed constitutional amendments, most of which called for the liberalization of rules governing the legislature and the management of public properties. Constituents in the arid northeastern counties expressed discontent over plans for completion of a massive irrigation project by replacing nearly half of the members of the Oahe Conservancy Sub-District Board.

Legislation. Important laws passed by the state legislature included an appropriations act envisioning expenditures of nearly $164 million —an increase of about $15 million over 1975 to raise the salaries of state employees, extend tax relief to the elderly and disabled, and provide more state aid for public education and social services. Other laws placed limits on premiums for malpractice insurance, reclassified prostitution and possession of small quantities of marijuana as petty offenses, and placed a student on the Board of Regents of Higher Education in a nonvoting capacity.

Tensions ran high during the session. Democratic Gov. Richard Kneip set a new record of vetoing 12 bills. Democrats in the legislature blamed their Republican colleagues for the rejection of many of Kneip's programs.

Economy. Although financial indicators reflected improvements in gross sales, employment opportunities, and tourism, many observers grew alarmed over the effects of a drought that cost farmers and ranchers nearly $750 million. Corn and grain crops were so poor in some areas that farmers did not bother to harvest them. Pasture and hay were also scarce. Little real estate changed hands, but experienced farmers and ranchers predicted that another dry year would drive hundreds from the land.

American Indian Affairs. South Dakota's eight tribes reported an enrolled population of approximately 46,350—an increase of more than 15,000 since the 1970 census. About 29,750 lived on reservations.

Tribal voters chose moderate officials during 1976. Expressing the belief that the occupation of Wounded Knee in 1973 had brought no salutary changes in their lives, those at Pine Ridge Reservation chose former Bureau of Indian Affairs Superintendent Albert Trimble as their president. Voters on Rosebud Reservation elected retired U. S. Army veteran Edward Driving Hawk. With nonmilitant leaders in charge, tribal councils on the eight reservations promoted plans for increases in public service careers, more federal housing and social programs, greater educational opportunities, and higher per capita incomes through the consolidation of land holdings and the establishment of industries.

HERBERT T. HOOVER
The University of South Dakota

SOUTH DAKOTA · Information Highlights

Area: 77,047 square miles (199,552 km²).
Population (1975 est.): 683,000.
Chief Cities (1970 census): Pierre, the capital, 9,699; Sioux Falls, 72,488; Rapid City, 43,836.
Government (1976): *Chief Officers*—governor, Richard F. Kneip (D); lt. gov., Harvey Wollman (D). *Legislature*—Senate, 35 members; House of Representatives, 70 members.
Education (1975–76): *Enrollment*—public elementary schools, 99,844 pupils; public secondary, 51,373; nonpublic (1976–77), 14,800; colleges and universities, 29,359 students. *Public school expenditures,* $157,656,000 ($1,050 per pupil).
State Finances (fiscal year 1975): *Revenues,* $424,938,-000; *expenditures,* $419,241,000.
Personal Income (1975): $3,365,000,000; per capita, $4,924.
Labor Force (July 1976): *Nonagricultural wage and salary earners,* 216,200; *insured unemployed,* 3,300 (4.4%).

SPACE EXPLORATION

The historic search for life on the red planet Mars by the U. S. spacecraft Viking 1 and 2 was the highlight of space activities in 1976. The Soviet Union continued its active manned space program with the launch of four Soyuz spacecraft and the launch of one Salyut space laboratory, all of which were pointed toward the development of permanent space stations in orbit around earth.

MANNED SPACE FLIGHT

Salyut 5, a new Soviet space station, based upon the Salyut 4 design but with the capability for docking two Soyuz spacecraft to facilitate operational resupply, was launched on June 22 from Baikonur Cosmodrome to await the arrival of manned Soyuz 21 and 23. The purpose of Salyut space station is to provide a laboratory for cosmonauts where they will be able to conduct scientific studies in the fields of astrophysics and geophysics and to survey a variety of earth resources.

Soyuz 21. On July 6, Soyuz 21 was launched with Commander Boris Volynov and flight engineer Vitali Zholobov onboard. On July 8, Soyuz 21 docked with Salyut 5; and the cosmonauts commenced what was to be a 45-day mission to study the earth's surface and its atmosphere and to conduct a few biological and space processing experiments. The earth resources experiments utilized black and white, color, and infrared photography. Many areas on the earth were photographed to help in the search for mineral deposits and to aid in locating geological faults. For example, photographs were taken of the Ukraine, Moldavia, the Altai territory in Soviet Central Asia, and the Caspian lowlands for geological studies that would be helpful in locating possible future sites for hydroengineering projects.

Areas in danger of mud slides were also photographed, as were locations in which new rail lines are planned. An infrared telescope-spectrometer was carried to measure ozone, nitrogen oxide, and water vapor at different levels of the atmosphere.

In addition to their other work, the cosmonauts conducted weightlessness experiments with guppies. In one of these experiments, the development of fish eggs was observed as part of the study of the behavior of fish in a weightlessness environment.

Limited space processing experiments involving the formation of crystals and the melting of metals under the condition of no gravity were also conducted by the Russians. Thus, in one experiment designed to study the growth of crystals, three containers were filled with potash-soda and alum. The cosmonauts placed seed crystals in each container to initiate crystal growth. After the crystals had matured, they were compared with crystals grown on the ground upon the completion of the mission. In another experiment, the crew evaluated the movement of liquid in containers as a function of the liquid surface tension.

All the experiments were completed on August 23, and the crew spent the next day placing the Salyut space station in an automatic mode and preparing the Soyuz for reentry. After all the photographic film, biological experiments, and the log of their work were transferred to Soyuz, the cosmonauts separated the spacecraft from the space station and reentered the atmosphere for a safe night landing at a point 125 miles (200 km) southwest of Kokchetav, Kazakhstan.

Soyuz 22. On September 15, the USSR launched Soyuz 22 in a cooperative Soviet/East Germany mission to photograph 30 geographical targets in both East Germany and the USSR in order to collect data for use by geologists, geodesists, oceanographers, and cartographers. The spacecraft carried an East German-built multispectral camera system (MKF-6) designed to take stereo photographs in six spectral bands —four visible and two near infrared. Soviet aircraft and ground crews collected surface truth information over the areas at approximately the same time as cosmonauts Valeri F. Bykovsky and Vladimir Aksenov photographed the areas from space.

NASA

UPI

The excellent photographs of the planet Mars taken by the Viking 1 and 2 spacecraft revealed a dune field (*above, left*) similar to many seen on the deserts of earth and a defrosted layered material on Mars' slopes (*below*). Soil samples (*above*) were collected to determine the possibility of life on the planet.

UPI

After almost eight days in orbit, Soyuz 22 landed safely in Kazakhstan 93 miles (150 km) northwest of Tselinograd. Soyuz 22 was the first manned Soviet craft to carry foreign-made equipment.

Soyuz 23. Three weeks after the return of Soyuz 22, Soyuz 23 was launched on the night of October 14 from the Baikonur Cosmodrome to rendezvous and dock with Salyut 5. Two rookie cosmonauts, Vyacheslav Zudov and Valeri Rozhdestvensky, were at the controls in what was perhaps planned to be a long-duration mission to continue the experiments performed by Soyuz 21. Before the launch, Colonel Zudov indicated that part of their scientific research would be space manufacturing experiments that would be the basis for future manufactory in space of metal, glass, and pharmaceutical materials. However, Soyuz 23 was unable to complete a successful docking with Salyut 5 on October 16 because of an equipment malfunction and was forced to land at night in Tengiz Lake during a snowstorm, 120 miles (195 km) southwest of Tselinograd.

PLANETARY AND LUNAR PROBES

Mars Probes. After a ten-month trip across interplanetary space, the United States Viking 1 spacecraft entered an orbit around Mars on June 19 to commence the most extensive exploration of the red planet ever attempted. The first task for Viking 1 was to survey the planned landing site on the large Martian plain called Chryse near the outlet of a network of Martian canyons. The result of this survey indicated that this site was much too rugged and hazardous and, hence, the landing originally planned for July 4 had to be cancelled. A new site 600 miles (960 km) to the northwest was chosen because of its smoother and more lightly cratered surface. On July 20, the 1,300-pound (600-kg) lander came safely to rest on the surface of Mars. By coincidence, the landing occurred seven years to the day after Neil Armstrong and Edwin Aldrin flew their historic Apollo 11 lunar module down to the surface of the moon.

The first photographs from the Martian surface were taken 25 seconds after touchdown and showed a surface strewn with boulders and smaller rocks interspersed by a fine-grain material resembling sand. A panoramic sweep of the surrounding Chryse Planitia terrain presented extraordinary detail of Martian surface features over an arc of about 340 degrees. The scene was desertlike with an array of shaped and structural rocks, some of which were highly pitted like a frothy lava on earth. The Martian surface had a reddish tint, which scientists attributed to long-term oxidization processes, while the sky appeared pink.

One of the first instruments on board the lander to report on the characteristics of the soil was the X-ray fluorescence spectrometer which identified abundant quantities of iron, calcium, silicon, titanium, and aluminum. It detected low concentrations, if any at all, of such trace elements as rubidium, strontium, and zirconium. These analyses suggested that the

Soviet cosmonauts Valeri Bykovsky and Vladimir Aksenov (*left*) completed the Soyuz 22 mission in September.

rusty red surface has a chemical makeup similar in many ways to deep ocean basalt deposits here on earth. A mass spectrometer on the lander measured the composition of the atmosphere and found it to be 95% carbon dioxide, 2 to 3% nitrogen, and 1 to 2% argon. This was the first time nitrogen had been detected on Mars, although its presence had been postulated. Water vapor was also identified in the atmosphere by a sensor on the orbiter.

Perhaps the most important experiment to be conducted by the Viking spacecraft was the testing for the evidence of life on the planet. The experiment found a surprisingly large amount of oxygen in the soil and also detected the formation of carbon dioxide by something, whether animate or inanimate, in that soil. These results, while very exciting, were not sufficient to prove that there is indeed some form of life on Mars. The third and critical test for evidence of complex organic molecules proved to be negative. Therefore, Viking 1 found insufficient evidence on which to base a claim that life exists on Mars.

The Viking 2 spacecraft, identical to Viking 1, entered Mars orbit in August and released its lander for a September 3 landing in the Utopia Planitia region. The picture from this lander showed a flat area that looked surprisingly like the rock-strewn terrain around the Viking 1 Chryse Planitia landing site. After the initial picture taking, Viking 2 commenced analyzing the soil and atmosphere at this new location and

gave results similar to Viking 1. The similarity between the surface materials at the widely separated Viking 1 and Viking 2 lander sites confirms the belief that the surface layers are products of weathering and do not necessarily reflect the primary material at each site. It also indicates that mixing of the weathered elements must take place on a global scale and at a fairly rapid rate. The life detector experiment on Viking 2 gave inconclusive results similar to those of Viking 1.

Solar Probes. Helios 2, the second of two spacecraft designed to fly closer to the sun than any previous man-made object, was launched by the United States on January 15. Helios, named after the ancient Greek sun god, was built by West Germany as part of a joint venture with the United States. Three of the ten experiments onboard were built by the United States and seven by the West Germans. These instruments are designed to measure the solar wind, magnetic fields, solar and galactic cosmic rays, electromagnetic waves, micrometeoroids, and the zodiacal lights. The approach to the sun, 93 days after launch and every 186 days thereafter, puts the spacecraft within a distance of 27,000,-000 miles (43,000,000 km), nearly 1,875,000 miles (3,000,000 km) closer than its predecessor, Helios 1.

Lunar Probes. On August 22, Luna 24 landed midway between the cities of Orenburg and Kuibyshev in the Soviet Union after a 13-day mission to the moon. Luna 24, the third successful lunar soil sample mission of the USSR, returned a core sample taken to a depth of 6.6 feet (2 meters) from the southeastern portion of the Sea of Crisis. This sample of the lunar surface is being analyzed by the USSR Academy of Science in hopes of shedding new light on theories regarding the formation and evolution of the lunar surface. Preliminary analysis provides evidence of a laminated structure, indicative of material that has been laid down in successive deposits.

EARTH SATELLITES

Communication Satellites. In 1976, a total of seventeen communication satellites was launched representing the largest number for any particular class. One hundred and seven countries, territories, or possessions on six continents are leasing communication satellite services full-time, enabling more than 1,000,000,000 people—one of every four persons on earth—to see an international event on television as it happens. In addition, a major portion of all long distance international communications and more than two thirds of all transoceanic communications are by satellite.

Only one satellite was launched in 1976 to maintain the global system of communications satellites: INTELSAT IVA-F-2 was lofted from the United States on January 29 for service over the Atlantic Ocean.

The USSR launched seven domestic communication satellites in 1976. Four were of the MOLNIYA 1 class (MOLNIYA 1–32, 1–33, 1–34, and 1–35 on January 29, March 11, March 19, and July 23); one was of the MOLNIYA 3 class (MOLNIYA 3–5 on May 12); one was the second geostationary communication satellite, RADUGA-2, launched on September 11 (RADUGA-1 was launched on December 22, 1975); and one, EKRAN, was a new geostationary television-broadcast satellite for relaying high-quality color programs from Moscow to Siberia.

The first communications satellite to be owned by a developing nation, the Indonesian satellite called PALAPA-1, was launched on July 8 and is providing transmission of television, voice, and data throughout Indonesia. Satellite communications are expected to be a boon for Indonesia's population of 135 million scattered through 5,000 inhabited islands spread across 3,300 miles (5,300 km) in the South Pacific.

Three maritime satellites (Marisat A, B, and C) were launched on February 19, June 10, and October 14. This new class of satellite is designed to enable merchant ships on the high seas to transmit voice, data, facsimile, and telex messages to shore stations at Southbury, Conn., and Santa Paula, Calif., which will be interconnected with existing domestic terrestrial networks. Marisat A is located over the Atlantic Ocean, Marisat B over the Pacific Ocean, and Marisat C over the Indian Ocean. Marisats are jointly owned by Comsat General Corporation; RCA Global Communications, Inc.; Western Union International, Inc.; and ITT World Communications, Inc.

Comstar I-A and I-B, the first two in a series of three domestic communication satellites of the Comsat General Corporation, were launched on May 13 and July 22, respectively. These satellites are leased by the American Telephone and Telegraph Company as part of a nationwide communication network. Each Comstar satellite has a capacity of more than 14,000 two-way high-quality voice circuits.

A communication satellite was launched to support the RCA-Globcom System in 1976: RCA Satcom II on March 26. (RCA Satcom III is to be launched in September 1977.) These spacecraft are capable of transmitting voice, data, facsimile, and telex messages to and from the continental United States, Alaska, and Hawaii.

The world's most powerful experimental communications satellite, CTS, was launched on January 17. A cooperative effort between NASA and Canada's Department of Communications, the CTS technology will make possible high quality color television reception and two-way voice communications with the use of small, low-cost ground terminals.

Research Satellites. A Laser Geodynamics Satellite (Lageos) that will serve as a tool for

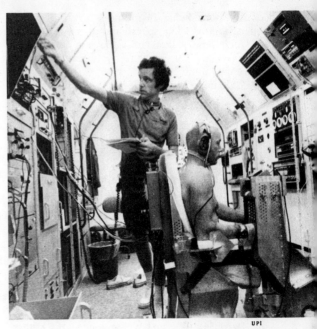

UPI

NASA scientists conduct experiments in a space shuttle Spacelab mockup. Development was on schedule.

obtaining information on the earth's crustal movements, polar motion, solid earth tides, and precise locations of various spots on the planet was launched by the United States on May 4. Lageos is 24 inches (60 cm) in diameter, weighs 906 pounds (411 kg), and will have a useful life of 50 years. Four hundred and twenty-six laser retroreflectors are mounted symmetrically over the entire outer surface for reflecting laser beams that may be directed toward the satellite from ground stations.

The Intercosmos Program of the USSR is now using a new generation of automated standardized satellites. These new satellites, larger and more sophisticated than previous ones, are capable of conducting experiments in space physics, biology, medicine, meteorology, and communications. The first test flight of this new class, Intercosmos 15, was initiated on June 19. This spacecraft also has the capability of transmitting data directly to the participating countries. Reception centers have been built in Czechoslovakia, East Germany, Hungary, and the Soviet Union. The planners have projected additional reception centers to be built in Poland, Bulgaria, and Cuba.

Intercosmos 16, a cooperative scientific satellite of USSR, East Germany, Czechoslovakia, and Sweden, was launched on July 27. The main objective of this satellite was to study ultraviolet and X-ray radiation emanating from the sun and to monitor its effects on the upper atmosphere.

On February 28, the Japanese launched the UME satellite (named for the flower of the Japanese apricot tree). This satellite was to observe worldwide distribution of critical frequencies in the ionosphere and to use the results of such observations in radiowave forecasting and warning for efficient operations of short-wave communications.

Late in 1975, the USSR launched Prognoz 4 and Prognoz 5 to study solar activity. These satellites will study corpuscular and electromagnetic emissions of the sun, flow of solar plasma, and magnetic fields.

Weather Satellites. The USSR launched three meteorological satellites in its Meteor series. Meteor 24, 25, and 26 were launched on April 7, May 15, and October 16. The United States launched NOAA-5 on July 29, the fifth in a series of polar orbiting satellites to obtain global cloud-cover data, both day and night, and to obtain global-scale quantitation measurements of the earth's atmospheric structure—data which then may be applied to numerical weather predictions.

ADVANCES IN SPACE TECHNOLOGY

Space Shuttle. The development by the United States of the new space shuttle, designed to move men, instruments, and automated satellites in and out of earth orbit at a lower cost than previously possible, made excellent progress in 1976. The first orbiter part of the space shuttle, Orbiter 101, christened the "Enterprise" by President Ford, underwent final systems checks following its formal rollout on September 17. Upon completion of these checkouts, the orbiter was to be transported to NASA's Dryden Flight Research Center in early 1977 for a series of approach and landing tests. A total of eight landing tests is planned with the orbiter being carried aloft atop a NASA/Boeing 747. The Orbiter 101 will then be used for vibration tests starting in 1978 after which it will be modified to an operational space configuration. Orbiter 102, which will be completed in mid-1978, is scheduled to be launched on the first manned orbital flight of the complete United States Space Transportation System in the spring of 1979. A total of five orbiters are scheduled to be built.

Spacelab. The development of the Spacelab, which is to fly in the space shuttle, also proceeded on schedule during 1976. Assembly was begun in Bremen, West Germany. Included is a hard mockup of the Spacelab being developed by 11 European nations. The flight version is being designed to make at least 50 flights and remain operational for a minimum of 10 years. Although only one flyable Spacelab will be built, through its modular design it will be able, on successive flights, to perform a wide range of missions. One of the engineering mockups will be sent to the United States in 1978 for test fitting in the orbiter. This will be followed by the flight unit, which is scheduled for shipment to the Kennedy Space Center in 1979. The first flight of the unit has been planned for sometime during 1980.

USSR Space Station. Soyuz 20, which was launched on November 17, 1975, and docked with Salyut 4 on November 19, was returned to earth on February 19, 1976, after testing its capability to remain in docked storage for a 90-day period before being reactivated for its return flight. This unmanned mission was a test of a resupply and rescue system needed for the development of permanent space stations. While no transfer of supplies actually took place during this mission, a vehicle of the Soyuz 20 type could serve as a rescue vehicle for the Salyut station crew in case of depressurization or sickness or for transporting food, water, and air supply to the station. This appears to be an important test for the Soviets in their development of a capability for permanent manned earth orbital stations.

PITT G. THOME
National Aeronautics and
Space Administration

The "Enterprise," the first orbiter part of the space shuttle, underwent final checks following its unveiling in September.

King Juan Carlos addressed a joint session of Congress on June 2 during his visit to the United States. Speaker of the House Carl Albert and Sen. Warren Magnuson (*right*) led the official welcome.

UPI

SPAIN

The year 1976, the first since the death of Generalissimo Francisco Franco, was a period of slow but steady change for Spain. King Juan Carlos attempted to preserve order and revive a floundering economy while seeking to modernize Franco's governmental structure.

The country took an important step toward democracy in November when the Cortes, the conservative and largely appointive parliament, approved general elections for 1977 and voted itself out of existence. The action, by a vote of 425 to 59 was a victory for Juan Carlos and Prime Minister Adolfo Suárez González. The reform bill provides for the election of a 350-member Congress and a less powerful Senate, with 207 elected members plus 40 appointed by the king. Voters overwhelmingly approved the reforms in a referendum on December 15.

--------- SPAIN • Information Highlights ---------

Official Name: Spanish State.
Location: Iberian Peninsula in southwestern Europe.
Area: 194,897 square miles (504,782 km²).
Population (1976 est.): 36,000,000.
Chief Cities (1975): Madrid, the capital, 3,500,000; Barcelona, 2,000,000; Valencia, 700,000.
Government: *Head of state,* Juan Carlos I, king (took office Nov. 1975). *Head of government,* Adolfo Suárez González, prime minister (took office July 1976). *Legislature* (unicameral)—Cortes.
Monetary Unit: Peseta (68.03 pesetas equal U. S.$1, Nov. 1976).
Gross National Product (1975 est.): $94,500,000,000.
Manufacturing (major products): Iron and steel, electrical machinery, automobiles, textiles, chemicals, ships, processed foods, leather.
Major Agricultural Products: Wheat, rye, barley, corn, citrus fruits, vegetables, almonds, olives, potatoes, fish, forest products, sheep.
Foreign Trade (1975): *Exports,* $7,691,000,000; *imports,* $16,097,000,000.

Politics. Juan Carlos stated his determination to create "a society that grows in prosperity, justice and authentic liberty." But such democratic rhetoric raised the hackles of diehard Francoists, known as the "Bunker," who view change as threatening to their privileged political and economic position. They also have regarded with disdain the shifting of the national day from July 18 (when Franco launched his 1936 uprising) to June 24 (the king's patron saint's day), the replacement of the old caudillo's portrait in government offices by that of Juan Carlos, and the government's refusal in May to allow civil war veterans to hold a mass rally in downtown Madrid to commemorate Franco's death.

More galling than these symbolic acts was the new regime's determination to make good on its pledge to institute political reforms. This commitment was evident on July 1 when the king dismissed Carlos Arias Navarro, an extremely cautious prime minister inherited from the previous government, and named Suárez to form a new cabinet. The new prime minister, a close friend of Juan Carlos, chose a cabinet composed of independent Christian Democrats and reformist officials of past administrations. The cabinet demonstrated a willingness to implement the king's reformist plans.

In addition, the Cortes agreed to eliminate many impediments to political meetings—in effect since the 1930's. In May it voted to allow all political organizations, except the Communist Party, to gather in nonpublic places, provided they give the government 72 hours notice; a 10-day prior authorization is necessary for street assemblies and outdoor demonstrations.

After protracted debate, the Cortes voted 338 to 91 in June to permit the formation of political parties as long as they win approval of the Ministry of the Interior. The right-wing National Movement had been the only legal political organization since 1939. Political parties are forbidden to receive funds from abroad. While scores of groups have sprung up, the Socialists and the Christian Democrats have the largest natural constituencies according to public opinion polls.

A revised penal code banned parties that "obeyed orders from abroad" and were "aimed at establishing a totalitarian regime." The provision was designed to apply to the Communist Party, which is anathema to the Bunker and the Spanish Army. The king has steadfastly opposed conferring legal status on the party, whose aging leadership strongly advocates ideological independence from the Soviet Union. Despite continuing restrictions on the political activities of the Communist Party, its members freely travel around the country as private citizens, holding meetings and giving lectures.

The role of Spain's Communists in public affairs is closely linked to proposed labor legislation. During Franco's dictatorship, Communist-dominated Worker Commissions sprang up alongside officially sanctioned syndicates. Legislation was drafted to create free labor unions, which would have the effect of legalizing the Worker Commissions and giving the Communists (and the Socialists) an even stronger position in the labor movement. Though strongly resisted by the right, this proposal is seen by some observers as a means to encourage leftist leaders to help fight the epidemic of strikes that have afflicted the country.

An amnesty was announced for individuals imprisoned for "politically motivated crimes or crimes of opinion." Although its procedures have not been fully defined, it was estimated that the decree will lead to the release of at least half of the 600 plus persons in jail for offenses related to political activity.

Economy. Official statistics reveal that 1.3 million workers took part in work stoppages during the first three months of the year, causing the loss of 49 million working hours. The strikes have contributed to the economic malaise besetting Spain. In the decade prior to 1971, Spain's real gross national product (GNP) increased 7.5% annually. However, the sharp rise in oil prices served to halve the growth rate in 1974 and lowered it to 1% in 1975. GNP grew 2.5% in 1976 and industrial output expanded 4%. However, unemployment remained high and prices rose 20% during the year.

The Bank of Spain announced on February 9 that the peseta's dollar equivalency was being lowered by 10%. The devaluation was made to dampen speculation, attract tourists, and stimulate exports. But speculative pressures continued, the tourist trade failed to recover, and imports rose, in part because of the structure of the Spanish economy and a poor harvest caused by a prolonged drought. The balance of payments deficit rose from $3,000,000,000 in 1975 to $3,500,000,000 in 1976.

Violence and worker unrest escalated throughout the year. Under Spanish law, wage increases are limited to rises in the cost of living, plus 3% (in unusual circumstances). Nonetheless, post office and transit workers secured much higher increases after prolonged strikes early in the year, and settlements in both public and private firms have averaged 25% to 30%. Neither a 23% boost in the minimum wage to 345 pesetas a day ($5.00) nor the threat of conscripting participating workers halted the spread of strikes by the workers.

Because of the "grave" economic crisis, the government published in October a stability plan under which (1) all prices would be frozen for two months and prices of selected items controlled thereafter, (2) pay increases would be limited to the rise in the cost of living, (3) the distribution of profits and dividends would be severely restricted, and (4) monetary and fiscal policy would be employed to invigorate the economy. Meanwhile, a balanced budget of 967,-000,000,000 pesetas ($14,200,000,000) was announced for 1977.

Foreign Relations. King Juan Carlos and Prime Minister Suárez reiterated their desire for Spain's eventual entry into the North Atlantic Treaty Organization (NATO) and the European Economic Community. But Western European leaders were hesitant to embrace a nation that was so recently under a dictator's sway and that, unlike neighboring Portugal, avoided a revolution destructive of the power base of its late strong man.

Juan Carlos and Queen Sofia paid a bicentennial visit to the United States on June 1–5. During his stay the king met with President Ford and addressed Congress. He was the first reigning Spanish monarch to visit America. During the trip the king visited the United Nations in New York.

Washington has come to Spain's aid with loans, grants, and other forms of assistance. In addition, a group of 17 banks provided $1,000,-000,000 in credits to the Madrid government, and the International Monetary Fund made a $340 million loan on extremely favorable terms.

On July 23 the Cortes approved a Treaty of Friendship and Cooperation with the United States. Under its terms the United States will continue to use three air fields and a Mediterranean naval base in return for $1,200,000,000 in loans and aid over five years. The United States is prohibited from storing nuclear matériel on Spanish soil.

See also MONARCHIES, pages 44–49; BIOGRAPHY: Adolfo Suárez González.

GEORGE W. GRAYSON
College of William and Mary

The XII Winter Olympiad opens in Innsbruck, Austria.

SPORTS:

THE OLYMPICS

The Winter Games

From Feb. 4 to Feb. 14, 1976, at Innsbruck, Austria, against a breathtaking backdrop of the Tyrolean Alps, the XII Winter Olympiad unfolded in an atmosphere that became notably more relaxed, more gentle, and more enjoyable as each day passed. In the first grim and uncertain days, the specter of terrorist attacks such as those that scarred the 1972 Olympics in Munich hung over the valley of the Inn River. Soon, however, all tension disappeared, and the hundreds of armed *polizei* and Austrian soldiers posted about Olympic sites began to smile, to nod, to wave their submachine guns amiably at passersby. The friendly presence of Lord Killanin, the pipe-smoking Irish peer who had replaced the austere and pontifical Avery Brundage as president of the International Olympic Committee, added immeasurably to the easygoing aura of these games.

The Tranquility and the Heroics. Despite the tranquility of it all, the heroics at Innsbruck were memorable, even inspiring. The feat of the young Austrian Franz Klammer, the world's premier downhill ski racer, would be long remembered, for few athletes ever perform under pressure as intense as he faced. On the first day of competition, more than 60,000 people watched the men's downhill. The pride of all Austria—both the Olympic host and the world's number 1 skiing nation—rested on young Klammer's performance. He was 15th out of the gate and he flung himself down the mountain with a recklessness that put him on the jagged edge of disaster. His speed soon reached 70 mph (112.6 kmph) and he seemed constantly out of control. Yet he flashed past the finish line upright and still gaining speed. By a scant .33 of a second he won over Bernard Russi, the Swiss veteran who had won the gold medal for the downhill in 1972.

Nothing quite matched the first-day drama of Klammer's singular victory. Ultimately the games belonged to a lovely, dimpled West German farm girl named Rosi Mittermaier (see also *Biography*). A veteran of ten years of World Cup skiing, this was Rosi's third Olympic Games, and although she was only 25, her teammates fondly referred to her as "Omi" (Granny). Thrillingly, it was

Granny who made Olympic history. Although she had never won a major downhill race in her career, Rosi got the gold in that event. Next, she produced two strong runs in the special slalom and won a second gold medal. That was the best any woman ski racer had ever done in the Olympics, but suddenly it was possible—even likely—that Rosi could win *three* golds. As she poised in the start of the giant slalom, the mountainside at Axamer Lizum was carpeted with 60,000 people, so many that hundreds were forced to climb trees to see. Rosi had a brilliant start, recorded the best time of all at the first interval, then faltered briefly on two turns. She recovered, but that eye-blink of time finally cost the race—and the golden sweep. She finished .12 of a second behind Kathy Kreiner of Canada. Still, Rosi's two golds and a silver were the best any woman ski racer had ever done.

Multiple Winners and Team Standings. Rosi was not the only multiple medal winner. Tatyana Averina, a grim and husky Russian speed skater, took two gold medals and two bronzes in the women's 500-, 1,000-, 1,500- and 3,000-meter races. And cheery Sheila Young of Detroit won a gold in the 500, a silver in the 1,500, and a bronze in the 1,000.

As usual, the rigidly disciplined and heavily government-funded teams from behind the Iron Curtain did by far the best: the Soviet Union

---

FINAL MEDAL STANDINGS

	Gold	Silver	Bronze	Total		Gold	Silver	Bronze	Total
Soviet Union	13	6	8	27	Netherlands	1	2	3	6
East Germany	7	5	7	19	Italy	1	2	1	4
United States	3	3	4	10	Canada	1	1	1	3
Norway	3	3	1	7	Britain	1	0	0	1
West Germany	2	5	3	10	Czechoslovakia	0	1	0	1
Finland	2	4	1	7	Liechtenstein	0	0	2	2
Austria	2	2	2	6	Sweden	0	0	2	2
Switzerland	1	3	1	5	France	0	0	1	1

GOLD MEDAL WINNERS

Alpine Skiing

Men's Downhill: Franz Klammer, Austria
Men's Slalom: Piero Gros, Italy
Men's Giant Slalom: Heini Hemmi, Switzerland
Women's Downhill: Rosi Mittermaier, West Germany
Women's Slalom: Mittermaier
Women's Giant Slalom: Kathy Kreiner, Canada

Biathlon

20-km Individual: Nikolai Kruglov, U. S. S. R.
30-km Relay: U. S. S. R.

Bobsled

Two-man: East Germany
Four-man: East Germany

Figure Skating

Men: John Curry, Britain
Women: Dorothy Hamill, U. S. A.
Ice Dancing: Ludmila Pakhomova and Alexander Gorshkov, U. S. S. R.
Pairs: Irina Rodnina and Alexander Zaitsev, U. S. S. R.

Ice Hockey

U. S. S. R.

Luge

Men's Singles: Detlef Guenther, East Germany
Men's Two-seater: East Germany
Women's Singles: Margit Schumann, East Germany

Nordic Skiing

Men's 15-km Cross Country: Nikolai Bajukov, U. S. S. R.
Men's 30-km Cross Country: Sergei Savelyev, U. S. S. R.
Men's 50-km Cross Country: Ivar Formo, Norway
Men's 40-km Cross Country Relay: Finland
Men's Combined: Ulrich Wehling, East Germany
Men's 70-m Special Ski Jump: Hans-Georg Aschenbach, East Germany
Men's 90-m Special Jump: Karl Schnabl, Austria
Women's 5-km Cross Country: Helena Takalo, Finland
Women's 10-km Cross Country: Raisa Smetanina, U. S. S. R.
Women's 20-km Cross Country Relay: U. S. S. R.

Speed Skating

Men's 500 m: Yevgeni Kulikov, U. S. S. R.
Men's 1,000 m: Peter Mueller, U. S. A.
Men's 1,500 m: Jan Egil Storholt, Norway
Men's 5,000 m: Sten Stensen, Norway
Men's 10,000 m: Piet Kleine, Netherlands
Women's 500 m: Sheila Young, U. S. A.
Women's 1,000 m: Tatyana Averina, U. S. S. R.
Women's 1,500 m: Galina Stepanskaya, U. S. S. R.
Women's 3,000 m: Averina

PHOTOS KEN REGAN, CAMERA 5

Austria's Franz Klammer, the world's finest downhill ski racer, captured a gold medal in dramatic fashion.

Dorothy Hamill of Riverside, Conn., won a gold medal, defeating the reigning women's figure skating champ.

won 27 medals (13 gold) and the East Germans 19 (7 gold). The United States and West Germany were next with 10 medals each. This made them relatively successful and very gratifying games for the Americans.

Other Stars. Peter Mueller of Madison, Wis., won a gold in the men's 1,000-meter speed skating race, and his fiancée, Leah Poulos of Northbrook, Ill., got a silver in the women's 1,000. Dan Immerfall of Madison took a bronze in the men's 500-meter skating race, and so did Cindy Nelson of Lutsen, Minn., in the women's downhill ski race. Of all the American medals, however, none was more welcome—or more astonishing—than that won by Billy Koch, 20, an ascetic Vermont farm boy, who stunned the world by taking the silver medal in the 30-km cross-country ski race. This grueling sport has been for years (and was again in 1976) almost totally dominated by Russians, Scandinavians, or East Germans. Indeed, no American had ever finished any Olympic cross-country race higher than 15th— and that happened in 1932. Thus some hailed Billy Koch's triumph as the greatest single Olympic upset ever accomplished by an American.

If Billy's medal was the most surprising, then Dorothy Hamill's was the most delightful. This smiling pixieish young figure skater from Riverside, Conn., so nearsighted that she could not even read the judges' scoreboard that recorded her victory, was the darling of the U.S. team.

She put together a perfectly disciplined performance in the rigid school figures, then finished off with a dazzling final free-skating program that brought a full-house crowd shouting to its feet, littering the ice with bouquets. Surprisingly, Dorothy had upset the reigning world champion, Dianne de Leeuw of Paramount, Calif., who was skating for the Netherlands.

As the games went on, the pattern was that of the expected. A superb Soviet hockey team easily won another gold medal. Other gold medalists included the magnificent Russian pairs figure skaters, Irina Rodnina and Alexander Zaitsev, England's fine figure skater, John Curry, and the men's and women's luge teams of East Germany. Finally it all came full circle in the last event of the games, the 90-m jump. As on the first day when Klammer was the Austrian favorite under pressure, so now on the last day two young Austrians—Karl Schnabl, 21, and Toni Innauer, 17—were expected to win. A capacity crowd of 70,000 jammed Bergisel stadium for the event, and it went wild with joy when Schnabl took the gold and Innauer the silver. The fans danced and sang and carried their two heroes off on their shoulders. It was the perfect climax for the citizens of Austria who had staged the loveliest and simplest Winter Olympics in many years.

WILLIAM OSCAR JOHNSON
Senior Writer, "Sports Illustrated"

Following two weeks of competition in Montreal, the XXI Olympiad closed with a colorful, televised ceremony.

The Summer Games

What probably will be remembered most about the XXI Olympiad in Montreal was the tightest security network seen anywhere in the world during peacetime. It cost in the neighborhood of $100 million, or about $12,500 for each of the nearly 8,000 athletes who participated.

Security, Cost, and Politics. The security was Canada's safeguard against a repeat of the tragedy that marred the XX Olympiad in Munich in 1972. The security at the Montreal games (July 17–Aug. 1, 1976) accomplished its objective. However, many athletes and coaches voiced complaints that security precautions had turned the Olympic Village into what resembled an armed camp, making a mockery of the friendship and international fellowship credo of the games. Some 18,000 policemen and members of the Canadian militia were unrelenting in their security pursuits, especially on the occasions of reports during the games that terrorists were headed to, or had entered, the country. But no incidents occurred, and afterward many team spokesmen credited the Canadians with a job well done in that respect.

That the games were held as scheduled was a relief to Canadian officials who had been concerned that the main stadium might not be completed in time and the games might have to be cancelled. Construction of the 72,000-seat arena —at a cost of $788 million—was finished just weeks before the scheduled start. Strikes, labor slowdowns, bad weather, and other factors contributed to the delay. The stadium was planned as a domed one, but when construction costs had virtually tripled from the original estimate, the addition of a retractable roof was postponed until after the games.

Including the $95 million Olympic Village, the $62 million Velodrome (site of swimming and cycling events), and numerous other facilities, the final cost of the Montreal games was estimated at $1.5 billion. The cost left the city of Montreal and the province of Quebec with a deficit of approximately $1 billion. It was no wonder that one of the major topics of discussion among international officials at the games concerned a plea that all future Olympics—after the 1980 games in Moscow—be rotated in cities where facilities already exist.

It was, of course, no surprise that politics came close to either canceling the games altogether or reducing them to a mere shadow of what they were intended to be. The main pressure was exerted on Taiwan. A few days before the opening ceremony, Canadian officials informed the Taiwanese delegation it could compete in the games only if it refrained from calling itself the Republic of China. The United States and Mexico threatened to boycott the games if

Nadia Comaneci, a 14-year-old Miss Perfection, delighted the audiences by becoming the first Olympic gymnast to gain a perfect score. She took three gold medals home to Rumania.

KEN REGAN, CAMERA 5

Taiwan did not compete, which made International Olympic Committee (IOC) members fear that such a withdrawal would ignite a walk-out by a multitude of countries. At this late stage, however, the IOC had almost no alternative but to back Canada's demands. Taiwan packed its bags and went home on the eve of the games' opening. The United States and Mexico remained, however.

That was only one of the headaches for IOC officials. A total of 32 nations, including more than 20 African countries, also pulled out on the eve of Queen Elizabeth's pronouncement opening the games. The African nations demanded that the IOC take action against New Zealand for permitting its national rugby team to tour South Africa. South Africa had been expelled from the Olympic movement for its past racist policies and the African nations insisted the IOC should take action against countries that persist in maintaining sports contact with South Africa. Nevertheless, the games opened on schedule in a sunlit stadium.

Incredible Performances. It did not take long for the sweetheart of the games to emerge: little Nadia Comaneci of Rumania, who was literally Miss Perfection during her performances in gymnastics at Montreal Forum. She recorded two perfect 10-point scores in her first day of competition. It was the first time any gymnast had ever posted a perfect score at the games, and the

FINAL MEDAL STANDINGS

	Gold	Silver	Bronze	Total
Soviet Union	47	43	35	125
East Germany	40	25	25	90
United States	34	35	25	94
West Germany	10	12	17	39
Japan	9	6	10	25
Poland	7	6	11	24
Bulgaria	6	7	9	22
Cuba	6	4	3	13
Rumania	4	9	14	27
Hungary	4	5	12	21
Finland	4	2	0	6
Sweden	4	1	0	5
Britain	3	5	5	13
Italy	2	7	4	13
France	2	2	5	9
Yugoslavia	2	3	3	8
Czechoslovakia	2	2	4	8
New Zealand	2	1	1	4
South Korea	1	1	4	6
Switzerland	1	1	2	4
Jamaica	1	1	0	2
North Korea	1	1	0	2
Norway	1	1	0	2
Denmark	1	0	2	3
Mexico	1	0	1	2
Trinidad	1	0	0	1
Canada	0	5	6	11
Belgium	0	3	3	6
Netherlands	0	2	3	5
Portugal	0	2	0	2
Spain	0	2	0	2
Australia	0	1	4	5
Iran	0	1	1	2
Mongolia	0	1	0	1
Venezuela	0	1	0	1
Brazil	0	0	2	2
Austria	0	0	1	1
Bermuda	0	0	1	1
Pakistan	0	0	1	1
Puerto Rico	0	0	1	1
Thailand	0	0	1	1

4-foot 5-inch 66-pounder (1.3 m; 30 kg) did it seven different times overall.

Comaneci, 14, won the balance beam, the uneven bars, and the individual all-around with a display of acrobatics that reminded spectators of the phenomenal performance of Russia's Olga Korbut in 1972. But Korbut, one of Comaneci's competitors, was simply an also-ran—very good but not great—this time around.

Other incredible performances were turned in by swimmers John Naber, a backstroker from the United States, and sprinter Kornelia Ender of East Germany who not only won gold medals but also turned in fantastic times that almost surely will remain world records for some time. Then, too, there was the world record-breaking effort by Soviet super-heavyweight weightlifter Vasili Alekseyev who hoisted 255 kilograms (562 pounds) over his head in the clean-and-jerk event. Other memorable performers included Alberto Juantorena of Cuba, who failed to make his country's basketball team, but won the 400- and 800-meter races, the latter in record time; Lasse Viren of Finland who won 5,000 and 10,-000 meters; and John Walker of New Zealand who captured the 1,500 meters.

Unpleasant Notes. But, as always, there was some unpleasant news. This was the case with Soviet pentathlete Boris Onischenko, 38, who was barred for using an épée wired to register a hit even when he failed to touch his opponent.

Hits are registered electronically in the fencing competition. Discovery of the illegal electronic device was made during a contest between Onischenko and Britain's Jim Fox, also a veteran pentathlon competitor. Onischenko was whisked back to his home town of Kiev, Russia, and a Soviet team spokesman said: "I fear his career as a sportsman is over."

Canada's Bob Martin was booted off the Olympic team for smuggling a former college teammate into the village to make use of an empty bed, a common occurrence at previous games. It was the only real embarrassment for security personnel.

Total Medals and Medalists. The Soviet Union was the team leader with 125 medals: 47 gold, 43 silver, and 35 bronze. Finishing a very respectable second in gold medals was East Germany with 40, although the United States, with 34 gold medals, had a 94–90 overall edge over the Germans in total medals.

American men swimmers were responsible for 12 of their nation's gold medals. Americans also won five of a possible 11 gold medals in boxing. The U. S. gold medal collection in track and field was the same as at Munich, six, and once again all were won by men.

Perhaps the biggest disappointment for the United States came in women's swimming where the team picked up only one gold—in the 400-m freestyle relay. In Munich the Americans were

With the United States dominating men's swimming competition, John Naber won four golds and a silver.

Kornelia Ender of East Germany took four gold medals, the most ever by a woman swimmer, and a silver.

PHOTOS KEN REGAN, CAMERA 5

PHOTOS KEN REGAN, CAMERA 5

On the last day of Olympic track, New Zealand's John Walker took the 1,500-meter race in 3:39.17.

Bruce Jenner scored an upset by winning the decathlon and did so with a record total of points.

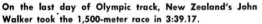

GOLD MEDAL WINNERS

Archery

Men: Darrell Pace, U. S. A.
Women: Luann Ryon, U. S. A.

Basketball

Men: United States
Women: U. S. R.

Boxing

Light Flyweight: Jorge Hernandez, Cuba
Flyweight: Leo Randolph, U. S. A.
Bantamweight: Yong Jo Gu, North Korea
Featherweight: Angel Herrera, Cuba
Lightweight: Howard Davis, U. S. A.
Light Welterweight: Ray Leonard, U. S. A.
Welterweight: Jochen Bachfeld, East Germany
Light Middleweight: Jerzy Rybicki, Poland
Middleweight: Michael Spinks, U. S. A.
Light Heavyweight: Leon Spinks, U. S. A.
Heavyweight: Teofilo Stevenson, Cuba

Canoeing

Men's 500-m Kayak Singles: Vasile Diba, Rumania
Men's 1,000-m Kayak Singles: Rudiger Helm, East Germany
Men's 500-m Kayak Pairs: East Germany
Men's 1,000-m Kayak Pairs: U. S. S. R.
Men's 1,000-m Kayak Fours: U. S. S. R.
Men's 500-m Canadian Singles: Alexander Rogov, U. S. S. R.
Men's 1,000-m Canadian Singles: Matija Ljubek, Yugoslavia
Men's 500-m Canadian Pairs: U. S. S. R.
Men's 1,000-m Canadian Pairs: U. S. S. R.
Women's Kayak Singles: Carola Zirzow, East Germany
Women's Kayak Pairs: U. S. S. R.

Cycling

1,000-m Time Trial: Klaus-Jürgen Grunke, East Germany
1,000-m Sprint: Anton Tkac, Czechoslovakia
4,000-m Individual Pursuit: Gregor Braun, West Germany
4,000-m Team Pursuit: West Germany
180-km Individual Road Race: Bernt Johansson, Sweden
100-km Team Time Trial: U. S. S. R.

Diving

Men's Springboard: Philip Boggs, U. S. A.
Men's Platform: Klaus Dibiasi, Italy
Women's Springboard: Jennifer Chandler, U. S. A.
Women's Platform: Elena Vaytsekhouskaya, U. S. S. R.

Equestrian

Individual Three-Day Event: Edmund Coffin, U. S. A.
Team Three-Day Event: United States
Individual Dressage: Christine Stueckelberger, Switzerland
Team Dressage: West Germany
Individual Jumping Grand Prix: Alwin Schockemoehle, West Germany
Team Jumping Grand Prix: France

Fencing

Men's Individual Foil: Fabio Dal Zotto, Italy
Men's Team Foil: West Germany
Men's Individual Épée: Alexander Pusch, West Germany
Men's Team Épée: Sweden
Men's Individual Sabre: Viktor Krovopovskov, U. S. S. R.
Men's Team Sabre: U. S. S. R.
Women's Individual Foil: Ildiko Schwarczenberger, Hungary
Women's Team Foil: U. S. S. R.

Field Hockey

New Zealand

considered the class of the world, but this time around the East Germans dominated the competition by capturing 11 of the 13 gold medals.

In team sports, the American basketball team made amends for its 1972 controversial loss to Russia. It won the gold medal with a 7–0 record and a convincing 95–74 victory over Yugoslavia in the final. The Soviet Union won in women's basketball and took both men's and women's titles in team handball. Poland won the men's volleyball championship and Japan won the women's competition. New Zealand was tops in field hockey; East Germany in soccer.

A surprise gold medal for the United States came in the decathlon when Bruce Jenner wound up with a record-breaking total of 8,618 points. Meanwhile, Frank Shorter was unsuccessful in his attempt to defend the marathon gold medal he won for the United States in Munich. An East German runner, Waldemar Cierpinski, finished less than a minute ahead of Shorter in the 26-mile, 385-yard (42.2 km) race, considered the most grueling of all Olympic events.

The Humorous, the Unforgettable, and a Suspenseful Ending. And, as always, the games had their humorous incidents. The New Zealand field hockey team, after winning its gold medal with a victory over Australia, did not show up for a press conference. It was learned that they decided to celebrate immediately and all team members headed for the nearest pub. British yachtsmen Alan Warren and David Hunt, annoyed at finishing 14th in a 16-team Tempest event, set their boat on fire and waded ashore. Unforgettable, also, was the performance of England's Princess Anne, who suffered minor injuries when thrown from her temperamental mount, Goodwill, during the cross-country portion of the equestrian event. Princess Anne, the only royal competitor at the games, finished 24th in a field of 28.

The games ended on a suspenseful note because of 17-year-old Soviet diver Sergei Nemtsanov, who decided to defect and remain in Canada.

Soviet team officials claimed Nemtsanov, a minor, had been "brainwashed" and ordered Canadian officials to return him to their delegation or they would pull out of the games with only a few days remaining. Furthermore, they warned they would break off all sports contact with Canada if their young diver was permitted to stay. But Nemtsanov still insisted he wanted to remain and was allowed to do so. The Russians, however, stayed until the games were completed, and participated in the closing ceremony. Later Nemtsanov returned to the Soviet Union. He said it was his "own decision."

ED CONRAD
Sports Department, "The Gazette," Montreal

Gymnastics

Men's All-Around: Nikolai Andrianov, U. S. S. R.
Men's Floor Exercises: Andrianov
Men's Horizontal Bars: Mitsuo Tsukahara, Japan
Men's Long Horse: Andrianov
Men's Parallel Bars: Sawao Kato, Japan
Men's Rings: Andrianov
Men's Side Horse: Zoltan Magyar, Hungary
Men's Team: Japan
Women's All-Around: Nadia Comaneci, Rumania
Women's Balance Beam: Comaneci
Women's Floor Exercises: Nelli Kim, U. S. S. R.
Women's Horse Vault: Kim
Women's Uneven Bars: Comaneci
Women's Team: U. S. S. R.

Handball

Men's Team: U. S. S. R.
Women's Team: U. S. S. R.

Judo

Lightweight: Hector Rodriguez, Cuba
Light Middleweight: Vladimir Nevzorov, U. S. S. R.
Middleweight: Isamu Sonoda, Japan
Light Heavyweight: Kazuhiro Ninomiya, Japan
Heavyweight: Sergei Novikov, U. S. S. R.
Open: Haruki Uemura, Japan

Modern Pentathlon

Individual: Janusz Pyciak-Peciak, Poland
Team: Britain

Rowing

Men's Single Sculls: Pertti Karppinen, Finland
Men's Double Sculls: Norway
Men's Quadruple Sculls: East Germany
Men's Coxed Pairs: East Germany
Men's Coxless Pairs: East Germany
Men's Coxed Fours: U. S. S. R.
Men's Coxless Fours: East Germany
Men's Coxed Eights: East Germany
Women's Single Sculls: Christine Scheiblich, East Germany
Women's Double Sculls: Bulgaria
Women's Coxed Quadruple Sculls: East Germany

Women's Coxless Pairs: Bulgaria
Women's Coxed Fours: East Germany
Women's Coxed Eights: East Germany

Shooting

Small Bore Rifle Prone: Karlheinz Smieszek, West Germany
Small Bore Rifle, Three-Positions: Lanny Bassham, U. S. A.
Trapshooting: Donald Haldeman, U. S. A.
Skeetshooting: Josef Panacek, Czechoslovakia
Free Pistol: Uwe Potteck, East Germany
Rapid Fire Pistol: Norbert Klaar, East Germany
Moving Target: Alexander Gazov, U. S. S. R.

Soccer

East Germany

Swimming

Men's 100-m Backstroke: John Naber, U. S. A.
Men's 200-m Backstroke: Naber
Men's 100-m Breaststroke: John Hencken, U. S. A.
Men's 200-m Breaststroke: David Wilkie, Britain
Men's 100-m Butterfly: Matt Vogel, U. S. A.
Men's 200-m Butterfly: Mike Bruner, U. S. A.
Men's 100-m Freestyle: Jim Montgomery, U. S. A.
Men's 200-m Freestyle: Bruce Furniss, U. S. A.
Men's 400-m Freestyle: Brian Goodell, U. S. A.
Men's 1,500-m Freestyle: Goodell
Men's 800-m Freestyle Relay: United States
Men's 400-m Individual Medley: Rod Strachan, U. S. A.
Men's 400-m Medley Relay: United States
Women's 100-m Backstroke: Ulrike Richter, East Germany
Women's 200-m Backstroke: Richter
Women's 100-m Breaststroke: Hannelore Anke, East Germany
Women's 200-m Breaststroke: Marina Koshevaya, U. S. S. R.
Women's 100-m Butterfly: Kornelia Ender, East Germany
Women's 200-m Butterfly: Andrea Pollack, East Germany
Women's 100-m Freestyle: Ender
Women's 200-m Freestyle: Ender
Women's 400-m Freestyle: Petra Thumer, East Germany
Women's 800-m Freestyle: Thumer
Women's 400-m Freestyle Relay: United States
Women's 400-m Individual Medley: Ulrike Tauber, East Germany
Women's 400-m Medley Relay: East Germany

With a 7–0 record, the U. S. basketball team recaptured the gold medal by defeating Yugoslavia in the finals.

Track and Field

Men's 100-m: Hasely Crawford, Trinidad
Men's 200-m: Donald Quarrie, Jamaica
Men's 400-m: Alberto Juantorena, Cuba
Men's 800-m: Juantorena
Men's 1,500-m: John Walker, New Zealand
Men's 5,000-m: Lasse Viren, Finland
Men's 10,000-m: Viren
Men's Marathon: Waldemar Cierpinski, East Germany
Men's 110-m Hurdles: Guy Drut, France
Men's 400-m Hurdles: Edwin Moses, U. S. A.
Men's 3,000-m Steeplechase: Anders Gaerderud, Sweden
Men's 400-m Relay: United States
Men's 1,600-m Relay: United States
Men's 20-km Walk: Daniel Bautista, Mexico
Men's Decathlon: Bruce Jenner, U. S. A.
Men's High Jump: Jacek Wszola, Poland
Men's Long Jump: Arnie Robinson, U. S. A.
Men's Triple Jump: Viktor Saneyev, U. S. S. R.
Men's Discus: Mac Wilkins, U. S. A.
Men's Shotput: Udo Beyer, East Germany
Men's Hammer Throw: Yuri Sedyh, U. S. S. R.
Men's Javelin: Miklos Nemeth, Hungary
Men's Pole Vault: Tadeusz Slusarski, Poland
Women's 100-m: Annegret Richter, West Germany
Women's 200-m: Baerbel Eckert, East Germany
Women's 400-m: Irena Szewinska, Poland
Women's 800-m: Tatyana Kazankina, U. S. S. R.
Women's 1,500-m: Kazankina
Women's 100-m Hurdles: Johanna Schaller, East Germany
Women's 400-m Relay: East Germany
Women's 1,600-m Relay: East Germany
Women's Pentathlon: Siegrun Siegl, East Germany
Women's High Jump: Rosemarie Ackermann, East Germany
Women's Long Jump: Angela Vogt, East Germany
Women's Discus: Evelin Schlaak, East Germany
Women's Shotput: Ivanka Christova, Bulgaria
Women's Javelin: Ruth Fuchs, East Germany

Volleyball

Men: Poland
Women: Japan

Water Polo

Hungary

Weightlifting

Flyweight: Alexander Voronin, U. S. S. R.
Bantamweight: Norair Nurikyan, Bulgaria
Featherweight: Nikolai Kolesnikov, U. S. S. R.
Lightweight: Zbigniew Kaczmarek[1], Poland
Middleweight: Yordan Mitkov, Bulgaria
Light Heavyweight: Valeri Shary, U. S. S. R.
Middle Heavyweight: David Rigert, U. S. S. R.
Heavyweight: Valentin Khristov[1], Bulgaria
Super Heavyweight: Vasili Alekseyev, U. S. S. R.

Wrestling, Freestyle

Light Flyweight: Khassan Issaev, Bulgaria
Flyweight: Yuji Takada, Japan
Bantamweight: Vladimir Yumin, U. S. S. R.
Featherweight: Jung-Mo Yang, South Korea
Lightweight: Pavel Pinigin, U. S. S. R.
Welterweight: Jiichiro Date, Japan
Middleweight: John Peterson, U. S. A.
Light Heavyweight: Levan Tediashvili, U. S. S. R.
Heavyweight: Ivan Yarygin, U. S. S. R.
Super Heavyweight: Soslan Andiyev, U. S. S. R.

Wrestling, Greco-Roman

Light Flyweight: Alekser Shumakov, U. S. S. R.
Flyweight: Vitali Konstantinov, U. S. S. R.
Bantamweight: Pertti Ukkola, Finland
Featherweight: Kazimier Lipien, Poland
Lightweight: Suren Nalbandyan, U. S. S. R.
Welterweight: Anatoli Bykov, U. S. S. R.
Middleweight: Momir Petkovic, Yugoslavia
Light Heavyweight: Valeri Rezantsev, U. S. S. R.
Heavyweight: Nikolai Bolboshin, U. S. S. R.
Super Heavyweight: Alexander Kolchinski, U. S. S. R.

Yachting

Class 470: West Germany
Finn: East Germany
Flying Dutchman: West Germany
Soling: Denmark
Tempest: Sweden
Tornado: Britain

[1]declared disqualified for drug use

INDIANAPOLIS MOTOR SPEEDWAY

Johnny Rutherford waves to the crowd after winning the Indianapolis 500 for the second time in three years. A heavy rainstorm caused the race to be stopped.

AUTO RACING

David Pearson won the 1976 Daytona 500-mile race in one of the wildest finishes in the history of auto racing. Pearson and Richard Petty were running almost side-by-side coming out of the final turn on the 200th lap. Their cars collided, hit the wall, and rolled into the infield. For a moment it looked as though Petty would cross the finish line backward, but the car stopped just short. Pearson limped home for his first victory in the prestigious event.

The 1976 season was spiced by the appearance of Arlene Hiss and Janet Guthrie. Mrs. Hiss became the first woman to compete in a United States Auto Club (USAC) event when she qualified at Phoenix. However, she did not do well in the race and did not enter another.

A 38-year-old physicist, Miss Guthrie was an experienced sports car driver but never before had tried the big leagues of American automobile racing. Miss Guthrie passed her rookie test at Indianapolis. She did not qualify for the race, but later was competitive in several USAC and National Association for Stock Car Auto Racing (NASCAR) events.

Texan Johnny Rutherford captured the Indianapolis 500-mile race for the second time in three years. Rutherford was building up a commanding lead on the field when a heavy rainstorm stopped it after 102 laps. His share of the $1 million purse was $256,121.

Brothers Al and Bob Unser won the other two events in USAC's "Triple Crown." Al won the Pocano "500" and Bobby took the Ontario "500." The two victories gave the Unsers a total of seven 500-mile race triumphs.

Austrian Niki Lauda, the defending Formula One champion, was injured seriously in a crash at the Nuerburgring course, W. Germany, but returned to racing six weeks later.

ROBERT J. COLLINS
Sports Editor
"The Indianapolis Star"

AUTO RACING

World Champion: James Hunt, England
USAC: Gordon Johncock, U.S.
NASCAR: Cale Yarborough, U.S.

Major Race Winners

Indianapolis 500: Johnny Rutherford, U.S.
Pocono 500: Al Unser, U.S.
Ontario 500: Bobby Unser, U.S.
Daytona 500: David Pearson, U.S.
Long Beach Grand Prix: Clay Regazzoni, Switzerland

Grand Prix for Formula I Cars, 1976

Austrian: John Watson, Ireland
Belgian: Niki Lauda, Austria
British: Niki Lauda
Brazilian: Niki Lauda
Canada: James Hunt
Dutch: James Hunt
French: James Hunt
Italian: Ronnie Peterson, Sweden
Japan: Mario Andretti, U.S.
Monte Carlo: Niki Lauda
South African: Niki Lauda
Spanish: James Hunt
Swedish: Jody Scheckter, South Africa
United States: James Hunt
United States (West): Clay Regazzoni
West German: James Hunt

BASEBALL

The Cincinnati Reds won their second consecutive world championship, but the most significant development of the 1976 baseball season was a revision of the sport's ancient reserve system which bound a player to one club until traded, sold, or released.

Off-Field News. For the first time in a century, baseball players were given freedom of movement. The dramatic change was presaged in December 1975 when an arbitrator resolved a dispute between major league club owners and the Major League Baseball Players Association. Arbitrator Peter Seitz declared pitchers Andy Messersmith and Dave McNally had become free agents by playing their "option year" of 1975 without signing contracts with their respective clubs—Messersmith with the Los Angeles Dodgers and McNally with the Montreal Expos. The arbitrator's decision was upheld in courts of law. McNally retired from the game, but Messersmith eventually signed with the Atlanta Braves, reportedly for three years and $1,000,000.

Then, on July 14, players and owners ended 13 months of negotiations by signing a four-year agreement. A major point was that a player with six years of major-league service could become a free agent and sign with another club. Additionally, as a carry-over from the Seitz decision, players not signed to 1976 or 1977 contracts could also become free agents at the conclusion of those seasons. Although owners feared mass defections, fewer than 25 players opted for their freedom in 1976. Top stars on the free-agent list included outfielder Reggie Jackson of the Baltimore Orioles, pitcher Rollie Fingers and outfielder Joe Rudi of the Oakland A's, and pitcher Don Gullett of the Reds.

An attempt to transfer the San Francisco Giants to Toronto was headed off when local interests purchased the National League club from Horace Stoneham. Subsequently, the American League voted to expand to 14 clubs in 1977 by granting franchises to Toronto and Seattle.

The start of spring training was made about two weeks late by the labor-management impasse; the camps opened only when the parties agreed to resume negotiations.

On June 15, Oakland owner Charles O. Finley sold pitcher Vida Blue to the New York Yankees for $1,500,000 and Fingers and Rudi to the Boston Red Sox for $1,000,000 each. Three days later baseball commissioner Bowie Kuhn voided the sales because "our efforts to preserve competitive balance would be greatly impaired."

Baseball deaths included those of Thomas A. Yawkey, 73, owner of the Red Sox for 43 years; Max Carey, 86, Hall of Fame outfielder with the Pittsburgh Pirates; Jimmy Dykes, 79, colorful player and manager; Urban (Red) Faber, 88, Hall of Fame pitcher for the Chicago White Sox, Earle Combs, 77, Hall of Fame outfielder for the Yankees, and Mrs. Babe Ruth, 76.

HERB SCHARFMAN, "SPORTS ILLUSTRATED"

Randy Jones of the San Diego Padres pitched extremely well, particularly during the first half of the season, winning a total of 22 games. He was named the National League's Cy Young award winner.

Fans enjoyed not only the pitching but also the antics of Mark Fidrych. The Detroit Tigers' star compiled a 19-9 record and was voted the American League's Rookie of the Year.

HERB SCHARFMAN, "SPORTS ILLUSTRATED"

The Season. On the field, it appeared the season might end without the semblance of a tight pennant race. The four divisional leaders —the Philadelphia Phillies (NL East), the Reds (NL West), the Yankees (AL East), and the Kansas City Royals (AL West)—all forged substantial leads. However, late-season slumps hit the Phillies and Royals. Both clubs staggered, then recovered to finish first.

Batting championships in both leagues went down to the final day. Bill Madlock of the Chicago Cubs won the NL title with four hits, finishing at .339 to .336 by the Reds' Ken Griffey. In the AL, the Royals' George Brett shaded teammate Hal McRae, .333 to .332, on a controversial hit. McRae charged that Minnesota Twins outfielder Steve Brye purposely let Brett's fly fall safely to give Brett the championship. The league office, though, absolved Brye. Mike Schmidt of the Phillies was the major leagues' home-run king with 38; George Foster of the Reds had the most runs batted in, 121, and Jim Palmer of the Orioles and Randy Jones of the Padres topped pitchers with 22 victories each.

The most fascinating personality to emerge was the Detroit Tigers' Mark (The Bird) Fidrych. The rookie talked to the baseball and groomed the mound while compiling a 19–9 record.

The season also marked the retirement of Henry Aaron, who slugged 755 homers to break Babe Ruth's career record of 714, and of Walter Alston, manager of the Brooklyn and Los Angeles Dodgers for 23 years.

The Play-off and Series. In the post season playoffs, the Reds swept the Phillies in three games to repeat as NL champions. The AL series went the limit; the Yankees defeated the Royals, three games to two. A dramatic homer by Chris Chambliss, snapping a 6–6 tie in the ninth inning of the fifth game, propelled the Yankees into their thirtieth World Series, but their first since 1964. The 1976 Yankees had none of the magic of their 20 previous world championship clubs. The Reds swept them aside in four straight games, leading winning manager Sparky Anderson to declare his club "one of the greatest in baseball history."

The Reds won the championship in New York's rebuilt Yankee Stadium as catcher Johnny Bench slammed two homers to drive in five runs. In fact, this was the World Series of the catcher. Bench batted .533 and Yankees backstop Thurman Munson hit .529. Only three batters had compiled higher averages in World Series history—Babe Ruth's .625 for the 1928 Yankees, Hank Gowdy's .545 for the 1914 Boston Braves, and Lou Gehrig's .545 for the 1928 Yankees.

The Cincinnati Reds' relief pitching was so outstanding—Pedro Borbon, Jack Billingham, and Will McEnaney did not allow a run in nine innings—that they did not call on their top bullpen pitcher, Rawley Eastwick. Cincinnati became the first National League club since the 1921–22 Giants to win consecutive World Series.

Bob Broeg, *"St. Louis Post-Dispatch"*

BASEBALL

Professional—Major Leagues

AMERICAN LEAGUE
(Final Standings, 1976)

Eastern Division	W	L	Pct.	Western Division	W	L	Pct.
New York....	97	62	.610	Kansas City....	90	72	.556
Baltimore.....	88	74	.543	Oakland.......	87	74	.540
Boston.......	83	79	.512	Minnesota.....	85	77	.525
Cleveland.....	81	78	.509	California......	76	86	.469
Detroit.......	74	87	.460	Texas.........	76	86	.469
Milwaukee....	66	95	.410	Chicago.......	64	97	.398

NATIONAL LEAGUE
(Final Standings, 1976)

Eastern Division	W	L	Pct.	Western Division	W	L	Pct.
Philadelphia..	101	61	.623	Cincinnati.....	102	60	.630
Pittsburgh.	92	70	.568	Los Angeles....	92	70	.568
New York....	86	76	.531	Houston.......	80	82	.494
Chicago......	75	87	.463	San Francisco..	74	88	.457
St. Louis.....	72	90	.444	San Diego.....	73	89	.451
Montreal.....	55	107	.340	Atlanta........	70	92	.432

Play-offs—American League: New York defeated Kansas City, 3 games to 2; National League: Cincinnati defeated Philadelphia, 3 games to 0

World Series—Cincinnati defeated New York 4 games to 0

First Game (Riverfront Stadium, Cincinnati, Oct. 15): Cincinnati 5, New York 1; second game (Riverfront Stadium, Oct. 17): Cincinnati 4, New York 3; third game (Yankee Stadium, New York, Oct. 19): Cincinnati 6, New York 2; fourth game (Yankee Stadium, Oct. 21): Cincinnati 7, New York 2; total attendance: 223 009.

All-Star Game (Philadelphia, July 13)—National League 7, American League 1

Most Valuable Players—American League: Thurman Munson, New York; National League: Joe Morgan, Cincinnati

Cy Young Memorial Awards (outstanding pitchers)—American League: Jim Palmer, Baltimore; National League: Randy Jones, San Diego

Rookie of the Year—American League: Mark Fidrych, Detroit; National League: Pat Zachry, Cincinnati and Butch Metzger, San Diego

Leading Batters—Percentage: American: George Brett, Kansas City, .333; National: Bill Madlock, Chicago, .339. Runs Batted In: American: Lee May, Baltimore, 109; National: George Foster, Cincinnati, 121. Home Runs: American: Graig Nettles, New York, 32; National: Mike Schmidt, Philadelphia, 38.

Leading Pitchers—(earned run average) American: Mark Fidrych, Detroit, 2.34; National: John Denny, St. Louis, 2.52. (Victories) American: Jim Palmer, Baltimore, 22; National: Randy Jones, San Diego, 22. (Strikeouts) American: Nolan Ryan, California, 327; National: Tom Seaver, New York, 235.

No-Hit Games Pitched: John Candelaria, Pittsburgh Pirates v. Los Angeles Dodgers; John Montefusco, San Francisco Giants v. Atlanta Braves; Larry Dierker, Houston Astros v. Montreal Expos; John (Blue Moon) Odom and Francisco Barrios, Chicago White Sox v. California Angels.

Hall of Fame Inductees—Oscar Charleston; Roger Connor; Cal Hubbard; Bob Lemmon; Fred Lindstrom; Robin Roberts.

Professional—Minor Leagues, Class AAA

American Association (play-offs): Denver defeated Omaha, 4 games to 2.

International League (play-off finals): Syracuse defeated Richmond, 3 games to 1.

Pacific Coast League (play-off championship): Hawaii defeated Salt Lake City, 3 games to 2.

Mexican League (championship): Mexico City Reds defeated Union Laguna 4 games to 2.

Amateur—N. C. A. A.

Division I: University of Arizona

BASKETBALL

In college basketball, 1976 belonged to the University of Indiana. In the professional ranks, it was the year that finally saw the merger of the American Basketball Association and the National Basketball Association.

THE COLLEGE SEASON

The NCAA. The University of Indiana captured the NCAA crown by avoiding the one big mistake made during the preceding season. In 1975, the Hoosiers had lost one game, in the play-offs, and this cost them the title. In 1976, however, they won all 32 of their games, most of them by good margins. Indiana, in regaining the title it had held in 1940 and 1953, became the

The play of center Kent Benson was a prime reason for Indiana's undefeated season and NCAA title.

INDIANA UNIVERSITY

seventh major team to complete a season unbeaten. Only North Carolina in 1957 had won as many games.

The Hoosiers capped their undefeated season with an 86–68 victory over Michigan at Philadelphia, March 29. The final was unusual because it pitted teams from the same conference against each other, a situation that was not possible until 1975. Michigan had almost ended the Indiana streak during the regular season, carrying the Hoosiers into overtime in their second meeting before losing, 72–67. The Wolverines also led at halftime in the final, 35–29, but could not sustain their threat and faded long before the finish of the game.

The starting lineup of the Indiana team, coached by Bobby Knight, was made up of four seniors and one junior. Scott May, 6 feet, 7 inches and 218 pounds (2 m, 98.8 kg) was the leader on offense and was named to most all-American teams. He was also voted the most valuable player in the Big Ten Conference. Quinn Buckner, a co-captain with May, was the leader on defense along with Kent Benson, the junior. At 6-11 and 245 pounds (2.1 m, 111 kg), Benson played center and defended so well that he, too, was named to most all-American teams. The other seniors were Tom Abernethy and Bobby Wilkerson.

Indiana went into the play-offs with a streak of 28 straight victories, winners of 57 regular season games without a loss and with 37 triumphs in a row in the Big Ten. They came out the champion with a record of 63 victories in 64 games. Their record for two years was marred only by a loss to Kentucky in the regional play-offs in 1975.

In the 1976 play-offs, Indiana routed St. John's, 90–70, then disposed of Alabama, 74–69. For the regional championship, Indiana played Marquette which had lost only once, to Minnesota by 4 points in overtime. Indiana won, 65–56, ending the Warriors' streak at 23 games and then prepared to face the University of California, Los Angeles, the defending champion. UCLA was playing in the play-offs for the first time since 1948 without John Wooden as coach.

The Hoosiers repeated an early season triumph over the Bruins, 65–51, and were in the final.

Michigan's route to the final was tougher. The Wolverines slipped past Wichita State, 74–73, stopped Notre Dame, 80–76, and brushed off Missouri, 95–88, after trailing late in the game. They next met Rutgers, the pride of the East, which had also come into the play-offs unbeaten, the 15th team in tournament history to do so. The Scarlet Knights, with 28 victories, were a fast-breaking team, paced by Phil Sellers. They turned back Princeton, Connecticut, and Virginia Military Institute before the Michigan defense halted their string at 31 games with an 86–70 victory.

Other Winners. Coppin State College of Maryland took the National Association of Intercollegiate Athletics championship, beating Henderson State in the final, 96–91. Puget Sound won the N. C. A. A. Division II title and the University of Scranton took Division III honors. Delta State, led by Luisa Harris, 6–3 (1.9 m), retained the Association of Intercollegiate Athletics for Women championship, beating Immaculata, 69–64, in the final. Kentucky won the National Invitation Tournament.

Phil Sellers led the fast-breaking Rutgers team to 31 victories before defeat in the NCAA semifinals.

COLLEGE BASKETBALL

Conference Champions

Atlantic Coast: Virginia
Big Eight: Missouri
Big Sky: Boise State
Big Ten: Indiana
East Coast—East Section: St. Joseph's; West Section: Lafayette
Ivy League: Princeton
Metro-6: Cincinnati
Mid-American: Western Michigan
Missouri Valley: Wichita State
Ohio Valley: Western Kentucky
Pacific-8: UCLA
Pacific Coast Athletic: Fullerton State
Southeastern: Alabama
Southern: VMI
Southwest: Texas Tech
West Coast Athletic: Pepperdine
Western Athletic: Arizona
Yankee: Massachusetts

The N.B.A.'s Rookie of the Year Alvan Adams of Phoenix and Boston's center Dave Cowens battle for a rebound in play-off action. The Celtics won the N.B.A. title, defeating the Suns 4 games to 2.

MANNY MILLAN, "SPORTS ILLUSTRATED"

THE PROFESSIONAL SEASON

Pro basketball lost one team just before its longest season opened, two more after a few weeks, and a fourth club and a league shortly after the finish in early June. The league was the American Basketball Association which succeeded in having four of its clubs absorbed by the National Basketball Association. A merger, which had been suggested by a federal court judge as a way of ending costly antitrust litigation, was agreed to on June 17. The N. B. A. accepted the Denver Nuggets, Indiana Pacers, New York Nets, and San Antonio Spurs but rejected two other clubs.

NBA Play-offs. Ten days before the merger, the Boston Celtics put down the challenge of the Phoenix Suns and won the N.B.A. championship. This was nearly a month after the A. B. A. season had ended with the Nets, led by Julius Erving, beating the Nuggets, 4 games to 2, to take the A. B. A. title.

In winning the championship for the 13th time, the Celtics eliminated the Buffalo Braves and Cleveland Cavaliers from Eastern Conference honors before meeting Phoenix. They were essentially the same team that had won the title in 1974 augmented by Charlie Scott, a high scorer obtained for Paul Westphal in a 1975 trade with Phoenix. The Celtics expected to meet the Golden State Warriors, the defending champion and the only team that had a better season record than Boston.

The Suns, however, refused to bow down, rallying three times to tie the Western Conference final series and then taking the deciding game on the champion's home court in Oakland, Calif., 94–86. Phoenix had come on late in the season with an effective blending of experienced players—Dick Van Arsdale, Keith Erickson, Curtis Perry, and Westphal—with Alvan Adams, a center who was named rookie of the year, and Ricky Sobers, a rookie guard. The team, calling itself the Sunderellas, was coached by John MacLeod.

The Celtics won the first two games of the final series only to have the Suns draw even. The fifth game, in Boston, went into triple overtime,

BRUCE CURTIS, PETER ARNOLD PHOTO ARCHIVES

Julius Erving, the A.B.A.'s Most Valuable Player, dominated action as the Nets won the crown. Later a contract dispute caused the Nets to sell "Dr. J."

The Merger. The merger was spurred late in May when CBS-TV indicated it would pay an additional $5 million in a four-year contract to televise N. B. A. games if four A. B. A. franchises were added to the league. An agreement with the Players Association in February on players' rights at the expiration of contracts, options, and salaries had eliminated a big obstacle in the way of a merger.

In the A. B. A., Baltimore, which had taken over the Memphis franchise, folded before play started in October; San Diego went under in November, and Utah in December. The Virginia Squires managed to last through the schedule, then died, and the St. Louis franchise was being moved to Salt Lake City when the league disappeared.

The new teams were to pay $3.2 million each for an N. B. A. franchise and receive no part of the TV cut for four years. They also paid large sums to Kentucky and St. Louis, the clubs that were left out.

BILL BRADDOCK
Sports Department, "The New York Times"

providing a wild TV spectacle and a near riot in which the referee was attacked by a spectator before Boston won. The Celtics took the sixth game in Phoenix, 87–80, and the title.

ABA Play-offs. The Nuggets and the Nets, the top teams in the A. B. A., each had to battle through a seven-game series to reach the final. The Nuggets beat Kentucky and the Nets eliminated San Antonio. Erving scored at the buzzer for the margin that beat the Nuggets, 120–118, in the opening game before 19,043 in Denver, the largest crowd in A. B. A. history. Erving, the league's most valuable player, led the Nets to victory in three of the next five games for the title. The Nuggets were paced by David Thompson, the rookie of the year, Ralph Simpson, and Dan Issel.

PROFESSIONAL BASKETBALL

National Basketball Association
(Final Standings, 1975–76)

Eastern Conference

Atlantic Division	W	L	Pct.
Boston Celtics	54	28	.659
Philadelphia 76ers	46	36	.561
Buffalo Braves	46	36	.561
New York Knickerbockers	38	44	.463

Central Division	W	L	Pct.
Cleveland Cavaliers	49	33	.598
Washington Bullets	48	34	.585
Houston Rockets	40	42	.488
New Orleans Jazz	38	44	.463
Atlanta Hawks	29	53	.354

Western Conference

Midwest Division	W	L	Pct.
Milwaukee Bucks	38	44	.463
Detroit Pistons	36	46	.439
Kansas City Kings	31	51	.378
Chicago Bulls	24	58	.293

Pacific Division	W	L	Pct.
Golden State Warriors	59	23	.720
Seattle Supersonics	43	39	.524
Phoenix Suns	42	40	.512
Los Angeles Lakers	40	42	.488
Portland Trail Blazers	37	45	.451

Most Valuable Player: Kareem Abdul-Jabbar, Los Angeles
Rookie of the Year: Alvan Adams, Phoenix
Coach of the Year: Bill Fitch, Cleveland
Leading Scorer: Bob McAdoo, 2,427 points; 31.1 per game
All Star Game: East 123, West 109

American Basketball Association
(Final Standings, 1975–76)

	W	L	Pct.
Denver Nuggets	60	24	.714
New York Nets	55	29	.655
San Antonio Spurs	50	34	.595
Kentucky Colonels	46	38	.548
Indiana Pacers	39	45	.464
Spirits of St. Louis	35	49	.417
Virginia Squires	15	68	.181

Most Valuable Player: Julius Erving, New York
Rookie of the Year: David Thompson, Denver
Coach of the Year: Larry Brown, Denver
Leading Scorer: Erving, 2,462 points, 29.3 per game
All Star Game: Denver 144, All Stars 138

BOXING

Muhammad Ali's penchant for controversies kept him involved in them from February through September. His choice of opponents for three of four bouts caused dissension. The decision of the officials in the fourth led to more controversy. Many fans thought Ken Norton had won.

Champions. Ali was one of 10 champions who retained his title. He was joined as the sole champion in a division by Carlos Monzon of Argentina, a middleweight, who is the longest reigning titleholder. In defense of the World Boxing Association title that Monzon won in 1970, he beat Rodrigo Valdes of Colombia, the World Boxing Council champion at Monte Carlo, June 26. It was Monzon's 61st straight victory and Valdes' first loss in six years.

Another long-reigning champion, Robert Duran of Panama, knocked out Lou Bizzarro of Erie, Pa., in the 14th round at Erie, May 23, and later stopped Alvaro Rojas of Costa Rica.

There were 14 new champions crowned in 1976. Two were in new classes and one, Saensak Muangsurin of Thailand, lost his title in June on a disqualification and got it back by knocking out Miguel Velasquez of Spain at Segovia.

Among the new champions were two young Californians, Carlos Palomino of Westminster and Danny Lopez of Los Angeles. Palomino, a student at Long Beach State, stopped John Stracey of Britain in the 12th round at Wembley, June 23, and took the WBC welterweight title. Lopez, a full-blooded Ute Indian, captured the WBC featherweight crown, November 6, outpointing David Kotey of Ghana at Accra.

Ali. In his first bout of the year, Ali knocked out Jean-Pierre Coopman of Belgium in the fifth round at San Juan, P. R. There was much clamor because no one had heard of the Belgian, who was suspended for accepting a title bout for which he was not qualified. Then Ali met a former sparring partner, Jimmy Young. After Ali won the decision there was controversy because he had done little fighting. The next controversial bout was with Richard Dunn of England who was knocked down five times before the referee stopped the bout in the fifth round at Munich, May 24. Then Ali engaged in a farce, called a draw, with a Japanese wrestler at Tokyo.

Norton was Ali's only qualified foe and he did so well that many in the crowd of 30,298 at Yankee Stadium, New York, September 28, booed the decision. There was so much controversy that the final round, which was decisive, was rerun on a special TV program so that fans could see what happened. It was generally agreed that Ali won that round and the fight.

BILL BRADDOCK

In a controversial decision at Yankee Stadium, Muhammad Ali defeats Ken Norton to retain heavyweight title.

UPI

BOXING

World Professional Champions
(Year of achieving title in parentheses)

Junior Flyweight—Yoko Gushiken, Japan (1976), World Boxing Association (WBA); Luis Estaba, Venezuela (1975), World Boxing Council (WBC).
Flyweight—Guty Espadas, Panama (1976), WBA; Miguel Canto, Mexico (1975) WBC
Bantamweight—Alfonso Zamora, Mexico (1975) WBA; Carlos Zarate, Mexico (1976) WBC
Junior Featherweight—Royal Kobayashi, Japan (1976) WBC
Featherweight—Alexis Arguello, Nicaragua (1974) WBA, announced retirement in November; Danny Lopez, Los Angeles (1976) WBC
Junior Lightweight—Samuel Serrano, Puerto Rico (1976) WBA; Alfredo Escalera, Puerto Rico (1975) WBC
Lightweight—Roberto Duran, Panama (1972) WBA; Esteban de Jesus, Puerto Rico (1976) WBC
Junior Welterweight—WBA declared vacant Nov. 1976; Saensak Muangsurin, Thailand (1976) WBC
Welterweight—José Cuevas, Mexico (1976) WBA; Carlos Palomino, Westminster, Calif. (1976) WBC
Junior Middleweight—Miguel Castellani, Argentina (1976) WBA; Eckhard Dagge, West Germany (1976) WBC
Middleweight—Carlos Monzon, Argentina (1970).
Light Heavyweight—Victor Galindez, Argentina (1974) WBA; John Conteh, England (1974) WBC
Heavyweight—Muhammad Ali, Chicago (1964 and 1974)

National AAU Champions
(Las Vegas, Nev., May 12–15)

106 Pounds—Brett Summers, Marysville, Wash.
112 Pounds—Leo Randolph, Tacoma, Wash.
119 Pounds—Bernard Taylor, Charlotte, N. C.
125 Pounds—Davey Armstrong, Puyallup, Wash.
132 Pounds—Howard Davis, Glen Cove, N. Y.
139 Pounds—Pete Seward, Columbus, Ohio
147 Pounds—Clinton Jackson, Nashville, Tenn.
156 Pounds—J. B. Williamson, Honolulu
165 Pounds—Keith Broom, Charlotte, N. C.
178 Pounds—Leon Spinks, St. Louis
Heavyweight—Marvin Stinson, Philadelphia
Team—Pacific Northwest

FOOTBALL

Led by Tony Dorsett, the University of Pittsburgh was the nation's number one college team. In the professional ranks, the Oakland Raiders won the Super Bowl game.

THE COLLEGE SEASON

Pittsburgh and the Bowl Games. The University of Pittsburgh lost its two top quarterbacks before midseason, filled in with an inexperienced substitute, kept its balance, and finished the season at the top of the polls as the number 1 major team. Most observers considered, however, that a first-class quarterback was a nonessential at Pitt—all the signal-caller had to do was face the team in the right direction and hand the ball to Tony Dorsett. That was not exactly the Pitt formula but it was the key. At the end of the regular season, Pitt had won all of its 11 games, and Dorsett had been awarded the Heisman Trophy as the leading player by a landslide vote. He broke all career rushing records.

UPI

Pitt's Tony Dorsett, who established a series of rushing records in 1976, wins the Heisman Trophy.

COLLEGE FOOTBALL

Intercollegiate and Conference Champions

National Press Polls—Pittsburgh
National Football Foundation Award (MacArthur Bowl)—Pittsburgh
Heisman Trophy—Tony Dorsett, Pittsburgh
Eastern (Lambert Trophy)—Pittsburgh
Eastern Small College—Lambert Bowl: C. W. Post; Lambert Cup: Delaware
Atlantic Coast—Maryland
Big Eight—Colorado, Oklahoma, Oklahoma State (tied)
Big Sky—Montana State
Big Ten—Michigan, Ohio State (tied)
Ivy League—Brown, Yale (tied)
Mid-American—Ball State
Missouri Valley—New Mexico State, Tulsa (tied)
Ohio Valley—East Kentucky
Pacific-8—Southern California
Southeastern—Georgia
Southern—East Carolina
Southwest—Houston, Texas Tech (tied)
Western Athletic—Brigham Young, Wyoming (tied)
Yankee—New Hampshire

Major Bowl Games

Tangerine Bowl (Orlando, Fla., Dec. 18)—Oklahoma State 49, Brigham Young 21
Liberty Bowl (Memphis, Tenn., Dec. 20)—Alabama 36, U.C.L.A. 6
Fiesta Bowl (Tempe, Ariz., Dec. 25)—Oklahoma 41, Wyoming 7
Gator Bowl (Jacksonville, Fla., Dec. 27)—Notre Dame 20, Penn State 9.
Astro-Bluebonnet Bowl (Houston, Dec. 31)—Nebraska 27, Texas Tech 24
Peach Bowl (Atlanta, Dec. 31)—Kentucky 21, North Carolina 0
Cotton Bowl (Dallas, Jan. 1)—Houston 30, Maryland 21
Orange Bowl (Miami, Jan. 1)—Ohio State 27, Colorado 10
Rose Bowl (Pasadena, Calif., Jan. 1)—Southern Cal 14, Michigan 6
Sugar Bowl (New Orleans, Jan. 1)—Pittsburgh 27, Georgia 3
Sun Bowl (El Paso, Tex., Jan. 2)—Texas A & M 37, Florida 14.

N. C. A. A. Championships

Division II: Montana State
Division III: St. John's, Minn.

N. A. I. A. Championships

Division I: Texas A & I
Division II: Westminster

Pitt, which had gained the top spot when Michigan was upset by Purdue, November 6, could not be acclaimed the national champion until the bowl games had been played. Maryland and Rutgers had won all of their games; Michigan, Southern California, and Georgia had lost only one. Rutgers, with 18 straight victories, had the longest major winning string but some of the Scarlet Knights' opponents were considered second-rate and Rutgers failed to get even one good bowl bid. There was also criticism of the potency of Maryland's foes, but the Terrapins got a spot in the Cotton Bowl against surprising Houston, a Southwest Conference co-champion. Michigan won the Big Ten role in the Rose Bowl with Southern Cal serving as the Pacific-8 host. Pitt chose the Sugar Bowl and a final test against the Southeastern Conference champions, Georgia, a fine defensive outfit that had lost only to Mississippi, 21–17.

Dorsett ran for 202 yards as Pitt routed Georgia, 27–3, and solidified its claim to the top ranking in the first of the New Years Day bowl games. Southern California beat Michigan, 14–6, in a dull defensive contest and took the runner-up spot away from the Wolverines. Houston scored 21 points in the first period and ended Maryland's unbeaten string at 15 games with a 30–21 victory. Ohio State rallied and defeated Colorado, 27–10, in the Orange Bowl.

The National Football Foundation voted the MacArthur Bowl to Pitt as the national champion and UPI and AP kept the Panthers at the top, with U. S. C. second and Michigan third.

The Season. The season started with a jolt for several of the usual high-ranking teams. Mississippi beat Alabama, 10–7; Pittsburgh romped over Notre Dame, 31–10; Boston College edged Texas, 13–12, Louisiana State tied Nebraska, 6–6, and Missouri in the first phase of a startling campaign, throttled Southern California, 46–25. Then Missouri was throttled by Illinois, 31–6, but rebounded by knocking off Ohio State, 22–21. Penn State lost to Ohio State, Iowa, and Kentucky in succession.

Amid the upsets, Michigan was being hailed as the best in the land and was being compared with the great teams of the past. The Wolverines, with Rob Lytle at fullback and Jim Smith at tight end, both all-American choices, and Rick Leach at quarterback, swamped all eight of their opponents except Navy. But Purdue did them in with a late field goal, 16–14. When the Big Ten showdown came, Michigan was again unbeatable and walloped Ohio State, 22–0, in their annual battle for the Rose Bowl spot. The Buckeyes, beaten twice and tied 10–10 by U. C. L. A., accepted a bid to play the Big Eight representative in the Orange Bowl.

Meanwhile, Pitt rolled along with the focus on Dorsett and his campaign to overhaul the career rushing mark of 5,177 yards set by Archie Griffin in 1975. The tailback from Aliquippa, Pa., reached his goal against Navy, October 23, with a 32-yard scoring run. In the next four regular season games he raised his four-year total to 6,082 yards and bettered or tied scads of records. His season rushing total of 1,948 yards bettered Ed Marinaro's mark of 1,881. With 356 points, Dorsett took the scoring record away from Glenn Davis of Army, who made 354 in 1946. Dorsett tied the Davis mark of 59 career touchdowns.

Torn knee ligaments put Robert Haygood, Pitt's quarterback, out for the season in the second game. Matt Cavanaugh was lost in the fifth game with a leg injury, and Coach Johnny Majors chose Tom Yewcic, a reserve who played seldom in four seasons, to start the next three games before Cavanaugh returned.

In the Big Eight, Oklahoma, Nebraska, Colorado, Oklahoma State, and Iowa State were tied for first with one game to go. Colorado and Oklahoma State won, leaving the Oklahoma-Nebraska game as the deciding contest for the Orange Bowl. The Sooners won in the final minute, 20–17. Because Colorado had beaten the other teams tied with Colorado for the title —Oklahoma and Oklahoma State—the Golden Buffalos won the trip to Miami.

The Pacific-8 situation again devolved into a showdown between Southern Cal and U. C. L. A.; the Trojans, paced by Ricky Bell, took the game, 24–14, and the Rose Bowl spot. Bell had given Dorsett a run for the Heisman Trophy until injuries slowed him in midseason. He was second in the voting. Houston, playing in the Southwest Conference for the first time, downed previously unbeaten Texas Tech, 27–19, and became the Cotton Bowl host.

Among coaches who were discharged or who resigned under pressure were Darrell Royal of Texas, Frank Broyles of Arkansas; Alex Agase

UPI

U. S. C.'s Charles White (12) runs for a first down as the Trojans defeat Michigan in the Rose Bowl game.

of Purdue; Jim Shofner of Texas Christian U., Bill Battle of Tennessee (Majors replaced him after the Sugar Bowl), and Bob Blackman of Illinois, who replaced George Seifert at Cornell.

Ove Johansson of Abilene Christian kicked a 69-yard field goal, the longest in either college or pro competition, at Abilene, October 16. Tony Franklin of Texas A.&M. had broken the record 20 minutes before at College Station with a 64-yarder.

THE PROFESSIONAL SEASON

Frustrations abounded during the march to the January 1977 Super Bowl game. The teams that made it to the final, the Minnesota Vikings and the Oakland Raiders, had had deep disappointments in the past. The Vikings, the Central Division winners, again blighted the hopes of Los Angeles in taking the National Conference title. The Rams, winners of the Western Division four straight times, have never gotten to the Super Bowl. Oakland thwarted the bid of the Pittsburgh Steelers, Super Bowl victors the preceding two years, to become the first three-time winner. In taking the American Conference title, the Raiders ended their own frustrations. They had tried six other times since 1968 (when they lost to Green Bay in the Super Bowl) to reach the final and had been accused of being unable to win the big games.

AFC play-off action: With seconds remaining in the game, Oakland quarterback Ken Stabler scores the winning touchdown as the Raiders defeat New England, 24–21.

UPI

Before 100,421 in Pasadena, Oakland won the Super Bowl, 32–14. The win compounded the frustrations of the Vikings and Fran Tarkenton. It was their fourth failure to win the title game. The Raiders, led by the running of Clarence Davis and Ken Stabler's passing, smothered the Minnesota ground game. Oakland gained a Super Bowl record of 429 yards, 180 on passes mainly to Fred Biletnikoff and Dave Casper.

Oakland, with 13 victories in 14 games, had the best regular-season record in the league that expanded to 28 teams. The Seattle Seahawks and Tampa Bay Buccaneers began play and the Bucs lost all of their games.

The Play-offs. When the Raiders played the Steelers at Oakland, December 26, each team had had a 10-game winning streak. Pittsburgh played without Franco Harris and Rocky Bleier, its best rushing backs, and had no ground game. Ken Stabler made effective use of the pass and the running of Clarence Davis as Oakland controlled the game from the start and won, 24–7.

Earlier in the day at Bloomington, Minn., the Vikings scored on a blocked field goal attempt and rolled to a 24–13 victory over Los Angeles. The Rams, with the ball inches from the goal line after Pat Haden had failed on a quarterback sneak, decided to try for a field goal on fourth down. Nate Allen blocked the kick, Bobby Bryant picked up the ball and ran 90 yards for a Viking touchdown. After Tarkenton and Chuck Foreman had increased the Minnesota lead to 17–0, the Rams rallied but could not overcome that early slippage.

In the first round of the play-offs, Los Angeles eliminated Dallas, the Eastern Division winner, 14–12, warding off a late Cowboy surge in which Roger Staubach's passes went awry because of an injured finger on his throwing hand. Minnesota routed the Washington Redskins who had gained the wild card berth, 35–20.

In the American Conference first round, Oakland scored with 10 seconds to play and ousted the New England Patriots, 24–21. The Patriots were the surprise team of the season. With Steve Grogan at quarterback, after they traded Jim Plunkett to San Francisco, they won 11 games, lost 3—the reverse of their preceding season's record. In the other game, Pittsburgh overpowered the Baltimore Colts, the Eastern Division victors, 40–14. Bert Jones, the Colt quarterback, acclaimed the best in the league, could find no way to break the strong Steeler defense, and the Baltimore defense had no success against the rushes of Harris and the passing of Terry Bradshaw to Lynn Swann.

The Season. The Steelers' stuttering start left an impression that the two-time champions had become too fat. They lost four of their first five games and faced the possibility of missing the play-offs. But in an important division test with Cincinnati, Pittsburgh returned to form with a 23–6 triumph. The Steelers took their nine remaining regular season games, holding five opponents scoreless and allowing only 28 points and no touchdowns by rushing.

Grogan was one of the four top scorers by rushing in the league and second only to Harris in the American Conference. He made 12 touchdowns by rushing and scored one on a kick return. By 6 points Grogan trailed Harris and Foreman, who led the league in scoring with 84 points. Grogan was tied with Walter Payton of the Chicago Bears, the season's surprise runner, who led the league in rushing yardage until overtaken by O. J. Simpson.

NFC Championship: Minnesota's Bobby Bryant (20) picks up a blocked Rams field goal attempt and runs for a touchdown. The Vikings went on to defeat Los Angeles, 24–13.

UPI

Simpson had sought to be traded to a California club and did not report to Buffalo until the start of the season. He was slow getting into shape but on Thanksgiving Day against Detroit O. J. ran for 273 yards, bettering his own game record by 23 yards. It was his fifth 200-yard game, one better than Jim Brown. On the final day, O. J. rushed for 171 yards and a season total of 1,503. This was 113 more than Payton, who was injured during the final game.

In the legal contests, the players made substantial gains against the owners but played another season without a union contract. The owners were set back when the courts decreed that the college draft procedure violated antitrust laws and that the Rozelle Rule (covering procedure after a player had served his option) was illegal. Both decisions were appealed.

Grey Cup. In the Canadian League, the Ottawa Rough Riders won the Grey Cup with a 23–20 victory over the Saskatchewan Roughriders at Toronto, November 28. Ottawa scored the deciding touchdown with 20 seconds left.

BILL BRADDOCK

PROFESSIONAL FOOTBALL

NATIONAL FOOTBALL LEAGUE

Final Standings

AMERICAN CONFERENCE
Eastern Division

	W	L	T	Pct.	For	Agst.
Baltimore	11	3	0	.786	417	246
New England*	11	3	0	.786	376	236
Miami	6	8	0	.429	263	264
Jets	3	11	0	.214	169	383
Buffalo	2	12	0	.143	245	363

Central Division

	W	L	T	Pct.	For	Agst.
Pittsburgh	10	4	0	.714	342	138
Cincinnati	10	4	0	.714	335	210
Cleveland	9	5	0	.643	267	287
Houston	5	9	0	.357	222	273

Western Division

	W	L	T	Pct.	For	Agst.
Oakland	13	1	0	.929	350	237
Denver	9	5	0	.643	315	206
San Diego	6	8	0	.429	248	285
Kansas City	5	9	0	.357	290	376
Tampa Bay	0	14	0	.000	125	412

*Won play-off berth

NATIONAL CONFERENCE
Eastern Division

	W	L	T	Pct.	For	Agst.
Dallas	11	3	0	.786	296	194
Washington*	10	4	0	.714	291	217
St. Louis	10	4	0	.714	309	267
Philadelphia	4	10	0	.286	165	286
Giants	3	11	0	.214	170	250

Central Division

	W	L	T	Pct.	For	Agst.
Minnesota	11	2	1	.821	305	176
Chicago	7	7	0	.500	253	216
Detroit	6	8	0	.429	262	220
Green Bay	5	9	0	.357	218	299

Western Division

	W	L	T	Pct.	For	Agst.
Los Angeles	10	3	1	.750	351	200
San Francisco	8	6	0	.571	270	190
Atlanta	4	10	0	.286	172	312
New Orleans	4	10	0	.286	253	346
Seattle	2	12	0	.143	229	429

*Won play-off berth

Play-offs
Oakland 24, New England 21
Pittsburgh 40, Baltimore 14
Conference Champion
Oakland 24, Pittsburgh 7

Play-offs
Minnesota 35, Washington 20
Los Angeles 14, Dallas 12
Conference Champion
Minnesota 24, Los Angeles 13

Super Bowl: Oakland 32, Minnesota 14

GOLF

Two of the more poignant golf sagas of the year were those of John Mahaffey and Severiano Ballesteros—neither one a winner. Mahaffey, who has won only one tournament in six years on the Professional Golfers' Association circuit, led the U. S. Open from the middle of the second round—by six strokes at one point —until the closing holes on the final day. His game went awry and he wound up tied for fourth. Ballesteros, a 19-year-old Spaniard, was a front-runner in the British Open for three rounds, faded in the fourth round but managed to tie for second place. Mahaffey had lost an 18-hole play-off for the U. S. Open title in 1975 to Lou Graham.

The U. S. Open. Another young player, Jerry Pate, 22, of Pensacola, Fla., took the U. S. Open away from Mahaffey. Pate, who had won the U. S. Amateur in 1974 while a student at the University of Alabama, had stayed in contention for the Open through the early rounds. He finally drew even with Mahaffey at the 16th on the closing day, went a stroke ahead with a par to the leader's bogey on the 17th and won with a birdie on the 18th (or 72nd) hole. That birdie also stymied the late bids of Al Geiberger and Tom Weiskopf. They slipped into the runner-up spot, two strokes back of the winner, when Mahaffey hit into the water and wound up with his third straight bogey. Pate had joined the tour at the start of the year.

The British Open. Johnny Miller snatched the British Open title with a six-under-par 66 on the

Johnny Miller displays his emotions during the British Open. Miller won the tournament on the final round.

Ray Floyd won the Masters with a record-tying score. Below, he putts for a birdie during the third round.

UPI

final round while Ballesteros was touring the rough. Miller's round, not quite so spectacular as the 63 he carded in running off with the U. S. Open in 1973, gave him a six-stroke margin. The Spaniard, after three bogeys, a double and a triple bogey, rallied for a birdie on the 72nd hole that gained him a tie with Jack Nicklaus for second place.

The Masters and Ray Floyd. The most remarkable performance in a major tourney was that of Ray Floyd. He led the Masters through all four rounds and finished with a 17-under-par total of 271 which equaled the record for the event made by Nicklaus in 1965. Floyd was continuing his resurgence begun the previous year. He also won the World open in a play-off with Jerry McGee, finished fourth in the British Open, and was tied for runner-up honors with Don January in the PGA title tourney, one stroke behind Dave Stockton. Stockton regained the championship he had won in 1970 by outlasting five others in a wild scramble through the final 18 holes.

The Money Winners. Nicklaus, playing in what he calls his last full competitive season, did not add to his list of 16 major victories. He did win the Tournament Players tourney, worth $60,000, and the expanded World Series of Golf, worth $100,000. His total of $266,438 held up as the top earnings through the final contests of the year which he skipped. Ben Crenshaw, 24, regained his 1973–74 touch, and was second with $257,759. He won three tourneys and was runner-up in three, including the Masters. Hale Irwin, a two-tourney winner, took third at $252,718 and Hubert Green, who won three tourneys in a row, was next at $228,031.

The Ladies PGA. Judy Rankin set a record for earnings in the Ladies Professional Golf Association by being the first to go over $100,000. She earned $150,734 and was named woman golfer of the year and took the Vare trophy for low average rounds. Mrs. Rankin won five tourneys including the $32,000 Colgate Winners Circle. The largest first-place purse in the history of women's golf, $35,000 at the Carlton Grand Prix in Los Angeles, was taken by Donna Caponi Young. JoAnne Carner captured the Open for the second time, beating Sandra Palmer, the defender, by two strokes in an 18-hole play-off.

The Amateurs. Dick Siderowf, of Westport, Conn., became the third American to win the British Amateur two times. He had won before in 1973 and joined Lawson Little and Frank Stranahan. Bill Sander of Kenmore, Wash., defeated Parker Moore, of Laurens, S. C., 8 and 6, in the final of the U. S. Amateur. Eddie Mudd of Morehead, Ky., won the Public Links title. Donna Horton of Jacksonville, Fla., captured the women's U. S. amateur.

BILL BRADDOCK

GOLF

Men's Individual Champions
U. S. Open—Jerry Pate (277)
British Open—Johnny Miller (279)
Masters—Ray Floyd (271)
PGA Tourney—Dave Stockton (281)
Canadian Open—Jerry Pate (267)
Tournament of Champions—Don January (277)
World Series of Golf—Jack Nicklaus (275)

Pro Team
Curtis Cup—United States
World Cup—United States

PGA Tournament Winners
Tucson Open—Johnny Miller (274)
Phoenix Open—Bob Gilder (268)
Bing Crosby Pro-Am—Ben Crenshaw (283)
Hawaiian Open—Ben Crenshaw (270)
Bob Hope Desert Classic—Johnny Miller (344)
San Diego Open—J. C. Snead (272)
Los Angeles Open—Hale Irwin (272)
Tallahassee Open—Gary Koch (277)
Nelson Classic—Mark Hayes (273)
Western Open—Al Geiberger (288)
Westchester Classic—David Graham (272)
Hartford Open—Rik Massengale (266)
Kaiser International—J. S. Snead (274)

Men's Individual Amateur Champions
British Amateur—Dick Siderowf
U. S. Amateur—Bill Sander
World Amateur—Britain-Ireland

Women's Individual Pro Champions
U. S. Open—JoAnne Carner (292)
LPGA Tourney—Betty Burfeindt (287)

Other LPGA Tour Winners
Orange Blossom—JoAnne Carner (209)
Colgate Winners Circle: Judy Rankin (285)

Women's Individual Amateur Champions
U. S. Amateur—Donna Horton
World Amateur—Nancy Lopez and Debbie Massey

HOCKEY

During 1976, the Montreal Canadiens won the Stanley Cup, two Soviet teams staged a series of exhibition games against National Hockey League (NHL) teams, the Winnipeg Jets took their first Avco Cup, and the first Canada Cup international hockey series was held.

NHL. In May 1976, another Stanley Cup championship banner—number 17—was hung from the rafters at the Forum in Montreal. It was fitting tribute to a Canadiens team that—statistically, at least—ranks as one of Montreal's best teams in NHL history. The Canadiens ended two years of frustration by setting several records and by defeating the defending champion Philadelphia Flyers in the championship round of the play-offs.

The Canadiens, who also had won two Stanley Cups prior to the official formation of the NHL, posted four consecutive victories over Philadelphia—4–3, 2–1, 3–2, and 5–3—to capture the best-of-seven series. Not only did it return Montreal to prominence as the league champion, but it also prevented the Flyers from becoming the first American team in history to win three consecutive cups.

Although the Stanley Cup had been the Canadiens' ultimate objective, coach Scotty Bowman's primary goal had been winning the Vezina Trophy for fewest goals allowed. And, when goalies Ken Dryden and backup Michel (Bunny) Larocque combined to allow the opposition only 174 goals in 80 regular-season games—an average of 2.17 goals-against—the Canadiens had breezed to their divisional title just as Bowman predicted.

But other honors came their way as well. Their 58 victories (against 11 losses and 11 ties) constituted a new league record as did their 127 total points in the league standings. Meanwhile, Guy Lafleur, their speedy winger, won the individual scoring championship with 125 points, six more than Bobby Clarke of the Flyers.

The Canadiens won 12 of 13 play-off games en route to victories in three consecutive best-of-seven series. After earning a bye in the opening round, Montreal proved too strong for the Chicago Black Hawks and beat them four straight. They continued their winning ways against the New York Islanders in the semifinals, clinching the series in five games after the Islanders had posted a victory in game four.

Then came the matchup against Philadelphia, which had won its best-of-seven quarter-final series in the full seven games over the Toronto Maple Leafs and its ensuing semifinal series in five games over the Boston Bruins. In the championship round, the Canadiens scored only 14 goals in the four games but their rugged defensive play kept the Flyers bottled up offensively. Philadelphia's only measure of consolation was having star forward Reggie Leach win the Conn Smythe Trophy as the most valuable

Canada and Czechoslovakia battle for the championship of the Canada Cup Series. Canada won the new tournament.

player throughout the playoffs. Leach wound up with 19 goals, breaking the record of 15 set by the Canadiens' Yvan Cournoyer in 1973.

In addition to Montreal, division champions during regular-season play had been Philadelphia, Boston, and Chicago. Boston was without the services of Bobby Orr, one of the game's most celebrated stars, who underwent knee surgery and played in only a handful of games. The Bruins' concern for his future prompted them to be involved in one of the most heralded player transactions in league history. The Bruins traded their super scorer Phil Esposito and Carol Vadnais to the New York Rangers in return for star defenseman Brad Park, Jean Ratelle, and minor leaguer Joe Zanussi. In June, Orr became a free agent and then agreed to sign a contract with the Chicago Black Hawks.

Soviet Tour. One of the highlights of the NHL season was a series of eight exhibition games between league members and two touring teams from the Soviet Union, the first time NHL clubs had played them. The Soviet Wings won three of four games—victories over the Chicago Black Hawks, Pittsburgh Penguins, and N. Y. Islanders—but suffered a defeat against the Buffalo Sabres. The Soviet Central Army defeated the Rangers and the Boston Bruins, tied the Canadiens, and was beaten by Philadelphia.

WHA. In the World Hockey Association, the Winnipeg Jets captured the Avco Cup by taking the play-off championship in the final series against the Houston Aeros, winning four straight games. It was the Jets' first title and ended at a pair the consecutive championships by the Aeros, who featured the father-sons

combination of the legendary Gordie Howe, 49, playing with sons Mark and Marty.

Marc Tardif of the Quebec Nordiques reigned as scoring champion with 148 points. However, he ended the season in a hospital bed with a brain contusion and other injuries. Tardif was assaulted during an opening round play-off game against Winnipeg in Quebec Coliseum. A Winnipeg player, Rick Jodzio, was scheduled to face criminal prosecution.

Canada Cup Series. Buoyed by Rogatien Vachon's goaltending and Bobby Orr's all-around play, Canada won the first international series involving North American professionals and European national teams.

Canada defeated Czechoslovakia two straight games in the best-of-three championship finals after finishing one-two in the five-game preliminaries. Orr's two goals triggered a 6–0 shutout in the opener and Darryl Sittler's overtime goal sparked a 5–4 victory in the deciding game. Earlier, Canada had beaten the U. S. S. R., Sweden, Finland, and the United States and had lost only to Czechoslovakia, 1–0. The Czechs had defeated Russia and Finland, lost to Sweden, and been tied, 4–4, by the United States.

Vachon, who allowed only 10 goals in seven games, was named the top Canadian in the tournament. Other teams' MVPs were Milan Novy, Czechoslovakia; Borje Salming, Sweden; Robbie Ftorek, United States; Matti Hagman, Finland; and goaltender Vladislav Tretiak, Russia. Despite poor knees, Orr was selected the top player in the tournament.

ED CONRAD

Sports Department, "The Gazette," Montreal

HOCKEY

National Hockey League
(Final Standings, 1975–76)
Prince of Wales Conference

Norris Division	W	L	T	Goals For	Goals Against	Pts.
Montreal	58	11	11	337	174	127
Los Angeles	38	33	9	263	265	85
Pittsburgh	35	33	12	339	303	82
Detroit	26	44	10	226	300	62
Washington	11	59	10	224	394	32
Adams Division						
Boston	48	15	17	313	237	113
Buffalo	46	21	13	339	240	105
Toronto	34	31	15	294	276	83
California	27	42	11	250	278	65

Campbell Conference

Patrick Division	W	L	T	Goals For	Goals Against	Pts.
Philadelphia	51	13	16	348	209	118
New York Islanders	42	21	17	297	190	101
Atlanta	35	33	12	262	237	82
N.Y. Rangers	29	42	9	262	333	67
Smythe Division						
Chicago	32	30	18	254	261	82
Vancouver	33	32	15	271	272	81
St. Louis	29	37	14	249	290	72
Minnesota	20	53	7	195	303	47
Kansas City	12	56	12	190	351	36

Stanley Cup: Montreal Canadiens

Individual Honors

Hart Trophy (most valuable): Bobby Clarke, Philadelphia Flyers
Ross Trophy (leading scorer): Guy Lafleur, Montreal Canadiens
Norris Trophy (best defenseman): Denis Potvin, New York Islanders
Lady Bing Trophy (sportsmanship): Jean Ratelle, Boston Bruins
Vezina Trophy (goalie): Ken Dryden, Montreal Canadiens
Calder Trophy (rookie of the year): Bryan Trottier, New York Islanders
Masterton Trophy (perserverance): Rod Gilbert, New York Rangers
Conn Smythe Trophy (most valuable in play-offs): Reggie Leach, Philadelphia Flyers

World Hockey Association
(Final Standings, 1975–76)

East Division	W	L	T	Goals For	Goals Against	Pts.
Indianapolis	35	39	6	245	247	76
Cleveland	35	40	5	273	279	75
N. England	33	40	7	255	290	73
Cincinnati	35	44	1	285	340	71
West Division						
Houston	53	27	0	341	263	106
Phoenix	39	35	6	302	287	84
San Diego	36	38	6	303	290	78
Canadian Division						
Winnipeg	52	27	2	345	254	106
Quebec	50	27	4	371	316	104
Calgary	41	35	4	307	282	86
Edmonton	27	49	5	268	345	59
Toronto	24	52	5	335	398	53

Avco Cup: Winnipeg Jets

Individual Honors

Most Valuable Player: Marc Tardif, Quebec
Defenseman of the Year: Paul Shmyr, Cleveland
Most Sportsmanlike: Vaclav Nedomansky, Toronto
Rookie of the Year: Mark Napier, Toronto
Gordie Howe Award (most valuable in play-offs): Ulf Nilsson, Winnipeg Jets
Goalie: Michael Tion, Indianapolis
Coach of the Year: Bobby Kromm, Winnipeg

Intercollegiate Champions

NCAA: University of Minnesota
Canadian: University of Toronto

Amateur Hockey Association of the United States
National Champions

Pee Wee: Chicago
Bantam: Ecorse, Mich.
Midget: Bloomfield, Mich.
Junior B: Springfield, Mass.
Junior A: Austin, Minn.

HORSE RACING

Forego, 6-year-old campaigner owned by the Lazy F Ranch, won six of eight starts during the season, en route to capturing Horse of the Year acclaim for the third straight year.

Forego came through with powerful stretch runs to win his final two starts of the year, the Woodward and Marlboro Cup handicaps. Ridden by Bill Shoemaker, he carried 135 pounds (60.7 kg) in the Woodward and 137 (61.6 kg) in the Marlboro Cup, conceding 18 pounds (13 kg) to runner-up Honest Pleasure in the latter race, which Forego won by a head in a dramatic finish. "It was one of the greatest horse races I've ever been in or seen," Shoemaker said after the Marlboro Cup. "I've ridden a lot of horses, but this has got to be the best."

Forego's 1976 earnings of $491,701 increased his career bankroll to $1,655,217, third on the all-time list of money winners behind Kelso ($1,977,896) and Round Table ($1,749,869).

Bold Forbes, winner of the Kentucky Derby and Belmont, ruled as the top 3-year-old colt of 1976. Ridden by Angel Cordero, Jr., Bold Forbes covered the Derby's mile and a quarter (2 km) in 2:01.6. Finishing second in the Churchill Downs classic was Honest Pleasure, who went off as the strongest favorite in the race since the Calumet Farm entry of Citation and Coaltown in 1948. Elocutionist, third in the Derby, won the Preakness.

HORSE RACING

Major U.S. Races of 1976

Alabama Stakes: Optimistic Gal, $48,555 (winner's prize)
Belmont Stakes: Bold Forbes, $117,000
Brooklyn Handicap: Forego, $67,860
Champagne Stakes: Seattle Slew, $82,350
Champions Invitational Handicap: King Pellinore, $240,000
Coaching Club American Oaks: Revidere, $68,640
Flamingo: Honest Pleasure, $85,605
Florida Derby: Honest Pleasure, $91,440
Hollywood Derby: Crystal Water, $152,750
Hollywood Gold Cup: Pay Tribute, $150,000
Hollywood Invitational Handicap: Dahlia, $120,000
Jockey Club Gold Cup: Great Contractor, $201,360
Kentucky Derby: Bold Forbes, $165,200
Marlboro Cup Handicap: Forego, $170,220
Metropolitan Handicap: Forego, $66,660
Preakness Stakes: Elocutionist, $129,700
Santa Anita Derby: An Act, $97,700
Santa Anita Handicap: Royal Glint, $155,900
Suburban Handicap: Foolish Pleasure, $65,280
Travers: Honest Pleasure, $65,040
United Nations Handicap: Intrepid Hero, $65,000
Washington, D.C., International: Youth, $100,000
Wood Memorial: Bold Forbes, $67,560
Woodward Handicap: Forego, $103,920

Major U.S. Harness Races of 1976

Adios: Armbro Ranger, $43,449
Cane Pace: Keystone Ore, $100,000
Fox Stake: Crash, $52,861
Hambletonian: Steve Lobell, $131,762
Kentucky Futurity: Quick Pay, $43,600
Little Brown Jug: Keystone Ore, $56,905
Messenger Stake: Windshield Wiper, $80,645
Monticello-OTB Classic: Oil Burner, $131,250
Roosevelt International: Equileo, $100,000
Yonkers Trot: Steve Lobell, $101,002

UPI

Bold Forbes (8), ridden by jockey Angel Cordero, Jr., wins the Belmont Stakes. McKenzie Bridge is second and Great Contractor finishes third.

Revidere won the 3-year-old filly championship with a 1976 record of eight victories, one second, and one third in 10 starts.

Cordero established a single-season record for earnings—his mounts earning $4,709,500. The old record was $4,251,060.

Harness Racing. Jade Prince, a 2-year-old pacer trained and driven by Jack Kopas, set an all-age world race record of 1:54.2 at the Lexington Red Mile in the Fayette Pace.

Quarter Horse Racing. Real Wind won the first prize of $330,000 in the All-American Futurity at Ruidoso Downs.

Sales. A yearling son of 1973 Triple Crown champion Secretariat sold for $1.5 million and Queen Sucree, dam of 1974 Kentucky Derby winner Cannonade, brought $1 million. Never before had a horse sold for seven figures at public auction.

JIM BOLUS, *"The Courier-Journal,"* Louisville

SAILING

The merging of three ocean races in late June filled the sea lanes between Bermuda and Newport, R. I., and led to the greatest assemblage of sailing ships in this century. One of the principal reasons for the armada was Operation Sail, designed to present a huge naval parade on the Hudson River in New York on July 4 as a segment of the U. S. bicentennial celebration. Its schedule intertwined with the biennial running of the Newport-Bermuda race and a trans-Atlantic single-handed race.

Operation Sail, aided by the American Sail Training Association, brought 16 tall ships, old windjammers, and 77 smaller craft (60 of them manned by 3,000 cadet trainees) across the Atlantic Ocean. The big ships ran from 241 feet (72 m) to the Russian 378-foot (113 m) Kruzenshtern. They left Plymouth, England, May 2, for the Canary Islands. They then sailed to Bermuda, reaching there between June 8–13. The ships were off for Newport, June 20.

En route to Newport they passed the fleet of 161 racing yachts which started the 635-mile (1,016 km) run to Bermuda, June 18. The only thing not in the area was a good sailing wind. The tall ships finished the passage by motor. *Tovarishch,* a Soviet vessel, was declared the overall winner. Al Van Metre's *Running Tide,* a 60-foot (18 m) sloop, won the race to Bermuda.

Meanwhile the first of the 125 single-handed sailers who left Plymouth, June 5, reached Newport, June 29. Eric Tabarly of France, in *Pen Duick VI,* won the 3,000-mile (4,800 km) race in 23 days, 20 hours, and 12 minutes.

BILL BRADDOCK

SOCCER

It was an excellent year for soccer. The year showed an overall commitment to the new concepts of total soccer—that is, versatility, adventure, and attack. The European Nations Cup final, held in Yugoslavia, was of special brilliance. Although the Dutch star was eclipsed, the Czechs, who beat them, played perhaps their best soccer ever. The Czech team added speed to their traditional short passing skill, and beat the West Germans, the title holders, in the final in Belgrade. They won by a series of penalty kicks in extra time. Both teams distinguished themselves enormously.

The West Germans, World Cup title holders, continued to use Franz Beckenbauer as a mobile sweeper behind the back four defenders. The Czechs, Yugoslavs, and Dutch were more orthodox, but perpetually threw defenders into the attack.

A few weeks previously Beckenbauer's club, Bayern Munich, had won its third consecutive European Cup, beating Saint Étienne, the French champions, 1–0, in a dazzling final in Glasgow. The only goal was scored after a free kick by Roth. The French team, the first to reach the final since Reims in 1959, hit the bar twice and was most unlucky to lose.

In the United States, where interest in soccer continued to increase at a surprising pace, a Bicentennial Tournament was played in May. It included teams from Italy, England, and Brazil. A hotchpotch Team America also participated. The tournament was watched by large crowds, was won by the Brazilians, and saw the revival of an England team that had been in the doldrums. Meanwhile, the New York Cosmos, backed by Warner Communications, were building a new stadium in New Jersey and added Giorgio Chianaglia, a center-forward, to their roster.

The qualifying tournament for the 1978 World Cup, to be held in Argentina, began. Johan Cruff of Holland announced that it was unlikely that he would participate.

BRIAN GLANVILLE, *"Sunday Times,"* London

SOCCER

British Champions

English Association Cup: Southampton
English League Cup: Manchester City
Scottish Association Cup: Glasgow Rangers
English League, First Division: Liverpool
English League, Premier Division: Glasgow Rangers

European Champions

European Federation Cup: Liverpool
European Nations Cup: Czechoslovakia
European Cup of Cups: Anderlecht, Belgium
European Supercup: Anderlecht, Belgium

North American Soccer League: Toronto Metros-Croatia

U. S. Champions

Amateur Cup: Bavarian Blue Ribbon
Challenge Cup: San Francisco AC

Collegiate Champions

N. C. A. A. Division I: University of San Francisco
N. C. A. A. Division II: Loyola, Baltimore
N. C. A. A. Division III: Brandeis
N. A. I. A.: Simon Fraser

SWIMMING

It seemed highly improbable after the complete inundation of records in the Olympics that any world marks would be made in the U. S. outdoor meet, August 11–14. But at Philadelphia, Jonty Skinner swam 100 meters freestyle in 49.44 seconds, bettering the incredible performance of Jim Montgomery, the first to go under 50 seconds with 49.99. Skinner of South Africa, who attends the University of Alabama, had tried unsuccessfully to become an American citizen so that he could compete in the Olympics.

Several records were smashed before the Olympic Games, especially by the East German women in their trials, June 1–5. All but two women's marks were broken as there were 25 swims under world record time. Two of these were by Roger Pytell, who wiped out Mark Spitz's record for the 100-meter butterfly, once in the preliminaries and again in the final with 1:59.63. His record lasted only until the Olympics. Those marks that survived the Montreal Games were: 1:01.5 in the 100-meter backstroke by Ulrike Richter; 2:12.47 in the 200-meter backstroke by Birgit Treiber, and 2:17.64 in the 200-meter individual medley by Kornelia Ender who broke one world record on each of the five days of the meet.

In the U. S. trials five records were set, two by Brian Goodell—400 and 1,500 meters freestyle, which he bettered in Montreal. The only trials record to remain was for 800 meters captured by Bobby Hackett. He swam 800-meters in 8:01.54 during the 1,500-meter race won by Brian Goodell.

See also OLYMPIC GAMES (pages 452–56).

BILL BRADDOCK

SWIMMING

Men's U. S. Long-Course Champions

100-Meter Freestyle: Jonty Skinner, Jacksonville, Fla.
200-Meter Freestyle: Mark Greenwood, Fresno, Calif.
400-Meter Freestyle: Casey Converse, Mission Viejo, Calif.
1,500-Meter Freestyle: Casey Converse
100-Meter Backstroke: John Naber, Ladera Oaks, Calif.
200-Meter Backstroke: John Naber
100-Meter Breaststroke: John Hencken, Santa Clara, Calif.
200-Meter Breaststroke: John Hencken
100-Meter Butterfly: Greg Janenberg, Newton Square, Pa.
200-Meter Butterfly: Bill Forrester, Jacksonville, Fla.
200-Meter Ind. Medley: Steve Furniss, Long Beach, Calif.
400-Meter Ind. Medley: Jesse Vassallo, Mission Viejo, Calif.
400-Meter Freestyle Relay: Central Jersey A. C.
400-Meter Medley Relay: Santa Clara Swim Club
800-Meter Freestyle Relay: Mission Viejo, Calif.
Team: Mission Viejo Nadadores

Women's U. S. Long-Course

100-Meter Freestyle: Jill Sterkel, El Monte, Calif.
200-Meter Freestyle: Kim Peyton, Portland, Ore.
400-Meter Freestyle: Rebecca Perrott, New Zealand
1,500-Meter Freestyle: Evie Kosenkranius, Seattle
100-Meter Backstroke: Linda Jezek, Santa Clara
200-Meter Backstroke: Linda Jezek
100-Meter Breaststroke: Dawn Rodighiero, Mission Viejo
200-Meter Breaststroke: Dawn Rodighiero
100-Meter Butterfly: Wendy Boglioli, Ocean City, N. J.
200-Meter Butterfly: Alice Browne, Mission Viejo
200-Meter Ind. Medley: Kathy Heddy, Summit, N. J.
400-Meter Ind. Medley: Donnalee Wennerstrom, West Valley, Calif.
400-Meter Freestyle Relay: El Monte (Calif.) A. C.
400-Meter Medley Relay: Central Jersey A. C.
800-Meter Freestyle Relay: Central Jersey A. C.
Team: Mission Viejo Nadadores

TENNIS

For tennis, 1976 was a year of consolidation. It has been eight years since tennis became open and the intervening period has been packed with polemic, political wars, player strikes, and an all-around selfishness that ill befit the game's image. As the year ended, the guns of struggle were silent and happily had been replaced by the arsenal of Bjorn Borg, Jimmy Connors, and Chris Evert. The next few years will determine the ultimate direction of all tennis.

The pro women dominated the news and not because of their on-court accomplishments. In the past, the men pros have noisily put their act together through a strong players' union (the ATP), and now the women are flexing their own muscle in the exact same union form, the WTA.

Led by Ms. Evert, the ladies insisted on prize money equal to the men at Wimbledon 1977 and received 75% of parity which avoided their threatened boycott. Forest Hills already had succumbed on the strength of Billie Jean King's 1974 efforts. The irony is that 1977 will be a sorry year for lady superstars. The distaff field once included Evert, King, Margaret Court, and Evonne Goolagong, but now only Chris Evert is available for all of the 1977 season, and she cannot play 52 weeks a year just to please fans and tournament directors.

The tour suffered its first setback when King retired, attempted a futile comeback, and quickly retreated to semiactive status as a doubles player for the New York Apples (née New York Sets) of World Team Tennis. Margaret Court has jumped back and forth several times from the land of the retired but she will never again commit herself to the full tournament grind. And Evonne Goolagong is pregnant and will not

be available until after midseason. The depth of talent on the women's tour after these magical four drops off rapidly.

Typical of the tone of consolidation for the year was the record of World Team Tennis which reduced its number of franchises from 16 to 10 and signed virtually every top woman player including two well known "rookies," Evert and Martina Navratilova. WTT was still unsuccessful in luring the top men to its ranks, although Ilie Nastase and Rod Laver both joined WTT rosters. Attendance grew uniformly around the league though surprisingly New York, which boasts the game's ranking senior citizen, Billie Jean King, floundered in the obscurity of the Nassau Coliseum. Financial losses by each team were cut drastically but they are losses nonetheless, and one wonders when sound business mentality will prevail among owners of sports franchises.

Chris Evert played only two of the Grand Slam Championships (Australian, Wimbledon, French and U.S. titles) because of her team tennis commitments. She won both Wimbledon and Forest Hills, and clearly established herself as the world's number one with Evonne Goolagong a bridesmaid's distance away.

One of the thorniest issues to confront any sport crashed onto the tennis scene at summer's end when Dr. Renee Richards, a 41-year-old transsexual, applied for entry to Forest Hills. Ironically, the women balked with matronly distress at the proposition that Richards be allowed in their tournaments. They insisted on a chromosome test at the Open to determine the sex of all women players. Dr. Richards refused on the grounds that chromosome patterns were the subject of limited laboratory study. The ladies remained stubborn and Ms. Richards was not allowed to compete.

UPI

Jimmy Connors captured the U. S. Open men's singles title and went on to be proclaimed "number one."

Victory was common for tennis star Chris Evert. In July she won the women's singles title at Wimbledon (*far right*); two months later she dominated the U. S. Open.

PHOTOS UPI

Jimmy Connors has never been less than number one in the world for the three years the ATP computer ranking list has existed. However, there were a number of year-end unofficial world rankings by the tennis magazines which for some unknown reason carry great authoritative weight with the fans. Prior to the Commercial Union Masters in December, the world's number one was a virtual toss of the racquet between Jimmy Connors and Bjorn Borg. The 20-year-old Swede won WCT and Wimbledon yet lost to Connors in a thrilling four set U. S. Open final. The dramatic showdown at the Masters in Houston never materialized and Connors was ranked number one all alone.

EUGENE L. SCOTT, *"Tennis Week"*

TENNIS

Major Tournaments

Davis Cup–Semi Finals: Chile defeated U. S. S. R. by default; Italy defeated Australia 3–2. (Italy won finals.)

Federation Cup (women): United States defeated Australia 2–1 in final.

U. S. Open: Men's Singles: Jimmy Connors*; Women's Singles: Chris Evert; Men's Doubles: Marty Riessen and Tom Okker, Netherlands; Women's Doubles: Linky Boshoff and Ilana Kloss, South Africa; Mixed Doubles: Billie Jean King and Phil Dent, Australia; Junior Men's Singles: Ricardo Ycaza, Ecuador; Junior Women's Singles: Marise Kruger, South Africa; Men's 35 Singles: Marty Riessen; Men's Hall of Fame Doubles: Bob Hewitt, South Africa and Ham Richardson.

National Men's Indoor Open: Singles: Ilie Nastase, Rumania; Doubles: Fred McNair and Sherwood Stewart.

National Women's Indoor Open: Singles: Virginia Wade, Great Britain; Doubles: Françoise Durr, France, and Rosemary Casals.

National Clay Court: Men's Singles: Jimmy Connors; Women's Singles: Kathy May; Men's Doubles: Brian Gottfried and Raul Ramirez, Mexico; Women's Doubles: Linky Boshoff and Ilana Kloss, South Africa.

National Amateur Grass Court: Men's Singles: Chris Lewis; Women's Singles: Diane Desfor; Men's Doubles: Tim Garcia and Colon Nunez; Women's Doubles: Barbara Hallquist and Barbara Jordan; Mixed Doubles: Cindy Thomas and Chris Lewis.

Other Countries

Wimbledon: Men's Singles: Bjorn Borg, Sweden; Women's Singles: Chris Evert; Men's Doubles: Brian Gottfried and Raul Ramirez, Mexico; Women's Doubles: Chris Evert and Martina Navratilova; Mixed Doubles: Françoise Durr, France and Tony Roche, Australia; Junior Men: Heinz Guenthardt, Switzerland; Junior Women: Natasha Chmyreva U. S. S. R.

Australian Open: Men's Singles: Mark Edmondson, Australia; Women's Singles: Evonne Goolagong, Australia; Men's Doubles: John Newcombe and Tony Roche, Australia; Women's Doubles: Evonne Goolagong and Helen Gourlay, Australia.

French Open: Men's Singles: Adriano Panatta, Italy; Women's Singles: Sue Barker, Great Britain; Men's Doubles: Fred McNair and Sherwood Stewart; Women's Doubles: Fiorella Bonicelli, Uruguay and Gail Lovera, France.

Italian Open: Men's Singles: Adriano Panatta, Italy; Women's Singles: Mima Jausovec, Yugoslavia; Men's Doubles: Brian Gottfried and Raul Ramirez, Mexico; Women's Doubles: Linky Boshoff and Ilana Kloss, South Africa.

Canadian Open: Men's Singles: Guillermo Vilas, Argentina; Men's Doubles: Bob Hewitt, South Africa and Raul Ramirez, Mexico.

Professional Champions

U. S. Championship: Bjorn Borg, Sweden.

World Championship Tennis Tour final: Singles: Bjorn Borg, Sweden; Doubles: Wojtek Fibak, Poland and Karl Meiler, Germany.

Virginia Slims Tour final: Singles: Evonne Goolagong, Australia; Doubles: Billie Jean King and Betty Stove.

World Team Tennis Championship: New York Sets defeated San Francisco Golden Gaters 3–0.

* Except as noted, players are U.S.

LEADING MONEY WINNERS IN 1976

World Championship Tennis Tour

Arthur Ashe	$287,813	Eddie Dibbs	$79,538
Ilie Nastase	275,362	Dick Stockton	77,975
Bjorn Borg	143,837	Harold Solomon	77,638
Raul Ramirez	105,900	Ken Rosewall	75,775
Guillermo Vilas	103,237	Bob Lutz	72,513

Virginia Slims

Evonne Goolagong	$133,675	Betty Stove	$45,425
Chris Evert	108,725	Mona Guerrant	31,000
Virginia Wade	59,100	Ann Kiyomura	27,750
Rosemary Casals	54,925	Olga Morozova	27,725
Martina Navratilova	54,575	Billie Jean King	26,200

Mac Wilkins, 25, of Portland, Oreg., set a discus record of 232 feet 6 inches (70.87 m).

UPI

TRACK AND FIELD

Performers in the field events regained the spotlight when the confrontations between Filbert Bayi and John Walker, milers, failed to materialize. The records for the pole vault and the high jump rose in exciting action, and discus and shotput marks were lengthened.

The best for the indoor pole vault was bettered five times in 42 days ending at 18 feet 3¾ inches (5.58 m) by Dan Ripley on February 20. Then outdoors, Earl Bell took the world record away from Dave Roberts with 18-7½ (5.68 m) on May 29. At the June Olympic Trials, Roberts broke his pole, borrowed Bell's, and regained the record at 18-8¼ (5.70 m). Meanwhile Dwight Stones raised the indoor high jump best to 7-6¼ (2.29 m) in New York on February 20 and to 7-6½ (2.30 m) the next night in San Diego, equaling the outdoor mark. In June he jumped the world mark to 7-7 (2.31 m). After his disappointment at the Olympics, Stones leapt 7-7¼ (2.32 m) in Philadelphia four days later.

Mac Wilkins bettered the discus record with a throw of 232 feet 6 inches (70.87 m) in June. Terry Albritton put the shot 71-8½ (21.86 m) in Honolulu in February, but his world mark was beaten by Alex Baryshnikov of the U.S.S.R. in Paris, July 10. Various factors kept Bayi and Walker apart, but Walker set a world mark of 4 minutes 51.4 seconds for 2,000 meters in Oslo, June 30. Bayi, who suffers from malaria, ran a 3:56.1 mile, third fastest indoors, at Madison Square Garden on February 27. But in Europe in late summer, he was beaten by lesser known runners.

The University of Tennessee relay team tied the world mark for 800 meters at 1:21.1 in April, and Harvey Glance, Steve Williams, and Don Quarrie equaled the 100-meter dash mark of 9.9.

Eastern European women shattered several records before and after the Olympics. Tatiana Kazankina, Soviet Union, ran 1,500 meters in 3:56; Lyudmila Bragina, U.S.S.R., bettered the June mark of 8:45.4 for 3,000 meters by Greta Waitz of Norway with 3:27.1 at College Park, Md., August 7. Rosemarie Ackerman of East Germany cleared 6-5¼ (1.96 m) in the high jump; Sigrun Siegl, a teammate hit 22-11¼ (6.99 m) in the long jump; and Ruth Fuchs, another East German, threw the javelin 226-9 (69.11 m). Faina Melnik, U.S.S.R., threw the discus 231-3 (70.49 m) in April, and Helena Fibingerova of Czechoslovakia put the shot 72-1¾ (21.99 m) in September bettering the 71-9¾ (21.89 m) of Ivanka Khristova of Bulgaria in July.

See also OLYMPIC GAMES (pages 452–57).

BILL BRADDOCK

TRACK AND FIELD

Men's U. S. Outdoor Champions

100-Meter Dash: Chris Garpenborg, Los Angeles
200-Meter Dash: Millard Hampton, San Jose, Calif.
400-Meter Dash: Maxie Parks, Los Angeles
800-Meter Run: James Robinson, Oakland, Calif.
1,500-Meter Run: Eamonn Coghlan, Ireland (Villanova)
5,000-Meter Run: Dick Buerkle, New York A. C.
10,000-Meter Run: Ed Leddy, Knoxville, Tenn.
3,000-Meter Steeplechase: Randy Smith, Striders
110-Meter Hurdles: Thomas Hill, U. S. Army
400-Meter Hurdles: Tom Andrews, Southern California
5,000-Meter Walk: Ron Laird, New York, A. C.
Pole Vault: Earl Bell, Arkansas State, Jonesboro, Ark.
High Jump: Dwight Stones, Los Angeles
Long Jump: Arnie Robinson, Los Angeles
Triple Jump: Tommy Hayes, U. S. Army
Hammer Throw: Larry Hart, New York A. C.
Javelin: Fred Luke, Seattle
Discus: Mac Wilkins, Portland, Ore.
Shotput: Terry Albritton, U. of Hawaii

Women's U. S. Outdoor Champions

100-Meter Dash: Chandra Cheeseborough, Tennessee State
200-Meter Dash: Brenda Morehead, Tennessee State
400-Meter Dash: Lorna Forde, Atoms T. C., Brooklyn
800-Meter Run: Madeline Jackson, Cleveland
1,500-Meter Run: Francie Larrieu, Long Beach, Calif.
3,000-Meter Run: Jan Merrill, Waterford, Conn.
100-Meter Hurdles: Jane Frederick, Los Angeles
400-Meter Hurdles: Arthurine Gainer, Prairie View, Tex.
Javelin: Kathy Schmidt, Los Angeles
Shotput: Maren Seidler, Chicago
Discus: Lynne Winbigler, Eugene, Ore.
Long Jump: Kathy McMillan, Raeford, N. C.
High Jump: Joni Huntley, Sheridan, Ore.
A. A. U. Pentathlon: Jane Frederick, Los Angeles

SPORTS SUMMARIES

ARCHERY—World: Men: Tommy Persson, Sweden; women: Anne-Marie Lehmann, West Germany; barebow: Jukka Virtanen, Finland; women's barebow: Shirley Sandiford, Britain. **National Archery Association:** Target: amateur: Darrell Pace, Cincinnati; professional: John Williams, Rialto, Calif.; crossbow: George Hall, Somerville, N. J.; women: amateur: Luann Ryon, Riverside, Calif.; professional: Marion Rhodes, Phoenix, Ariz.; crossbow: Carol Pelosi, Greenbelt, Md. Field: freestyle: Darrell Pace; barebow: Franklin Ditzler, Lebanon, Pa.; women: freestyle: Luann Ryon; barebow: Eunice Anderson, Tijeras, N. M. **National Field Archery Association:** Open: Kenneth Cranberg, Dallas City, Ill.; open limited: Terry Frazier, Houston, Tex.; amateur: Barry Velarde, Fort Knox, Ky.; amateur, limited: Edwin Eliason, Seattle; women: open: Janet Boatman, Alden, N. Y.; open, limited: Millie Foster, Kansas City, Mo.; amateur: Michelle Sanderson, Hastings, Minn.; amateur, limited: Valerie Gramzow, Creswell, Ore.; bowhunter: open: Hugh McConnell, Hiltons, Va.; amateur: John Saporiti, Rockford, Ill.; women: June Hardy, Houston, Tex.; barebow: open: David Hughes, Irving, Tex.; amateur: Donald Morehead, Wheaton, Ill.; women: open: Frozine Greene, Liberal, Kan.; amateur: Patricia Kramer, Fort Lauderdale, Fla.

BADMINTON—U. S. Championships: men's singles: Chris Kinard, Pasadena, Calif.; women's singles: Pam Bristol, Flint, Mich.; doubles—Don Paup, Vienna, Va., and Bruce Pontow, Chicago; women's doubles: Pam Bristol and Rosine Lemon, New York; mixed doubles: Mike Walker, Manhattan Beach, Calif., and Judianne Kelly, Norwalk, Calif.; senior singles: Jim Poole, Westminster, Calif. U. S. Open: men's singles: Paul Whetnall, England; women's singles: Gillian Gilks, England.

BOWLING—American Bowling Congress: Regular Division: singles: Mike Putzer, Oshkosh, Wisc.; doubles: Fred Willen, Sr., and Gary Voss, St. Louis; all-events: Jim Lindquist, Minneapolis; team: Andy's Pro Shop, Tucson, Ariz. Classic Division: singles: Jim Schroeder, Buffalo, N. Y.; doubles: Don Johnson, Las Vegas, Nev., and Paul Colwell, Tucson, Ariz.; all-events: Gary Fust, Des Moines, Iowa; team: Munsingwear No. 2, Minneapolis.

BRIDGE—World Team Olympiad: Brazil (Gabriel Chagas, Pedro-Apulo Assumpcaco, Gabino Cintra, Christiano Fonseca, Pedro Branco, Sergio Barbosa). Final standing: Brazil, Italy, Britain, Poland.

CANOEING—Flat water: Kayak: 500 and 1,000 meters: Steve Kelly, New York; 10,000 meters: Brent Turner, St. Charles, Ill.; women: 500 and 5,000 meters: Ann Turner, St. Charles, Ill. Canoe: 500, 1,000 and 10,000 meters: Andy Weigand, Arlington, Va.

CHESS—U. S. Championships: Open: Anatoly Lein, New York, and Leonid Shamkovich, New York (tied); women's open: Diane Savereide, Culver City, Calif.; amateur: Laszlo Ficsor, Minneapolis; women's amateur: Gwen Ratte, Norwood, Mass.; national open: Edward Formanek, Chicago, and Anthony Miles, England (tied); junior open: Steven Odendahl, Chevy Chase, Md.

CROSS-COUNTRY—AAU (10,000 meters): Rick Rojas, Los Alamos, N. M.; team: Jamul Toads, San Diego, Calif. **NCAA:** Division I (10,000 meters): Henry Rono, Washington State; team: Texas-El Paso; Division II (10,000 meters): Ralph Serna, California-Irvine; team: California-Irvine; Division III (8,000 meters): Dale Kramer, Carleton; team: North Central Illinois. **NAIA:** (5 miles): John Kebiro, Eastern New Mexico; team: Edinboro State; IC4A (5 miles): Curt Alitz, Army; women: AAU (3 miles): Janice Merrill, Waterford, Conn.; team: Los Angeles T. C.

CURLING—World: United States (defeated Scotland, 6–5, in final); **U. S. Championships:** Men: Hibbing, Minn.; women: Highland Park, Ill.; mixed: Grafton, N. D.

CYCLING—World: men's pro: Freddy Maertens, Belgium; men's pro pursuit: Francesco Moser, Italy; women's sprint: Sheila Young Ochowicz, Detroit; women's road: Kornelia Van Oosten-Hage, Netherlands. **U. S. Championships:** Track: men: sprint: Leigh Barszewski, West Allis, Wisc.; kilometer: Bob Vehe, Mount Prospect, Ill.; 10-mile: Ron Skarin, Van Nuys, Calif.; 4,000-meter pursuit: Leonard Nitz, Sacramento, Calif.; team pursuit: Southern California; women: sprint: Connie Carpenter, Madison, Wisc.; 3,000-meter pursuit: Connie Carpenter. Road: men (114 miles): Wayne Stetina, Indianapolis; women (37 miles): Connie Carpenter; veterans (41 miles): Jim Meyers, Costa Mesa, Calif.

DOG SHOWS—Westminster (New York); Best: Ch. Jo-Ni's Red Baron of Crofton, Lakeland terrier, owned by Virginia Dickson, La Habra, Calif. (3,098 dogs entered);

International (Chicago): best: Ch. Marinebull's All the Way, bulldog, owned by Karl and Joyce Dingman, Richfield, Minn. (3,206 dogs entered).

FENCING—U. S. Champions: foil: Lt. Ed. Donofrio, U. S. Marines; épée: George Masin, New York Athletic Club; saber: Thomas Losonczy, New York A. C.; women's foil: Ann O'Donnell, Salle Santelli, New York; team: foil: Wauwautosa, Wisc.; épée: New York A. C.

GYMNASTICS—AAU: Men: All-Around: Coje Saito, Mobile, Ala.; floor exercise: Ron Galimore, Tallahassee, Fla.; vault: Mike Carter, Louisiana State; rings: Vic Randozzo, New York A. C., and Todd Kuoni, Baton Rouge, La. (tied); horizontal bar: Saito; pommel horse: Ed Paul, Penn State. Women: All-Around: Roxanne Pierce, Philadelphia; floor exercise: Janice Baker, Syracuse, N. Y.; balance beam: Roxanne Pierce; vault: Ann Woods, Red Bank, N. J.; uneven parallel bars: Ann Carr, Philadelphia. NCAA: Division I: All-Around: Peter Kormann, Southern Connecticut; floor exercise: Bob Robbins, Colorado State; vault: Sam Shaw, California State-Fullerton; parallel bars: Gene Whelan, Penn State; rings: Doug Wood, Iowa State; horizontal bar: Tom Beach, California; pommel horse: Ted Marcy, Stanford; team: Penn State.

HANDBALL—United States Handball Association Champions: 4-wall: singles: Vern Roberts, Jr., Lake Forest, Ill.; doubles: Gary Rohrer, Minneapolis, and Dan O'Connor, St. Paul; masters singles: Jack Scrivens, Portland, Ore.; masters doubles: Arnold Aguilar and Gabe Enriquez, Los Angeles; golden masters singles: Murray Marcus, Miami, Fla.; golden masters doubles: Rudy Stadlberger and Tom Kelly, San Francisco.

HORSE SHOWS—American Horse Show Association Equitation Medals: saddle seat: Virginia Cable, Lima, Ohio; hunter seat: Francis C. Steinwedell, Pasadena, Calif.; stock seat: Lisa Acquire, San Juan Capistrano, Calif.; dressage: overall: Bodo Hangen, Wayne, Ill.; senior medal: Lendon Gray, Dixmont, Me.; junior medal: Kris Bobo, Cohasset, Mass.

ICE SKATING, FIGURE—World: men: John Curry, Britain; women: Dorothy Hamill, Riverside, Conn.; pairs: Irina Rodnina and Alexandr Zaitsev, U. S. S. R.; dance: Ludmila Pakhomova and Alexandr Gorshkov, U. S. S. R. **U. S. Championships:** men: Terry Kubicka, Cypress, Calif.; women: Dorothy Hamill, pairs: Tai Babilonia and Randy Gardner, Los Angeles; dance: Colleen O'Connor and Jim Millns, Colorado Springs.

ICE SKATING, SPEED—World Champions: men's all-around: Piet Kleine, Netherlands; women's all-around: Sylvia Burka, Canada; sprints: men's all-around: Johann Granath, Sweden; women's sprint: Sheila Young, Detroit. **U. S. Champions:** outdoor: men's all-around: John Wurster, Ballston Spa, N. Y.; women's all-around: Connie Carpenter, Madison, Wisc.; national indoor: men's all-around: Alan Rattray, Los Angeles; women's all-around: Celest Chlapaty, Skokie, Ill., and Peggy Hartrich, St. Louis (tied).

LACROSSE—NCAA: Division I: Cornell; Division II: Hobart. **Club:** Mount Washington L. C., Baltimore.

MOTORBOAT—World: offshore racing: Tom Gentry, Hawaii; **U. S. Champions:** offshore racing: Joel Halpern, Bronxville, N. Y.; unlimited hydroplanes: Atlas Van Lines, owned and driven by Bill Muncey, LaMesa, Calif.; distance races: Swift Hurricane; classic: Halpern; Bacardi Trophy: Preston Henn, Fort Lauderdale, Fla.; Benihana Grand Prix: Roger Penske, Reading, Pa., and Bob Magoon, Miami; Bahamas 500: Rocky Aoki, Englewood Cliffs, N. J. **Hydroplane races:** President's Cup: Olympia Beer, Billy Schumacher; Gold Cup: Miss U. S., Tom D'Eath.

MOTORCYCLE RACING—Grand U. S. Championship (Camel Pro Series): Jay Springsteen, Flint, Mich. **Motocross Champions:** 125 cc: Bob Hannah, Whittier, Calif.; 250 cc: Tony DiStefano, Morrisville, Pa.; 500 cc: Kent Howerton, San Antonio, Tex.

PARACHUTING—World: men: overall: Greg Surabko, U. S. S. R.; team: accuracy: U. S. S. R.; women: overall: Rita Klaburn, East Germany; team: accuracy: U. S.; combined: U. S. **U. S. Champions:** men: overall: Jack Brake, U. S. Army, Fort Bragg, N. C.; accuracy: Frank Paynter, Warrenton, Va.; style: Jack Brake; 10-man team: Captain Hook and His Sky Pirates, Elsinore, Calif.; women: overall: Cheryl Stearns, Scottsdale, Ariz.; accuracy: Debbie Schmidt, Joliet, Ill.; style: Marie Ledbetter, Mesa, Ariz.; 4-member team: Rainbow Flyers, Flint, Mich.

European Figure Skating Championships: Dianne de Leeuw of the Netherlands wins in free skating.

POLO—U. S. Championship: open: Willow Bend, Dallas, Tex.; Gold Cup (18–22 goals): Willow Bend; America Cup (16 goal): Boca Raton, Fla.; Continental Cup (14 goals): Jay Farm, Milwaukee; Copper Cup (10 goals): Village Farm.

RODEO—World: all-around: Tom Ferguson, Miami, Okla.; saddle bronc riding: Monte Henson, Mesquite, Tex., and Mel Hyland, Surrey, B. C. (tied); bareback bronc: Chris Ledoux, Kaycee, Wyo.; calf roping: Roy Cooper, Durant, Okla.; steer wrestling: Rick Bradley, Burkburnett, Tex.

ROWING—U. S. Champions: singles: Sean Drea, Ireland and Undine Barge Club, Philadelphia; singles dash: Jim Dietz, New York A. C.; double sculls: Dietz and Dr. Larry Klecatsky, New York A. C.; pairs: Bob Blakeley and Mike Borchelt, Potomac B. C., Washington; pairs with coxswains: John Matthews, Mark Norelius, and Ken Dreyfuss, coxswain, Vesper B. C., Philadelphia; fours: Vesper B. C.; fours with coxswains: Vesper; quads: New York A. C.; eights: Vesper; intercollegiate champions: I. R. A.; varsity: California; second varsity: Pennsylvania; pairs with coxswains: Navy; pairs without coxswains: Rutgers; fours with coxswains: Navy; fours without coxswains: Wisconsin; team (Jim Ten Eyck Trophy): Pennsylvania. **Dad Vail Trophy:** eights and overall: Coast Guard Academy. **Eastern Sprints:** varsity: Harvard; team: Rowe Cup (heavyweights): Harvard; Jope Cup (lightweights): Harvard. **Midwest Championships:** varsity: Wisconsin; women's varsity: Wisconsin; singles: Neil Helein, Wisconsin. **Western Sprints:** varsity: Washington; women: U. C. L. A. **Dual regattas:** Harvard defeated Yale; Washington defeated California; Oxford defeated Cambridge. **British Royal Henley:** diamond sculls: E. O. Hale, Australia; silver goblets (pairs): I. A. Luxford and C. D. Shinners, Australia; stewards cup (fours): British Columbia University; Wyfold cup (fours): London R. C.; ladies plate (eights): Trinity College, Hartford, Conn.; Princess Elizabeth cup (schoolboy eights): Holy Spirit High School, Absecon, N. J.; Thames cup (eights): Harvard; grand challenge cup (eights): Thames Tradesmen, London. **U. S. Women:** singles: Joan Lind, Long Beach (Calif.) R. A.; doubles: Joan Lind and Lisa Hansen, Long Beach; eights: College B. C.

RUGBY—World: British Lions. **Europe:** Wales.

SHOOTING—Grand American Trapshooting Champions: handicap: men: Frank Crevatin, Tecumseh, Ontario; women: Judith Whittenberger, Fort Wayne, Ind.; junior: James Linke, Woonsocket, S. D.; veterans: Ronald Cornwell, Washington Court House, Ohio; senior: Kenneth Kummer, Columbus, Ohio; doubles: men: Larry McKinley, Rich Hill, Mo.; women: Nyla Johnson, Chattaroy, Wash.; overall: Gene Sears, El Reno, Okla.; women: Susan Nattrass, Hamilton, Ont.; all-around: Frank Little; women: Susan Nattrass. **National Skeet Shooting Association Champions:** men: Charles Parks, Alliance, Ohio; women: Valerie Johnson, San Antonio, Tex.; junior: Alan Clark, Delmar, Calif.; junior women: Kathryn Drennan, Ada, Okla.; collegiate: Tito Killian, Trinity of Texas.

SKIING—World Cup: men: Ingemar Stenmark, Sweden; women: Rosi Mittermaier, West Germany. **U. S. Champions:** alpine: men: downhill: Greg Jones, Tahoe City, Calif.; slalom: Cary Adgate, Boyne City, Mich.; giant slalom: Geoff Bruce, Corning, N. Y.; combined: Adgate; women: downhill: Susie Patterson, Sun Valley, Idaho; slalom: Cindy Nelson, Lutsen, Minn.; giant slalom: Lindy Cochran, Richmond, Vt.; combined: Viki Fleckenstein, Syracuse, N. Y.; nordic: jumping: Jim Denney, Duluth, Minn.; veteran: Earl Murphy, Brattleboro, Vt.; junior: John Broman, Duluth, Minn.; cross-country: men: 15 and 30 kilometers: Devin Swigert, Sun Valley, Idaho; 50

kilometers: Stan Dunklee, Brattleboro, Vt.; veterans: Ole Kristensen, Alaska; women: 5, 10 and 20 kilometers: Jana Hlavaty, Chicago. **Collegiate:** (NCAA): slalom: Mike Meleski, Wyoming; giant slalom: Dave Cleveland, Dartmouth; alpine combined: Meleski; cross-country: Stan Dunklee; jumping: Kip Sungaard, Utah; nordic combined: Jack Turner, Colorado; team: Colorado and Dartmouth (tied).

SOFTBALL—U. S. Amateur Softball Association Champions: Men: fast pitch: Raybestos Cardinals, Stratford, Conn.; slow pitch: Warren Motors, Jacksonville, Fla.; 16-inch slow pitch: Republic Bank Bobcats, Chicago; modified fast pitch: Clinica, Miami, Fla. Women: fast pitch: Raybestos Brakettes, Stratford, Conn.; slow pitch: Sorrento's Pizza, Cincinnati.

SQUASH RACQUETS—U. S. Squash Racquets Association Champions: Men: singles: Peter Briggs, New York; veterans singles: Richard Radloff, Seattle; senior singles: Bob Stuckert, Milwaukee; doubles: Briggs and Ralph Howe, New York; veterans doubles: Charles Wright, Toronto, and Don Leggat, Hamilton, Ont.; senior doubles: Gordon Guyett and Eric Wiffen, Toronto.

TABLE TENNIS—U. S. Champions: Open singles: Dragutin Surbak, Yugoslavia; closed singles: Ray Guillen, Los Angeles; women's open singles: Kim Soon Ok, South Korea; women's closed singles: In Sock Bhusan, Columbus, Ohio; doubles: Surbak and Milivoj Karakasevic, Yugoslavia; women's doubles: Kim Soon Ok and Son Hye Soon, South Korea; mixed doubles: Desmond Douglas and Jill Hammersley, England.

VOLLEYBALL—U. S. Volleyball Association: Men's open: Maccabi Union, Los Angeles; Women's open: Pasadena (Tex.) Volleyball Club; senior: Olyrollers,, Long Beach, Calif.; collegiate: Penn State. **NCAA:** U. C. L. A.

WATER POLO—U. S.: Men: Concord (Calif.) Aquatics.

WATER SKIING—U. S. Champions: Men's Open: overall: Chris Redmond, Canton, Ohio; slalom: Bob LaPoint, Castro Valley, Calif.; tricks: Tony Krupa, Jackson, Mich.; jumping: Bob LaPoint; Senior: overall: Dr. J. D. Morgan, Norfolk, Va.; slalom: Morgan; tricks: Jerry Hosner, Fenton, Mich.; jumping: Morgan; Women: Open: overall: Cindy Todd, Pierson, Fla.; slalom: Cindy Todd; tricks: Cindy Todd; jumping: Linda Giddens, Eastman, Ga.; Senior: overall: Thelma Salmas, Canyon Lake, Calif.

WEIGHT LIFTING—National AAU: 114 pound class: Joel Widdell, Dewar, Iowa (424¼ pounds total); 123: John Yamauchi, Honolulu (479½); 132: Dane Hussey, St. Louis (534½); 148: Dan Cantore, Pacifica, Calif. (628); 165: Fred Lowe, East Lansing, Mich. (672¼); 181: Sam Bigler, Lancaster, Pa. (705¼); 198: Lee James, Manchester, Pa. (782½); 242: Mark Cameron, Middletown, R. I. (843¾); super-heavyweight: Bruce Wilhelm, Los Altos, Calif. (848¾).

WRESTLING—National AAU Champions: Freestyle: 105.5 pound class: Bill Rosado, Arizona W. C.; 114.5: Jim Haines, Wisconsin W. C.: 125.5 Jan Gitcho, Hawkeye W. C.; 136.5: Kiyoshi Abe, New York A. C.; 149.5 Lt. Lloyd Keaser, U. S. Marines; 163: Stan Dziedzic, New York A. C.; 180.5: Brady Hall, Los Angeles; 198: Ben Peterson, Comstock, Wisc.; 220: Russ Hellickson, Wisconsin W. C.; Heavyweight: Mike McCready, Hawkeye W. C.; outstanding wrestler: Keaser. Greco-Roman: 105.5: Karoly Kancsar, San Francisco; 114.5: Chris Sones, Hawkeye W. C.; 125.5: Bruce Thompson, Minnesota W. C.; 136.5: Hachiro Oishi, New York A. C.; 149.5: Larry Morgan, Hawkeye W. C.; 163: John Matthews, Michigan W. C.; 180.5: Dan Chandler, Minnesota W. C.; 198: Willie Williams, Mayor Daley Youth Foundation, Chicago; 220: Brad Rheingans, Minnesota W. C.; Unlimited: Mike McCready; outstanding wrestler: Thompson.

YACHTING—U. S. Yacht Racing Union Champions: Mallory Cup (men): David Crockett, Las Alamitos Y. C., Long Beach, Calif; O'Day Trophy (single-handed): Buzz Reynolds, Notre Dame University; Prince of Wales Bowl (club): Coronado (Calif.) Y. C.; Women: Adams Trophy: Galveston Bay (Tex.) Cruising Assn.; Mertz Trophy (single-handed): Kiki Saltmarsh, Little Compton, R. I.; Adams Memorial Trophy (double-handed): Diane Greene and Jennifer Lawson, Annapolis, Md. Juniors: Sears Cup (single-handed): Potomac River S. A., Washington; Smythe Trophy (single-handed): Scott Young, White Rock B. C., Dallas, Tex.; Bemis Trophy (double-handed): Chris Lloyd and Mark Perkins, Shrewbury, Y. C., Fair Haven, N. J.; National Sea Exploring Championship: Brian Kfoury and Wesley Stillwell, Newport Beach, California. College: Fowle Trophy (overall): Tufts; Foster Trophy (single-handed): James McCreary, Tufts; women: Princeton. **Distant Races:** Newport to Bermuda (635 miles): Running Tide (Class A) Al Van Metre, Alexandria, Va., 3 days, 14 hours; Trans-Atlantc single-handed (Plymouth, England to Newport, R. I., 3,000 miles): Pen Duick VI, Eric Tabarly, France; 23:20:12; Trans-Pacific (Los Angeles to Tahiti, 3,571 miles): Bravura, Irving Loube, Oakland, Calif.; 21:13:37:37; Trans-Pacific (Victoria, B. C. to Maui, Hawaii, 2,310 miles): Race Passage, Paul McCullough, Bremerton, Wash.; 10:19:37:14.

Sri Lanka's Prime Minister Bandaranaike was president of the nonaligned nations conference held in Colombo.

SRI LANKA (Ceylon)

The highlight of 1976 in Sri Lanka was the hosting of the summit conference of nonaligned nations in August. The economy, already in bad shape, steadily deteriorated.

The Summit. The Fifth Conference of Heads of State or Government of Non-Aligned Countries was held in Colombo, August 16–19. It was the largest one so far and the first to be held in Asia. In her inaugural address as president of the conference Prime Minister Sirimavo Bandaranaike endorsed the concept of a more equitable economic and political order, called for "resolute opposition to imperialism" and for the expansion of détente "to all the regions of the world," and proposed a commercial bank for the third world.

Foreign Affairs. Sri Lanka and China concluded an agreement in January, providing for

---
SRI LANKA · Information Highlights

Official Name: Republic of Sri Lanka.
Location: Island off the southeastern coast of India.
Area: 25,332 square miles (65,610 km²).
Population (1976 est.): 14,000,000.
Chief City (1973 est.): Colombo, the capital, 890,000.
Government: *Head of state,* William Gopallawa, president (took office May 1972). *Head of government,* Mrs. Sirimavo Bandaranaike, prime minister (took office May 1970).
Monetary Unit: Rupee (8.68 rupees equal U. S.$1, Aug. 1976).
Gross National Product (1975 est.): $3,300,000,000.
Manufacturing (major products): Milled rice, chemicals.
Major Agricultural Products: Tea, rubber, coconuts.
Foreign Trade (1975): *Exports,* $559,000,000; *imports,* $745,000,000.

Chinese aid for flood protection and river-valley development projects. China also agreed to export 200,000 tons of rice in exchange for 67,000 tons of Sri Lankan rubber, and to trade in tea and other commodities.

On March 23 representatives of Sri Lanka and India signed an agreement on their maritime boundaries, the first to incorporate formally the concept of a 200-mile economic zone.

Economy. Inflation remained very high, and the trade deficit rose to record proportions. The dismal economic picture was made even worse by widespread strikes in March and the worst drought in living memory. The government fixed prices of 75 essential commodities, including rice and other food items, and launched an anti-profiteering and anti-hoarding campaign.

Politics. Prime Minister Bandaranaike was faced with mounting opposition in the parliament from the Trotskyite Lanka Sama Samaj party, with which she had been allied in a United Front until September 1975, as well as from the major opposition group, the United National party. Her own Sri Lanka Freedom party seemed to be losing support, leaving the results of the next general election, scheduled in 1977, very much in doubt.

NORMAN D. PALMER
University of Pennsylvania

STAMP COLLECTING

The U. S. Postal Service's 1976 stamp program, devised to commemorate the nation's 200th birthday, provoked collectors to vehement charges of exploitation and "rip-off".

Contrary to a promise in February that Washington would adopt more conservative stamp-issuing policies, the number of costly issues exceeded that of previous years. Especially "abusive" were the multiple-stamp units, featuring designs that spread over three or more stamps. Among these issues were the triptych of three *se tenant* (joined together) 13-cent stamps to accommodate the "Spirit of '76" painting. It took four jumbo-size stamps to reproduce John Trumbull's "Signing of the Declaration of Independence." In 1869 that masterpiece was engraved on a single stamp measuring less than a square inch. The Olympics commemoratives also required four 13-cent stamps. Those honoring the states of the Union made up a pane of 50 13-cent stamps, each showing a state flag.

Most complaints, however, were leveled at the four souvenir sheets issued in connection with the INTERPHIL '76 stamps show in Philadelphia. These comprised four reproductions of revolution-period paintings, in each of which five stamps (13, 18, 24, and 31 cents) were placed in jigsaw-puzzle fashion. The sheets were deliberately so designed that their large size of 8 x 6 inches (20 x 15 cm) did not fit on any normal envelope. Furthermore, one had to buy complete sets of four sheets at $4.30.

SELECTED U. S. COMMEMORATIVE STAMPS, 1976

Subject	Denomination	Date
Spirit of '76	3x13¢	Jan. 1
Air Mails	25¢,31¢	Jan. 2
INTERPHIL	13¢	Jan. 17
State Flags	50x13¢	Feb. 23
Freedom (coil)	9¢	March 5
Telephone Centenary	13¢	March 10
Farmers (envelope)	13¢	March 15
Aviation Jubilee	13¢	March 19
Chemistry Centenary	13¢	April 6
Bulk Mail	7.9¢	April 23
Bicentennial sheets	$4.30	May 29
Franklin Bicentennial	13¢	June 1
American Doctors (envelope)	13¢	June 30
Declaration Bicentennial	4x13¢	July 4
Montreal Olympics	13¢	July 16
American Craftsmen (envelope)	13¢	Aug. 6
Bicentennial (envelope)	13¢	Oct. 15
Christmas	2x13¢	Oct. 27

The INTERPHIL '76 show was the 7th international philatelic competition held in the United States since 1913 and, with some 20,000 American and foreign collectors, the 3d largest in 61 years. Other international shows were staged in Switzerland, Denmark, and Italy.

During 1976 the United Nations marked the 25th anniversary of its first stamps, an event which both the organization and member countries commemorated with special issues. Other commemoratives observed the telephone centenary, the U. S. Bicentennial, and the Olympics.

ERNEST A. KEHR, *Stamp News Bureau*

STOCKS AND BONDS

The stock market moved higher in 1976, extending the rally that got under way the prior year. To be sure, the advance was not as spectacular as the rally of 1975—a rally that ranked as one of the sharpest in modern history. Nevertheless, the Standard & Poor's 500-Stock Composite Index managed to post a respectable 19% year-to-year gain. Most of the increase came within the first two months of the year. In subsequent months, stock prices backed and filled within a fairly narrow range.

The bond market staged one of the sharpest rallies in post-depression history. The advance reflected the Federal Reserve Board's loosening of the monetary reins. Interest rates and bond yields declined dramatically.

Stock Prices. The stock market began 1976 on an optimistic note. After moving back and forth in a broad trading range for the last five months of 1975, stock prices began to rise toward the end of December and gathered momentum in January. Led by better-grade issues, stock prices participated in a broad advance. Volume was some of the heaviest on record. By the end of January, the S&P 500-index had posted a 12% gain in just one month. This was the best showing for this index since October 1974—a month that represented the list's initial rebound from the 1973–1974 bear market. It is interesting to note that the rally occurred despite concern over the viability of the

economic recovery. On the other hand, the Federal Reserve Board was loosening the reins on the money supply, and monetary conditions were generally conducive to investment.

While stock prices were able to make some headway in February and March, some profit taking began to appear. Trading remained at exceptionally high levels, in part reflecting the increased activity in the options market. The market's ability to gain ground was impressive, especially in view of the bankruptcy of W. T. Grant, reports of political payoffs by Lockheed Corp., and the proposed dismemberment of major integrated oil companies. All of this caused some localized pressure. The Dow Jones Industrials broke through the "1,000" barrier in mid-March. The "1,000" mark had been penetrated by the final upthrust of the 1970–1973 bull market; twice earlier, in 1966 and 1968, this level halted major bull markets. And 1976 proved to be no exception. Although the "1,000" barrier was broken a dozen or so times in 1976, the market failed to hold above that level for any extended period.

For the next few months, stock prices went through a rolling consolidation. Investor patience was stretched by rallies that aborted and were followed by mild pullbacks. Developments during this period that may have contributed to the market's inability to make further headway include: concern over the slowdown in the economy following the strong first-quarter showing, a heavy outpouring of new stock offerings, election-year politics, and tremors in several

William M. Batten, former chairman of J. C. Penney, became president of the New York Stock Exchange in April.

UPI

On March 11, the news display at New York City's Times Square informs the public that the Dow Jones Industrial Average has broken the 1,000 mark for the first time since January 1973.

UPI

foreign currencies. After an extended period of backing and filling within a fairly narrow range, stock prices rose to new highs for the year in mid-September. However, subsequent unsettling economic news left investors edgy, and stock prices dropped sharply for four consecutive weeks. This selling culminated around the time of the November elections.

From early November until the end of the year, stock prices improved markedly. Investors were apparently relieved that President-elect Carter's initial actions and appointments placed him in the mainstream of political thinking. Another factor contributing to the salutary environment for stock prices at year-end was the adoption of a reasonable posture by the Organization of Petroleum Exporting Countries (OPEC) cartel. This group of oil producing countries met on December 15 and adopted a complicated "two-tier" oil price increase. Some countries, led by Saudi Arabia, opted for a 5% price increase; other countries raised the price of crude oil by 10%. Despite the complexity, the market viewed this move as only modestly inflationary. This was a plus in the investment equation, because inflation, or, to be more precise, inflationary expectations, is one of the dominant determinants of the level at which investors are willing to capitalize current and future earnings. The lower the level of inflation, the more liberally investors are willing to appraise common stocks, and, hence, the market.

Earnings and Dividends. For most companies, earnings made a strong recovery in 1976. In terms of Standard & Poor's industrial-stock price index, net income (partly estimated) jumped to $10.87 a share, up from $8.68 in 1975, which was, in turn, down from $9.69 in 1974. Dividends trended higher, averaging $4.31 (indicated) a share on Standard & Poor's 500-index, up from $3.78 in 1975 and $3.72 in 1974. These stocks sold at an average price of 10.2 times partly estimated earnings and had an average return of 3.91% (indicated) in 1976, compared with a 1975 average multiple of 10.7 and a yield of 4.21%.

Volume. Trading on the New York Stock Exchange hit a record, totaling 5,360,116,438 shares, up from 4,693,426,508 in 1975.

Bond Prices. The year 1976 saw one of the most dramatic rallies in bond prices in modern history. The surge was fueled by the Federal Reserve Board's accommodative stance in relation to the money supply. Yields on highest-grade industrials were at a high of 8.47% on May 26, and dropped to 7.84% in late December. This compares with a high of 8.62% and a low of 8.31% in 1975. Bond prices move inversely to their yields; in other words, bond prices move up as yields drop. Each one-hundredth of a percent is called a "basis point." A decline of this magnitude, roughly 65 basis points, in bond yields means that bond prices rose fairly substantially, on the average order of 10%. In some cases, there were even more dramatic surges. The dramatic reduction in interest rates and, hence, bond yields, led to an interesting development. By the end of 1976, many corporations were moving to refund some of their high-interest-cost debt into lower-coupon issues (a coupon indicates the interest a company must pay to its bond, or debt, holders).

The growth of the bond market over the last ten years is one of the more significant aspects of modern market history. This can be traced to a subtle, but equally significant, shift in investor psychology. Many investors seem to be more interested in maximizing current, or nearly current, returns than in looking at the longer-term picture. Again, the major factor behind this indicated shift in psychology is the impact of inflation. The memory of double-digit inflation is fresh enough in most investors' minds to underscore their interest in current income—income that can be spent before prices rise. Hence, they turn to bonds. In 1966, the yield on stocks and bonds was about the same. By 1976, bond yields were nearly double those of stocks. Moreover, liquidity in the bond market improved dramatically.

CAROLYN J. COLE, *Vice President, Research Paine, Webber, Jackson & Curtis, Inc.*

SUDAN

A bloody abortive coup dominated events in Sudan in 1976. President Jaafar al-Numeiry narrowly escaped assassination in the coup attempt on July 2, which was timed to coincide with his return from state visits to Washington and Paris. The attempt occurred amid evidence of growing discontent with the government's economic setbacks.

Coup Attempt. The failed coup was the fourth major assault on his regime that Numeiry has survived. As in the previous attempt in September 1975, the army remained loyal to the government and put down the rebels in battles throughout Khartoum. Some 800 people were killed in heavy fighting. All together, 300 persons were tried for involvement in the plot, and 98 were executed by firing squad in August.

Numeiry laid the blame for the coup attempt on Libya's leader, Col. Muammar el-Qaddafi, alleging that Libya spent some $20 million to arm and train about 1,500 men from Ethiopia, Chad, and other African nations. The bulk of the force, however, was reliably reported to have been composed of Mahdists, Sudanese émigrés affiliated with a right-wing Muslim sect led by former Prime Minister Sadik al-Mahdi. Mahdi charged from London that the executions following the coup attempt would lead to more determined and widespread activity against the Numeiry regime. But observers in Khartoum said the plotters had experienced a distinct lack of popular support.

Economy. Although the first phase of a vast $2,000,000,000 Arab-financed project to make Sudan self sufficient in major foodstuffs got under way in 1976, problems still plagued the agricultural industry. At midyear, the government disclosed that over half the cotton and wheat crops in the Gezira, the richest and most highly mechanized farming area, had been lost, partly because of a burgeoning rat population. Sudan earns most of its foreign exchange from the Gezira farming area.

Critics said that the rat plague resulted from government-managed schemes that, in order to meet production quotas, have not permitted land to lie fallow. There was also a failure to distribute sufficient quantities of rat poison. Angry farmers marched through the Gezira on May Day protesting the government's agricultural policies.

The cotton output for the 1975–76 season was only 310,000 bales, less than a third of the normal annual crop in the previous five years. But total earnings from cotton exports in 1976 were still expected to be higher than those in 1975 because of large cotton stockpiles and a 60% rise in the world cotton price.

Sudan, Africa's biggest country, continued in 1976 to import huge quantities of food simply to feed its population. Some 20% of imports were basic food items, which could be grown domestically. A project to turn Sudan into a breadbasket for the Arab world aims to cultivate the country's 200 million acres (81 million hectares) of arable land, only 10% of which is now being farmed.

Foreign Relations. After the coup attempt, Sudan broke off relations with Libya and Numeiry and President Anwar Sadat of Egypt concluded a military defense pact clearly aimed at Libya. It was believed that the two leaders also secretly agreed to work to oust Qaddafi by supporting a coup within Libya.

JOSEPH MARGOLIS
"African Update," African-American Institute

SWEDEN

The loss of power by the long-governing Social Democrats, Ingmar Bergman's self-imposed exile, and a royal wedding were the top stories from Sweden in 1976.

Elections. A total of 5,985,000 out of Sweden's 8,200,000 people held the franchise in the parliamentary elections on September 19, the voting age having been lowered from 20 to

--------- **SUDAN • Information Highlights** ---------

Official Name: Democratic Republic of Sudan.
Location: Northeast Africa.
Area: 967,497 square miles (2,505,813 km²).
Population (1976 est.): 18,200,000.
Chief Cities (1973 est.): Khartoum, the capital, 322,-000; Omdurman, 305,000.
Government: *Head of state,* Gen. Jaafar Mohammed al-Numeiry, president (took office Oct. 1971). *Legislature* (unicameral)—People's Assembly.
Monetary Unit: Pound (0.35 pound equals U. S.$1, June 1976).
Gross National Product (1975 est.): $2,800,000,000.
Manufacturing (major products): Vegetable oil, processed foods, textiles, shoes, pharmaceuticals.
Major Agricultural Products: Cotton, oilseeds, gum arabic, sorghum, sesame seeds, groundnuts, wheat, livestock.
Foreign Trade (1975): *Exports,* $443,000,000; *imports,* $887,000,000.

Sweden's new Prime Minister Thorbjörn Fälldin outlines his government's policy to Parliament.

UPI

18 years. The result was that the three so-called bourgeois parties—Center, Moderate, and Liberal—ousted the Social Democrats, who almost uninterruptedly had held power for 44 years. The new governing parties gained a 180–169 majority. The leader of the Center party, Thorbjörn Fälldin, was nominated prime minister. He presented a 20-member cabinet to the Riksdag on October 8. It includes five women, among them Foreign Minister Karin Söder, vice chairman of the Center party. The Finance Ministry was divided into two sections: an Economics Ministry led by Gösta Bohman, head of the Moderate party, and a Budget Ministry under Liberal party tax expert Ingemar Mundebo.

The main issues in the election campaign were taxes, a vast and powerful bureaucracy, and a union-sponsored plan to allocate 20% of annual business profits before taxes to workers' funds in the form of company shares. This would give the workers majority control of all concerns in 20 years and effective control in five or six. Additional controversy arose over the outgoing government's nuclear energy program.

Economy. A long-term prognosis made public by a government bureau in the summer of 1976 forecast an industrial production increase until 1980 of 5.7% annually. Unemployment totaled 1.5% of the labor force during most of 1976. Swedish industry had a total of 1,800 foreign subsidiaries which employed 291,000 people.

Consumer prices rose 3.8% during the first four months of the year. Between March 1975 and March 1976 consumer prices went up by 11.1%. Sweden's foreign debts were approximately $5,000,000,000 in 1976.

Star Exodus. In early February the world-famous stage and film director Ingmar Bergman was arrested at the Royal Dramatic Theater in Stockholm where he was busy rehearsing a Strindberg play. The alleged offense was income tax evasion. Bergman's passport was confiscated

King Carl XVI Gustaf and the new Queen Silvia wave to the crowd following their June 19 wedding.

and he was forbidden to leave Stockholm. As a result, he suffered a nervous collapse. Upon his recovery and the withdrawal of all charges against him, Bergman and his wife left Sweden; they are now living in Munich, West Germany.

Royal Wedding. In April King Carl XVI Gustaf made a four-week tour of the United States, the first by a reigning Swedish monarch. In June the king was wed, with pomp and ceremony, to West German commoner Silvia Sommerlath.

MAC LINDAHL, *Harvard University*

--------- **SWEDEN · Information Highlights** ---------

Official Name: Kingdom of Sweden.
Location: Northern Europe.
Area: 173,649 square miles (449,750 km²).
Population (1976 est.): 8,200,000.
Chief Cities (1974 est.): Stockholm, the capital, 671,000; Göteborg, 446,000; Malmö, 247,000.
Government: *Head of State,* Carl XVI Gustaf, king (acceded Sept. 1973). *Head of government,* Thorbjörn Fälldin, prime minister (took office Oct. 1976). *Legislature* (unicameral)—Riksdag.
Monetary Unit: Krona (4.27 kronor equal U. S.$1, Oct. 1976).
Gross National Product (1975 est.): $71,610,000,000.
Manufacturing (major products): Pulp and paper, iron and steel, machinery and equipment, ships.
Major Agricultural Products: Oats, sugar beets, potatoes, wheat, livestock, forest products.
Foreign Trade (1975): *Exports,* $17,439,000,000; *imports,* $17,874,000,000.

The new prime minister is surrounded by members of his cabinet, consisting of members of the Center, Moderate, and Liberal parties. The new government also included five women.

Swiss soldiers, carrying full field packs and weapons, participate in a 25-mile (40-km) race in Frauenfeld in November.

SWITZERLAND

Economic stability and political conservatism dominated Swiss life in 1976.

Economy. Economic controls implemented in 1974 and 1975 led to a stabilization of the inflation rate at about 2% by the fall of 1976, a major change from the 9.5% of two years earlier. The long-sought favorable balance of exports over imports, achieved in the last quarter of 1975, was maintained during the first half of 1976. The change was highlighted by a sharp increase in arms sales abroad, a development that promised to be partially counterbalanced by a March 1976 government decision to purchase 6 F-5 and 66 F-5E American-manufactured fighter planes.

International Loans. In a national referendum on June 13, Swiss voters rejected a proposal (which had received parliamentary approval) for an interest-free 50-year loan of $80,000,000 to the International Development Association, a subsidiary of the World Bank. Conservative opponents claimed that these organizations were dominated by the United States, that contributing to them would constitute the first step toward Swiss membership in the United Nations, and that the Swiss economy could not support such a loan. Proponents pointed to Switzerland's high per capita income and its very low contribution to aid for developing nations. The Swiss government did affirm its willingness to support developing nations when it joined the Inter-American Development Bank on July 9.

Political Issues. The conservative nature of the Swiss electorate was further evidenced by the defeat on March 21 of referenda items that would have changed the tax structure and given workers greater participation in industrial management. In an effort to overturn a very restrictive law passed in 1975, the Swiss Union for the Decriminalization of Abortion gathered enough signatures in January to ensure a national referendum on the issue. In April, the first Constituent Assembly of Jura was installed, bringing a separate Jurassian canton one step nearer to realization.

PAUL C. HELMREICH, *Wheaton College, Mass.*

SWITZERLAND · Information Highlights

Official Name: Swiss Confederation.
Location: Central Europe.
Area: 15,941 square miles (41,288 km²).
Population (1976 est.): 6,500,000.
Chief Cities (1974 est.): Bern, the capital, 156,100; Zurich, 404,300; Basel, 201,000.
Government: *Head of state,* Rudolf Gnägi, president (took office Jan. 1976). *Legislature*—Federal Assembly: Council of States and National Council.
Monetary Unit: Franc (2.43 francs equal U.S.$1, Oct. 1976).
Gross National Product (1974 est.): $45,000,000,000.
Manufacturing (major products): Machinery, chemicals, textiles, watches, clocks, clock parts.
Major Agricultural Products: Potatoes, sugar beets, wheat, barley, dairy products, forest products.
Foreign Trade (1975): *Exports,* $12,957,000,000; *imports,* $13,305,000,000.

SYRIA

Syria's involvement in the Lebanese civil war provided President Hafez Assad with one of his most severe tests of nerve since he seized power in 1970. Accused in 1975 of trying to impose a *Pax Syriana* on Lebanon because of Syria's leadership in the countless truce negotiations, President Assad in 1976 became the target of scathing condemnations for his massive, direct military intervention.

Lebanon. Above all, Assad's preoccupation with Lebanon's civil war was based on his fear that continued fighting would perpetuate the divisiveness of the Arab world and prevent positive steps toward an overall peace settlement in the Middle East.

Specifically, Assad feared that the war could lead to a partition of Lebanon into Muslim and Christian sectors, or, should the Muslim left achieve its objective of a secular and democratic government, the emergence of a radical socialist Arab state. While he had always supported the left's demand for political reforms to reflect the country's Muslim majority, Assad did not want Lebanon to lose its conservative character, nor did he want to upset the region's tenuous balance of power.

Syria's attempts to end the conflict in 1975 were almost entirely diplomatic, but after months of fruitless negotiations it became clear that both diplomatic and military means would be used in 1976. To break the stalemate that had prevailed since December 1975, Assad allowed Syrian-trained units of the Palestine Liberation Army (PLA) to reinforce the left on Jan. 20, 1976. When the resulting cease-fire collapsed a few weeks later and the Palestine Liberation Organization (PLO) had joined the Muslim left, Assad realized that that side would not settle for its original demands. In mid-March, consequently, he cut off the arms flow to the left and ordered the PLA forces, which numbered some 9,000 troops, to assist the badly beleagured Christian right. During the next two and a half months, President Assad gradually increased his military support for the right while continuing to exercise a diplomatic role through a negotiating team headed by Foreign Minister Abdel Halim Khaddam.

Syrian-Egyptian Rift. When Assad shifted his support to the right, Egyptian President Anwar Sadat saw an opportunity to attack Assad, who, since the conclusion of the second Egyptian-Israeli Sinai Agreement, had accused President Sadat of selling out. Sadat's subsequent vocal support for the PLO and his accusation that Assad was planning to liquidate the Palestinian resistance exacerbated the feelings between the former allies and paralyzed all Middle East peace efforts.

Massive Intervention. Despite Israeli warnings that a direct Syrian intervention might provoke an Israeli reaction, Assad, on June 1, ordered Syrian infantry and armor into Lebanon to curb the leftist-PLO coalition and to impose a peace. Syrian forces, which by October had grown to more than 22,000 troops and 500 tanks, successfully changed the tide of the war.

From June to October, the Christian right, supported by the Syrians, was indisputably on the offensive.

In the wake of the intervention, the Arab League dispatched a peace-keeping force and a special envoy not only to attempt to separate the warring factions but also to complement the efforts of Saudi Arabia and the oil-rich Gulf states to end the war and heal the breach in Syrian-Egyptian relations.

Saudi Mediation. In August, Assad declared that if negotiations could not resolve the conflict by September 15, Syria would not limit its military efforts to support operations. As the deadline passed, two massive offensives were ordered to drive the PLO out of the Matn Mountains east of Beirut and to isolate the leftist-held port city of Sidon. By mid-October, however, Assad's inability to produce a quick success and the $1-million-a-day drain on his economy paved the way for a Saudi initiative. Assad then gave his assent to a Saudi plan to end the war and to save Syria's face. Later ratified by the Arab League, the key feature of the plan was to provide a 30,000-member Arab peace-keeping force under the command of Lebanese President Elias Sarkis. The force was to be made up of at least 15,000 Syrian troops and was empowered, at Sarkis' choice, to strike against anyone who broke the cease-fire established October 21. In this way, Syria's prominent role was recognized and confirmed by the Arab League and, more important, by Egypt's President Sadat.

Consequences. The Lebanese war imposed a heavy burden on the Syrian economy, and early in the year, many observers were calling Lebanon Syria's "Vietnam." If a lasting peace is achieved in Lebanon, however, President Assad will have emerged a success.

F. NICHOLAS WILLARD
Georgetown University

Syria's President Hafez Assad urges the Arab summit conference to find a way to stop Lebanon's civil war.

UPI

----------- SYRIA • Information Highlights -----------

Official Name: Syrian Arab Republic.
Location: Southwest Asia.
Area: 71,498 square miles (185,180 km²).
Population (1976 est.): 7,600,000.
Chief Cities (1974): Damascus, the capital, 835,000; Aleppo, 500,000; Homs, 164,000.
Government: *Head of state,* Lt. Gen. Hafez al-Assad, president (took office March 1971). *Head of government,* Abdel Rahman Khleifawi, prime minister (took office Aug. 1976). *Legislature* (unicameral)—People's Council.
Monetary Unit: Pound (3.70 pounds equal U. S.$1, July 1976).
Gross National Product (1975 est.): $4,700,000,000.
Manufacturing (major products): Petroleum products, textiles, cement, glass, soap.
Major Agricultural Products: Wheat, barley, sugar beets.
Foreign Trade (1975): *Exports,* $930,000,000; *imports,* $1,686,000,000.

TANZANIA

Tanzania figured prominently on the world stage in 1976. Both the difficulties of economic development for the poorest countries of what experts now call "the fourth world" and the political situation in southern Africa thrust Tanzania into world politics.

Internal Affairs. The Tanzanian government announced in May that it would free more than 400 members of the Barbaig tribe detained since the January 6 assassination by Barbaigs of 21 members of the Nyaturu tribe. The killings occurred during a feud between the rival tribes in the south central Singida region. The Chinese-built Tanzam railroad was formally turned over to Tanzania and Zambia in July.

International Affairs. In May, the World Bank suspended loans of several million dollars to the East African community—composed of Tanzania, Kenya, and Uganda—because of significant delay in their repayment of loans. Although the default was largely Uganda's, the economic development plans of Tanzania were severely affected by the lack of funds.

Tanzania was the first African country to withdraw its athletes from the summer Olympic games in Montreal. The withdrawal was initiated as a protest against the participation of New Zealand, which earlier in the year had sent its rugby team on a tour of South Africa, in disfavor with Organization of African Unity states because of its system of apartheid.

President Julius Nyerere assumed a leadership position in the coalition of African states calling for black majority rule in southern Africa. He defended the Cuban and Soviet presence in Angola, and castigated the United States for pressuring African countries to reject Communist intervention in Angola.

U. S. Secretary of State Henry Kissinger traveled to Dar es Salaam in September to begin a series of talks with African leaders aimed at a peaceful settlement of the southern African racial crisis. The Tanzanian government called upon the United States to support liberation forces in South West Africa (Namibia).

JEAN O'BARR, *Duke University*

TANZANIA • Information Highlights

Official Name: United Republic of Tanzania.
Location: East Africa.
Area: 364,899 square miles (945,087 km²).
Population (1976 est.): 15,600,000.
Chief City (1974 est.): Dar es Salaam, the capital, 300,-000.
Government: *Head of state,* Julius K. Nyerere, president (took office 1964). *Chief Minister,* Rashidi Kawawa, premier (took office 1972). *Legislature* (unicameral) —National Assembly.
Monetary Unit: Shilling (8.38 shillings equal U. S.$1, Sept. 1976).
Gross National Product (1974): $1,900,000,000.
Manufacturing (major products): Textiles, cement, petroleum products, refined sugar, aluminum.
Major Agricultural Products: Cloves, sisal, cotton, coffee, oilseeds, groundnuts, tea, tobacco, sugarcane.
Foreign Trade (1975): *Exports,* $349,000,000; *imports,* $714,000,000.

TAXATION

Serious policy questions are raised whenever both unemployment and inflation rates are high. Choices have to be made as to which problem should be solved first. Such was the situation in the United States during 1976.

Federal Budget. In the fiscal 1977 federal budget, President Ford emphasized inflation as the first problem to be solved. In January, he proposed to restrict federal spending to $394,-200,000,000, and to limit the size of the deficit to $43,000,000,000. The Congress, however, felt unemployment was the bigger problem, and increased federal spending beyond Ford's request to $413,100,000,000. The federal deficit was increased to a projected $50,600,000,000.

Federal Tax Reform. The Tax Reform Act of 1976 was signed into law on October 4, after nearly three years of hearings, testimony, and debate. Hundreds of changes were made in the federal tax code, and the act thus affects almost all American taxpayers.

One of the major decisions was to extend certain tax cuts enacted in 1975. Increases in the personal standard deduction were extended permanently. The $35 per person tax credit and the tax credit for taxpayers earning less than $8,000 annually were extended through 1977.

Certain corporate tax cuts also were extended—the 11% investment tax credit through 1980 and the temporary tax reduction for small businesses through 1977. In addition, the period that businesses may choose to carry forward losses was extended to seven years.

The tax reform act made important changes in the use of so-called "tax shelters," which are investments wealthier taxpayers often make in order to avoid paying taxes. Tax shelters include farming and ranching operations, real estate investments, gas and oil exploration, and sports franchises. The act sharply restricts the use of these shelters by limiting the amount of the investment that may be deducted from tax payments. In making these changes, the Congress was responding to public pressures to close tax loopholes used by the wealthy.

The tax reform act also made major changes in the taxing of gifts and estates, the first such adjustments in over 30 years. The tax exemption for gifts was increased, lowering the amount taxpayers owe the federal government when making large gifts. Estate taxes also were lowered by increasing the basic exemption. An important provision, included to help farmers, limited the estate tax on family-owned farms to $500,000.

The Congress also attempted to simplify income tax forms. The number of tax tables was reduced from 12 to 4 and the calculation of deductions was made simpler by lumping together certain types of deductible expenses.

Presidential Campaign. The state of the economy received a great deal of attention during the presidential campaign. President Ford emphasized inflation and big government as the nation's major problems, promising to reduce federal spending and taxes. Gov. Jimmy Carter emphasized the problem of high unemployment, promising to increase federal spending in order to get people back to work, and to cut taxes. Both presidential candidates promised a balanced federal budget.

Shortly after the election, President-elect Carter and several of his advisers indicated that a major federal tax cut was being considered for congressional action early in 1977. Many economists and business leaders later urged a tax reduction of about $15,000,000,000.

New Federal Fiscal Year. Under provisions of the Congressional Budget Reform Act of 1974, the fiscal year for the federal government was changed in 1976 to October through September of each year. A special transition quarter was used to bridge the old fiscal reporting year, which ran from July to June.

Internal Revenue Service. The IRS was embroiled in several controversies during 1976. Early in the year IRS Director Donald C. Alexander was criticized for allegedly helping friends avoid a tax investigation. He was later cleared of these charges.

It also was alleged that the IRS tended to audit the tax returns of private citizens more frequently than those of multimillion dollar corporations. By the end of the year, an investigation was being made into this charge.

State and Local Revenue. High rates of inflation and unemployment affect state and local governments. When unemployment is high, governmental expenses increase because some of the unemployed turn to welfare and other programs designed to help the poor. Inflation also causes problems at the state and local levels, since the cost of delivering public services increases with the overall inflation rate.

In fiscal 1976, ending June 30, total state-local tax revenues increased to $156,200,000,-000, 10.4% above 1974 revenue. General sales taxes, gross receipts taxes, and individual income taxes registered the highest gains. Gasoline tax revenues increased by less than 1%.

Several states increased taxes during the year. The New Jersey legislature, under court order to find an equitable method of financing public education, enacted a state income tax. Nebraska, Maine, and the District of Columbia increased sales, use, and income taxes. Connecticut increased the gasoline tax from 10¢ to 11¢; Colorado increased the beverage tax; Tennessee increased the sales and use tax from 3½ to 4½%; and Massachusetts increased the state sales tax to 5%.

Several states lowered taxes during 1976. Utah lowered the personal income tax rate by one fourth of 1% in each rate bracket, and Kentucky increased the personal standard deduction for state income taxes. Hawaii changed the state income tax credit schedules for low income taxpayers and doubled credits for taxpayers over 65. Ten states reduced inheritance or estate taxes.

U. S. Supreme Court. Several important Supreme Court decisions involving tax issues were handed down in 1976. In three related cases, commuter income taxes were held to be unconstitutional. The court ruled that commuter taxes enacted by the states of New Jersey and New Hampshire on workers living in other states could not be imposed.

In another important case, *Michelin Tire Corp.* v. *Wages,* the Supreme Court ruled that business inventories temporarily stored in a Georgia warehouse may be taxed by the state. The court decision overturned an 1871 court ruling that such taxes may not be collected from businesses.

In *Buckley* v. *Valeo,* the Supreme Court held that the presidential campaign contribution check-off system on income tax returns was constitutional. The decision thus ensured the continuance of public financing of presidential elections.

Canada. Canada adopted an indexing system for personal income taxes during 1976. Under this plan tax rates are automatically tied to rising income, so that no taxpayer suffers increased tax payments. As a result, $1,000,000,000 in new revenues were lost. In the budget proposal for fiscal 1977, Prime Minister Trudeau placed emphasis on lowering the inflation rate.

Other Countries. Western European countries continued to experience high inflation and relatively high unemployment during 1976. The most dramatic tax change occurred in France, with the enactment of a major capital gains tax. The law enacted was very complex, with numerous loopholes and complicated language, the result of political bargaining in the National Assembly. A considerable amount of public controversy was created when the bill was signed. The intent of the law is to tax the wealthy more and the poor less.

Denmark enacted an emergency tax measure. Taxes were sharply increased on various types of insurance policies. Excise duties were increased for tobacco, alcohol, tea, coffee, motor vehicles, and gasoline.

In Britain, a proposal was made to reduce taxes on income in the highest brackets. But the proposal was dependent upon the achievement of satisfactory pay limits with labor unions.

Business taxes were increased in Portugal. The corporate income tax was increased by 66%, the business tax by 33%, and the tax rate on income from loans was increased by 22%. Taxes on the income of workers were increased only slightly. To enforce the new taxes, a decree was issued in July imposing stiff penalties for tax fraud.

CHARLES KNERR
University of Texas at Arlington

TELECOMMUNICATIONS

Without question, the most significant development in the telecommunications field during 1976 was the introduction in the U. S. Congress of the Consumer Communications Reform Bill. But because the proposed legislation seemed heavily weighted in favor of the telephone establishment and would reduce the Federal Communications Commission's (FCC) regulatory powers over American Telephone & Telegraph Co. (AT&T) and independent telephone carriers, its critics labeled it the "Bell bill" and even the "Monopoly Protection Act of 1976."

Provisions of Legislation. The bill would not only bar competition in present telephone and future network communications services but also transfer jurisdiction over telephone terminals to state agencies. It would prevent regulatory agencies from declaring a carrier's rates too low so long as they cover its service costs, and give the FCC the power to approve the acquisition by one carrier of competing ones in order to guarantee service if competitors fail.

Indeed, one competitor did fail. In August, Data Transmission Co., an early entry in the domestic communications field after the FCC issued its "specialized common carrier" decision to foster competition to the telephone industry in the private line communications field, said it went bankrupt because of the "anticompetitive nature of the marketplace." Customers were transferred to other carriers.

AT&T's competitors say the proposed legislation is "inherently anticompetitive and anticonsumer in nature and impact." They charge AT&T with attempting to kill competition "which is providing U. S. business and government users with lower-cost, technically superior communications via domestic satellite" and other advanced systems. As the bill also calls for erosion of the FCC's role, commission chairman Richard Wiley and chief of its Common Carrier Bureau Walter Hinchman, have both spoken out sharply against its passage by Congress.

AT&T's main argument for the bill is that home telephone rates will climb drastically unless competition is reduced. The Bell system says home telephone service is a money loser made possible by high revenues from other services, including long-distance tolls, an area where competing specialized carriers and private satellite communications services are just beginning to make a dent in AT&T's revenues.

Despite the intensity of the initial hearings before congressional committees, no action on the bill was expected before 1977.

AT&T Troubles. The "Bell bill" may have been influenced by a 535-page study of the Bell telephone system, written by FCC administrative law judge David I. Kraushaar. The study portrays the Bell system as needing tighter management and more competition, rather than the breakup of AT&T called for in an antitrust suit brought by the Justice Department in 1974. The opinion was written after a four-year review of the technology and economies of the Bell system.

Meanwhile, three subsidiaries of Litton Industries filed a $330-million suit against AT&T, charging antitrust violations in the telephone terminal equipment market. The suit alleges that AT&T, in restraint of trade, conspired to prevent subscribers from connecting their own terminals to the Bell system.

Other Developments. A report to the White House Office of Telecommunications Policy warned of a possible breakdown of the federal regulatory system in the face of rapidly developing telecommunications technology. Prepared by Arthur D. Little Inc., a research and consulting firm, the report foresees the headlong growth of citizens band (CB) radio resulting in new criminal techniques and a threat of obsolescence to the postal service. A monopoly by AT&T of all broadband distribution to the home is another possible impact of technological change described in the report.

The Little study indicates that the many new users and uses of CB radio could in the not-too-distant future turn the present situation into sheer chaos unless a workable policy is developed. Indeed, the FCC was so concerned about overcrowding of CB frequencies that it authorized expansion of CB radio service from 23 to 40 channels, effective Jan. 1, 1977.

RONALD A. SCHNEIDERMAN
Consumer Electronics Daily

TELEPHONES IN MAJOR COUNTRIES

Country	Telephones Jan. 1, 1975	% increase over 1974	No. per 100 population
Argentina	2,373,665	14.9	9.41
Australia	4,999,982	7.3	37.49
Austria	1,986,733	7.9	26.37
Belgium	2,666,701	6.4	27.32
Brazil	2,651,728	9.8	2.50
Bulgaria	718,325	12.1	8.18
Canada	12,454,331	6.7	54.96
China, Nationalist	900,605	21.3	5.68
Colombia	1,186,205	9.9	4.74
Czechoslovakia	2,480,801	5.4	16.83
Denmark	2,183,847	6.7	42.48
Egypt	503,200	6.7	1.37
Finland	1,678,873	9.3	35.78
France	12,405,000	9.4	23.52
Germany, East	2,451,011	5.4	15.04
Germany, West	18,767,033	5.4	30.25
Greece	1,862,050	11.5	20.71
Hong Kong	988,545	8.2	22.75
Hungary	1,013,731	4.7	9.65
India	1,689,528	6.3	0.29
Iran	805,560	45.8	2.40
Israel	735,156	7.3	21.57
Italy	13,695,006	8.6	24.62
Japan	41,904,960	10.2	37.88
Mexico	2,546,186	14.6	4.37
Netherlands, The	4,678,945	8.4	34.41
New Zealand	1,494,587	6.0	48.12
Norway	1,355,142	3.6	33.90
Poland	2,399,249	7.2	7.09
Portugal	1,011,177	6.7	11.67
Rumania	1,076,566	21.5	5.10
South Africa	1,935,831	6.6	7.77
Spain	7,042,968	11.2	19.96
Sweden	5,178,082	3.9	63.32
Switzerland	3,790,351	5.2	59.46
Turkey	899,923	11.5	2.30
United Kingdom	20,342,457	6.5	36.26
U.S.S.R.	15,782,000	10.7	6.23
United States	143,972,000	4.1	67.65
Venezuela	554,197	10.0	4.65
Yugoslavia	1,142,883	13.9	5.38

Source: AT&T

TELEVISION AND RADIO

Every four years the news, sports, and engineering staffs of the television and radio networks are required to put forth enormous effort in order to cover the Olympic Games and the U. S. presidential campaigns. The task in 1976 was made even more difficult by the addition of the bicentennial celebration, concentrated of course on the Fourth of July, and by an increased number of political primaries. The year also saw the emergence of ABC, the American Broadcasting Company, as the leader in the networks' ratings race.

News. Never in history, it seems safe to say, have so many reporters covered so extensively what is essentially a single, though drawn-out, event, the election in November of a new president. The magazine *Broadcasting* estimated that 3,600 to 3,800 news staffers, technicians, and other personnel were used in television and radio coverage of each convention. In fact, the people involved in broadcasting the conventions far outnumbered the delegates. The cost to the networks alone was estimated to be between $25 and $30 million, not counting the millions of dollars lost through the preemption of regular programs.

Early in the year speculation arose about the need to increase network evening news programs from 30 to 60 minutes in order to achieve greater depth in news coverage. Serious concern was focused on the idea with ABC's announce-

NBC

Sada Thompson and Hal Holbrook were Mary and Abe Lincoln in the bicentennial series *Sandburg's Lincoln*.

Episodes from Book 1 of *Rich Man, Poor Man* featured Peter Strauss *(left)*, Susan Blakely, and Nick Nolte.

AMERICAN BROADCASTING COMPANIES, INC.

ment in April that it had signed Barbara Walters to a five-year "million dollar a year" contract, to be coanchor with Harry Reasoner of the *ABC Evening News*. Long a fixture of the NBC *Today* program, Walters began her association with ABC in September. The million-dollar figure was misleading: about half that amount was salary for the evening news stint, the remainder contingent on her involvement in many other ABC programs. As for 60-minute network evening news, the idea was shelved in November because of sharp affiliate resistance.

Sports. With all three networks contending for the top position in sports, it was a rich year for the fans. Baseball, basketball, golf, tennis, racing, and sundry other sports were available often, along with a grand total of 266 collegiate and professional football games, preseason, season, playoff, and bowl.

In addition, there were the Olympics—the Winter Games from Innsbruck, Austria, the Summer Games from Montreal, Canada. ABC's coverage of the Winter Games was good, but its coverage of the Summer Games was remarkable, in the face of the wide physical separation of events and the extraordinary number of them. ABC afforded American viewers some 75 hours of airtime in the 17 days of the games.

WNET/13

Ed Flanders is Harry Truman in TV's adaptation of Merle Miller's book Harry S. Truman Plain Speaking.

Ratings. The audience responded markedly to this effort, and the Olympic ratings went far to lock up ABC's position as the leader for the year in the ratings race. The second week of the Summer Games saw ABC winning almost 50% of the audience every night of the week. This, along with strong showings by three or four regular series introduced in January, confirmed ABC as the leader for the first time in its history, replacing CBS in the position it had occupied for the previous 20 years.

Entertainment. Television's "second season" —the January cancellation of unsuccessful shows and the introduction of new hopefuls—brought in several successes. They included reunited *Sonny and Cher* and Norman Lear's *One Day At a Time*, both on CBS; and on ABC *The Bionic Woman*, spun off from *Six Million Dollar Man; Laverne and Shirley*, out of *Happy Days*; the *Donnie and Marie Show*; and *Rich Man, Poor Man*, the dramatization in 12 weekly hours of the Irwin Shaw novel.

The new season, introducing the 1976–77 prime time schedule, brought 22 new programs into view, 9 from ABC, 7 from NBC, and 6 from CBS. With the addition overall of three comedy-variety shows, a western, and only one new police show, the normal program mix was somewhat better balanced than in recent years. It is notable that, with the cancellation, after seven years, of *Marcus Welby, M. D.*, there were no doctor/hospital dramatic programs regularly represented.

The springtime success of the 12-episode *Rich Man, Poor Man* prompted a trend. NBC presented a multi-episode dramatization of the Taylor Caldwell novel, *The Captains and the Kings*, as the first element in a regular new series called *Best Sellers*. *Rich Man, Poor Man, Book*

II appeared on ABC as a regular series based on the original *Rich Man, Poor Man* material. ABC also announced a forthcoming 12-part dramatization of Alex Haley's book, *Roots*.

The extraordinary successes of the year, however, were two quite disparate programs, alike only in owing nothing to ABC, CBS, or NBC. Public Television's own, home-produced series, *The Adams Chronicles*, was a smashing success. Offered as part of the bicentennial celebration, it was played and replayed on the public television network and by many commercial stations in markets not served by PBS. Norman Lear's *Mary Hartman, Mary Hartman*, a wildly comic mockery of the soap-opera form, was turned down by all three networks. Lear then undertook to syndicate it directly to local stations. By year-end it was playing to large and enthusiastic audiences on over 125 independent stations. Nothing like *Mary Hartman, Mary Hartman* had ever before happened in the history of television.

Words of praise also must go to David Brinkley's three-part bicentennial essay on *Life, Liberty, and the Pursuit of Happiness*, and to the "tall ships" segment of the networks' day-and-night-long coverage of the bicentennial Fourth of July.

Family Hour. The television networks' "family hour" agreement was ruled unconstitutional by a federal district judge in Los Angeles on November 3. The networks had initiated the family hour in September 1975 in response to mounting

Louise Lasser played the title role in Norman Lear's hit of the 1976 season, *Mary Hartman, Mary Hartman*.

UPI

Thames, Britain's leading television production company, presented a series of programs on WOR, New York City, in September. The top-rated shows, intended to "introduce New Yorkers to London," included *Father, Dear Father* (below) and *Rock Follies*.

criticism of television sex and violence, agreeing to show only material appropriate for viewing by the whole family between 7 and 9 P. M. But the judge ruled that the agreement violated the first amendment guarantee of free speech. CBS said it would appeal the decision.

Federal Communications Commission. The FCC continued its careful progress through the minefield of license renewal requirements, the fairness doctrine, media cross-ownership, cable and pay-cable regulations, and other matters that have been its major concerns over the past years. It looked to Congress, always slow to act, to defuse some of these issues. But there were two new land-bombs to deal with; one a series of court orders that the FCC move closer to participation in local station programming decisions, another the intensifying problem of citizens' band radio. And, as always in an election year, there were ever more pressing problems of "reasonable access" for politicians to radio and TV and of equal time requirements.

In the fall of 1975 the FCC issued a reinterpretation of its equal time rules, classifying news conferences and debates between presidential and vice-presidential candidates as news events and therefore not subject to equal time requirements. Promptly challenged, the commission was upheld in April by a 2–1 vote of a U. S. Court of Appeals panel in Washington, D. C. As a result, the widely awaited television-radio debates between the major parties' candidates for the presidency and vice presidency were held, despite further court challenges by minor party candidates, chief among them former Sen. Eugene McCarthy.

The three presidential debates were the first since the 1960 Kennedy-Nixon debates; the vice presidential debate was the first in history. What the debates added in a substantive way to the campaign will be discussed for a long time to come. They drew good audiences, some 80 to 90 million TV viewers. But perhaps the most striking feature of them was the 26-minute loss of sound during the first debate, caused by the malfunctioning of a tiny capacitor in the audio distribution system.

For seven years past the FCC had approved without public hearings the sale of a number of radio stations, despite local citizens' objections to proposed changes in format. In general, the stations had switched from classical music (in one instance from jazz, in another from progressive rock) to top-40 or country and western. The U. S. Court of Appeals in Washington had overturned all these FCC decisions, ruling that the commission must address "the public interest in a diversity of broadcast entertainment formats" in a given market. Troubled by the constitutional question, the FCC in early January issued a notice of inquiry. Strengthened by responses to its inquiry, it issued a policy statement in August, claiming that broadcasters have the right to decide on their own formats and

WORLD TELEVISION STATIONS AND SETS
(as of mid-1976)

Country	Stations	Number of TV sets	Country	Stations	Number of TV sets	Country	Stations	Number of TV sets
Albania	1	3,000	Honduras	7	47,000	Paraguay	1	52,000
Algeria	7	410,000	Hong Kong	4	839,000	Peru	19	750,000
Angola	1		Hungary	26	2,540,000	Philippines	23	650,000
Antigua	1	15,000	Iceland	7	50,900	Poland	50	5,695,300
Argentina	33	4,550,000	India	8	400,000	Portugal	14	723,000
Australia	128	4,917,000	Indonesia	18	370,000	Qatar	2	28,000
Austria	273	1,916,000	Iran	17	2,018,000	Rhodesia	2	67,600
Bangladesh	3	25,000	Iraq	7	500,000	Rumania	24	2,700,000
Barbados	1	40,000	Ireland	23	720,000	Samoa (American)	6	5,700
Belgium	16	2,575,000	Israel	11	475,000	Saudi Arabia	8	300,000
Bermuda	2	27,000	Italy	93	12,580,000	Senegal	1	1,700
Bolivia	1	100,000	Ivory Coast	6	87,500	Sierra Leone	1	6,000
Brazil	98	8,700,000	Jamaica	10	120,000	Singapore	2	250,000
Bulgaria	13	1,530,000	Japan	212	26,400,000	South Africa	18	500,000
Cambodia	2	30,000	Jordan	6	171,000	Spain	35	6,640,000
Canada	338	8,100,000	Kenya	5	50,000	Sudan	2	90,000
Chile	42	1,200,000	Korea (South)	12	2,300,000	Surinam	1	33,000
China (mainland)	40	3,200,000	Kuwait	3	130,000	Sweden	266	4,363,000
Colombia	18	1,200,000	Lebanon	9	410,000	Switzerland	87	1,781,000
Costa Rica	4	155,000	Liberia	1	10,000	Syria	8	224,000
Cuba	25	575,000	Libya	11	15,000	Tanzania	1	4,152
Cyprus	2	82,000	Luxembourg	1	85,000	Thailand	9	720,000
Czechoslovakia	28	3,700,000	Malaysia	32	738,000	Trinidad & Tobago	3	110,000
Denmark	30	1,725,000	Malta	1	76,000	Tunisia	9	250,000
Dominican Republic	8	305,000	Martinique	1	20,100	Turkey	28	650,000
Ecuador	10	250,000	Mauritius	1	55,000	Uganda	6	65,000
Egypt	18	1,000,000	Mexico	80	5,480,000	United Arab Emirates	3	92,000
El Salvador	5	109,300	Monaco	3	20,000	United Kingdom	263	18,000,000
Ethiopia	3	28,000	Mongolia	1	2,000	United States	964	125,000,000
Finland	91	1,608,000	Morocco	17	500,000	Upper Volta	1	7,700
France	225	13,930,000	Netherlands	20	5,081,100	Uruguay	18	350,000
Germany (East)	28	5,170,000	Netherlands Antilles	3	40,000	USSR	167	50,000,000
Germany (West)	182	19,226,000	New Zealand	32	812,000	Venezuela	31	1,460,000
Ghana	4	35,000	Nicaragua	2	72,200	Yemen	3	30,000
Greece	20	1,050,000	Nigeria	6	100,000	Yugoslavia	62	3,345,000
Guadeloupe	2	13,000	Norway	95	868,200	Zaire	2	7,500
Guam	1	20,000	Pakistan	9	255,000	Zambia	3	22,000
Guatemala	3	145,000	Panama	12	206,000			
Haiti	3	13,000						

Source: Television Factbook, 1976–1977.

that governmental involvement in such decisions is unconstitutional under the First Amendment and highly impracticable in administration. The commission looks to an ultimate decision by the Supreme Court.

There were several changes in personnel among the commissioners. Democrat Glen O. Robinson's term came to an end and he did not want reappointment to another seven-year term. Republican Charlotte Reid resigned in June, leaving two years of her term unfilled. President Ford unexpectedly nominated Republican Margita White, assistant news secretary and director of the White House Office of Communications, to the full, seven-year term and, shortly after, nominated Democrat Joseph Fogarty, counsel to the Senate Communications Subcommittee, to the two-year remainder. White's nomination was promptly questioned on grounds of possible conflict of interest because her husband, a tax specialist, was a member of a law firm that handled some broadcasting business. The "situation" was resolved by the acceptance of Sen. Wendell Ford's suggestion that the appointments be reversed, that Democrat Fogarty be given Democrat Robinson's seven-year term and Republican White Republican Reid's remaining two years. Benjamin Lawson Hooks, the first black member of the commission, resigned late in the year following his appointment as executive director of the NAACP.

Citizens' Band Radio. CB radio, sparked by a couple of amusing phonograph records, the American love of new toys, and the fact that no technical skills are required in its operation, grew at an amazing rate during the year, by hundreds of thousands a month. There were over 5 million units in use by year-end.

Licensed and regulated by the FCC, CB radio came to be the commission's worst headache and workload, with something like 3.5 million applications to process. With increasing numbers of sets in use there came to be, predictably, an increasing demand for more channels and, less predictably, increasing instances of widespread CB interference with television and radio signals. In midsummer the FCC added 17 new CB channels to the existing 23, made provisions for easing the problem of interference, and began studies to determine where better to place the whole CB operation.

Television and Congress. After labors extending over the past decade, Congress finally passed the first reform of the copyright laws since 1909, and President Ford signed the bill into law on October 19. In brief, the bill requires both cable and public television to pay copyright royalties, denies to cable systems any right to substitute its own commercials on imported broadcast signals, and creates the American Television and Radio Archives in the Library of Congress, thus making news and entertainment programs avail-

For the increasing number of dance enthusiasts, public television presented "Dance in America" programs. Yuriko Kimura (left) was the soloist in "Appalachian Spring" and Twyla Tharp starred in "Sue's Leg."

MAJOR 1976 U. S. TELEVISION PROGRAMS

The Adams Chronicles—A 13-part dramatization of four generations of the Adams family, with George Grizzard, Kathryn Walker. PBS, beginning Jan. 20.

America Salutes Richard Rodgers—Tribute to the composer and his music; with a cast including Gene Kelly, Henry Winkler, Cloris Leachman, Sandy Duncan, Sammy Davis, Jr., Diahann Carroll. CBS, Dec. 9.

Bell Telephone "Jubilee"—Musical-variety special saluting the 100th anniversary of the telephone, hosted by Liza Minnelli, Bing Crosby. NBC, March 26.

The Bolshoi Theater: Romeo and Juliet—Presentation from Russia commemorating the bicentennial of the Bolshoi Ballet, with Mary Tyler Moore as hostess. CBS, June 27.

Eleanor and Franklin—A 2-part dramatization of Joseph P. Lash's biography, with Jane Alexander and Edward Herrmann. ABC, Jan. 11, 12.

Farewell to Manzanar—TV-movie about the internment of Japanese-Americans during World War II, based on the book by Jeanne Wakatsuki Houston and James Houston; with Nobu McCarthy, Yuki Shimoda. NBC, March 11.

Fight Against Slavery—A 6-part series dramatizing the fight to abolish slavery in the British Empire, introduced by Ruby Dee. PBS, beginning Nov. 29.

The First Breeze of Summer—Negro Ensemble Company production of Leslie Lee's play, with Moses Gunn, Frances Foster, Douglas Turner Ward. PBS, Jan. 28.

The First 50 Years—Special celebrating NBC's golden anniversary in radio and television, narrated by Orson Welles. NBC, Nov. 21.

Fourth of July Celebrations—All-day coverage of events throughout the United States in honor of the nation's 200th birthday. ABC, CBS, NBC, July 4.

Gone with the Wind—The 1939 movie, starring Vivian Leigh, Clark Gable, Olivia de Havilland, Leslie Howard, Hattie McDaniel. NBC, in two parts, Nov. 7, 8.

Gypsy in My Soul—Musical special starring Shirley MacLaine, guest star Lucille Ball. CBS, Jan. 20.

Harry S. Truman: Plain Speaking—Adaptation of Merle Miller's book, with Ed Flanders. PBS, Oct. 5.

Helter Skelter—A 2-part TV-movie based on the book by Vincent Bugliosi and Curt Gentry about the murder trial of the Charles Manson "family." CBS, April 1, 2.

John Denver and Friend—Denver and Frank Sinatra in a tribute to the big band era. ABC, March 29.

Judge Horton and the Scottsboro Boys—TV-movie dramatizing the 1931 trial, with Arthur Hill, Vera Miles, Lewis J. Stadlin, Ken Kercheval. NBC, April 22.

Just an Old Sweet Song—Drama by Melvin Van Peebles about an urban black family vacationing in the South, with Cicely Tyson, Robert Hooks. CBS, Sept. 14.

The Last of Mrs. Lincoln—Production of the James Prideaux play, with Julie Harris recreating her original stage role. PBS, Sept. 16.

Life Goes to the Movies—Famous scenes from 36 years of motion-picture history, hosted by Henry Fonda, Shirley MacLaine, Liza Minnelli. NBC, Oct. 31.

Mr. Rooney Goes to Dinner—A look at the gastronomic habits of Americans, with Andrew A. Rooney. CBS, April 20.

Olympic Games—Opening, closing, and sporting events of the 1976 Winter Olympics in Innsbruck, Feb. 4–15; and Summer Olympics in Montreal, July 17–Aug. 1. ABC.

Presidential Debates—Between President Gerald Ford and Jimmy Carter, Sept. 23, Oct. 6, Oct. 22. Vice presidential debate between Sen. Walter Mondale and Sen. Robert Dole, Oct. 15. Televised live. ABC, CBS, NBC, PBS.

Rich Man, Poor Man—A nine-part dramatization of Irwin Shaw's novel, with Nick Nolte, Susan Blakely, Peter Strauss. ABC, beginning Feb. 1.

Sills and Burnett at the Met—Beverly Sills and Carol Burnett in concert at the Metropolitan Opera House in New York City. CBS, Nov. 25.

Song of Myself—Portrait of Walt Whitman, written by Jan Hartman; with Rip Torn. CBS, March 9.

A State Dinner for Queen Elizabeth II—The formal White House festivities honoring the visiting British royalty. PBS, July 7.

Suddenly An Eagle—Stories of people and events that triggered the American Revolution, with Lee J. Cobb, Kenneth Griffith. ABC, Jan. 7.

Swan Lake—Live from Lincoln Center presentation of the Tchaikovsky ballet; performed by the American Ballet Theater, with Natalia Makarova and Ivan Nagy. PBS, June 30.

Truman at Potsdam—Hallmark Hall of Fame dramatization based on the book by Charles L. Mee, Jr.; with Ed Flanders as President Harry Truman, John Houseman as Prime Minister Churchill, José Ferrer as Premier Stalin. NBC, April 8.

able to the public for private, nonprofit use.

The move to open regular House sessions to live broadcast coverage ran into heavy opposition. But the President did sign a "sunshine" bill opening to the public most meetings of some 50 government agencies.

Having passed a five-year funding bill for public television, Congress then authorized specific amounts for the next three years, as part of a large appropriations bill for health, education, welfare, and labor. In round numbers the figures are $103 million for 1977, $107 million for 1978, and $120 million for 1979. Under the terms of the funding arrangement public television must raise $2.50 to match each $1 of federal funds.

Television and South Africa. South Africa, the last holdout among developed nations, finally accepted television in 1976. On January 5 it began regular broadcasts of 37 hours a week, in Afrikaans and English. A Bantu network, broadcasting in two main African languages, will be instituted later, staffed largely by Africans. The cost of TV sets was extraordinarily high, ranging from $450 for a 19-inch black and white, the smallest set available, to $1,500 for a 24-inch color receiver.

Radio. Although television and its problems got most of the headlines, radio continued to grow at a remarkable pace. In the first few months of the year there were so many applications to the FCC for new AM and FM stations that the commission was forced to declare a six-month "freeze" on applications in order to clear up an existing backlog of 257 AM and 467 FM applications. As the figures indicate, FM is no longer the stepsister of AM. In the past few years its numbers have doubled in the United State alone, and there are now over 3,500 FM stations (with an added 850 educational) on the air as compared with approximately 4,500 AM. And in the same time period FM's revenues have increased sevenfold.

Footnote. In January the National Broadcasting Company unveiled a new logo, a stylized letter "N," to replace the familiar peacock and to mark NBC's 50th anniversary. The cost of the design (plus a "corporate identity" campaign) was reported to be in the hundreds of thousands of dollars. NBC soon discovered that the identical "N" had been in use for six months by the Nebraska Educational Television Network as its logo, and was being seen nationally on PBS. It had been designed "in house" for under $100. Discussions ensued between the two networks, without result, and so in February Nebraska ETV sued, asking for a permanent injunction against NBC's use of the logo. NBC then capitulated, acquiring sole TV use of the "N" in return for cash and color TV equipment totalling about $600,000.

JOHN M. GUNN
Formerly, Professor of Radio-TV-Film
State University of New York at Albany

TELEVISION AND RADIO ENGINEERING

During 1976, there was little expansion of television broadcasting in the United States. However, cable TV systems and citizens' band (CB) radio continued to grow steadily. In fact, CB radio became a major trend.

Television Broadcasting. At year-end, there were 708 commercial and 253 public (educational) stations in regular service in the United States. Sets in use totaled 125 million, of which almost half were color. TV receiver improvements featured increased use of push-button (digital) tuning, improved color picture tubes, and large-screen projection receivers.

Home video tape machines were increasingly used and two developmental home video disk players were demonstrated.

Systems for captioning TV pictures for the deaf were demonstrated, and the Federal Communications Commission (FCC) required visual captioning to accompany all emergency warning messages.

Cable Television. According to the National Cable Television Association (NCTA), 12 million homes were being served in 1976 by cable TV systems, representing 17% of all television homes in the United States. The largest expansion was in the distribution of pay-cable TV programs. Earth-orbiting satellites were employed for pay-cable TV relaying, with approximately 100 satellite receiving stations in operation at year-end. The number of homes in the United States subscribing to pay-cable TV service more than doubled during the year, to reach a total of 800,000 subscribers.

The first regular use of fiber optics for cable TV distribution was made during 1976 in both the United States and Great Britain. A large cable system in Japan employing fiber optics was under construction, with completion expected beginning in 1978.

Plans were also completed for an elaborate earth satellite relaying system for interconnecting public TV broadcast stations. Completion of this system is expected by 1979.

Radio Broadcasting. In radio broadcasting, there were 4,520 AM stations on the air in the United States at year-end, and 3,780 FM stations (including 887 noncommercial educational FM stations). Systems to permit stereophonic AM broadcasting were tested during the year, and a decision from the FCC was awaited on a standard system to permit the use of quadraphonic sound for FM broadcasting.

Citizens' Band (CB) Radio. Over 5 million new CB transceivers were put into service in 1976. The FCC expanded from 23 to 40 the number of channels available in the popular Class D CB service at 27 MHz. The ruling became effective Jan. 1, 1977.

See also Industrial Production.

HOWARD T. HEAD
A. D. Ring & Associates

Tennessee's newly elected Democratic Senator James Sasser (*center*) confers with Senate Sergeant at Arms Frank Nordy Hoffman (*left*) and Secretary of the Senate Francis R. Valeo. The Nashville lawyer defeated Sen. William Brock.

WIDE WORLD

TENNESSEE

Changes in voting patterns, new legislation, and bicentennial activities dominated the interests of Tennesseans during 1976.

Elections. For the second time since 1948, a Democratic presidential candidate carried Tennessee, this time by a 55.8% margin. Nashville lawyer James Sasser defeated incumbent Republican Sen. William Brock, but Rep. Robin Beard (R) turned back a strong Democratic thrust by former Sen. Ross Bass. Democrats again captured control of the state legislature.

In August, Tennesseans approved the call of a limited constitutional convention scheduled for summer 1977. The most controversial item designated for consideration limits interest rates on loans to 10%. Bankers have contended for years that the limitation is archaic and inhibits economic growth.

Legislation. The general assembly increased the sales tax by 1%; it is now 4.5%. This increase, the largest in the state's history, is expected to bring in more than $160 million. Also approved was a record state budget of $2,400,-000,000.

Economy. Declining agricultural prices and rising rates of inflation and unemployment continued to trouble Tennesseans. The collapse of Hamilton Bankshares, Inc., of Chattanooga, the third largest banking failure in the nation's

history, sent shock waves through the state's business communities. Other banks and holding companies also experienced difficulties and loss of public confidence. Economists blamed these problems upon the severity of the 1974–75 recession, inflated real estate values, and the state's 10% usury law.

Cities. Crime in the cities continued to be a matter of concern in some areas. Knoxville had a 14% rise in the number of serious crimes. Nashville, Chattanooga, and Memphis, however, showed modest declines in the rate.

In June, Gov. Ray Blanton welcomed to Nashville more than one hundred UN delegates who came for a one-day visit. This marked the first time that the United Nations, as a body, had gathered in the United States outside New York City.

In January, Gov. Blanton signed a $31-million contract for the construction in Nashville of a Cultural Complex and Office Building. Plans for the structure include a 2,400-seat music hall and a museum. The building, to be completed in 1979, will strengthen Nashville's position as a major cultural center of the South.

Education. A 9% pay increase for teachers helped avert strikes threatened in several parts of the state. Enrollment patterns tended to stabilize. The state's 10 community colleges had a 3% enrollment gain as compared with 30% in 1975. The senior colleges and universities sustained a 1% decline. Dr. Walter J. Leonard, erstwhile assistant to the president of Harvard University, was chosen as the 8th president of Fisk University of Nashville.

Transition. Rep. Joe L. Evins (D) retired after 30 years in Congress. Evins held membership on several important committees and was considered the most influential Democrat in the state.

The year marked the death of one of Tennessee's most colorful governors and also of one of the South's best known newspaper publishers. Gordon W. Browning, 87, controversial governor of the late 1930's and early 1950's, died in May. James G. Stahlman, 83, publisher of the Nashville *Banner,* 1930–1973, also died in May.

ROBERT E. CORLEW
Middle Tennessee State University

─────── **TENNESSEE** · Information Highlights ───────

Area: 42,244 square miles (109,412 km²).
Population (1975 est.): 4,188,000.
Chief Cities (1970 census): Nashville, the capital, 447,-877; Memphis, 623,530; Knoxville, 174,587.
Government (1976): *Chief Officers*—governor, Ray Blanton (D); lt. gov., John S. Wilder (D). *General Assembly*—Senate, 33 members; House of Representatives, 99 members.
Education (1975–76): *Enrollment*—public elementary schools, 537,793 pupils; public secondary, 339,133; nonpublic (1976–77), 44,700; colleges and universities, 169,050 students. *Public school expenditures,* $803,691,000 ($915 per pupil).
State Finances (fiscal year 1975): *Revenues,* $2,234,-018,000; *expenditures,* $2,417,217,000.
Personal Income (1975): $20,501,000,000; per capita, $4,895.
Labor Force (July 1976): *Nonagricultural wage and salary earners,* 1,516,600; *insured unemployed,* 54,-200 (4.4%).

TEXAS

Politics dominated events in Texas in 1976, but a U. S. Supreme Court decision upholding the state's death penalty also made big headlines.

Politics. In eking out his November 2 presidential election victory, Democrat Jimmy Carter garnered the 26 Texas electoral votes. His popular vote was 1.8 million to President Ford's 1.59 million. But what went on in the state prior to the election had great bearing on the national outcome.

Early in the year, Texas Democratic Sen. Lloyd Bentsen announced himself a candidate for the Democratic presidential nomination. His candidacy got sidetracked, however, by poor showings in early primaries in Oklahoma and Mississippi. On February 10, Bentsen withdrew and became a favorite son candidate in Texas only, hoping to salvage some political clout for the Democratic national convention in New York City in July. In the May 1 Texas primary, however, Jimmy Carter captured 124 of the 130 Texas delegates to the convention, leaving Bentsen to run for reelection against Republican Congressman Alan Steelman of Dallas. Bentsen won handily.

According to local experts, Carter's victory in Texas proved once again that only in unusual circumstances can Texas be expected to support a Republican for president. Texas, they say, remains firmly a one-party state.

Sen. Lloyd Bentsen (D-Tex.) was unsuccessful in his bid for the White House but won reelection on Nov. 2.

UPI

Other Election Results. In that May 1 Texas primary, Ronald Reagan took all the Republican delegates in his unsuccessful challenge to President Gerald Ford.

In the November 2 election all incumbent U. S. congressmen were reelected, as were most incumbent state legislators. One of the closest congressional races in the nation was in Houston's District 22, where Rep. Ron Paul (R), in office only seven months, lost to Democrat Bob Gammage by 250 votes out of nearly 200,000 cast. Paul asked for a recount.

Unopposed Democrat Don Yarbrough won his seat on the Texas Supreme Court, but faces a disbarment suit by the State Bar of Texas. The suit lists 53 allegations that Yarbrough, 35, violated the Texas Securities Act, federal and state fraud laws, and the Code of Professional Responsibility for Attorneys.

Debate. The single debate between the vice-presidential candidates was held on October 15 in Houston. Pundits generally agreed that the debate, laced with humor and sarcasm, tended to benefit Democrat Walter Mondale more than Republican Robert Dole.

Electric Chair Reinstated. On July 1, the U. S. Supreme Court upheld the constitutionality of the state's death penalty. At year's end there were more than 40 persons on death row in the state penitentiary at Huntsville.

Training Fatality. On April 16 marine recruit Lynn McClure of Lufkin died in Houston a month after suffering head injuries during pugil stick drills at the Marine Corps training depot at San Diego, Calif. An investigation resulted in widespread publicity and an examination of marine recruiting and training practices throughout the United States.

Desegregation. A federal judge on March 10 ordered Dallas to implement a school integration plan involving the busing of 20,000 pupils and the creation of magnet schools.

Death. Rep. Wright Patman, 82, died March 7 of cardiac arrest. He had served as chairman of the House Banking and Currency Committee.

MICHAEL LONSFORD
"The Houston Chronicle"

——— TEXAS · Information Highlights ———

Area: 267,338 square miles (692,405 km²).

Population (1975 est.): 12,237,000.

Chief Cities (1970 census): Austin, the capital, 251,-808; Houston, 1,232,802; Dallas, 844,401; San Antonio, 654,153.

Government (1976): *Chief Officers*—governor, Dolph Briscoe (D); lt. gov., William P. Hobby (D). *Legislature*—Senate, 31 members; House of Representatives, 150 members.

Education (1975–76): *Enrollment*—public elementary schools, 1,517,060 pupils; public secondary, 1,295,-828; nonpublic (1976–77), 135,300; colleges and universities, 550,002 students. *Public school expenditures,* $2,772,485,000 ($1,016 per pupil).

State Finances (fiscal year 1975): *Revenues,* $6,709,-260,000; *expenditures,* $6,106,543,000.

Personal Income (1975): $68,903,000,000; per capita, $5,631.

Labor Force (July 1976): *Nonagricultural wage and salary earners,* 4,531,100; *insured unemployed,* 57,-900 (1.6%).

Students staged an anti-U.S. demonstration in Bangkok in March. The last officially designated U.S. combat soldier left the country by midyear.

UPI

THAILAND

Thailand's three-year-old democratic experiment floundered in confusion and violence during 1976. It ended with a bloody military coup in October.

Political Developments. January opened with a crisis in rice-pricing and a consequent general strike in Bangkok. On January 12, the government of Premier Kukrit Pramoj collapsed, resulting in the dissolution of parliament and the scheduling of new elections. Following a period of unprecedented electoral strife, including more than a dozen assassinations, the elections were held in early April. About 40 parties, with nearly 2,400 candidates, competed for the 279 parliamentary seats. Kukrit lost his seat in the assembly. His brother Seni Pramoj (a political opponent) became premier, heading a four-party coalition.

But government stability was short lived. In mid-September Field Marshal Thanom Kittikachorn, whose government had been overthrown by a student-led revolt in 1973, returned from exile, ostensibly to visit his ailing father. Thanom's return was strongly opposed by the government, but it did not feel strong enough to prevent his entry. To emphasize his nonpolitical role, Thanom was ordained as a Buddhist monk. Nevertheless, he was greeted by many old military colleagues.

--------- **THAILAND · Information Highlights** ---------

Official Name: Kingdom of Thailand.
Location: Southeast Asia.
Area: 198,456 square miles (514,000 km²).
Population (1976 est.): 43,300,000.
Chief Cities (1975 est.): Bangkok, the capital, 4,000,-000; Chiang Mai, 100,000.
Government: *Head of state,* Bhumibol Adulyadej, king (acceded June 1946). *Head of government,* Thanin Kraivichien, premier (took office Oct. 1976). *Chairman of the Administrative Reform Council,* Sa-ngad Chaloryu. *Legislature*—National Assembly: Senate and House of Representatives (suspended Oct. 1976).
Monetary Unit: Baht (20.40 baht equal U.S.$1, Aug. 1976).
Gross National Product (1975 est.): $14,700,000,000.
Manufacturing (major products): Processed foods, textiles, clothing.
Major Agricultural Products: Rice, rubber, tapicoa, corn, tobacco, fruits, sugarcane, kenaf and jute, forest products.
Foreign Trade (1974): *Exports,* $2,466,000,000; *imports,* $3,143,000,000.

Thanom's return sparked student demonstrations demanding his deportation. The government collapsed on September 23, but King Bhumibol Adulyadej asked Seni to form another government with the same coalition. Student demonstrations continued, and the situation deteriorated.

Military Coup. On October 6 the military mounted a bloody coup against what it termed Communist-inspired student rioters. The junta, known as the Administrative Reform Committee, was led by Adm. Sa-ngad Chaloryu, who suspended the 1974 constitution, banned newspapers, and established a curfew. It quickly purged the government, both civilian and military, of potentially unreliable persons and followed up with a general roundup of "leftist subversives," estimated to number over 4,000.

The king officially approved the military coup and appointed a civilian premier, Thanin Kraivichien, who had been a supreme court justice. Although Sa-ngad at first promised a quick return to "civilian" government, it was apparent that a return to parliamentary rule had been postponed indefinitely.

By the end of the year there was much uncertainty about the nature of the government and its prospects. It seemed a bit more pro-United States than its predecessor, but little of its ultimate policies seemed very certain. In the meantime, the old subversive-guerrilla movements in the interior continued.

Foreign Affairs. Perhaps the main foreign policy problem Thai governments have had to face in the last several years has been the presence of U.S. military forces in the country. In 1975 the United States and Thailand agreed that the final exodus of U.S. forces would occur by spring 1976. Major installations were in fact closed in June, but the United States continued to negotiate the possibility of retaining electronic surveillance crews in Thailand. However, the officially designated "last" U.S. combat soldier left Thailand on July 20.

Thailand and Vietnam agreed to open diplomatic relations in August. Relations with Cambodia slowly returned to normal.

CARL LEIDEN, *The University of Texas, Austin*

Joseph Papp's revival of Bertolt Brecht's "Threepenny Opera" was a highlight of the theatrical season.

THEATER

New York's theatrical activity in 1976 continued to be dominated by the indefatigable Joseph Papp. He broke with all precedent by keeping two highly successful productions running far beyond their original commitments at Lincoln Center's Vivian Beaumont and Mitzi E. Newhouse theaters, and he announced that he would install a permanent acting company at Lincoln Center early in 1977.

Joseph Papp's Productions. Papp continued to monopolize the annual honors in the theater. *A Chorus Line,* a musical produced by Papp in 1975, won the 1976 Pulitzer Prize for drama (although no one ever claimed great distinction for its literary qualities), the Tony Award for the best Broadway musical, an additional Tony for its director, and three out of four possible Tonys for the best individual performances in musicals.

Another Papp production, David Rabe's *Streamers* at the Newhouse Theater, won the award of the Drama Critics Circle for the best

American play. Papp's revival of Bertolt Brecht's *Threepenny Opera* at the Beaumont was so striking that the annual *Best Plays* volume departed from its usual practice of ignoring revivals and published a detailed summary. In addition, Papp brought to Broadway the best black show of the year—it cannot precisely be called a play because it is, in fact, a poetry reading—*For Colored Girls Who Have Considered Suicide/ When the Rainbow is Enuf,* by Ntozake Shange.

Other producers are fearful and inclined to trust only American revivals and British importations. A few of the bolder ones look to off-Broadway or the regional theaters for plays they can transfer to Broadway. Papp, on the other hand, benefits not only from his own good judgment but also from the support provided by his ongoing organizations at the Public Theater and Lincoln Center, from the financial support provided by both private and federal foundations, and, lately, from the profits that *A Chorus Line* has been earning. He can be in at the start of a production, as in the case of *A Chorus Line* and *Threepenny Opera,* but he too has had to scramble for scripts. Although Papp has fostered Rabe's professional career from its very beginning, *Streamers* opened at the Long Wharf Theater of New Haven; *For Colored Girls* came from the New Federal Theater of the Henry Street Settlement.

At the Beaumont Theater, Papp began the year with George Bernard Shaw's *Mrs. Warren's Profession,* memorable mainly for an eccentric performance by octogenarian Ruth Gordon as Mrs. Warren and a vigorous impersonation of her rebellious daughter by Lynn Redgrave. *Threepenny Opera* followed, in the harsh-sounding but scrupulously faithful new translation by Ralph Manheim and John Willett. Avant-garde director Richard Foreman, working on Broadway for the first time, projected his own distinctive, rather sinister vision of the play's world. If Foreman's vision was not identical with Brecht's conception, it nevertheless worked on its own terms and became the most popular production the Beaumont had ever housed.

The Beaumont's smaller sister theater at New York's Lincoln Center, the Newhouse, first offered Michael Dorn Moody's *The Shortchanged Review,* a violent melodrama of no great interest. It was followed by Rabe's *Streamers,* which made better use of its violence by saving it for the evening's final, climactic moments. Set in a stateside army barracks in 1965, *Streamers* exploits an explosive situation that is plentifully supplied with racial and sexual tensions. The play's concern is not just the Vietnamese war or military life in general; its real subject is the immanent violence of our daily lives. *Streamers* is surely Rabe's best play to date, and it benefits enormously from the resourceful direction of Mike Nichols.

For Colored Girls is a program of angry, highly theatrical poetry, movingly declaimed, danced, and acted out by seven actresses who originally included the author herself. Some of the poems are lyrical and others are narrative. All vividly convey the courage of black women as well as the tragedies they suffer, mostly at the hands of their men.

Papp's Public Theater was alive with activity early in the year, offering plays that were colorful and curious, but most fell short of their aspirations: John Guare's *Rich & Famous,* about a playwright's first opening night; Myrna Lamb's *Apple Pie,* a musical with a feminist theme; Neil Harris' *So Nice, They Named it Twice,* a comedy of black life; Thomas Babe's *Rebel Women,* which humanizes General Sherman by providing a romantic interlude during his march to the sea. There were also two plays by resident companies, the Manhattan Project and Shaliko, the latter represented by Georg Büchner's *Woyzeck.* Later in the year, things were quieter at the Public. Throughout most of the fall the only show on view there was *Cascando,* a radio play by Samuel Beckett brought to the stage by the Mabou Mines, an experimental company that has shown great skill in its productions of Beckett.

Broadway Theater. Not many native plays of real quality reached Broadway, and the few that made it generally had arrived by way of off-Broadway or the regional theater. One of the few new works of value was Jules Feiffer's *Knock Knock,* which originated off-Broadway with the Circle Repertory Company. The play traded profitably in the comic value of incongruity, presenting the story of two complacent middle-aged Jewish intellectuals, naggers straight out of Feiffer's cartoons, who are surprised, as well they might be, at being visited by Joan of Arc in full armor and told, in effect, to get out of the house. Marshall W. Mason's engaging production moved to Broadway with its cast of relatively unknown actors, but the producers soon decided to bolster business by substituting a new cast of better-known actors, led by Lynn Redgrave as Joan, with José Quintero as director. Even with this change, *Knock Knock* did not last long on Broadway.

Preston Jones' *A Texas Trilogy* comprises three full-length plays, which were performed on alternating nights. The *Trilogy* went to Broadway from the Kennedy Center in Washington, but individual components had been seen at various regional theaters during the previous two years, beginning with the Dallas Theater Center in 1974. Although the three plays have overlapping characters and are set in the same imaginary town in Texas, each one can stand by itself. Each tells a plain tale of recognizably real people. In *Lu Ann Hampton Laverty Oberlander,* Diane Ladd played a lively high school girl who passes, over a number of years, from hope to despair. In *The Last Meeting of the Knights of the White Magnolia,* an organization resembling the Ku Klux Klan far-

cically comes to its end. *The Oldest Living Graduate,* which is probably the weakest of the three, shows the town's patriarch suffering a stroke that is likely to be fatal. Broadway was less enthusiastic than the regional audiences had been. There was a plan to save *Lu Ann* and close the other plays, but all three went down together.

The principal nonmusical commercial success on Broadway was Neil Simon's *California Suite,* which is composed of four one-act plays that take place in a room at the Beverly Hills Hotel. Simon is funnier and more at home with his two lowbrow characters (played by Barbara Barrie and Jack Weston) in a sketch about a husband who must hide from his wife the girl he has spent the night with and another about a wife crippled by a tennis ball. He is less successful with the two others (played by Tammy Grimes and George Grizzard), with whom he tries to deal more seriously.

Ronald Ribman's *The Poison Tree,* a play of prison life, was admirably serious and beautifully acted but lacking in dramatic construction. Equally solemn but less immediate in its appeal was Milan Stitt's *The Runner Stumbles* (which came from the Hartman Theater of Stamford), about a priest accused of killing a nun with whom he is in love. Julie Harris had a personal success with her one-woman show about Emily Dickinson, *The Belle of Amherst,* which played briefly on Broadway and then went on national tour.

Pride of place among the imported Broadway plays must be given to Harold Pinter's beguiling but puzzling *No Man's Land.* Sir John Gielgud and Sir Ralph Richardson were seen as two writers, a failure and a success respectively, who seem to be total strangers in the first act and old acquaintances in the second. However the relationship is to be explained, if it can be ex-

Jack Weston and Tammy Grimes star in Neil Simon's "California Suite." The comedy was a commercial hit.

Of the musical revivals, "Porgy and Bess" was the most notable. The Sherwin M. Goldman Houston Grand Opera produced the work as originally conceived by its author, George Gershwin.

plained at all, the knights' performances were riveting.

Trevor Griffiths' *Comedians*, also imported from Britain, showed several novice comedians competing for a chance to become professionals. Their teacher wants them to be conscientious critics of society, but two of them sell out and a third over responds to his instruction, totally sacrificing comedy to bitter social criticism. In this slightly toned down Broadway version, Griffiths entertains us and conveys the seriousness of his ideas about comedy without entirely selling us on their merit. It was directed by Mike Nichols.

Monty Python Live! imported an all-British cast for a limited engagement to recreate episodes of a zany television program that enjoys great international popularity. Enid Bagnold's *A Matter of Gravity* was represented as a new play, although an earlier version, with Dame Sybil Thorndike in the lead, was presented in England in 1968 and closed in the provinces without reaching London. On Broadway, the chief attraction was Katharine Hepburn, essentially playing herself but nominally playing an old lady who startles young people by expressing haughty tolerance of their misbehavior.

Elie Wiesel's *Zalmen, or the Madness of God*, translated from the French, criticized Soviet mistreatment of the Jews. In Pavel Kohout's

Poor Murderer, a Czech dramatization of a story by Leonid Andreyev, an actor reenacts, for therapeutic reasons, a murder he planned but could not commit. Political considerations won both of these plays more attention than they would otherwise have earned. Few attributed any political theme to *Poor Murderer*, but Kohout is in trouble with the authorities in Czechoslovakia and was not permitted to go to New York for the opening.

To observe the bicentennial, American plays of all periods were revived on Broadway, off-Broadway, and in the regional theaters. New York's most successful revival of a straight play was Edward Albee's own staging of his *Who's Afraid of Virginia Woolf?*, which carefully reproduced all of the play's original tensions, especially in Colleen Dewhurst's boisterous performance as Martha. The year's most disappointing revival of a great play was surely Eugene O'Neill's powerful autobiographical work, *Long Day's Journey into Night*. A tepid production directed by Jason Robards, it traveled from Washington's Kennedy Center to the Brooklyn Academy of Music. Zoe Caldwell's moving portrait of the mother was its only redeeming element.

Revivals also figured prominently among the musicals presented on Broadway in 1976. The most notable was George Gershwin's *Porgy and*

Bess, spectacularly performed, uncut, in operatic style, as Gershwin intended, by the Houston Grand Opera. Also reappearing on Broadway were *Guys and Dolls* (with an all-black cast), *My Fair Lady* (highlighted by George Rose as Alfred Doolittle), *Pal Joey* (which had a secondary drama of its own with its much publicized problems of casting), and *Going Up* (first seen in 1917). The musicals *Godspell* and *The Robber Bridegroom* were presented on Broadway after previous off-Broadway productions. In addition, *Bubbling Brown Sugar* was a revue that revived the songs and dances of Harlem in the 1920's and 1930's.

Take away the revivals, and Broadway was left with several extraordinarily expensive disasters, such as *Home Sweet Homer* and *1600 Pennsylvania Avenue*. *Pacific Overtures* was a critical success but a commercial failure. A highly original show, it used something like Kabuki music and stage technique to interpret Commodore Perry's opening of Japan to the world in 1853 and its consequences. The music, text, direction, and sets conspired to create a Japanese context from which the events were seen. How authentic were the Kabuki elements? As authentic as a Broadway audience could stand.

Pal Joey was presented by the Circle in the Square, a Broadway operation mainly concerned with reviving theatrical classics. Its other productions were Ibsen's *The Lady from the Sea,* whose languor was not arrested even by the presence of Vanessa Redgrave in the title role; Marguerite Duras' *Days in the Trees,* a contemporary French classic getting its first American staging and benefiting from Mildred Dunnock's unsparing portrait of a selfish, self-indulgent mother; and Tennessee Williams' *The Night of the Iguana.*

Off-Broadway. To see a new American play it was generally necessary to go off Broadway. Highlights of the off-Broadway year included David Mamet's double bill, *Duck Variations* and *Sexual Perversity in Chicago,* memorable portraits of trivial people in peppery dialogue; Israel Horovitz's *The Primary English Class,* with Diane Keaton giving a hilarious performance as a neurotic teacher; Tom Cole's *Medal of Honor Rag,* based on the story of a medal-of-honor winner who was killed committing a robbery; Jack Heitner's *Vanities,* from the Chelsea Center, about the changes in the lives of three girls over a decade; Heinrich von Kleist's *The Prince of Homburg,* also from Chelsea, the 19th-century German classic getting its professional American première in an ambitious production; and Steve Carter's *Eden,* from the Negro Ensemble Company, about hostilities between West Indians and other blacks.

One other American production is unclassifiable, Robert Wilson's *Einstein on the Beach,* with a musical score by Philip Glass. This symbolic, pictorial, controversial work toured Europe and then came home for two performances at the Metropolitan Opera House.

International Theater. In England, most attention and most controversy were drawn to the National Theatre, which opened two of its three new playhouses, the Lyttelton and the Olivier. Peter Hall, who runs the National, was under fire for requiring so much money that other subsidies (in particular the one paid to the Royal Shakespeare Theater) were endangered. He was also criticized for failing to maintain a permanent company and for presenting several

Yale Repertory Theater in New Haven, Conn., opened its fall season with "Julius Caesar," starring Robert Drivas as Mark Antony and Jeremy Geidt as Julius Caesar. During the year, more and more playwrights, producers, and actors turned their attention to regional theater.

Mermaid Theatre
Puddle Dock, Blackfriars, London, EC4V 3DB. Tel: 01 236 9521.

THE MERMAID THEATRE IN ASSOCIATION WITH
H. M. TENNENT LIMITED CAMERON MACKINTOSH
AND BY ARRANGEMENT WITH THE INCOMES COMPANY (THEATRE) LTD
present

SIDE BY
SIDE BY
SONDHEIM

with

MILLICENT MARTIN
JULIA McKENZIE
DAVID KERNAN
NED SHERRIN

Directed /
NED SHERRIN
Musical Numbers Staged /
BOB HOWE
Musical Supervisor /
RAY COOK
Setting /
PETER DOCHERTY
Costumes /
GINA FRATINI
Lighting /
JOHN WOOD
Keyboards /
TIM HIGGS &
STUART PEDLAR

OPENS TUES.
MAY 4th

(Public previews
April 27th - May 3rd)
Nightly at 8.15 pm
(May 4th at 7.0 pm)
Saturday matinees at 5.0 pm
Seats from 75p
Combined Theatre Dinner
ticket £5.95
ALL BOOKINGS
01-248 7656

Cannan was also represented by *The Ik*, which he adapted with Colin Turnbull and Colin Higgins from Turnbull's *The Mountain People*, an anthropological study of a tribe in Uganda that lost its normal sustenance and developed a streak of moral viciousness. Brilliantly directed by Peter Brook, this simple but harrowing play was first performed in French in 1975, but in 1976 was at last seen in English and in England. The English-language version later journeyed to the Theater of the Nations in Belgrade, Yugoslavia, and then toured university centers in the United States. At Belgrade, it shared the festival's three equal prizes with Wilson's *Einstein on the Beach* and Yuri Lyubimov's *Hamlet* from the Taganka Theater of Moscow. The *Hamlet* production goes back to 1972, but its achievement of recognition at Belgrade was important because this was the first visit to a foreign theater festival by this innovative Soviet company. The awards made in Belgrade confirmed an impression that was growing in the theater capitals of Europe that the theater of today is primarily a directors' theater.

See also PRIZES AND AWARDS.

HENRY POPKIN
State University of New York at Buffalo

London offered "Side by Side by Sondheim," a revue based on Stephen Sondheim lyrics and music, and "Banana Ridge," a comedy about a paternity issue. The latter featured Anthony Dawes, George Cole, and Robert Morley.

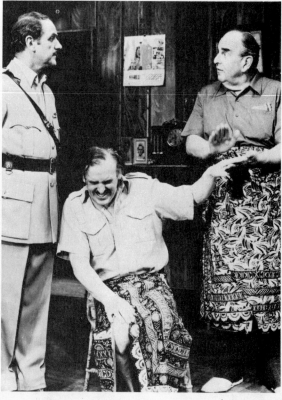

plays that seemed unworthy of the National.

Some of the criticism was softened after the Olivier opened with Hall's impressive production of the two parts of Marlowe's *Tamburlaine,* in which Albert Finney played the title role. (See Special Report following this article.)

The Royal Shakespeare struggled valiantly on a tight budget. It continued to specialize in Russian drama at its London outpost, the Aldwych, and added a new theater at Stratford-on-Avon, the Other Place, where Trevor Nunn's much admired *Macbeth* was seen. Terry Hands' imaginative Royal Shakespeare production of *Henry V* won praise when it was presented at the Brooklyn Academy of Music.

Some indication of what the British valued in their commercial theater was provided by the first awards of the Society of West End Theater. The prize for best musical went to an American importation, *A Chorus Line;* the "best play" was Denis Cannan's *Dear Daddy,* about an explosive family reunion; and the "best comedy" was Michael Frayn's *Donkey's Years,* a farcical treatment of a reunion of Cambridge University graduates. Frayn also provided another, somewhat meatier, comedy about English journalists in Cuba, *Clouds.*

BROADWAY OPENINGS OF 1976

PLAYS

The Belle of Amherst, by William Luce; directed by Charles Nelson Reilly; with Julie Harris; April 28–August 8.

Best Friend, by Michael Sawyer; directed by Marty Jacobs; with Barbara Baxley; October 19–23.

California Suite, by Neil Simon; directed by Gene Saks; with Tammy Grimes, George Grizzard, Jack Weston, Barbara Barrie; June 10–.

Comedians, by Trevor Griffiths; directed by Mike Nichols; with Milo O'Shea; November 28–.

Days in the Trees, by Marguerite Duras, translated by Sonia Orwell; directed by Stephen Porter; with Mildred Dunnock; September 26–November 21.

The Eccentricities of a Nightingale, by Tennessee Williams; directed by Edwin Sherin; with Betsy Palmer; November 23–December 12.

For Colored Girls Who Have Considered Suicide/When the Rainbow is Enuf, by Ntozake Shange; directed by Oz Scott, September 15–.

The Heiress, by Ruth and Augustus Goetz, based on the novel by Henry James; directed by George Keathley; with Jane Alexander and Richard Kiley; April 20–May 9.

Herzl, by Dore Schary and Amos Elon; based on the biography by Elon; directed by J. Ranelli; with Paul Hecht; November 30–December 5.

I Have a Dream, based on the life of Dr. Martin Luther King, Jr., conceived and directed by Robert Greenwald; with Billy Dee Williams; September 20–December 5.

The Innocents, by William Archibald, based on Henry James' story *The Turn of the Screw;* directed by Harold Pinter; with Claire Bloom; October 21–30.

Knock, Knock, by Jules Feiffer; directed by Marshall W. Mason (and subsequently redirected by José Quintero); February 24–July 3.

The Lady from the Sea, by Henrik Ibsen, translated by Michael Meyer; directed by Tony Richardson; with Vanessa Redgrave; March 18–May 23.

A Matter of Gravity, by Enid Bagnold; directed by Noel Willman; with Katharine Hepburn; February 3–April 10.

Monty Python Live!, conceived, written, directed, and acted by the *Monty Python* team; April 14–May 2.

Mrs. Warren's Profession, by George Bernard Shaw; directed by Gerald Freedman; with Ruth Gordon and Lynn Redgrave; February 18–April 14.

The Night of the Iguana, by Tennessee Williams; directed by Joseph Hardy; with Richard Chamberlain, Dorothy McGuire, and Sylvia Miles; December 17–.

No Man's Land, by Harold Pinter; directed by Peter Hall; with John Gielgud and Ralph Richardson; November 9–December 18.

The Poison Tree, by Ronald Ribman; directed by Charles Blackwell; with Cleavon Little; January 8–11.

Poor Murderer, by Pavel Kohout, translated by Herbert Berghof and Laurence Luckinbill; directed by Berghof; with Luckinbill, Maria Schell, and Kevin McCarthy; October 20–January 2, 1977.

The Runner Stumbles, by Milan Stitt; directed by Austin Pendleton; with Stephen Joyce and Nancy Donohue; May 18–October 31.

Sly Fox, by Larry Gelbart, based on Ben Johnson's *Volpone;* directed by Arthur Penn; with George C. Scott, Trish Van Devere, and Jack Gilford; December 14–.

A Texas Trilogy (three plays), by Preston Jones; directed by Alan Schneider; with Fred Gwynne and Diane Ladd; September 21–October 31.

Who's Afraid of Virginia Woolf? by Edward Albee; directed by Albee; with Colleen Dewhurst and Ben Gazzara; April 1–August 1.

Zalmen, or the Madness of God, by Elie Wiesel, adapted by Marion Wiesel; directed by Alan Schneider; with Joseph Wiseman; March 17–April 4.

MUSICALS

Bubbling Brown Sugar, revue based on a concept by Rosetta LeNoire, book by Loften Mitchell, music and lyrics by many authors of the last 50 years, new music by Danny Holgate, Emme Kemp, and Lillian Lopez; directed by Robert M. Cooper; with Josephine Premice and Vivian Reed; March 2–.

Fiddler on the Roof, book by Joseph Stein, music by Jerry Bock; directed and choreographed by Jerome Robbins; with Zero Mostel; December 28–.

Godspell, based on the Gospel according to St. Matthew, conceived by John-Michael Tebelak, music and lyrics by Stephen Schwartz; directed by Tebelak; June 22–.

Going Up, based on a play by James Montgomery, book and lyrics by Otto Harbach, music by Louis A. Hirsch; directed by Bill Gile; with Brad Blaisdell and Kimberly Farr; September 19–October 31.

Guys and Dolls, based on a story by Damon Runyon, book by Jo Swerling and Abe Burrows, music and lyrics by Frank Loesser; directed and choreographed by Billy Wilson; with Norma Donaldson, Robert Guillaume, Ernestine Jackson, James Randolph, and Ken Page; July 21–.

Home Sweet Homer, based on Homer's *Odyssey,* book by Roland Kibbee and Albert Marre, lyrics by Charles Burr and Forman Brown, music by Mitch Leigh; directed by Marre; with Yul Brynner and Joan Diener; January 4.

Music Is, based on Shakespeare's *Twelfth Night,* book by George Abbott, music by Richard Adler, lyrics by Will Holt; choreography by Patricia Birch; directed by Abbott; December 20–26.

My Fair Lady, based on George Bernard Shaw's *Pygmalion,* book and lyrics by Allan Jay Lerner, music by Frederick Loewe; directed by Jerry Adler (based on the original production by Moss Hart); with Ian Richardson, George Rose, Christine Andreas, and Robert Coote; March 25–.

Pacific Overtures, book by John Weidman, lyrics and music by Stephen Sondheim, additional material by Hugh Wheeler; directed by Harold Prince; January 11–June 27.

Pal Joey, book by John O'Hara, based on his stories, lyrics by Lorenz Hart, music by Richard Rodgers; directed by Theodore Mann; with Joan Copeland and Christopher Chadman; June 27–August 29.

Porgy and Bess, libretto by DuBose Heyward, based on his novel and on his play with Dorothy Heyward, lyrics by Heyward and Ira Gershwin; music by George Gershwin; September 26–.

Rex, book by Sherman Yellen, lyrics by Sheldon Harnick, music by Richard Rodgers; directed by Edwin Sherin; with Nicol Williamson and Penny Fuller; April 25–June 5.

The Robber Bridegroom, based on a novel by Eudora Welty, book and lyrics by Alfred Uhry, music by Robert Waldman; directed by Gerald Freedman; with Barry Bostwick; October 9–.

Rockabye Hamlet, based on Shakespeare's *Hamlet,* book, lyrics, and music by Cliff Jones; directed and choreographed by Gower Champion; February 17–21.

1600 Pennsylvania Avenue, book and lyrics by Allan Jay Lerner, music by Leonard Bernstein; directed and choreographed by Gilbert Moses and George Faison; with Ken Howard, Patricia Routledge, Gilbert Price, and Emily Yancy; May 4–8.

So Long, 174th Street, book by Joseph Stein, based on his play (which was based on a novel by Carl Reiner), lyrics and music by Stan Daniels; directed by Burt Shevelove; with Robert Morse; April 27–May 9.

Threepenny Opera, book and lyrics by Bertolt Brecht, newly translated by Ralph Manheim and John Willett, music by Kurt Weill; directed by Richard Foreman; with Raul Julia; May 1–.

SPECIAL REPORT:

Britain's New National Theatre

Britain's new National Theatre stands proudly on the South Bank of the Thames, face to face with the eighteenth century splendor of Somerset House and within earshot of Big Ben and the bustle of Waterloo Station. Conceived in 1848 and given the go-ahead by Parliament 100 years later, it was not until March 1976 that the dream became reality when the National opened its doors to the public.

Design. The theater is an angular, powerful building of white concrete, starkly modern and dominated by two squat, windowless towers. Outside are terraces and riverside walks with superb views of the Thames curving away toward St. Paul's Cathedral in the distance. Inside are three theaters, each of completely different character, eight bars, two cafes, a restaurant which seats 100 people, and ample space for mingling. An underground car park can accommodate 400 vehicles.

The biggest of the three theaters is the Olivier, with 1,160 seats. Designed on the lines of a Greek amphitheater, the auditorium relates like a fan to the vast open stage. The focal point on stage is a split, revolving drum, 40 feet (12 m) in diameter, each half of which can be raised or lowered through 45 feet (13.5 m) on separate lifts, simplifying changes from one play to another. The revolving stage can carry five tons of scenery and armies of performers. Computerized machinery enables scenery and lighting patterns to be changed rapidly. It is in the Olivier that the resident National Theatre Company will present its year-round repertoire of six plays. These will include a Shakespeare, a classic comedy of the 17th or 18th century, and a 19th century play by writers such as Ibsen and Shaw.

Next in size is the Lyttleton Theatre, which seats 890 persons. This is a proscenium theater with a picture frame type of stage, part of which can be lowered to form an orchestra pit.

Visiting companies from home and abroad will be invited here. It aims to produce both modern work and revivals by forgotten writers.

Lastly, the small Cottesloe holds only 400 people. It is a simple, rectangular box that can be adapted for all types of experimental drama. It is this theater that will stage new ideas from "fringe" groups, operating on the threshold of dramatic innovation.

Backstage are two rehearsal rooms and 135 air-conditioned dressing rooms. Through a relay system each performer can tune to the auditorium of his choice. Two floors of offices house the 500-strong administrative staff.

Denys Lasdun, the architect who designed the complex, claims that its vast public areas and outside terraces are in themselves a fourth theater. Street traders will be encouraged to set up stalls; street performers can stage impromptu shows; and visitors will enjoy such activities as kite flying and firework displays.

Costs. Peter Hall, founder of the Royal Shakespeare Company, and now the National's director, says that it is essential that the center be popular with everyone. Seat prices will be kept as low as possible by means of an annual subsidy from public funds of about £2 million. The building itself has cost the public over £16 million. Much of this high cost can be blamed on strikes and other industrial unrest which caused delays when building work finally started in 1969.

Construction was held up to such an extent that the complex opened the three theaters one by one over a 12-month period. By the end of 1976 the Olivier and Cottesloe were still not completely finished. To add to the problems, performances at the Lyttleton were halted for a week by a wildcat strike of stagehands, who were demanding more money.

DAVID NORRIS
"Sunday Telegraph"

TOKYO

Once known as the most polluted and populous city in the world, the capital of Japan has become a little more livable. Stringent control over industrial waste and other pollutants has made Tokyo Bay less muddy; fish are back in the rivers, and the air is cleaner.

Population. The population of the city proper, the world's largest until Shanghai overtook it some years ago, has shrunk by 2% in the last four years. In what is known as the "doughnut" phenomenon, people are moving out to suburbs and surrounding prefectures.

Finance. The city in 1976 was facing financial difficulties. Snowballing expenditures and declining tax revenues from corporations were expected to make the annual shortfall $1,000,000,000 by March 1977. The city's buses and subways alone suffered a deficit amounting to $345 million. To reduce expenditures the municipal government cut down the number of its bureaus and employees. It also decided (for the first time) not to recruit any college graduates for the fiscal year starting in April 1977. It suspended chauffeur service for high officials of the city government and also gave up mailing New Year's cards. Governor Ryokichi Minobe, who runs both the city and the province of Tokyo, even revived the city-sponsored horse races, a source of revenue he had banned three years before as "dishonorable."

Prices. Though the inflation has slackened a little, some items jumped in 1976. Tuition in the city government's high schools and universities more than doubled. Electricity went up 21%. Admission to public baths rose 20%. And a worldwide survey showed that Tokyo was still the costliest city in the world.

Crime. Despite all its problems, Tokyo remained one of the safest cities on earth, with only about 175 murders and 400 rapes per year.

HIROTAKA YOSHIZAKI
"The New York Times," Tokyo

TORONTO

Numerous problems plagued Metropolitan Toronto in 1976. In July an inquiry into charges of police brutality turned up positive evidence of the use of torture and of attempts to cover up the facts, thus seriously tarnishing the force's respected past record. A bitter two-month strike of Metro secondary school teachers finally ended on January 19 with a provincial back-to-work order. And throughout the year the city had to face growing financial difficulties.

Government. The year-long problems of revenue and expenditure that confronted the city in 1976 were brought on, in part, by cutbacks in provincial funding for municipal governments. The Metro Council instituted a $41-million spending cut, including a freeze on police hiring, and raised taxes on property owners. The Royal

UPI

In Tokyo, the $12,500,000 U. S. Embassy replaces four pre-World War II buildings which had become too small.

Commission established in 1975 to study the problems of the city's two-tiered administration continued through 1976.

Transportation. In February the Toronto Transit Commission increased fares on public transport from 33¢ to 40¢—the second such increase in less than a year—and there was debate over returning to a system of zone fares and transfers in order to ease chronic financial problems. Concern also grew over subway safety following an outbreak of assaults, though over the year the number of incidents remained extremely small in comparison with other large North American cities. Furthermore, major crime on all of Toronto's public transit facilities actually decreased from 1975.

General. A provincial court ordered the Doctor's Hospital to reopen after the Ontario government had closed it as part of a policy to hold down the province's soaring health costs. An American League baseball franchise was awarded to the city for 1977 after an attempt to purchase the National League's San Francisco Giants fell through at the last minute.

ERIC JARVIS
University of Western Ontario

In 1976 the famous double-decker bus went back into service in New York City and the electric trolly was reintroduced in Detroit.

TRANSPORTATION

Survey

Almost all areas of transportation showed advances in 1976. Equipment and revenue continued to grow and safety continued to improve.

Airlines. The most dramatic development in transportation was the advent of supersonic transportation. On January 21, Concordes simultaneously took off from Paris and London for flights to Bahrain and Rio de Janeiro respectively. Estimates of the cost to develop this aircraft run as high as $4,000,000,000

Air Freight. The Civil Aeronautics Board (CAB) announced that international air freight increased its share of all U. S. two-way foreign trade to 11–12% in 1974 with a total value of $22,400,000,000. Such traffic has been growing at a yearly rate of 18% since 1970. U. S. air carriers moved 38% of the 2,600,000,000 pounds (1,180,000,000 kg) of air freight.

Commuter Airlines. The CAB reported that in 1975 commuter airlines flew 1,480,561 flights, or approximately 24% of all flights by scheduled and commuter air carriers. But they flew only 253,836,000 miles (408,510,000 km) or 10% of the total distance flown by scheduled and commuter air carriers. This reflects the fact that these carriers fly shorter routes as compared with the domestic trunk airlines.

Oil Pipelines. The Interstate Commerce Commission (ICC) reported that oil pipelines have grown annually over the past two decades. They have grown from total revenues of $677.6 million in 1955 to a total of $1,582,000,000 in 1974. Like railroads and water carriers, they have seen their share of the total traffic decline from 4.5% in 1955 to 3.9% in 1974. Rail traffic has declined from 57.0% to 39.0%. Water traffic has declined from 2.1% to 1.8%. Motor carriers, on the other hand, have increased their market share from 36.4% to 55.3%.

Railroads. In spite of the fact that U. S. railroads did substantially better in 1976 than in

1975, the U. S. Department of Commerce expected that capital investment in equipment and facilities would total only $2,180,000,000 in 1976 as compared with $2,550,000,000 in 1975 and $2,540,000,000 in 1974.

During the first nine months operating revenues increased to $13,800,000,000 from $11,900,000,000 for a gain of 16%. Operating expenses increased only 13% from $9,800,000,000 to $11,100,000,000. After allowing for taxes and other nonoperating expenses the system earned $253,100,000, as compared with a loss of $128,500,000 during the same period of 1975. This amounted to only a 2.05% return on investment. One of the bright spots in railroad traffic continued to be piggyback. It is projected that this traffic will account for 1,420,000 carloadings in 1976 of a total of 23.8 million carloadings or 6.0% of the total. Over the past decade this total has been increasing each year starting from 3.9%, with setbacks marked only in 1970 and 1975.

Vehicles. The Deparment of Transportation expected 137,287,000 motor vehicles to be registered in the United States at the end of 1976. The increase of 3.3% is up from 2.3% in 1975. The registration figures include 109,675,000 automobiles and 27,612,000 trucks.

California leads the nation with 14.1 million vehicle registrations, followed by Texas with 8.7 million, Pennsylvania with 8 million, New York with 7.8 million, and Ohio with 7.5 million. In addition, Illinois, Michigan, and Florida each registered more than 5 million vehicles. These 8 states registered 46% of all vehicles in the country.

Not included in the above total are some 5,110,000 motorcycles, motor scooters, and motorized bicycles and 12,834,671 trailers. Motorcycle registrations showed an increase of only 2.9%.

Safety. The National Transportation Safety Board announced that the transportation death toll continued to decline in 1975 to 49,502, a decline of 2% from 1974. Highway fatalities accounted for 44,690, recreational marine 1,480, general aviation 1,324, rail-highway grade crossing 910, railroad 564, commercial marine 380, commercial aviation 124, and pipeline 30.

JAMES R. ROMAN, JR.
The George Washington University

Aviation

The long-awaited turnaround in traffic and profits for commercial airlines appeared well under way in 1976.

Profits. For U. S. airlines, the first six months of 1976 generally were encouraging, with many showing a profit for the period, or at least for the second quarter. Pacing the recovery were Eastern Airlines and the well-managed, perennially profitable Delta Airlines. For Eastern, the $38 million earned in the first half represented a 12-fold increase over that period a year earlier. Braniff and American also posted profits. The nation's largest domestic carrier, United, turned a profit in the second quarter, but had a loss for the six months overall. Trans World Airlines showed a similar pattern, although TWA's loss for the half was only one-quarter of that experienced in the first half of 1975. Pan American World Airways showed a gain of $50 million for the six months, although this included gains on the exchange of debentures in May.

The results for the first half also compare very well with those for the first year of 1975, when U. S. domestic trunk airlines lost $49.1 million on operating revenues of $10,300,000,000, and U. S. international carriers lost $36.4 million on $3,100,000,000 in revenues.

Passenger Traffic. For the first half of 1976, boardings showed increases, helping to pull the carriers into the black. The traffic upswing, averaging about 10% over the like period of 1975, stemmed from the improved U. S. economy, which increased both business travel—the bread and butter of most airlines—and leisure travel. In contrast, 1975 saw a 0.2% decrease in domestic passenger boardings over 1974 and a 9.2% drop in international passengers.

Fares. Only moderate increases in fares occurred in 1976, compared with the large hikes the carriers obtained in 1974 to offset the rise in fuel costs. Domestic carriers had received slight rises early in 1976, amounting to about 5% in small steps, and in September banded together in near-unanimity to ask a further 2% average increase from the Civil Aeronautics Board (CAB). A number of carriers appear to have adopted the tactic of asking for small increases several times a year, to keep up with the ongoing inflation. A number of airlines also moved to limit discount fares. They had found that some, instead of generating new traffic, had merely diverted traffic from regular services. The "Freedom Fare," the principal domestic discount tariff, was limited to a 15% cut during peak periods and 20% offpeak.

North Atlantic fares always are the cause for much haggling. During the International Air Transport Association fare meeting in Miami, several new fare types were proposed. Air Canada came up with its "charter-competitive fare," which would cut as much as 50% from regular economy fares, and TWA proposed an "advance-purchase inclusive tour" fare, which would reduce the New York-London roundtrip fare to $325 off-peak, plus a minimum $100 package of ground services. Both innovations were hotly contested.

Labor. Almost complete labor peace reigned in the air transportation field during 1976. The exceptions were a week-long strike by TWA mechanics, and an air traffic controllers' slowdown. The latter, which occurred in July, resulted in many delayed flights. Members of the Professional Air Traffic Controllers Organiza-
Continued page 512

SPECIAL REPORT:

The Concorde

The biggest technological jump in air transportation since the introduction of the first jets occurred during 1976, with the inauguration of scheduled flights of the Anglo-French Concorde supersonic transport from Europe to the Middle East, South America, and the United States.

The sleek, arrowhead-shaped Concorde, which gives the appearance of being almost all wing, nearly triples the speed of the most advanced jet transports, cruising at 2.2 times the speed of sound or about 1,400 mph (2,250 kmph). It is built by Aerospatiale-France and British Aircraft Corp., with afterburning Rolls-Royce Olympus turbojets as powerplants. But it is not capacious: there are just 100 seats, all first class.

The Concorde operators, both government-owned, are British Airways and Air France. They began commercial service with the Concorde Jan. 21, 1976, after more than three years of trial flights. British Airways flies to the oil-rich sheikhdom of Bahrain on the Persian Gulf in about 3 hrs. 40 mins. The airline is using this route to obtain passenger reaction and to feed subsonic services from there to Australia and Singapore. Flights to Australia and Singapore may be added to the Concorde itinerary if overflight rights from intervening nations can be obtained.

Air France inaugurated service to Rio de Janeiro, Brazil, with an intermediate refueling stop in Dakar, Senegal, on the West African coast. Total flight time is about 7 hours, including the stop. On April 9, Air France began scheduled flights to Caracas, Venezuela, with a stop in the Azores. It takes about 6 hours.

But the North Atlantic market is the biggest plum for both airlines. The U. S. Department of Transportation (DoT) held public hearings in January 1976 to determine the pros and cons of Concorde service to the United States. Representatives of the British and French governments argued in favor, whereas some U. S. federal and state agencies, including the U. S. Environmental Protection Agency, turned thumbs-down on the proposal.

After mulling the testimony for several weeks, Transportation Secretary William T. Coleman, Jr., rendered his decision: the two carriers would be allowed to operate up to six flights per day to Washington's Dulles Airport and to New York's Kennedy Airport, for a trial period of 16 months. During that time, noise, pollution, and vibration would be monitored closely. The flights could operate only between 7:00 AM and 10:00 PM, and the Concorde might not be flown supersonically over U. S. territory. Essentially, Secretary Coleman decided to let the Concorde fly or flop on its economic merits, while the

environmental questions are being worked out.

Since DoT "owns" Dulles, there was little question about landing rights, although the Virginia counties near the airport sued unsuccessfully to stop the Concorde.

Kennedy Airport, operated by the Port Authority of New York and New Jersey, was a different matter. Angry residents of nearby communities demonstrated noisily at the airport; New York Gov. Hugh Carey inveighed against Concorde; and the New York legislature passed an airport noise bill that would rule out Concorde operations at Kennedy. The Port Authority entered the fracas in March by denying Concorde landing rights at Kennedy for at least six months.

British Airways and Air France immediately slapped a suit on the Port Authority. They alleged that the Port had unconstitutionally invaded regulatory authority that is vested in the federal government, and had interfered in an area of foreign affairs, which is the sole prerogative of the federal government. (The carriers' operations to the United States are the subject of bilateral agreements, which have the force of treaties.) The case was to have been argued September 13, but the plaintiffs had it continued to January 1977, to see what the Port would do after the six months expired. DoT did not move to intervene.

Concorde operations by both airlines began May 24 to Dulles, with British Airways flying twice a week from London's Heathrow Airport and Air France thrice weekly from the Charles de Gaulle Airport near Paris. Fare is first class plus 20% surcharge, or $1,654 round trip to Paris and $1,267 to London. Flying time is

Secretary Coleman presides at hearings to determine whether the Concorde will fly in the United States.

UPI

PHOTOS UPI

British Airways and Air France began commercial service with the Concorde in January 1976.

about 3½ hours, about half that for a subsonic jetliner.

Environmental concerns regarding the Concorde were especially strong in the area of noise. On landing, when the engines are throttled back, Concorde is no noisier than a Boeing 707, Dulles measurements showed. But, according to the Federal Aviation Agency, it is twice as loud on takeoff. This writer witnessed a Concorde prototype take off from Boston in 1974, and estimated that it was about as loud as a brace of F-4 Phantom 2 fighters on takeoff. This is because the aircraft must use its afterburners, which are lit for about 70 seconds on takeoff. But since the aircraft climbs faster than a subsonic jet, the time of exposure on the ground is lessened. Only one sonic boom has been recorded in the United States, an accidental one from an Air France Concorde which was slowing to subsonic speed off New Jersey.

Pollution in the vicinity of airports, given the small number of Concordes that will be operating—only 16 have been approved for production—is not likely to be increased measurably. The World Meteorological Organization and the Livermore Laboratory have both indicated that a 50-aircraft fleet is not likely to impact adversely the atmospheric ozone layer.

Fuel consumption in the Concorde also has given rise to some concern. The amount of fuel consumed at supersonic speed is more per seat-mile than most subsonic jets, simply because it requires more energy to travel faster, as in an automobile. But the fuel being burned is the property of two foreign airlines, and so banning the Concorde would not affect the U. S. energy situation.

WARREN WETMORE
Aviation Week & Space Technology

New York motorists demonstrate against the Concorde.

tion "worked to rules" in an attempt to prevent the U. S. Civil Service Commission from downgrading their job ratings.

Canada's air transportation system was shut down for more than a week in June when many controllers stayed off the job to protest the planned introduction of bilingual English-French air traffic control at Montreal's two major airports. The issue nominally was one of safety —controlling aircraft in two different languages, when pilots may be fluent only in one, is considered complicated and hazardous—but the English-speaking Montreal controllers also would have to become fluent in French or be transferred elsewhere. The Canadian airline pilots also were upset, and struck after the controllers were ordered back to work; they also enlisted the aid of a number of foreign pilot associations in temporarily "quarantining" Canadian airspace.

Service was restored when the Canadian government backed down, agreeing to create a three-man commission to study the safety aspects of bilingualism and to permit members of parliament to vote on the eventual report according to conviction, not strict party line.

New Aircraft. The introduction of the Anglo-French Concorde supersonic transport into commercial service was the highlight of the year in new aircraft (see pages 510–511). The Boeing 747SP (Special Purpose), a new, slightly smaller but longer-range version of the jumbo jet, also entered service and set a round-the-world speed record of 46 hours, 56 seconds.

The next generation of transport aircraft was a subject much considered by the airlines and the manufacturers. Eastern Airlines tried to interest other airlines in drawing up the specifications of a new passenger aircraft, but found little enthusiasm for this approach. Boeing and McDonnell Douglas also appeared to reverse the trend toward ever-larger aircraft with their 7N7 and DC-X-200 designs, both 200-passenger aircraft employing fuel-saving technology and intended to replace eventually the Boeing 727 trijet. Boeing also is continuing studies on the larger 7X7, which would be in the same general class as the DC-10.

Lockheed, under contract from NASA, also delved into fuel-economic aircraft with its RECAT design. This would be a four-engined, 200-passenger transport employing "propfan" engines—essentially advanced turboprop engines with smaller-diameter, eight-bladed propellers.

WARREN C. WETMORE
Aviation Week & Space Technology

Highways

During 1976 all parts of the highway system expanded.

Roads and Streets. The U. S. Department of Transportation announced that there are now 3,838,146 miles (6,176,898 km) of roads and streets in the United States. Seventeen percent is municipal roads and streets while the balance is rural mileage. About 48% of the mileage has bituminous or portland cement concrete surfaces, which the public thinks of as "paved." About 33% has surfaces of gravel or crushed stone, while the balance is unsurfaced. Texas leads with 255,887 miles (411,810 km).

Interstate Highway System. The Department of Transportation revealed that based on current cost estimates 72.4% of the funds required to complete the 42,500-mile (68,000-km) Interstate System have been obligated. If inflation continues at its present rate only 65.4% of the system can be considered to be funded. So far, some $61,660,000,000 has been invested in the system since 1956. As currently designated, the system consists of 33,664 miles (54,177 km) of rural and 8,836 miles (14,420 km) of urban highways. Presently 37,717 miles (60,700 km) are open to traffic, but only 11,295 miles (18,178 km) can be considered complete. The balance requires work, including rest areas, lighting, and fencing. Currently, construction or improvement is under way on 4,214 miles (6,782 km) including 2,160 miles (3,476 km) which are already in use and 2,054 miles (3,306 km) being built in new locations.

Appalachian System. The Appalachian Development Highway System, authorized in 1965 to help develop the region, approved a total of $2,930,000,000 for the construction of up to 2,900 miles (4,665 km) of development highways and up to 1,600 miles (2,575 km) of local access roads. This is administered by the Appalachian Regional Commission consisting of the governors of the 13 states involved, a cochairman appointed by the U. S. president in cooperation with the Federal Highway Administration.

By year-end a total of $2,885,000,000 had been obligated including the federal share of $1,-655,000,000. Highways and access roads completed or under construction total 2,032 miles (3,270 km), with engineering and right-of-way acquisition under way on an additional 430 miles (692 km). Design has been approved or hearings held on 152 miles (245 km), while locations have been approved and design is under way on 173 miles (278 km).

Financing. The Department of Transportation reported that state highway departments and related agencies spent a total of $21,100,000,000, including $1,400,000,000 in borrowed funds and $6,000,000,000 in federal aid. Some $3,800,-000,000 was spent on the Interstate system.

JAMES R. ROMAN, JR.

Mass Transit

Urban mass transit took several steps forward in many major cities.

Washington, D. C. The most important development in urban mass transit occurred on March 29 when the Washington Metropolitan Area Transit Authority began operating on a 4.6-mile (7.4-km) segment of a planned 98-mile (157-km) system. Serving only 5 stations out of an eventual 86-station system, it surpassed all initial expectations. Operating only from 6 A. M. to 8 P. M. not including holidays or weekends, the system carried about 21,000 daily passengers as compared with a projected 8,000. This means that it transports over 4.0% of the 2.5 million passengers carried weekly by the Metrobus system which operates around the clock all week. With an $80,000 a day operating cost, farebox revenue is providing only about 50% of the revenue necessary to break even.

Late in the year it was estimated that the entire system, which was to cost a projected $2,500,000,000 when completed, would cost $5,250,000,000 because of inflation. Construction contracts of $2,174,000,000 had been awarded for 46.2 miles (74.4 km) of new rail and for 44 new stations. In addition, $102 million has been awarded design contracts on 27.3 more miles (43.9 km) and 20 new stations.

San Francisco. The Bay Area Rapid Transit System (BART) continued to experience technical and financial difficulties. Too many of BART cars are out for repair at a given time, resulting in service not up to the quality that was expected. At the same time fare increases have been implemented to reduce the operating deficit. On the positive side, BART increased service on some lines from an 8 PM ending to midnight, so in spite of the fare increase, the number of daily riders was averaging about 125,000.

The BART Impact Program Study produced some preliminary results, including the facts that BART delivers 10 times as many passenger miles as the automobile during peak periods, and that more than one third of the BART riders are former automobile riders.

Atlanta. The Metropolitan Atlanta Rapid Transit Authority plans to open service on a 7.1 mile (11.3 km) east line in December 1978. The system will have 53 miles (85 km) of heavy rail line. Atlanta is the first U. S. city to contract with a foreign car builder for its system. Société Franco-Belge won the contract with a bid of $54.3 million for 100 cars.

Buffalo. The Niagara Frontier Transportation Authority received a tentative $269 million from the Urban Mass Transportation Administration to develop a 6.4 mile (10.2 km), 14-station light rail line from downtown Buffalo to the campus of the State University of New York at Buffalo. It would be the first stage of a multiphase rapid transit project for the area.

JAMES R. ROMAN, JR.

Railroads

A new name entered the railroad lexicon in 1976: Conrail. Pieced together from the ruins of six bankrupt railroads in the Northeast and the Midwest, Conrail (for Consolidated Rail Corp.) came into being April 1—a 17,000-mile (27,000-km) carrier whose lines lace 17 states and two provinces of Canada. Conrail was created, by a special act of Congress, as a private

UPI

Britain's first high speed rail service—London to Bristol in 1 hr. 32 mins.—began operating in October.

railroad heavily funded by the U. S. government. Under the Railroad Revitalization and Regulatory Reform Act of 1976, Conrail received $2,-100,000,000 to help pay for a $7,000,000,000 modernization and rehabilitation program. In return, the U. S. government will have a strong say in Conrail's affairs until the obligations are paid off. When (and if) that day arrives, the threat of nationalization of the U. S. railroad industry may have been averted. Many observers, however, both within and without the industry, saw the Conrail experiment as *de facto* nationalization which would inevitably spread to other railroads. Two neighboring railroads, the Chessie System (composed of the Chesapeake & Ohio and the Baltimore & Ohio railroads), and the Norfolk & Western Railway, were especially fearful of what they perceived to be government-subsidized competition. After six months of operation, however, Conrail was operating to the satisfaction of most of its shippers. By the end of 1976 it had invested $1,000,000,000 in the rehabilitation of roadway and other fixed facilities, and in heavy repairs to about 12,000 freight cars and 500 locomotives.

Legislation. The act which provided funding for Conrail also promised financial relief for the nation's other 50-odd Class I railroads (those with operating revenues in excess of $5 million a year). The 4R Act, as it is known, authorized an additional $1,600,000,000 in federal aid to all railroads for equipment and roadway modernization. On top of this, $1,750,000,000 was authorized for upgrading the Northeast Corridor lines of Amtrak (Washington to Boston) for high-speed passenger service.

Congress also authorized the expenditure of $485 million for the continuation of service on lightly-patronized branchlines, which otherwise

An electric locomotive leased from Sweden made its inaugural run from Washington for Amtrak in October.

would have been abandoned under the Conrail reorganization plan. All together, the 4R Act provided nearly $6,400,000,000 in federal aid to railroads.

Finances. Generally, the railroads made a strong recovery in 1976 from the deep recession of 1975. In the first half of 1976 the industry posted ordinary (net) income of $176 million, compared with a deficit of $243 million in 1975. This was due partly to a modest recovery in traffic, which averaged about 6% until the fourth-quarter stagnation set in, and partly to rate increases. During 1975, railroad freight rates rose in three stages by a total of 13%. Increases of about the same magnitude were sought in 1976. Capital expenditures for all Class I railroads for 1976 were estimated just short of $2,200,000,000, compared with $2,500,-000,000 in each of the two preceding years.

Passenger Service. Amtrak, the government-subsidized corporation that now operates around 250 inter-city passenger trains a day, continued to post mounting deficits in 1976—and Congress continued to come through with the necessary subsidies. The Rail Transportation Improvement Act of 1976, which became law on October 1, provided Amtrak with a $430-million operating subsidy for fiscal 1977 and a $470-million one for fiscal 1978, plus capital grants of $130 million for each of those years. Dissatisfied with the railroad passenger equipment available in the United States, Amtrak was looking abroad for both locomotives and cars. An electric locomotive was brought over from Sweden in mid-1976 for testing in the Northeast Corridor, and a French-built locomotive was to arrive for similar tests in 1977. Meanwhile, Amtrak was negotiating with a Canadian firm, Bombardier-MLW Ltd., for the lease of two "LRC" (light, rapid, comfortable) passenger trains for a two-year test period; it was anticipated that test trains would also be leased from British and French manufacturers.

LUTHER S. MILLER, *Editor, "Railway Age"*

Shipping

In 1976 the American Bureau of Shipping recognized a total of 12,986 vessels operating in international commerce under the flags of 75 nations. The United States led with 7,718 vessels, followed by Liberia with 1,083. Panama (615 vessels) and Greece (571) are the only other nations with more than 500 vessels. These four nations control 77% of the world's vessels.

U. S. Inland Water. The inland waterway system of the United States is divided into five segments: (1) The Atlantic and Gulf Coast, (2) the Great Lakes, (3) the Mississippi and tributaries, (4) the Pacific Coast, and (5) Intercoastal. According to Interstate Commerce Commission (ICC) figures, the Mississippi and its tributaries are the most important segment of the shipping industry. In 1975 operators on this system had revenues of $314,360,000, down 2.6% from 1974 while freight decreased by 7.8% to 107,720,000 tons. The revenue was 51.1% of the total $615,488,000 generated by the entire system, while the tonnage was 71.6% of the total 150,364,000 for the entire system. In 1975 freight revenue on the entire system was up 1.2% while tons of freight decreased by 5.0%. This reflects higher freight rates.

In terms of freight revenue the Intercoastal traffic was the next most important with $174,-070,000. The balance was almost equally divided among the other three segments of the system. In light of the foregoing, 3,224,000 tons of freight handled in Intercoastal traffic looks small. The difference is explained when one considers the difference in the length of the average haul. On the Mississippi this is only 553 miles (885 km) while on the Intercoastal system it is 2,775 miles (4,640 km). The shortest hauls are found on the Pacific coast where they average 129 miles (206 km).

Fishyback. In the last several years the cartage of loaded trailers and containers by ship in international commerce has been one of the best growth segments of the shipping industry. In 1975, no matter what measure of growth is used, such cartage was down. The numbers of trailers and containers (102,776 in 1972) grew 14.1% in 1973 and 8.2% in 1974 reaching a total of 126,903. In 1975 only 115,992 trailers and containers were carried fishyback, a decrease of 8.6%.

Net tons of freight carried in trailers and containers (1,779,981 in 1972) increased by 15.4% in 1973 and 26.6% in 1974, reaching a high of 2,600,775 tons. In 1975 net tonnage dropped 15.4% to 2,201,112 tons.

Gross revenues for fishyback did not suffer so badly as the other categories primarily because of freight rate increases. Revenues of $99,533,000 in 1972 grew by 4.7% in 1973 and 44.9% in 1974, reaching a level of $150,491,-100. In 1975 revenue fell by only 1.7%.

JAMES R. ROMAN, JR.

The Revolutionary War battle of Lexington is reenacted. U. S. travel received a boost from such events.

TRAVEL

For travelers, 1976 was the year the United States turned 200 years old and the introduction of the supersonic Anglo-French Concorde turned the Atlantic Ocean into a pond.

The bicentennial stimulated worldwide interest in U. S. travel, and generated efforts to preserve historic buildings and sites or develop new attractions. In most American communities, bicentennial projects were modest but meaningful. People fixed up historic houses or turned old railroad depots into local museums.

But the bicentennial also produced major travel attractions. As part of the Fourth of July observance, the Smithsonian Institution in Washington, D. C., opened its massive new Air and Space Museum on The Mall. The museum, which is the largest of its kind in the world, is jammed with historic aircraft ranging from ancient Chinese battle kites to the latest space capsule. One of the more imaginative—and economical—bicentennial projects was the Trans-America Bicycle Trail, a 4,500 mile (7,200 km) route running from Williamsburg, Va., to Astoria, Ore. The Trans-America is the longest recreational bicycle trail in the world, and has a system of low-priced "bike inns" located at various points along it. The long bicycle journey proved to be a popular vacation activity with American and visiting cyclists.

The focal point of the bicentennial celebration was the "Colonial Corridor," the East Coast states that made up the 13 original colonies. However, the historic cities of Boston, Philadel-phia, and Washington did not attract the expected crowds. The visitors may have stayed away because of the advance publicity predicting vast mob scenes.

European Travel and the Concorde. Predictions that international visitors would travel to the United States in record numbers, however, proved to be accurate. Approximately 18 million foreign visitors, spending about $7 billion—a 15% increase over 1975—came to America in 1976.

Because of the new Concorde aircraft, no place in the world was more than 12 hours' flying time from any other place. The supersonic plane, capable of cruising at 1,400-miles (2,200 km) per hour, can make the trip from Paris or London to Washington, D. C., in 3 hours and 50 minutes.

Traffic between the United States and Europe was very much two-way in 1976. American tourism to Europe, which fell off drastically in 1973, revived, with travel to the continent up more than 10% for the year. In August alone, nearly 400,000 U. S. citizens went to Europe. This was an increase of 19% over the same time the previous year.

European visitors were attracted to North America not only by the bicentennial, but also by the Summer Olympic Games that were held in Montreal at a spectacular new sports complex. The opening of the games was marred by a boycott of Third World countries protesting the presence of New Zealand because of that country's sports relations with South Africa. Because of the boycott, the games drew fewer visitors than expected.

Mexican Travel. A boycott also had a major effect on travel to Mexico. Because of Mexican support of anti-Zionist resolutions in the United Nations, Jewish groups began to cancel travel plans to Mexico in the fall of 1975. The matter was not resolved until January 1976, when the presidents of major Jewish organizations met with Mexican officials and agreed to lift the travel ban.

The boycott, a word never used by Jewish groups, cost Mexico about 350,000 tourists and some $10 million. Although the dispute was settled early in the year, the effects of the boycott lingered for several months. For the Mexicans, who had invested large sums of money in the development of new vacation resorts, such as Cancun in Yucatan, the timing of the boycott could not have been worse.

Later, to stimulate a generally sluggish economy, the Mexican government "freed" the peso, which immediately went from 12.5 pesos to the dollar to around 20 to the dollar—a bonus for travelers.

Better exchange rates were also one of the reasons American travelers were flocking to Europe. The British pound dropped to below $2 and signaled a new—and cheaper—era. Toward the end of the year, the pound began declining even further, falling to an historic low of less than $1.60.

The Airlines. Despite an increase in the number of passengers, airlines flying the North Atlantic reported little or no profit on scheduled service. Carriers such as Pan American Airlines and Trans World Airways (TWA) continued to experience massive deficits. In an effort to help the airlines, the British government called for new agreements to restrict capacity on North Atlantic routes. Under the British plan, the governments, not the airlines, would allocate the number of seats available. The U. S. Civil Aeronautics Board (CAB), however, favored more of a free enterprise approach, and proposed adding Delta and Northwest Orient to the 49 scheduled and supplemental airlines already flying to Europe.

The CAB rejected an airline agreement that called for a 6% fare increase. The CAB insisted that carriers hold the line on their present economy fare prices and increase the popular, but marginally profitable, discount fares. Pan Am and TWA later proposed simplifying the North Atlantic fare structure, replacing 22 existing fares with 8 new ones, eliminating seasonal, youth and most excursion fares.

Travelers were offered some flight bargains in 1976. Encouraged by the success of "one stop tour charters" (OTC's), packages that combine charter airfares with discount land arrangements, the CAB approved "advanced booking charters" (ABC's). Under this new plan, which must be purchased 30 to 45 days in advance, depending on the destination, passengers are not required to belong to the same organization, and no land package has to be purchased. The ABC's revolutionized European travel, and such charters are expected to be very popular in the United States.

Cruise Ships and the U. S. Passport. Cruise ships continued popular in 1976, a year which saw a spectacular new arrival and a delay in the departure of an older vessel. *The Mississippi Queen,* the first paddlewheel passenger ship built in the United States in more than 50 years, went into service. She is a larger and more luxurious version of her sister ship *The Delta Queen.* The Italian Line was scheduled to cease all North American operations, but decided to let the *Leonardo Da Vinci* carry out a fall program of Caribbean cruising.

The U. S. passport, official emblem of the American traveler, received a facelift in 1976, which was a prelude to things to come. The old sage green cover was replaced by a dark blue one bearing the bicentennial seal. At the end of the year, the Passport Office announced that a smaller version of the bicentennial passport, one that complies with new international standards, becomes the official U. S. passport on Jan. 1, 1977.

WILLIAM A. DAVIS
Travel Editor, The Boston Globe

UPI

The *Hokule'a,* a 60-foot (18-m) replica of an ancient Polynesian double hulled canoe, sailed from Hawaii July 4 for a round-trip voyage to Tahiti. The journey was staged to mark the U. S. bicentennial.

In March, Tunisia's President Habib Bourguiba (*center*) joined other government officials in ceremonies marking the nation's 20th anniversary of independence. The festivities were marred by the attempted assassination of Premier Hedi Nouira.

RICHARD MELLOUL, SYGMA

TUNISIA

Tunisia celebrated 20 years of independence in 1976, a period marked by the political stability of President Habib Bourguiba's regime and steady economic development based on attracting foreign investment. Unemployment, however, remained the most intractable problem.

Economy. Two large projects relying on foreign investment, an oil refinery and an integrated sponge iron and steel complex, were shelved temporarily in 1976. But work went ahead on a $400 million fertilizer plant financed partly by Abu Dhabi.

Phosphates, used in fertilizer, and oil continued to be the pillars of Tunisia's exports. The production of oil covers all domestic needs and gains Tunisia some $300 million annually in export earnings. In a country where skill in textiles is traditional and labor is cheap, foreign investment in denim production boomed.

The fastest growing industry in 1976 was tourism, which jumped 50% over 1975. Tunisia's tourism agency, backed by the Arab Investment Company, was building a $300 million resort complex containing hotels, condominiums, and sports facilities in an effort to attract wealthy European and Arab tourists.

--------- **TUNISIA · Information Highlights** ---------

Official Name: Republic of Tunisia.
Location: North Africa.
Area: 63,170 square miles (164,150 km²).
Population (1976 est.): 5,900,000.
Chief City (1972 est.): Tunis, the capital, 750,000.
Government: *Head of state,* Habib Bourguiba, president (took office 1957). *Chief minister,* Hedi Nouira, premier (took office Nov. 1970). *Legislature* (unicameral)—National Assembly.
Monetary Unit: Dinar (0.42 dinar equals U. S.$1, Sept. 1976).
Gross National Product (1975 est.): $4,800,000,000.
Manufacturing (major products): Processed foods, wines, petroleum products, olive oil, pulp and wood products.
Major Agricultural Products: Wheat, olives, vegetables, grapes, citrus fruits, forest products.
Foreign Trade (1975): *Exports,* $855,000,000; *imports,* $1,422,000,000.

Unemployment. An estimated 50,000–60,000 new jobs are needed every year to stem unemployment, running at more than 10% of the work force. Under the four-year plan that ended in 1976, only some 150,000 new jobs were created. Experts suggested that to eliminate high unemployment a 10% annual growth rate was necessary, compared with the actual rate of 6.2%. Before Western Europe's economy slowed down, Tunisians by the thousands crossed the Mediterranean seeking work.

Social Unrest. President Bourguiba's economic and social policies have not found universal favor. The University of Tunis was ringed by a police guard in April and May after demonstrations by students demanding university reforms and agitating for socialist policies. Reportedly, at least one student was killed and dozens were wounded in clashes with the police.

In a cabinet reshuffle on May 31, Minister of National Education Driss Guiga, who was responsible for carrying out educational policies the students had demonstrated against, was dropped from the government.

Wildcat strikes by postal employees, rail and bus transport workers, and bakers were also a feature of life in 1976. In June, 700 miners at the Jerissa phosphate mines struck for two days over low pay and poor working conditions. Eleven miners were tried and given prison terms ranging from three months to three years.

Foreign Relations. Diplomatic ties between Tunisia and neighboring Libya were friendlier at the end of the year after hitting an all-time low in March, when Tunisia uncovered an alleged Libyan plot to assassinate prominent political figures. Libya denied the charge and responded by expelling thousands of Tunisian workers. A point of contention was ownership of the rich offshore oil deposits in the Gulf of Gabès. Libya was exploring for oil on the part of the continental shelf claimed by Tunisia.

JOSEPH MARGOLIS, *"African Update"*
The African-American Institute

UPI

The Greek (*right*) and Turkish foreign ministers met in New York in 1976 to arrange bilateral talks between their nations.

TURKEY

Turkey faced serious domestic and foreign problems in 1976. The Cyprus issue plagued Turco-Greek relations, as did that of the continental shelf in the Aegean Sea, over which Greece claimed sovereignty. While the conservative coalition headed by Prime Minister Süleyman Demirel moved toward political stability, student and labor unrest persisted, and the rate of inflation remained high (20%). Some 2,000,-000 were out of work, and there was the possibility that additional thousands of workers in western Europe might be forced to return home.

Domestic Issues. The Demirel government, formed in 1975, gained strength and seemed likely to endure until the elections in October 1977. Its primary achievement was rapid economic growth. The gross national product increased by almost 8% during 1975–76, although there were enormous repayment problems. The chronic balance-of-payments deficit has been much aggravated by the increases in the price of oil. Turkey's import bill rose to $4,640,000,-000—almost 25%—in 1975, while exports fell to $1,400,000,000. The deficit will exceed $3,-000,000,000 in 1976. The great need is for restructuring of Turkish industry. Turkey has sought direct investments from abroad. In 1975 the USSR pledged more than $500,000,000 in credits, and arrangements were signed with Iran and Libya. In the fall of 1976 Turkey demanded drastic changes in its relations with the European Common Market, covering the issues of Turks working abroad, preferences for Turkish farm products, and financial aid.

Foreign Affairs. Turkey continued its policies of seeking more friendly relations with its Balkan neighbors, the Arab states, Iran, and the USSR. The country had very serious problems with its NATO ally, Greece, concerning Cyprus and the prospecting for oil and other resources on the Aegean continental shelf. The Cyprus problem defied solution, threatening to shatter the southeastern NATO flank and to unhinge the much troubled Turco-American alliance. The United States embargoed the shipment of arms to Turkey in response to the landing of some 40,000 Turkish troops on Cyprus in July 1974, after an attempted Greek military coup. Although there was no solution of the problem, the United States and Turkey on March 26, 1976, signed a four-year agreement, allowing U. S. military installations in Turkey to reopen in return for some $1,000,000,000 in grants and credits. (It was noteworthy that on April 15 the United States and Greece announced a similar four-year agreement, granting Greece $700,000,-000 in American military aid. Congressional approval of both pacts, however, was stalled.) While the United States could not dictate terms, it suggested some points that a settlement should include. But there was little indication of any basic change in the situation; while the Greeks seemed to have tacitly accepted the Turkish view that the future government must be a federation with separate states, the agreement ended there.

The Aegean question flared up in July 1976, when a Turkish research vessel was sent into the Aegean Sea to conduct a seismic survey. The Greeks took their complaint to the UN Security Council which, on August 25, urged the parties to relax tensions and resume direct negotiations.

Disaster. In late November eastern Turkey was hit by an earthquake that left some 4,000 people dead and thousands of others homeless.

HARRY N. HOWARD
The American University, Washington, D. C.

─────── **TURKEY · Information Highlights** ───────

Official Name: Republic of Turkey.
Location: Southeastern Europe and southwestern Asia.
Area: 301,381 square miles (780,576 km²).
Population (1976 est.): 40,200,000.
Chief Cities (1974 est.): Ankara, the capital, 1,522,000; Istanbul, 2,487,000; Izmir, 619,000.
Government: *Head of state,* Fahri Korutürk, president (took office April 1973). *Head of government,* Süleyman Demirel, prime minister (took office March 1975). *Legislature*—Grand National Assembly: Senate and National Assembly.
Monetary Unit: Lira (16.16 liras equal U. S.$1, Aug. 1976).
Gross National Product (1975 est.): $33,100,000,000.
Manufacturing (major products): Textiles, petroleum products, cement, iron and steel, fertilizers, processed foods.
Major Agricultural Products: Raisins, wheat, cotton, rye, sugar beets, barley, fruit, tobacco, hazelnuts, sheep, cattle.
Foreign Trade (1975): *Exports,* $1,400,000,000; *imports,* $4,640,000,000.

UGANDA

World attention focused on Uganda in 1976 as a result of the Entebbe incident and the continued deteriorating state of domestic affairs.

Entebbe Incident. The country attracted global attention for its role in the hijacking on June 27 of an Air France jetliner by seven pro-Palestinian guerrillas. Seized on a flight between Athens and Paris, the plane, carrying 258 passengers and 12 crew members, was forced to land at the Entebbe airport in Uganda. The hijackers threatened to blow up the plane and kill all the hostages unless 53 Palestinian and pro-Palestinian terrorists were released from prisons in Israel and four other countries. President Idi Amin assumed the role of mediator, denying any collaboration with the hijackers.

The drama came to an end on July 3–4, when Israeli commandos raided the airport and rescued 91 passengers and 12 crew members still being held at the airport. In the course of the fighting 20 of the Ugandan soldiers guarding the field were killed, and the Israelis destroyed 11 Ugandan MiG's on the ground. Amin threatened to take reprisals for the raid and called on the United Nations and the Organization of African Unity to condemn Israel. Israeli Premier Itzhak Rabin accused Amin of having cooperated with the hijackers.

Break With Britain. Britain broke diplomatic relations with Uganda on July 28. The break was precipitated by Uganda's failure to explain the disappearance of 73-year-old Dora Bloch, a British subject left behind in a Kampala hospital where she had been taken for treatment shortly before the Israeli raid. Britain's move followed four years of strained relations between the two countries and was the first time that Britain had cut ties with a member of the Commonwealth of Nations.

Relations with Kenya. The year saw the further deterioration of already strained relations between Uganda and Kenya. Charges of troop build-ups along the border were made by each country. Uganda accused Kenya of complicity in the Israeli raid, but denied allegations that Kenyans in Uganda were killed in retaliation.

President Amin declared that Kenya had imposed a deliberate oil blockade, and on July 28 publicly accused Kenyan President Jomo Kenyatta of being "not African."

In August, Amin and Kenyatta signed a communiqué in Nairobi, Kenya, agreeing to end the state of tension between their two countries. The agreement outlined each country's obligations to the other and called for a six-nation committee to assist in the normalization of relations. But the Kenyan foreign minister expressed doubt that the agreement would be successful. The tension between Uganda and Kenya worsened the already poor state of the Ugandan economy.

Domestic Affairs. Amin was declared president for life on June 25 by the Defense Council, the ruling body of the government since Amin's 1971 coup. Amin escaped injury earlier in June when would-be assassins hurled three grenades at him as he was leaving a parade of police force graduates near Kampala.

Uganda suffered a serious oil shortage, which Amin blamed on a Kenyan blockade. On July 22, Uganda announced a ban on the sale of gasoline for private use.

Emmanuel Nsubuga, archbishop of Kampala, became Uganda's first cardinal, following his elevation by Pope Paul VI on April 27.

JEAN O'BARR
Duke University

─────── UGANDA • Information Highlights ───────

Official Name: Republic of Uganda.
Location: East Africa.
Area: 91,134 square miles (236,036 km²).
Population (1976 est.): 11,900,000.
Chief City (1976 est.): Kampala, the capital, 410,000.
Government: *Head of state and government,* Gen. Idi Amin, president (assumed power Feb. 1971). *Legislature* (unicameral)—National Assembly (dissolved Feb. 1971).
Monetary Unit: Shilling (8.42 shillings equal U. S.$1, July 1976).
Gross National Product (1974 est.): $2,000,000,000.
Manufacturing (major products): Processed agricultural products, steel, textiles.
Major Agricultural Products: Coffee, tea, millet, cotton, sisal, tobacco, sweet potatoes, cassava.
Foreign Trade (1975): *Exports,* $273,000,000; *imports,* $133,000,000.

UPI

Presidents Mobutu Sese Seko of Zaire *(left),* Idi Amin of Uganda, and Jean Bokassa of the Central African Republic (later Bokassa I of the Central African Empire) watch a military parade marking the fifth anniversary of Amin's takeover.

Photos of Politburo members line a Moscow street as the USSR marks the anniversary of the Bolshevik Revolution.

USSR

U. S.-Soviet détente slowed in 1976 because of bomb and rifle damage to Soviet offices in the United States, bomb threats to U. S. missions in the Soviet Union, U. S. suspicion of Soviet aggressiveness in Africa, and the unwillingness of either candidate for the U. S. presidency to endorse détente strongly. But the United States and the USSR did conclude a shipping pact and three minor agreements lessening the danger of nuclear war.

Soviet relations with China remained hostile, and links with Japan, Syria, and Egypt deteriorated. Four West European and two East European Communist parties publicly declared their independence of Soviet control, while USSR leader Leonid Brezhnev grudgingly accepted this loss of international power. In the world of sport the Soviet Union retained its strength, winning both the winter and summer Olympic Games.

The USSR 1976 grain harvest was good, but more than 10 million tons of cereals were still imported, mostly from the United States. Early in the year the Soviet government issued a new Five-Year Plan for 1976–80, slowing the planned growth rates for industry, transport, urban wages, retail, and foreign trade. The Communist party congress that adopted this plan reelected the entire party Politburo, except for the minister of agriculture, and reappointed Brezhnev as secretary general of the party.

FOREIGN AFFAIRS

United States. In the period from February to May 1976 rifle shots were fired into the Soviet UN mission and its residence in New York City; bombs blew outside the Soviet airline office and bookstore there, and unexploded bombs were found at the bookstore and the local Soviet trade office. Militant American Jewish organizations took credit for the shooting and bombing, which caused little damage and no injuries. The Soviet government protested several times, complaining of poor police protection of USSR buildings in New York. Apparently in retaliation, the U. S. embassy in Moscow and the consulate in Leningrad received bomb threats by telephone during March, and so did the U. S. exhibition in Moscow during November. In August, the United States revoked the visa of a counselor in the Soviet UN mission for "improper activities." The USSR retaliated in November with identical action against a U. S. counselor in Moscow.

Yakov A. Malik, who late in 1976 announed his resignation as the Soviet ambassador to the United Nations, and his wife were injured in March by an accidental auto collision on Long Island. Two other unpleasantnesses occurred during August: a Soviet nuclear submarine rammed the stern of the U. S. frigate *Voge* in the Ionian Sea, and three young U. S. citizens were sentenced to 5–8 years of Soviet imprisonment for attempting to smuggle heroin through the USSR en route from Malaysia to France.

Because the USSR provided armament to the left-wing Popular Movement for the Liberation of Angola, which won the civil war in that country early in 1976, U. S. President Ford on March 17 postponed planned U. S.-Soviet cabinet-level conferences on trade, housing, and energy, thus violating earlier détente treaties.

Despite all these frictions, the two superpowers on May 28 signed a five-year agreement limiting underground nuclear explosions for peaceful purposes to 150 kilotons and group explosions to 1.5 megatons. An unprecedented feature of this agreement is that each side, in certain cases, may witness the other's blasts. By another pact (July 19) the Soviet government promised that its cargo ships serving U. S. ports would stop charging freight rates 15–20% lower than U. S. ships.

Two further U. S.-Soviet treaties in September limited the modernization of their antiballistic missile systems and created a short code for warning each other of accidents that could be interpreted as the start of atomic war.

Europe. Soviet relations with most West European nations were harmonious in 1976. The USSR concluded trade accords with Sweden and West Germany, an agreement with Denmark on annual consultations, a pact with France on mutual prevention of accidental or unsanctioned use of nuclear weapons, and treaties with Belgium providing for cultural exchange, growth of tourism, and mutual establishment of consulates.

Unpleasantnesses included the expulsion of a Soviet trade official from France for attempted espionage, and the arrest in Switzerland of a retired general as a long-time Soviet spy. USSR athletes refused to participate in the world speed-skating races in West Berlin in March because their invitation had been issued by West Germany rather than the city itself. During August the Soviet government protested to France, Great Britain, and the United States (the three occupying powers in West Berlin) against the city's plan to send deputies to the European parliament.

But the main Soviet troubles in Europe during 1976 were with other Communist parties. At an all-European Communist party conference in East Berlin in June, leaders of the parties of France, Great Britain, Italy, Rumania, Spain, and Yugoslavia declared their independence of Soviet control. The conference, which Albanian Communist leaders did not even attend, issued a declaration approving autonomy for all Communist parties, despite Soviet objections.

During 1976 the Soviet Union rendered technical aid to Portugal and exchanged such aid with the nations of Finland, Czechoslovakia, Bulgaria, Hungary, East Germany, Poland, Rumania, and Yugoslavia.

Middle East. Soviet policy toward the Middle East was more active in the economic than the political sphere. Technical aid pacts were concluded with Iraq, Jordan, and Syria and a new trade agreement with Iran. The USSR also rendered technical aid to Afghanistan, Bangladesh, India, Kuwait, Nepal, Pakistan, Southern Yemen, Sri Lanka, Turkey, and Yemen.

Politically, the USSR largely confined itself to protesting events over which it lacked control. Thus, Soviet spokesmen disapproved the presence of Turkish troops in Cyprus, the Syrian armed intervention in the Lebanese civil war, and the Israeli raid that freed French airplane hostages from Palestinian guerrillas in Uganda.

In October, Soviet and Cuban leaders, including party leader Brezhnev and Cuba's Defense Minister Raul Castro (*second from left*) discussed "further deepening and expansion" of USSR-Cuban relations.

UPI

Some 80 million Soviets participated in the 6th People's Games of the USSR. Physical culture and sport activities play a major role in Soviet life.

In September Lt. Valentin I. Zasimov of the Soviet air force landed his small mail plane in Iran and asked for asylum in the United States. A month later the Iranian government returned him to the USSR in compliance with an existing Soviet-Iranian treaty on air piracy.

Far East. Soviet-Chinese relations remained poor during 1976. In April a bomb exploded at the gatehouse of the USSR embassy in Peking, wounding two Chinese guards. Soviet Communist party messages of condolences upon the death of Mao Tse-tung and of congratulations on Hua Kuo-feng's promotion to party chairman were both rejected by the Chinese Communist party.

Soviet-Japanese relations deteriorated. First, in May, Japan expelled a Soviet news correspondent for spying on U.S. naval ships in Japanese harbors. Then, on September 6, Lt. Viktor I. Belenko of the Soviet air force defected to Japan with his new MiG-25 jet fighter plane. He requested asylum in the United States, which he immediately received. The Soviet government demanded the return of both plane and pilot, and was angry that the plane was returned only after a long delay, during which Japanese and U.S. experts carefully examined it.

Despite the incident in March, when two grenades were hurled into the grounds of the Soviet embassy in Laos, wounding four people, the USSR in April concluded treaties of trade, technical aid, and cultural exchange with the new Laotian Communist government.

In June the USSR established diplomatic relations and concluded a trade pact with the Republic of the Philippines. Soviet border and technical-aid treaties with Mongolia were signed in October.

Africa. Soviet-Egyptian relations deteriorated further when, on March 15, Egypt unilaterally abrogated the 15-year Soviet-Egyptian treaty of friendship, concluded in 1971. Egypt's reason was the Soviet refusal to supply spare parts for USSR armament purchased earlier by the Egyptian government.

In contrast, Soviet arms shipments helped the left-wing Popular Movement for the Liberation of Angola to win the civil war in that country in March 1976. Trade, technical-aid, and cultural-exchange treaties with the new Angolan government were signed in May and a 20-year treaty of friendship in October.

USSR • Information Highlights

Official Name: Union of Soviet Socialist Republics.
Area: 8,649,412 square miles (22,402,000 km²).
Population (1976 est.): 257,000,000.
Chief Cities (1975 est.): Moscow, the capital, 7,635,000; Leningrad, 4,300,000; Kiev, 1,947,000.
Government: *Head of state,* Nikolai V. Podgorny, president (took office Dec. 1965). *Head of government,* Aleksei N. Kosygin, premier (took office Oct. 1964). *Secretary general of the Communist party,* Leonid I. Brezhnev (took office 1964). *Legislature*—Supreme Soviet: Soviet of the Union, Soviet of Nationalities.
Monetary Unit: Ruble (0.75 ruble equals U. S.$1, 1976).
Gross National Product (1975 est.): $655,000,000,000.
Manufacturing (major products): Steel, cement, chemical fertilizer, machine tools, electric power.
Major Agricultural Products: Grain, sugar beets, sunflower seeds, potatoes, cotton.
Foreign Trade (1975): *Exports,* $33,310,000,000; *imports,* $36,969,000,000.

During 1976 Soviet technical aid helped build 400 industrial and other economic projects in some 24 African countries, and Soviet arms were supplied to guerrillas in South West Africa and Rhodesia.

Latin America. By 1976, at least 17 of the 27 Western Hemisphere countries south of the United States had diplomatic relations with the USSR, which rendered technical aid to 6 of the 17. As before, Cuba obtained the largest share, receiving about $2,000,000 worth per day. As a result, Cuba was in debt to the USSR to the extent of at least $5,000,000,000.

Canada. During May a Canadian-Soviet treaty limited the USSR fish catch within 200 miles from the Canadian coast.

Soviet victory in the summer Olympic Games at Montreal was marred by two incidents: Boris Onischenko, a Soviet fencer, was disqualified from participating after the discovery of an illegal electronic device in his epée. Then Sergei Nemtsanov, a 17-year-old diver, temporarily defected from the Olympic team, and asked for asylum in Canada. But he later changed his mind and returned home.

SPACE AND DEFENSE

Space Program. By August 1976, the USSR had launched 847 space satellites since the first Soviet sputnik went aloft in 1957. Of this total, 111 were lofted in 1975 alone.

On June 22, 1976, an unmanned orbital research station, Salyut 5, was launched into space. Soyuz 21, a manned spaceship, was lofted on July 6, docked with Salyut 5 on July 7, and returned to earth with its 2-man crew on August 24.

During August the unmanned Luna 24 rocket landed on the moon, took soil samples, and returned, landing in a west Siberian forest.

From September 15 to 23, the Soyuz 22 spaceship circled the world with a 2-man crew, who took pictures with new East German cameras which more distinctly photograph the earth surface. During October Soyuz 23 was lofted with a 2-man crew, who planned to dock with Salyut 5. A mechanical failure, however, prevented the docking, and Soyuz 23 was ordered back to earth, landing in a Central Asian lake.

Armed Forces. In 1976 the Soviet armed forces totaled about 4,780,000 men, including 430,000 police troops. Much of their equipment was numerically first in the world, such as their ballistic missiles, submarines, and tanks. In contrast, Soviet armament lagged far behind the United States in aircraft carriers, long-range bombers, and total nuclear warheads.

The land and air forces conducted large-scale maneuvers in the Caucasus and near Leningrad during the year. For the first time in Soviet history, military observers from nearby non-Communist countries were permitted to watch these war rehearsals. Displaying Soviet sea power, USSR naval ships visited more than 100 foreign ports in 1976.

On April 26, Soviet Defense Minister Andrei A. Grechko died in Moscow of a heart attack at age 72. He was replaced three days later by Dmitri F. Ustinov, a 67-year-old armament production expert who, though a civilian, in July was given the rank of marshal.

GOVERNMENT AND POLITICS

The 25th Soviet Communist party congress met in Moscow from February 24 to March 5, electing a 426-man Central Committee which reappointed Leonid Brezhnev as secretary general. All party Politburo members were also reappointed, except for Dmitri S. Polyanski, who shortly thereafter was dismissed as minister of agriculture and appointed Soviet ambassador to Japan. The Central Committee also promoted Ustinov and Grigori V. Romanov, the Leningrad party chief, from Politburo candidacy to full membership, and chose Geidar A. Aliyev, the party chief of the Azerbaidzhan republic, as a new Politburo candidate.

The congress revealed that the party in 1976 had 15,694,000 members, of whom 44% were by origin upper and middle class, 42% workers, and 14% collective farmers.

Brezhnev Ascendancy. The party congress praised Leonid Brezhnev as an "outstanding leader of our day." During the year Brezhnev promoted himself to the military rank of marshal. A new book glorified his World War II record, and he was honored by a statue in his home city of Dneprodzerzhinsk.

Nikolai Tikhonov, an economic specialist, serves as first deputy chairman of the USSR Council of Ministers.

UPI

Minority Problems. At party congresses in the non-Russian Soviet republics, speakers accused the minorities of excessive nationalism. In April a bomb broke windows of the government building in Tbilisi, capital of the Georgian republic.

Dissidents. The government continued its policy of exiling troublesome dissident intellectuals. Among the prominent 1976 exiles were the scholar Leonid Plyushch, the sculptor Ernst Neizvestny, the historian Andrei Amalrik, and civil rights activist Vladimir K. Bukovsky, who was exchanged for Chilean Communist party leader Luis Covalan Lepe. Meanwhile, Jews seeking to emigrate were often dismissed from their jobs, occasionally arrested, and sometimes sentenced to prison.

Natural Disasters. During April–June, three severe earthquakes struck south-central Asia. They destroyed the gas-mining town of Gazli, wrecked many buildings in Bukhara and Chardzhou, and caused mud slides that damaged crops, buildings, and roads in the Tadzhik republic. In July another earthquake caused damage in the Azerbaidzhan republic. In October large-scale forest fires raged in the Khabarovsk territory.

CULTURE

The USSR in 1976 was engaged in cultural exchange programs with 120 foreign countries. Though the Soviet educational system has produced three times as many engineers as the American and one of every four physicians in the world, in 1976 one third of Soviet industrial workers and one half of the peasants still had only a grade-school education.

ECONOMY

Planning. The Five-Year Plan of 1971–75 ended short of its quota of industrial growth, agricultural production, farm wages, transport and housing construction, and industrial labor productivity, but exceeded expectations of transport freight haulage and foreign trade. Despite the many underfulfillments, the USSR by 1976 outproduced the United States in iron ore, iron, steel, oil, coal, chemical fertilizer, cement, potash, phosphates, manganese, chrome, timber, sugar, tractors, and machine tools.

Perhaps because of the troubles of the 1971–75 plan, the new plan for 1976–80 has lower growth targets (1971–75 actual growth in parentheses): industry, 36% (37.2%); transport freight haulage, 32% (36%); foreign trade, 30–35% (over 100%), national income 26% (28%), urban wages 17% (20%), and retail trade 28.7% (36%). Only agriculture is higher, 16% (12%).

Planned capital investments are 48% for heavy industry and transport, 28% for agriculture, 16% for housing and urban utilities, 5% for light consumer-goods industry, and 3% for hospitals, schools, and cultural institutions.

Agriculture. The 1976 USSR grain harvest totaled more than 220 million metric tons, far exceeding the 140 million tons reaped in 1975 and a good deal more than the planned 206 million. Nevertheless, the USSR in 1976 spent about $1,000,000,000 importing more than 10 million tons of grain.

ELLSWORTH RAYMOND, *New York University*

Western Europe experienced an extremely dry summer; tropical summer rains were quite common in Moscow.

Soviet youths, dressed in much sought-after Western-style blue jeans, walk through Moscow's Red Square.

PHOTOS UPI

UNITED NATIONS

The process of adjustment to new factors in international relations, through which the world is passing, dominated the proceedings at the United Nations in 1976. The hard facts of international politico-economic life, which were responsible for the beginnings of a new willingness by both newer and older countries to reach accommodations in certain areas toward the end of 1975, exerted an even stronger influence in 1976. Yet there remained a number of questions on which there was little change in attitudes. Thus, the Middle East, southern Africa, the problems caused by the disparity in living standards between the rich and poor nations, and the differences in approach and ideology they demonstrated dominated the discussions in all the organization's component bodies.

Perhaps the outstanding example of the interplay of politics and socio-economic problems was the Conference on Human Settlement (Habitat) at Vancouver in June. Dominated by representatives of the Third World, the conference produced recommendations which in many cases reflected Third World situations and ideologies, such as the resolution which called for restrictions on the private ownership of land. And the closing hours of the conference saw parliamentary maneuvering by the Arab bloc to place on record resolutions critical of Israel, two of which were passed. Similarly, Panama, in an effort to provoke a debate with the United States, introduced an amendment which, while not directly referring to the Canal Zone, was generally understood to allude to it. The United States proposed that the amendment be adopted by consensus, thus successfully countering the Panamanian move.

By the opening of the General Assembly the atmosphere was calmer, in contrast to the 1974 and 1975 sessions, which had provoked the U. S. representative to speak of the "tyranny of the majority." *The New York Times* on September 26 ascribed this change in atmosphere to a number of factors, including the American presidential election. It pointed out that Arab unity had cracked, largely because of Lebanon, and that the developing countries seemed to be adopting a more pragmatic approach as their representatives faced the task of implementing their demands. The industrial countries, for their part, were divided over their response to the developing nations, while the United States, deliberately keeping a low profile, was holding back on a number of issues which could disrupt the assembly's meetings.

The principal activities of the United Nations in its 31st year are summarized below under the following headings: General Assembly; Security Council; Economic and Social Council; Trusteeship and Decolonization; and Legal Activities.

GENERAL ASSEMBLY

The 31st session of the General Assembly opened in New York on September 21, when the Seychelles were admitted as the 145th member state. Hamilton Shirley Amerasinghe of Sri Lanka was elected president and in his inaugural address called for a new approach to disarmament. There were 125 items on the assembly's agenda, about 13 of them relating to southern Africa. The general debate, in which about 130 states expressed their views on various aspects of the world situation, lasted until October 14.

In the week following the general debate, the assembly turned its attention to southern Africa. In a resolution approved without opposition on October 26 the assembly strongly condemned the establishment by South Africa of Bantustans (homelands), of which the Transkei was one, and called on all governments to deny any form of recognition to "the so-called independent Transkei." The vote was 134 to 0; the United States abstained.

The debate on apartheid, which followed, centered on the report of the apartheid special committee, which urged measures to isolate the South African regime. The committee also recommended that a world conference be held in 1977 in "the capital of an African state totally committed to the liberation of South Africa."

Other matters considered by the assembly included the Cyprus problem and a draft treaty on the nonuse of force in international relations. These discussions were followed by the adoption of a resolution welcoming the efforts of the Organization of African Unity (OAU) to find "African solutions" to important international issues. Consideration of the Middle East situation involved the assembly in a discussion of a report outlining a two-phase program for the return of displaced Palestinians and Israeli withdrawal from occupied Arab territories by June 1, 1977. The endorsement of the report by a vote of 90 to 16, with 30 abstentions, was followed in November by five resolutions dealing with Palestinian refugees.

Concern over the lack of results at the Paris Conference on International Economic Cooperation was expressed in a resolution passed by a vote of 96 to 0, with 30 abstentions.

On December 1 the assembly voted, 116 to 0, to admit Angola as the 146th member of the United Nations. The United States abstained. On December 15 Western Samoa was accepted, by a vote of the General Assembly, as the organization's 147th member.

SECURITY COUNCIL

The question of a settlement in the Middle East remained, as in previous years, one of the major concerns of the Security Council in 1976.

An equally complex question, southern Africa, also occupied much of the council's attention.

Middle East. The first U. S. veto of the year was cast on January 26, when a resolution calling on the council to affirm the right of the Palestinian people to establish an independent state was defeated by the veto on a 9 to 1 favorable vote. Again on June 21 the United States vetoed a resolution which would have affirmed the Palestinians' right to self-determination and their right to national independence in Palestine. Another U. S. veto on March 25 prevented the council from deploring Israel's failure to put a stop to actions and policies that tend to change the status of Jerusalem. On May 26, however, a majority of the members of the council deplored the measures taken by Israel in the occupied territories and called on it to comply with the provisions of the Fourth Geneva Convention, relating to the protection of civilians in time of war.

A debate on the situation in Israeli-occupied Arab territories in the first part of November resulted in a consensus statement deploring such measures as the establishment of Israeli settlements in them. On October 22 the council extended the mandate of the UN peace-keeping force in the Sinai for one year.

Southern Africa. On January 30 the council called on South Africa to prepare the transfer of power to the people of South West Africa (Namibia) and allow free elections under UN supervision and control. Another unanimous resolution on April 6 expanded sanctions against Rhodesia. South Africa was again unanimously condemned on June 19 for the killing of Africans during the disturbances at Soweto. Further strong condemnation of South Africa for an armed attack on a Zambian village on July 11 was contained in a resolution, passed 14 to 0, on July 30, with the United States abstaining. Finally, on October 19, a resolution concerning South Africa failed to pass. Aimed at forcing the country to surrender control of South West Africa, a proposed arms embargo was vetoed by Britain, the United States, and France.

The aftermath of the Angolan civil war was taken up by the council in a special session which opened on March 26. It resulted in a resolution on March 31, passed by 9 to 0, with 5 abstentions, condemning South African aggression against Angola and calling on the South African government to compensate for damages resulting from its intervention in the civil war.

Mozambique appeared briefly in deliberations on March 17, when the council unanimously commended the country's government on its decision to impose sanctions on Rhodesia.

Cyprus. On June 15 the mandate of the UN peace-keeping force in Cyprus was extended to Dec. 15, 1976.

Air Hijacking. The council met from July 9 to 14 to consider a complaint made by the OAU arising from the landing by Israeli military forces at Entebbe, Uganda, after the hijacking of an Air France plane which landed there, but two resolutions failed to secure a majority.

Aegean Sea Dispute. Following a complaint by Greece about Turkish exploration on the Aegean continental shelf, a resolution was adopted by consensus on August 25, calling on both parties to reduce tensions in the area. The council urged both governments to take into account the contribution that the International Court could make toward a settlement, and to resume direct negotiations.

Angola. After vetoing the admission of Angola to the United Nations on June 23, the United States abstained when the application came before the council again in November, and Angola's admission was recommended by a vote of 13 to 0.

The Chief Executive. Secretary General Kurt Waldheim on December 7 won the approval of the council for a second five-year term. The vote, on the second ballot, was 14 to 0, with one abstention.

ECONOMIC AND SOCIAL COUNCIL

At the organizational meeting of the Economic and Social Council, held in New York from January 13 to 15, Simeon Ake of the Ivory Coast was elected president for 1976. The council also met in New York from April 13 to May 14 and adopted measures aimed at combating racism and protecting human rights.

The first meeting of the council to take place in Africa was held at Abidjan, the Ivory Coast, from June 30 to July 9; it was followed by a continuation of the session in Geneva, Switzerland, from July 12 to August 5. On July 9 the council adopted the Declaration of Abidjan, a general statement of the council's principles and objectives.

The Conference on Human Settlement (Habitat) that met in Vancouver from May 31 to June

In December, Kurt Waldheim of Austria was elected to a second five-year term as secretary general of the UN.

UPI

The Middle East, southern Africa, and the disparity between the rich and poor nations dominated Security Council debate.

11 made 64 recommendations to governments, suggesting concrete measures for meeting the basic requirements of human habitation.

A report on "The Future of the World Economy," compiled by a team of economists under the leadership of Wassily Leontief, professor of economics at New York University, was published on October 13. The report concluded that it should be possible to lessen by half the gap between rich and poor countries by the end of this century. The principal limits to growth, it said, were "political, social, and institutional rather than physical."

TRUSTEESHIP AND DECOLONIZATION

The Trusteeship Council met in New York from June 29 to July 13, when it discussed the future of the Trust Territory of the Pacific Islands (Micronesia), the sole remaining trust territory, administered by the United States. It reaffirmed the right of the peoples of Micronesia to self-determination and felt that the political unity of the Caroline and Marshall Islands should be maintained.

At the opening of the 1976 session of the Special Committee of 24 on decolonization, on January 30, Salim A. Salim of Tanzania was elected chairman for the fifth successive year.

Six members of the committee visited Tanzania, Zambia, Botswana, Mozambique, and Ethiopia from April 14 to May 4 on a fact-finding mission. Summing up the mission's impressions, Salim stated that the people of the area were unanimous in the view that illegal racist minority regimes had forced intensified armed struggles upon them.

On June 16 the committee adopted two resolutions on Rhodesia and a consensus on South West Africa, condemning the terror tactics of South Africa. On September 7 the committee reaffirmed the inalienable right of Puerto Ricans to self-determination and independence.

The Special Committee concluded its work for the year on September 17. On that date it condemned, by a vote of 21 to 0, the policies of governments which continued to support or collaborate with foreign economic or other interests engaged in exploiting the natural and human resources of dependent territories. A resolution on military activities by colonial powers, nuclear cooperation with South Africa, and the alienation of land in colonial territories for military installations, was passed by the same vote.

LEGAL ACTIVITIES

The Greco-Turkish dispute over the continental shelf in the Aegean Sea was taken before the International Court of Justice by Greece on August 10. The International Court made an order on September 11, ruling against interim measures of protection for Greece but refusing Turkey's request that the case be removed from the court's list.

The fourth session of the Conference on the Law of the Sea was held in New York from March 15 to May 7. After meeting again from August 2 to September 17, it adjourned until May 23, 1977. (See special feature pp. 50–60.)

The Commission on International Trade Law met in New York from April 12 to May 7. It approved a 25-article draft convention governing the liability of shipping carriers for goods transported by sea.

RICHARD E. WEBB
Formerly, British Information Services,
New York

ORGANIZATION OF THE UNITED NATIONS

THE SECRETARIAT

Secretary General: Kurt Waldheim (until Dec. 31, 1981)

THE GENERAL ASSEMBLY (1976)

President: Hamilton Shirley Amerasinghe (Sri Lanka). The 147 member nations were as follows:

Afghanistan	Germany, Federal	Nigeria
Albania	Republic of	Norway
Algeria	Ghana	Oman
Angola	Greece	Pakistan
Argentina	Grenada	Panama
Australia	Guatemala	Papua-New Guinea
Austria	Guinea	Paraguay
Bahamas	Guinea-Bissau	Peru
Bahrain	Guyana	Philippines
Bangladesh	Haiti	Poland
Barbados	Honduras	Portugal
Belgium	Hungary	Qatar
Belorussian SSR	Iceland	Rumania
Benin	India	Rwanda
Bhutan	Indonesia	São Tomé and
Bolivia	Iran	Príncipe
Botswana	Iraq	Saudi Arabia
Brazil	Ireland	Senegal
Bulgaria	Israel	Seychelles
Burma	Italy	Sierra Leone
Burundi	Ivory Coast	Singapore
Cambodia	Jamaica	Somalia
Cameroon	Japan	South Africa
Canada	Jordan	Spain
Cape Verde	Kenya	Sri Lanka (Ceylon)
Central African	Kuwait	Sudan
Republic	Laos	Surinam
Chad	Lebanon	Swaziland
Chile	Lesotho	Sweden
China, People's	Liberia	Syrian Arab Republic
Republic of	Libyan Arab	Tanzania, United
Colombia	Republic	Republic of
Comoros	Luxembourg	Thailand
Congo	Madagascar	Togo
Costa Rica	(Malagasy	Trinidad and Tobago
Cuba	Republic)	Tunisia
Cyprus	Malawi	Turkey
Czechoslovakia	Malaysia	Uganda
Denmark	Maldives	Ukrainian SSR
Dominican Republic	Mali	USSR
Ecuador	Malta	United Arab Emirates
Egypt	Mauritania	United Kingdom
El Salvador	Mauritius	United States
Equatorial Guinea	Mexico	Upper Volta
Ethiopia	Mongolia	Uruguay
Fiji	Morocco	Venezuela
Finland	Mozambique	Western Samoa
France	Nepal	Yemen
Gabon	Netherlands	Yemen, Democratic
Gambia	New Zealand	Yugoslavia
German Democratic	Nicaragua	Zaire
Republic	Niger	Zambia

COMMITTEES

General: Composed of 25 members as follows: The General Assembly president; the 17 General Assembly vice presidents (heads of delegations or their deputies of Australia, Chad, China, Dominican Republic, France, German Democratic Republic, Guinea, Japan, Nicaragua, Oman, Panama, Sudan, Turkey, USSR, United Kingdom, United Republic of Tanzania, United States); and the chairmen of the following main committees, which are composed of all 147 member countries:

First (Political and Security): Henryk Jaroszek (Poland)

Special Political: Mooki V. Molapo (Lesotho)

Second (Economic and Financial): Jaime Valdes Hertzog (Bolivia)

Third (Social, Humanitarian and Cultural): Dietrich von Kyaw (West Germany)

Fourth (Trust and Non-Self-Governing Territories): Tom E. Vraalsen (Norway)

Fifth (Administrative and Budgetary): Ali Sunni Muntasser (Libya)

Sixth (Legal): Estelito P. Mendoza (Philippines)

THE SECURITY COUNCIL

*(Membership ends on December 31 of the year noted; asterisks indicate permanent membership).

Benin (1977)	India (1978)	Rumania (1977)
Canada (1978)	Libya (1977)	USSR*
China*	Mauritius (1978)	United Kingdom*
France*	Pakistan (1977)	United States*
Germany, Fed.	Panama (1977)	Venezuela (1978)
Rep. of (1978)		

Military Staff Committee: Representatives of chief of staffs of permanent members.

Disarmament Commission: Representatives of all UN members.

THE ECONOMIC AND SOCIAL COUNCIL

President: Simeon Ake (Ivory Coast), 60th and 61st sessions (1976). Membership ends on December 31 of the year noted.

Membership of ECONOMIC AND SOCIAL COUNCIL

Afghanistan (1978)	Ecuador (1977)	Nigeria (1978)
Algeria (1978)	Egypt (1976)	Norway (1977)
Argentina (1977)	Ethiopia (1977)	Pakistan (1977)
Australia (1976)	France (1978)	Peru (1977)
Austria (1978)	Gabon (1977)	Portugal (1978)
Bangladesh (1978)	Federal Republic	Rumania (1976)
Belgium (1976)	of Germany (1978)	Thailand (1976)
Bolivia (1978)	German Democratic	Togo (1978)
Brazil (1978)	Republic (1976)	Tunisia (1977)
Bulgaria (1977)	Greece (1978)	Uganda (1978)
Canada (1977)	Iran (1976)	USSR (1977)
China (1977)	Italy (1976)	United Kingdom
Colombia (1976)	Ivory Coast (1976)	(1977)
Congo (1976)	Jamaica (1976)	United States
Cuba (1978)	Japan (1977)	(1976)
Czechoslovakia	Jordan (1976)	Venezuela (1978)
(1977)	Kenya (1977)	Yemen (1977)
Democratic Yemen	Liberia (1976)	Yugoslavia (1978)
(1976)	Malaysia (1978)	Zaire (1977)
Denmark (1977)	Mexico (1976)	Zambia (1976)

THE TRUSTEESHIP COUNCIL (1976–77)

President: Guy Scalabre (France), 43d session (1976).

Australia[1]	France[2]	United Kingdom[2]
China[2]	USSR[2]	United States[1]

[1] Administers Trust Territory. [2] Permanent member of Security Council not administering Trust Territory.

THE INTERNATIONAL COURT OF JUSTICE

(Membership ends on February 5 of the year noted)

President: Eduardo Jiménez de Aréchaga (Uruguay, 1979)
Vice President: Nagendra Singh (India, 1982)

Isaac Forster (Senegal, 1982)	Federico de Castro (Spain, 1979)
André Gros (France, 1982)	Platon Morozov (USSR, 1979)
Taslim Olawale Elias (Nigeria, 1985)	Manfred Lachs (Poland, 1985)
Herman Mosler (Federal Republic of Germany, 1985)	Sir Humphrey Waldock (United Kingdom, 1982)
Shigeru Oda (Japan, 1985)	José María Ruda (Argentina, 1982)
Salah El Dine Tarazi (Syrian Arab Republic, 1985)	Hardy C. Dillard (U. S., 1979)
Louis Ignacio-Pinto (Benin, 1979)	

SPECIALIZED AGENCIES

Food and Agriculture Organization (FAO); Intergovernmental Maritime Consultative Organization (IMCO); International Atomic Energy Agency (IAEA); International Bank for Reconstruction and Development (World Bank, IBRD); International Civil Aviation Organization (ICAO); International Development Association (IDA); International Finance Corporation (IFC); International Labor Organization (ILO); International Monetary Fund (IMF); International Telecommunication Union (ITU); United Nations Educational, Scientific and Cultural Organization (UNESCO); Universal Postal Union (UPU); United Nations International Children's Emergency Fund (UNICEF); World Health Organization (WHO); World Meteorological Organization (WMO).

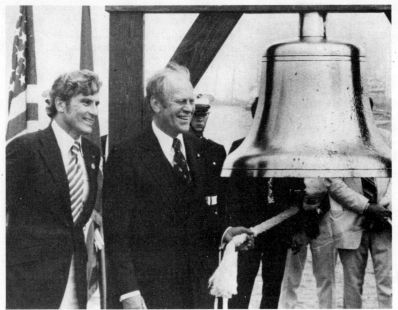

UNITED STATES

On board the "USS Forrestal" during Operation Sail, President Gerald Ford commemorates the ringing of the Liberty Bell, July 4, 1776. John W. Warner, administrator of the American Revolution Bicentennial Commission, assists the President.

Coverage of developments in the United States is divided into four sections: Domestic Affairs, the Carter cabinet, Foreign Affairs, and the 95th Congress: First Session.

Domestic Affairs

In 1976 the United States was 200 years old. Though that is a modest age in comparison with many other nations, the country celebrated from coast to coast, flying more flags, hanging more bunting, exploding more fireworks on the Fourth of July than at any other time in its history. While there were joy and pride in the nation and in its principles and accomplishments, there was also a more subdued recognition of work yet undone, goals not yet reached, and failures recently and often bitterly experienced.

The bicentennial year was a time for starting over. The social and political upheavals of the 1960's and early 1970's seemed to have exhausted the nation and its leaders and even many of its ideas. The election of a new president, Jimmy Carter, was a key part of the country's attempt to set a new course. But throughout the year cases of corporate bribery, foreign payments to congressmen, and scandals involving the sexual lives of public officials kept emerging. The full-scale Congressional investigation of the national intelligence community disclosed abuses that seemed to typify the errors and misdirections of the previous decade of national life.

The Administration. President Ford began his second full year in office hoping that in November he would win a full term as an elected rather than as an appointed president. Most of his year was, indeed, devoted to his campaign efforts. He faced first a difficult test from his own party's right wing in the person of former California

Gov. Ronald Reagan and then fought a close but futile campaign with Carter.

The President began the year by calling, in his State of the Union message, for "a new realism" in national affairs. His message was one of moderation, especially in economic matters. Unlike the previous year, the economy of the country was moving back toward prosperity and the President and his economic advisers, ever fearful of re-igniting inflation, urged that the federal government go slow in stimulating new economic growth.

This course not only served the President's economic philosophy, but also was designed to blunt the attacks of conservative Ronald Reagan, who was criticizing the size of the federal deficit. Ford urged the Congress to cut taxes and to match those cuts with reductions in federal spending. He wanted a consolidation of a variety of social service programs.

On January 2, Ford vetoed a bill that gave broader picketing rights to striking construction workers. His own labor secretary, John Dunlop, had carefully shepherded the bill through Congress, and the veto broke a promise Ford had made to Dunlop. On January 14, Dunlop, an expert of long standing on labor matters, resigned to return to Harvard University. The veto of the so-called common situs picketing bill was another concession to conservative Republican interests dictated by the Reagan challenge. That political necessity, coupled with Ford's own conservative bent, put him in constant conflict with the Congress, which was controlled by a large Democratic majority. In fact, the Ford administration and the Democratic Congress spent the entire year jockeying for political position and, in the end, accomplished very little.

The President, having already had the hard task of presiding over the final collapse of South Vietnam, attempted early in the year to persuade Congress to vote money to aid the U.S.-backed factions in the Angolan civil war. Congress, reasserting its role in foreign affairs and mindful of the Vietnam experience, turned the President down cold.

In February, President Ford moved again to get ahead of the Congress when he issued an executive order reorganizing the control of American intelligence agencies. He appointed a citizens' independent advisory board to review intelligence-gathering efforts and drew direct authority for covert operations into the National Security Council at the White House. The President also urged Congressional passage of a "critical intelligence secrets act" to prevent disclosure of sensitive national security information. But that proposal too was ignored by the houses of Congress. Disclosure of abuses in the intelligence agencies led to a fear that a major weakening of those agencies was in store. President Ford vowed: "I will not be a party to the dismantling of the CIA or other intelligence agencies."

The Ford domestic program, in keeping with his State of the Union speech, amounted to an attempt to limit government involvement rather than to expand it. He vetoed bill after bill sent to him by the Democratic Congress, especially those aimed at directly creating jobs by initiating public works projects. He also attempted to reduce the scope of the food stamp program by saving $1,200,000,000 by cutting out 5 million of the approximately 19 million Americans who received that relief.

While much of Ford's activity in the White House was clearly in keeping with his Republican philosophy, he also seemed to have a sense of a new national mood distrustful of efforts to concoct elaborate federal solutions to complex social problems. In March, a little noticed report issued by the Rockefeller Commission on Critical Choices gave support to the "go-slow" philosophy Ford was following. The commission, organized by Nelson Rockefeller before Ford had named him vice president, commissioned a long series of papers by prominent national experts in a variety of fields. In paper after paper, the experts admitted an exhaustion of the great liberal optimism of the 1960's that had been the underpinning of Lyndon Johnson's Great Society. Bold solutions were in short supply in 1976.

The Congress. Politics dominated much of the second session of the 94th Congress as the Democrats tried to position themselves for the fall elections. They began the year by voting for budget levels higher than President Ford had proposed, a total of $394,200,000,000. With the economy still attempting to recover from the previous year's recession, the federal budget deficit was expected by the Congress to reach $43,000,000,000. A number of Congressional proposals failed because sponsors anticipated a presidential veto. Some, like a plan approved by the Senate Judiciary Committee to break up the largest American oil companies, were never considered by the Congress since they involved sweeping changes and were largely designed for political effect.

For the first time in its history, the Congress used new budget procedures that had been created to give the legislators a comprehensive look at the economic impact of their spending decisions and to increase their power to direct the economy. On September 16 the Congress completed the most extensive revision of the tax code since 1969. The tax reform bill restricted use of a variety of tax shelters and loopholes, made the first significant change in estate tax laws in three decades, and increased taxes on very wealthy taxpayers by stiffening minimum tax payment requirements.

The Congress, waiting hopefully for a new, Democratic president, settled into a stalemate with President Ford. In spite of heavy Democratic majorities in both houses, it managed to override only 4 of President Ford's 15 vetoes. The anti-military-spending mood that had been strong in the Congress for several years nearly vanished. But the Congress rejected aid for military forces in Angola and conducted exhaustive investigations of national intelligence gathering agencies.

In April, the Senate Select Intelligence Committee published the results of its 15-month investigations of abuses by and illegal actions of the Central Intelligence Agency, the Federal Bureau of Investigation, the National Security Agency, and other intelligence agencies of the federal government. Its findings documented a pattern of illegal conduct stretching through the administrations of past presidents, including both Democrats and Republicans. The committee concluded that both the FBI and the CIA as well as other agencies had been operating outside the law for decades.

The committee counted some 900 "major or sensitive" covert actions conducted by the CIA

—— **UNITED STATES · Information Highlights** ——

Official Name: United States of America
Area: 3,615,123 square miles (9,363,169 km²).
Population (1976 est.): 215,300,000.
Chief Cities (1970 census): Washington, D. C., the capital, 756,510; New York, 7,895,563; Chicago, 3,369,-359; Los Angeles, 2,816,061; Philadelphia, 1,950,098.
Government: Head of state and government, Gerald R. Ford, president (took office Aug. 9, 1974). *Legislature*—Congress: Senate and House of Representatives.
Monetary Unit: Dollar
Gross National Product (3d quarter 1976 est.): $1,709,-700,000,000.
Manufacturing (major products): Motor vehicles, aircraft, ships and railroad equipment, industrial machinery, processed foods, chemicals, electrical equipment and supplies, fabricated metals.
Major Agricultural Products: Wheat, rye, corn, barley, oats, soybeans, tobacco, cotton, sorghum.
Foreign Trade (1975): Exports, $106,157,000,000; imports, $102,984,000,000.

CIA Director George Bush (*left*) prepares to testify before the Senate select committee on intelligence, chaired by Sen. Frank Church.

UPI

since 1961, along with several thousand "smaller actions" that seemed to violate "the open and democratic assumptions on which our government is based." Of special concern to the senators was the involvement of U. S. citizens in CIA operations. According to the committee report: "The CIA is now using several hundred American academics who, in addition to providing leads and sometimes making introductions for intelligence purposes, occasionally write books and other materials to be used for propaganda purposes abroad." The CIA's use of journalists was also criticized, with more than a dozen U. S. news organizations and commercial publishing houses found to have provided cover for agency employees abroad. Further, the committee disclosed that well over 1,000 books were produced, subsidized, or sponsored by the CIA before the end of 1967. Many of these were circulated in the United States, leading the committee to conclude that the agency was engaging in influencing public opinion at home.

In addition, the committee found that the FBI under J. Edgar Hoover was equally at fault. The bureau had infiltrated such organizations as the Women's Liberation Movement, church groups that had opposed the war in Vietnam, and civil rights organizations, including the National Association for the Advancement of Colored People and Dr. Martin Luther King's Southern Christian Leadership Conference. Hoover had conducted a particular program of harassment and wiretapping against King himself. At one point, the bureau concluded that King was "the most dangerous and effective Negro leader in the country."

The committee report concluded that the FBI had frequently gone beyond intelligence gathering. Arrangements were often made to have political dissidents fired or transferred from jobs. Anonymous letters had been sent by the bureau to disrupt marriages. Some 500,000 files had been collected in the name of domestic intelligence.

The Army, employed to help control urban riots in the 1960's, also had developed its own domestic intelligence apparatus, eventually setting up files on 100,000 Americans. The Internal Revenue Service, especially during the Nixon administration, had turned its investigative efforts to political purposes and had established secret files on 11,000 individuals and organizations. In one year alone, tax returns of 25,000 Americans had been turned over to other agencies with no interest in the enforcement of revenue laws.

The main impact of the Senate investigation came from the disclosures themselves. But agency chiefs issued new orders and FBI Director Clarence Kelley, who had succeeded Hoover, issued a public apology. Attorney General Edward Levi issued new rules to enable the Justice Department to gain control over the FBI. And the Senate itself set up a permanent intelligence oversight committee.

While the Congress was busy investigating the executive departments, it was finding much to be concerned about among its own members. The most spectacular scandal erupted in the early summer when Elizabeth Ray, an employee of Democratic Rep. Wayne L. Hays, accused him of having put her on the payroll in compensation for sexual favors. She claimed she had none of the skills necessary to perform her secretarial duties.

After first denying any wrongdoing, Hays admitted he had had sexual relations with Ray, but then denied having misused public funds. The leadership of the House of Representatives finally forced Hays to resign the two powerful committee chairmanships he held. On September 1, Hays resigned from the House of Representatives after 28 years of service, but with a $30,000 annual pension.

The Hays affair became a symbol of what was called the "post-Watergate morality." Public officials at all levels recognized a widespread public disenchantment with and distrust of government. Indeed, that theme became dominant in the election campaign and partially accounted for the election of Jimmy Carter, who structured his appeal to the voters around discontent with official Washington.

Other Congressmen also were in trouble. Rep. Robert Sikes, a Democrat from Florida, was accused of financial misdealings and received a reprimand from the House of Representatives, the first such action, albeit mild, since 1969. Like some others accused of misdeeds, however, Representative Sikes was reelected. Throughout the year there were sporadic attempts to define just what sort of conduct was to be condoned. A nasty divorce and an affair with a secretary were made issues in Congressman Donald Riegle's Senate campaign in Michigan, but he too won election.

The number of retirements from the Congress was the highest in 30 years. Both the Senate majority leader, Mike Mansfield, and the minority leader, Hugh Scott, retired. In the House, Speaker Carl Albert announced his decision to leave the Congress. This exodus of Congressional leadership was the most complete in memory. By year's end, the House had chosen Rep. Thomas P. "Tip" O'Neill as its new speaker amid speculation that he would become the most powerful occupant of that post since Sam Rayburn. The Democrats chose Rep. James Wright of Texas to fill O'Neill's post as majority leader. In the Senate, Robert Byrd of West Virginia was selected to succeed Mansfield as majority leader and Howard Baker of Tennessee took over the minority leader's job vacated by Scott.

After his selection as speaker of the House, O'Neill vowed a toughening of ethical standards for members of Congress. His warnings were timely because of revelations that a representative of the Korean intelligence agency had been doling out money to members of Congress for some years. Tongsun Park, a Korean businessman living in Washington, allegedly distributed between $500,000 and $1 million a year in cash, gifts, and campaign contributions. A number of investigations of these allegations were begun by the Department of Justice and several committees of the House. The allegations spread concern on Capitol Hill about a "Congressional Watergate," and the problem was seen as a critical test of whether the Congress could police its own standards of conduct with the same thoroughness as it had those of the executive branch in recent years.

The Carter Administration. Partly as a product of the kinds of national doubts and frustrations that were apparent throughout 1976, Jimmy Carter was elected to succeed Gerald Ford as president (see feature article pages 24–31). The election result was hardly an overwhelming mandate for anything, but did seem to express a feeling that the nation wanted new people running the government in Washington. Carter will begin his four-year term as leader of a nation still unsure of what it wants or where it is going.

Though something of an enigma to voters throughout the election campaign, Governor Carter appeared to be a new sort of Democrat, a kind of "managerial liberal" who professed concern about poverty and other domestic social problems, but whose own background as a military officer and a successful businessman gave him a deep appreciation of careful economic management. The question about Carter immediately focused on what balance he would strike between these two concerns.

One measure of that balance was seen in late 1976 as Carter began his transition to power. As early as midsummer, he had set aside $150,-000 from campaign funds to pay for a planning effort to prepare him to assume office. Although such an effort was regarded as presumptuous by some, it was a sign of the importance Carter placed on gathering information and on being prepared. After his election, the transition group moved to Washington with a budget of $2 million that had been appropriated by Congress. More than 200 people were involved in an extensive talent hunt and in the preparation of exhaustive analyses of problems and options

BOB ENGLEHART, "THE JOURNAL HERALD," DAYTON, OHIO

A cartoonist's view of the series of sex scandals that involved members of Congress during the year.

Reps. Thomas O'Neill (*above, left*) and James Wright are the new House speaker and majority leader. Senators who did not seek reelection in 1976 included (*l-r*): Fannin, Hruska, Symington, Scott, and Pastore.

Carter would need once he took over the White House.

Carter, the political outsider and the new-breed liberal, began at the same time a patient screening of the candidates for top positions in his government. He and his staff had promised throughout the campaign that the Carter administration would be a blend of new and old faces, of establishment figures and of outsiders. The aim, they said, was to divest the policy planning functions that gradually had been gathered into the president's executive office and to return that power to the cabinet. In addition, Carter wanted to reorganize the White House staff itself, to reduce its size and make it more efficient.

Carter's appointments were indeed a blend. He quickly named his long-time associate Jody Powell as White House press secretary and Bertram Lance, a Georgia banker and old friend, as chief of the critically important Office of Management and Budget. At the same time, Carter turned to the "Eastern liberal establishment" in the person of Cyrus R. Vance, a former official in the Kennedy and Johnson administrations, as his secretary of state. Other Carter appointments included W. Michael Blumenthal, chief executive of the Bendix Corporation, as treasury secretary and Rep. Brock Adams (D-Wash.) as transportation secretary.

On balance, the Carter cabinet was more heavily weighted toward proven talents from past Democratic administrations than it was toward unproven outsiders. Indeed, as the cabinet selection process went on from Carter's home in Plains, the expectations he and his staff had raised over the number of women and minorities in the cabinet caused him some political problems, and in the end both groups felt somewhat shortchanged.

Yet Carter was as eclectic in cabinet selections as he was with ideas and policies. He overrode the objections of labor by putting Dr. Harold Brown of Cal Tech into the top defense job. He ignored George Meany's demand that John Dunlop of Harvard be returned to the Labor Department where he had served Gerald Ford. Yet Carter chose former Nixon and Ford administration stalwart James Schlesinger to lead a planned consolidated energy agency.

Moral Questions. Throughout 1976, there were reminders of moral and political problems as yet unsolved. On January 15, Sara Jane Moore was sentenced to life in prison for her attempt to shoot President Ford the preceding fall. Patty Hearst, the daughter of a wealthy newspaper publisher, who had been kidnapped by a small band of political radicals, was convicted on March 20 of having assisted her captors in a bank robbery.

In November, a convicted murderer named Gary Gilmore pleaded with the courts in Utah to permit the carrying out of his sentence of death before a firing squad. His bizarre case again raised questions about the government's use of death as a punishment for crimes. The problem had been addressed earlier in the year by the U. S. Supreme Court, which by a vote of 7–2 reversed a 1972 decision against the death penalty. The issue was typical of the kind of quandary public leaders faced on a variety of social questions in 1976.

JOHN F. STACKS
Washington Correspondent, "Time" Magazine

THE CARTER CABINET

President-elect Jimmy Carter met with his full prospective cabinet on St. Simons Island, Ga., on December 28. He stressed his intention to elevate the vice presidency by calling Vice President-elect Mondale his "chief staff person." Other important appointments by President-elect Carter were those of Charles L. Schultze as chairman of the Council of Economic Advisers; Bert Lance as director of the Office of Management and Budget; Zbigniew Brzezinski as national security adviser; and Theodore Sorensen as CIA director (withdrawn in mid-January). Andrew J. Young, Jr., was named U. S. ambassador to the United Nations, a cabinet-level post. The cabinet proper consists of:

State. Cyrus R. Vance was a deputy secretary of defense and diplomatic troubleshooter in the Johnson administration. He has been described as a liberal-moderate Democrat who favors arms control and détente with the Soviet Union, a skilled negotiator, and a realist who works within a consensus but has a streak of moral idealism. Vance was born in Clarksburg, W. Va., on March 27, 1917. He was graduated from Yale Law School in 1942 and is a partner in the law firm of Simpson, Thacher and Bartlett in New York City.

Treasury. W. Michael Blumenthal joined the Bendix Corporation in 1967 and served as chairman, president, and chief executive officer. He was born in Berlin, Germany, on Jan. 3, 1926, and went to the United States in 1947 to study international economics at the University of California. As deputy assistant secretary of state in the Kennedy Administration, he negotiated the Kennedy Round of tariff agreements, with the rank of ambassador. After completing the negotiations, he left government service.

Defense. Harold Brown, the first scientist to fill the post of defense secretary, was born in New York City on Sept. 19, 1927. Having graduated from Columbia in 1945, with honors in physics, he worked for the Atomic Energy Commission, the protegé of Edward Teller. After a stint in various governmental advisory jobs he became director of research and engineering at the Pentagon. Secretary of the Air Force from 1965 to 1969, he served after that as president of the California Institute of Technology.

Justice. Griffin B. Bell, Carter's most controversial appointee, was born in Americus, Ga., on Oct. 31, 1918. He began practicing law in Savannah, then moved to Rome, Ga., where he joined the firm of King and Spalding. In 1960 he was one of the state campaign chairmen for John F. Kennedy, who later appointed him to the U. S. Court of Appeals for the Fifth Circuit. Described by some as "no legal scholar," as a federal judge he was often criticized for his middle-of-the-road civil rights decisions.

Interior. Cecil D. Andrus, governor of Idaho since 1971, is regarded as a pragmatist who manages to remain in good standing with both conservation and business interest. His reputation rests on strong environmental stands and advocacy of land-use planning, but he is probably best known nationally as the man who promotes Idaho potatoes in television commercials. Born in Hood River, Oreg., on Aug. 25, 1931, he attended Oregon State University and served in the Idaho State Senate before he became governor.

WIDE WORLD

Agriculture. Bob Bergland, who served three terms in the House of Representatives before joining the Carter administration, is known as a friend and advocate of farmers. He was born on July 22, 1928, in Roseau, Minn., and was graduated from the University of Minnesota's School of Agriculture. He worked for a time as a Midwest regional director in the Agricultural Stabilization and Conservation Service, and he still operates a 600-acre farm near Roseau, Minn., raising spring wheat and lawn seed.

UPI

Commerce. When appointed to the Carter cabinet, the first of two women, Juanita Morris Kreps was a professor of economics and vice president of Duke University, the first woman director of the New York Stock Exchange, and a member of several corporate boards. She was born in Lynch, Ky., on Jan. 11, 1921, and attended Berea College and Duke University. Mrs. Kreps feels that, as secretary of commerce, she should "encourage business to perform well all those activities which serve to improve human welfare."

UPI

Labor. F. Ray Marshall, at the time of his appointment a labor economist at the University of Texas, has been described as "one of the few American professors who understands the working people." Born on Aug. 22, 1928, in Oak Grove, La., Marshall was educated at Louisiana State University and the University of California at Berkeley. His principal interest has been in the expansion of employment opportunities, especially for women and members of minority groups, and he has written numerous books on the subject.

UPI

Health, Education and Welfare. Joseph A. Califano, Jr., was a New York City lawyer before joining the Defense Department in the Kennedy administration. He became special assistant to Defense Secretary Robert McNamara and later held the post of assistant in charge of domestic programs under Lyndon Johnson. He was generally credited with the "conception, formulation, and implementation of the programs for the Great Society." Califano, born in Brooklyn, N.Y., on May 15, 1931, is a partner in a Washington law firm.

UPI   KEN HAWKINS, SYGMA

Housing and Urban Development. Patricia Roberts Harris, the second woman and first black named to the Carter cabinet, was born in Mattoon, Ill., on May 31, 1924. She is a graduate of George Washington University Law School and has served as a delegate to the UN General Assembly, ambassador to Luxembourg, a board member of several corporations, and professor of law at Howard University. As secretary of housing and urban development, she is expected to stress equal treatment for blacks and women.

Transportation. A six-term member of the U.S. House of Representatives, Brock Adams was born in Atlanta, Ga., on Jan. 13, 1927, but grew up in the Pacific West. President John F. Kennedy appointed him U.S. attorney for the Western District of Washington state. As a congressman, Adams sponsored many bills beneficial to the transportation industry and was the chief author of the legislation that consolidated the bankrupt Northeastern railroads into the government-backed Conrail system.

FOREIGN AFFAIRS

During the bicentennial year the United States was at peace in the world and turned to defining and refining its strategies to deal with a broad spectrum of international problems. Fundamental, long-range objectives and policies were reconfirmed, and new, more precise positions were formulated to deal with such worldwide matters as relations with the United Nations, human rights, weapons proliferation, terrorism, the law of the sea, and the developing countries.

Two new countries—the Seychelles in the Indian Ocean and Transkei, a portion of South Africa—gained independence, and the two Vietnams were combined. More than half of the 156 members of the community of nations have populations of less than 5 million, and 17 microstates have less than 300,000. The number of small states continued to grow, evidencing the dramatic change under way in the international community. The United States engages in regularized bilateral relations with 138 governments, including the special mission to China, and maintains approximately 130 consular establishments throughout the world.

Two dozen foreign leaders came to Washington on official visits, including the monarchs, princes, presidents, and prime ministers of 11 friendly powers who arrived as bicentennial celebrants. President Ford ventured abroad on only one trip—to attend the Puerto Rican summit meeting of western powers on economic matters. Secretary of State Henry Kissinger undertook 11 official trips. While five of these were to Europe and three to Latin America, he reori-

African affairs were a major concern of U. S. foreign policy in 1976. In September, Secretary of State Kissinger met with South African Prime Minister J. B. Vorster.

UPI

ented his shuttle diplomacy and became directly involved with affairs in southern Africa.

The United States sent negotiating missions to 828 sessions of international organizations and international conferences, including important meetings of the UN Conference on Trade and Development (UNCTAD) and the Conference on International Economic Cooperation (CIEC), the conclave on the law of the sea, and a special UN-sponsored meeting on the human habitat. At the beginning of the year the country was party to 3,459 bilateral treaties and 431 multilateral conventions. During 1976 another 13 treaties and 380 executive agreements were signed, including those on the release of American prisoners (with Mexico) and on nuclear explosion (with the Soviet Union).

National Election. The fact that 1976 was an election year had an impact on foreign relations. Early in the year Secretary Kissinger intimated that the administration would avoid dramatic policy moves that might be viewed as politically motivated. A slowdown in new initiatives ensued, and fewer new starts and consummations were visible.

As the political campaign progressed, differences over foreign relations among candidates and major political parties centered less on basic objectives and principles than on emphasis, procedures, and priorities. The president-elect received no clear mandate to alter foreign policy, but he intimated firmer presidential control over foreign affairs.

General Policy. Early in the year Secretary Kissinger epitomized persisting problems in their broader-range context when he said that the principal issues confronting the United States abroad were global in nature, that their complexity eluded the conventional solutions of the past, and that their pace outstripped the measured process of traditional diplomacy. The imperative of peace, he said, requires the maintenance of global stability, the resolution of conflict, and the easing of tension. The newer challenges embrace the improving of the world's economy and the devising of international solutions to such problems as energy, the environment, food, population, and trade—"the agenda of the modern period."

Addressing the UN General Assembly in September, Secretary Kissinger posed a dual equation. He assured the world of American resolve to vindicate mankind's positive goals and help nations frame a nobler international community. But he also warned that the task has been impeded by resurgent nationalism, erosion of moral and political cohesion, politicization and confrontation, escalation of peremptory demands, stridency of rhetoric, rigid ideologies, appeals to hatred, and resort to tests of strength. The very states that have most to gain from consensual and cooperative ventures, he added, have most to lose from retrogression of the diplomatic process.

At the United Nations, U. S. Ambassador William Scranton vetoes a Security Council resolution condemning Israel's annexation of Jerusalem. Although it was suggested that the United States might withdraw from the world body, the subject did not come up during the presidential campaign.

UPI

International Organizations. Responding to public comments on some of the actions of the United Nations and other international organizations, President Ford declared that "the United States retains the idealism that made us the driving force behind the creation of the UN system . . . to promote peace and progress." The Department of State reemphasized interdependence in remolding the international community and counseled against withdrawal from the United Nations or curtailment of involvement in constructive discussions and projects. While the matter of continuing participation did not become an issue in the presidential election, a deterioration of partnership was readily discernible in arbitrary UN resolutions, wanton attacks on the United States, and procedural abuses.

Secretary Kissinger indicated that the United States would not react emotionally to such retrogression and would continue to promote positive programs. However, he warned that the dissatisfied and impatient cannot have it both ways—they cannot brazenly confront the United States while demanding its enthusiastic cooperation and assistance. He defined American strategy as selective refusal to join in irresponsible measures, rejection of vindictive and unreasonable motions which lacked legal effect, and, when a consistent pattern of hostility toward the United States is discerned, a shifting to alternative direct responses. To counter a growing "tyranny of the majority" he proposed decision-making by consensus rather than formal vote. The United States made several moves to implement its strategy, such as withholding most of its contributions to UNESCO (United Nations Educational, Scientific, and Cultural Organization) in the past three years, intimating withdrawal from the International Labor Organization, and vetoing the admission to UN membership of North Korea and Vietnam until specific conditions are met.

Human Rights. The United States evidenced mounting concern about deterioration of human rights in large parts of the world. Internal self-determination and freedom was eroding, while more governments were becoming authoritarian if not dictatorial. Addressing the United Nations on the subject in unusually strong language, Secretary Kissinger condemned the hypocrisy, double standards, and strident rhetoric by some of the worst transgressors, passing pharisaical judgments on others. He prosposed programs to lessen officially sanctioned torture, protect the rights of those under detention, and improve the treatment of political refugees around the world.

A related issue flowed from congressional policy requiring the executive to reduce or terminate U. S. security assistance to governments that consistently violate international standards of human rights. The Department of State countered that withdrawal of such assistance would hurt other basic objectives and weaken mutual defense, without any guarantee of improving human rights abroad.

Weapons Proliferation. Armaments suppliers, including the United States, are providing a growing number of countries with quantities of sophisticated weaponry. While 1976 did not produce any major attempt to grapple with this general problem, attention was paid to policies on nuclear proliferation.

Approximately 100 states subscribed to the Non-Proliferation Treaty, but there were significant exceptions. Fearful of the expansion of the nuclear fraternity and the potentiality of nuclear war, the United States pressed for specific action to restrain nuclearization. It urged vigorous implementation of the International Atomic Energy Agency safeguard system, negotiation of agreed standards for protecting the physical security of nuclear materials, and the establishment of controls on reprocessing and enrichment plants in order to prevent the theft or diversion of nuclear material for weapons production.

International Terrorism. Secretary Kissinger reiterated U. S. concern with the spread of international terrorism—hijackings, kidnappings, armed attacks, and bombings—which he branded "a new, brutal, cowardly, and indiscriminate form of violence." He urged the United Nations to formulate programs to deny terrorists sanctuary and protect passengers in transit and in terminals. He also solicited universal implementation of the security measures adopted by the International Civil Aviation Organization and endorsed the initiative of West Germany to achieve a global agreement to stop the taking of hostages by terrorists. He warned that if international action was not forthcoming, the United States would adopt its own measures.

Law of the Sea. The complex international conference on the law of the sea, commenced under UN auspices in 1973, held its fifth session in 1976. Secretary Kissinger described it as "one of the most significant negotiations in diplomatic history" which, if successful, would provide "the first truly global solution to a global problem." (See feature article on the conference, beginning on page 50.)

Certain matters, agreed to by the United States, achieved widespread acceptance, such as extending the territorial sea to 12 miles, unimpeded transit through international straits, control by coastal states over a 200-mile-wide economic zone, and protection of the marine environment. Issues more difficult to negotiate include marine research within the areas of interest of coastal states, machinery for the impartial settlement of disputes, an international regime for exploiting the resources of the deep seabed, and the economic benefits that would accrue to poorer countries.

Integrating the vast array of conflicting interests into a practicable package of compromises and advantages is both difficult and necessary. In view of the developing vested interests, the Department of State was fearful that, in the absence of early international agreement, unrestrained commercial rivalry and political turmoil could result.

Regional and Territorial Policy and Issues. Negotiations continued with Panama on a new canal treaty, but, partly because the matter became an issue in the Republican presidential primary, little progress was made. While the United States was moving toward negotiations to normalize relations with the Castro government, Cuba's maneuvering to undo Puerto Rico's relations with the United States and its military intervention in Angola revived the specter of Cuban adventurism, militance, and export of revolution.

In the Middle East the United States reiterated its commitments to the survival of Israel, improvement of relations with the Arab countries and Turkey, and continuance of negotiations on the Arab-Israeli conflict. The United States remained aloof from the civil strife in Lebanon, and following the June murders of Ambassador Francis E. Meloy, Jr., and Economic Counselor Robert O. Waring, President Ford ordered the evacuation of all Americans who elected to leave the country.

After the Vietnam War, the United States demanded information on Americans missing in action as a precondition to reviving discussions with Hanoi. The death of Mao Tse-tung and the American election produced some pause in developing U. S.-Chinese détente. During the year Congress approved the establishment of the Commonwealth of the Northern Marianas in the Pacific, which had previously been approved by the Marianas legislature and by a UN-administered popular referendum.

The main crisis in the Asian-Pacific area occurred at Panmunjom, Korea, in August, when two U. S. army officers were killed and several enlisted men were wounded. Washington responded with a series of substantial military moves, and when the North Korean government expressed its regrets and agreed to new security measures at the site, the crisis receded.

Policies toward the Soviet Union include constraining its expansion, maintaining a reasonable balance of power, and détente. Negotiations on strategic arms continued, and during the year the principal issues in U. S.-Soviet relations involved the microwave bugging of the American embassy in Moscow and Soviet intervention in Angola.

When Portugal decided to withdraw from Angola, local factions fought for control. The Soviet government intervened—with some $200 million in arms, and sea and airlift support—and Cuba supplied 11,000 combat troops. This was the first time the Soviets moved militarily at long range to impose a political regime of their choice in a foreign land, the first time that United States failed to react forcefully, and the first time that Congress forestalled executive action to meet such a Communist challenge. The Soviets thereby tilted the geopolitical balance in southern Africa and gained a base in the southeast Atlantic.

This caused apprehension that external interposition would spread to other portions of southern Africa. Secretary Kissinger went to Africa on two missions, late in April and in September, to try to help resolve the Rhodesian and South West African (Namibian) problems. The United States worked closely with Great Britain and backed London's proposal for transition to majority rule in Rhodesia within two years, to be negotiated by local leaders. Such discussions were launched, and agreement was reached on the principle of majority rule and a compromise on timing. Secretary Kissinger also met with leaders of southern Africa on the problem of Namibia. While South Africa negotiated arrangements at a multiracial conference to grant independence at the end of 1978, local leaders and the United Nations demanded more rapid progress.

ELMER PLISCHKE
University of Maryland

UNITED STATES: 95TH CONGRESS

SENATE MEMBERSHIP

(As of January 1977: 62 Democrats, 38 Republicans)

Letters after senators' names refer to party affiliation—D for Democrat, R for Republican. Single asterisk (*) denotes term expiring in January 1979; double asterisk (**), term expiring in January 1981; triple asterisk (***), term expiring in January 1983; (a) appointed to fill vacancy; (1) ran as independent.

ALABAMA
*J. Sparkman, D
**J. B. Allen, D

ALASKA
*T. Stevens, R
**M. Gravel, D

ARIZONA
**B. Goldwater, R
***D. DeConcini, D

ARKANSAS
*J. L. McClellan, D
**D. Bumpers, D

CALIFORNIA
**A. Cranston, D
***S. I. Hayakawa, R

COLORADO
*F. K. Haskell, D
**G. Hart, D

CONNECTICUT
*A. A. Ribicoff, D
***L. P. Weicker, Jr., R

DELAWARE
*J. R. Biden, Jr., D
***W. V. Roth, Jr., R

FLORIDA
**R. Stone, D
***L. Chiles, D

GEORGIA
*S. A. Nunn, D
**H. E. Talmadge, D

HAWAII
**D. K. Inouye, D
***S. Matsunaga, D

IDAHO
*J. A. McClure, R
**F. Church, D

ILLINOIS
*C. H. Percy, R
**A. E. Stevenson, III, D

INDIANA
**B. Bayh, D
***R. Lugar, R

IOWA
*R. Clark, D
**J. C. Culver, D

KANSAS
*J. B. Pearson, R
**R. Dole, R

KENTUCKY
*W. Huddleston, D
**W. H. Ford, D

LOUISIANA
*J. B. Johnston, Jr., D
**R. B. Long, D

MAINE
*W. D. Hathaway, D
***E. S. Muskie, D

MARYLAND
**C. M. Mathias, Jr., R
***P. S. Sarbanes, D

MASSACHUSETTS
*E. W. Brooke, R
***E. M. Kennedy, D

MICHIGAN
*R. P. Griffin, R
***D. W. Riegle, Jr., D

MINNESOTA
***H. H. Humphrey, D
*aWendell Anderson, D

MISSISSIPPI
*J. O. Eastland, D
***J. C. Stennis, D

MISSOURI
**T. F. Eagleton, D
***J. C. Danforth, R

MONTANA
*L. Metcalf, D
***J. Melcher, D

NEBRASKA
*C. T. Curtis, R
***E. Zorinsky, D

NEVADA
**P. Laxalt, R
***H. W. Cannon, D

NEW HAMPSHIRE
*T. J. McIntyre, D
**J. Durkin, D

NEW JERSEY
*C. P. Case, R
***H. A. Williams, Jr., D

NEW MEXICO
*P. V. Domenici, R
***H. Schmitt, R

NEW YORK
*J. K. Javits, R
***D. P. Moynihan, D

NORTH CAROLINA
*J. Helms, R
**R. Morgan, D

NORTH DAKOTA
**M. R. Young, R
***Q. N. Burdick, D

OHIO
**J. H. Glenn, Jr., D
***H. M. Metzenbaum, D

OKLAHOMA
*D. F. Bartlett, R
**H. Bellmon, R

OREGON
*M. O. Hatfield, R
**B. Packwood, R

PENNSYLVANIA
**R. S. Schweiker, R
***H. J. Heinz, III, R

RHODE ISLAND
*C. Pell, D
***J. H. Chafee, R

SOUTH CAROLINA
*S. Thurmond, R
**E. F. Hollings, D

SOUTH DAKOTA
*J. G. Abourezk, D
**G. S. McGovern, D

TENNESSEE
*H. H. Baker, Jr., R
***J. Sasser, D

TEXAS
*J. G. Tower, R
***L. M. Bentsen, D

UTAH
**J. Garn, R
***O. Hatch, R

VERMONT
**P. J. Leahy, D
***R. T. Stafford, R

VIRGINIA
*W. L. Scott, R
***H. F. Byrd, Jr., D (1)

WASHINGTON
**W. G. Magnuson, D
***H. M. Jackson, D

WEST VIRGINIA
*J. Randolph, D
***R. C. Byrd, D

WISCONSIN
**G. Nelson, D
***W. Proxmire, D

WYOMING
*C. P. Hansen, R
***M. Wallop, R

HOUSE MEMBERSHIP

(As of January 1977: 289 Democrats, 143 Republicans, 3 vacancies)

"At-L." in place of congressional district number means "representative at large." Asterisk (*) before name indicates elected Nov. 2, 1976; all others were reelected.

ALABAMA
1. J. Edwards, R
2. W. L. Dickinson, R
3. W. Nichols, D
4. T. Bevill, D
5. *R. Flippo, D
6. J. H. Buchanan, Jr., R
7. W. Flowers, D

ALASKA
At-L. D. Young, R

ARIZONA
1. J. J. Rhodes, R
2. M. K. Udall, D
3. *B. Stump, D
4. *E. Rudd, R

ARKANSAS
1. W. V. Alexander, Jr., D
2. *J. G. Tucker, D
3. J. P. Hammerschmidt, R
4. R. H. Thornton, Jr., D

CALIFORNIA
1. H. T. Johnson, D
2. D. H. Clausen, R
3. J. E. Moss, D
4. R. L. Leggett, D
5. J. Burton, D
6. P. Burton, D

7. G. Miller, D
8. R. V. Dellums, D
9. F. H. Stark, D
10. D. Edwards, D
11. L. J. Ryan, D
12. P. N. McCloskey, Jr., R
13. N. Y. Mineta, D
14. J. J. McFall, D
15. B. F. Sisk, D
16. *L. E. Panetta, D
17. J. Krebs, D
18. W. M. Ketchum, R
19. R. J. Lagomarsino, R
20. B. M. Goldwater, Jr., R
21. J. C. Corman, D
22. C. J. Moorhead, R
23. *A. C. Beilenson, D
24. H. A. Waxman, D
25. E. R. Roybal, D
26. J. H. Rousselot, R
27. *R. K. Dornan, R
28. Y. B. Burke, D
29. A. F. Hawkins, D
30. G. E. Danielson, D
31. C. H. Wilson, D
32. G. M. Anderson, D
33. D. Clawson, R
34. M. W. Hannaford, D
35. J. Lloyd, D
36. G. E. Brown, Jr., D
37. S. N. Pettis, R

38. J. M. Patterson, D
39. C. E. Wiggins, R
40. *R. Badham, R
41. B. Wilson, R
42. L. Van Deerlin, D
43. C. W. Burgener, R

COLORADO
1. P. Schroeder, D
2. T. E. Wirth, D
3. F. E. Evans, D
4. J. P. Johnson, R
5. W. L. Armstrong, R

CONNECTICUT
1. W. R. Cotter, D
2. C. J. Dodd, D
3. R. N. Giaimo, D
4. S. B. McKinney, R
5. R. A. Sarasin, R
6. T. Moffett, D

DELAWARE
At-L. *T. B. Evans, Jr., R

FLORIDA
1. R. L. F. Sikes, D
2. D. Fuqua, D
3. C. E. Bennett, D
4. W. V. Chappell, Jr., D
5. R. Kelly, R

6. C. W. Young, R
7. S. M. Gibbons, D
8. *A. Ireland, D
9. L. Frey, Jr., R
10. L. A. Bafalis, R
11. P. G. Rogers, D
12. J. H. Burke, D
13. W. Lehman, D
14. C. Pepper, D
15. D. B. Fascell, D

GEORGIA
1. R. B. Ginn, D
2. M. D. Mathis, D
3. J. Brinkley, D
4. E. H. Levitas, D
5. Vacant
6. J. Flynt, Jr., D
7. L. McDonald, D
8. *B. L. Evans, D
9. *E. Jenkins, D
10. *D. Barnard, D

HAWAII
1. *C. Heftel, D
2. *D. Akaka, D

IDAHO
1. S. D. Symms, R
2. G. Hansen, R

ILLINOIS
1. R. H. Metcalfe, D
2. M. F. Murphy, D
3. M. A. Russo, D
4. E. J. Derwinski, R
5. J. G. Fary, D
6. H. J. Hyde, R
7. C. Collins, D
8. D. Rostenkowski, D
9. S. R. Yates, D
10. A. J. Mikva, D
11. F. Annunzio, D
12. P. M. Crane, R
13. R. McClory, R
14. J. N. Erlenborn, R
15. *T. Corcoran, R
16. J. B. Anderson, R
17. G. M. O'Brien, R
18. R. H. Michel, R
19. T. Railsback, R
20. P. Findley, R
21. E. R. Madigan, R
22. G. E. Shipley, D
23. C. M. Price, D
24. P. Simon, D

INDIANA
1. *A. Benjamin, Jr., D
2. F. J. Fithian, D
3. J. Brademas, D
4. *J. D. Quayle, R
5. E. H. Hillis, R
6. D. W. Evans, D
7. J. T. Myers, R
8. *D. L. Cornwell, D
9. L. H. Hamilton, D
10. P. R. Sharp, D
11. A. Jacobs, Jr., D

IOWA
1. *J. Leach, R
2. M. T. Blouin, D
3. C. E. Grassley, R
4. N. Smith, D
5. T. Harkin, D
6. B. Bedell, D

KANSAS
1. K. G. Sebelius, R
2. M. Keys, D
3. L. Winn, Jr., R
4. *D. Glickman, D
5. J. Skubitz, R

KENTUCKY
1. C. Hubbard, Jr., D
2. W. H. Natcher, D
3. R. L. Mazzoli, D
4. M. G. Snyder, R
5. T. L. Carter, R
6. J. B. Breckinridge, D
7. C. D. Perkins, D

LOUISIANA
1. *R. Tonry, D
2. C. C. Boggs, D
3. D. C. Treen, R
4. J. D. Waggonner, Jr., D
5. *J. Huckaby, D
6. W. H. Moore, R
7. J. B. Breaux, D
8. G. W. Long, D

MAINE
1. D. F. Emery, R
2. W. S. Cohen, R

MARYLAND
1. R. E. Bauman, R
2. C. D. Long, D
3. *B. Mikulski, D
4. M. S. Holt, R
5. G. N. Spellman, D
6. G. E. Byron, D
7. P. J. Mitchell, D
8. *N. Steers, Jr., R

MASSACHUSETTS
1. S. O. Conte, R
2. E. P. Boland, D
3. J. D. Early, D
4. R. F. Drinan, D
5. P. E. Tsongas, D
6. M. J. Harrington, D
7. *E. J. Markey, D
8. T. P. O'Neill, Jr., D
9. J. J. Moakley, D
10. M. M. Heckler, R
11. J. A. Burke, D
12. G. E. Studds, D

MICHIGAN
1. J. Conyers, Jr., D
2. *C. D. Pursell, R
3. G. Brown, R

4. *D. Stockman, R
5. *H. Sawyer, R
6. B. Carr, D
7. *D. E. Kildee, D
8. B. Traxler, D
9. G. A. Vander Jagt, R
10. E. A. Cederberg, R
11. P. E. Ruppe, R
12. *D. E. Bonior, D
13. C. C. Diggs, Jr., D
14. L. N. Nedzi, D
15. W. D. Ford, D
16. J. D. Dingell, D
17. W. M. Brodhead, D
18. J. J. Blanchard, D
19. W. S. Broomfield, R

MINNESOTA
1. A. H. Quie, R
2. T. Hagedorn, R
3. B. Frenzel, R
4. *B. Vento, D
5. D. M. Fraser, D
6. R. Nolan, D
7. Vacant
8. J. L. Oberstar, D

MISSISSIPPI
1. J. L. Whitten, D
2. D. R. Bowen, D
3. G. V. Montgomery, D
4. T. Cochran, R
5. T. Lott, R

MISSOURI
1. W. L. Clay, D
2. *R. A. Young, D
3. *R. A. Gephardt, D
4. *I. Skelton, D
5. R. Bolling, D
6. *E. T. Coleman, R
7. G. Taylor, R
8. R. H. Ichord, D
9. *H. L. Volkmer, D
10. B. D. Burlison, D

MONTANA
1. M. S. Baucus, D
2. *R. Marlenee, R

NEBRASKA
1. C. Thone, R
2. *J. J. Cavanaugh, D
3. V. Smith, R

NEVADA
At-L. J. Santini, D

NEW HAMPSHIRE
1. N. E. D'Amours, D
2. J. C. Cleveland, R

NEW JERSEY
1. J. J. Florio, D
2. W. J. Hughes, D
3. J. J. Howard, D
4. F. Thompson, Jr., D
5. M. Fenwick, R
6. E. B. Forsythe, R
7. A. Maguire, D
8. R. A. Roe, D
9. *H. Hollenbeck, R
10. P. W. Rodino, Jr., D
11. J. G. Minish, D
12. M. J. Rinaldo, R
13. H. S. Meyner, D
14. *J. A. Le Fante, D
15. E. J. Patten, D

NEW MEXICO
1. M. Lujan, Jr., R
2. H. Runnels, D

NEW YORK
1. O. G. Pike, D
2. T. J. Downey, D
3. J. Ambro, Jr., D
4. N. F. Lent, R
5. J. W. Wydler, R
6. L. L. Wolff, D
7. J. P. Addabbo, D
8. B. S. Rosenthal, D
9. J. J. Delaney, D
10. M. Biaggi, D
11. J. H. Scheuer, D
12. S. A. Chisholm, D
13. S. J. Solarz, D
14. F. W. Richmond, D
15. L. C. Zeferetti, D
16. E. Holtzman, D
17. J. M. Murphy, D
18. E. I. Koch, D
19. C. B. Rangel, D
20. *T. S. Weiss, D
21. H. Badillo, D

22. J. B. Bingham, D
23. *B. F. Caputo, R
24. R. L. Ottinger, D
25. H. Fish, Jr., R
26. B. A. Gilman, R
27. M. F. McHugh, D
28. S. S. Stratton, D
29. E. W. Pattison, D
30. R. C. McEwen, R
31. D. J. Mitchell, R
32. J. M. Hanley, D
33. W. F. Walsh, R
34. F. Horton, R
35. B. B. Conable, Jr., R
36. J. J. LaFalce, D
37. H. J. Nowak, D
38. J. F. Kemp, R
39. S. N. Lundine, D

NORTH CAROLINA
1. W. B. Jones, D
2. L. H. Fountain, D
3. *C. Whitley, D
4. I. F. Andrews, D
5. S. L. Neal, D
6. L. R. Preyer, D
7. C. G. Rose, D
8. W. G. Hefner, D
9. J. G. Martin, R
10. J. T. Broyhill, R
11. *L. Gudger, D

NORTH DAKOTA
At-L. M. Andrews, R

OHIO
1. W. D. Gradison, Jr., R
2. *T. A. Luken, D
3. C. W. Whalen, Jr., R
4. T. Guyer, R
5. D. L. Latta, R
6. W. H. Harsha, R
7. C. J. Brown, R
8. T. N. Kindness, R
9. T. L. Ashley, D
10. C. E. Miller, R
11. J. W. Stanton, R
12. S. L. Devine, R
13. *D. J. Pease, D
14. J. F. Seiberling, D
15. C. P. Wylie, R
16. R. S. Regula, R
17. J. M. Ashbrook, R
18. *D. Applegate, D
19. C. J. Carney, D
20. *M. R. Oakar, D
21. L. Stokes, D
22. C. A. Vanik, D
23. R. M. Mottl, D

OKLAHOMA
1. J. R. Jones, D
2. T. M. Risenhoover, D
3. *W. Watkins, D
4. T. Steed, D
5. *M. Edwards, R
6. G. English, D

OREGON
1. L. AuCoin, D
2. A. Ullman, D
3. R. Duncan, D
4. J. Weaver, D

PENNSYLVANIA
1. *M. Myers, D
2. R. N. C. Nix, D
3. *R. F. Lederer, D
4. J. Eilberg, D
5. R. T. Schulze, R
6. G. Yatron, D
7. R. W. Edgar, D
8. *P. H. Kostmayer, D
9. E. G. Shuster, R
10. J. M. McDade, R
11. D. J. Flood, D
12. J. P. Murtha, D
13. L. Coughlin, R
14. W. S. Moorhead, D
15. F. B. Rooney, D
16. *R. S. Walker, R
17. *A. E. Ertel, D
18. *D. Walgren, D
19. W. F. Goodling, R
20. J. M. Gaydos, D
21. J. H. Dent, D
22. *A. J. Murphy, D
23. *J. Ammerman, D
24. *M. Marks, R
25. G. A. Myers, D

RHODE ISLAND
1. F. J. St Germain, D
2. E. P. Beard, D

SOUTH CAROLINA
1. M. J. Davis, D
2. F. D. Spence, R
3. B. Derrick, Jr., D
4. J. R. Mann, D
5. K. L. Holland, D
6. J. W. Jenrette, Jr., D

SOUTH DAKOTA
1. L. Pressler, R
2. J. Abdnor, R

TENNESSEE
1. J. H. Quillen, R
2. J. J. Duncan, R
3. M. Lloyd, D
4. *A. Gore, Jr., D
5. C. R. Allen, D
6. R. L. Beard, Jr., R
7. E. Jones, D
8. H. E. Ford, D

TEXAS
1. S. B. Hall, Jr., D
2. C. Wilson, D
3. J. M. Collins, R
4. R. Roberts, D
5. *J. Mattox, D
6. O. E. Teague, D
7. B. Archer, R
8. B. Eckhardt, D
9. J. Brooks, D
10. J. J. Pickle, D
11. W. R. Poage, D
12. J. C. Wright, Jr., D
13. J. Hightower, D
14. J. Young, D
15. E. de la Garza, D
16. R. C. White, D
17. O. Burleson, D
18. B. C. Jordan, D
19. G. H. Mahon, D
20. H. B. Gonzalez, D
21. R. Krueger, D
22. *B. Gammage, D
23. A. Kazen, Jr., D
24. D. Milford, D

UTAH
1. G. McKay, D
2. *D. Marriott, R

VERMONT
At-L. J. M. Jeffords, R

VIRGINIA
1. *P. S. Trible, Jr., R
2. G. W. Whitehurst, R
3. D. E. Satterfield, III, D
4. R. W. Daniel, Jr., R
5. W. C. Daniel, D
6. M. C. Butler, R
7. J. K. Robinson, R
8. H. E. Harris, II, D
9. W. C. Wampler, R
10. J. L. Fisher, D

WASHINGTON
1. J. M. Pritchard, R
2. L. Meeds, D
3. D. Bonker, D
4. M. McCormack, D
5. T. S. Foley, D
6. *N. Dicks, D
7. Vacant

WEST VIRGINIA
1. R. H. Mollohan, D
2. H. O. Staggers, D
3. J. Slack, D
4. *N. J. Rahall, D

WISCONSIN
1. L. Aspin, D
2. R. W. Kastenmeier, D
3. A. Baldus, D
4. C. J. Zablocki, D
5. H. S. Reuss, D
6. W. A. Steiger, R
7. D. R. Obey, D
8. R. J. Cornell, D
9. R. W. Kasten, Jr., R

WYOMING
At-L. T. Roncalio, D

PUERTO RICO
Resident Commissioner
*B. Corrada del Rio

DISTRICT OF COLUMBIA
Delegate
W. E. Fauntroy, D

URUGUAY

During 1976 the military-controlled regime, in power since 1973, was "institutionalized." President Juan María Bordaberry was deposed, and a government supposed to last five years was substituted.

Government. Controversy during the first few months of 1976 between the military and President Bordaberry ended on June 12, when the armed forces ousted the president, putting in his place Vice President Alberto Demichell. They announced that Demichell would remain in office for 60 days.

On June 27 a National Council of 25 civilians and 21 military officers was appointed to choose a new president. Its chairman was Aparicio Méndez, an old politician of the conservative Blanco party. Some two weeks later the National Council announced the choice of Aparicio Méndez as president for five years. He took office on September 1, proclaiming a "civic purge" of Marxists and the establishment of a "new order," which would have some role for the two traditional parties, the Colorados and Blancos. He also promised a new constitution.

Economy. The country's economic problems were severe throughout the year. During the 12 months ending May 31, the cost of living had increased 44%. Wages were frozen during the first half of the year, but a general 20% wage increase was granted July 1. Rises in prices of essential goods, ranging from 4.6% to 22% were granted at the same time. The foreign exchange situation also remained precarious, but the International Monetary Fund provided $29.8 million to stabilize the peso and the general economy.

Foreign Affairs. The Soviet Union protested in January against the persecution of Communists. In February, Amnesty International accused the country of keeping 6,000 political prisoners, the largest number per capita of any country in the world. These charges were later repeated by the International Commission of Jurists. The U. S. House of Representatives also held hearings on Uruguayan human rights, as a result of which Congress ended military aid.

ROBERT J. ALEXANDER, *Rutgers University*

─────── **URUGUAY · Information Highlights** ───────

Official Name: Eastern Republic of Uruguay.
Location: Southeastern coast of South America.
Area: 68,536 square miles (177,508 km²).
Population (1976 est.): 2,800,000.
Chief City (1975 census): Montevideo, the capital, 1,230,000.
Government: *Head of state and government,* Aparicio Méndez, president (took office Sept. 1976). *Legislature*—General Assembly (suspended June 1973).
Monetary Unit: Peso (3.43 pesos equal U. S.$1, July 1976).
Gross National Product (1975 est.): $2,800,000,000.
Manufacturing (major products): Meat products, textiles, construction and building materials, beverages, chemicals.
Major Agricultural Products: Wheat, corn, rice, livestock, wool.
Foreign Trade (1975): *Exports,* $384,000,000; *imports,* $557,000,000.

UTAH

Political scandal, elections, and initiative proposals held Utahans' attention in 1976.

Politics. In June, following the Salt Lake County Democratic party convention, Rep. Allan T. Howe was arrested on a sex solicitation charge. He was convicted of the charge in July by a four-member jury in Salt Lake City Court, and again in August by a Third District Court jury. Throughout the trial period the question whether Howe should withdraw as a Democratic candidate for Congress was publicly debated. Rep. Howe chose to run despite the withdrawal of support by the state Democratic party. A write-in candidate, Daryl McCarty, was supported by officials of the party.

Elections. Approximately 540,000 Utahans voted in the 1976 general election. This represented slightly more than 80% of the registered voters in the state and exceeded by 60,000 the votes cast in 1972. Utah continues to rank at or near the top among the 50 states in voter turnout. In the presidential race, the Ford-Dole ticket received 62.4% of the votes cast. In a hotly contested race for the Senate, newcomer Republican Orrin G. Hatch defeated incumbent Democratic Sen. Frank E. Moss, who had held the office for 18 years. Rep. Allan

Gary Gilmore is wheeled into a Salt Lake City hospital on November 16. Sentenced to death by firing squad, the condemned murderer attempted suicide when the state of Utah delayed his execution.

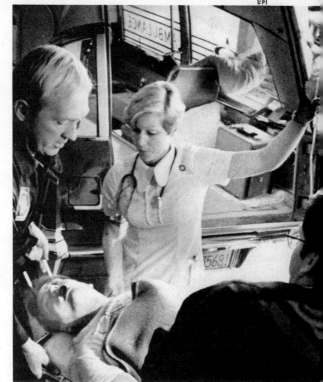

UPI

Howe was defeated by another newcomer to Utah politics, Republican Dan Marriott. Three-term Democratic incumbent Gunn McKay won reelection.

In spite of the strong support for President Ford, Utahans picked a Democrat, Scott M. Matheson, for the state's highest office; he succeeds three-term Gov. Calvin Rampton, also a Democrat. The political alignment of the legislature will be split. The state Senate will have a Democratic majority of 17–12, whereas the Utah House of Representatives will be dominated by the Republicans, 40–35. The election of state representatives was marked by the seating of a black minister from Ogden and a Chicano for the first time in the state's history.

Initiative Proposals. Three initiative proposals were placed on the Utah ballot by petition. All three were extremely controversial and generated heated public debate throughout the campaign. The first was entitled "Freedom from Compulsory Fluoridation and Medication Act." This proposal would "expressly prohibit" the state Board of Health from "compelling additives of fluorides or any other medications to any public water supplies," state, county, or municipal. The issue has long been an emotional one in Utah, and for the third time fluoridation at the state level was defeated by a 52 to 48% margin. A second initiative petition, entitled "Budgetary Procedures Ceiling Act" would have imposed limitations on the state budget for the five-year period beginning with fiscal 1977–78 at the current level of $915 million and would have phased out all federal spending in Utah at the rate of 20% a year. This proposal was overwhelmingly defeated by a 78 to 22% margin. The third initiative petition entitled "Utah Recall and Advisory Recall Act" provided for special elections to recall elected or appointed officials on certification of petitions signed by a designated number of qualified voters. The proposed law provided that "any reason causing voter dissatisfaction" with a public official was legal basis for circulating a recall petition. Utah voters rejected this proposal by a 52 to 48% margin.

LORENZO K. KIMBALL, *University of Utah*

UTAH • Information Highlights

Area: 84,916 square miles (219,932 km²).
Population (1975 est.): 1,206,000.
Chief Cities (1970 census): Salt Lake City, the capital, 175,885; Ogden, 69,478; Provo, 53,131.
Government (1976): *Chief Officers*—governor, Calvin L. Rampton (D); secy. of state, Clyde L. Miller (D). *Legislature*—Senate, 29 members; House of Representatives, 75 members.
Education (1975–76): *Enrollment*—public elementary schools, 163,453 pupils; public secondary, 146,255; nonpublic (1976–77), 3,900; colleges and universities, 74,295 students. *Public school expenditures,* $314,578,000 ($1,020 per pupil).
State Finances (fiscal year 1975): *Revenues,* $907,865,-000; *expenditures,* $895,403,000.
Personal Income (1975): $5,937,000,000; per capita, $4,923.
Labor Force (July 1976): *Nonagricultural wage and salary earners,* 465,000,000; *insured unemployed,* 10,800 (3.2%).

VENEZUELA

The year 1976 in Venezuela was marked by increasing political problems for President Carlos Andrés Pérez and the nationalization of foreign oil companies. The leaders of European and Latin American Social Democratic parties met in Caracas in May.

Domestic Affairs. President Andrés Pérez completed his second year in office in March in a deteriorating political climate. The opposition Social Christian party (COPEI), a coalition partner of his own Democratic Action party (AD) in a previous administration, called in May for the censure of five AD ministers and criticized Andrés Pérez for violations of free speech. Later COPEI gave vent to its "deep frustration" with the president's inability to deliver on his promises. AD had begun the year with a promise of full debate on several controversial issues, including tax reform to reduce government reliance on oil revenues and a long term indebtedness that would enable the government to borrow up to 60 billion bolivars.

The magazine *Elite* commented in July that a military coup seemed imminent in view of the hostilities between the two major parties. In September the government confiscated an issue of the leftist *Punto* because it contained an article highly critical of the president and the armed forces.

Widespread student riots broke out in 13 cities in February following the deaths of two students during a demonstration in San Felipe, Yaracuy state. The auditor general resigned in June, charging government officials with irregularities and corruption, and with ignoring his reports.

A bizarre chain of events was set in motion in February with the kidnapping of William Niehous, manager of the U. S. firm of Owens-Illinois in Venezuela. The Group of Revolutionary Commandos said the abduction was a protest against the company's interference in Venezuelan politics. The government later nationalized Owens-Illinois, claiming the company was secretly negotiating with the kidnappers. Two congressmen were implicated and later arrested. In all, 16 persons have been detained in connection with the crime. During the investigation the government was embarrassed by the death of an extreme leftist who suffered a heart attack after being questioned by the security police.

To cut down on high crime and accident rates the government forbade the sale of beer in public places on Sundays and holidays.

Venezuela suffered its worst floods in 30 years in July. More than 50,000 persons were made homeless and $35-million worth of damages resulted from the rising waters of the Orinoco and Caroní rivers.

Economy. Venezuela, the most important oil producing country in Latin America, nationalized foreign oil companies. The companies have

Carlos Andrés Pérez (left) and Italy's President Giovanni Leone review the presidential bodyguard in the Quirinale courtyard. The Venezuelan president was on an official visit to Italy and the Vatican.

UPI

agreed to furnish technical assistance for all phases of production and distribution as well as parts and equipment. They will be paid 15¢ for each barrel of crude and refined oil produced. They have also agreed to buy 1.5 million barrels a day at OPEC prices. The government corporation, Petroven, will need to sell a total of 2.2 million barrels a day if it is to meet its budgeted revenues for the year.

In January, Venezuela entered into a complicated economic agreement with Argentina that included an exchange of Venezuelan iron ore for Argentine wheat.

Foreign Affairs. Venezuela was visited by Canadian Prime Minister Pierre Elliott Trudeau

--- **VENEZUELA · Information Highlights** ---

Official Name: Republic of Venezuela.
Location: Northwestern South America.
Area: 352,143 square miles (912,050 km²).
Population (1976 est.): 12,300,000.
Chief Cities (1974): Caracas, the capital, 2,400,000; Maracaibo, 900,000; Barquisimeto, 350,000.
Government: *Head of state and government,* Carlos Andrés Pérez, president (took office March 1974). *Legislature*—Congress: Senate and Chamber of Deputies.
Monetary Unit: Bolivar (4.20 bolivares equal U. S.$1, Sept. 1976).
Gross National Product (1975 est.): $28,900,000,000.
Manufacturing (major products): Processed foods, paper and paperboard, petroleum products, beverages, metal products, furniture, clothing.
Major Agricultural Products: Coffee, cacao, bananas, sugarcane, cotton, rice, corn, dairy products.
Foreign Trade (1975): *Exports,* $10,040,000,000; *imports,* $5,401,000,000.

in January, by U. S. Secretary of State Henry Kissinger in February, and by President Tito of Yugoslavia in March. Secretary Kissinger's cool reception was underlined by student demonstrations against his visit.

President Andrés Pérez met with Colombian President López in January to discuss border problems caused by the shifting Arauca River and their conflicting claims to part of the oil rich Gulf of Venezuela. In July, Venezuela broke diplomatic relations with Uruguay over the issue of violation of sovereignty in the Venezuelan embassy in Montevideo. The government concluded a $2.3 million banking agreement with Cuba and promised to send oil and steel trade missions to visit Castro. Relations with Brazil worsened during the year, and Venezuela became increasingly concerned by border incidents involving Brazilian troops on its extreme southern frontier. It also expressed dissatisfaction with Kissinger's promise to consult with Brazil on a regular basis.

At a meeting with Panamanian Gen. Omar Torrijos, President Andrés Pérez announced his firm and full support for Panama's efforts to secure revision of the canal treaty, and his willingness to play an important role toward that end. Relations with the United States improved after Washington recalled its unpopular ambassador and repealed a clause of the U. S. trade act that discriminated against OPEC countries.

LEO B. LOTT, *University of Montana*

VERMONT

Bicentennial celebrations were held in virtually every town of Vermont in 1976. However, the principal bicentennial project, a steam passenger train, was a financial disaster. Planned to run in 1976 and 1977 from late spring through the fall foliage season, the train failed to attract enough passengers and was stopped after the Labor Day weekend. Its deficit, exceeding $800,000, will be assumed by the state.

Elections. A nonbinding presidential primary gave a plurality among 3 Democratic contenders to Jimmy Carter. President Ford was unchallenged. Democratic national convention delegates chosen by the state convention remained divided; Republicans were solidly pro-Ford.

The gubernatorial campaign was highlighted by a split in the Democratic party, when conservative State Treasurer Stella Hackel defeated liberal Lt. Gov. Brian D. Burns in the September primary. Hackel was soundly defeated by Republican House Majority Leader Richard A. Snelling, 92,232 to 71,053. The Democrats held the state attorney generalship and won the office of secretary of state. They led for the lieutenant governorship, but without a majority, necessitating a decision by the new legislature. Republicans tightened their hold on the state Senate, while the House swung narrowly Democratic. An advisory referendum on a state lottery was approved by a margin of almost 3 to 1.

State House Majority Leader Richard A. Snelling, 49-year-old Republican, was elected governor of Vermont.

WIDE WORLD

In the U. S. Senate race, retiring Democratic Gov. Thomas P. Salmon lost to incumbent Sen. Robert Stafford (R). Vermont's lone Congressman, James Jeffords (R), was reelected. President Ford won the state's three electoral votes.

Legislation. Environmental protection efforts were frustrated with the one-vote defeat of a ban on phosphate detergents and the failure of a land-use plan to get out of committee. Health problems were addressed by a package of bills dealing with malpractice insurance rates and the creation of a Health Policy Council.

Continuing to reject the notion of tax increases, Vermont was able to avoid the appearance of a deficit through accounting transfers and accelerated tax collections.

A five-member state Senate committee was created, with the implicit purpose of investigating the Korean-based Unification Church of the Rev. Sun Myung Moon. The Vermont chapter of the American Civil Liberties Union (ACLU) labeled the investigation proceedings "clearly unconstitutional and unreasonable," and the committee chairman countered with a threat to expand his probe to include the ACLU.

Legal. The Vermont Supreme Court ruled that the power of lay assistant judges in county courts to decide questions of law was contrary to the U.S. Constitution.

Following complaints to the House Judiciary Committee by the attorney general's office, the Vermont House of Representatives, for the first time in history, voted articles of impeachment against a county sheriff. The sheriff was narrowly acquitted by the state Senate.

Education. Most news stories featuring higher education headlined the resignation or inauguration of presidents. Among institutions receiving new presidents were the University of Vermont, Middlebury College, and Bennington College.

The Miller Formula, governing distribution of state aid for elementary and secondary education, came under attack for failing to reflect low average income in certain land-rich towns. However, no substitute could be agreed upon.

SAMUEL B. HAND AND ROBERT V. DANIELS
University of Vermont

——— **VERMONT · Information Highlights** ———

Area: 9,609 square miles (24,887 km²).
Population (1975 est.): 471,000.
Chief Cities (1970 census): Montpelier, the capital, 8,609; Burlington, 38,633; Rutland, 19,293; Bennington, 14,586.
Government (1976): *Chief Officers*—governor, Thomas P. Salmon (D); lt. gov., Brian D. Burns (D). *General Assembly*—Senate, 30 members; House of Representatives, 150 members.
Education (1975–76): *Enrollment*—public elementary schools, 63,090 pupils; public secondary, 41,784; nonpublic (1976–77), 9,800; colleges and universities, 27,977 students. *Public school expenditures,* $139,306,000 ($1,342 per pupil).
State Finances (fiscal year 1975): *Revenues,* $452,957,-000; *expenditures,* $471,815,000.
Personal Income (1975): $2,336,000,000; per capita, $4,960.
Labor Force (July 1976): *Nonagricultural wage and salary earners,* 165,200; *insured unemployed,* 7,000 (5.4%).

Large posters encourage Vietnamese citizens to vote in April 25 elections for a 492-member National Assembly. In honor of the event, a massive parade was held in Saigon (below). About 99% of the eligible voters cast their ballots.

VIETNAM

Vietnam's 22-year-long struggle for reunification ended on July 2, 1976, with the official establishment of a single state structure joining once warring North and South Vietnam. Elections were held on April 25 to choose a national legislature. Problems persisted, however, from the two decades of division and from the differing development of the two Vietnams.

Politics. The April elections were held on the eve of the anniversary of the 1975 Communist victory in Vietnam. The government claimed that 99% of eligible voters, in both North and South Vietnam, went to the polls to choose a 492-member National Assembly (249 deputies from the North and 243 from the South). There was no non-Communist opposition.

The reunification of the two Vietnams as the "Socialist Republic of Vietnam" was officially proclaimed during the first session of the new Assembly, held from June 24 to July 3. The state consists of 35 provinces, three of which are cities—Hanoi, Haiphong, and Saigon. Hanoi was designated the capital, and the national flag, emblem, and anthem of North Vietnam were adopted for the whole country. Saigon, capital of the former South Vietnam, was renamed "Ho Chi Minh City." The 1959 North Vietnamese

constitution was to be the law of the land until a new constitution was drawn up.

The National Assembly also chose the leaders of the government of the reunified state—most of them officials of the old North Vietnam. Pham Van Dong, North Vietnam's premier and long one of its real ranking leaders, was named premier of the new republic. Ailing 88-year-old figurehead North Vietnamese President Ton Duc Thang was made chief of state of the unified country. Two vice presidents were designated: Nguyen Huu Tho, previously president of the Provisional Revolutionary Government of South Vietnam, and North Vietnamese Vice President Nguyen Luong Bang. Truong Chinh, doctrinaire theoretician of the Hanoi regime, was elected president of the Standing Committee of the Assembly, which carries on the Assembly's work between its brief annual sessions.

The governing Workers' party was renamed the Communist party in December. Meeting in its first congress since 1960, the party also expanded its Politburo to include new members from the South. In addition, the party's Central Committee was expanded.

Party Secretary General Le Duan and Premier Pham Van Dong remained the two most powerful political figures in the country. The ideologue Truong Chinh, emphasizing such theory-derived goals as the development of "Socialist man," was also important. But there was no evidence that Chinh was in any kind of conflict with Premier Dong, principal advocate of the practical objectives of economic development and reconciliation with the Western group of nations. There were, however, some residual tensions between the former North Vietnamese leadership, which dominated the new national government, and various members of the short-lived provisional government of the South, whose political importance was progressively eclipsed by the Hanoi politicians.

The chief political problem of Communist-ruled Vietnam may have been what was described in official organs as an erosion of the "revolutionary quality" of party military and civilian personnel.

There was no widespread bloodletting in the first full year of Communist governance of all of Vietnam, as once had been predicted and feared. This was partly because so many persons associated with the former anti-Communist regime had fled with the Americans in April 1975. But a quarter of a million persons were in political reeducation camps—not only military and civilian officials of the former Nguyen Van Thieu government but also many former "third force" politicians. It was indicated in late 1976 that they probably would not be released for another two years.

Economy. The economic situation in Vietnam modestly improved during the year. Prices in the southern part of the country tripled between the Communist take-over in April 1975 and the end of 1976. Jobs were scarce, with 2 million persons unemployed. Civil servants, generally resident in cities, had their salaries cut despite the continuing rise in the cost of living. Both farming implements and draught animals were in short supply, while many manufacturing plants, previously dependent on the import of raw materials, closed down.

Vietnam's foreign friends provided aid to assist the country with its economic problems. The Soviet Union and the Eastern European states supplied heavy machinery and industrial raw materials. China provided, on an interest-free-loan basis, rice, petroleum, textiles, and different consumer goods. Such help, combined with a thriving black market, helped the country to limit the effects of its economic difficulties.

Despite its problems (and unlike neighboring Cambodia), Vietnam did not experience starvation. The movement of as many as 1.5 million persons from Saigon and other cities to rural areas probably helped avert famine and provided new farm workers.

Vietnam's leaders clearly appreciated the economic value of trade, aid, and investment from Western countries. In September the nation became a member of the World Bank and International Monetary Fund. Various government figures openly solicited foreign investment and even the return of Western oil companies to engage in offshore exploration.

Foreign Affairs. The influence of the Soviet Union was clearly greater than that of China on the Vietnamese government. Hanoi and Peking had differences over their common frontier as well as over sovereignty of the Paracel and Spratly islands. Various actions of the Vietnamese regime indicated that it valued Soviet friendship not only as a counterweight to China but also for the type of capital and technological aid that Moscow was more able to supply. But, at the 25th Soviet Party Congress in Moscow, Workers' Party Secretary General Le Duan sided with the independence-advocating Western European Communist parties.

In a major turn-about, Hanoi reestablished diplomatic relations with the members of the non-Communist Association of Southeast Asian Nations—the Philippines, Thailand, Indonesia, Malaysia, and Singapore. A five-man delegation visited the Philippines in July, after which the two governments agreed not to allow third countries to use military bases on their soil against one another. The United States had both air and naval bases in the Philippines, while the Soviet Union reportedly was seeking use of the former U. S. Navy facility at Cam Ranh Bay in Vietnam.

Despite earlier attempts to improve relations with Thailand, Hanoi's leaders strongly criticized the October military coup in that country, charging U. S. sponsorship of the action. Hanoi also maintained 30,000 troops in neighboring Laos as well as an unknown number of forces in the northeastern part of Cambodia.

U. S.-Vietnamese Relations. The United States took the initiative in March in trying to open talks with Hanoi on improved relations. Representatives of the two nations met in Paris on November 12 to begin their first formal talks since the fall of Saigon. Major obstacles to negotiations were Washington's unwillingness to provide reconstruction aid and Hanoi's refusal to account for some 800 Americans listed as missing in action. The United States vetoed Vietnam's bid for UN membership in November.

RICHARD BUTWELL
State University of New York College at Fredonia

VIETNAM • Information Highlights

Official Name: Socialist Republic of Vietnam.
Location: Southeast Asia.
Area: 128,402 square miles (332,535 km²).
Population (1976 est.): 46,400,000.
Chief Cities (1974): Hanoi, the capital, 643,000; Saigon, 3,500,000; Da Nang, 500,000.
Government: *Head of state,* Ton Duc Thang, president (took office 1969). *Head of government,* Pham Van Dong, premier (took office 1954). *First secretary of Communist party,* Le Duan. *Legislature* (unicameral) —National Assembly.
Monetary Unit: Dong (2.41 dong equal U. S.$1, Dec. 1976).
Manufacturing (major products): Processed foods, cement, textiles, chemicals, rubber products.
Major Agricultural Products: Rice, sugarcane, tea, sweet potatoes, cassava, rubber, corn, fruits.

VIRGIN ISLANDS

The Virgin Islands ushered in 1976 with a month-long teachers' strike, beginning on January 8 and not ending until mid-February. One cause of the strike was the overcrowding of the school system, brought about by the decision to provide education for the children of some 7,352 resident aliens. Another cause was the lack of government funds. The system already ranks behind only California and New York as the most costly in the United States. The teachers returned to their classrooms without any substantial increase in pay but won recognition of the normal increments resulting from years of service.

Air Tragedy. On April 27 a passenger jet airplane on a scheduled direct flight from a northeastern city crashed and burned while trying to land in clear weather at the Harry S. Truman Airport on St. Thomas. The airport has long been recognized as one of the most dangerous in the world because of its short 4,658-foot (1,420-m) runway, which begins at the beach and terminates just below a small hill. A nearby gasoline station, where the plane finally came to rest, added further horror to the accident, in which 37 people lost their lives. The tragedy provoked such a public outcry that swift action was taken to assign funds for the improvement of the airports on both St. Thomas and St. Croix. The St. Thomas airstrip will be length-ened 2,400 feet (730 m) by partially leveling the hill and extending the runway out into the ocean. Construction will take more than five years and cost some $60 million.

Economy and Politics. The impact of the economic recession on the Virgin Islands has been devastating. The unemployment rate is officially placed at more than 11% of the labor force, much of which comes from outside the islands. The government was forced to borrow $10 million to provide unemployment compensation, and for the first time it ended the fiscal year with a sizable debt. Since this is not permitted by the organic act of the Virgin Islands, the governor had to seek permission from Congress for a loan to meet the obligations.

The friction previously noted between the various branches of the Virgin Islands government continued during 1976. On November 2 Virgin Islanders had an opportunity to correct this situation by electing a different delegate to Congress and a legislature more compatible with the governor. The elections produced a decisive defeat for Gov. Cyril King and his Independent Citizens' Movement. The Democratic party elected 13 out of the 15 representatives to the island legislature. Ron DeLugo, Democratic resident commissioner to the U. S. House of Representatives, defeated his opponent by a landslide: 12,156 to 5,085.

THOMAS G. MATHEWS
University of Puerto Rico

The tail section of a jet lies at the end of the runway after crashing while landing at St. Thomas' airport in April.

UPI

VIRGINIA

Environmentalists were alternately elated and appalled by two separate developments in Virginia during 1976.

New River Controversy. The 14-year quarrel over construction of New River dams was finally resolved. At issue was a hydroelectric project to be located on the New River in Virginia near the North Carolina border. Because the electricity generated would have gone mainly to Virginia consumers, while most of the land to be flooded lay in North Carolina, most Virginians supported the project; North Carolinians opposed it. In 1976 the issue reached Congress which passed a law preserving portions of the river as a scenic waterway, thereby finally blocking dam construction.

Kepone Case. A major ecological disaster unfolded when it was discovered that for 16 months large quantities of the highly toxic Kepone had been illegally discharged into the James River. The insecticide had been manufactured at an abandoned Hopewell service station by a small subsidiary of the Allied Chemical Corporation. When the discharges were discovered, a state pollution agency ordered the plant closed, and Gov. Godwin subsequently banned fishing in the James River. Studies indicated the fishing ban might be required indefinitely and that Virginia's waters would be seriously polluted for decades. In the fall a federal judge levied a fine exceeding $13 million against Allied Chemical.

Elections. The Kepone case affected the 1976 senatorial election in Virginia. Adm. Elmo Zumwalt, the Democratic nominee who attempted to unseat independent Sen. Harry F. Byrd, Jr., charged that neither Byrd nor Gov. Godwin had acted with energy in coping with the crisis. Republicans failed to entice Byrd to run on their ticket, and the party fielded no candidate of its own. Byrd easily triumphed, with 57% of the total vote.

In the pre-nomination period Virginia Republicans predominantly favored Ronald Reagan over Gerald Ford, but later closed ranks to support the president. Virginia Democrats were originally divided, but eventually coalesced behind Jimmy Carter's bandwagon. Ford narrowly carried Virginia in November, making the state the only exception to Carter's sweep of the South. In the races for Congress, Virginia returned six Republicans and four Democrats to the House, a gain of one seat for the Republicans.

State Legislation. The General Assembly met early in the year. The biggest controversy arose over Gov. Godwin's recommendation that a $97 million list of capital outlay projects be added to the budget to be financed mainly by a 4% coal severance tax. The Senate supported the governor, but the House of Delegates rejected the coal tax. Because of the impasse only $25 million in miscellaneous new revenues were raised, mainly for air conditioning in state hospitals.

Otherwise, the record of the assembly was more of measures rejected than of legislation adopted. Advocates of the women's equal rights amendment met defeat in committee for the fourth time, and proponents of parimutuel betting, collective bargaining by public employees, and "death with dignity" were similarly disappointed. After the Democratic assembly adjourned, Republican Godwin vetoed an unusually large number of its bills.

The state continued to feel the nationwide financial pinch. As in 1975, Gov. Godwin was forced to mandate another 5% reduction in spending for many state agencies.

WILLIAM LARSEN, *Radford College*

WASHINGTON

Political feuds and a struggle over schools and teachers marked Washington in 1976.

Legislative Wrangle. The second special session of the 44th legislature saw bitter Democratic infighting force the resignation of Rep. Leonard Sawyer as speaker. Only after two weeks of struggle could the legislature turn to the principal problems—school funding, teacher accountability, and the budget. The public school budget was debated during the entire 75-day session. Temporary financial relief was finally provided, but no long-range plan was adopted.

Caught up in the school-budget wrangle was a controversial teachers' tenure bill. The legislature adopted a bill which provides a one-year probationary period for new teachers and a tough procedure for appealing dismissals.

Following the double levy loss by Seattle schools in 1975, teachers voluntarily gave up salary increases so that more laid-off staff could be rehired. But disenchantment with the rehiring procedure and a desire to catch up on the foregone pay raise caused the Seattle Teachers Association to strike for the first time in history. The 14-day strike was settled when both sides agreed to a 16% pay raise and a modified agency shop with a prescribed reduction-in-force and recall policy.

--------- **VIRGINIA · Information Highlights** ---------

Area: 40,817 square miles (105,716 km²).

Population (1975 est.): 4,967,000.

Chief Cities (1970 census): Richmond, the capital, 249,-430; Norfolk, 307,951; Virginia Beach, 172,106.

Government (1976): *Chief Officers*—governor, Mills E. Godwin, Jr. (R); lt. gov., John N. Dalton (R). *General Assembly*—Senate, 40 members; House of Delegates, 100 members.

Education (1975–76): *Enrollment*—public elementary schools, 665,606 pupils; public secondary, 438,063; nonpublic (1976–77), 89,800; colleges and universities, 220,231 students. *Public school expenditures,* $1,207,672,000 ($1,111 per pupil).

State Finances (fiscal year 1975): *Revenues,* $3,281,-811,000; *expenditures,* $3,374,150,000.

Personal Income (1975): $28,732,000,000; per capita, $5,785.

Labor Force (July 1976): *Nonagricultural wage and salary earners,* 1,792,400; *insured unemployed,* 26,-600 (1.9%).

UPI

Seattle's new $60 million multipurpose arena, the Kingdome, was dedicated early in 1976. The publicly owned structure will serve primarily as a sports complex.

Indian Affairs. A decision by U. S. District Judge George Boldt, giving treaty Indians the right to catch 50% of the salmon returning to traditional off-reservation Indian fishing grounds, continued to spawn trouble. Attempts to allocate the catch between Indians and non-Indian commercial fishermen set off many clashes between enforcement officers and fishermen. In one confrontation, a fisherman was seriously wounded. An appeal to the U. S. Supreme Court to review the Boldt decision was rejected.

Late in October members of the Puyallup Indian tribe seized control of a juvenile center in Tacoma and demanded it be converted to an Indian medical center. Title to the land and facility, formerly the Cushman Indian Hospital, had been transferred from the tribe to the federal government in 1940 for use as an Indian hospital. The medical facility was phased out in 1959, and in 1961 the federal government turned the property over to the state to house troubled juveniles. Indians surrendered the center on October 30 after representatives of the federal government had agreed to work with the tribe and the state to reacquire the property and develop an Indian medical center and a reservation school.

Elections. In the general elections, Dixy Lee Ray, scientist and former chairman of the Atomic Energy Commission, defeated King County Executive John Spellman by a surprising margin and became the first woman governor of a western state. Otherwise, the elections produced few surprises. Democratic Sen. Henry M. Jackson easily won a fifth term with some 70% of the vote, and Washington's congressional delegation remained solidly Democratic.

Voters rejected an initiative that would have imposed strict safety and insurance requirements on the development of nuclear energy facilities and turned back a proposal to prohibit the fluoridation of public water supplies. They approved a requirement that all appointed officials disclose their personal finances and business associations.

WARREN W. ETCHESON
University of Washington

───── **WASHINGTON · Information Highlights** ─────

Area: 68,192 square miles (176,617 km²).
Population (1975 est.): 3,544,000.
Chief Cities (1970 census): Olympia, the capital, 23,-111; Seattle, 530,831; Spokane, 170,516; Tacoma, 154,581.
Government (1976): *Chief Officers*—governor, Daniel J. Evans (R); lt. gov., John A. Cherberg (D). *Legislature*—Senate, 49 members; House of Representatives, 98 members.
Education (1975–76): *Enrollment*—public elementary schools, 398,825 pupils; public secondary, 386,624; nonpublic (1976–77), 44,500; colleges and universities, 173,165 students. *Public school expenditures,* $1,050,675,000 ($1,350 per pupil).
State Finances (fiscal year 1975): *Revenues,* $3,306,-685,000; *expenditures,* $3,195,846,000.
Personal Income (1975): $22,158,000,000; per capita, $6,247.
Labor Force (July 1976): *Nonagricultural wage and salary earners,* 1,229,900; *insured unemployed,* 70,-400 (7.1%).

WASHINGTON, D. C.

The U. S. bicentennial was celebrated with spectacular fireworks in the capital. More than a million people crowded onto the monument area, the highways, and rivers to witness the hour-long show on Independence Day. It was the highlight of events that included special museum displays and the summer-long American Folklife Festival. The activities attracted American and foreign tourists and dignitaries from many nations.

New Attractions. The $42-million National Visitor Center opened in the restored Union Station. Its chief attraction is the 9½-minute "Welcome to Washington" slide show. The Constitutional Gardens replaced the temporary Navy Buildings which had stood on the site near the Washington Monument since World War I. The Smithsonian Institution's National Air and Space Museum, dedicated to 500 years of man's aerial endeavors, was completed ahead of schedule and within the budget. The history of the National Guard is traced in its new Heritage Gallery. Pine trees and granite slabs in the Lyndon B. Johnson Memorial Grove comprise the national memorial to the late president. The Hyatt Regency Hotel, the first new one in 11 years, was opened near the Capitol.

Transportation. Metro subway opened March 27. The 4.6-mile (7.4-km) line extends from Farragut Square to Rhode Island Avenue. Five stations are in service; a sixth was closed by court action pending installation of facilities for handicapped passengers. The subway operates on a 14-hour, 5-week-day schedule, the trains controlled by computers. The next segment, running north to Dupont Circle as of January 1977, is to be followed by an extension to Silver Spring, Md., in November. A new subway line between the Stadium and Armory through the downtown area to National Airport is scheduled for opening in July 1977. The new lines will lengthen the subway by 14 miles (22.5 km).

Government. A new gun-control law bans possession of all handguns not already registered unless they belong to policemen or security guards. This was the most controversial piece of legislation passed by the city council in 1976. Elections were held to fill the seats on 30 Advisory Neighborhood Commissions, the unique experiment in grass-roots democracy. Each ANC will advise the city government on proposed actions that involve its neighborhood.

Congress established a commission to audit the city's books and to coordinate improvements in the financial system after hearings and study showed disarray in city finances.

Education. Vincent Reed was appointed superintendent of education. The school system has faced declining student enrollment and a consequent excess of classroom spaces.

MORRIS J. LEVITT
Howard University

The first link of Washington's new Metro subway was opened in March 1976. It extends 4.6 miles (7.4 km) from Farragut Square to Rhode Island Avenue.

UPI

Jay Rockefeller won the West Virginia gubernatorial election on November 2. It was his second try for the office.

WEST VIRGINIA

Democrat John D. ("Jay") Rockefeller, IV won a smashing victory over former Republican Gov. Cecil H. Underwood in West Virginia's gubernatorial race November 2, and fellow Democrats swept all major offices. U. S. Sen. Robert Byrd was unopposed for his seat, and Democratic incumbents Robert Mollohan, Harley Staggers, and John Slack were returned to the U. S. House of Representatives. In the Fourth District, Democratic newcomer Nick Joe Rahall replaced veteran Ken Hechler (D), who had passed up an almost certain nomination in May to oppose Rockefeller in the primary. As a write-in congressional candidate, Hechler ran second, ahead of Republican opposition, but lost to Rahall.

Incumbent Republicans in the office of secretary of state, treasurer, and auditor all lost to Democratic opponents, while Atty. Gen. Chauncey Browning, Jr., and Secretary of Agriculture Gus Douglass were unopposed.

Democratic Supreme Court candidates won one vacant spot and defeated two other Republican incumbents. The state's heavily Democratic legislature showed little change in political alignment.

Moore's Troubles. Underwood had won the nomination in May after two-term Gov. Arch A. Moore, Jr., had been denied the right to seek a third term by the State Supreme Court. Nor was it Moore's only ordeal during a politically active year: he was acquitted by a federal jury May 5 (along with former aide William H. Loy) of charges of extortion. By November, he still had not won his fight to regain possession of the telephone and secretarial records which had been used by the prosecution, federal attorneys insisting that they were "vital to continuing investigations."

Moore's eight-year duel with Democratic legislators followed its familiar pattern, with the regular January-to-March session continued until after the May primary, a special session called in June, another in July, and a final four-day session following the November election. The June session appropriated $28 million for road work (Moore requested double that amount) and authorized the expenditure of $2.5 million in federal money (instead of the $17.5 million the governor asked). The July session awarded $1,000 across-the-board pay raises to public school teachers, $200 below his recommendation.

Moore's firm control over the state's Republican machinery was evident at the party's national convention, however, when his delegation's vote formally put the president over the top for the nomination.

Economy. The economy continued to be brighter than that of much of the country. Unemployment was substantially lower than the national average and in some counties matched the nation's lowest figures. But coal production was badly curtailed by a four-week wildcat strike in July and August.

Toward the end of the year the rosy future extolled by all candidates during the campaign could be most clearly seen in West Virginia's highways, as the ambitious interstate construction program continued to surpass completion goals. On the day before the general election, the last piece of steel was welded into place in the high bridge spanning the New River Gorge near Fayetteville. The bridge, 1,700 feet (523 m) long, is the longest main-arch single span in the world.

DONOVAN H. BOND, *West Virginia University*

——— WEST VIRGINIA · Information Highlights ———

Area: 24,181 square miles (62,629 km²).
Population (1975 est.): 1,803,000.
Chief Cities (1970 census): Charleston, the capital, 71,505; Huntington, 74,315; Wheeling, 48,188.
Government (1976): *Chief Officers*—governor, Arch A. Moore, Jr. (R); secy. of state, James R. McArtney (R). *Legislature*—Senate, 34 members; House of Delegates, 100 members.
Education (1975–76): *Enrollment*—public elementary schools, 229,919 pupils; public secondary, 174,200; nonpublic (1976–77), 12,700; colleges and universities, 70,378 students. *Public school expenditures,* $393,400,000 ($1,015 per pupil).
State Finances (fiscal year 1975): *Revenues,* $1,555,099,-000; *expenditures,* $1,459,362,000.
Personal Income (1975): $8,867,000,000; per capita, $4,918.
Labor Force (July 1976): *Nonagricultural wage and salary earners,* 580,200; *insured unemployed,* 19,100 (4.2%).

WISCONSIN

The desegregation of Milwaukee schools became the focus of statewide attention in 1976.

Integration. Milwaukee eased into an integration plan in 1976 after Federal Judge John W. Reynolds ruled that its schools were unconstitutionally segregated. Judge Reynolds ordered that a third of the schools—58 of 158—be integrated in the fall. The remaining two thirds are to be integrated in 1977 and 1978.

Unlike other cities, Milwaukee decided on a voluntary plan, and this was approved by John Gronouski, the special master in the case appointed by Judge Reynolds. There was a threat of mandatory transfers if not enough voluntary transfers were made. Eighteen specialty schools were set up to encourage voluntary transfers. In the fall, the integration went smoothly, and 67 schools actually met the integration goals. It was evident, however, that the burden had been on blacks. Of the 8,024 students who transferred under threat of mandatory reassignment, 92% were black. The real test of the voluntary plan will come in the next two years, when the burden will shift to white pupils. A third of the city's schools remain more than 90% white or 90% black.

Despite the integration plan, the Milwaukee School Board is still officially balking at Judge Reynolds' order. By an 8–7 vote it is appealing the order to the U.S. Supreme Court, even

Democrat William Proxmire was elected to his fourth full term in the U.S. Senate by a majority of 73%, beating even his own previous record. He has served since 1957.

UPI

though an earlier appeal was rejected by a Circuit Court of Appeals.

Legislature. Integration was also the topic for debate in the spring legislative session, and lawmakers passed a bill providing extra state money to school districts that voluntarily engage in racial and cultural integration projects. The bill was pushed as a means to encourage racial integration between Milwaukee and its suburbs. Another major bill passed revised the state's rape law, establishing four degrees of sexual assault. Supporters said the new law would place the criminal, not the victim, on trial.

Elections. The November 2 elections gave another warning to Wisconsin Republicans that their party was in a declining condition, as Democrats won significant victories. They gained two-thirds majorities in both the state Assembly and the Senate, giving them power in procedural moves. They also retained 7 of 9 congressional seats and returned William Proxmire to the U.S. Senate with 73% of the vote, a figure that beat his own record. Most significantly, Wisconsin voted for Jimmy Carter over President Ford, the first time in 12 years the state had gone Democratic.

Drought. Like other midwestern states, Wisconsin suffered from severe drought in 1976 and the State Agriculture Department called it even worse than the Dust-Bowl era of the Depression. The results were the smallest hay crop since 1958, the poorest corn harvest since 1967, and the smallest oat yield since 1907. The department estimated that farmers' loss to the drought would total at least $625 million.

Population. The state's population estimates for 1976 showed a growth in suburban counties north and west of Milwaukee and in resort and vacation home regions. Milwaukee County experienced the largest population loss since 1970 —50,030 persons or 4.8%. However, neighboring Washington County went up 23% and Ozaukee County 22%. Elsewhere, Adams County in the central part of the state grew 27%, and in the north Vilas grew 22% and Oneida 18%.

PAUL SALSINI
The Milwaukee "Journal"

-------- **WISCONSIN • Information Highlights** --------

Area: 56,154 square miles (145,439 km²).
Population (1975 est.): 4,607,000.
Chief Cities (1970 census): Madison, the capital, 172,-007; Milwaukee, 717,372; Racine, 95,162.
Government (1976): *Chief Officers*—governor, Patrick J. Lucey (D); lt. gov., Martin J. Schreiber (D). *Legislature*—Senate, 33 members; Assembly, 99 members.
Education (1975–76): *Enrollment*—public elementary schools, 541,563 pupils; public secondary, 422,656; nonpublic (1976–77), 189,400; colleges and universities, 179,444 students. *Public school expenditures,* $1,393,696,000 ($1,518 per pupil).
State Finances (fiscal year 1975): *Revenues,* $3,647,-105,000; *expenditures,* $3,695,146,000.
Personal Income (1975): $26,109,000,000; per capita, $5,669.
Labor Force (July 1976): *Nonagricultural wage and salary earners,* 1,701,700; *insured unemployed,* 58,-700 (3.7%).

WOMEN

The U. S. service academies admitted women for the first time in 1976. Of 1,475 cadets admitted to West Point (*left*), 118 were women; the Naval Academy had 81 women; and 157 women enrolled at the Air Force Academy in Colorado (*above*).

The U. S. bicentennial year was marked by continued dialogue about the rights of women and by no dramatic changes in women's political, economic, and social status. Two women were appointed to President-elect Carter's cabinet.

Politics. In 1976 a lower proportion of women participated as delegates to the Democratic presidential nominating convention than in 1972 (34% in 1976; 40% in 1972). Women delegates to the Republican convention increased by an insignificant 1% (31% in 1976; 30% in 1972). The Democratic convention featured Congresswoman Corrine (Lindy) Boggs of Louisiana as the first female chairperson of a presidential nominating convention, and Texas Congresswoman Barbara Jordan became the first woman and black person to keynote a major party convention. Republicans met under the leadership of Iowa's Mary Louise Smith.

Both party platforms supported ratification of the federal Equal Rights Amendment (ERA) and endorsed equal job opportunities, increased part-time work and flexible schedules, equal credit and mortgage availability, and reform of discriminatory estate and gift tax laws. Party platforms differed on the abortion issue. Democrats opposed a constitutional amendment banning abortion and Republicans supported the prohibition of abortion. Efforts of Democratic Women's Caucus leaders to guarantee women equal representation at future conventions was defeated in the Rules Committee. Democratic nominee Jimmy Carter named prominent women to a "Committee of 51.3 Percent" for campaign advice on women's issues.

In 1976 women held roughly 5% of all public offices in the United States. In federal appointive positions, Anne L. Armstrong became the first female U. S. ambassador to the United Kingdom, and Shirley Temple Black is the first woman chief of protocol.

Among candidates for federal and state legislative offices, women showed a slow but steady increase over recent years. Major party nominees for the U. S. House and Senate in 1976 totaled 52 women, compared with 47 women in 1974. Races for state legislative office included 1,241 women, compared with 1,125 in 1974. In statewide races two women, Stella Hackel in Vermont and Dixy Lee Ray in Washington, won Democratic primaries for gubernatorial nominations. Hackel lost; Ray won.

Governmental Activities. The National Commission on the Observance of International Women's Year (IWY) presented its report to President Ford on July 1. Entitled "...*To Form a More Perfect Union*..." *Justice for American Women,* the report contained a 115-point program to end much of the "sexism still so rampant throughout our country." Recommendations included support for homemakers' work, improved quality of life for older women, revision of state divorce laws, reform of rape laws, increased child care services for working parents, greater participation of women in government and policy making, and the creation of a cabinet-level office responsible for governmental programs affecting women.

On July 1 Elizabeth Athanasakos, an attorney from Florida, succeeded Jill Ruckelshaus as presiding officer of the IWY Commission. Its life was extended by Congress through March 1978 to serve as the instrument for implementing Public Law 94–167 mandating 56 state and territorial meetings in 1977 and culminating in a National Women's Conference. Intended to reexamine the barriers women face, develop recommendations for ending barriers, and establish timetables for achieving recommendations, the conferences were funded by a controversial $5 million appropriation.

Equal Rights Amendment. No additional states ratified ERA in 1976, leaving the amendment 4 states short of the 38 required for ratification before the March 1979 deadline. In May 8,000 supporters of ERA from 30 states convened in Springfield, Ill., to rally for passage in Illinois and neighboring Indiana and Missouri.

ERAmerica, an organization formed to spearhead a nationwide campaign to ratify ERA, was launched in January and cochaired by two prominent women, Democrat Liz Carpenter and Republican Elly Peterson. ERAmerica grew from recommendations made by the IWY Commission's ERA Committee. As an educational effort, 35 magazines with a combined readership of 60,000,000 printed ERA information in their July issues.

Economic Picture. Census Bureau figures for 1976 showed the earnings gap between women and men widening over nearly two decades. Concurrently, increasing proportions of women sought employment and comprised almost 41% of the labor force in 1976 compared with 33% in 1960. From 1974 to 1976, 2,800,000 newly employed women accounted for two thirds of the increase in the U. S. labor force. Almost 45% of married women with children under 18 were employed, and over 13% of all families had female heads of household. Many female job seekers with children to support came from the group of approximately 1 million women divorced in 1975.

In collective bargaining associations only 7% of positions in top union governing boards were held by women. While 60% of all bank employees were women, nine tenths held clerical jobs. In elementary and secondary schools over 64% of all teachers were women, but only 15% of all principals were women. A study of private philanthropy indicated that of $2,000,000,000 awarded in grants yearly, less than 1% was designated to promote women's equality.

Education. Final regulations for awarding funds under the Women's Educational Equity Act of 1974 (WEEA) were published. WEEA authorized the U. S. commissioner of education to award grants and contracts for projects contributing to educational equity for American women. Awards for 67 projects were made.

Women were chief administrative officers of 6% of the nation's institutions of higher education. Of only 2 women heading large universities, Mary Berry was appointed chancellor of the University of Colorado at Boulder in 1976. Among new presidents of small women's schools, Wells College appointed Frances (Sissy) Farenthold; Barnard College named Jacquelyn Mattfeld; and Mills College selected Barbara White.

Religion. After debate, the 2,900,000 member Episcopal Church approved the ordination of women to be priests and bishops. Pope Paul VI reaffirmed the Roman Catholic Church's opposition to ordaining women as priests.

International. The *World Plan of Action* adopted in 1975 was endorsed by the UN General Assembly, which called on governments to establish goals, strategies, and timetables for improving women's opportunities and status. The plan provides guidelines for national action during the 1975–1985 Decade for Women.

In Italy, Tina Anselmi became the first female Cabinet minister. Ms. Anselmi, a Christian Democrat appointed as minister of labor, had served in the Italian Parliament since 1958.

RUTH B. MANDEL, *Director*
Center for the American Woman and Politics
Eagleton Institute of Politics, Rutgers University

WYOMING

Issues involving natural resources were dominant in Wyoming in 1976. The state sued the U. S. Department of the Interior concerning reclamation standards on mined public lands. Gov. Ed Herschler charged that the rules give the Secretary of the Interior discretion to impose federal standards over state environmental quality standards.

Natural Resources. The fededal moratorium on coal leasing was lifted and new natural gas fields were being planned. But approval of a coal-slurry pipeline was still being sought. Construction was begun on the $1,400,000,000 Laramie River Station of the Missouri Basin power projects, although strong opposition was voiced by the Laramie River Conservation Council.

Several pieces of federal legislation bearing directly on Wyoming's natural resources problems were enacted during the year. In August, Congress overrode President Ford's veto of a coal leasing law that increases the states' share of royalties from federal minerals from 37½% to 50%. The new law meant an additional $13 million for 1976 to be used in coal development areas. Another bill provides for "payments in lieu of taxes" to those counties where federally-owned, tax-exempt land places considerable burden on local tax structures. Over 50% of Wyoming is federally owned, and this bill will provide $6.1 million annually for the state's counties. A provision in the Bureau of Land Management organic act authorizes western states to borrow federal money to finance impact aid projects, repaying the loans later by forfeiting a portion of future mineral royalty income.

Elections. President Ford outpolled Jimmy Carter in Wyoming 92,831 to 62,267. Laramie County, a bellwether county that had voted for the successful presidential candidate in every election since 1896, lost that status by supporting President Ford in 1976.

Democratic incumbent U. S. Senator Gale McGee was upset in his bid for a fourth term by state Senator Malcolm Wallop, who won by a vote of 84,824 to 70,464. McGee, chairman of the Post Office and Civil Service Committee and a member of the Appropriations and Foreign Relations committees, emphasized his seniority or "clout" during the campaign. Wallop, capitalizing on a heavy turnout in a state with a 10,000-Republican voter registration edge, relied on anti-Washington sentiment, suggesting that McGee had lost touch with Wyoming. In the only other statewide race incumbent Democrat Teno Roncalio defeated political newcomer Larry Hart, 85,725 to 66,178, for Wyoming's congressional seat.

Republicans swept both houses of the state legislature. They will control the Senate by a margin of 18–12 and the House by 32–29, with 1 independent. Two amendments to the state constitution passed: one removing the requirement of prior approval by the judicial nominating commission before a vote on retention of a judge is held; and the other permitting trials in counties where evidence is collected even though location of a crime is impossible to determine. An amendment that would have permitted a rise in local governmental debt ceilings failed. Three supreme court judges and eight district judges were retained. Voters in 10 counties approved an additional local sales tax of 1%, while voters in 8 other counties rejected the increase.

JOHN B. RICHARD
University of Wyoming

WYOMING · Information Highlights

Area: 97,914 square miles (253,597 km²).
Population (1975 est.): 374,000.
Chief Cities (1970 census): Cheyenne, the capital, 40,-914; Casper, 39,361; Laramie, 23,143; Rock Springs, 11,657.
Government (1976): *Chief Officers*—governor, Ed Herschler (D); secy. of state, Thyra Thomson (R). *Legislature*—Senate, 30 members; House of Representatives, 62 members.
Education (1975–76): *Enrollment*—public elementary schools, 44,140; public secondary, 44,044; nonpublic (1976–77), 3,100; colleges and universities, 15,539 students. *Public school expenditures*, $117,093,000 ($1,433 per pupil).
State Finances (fiscal year 1975): *Revenues*, $389,247,-000; *expenditures*, $330,849,000.
Personal Income (1975): $2,294,000,000; per capita, $6,131.
Labor Force (July 1976): *Nonagricultural wage and salary earners*, 166,900; *insured unemployed*, 1,600 (1.5%).

YUGOSLAVIA

President Tito's acute liver disease in the early fall of 1976 underscored the political uncertainties in Yugoslavia. While the ruling League of Communists was in ful control of the situation, the potentiality for unrest was evident in arrests and trials of Cominformists, Croatian and Serbian nationalists, and Albanian secessionists. A Belgrade court found former Col. Vlado Dapčević guilty of "Cominformist activities," and sentenced him to death on July 5 (sentence commuted to 20 years imprisonment). Blows to the independence of the courts included the cases of a Serbian lawyer, Srdja Popović, tried in March for sharing his client's views, and that of a Slovenian judge, Franc Miklavčič, a champion of civil rights, who was sentenced in October to six years' imprisonment for treason.

Economy. Domestic measures of economic stabilization and a revival of economic activity on a worldwide scale brought some positive results in 1976. The rate of inflation was reduced, as well as the external payments deficit. During the first 10 months of 1976 exports increased by 21% and imports decreased by 7.6% compared to the same period of 1975. The 1976 grain harvest was highly satisfactory, with 5,-980,000 tons of wheat produced (surpassing the 1975 crop by 36%). The corn harvest equaled that of 1975. On the other hand, industrial out-

UPI

UPI

Yugoslavia's President Tito met twice with Soviet Communist Party Secretary Brezhnev during 1976. In June they conferred in East Berlin (above) prior to the opening of the summit meeting of the European Communist parties, and in November they discussed Yugoslavia's independence of the Soviet-bloc alliance in Belgrade.

put was stagnating, labor productivity was low, and the cost of living high. The 1976–80 economic plan was approved in July. A new 296-mile (476-km) rail link between Belgrade and Bar on the Adriatic coast was inaugurated.

The largest U. S. investment ever made in Yugoslavia was concluded on March 26, with an agreement between Dow Chemical Co. of Minnesota and the largest Yugoslav oil company for

------ YUGOSLAVIA · Information Highlights ------

Official Name: Socialist Federal Republic of Yugoslavia.
Location: Southeastern Europe.
Area: 98,766 square miles (255,804 km²).
Population (1976 est.): 21,500,000.
Chief Cities (1974 est.): Belgrade, the capital, 845,000; Zagreb, 602,000; Skopje, 389,000.
Government: *Head of state,* Tito (Josip Broz), president (took office 1953). *Head of government,* Džemal Bijedić, prime minister (took office 1971). *Legislature*—Federal Assembly: Federal Chamber and Chamber of Republics and Provinces.
Monetary Unit: Dinar (18.30 dinars equal U. S.$1, Aug. 1976).
Gross Domestic Product (1975 est.): $30,200,000,000.
Manufacturing (major products): Iron and steel, processed foods, chemicals, machinery, textiles.
Major Agricultural Products: Corn, wheat, fruits, potatoes, sugar beets, forest products, livestock.
Foreign Trade (1975): *Exports,* $4,061,000,000; *imports,* $7,697,000,000.

the joint construction and operation of a $700-million petrochemical complex in Dalmatia. In May and June the World Bank loaned Yugoslavia $153 million for various industrial projects.

Foreign Relations. Tito's extensive foreign travels, international contacts, and public statements reflected Yugoslavia's foreign political line in 1976. Premier Fidel Castro of Cuba visited Yugoslavia (March 6–8) and obtained Tito's approval of the country's military intervention in Angola. In March Tito visited Mexico, Panama, Venezuela, and Portugal, in May Greece, and in June Turkey. He also headed the Yugoslav delegation to the fifth conference of nonaligned nations in Colombo, Sri Lanka, August 16–19. Tito and Leonid Brezhnev met in East Berlin on June 28, a day before the opening of the summit meeting of European Communist parties; Tito's presence on that occasion ended Yugoslavia's 19-year-old boycott of international Communist conferences.

Yugoslav-U. S. relations deteriorated. Tito openly criticized U. S. Ambassador Laurence Silberman for "interference" in Yugoslav domestic affairs. The hijacking of a U. S. jet, flown to Paris in September by a group of Croatian terrorists to foster the cause of Croatian independence, provoked strong official Yugoslav reaction.

Yugoslav-Austrian tension grew over the Austrian minority-rights bill and ethnic census. In the Communist realm, Yugoslav-Czechoslovak relations became strained, and the Macedonian issue continued to perturb Belgrade-Sofia ties. The persecution of "Cominformists" in Yugoslavia pointed to the other side of the officially correct Yugoslav-Soviet relations.

MILORAD M. DRACHKOVITCH
Stanford University

YUKON

Strikes in the mining industry, speculation about constitutional changes and native land claims, plus possible pipeline developments were key issues for Yukoners in 1976.

Government and Politics. James Smith left office in July after serving 10 years as Yukon commissioner. Dr. Arthur M. Pearson, a wildlife biologist was appointed as the new commissioner. Merv Miller resigned his post as a federally appointed member of the Yukon Executive Committee (cabinet), leaving the three elected members in a majority position. Debate continued on what further steps toward responsible government and provincial status may be initiated by the federal and territorial governments. Paul Lucier, former Whitehorse mayor, became the first Yukon senator and the first from "north of 60" in the Canadian Parliament. Governor General Jules Léger opened the new Yukon Territorial Administration Building, which houses the Legislative Council chambers and all territorial departments of administration.

Indian Land Claims. Negotiations between the federal government and the Council of Yukon Indians (CYI) were temporarily adjourned in the spring. The CYI reorganized its negotiating committee, and a new chief negotiator for the federal government, Dr. John Naysmith, was named to replace Digby Hunt. Negotiations were scheduled to resume early in 1977.

Economy. The Yukon economy was severely affected by strikes in the mining and transportation industries. Wage agreements were successfully negotiated at Whitehorse Copper Mines and at United Keno Mines, but the Cyprus Anvil Mine contract was rolled back by the federal Anti-Inflation Board, leading to a prolonged

strike at Faro. The strike forced the White Pass and Yukon Route Company to shut down most highway operations and partially curtail rail and sea services. Hopes remain high that new mines will be developed in the near future, possibly one at Minto, and another in the Faro area. Speculation also continues on the possible routing of an Alaska pipeline via the Alaskan Highway through the Yukon.

LINDA JOHNSON
Acting Territorial Archivist

ZAIRE

The year 1976 was a difficult one for the regime of President Mobutu Sese Seko, which faced economic bankruptcy, diplomatic embarrassment, and domestic unpopularity.

Economy. Economic storm signals had been up since copper prices began to decline in 1974, but the government's over-ambitious spending and borrowing practices continued. By the end of 1975, Zaire's debt repayment had come to a complete halt and the country was technically bankrupt, with foreign exchange and gold reserves down to $25 million (equivalent to less than two weeks' imports). Total indebtedness was believed to be close to $3,000,000,000.

The International Monetary Fund (IMF) dispatched a team of experts to Kinshasa and laid down the terms of Zaire's rescue. On March 12, Zaire announced a 42% devaluation of its currency, combined with major budgetary cuts and the application of stringent import quotas. The government also took steps to dismantle the nationalization policy it had initiated in 1973, announcing that former owners would be allowed to regain up to 60% control. Marred by corruption, mismanagement, and political favoritism, the "Zairianization" of small- and medium-sized foreign firms had seriously disrupted some sectors of the economy.

Having persuaded Zaire to accept its recommendations, the IMF on March 23 negotiated new credits of $150 million for immediate financial relief and took steps to arrange for the rescheduling of the nation's debts. Zaire reached

─────── YUKON • Information Highlights ───────

Area: 207,076 square miles (536,327 km²).
Population (April 1976 est.): 21,000.
Chief City (1971 census): Whitehorse, the capital, 11,600.
Government (1976): *Chief Officers*—commissioner, James Smith; exec. asst. commissioner, Peter J. Gillespie. *Legislature*—Territorial Council, 12 members.
Education (1976–77): *Enrollment*—public elementary and secondary schools, 4,990 pupils.
Personal Income (1974): $259,000,000; $4,544 per person.

─────── ZAIRE • Information Highlights ───────

Official Name: Republic of Zaire.
Location: Central equatorial Africa.
Area: 905,565 square miles (2,345,409 km²).
Population (1976 est.): 25,600,000.
Chief Cities (1974 est.): Kinshasa, the capital, 2,008,000; Kananga, 601,000.
Government: *Head of state and government,* Mobutu Sese Seko, president (took office Nov. 1965). *Legislature* (unicameral)—National Legislative Council.
Monetary Unit: Zaire (0.87 zaire equals U. S.$1, Sept. 1976).
Gross National Product (1974 est.): $3,500,000,000.
Manufacturing (major products): Processed foods, clothing, textiles, soap.
Major Agricultural Products: Palm oil and kernels, coffee, rubber, tea, cacao, groundnuts, bananas, cassava.
Foreign Trade (1975): *Exports,* $904,000,000; *imports,* $827,000,000.

agreement on June 17 with 11 Western government creditors, pledging to pay 15% of the sums due for 1975 and the first half of 1976. After a three-year grace period, it will pay the remaining 85% over a period of seven years.

Zaire also had to contend with a steady decline of its agricultural output. It has become a massive importer of foodstuffs, which absorb over 30% of its foreign exchange earnings, and its agricultural exports are now negligible.

Although the hoped-for recovery of copper prices failed to materialize, Zaire has continued to depend on its mineral exports for survival. But in January, the international consortium that had started to develop the huge Tenke-Fungurume copper deposits decided to suspend its operations until world market conditions looked more attractive.

Foreign Affairs. Zaire was embroiled in the Angolan civil war, and Mobutu's troops suffered a swift defeat in their covert efforts to assist the U. S.-backed Nationalist Front for the Liberation of Angola (FNLA). Zaire found itself in the invidious position of being involved in a partnership with South Africa. Mobutu's awkward position turned into humiliation in January when the northern front manned by his troops caved in. As the Zairian contingent retreated, it reportedly looted the towns it was supposed to defend. In addition, the interruption of traffic on Angola's Benguela Railroad, which traditionally carried most of Zaire's mineral output, placed an added burden on the ailing economy.

Mobutu therefore executed a swift about-face. On February 28 he reached an agreement with Agostinho Neto, president of the People's Republic of Angola, designed to normalize relations between their countries. Although the two leaders pledged not to interfere with each other's domestic affairs, relations have remained uncomfortable. Under the terms of the agreement Mobutu closed down the FNLA's headquarters in Kinshasa.

Zaire's intervention in the Angolan civil war undermined the influence that it had tried to acquire on the continent. Also, the country's increasingly close relations with the United States, strengthened by mutual interests in Angola, did not help to restore the image of nonalignment that Zaire had been trying to develop in past years. As a result of increased U. S. military assistance, Zaire's military expenditures will not be affected by budget cuts.

Domestic Events. In spite of the economic and diplomatic setbacks suffered by the regime, active opposition was relatively limited. In February, President Mobutu reshuffled the national Executive Council (cabinet), dismissing or shifting 15 ministers. The president also reduced the membership of the Political Bureau of the ruling Mouvement Populaire de la Révolution from 32 to 20.

In January, former Vice Premier Antoine Gizenga announced, unconvincingly, that he would return to Zaire during the year to lead an armed struggle against the regime.

In an attempt to consolidate domestic support, the government rescinded its decision to take over all church-related schools. This was only the latest step in a gradual process of reconciliation with the powerful Roman Catholic establishment, which had been alienated from the regime as a result of Mobutu's policy of *authenticité*.

EDOUARD BUSTIN
Boston University

Zaire's President Mobutu and other African chiefs of state watch a military parade in Kinshasa in November, held in honor of the 11th anniversary of the Mobutu regime.

ZOOLOGY

Several thousand books and research reports on animals were published in 1976. A few were filled with misinformation. Most were so technical that they were of interest only to another specialist in the same subdiscipline of zoology. Some were fascinating, even to the public.

Although studies of rare and endangered species constituted only a fraction of the research activities in zoology, they continued to be featured in the popular press. The destruction of natural habitats by ever-increasing human populations throughout the world put further pressures on many species. Not only do such imposing animals as whales, sea lions, mountain lions, and golden eagles suffer from this pressure but also uncounted thousands of tiny species, such as insects, mites, and nematodes. In fact, any creature that requires a specialized natural habitat is being subjected to actual or potential extermination.

On the other hand, many animal species benefit from man-made changes in the environment. Certainly, the various household, garden, and agricultural insects have more available habitats. English sparrows, house mice, barn rats, and other commensals of man have thus increased, as have domestic animals and pets. Even some wild animals have more food and shelter available in a man-modified environment. Rabbits, opossums, coyotes, spotted skunks, and even deer generally increase when forests are cleared, prairies fenced, and swamps drained.

Fur trappers. In the past, and in some cold regions even today, furs were necessary human clothing. The use of furs as decorative costumes, especially by women in temperate and tropical regions, became common in the 18th century. The role of fur trappers in the early exploration of the North American West has been recounted many times. Shortly after World War II, furs became unpopular as decorative wear for women in most parts of the world. To a large degree, this was the result of widespread realization of the effect of fashion on the populations of many wild animals. However, as underscored in *Audubon Magazine* (June 1976), a major shift in human attitudes has recently occurred. Suddenly, pelts of the bobcat (*Lynx rufus*) are in demand. A pelt in prime condition is now worth as much as $165. Since bobcats are relatively easy to trap, a "good" trapper could essentially exterminate the animal in a small region.

Pesticides. As reported in *Nature* (Nov. 27, 1975), debates continue on the place of pesticides in the future. Dr. Cleve Goring, director of research in plant sciences for Dow Chemical Company, contends that the continuing growth of human populations will necessitate a threefold gain in food production by the year 2000. To accomplish this, a five-fold increase in the use of pesticides will be required. Dr. Goring bemoans the lack of any international agreement on the "unjustifiable elimination" of many pesticides and warns that people must "develop some perspective on the largely imaginary horror of a 'Silent Spring' and the minute amounts of pesticide chemicals that occur in our food." Dr. Goring points out that many items on the U. S. Environmental Protection Agency (EPA) list of cancer-causing substances include "many of the natural materials essential to living systems."

Thomas H. Jukes (*Nature,* Feb. 12, 1976) has summarized a series of studies showing that DDT may well not be the villain it has been made out to be in the past. Laboratory tests at Cornell University have shown that DDT fed to laying hens has no effect on egg production or hatchability of eggs. In contrast, the polychlorinated biphenyls (PCB), and methyl mercury generally, did adversely affect egg production, shell strength, and hatchability of eggs. These chemicals have been associated with a series of detrimental effects on humans and wild animals.

UPI

A Speke's gazelle was born at the St. Louis Zoo in January. The species, native to the East Africa highlands, is very rare.

Jukes points out that DDT has never been recorded as having poisoned humans, either through food supply or industrial exposure. He and other experts are of the view that PCB and mercury—not DDT—may well be the culprits in many past cases of wildlife poisoning. Some chemical tests involving PCB give results similar to those of DDT.

Preservation of Genetic Materials. Many zoologists have expressed concern that genetic diversity is being lost by the actual and potential extinction of various animal species and varieties. A few are doing something about it. Thus, as reported in *Nature* (Nov. 20, 1975), The Rare Breeds Survival Trust, an English group, maintains breeding populations of endangered breeds of domestic animals, and the UN Food and Agriculture Organization is currently sponsoring efforts to preserve certain rare breeds of cattle in West Africa.

Zoological gardens throughout the world are also assuming an important role in preserving breeding populations of some species currently in danger of extinction. The Arizona-Sonora Desert Museum in Tucson is trying to establish a breeding colony of the margay, a small, spotted New World wild cat, and the thick-billed parrot—both on the Rare and Endangered Species list. The successful efforts of the Phoenix (Ariz.) Zoological Gardens in establishing breeding populations of the Arabian oryx (a gazelle now almost extinct in nature) are considered by some experts to be "classical" and worthy of close examination by anyone interested in the problem. The San Diego (Calif.) Zoo has also done an outstanding job in establishing a breeding colony of the endangered large land tortoise, native to the Galapagos Islands. The Zoological Gardens in Tunis, Tunisia, has a breeding colony of the almost extinct Barbary stag. Still other parks are working with other species.

Behavior. Animal behavior continues to interest many zoologists. According to Nechemia Meyers (*Nature,* Dec. 4, 1975), Syrian woodpeckers in northern Israel are striking back at modern civilization. They have been puncturing above-ground plastic irrigation pipes, apparently because the water passing through sounds like insects in trees.

W. Cade of the University of Texas, Austin, has reported (*Science,* Dec. 26, 1975) a parasite that locates its host by the latter's song. He proved that female tachinid flies are attracted to singing male crickets. The female then deposits larvae on the cricket. The larvae burrow into the cricket, feeding on its tissues. Once parasitized, the cricket no longer sings; thus, multiple parasites in one cricket are uncommon. Further, not all male crickets sing. These so-called "satellite males" have a much lower incidence of parasitism than the singing males of their species.

Elephants. Most of us have heard of the grade school boy who, when asked to write a review of a book about elephants, produced the classic, "This book contains more about elephants than I care to know." R. M. Laws of Cambridge University, England, and his associates have just published a book that might have changed the young boy's mind. Encumbered with the laborious title *Elephants and Their Habitats: The Ecology of Elephants in North Bunyoro, Uganda,* the book, however, gives a realistic overview of elephants, their lives, and their competitive relationship with man.

E. LENDELL COCKRUM
University of Arizona

UPI

Boston's Franklin Park Zoo welcomed its latest arrival, a female black rhinoceros, in July. In the previous three years, only a dozen rhinos were born in captivity.

A

Aalto, Alvar (Fin. arch.) 377, 97
Aaron, Henry (Amer. athl.) 460
Abalone (zool.) 317
Abdul Razak (Mal. prime minis.) 377
Abel's Island, bk. (Steig) 304
ABM: *see* Antiballistic Missiles
Abortion 167, 294, 436, 437
　Connecticut 170
　Morgentaler Case 143
　Political Parties, U.S. 553
Abu Dhabi 517
Abu Rudeis Oilfields, Egy. 333
Academy of American Poets Awards 413
Academy of Motion Picture Arts and Sciences Awards 413
Accelerators (phys.) 404
ACCIDENTS AND DISASTERS 72
　Earthquakes 227, 228
　Transportation 509
　Weather 327
Acheampong, I. K. (Ghanaian gen., pol.) 234
Acid Rain 135
ACLU: *see* American Civil Liberties Union
Acrylonitrile (plastic) 219
Adams, Alvan (Amer. athl.) 463
Adams, Brock (Amer. pub. offi.) 535, 533
Adams Chronicles, The (TV program) 492
Addiction, Drug: *see* Drug Addiction and Abuse
Administration on Aging (U.S.) 390, 391
ADVERTISING 73
　Eyeglasses 216
　Magazines and Newspapers 416
　Prescription Drugs 151, 171
AEC: *see* Atomic Energy Commission
Aegean Sea Dispute (Gr.-Turk.) 240, 518
　United Nations 526, 527
Aerosol Spray Cans 154
Aerospace Industry 258
Afars and Issas: *see* French Territory of the Afars and Issas
AFGHANISTAN 74
AFRICA 75
　Agriculture 83
　Archaeology 93
　Cuba 176
　Islam 428
　Natural Gas 198
　Olympic Games 453
　Petroleum 200
　Population 407
　USSR 522
　United States 538
African Party for the Independence of Guinea and Cape Verde 241
Afrikaans (lang.) 440
Afro-Americans: *see* Negroes, American
Agency for Consumer Advocacy (U.S.) 171
Agency for International Development (U.S.) 153
AGRICULTURE 81, 107, 327
　Caribbean 149
　Europe 210
　Foreign Aid 220
　International Trade 263
　Migrant Farmworkers 209
　Soviet Grain Imports 524
　See also specific crops; and articles on countries, provinces of Canada, and states of the U.S.
Agriculture, Department of (U.S.) 81, 84, 171, 218
AIB: *see* Anti-Inflation Board
Aid India Consortium 253
Aid to Families with Dependent Children (U.S.) 435, 436
Ailey, Alvin (Amer. choreog.) 179, 180
Air and Space Museum, Washington, D.C. 515
Air Canada 420, 509
Air Force (U.S.) 335 fol.
Air France 510
Air Pollution 206, 204, 326
　Coal 197
　Italy 274
Air Traffic Controllers' Slowdown (U.S.) 509
Air Traffic Controllers' Strike (Can.) 142, 512
Air Transportation 508, 509, 516
　Accidents 72
　Concorde 510, 515
　Hijackings 519, 556
　Language Controversy, Quebec 420
　Nader Case 294
　Territorial Seas 56
Airplane Crashes 72
Airplanes 335 fol., 512
　Concorde 510
Ake, Simeon (Iv. Cst. states.) 526
Aksenov, Vladimir (Sov. cosmonaut) 442
　Illus. 444
ALA: *see* American Library Association
ALABAMA 85
　Bridge 201
　Prisons 166, 411
ALASKA 86
　Bridge 201
　Pipeline 200, 207
　Weather 327
ALBANIA 87
　Television 494
Albert, Carl (Amer. cong.) 389
　Illus. 447
Albert Lasker Medical Research Awards 414
ALBERTA, prov., Can. 87, 145
　Archaeology 93
Albuquerque, N. Mex. 362
ALGERIA 88, 77, 78
　Spanish Sahara 346
　Television 494
Ali, Muhammad (Amer. athl.) 465
Alia Toukan (wife of King Hussein):
　Illus. 49
Aliens, Rights of 293
All Nippon Airways 278
All the President's Men (film) 348
　Illus. 347
Allergic Eczema (med.) 322
Allied Chemical Corporation 204, 548
Allott, Kenneth (Brit. poet) 309
Alvin Ailey City Center Dance Theater 180
　Television 494
Amalrik, Andrei (Sov. hist.) 524
Amerasinghe, Hamilton Shirley (Sri Lankan states.) 118, 525
　Illus. 50
American Anthropological Association 91
American Ballet Theater 180
American Basketball Association 463, 464
American Broadcasting Company 491, 492
American Chemical Society Awards 414
American Civil Liberties Union 544
American Council of Life Insurance 260
American Library Association 298
American Literature 300
　Bellow, S. 119
　Prizes and Awards 413
　Publishing 415
　Warren, R. P. 132
American Motors Corporation 112

American Telephone & Telegraph Company 445, 490
American Television and Radio Archives 494
Amin, Idi (Ugandan pres.) 519, 77
Amino Acids (biochem.) 92
Ammonia Tank Truck Crash, Houston, Tex. 247
Amnesty International 541
Amtrak (R. R. corp.) 514
Andean Pact Countries 289
　Chile 156
Anderson, Wendell R. (Amer. sen.) 341
Andreotti, Giulio (It. premier) 273, 274
Andrus, Cecil D. (Amer. pub. offi.) 534, 249
Anglican Church of Canada 425
ANGOLA 89, 75 fol.
　Cuba 175, 176
　South Africa 439
　Television 494
　USSR 522
　United Nations 526
　United States 538
　Zaire 558
Anguilla, isl., Carib. 150
Animal Feed 81
Animals: *see* Livestock; Zoology
Anne (Brit. princess) 456
Annuities 260
Anselmi, Tina (It. pub. offi.) 275, 554
　Illus. 273
Antarctica 406
ANTHROPOLOGY 91, 92
　Inuit of Canada 146
Antiballistic Missiles 337, 521
Anti-Communist Alliance of Brazil 290
Anticonvulsant Drugs 321
Antigua 150
　Television 494
Anti-Hijacking Agreement (Cuba-U.S.) 290
Anti-Inflation Board (Can.) 141, 286
Antiochene Church 427
Anti-Semitism 427
Antitrust Laws 171, 490
Apartheid 525
Aperture (phot. jour.) 402
Appalachian Development Highway System (U.S.) 512
Arab-Israeli Conflict 272, 332
　Egypt 194
　Hijacking of French Jetliner 519
　Jordan 280
　Religion 428
　Rumania 431
　United Nations 525, 526
　United States 538
Arab League 296
Arabian American Oil Company 432
Arafat, Yasir (Arab leader) 295, 296

ARAMCO: *see* Arabian American Oil Company
ARCHAEOLOGY 92
　Buddha's Remains Discovered 428
Archery (sport) 479, 455
ARCHITECTURE 95
　Britain's National Theatre 506
　Interior Design 261
　Prizes and Awards 412
Arctic Ice Dynamics Joint Experiment 406
Arctic Region 406
ARGENTINA 98, 290
　Agriculture 82, 83
　Anti-Semitism 427
　Automobiles 113
　Bridge 201
　Labor 287
　Literature 312
　Paraguay 396
　Telephones 490
　Television 494
　Videla, J. R. 130
Argentine Anti-Communist Alliance 290
ARIZONA 100
　Central Arizona Project 201
Arizona-Sonora Desert Museum 560
ARKANSAS 101
　Archaeology 92
Arlington Heights, Ill. 165
Armenia, rep., USSR 94
Arms Control: *see* Disarmament and Arms Control
Arms Sales 183, 338, 537
　Chile 156
　Egypt 195
　Ethiopia 207
　Iran 269
　Jordan 280
　Kenya 76, 282
　Saudi Arabia 433
　Zaire 558
Armstrong, Anne (Amer. ambassador) 118
Army (U.S.) 531
ART 102
　Calder, A. 376
　Canada 149
Arthritis (med.) 320, 324
Artificial Genes (biol.) 117
Asbestos (min.) 340, 341
ASEAN: *see* Association of Southeast Asian Nations
Ashbery, John (Amer. poet) 300
ASIA 106
　Agriculture 82, 83
　Archaeology 93, 94
　Food 217
　Natural Gas 198
　Petroleum 200
　Weather 327
Askew, Reubin (Fla. gov.) 216
Aspin, Lee (Amer. cong.) 337
Aspirin (drug) 321
Assad, Hafez al- (Syr. pres.) 486, 487
　Lebanon 296

Main article headings appear in this index as bold-faced capitals; subjects within articles appear as lower-case entries. Main article page numbers and general references are listed first under each entry; the subentries which follow them on separate lines direct the reader to related topics appearing elsewhere. Both the general references and the subentries should be consulted for maximum usefulness of this index. Illustrations are indexed herein. Cross references are to the entries in this index.

Association of Southeast Asian Nations 546
  Illus. 106
Asthma (med.) 324
Astronauts (Cosmonauts) 442
ASTRONOMY 108
Athanasakos, Elizabeth (Amer. attorney) 554
Athfield, Ian (N.Z. arch.) 95
Atlanta, Ga. 513
Atlantic City, N.J. 361
Atlantic Ocean 52
Atmosphere 325, 326
Atomic Energy Commission (U.S.,) 411
Atomic Weapons: *see* Nuclear Weapons
Atopic Dermatitis (med.) 322
Attica Prison, N.Y. 410
Atwood, Margaret (Can. writ.) 306
Auden, W. H. (Brit. poet) 308
Audio Equipment 423
Audio-Visual Education 41
  Illus. 42
Austin, Tex. 202
AUSTRALIA 109
  Agriculture 82
  Archaeology 93
  Automobiles 113
  Education 193
  Fraser, J. M. 125
  Mining 339
  Oceania 385
  Olympic Games 453
  Petroleum 200
  Telephones 490
  Television 494
  Weather 327
Australian Ballet 180
AUSTRIA 111
  Art Exhibition in U.S. 102
  Automobiles 113
  Music 354, 355
  Olympic Games 449, 450, 453
  Telephones 490
  Television 494
  Yugoslavia 556
Auto Racing 458
AUTOMOBILES 112, 509
  Economy, U.S. 186
  Emission Standards 206
  Gas Mileage 196
  Industrial Review 257, 258
  Labor 285, 330
  Recall of Defective Vehicles 294
Avco Cup (hockey) 472
Averina, Tatiana (Russ. athl.) 450
Avery Fisher Hall, New York, N.Y. 353
  Illus. 364
Aviation: *see* Air Transportation
Awards: *see* Prizes and Awards
Awoonor, Kofi (Ghanaian writ.) 234

B

B-1 Bomber (airplane) 335, 336
Baader-Meinhof Group (Ger. guerrillas) 230
Baby Foods 219
Back-to-Basics Movement (educ.) 43
Backfire Bomber (airplane) 183, 338
Bacteria 117, 331
  Oceanic 325
Badminton 479
Bahamas 168
Baker, James A. (Amer. law., pol.) 247
Balance of Payments 263, 265, 266
Balanchine, George (Amer. choreog.) 180
Ballard, Florence (Amer. singer) 377
Ballet: *see* Dance

Ballistic Missiles 183
Baltic Sea 387
Baltimore, Md. 165, 318
Banaban (people) 385
Bandaranaike, Sirimavo (Sri Lankan prime minis.) 481
BANGLADESH 114, 107
  India 254
  Television 494
  Weather 327
Bank of America 189
BANKING 114
  Canada 145
  International Finance 264
  Irish Strike 270
Bantu (Afr. people) 496
Banzer Suárez, Hugo (Bol. pres.) 133
Baptists (rel.) 524
Barbados 150, 291
  Television 494
Barbaigs (Afr. people) 488
Barcelona Conference on Ocean Pollution 387
Barre, Raymond (Fr. prime minis.) 221, 223
Baryshnikov, Mikhail (Russ. dancer) 119, 179
Baseball 459
  Toronto 507
  Illus. 279
Basketball 461
  Erving, J. 123
  Olympic Games 455, 456, 457
Baudouin (Belg. k.) 47, 116
  Illus. 45
Baum, William (Amer. card.) 426
Bay Area Rapid Transit System 513
Bayano Dam, Pan. 395
Bayi, Filbert (Tanz. athl.) 478
Bayreuth Festival, Ger. 354
  Illus. 353
Beaux Arts Architecture Exhibition, New York 95
Bechtel International 88
Bedford-Stuyvesant, New York City 96
Beef (meat) 81 fol.
Beirut, Leb. 296, 333
  Illus. 295
Belaúnde Terry, Fernando (Peruv. pres.) 398
Belenko, Viktor (Sov. pilot) 276, 522
  Illus. 337
BELGIUM 116
  Automobiles 113
  International Finance 264
  Monarchy 47
  Olympic Games 453
  Telephones 490
  Television 494
  USSR 521
Belize 153, 291
Bell, Griffin B. (Amer. pub. offi.) 534
Bell Bill (U.S.) 490
Bellow, Saul (Amer. writ.) 119, 300
Bench, Johnny (Amer. athl.) 460
Benham, Dorothy Kathleen (Miss America) 341
Benin (Dahomey) 79
Benson, Kent (Amer. athl.) 462, 461
Bentsen, Lloyd (Amer. sen.) 498
Bergland, Bob (Amer. pub. offi.) 535
Bergman, Ingmar (Swed. dir.) 535
Berkeley, Busby (Amer. choreog.) 377
Berlinguer, Enrico (It. pol.) 119, 274, 275
Bermuda 453, 494
Bernhard (Neth. pr.) 66, 358
  Illus. 45
Berry, Mary (Amer. educ.) 554
Bersianik, Louky (Can. writ.) 306
Bert Breen's Barn, nov. (Edmonds) 303

Best Sellers (books) 415
Bhumibol Adulyadej (Thai k.) 499
Bhutto, Zulfikar Ali (Pak. prime minis.) 393, 394
Biathlon (sports) 450
Bicentennial (U.S.) 32, 529
  Architecture 97
  Art 102
  Austria 111
  Boston 134
  Children's Literature 303
  Cities 165
  Coins 167, 168
  Dance Productions 179
  Germany, West 231
  Stamps 481
  Television 492
  Travel 515
Bicentennial Wagon Trains 396
Bicycling 515
Big Bang Theory (astron.) 109
Big Ben, clock, London, Eng. 236
Bilingualism: *see* Language Controversies
BIOCHEMISTRY 117
BIOGRAPHIES 118
Biology 117, 226, 317, 331, 444, 559
Birth Control 436, 107
  Bangladesh 114
  India 253
  Pakistan 394
Birth Defects (med.) 321
Birth Rates 407
Black Family in Slavery and Freedom 1750-1925, The, bk. (Gutman) 302
Blackmun, Harry (Amer. justice) 292
Blacks: *see* Negroes, American
Bloomgarden, Kermit (Amer. theat. prod.) 377
Blue Laws 170
Blumberg, Baruch S. (Amer. sci.) 412
Blumenthal, W. Michael (Amer. pub. offi.) 534, 533
Bobcat (zool.) 559
Bobsledding (sport) 450
Boeing 747SP (airplane) 512
Bokassa, Jean (C. Afr. Rep. pres.):
  Illus. 519
Bolan Dam, Pak. 394
Bold Forbes (horse) 473
BOLIVIA 133
  Chile 156
  Labor 287
  Television 494
Bolles, Don (Amer. jour.) 100, 418
Bombers (airplanes) 335 fol.
  Disarmament 183
Bonds: *see* Stocks and Bonds
Book of Common Prayer 425
Books: *see* Literature; Publishing
Boorstin, Daniel (Amer. schol.) 297
Bordaberry, Juan María (Uru. pres.) 541
Borg, Björn (Swed. athl.) 120, 477
BOSTON, Mass. 134, 165
  Quincy Market 95
  School Integration 190
  Illus. 34, 35
Boston Affirmations (rel. manifesto) 425
Boston Celtics (basketball team) 463, 464
Boston Pops Orchestra 134
Boswell, Connee (Amer. singer) 377
BOTANY 134
  Gardening and Horticulture 225
Botswana 79
Bougainville, prov., Papua New Guinea 385
Boulez, Pierre (Fr. cond.) 353, 354

Boumédienne, Houari (Alg. pres.) 88
Bound for Glory (film) 347
Bourassa, Robert (Can. pol.) 142
Bourguiba, Habib (Tun. pres.) 517
Bowen, Otis R. (Ind. gov.) 255
Bowl Games (football) 466
Bowling 479
Boxing (sport) 465
  Olympic Games 455
Brailowsky, Alexander (Russ. pianist) 377
Brain (anat.) 117
Brandt, Willy (Ger. pol.) 230
BRAZIL 135, 289, 290
  Agriculture, 82, 83
  Automobiles 113
  Industrial Review 257
  Itaipu Dam 202
  Labor 287
  Mining 339
  Olympic Games 453
  Telephones 490
  Television 494
  Venezuela 543
  Illus. 291
Breast Cancer (med.) 320
Brennan, William J. (Amer. justice) 292
Brezhnev, Leonid (Sov. pol.) 523
  Disarmament 183
  Rumania 431
  Illus. 521
Bribery (crime) 65, 67
Bridge (game) 479
Bridges 201
  Reichsbrücke Collapse, Austria 111
British Aircraft Corporation 268
British Airways 510
BRITISH COLUMBIA, prov., Can. 137, 145
  Cultural Activities 148, 149
British Commonwealth: *see* Commonwealth of Nations
British Honduras: *see* Belize
Britten, Benjamin (Brit. comp.) 377
Broadcasting: *see* Television and Radio
Bronx, borough, N.Y. 364
Brown, Edmund G., Jr. (Calif. gov.) 28, 138
  Farmworkers 209
Brown, George S. (Amer. gen.) 338
Brown, Harold (Amer. pub. offi.) 534
Brüsewitz, Oskar (Ger. cler.) 233
Brzezinski, Zbigniew (Amer. pub. offi.) 534
Buckley, James L. (Amer. sen.) 363, 364
Buckley v.Valeo (U.S. case) 489
Buddhism 428
  Archaeology 94
Buffalo, N.Y. 96, 513
Building and Construction 95, 244, 258
  Labor 286
Bukovsky, Vladimir (Sov. diss.) 524
BULGARIA 137
  Olympic Games 453
  Telephones 490
  Television 494
Burger, Warren (Amer. justice) 292, 293
  Church and State 166
Burger Chef Restaurants 63
Burger King Restaurants 61, 63, 64
Burglary (crime) 174
Burgtheater, Vienna, Aus. 111
BURMA 138, 107
Burns, Arthur F. (Amer. pub. offi.) 115
Burns, George (Amer. comedian) 413
Burundi 79
Buses 509, 508

Bush, George (Amer. offi.) 417, 531
Business Cycles (econ.) 188
Business Ethics 65
Business Roundtable 164
Busing of School Children 165, 166, 208
  Boston 134, 190
  Dallas 498
  Louisville 281
  Ohio 388
  Supreme Court 293
Butz, Earl (Amer. offi.) 83
Bykovsky, Valeri F. (Sov. cosmonaut) 442
  Illus. 444
Byrd, Harry F., Jr. (Amer. sen.) 548
Byrd, Robert (Amer. sen.) 532
  Illus. 344
Byrne, Brendan (N.J. gov.) 361

C

C-130 Airplanes 406
Cabinet Members, U.S. 534
Cable Television 494, 496
Caffeine (drug) 322
Cahokia Archaeological Site, Ill. 92
Calculators 42, 259
Caldecott Medal 298
Calder, Alexander (Amer. art.) 376
Caldwell, Sarah (Amer. cond.) 120, 354
Califano, Joseph A., Jr. (Amer. pub. offi.) 535
CALIFORNIA 138
  Archaeology 92
  Farmworkers 209
  Illegal Aliens, Hiring of 293
  Los Angeles 313
  Motor Vehicles 509
  Nuclear Energy 199, 339
  Offshore Oil and Gas 206
  Weather 327
  Zoning Regulations 294
  Illus. 244, 340
California, Gulf of 329
California Suite, play (Simon) 501
Call to Action (R.C. assembly) 426
Callaghan, James (Brit. prime minis.) 121, 236, 237
  Illus. 15, 235
Calloway, Howard ("Bo") (Amer. pol.) 27
CAMBODIA 139, 107
  Television 494
  Vietnam 546
Cambridge, Godfrey (Amer. act.) 377
Cameras 400, 442
Cameroon 79
Cámpora, Héctor (Arg. pres.) 98
CANADA 141
  Advertising 74
  Agriculture 82
  Air Traffic Controllers' Strike 512
  Anglican Church 425
  Archaeology 93
  Automobiles 113
  Capital Punishment 174
  Clark, C.J. 123
  Coins 168
  Consumerism 171
  Cuba 176
  Education 192
  Food 218
  Housing 246
  India 254
  Industrial Review 257
  International Trade and Finance 263
  Inuit 146
  Labor 286
  Literature 305, 306
  Mining 339, 340
  Motion Pictures 352

Olympic Games 450, 452, 453
  Petroleum 200
  Population 407
  Taxation 489
  Telephones 490
  Television 494
  USSR 523
  Weather 327
Canada Council's Art Bank 149
Canada Cup (hockey) 472
Canadian-American Committee 144
Canadian Food and Drug Directorate 218
Canadian Labour Congress 141, 286
Canadian Library Association 298
Canadian Opera Company 148
Canals 201
Cancer (med.) 320, 321
  Oncogenes 117
Cannes International Film Festival Awards 414
Canoeing 479, 455
Cape Verde 79, 241
Capital Punishment 174, 166, 292
  Canada 143
  Gilmore Case 533
  Oklahoma 389
  Texas 498
Caramanlis, Constantine (Gr. premier) 240
Carbon Black (chem.) 206
Carbon Dioxide (chem.) 325
Carey, Hugh (N.Y. gov.) 510
CARIBBEAN 149
Caribbean Common Market 289
Caribbean Development Bank 149, 150
Caribbean Sea 386
Carl XVI Gustaf (Swed. k.) 121, 485
  Illus. 45
Carlsberg-Indian-Antarctic Ridge (ocean.) 52
Carnegie Hall, New York, N.Y., 355
Carter, James Earl ("Jimmy"), Jr. (Amer. pres.) 121, 24 fol., 229, 532
  Consumerism 171
  Environment 204
  Ethnic Groups 208
  Taxation 489
  Illus. 534, 20, 22, 85
Carter, Lillian (mother of pres.):
  Illus. 28
Carter, Rosalynn (wife of pres.) 26, 27
Cassin, René (Fr. jur.) 377
Castro, Fidel (Cuban prime minis.) 175, 176, 556
Castro, Raul (Cuban offi.) 521
CAT Scanning (med.) 322
Catholicism 426, 424
  Abortion 437
  Chile 156
  Ecuador 189
  Paraguay 396
  Poland 405
  Zaire 558
Cattle 145, 280
Cayman Trough, Caribbean Sea 386
CB Radio: *see* Citizens' Band Radio
Ceauşescu, Nicolae (Rum. pres.) 431
Cement 340
CENSORSHIP 151
  Brazil 136
  India 251, 252
  Motion Pictures 351
Center for Disease Control, Atlanta, Ga. 229
Central African Republic 79
CENTRAL AMERICA 152
Central American Common Market 289
Central Arizona Project 100

Central Intelligence Agency (U.S.) 530, 531
  Daniel Schorr Case 417
  Italy 275
Cerro Colorado Copper Project, Pan. 395
Ceylon: *see* Sri Lanka
Chad 79
  Libya 299
Chamberlain Basin, Idaho 249
Champion Paper Company 86
Charles (Prince of Wales) 47
Charm (phys.) 404
Charmonium (phys.) 404
Chase Sardi, Miguel (Para. anthro.) 396
Chavez, Cesar (Amer. labor leader) 209
Chea, Muon (Camb. premier) 140
Chellini Madonna, bronze tondo (Donatello) 104
CHEMISTRY 154
  Prizes and Awards 412, 414
  Superheavy Elements 403
Chess (game) 479
Chevrolet (auto.) 112
Chiang Ch'ing (widow of Mao Tse-tung) 158
Chiang Ching-Kuo (Chin. premier) 161, 162
CHICAGO, Ill. 155, 167, 203
Chicago Lyric Opera 354
Chicanos (Mex.-Amer.) 209
Child Abuse 436
Child Welfare: *see* Social Welfare
Children and Youth:
  Crime 363
  Education 37
  Literature 303
  Unemployment 208
Children's Literature 303, 298
CHILE 155, 289
  Agriculture 83
  Bolivia 133
  Labor 287
  Literature 312
  Religion 425
  Television 494
Chiles, Lawton (Amer. sen.) 216
CHINA, People's Republic of 157, 106, 107, 71
  Agriculture 82
  Cambodia 140
  Chou En-lai 372
  Earthquakes 227, 228
  Foreign Aid 220
  Hua Kuo-feng 125
  India 254
  Japan 277
  Mao Tse-tung 375
  Mining 339, 340
  Natural Gas 198
  Nuclear Tests 199
  Petroleum 200
  Population 407
  Singapore 434
  Sri Lanka 481
  Television 494
  USSR 522
  Vietnam 546
CHINA, Republic of 161
  Industrial Review 257
  Japan 277
  Olympic Games 452
  Telephones 490
Chinh, Truong (Viet. pub. offi.) 545
Chirac, Jacques (Fr. pol.) 221, 222
Chlorofluorocarbons (chem.) 154, 326
Chomsky, Noam (Amer. schol.) 302
Chorus Line, A, musical 300, 500
Chou En-lai (Chin. premier) 372
Chowchilla School Bus Kidnapping, Calif. 174, 139, 173
Christian-Democratic Union (Ger. pol.) 230, 234
Christian Democrats (It. pol.) 274

Christian-Social Union (Ger. pol.) 230
Christianity 424 fol., 207
Christie, Agatha (Brit. writ.) 378
  Illus. 308
Chromosomes (genetics) 226
CHRONOLOGY 11
Chrysler Corporation 112, 113, 204
Chu Teh (Chin. mil. leader) 378
Church, Frank (Amer. sen.) 28
  Illus. 69, 316, 531
Church and State 166, 167
  Grants to Church Colleges 294, 318
  Poland 405
CIA: *see* Central Intelligence Agency
Cierpinski, Waldemar (Ger. athl.) 456
Cigarettes 154
Cincinnati, Ohio 96
Cincinnati Reds (baseball team) 459 fol.
Citadel Theatre, Edmonton, Can. 148
CITIES AND URBAN AFFAIRS 163, 95
  Crime 172
  Employees Required to Live in City 155
  Mass Transit 96
Citizens' Band Radio 490, 494, 496
  Illus. 259
City University of New York 190, 363, 364
Civil Aeronautics Board 508, 516
CIVIL LIBERTIES AND CIVIL RIGHTS 166, 537
  Censorship 151
  Chile 155, 156
  Ethnic Groups 209
  School Integration 190
  Supreme Court Rulings 292 fol.
Clark, Charles Joseph (Can. pol.) 123, 141
  Illus. 142
CLC: *see* Canadian Labour Congress
Clean Air Act (U.S.) 206
Clerides, Glafkos (Cypriot pol.) 177
Cleveland, Ohio 388
Cleveland Museum, Ohio 104
Climate: *see* Meteorology
Cloud Seeding (meteorol.) 325
Coal 196, 257, 339
  Alaska 86
  Canada 145
  Strip Mining 294
  West Virginia 551
Coal Leasing Law (U.S.) 555
Coast Guard (U.S.) 406
Coastal Energy Impact Bill (U.S.) 206
Coastal Upwelling Ecosystems Analysis (ocean.) 386
Cobalt 53
Cobb, Lee J. (Amer. act.) 378
Cocoa 234
Cod Wars (Ice.-Brit.) 56, 248
Coffee 83, 90, 168, 290
COINS AND COIN COLLECTING 167
Coleman, James S. (Amer. educ.) 208
Coleman, William T. (Amer. pub. offi.) 510
College Entrance Examination Board 37, 43
Colleges and Universities 191
COLOMBIA 168, 291
  Literature 312
  Telephones 490
  Television 494
  Venezuela 543
COLORADO 169
  Weather 327
  Illus. 339
Colossus (warship) 94

Columbia Broadcasting System 492, 464
Columbia River Compact 249
Columbus, Ind. 97, 95
Comaneci, Nadia (Rum. athl.) 453
COMECON: see Council for Mutual Economic Assistance
Comet West (astron.) 109
Commerce Power (U.S. Congress) 294
Commercial speech (law) 73
Commission on Civil Rights (U.S.) 190
Common Situs Picketing Bill (U.S.) 529
Commonwealth of Nations 48
Communication Satellites 444, 496
Communism 211
Berlinguer, E. 119
Castro, F. 176
European Conference, East Berlin 232, 521
France 222, 223
Italy 273 fol.
Paraguay 396
Philippines 399
Portugal 407, 408
Rumania 431
Spain 447, 448
USSR 523
Vietnam 545, 546
Yugoslavia 556
Communist China: see China, People's Republic of
Community Standards for Obscenity 151
Commuter Airlines 508
Comoro Islands 79
Computers 323, 423
Comsat General Corporation 445
Comstar (communication satellite) 445
Concorde (airplane) 510, 508, 515, 224
Conference of Latin American Bishops 189
Conference of Mayors (U.S.) 163, 164
Conference of Nonaligned Countries, Sri Lanka 481
Afghanistan 74
India 254
Conference on Human Settlement, Vancouver, B.C., Can. 205, 95, 525, 526
Congaree Swamp, S.C. 441
Congo 79
Congress, U.S. 530, 529
Banking 114
Cities 164
Consumerism 171, 490
Elections 31
Foreign Affairs 537, 538
Foreign Aid 220
Membership 539
Military Forces 335
Oil and Gas Prices 207
Older Population 390
Postal Service 409
Taxation 488
Television and Radio 494, 496
Congress of Racial Equality:
Angola 76
Congress Party (India) 251, 252
CONNECTICUT 170
Connors, Jimmy (Amer. athl.) 477, 476
Conrail (Consolidated Rail Corporation) 513
Conservation 134, 204
Nunavut (Inuit territory) 147
Conservative Party (Can.) 141
Construction: see Building and Construction
Consumer Communications Reform Bill (U.S.) 490
Consumer Goods 259
Consumer Price Index 285

Canada 145, 286
Graph 187
Consumer Product Safety Commission (U.S.) 171
Consumer Spending 185
CONSUMERISM 171
Banking 115
Mexico 328
Containers, Food 218
Contiguous Zone (ocean.) 57
Continental Shelf (ocean.) 51, 55, 57
Continental Slope (ocean.) 51
Conventions, Political 28, 553
Illus. 24, 25
Cooper, Susan (Amer. writ.) 303
Cooper-Hewitt Museum, New York, N.Y. 105
Cooperman, Stanley (Can. poet) 306
Copenhagen, Den. 182
Copper 339, 53, 156, 268, 558
Coptic Church 424
Copyright Law 297, 494
Cordelier, Jeanne (Fr. writ.) 309
CORE: see Congress of Racial Equality
Corn 83, 84, 250, 267, 280
Corn Syrup (food) 219
Coronary Arteries (anat.) 321
Coronary Thrombosis (med.) 320
Corporate Taxes 488
Corvalán, Luís (Chil. pol.) 524
Cosmology 109
Cosmonauts (astronauts) 442
Costa Rica 152, 494
Cottesloe Theatre, London, Eng. 506
Cotton 484
Council for Mutual Economic Assistance 431
Council of Yukon Indians 557
Council on Environmental Quality (U.S.) 204, 206
Country Music 356, 412
Crickets (entom.) 560
CRIME 172, 165
Art Thefts 103
Bolles Murder, Arizona 100
California 139
Canada 143
Detroit 330
Drug Dealing 184
Hong Kong 243
Houston 247
Medicaid Frauds 437
New York 363
Prisons 405
Tokyo 507
Criminal Defendants, Rights of 166, 293
Croatia, rep., Yugos. 555, 556
Crossman, Richard (Brit. pub. offi.) 307
Cruise Missile 337
Cruise Ships 516
Cryogenics (phys.) 197
CUBA 175, 289, 290
Africa 75 fol., 80
Angola 89, 90
Canada 144
Caribbean, Influence in 150
Central America 152, 153
Ethiopia 207
Olympic Games 453
Television 494
USSR 523
United States 538
Venezuela 543
Cunningham, Imogen (Amer. phot.) 378, 402
Illus. 401
CUNY 190, 363, 364
Curling (sport) 479
Cy Young Memorial Awards (baseball) 461
Cycling (sport) 479, 455
Cyclones 72
CYPRUS 177, 518, 526
Television 494
CZECHOSLOVAKIA 178

Automobiles 113
Olympic Games 450, 453
Space Exploration 445
Telephones 490
Television 494

D

Dahomey: see Benin
Dalai Lama (Tibetan rel. leader) 428
Daley, Richard J. (Amer. mayor) 378, 155, 250
Dallas, Tex. 165, 498
Dallas Symphony 353
Dalton Period (archaeo.) 92
Dam, (Carl Peter) Henrik (Dan. biochem.) 378
Dams 202
Bolan Dam Collapse, Pak. 394
Teton Dam Disaster 249
DANCE 179
Baryshnikov, M. 119
Canada 148
Makarova, N. 127
Prizes and Awards 412
Illus. 495
Danson, Barnett J. (Can. pub. offi.) 205
Data Transmission Company 490
Dating Methods (archaeo.) 92
Daud Khan, Mohammed (Afg. pres.) 74
Davis, Bernard D. (Amer. educ.) 209
Davis, Meyer (Amer. cond.) 378
Day-Care Centers 436
Daytona 500-Mile Race 458
DDT (insecticide) 559, 560
Death, Determination of 436
Death Penalty: see Capital Punishment
Death Rates 407
Deaths: see Obituaries
Debates (U.S. elections) 30, 498
Illus. 28
Decatur, Ga. 96
Decolonization, Special Committee on (U.N.) 527
DeCrow, Karen (Amer. feminist) 173
Deep-Sea Exploration: see Oceanography
Defendants' Rights: see Criminal Defendants, Rights of
Defense Forces: see Military Forces
DELAWARE 181
Del Mar Skull (archaeo.) 92
Delta Airlines 509
Demirel, Süleyman (Turk. prime minis.) 518
Democratic Party (U.S.) 24 fol.
Ethnic Groups 208
Social Welfare 435
Women 553
Dene (Can. Indians) 369
DENMARK 182
Archaeology 93
International Finance 264
Olympic Games 453
Taxation 489
Telephones 490
Television 494
Dennis, Patrick (Amer. writ.) 378
Denver Center for the Performing Arts, Colo. 169
Denver Nuggets (basketball team) 463, 464
Deoxyribonucleic Acid (DNA) 226, 331
Oncogenes 117
Dermatology (med.) 321
Detroit, Mich. 165, 330
Catholic Assembly 426
Trolleys 96
*Illus.*163, 508
Detroit Public Library, Mich. 298
Deutschmark (Ger. currency): see Mark
Devaluation of Currencies: see Revaluation of Currencies

Developing Countries (Third World):
Asia 107
Censorship 151
Cuba 176
Environment 204
Food 81, 217
Foreign Aid 220
Industrial Review 257
International Trade and Finance 264, 266
Development Assistance Committee (DAC) 220
Diamond (min.) 340
Diego Garcia, isl., Ind. O. 106
Diet: see Nutrition
Dillon, Leo and Diane (Amer. illustrators) 303
Dioxin (chem.) 274
Direct Mail Advertising 74
DISARMAMENT AND ARMS CONTROL 183, 537
Disasters: see Accidents and Disasters
Disco Music 356, 422
Discount Rate (fin.) 115
Discus Throw (sport) 478, 457
Dividends (fin.) 483
Diving (sport) 455
Divorce 407
Djibouti, Fr. Terr. of the Afars and Issas 78
DNA: see Deoxyribonucleic Acid
Doctorow, E. L. (Amer. writ.) 300
Dog Shows 479
Dole, Robert Joseph (Amer. sen.) 123, 29
Illus. 26, 28
Domenici, Pete (Amer. sen.):
Illus. 437
Dominican Republic:
Television 494
Dong, Pham Van (Viet. prime minis.) 545
Dorsett, Tony (Amer. athl.) 466, 467
Douglas, Paul H. (Amer. sen.) 378
Dow Chemical Company 556
Dow Jones Industrials (stocks) 482
Dowling, Eddie (Amer. act., dir. (378)
Drama: see Theater
Drama Critics Circle Award 500
Dress: see Fashion
Drew Pearson Award 412
Drought (meteorol.) 327
Agriculture 82
Caribbean 149
Europe 210
Illus. 326
DRUG ADDICTION AND ABUSE 184
New York 363
Drugs (pharm.) 321, 324
Advertising 171
Generic Names 216
Drumm, Maire (N. Ire. pol.) 238
Dry Valley Drilling Project 406
Due Process Clause (law) 294
Dukakis, Michael S. (Mass. gov.) 319
Dulles Airport, Washington, D.C. 510
Dunlop, John (Amer. pub. offi.) 529
Du Pont, Pierre S., IV (Del. gov.) 181
Duran, Robert (Pan. athl.) 465
Durand, Lucille (Can. writ.) 306
Dutch National Ballet 180
Dyes, Food 218
Dykes, James J. (Amer. athl.) 379

E

Eanes, António Ramalho (Port. pres.) 407
Illus. 408
Earthquakes, 227, 228

Eathquakes (con't.)
  Central America, 152, 153, 291
  China 158
  Italy 274
  Mexico 328
  Oceanic 52
  Turkey 518
  USSR 524
East African Community 488
East Germany: *see* German Democratic Republic
East Pacific Rise (ocean.) 52
East Timor, prov., Indon. 256
Eastern Airlines 509
Eastern Caribbean Currency Commission 150
Eastern Orthodox Church: *see* Orthodox Eastern Church
Eblalite (lang.) 94
Echeverría, Luis (Mex. pres.) 329, 289, 291
  Habitat Conference 205
  Illus. 328
Echternach, Luxem. 94
Éclipse (astron.) 109
École des Beaux Arts Exhibition, New York 379
Ecology: *see* Environment
Economic and Social Council (U.N.) 526, 528
Economic Conference, Puerto Rico 210
  Japan 276
Economic Cooperation and Development, Organization for 70
Economics, Nobel Prize in 412
ECONOMY, U.S. 185, 529
  Automobiles 112
  Banking 114
  Blacks 208
  Cities 163
  Civil Liberties and Civil Rights 167
  Food 218
  Housing 244
  Industrial Review 258, 257
  Insurance 260
  International Trade and Finance 263 fol.
  Quick Food Chains 61
  Stocks and Bonds 482
ECUADOR 189, 291
  Catholicism 426
  Literature 312
  Television 494
Eczema (med.) 322
Edmonds, Walter D. (Amer. writ.) 303
Edmonton, Alta, Can. 148
EDUCATION 190, 37
  Chicago's Early School Closing 155
  Ethnic Groups 208
  Inuit of Canada 146
  Librarianship 298
  Montreal Language Controversy 345
  Nonpublic Schools, Aid to 167, 318
  Ontario 391
  Women 554
  See also Information Highlights section in articles on provinces of Canada and states of the U.S.
Education, Office of (U.S.) 38
Edwards, Edwin (La. gov.) 314
EEC: *see* European Economic Community
Eggleston, William (Amer. phot.) 400
EGYPT 194, 332 fol
  Agriculture 83
  Bridge 201
  China 161
  Coptic Church 424
  Foreign Aid 220
  Libya 299
  Saudi Arabia 433
  Sudan 484

Syria 487
Telephones 490
Television 494
Tunnels 202
USSR 522
Elbe Lateral Canal, Ger. 201
Elcaset Tape Format 423
Election Campaign Act (U.S.) 294, 167, 489
Elections 24, 536
  Campaign Financing 167, 294, 489
  Caribbean 150
  Catholicism 426
  Cities 164
  Ethnic Groups 208
  Europe 211
  Taxation 488
  Television 491, 493
  Women 553
  See also articles on countries, provinces of Canada, and states of the U.S.
Electrical Machinery 259
Electricity 197, 198, 200
Electronics:
  Audio Equipment 423
  Calculators 259
  Education 42
  Photography 400
  Postal Service 409
Elementary Particles (phys.) 403, 404
Elements (chem.) 403
  Superheavy Elements 154
Elephants (zool.) 560
Eliasberg Coin Collection 168
Elizabeth II (Brit. q.) 48
  Illus. 11, 46
Ellen, Typhoon 243, 327
Ellington, Duke (Amer. comp.) 179, 180
El Salvador 152
  Television 494
Embezzlement (crime) 172
Emission Standards (auto.) 206
Emmy Awards (TV) 414
Employee Stock Ownership Plans 286
Employment: *see* Labor
Endangered Species (biol.) 134, 559, 560
Ender, Kornelia (Ger. athl.) 454, 475
ENERGY 195, 207
  Canada 144
  Concorde 511
  Conservation 95
  Thermonuclear Fusion 404
  USSR 257
Energy Research and Development Administration (U.S.) 195, 199, 200
ENGINEERING, Civil 201
England: *see* Great Britain
English Literature 307
Entebbe Airport Raid, Uganda 272, 519
  Kenya 282
Enterprise (space-shuttle orbiter) 446
ENVIRONMENT 203
  Acid Rain 135
  Alaska 86
  Animals 559
  Arctic Research 406
  Concorde 511
  Energy 197 fol.
  Florida 216
  Italy 274
  Kepone Case, Va. 548
  New Hampshire 360
  New Mexico's Uranium Belt 362
  Nunavut (Inuit territory) 147
  Ocean Pollution 54, 60
  Ocean's Upwelling Regions 386, 387
  Plants 134
  Supreme Court Rulings 294
  Toxic Substances 154

Environmental Protection Agency (U.S.) 206, 154
Environmental Quality, Council on: *see* Council on Environmental Quality
Episcopal Church, 424, 554
Equal Protection (law) 293
Equal Rights Amendment (U.S.) 553, 554
Equal Time Rules (broadcasting) 493
Equatorial Guinea 79
Equestrian Events (sports) 455
ERA: *see* Equal Rights Amendment
ERAmerica (organ.) 554
ERDA: *see* Energy Research and Development Administration
Eritrea, prov., Eth. 207
Ernst, Max (Ger. art.) 379
Ernst, Morris L. (Amer. law.) 379
Erving, Julius (Amer. athl.) 123, 464
Eskimos: *see* Inuit
Estado de São Paulo (Braz. news.) 136
Estate Tax 390, 488
Estrogen (hormone) 320
Ethics Committee (House of Representatives) 417
ETHIOPIA 207, 78, 80
  Anthropology 91
  Libya 299
  Television 494
ETHNIC GROUPS 208
  Great Britain 238
  Hawaii 242
  Inuit of Canada 146
  New York City 364
  USSR 524
Eucharistic Congress, Philadelphia, Pa. 424, 426
EUROPE 210
  Agriculture 82
  Archaeology 93, 94
  Labor 287
  Natural Gas 198
  Petroleum 200
  Weather 327
European Economic Community 210, 211
  Canada 144
  Food Harvest 217
  International Finance 265
  Ireland 270
  Italy 273
  Luxembourg 315
  Tindemans, Leo 116
European Investment Bank 408
European Nations Cup (soccer) 475
European Parliament 210, 211
Evans, Dame Edith (Brit. act.) 379
Evensen, Jens (Nor. law.) 56
Evert, Chris (Amer. athl.) 476
  Illus. 477
Evidence (law) 166, 293
Evolution (biol.) 91
Ewart-Biggs, Christopher (Brit. ambassador) 270
Excelsior (Mex. news.) 328
Exchange Rates (fin.) 264, 263
  See also Information Highlights section in articles on countries
Exclusionary Rule (law) 166, 293
Exclusive Economic Zone (ocean.) 57
Exon, J. James (Neb. gov.) 357
Expanding Universe Theory (astron.) 109
Explosions 72
Exports: *see* International Trade and Finance
Extraterrestrial Life 108, 154, 444
Eye (anat.) 324
Eye of Jefferson, The, exhibition (National Gallery) 102
  Illus. 103
Eyeglasses:
  Advertising 216

F

Fabiola (Belg. q.) 47
  Illus. 45
Face to Face (film) 351
Fair Labor Standards Act (U.S.) 165, 167
Fair Trading, Office of (Brit.) 171
Faith, Percy (Can.-Amer. cond.) 379
Falkland Islands (Islas Malvinas), S.Atl.O. 99
Fälldin, Thorbjörn (Swed. prime minis.) 124, 485
  Nuclear Power Plants 198
  Illus. 484
Family Hour Agreement (TV) 492
Family Plot (film) 350
  Illus. 349
Family Weekly (mag.) 416
FAO: *see* Food and Agriculture Organization
Farley, Carol (Amer. writ.) 303
Farley, James A. (Amer. pol.) 379
Farming: *see* Agriculture
FASHION 212
  Clothing Industry 259
  Furs 559
FBI: *see* Federal Bureau of Investigation
FCC: *see* Federal Communications Commission
FDA: *see* Food and Drug Administration
FDIC: *see* Federal Deposit Insurance Corporation
Federal Aid:
  Housing 246
  Libraries 298
  Postal Service 409
  Railroads 513, 514
Federal Bureau of Investigation (U.S.) 530, 531
Federal Communications Commission (U.S.) 493, 490, 494
Federal Deposit Insurance Corporation (U.S.) 114
Federal Energy Act (U.S.) 112
Federal Power Commission (U.S.) 197
  Oil and Gas Prices 207
Federal Reserve System (U.S.) 115, 265
  Industrial Production Index 258
Federal Trade Commission (U.S.) 171
  Advertising 73
  Holder-in-Due-Course Doctrine 115
Fencing (sport) 479
  Olympic Games 455
Fernández Maldonado, Jorge (Peruv. prime minis.) 398
Ferryboat-Tanker Collision, La. 314
Fertilizers (agr.) 340
Festivals:
  Motion Pictures 352
  Music 354
Fiber-Containing Foods 219
Fiber Optics (phys.) 496
Fiction: *see* Literature
Fidrych, Mark (Amer. athl.) 460
Fiedler, Arthur (Amer. cond.) 134
Field Hockey (sport) 455
Fighter Planes 337
Figure Skating 479, 450, 451
Film (phot.) 400
Films: *see* Motion Pictures
Finance: *see* Banking; Economy, U.S.; International Trade and Finance
FINLAND 215
  Olympic Games 450, 453
  Telephones 490
  Television 494
Firearms 165
Firemen 163

Fires 72
  Forest Fires 325
  Manitoba 317
  Michigan's National Wildlife Refuge 330
  Minnesota 341
  Polyvinyl Chloride (PVC) 324
  Tenneco Oil Co., La. 314
  Illus. 243
First Admendment (U.S. constitution) 151, 166, 294
  Advertising 73
Fisheries:
  Continental Shelf 52
  Iceland 248
Fishery Conservation and Management Act (U.S.) 57
Fishing-Zone Claims 55, 57
  Canada 144
  Iceland 248
  Oceania 385
Fjords (geog.) 317
Flemings (Belg. people) 116
Fletcher, Louise (Amer. act.) 413
Floating Currencies (fin.) 264, 265
Floods 72, 327
  Houston 247
  North Dakota 369
  Venezuela 542
  Illus. 169
FLORIDA 216
  Death Penalty 293
  Education 43
  Elections 26, 27
  Motor Vehicles 509
Floyd, Ray (Amer. athl.) 470
Flu (med.): *see* Influenza
Fluoridation of Water 542
Fluorocarbons (chem.) 154, 204
Flynt, John J. (Amer. cong.) 417
Folic Acid (chem.) 321
FOOD 217
  Agriculture 81
  Asia 107
  International Trade 264
  Microbial Protein 331
  Quick Food Chains 61
  U.S. Consumption 84
Food Additives 218
Food and Agriculture Organization (U.N.) 81
Food and Drug Administration (U.S.) 218, 219
  Regulation of Medical Devices 171
Food Stamp Program (U.S.) 435, 530
  Puerto Rico 419
Football 466
For Colored Girls Who Have Considered Suicide/When the Rainbow is Enuf, play (Shange) 500
Foraker, Mount, Alas. 86
Ford, Elizabeth (wife of pres.): *Illus.* 26
Ford, Gerald Rudolph (Amer. pres.) 124, 529 fol.
  Africa 75
  Busing of School Children 190
  Cities 164
  Consumerism 171
  Disarmament 183
  Elections 25, 27 fol.
  Environment 204, 206, 207
  Foreign Aid 220
  Military Forces 335
  Older Population 390
  Social Welfare 435
  Taxation 488, 489
  United Nations 537
  Illus. 16, 20
Ford Motor Company 112, 113
  Strike 330
Forego (horse) 473
FOREIGN AID 220
  Africa 75
  Caribbean 149, 150
  Central America 152, 153
  Europe 210, 211
  Middle East 332

USSR 521 fol.
  See also articles on countries
Foreign Trade: *see* International Trade and Finance
Forest Fires 325
  Manitoba 317
  Michigan 330
  Minnesota 341
Forward Based Systems (mil.) 336
Fossils 91
FPC: *see* Federal Power Commission
Fran, Typhoon 327
Franc (Fr. currency) 210
FRANCE 221, 210
  Africa 78
  Automobiles 113
  Capital Punishment 174
  Concorde 510
  Education 193
  Food Costs 218
  Industrial Review 257
  International Trade and Finance 263, 265
  Iran 268
  Labor 288
  Literature 309
  Mining 339
  Music 355
  Olympic Games 450, 453
  Taxation 489
  Telephones 490
  Television 494
  USSR 521
  Weather 327
  Illus. 192
Franchising (business) 63
Francis, Connie (Amer. singer) 174
Franconia Notch, N.H. 360
Franjieh, Suleiman (Leb. pres.) 296
Frankfurt International Book Fair, Ger.:
  Illus. 415
Fraser, John Malcolm (Austr. prime minis.) 125, 109, 110
Free Democrats (Ger. pol.) 230
Free State of Christiania, Copenhagen, Den. 182
Freedom of Information Act (U.S.) 151, 418
Freedom of the Press, Speech, etc.: *see* Press, Freedom of the; Speech, Freedom of, etc.
French-Canadian Literature 306
French Territory of the Afars and Issas 78, 80
Frenz, Helmut (Chilean bp.) 425
Freons: *see* Chlorofluorocarbons
Fresno Bee (news.) 418
Friedman, Milton (Amer. econ.) 412
Frisch, Max (Ger. writ.) 310
Front, The (film) 347
  Illus. 349
Fronts (meteorol.) 325
Frozen Foods 219
Fruits:
  USDA Standards 171
FTAI: *see* French Territory of the Afars and Issas
FTC: *see* Federal Trade Commission
Fuels: *see* Coal; Energy; Natural Gas; Nuclear Energy; Petroleum
Fugate, Caril Ann (Amer. paroled convict) 357
Fundamental Schools 43
Fur Trapping 559
Fusion, Thermonuclear (phys.) 404

G

Gabin, Jean (Fr. act.) 379
Gabon 79
Gaddis, William (Amer. writ.) 300

Gag Orders (law) 151, 294, 418
Gajdusek, D. Carleton (Amer. sci.) 412
Galaxies (astron.) 109
Galleries: *see* Museums and Galleries
Gallico, Paul (Amer. writ.) 379
Gambia, The 79
Gambling:
  Connecticut 170
  Massachusetts 319
  Nevada 359
  New Jersey 361
Gandhi, Indira (Indian prime minis.) 251, 254
  Illus. 253
Gandhi, Sanjay (Indian pol.) 254
  Illus. 252
Ganges River, Asia 254
Gannett Newspapers 416
Garden is Doing Fine, The, bk. (Farley) 303
GARDENING AND HORTICULTURE 225
Garrison River Diversion Project, N. Dak. 201, 369
Garton Slack, archaeo. site, Eng. 94
Gas, Natural: *see* Natural Gas
Gasoline 112, 113, 196
Gathright Dam, Va. 202
Gaullists (Fr. pol.) 221, 222
Geiger-Torel, Herman (Can. opera dir.) 149
Geisel, Ernesto (Braz. pres.) 135, 136, 290
General Assembly (U.N) 525, 528, 333, 536
  Amerasinghe, H.S. 118
  Habitat Conference 205
  Illus. 405
General Electric Company 204
General Labor Confederation (CGT) (Arg.) 99
General Motors Corporation 112, 113
Generic Names of Drugs 216
GENETICS 226, 117
  Microorganisms 331
Geneva Conference on Rhodesia 430, 80
  Illus. 21
Geneva Conference on the Middle East 333
GEOLOGY 227
  Ice Age Climate 325
  Oceanography 52, 386
George Foster Peabody Awards 414
GEORGIA 229
  Death Penalty 292
Geothermal Energy 248
Geriatrics: *see* Older Population
GERMAN DEMOCRATIC REPUBLIC (East Germany) 232
  Automobiles 113
  East-West German Relations 233
  Literature 310
  Music 353
  Olympic Games 450, 453
  Space Exloration 442, 445
  Telephones 490
  Television 494
GERMANY, Federal Republic of (West Germany) 230, 210, 211
  Archaeology 93
  Automobiles 113
  China 161
  East-West German Relations 233
  Education 193
  Elbe Lateral Canal 201
  Food Costs 218
  Industrial Review 257
  International Trade and Finance 263 fol.
  Italy 274
  Labor 288
  Literature 310
  Mining 339

Music, 354, 355
  Olympic Games 450, 453
  Poland 405
  Portugal 408
  Space Exploration 444
  Telephones 490
  Television 494
  USSR 521
  Illus. 81
Gerontology: *see* Older Population
Getty, J. Paul (Amer. fin.) 379
GHANA 234
  Agriculture 83
  Television 494
Giant Halos (phys.) 403
Gibson, Ralph (Amer. phot.) 400
Gift Tax 490, 488
Gilbert Islands, Pac. O. 385
Gilmore, Gary (Amer. convict) 533
  Illus. 541
Giroud, Françoise (Fr. pub. offi.) 221, 222
Giscard d'Estaing, Valéry (Fr. pres.) 221 fol.
  Illus. 16
Gizenga, Antoine (Zaire pol.) 558
GNP: *see* Gross National Product
Gold 266, 267, 340
  Coins 168
Golf 470
Goulart, João (Braz. pres.) 380
Government Employees 286
  Australia 109
  Supreme Court Rulings 167
Government Spending 186, 530
  Australia 109
  Canada 145
  Cities 163
  Education 191
  Foreign Aid 220
  Mexico 329
  Taxation 488
Governor General's Literary Awards (Can.) 413
Goya, Francisco (Sp. art.) 102
Grain (agr.) 81 fol., 217
  Korea, North 284
  Manitoba 317
  USSR 524
Grain Elevator Explosion, Houston, Tex. 247
Grammy Awards 412
Granada (auto.) 112
Grand Jury 293
Grant, Lee (Amer. act.) 413
Grants, N. Mex. 362
Grasso, Ella (Conn. gov.) 170
GREAT BRITAIN 235, 210, 211
  Air Transportation 516
  Archaeology 94
  Argentina 99
  Automobiles 113
  Bridge 201
  Callaghan, J. 121
  Concorde 510
  Consumerism 171
  Crime 174
  Education 192
  Food Costs 218
  France 224
  Housing 246
  Iceland 248
  Industrial Review 257
  International Trade and Finance 263
  Labor 287
  Literature 307
  London 313
  Monarchy 48
  Music 354, 355
  Northern Ireland's Peace Movement 270
  Olympic Games 450, 453
  Telephones 490
  Television 494, 496
  Theater 503, 506
  Uganda 519
  Weather 327
  Illus. 326

Great Britain, Library Association of 298

Grechko, Andrei A. (Sov. pub. offi.) 523

GREECE 240, 211
Aegean Sea Dispute 526, 527
Shipping 514
Telephones 490
Television 494
Turkey 518

Greek Orthodox Church 427

Green Revolution (agr.) 83

Grey Cup (football) 469

Grey King, The, bk. (Cooper) 303
Illus. 304

Griffin, Archie (Amer. athl.) 467

Griffin, Robert (Amer. sen.) 532

Grolier Award 298

Grooms, Red (Amer. art.) 105

Gross National Product 185, 188, 220
Canada 145
Education Expenditures 191
Energy 196
International Trade and Finance 263
Graph 187
See also Information Highlights section in articles on countries

Guadeloupe, isl., Carib.:
Soufrière, volcano 149
Television 494

Guam:
Television 494
Weather 327

Guatemala 152
Earthquake 227, 228, 246, 386
Television 494
Illus. 13, 153

Guerrilla Activities:
Africa 77, 78
Argentina 98
Croatian Nationalists 556
Ireland 270
Latin America 290, 291
Mozambique 352
Nicaragua 153
Palestinian Hijacking of French Jetliner 519
Paraguay 396
Rhodesia 430, 431
Spanish Sahara 346
Thailand 499

Guggenheim Museum, New York 105

Guinea 79, 75

GUINEA-BISSAU 241

Gulf Oil Corporation 70
Angola 90
Ecuador 189

Gun-Control Law 550

Gur, Mordechai (Isr. gen.) 18

Gurney, Edward, J. (Amer. pol.):
Illus. 216

Gush Emunim Movement (Judaism) 427

Guthrie, Janet (Amer. phys., racer) 458

Gutman, Herbert (Amer. hist.) 302

GUYANA 241

Gymnastics 479, 453, 456

H

Habeas Corpus Review (law) 293

Habitat Conference: *see* Conference on Human Settlement

Hackett, Bobby (Amer. mus.) 380

Haedens, Kleber (Fr. writ.) 309

Hail (meteorol.) 325

Haiti:
Drought 149
Television 494

Haley, Alex (Amer. writ.) 303

Halifax, N.S., Can. 147

Hall, Peter (Brit. theat. dir.) 506, 503

Hall of Fame (baseball) 461

Hall of Fame for Great Americans 414

Hamill, Dorothy (Amer. athl.) 451

Hamilton National Bank, Chattanooga, Tenn. 114

Handball, 479, 456

Handguns 165, 174

Hanoi, Viet. 545

Harness Racing 474

Harris, Patricia Roberts (Amer. pub. offi.) 535

Harris, William and Emily (Amer. revol.) 139
Illus. 172

Harry S. Truman Airport, V.I. 547

Hartford Times (news.) 170

Harvard University, Mass. 91

Hassan II (Mor. k.) 346

HAWAII 242

Hayakawa, S. I. (Amer. sen.) 138

Hays, Wayne L. (Amer. cong.) 531

Healey, Denis (Brit. pub. offi.) 239

Health and Welfare: *see* Medicine; Nutrition; Social Welfare

Health, Education, and Welfare, Department of (U.S.) 435

Health Insurance 260

Health Systems Agencies (U.S.) 437

Hearst, Patricia (Amer. kidnap victim) 139, 174, 533

Heart Disease 321, 320

Heavy Ions (phys.) 404

Hébert, Anne (Can. writ.) 307

Heidegger, Martin (Ger. philos.) 380

Heisenberg, Werner (Ger. phys.) 380

Heisman Trophy (football) 466

Helios (spacecraft) 444

Hemingway, Mary (Amer. writ.) 303

Herpes Infections (med.) 324

High Density Polyethylene (plastic) 219

High Seas (internat. law) 56

Highways 512
West Virginia 551

Hijacking of Airplanes:
Air France Jetliner 519
Croatian Terrorists 556
Entebbe 272, 519
USSR 522

Hillery, Patrick J. (Ire. pres.) 270

Hills, Carla (Amer. pub. offi.) 205

Hirohito (Jap. emp.) 279
Illus. 48, 276

Hiss, Arlene (Amer. racer) 458

Historiography: *see* Literature

Ho Chi Minh City, Viet. 545

Hockey (sport) 471
Olympic Games 450

Hogs 82

Hoijer, Harry (Amer. anthro.) 91

Hokule'a (canoe) 242
Illus. 516

Holder-in-Due-Course Provision (com.) 115, 171

Homosexuality 167, 294

Honduras 152, 153
Television 494

Honecker, Erich (Ger. pol.) 232

HONG KONG 242
Telephones 490
Television 494
Weather 327
Illus. 12

Hooks, Benjamin Lawson (Amer. civil rights leader) 209, 494

Hoover, J. Edgar (Amer. pub. offi.) 531

Horn & Hardart (restaurant chain) 64

Horse Racing 473

Horse Shows 479

Horticulture: *see* Gardening and Horticulture

Hospital Insurance: *see* Health Insurance

Hospital Workers' Strike (N.Y.) 163

Houdon, Jean-Antoine (Fr. art.):
Illus.: sculpture of Robert Fulton 103

Hours of Labor 294
Government Employees 165

House of Representatives (U.S.) 531
Copyright Law 297
Daniel Schorr Case 417
Medicaid Funds for Abortion 437
Membership 539
Open Committee Meetings 151

HOUSING 244
Federal Subsidies 166
Germany, East 233
Industrial Review 258
Older Population 390

Housing and Urban Development, Department of (U.S.) 246, 390
Solar Energy 200

HOUSTON, Tex. 247

Howe, Allan T. (Amer. cong.) 541, 542

Howe, Irving (Amer. writ.) 301

Howe, James Wong (Chin.-Amer. cinematographer) 380

Howlin' Wolf (Chester A. Burnett) (Amer. mus.) 377

Hoxha, Enver (Alban. pol.) 87

Hua Kuo-feng (Chin. premier) 125, 158

HUD: *see* Housing and Urban Development, Department of

Hudson River, U.S. 204

Hughes, Howard (Amer. indus.) 374

Hughes, Richard (Eng. nov.) 380

Human Organization (anthro. jour.) 91

Human Rights: *see* Civil Liberties and Civil Rights

Human Settlement, Conference on: *see* Conference on Human Settlement

Humboldt's Gift, nov. (Bellow) 300

Hume, George Basil (Brit. card.) 426

Humphrey, Hubert H. (Amer. sen.) 341
Illus. 319

Humphrey-Hawkins Bill (U.S.) 435

HUNGARY 247
Automobiles 113
Catholicism 426
Olympic Games 453
Telephones 490
Television 494

Hunter Island, Tas., Austr. 93

Hurricanes 72, 327
Mexico 291, 328

Husák, Gustav (Czech. pres.) 178

Hussein (Jor. k.) 280
Illus. 49

Hydantoin Anticonvulsant Drugs 321

Hydrocarbons (chem.) 317

I

ICBM: *see* Intercontinental Ballistic Missiles

Ice Age (geol.) 325

Ice Skating 479, 450, 451

ICELAND 248
Earthquake 228
Television 494
Volcanoes 52

IDAHO 249
Teton Dam 202

Ik, The, play (Cannan) 504

Illegal Aliens 293

ILLINOIS 250

Archaeology 92
Chicago 155
Motor Vehicles 509
Illus. 166

Illiteracy 38

IMF: *see* International Monetary Fund

Immunization (med.) 322, 331, 436

Imports: *see* International Trade and Finance

In the Realm of the Senses (Jap. film) 352

Incinerators, Municipal 326

Income: *see* Wages and Salaries; and Information Highlights section in articles on provinces of Canada and states of the U.S.

Income Taxes 489
New Jersey 190, 361

Indeterminate Sentence (law) 138, 411

INDIA 251, 106, 107
Archaeology 94
Automobiles 113
Bangladesh 114
Birth Control 436
Censorship 151
China 161
Industrial Review 257
Mining 339
Pakistan 394
Population 407
Religion 428
Sri Lanka 481
Telephones 490
Television 494
Weather 327

Indian Ocean 52

Indian Pueblo Cultural Center, Albuquerque, N. Mex. 362

INDIANA 255

Indianapolis 500-Mile Race 458

Indians, American:
Archaeology 92
Maine 315
New Mexico 362
Northwest Territories 369
South Dakota 441
Washington, state 549
Yukon 557

Individual Retirement Account 260

INDONESIA 256
Agriculture 82
Communication Satellite 445
Earthquake 228
Television 494

Industrial Production Index 258

INDUSTRIAL REVIEW 257, 186
Advertising 73
Automobiles 112
Business Ethics 65
Canada 145
Energy 195
Food Industry 218
Housing 244
Labor 285
Mexico 329
Mining 339
Publishing 415
Quick Food Chains 61
Graph 187

Inflation 188
Asia 107
Consumerism 171
Europe 210
Food 218
Housing 244
International Trade and Finance 263
Labor 285 fol.
Stocks and Bonds 483
Taxation 488, 489
See also articles on countries

Influenza (med.) 322, 331, 436

Information, Freedom of 151

Innauer, Toni (Aus. athl.) 451

Innocent Passage (internat. law) 55, 56

INSURANCE 260

Integration: *see* Civil Liberties and Civil Rights; School Integration
Intelligence Agencies (U.S.) 530
INTELSAT (communication satellite) 444, 445
Inter-American Affairs: *see* Latin America
Inter-American Development Bank 486
Intercontinental Ballistic Missiles 335, 336, 338
  Disarmament 183
Intercosmos (research satellite) 445
Interest Rates (econ.) 115
  Great Britain 235
  Housing 244, 245
  Italy 274
INTERIOR DESIGN 261
Interlibrary Loans 297
Internal Revenue Service (U.S.) 489, 531
International Bank for Reconstruction and Development: *see* World Bank
International Corporations: *see* Multinational Corporations
International Court of Justice 528
  Greco-Turkish Aegean Sea Dispute 240, 527
International Energy Agency 196
International Finance: *see* International Trade and Finance
International Monetary Fund 266
  Argentina 99
  Great Britain 210, 239
  Italy 274
  Spain 448
  Zaire 557
International Relations:
  Asia 106
  Balkan Countries 431
  Cuba's International Role 176
  Europe 210
  Latin America 289
  Middle East 332
  Law of the Sea Conference 50
  United Nations 525
INTERNATIONAL TRADE AND FINANCE 263
  Automobiles 113
  Books 416
  Caribbean 150
  China 159, 161
  Europe 210
  Foreign Aid 220
  Hong Kong 242
  Meat 81
  Multinational Corporations 65
  Petroleum 195
  Soviet Grain Purchases 218
  Taxation of Imports by States and Cities 294
  Transportation 508, 514
  See also Information Highlights section in articles on countries
International Trade Law, Commission on (U.N.) 527
International Women's Year 554
INTERPHIL '76 Stamp Show, Philadelphia, Pa. 481, 482
Interstate Highway System (U.S.) 512
Interstellar Matter (astron.) 109
Inuit (Eskimos) (people) 146
  Northwest Territories 369
Investment Tax Credit 488
Investments (econ.) 186, 188
  Insurance Companies 260
  OPEC Countries 264
  Stocks and Bonds 482
IOWA 267
  Elections 25
  Weather 327
IRA (Individual Retirement Account) 260

IRAN 268, 106, 107
  Agriculture 83
  France 224
  Iraq 269
  Libya 299
  Mining 339
  Olympic Games 453
  Soviet Pilot's Defection 522
  Telephones 490
  Television 494
  U.S. Arms Sales 338
IRAQ 269, 334
  Agriculture 83
  Television 494
IRELAND 270
  Television 494
Irish Republican Army 270
  Libya 299
Iron 339
  Ocean Deposits 53
Islam 428
Islas Malvinas (Falkland Islands), S. Atl. O. 99
ISRAEL 271, 332 fol.
  Agriculture 83
  Coins 168
  Education 193
  Egypt 194
  Entebbe Airport Incident 519
  Ethiopia 80
  Foreign Aid 220
  Habitat Conference 205
  Lebanon 295
  Rabin's Resignation 23
  Religion 427, 428
  Rumania 431
  South Africa 439
  Telephones 490
  Television 494
  United Nations 525, 526
  U.S. Arms Sales 338
Itaipu Dam, Braz.-Para. 202
ITALY 273, 210, 211
  Archaeology 94
  Automobiles 113
  Berlinguer, E. 119
  Earthquake 228
  Industrial Review 257
  International Trade and Finance 263
  Labor 288
  Literature 310
  Lockheed Scandal 66
  Music 355
  Olympic Games 450, 453
  Telephones 490
  Television 494
  Weather 327
Item Pricing (com.) 171
Ivory Coast 79
  Television 494
IWY: *see* International Women's Year

J

Jack-In-The-Box Restaurants 61, 63
Jagan, Cheddi (Guyana pol.) 242
  Illus. 241
Jai Alai (sport) 170
Jakarta, Indon.:
  Illus. 256
Jallud, Abdul Salam (Lib. prime minis.) 299
Jamaica:
  Cuba 175
  Drought 149
  Election 23, 150
  Olympic Games 453
  Television 494
  Violence 150
James River, Va. 204, 548
Jamison, Judith (Amer. dancer) 179, 180
JAPAN 276, 107
  Australia 110
  Automobiles 113
  China, People's Republic of 159, 161
  China, Republic of 162

  Food Costs 218
  Industrial Review 257, 258
  International Trade and Finance 263
  Labor 286
  Lockheed Scandal 66
  Mining 339
  Monarchy 49
  Olympic Games 453
  Papua New Guinea 385
  Soviet Pilot's Defection 522
  Space Exploration 445
  Telephones 490
  Television 494, 496
  Tokyo 507
  Weather 327
Javelin Throw (sport) 478, 457
Jazz (mus.) 423
Jefferson, Thomas (Amer. pres.) 102
Jenkins, Roy (Brit. pub. offi.) 211
Jenner, Bruce (Amer. athl.) 456
  Illus. 455
Jerusalem, Isr. 428
Jewelry 214
Job Discrimination 166
Job Qualification Tests 293
Joffrey Ballet 180
Joint North Sea Informative Service (JONSIS) 387
Joint Oceanographic Assembly, Edinburgh, Scot. 386
Jones, Randy (Amer. athl.):
  Illus. 459
JONSDAP 76 Program (ocean.) 387
Jordan, Barbara (Amer. pol.) 126, 208
JORDAN 280
  Agriculture 83
  Television 494
  Illus. 427
Jour, Le (Can. news.) 345
Journalism 415, 418
  Asia 107
  Bolles Murder, Arizona 100
  Brazil 136
  Censorship 151
  CIA's Use of Journalists 531
  India 251, 252
  Mexico 328
  Montreal 345
  Prizes and Awards 412, 413
  Television 491
JR, nov. (Gaddis) 300
Juan Carlos I (Sp. k.) 47, 447, 448
  Latin America 291
  Illus. 44
Juantorena, Alberto (Cuban athl.) 454
Judaism 427, 424
  Mexico 329, 516
Judo (sport) 456
Juliana (Neth. q.):
  Illus. 45
Jumblat, Kemal (Leb. pol.) 295, 296
Jumping (sport) 478, 457
Jupiter (planet) 108, 109
Justice, Department of (U.S.) 277
Juvenile Crime 363

K

Kachemak Bay, Alas. 86
Kaimai Tunnel, N.Z. 202
  Illus. 365
Kaleidoscope, museum, Kansas City, Mo. 262
Kamm, Robert (Amer. pub. offi.) 389
KANSAS 280
Kansas City, Mo. 262
Kansas City Royals (baseball team) 460, 461
Kazankina, Tatiana (Sov. athl.) 478
Kaunda, Kenneth (Zambian pres.) 80
Kaysone Phoumvihan (Laotian prime minis.) 288
Kearns, Doris (Amer. writ.) 302

Kekkonen, Urho K. (Finn. pres.) 215
Kelley, Clarence (Amer. pub. offi.) 531
  Illus. 174
Kempe, Rudolf (Ger. cond.) 380
Kennedy, Edward M. (Amer. Sen.) 319
Kennedy Airport, New York, N.Y. 510
Kenneth Parker Associates (arch.) 262
  Illus. 261
KENTUCKY 281
Kentucky Derby (horse race) 473
Kentucky Fried Chicken Restaurants 62
KENYA 282, 76
  Agriculture 83
  Anthropology 91
  Archaeology 93
  Television 494
  Uganda 519
Kenyatta, Jomo (Kenyan pres.) 282, 519
Kepone (chem.) 204, 548
Kerner, Otto (Amer. pub. offi.) 380
Keynes, John Maynard (Eng. econ.) 188
Khalid (Saudi Ar. k.) 296, 433
  Illus. 49
Khashoggi, Adnan (Saudi Ar. bsman.) 67
Khorana, Har Gobind (Amer. sci.) 117
  Illus. 226
Kidnappings:
  California School Children 139, 174
  Chilean Political Refugees 156
  French Children in Africa 78
  Mexico 328
  Venezuela 542
Kiev (Sov. ship) 338
Killer Satellites (Sov.) 338
Kim Il Sung (Kor. pres.) 284
Kim Chong Il (Kor. pol.) 284
Kim Dae Jung (Kor. pol.) 277
King, Clennon (Amer. cler.):
  Illus. 229
King, Martin Luther, Jr. (Amer. civil rights leader) 531
King Kong (film) 348
Kingdome, arena, Seattle, Wash.:
  Illus. 549
Kingston, Jam. 150
Kip (Laotian currency) 288
Kissinger, Henry (Amer. pub. offi.) 536 fol.
  Africa 76
  Brazil 136
  Central America 152
  Chile 156
  China 160
  Greece 240
  Iran 269
  Italy 275
  Kenya 282
  Latin America 289
  Luxembourg 315
  Peru 398
  Rhodesia 430
  South Africa 439
  Venezuela 543
Klammer, Franz (Aus. athl.) 450
  Illus. 451
Knebel, John (Amer. pub. offi.):
  Illus. 83
Knock Knock, play (Feiffer) 501
Knoxville, Tenn. 497
Knud (Dan. pr.) 182
Koch, Billy (Amer. athl.) 451
Kodama, Yoshio (Jap. pol.) 278
Kohl, Helmut (Ger. pol.) 230
Komische Oper, opera house, East Berlin, Ger. 354
KOREA, North 284
  Olympic Games 453
  United States 537, 538

KOREA, South 283
  Industrial Review 257
  Japan 277
  Olympic Games 453
  Religion 425, 428
  Television 494
Korean Intelligence Agency 532
Kosaka, Zentaro (Jap. pub. offi.) 276
Kotchian, A. Carl (Amer. bsman.) 277
Kreisky, Bruno (Aus. chancellor) 111
Kreps, Juanita Morris (Amer. pub. offi.) 535
Krone (Dan. currency) 182
Krupp (Ger. indus. firm) 268
Kubitschek, Juscelino (Braz. pres.) 380, 136
Kukrit Pramoj (Thai premier) 499
Kurds (people) 269
Kuwait:
  International Trade and Finance 264
  Mining 339
  Television 494

L

Labeling of Foods 219
LABOR 285, 188
  Air Transportation 509
  Cities 163
  Common Situs Picketing Bill 529
  Economy, U.S. 186
  Elections, U.S. 28, 29
  Ethnic Groups 208, 209
  Europe 210, 211
  Job Discrimination 166
  New York City 364
  Newspapers 418
  Prisons 411
  Public Employment Programs 435
  Supreme Court Rulings 167, 293, 294
  Unemployment Rate, *Graph* 187
  Women 554
  See also articles on countries, provinces of Canada, and states of the U.S.
Labor Unions: *see* Labor; and names of specific unions
Labour Party (Brit.) 235 fol.
Labrador, Can.:
  Inuit 146
Lacrosse (sport) 479
LAES *see* Latin American Economic System
Lageos (research satellite) 445
Lagos, Nig. 367
Lamaism (rel.) 428
Lamm, Richard D. (Colo. gov.) 169
Lamont, Donal (Rhod. bp.) 426
Lance, Bert (Amer. pub. offi.) 534, 533
Land Reform:
  Algeria 88
  Habitat Conference 205
  Honduras 153
Lang, Fritz (Aus. film dir.) 380
Language Controversies:
  Belgium 116
  Canada 142, 192, 393
  South Africa 440
LAOS 288, 107
  China 161
  USSR 522
  Vietnam 546
Laramie River Station, power project, Wyo. 555
Larceny (crime) 174
Lasdun, Denys (Brit. arch.) 506
Laser Geodynamics Satellite 445
Lastiri, Raul (Arg. pres.) 98
Las Vegas Nights (gambling) 363
LATIN AMERICA 289, 152

Agriculture 82
Catholicism 426
Labor 287
Natural Gas 198
Population 407
USSR 523
Latin American Bishops, Conference of: *see* Conference of Latin American Bishops
Latin American Economic System 289
Lauda, Niki (Aus. racer) 458
Laurence, Margaret (Can. writ.) 305
Lavon, Pinhas (Isr. pol.) 380
LAW 292
  Canada 143
  Copyrights 297
  Crime 173, 174
  Indiana's Recodification 255
  Prisons 411
Law Enforcement Assistance Program (U.S.) 164
Law of the Sea Conference (U.N.) 50
  Amerasinghe, H.S. 118
  United States 538
Lead (chem.) 317
Leakey, Mary (Kenyan anthro.) 91
Leather Goods 259
LEBANON 295, 333
  Egypt 194
  France 224
  Israel 272
  Jordan 280
  Libya 299
  Maronite Christians 424
  Syria 486, 487
  Television 494
  United States 538
  Illus. 332
Lechín Oquendo, Juan (Bol. labor leader) 133
Lee, William C. (Amer. gen.) 368
Lee Kuan Yew (Singapore prime minis.) 434
Lefebvre, Marcel (Fr. archbp.) 424, 426
Legion Disease (med.) 320, 397
Lehmann, Lotte (Ger. singer) 380
  Illus. 381
Leighton, Margaret (Brit. act.) 381
Lekai, Laszlo (Hung. card.) 426
Lenin Prize (Sov. lit.) 311
Lens (optics) 400
Leone, Giovanni (It. pres.):
  Illus. 273, 543
Leontief, Wassily (Amer. econ.) 527
Lesotho 79
Letelier, Orlando (Chil. pub. offi.) 381, 156
  Venezuela 290
Lévesque, René (P.Q. premier) 143, 420
Levi, Edward (Amer. pub. offi.) 531
Lewisburg Penitentiary, Pa. 410
Liability Insurance 260
  Swine Flu Vaccine 322
Libel (law) 294
Liberal Party (Brit.) 237
Liberal Party (Can.) 141
Liberal-Democratic Party (Jap.) 279
Liberia 79
  Shipping 514
  Television 494
Liberty Bell:
  Illus. 397
Liberty Bell Pavilion, Philadelphia, Pa. 97
LIBRARIES 297
  School Libraries 41, 151
Library Association of Great Britain 298
Library of Congress 297, 298, 415
  Television and Radio Archives 494

LIBYA 299, 334
  Egypt 195
  Mining 339
  Spanish Sahara 346
  Sudan 484
  Television 494
  Tunisia 517
Liechtenstein:
  Olympic Games 450
Life, Extraterrestrial 108, 154, 444
Life Insurance 260
Limonite (min.) 108
Lin Yutang (Chin. schol.) 381
Linear Ware People (archaeo.) 93
Lippincott Award 298
Lipscomb, William N., Jr. (Amer. chem.) 412
Lira (It. currency) 210, 273
Lisagor, Peter (Amer. jour.) 381
Literacy 38
LITERATURE 300
  Prizes and Awards 412, 413
Litton, Jerry (Amer. cong.) 381, 343
Litton Industries 490
Livestock 82 fol.
  Canada 145
  Kansas 280
Living Will 436
Liza, Hurricane 327, 328
Loans (econ.) 115
  Cities 164
  International Finance 264
  See also Mortgages
Local Taxes 489
Lockheed Aircraft Corporation 66
  Japan 277
  Netherlands 358
LONDON, Eng. 313
  Theater, 504, 506
  Illus. 237, 238
López Michelsen, Alfonso (Colom. pres.) 168
López Portillo, José (Mex. pres.) 126, 328
  Illus. 23
LOS ANGELES, Calif. 313
  Air Pollution 206
  Education 43
Lotteries:
  Connecticut 170
  Massachusetts 319
LOUISIANA 314
  Death Penalty 293
  State Employees Retirement Law 293
Louisiana Building and Construction Trades Council 314
Louisville, Ky. 208, 281
  Illus. 191
Lourenço Marques, Moz.: *see* Maputo
Lowari Pass Tunnel, Pak. 202
Lugar, Richard G. (Amer. sen.) 255
Luge (sport) 450
Lumber Industry 258
  Alaska 86
  Laos 288
Lumière (film) 352
Lummus Company 269
Luna (spacecraft) 444, 523
Lunar Probes 444
Lutheran Church 425
LUXEMBOURG 315
  Archaeology 94
  International Finance 264
  Television 494
Lyme Arthritis (med.) 320
Lyons, Leonard (Amer. jour.) 381
Lysenko, Trofim D. (Sov. geneticist) 381
Lyttleton Theatre, London, Eng. 506

M

McBride, Mary Margaret (Amer. broadcaster) 381

McCarthy, Eugene (Amer. pol.) 31
McCloy, John J. (Amer. bank., pub. offi.) 69, 70
McClure, Lynn (Amer. marine) 498
McDonald's Restaurants 62, 64
McGee, Gale (Amer. sen.) 555
Machel, Samora (Moz. pres.) 352
McKinley, Mount, Alas. 86
McNally, Dave (Amer. athl.) 459
Madagascar: *see* Malagasy Republic
Maddox, Lester (Amer. pol.) 229
Madeleine, Hurricane 327
Magazines 416, 73, 74, 401
Magnetic Monopole (phys.) 404
Magnetohydrodynamics (MHD) (phys.) 197
Mahdists (Sud. pol.) 484
Mail-Order Industry 171
MAINE 315
  Prisons 411
Major, André (Can. writ.) 306
Makarios III, Archbishop (Cypriot pres.) 177
Makarova, Natalia (Russ. dancer) 127, 179
Malagasy Republic 79
Malaria (med.) 331, 407
Malawi 79
MALAYSIA 316, 494
Mali 79
Malik, Yakov (Sov. ambassador) 520
Malpractice (med.) 436, 229
Malraux, André (Fr. writ.) 381
Malta 494
Mammography (med.) 320
Mandel, Marvin (Md. gov.) 318
Manganese 53, 55
Manila, Philipp. 398
MANITOBA, prov., Can. 317, 145, 148, 149
Manley, Michael (Jam. prime minis.) 23, 150
Mansfield, Mike (Amer. sen.) 344
Manufacturing: *see* Industrial Review; and Information Highlights section in articles on countries
Mao Tse-tung (Chin. pol.) 375, 157
Maputo, Moz. 352, 75
Marathon Man (film) 350, 349
Marcona Mining Corporation 398
Marcos, Ferdinand E. (Philipp. pres.) 398, 399, 266
Margarethe II (Dan. q.) 182
MARINE BIOLOGY 317, 386, 387
Marine Corps (U.S.) 498
Marisat (maritime satellite) 445
Mark (Ger. currency) 231, 265
Markov, Georgi (Sov. writ.) 311
Maronite Christians 424
Mars (planet) 443, 108, 154, 227, 331
Marshall, F. Ray (Amer. pub. offi.) 535
Marshall, Thurgood (Amer. justice) 292
Martin, James S., Jr. (Amer. eng.) 127
Martinez School Bus Crash, Calif. 72
Martinique 494
Marubeni (Jap. business) 277, 278
Mary Hartman, Mary Hartman (TV program) 492
MARYLAND 318
  Church College Aid 167, 191, 294
  Public School Tests 43
Mass Transit: *see* Urban Mass Transit
MASSACHUSETTS 319
  Boston 134
  Indian Suits 315
  State Police Retirement Law 293

Matanzima, Kaiser (Transkei prime minis.) 77
Illus. 78
Mathematics 38, 41
Matheson, Scott M. (Utah gov.) 542
Mauna Loa Volcano, Haw. 228
Mauritania 79, 77
Mauritius 79, 494
May, Scott (Amer. athl.) 462
Mayors, Conference of (U.S.) 163, 164
Meat (food) 81 fol., 218
Medals of Freedom (U.S.) 414
Medicaid 437
Medicare 390
MEDICINE 320, 436
　Drug-Abuse Treatment 184
　High Fiber Diet 219
　Influenza Immunization 331
　Legion Disease 397
　Malaria 407
　New York-Israeli Educational Program 193
　Older Population 390
　Prizes and Awards 412, 414
Mediterranean Sea 204, 387
Mehta, Zubin (Amer. cond.) 313
Meinhof, Ulrike (Ger. guerrilla) 230
Melgar Castro, Juan Alberto (Hond. pres.) 153
Memory of Justice, The (film) 348
Méndez, Aparicio (Uru. pres.) 541, 291
Menopause (physiol.) 320
Mercer, John H. (Amer. comp.) 382
Mercury (chem.) 340, 559, 560
Messersmith, Andy (Amer. athl.) 459
Metals 259, 339, 340, 263
Meteor (weather satellite) 446
METEOROLOGY 325
　Agriculture 81, 82
　Britain's Drought 238
　Caribbean Weather 149
　European Drought 210
　Ocean's Effect on Weather 386
　Weather Satellites 446
Methadone (drug) 184
Metropolitan Museum, New York City 105
Metropolitan Opera, New York, N.Y. 354
Metzenbaum, Howard (Amer. sen.) 388
Mexican-Americans 209
MEXICO 328, 289, 291
　Agriculture 83
　Anti-Semitism 427
　Automobiles 113
　Industrial Review 257
　International Finance 265
　Labor 287
　Literature 312
　López Portillo, J. 126
　Olympic Games 453
　Telephones 490
　Television 494
　Travel 516
　Weather 327
Michaux, Lewis (Amer. book-seller) 382
Michelangelo (It. art.) 104
Michelin Tire Corp. v. Wages (U.S. case) 489
MICHIGAN 330
　Elections 28
　Motor Vehicles 509
　Rape Law 173
MICROBIOLOGY 331
Microwave Ovens 219
Mid-Atlantic Ridge (ocean.) 52
MIDDLE EAST 332
　Foreign Aid 220
　Military Forces 338
　Natural Gas 198
　Petroleum 200
　USSR 521
　United States 538

Mid-Ocean Dynamics Experiment 386
Mid-Ocean Ridges 51, 52
Mielziner, Jo (Amer. theat. designer) 382
Miettunen, Martti (Finn. prime minis.) 215
MiG-25 (Sov. airplane) 276, 337, 522
Migrants 135, 209, 231
Miki, Takeo (Jap. premier) 278, 279, 277
Mikodom (Russ. prelate) 428
Milan, It. 355
MILITARY FORCES 335
　Africa 75
　Asia 106
　Australia 110
　Canada 144
　Disarmament 183
　Foreign Aid 220
　India 253
　Korea, North 284
　Middle East 332
　Philippines 399
　Thailand 499
　USSR 523, 257
　U.S. forces in Germany 231
Miller, Johnny (Amer. athl.) 470
Milliken, William C. (Mich. gov.) 330
Milwaukee, Wis. 208, 552
Mineo, Sal (Amer. act.) 382
Miners' Federation (Bol.) 133
Minimum Wages:
　Brazil 135
　Government Employees 165
　Mexico 329
　Philippines 399
　Spain 448
MINING 339
　Antarctica 406
　Coal Leasing Law 555
　Industrial Review 257 fol.
　Kentucky Disaster 281
　Mexico 329
　Ocean Floor 52, 53
　Yukon Strikes 557
MINNESOTA 341, 92
Minnesota Vikings (football team) 467, 468
Minority Groups: *see* Ethnic Groups
Minot, N. Dak. 369
Minuteman Missiles 337
Miranda Rules (law) 293
Miron, Gaston (Can. poet) 307
MIRV (Multiple Individually Targeted Reentry Vehicles) 183
Miss America 341
Missiles 335 fol., 183
Missing in Action (mil.) 546
MISSISSIPPI 342, 30
Mississippi Queen (ship) 516
Mississippi River, U.S. 514
MISSOURI 343, 327
Missouri Synod (Lutheran Church) 425
Mitchell, Martha (wife of attorney general) 382
Mittermaier, Rosi (Ger. athl.) 128, 450
Mobile, Ala. 85
Mobile (art) 376
Mobile Homes 244
Mobutu Sese Seko (Zaire pres.) 557, 558, 519
Modern Pentathlon (athl.) 456
Moldavia, rep., USSR 431
Molecular Biology 117
Molina, Arturo Armando (Salv. pres.) 152
Monaco 494
Monarchies (govt.) 44
Moncton, N.B., Can. 359
Mondadori, Alberto (It. publ.) 311
Mondale, Walter Frederick (Amer. vice pres.) 128, 29
Illus. 27, 28
Money: *see* Banking; Inflation;

International Trade and Finance; and Information Highlights section in articles on countries
Mongolia 453, 494, 522
Monod, Jacques (Fr. biol.) 382
Monroe, La. 163
MONTANA 344, 327
Monterey, Tenn. 262
Montgomery of Alamein, 1st Viscount (Brit. field marshal) 382
Montoneros (Arg. terrorists) 98
Montoya, Joseph (Amer. sen.) 362
MONTREAL, P.Q., Can. 345, 147
　Olympic Games 452
Montreal Canadiens (hockey team) 471
Monzon, Carlos (Arg. athl.) 465
Moon, Sun Myung (Kor. cler.) 424, 544, 425
Moon (astron.) 444
Moore, Arch A., Jr. (W. Va. gov.) 551
Moore, Sara Jane (Amer. convict) 533
Morales Bermúdez, Francisco (Peruv. pres.) 398, 291
Morand, Paul (Fr. writ.) 309
Moreau, Jeanne (Fr. act., dir.) 352
Morgentaler, Henry (Can. phy.) 143
Morison, Samuel Eliot (Amer. hist.) 382
Moro, Aldo (It. premier) 273, 274
MOROCCO 346, 77, 78, 494
Mortgages 244 fol.
Moscow, USSR 524
Moss, Frank (Amer. sen.) 437
MOTION PICTURES 347, 364
　Prizes and Awards 413, 414
Motor Vehicle Registrations 509
Motorboating 479
Motorcycle Racing 479
Motorcycles 509
Mountain Climbing 86
Mouse River, N. Dak. 369
Moynihan, Daniel Patrick (Amer. sen.) 363, 364, 31
MOZAMBIQUE 352, 75
　Rhodesia 430, 431
　United Nations 526
Illus. 77
Mugabe, Robert (Rhod. leader) 430
Muhammad, Murtala (Nig. gen., pol.) 366
Muldoon, Robert (N.Z. prime minis.) 365
Multinational Corporations 65
Multiple Individually Targeted Reentry Vehicles: *see* MIRV
Munrow, David (Eng. mus.) 421
Munson, Thurman (Amer. athl.) 460
Murchison, Ruby (Amer. educ.) 368
Murder (crime) 165, 174, 507
Murder by Death (film) 351
Murdoch, Iris (Brit. writ.) 308
Museum of Fine Arts, Montreal, Can. 149
Museum of Modern Art, New York, N.Y. 103, 105
　Architecture Exhibition 95
　Photography Show 400
　Taxi Exhibit 96
Museums and Galleries 102 fol.
　Canada 149
　Photography 402
　Smithsonian's Air and Space Museum 550
MUSIC 353
　Caldwell, S. 120
　Canada 148
　Prizes and Awards 412
　Radio 493
　Recordings 421
Muskie, Edmund (Amer. sen.)

315, 316
Muslim Brotherhood (Egy. extremists) 194
Muslims: *see* Islam
Mussel (zool.) 317
Muzorewa, Abel (Rhod. bp.) 430
M-X Missle 336

N

NAACP: *see* National Association for the Advancement of Colored People
Naber, John (Amer. athl.) 454
Nader, Ralph (Amer. law.) 115, 294
Nagako (Jap. emp.):
Illus. 48, 276
Nambe Falls Dam. New Mexico 202
Illus. 201
Namibia: *see* South West Africa
Narayan, Jayaprakash (Indian pol.) 252
Nashville, Tenn. 497
National Air and Space Museum, Washington, D.C. 550
National Archives, Washington, D.C.:
Illus. 34
National Arts Centre, Ottawa, Can. 148
National Assessment of Educational Progress 38
National Association for the Advancement of Colored People 209, 342
National Ballet of Canada 180
National Basketball Association 463, 464
National Book Awards 413
National Book Critics' Circle Awards 300
National Broadcasting Company 492, 496
National Cancer Institute 154
National Center for the Humanities 368
National Gallery, Washington, D.C. 102
Illus. 103
National Gallery of Canada 149
National Institute of Arts and Letters Awards 412, 413
National Institutes of Health (U.S.) 117
National Magazine Awards 412
National Medals of Science 414
National Oceanic and Atmospheric Administration (U.S.) 54
National Security Agency (U.S.) 530
National Teacher of the Year 368
National Theatre, London, Eng. 506, 503
National Visitor Center, Washington, D.C. 550
National Women's Conference 554
Nationalist China: *see* China, Republic of
Nationalization:
　Guyana 241
　Pakistan 393
　Panama 395
　Peru 398
　U.S. Railroads 513
　Venezuela 542
　Zaire 557
NATO: *see* North Atlantic Treaty Organization
Natural Gas 197, 207, 257, 268, 339
　Algeria 88
　Offshore Gas Fields 206
Navy (U.S.) 337
N.B.A.: *see* National Basketball Association
NBC: *see* National Broadcasting Company
Ne Win (Bur. pres.) 138

NEBRASKA 357
  Gag Order Case 151, 294
  Weather 327
Necrology: *see* Obituaries
Negroes, American 208, 165
  Elections 30
  New York City 364
  Supreme Court Rulings 293
Neizvestny, Ernst (Sov. sculp.) 524
Nemtsanov, Sergei (Sov. athl.) 456, 523
Nepal 107
Neptune Theatre, Halifax, Can. 147
NETHERLANDS 357
  Automobiles 113
  International Finance 265
  Lockheed Scandal 66
  Olympic Games 450, 453
  Telephones 490
  Television 494
Netherlands Antilles:
  Gold Coin 168
  Television 494
Neto, Agostinho (Ang. pres.) 89
  Cuba 176
  Illus. 76
Network (film) 348
NEVADA 359
  Water Diversion Case 294
NEW BRUNSWICK, prov., Can. 359
New Delhi, India:
  Illus. 252
New Guinea 228
NEW HAMPSHIRE 360
  Elections 25
NEW JERSEY 361
  Cities 163
  Education 190
  Prisons 410, 411
  Quinlan Case 324
  Taxation 489
New Math (educ.) 41
NEW MEXICO 362
  Nambe Falls Dam 202
  Illus. 201
New Orleans, La. 96
New River Dams Controversy (N.C.-Va.) 548
New River Gorge Bridge, W. Va. 551
New Towns 246
New World Records 421
NEW YORK, state 363
  Education 190, 193
  Fair Campaign Code 294
  Motor Vehicles 509
  New York City 364
  Nonpublic Schools, Aid to 167
  Prisons 410
  Weather 327
NEW YORK CITY, N.Y. 364, 163, 164, 363
  Acid Rain 135
  Air Pollution 206
  Anti-Soviet Activities 520
  Architecture 95, 96
  Art Exhibitions 102, 103, 105
  Day-Care Centers 436
  Education 190
  Medicaid Frauds 437
  Music 353, 354
  Operation Sail 36
  Theater 500
  Illus. 164, 297, 508
New York City Ballet 179, 180
New York City Opera 354
New York Cosmos (soccer team) 475
New York Drama Critics' Circle Theater Awards 414
New York Nets (basketball team) 463, 464
New York Philharmonic 353
New York Yankees (baseball team) 460, 461
NEW ZEALAND 365, 385
  Caribbean Development Bank 150
  Olympic Games 453, 456

Telephones 490
Television 494
Tunnel 202
Newbery Medal 303
NEWFOUNDLAND 366
Newport, R.I. 429
  Operation Sail 36
Newspapers 416
  Advertising 73, 74
  Asia 107
  Brazil 136
  Hartford *Times* 170
  India 253
  Mexico 328
  Montreal 345
  Photographic Publications 401
  Prizes and Awards 412
Newsprint (paper) 416
Ngo Dinh Thuc, Pierre Martin (Viet. archbp.) 426
Nicaragua 152, 153
  Television 494
Nicholson, Jack (Amer. act.) 413
Nickel (metal) 340
  Ocean Deposits 53
Nicklaus, Jack (Amer. athl.) 470
Niehous, William (Amer. bsman.) 542
Niger 79
NIGERIA 366
  Agriculture 83
  Industrial Review 257
  Mining 339
  Television 494
NIH: *see* National Institutes of Health
Nitrogen (chem.) 340
  Mars 444
Nixon, Richard M. (Amer. pres.) 159
Nkomo, Joshua (Rhod. leader) 430
NOAA (weather satellite) 446
Nobel Prizes 412
No-Deposit Containers 330
Noise 218, 511
Nonaligned Countries 481
  Afghanistan 74
  Cuba 176
  India 254
Non-Proliferation Treaty 183, 537
Nordic Investment Bank 215
Nordli, Odvar (Nor. prime minis.) 371
Norris, Clarence (Scottsboro defendant) 85
North Atlantic Treaty Organization 223, 315
NORTH CAROLINA 368
  Death Penalty 293
  Elections 27
  Illus. 411
NORTH DAKOTA 369
  Garrison River Diversion Project 201
North Sea 55, 199, 387
North Solomons, Pac. O. 385
Northern Ireland: *see* Great Britain
Northern Marianas, Commonwealth of the 538
NORTHWEST TERRITORIES, Can. 369
  Inuit 146
Norton, Ken (Amer. athl.) 465
NORWAY 370
  Fjords 317
  International Finance 265
  Olympic Games 450, 453
  Portugal 408
  Telephones 490
  Television 494
NOVA SCOTIA, prov., Can. 371
Novels: *see* Literature
Nsubuga, Emmanuel (Ugandan card.) 519
Nuclear Energy 198, 339
  Denmark 182
  Environment 204
  Iran 268

New Hampshire 360
Nuclear Explosions Agreement (U.S.-USSR) 521
Nuclear Fusion (phys.) 199
Nuclear Physics 404
Nuclear Regulatory Commission (U.S.) 198
Nuclear Tests:
  China 161
  Oceania 385
Nuclear Weapons 183, 537
  Israel 332
Numeiry, Jaafar al- (Sud. pres.) 484
Numismatics: *see* Coins and Coin Collecting
Nunavut (Our Land) (Inuit territory) 147, 369
Nutrition 219
  Asia 107
  Quick Food Chains 64
Nyerere, Julius (Tanz. pres.) 488
  Illus. 282

O

Oakland Raiders (football team) 467, 468
OAS: *see* Organization of American States
OAU: *see* Organization of African Unity
Obasanjo, Olusegun (Nig. gen., pol.) 366
OBITUARIES 372
Obscenity (law) 151, 294
  Motion Pictures 351
Occupational Safety and Health Administration (U.S.) 218
Ocean Island, Pac. O. 385
OCEANIA 385
OCEANOGRAPHY 386
  Deep Sea Drilling 228
  Law of the Sea Conference 51, 58
  Polar Research 406
Ochs, Phil (Amer. singer) 382
Ó Dálaigh, Cearbhall (Ire. pres.) 270
Oduber, Daniel (Costa R. pres.) 152
O.E.C.D.: *see* Economic Cooperation and Development, Organization for
Office Buildings 262
Office of Economic Opportunity (U.S.) 39
Office of Fair Trading (Brit.) 171
Official Development Assistance (ODA) 220
Offshore Oil and Gas 52, 56, 199, 206, 370
Oh, Sadaharu (Jap. athl.):
  Illus. 279
OHIO 388
  Motor Vehicles 509
Oil: *see* Petroleum
OKLAHOMA 389
  Death Penalty 293
Older Americans Act (U.S.) 390, 391
OLDER POPULATION 390
  Employment Discrimination 293
Oleanic (oil spillage recovery system):
  Illus. 206
Olivier Theatre, London, Eng. 506
Olympic Games 449
  China, Republic of 162
  Commemorative Coins 168
  Germany, East 233
  Guyana 242
  New Zealand 365
  Tanzania 488
  Television 491, 492
  Travel 515
  USSR 523
  Illus. 111
Olympic Stadium and Velodrome, Montreal, P.Q.,

Can. 97
Olympics Cultural Program, Can. 147
Omaha, Neb. 165, 357
Oncogene (biochem.) 117
One Flew Over the Cuckoo's Nest (film) 413
One Stop Tour Charters (air travel) 516
O'Neill, Thomas P. (Amer. cong.) 532
  Illus. 533
Onischenko, Boris (Sov. athl.) 454, 523
Onn, Datuk Hussein bin (Malay. prime minis.) 316
Onsager, Lars (Nor.-Amer. chem.) 382
ONTARIO, prov., Can. 391
  Archaeology 93
  Education 193
  Ottawa 393
  Toronto 507
Ontario 500-Mile Race 458
OPEC: *see* Organization of Petroleum Exporting Countries
Open Classroom (educ.):
  Illus. 40
Open Universe Theory (astron.) 109
Opera 354, 353
  Canada 148, 149
  Recordings 421
Operation Sail 36, 474
  New York City 364
  Newport, R.I. 429
  Illus. 529
Oral Contraceptives 320
Orange Bowl (football) 466
Orchid Archaeological Site, Ont., Can. 93
OREGON 392
  Education 43
Organization of African Unity 77
  Angola 89
  Spanish Sahara 346
Organization of American States 289, 396
  Chile 155
Organization of Petroleum Exporting Countries 199, 200, 264
  Foreign Aid 220
  Oil Prices 23, 334, 483
  Illus. 196
Orr, Bobby (Can. athl.) 472
Orthodox Eastern Church 427
  Ethiopia 207
  USSR 524
Oscars (motion picture awards) 413
OSHA: *see* Occupational Safety and Health Administration
Ospina Pérez, Mariano (Colom. pres.) 383
OTTAWA, Ont., Can. 393
  National Arts Centre 148
Ottawa Rough Riders (football team) 469
Overseas Press Club Awards 412
Owens-Illinois (corp.) 542
Ozone Layer (atmosphere) 154, 204, 326

P

Paci, Enzo (It. philos.) 311
Pacific Ocean 52, 53
Pahlavi, Mohammed Reza (shah of Iran) 268, 269
PAKISTAN 393, 107
  Afghanistan 74
  India 254
  Malaria 407
  Olympic Games 453
  Television 494
  Tunnel 202
  Weather 327
Palestine Liberation Army 487
  Lebanon 295
Palestine Liberation Organization 334

Israel 272
Lebanon 295, 296
Libya 299
Syria 487
Palestinian Guerrillas 519
Pamela, Typhoon 327
PANAMA 395, 176, 494, 514, 543
Panama Canal 289, 396, 27, 395
Panmunjom Incident, Kor. 283, 284, 538
Paper Industry 259, 415, 416
Papp, Joseph (Amer. theat. prod.) 500
Papua New Guinea 385
Parachuting (sport) 480
PARAGUAY 396, 202, 494
Parasites (biol.) 317
Paris, Fr. 222, 223, 224, 355
Park Chung Hee (Kor. pres.) 283
Park, Tongsun (Kor. lobbyist) 277, 532
Edwards, E. 314
Parole System (penology) 411
Particles, Elementary (phys.) 403, 404
Pas de Duke (ballet) 179
Pasadena, Calif. 43
Passamaquoddy Indians 315
Passport 516
Pate, Jerry (Amer. athl.) 470
Patman, Wright (Amer. cong.) 383, 498
Paul VI (pope) 428, 275
Paul (Yugos. pr.) 383
Paulus, Norma (Amer. pub. offi.) 392
Pay Television 496
PCB (chem.): *see* Polychlorinated Biphenyls
Pearson, David (Amer. racer) 458
Peking, China 158
PENNSYLVANIA 396
Elections 28
Motor Vehicles 509
Pennsylvania Academy of Fine Arts 95, 96
Penobscot Indians 315
Pentathlon (athl.) 456
People Mover Transit System 341
Peoria, Ill. 297
Pérez, Carlos Andrés (Venez. pres.) 289, 290
Periodicals 73, 74, 401, 412
Perón, Isabel Martínez de (Arg. pres.) 98, 14
Perpich, Rudy (Minn. gov.) 341
Persian Gulf 268, 269
PERU 398, 291
Labor 287
Literature 312
Television 494
USSR 338
Peseta (Sp. currency) 448
Peso (Chilean currency) 156
Peso (Mex. currency) 265, 287, 291, 329, 516
Pesticides 559
Petroleum 199, 195, 196, 207, 257
Alaska 86
Algeria 88
Angola 90
Canada 144, 145
Ecuador 189
Europe 210
International Trade and Finance 263, 266
Iran 268
Iraq 269
Ireland 270
Libya 299
Mexico 329
Mining 339
Nigeria 367
Norway 370, 371
Ocean Floor 52
Offshore Oil Fields 206
Oil Spills 86; *illus.* 59
Prices 23, 334, 483
Saudi Arabia 432, 433

Tunisia 517
Venezuela 543
Philadelphia, Pa. 165
Architecture 96, 97
Art Exhibition 102
Interior Design 262
Legion Disease 320
Police Department 293
Illus. 34, 104, 115, 397
Philadelphia Phillies (baseball team) 460, 461
Philip, Prince (Duke of Edinburgh) 11, 46
PHILIPPINES 398
Earthquake 228
Libya 299
Television 494
USSR 522
United States 106
Vietnam 546
Weather 327
Phillips Curve (econ.) 188
Phillips Petroleum Company 389
Phnom Penh, Camb. 139
Phoenix Suns (basketball team) 463
Phoenix Zoological Gardens, Ariz. 560
Phosphates (min.) 78, 346, 517
PHOTOGRAPHY 400
Pulitzer Prizes 413
Space Exploration 442
Photosynthesis (bot.) 117
PHYSICS 403
Prizes and Awards 412
Physiology:
Prizes and Awards 412
Piatigorsky, Gregor (Amer. mus.) 383
Picketing (labor) 294
Picon, Gaetan (Fr. writ. 309
Picts (people) 94
Pinochet Ugarte, Augusto (Chilean pres.) 155, 156, 289
Pipelines 508
Alaska 86, 200, 207
Canada 144
China-Korea 284
Piprahwa, India 94
Piston, Walter (Amer. comp.) 383
Placer Deposits (min.) 52
Plains, Ga. 229
Plants: *see* Botany
Plastics 219, 324
Plate Tectonics (geol.) 227
Platinum (metal) 340
PLO: *see* Palestine Liberation Organization
Pluto (planet) 109
Plutonium (chem.) 183
Plyushch, Leonid (Sov. schol.) 524
Pocano 500-Mile Race 458
Podgorny, Nikolai (Sov. pres.) 76
Poetry: *see* Literature
Poisoning 560
POLAND 405
Automobiles 113
Olympic Games 453
Telephones 490
Television 494
POLAR RESEARCH 406
Polar Star (icebreaker) 406
Pole Vault (sport) 478, 457
Police 163 fol.
Chicago 155
Detroit 330
Hong Kong 243
New York City 364
Supreme Court Rulings 293
Polisario (Saharan rebels) 77, 78, 88, 80
Political Prisoners:
Asia 107
Brazil 135
Chile 156
Ethiopia 207
India 251
Korea, South 283
Pakistan 393
Uruguay 541

Polls, Public Opinion 29, 28
Polo 480
Polychlorinated Biphenyls (chem.) 204, 559, 560
Polyvinyl Chloride (plastic) 324
Pompeii, It. 94
Pons, Lily (Fr.-Amer. singer) 383
Popular Movement for the Liberation of Angola 89, 75, 176
POPULATION 407, 84, 107, 114, 217, 436
See also Information Highlights section in articles on countries, provinces of Canada, and states of the U.S.
Porgy and Bess, musical (Gershwin) 503
Pornography 351
Port Authority of New York and New Jersey 510
Port Gibson, Miss. 342
PORTUGAL 407, 211
Automobiles 113
Guinea-Bissau 241
Olympic Games 453
Refugees 246
Soares, M. 129
Taxation 489
Telephones 490
Television 494
POSTAL SERVICE 409, 481
Potash (min.) 432
Potter, David M. (Amer. hist.) 302
Poultry 84
Pound, Ezra (Amer. poet) 303
Pound (Brit. currency) 210, 235, 265, 516
Poveda, Alfredo (Ecua. pres.) 189
Poverty: *see* Social Welfare
Powell, Jody (Amer. pub. offi.) 533
Powell, Lewis F. (Amer. justice) 292
Power Plants, Nuclear 198, 199, 204, 339
Denmark 182
Iran 268
New Hampshire 360
Oregon 392
Precipitation (meteorol.) 325
Press, Freedom of the 151, 418
Asia 107
Brazil 136
Daniel Schorr Case 417
India 251, 252
Mexico 328
Supreme Court Rulings 294
Pretrial Publicity 151, 294
Preus, J. A. O. (Amer. cler.) 425
Prices 171, 188
Air Fares 509
Automobiles 113
Canada 145
Copper 156
Europe 210
Food 218
Gold 267
Great Britain 239
Housing 244
International Trade and Finance 263 fol.
Natural Gas 197, 198, 207
Petroleum 23, 88, 196, 199, 207, 334
Postal Rates 409
Railroad Freight Rates 514
Stocks and Bonds 482, 483
Sugar 289
Television Advertising 73
Primary Elections (U.S.) 25
Prime Rate (fin.) 115
PRINCE EDWARD ISLAND, prov., Can. 410
PRISONS 410
Alabama 85, 166
Canada 143
Mexican-U.S. Exchange of Prisoners 329
Privacy (law) 294, 293

Private Schools 191
Integration 166, 190, 292, 293
State Aid to Church Colleges 318
PRIZES AND AWARDS 412
Baseball 461
Basketball 464
Library Awards 298
Literature 300, 303, 310 fol.
Pulitzer Prize for Music 353
Theater 500, 504
Product Liability Insurance 260
Professional Employees 286
Profits (econ.) 185, 145, 509
Progressive Conservative Party (Can.) 141
Property Insurance 260
Property Taxes 134, 190
Protein (food) 331
Protestantism 424
Proxmire, William (Amer. sen.) 69, 552
Pryor, David H. (Ark. gov.) 101
Psi Particles (phys.) 403, 404
Psoriasis (med.) 321, 324
Public Health Service (U.S.) 323
Public Housing 166, 245
Public Lands 555
Public Schools 43, 190, 191
Chicago 155
Detroit 330
Interior Design 262
Vermont 544
See also Busing of School Children; School Integration
Public Service Awards 414
Public Service Jobs Program (U.S.) 164
Public Television 492, 496
PUBLISHING 415
Censorship 151
CIA's Involvement 531
Italy 310
Photographic Publications 401
Quebec 306
Pueblo Indians 362
PUERTO RICO 419
Economic Conference 210, 276
Olympic Games 453
United Nations 527
Pulitzer Prizes 412 fol., 300, 353
PUVA Therapy (med.) 321
Puyallup Indians 549
PVC: *see* Polyvinyl Chloride

Q

Qaddafi, Muammar el- (Lib. pres.) 299, 484
Qatar:
International Trade and Finance 264
Television 494
Quarks (phys.) 404
QUEBEC, prov., Can. 420, 142, 143, 147 fol.
Advertising 74
Inuit 146
Montreal 345
Olympic Games 452
Quick Food Chains 61
Quincy Market, Boston, Mass. 95
Quinlan Case (law) 324, 436

R

Rabin, Itzhak (Isr. premier) 271, 272, 23
Racial Violence:
Boston 134
Chicago 155
Great Britain 238
South Africa 438
Racing: *see* specific sport, such as Horse Racing
Radiation (phys.) 404
Radio: *see* Television and Radio
Radioactive Fallout 199

Radioactive Wastes 198
RADUGA (communication satellite) 445
Ragtime, nov. (Doctorow) 300
Rahway Prison, N.J. 410, 411
Rail Transportation Improvement Act (U.S.) 514
Railroad Revitalization and Regulation Reform Act (U.S.) 513
Railroads 508, 513
  Accidents 72
  Hong Kong 243
Rain (meteorol.) 325, 327
  Acid Rain 135
Rankin, Judy (Amer. athl.) 471
Rape (crime) 173, 507
Rare Breeds Survival Trust (Eng.) 560
Ray, Dixy Lee (Wash. gov.) 549
  Illus. 31
Ray, Man (Amer. paint., phot.) 383
RCA Global Communications, Inc. 445
Reading (educ.) 38, 41
Reagan, Ronald (Amer. pol.) 25, 27 fol., 529
  Social Welfare 435
Recession (econ.) 185, 210
Reclamation, Bureau of (U.S.) 201, 202
RECORDINGS (mus.) 421
Red Dyes (food additives) 218
Red Fox (Amer. Indian chief) 383
Redlight Theatre, Toronto, Can. 147
Reed, Sir Carol (Eng. film dir.) 383
Re-Education Centers (Laos) 288
Refugees:
  Portugal 246
Reggae (mus.) 356, 422
Rehnquist, William H. (Amer. justice) 292
Reichsbrücke, bridge, Vienna, Aus. 111
RELIGION 424
  Aid to Church Colleges 294, 318
  Books 415
  Ethiopia 207
  USSR 524
  Women, Ordination of 554
Remedial Programs (educ.) 39
Reno, Nev. 359
Republican Party (U.S.) 25 fol.
  Women 553
Reserve Mining Company 341
Restaurants 61
Rethberg, Elisabeth (Ger. singer) 383
Retirement Age 293
Retirement Income Credits 390
Revaluation of Currencies 263, 265, 287
  Chile 156
  Denmark 182
  Germany, West 231
  Great Britain 235
  Israel 271
  Italy 273
  Mexico 287, 291, 329
  Peru 291, 398
  Spain 448
  Zaire 557
Revenue-Sharing Program (U.S.) 164, 390
Rexburg, Idaho 249
RHODE ISLAND 429
RHODESIA 430, 76, 80
  Catholicism 426
  Mozambique 352
  Smith, I.D. 129
  South Africa 439
  Television 494
  USSR 523
  United States 538
Ribosomes (biol.) 117
Rice (grain) 81 fol., 217
Rich Man, Poor Man (TV program) 492

Illus. 491
Richard, Ivor (Brit. ambassador) 430
  Illus. 21
Richards, Renee (Amer. athl.) 476
Richardson, Bobby (Amer. athl., pol.):
  Illus. 440
Rich's Inc. (dept. store) 229
Richter, Burton (Amer. phys.) 412
Richter, Hans (Ger. art., film dir.) 383
Richter Scale (seismol.) 228
Right to Die (med.) 436
Right to Life Movement 436
Risser, James (Amer. jour.) 413
Rizzo, Frank (Amer. mayor) 165, 397
Roads: *see* Highways
Robbins, Jerome (Amer. choreog.) 179
Roberto, Holden (Ang. pol.) 89
Robeson, Paul Bustill (Amer. singer, act.) 373
Roche and Dinkeloo (arch.) 97
Rock Music Awards 412
Rockefeller, John D. ("Jay"), IV (W. Va. gov.) 551
Rockefeller, Nelson (Amer. vice pres.) 27
Rockefeller Commission on Critical Choices 530
Rockwell International 268, 335
Rocky (film) 352
Rodeo 480
Rodrique, Norbert (Can. labor leader) 420
Rodríguez, Manuel Alfonso (Salv. mil. off.) 152
Rodríguez Lara, Guillermo (Ecua. pres.) 189
Rolling Thunder Revue (mus.) 355
  Illus. 356
Roman Catholic Church: *see* Catholicism
Rome, It. 275
Rookie of the Year (baseball) 461
Rookie of the Year (basketball) 464
Roots, bk. (Haley) 303, 492
Rorem, Ned (Amer. comp.) 353
Rose (bot.) 225
Rose Bowl (football) 466
  Illus. 467
Rothko, Mark (Amer. art.) 105
Rowing 480, 456
Roy, Gabrielle (Can. writ.) 307
Royal Ballet (Brit.) 179
Royal Danish Ballet 179
Rozhdestvensky, Valeri (Sov. cosmonaut) 443
Rubber Workers' Strike 285, 388
Rubinstein, Arthur (Pol.-Amer. mus.) 421
Ruckus Manhattan 1975-76, art show (Grooms) 105
Rugby (sport) 480
RUMANIA 431
  Automobiles 113
  Jordan 280
  Olympic Games 453
  Telephones 490
  Television 494
Rumsfeld, Donald (Amer. pub. offi.) 337, 338
  Africa 76, 282
  Illus. 335
Running (sport) 478, 457
Russell, Rosalind (Amer. act.) 383
Russia: *see* Union of Soviet Socialist Republics
Ruth, Mrs. Babe (widow of athl.) 459
Rutherford, Johnny (Amer. racer) 458
Ružička, Leopold (Swiss chem.) 383
Rwanda 79

S

Sadat, Anwar el- (Egy. pres.) 194, 296, 484
Sagan, Françoise (Fr. writ.) 309
Saigon, Viet. 545
Sailing 474
Saint Paul, Minn. 341
Saint Pierre and Miquelon, Fr. isls., N. Amer. 224
Saint Thomas, Virgin Islands 547
Salem, Mamdouh (Egy. prime minis.) 194
Sales 112, 113, 415
Salim, Salim A. (Tanz. states.) 527
SALT Agreements (U.S.-USSR) 183, 337, 338
Salyut (Sov. spacecraft) 442, 523
Salzburg Easter Festival, Aus. 354
Samoa, American 494
Samphan, Khieu (Camb. pres.) 140
Sampson, Nicos Giorgiades (Cypriot pres.) 177
Sanders, Harland (Amer. bsman.) 62
Sandia Laboratories, Albuquerque, N. Mex. 200
San Diego Zoo, Calif. 560
San Francisco, Calif. 96, 165, 513
San Francisco Giants (baseball team) 459
San Francisco Opera 354
San Francisco Symphony 353
Sa-ngad Chaloryu (Thai adm., pol.) 499
Santucho, Mario Roberto (Arg. pol.) 98
São Tomé and Príncipe 79
Sarbanes, Paul (Amer. sen.) 318
Sarkis, Elias (Leb. pres.) 296
Sarmatians (people) 94
SASKATCHEWAN, prov., Can. 432, 145
Sasser, James (Amer. sen.) 497
Satellites, Artificial 444, 338, 523
Saturn (planet) 108, 109
SAUDI ARABIA 432
  China, Republic of 162
  International Trade and Finance 264
  Lebanon 296
  Lockheed Scandal 67
  Mining 339
  Oil Prices 23, 334
  Television 494
Savings 188
Saxbe, William (Amer. ambassador) 254
Scala, La opera house, Milan, It. 355
  Illus. 354
Scheel, Walter (Ger. pres.) 230
Schistosomiasis (med.) 331
Schlesinger, Arthur (Amer. hist.) 172
Schmidt, Helmut (Ger. chancellor) 230, 231, 275, 221
Schmitt, Harrison H. (Amer. sci., sen.) 362
Schnabl, Karl (Aus. athl.) 451
Scholastic Aptitude Tests 37
School Buildings 262
School Integration 166, 292, 293
  Boston 134, 190
  Dallas 498
  Houston 247
  Los Angeles 313
  Louisville 281
  Milwaukee 552
School Libraries 151
Schools: *see* Education; Private Schools; Public Schools; and Information Highlights section in articles on provinces of Canada and states of the U.S.
Schorr, Daniel (Amer. TV correspondent) 417

Schultze, Charles L. (Amer. pub. offi.) 534
Schweiker, Richard (Amer. sen.) 29
Scientific Committee on Oceanic Research (SCOR) 387
Scotia Coal Mine, Ky. 281
Scotland: *see* Great Britain
Scottsboro Trials (U.S.) 85
Seabrook, N.H. 360
Securities and Exchange Commission (U.S.) 115
Security Council (U.N.) 525, 528
  Greco-Turkish Aegean Sea Dispute 240
  Middle East 332, 333
  South Africa 439
Seismology: *see* Earthquakes
Sellers, Phil (Amer. athl.) 462
Senate, U.S.:
  Copyright Law 297
  Intelligence Committee 530
  Medicaid Funds for Abortion 437
  Membership 539
  Nutrition and Health Report 219
  Open Committee Meetings 151
Senegal 79, 494
Seni Pramoj (Thai premier) 499
Senior Service Corps (U.S.) 390
Sentencing (law) 138
Seoul, Kor. 283
Serbian Orthodox Church 427
Seven Beauties (film) 348
SEYCHELLES 433
Shapp, Milton J. (Pa. gov.) 397, 321
Shipping 514
Shoemaker, Bill (Amer. jockey) 473
Shomron, Dan (Isr. gen.):
  Illus. 272
Shooting (sport) 480, 456
Shore, Dinah (Amer. singer) 414
Shot Put (sport) 478, 457
Siderowf, Dick (Amer. athl.) 471
Sierra Leone 79, 494
Sihanouk, Norodom (Camb. pol.) 139
Sikes, Robert (Amer. cong.) 532
Silberman, Laurence (Amer. ambassador) 556
Silkwood, Karen (Amer. nuclear plant employee) 389
Silva Henríquez, Raúl (Chilean card.) 156
Silver (metal) 340
Silver Dollar (Can.) 168
Silver Dollar (U.S.) 167
Sim, Alastair (Brit. act.) 383
Simon, William (Amer. pub. offi.) 156, 195, 289
Simpson, O.J. (Amer. athl.) 468, 469
Sinai Accords (Egy.-Isr.) 194, 332
SINGAPORE 434
  Book Production 416
  Great Britain 106
  Television 494
Sithole, Edson (Rhod. leader) 431
Sithole, Ndabaningi (Rhod. leader) 430
Skating 479, 450
Skiing 480, 450, 451
  Mittermaier, R. 128
Skin (anat.) 321
Skinner, Jonty (S. Afr. athl.) 475
SLBM: *see* Submarine Launched Ballistic Missiles
Slonim, Marc (Russ.-Amer. crit.) 383
Slovenes (people) 111
Smith, Gerald L.K. (Amer. crusader) 384
Smith, H. Allen (Amer. humorist) 384
Smith, Howard Worth (Amer. pol.) 384
Smith, Ian Douglas (Rhod. prime minis.) 129, 430, 431

Smithsonian Institution, Washington, D.C. 550
  Air and Space Museum 515
  Cooper-Hewitt Museum 105
  Jazz Recordings 423
Smoking 154
Snake Arrangement (Eur. fin.) 265
Snelling, Richard A. (Vt. gov.) 544
Snowstorms 327
Soares, Mário (Port. prime minis.) 129, 408
Soccer 475, 456
Social Democrats (Ger. pol.) 230
Social Security 435, 390
SOCIAL WELFARE 435
  Brazil's Abandoned Children 135
  Denmark 182
  Germany, West 231
  Older Population 390
  Ontario 391
Socialism 211
  Austria 111
  France 222
  Germany 232
  Italy 274
Sofia (Sp. q.) 44
Softball 480
Sol (Peruv. currency) 398
Solar Cells (phys.) 200
Solar Eclipse (astron.) 109
Solar Energy 200, 95
Solar Probes (space expl.) 444
Solar System (astron.) 108
Soleri, Paolo (Amer. arch.) 95
Solzhenitsyn, Aleksandr (Russ. writ.) 312, 311
Somalia 79, 75, 78, 80
Somare, Michael (PNG prime minis.) 385
Somoza, Anastasio (Nicar. pres.) 153
Sonic Boom (phys.) 511
Sorensen, Theodore (Amer. pub. offi.) 534
Sorghum (agr.) 280
Soufrière, volc., Guadeloupe 149, 228
Souphanouvong (Laotian pres.) 288
SOUTH AFRICA 438, 76, 77, 80
  Angola 89, 90
  Israel 272
  Mexico 329
  Mining 339, 340
  Olympic Games 453
  Religion 425
  Telephones 490
  Television 494, 496
  United Nations 525, 526
  Vorster, J. 131
SOUTH CAROLINA 440
SOUTH DAKOTA 441
South Pacific Forum 385
South West Africa (Namibia) 76, 80, 439
  USSR 523
  United Nations 526, 527
  United States 538
South West Africa People's Organization 80
Soweto, S. Afr. 438, 439
Soybeans (agr.) 83, 250, 267, 280
Soyuz (Sov. spacecraft) 442, 443, 446, 523
SPACE EXPLORATION 442, 108
  Martin, J.S., Jr. 127
  USSR 523
  Viking Missions to Mars 154, 227
Space Shuttle 446, 445
Space Station 442
Spacelab 446, 445
SPAIN 447, 211
  Art Exhibition in U.S. 102
  Automobiles 113
  Literature 312
  Monarchy 47
  Olympic Games 453
  Spanish Sahara 346

Suárez González, A. 130
  Telephones 490
  Television 494
Spanish Sahara (Western Sahara) 76, 77, 88, 346, 80
Spark, Muriel (Brit. writ.) 308
Special Drawing Rights (fin.) 263, 266
Speech, Freedom of 294, 73, 493
Speed Skating 479, 450
SPORTS 449, 491
Squash Racquets 480
SRI LANKA (Ceylon) 481, 107, 254
Stabile (art) 376
Stagflation (econ.) 188
Stallone, Sylvester (Amer. act.) 352
STAMP COLLECTING 481, 385
Standard & Poor's Index 482, 483
Stanley Cup (hockey) 471
Stars (astron.) 109
State of the Union Message 529
State Taxes 489
Steel, David (Brit. pol.) 237
  Illus. 235
Steel 257, 259, 329, 339
Steig, William (Amer. writ., illus.) 304
Sterilization (surg.) 253, 436
Steroid Drugs (med.) 324
Stevens, John Paul (Amer. justice) 292
Stewart, Potter (Amer. justice) 292
STOCKS AND BONDS 482, 186
  Banks' Brokerage Services 115
  Employee Ownership Plans 286
  Frauds 294
Stokowski, Leopold (Amer. cond.) 421
Storms (meteorol.) 325, 72
Strand, Paul (Amer. phot.) 384, 402
  Illus. 401
Strategic Arms Limitation Talks: see SALT Agreements
Stratford Festival, Can. 147, 149
Stratosphere 326, 154
Streamers, play (Rabe) 500
Strega Prize (It. lit.) 310
Streisand, Barbra (Amer. singer, act.) 352
Strikes 285 fol., 163
  Air Transportation 509, 512
  Automobile Workers 330
  Bolivia 133
  Canada 141, 142
  Denmark 182
  Ecuador 189
  Finland 215
  France 222
  Irish Bank Officials 270
  Israel 271
  Massachusetts State Employees 319
  Poland 405
  Prince Edward Island 410
  Rubber Workers 388
  Saskatchewan 432
  Tunisia 517
  Virgin Islands 547
  West Virginia 551
  Yukon Mines 557
Strip Mining 294
Stroessner, Alfredo (Para. pres.) 396
Student Demonstrations 517
  Bolivia 133
  Burma 138
  Colombia 168
  Ecuador 189
  Egypt 195
  France 193
  Ghana 234
  Panama 395
  Thailand 499
  Venezuela 542, 543
  Illus. 177, 192
Suárez González, Adolfo (Sp. prime minis.) 130, 447

Submarine Launched Ballistic Missiles 335, 336, 183
Submarines 336, 337, 56
Subways 96, 222, 318, 550
SUDAN 484, 76, 80, 299, 334
  Television 494
Sugar:
  Cuba 175
  Guyana 241
  Hawaii 242
  Latin America 289
  Maine 315
  Philippines 399
Sugar City, Idaho 249
Suharto (Indon. pres.) 256
Sulfur (chem.) 340
Sulfuric Acid (chem.) 326
Sullivan, Frank (Amer. humorist) 384
Sumerians (people) 94
Sun: see entries beginning with Solar
Sunset Laws 85, 267
Sunshine Laws 151, 318, 418
Superheavy Elements (chem.) 154, 403
Superior, Lake, N. Amer. 341
Supplementary Security Income 390, 435
Supreme Court, U.S. 292
  Advertising 73
  Capital Punishment 174
  Censorship Rulings 151
  Church College Aid 191, 318
  Cities 164, 165
  Civil Liberties and Civil Rights 166
  Consumerism 171
  Environment 206
  School Integration 190, 208
  Taxation 489
Surgery 321
Surinam 494
Swaziland 79
SWEDEN 484, 211
  Automobiles 113
  Carl XVI Gustaf 121
  Fälldin, T. 124
  International Finance 265
  Mining 339
  Nuclear Power Plants 198
  Olympic Games 450, 453
  Telephones 490
  Television 494
Swimming 475, 454, 456
Swine 82
Swine Flu (med.) 322, 320, 331, 436
SWITZERLAND 486
  Automobiles 113
  Olympic Games 450, 453
  Portugal 408
  Telephones 490
  Television 494
SYRIA 486
  Archaeology 94
  Egypt 195
  Iraq 269
  Jordan 280
  Lebanon 295, 296, 333
  Libya 299
  Television 494

T

Table Tennis 480
Tachinid Flies (entom.) 560
Taft, Robert A., Jr. (Amer. sen.) 388
Taiwan: see China, Republic of
Tanaka, Kakuei (Jap. premier) 277, 278, 66
Tangshan, China 159
Tanzam Railway 80
TANZANIA 488
  Anthropology 91
  Mozambique 352
  Television 494
Target Projects Program (housing) 245
Tasmania, state, Austr. 93
Tax Reform Act (U.S.) 488

Older Population 390
Tax Shelters 488
TAXATION 488, 530
  Australia 110
  Boston 134
  Imported Goods 294
  Israel 271
  Italy 273
  School Financing 190
Taxi Driver (film) 348
Taylor, Elizabeth (Brit. writ.) 308
Teacher of the Year Award 368
Teachers 191
  Australia 193
  New Methods of Teaching 39
  Women 554
Teachers' Strikes 163
  Canada 142
  Virgin Islands 547
Teasdale, Joseph (Mo. gov.) 343
Teen-Agers: see Children and Youth
Teheran, Iran 268
Tel Aviv University, Isr. 193
TELECOMMUNICATIONS 490
Telephones 490
Telescope:
  Illus. 108
TELEVISION AND RADIO 491
  Advertising 73, 74
  CB Radio 490
  Communication Satellites 444
  Elections 24
  Inuit of Canada 146
  Learning Abilities, TV's Effect on 41
  Prizes and Awards 412, 414
  Voice of Islam 428
  Walters, B. 131
Teng Hsiao-p'ing (Chin. pol.) 158, 159
Tenneco Oil Company 314
TENNESSEE 497
  Illus. 198
Tennis 476
  Borg, B. 120
Teresa, Mother (Alban. nun):
  Illus. 426
Territorial Seas (internat. law) 56, 55
  Australia 110
  Canada 144
  Costa Rica 152
  Greco-Turkish Dispute 240
  Iceland 248
  Korea, North 284
  Mexico 329
  Norway 371
  Oceania 385
  United States 538
Terrorism:
  Africa 78
  Argentina 98
  Bolivia 133
  Brazil 136
  Chile 156
  Croatian Nationalists 556
  Egypt 195
  Hijacking of French Jetliner 519
  Iran 268
  Ireland 270
  Israel 272
  Jamaica 150
  Kissinger, H. 537
  Latin America 289
  Libya 299
  Mexico 328
  Middle East 334
  Northern Ireland 238
Tests (educ.) 37 fol.
Teton Dam, Idaho 202, 249
TEXAS 498
  Austin Tunnel 202
  Death Penalty 293
  Houston 247
  Motor Vehicles 509
Texas, University of 38
Texas Trilogy, A, plays (Jones) 501
Textbook Censorship 151
Textiles 259, 162

THAILAND 499, 107
Agriculture 82
Archaeology 93
Malaysia 316
Military Forces 337
Olympic Games 453
Television 494
United States 106
Vietnam 546
Thang, Ton Duc (Viet. pres.) 545
Thanin Kraivichien (Thai premier) 499
Thanom Kittikachorn (Thai sol., pol.) 499
Tharp, Twyla (Amer. choreog.) 179
Illus. 495
THEATER 500
Austria 111
Britain's National 506
Canada 147
Germany 310
Prizes and Awards 414
Spain 312
Théâtre du Nouveau Monde, Montreal, Can. 147
Theft (crime) 103, 174
Theophilos, Abuna (Eth. patriarch) 207
Thermonuclear Fusion (phys.) 404
Third World: *see* Developing Countries
Thompson, David (Amer. athl.) 464
Thompson, James R. (Ill. gov.) 250
Thompson, Stith (Amer. schol.) 384
Thomson, Meldrim (N.H. gov.) 360
Thomson of Fleet, 1st Baron (Brit. publ.) 384
Thorium (chem.) 86
Thorn, Gaston (Luxem. prime minis.) 315
Thorndike, Dame Sybil (Brit. act.) 384
Thorpe, Jeremy (Brit. pol.) 237
Threepenny Opera, play (Brecht) 500
Throwaway Containers 330
Thuburbo, Tun. 94
Thunderstorms (meteorol.) 325
Tin 316
Tindemans, Leo (Belg. prime minis.) 116
Ting, Samuel C.C. (Amer. phys.) 412
Tito (Yugos. pres.) 555, 556
Tobago: *see* Trinidad and Tobago
Tobey, Mark (Amer. art.) 384
Todd, Garfield (Rhod. prime minis.) 431
Togo 79
TOKYO, Jap. 507
Illus. 278
Tokyo Symphony Orchestra 148
Tony Awards (theater) 414
Tornadoes 72, 325, 327, 389
TORONTO, Ont., Can. 507, 147, 148
Film Festival 352
Torres, Juan José (Bol. pres.) 133
Torrijos Herrera, Omar (Pan. gen., pol.) 395
Cuba 176
Tourism: *see* Travel
Tovarishch (Sov. ship) 474
Toxic Substances Act (U.S.) 154, 171, 206
Track and Field (sports) 478, 454, 457
Trade: *see* International Trade and Finance
Trade and Development, United Nations Conference on: *see* United Nations Conference on Trade and Development
Trade Unions: *see* Labor
Trains: *see* Railroads

Tramway, N.Y.C.:
Illus. 164
Trans-America Bicycle Trail 515
Transit Passage (internat. law) 56
Transkei 77, 439, 440
United Nations 525
Illus. 78
Transnational Corporations: *see* Multinational Corporations
TRANSPORTATION 508, 258
Accidents 72
Air 516
Cruise Ships 516
See also Urban Mass Transit
Transportation, Department of (U.S.):
Concorde 510
Trans World Airlines 509
TRAVEL 515
East-West Germany 233
Hawaii 242
Hungary 247
Mexico 329
Rhode Island 429
Seychelles 434
Transportation 508
Tunisia 517
Trenton Prison, N.J. 410
Triad Concept (mil.) 335
Trials (law):
Press Restrictions 151
Trichlorophenol (chem.) 274
Trident Submarine 336, 337
Trin Nhu Khue, Joseph Marie (Viet. card.) 426
Trinidad and Tobago:
Elections 150
Olympic Games 453
Television 494
Trucks 258, 509
Trudeau, Pierre Elliott (Can. prime minis.) 141, 142, 144
Cuba 176
Illus. 143, 175, 287
Trumbo, Dalton (Amer. writ.) 384
Trust Territory of the Pacific Islands 527
Trusteeship Council (U.N.) 527, 528
Tulsa, Okla. 389
Tumor (med.) 117
TUNISIA 517
Archaeology 94
Television 494
Tunnels 202
Illus. 365
TURKEY 518
Aegean Sea Dispute 526, 527
Agriculture 83
Cyprus 177
Greece 240
Religion 428
Telephones 490
Television 494
TV Guide (mag.) 416
23d of September League (Mex. terrorists) 328
Two-Dollar Note (U.S.) 167
200-Mile Resources Zone (ocean.) 57
Canada 144
Costa Rica 152
Norway 371
Typhoons 72, 327
Hong Kong 243

U

UAW: *see* United Automobile Workers
Uffelman Elementary School, Monterey, Tenn. 262
UGANDA 519, 77
Kenya 282
Television 494
Ullman, Al (Amer. cong.) 392
Ultraviolet Light 321
UME (research satellite) 445
U.N.: *see* United Nations
UNCTAD: *see* United Nations

Conference on Trade and Development
Underwater Archaeology 94
Unemployment: *see* Labor
Unemployment Insurance 435
UNEP: *see* United Nations Environmental Program
UNESCO:*see* United Nations Educational, Scientific and Cultural Organization
Unification Church 424, 544
Union Jack (ballet) 180
UNION OF SOVIET SOCIALIST REPUBLICS 520
Africa 75, 76
Agriculture 82
Angola 89
Archaeology 94
Asia 106
Automobiles 113
Bulgaria 137
China 160
Cuba 176
Disarmament 183
Earthquake 228
Education 193
Egypt 195
Food Costs 218
Foreign Aid 220
France 224
Germany, West 231, 232
Grain Purchases 218
Hockey 472
Hungary 247
India 254
Industrial Review 257
Japan 276
Laos 288
Literature 311
Luxembourg 315
Middle East 334
Military Forces 337
Mining 339, 340
Natural Gas 198
Olympic Games 450, 453
Petroleum 200
Philippines 399
Poland 405
Population 407
Religion 424, 427
Rumania 431
Space Exploration 442 fol., 108
Taganka Theater 504
Telephones 490
Television 494
Turkey 518
United States 538
Vietnam 546
Unions, Labor: *see* Labor
United Arab Emirates 264
Oil Prices 23, 334
Television 494
United Automobile Workers 285
Elections, U.S. 28
Energy Conservation Project 95
Strike 330
United Farm Workers 209
United Kingdom of Great Britain and Northern Ireland: *see* Great Britain
UNITED NATIONS 525
Amerasinghe, H.S. 118
Cyprus 177
Environment 203
Greco-Turkish Aegean Sea Dispute 240
Habitat Conference 205, 95
Law of the Sea Conference 50
Middle East 332, 333
Multinational Business Ethics 70
Ocean Pollution 387
South Africa 439
Stamps 482
United States 536 fol.
Women's Rights 554
Illus. 405
United Nations Conference on Trade and Development 220, 264

United Nations Educational, Scientific and Cultural Organization 387
United States 537
United Nations Environmental Program 203, 204
United Parcel Service 409
United Rubber Workers 285
UNITED STATES 529
Africa 76, 80
Angola 89, 90
Arms Sales 183
Asia 106
Bicentennial: *see* Bicentennial
Brazil 136
Canada 144
Caribbean Development Bank 149
Carter, J. 121
Central America 152, 153
China 159, 160, 162
Cuba 176
Disarmament 183
Economy: *see* Economy, U.S.
Egypt 195
Elections 24
Energy 195 fol.
Ethiopia 207
Ford, G. R. 124
Foreign Aid 220
France 224
Germany 231, 233
Greece 240
Guyana 242
International Trade and Finance 263 fol.
Iran 269
Iraq 269
Israel 272
Italy 275
Japan 276, 277
Jordan 280
Korea, North 284
Latin America 289, 290
Law of the Sea 56, 57
Mexico 329
Middle East 332 fol.
Military Forces 335, 338
New Zealand 365
Oceania 385
Olympic Games 450, 453
Panama 396
Philippines 399
Population 407
Portugal 408
Shipping 514
Soviet Grain Purchases 218, 524
Space Exploration 443 fol.
Spain 448
Thailand 499
Turkey 518
USSR 520
United Nations 525, 526
Uruguay 541
Venezuela 543
Vietnam 546
Yugoslavia 556
Zaire 558
See also states, territories and principal cities
United States Air Force Academy, Col.:
Illus. 553
United States Military Academy, West Point, N.Y. 191
Illus. 553
Unser, Al (Amer. racer) 458
Unser, Bob (Amer. racer) 458
Upper Volta 79
Television 494
Uranium (chem.) 86, 362
Urban Affairs: *see* Cities and Urban Affairs
Urban Mass Transit 512, 96
Hong Kong 243
People Mover 341
Toronto 507
Washington's Subway 550
Uris, Leon (Amer. writ.):
Illus. 301
URUGUAY 541, 291

Argentina 99
Bridge 201
Literature 312
Television 494
Venezuela 543
USDA: *see* Agriculture, Department of
USSR: *see* Union of Soviet Socialist Republics
Ustinov, Dmitri F. (Sov. pub. offi.) 523
Uterine Cancer (med.) 321
UTAH 541
Gilmore Case 533

V

Vaccination (med.): *see* Immunization
Vance, Cyrus R. (Amer. pub. offi.) 534, 533
Vancouver, B.C., Can. 148, 149
Habitat Conference 205
Vegetables 171
Venera Space Probes (USSR) 108
VENEZUELA 542, 289, 290
Mining 339
Olympic Games 453
Telephones 490
Television 494
Veniaminov, John (Russ. miss.) 428
Venus (planet) 108
VERMONT 544
Vezina Trophy (hockey) 471
Viareggio Prize (It. lit.) 310
Videla, Jorge Rafael (Arg. pres.) 130, 98, 99, 289
Illus. 14
Vienna, Aus. 111
VIETNAM 545, 106, 107
Catholicism 426
Laos 288
Religion 428
United States 537, 538
Viking (spacecraft) 443, 108, 154, 227
Martin, J.S., Jr. 127
Village Voice, The (news.) 417
Vinca Culture (archaeo.) 93
Violence: *see* Crime; Racial Violence; Terrorism
Violet Dye (food additive) 218
VIRGIN ISLANDS 547
VIRGINIA 548
Dams 202
Virus:
Eye Infections 324
Oncogenes 117
Swine Flu 322
Visconti, Luchino (It. film dir.) 384
Vladivostok Declaration (1974) 183
Voge (U.S. frigate) 520
Voice of Islam (radio station) 428
Volcanoes 228
Climate, Effect on 325
Oceanic 52
Volkswagen (auto.) 113, 257, 397
Volleyball 480, 457
Volvo (auto.) 113, 257

Volynov, Boris (Sov. cosmonaut) 442
Vorster, Balthazar Johannes ("John") (S. Afr. prime minis.) 131, 80, 438 fol.
Vouel, Raymond (Luxem. states.) 315

W

Wages and Salaries 186, 188, 285 fol.
Australia 109
Blacks 208
Brazil 135
Canada 145
Farm Income 84
Federal Standards 294
Government Employees 165
Great Britain 239
Manufacturing 257
Mexico 329
New Zealand 365
Philippines 399
Spain 448
Women 554
Waldheim, Kurt (Aus. states.) 526
Illus. 50
Wales: *see* Great Britain
Walker, Daniel (Ill. gov.) 250
School Aid Veto 155
Walker, John (N.Z. athl.) 454, 478
Illus. 455
Wallace, George C. (Ala. gov.) 26
Illus. 85
Walloons (Belg. people) 116
Wallop, Malcolm (Amer. sen.) 555
Walpole, N.H. 360
Walters, Barbara (Amer. broadcaster) 131, 491
Warner, John W. (Amer. pub. offi.) 529
Warren, Robert Penn (Amer. writ.) 132
WASHINGTON, state 548
WASHINGTON, D.C. 550, 165
Art Exhibitions 102
Mass Transit 512
Metro 96
Illus. 354
Wastes, Industrial 198
Water Day Rally 205
Water Pollution 206, 204, 317
James River, Va. 548
Oceans 54, 60, 387
Superior, Lake 341
Water Polo 480, 457
Water Skiing 480
Water Supply:
Arizona 100
Bangladesh 114
Nevada Diversion Case 294
Waterloo-Columbia, Ill. 250
Waugh, Evelyn (Brit. writ.) 307
Weather: *see* Meteorology
Weather Satellites 446
Weicker, Lowell P. (Amer. sen.) 170
Weight Lifting 480, 454, 457
Welfare: *see* Social Welfare

West, Comet (astron.) 109
West Berlin, Ger. 233, 232
USSR 521
West Germany: *see* Germany, Federal Republic of
West Indies: *see* Caribbean; and specific islands and political divisions
West Point: *see* United States Military Academy
WEST VIRGINIA 551
Western Sahara: *see* Spanish Sahara
Western Somoa 338, 525
Wheat 81 fol., 217
Argentina 99
Kansas 280, 281
North Dakota 369
Yugoslavia 555
Whipple, George Hoyt (Amer. phy.) 384
White, Byron (Amer. justice) 292
White, Kevin H. (Amer. mayor) 134
White, Minor (Amer. phot.) 403, 384
Illus. 401
Whitney Museum, New York 102
Wholesale Price Index 285
Who's Afraid of Virginia Woolf?, play (Albee) 502
Why Mosquitoes Buzz in People's Ears, story 303
Illus. 304
Wilderness Preservation 204
Wilkins, Mac (Amer. athl.) 478
Wilkins, Roy (Amer. civil rights leader) 209
Willow, Alas. 86
Wilson, Harold (Brit. prime minis.) 236
Illus. 235
Wilson, Louis Round (Amer. schol.) 368
Wind Power 95
Wine-Growers' Demonstrations (Fr.) 222
Winnipeg, Man., Can. 148, 149, 317
Winnipeg Jets (hockey team) 472
Whipple, George Hoyt (Amer. phy.) 384
WISCONSIN 552
WOMEN 553
Auto Racing 458
Crime 172
France 222
Medicine 320
Ordination to the Priesthood 425
Women's Educational Equity Act (U.S.) 554
Women's Hall of Fame 414
Women's International Film Festival 352
Woodcock, Leonard (Amer. labor leader) 26
Woodpeckers (birds) 560
Woolf, Virginia (Brit. writ.) 307
Workers' Party (Viet.) 545, 546
Workmen's Compensation Scandal, Ohio 388

World Bank 220
East African Community 488
India 253
Yugoslavia 556
World Court: *see* International Court of Justice
World of Our Fathers, The, bk. (Howe) 301
World Series (baseball) 460, 461
World Trade: *see* International Trade and Finance
Wrestling 480, 457
Wright, James (Amer. cong.) 532
Illus. 533
Writing (edu.) 38
WYOMING 555

X, Y, Z

X-Rays:
Astronomy 109
CAT Scanning 323
Yachting 480, 457
Yale University Art Gallery, Conn. 102
Yankee Stadium, N.Y. 364
Yemen:
Television 494
Yen (Jap. currency) 276
Yevtushenko, Yevgeni (Russ. poet) 312
Young, Andrew J., Jr. (Amer. pub. offi.) 208, 534
Young, Sheila (Amer. athl.) 450
YUGOSLAVIA 555
Archaeology 93, 94
Austria 111
Automobiles 113
Czechoslovakia 178
Olympic Games 453
Telephones 490
Television 494
YUKON, terr., Can. 557
ZAIRE 557, 76
Angola 89
Television 494
Zambia 79, 80
Angola 90
Rhodesia 430, 431
Television 494
Zarb, Frank (Amer. pub. offi.) 195, 196
Zasimov, Valentin I. (Sov. pilot) 522
Zhivkov, Todor (Bulg. pol.) 137
Zholobov, Vitali (Sov. cosmonaut) 442
Ziaur Rahman (Bangladesh sol., pol.) 114
Zinc 339
Zionism 427
Guyana 242
Mexico 329
Zoning (law) 151, 167, 294
Zoological Gardens 560
ZOOLOGY 559
Zorinsky, Edward (Amer. sen.) 357
Zudov, Vyacheslav (Sov. cosmonaut) 443
Zukofsky, Louis (Amer. poet) 301
Zukor, Adolph (Amer. film prod.) 384